The Women's Suffrage Mo[v

CLARK, Alice
CLARK, Helen
See: - HOUSMAN, L

Women's and Gender History
Edited by June Purvis

Child Sexual Abuse in Victorian England
Louise A. Jackson

Crimes of Outrage: Sex, Violence and Victorian Working Women
Shani D'Cruze

Feminism, Femininity and the Politics of Working Women: The Women's Co-operative Guild, 1880s to the Second World War
Gillian Scott

Gender and Crime in Modern Europe
Edited by Margaret L. Arnot and Cornelie Usborne

Gender Relations in German History: Power, Agency and Experience from the Sixteenth to the Twentieth Century
Edited by Lynn Abrams and Elizabeth Harvey

Imaging Home: Gender, 'Race' and National Identity, 1945–64
Wendy Webster

Midwives of the Revolution: Female Bolsheviks and Women Workers in 1917
Jane McDermid and Anna Hillyar

No Distinction of Sex? Women in British Universities 1870–1939
Carol Dyhouse

Policing Gender, Class and Family: Britain, 1850–1945
Linda Mahood

Prostitution: Prevention and Reform in England, 1860–1914
Paula Bartley

Sylvia Pankhurst: Sexual Politics and Political Activism
Barbara Winslow

Votes for Women
Edited by June Purvis and Sandra Holton

Women's History: Britain 1850–1945
Edited by June Purvis

The Women's Suffrage Movement: A Reference Guide, 1866–1928
Elizabeth Crawford

Women and Teacher Training Colleges 1900–1960: A Culture of Femininity
Elizabeth Edwards

Women, Work and Sexual Politics in Eighteenth-Century England
Bridget Hill

The Women's Suffrage Movement
A Reference Guide 1866–1928

Elizabeth Crawford

London and New York

First published 1999 by UCL Press

First published in paperback 2001
by Routledge
11 New Fetter Lane, London EC4P 4EE

Simultaneously published in the USA and Canada
by Routledge
29 West 35th Street, New York, NY 10001

Routledge is an imprint of the Taylor & Francis Group

© 1999, 2001 Elizabeth Crawford

Typeset in Hong Kong by Graphicraft Ltd
Printed and bound in Great Britain by
TJ International Ltd, Padstow, Cornwall

All rights reserved. No part of this book may be reprinted or reproduced or utilised in any form or by any electronic, mechanical, or other means, now known or hereafter invented, including photocopying and recording, or in any information storage or retrieval system, without permission in writing from the publishers.

British Library Cataloguing in Publication Data
A catalogue record for this book is available from the British Library

Library of Congress Cataloging in Publication Data
A catalog record for this book has been requested

ISBN 0–415–23926–5

Contents

List of Illustrations	vi
Introduction	ix
Reference Guide A–Z	1
Appendix: The Radical Liberal Family Networks	767
Acknowledgements	769
Archival Sources	771
Select Bibliography	774

List of Illustrations

Artists' Suffrage League postcard.	17
Portrait of Lydia Ernestine Becker, in its original state as painted by Susan Isabel Dacre *c*. 1886.	44
Cup and saucer from one of the tea sets commissioned by the WSPU from the Diamond China Co. for use at the Scottish WSPU Exhibition, held in Glasgow in April 1910.	108
Derby Day, 4 June 1913. Emily Wilding Davison lies on the ground after being kicked by horses' hooves.	162
Charlotte Despard (1844–1939), president of the Women's Freedom League.	167
In Hyde Park on "Woman's Sunday", 21 June 1908, Elizabeth Wolstenholme Elmy, wearing a "Votes for Women" sash and carrying her bouquet of ferns, purple lilies, and lilies of the valley, stands with Mrs Pankhurst.	202
Mrs Millicent Garrett Fawcett, president of the National Union of Women's Suffrage Societies.	215
The WSPU's "Holloway" badge, designed by Sylvia Pankhurst.	306
WSPU hunger strike medal, presented to Edith Downing.	307
With their hats prepared for motoring, Mrs Pankhurst and Annie Kenney sit in the back of the WSPU car. Mrs Pethick-Lawrence, to whom the car was presented in 1909, stands alongside.	317
The WSPU fife and drum band prepares to march to advertise the May 1909 Exhibition at the Prince's Skating Rink.	339
E.M. Gardner's caravan in Yorkshire with NUWSS banner.	439
Christabel Pankhurst (1880–1958), photographed *c*. 1908.	491
Mrs Emmeline Pankhurst (1858–1928) photographed *c*. 1909.	506
The west-country contingent of the NUWSS Pilgrimage, July 1913.	550
Taken on the occasion of the "Grand Demonstration" held in Sheffield in 1882.	630
The International Suffrage Shop, 15 Adam Street, Strand, London.	633
The Street Women's Suffrage Association, possibly photographed around the time of the NUWSS Pilgrimage, July 1913.	660
Clementia Taylor (1810–1908).	675

LIST OF ILLUSTRATIONS vii

Vera Wentworth wearing an apron to advertise a WSPU London procession, probably that of 21 June 1908. 705

The "Arts" banner carried by university graduates in the West Procession, 23 July 1910. 743

The Women's Social and Political Union Christmas Bazaar in the Portman Rooms, 4–9 December 1911. 747

A neat corner of a WSPU office/shop. 752

Introduction

The women's suffrage campaign was a single-issue political campaign. Its first petition to parliament, presented by John Stuart Mill on 7 June 1866, was only one, passing virtually unnoticed, amongst that day's muster. Throughout the course of the next 62 years, until women achieved full enfranchisement in 1928, the women's suffrage campaign competed for attention in the lives of successive parliaments and, indeed, in the lives of the campaigners themselves. Using the *Personal Rights Journal,* the advocate of radical causes, as a lens through which to view the world of political lobbying in the 1880s, it is clear that, 20 years after it was launched, the aim and activity of the women's suffrage campaign was not expected to be of any greater interest, nor was it considered of intrinsically greater merit, to political activists of the day than any of the other issues of concern, such as land reform, Ireland, anti-vaccination (which if anything had greater exposure), compulsory education and early closing. Doubtless reference works similar to this one could be compiled for any of these issues and, indeed, would contain many of the same names. It is to us, looking back over the past 150 years, that the campaign for women's enfranchisement has a particular resonance. By tracing, from its faltering beginnings, the process in its various strands, constitutional and militant, we map women's journey not only into citizenship but also into a society which that citizenship has progressively feminized. The journey's winding path has been obscured by the knowledge that the goal was, eventually, attained. The byways and wayside dallyings of the campaign are of intrinsic interest as stages in its development, fuelling spurts of growth or new lines of attack. The women making this journey had the company of friends and relations to sustain them, and to guide them the compass of principle – that women were as equal in value to society as were men. It soon became clear, as parliament ignored the argument, that principle was not enough. Although other feminist campaigns, such as that to give married women control over their own property, that to repeal the Contagious Diseases Acts, that to give widows joint guardianship of their children, and that to give suitably qualified women local government enfranchisement, were successfully manoeuvred through parliament, the machinery of government was engineered to exclude women from its workings and again and again was activated to do so. When it very quickly became clear that the argument would not be won on principle, it moved to one of mechanics. It was the use to which a vote might be put that became the rationale given to answer those defending the *status quo* – that the interests of women would never be protected until they were in charge of their own destiny. It is clear, however, when reading the biographies of the campaigners, how strong a motivation was the feeling that the vote was a symbolic proof of self-worth and, conversely, that without the talisman of full citizenship, women were unprotected from shame in all its social and economic manifestations. The campaign reveals in so many ways the tension between the expectations of individual women and the position to which evolving society had assigned them. It was no coincidence that as the industrial, educational and social status of women "improved" (that is, became closer to that enjoyed by men) so the struggle for the vote became more determined. A study of the women's suffrage campaign highlights the tension between the "masculinity" of the political goal and the efforts to achieve it, both the "feminine" (spectacle and fund-raising, which employed a wide range of womanly skills), and the "masculine" (from speaking from platforms in public in the nineteenth century to terrorism in the twentieth).

Parliament was a machine that had evolved to run a patriarchal society. Women's interests were deemed to be subsumed in those of men. There is benefit to be gained in studying how women, peculiarly at a disadvantage as a parliamentary pressure group, employed a variety of strategies in order to influence the body from which they were barred. The image conjured up is of watching a game of chess in which one participant stands at a considerable distance from the board and, with concentration and dexterity that improves with practice, operates her pieces by nudging them into position with a length of shaky cane. The other player has little need to pay much attention to the board, other than to slam down a winning piece when the occasion arises. Successive governments had no difficulty in using parliamentary procedure to obstruct the introduction of any measure of full enfranchisement. Modern biographies of Gladstone, Asquith and Lloyd George, by omission, highlight how little, despite women's best efforts, the campaign impinged on the workings of government. Indeed, the goal was only achieved in 1918 when, as Martin Pugh has pointed out in *Electoral Reform in War and Peace* (1978), "it mattered very much less who had a vote than it had in 1832 because it was becoming less important to sit in Parliament whose Members were increasingly spectators in the drama of politics".

In its beginning the women's suffrage campaign aimed to influence parliament by following the "usual channels", that is by petitioning, which was relatively cheap, although time-consuming to organize, and easily ignored by MPs. The next stage was to invite a sympathetic MP to introduce a private member's bill. The movement did from its beginning have spokesmen, mainly Radical Liberals, in parliament, and gathered increasing cross-party support as the years went by. However, the days had gone when such a bill, if it had attracted the opposition of the government, could hope to obtain sufficient parliamentary time to pass through all the necessary stages. The energy expended by such women as Elizabeth Wolstenholme Elmy and Helen Blackburn on compiling tables of parliamentary supporters and carefully balancing the parliamentary arithmetic was, we can now sadly recognize, futile in the face of the intractable opposition of the Cabinet. Christabel Pankhurst's main service to the suffrage cause was to recognize this fact and to move the point on which pressure should be exerted from the individual MP to the Cabinet. By 1906 it was clear that only a government measure could enfranchise women and it was only through the (male) electorate that the government could be pressurized. The WSPU's election policy, of opposing all government candidates, was a bold and imaginative tactic. Six years later the NUWSS Election Fighting Fund policy, of supporting Labour Party candidates in preference to those of any other party, however deeply the latter might individually be committed to women's enfranchisement, demonstrated a similar political flair. This analytical astuteness has until recently been buried by accretions of spectacle and martyrdom. The vote was gained by no single tactic but by the force of changing circumstances, one of which was that women had for 60 years been involved in an increasingly public political campaign.

The amazing siege engine of the women's suffrage campaign was constructed to take advantage of any breaches that could be spotted in the bastion of male privilege. The fact that the campaign developed on an *ad hoc* basis, dynamic, interactive and reactive, has obscured many of the societies and individuals who devoted to it lifetimes of thought, time and energy. The suffrage movement was at no time typified by steady progress, but developed through a series of actions and reactions, leaving in its wake a bewildering variety of groupings. Membership shifted between groups, as women reacted to their own life events or to each other (feuding was a natural hazard) as well as to political developments. One can best make sense of the evolution of the campaign by knowing who the people were who set it in motion and by understanding something of the dynamics of the kinship and friendship networks that underlay the campaign.

The 1866 women's suffrage petition acted as a hinge, linking, through its signatures, past campaigns and societies, such as the anti-slavery movement, the anti-Corn Law League, Chartism, the National Association for Promoting Political and Social Improvement of People, and the Law Amendment Society, with one that would only end in 1928. Analysis of the names and addresses on the petition discloses the circles of influence that could, in around two weeks in May 1866, persuade 1499 women to make such a public commitment to a political cause. The wives and daughters of Chartists, Philosophic Radicals, and the Radical Liberals, drawn to a large degree from families of Unitarians and Quakers, such as the Courtaulds/Taylors, Leigh Smiths, Penningtons, Thomassons and Brights (*see* Appendix), in all their ramifications, had the experience of observing and themselves being involved in the running of past campaigns. Reform was in the air; two years previously the men who had led the Anti-Corn Law League, Bright, Cobden, Stansfeld, P.A. Taylor, and George Dawson, had, with Henry Fawcett, founded in Manchester the National Reform Union to campaign for household suffrage. By early 1865 this campaign, lobbying for manhood suffrage only, had been taken up in London by a new generation of working-class radicals, drawing on the experience of Chartists such as George Holyoake. John Stuart Mill, a philosopher rather than a practical politician, in his electoral addresses, both published and in person, in the summer of 1865 took the subject to its logical conclusion and included women in the sweep of enfranchisement. In parallel, movements for the improvement of the education of girls and women and for providing them with better opportunities for employment, had widened the circles of acquaintance and influence. The subsequent interaction between personalities and philosophies, the pragmatic reaction to differing priorities and methods of campaigning, as well as to political developments, provided the dynamic that drove the suffrage campaign.

In *The Unexpected Revolution* (1979), Margaret Bryant, writing about the history of the women's education movement, suggested, "What is needed is closer, more critical, and more balanced study of individuals and of the interplay between those able to take a leading part and those, sometimes equally active, taking a subordinate role." As for education, so for suffrage, it is only by having before one the facts of individual lives and details of individual involvement, that one can "read" the shape of the whole campaign. Societies did not arise spontaneously, but were formed to press for the aims of individuals, and took shape around the personalities involved. It was not a campaign only of leaders. When it was considered politic to move the masses, as in the "Grand Demonstrations" of the 1880s, they could be moved. Between the leaders and the masses was, throughout the whole campaign, a dedicated body of what Elizabeth Wolstenholme Elmy termed "earnest workers". The purpose of this reference work is to give a corporeal presence to these workers, placing them in their context in the campaign. Until now many of these women have been only ciphers, the details of their lives unremarked.

Lilias Ashworth Hallett, speaking of the nineteenth-century movement, valued the early annual reports of the various suffrage committees, "for they have lists of all the early workers and early subscriptions and I believe that these will be of lasting interest. There will always be a few women who will look back through the years with interest and gratitude to the struggles of the early workers." Teresa Billington-Greig, discussing the early days of the twentieth-century Women's Social and Political Union, wrote, "I cannot even begin to give lists of names, but somewhere, at some time, this should be done, for there were women who enlisted then who served the movements heroically and gave us immediate hope and status and women who were handmaids in our service expecting no recognition, and men whose staunch support lasted through the years until the fight ended – and after." It is not only the handmaids who have slipped from view but even women, such as Florence Balgarnie, who for a time held positions of some authority in the movement. Similarly the involvement in the women's suffrage campaign of men whose lives are recorded, such as Israel Zangwill, has been overlooked in the conventional biographical source, the *Dictionary of National Biography*. My intention has been to give the women's suffrage campaign a social, physical and geographical, as well as a political reality and, by plotting an alternative cartography, highlighting family and friendship connections, to lay out a fresh and convincing map of that journey into citizenship.

I have used a wide range of sources to build up a snapshot of these individual lives, angled, of course, to their involvement in the women's suffrage campaign. As Lilias Ashworth Hallett, a very practical woman, suggested, the annual reports of all the myriad suffrage societies, as well as some from the parallel women's education and women's medical movements, have been culled to construct a picture of practical involvement. The suffrage and feminist journals of the nineteenth and twentieth centuries have been combed for references to the "workers". I have given firm specific dates for known membership of societies, although lack of continuous records means that membership may have begun before that date and continued after. Although women may be "hidden from history" they are not, on the whole, hidden from the Registrar of Births, Marriages, and Deaths, nor from the Principal Registry of the Family Division (in England and Wales) or the General Register Office in Scotland. A determined effort, some minimal information, and some luck, has resulted in firm birth and death dates for the majority of the entrants, queries about a few, who have perhaps married or remarried and been lost from view, and a complete blank on a handful, possibly because they have emigrated or died abroad. Each of these dates does, of course, carry with it the possibility of inspecting a birth or death certificate that will in itself supply further details. I have found wills to be invaluable in building up a picture of feminist networks. As one might expect, unmarried women, particularly, tended to leave money and possessions to other women, many of whom were those with whom they had been associated in the suffrage campaign, and to feminist-orientated organizations, such as housing associations or hospitals for women. As many of the women have left no other public written testimony, their wills are the only documentary evidence of what they thought important.

Wherever possible, I have given firm addresses in each entry in order to facilitate further local research. I do feel that one can reanimate a life by lifting it off the printed page and placing it back in its earthly context. When serendipity brought me in front of, for instance, the Priestmans' house in Bristol and Christabel Pankhurst's first home in Paris, the reality of past lives, all those letters, meetings and speeches, were given another dimension by visual evidence of the surroundings in which were carried out the daily round and practicalities of life. In a similar manner I have been at pains to track down likenesses of the subjects; a knowledge of the physical presence informs the politics. Connections between artist and sitter, between architect and patron, between novelist and dedicatee, between playwright and actor, between writer and publisher, between publisher and printer, have all been brought into play to give depth to the network. There is plenty of scope for broadening the research on any of the subjects I have treated.

Most of the research for this reference work has been based on archival sources, relying as little as possible on secondary material. It is interesting to consider in what manner the availability and the nature of archival material shapes the writing of suffrage history. Many of the campaigners had been "written out" because there was no obvious collection of letters or a diary with which to write them in. I trust that I have demonstrated that such a lack of material should not preclude any attempt to build up a picture of a life of involvement. The personal archives are of two types, collections of letters (such as those of Minnie Baldock, Helen Taylor, or Elizabeth Wolstenholme Elmy) and diaries (Mary Blathwayt's) that have been preserved as they were written, unconscious (except in their retention) of any potential to shape history, and scrapbooks, such as those of Helen Blackburn or Maud Arncliffe Sennett that were put together with the purpose of presenting a "history". The Suffragette Fellowship Collection, consisting of autobiographical and biographical details of those who had belonged to the WSPU, is the largest example of the latter type of archive. It is necessary to bear in mind when using it that writers were responding, many years after the events, to a specific request for details of their militant activities and imprisonment. The respondents were a self-selected group, writing in the knowledge that their goal had been attained. Little is revealed of past doubt and disagreement. Because all the records of the WSPU have disappeared, apparently in police raids, there is little original written (as opposed to published) material relating to the conduct of the campaign. The Suffragette Fellowship collection has filled this vacuum, its easy accessibility, fleshed out by radio and television interviews and dramatizations, shaping, for a time, the history of the suffrage campaign. The original Suffragette Fellowship collection is augmented by material that is still being donated from families of former WSPU members. This material tends to consist of prison diaries and letters written from prison, these being the relics that have been thought most worthy of preservation, while personal correspondence that might have provided a more rounded picture has been destroyed. Fortunately for us there are collections of papers, such as those of Janie Allan (Edinburgh), Caroline Phillips (Aberdeen) and Mary Phillips (Camellia) that reveal rather more of the reality of working for the WSPU. The National Union of Women's Suffrage Societies has, of course, left a vastly greater reservoir of much less dramatic documentary evidence, held not only in the main collections in Manchester Central Library and the Fawcett Library, but in record offices throughout the country. The minute books of a NUWSS branch, containing the records of monthly meetings, presumably looked sufficiently important (in a similar manner to WSPU prison diaries) to be kept by the descendants of its last trustee. I am aware that many more pieces of the jigsaw, individual diaries and letters, and minute books of complementary societies, for instance, of the National Union of Women Workers, lie in record offices and could be used to give a more rounded picture of local involvement.

Although *The Women's Suffrage Movement* is primarily a work of reference, a map to guide the reader, I trust that the individual lives and groupings, with all their foibles and contradictions, give depth and colour to build up, with a "pointillist" effect, a landscape teeming with life and incident.

A

ABADAM, ALICE (c. 1856–1940) Daughter of the High Sheriff of Carmarthen. She subscribed to the CENTRAL SOCIETY in 1905 and 1906–7. She signed, as an "Independent Socialist", the joint WOMEN'S SOCIAL POLITICAL UNION/Independent Labour Party manifesto issued at the January 1906 general election, subscribed to the WSPU in 1906–7, and attended the banquet given at the Savoy on 11 December 1906 to celebrate the release of the WSPU prisoners. She left the WSPU in 1907 to become a member of the first committee of the WOMEN'S FREEDOM LEAGUE. However, by 1908 she appears to have left the militant wing of the suffrage movement to become the president of the Beckenham branch of the LONDON SOCIETY FOR WOMEN'S SUFFRAGE and was president of the Norwood and District Women's Suffrage Society in 1913.

Alice Abadam was a peripatetic speaker to a variety of suffrage societies. In 1908 she addressed, over the course of a fortnight, a series of "women only" meetings arranged by the BIRMINGHAM SOCIETY FOR WOMEN'S SUFFRAGE (NUWSS) on the moral aspects of women's suffrage and on 21 August was speaking for the NUWSS in Whitby. *Votes for Women* described her in its 13 January 1911 issue as "that well-known speaker on social subjects". On that occasion she had been addressing the ACTRESSES' FRANCHISE LEAGUE. The next week she was speaking at a meeting of the WOMEN WRITERS' SUFFRAGE LEAGUE. She spoke to the MANSFIELD NUWSS in April 1909 and again in 1913 – on "How the Vote will affect the White Slave Traffic". She spoke to the BEDFORD NUWSS in December 1912. She was a speaker for the CHURCH LEAGUE FOR WOMEN'S SUFFRAGE after its formation in 1909, a supporter of the NEW CONSTITUTIONAL SOCIETY after it was founded in 1910, and was a prominent member and regular speaker for the CATHOLIC WOMEN'S SUFFRAGE SOCIETY after its formation in 1911. On 29 June 1914 she was the hostess of one of the tables for the Costume Dinner organized by the Actresses' Franchise League and the Women Writers' Suffrage League held at the Hotel Cecil. Evelina HAVERFIELD was among those sitting at her table. By 1916 Miss Abadam was chairman of the FEDERATED COUNCIL OF SUFFRAGE SOCIETIES.

In a pamphlet, *The Feminist Vote, Enfranchised or Emancipated?*, published in 1918, she wrote "The Constructive Feminist has to be no man's shadow. She must be herself – free to the very soul of sex servility. So, and only so, can she save a stricken world." In later years she was chairman on the sub-committee on art in the University of Wales.

When she died Alice Abadam was living at Brynmyrddin, Abergwili, Carmarthenshire. She left most of her estate to her niece, Mary Edith Morris, and the remainder for "the education advancement" of a great-niece, Margaret Morris. One of the founders of the CARMARTHEN Women's Suffrage Society in 1911 was Miss Morris of Brynmyrddin. The minutes of that society show that Miss Abadam was asked to speak at a meeting (but declined) and was to be held in reserve as president if the first choice refused.

Address: (1908) 97 Central Hill, Upper Norwood, London SE; (1940) 70 Hamilton Terrace, St John's Wood, London N.
Photograph: by Edringtons Ltd, 29 Bold St, Liverpool issued as a postcard; in E. Hill and O.F. Shafer, *Great Suffragists – and Why*, 1909; in Fawcett Library Collection.
Bibliography: E. Hill and O.F. Shafer (eds), *Great Suffragists – and Why*, 1909.

ABBOTT, ELIZABETH, MRS (1883–1957) Born Wilhelmina Hay Lamond, in Scotland; she later adopted the name Elizabeth. She was educated at the City of London School for Girls, in Brussels, and at University College, London. Between 1903 and 1906 she trained as a secretary and accountant.

In 1909 she became ORGANIZER for the EDINBURGH NATIONAL SOCIETY FOR WOMEN'S SUFFRAGE, carrying out a suffrage campaign in the Highlands in August, and in 1910 became a member of the executive committee of the SCOTTISH FEDERATION OF WOMEN'S SUFFRAGE. In 1910 she was also a member of the Scottish Committee that produced a Minority Report on Poor Law Reform. In 1911 she married George Frederick Abbott and became the mother of a son.

Between 1916, when she was released from her position with the Women's Municipal Party Committee, and 1918, she gave lecture tours in India, Australia and New Zealand on behalf of the Scottish Women's Hospital; almost single-handedly she raised over £60 000. In 1920 she was secretary of the INTERNATIONAL WOMAN SUFFFRAGE ALLIANCE and editor of its paper, *Jus Suffragii*. In 1923 she was a delegate from the NATIONAL UNION OF SOCIETIES FOR EQUAL CITIZENSHIP to the International Alliance of Women for Suffrage and Equal Citizenship. In 1926, with Chrystal MACMILLAN, she founded the Open Door Council, and eventually the Open Door International. She also worked for the Association for Moral and Social Hygiene for 40 years, for 10 of which she was its chairman. She was the executor of Chrystal MacMillan's will and Cicely HAMILTON left to her the copyright of all her books and plays. In her own will Elizabeth Abbott left to her daughter-in-law letters to Josephine Butler that had been given to her by the latter's grandson.

Address: (1913) 96 Church Street, Chelsea, London SW; (1923) 1 Burgess Hill, London NW2; (1934) Penbury Grove, Penn, Buckinghamshire; (1957) Freemans Farm, Thaxted, Essex.

Bibliography: L. Leneman, *In the Service of Life: The Story of Elsie Inglis and the Scottish Women's Hospitals*, 1994.

ABERDARE (WFL) Secretary (1913) Miss J. Phillips, BA, 8 Elm Grove, Aberdare.

ABERDEEN branch of the NATIONAL SOCIETY FOR WOMEN'S SUFFRAGE Founded by 1871, when the secretary was Mrs Bain of Ferry Hill Lodge. The society was in 1913 a member of the SCOTTISH FEDERATION OF WOMEN'S SUFFRAGE SOCIETIES. Secretary (NUWSS) (1909) Miss L.M. Murray, 626 King Street, Aberdeen; (1913) Mrs Firth, 65 Forest Avenue, Aberdeen. Office, 214 Union Street, Aberdeen.

ABERDEEN branch of the SCOTTISH UNIVERSITY WOMEN'S SUFFRAGE UNION Secretary (1913) Miss Rudmore Brown, 52 Beconsfield Place, Aberdeen.

ABERDEEN (WSPU) Organizer (1907) Miss Caroline PHILLIPS, 61 Albury Road, Aberdeen; (1913) Miss Fussell, 7 Bon Accord, Aberdeen.

ABERDEEN, ISHBEL MARIA GORDON, COUNTESS OF (1857–1939) (from 1916 Marchioness of Aberdeen and Temaire) née Ishbel Marjoribanks Educated privately, married the 7th Earl of Aberdeen in 1877, and became the mother of five children. By 1889 she was chairman of the WOMEN'S LIBERAL FEDERATION, becoming president of the WLF, in both England and Scotland, in 1900. She resigned from her membership of the Women's Council of the Scottish Liberal Federation only a few days before her death. She was a firm supporter of women's suffrage, being particularly aware of its importance to working women. She was a member of the SPECIAL APPEAL COMMITTEE in 1892–6. In 1906 she did, however, in a letter to the Prime Minister, Campbell-Bannerman, disassociate the WLF from any support for the growing militant suffrage movement. She was involved in many projects to give practical educational and social help to women and young girls, both on the Aberdeen estate and in London. In 1888 she was president of the SOCIETY FOR PROMOTING THE RETURN OF WOMEN AS COUNTY COUNCILLORS, remaining in that position with its successor, the WOMEN'S LOCAL GOVERNMENT SOCIETY. In 1888, at Washington, she was elected president of the newly formed International Council of Women. In 1893 she attended the World's Congress of Representative Women in Chicago and reported on the progress made by the Society for Promoting the Return of Women to all Local Governing Bodies (as the Women's Local Government Society was for a short period cumbrously named). In June 1899 she was the impetus behind the very successful International Council of Women quinquennial congress that was held in London, editing the seven volumes of the published transactions. She was present, and repeatedly re-elected as president, at subsequent ICW congresses, in Berlin in 1904, in Toronto in 1909, and in Rome in 1914.

Address: (1885) Dollis Hill, Kilburn, London NW; Haddo House, Aberdeen; (1907) 58 Grosvenor Street, London W.
Bibliography: Lord and Lady Aberdeen, *"We Twa": reminiscences*, 1925; M. Pentland, *A Bonnie Fechter: The Life of Ishbel Marjoribanks, Marchioness of Aberdeen and Temair, 1857–1939*, 1952.

ABERDEEN UNIVERSITY WOMAN SUFFRAGE ASSOCIATION

Formed in 1908, as the Aberdeen Women's Social and Franchise League, and was open to men and women students. In 1909 it joined the SCOTTISH UNIVERSITY WOMEN'S SUFFRAGE UNION and in March 1912 published a newsletter, perhaps the only issue. Secretary (1913) Miss M.L. Leitch, Aberdeen University Woman Suffrage Association, The University, Aberdeen.
Bibliography: L. Moore, *Bajanellas and Semilinas: Aberdeen University and the Education of Women, 1860–1920*, 1991.

ABERGAVENNY (NUWSS)

In 1913 the society was a member of the SOUTH WALES AND MONMOUTH FEDERATION OF THE NATIONAL UNION OF WOMEN'S SUFFRAGE SOCIETIES. Secretary (1913) *pro tem* Miss Gardner, Hawkhurst, Western Road, Abergavenny.

ABERNETHY (NUWSS)

In 1913 the society was a member of the SCOTTISH FEDERATION OF WOMEN'S SUFFRAGE SOCIETIES. Secretary (1913) Miss Williamson, Ochil View, Abernethy, Perthshire.

ABERYSTWYTH (NUWSS)

In 1913 the society was a member of the SOUTH WALES AND MONMOUTH FEDERATION OF THE NATIONAL UNION OF WOMEN'S SUFFRAGE SOCIETIES. Secretary (1913) Miss Miles Thomas, Somerville, South Terrace, Aberystwyth.

ACCRINGTON (NUWSS)

In 1913 the society was a member of the MANCHESTER AND DISTRICT FEDERATION OF THE NATIONAL UNION OF WOMEN'S SUFFRAGE SOCIETIES. Secretary (1913), Miss Florence Hoare, 5 Christ Church Terrace, Accrington, Lancashire.

ACOMB (NUWSS)

In 1913 the society was a member of the NORTH AND EAST RIDINGS OF YORKSHIRE FEDERATION OF THE NATIONAL UNION OF WOMEN'S SUFFRAGE SOCIETIES. Secretary (1909) Miss H. Westrope, Wayside, Poppleton Road, York; (1913) Mrs Beecroft, 6 Howe St, Acomb, York.

ACTIVE SERVICE LEAGUE (NUWSS)

On 12 February 1914 a suggestion was made at the Council meeting of the NATIONAL UNION OF WOMEN'S SUFFRAGE SOCIETIES, held in the Horticultural Hall in Westminster, that an Active Service Corps should be formed to revitalize the constitutional suffrage movement by bringing it to the attention of fresh categories of women; shop assistants were mentioned. The OXFORD WOMEN STUDENTS' SOCIETY, supported by many others, objected to the military terms suggested and it was finally agreed that the organization should be formed, but with the less militaristic title, "Active Service League", with Mrs FAWCETT as their "chief". It is more than likely that the idea for the ASL emanated from Katherine HARLEY, the instigator of the 1913 NUWSS PILGRIMAGE. The badge adopted by the ASL, an example of which is held in the Fawcett Archive Collection, is identical to the cockade worn during the Pilgrimage. A statement issued in May 1914 explained that "This League has been formed as an outcome of the Pilgrimage to combine the efforts of those who are willing to devote some time to openair propaganda in the cause of Women's Suffrage." It was suggested that "professional" women might like to devote a portion of their holidays to a healthy outdoor campaign. The aim was to speak at open-air meetings, sell the *Common Cause*, develop the FRIENDS OF WOMEN'S SUFFRAGE scheme, and distribute suffrage literature. It was suggested that "Saturday Afternoon Tramps and Bicycling Parties to villages and hamlets" might be undertaken. Maude ROYDEN was in charge of the ASL's *Common Cause* campaign. Under its "chief" and "League Leader", the ASL was the responsibility of "Federation Section Leaders", to whom reported a representative from each NUWSS society, the "Group Leader", who was in charge of her cohort of Leaguers. Uniform, probably very close to Mrs Harley's heart, was optional but recommended. It was suggested that it should comprise a dark green coat and skirt, white blouse, a tie in the colours of the NUWSS, a hat of soft felt in green, with the pilgrim's badge. A small haversack, of light brown waterproof with "NUWSS" in red lettering, was also recommended "to be worn at the back"; *Common Cause* sellers had special bags. A sample uniform was on display that summer at the Women's

Kingdom Exhibition. The coat and skirt could be obtained for £2 2s from Swan and Edgar and the rest of the uniform from Parnell in Victoria Street.

In this last summer before the war, the Oxford branch of the ASL had Tuesday Afternoon Expeditions planned for July and August "to visit from house to house giving away leaflets, making 'Friends of WS', selling the *Common Cause*", and preparing the way for an evening meeting. The NORTH-EASTERN FEDERATION reported that in June and July they carried on a very active campaign, their object being to ensure that before the next general election every village in the area should have heard a suffrage speaker at least once. They sold over 2000 copies of the *Common Cause* and acquired signatures to more than 1900 "Friends of Women's Suffrage" cards. The ASL did not survive the outbreak of war; many of the Leaguers were then able to involve themselves in even more active service.

Chief: Millicent Garrett Fawcett; The League Leader, Katherine Harley.

Archival source: NUWSS Annual report, 1914, Fawcett Library.

ACTRESSES' FRANCHISE LEAGUE Founded by Gertrude Elliott, Winifred MAYO, Sime SERUYA, and Adeline BOURNE when, in December 1908, they called 400 members of the London stage to a meeting in the Criterion Restaurant at Piccadilly Circus. The AFL neither supported nor condemned militancy. The League was open to anyone involved in the theatrical profession and its aim was to work for women's enfranchisement by educational methods, such as by holding propaganda meetings, selling suffrage literature, staging propaganda plays, and giving lectures. It was willing to assist all other suffrage societies. Members of the AFL were initially asked to send the League's secretary their touring lists, so that provincial suffrage societies could be told in advance of their presence in order to avail themselves of their services – such as reciting, singing, or speaking at meetings. In 1910–11 the League opened its own provincial branches in Edinburgh, Glasgow, Liverpool and Eastbourne and the local honorary secretaries of these branches then kept in touch with touring members of the League. The AFL charged a small amount to suffrage societies for supplying them with singers and reciters. AFL members on occasion gave the benefit of their experience to WSPU ORGANIZERS as to the best digs in which to stay when they arrived in a new area.

Besides committed activists such as Elizabeth ROBINS, Cicely HAMILTON, and Edith CRAIG, the AFL also had among its members many well-known performers of the Edwardian stage, including Ellen Terry, Lillah McCARTHY, Lena ASHWELL, Lillie Langtry, Nina Boucicault, Decima and Eva MOORE, Irene and Violet Vanbrugh, Athene Seyler, Sybil Thorndike and May Whitty. The husband of the AFL's president, Johnson Forbes Robertson, was the godson of David MASSON, and was himself a very active supporter of the campaign.

AFL members began their involvement in the suffrage campaign by reciting suffragist poetry, but soon began to compose suitable monologues and duologues. The play department was then placed under the control of Inez BENSUSAN who oversaw the writing, collection and publication of AFL suffrage drama (*see* PLAYS). In May 1909 the AFL provided the WSPU Prince's Skating Rink Exhibition with a very full programme of entertainments. Over the course of a week, 18 different entertainments were presented and over £360 raised for WSPU funds. The AFL's first fund-raising matinée, in conjunction with the WOMEN WRITERS' SUFFRAGE LEAGUE, was held in November 1909 at the Scala Theatre. For this Edith Craig produced Cicely Hamilton's *Pageant of Great Women*. By 1910 the League had its own offices in London, decorated in the AFL colours of pink and green (with blinds embroidered with the League's badge and name).

The League held monthly meetings at the Criterion Restaurant as well as drawing-room meetings and, from 1911, "East End meetings". At the first of these, held in April 1911 at Bow Baths Hall, the AFL after an agenda of speeches, songs, and recitations staged Henry Arncliffe Sennett's *An Englishwoman's Home*. In 1912 the League affiliated to the FEDERATED COUNCIL OF SUFFRAGE SOCIETIES and in April 1913 presented its own suffrage petition to the House of Commons. From 1913 men were able to join a "Men's Group" of the AFL, so that actors, dramatists and other men connected with the theatre were able to show active sympathy with the women's cause. Maud Arncliffe SENNETT's husband,

Henry, had already had his play, *An Englishwoman's Home*, published by the League. The AFL's membership rose from 360 in 1910, to 550 in 1911, and by 1914 stood at 900.

After the outbreak of war in August 1914 the AFL, at the instigation of Lena AsHWELL, launched the "Women's Theatre Camps Entertainments", which travelled round camps and hospitals. The AFL annual report recorded that, "Over and over again we are told what a treat it is to perform for the Woman's Theatre, because it is the quality of the artist's work that procures the engagement, and not the accident of having found grace in the managerial eye." AFL members, such as Kitty MARION, in the years before the war had protested against the tactics used by theatrical employment agencies. From August 1915 the AFL also organized the "British Women's Hospital". On 13 March 1918 the AFL took part in the NATIONAL UNION OF WOMEN'S SUFFRAGE SOCIETIES' victory celebration at the Queen's Hall and was still in existence in 1934. The AFL's banner, "hanging masks of comedy and tragedy framed by wreaths of ribbons stencilled in the AFL colours of pink and green", was carried in the Coronation Procession of 17 June 1911 and is now held in the collection of the Museum of London.
President (1913) Mrs Forbes Robertson; honorary secretary (1913) Adeline Bourne; honorary treasurer (1913) Mrs Carl Leyel; organizing secretary (?–1911) Joan Dugdale (*see* Una DUVAL); (1911, 1913) Gertrude CONOLAN.
Address: (1913) 2 Robert Street, Strand, London WC; (1917) 93 Oakley Street, London SW3.
Archival source: Annual reports of the Actresses' Franchise League, Fawcett Library.
Bibliography: J. Holledge, *Innocent Flowers: women in the Edwardian theatre*, 1981; D. Spender and C. Hayman, *How the Vote Was Won and Other Suffragette Plays*, 1985; S. Stowell, *A Stage of Their Own: Feminist Playwrights of the Suffrage Era*, 1992.

AINSWORTH, LAURA FRANCES (1885–1958) Born at Blything, Northumberland, the daughter of a school inspector. She was educated in Salisbury and became a teacher, eventually resigning her position in order to work full-time for the WOMEN'S SOCIAL AND POLITICAL UNION. She was working for the WSPU in London in the spring of 1909 and then joined Gladice KEEVIL in June as a much-needed additional ORGANIZER in the Midlands, based in Birmingham. On 22 September 1909 she was sentenced to two weeks' imprisonment as a result of her part in the disruption of Asquith's meeting at the Bingley Hall. She and the others involved, who included Charlotte MARSH and Mary LEIGH, immediately began a hunger strike, the militant tactic that had recently been adopted for the first time by a WSPU prisoner, Marion Wallace-DUNLOP. The governor of Winson Green Prison was willing to feed the hunger-strikers by force; Marion Wallace-Dunlop had been released from Holloway before completing her sentence. The Prison Visitors' minutes noted of Laura Ainsworth that "she is very determined and it is necessary still to administer food through the tube". She made a formal complaint about having food forced upon her but, according to the Visiting Committee, had no complaint about how it was done. She gave a description of her experience in *Votes for Women*, 8 October 1909, and in a letter to Marion Wallace-Dunlop. She was taken to a nursing home on her release and criminal proceedings, alleging assault, were instigated on her behalf against the prison authorities. The case ensured that maximum publicity was given to the new level of militancy. In *Prisons and Prisoners*, 1914, Lady Constance LYTTON recorded that it was a meeting with Laura Ainsworth (whom, although she does not name her, she likened on this occasion to a Fra Angelico angel) in the nursing home, that inspired her to "take the very next opportunity of making my protest with a stone". In January 1910 Laura Ainsworth worked with Mary PHILLIPS in Bradford during the general election campaign. In February 1910 she was the WSPU organizer in Bolton and Bury, was then based at the new WSPU shop in Charing Cross Road, organizing poster parades to advertise *Votes for Women*, and in September she ran a holiday campaign in Southend. In February 1911 she was the organizer in Maidstone and North Kent, based first at 22 Stuart Road, Gillingham and then at 21 Oxford Street, Margate. She moved back to Newcastle in July 1911, taking over as organizer from Annie WILLIAMS.

In September 1912, after the split between the Pankhursts and the Pethick-Lawrences, Laura Ainsworth, with Mona TAYLOR, resigned from the WSPU in Newcastle. In 1913 she became honorary

secretary and organizer of the north-eastern branch of the NATIONAL POLITICAL LEAGUE. In 1934 she was a member of the central committee and chairman of the North-East Area of the Women's Section of the British Legion and honorary secretary of the League of Nations Union in the north-east.
Address: (1934) Chipchase, Wark-on-Tyne.
Photograph: in *Votes for Women*, 8 October 1909.
Archival source: Suffragette Fellowship Collection, Museum of London; Birmingham Archives and Local History Library.

AINTREE (WFL) Secretary (1913) Mrs Shaw, 15 Chatsworth Ave, Aintree, Lancashire.

ALDEBURGH (NUWSS) In 1913 the society was a member of the EASTERN COUNTIES FEDERATION OF THE NATIONAL UNION OF WOMEN'S SUFFRAGE SOCIETIES. Secretary (1913) Mrs Sharp, Whitebays, Aldeburgh, Suffolk.

ALDERSHOT (NUWSS) In 1913 the society was a member of the SURREY, SUSSEX, AND HANTS FEDERATION OF THE NATIONAL UNION OF WOMEN'S SUFFRAGE SOCIETIES. Secretary (1913) Mrs Elise C. Garrett, Sherwood, Church Lane, Aldershot, Hampshire.

ALIASES On occasion women involved in the suffrage movement used aliases, either to protect their family from obloquy by association, or, more commonly, in their attempts to evade the police. Home Office papers reveal that officials were usually able to penetrate the aliases. However, the SUFFRAGETTE FELLOWSHIP was less successful and its *Roll of Honour of Suffragette Prisoners* includes aliases in addition to the real women, thereby inflating the number of those imprisoned. The following women and their aliases have been identified; doubtless there were others.

Name	Alias
Mary Aldham	Mary Wood
Olive BARTELS	Margaret Cunningham
Frances BARTLETT	Frances Satterly
Olive BEAMISH	Phyllis Brady
Annie Bell	Hannah Booth; Elizabeth Bell
Hilda BURKITT	Byron
Kate E.G. Cardo	Catherine Swain
Eileen CASEY	Eleanor Cleary; Irene Casey
Evelyn Cheshire	Evelyn Taylor
Gwendoline Cook	Ethel Cox
Helen CRAGGS	Helen Millar
Ethel Crawley	Mary Carlyn
Emily Wilding DAVISON	Mary Brown
Elsie Duval	Millicent Dean; Eveline Dukes
Emily Fussell	Georgina Lloyd
Theresa GARNETT	Annie O'Sullivan
Florence Graves	Frances Gordon
Nellie HALL	Marie Roberts
Helen HANSON	Helen Rice
Edith Hudson	Mary Brown
Florence Hull	Mary Gray
Jessie KENNEY	Constance Burrows; Mary Fordyce
Lilian LENTON	Ida Inkley
Leslie McMurdo	Leslie Lawless
Kitty MARION	Aunt Maggie
Selina Martin	Mary Richards
Ethel MOORHEAD	Margaret Morrison; Edith Johnson; Mary Humphreys
Elsie MYERS	Marjorie Manners
Christabel PANKHURST	Amy Richards
Frances PARKER	Janet Arthur
Rachel Peace	Jane Short
Mary PHILLIPS	Margaret Paterson
Grace ROE	Grace Courtenay
Grace Scholey	Freda Graham
Arabella SCOTT	Catherine Reid
Muriel SCOTT	Jane C. Dark; Ellen Smith
Ella Stevenson	Ethel Slade
Geraldine Stevenson	Grace Stuart
Grace Cameron Swan	Greta Cameron
Mary Ellen (Nellie) Taylor	Mary Wyan
Olive WHARRY	Joyce Lock(e); Phyllis North
Laetitia Withall	Leslie Hall
Gertrude Wilkinson	Jessie Howard

ALLAN, JANIE (*c.* 1868–1968) Daughter of Alexander Allan, the owner of the Allan Shipping Line.

The family was known for its socialist principles. She was one of the founder members of the GLASGOW AND WEST OF SCOTLAND ASSOCIATION FOR WOMEN'S SUFFRAGE when it was formed in May 1902. She gave generous financial support to the society, was one of its vice-presidents, a member of its executive committee, and in 1903 agreed to represent the society on the committee of the NATIONAL UNION OF WOMEN'S SUFFRAGE SOCIETIES. However, in December 1905 she asked that her name be deleted from the list of vice-presidents as she did not feel able to give as much help to the society as she would like. Although she was still a member of the executive committee, she attended very few committee meetings after that, but was present at that held on 11 December 1906 at which Helen FRASER, ORGANIZER for the WOMEN'S SOCIAL AND POLITICAL UNION, explained that society's policy of militancy. At a meeting in January Janie Allan backed a motion that regretted that officials of the GWSAWS had not appeared on a WSPU platform. In March 1907 she herself arranged a meeting at St Andrew's Hall "at which officials of the WSPU and others [were] to speak". The Association eventually agreed to help. She subscribed to the WSPU in 1907 but did not actually resign from the NUWSS committee until February 1909 "as her sympathies were more with the militant section of the movement, but as she knew that this Association had done and was still doing good work she would still remain a member [of the Association]". She gave £50 to the WSPU Scottish Campaign Fund in September 1909, £50 to its General Election Fund in December 1909, and £250 to the WSPU "War Chest" in November 1910. She also gave financial support to the WOMEN'S FREEDOM LEAGUE until 1912.

On 27 March 1912 she was sentenced to four months' imprisonment in Holloway after taking part in the London window-smashing campaign. At her trial she drew attention to white slave traffic, the "sweating" of women workers, and the shamefully short punishments given to those who had "outraged" little girls. About these, she said, there was no outcry; that was reserved for broken glass. She maintained an interest in this aspect of the women's movement, leaving in her will a bequest to the Glasgow branch of the National Vigilance Association. A petition protesting against her imprisonment in 1912 was signed by 10 500 Glaswegians. While in prison she was generous in distributing small comforts to her fellow prisoners; Mary D. THOMPSON noted that she was given cake, strawberries and cherries by Janie Allan. Zoe PROCTER recorded that Janie Allan was "always correctly dressed for Exercise in hat and lemon kid gloves". In May she barricaded herself in her cell and it took three men, using crowbars, 45 minutes to force an entrance. She went on hunger strike and was forcibly fed for one week. She wrote in a letter "I did not resist at all, but sat quite still as if it were a dentist's chair, and yet the effect on my health was most disastrous – I am a very strong woman and absolutely sound in heart and lungs, but it was not till five months later, that I was able to take any exercise or begin to feel in my usual health again". She was released on the completion of her sentence at the end of June. Margaret McPHUN wrote a poem, "To a Fellow Prisoner (Miss Janie Allan)", that was included in *Holloway Jingles*, published by the Glasgow branch of the WSPU; it begins "Upon thy pure and stedfast brow there lies/ A tender sorrow".

Janie Allan was a supporter of the TAX RESISTANCE LEAGUE; in March 1913 she refused to pay her supertax, and lost the subsequent case. In 1913 she was a vice-president of the NATIONAL POLITICAL LEAGUE. By 1914 she appears to have been for a time WSPU organizer in the west of Scotland, conducting much of her suffrage business from the premises of the Society of Lady Artists' CLUB at 5 Blythswood Square in Glasgow. She also supported the NORTHERN MEN'S FEDERATION FOR WOMEN'S SUFFRAGE after it was formed in mid-1913. In St Andrew's Hall, Glasgow on 9 March 1914 she fired a blank from a pistol at a policeman who attempted to arrest Mrs PANKHURST. There is no mention of this action in the official reports of the event, although one of the women who completed a form of evidence organized by Janie Allan noted that she had seen one woman there with a pistol. She does not name her but notes "She was defending the platform from a band of police with drawn batons." Gertrude Harding, in a report of the meeting quoted in A. Raeburn, *The Militant Suffragettes*, 1973, does name the woman as Janie Allan. From Paris Janie Allan received a very supportive letter from Christabel Pankhurst, congratulating her on the events at St Andrew's Hall. After the WSPU's allegations of ill-treatment by the police at this meeting were dismissed, Janie Allan was determined that there should be an official inquiry. Her advisers, however, were unhappy when in May, during the preparations, she went to London to take part in the deputation to the King. One of them wrote to her "I am told that the Lord Provost asked for your present address today. It is just as well that it did not happen to be Holloway." She was arrested during the deputation and was imprisoned; nothing came of the demand for an inquiry.

Janie Allan was extremely concerned about forcible feeding in Scottish prisons, which only began in February 1914 with the case of Ethel MOORHEAD. She exchanged clothes with Ethel Moorhead while visiting her at the doctor's home where she was recovering from her ordeal, in order that her escape might be effected, under the eyes of the police, in Janie Allan's car. Among Janie Allan's papers in the National Library of Scotland is a file solely devoted to newspaper cuttings relevant to forcible feeding. In June she wrote to the Chairman of the Prison Commission reminding him that Whitekirk had been burnt down in reprisal for the forcible feeding of Ethel Moorhead, and now that Arabella SCOTT and "Frances Gordon" were likely to be force fed in Perth prison it was not difficult to imagine what the result might be. "It seems a pity to enter upon such a course especially in view of the Royal visit to Scotland [the King and Queen were to tour in July] which would, of course, present many opportunities for protests of a memorable and disastrous nature." The Director of Public Prosecutions advised that she should not be prosecuted for making such threats. Janie Allan was one of Mrs Pankhurst's most important financial supporters, although at this time she was in correspondence about the forcible feeding of Arabella Scott both with the WSPU at Lincoln's Inn House and with Mrs PETHICK-LAWRENCE and the VOTES FOR WOMEN FELLOWSHIP.

After the August 1914 amnesty Janie Allan went to considerable lengths to get answers from the Scottish Office about the position of both those women who were on licence and those who, like Frances PARKER, were unconvicted. In August 1914 she refused Maud Arncliffe SENNETT's suggestion that she should take over the organization of the Northern Men's Federation for Women's Suffrage, noting that she was exhausted.

In September 1914 she sent money to Louisa Garrett ANDERSON and Flora MURRAY to provide the initial funding of the Women's Hospital Corps. During the First World War she was associated with the Scottish Council for Women's Trades and in 1939 was still a member of its general council. In 1923 she was chairman of the Glasgow-based Women's Watch Committee, which aimed to monitor the treatment of women's interests by public bodies. After the First World War she kept in touch with Ethel Moorhead and Frances Parker, giving the confirmation to the Scottish authorities of the latter's death and acting as executrix to her will. In 1918 Janie Allan was a member of the SUFFRAGETTES OF THE WSPU but when, in 1931, she was asked by the SUFFRAGETTE FELLOWSHIP to furnish them with details of her suffrage activities she declined, replying that she did not think them of any interest. Her will, although detailing many individual bequests, makes no mention of any mementos of the suffrage movement. She did, however, hold at the time of her death five £1 shares in the "Time and Tide Publishing Co" and had in 1963 subscribed to the Pethick-Lawrence Memorial Appeal Fund.

Address: (1913) Greystone, Prestwick, Ayrshire; (1934) Invergloy House, Invergloy, Inverness; (1968) East Lodge, Invergloy, Inverness.

Archival sources: Janie Allan Collection, National Library of Scotland; Scottish Record Office.

ALLEN, MARY SOPHIA (1878–1964) OBE Born in Cardiff, educated at Princess Helena College, Ealing. Her father was manager of the Great Western Railway. According to the account in her autobiography, *Lady in Blue*, she was inspired by Annie KENNEY's oratory and was then given an ultimatum by her father, either to give up her involvement in the suffragette movement or to leave his house. So she left, although her father continued to support her financially. She volunteered to take part in the February 1909 deputation from the Women's Parliament in Caxton Hall to the House of Commons, was arrested, with 28 others, and sentenced to a month's imprisonment in Holloway. After her release she worked for the West of England branch of the WOMEN'S SOCIAL AND POLITICAL UNION in Newport and Cardiff as an honorary ORGANIZER (she stressed that she was not paid) until 29 June when she was arrested after breaking a window in the Home Office while taking part in another deputation. With ten others, she was released early from her sentence after hunger-striking, while demanding political prisoner status. Marion Wallace-DUNLOP had, a few days before, initiated this form of militancy. Mary Allen was the first woman to receive a hunger-strike medal from the hands of Mrs PETHICK-LAWRENCE at St James's Hall in August 1909. In November 1909, with Vera WENTWORTH, she broke the windows of the Bristol Liberal Club during a visit made by Winston Churchill to the city and was sentenced to two weeks' imprisonment. She went on hunger strike and this time was forcibly fed. A fellow prisoner, Nurse Pitman, reported in *Votes for Women* that she had heard "the cries and deep moans of Miss Mary Allen, who was in a cell not very far from her own". Mary Allen was released early from her sentence and recorded that her digestion had been permanently affected. She was forbidden by Mrs Pankhurst and her doctors to take part in any further militant activity. In an interview in 1974 Grace ROE remarked that at this time Mary Allen was "very feminine, very delicate". In February 1912 she took over from Dorothy BOWKER as organizer in Eastbourne, Bexhill, and Hastings and St Leonards. In early 1914 she was moved to Scotland, succeeding Lucy BURNS as organizer in Edinburgh. On 6 May Christabel Pankhurst, writing from Paris to Janie ALLAN, remarked that "in Edinburgh a small handful of people . . . are decidedly cantankerous, and the person who is organising for the time being is made to feel the effect of this. These people criticise Miss Mary Allen at the present time". The lot of the organizer was never smooth. There appears to have been a suggestion that the Scots did not care to have an English organizer.

With the outbreak of war, chance led Mary Allen to hear of the work of Margaret Damer Dawson in setting up a band of Women Police Volunteers. She stressed in her books that it was through her experience in the militant suffrage movement, which brought her into contact with police and prisons, that she realized how necessary it was that women culprits should not "be handled by men". She was appointed sub-commandant of the Women Police Service and, in 1919, commandant, a rank she held until 1938, and was the founder and editor of the *Policewoman's Review*. She was awarded the OBE at the end of the war. She stood, unsuccessfully, as an Independent Liberal candidate for St George's Westminster at the election in November 1922. In 1925 she was a member of the executive committee of the Forum Club, the London centre for Women's Institute members (*see under* CLUBS). She aroused controversy in the 1930s by speaking in praise of Hitler, whom she actually visited in 1934. Her interest in fascism brought criticism from MPs in 1940 when she was head of the Women's Auxiliary Service, following which that movement's association with Civil Defence ended. She worked as a journalist, contributing articles to *Good Housekeeping*, *Pearsons* and daily and weekly papers in London and the provinces and died, almost penniless, in a Croydon nursing home.

Address: (1911) Bowry House, Wraysbury, Bucks; (1912) 46 Hurlingham Court, London SW; (1934) 1 Morpeth Terrrace, London SW1.
Photograph: in her books.
Bibliography: M. Allen, *The Pioneer Policewoman*, 1925; *Woman at the Cross Roads*, 1934; *Lady in Blue*, 1936.

ALLOA committee of the NATIONAL SOCIETY FOR WOMEN'S SUFFRAGE Formed in 1872. In 1913 the society was a member of the SCOTTISH FEDERATION OF WOMEN'S SUFFRAGE SOCIETIES. Secretary (1913) Mrs Andrew, 20 Fenton Street, Alloa, Clackmannanshire.

ALTRINCHAM (NUWSS) In existence by 1908. In 1910 it became a member of the MANCHESTER AND DISTRICT FEDERATION OF THE NATIONAL UNION OF WOMEN'S SUFFRAGE SOCIETIES. Secretary (1909) Miss M. Sugden, Beevor House, Bowdon, Cheshire; (1913) Miss A. Uttley, Sidcot, Hale, Altrincham, Cheshire.

ALVA (NUWSS) In 1913 the society was a member of the SCOTTISH FEDERATION OF WOMEN'S SUFFRAGE SOCIETIES. Secretary (1913) Miss Mary J. Lodge, Strude Cottage, Alva, Clackmannanshire.

AMBERLEY, KATHERINE LOUISA, VISCOUNTESS (1842–74) Fourth daughter of Lord and Lady

Stanley of Alderley, and sister of Rosalind Howard, Countess of CARLISLE. Her mother was a passionate supporter of Italian unification and one of the founders of Girton College. In 1864 Kate Stanley married Viscount Amberley, son of Lord John Russell, a former Liberal prime minister. She was introduced to Helen TAYLOR in 1865 by Harriet GROTE and in 1866 signed the women's suffrage petition, stressing, when she returned it, that she was only in favour of women of property having the vote. Her husband, a Radical Liberal much influenced by John Stuart MILL, was from 1867 briefly MP for Nottingham. Emily DAVIES, who met her for the first time in June 1866, wrote "I like Lady Amberley very much. She seems very simple and good and alive." The liking was mutual. Kate Amberley became part of the circle of women that included Elizabeth Garrett (see Elizabeth Garrett ANDERSON), who became her doctor, and Frances Power COBBE, working together for a variety of women's causes. In 1866, with her husband, she was a member of the first general committee of Elizabeth Garrett's St Mary's Dispensary for Women and Children. With her husband, she spent several months in 1867 in America, where she met Lucretia Mott (after whom she later named her daughter), Harriet Beecher Stowe, and Elizabeth Cady Stanton, "a lady who lectures and speaks on women suffrage and prostitution".

In 1868 she became the first president of the BRISTOL AND WEST OF ENGLAND branch of the NATIONAL SOCIETY FOR WOMEN'S SUFFRAGE. On 25 May 1870 she gave a lecture, later published as "The Claims of Women", to a large audience in the Subscription Rooms at Stroud. She wrote in her Journal "There was hardly any applause & it seemed to fall very flat ... I had written my lecture last October and shown it to Miss Taylor at Avignon who persuaded me to give it as a lecture." She remarked in a letter to Helen Taylor that people had expressed surprise to her afterwards that a woman could lecture and still look like a lady. She added that the idea of women's suffrage seemed new to her audience. This is a little surprising; a noticeable clutch of women from Stroud, including the wives of the blacksmith, outfitters, and brush-maker, had signed the 1866 petition. One might conclude that this was not the class of women invited to comprise the audience for Kate Amberley's lecture. It did, however, cause a considerable stir in the correspondence columns of *The Times* and, we now know, the opprobrium of Queen Victoria, who wrote to Theodore Martin, "The Queen is most anxious to enlist everyone who can speak or write or join in checking this mad, wicked folly of 'Women's Rights' with all its attendant horrors, on which her poor feeble sex is bent, forgetting every sense of womanly feeling and propriety. Lady Amberley ought to get a *good whipping*." Lady Amberley received many congratulatory letters from her own circle and from Harriet Beecher Stowe, to whom she had sent the text, who wrote "there are weak fashionables here in America who will hear a Viscountess or Duchess when they would scoff at Miss Stanton and Susan Anthony".

Lady Amberley worked hard to set up a Suffrage Committee in Stroud and by June 1870 it had 12 members. In 1872 she became president of the Monmouthshire Society for Women's Suffrage and the mother of Bertrand Russell, to whom Helen Taylor stood godmother. In addition to her work for the women's suffrage campaign she was, from 1871 until her death from diphtheria (caught while nursing her daughter), a member of the executive committee of the Married Women's Property Committee.

Address: (1865) Rodborough Manor, Stroud, Gloucestershire; (1872) Ravenscroft, Chepstow, Monmouthshire.
Portrait: with her sister Rosalind, by Lowes Cato Dickinson, no date, but pre-1864, in private collection (photograph in National Portrait Gallery archive); posthumous portrait by Elizabeth Guinness, from a photograph of 1872, in Helen Blackburn collection, Girton College archive, reproduced in H. Blackburn, *Record of Women's Suffrage*, 1902.
Archival source: Mill–Taylor Papers, London School of Economics.
Bibliography: Lady Amberley, "The claims of women", *Fortnightly Review*, 1870; B. & P. Russell (eds), *The Amberley Papers: The Letters and Diaries of Lord and Lady Amberley*, 1937; R. Fulford, *Votes for Women*, 1957.

AMBLESIDE AND DISTRICT (NUWSS) In 1913 the society was a member of the NORTH-WESTERN FEDERATION OF THE NATIONAL UNION OF WOMEN'S SUFFRAGE SOCIETIES. President (1909) Mrs Cunliffe, Croft, Ambleside; Secretary (1913) Charles G. Boullen, Roselands, Ambleside, Westmorland.

AMERSHAM branch of the UNITED SUFFRAGISTS Founded in mid 1914. Honorary secretary: Mrs Drinkwater, Fieldtop, Amersham on the Hill.

AMOS, SARAH MACLARDIE, MRS (c. 1833–1908) Born in Manchester, granddaughter of Jabez Bunting, who was the leading figure in Weslyan Methodism in the first half of the nineteenth century, a prominent supporter of Catholic Emancipation, of the 1832 Reform Bill, and a member of the Anti-Slavery Committee. Her brother, Percy Bunting, was editor from 1882 of the *Contemporary Review*. Sarah Bunting joined the executive committee of the LONDON NATIONAL SOCIETY FOR WOMEN'S SUFFRAGE in 1867. She was, apparently, superintendent of the College for Working Women in Queen Square, retaining her post for a time after her marriage to Sheldon Amos in 1870. They had two children. She was an active member of the National Vigilance Association and of the WOMEN'S LOCAL GOVERNMENT SOCIETY, which, as the SOCIETY FOR PROMOTING THE RETURN OF WOMEN AS COUNTY COUNCILLORS, was founded at a meeting held at her brother's house in 1888. A Radical, she was returned as a member of the Marylebone vestry in 1894 and was a member of the executive committee of the WOMEN'S LIBERAL FEDERATION in 1898. She was also a founding member, in 1889, of the Women's Trade Union Association, was a member of the committee of the Women's Temperance Association and on that of the National Union of Women Workers. She subscribed to the CENTRAL SOCIETY FOR WOMEN'S SUFFRAGE from 1905 until her death in Cairo, where the family spent much of the time and where her son was a judge. In June 1892 an article by her on "The Woman's Suffrage Question" was published in the *Contemporary Review*.
Address: (1876) 27 Cheyne Walk, Chelsea, London; (1901) 14 Grosvenor Road, Westminster, London; (1902) St Ermin's Hotel, Westminster, London.
Photograph: carte de visite in Josephine Butler Collection, Fawcett Library.
Bibliography: obituary in *Englishwoman's Review*, 15 April 1908.

AMOS, SHELDON, PROFESSOR (1835–86) Son of the first professor of law at University College, London, and then Downing Professor of the Laws of England at Cambridge, he himself was educated at Clare College, Cambridge, and, in 1869, became professor of jurisprudence at University College, London. He was a friend of P.A. and Clementia TAYLOR and taught law at the Men and Women's College, where Sarah Bunting, whom he married in 1870, was superintendent. He was an advocate of the higher education and the political emancipation of women. He was a member of the executive committee of the LONDON NATIONAL SOCIETY FOR WOMEN'S SUFFRAGE until 1871 when, as an opponent of the Contagious Diseases Acts, he joined Jacob BRIGHT in founding the CENTRAL COMMITTEE OF THE NATIONAL SOCIETY, the executive committee of which he was then a member for many years. He was a founding member of the Vigilance Association, an active member of the National Association for the Repeal of the Contagious Diseases Acts, and wrote the legal history of regulated prostitution, *Laws for the Regulation of Vice*, 1877. He was also the author of *Difference of Sex Considered as a Topic of Jurisprudence and Legislation*, 1870.
Photograph: carte de visite in Josephine Butler Collection, Fawcett Library.

ANDERSON, ELIZABETH GARRETT, MRS (1836–1917) Daughter of Newson Garrett, a malter in Aldeburgh. Among her sisters were Agnes GARRETT and Millicent Garrett FAWCETT. From the age of 15, with another sister, Louisa (*see* SMITH), she attended a school in Blackheath. In 1854 on a visit to friends in Northumberland, Jane and Annie Crow, she met Emily DAVIES. A friendship developed that lasted their lifetimes and from this friendship spread a network that effected the entrance of women into higher education, medicine, and politics. Millicent Fawcett later identified this visit as a turning point in history. In 1865 Elizabeth Garrett, having received constant support from her father and from Emily Davies, was the first woman in England to become a licentiate of the Society of Apothecaries. In the same year she was a founding member of the KENSINGTON SOCIETY. In 1866 as Elizabeth Garrett, LSA, she signed the petition for the enfranchisement of women householders that she, with Jane Crow (who was living with her at the time), Emily Davies, Bessie Raynes PARKES, Jessie BOUCHERETT, and Barbara BODICHON initiated and which she, with Emily Davies, presented in person to John

Stuart MILL on 7 June. In October 1866 she was present at the meeting that proposed to form itself into a provisional committee to carry on the struggle to obtain the parliamentary franchise for duly qualified women (*see* LONDON PROVISIONAL PETITION COMMITTEE). However, like Barbara Bodichon, it was probably at this stage that she withdrew from direct involvement in the suffrage cause, although she did subscribe to the ENFRANCHISEMENT OF WOMEN COMMITTEE, 1866–7. Her name was not included in the proposed permanent committee. She was never, until 1910, a member of the executive committee of any of the suffrage societies. Louisa Garrett ANDERSON notes in the biography of her mother that she thought "it would be unwise to be identified with a second unpopular cause. Nevertheless she gave her whole-hearted adherence".

In 1870 Elizabeth Garrett was the first woman to be elected to a London School Board, the body newly devised to supplement the voluntary education system and for which women rate-payers were eligible to vote. She polled three times as many votes as the next highest candidate, T.H. Huxley. She was one of the first women in England ever to face public election, the others being Emily Davies, Lydia BECKER, and Maria Grey. Her campaign team included Henry FAWCETT; the Revd Llewelyn Davies, brother of Emily; John and Alice WESTLAKE; Prof. Norman Lockyer, brother-in-law of Annie Leigh BROWNE, and her future husband, J.G.S. Anderson. Although never a member of the works committee of the London School Board, her medical experience on the effects of bad drainage and ventilation led to her acceptance as an *ex officio* expert. Interestingly J.J. Stevenson, brother of Flora and Louisa STEVENSON, and cousin of J.G.S. Anderson, was the co-architect of many of the new LSB schools. As well as her school board activities, which lasted until 1873, she continued to develop her own medical practice, launched a new hospital for women, promoted the medical education of women, and gave birth to three children.

Out of the public gaze her support of the suffrage cause continued. On 17 June 1884 she chaired a large suffrage meeting in the St James's Hall and certainly in 1889 she was a member of the CENTRAL COMMITTEE OF THE NATIONAL SOCIETY FOR WOMEN'S SUFFRAGE of which her sister, Millicent Fawcett, was the honorary secretary, and she subscribed to the LONDON SOCIETY FOR WOMEN'S SUFFRAGE in 1906–7. By 1908, the year in which she became the first woman to be elected mayor, of Aldeburgh, despite ties of sisterly loyalty, she left the NATIONAL UNION OF WOMEN'S SUFFRAGE SOCIETIES for the WOMEN'S SOCIAL AND POLITICAL UNION, took part in a "raid" on the House of Commons, was visited by Mrs PANKHURST, and, for good measure, gave a small donation to the WOMEN'S FREEDOM LEAGUE. In May 1909 her involvement became quite public when she opened the first day of the WSPU's Exhibition at the Prince's Skating Rink with a speech, reported in *Votes for Women*, 21 May 1909, in which she set out her reasons for being a suffragette and, to shouts of "Bravo", stressed that she now supported militant methods. In October 1909 she undertook a short tour of the west country with Annie KENNEY. In December 1909 she gave £50 to the WSPU's General Election Fund and in April 1910 opened the first day of the Scottish WSPU Exhibition in Glasgow. On 11 June she wrote to her sister, Millicent Fawcett, that she was going to London on 18 June to take part in the WSPU procession and "shall for once walk all the way by way of special protest". On 18 November 1910 she was present at the centre of the militant cause when she appeared with Mrs Pankhurst at the head of a deputation to the prime minister. She, Hertha AYRTON and Mrs Pankhurst stood on the steps of the St Stephen's entrance to the House of Commons from 1.30 pm to 3.30 pm until conducted inside by Asquith's secretary, who then told them that the prime minister would not receive them. As a protest they remained standing on the steps until 6 pm when the House rose. The surrounding debacle quickly gave the day the sobriquet "Black Friday". It is interesting to contrast two images, both created in 1910, in which Elizabeth Garrett Anderson is a central player. One is *The Apple Seller*, the oil painting by Bertha NEWCOMBE, which depicts Emily Davies and Elizabeth Garrett, in crinolines, coyly revealing the 1866 suffrage petition to J.S. Mill in Westminster Hall. The other treats the reality of events 44 years later. On one side of a double spread of the 25 November 1910 issue of *Votes for Women*, Elizabeth Garrett Anderson stands, looking decidedly truculent, barred, with Emmeline Pankhurst, from the House of Commons; on the facing page Ada WRIGHT lies, having been struck to the ground, shielding her face. However, after the violence and window-smashing following the failure of the Conciliation Bill at the end of 1911 she was no longer able to support militancy. In July 1912 she signed, with Millicent Fawcett, Sir Edward Grey and Elizabeth Wolstenholme ELMY, among others, a public protest against the militancy of the WSPU. In 1910 she was asked if she would be president of the TAX RESISTANCE LEAGUE, but declined, offering instead to sit on its committee, of which she was still a member in 1913. Increasing frailty of mind did, however, soon lead to her retirement from public life.

Address: (1866) 20 Upper Berkeley Street, London W; (1874) 4 Upper Berkeley Street, London W; (1917) Alde House, Aldeburgh, Suffolk.

Portrait: by Laura Herford, Girton College; by J.S. Sargent, exhibited at Sargent exhibition held at the Royal Academy in 1926 (illustrated in its catalogue), Elizabeth Garrett Anderson Hospital; by unknown artist, British Medical Association; by unknown artist, Wellcome Institute.

Bibliography: B. Stephen, *Emily Davies and Girton College*, 1927; L. Garrett Anderson, *Elizabeth Garrett Anderson*, 1939; J. Manton, *Elizabeth Garrett Anderson*, 1965; P. Hollis, *Ladies Elect: Women in English Local Government, 1865–1914*, 1987.

ANDERSON, LOUISA GARRETT (1873–1943) CBE Daughter of Elizabeth Garrett ANDERSON, niece of Agnes GARRETT and of Millicent Garrett FAWCETT, and named for their dead sister, Louisa (*see* SMITH). She was educated at home (among her teachers was Hertha AYRTON – then Hertha Marks); at St Leonards School, St Andrews; Bedford College, London; and the London School of Medicine for Women, qualifying as a surgeon in 1897. She was chairman of a meeting of the Fulham branch of the CENTRAL SOCIETY FOR WOMEN'S SUFFRAGE in 1903, subscribed to the LONDON SOCIETY FOR WOMEN'S SUFFRAGE in 1906–7, was a member of the WOMEN'S SOCIAL AND POLITICAL UNION in 1907, and gave at least £200 to the WSPU in 1908–9. In 1908, still also a member of the NATIONAL UNION OF WOMEN'S SUFFRAGE SOCIETIES, she protested with others against Mrs Fawcett's manifesto against militancy following Muriel MATTERS's protest in the Ladies' Gallery of the House of Commons. It is probable that at this point she finally left the NUWSS. In October 1909 the TAX RESISTANCE LEAGUE was founded at a meeting at her flat in Harley Street, and in 1910 she was a member of its executive committee. In January 1910 she gave £60 to the WSPU General Election campaign fund and was in charge of the Medical Women Graduates section of the WSPU Procession held on 21 June 1910. On 14 November 1910 she wrote to the chairman of the committee of the New Hospital, where she was employed, to tell him "that I have decided, after long and very serious consideration, to go on the deputation to the Prime Minister". She was expecting to be arrested and probably imprisoned and apologized that, because the date of the deputation had been brought forward, she had not been able to organize cover for her hospital work. In the event, although she was arrested, she, along with many others, was discharged. In January 1911 she was elected to the committee of the Kensington WSPU. She was a close friend of Evelyn SHARP, meeting her at the gates of Holloway when the latter was released in December 1911. In March 1912, although, in a letter to Evelyn Sharp, she had hinted at some misgivings, she herself was arrested after the window-smashing raid and sentenced to six weeks in Holloway, from where she was released two weeks before the due date. In a speech at Steinway Hall on 18 April 1912 she drew attention to the anomaly that, because she was of some social standing, "the Home Office found that I might like to spend Easter with my family", while allowing no such concessions to the less well connected. She herself had left prison by the time the hunger strike started but wrote a letter of protest about it to the *British Medical Journal*. In October 1912 she was shaken by the split between the Pankhursts and the Pethick-Lawrences. She was involved with Dr Flora MURRAY and Nurse PINE in the running of the Notting Hill nursing home to which many suffragettes were taken on release from prison under the "Cat and Mouse" Act. In 1912, with Dr Murray, she founded the Women's Hospital for Children in the Harrow Road. In July 1913 she resigned from the committee of the Kensington WSPU, joined the NATIONAL POLITICAL LEAGUE, and in 1914 was a vice-president of the UNITED SUFFRAGISTS.

Soon after the outbreak of war she and Dr Flora Murray were the first women to break down the prejudice of the British War Office and, after successfully forming the Women's Hospital Corps (the motto of which was the WSPU's "Deeds Not Words"), and running a hospital in Claridge's Hotel in Paris, they were invited to organize a hospital at Wimereux near Boulogne. In February 1915 they were asked to take entire charge of the Endell Street Military Hospital in London. Louisa Garrett Anderson was chief surgeon; the hospital treated 26 000 patients before it closed in 1919. When the limited suffrage bill was passed in February 1918 WSPU and other flags were run up at the hospital. She was made a CBE at the end of the war. She and Flora Murray were constant companions. Flora Murray dedicated *Women as Army Surgeons* to Louisa Garrett Anderson – "Bold, courageous, true and my loving comrade" – and Louisa Garrett Anderson in her will refers to Flora's nieces as her own "nieces in love". In 1934 she was a justice of the peace, secretary of the Penn branch of the Conservative Association and chairman of her local branch of the League of Nations Union. In 1939 she published a biography of her mother.

Address: (1907) 14B Hyde Park Mansions, Marylebone Road, London; (1910) 114a Harley Street, London; (1934) Paul End, Penn, Buckinghamshire.
Portrait: Francis Dodd, *An Operation at the Military Hospital, Endell Street*, 1920, in Imperial War Museum; pencil drawing by Francis Dodd (photograph in National Portrait Gallery Archives); portrait by Annie Swynnerton (photograph in National Portrait Gallery Archives).
Bibliography: F. Murray, *Women as Army Surgeons*, 1920.

ANERLEY (WFL) Secretary (1913) Miss J. Fennings, 149 Croydon Road, Anerley, London SE.

ANSELL, GERTRUDE MARY (1861–1932) Born in central London. After the death of her father she ran her own business, a successful typing bureau; in the 1908 London Post Office directory she is described as a "typewriter". She was honorary secretary of one animal society and honorary treasurer of another, and (she obviously thought, 20 years later, that this was worth noting) made most of her own clothes. She had become convinced, from her own experience as a businesswoman, that the economic position of women would never be satisfactory without political freedom. In December 1906 she was inspired to join the WOMEN'S SOCIAL AND POLITICAL UNION after seeing the effects wrought by militancy, the arrest of Mrs PETHICK-LAWRENCE, Mrs Cobden SANDERSON and Annie KENNEY. In February 1907 she joined the "Mud March" organized by the NATIONAL UNION OF WOMEN'S SUFFRAGE SOCIETIES and a few days later, on 13 February, took part in the demonstrations surrounding the WSPU's Women's Parliament in Caxton Hall. In February 1908 she gave a small donation to the WSPU. On 27 May 1908 she apparently sold her business. On 13 October 1908 she was arrested after taking part in the "raid" on the House of Commons. She estimated that there were 6000 police there to restrain the deputation. She was sentenced to a month in Holloway and described the sound of the huge crowd that gathered, singing the "Women's Marseillaise" outside the prison in support of the prisoners, who by then also included Mrs PANKHURST, Christabel PANKHURST, and Mrs DESPARD. On her release, with the others, she was met by Mrs Pethick-Lawrence and taken to a triumphal breakfast at the Inns of Court Hotel. In her speech on this occasion her veneration for Mrs Pankhurst is obvious. She was present with other members of the WSPU, dressed in prison clothes, at the Women's Liberal Association meeting, chaired by Lady McLaren (*see* Laura McLAREN), in the Albert Hall on 5 December 1908. Such was the heckling at this meeting that Lloyd George took two hours to say very little, Helen OGSTON wielded her dog-whip against Liberal stewards, and the effect as reported in the daily press was that the militants had given impressive proof that their demand for the vote was in earnest. From the Albert Hall Gertrude Ansell and her fellow rioters went to have tea at the Lyceum Club (*see under* CLUBS).

Gertrude Ansell was a member of the FABIAN WOMEN'S GROUP in 1910 and continued her work for animal societies. In July 1909 she was one of the organizers of the International Anti-Vivisection and Animal Protection Congress at the Caxton Hall, which advertised in *Votes for Women*, promising a Great Procession, with 200 banners, from the Embankment to Hyde Park. Although she took part in all the big WSPU marches, meetings and breakfasts, she had given an undertaking to one of these animal committees to abstain from militancy. However in the summer of 1913 the Dogs Exemption Bill and the Plumage Bill, two acts for which she had been working, were defeated in the House of Commons and she was released from her promise. On 31 July she smashed a window at the Home

Office and was sentenced on 2 August to a month's imprisonment. She described the horror of being locked in the Black Maria as it took two hours to complete the journey to Holloway, picking up "the flotsam and jetsam of the night" on its way. She immediately went on a hunger-and-thirst strike and was released on 6 August under the "Cat and Mouse" Act. Her licence for release is now in the Museum of London collection. She escaped rearrest, although she can hardly be said to have been in hiding, because she was recaptured on 30 October while selling the *Suffragette* at Holborn Tube Station. The Criminal Record Office had circulated her photograph and description (5' 4", grey eyes, hair turning grey) as a "Known Militant Suffragette". She repeated the hunger-and-thirst strike, was released, caught again in Kingsway on 18 November, again went on strike, again was released, and then escaped from the house to which she had been taken. On 19 January 1914 she was recaptured in Knightsbridge and again went on hunger-and-thirst strike.

On 12 May 1914 she smashed Herkomer's picture of the Duke of Wellington in the Royal Academy (for a cartoon inspired by this action see *Punch*, 13 May 1914) and was sentenced to six months' imprisonment. By the end of the month the National Gallery, Tate Gallery and the Wallace Collection had all been closed. This time she was not released, but because she carried on with her hunger-and-thirst strike was forcibly fed. She was released under the amnesty on 10 August, having been forcibly fed 236 times.

A businesswoman to the last, her will, leaving her small estate to her nephew and niece, noted "I am hoping to get my investments settled into good securities before I die . . . It is my habit to keep everything paid up."

Address: (1908) 70 Chancery Lane, London WC; (1932) Elm Cottage, Finchingfield, Essex.
Photograph: Criminal Record Office.
Archival source: Suffragette Fellowship Collection, Museum of London.

APPLEBY (NUWSS) In 1913 the society was a member of the NORTH-WESTERN FEDERATION OF THE NATIONAL UNION OF WOMEN'S SUFFRAGE SOCIETIES. Secretary (1913) Mrs Baker, Battlebarrow, Appleby, Westmorland.

APPLEDORE (NUWSS) In 1913 the society was a member of the SOUTH-WESTERN FEDERATION OF THE NATIONAL UNION OF WOMEN'S SUFFRAGE SOCIETIES. Secretary (1913) Miss E. Martin, Torridge House, Appledore, North Devon.

ARBROATH (a branch of the EDINBURGH NATIONAL SOCIETY FOR WOMEN'S SUFFRAGE, NUWSS) Secretary (1909) Miss Lowson, Woodville, Arbroath, Angus.

ARCHDALE, HELEN ALEXANDER, MRS (1876–1950) née Russel Daughter of the editor of the *Scotsman*, who had backed Sophia Jex-Blake's campaign for the entry of women into the medical school in Edinburgh and had married one of these medical students in 1871. Their daughter was educated at St Leonards School, St Andrews and at St Andrews University, where she attended sessions in 1892–3 and 1893–4. In 1901 she married Lt Col T.M. Archdale, who was stationed in India. She became the mother of two sons and one daughter. In September 1908, having returned from India, she joined the WOMEN'S SOCIAL AND POLITICAL UNION. She took part in the Scottish Demonstration in Edinburgh on 9 October 1909. Later that month, with Adela PANKHURST, Maud JOACHIM, Catherine CORBETT (*see* Marie CORBETT) and Laura Evans, she was convicted of breach of the peace, following a disturbance at a meeting attended by Winston Churchill in Dundee. On 20 October all five went on hunger strike. This was barely a month after the first English hunger-strikers, Laura AINSWORTH, Mary LEIGH and Charlotte MARSH, had been force-fed in Winson Green Prison; in fact suffragettes were at that very time being force-fed in Newcastle gaol, and the Dundee authorities were prepared to follow suit. However, Helen Archdale and Catherine Corbett, perhaps because of their married status or perhaps because of their connections, and Adela Pankhurst, ostensibly on the grounds of her mental state, were immediately exempted. In fact, on this occasion, none of the hunger-strikers was force-fed, but all were released after four days. Helen Archdale was said to have lost one-and-a-half stone during this imprisonment. Much was made at the time between the difference in attitude to force-feeding between the English and Scottish authorities. It has, however, become clear that the Scottish prison commissioners were quite prepared to resort to this "treatment" if necessary.

In March 1910 she was working as a WSPU ORGANIZER in Sheffield, but became ill, and was succeeded by Adela Pankhurst. By February 1911 she had returned to Sheffield, but later in the year moved to London to act as the WSPU prisoners' secretary, organizing information and comforts. In December 1911 she herself became a prisoner, having been sentenced to two months in Holloway for breaking a window in London. After her release she again acted as prisoners' secretary and later worked, as a sub-editor and even occasionally as a printer, on the *Suffragette* when it was published under cover. She worked for the Ministry of National Service from 1917 to 1918, was editor of *Time and Tide* from 1922 to 1926, International Secretary of the Six Point Group of Great Britain until 1933, and chairman of Equal Rights International. After 1927 she worked for the Liaison Committee of the Women's International Organizations in Geneva. In the 1920s she lived for some years with Lady RHONDDA. In 1934 she was a member of the Open Door International, Open Door Council, International Federation of Business and Professional Women, British Institute of Journalists and Women's Electrical Association, and contributed articles to *The Times*, *Daily News*, *Christian Science Monitor*, the *Scotsman*, and papers in the USA, Canada and Australia. Her daughter, Betty Archdale, shared her feminist interests, was political secretary of the Six Point Group, and studied for the Bar, in 1934 the only woman to enter for the examination in International Law, passed at the head of all the male candidates. After the Second World War, in which Betty Archdale served in the WRNS, she became principal of the Women's College in the University of Sydney.

Address: (1934) 3 rue Butini, Geneva, Switzerland; (1930s) Stilestone, Crouch Borough Green, Kent.
Portrait: photograph by Lafayette taken on 3 February 1928, in National Portrait Gallery Archives.
Archival sources: Scottish Record Office; Suffragette Fellowship Collection, Museum of London.
Bibliography: S.M. Eoff, *Viscountess Rhondda: Equalitarian Feminist*, 1991; L. Leneman, *A Guid Cause: The Woman's Suffrage Movement in Scotland*, 1991; *Martyrs in Our Midst*, 1993.

ARDROSSAN AND SALTCOATS (NUWSS) In 1913 the society was a member of the SCOTTISH FEDERATION OF WOMEN'S SUFFRAGE SOCIETIES. Secretary (1913) Mrs Kerr, 38 Sydney Street, Saltcoats, Ayrshire.

ARLECDON AND FRIZINGDON (NUWSS) In 1913 the society was a member of the NORTH-WESTERN FEDERATION OF THE NATIONAL UNION OF WOMEN'S SUFFRAGE SOCIETIES. Secretary Miss Annie Lawrence, 17 Parks Road, Arlecdon, Cockermouth, Cumberland.

ARTISTS' SUFFRAGE LEAGUE Founded in January 1907 by professional women artists to help with the preparations for the first large-scale public women's suffrage demonstration, later known by the sobriquet the "Mud March", which the NATIONAL UNION OF WOMEN'S SUFFRAGE SOCIETIES was planning to hold the next month. The League's founder and chairman was Mary LOWNDES; Emily FORD was vice-chairman, Barbara Forbes, Mary Lowndes' companion, was secretary, and Sara Anderson was treasurer. Among the committee members were May H. Barker, Clara Billing, Dora Meeson COATES, Violet Garrard, Bertha NEWCOMBE, Bethia Shore, Bessie Wigan and Mary V. Wheelhouse. The League explained in the *Suffrage Annual and Women's Who's Who*, 1913, that its object "was to further the cause of Women's Enfranchisement by the work and professional help of artists ... by bringing in an attractive manner before the public eye the long-continued demand for the vote". Unlike the members of the SUFFRAGE ATELIER, those of the ASL worked only for the NUWSS and did not charge for their work. The ASL does not appear to have had a formal structure; there is no suggestion that it had a constitution and no membership lists survive, if they ever existed. In 1907 the NUWSS annual report noted that the League had been of great assistance, having contributed both posters (two of which had since been printed) and many workers who had campaigned at the Wimbledon by-election. Members of the League had coloured posters by hand, in order that the NUWSS might not be put to the heavy expense of colour printing. The League also delegated such work; in 1908 it sent a number of "John Bull" posters to NEWNHAM and members of the college suffrage society then painted them in coloured inks. This poster was

IS THIS RIGHT?

Woman. Why can't I have an umbrella too?
Voter. You can't. You ought to stop at home.
Woman. Stop at home indeed! I have my Living to earn.

Artists' Suffrage League postcard. (Author's collection)

probably the design with which Dora Meeson Coates had won a poster competition organized for the NUWSS by the Artists' Suffrage League ("Mrs John Bull: Now you greedy boys. I shall not give you any more until I have helped myself"). In 1909 Duncan Grant, with his poster "Handicapped", was the winner of a similar competition. Among the other posters, all published in colour by the ASL, are "Bugler Girl" by Caroline Watts, "The Factory Girl" by Emily Ford (sold for 4d), and "What's Sauce for the Gander is Sauce for the Goose" by Mary Sargant Florence (also 4d). The League sent out its publications to suffrage societies and their attendant shops in all parts of the country and its material was used as propaganda at all the pre-war general and by-elections.

The League was responsible for designing and, with the help of outworkers, the making of around 80 embroidered BANNERS carried in the 13 June 1908 NUWSS procession. The album in which Mary Lowndes sketched many of these designs is preserved in the Fawcett Library. In 1909 the League provided the decorations for the Pageant of Trades and Professions organized by the NUWSS to entertain the delegates to the quinquennial meeting of the INTERNATIONAL WOMAN SUFFRAGE ALLIANCE at the Albert Hall. The League also designed many of the banners for the NUWSS and its branches, Christmas cards, and at least 16 designs for postcards. The Christmas card for 1910 made use of a quote from Shelley, "And women, too, frank, beautiful, and kind..."; that for 1912 depicts a blindfolded baby flying on Mother Goose, dispensing feathery votes onto the snowy townscape – Mother Goose's ribbon carries the message "Equal Liberty 1912". Mounted on a larger sheet, this card also doubled as a calendar. In addition to members of the ASL already mentioned, other artists whose work was thus produced were C. Hedley Charlton, Emily J. Harding Andrews, Harriet S. Adkins, K.F. Powell, Joan Harvey Drew and Mrs E.L. Shute. One of the colour printers used by the League to print its Christmas cards and calendars was Carl Hentschel, who was a regular advertiser in *The Common Cause* (*see* PUBLISHERS AND PRINTERS). All the ASL postcards, which were sold for 1d each, were printed in black and white only. The ASL also published two witty rhyme books: *Beware! A Warning to Suffragists*, written by Cicely HAMILTON with illustrations by Mary Lowndes, Dora Meeson Coates and C. Hedley Charlton, c. 1909, and *A.B.C. of Politics for Women Politicians* written by Mary Lowndes and illustrated by C. Hedley Charlton and Dora Meeson Coates, c. 1910. By 1913 the ASL was able to record that its posters had also been supplied to America for the use of the National Association for Women's Suffrage. In March 1918 the ASL decorated the Queen's Hall for the NUWSS "victory" celebration. The society's banner, probably designed by Mary Lowndes in 1908, with its motto "Alliance Not Defiance" is now held in the Museum of London.

Address: (1913) Brittany Studios, 259 King's Road, Chelsea; (1917) Brittany Studios, 27 Trafalgar Square, Chelsea.
Archival source: Annual reports of the ASL, 1909, 1910, Fawcett Library; The Fawcett Collection and those in the Museum of London and the Communist Party Archives all include ASL posters; The John Johnson Collection, Bodleian Library, includes some ASL postcards.

Bibliography: L. Tickner, *Spectacle of Women: Imagery of the Suffrage Campaign, 1907–14*, 1987.

ASCOT (NUWSS) In 1913 the society was a member of the Oxon, Berks, Bucks, and Beds Federation of the National Union of Women's Suffrage Societies. Secretary (1913) Miss Violet Hanbury, Holmwood Lodge, Ascot, Berkshire.

ASHBY, MARGERY IRENE CORBETT, MRS (1882–1981) DBE, 1967   Daughter of C.H. Corbett, who was from 1906 to 1910 Liberal MP for East Grinstead, a supporter of women's suffrage, and of Marie Corbett. Educated at home where her German governess was Lina Eckenstein (author of *Women Under Monasticism*, 1896, sometime member of the Men and Women's Club and, later, member of the Fabian Women's Group), she then went to read classics, 1901–3, attended the Training College in Cambridge (now Homerton) and in 1904 was taken to Berlin, with her sister, by their mother to attend the first meeting of the International Woman Suffrage Alliance. (She was to become its president from 1923 to 1946; after 1926 it was renamed the International Alliance of Women.) In 1906 and 1907 she ran vacation courses, organized by Mary Murdoch, for Hull dockside children. She was secretary of the National Union of Women's Suffrage Societies (paid £100 per annum) from 1907 until dismissed in 1909. She was then elected a member of its executive committee. In 1909 she was co-opted onto the executive committee of the Cambridge Women's Suffrage Association. In November 1909, with her mother, she attended a Fabian Women's Group meeting and in 1910, the year in which she married, she was an organizer for the Liberal Party. In 1912 she became a poor law guardian in Wandsworth and in 1914 was the chairman of the Barnes, Mortlake, and East Sheen branch of the London Society for Women's Suffrage. She resigned in 1914 from the NUWSS executive committee, too committed a Liberal to support the Election Fighting Fund policy. Her only child, a son, was born the same year.

After the First World War she was a substitute for Mrs Fawcett, who did not wish to attend, at the Versailles Peace Conference. With Mary Allen she advised Germany on the founding of its women's police force. In 1918 she lost her deposit when she stood as a Liberal candidate at Birmingham Ladywood. The Birmingham Society for Women's Suffrage was criticized for supporting her rather than the Labour candidate, as the latter party had, unlike the Liberals, traditionally supported the suffrage movement. She stood, unsuccessfully, at every inter-war election except that of 1931. She succeeded Eleanor Rathbone as president of the National Union of Societies for Equal Citizenship and in the late 1920s she was co-founder, with Eva Hubback, of the Townswomen's Guild, having, in order to be permitted to accept this, resigned as president of the Women's Liberal Federation. When she stood as a Liberal candidate in 1935 she was forced to stand down as president of the Townswomen's Guild but immediately accepted the presidency of the Women's Freedom League, succeeding Emmeline Pethick-Lawrence. She was a vice-president of the Fawcett Society. At various times she was also president of the British Commonwealth League, member of the executive committee of the Family Endowment Society and chairman of the Association of Moral and Social Hygiene.

Address: (1908) Woodgate, Danehill, Sussex; (1934) 33 Upper Richmond Road, London SW 15; (1960s) Wickens, Birch Grove, Haywards Heath, Sussex.

Bibliography: A. Whittick, *Woman Into Citizen*, 1979; B. Harrison, *Prudent Revolutionaries: Portraits of British Feminists between the Wars*, 1987; M. Bosch, *Politics and Friendship: Letters from the International Woman Suffrage Alliance, 1902–1942*, 1990; Dame M. Corbett Ashby, *Memoirs*, with additional material by Dr M. Corbett Ashby, 1996.

ASHFORD (NUWSS) In 1913 the society was a member of the Kentish Federation of the National Union of Women's Suffrage Societies. Secretary (1913) Mrs X. Willis, 1 Wellesley Villas, Ashford, Kent.

ASHFORD branch of the United Suffragists Formed in 1917. Honorary secretary: Mr John Marsh, 45 Royd's Road, Willsborough, Kent. Organizer: Maude White, Magazine House, Winchelsea, Sussex (see Winchelsea, Ashford, and Rye branches of the New Constitutional Society for Women's Suffrage).

ASHTON, MARGARET (1856–1937)   A Unitarian, daughter of Thomas Ashton, a Liberal, educated at Manchester University. Eleanor RATHBONE was nearly a cousin (her father's first wife was Margaret Ashton's sister) and James Bryce, Liberal MP (1880–1907) although a stalwart supporter from the earliest days of Emily DAVIES and GIRTON COLLEGE, an anti-suffragist, was her brother-in-law. Her brother was a Liberal MP from 1895 to 1911. Her father refused her request to be taken into the family business, although she was able to concern herself with its welfare policy. She herself was a school manager from 1875, served on three education committees and was chairman of the Withington Urban District Council from 1900 for the whole of its existence. In the 1880s she formed a federation of local groups into the North of England Women Guardians Society. In February 1902 she visited Elizabeth Wolstenholme ELMY who reported to Harriet McILQUHAM that "she came over to see me about the new works that her committee has undertaken. She is, you know, the Hon. Sec. and the only U.D.C. in the 6 northern counties. She *is* very much in earnest". She was a supporter, with Bertha MASON and the Rev. S. STEINTHAL, of the Manchester and Salford Women's Trade Council, of which Eva GORE-BOOTH was the secretary. In 1903 she left the Women's National Liberal Association and joined the WOMEN'S LIBERAL FEDERATION, of which she became chairman of the Lancashire and Cheshire Union. A practitioner of, and respecter of, the due political processes, she repudiated the actions, which she witnessed, of Christabel PANKHURST and Annie KENNEY at the Free Trade Hall in Manchester in October 1905. In 1906 she took part in the suffrage deputation to Campbell-Bannerman, noting that she represented over 99 000 women and that "We ask it as Liberals from a Liberal government, and as Liberal women we ask it from the present Parliament". She then resigned from the Liberal Party after the prime minister refused to introduce a suffrage bill. On 11 December 1906 she was present at the banquet at the Savoy organized by Mrs FAWCETT to celebrate the release of the WOMEN'S SOCIAL AND POLITICAL UNION prisoners. In 1908 she became Manchester's first woman councillor, standing as an independent of liberal principles. In the same year she attended the INTERNATIONAL WOMAN SUFFRAGE ALLIANCE Conference in Amsterdam.

From 1906 until 1915 she was chairman of the NORTH OF ENGLAND SOCIETY FOR WOMEN'S SUFFRAGE (after 1911 renamed the Manchester Society for Women's Suffrage) and was that society's representative to the NATIONAL UNION OF WOMEN'S SUFFRAGE SOCIETIES. In 1912 she was what Sandra Holton has termed "a democratic suffragist", and was until 1916 an active supporter of the NUWSS Election Fighting Fund, determined to put the suffrage cause before any party interest. In 1913 she was a member of the Manchester and Salford Women's Trade Union Council, of which she had been unofficial treasurer in 1895, and was honorary secretary of the Manchester branch of the WOMEN'S LOCAL GOVERNMENT SOCIETY. In July 1912 she signed a public letter protesting against the militancy of the WSPU.

In 1914 she signed the Open Christmas Letter to the Women of Germany and Austria. She resigned in April 1915 from the NUWSS executive after the rejection of a resolution to send delegates to the International Women's Congress at the Hague. In June the Manchester society repudiated the anti-war policy and, as a corollary, Margaret Ashton. In 1917 she was removed from the Education Committee of Manchester City Council on account of her support for pacifism. In 1919 she became one of the founding members and vice-chairman of the Women's International League for Peace and Freedom. In the 1930s she was a vice-president of the National Council for Equal Citizenship.

We have to thank Margaret Ashton for having the foresight to present, in 1922, the papers of the Manchester branch of the NUWSS to the Manchester Central Library. In her will she left bequests to the Manchester branch of the Women's International League, to the Association of University Women and to the Manchester High School for Girls.

Address: (1907) Fairfax House, Didsbury, Manchester; (1912) 8 Kinnaird Road, Withington, Manchester; (1934) 12 Kingston Road, Didsbury, Manchester.
Portrait: by Henry Lamb in City Art Gallery, Manchester, despite the fact that, in 1926, the Gallery refused to accept the portrait because of her "pacifist opinions". It was then presented to Manchester University and hung in the Debating Hall for many years.
Archival source: Women's Suffrage Collection, Manchester City Library; Elizabeth Wolstenholme Elmy Papers, British Library.

Bibliography: Lady Simon of Wythenshawe, *Margaret Ashton and Her Times*, 1949; P. Hollis, *Ladies Elect: Women in English Local Government, 1865–1914*, 1987; S. Holton, *Feminism and Democracy: Women's Suffrage and Reform Politics in Britain, 1900–1918*, 1986; G. Lewis, *Eva Gore Booth and Esther Roper*, 1988.

ASHTON-UNDER-LYNE (NUWSS) Formed in 1910, a member of the MANCHESTER AND DISTRICT FEDERATION OF THE NATIONAL UNION OF WOMEN'S SUFFRAGE SOCIETIES. Secretary (1913) Miss K. Dyson, Waterloo, Ashton-under-Lyne, Lancashire.

ASHTON-UNDER-LYNE (WSPU) Organizer (1906) Mrs M. (Hannah) MITCHELL, 43 Elizabeth St, Ashton-under-Lyne, Lancashire.

ASHWELL, LENA (1872–1957) (Lady Simson, OBE) Born on a ship on the Tyne, one of seven children of the captain of a training ship. When she was a child the family emigrated to Canada, but in her late teens, after her mother's death, she returned to Europe to study first French at Lausanne and then singing in London at the Royal Academy of Music. She became a successful actress and, ambitious to have control of a theatre, was gratified when in 1907 the opportunity was given to her. In her memoir she clouds the leading characters in this melodrama in pseudonyms. One, "Jane", is a wealthy American, a long-standing acquaintance. The other, "Lady Caroline", is predatory, interested in power and control, and Lena Ashwell intimates that she had already repulsed her advances. "Lady Caroline" had recently moved into "Jane's" home, ousting a previous female incumbent, when "Jane" made Lena Ashwell the offer of setting her up in a theatre of her own. Thrilled, she took out a long lease on the Kingsway theatre and engaged a company for a year, intending to give actors stability by guaranteeing long-term employment and to produce plays by new young writers. She then discovered that it was not "Jane" but "Lady Caroline" who was putting up the money and who, in return, wished to wield unacceptable power over her life. After this rejection, although the first instalment of £3000 had been paid, no further money was forthcoming and she had to fund her theatre and company in a rather more conventional way. It is tempting to decode the pseudonyms; "Jane" could be Mary Dodge and "Lady Caroline" Lady DE LA WARR. Lena Ashwell's Kingsway theatre season opened in 1908 and the second play she staged, and starred in, was Cicely HAMILTON's *Diana of Dobson's*. She was a vice-president of the ACTRESSES' FRANCHISE LEAGUE. As a tax resister, she took part in a deputation to Lloyd George, protesting that as sole proprietor and licensee of the Kingsway theatre, liable for taxes on income she had herself earned, her income tax return had to be signed by her husband who, as a doctor, knew nothing about her business. She took part in the suffrage procession of 18 June 1910 and subscribed to Mrs DE FONBLANQUE's "Woman's March" in 1912.

During the First World War Lena Ashwell was one of the founders of the Women's Emergency Corps, honorary treasurer of the British Women's Hospitals, and then took the "Lena Ashwell Players" to "Concerts at the Front". Cicely Hamilton while working in Abbeville wrote *The Child in Flanders* for the Players. After the war the Lena Ashwell Players continued as a company, with the intention of bringing plays dealing with social issues to audiences in town halls and baths. The company, latterly subsidized by her husband, eventually found a base at Kensington's Century Theatre.

Address: (1907) 4M Portman Mansions, Marylebone Road, London NW; (1913) 50 Grosvenor Street, London W; (1934) 48 Grosvenor Square, London W1.

Photograph: in her autobiography; by Mrs Albert Broom (National Portrait Gallery Archive); portrait by Glyn Philpot "as I appeared in 'the Great Mrs Alloway'", whereabouts unknown (photograph in National Portrait Gallery Archive).

Bibliography: L. Ashwell, *Myself a Player*, 1936; J. Holledge, *Innocent Flowers: Women in the Edwardian Theatre*, 1981; S. Stowell, *A Stage Of Their Own: Feminist Playwrights of the Suffrage Era*, 1992.

ASHWORTH, ANNE FRANCES (1842–1921) (later Mrs Joseph Cross) Quaker, daughter of Thomas Ashworth, who was a close friend of Richard Cobden, sister of Lilias Ashworth HALLETT, and niece of John and Jacob BRIGHT (*see* Appendix). She signed the 1866 suffrage petition. In July 1867, when the LONDON NATIONAL SOCIETY was formed, Clementia TAYLOR wrote to Anne and Lilias Ashworth, asking them to form a committee of this society, of which they were already members, at Bath. They agreed to do so, although the first record of the Bath Society dates from 1871; Anne

Ashworth was on its executive committee. She was a member of the executive committee of the CENTRAL COMMITTEE OF THE NATIONAL SOCIETY FOR WOMEN'S SUFFRAGE when it was formed in 1872. She and her sister together gave £100 to the Central Committee in May 1873. She had already subscribed to the EDINBURGH NATIONAL SOCIETY FOR WOMEN'S SUFFRAGE in 1870 (Priscilla Bright McLAREN being her aunt) and to the BRISTOL AND WEST OF ENGLAND SOCIETY in 1871. In the same year she also supported the Ladies' National Society and was elected to the School Board in Bath, although she did not stand for re-election at the end of her term. At this time the *Woman's Suffrage Journal* noted that she was the first honorary treasurer of an association formed "to diffuse amongst women accurate information as to the nature and working of the [Elementary Education] Act, 1870". In 1873 she was a member of the executive committee of the Married Women's Property Committee. In March 1871 she addressed a women's suffrage meeting in Bath, at which Mrs FAWCETT was the main speaker; in the summer of 1874, with her sister, gave a Suffrage Garden Party for members of the British Association whose meeting was addressed that year in Bristol by their kinswoman, Anna Maria PRIESTMAN; and in December 1874 spoke at a public meeting in the Hanover Square Rooms in London. Caroline Ashurst BIGGS in her chapter "Great Britain" in Stanton, Anthony and Gage (eds) *History of Woman Suffrage*, 1886, notes that Anne Ashworth did not speak at meetings, in contrast to her sister. In her autobiography, *What I Remember*, Millicent Fawcett also remarked that Anne Ashworth "never spoke or took part in public work of any kind". Millicent Garrett Fawcett added "But she helped and supported the movement in every other way in her power", remarking on the pleasure of relaxing at Claverton Lodge after the rigours of a public-speaking tour. One way in which Anne Ashworth supported the cause at this time was with her financial support. In September 1871 she gave to the MANCHESTER SOCIETY £100, specifically in order to relieve it of the necesssity of raising funds by running a bazaar. In 1872 she, with her sister, gave the same society another £100. In 1873 they gave £100 to the CENTRAL COMMITTEE, which had been formed at the instigation of their uncle, Jacob Bright. In 1874 she gave, with her sister, £150 to the Bristol and West of England Society, £20 to the BIRMINGHAM SOCIETY, and another £100 to the Central Committee. Similar funding was carried on over a period of years.

In September 1877 Anne Ashworth married Joseph Cross, youngest son of John Cross of Bolton. His brother was J.K. Cross, a Liberal MP, who had been present in 1872 at a suffrage meeting in Bolton at which Rhoda GARRETT spoke. Anne Ashworth was given away by her uncle by marriage, Duncan McLaren, and the wedding breakfast was at the London home of the McLarens, in The Boltons, Kensington. The wedding was held at the parish church; Anne Ashworth obviously married out of the Quaker community. Agnes and Rhoda Garrett were among the small number of guests invited. Mr and Mrs Joseph Cross went to live in Bolton, and had one son, Elward Guy Kynaston Cross. From 1877 to 1892 Mrs Joseph Cross was a member of the executive committee of the Manchester National Society for Women. From its institution in 1893 until 1907 she was on the general committee of the Manchester Society (after 1897 the NORTH OF ENGLAND SOCIETY). She was present, with Lilias Ashworth Hallett and Lady Frances BALFOUR in the Ladies' Gallery on 3 February 1897 when the suffrage bill presented by Mr Faithfull Begg passed its second reading, an event that those present thought presaged imminent enfranchisement. It was not to be and Mrs Joseph Cross was still a vice-president of the North of England Society in 1907.

Address: (1870) Claverton Lodge, Bath; (1913) Great Glenn House, Leicester; (1921) died at 8 Eccleston Square, London SW1.

Photograph: carte de visite in Josephine Butler Collection, Fawcett Library.

ATKINSON, MABEL (1876–1958) (later Mrs Palmer) Born in Northumberland, she graduated from Glasgow University, and continued her studies as a postgraduate at LSE and at Bryn Mawr. In September 1909 she gave one guinea to the WOMEN'S SOCIAL AND POLITICAL UNION Prisoners' Fund and in October was a speaker for the WOMEN'S FREEDOM LEAGUE. She spoke on behalf of the WSPU during the January 1910 general election campaign. She was a member of the executive committee of the Fabian Society, 1909–15 and was chairman of the

Suffrage Section of the FABIAN WOMEN'S GROUP from its formation in October 1911. She was involved, with Mary HANKINSON, in the development of the Fabian Summer School. She took part in the tax resistance campaign as means of supporting the cause of women's suffrage. At the end of the First World War she emigrated first to Australia and then to South Africa.

AUSTRALIAN AND NEW ZEALAND WOMEN VOTERS' ASSOCIATION The society's BANNER, painted by Dora Meeson COATES, was carried in the June 1908 NATIONAL UNION OF WOMEN'S SUFFRAGE SOCIETIES procession. It depicts a daughter figure, "Commonwealth of Australia", addressing mother Britannia with the message, "Trust the Women Mother as I have done" and is now in the Parliament Building, Canberra, having been bought from the Fawcett Collection in 1987.
Address: (1913, 1917) c/o International Women's Franchise Club, 9 Grafton Street, London, W.

AXMINSTER (WSPU) Secretary (1913) Miss Tuker, Ashe House, nr Axminster, Devon.

AYR committee of the National Society for Women's Suffrage Formed in 1872. In 1913 the society was a member of the SCOTTISH FEDERATION OF THE NATIONAL UNION OF WOMEN'S SUFFRAGE SOCIETIES. Secretary (1913) Mrs Harvey, Hay Lodge, Peebles; president Mrs Jean Muir, St Monenna, Troon, Ayrshire.

AYRTON, HERTHA, MRS (1854–1923) Jewish, born Phoebe Sarah Marks in Portsea in Hampshire, where her father became a watchmaker. She received her first education in London from an aunt, in the company of her cousins who included Rosa LEO. From the age of 16 she worked as a governess, at first in a residential post and then as a daily tutor, living in lodgings. In 1875 Eliza ORME wrote to Helen TAYLOR, who had previously expressed a wish to sponsor a needy student, to tell her about a girl who wanted to study at Girton. Eliza Orme had taught Hertha Marks mathematics and Barbara BODICHON had paid for further teaching and was willing to pay what was necessary for her to attend Girton, but Hertha Marks wished to sit for the Gilchrist scholarship, a London University examination that would pay for half her expenses as Girton. She therefore required a loan or gift of £92 a year until October 1876 to enable her to live without teaching and devote herself to her work. Helen Taylor gave £25, Lady GOLDSMID, George Eliot and others gave enough to make up the amount. She did not win the scholarship but did attend Girton, studying mathematics, from 1877 until 1881. On leaving, she taught for a time at Notting Hill and Ealing High School. In 1872 Hertha Marks had joined the Hampstead branch of the CENTRAL SOCIETY FOR WOMEN'S SUFFRAGE. In 1885 the line divider she had invented and patented was shown at the Exhibition of Women's Industries organized in Bristol by Helen BLACKBURN. In that year she married Professor William Ayrton, a widower whose first wife, his cousin Matilda Chaplin Ayrton, had been a doctor and in 1867 a member of the LONDON NATIONAL SOCIETY; her mother had signed the 1866 petition. From this first marriage there was one daughter, Edith (see Edith ZANGWILL). William Ayrton was the nephew of Acton Smee Ayrton, who had been a Radical Liberal MP, a champion of the working classes, and had in 1866 been the first MP to protest about the Contagious Diseases Acts in the House of Commons. The Ayrtons acted as guardians for a time to Ernestine Evans Bell (see Ernestine MILLS), the orphaned daughter of another radical. Their own daughter (see Barbara Ayrton GOULD) was born in 1886. Hertha Ayrton continued with her scientific research, working from a laboratory in her house, and was awarded the Hughes medal by the Royal Society in 1906, the first woman to have received it for work that was exclusively her own.

Hertha Ayrton still subscribed to the Central Society in 1900, spoke in Hull at the 1905 Annual Convention of the NATIONAL UNION OF WOMEN'S SUFFRAGE SOCIETIES, and subscribed to the LONDON SOCIETY FOR WOMEN'S SUFFRAGE in 1906. She was present at the banquet given at the Savoy on 11 December 1906 to celebrate the release of the Women's Social and Political Union prisoners. She joined the WSPU in 1907, of which, in the *Girton Register*, she is described as having been an "ardent and active member", and gave very generously of the money, left to her by Barbara Bodichon, that she felt she held in trust for the woman's movement.

The 1909–10 WSPU accounts show that she gave £1060 in that year. Of this amount £500 was to be devoted to the WSPU Legal Defence Fund. In June 1910 she gave £500 in memory of Barbara Bodichon. In May 1909 she opened the second day of the Prince's Rink WSPU Exhibition and noted that she was wholly in favour of militant methods. In November 1910 she was, with Mrs PANKHURST and Elizabeth Garrett ANDERSON, a member of the "Black Friday" deputation. She was a supporter of the TAX RESISTANCE LEAGUE from its formation in 1910. In 1911 she gave a generous donation to the Hawkins Legal Fund (see Alice HAWKINS) organized by the MEN'S POLITICAL UNION FOR THE ENFRANCHISEMENT OF WOMEN, in April she gave hospitality in her house to over 40 census resisters, and on 7 June walked with the "Science" section in the Coronation Procession. Evelyn SHARP related that, although Hertha Ayrton took no further part in the increasing militancy, she did "launder" through her bank account the funds of the WSPU when it became clear in March 1912 that the government intended to seize them. The WSPU bank manager was subpoenaed to appear at the conspiracy trial and revealed that £7000 had been paid to "someone named Ayrton" on 6 March. Hertha Ayrton herself added a further £1000 to these funds that same month. She was very concerned in October 1912 by the split in the WSPU but for the next 18 months did offer refuge in her own house to suffragettes, including Mrs Pankhurst, when they were released from prison under the "Cat and Mouse" Act. In September 1913, in a letter in reply to Maud Arncliffe SENNETT's request for a donation to the newly formed NORTHERN MEN'S FEDERATION FOR WOMEN'S SUFFRAGE, Hertha Ayrton wrote, "I made up my mind some time ago that as I am unable to be militant myself, from reasons of health, and as I believe most fully in the necessity for militancy, I was bound to give every penny I can afford to the militant union that is bearing the brunt of the battle, namely the WSPU". Evelyn Sharp surmised that, in the new year, Hertha Ayrton felt the WSPU tactics had become ineffective and it was probably with some relief that she joined the UNITED SUFFRAGISTS in 1914. She gave the first donation, £100, to the new society's funds and became one of its vice-presidents.

In 1915 she devised a simple anti-gas fan that could be used in the trenches and carried out experiments to test it in Ernestine Mills's back garden in Kensington. She met with opposition and lethargy from the War Office, an episode used by Edith Zangwill in her "suffrage novel" *The Call*, with the fan transmuted into an extinguisher. Hertha Ayrton was present in the Queen's Hall for the NUWSS Victory Celebrations and at those held by the United Suffragists in Caxton Hall and by the Women's International League for Peace and Freedom. After her death a science scholarship in her name was established at Girton and five pictures painted by Barbara Bodichon and given to Hertha Ayrton were presented to the College by her daughter.
Address: (1908) 41 Norfolk Square, London W.
Portrait: by her cousin, Helena Darmesteter, in Girton, given by Barbara Ayrton Gould; photograph: in her laboratory (a very domestic scene) as frontispiece of E. Sharp, *Hertha Ayrton*, 1926.
Bibliography: E. Sharp, *Hertha Ayrton*, 1926; *Girton College Register, 1869–1946*, 1948.

AYRTON, PHYLLIS ALSAGER (1884–1975)   Born in China, daughter of the British Consul at Wenchow. She joined the WOMEN'S SOCIAL AND POLITICAL UNION in 1909 and with Cynthia MAGUIRE formed the CLERKS' WSPU. Together, they carried on the campaigning during holidays; August 1910 was spent converting Sheringham. Phyllis Ayrton helped organize the Clerks' and Civil Servants' contingent in the Coronation Procession in June 1911 and was a group captain of Section B at Emily Wilding Davison's funeral. In May 1914 she went to Birmingham as the WSPU ORGANIZER, succeeding Lilias MITCHELL whose health had broken down. During the First World War she worked for the Pankhursts' WOMEN'S PARTY, speaking with Elsie BOWERMAN on anti-strike campaigns in South Wales and on Clydeside. In 1918 she was a member of the "Meetings Department", supporting Christabel PANKHURST's election campaign in Smethwick in 1918. She was working in Liverpool for the Women's Guild of Empire in 1920.
Address: (1913) 62 Edith Road, West Kensington, London W.
Photograph: in D. Mitchell, *Women on the Warpath*, 1966.
Archival source: Suffragette Fellowship Collection, Museum of London.

B

BABB, CHARLOTTE (1830–1906) An artist, from 1859 she campaigned for the admission of women students to the Royal Academy Schools and in 1861 was one of the first to be admitted, recommended by the Heatherley School of Art. She painted all her life and exhibited widely. In 1866 she signed the petition for women's suffrage. She was a member, and with her brother a generous supporter, of the CENTRAL COMMITTEE OF THE NATIONAL SOCIETY FOR WOMEN'S SUFFRAGE from its formation in 1871. In 1871, wearied by what she conceived as the futility of suffrage petitions, she launched a campaign for "no taxation without representation". She allowed her goods to be distrained and sold in lieu of tax and repeated this resistance on 12 occasions over a period of a further 13 years. She wrote many leaflets, including *A Word to Woman Householders; Practical Protests; Political Outcasts*, 1874. Although she did not achieve much of a following she was friendly with at least one fellow resister, Rose Anne Hall (*c.* 1823–92), who had signed the 1866 petition while living at Orange Hill, near Edgware and in 1877 was a fellow member of the West Middlesex branch of the NATIONAL SOCIETY FOR WOMEN'S SUFFRAGE. Miss Hall had been in correspondence with Helen TAYLOR, enthusiastically supported the LONDON NATIONAL SOCIETY, the Central Committee of the National Society from its formation (she addressed its annual general meeting in 1877), the MANCHESTER NATIONAL SOCIETY (1870–78), and from 1888 the CENTRAL NATIONAL SOCIETY. In 1871 Miss Hall refused to pay state taxes and her goods were seized; she continued the protest until her marriage with Charles Anderson, who himself had subscribed to the Central Committee in 1872–3. The connection between Charlotte Babb and Rose Anne Hall (which exists in a corrupt printed form in a footnote to C.A. Bigg's chapter "Great Britain" in Stanton, Anthony and Gage (eds), *History of Woman's Suffrage*, 1886, which refers to "Charlotte Hall") is made in a studio photograph taken of the two of them together, which forms part of Helen BLACKBURN's collection in Girton College archives.

In an obituary of his sister in the January 1907 issue of the *Englishwoman's Review*, John Staines Babb, who was also an artist, wrote that Charlotte Babb had maintained that tax resistance was the most peaceable and practical way of asserting the right to the parliamentary vote. She thought a great opportunity had been lost because her movement had not had more widespread support, "because a measure of a reasonable character [presumably the 'reasonable' qualification was the exclusion of married women] extending the franchise to women in the same terms as to men might have prevented the lowering of the franchise to the male voter of an inferior description, an unfortunate event which came about later, and has thrown back all women's chances indefinitely". Charlotte Babb was also, in the 1880s, a member of the Vigilance Association for the Defence of Personal Rights. In December 1884 she, with Henrietta MULLER, who had also in that year refused to pay her taxes, Viscountess HARBERTON and Mrs Ashton DILKE, spoke at a meeting of support of the claim of women ratepayers for the parliamentary franchise which was held at Bromley Town Hall. She signed the Women Householders' Declaration in favour of women's suffrage of 1889–90. A few days before she died she sent a donation of £5 and a message of good will to the WOMEN'S SOCIAL AND POLITICAL UNION.

Address: (1866) Hotel D'Antin, rue Biot, Paris; (1903) 12 Albert Square, Clapham Road, London SW.
Photograph: in Blackburn Collection, Girton College.
Bibliography: obituary in *Englishwoman's Review*, January 1907; D. Cherry, *Painting Women*, 1993.

BAINES, [SARAH JANE] JENNIE, MRS (1866–1951) Born in Birmingham, daughter of James Hunt, gunmaker, and his wife Sarah Ann. At the age of

11 she worked with her mother in a gun factory belonging to Joseph Chamberlain. She later observed that she had been schooled by the Salvation Army from earliest childhood in the spirit of rebellion. Mrs PANKHURST is quoted by A.E. Metcalfe in *Woman's Effort*, 1917, as saying that it was Salvation Army methods that the WOMEN'S SOCIAL AND POLITICAL UNION adopted from its earliest days, "Just as the Booths took religion to the street crowds, so we took suffrage to the general public". Jennie Baines was well practised in these methods. She recorded that she had at this early age been arrested "for free speech" and in prison had her first glimpse of social degradation. On 16 September 1888 she married a bootmaker, George Baines, and spent 16 years bringing up their children. During this time she worked for the temperance movement in Bolton, was an active member of the Independent Labour Party and for two years was a member of the Stockport Unemployed Committee. She says that in 1903 she met and was influenced by Mrs Pankhurst and was present at the meeting at Manchester Free Trade Hall on 13 October 1905, witnessed the brutal treatment (as she termed it) meted out to Christabel PANKHURST and Annie KENNEY, and immediately joined the WSPU. In 1906 Mrs Pankhurst asked her to go to London as an ORGANIZER. She went on her own to London, with her husband's support and leaving a daughter to manage the home. She was arrested on 13 December 1906 while speaking outside one of the entrances to the House of Commons and served a sentence of 14 days' imprisonment in Holloway, an experience that reinforced her concern for the treatment of women prisoners, which left her, she said, more of a rebel than ever. In particular she cites the case of Daisy Lord, who had been convicted of infanticide, and whose fate invoked much correspondence in the pages of *Votes for Women*. In 1907 Jennie Baines went to Birmingham as a temporary organizer and in April 1908 was made a full-time organizer, at £2 a week, in the Midlands and North of England. She was the main speaker on one of the platforms at the WSPU June 1908 Hyde Park demonstration and her short biography in *Votes for Women*, 7 May 1908, noted "She has the power of holding a very large audience." In 1908 she wrote a handbill, published by the Woman's Press, titled "The Labour of Married Women: a working woman's reply to Mr John Burns". In November 1908 she was the first suffragette to be tried by a jury, on a charge of "unlawful assembly" in Leeds. She was defended by Frederick PETHICK-LAWRENCE, who attempted, without success, to subpoena Herbert Gladstone and Asquith, as Christabel Pankhurst had done at her trial in London the previous month. Jennie Baines was found guilty, spent six weeks in Armley Gaol, and on her release was drawn in a carriage for three miles by women dressed as mill-hands in clogs and shawls. She then went to London where she was met by a triumphal procession and taken to a meeting in Trafalgar Square.

In 1909 she was one of the first hunger-strikers and by mid-1910 she had been in prison four times. In December 1909 she organized the demonstration outside Walton Gaol in Liverpool, during the course of which Constance LYTTON was arrested as "Jane Warton". In February 1910 she was WSPU organizer in Oldham and was one of the platform speakers at the 23 July 1910 Hyde Park rally. In August 1912 she was arrested, as "Lizzie Baker", in Dublin with Mary LEIGH, Gladys Evans, and Mabel CAPPER. She pleaded guilty to a lesser charge than that of arson, of which two of the others were convicted, and was sentenced to seven months' imprisonment. She immediately went on hunger strike and was released. In November 1913 she was charged with blowing up an empty railway carriage, hunger struck on remand, and was released. The Criminal Record Office circulated her photograph and description (4' 10", brown eyes, dark brown hair) as a "Known Militant Suffragette". She was advised that her health had been so weakened that she could not undergo another hunger strike. So, a week before she was due to appear at Manchester assizes, armed with letters of introduction from Keir HARDIE and John SCURR, she and her family, under the assumed name of "Evans", escaped to Australia. In June 1914 she became an organizer for the Women's Political Association, which had links with the WSPU, supporting Vida GOLDSTEIN's candidacy in the Australian federal election.

During the First World War she joined the Women's Peace Army and was elected an officer in 1917. She and her husband joined the Socialist party in 1916 and she spoke at anti-conscription rallies. In 1917 she and Adela PANKHURST, a fellow exile, led marches to protest against war profiteering. The two were arrested and sentenced to nine months' imprisonment, although the sentence was quashed on a technicality. In 1919, in Melbourne, she was sentenced to six months' imprisonment for having flown the Red Flag in Flinders Park. She went on hunger-and-thirst strike and was released after four days. To her career as a rebel she could add the accolade of being Australia's first hunger-striker. In 1928 she was appointed a Children's Court magistrate in Melbourne. In 1946 she was an active member of the Australian branch of the SUFFRAGETTE FELLOWSHIP.

Address: (1912) 194 Oldham Road, Failsworth, Manchester; (1913) 762 Oldham Road, Newton Heath, Manchester.
Photograph: in *Votes for Women*, 7 May 1908.
Archival source: Suffragette Fellowship Collection, Museum of London.
Bibliography: *Votes for Women*; *Australian Dictionary of National Biography*.

BALDOCK, [LUCY] MINNIE, MRS (c. 1864–1954) One of the earliest London supporters of the WOMEN'S SOCIAL AND POLITICAL UNION. As a girl she had worked in a shirt factory and later noted that if her parents had not helped her she could not have earned enough to support herself. She was a member of the Independent Labour Party, married to a local councillor in West Ham, who was a fitter and also a member of the ILP, and they had two sons, Jack and Harry. In 1892 Keir HARDIE was elected in West Ham as the first ILP MP. In 1903 Minnie Baldock had held a meeting for women to protest against the low wage that West Ham Council was proposing to pay women in its tramway department. She had been very much involved in the administration of the West Ham Unemployed Fund and in organizing deputations of working women in support of the Unemployed Workmen's Act. Dora MONTEFIORE and Charlotte DESPARD were also both involved at this time in organizing similar Distress Committees. In April 1905 Minnie Baldock was asked by West Ham ILP to stand as a candidate in the election for the West Ham Board of Guardians.

Dora Montefiore, in *From a Victorian to a Modern*, 1927, corrects a "mis-statement" by Sylvia PANKHURST "in what she calls her 'History of the Suffrage Movement'". The mis-statement (if it is so) is that Annie KENNEY came to London in early 1906 (with £2 in her pocket) and immediately sought out Sylvia Pankhurst and stayed with her in her lodgings in Chelsea. It was first put in print by Sylvia Pankhurst in *Votes for Women* on 5 November 1908, then repeated in *The Suffragette*, 1911 and *The Suffragette Movement*, 1931, and has now become mythology. Mrs Montefiore was adamant that it was to her that Annie Kenney came and that she put her in touch with Mrs Baldock, with whom Annie then lived during her first weeks in London. Mrs Montefiore noted that when, years later, she tackled Sylvia Pankhurst about her version, she was given what she considered an inadequate reply – that Sylvia was under her mother's influence and that Mrs Pankhurst had wanted to suppress Mrs Montefiore's name. There can be no doubt, however, that Annie Kenney had, on a previous occasion, been in touch with Mrs Baldock. With Mrs Montefiore, the three had heckled Asquith at the Queen's Hall on 19 December 1905 and Annie Kenney and Minnie Baldock, who was disguised as her maid, repeated the performance for Campbell-Bannerman at a Liberal party rally in the Albert Hall on 21 December 1905. They were ejected to the accompaniment of loud cries of "Shame". In her autobiography Mrs Pankhurst, and Sylvia Pankhurst in *The Suffragette Movement*, both give the glory of this interruption to Annie Kenney and Teresa Billington (*see* Teresa BILLINGTON-GREIG) who was also there. On 22 December Minnie Baldock, with Annie Kenney, Teresa Billington, and a Mrs Fennell (who later became a member of the CANNING TOWN branch of the WSPU) called on Campbell-Bannerman at his house at 39 Belgrave Square, asking for an interview with him. He replied that he would be dealing soon with the question of women's suffrage. Annie Kenney was finally sent to "rouse" London in early 1906. It is clear that Minnie Baldock had the capability and opportunity of interesting and mobilizing numbers of women from the East End of London in the suffrage cause. It would have seemed sensible for Annie Kenney to have stayed in the midst of this community, rather than commuting each day from Sylvia Pankhurst's lodgings in Chelsea. However,

Annie Kenney in her autobiography, *Memories of the Militant*, 1924, does state that she lived at this time with Sylvia Pankhurst. She may have spent a few days before the Caxton Hall demonstration on 19 February staying with Minnie Baldock in Canning Town. Certainly when she was arrested on 9 March Annie Kenney gave the Park Walk address to the police. Dora Montefiore considered that, nearly 20 years after the event, there was a conspiracy to write her, and by association Mrs Baldock, out of this particular part of history. In fact in *The Suffragette Movement* Sylvia Pankhurst makes only two, extremely brief, references to Mrs Baldock by name. She does say that a little later "Annie Kenney now spent most of her time in the East End" and it is not impossible that, having spent a short time in Chelsea, she then went to stay with Mrs Baldock.

Proof of Annie Kenney's close association with Minnie Baldock can be found in the latter's voluminous papers, now in the Museum of London. On 29 January 1906 a new group, the Unemployed Women of South-West Ham, was formed, with Mrs Baldock as chairwoman, in order to put pressure on the Local Distress Committee to make provision for unemployed women. This group was addressed on 6 February by Annie Kenney who urged them to take up the cause of women's suffrage. Very sensibly the embryonic London WSPU took advantage of existing political organization and awareness. On 19 February 1906, the day of the opening of the new parliament, what Sylvia Pankhurst describes as "a procession of East End women in the unemployed movement" came to Caxton Hall and joined Mrs Pankhurst in lobbying the House of Commons. On 27 February 1906 this group voted to become the Canning Town branch of the WSPU – the first in London.

On 2 March 1906 Mrs Baldock was a member of a deputation to Downing Street. The other members included Dora Montefiore, Flora DRUMMOND and Annie Kenney. She was still closely in touch with Dora Montefiore, who does not appear to have been a member of the WSPU London Committee, and who conducted her own, much self-publicized, campaign of tax resistance in May 1906. Dora Montefiore sent Minnie Baldock a postcard on 23 May: "Am resisting bailiff who has come to distrain for income tax, and the house is besieged. Tell the poor women I am doing it to help them." Along with Annie Kenney, Irene MILLER, and 50 women from Canning Town, Minnie Baldock joined a demonstration outside Mrs Montefiore's barricaded house in Hammersmith. She kept among her papers many newscuttings about Dora Montefiore's campaign.

In June 1906 Minnie Baldock was present at, and has left a first-hand description of, the events in Cavendish Square surrounding the arrest and subsequent imprisonment of Teresa Billington and she spoke at a demonstration to protest against this in Trafalgar Square on 1 July. She became an official WSPU ORGANIZER, with her name on the notepaper, fourth on the list, along with Annie Kenney, Mary GAWTHORPE, Mrs MARTEL, Helen FRASER, Adela PANKHURST and Flora Drummond. Her organizing activities were obviously taking her further afield; in October Mrs PETHICK-LAWRENCE sent her a postal order for 30/- to cover her expenses while holding meetings in Long Eaton in Derbyshire. The rising involvement in militancy led to the arrest of Mrs Baldock on 23 October on a charge of disorderly conduct in Old Palace Yard at Westminster on the occasion of the opening of parliament, and, having been refused to be bound over, she was sentenced to two months' imprisonment. Her husband spoke in her support at a meeting in Hyde Park. "I am proud to be the husband of such a woman as Mrs Baldock, and I glory in her courage and that of the other ten women who have been imprisoned for the sake of the faith that is in them". She suffered from recurring appendicitis and Mr Baldock, on the advice of Keir Hardie, wrote to Herbert Gladstone, the Home Secretary, asking "if you would kindly see that she receives proper treatment for this". By 2 November Mrs Baldock, along with the other suffrage prisoners, was placed in the first division prison category. On 6 November she wrote "A Miss Robins A Lady from America visited us the other day and promised she would write to Jack. Tell him that he must answer it very nicely." Elizabeth ROBINS also commented with approval on Mr Baldock's speech. Mrs Baldock mentions that Dr Stanton COIT had sent her a copy of *Women and Economics* by Charlotte Perkins Gilman. On their release she and her fellow prisoners were entertained at a banquet organized by Mrs Fawcett at the Savoy Hotel on 11 December 1906. Rather poignant in retrospect is her worry, mentioned in her correspondence with Mrs Pethick-Lawrence, that her dress might not be suitable for a banquet. Rather sadly too, in view of her husband's support, her name is given on the table plan of the banquet as "Miss Baldock".

In November 1906, while she was in prison, she was reappointed as manager of the Council Schools in a district of West Ham. By mid-1907 the WSPU was concentrating on attracting the monied middle-classes and used Mrs Baldock to articulate the claim of respectable working-class women for the vote. Louise EATES wrote to her on 7 June, asking her to speak at a Drawing-Room Meeting to be held at 71 Knightsbridge "to an audience of ladies". The invitation runs "Mrs Macdonald is anxious to put before her friends the case for women's suffrage as it is seen by Working Women and I felt that your long experience as guardian would supply what she wants. She is anxious to have a *real* Working Woman to speak so I thought that perhaps you would bring Mrs Sparborough [*see* SBARBORO] with you. . . . Mrs Macdonald is a rich woman and I hope to get a Collection for our funds. All expenses will be paid by Mrs Macdonald." It is not clear if Mrs Sbarboro did go, in order to bring the necessary touch of realism, but Mrs Baldock certainly did. Louise Eates sent her a postal order for 1/6 out of the money Mrs Macdonald had provided for expenses and "I had ever so many nice compliments for you." It is clear that Mrs Baldock acted as an acceptable intermediary between upper- and middle-class women and the working-classes. Correspondence to her invariably contained a delicate allusion to the fact that her expenses would be paid. A couple of months later Mrs Eates again invited her to a meeting in Kensington "to make the rich and idle women realize the difficulties that drive poor women to demand the Vote". At this meeting her co-speakers were to be Mrs PANKHURST and Gertrude CONOLAN.

In February 1908 Minnie Baldock was arrested, with Mrs Pankhurst and Annie Kenney among others, and imprisoned after the "rush" on parliament from Caxton Hall. She had driven round Parliament Square, shouting exhortations through a megaphone. As a previous offender she received a sentence of one month. When she was in prison Maud Arncliffe SENNETT sent a parcel of toys to Jack Baldock, and Mrs Macdonald of Knightsbridge sent him 5/– to buy something to pass the time while his mother was away. In May 1908 Emily Cobb of Hove, a member of the Brighton WSPU (she had previously belonged to the Brighton branch of the National Union of Women's Suffrage Societies) wrote to Minnie Baldock, suggesting that she pay her £1 a week for four weeks so that Mrs Baldock could get someone to do "your home work and so set you free to do work which you *can* do and many of us can not". This was so that she could spend time helping with the organization of the June Hyde Park Demonstration, at which she was a platform speaker. Life working for the WSPU was obviously much more interesting than doing the housework. A few days before the Demonstration she received a letter from the Graphic Cinematographic Company of 154 Charing Cross Road, confirming that they would be present at a "dinner-hour meeting" she was to hold the next day at Waterlows printing works in Shoreditch. In early August she was ejected from the Queen's Hall after jumping onto the platform and attempting to question Lloyd George, while he was addressing a meeting in connection with the Peace Congress. Later that month she was lent a cottage in Kent and in the autumn returned to the round of London speaking engagements.

She went to Bristol in February 1909, staying in the same digs as Mary BLATHWAYT, speaking at meetings, organizing the new shop and sales of *Votes for Women*, and in the course of the next few months also went to work with Annie Kenney in Cardiff. The issue of *Votes for Women* of 4 June notes that Mrs Baldock was expected to return to Bristol from London but it became clear that she was unable to do so. On 16 June Emmeline Pethick-Lawrence wrote to her, "I brought your difficulty to the Finance committee and after giving the matter very careful consideration, the committee decided to give you a month's holiday from the day you left Bristol and returned home, at full salary. . . . The committee have [*sic*] decided that at the end of the month it would consider your connection with the Movement at an end for the present. That will give you the whole summer to recruit and to make your domestic arrangements." It seems that the fact that she was working full-time for the WSPU did cause her family financial difficulties, but in the autumn she was helping at the Bermondsey by-election. Her husband was also involved with the WSPU; in December 1909 Flora Drummond wrote to him from Glasgow, inviting him when she was next in London to have lunch with her at the Writers' Club (*see under* CLUBS). In the January 1910 general election campaign Minnie Baldock was busy speaking at meetings all over London. It is interesting to note in the correspondence the intricacy and delicacy of the arrangements that were employed in order to make it possible for her to carry out this work. On 1 February 1910 Mrs Penn GASKELL wrote asking her to speak at the north-west London branch of the WSPU: "we would pay fares or would gladly put you up with Mrs CULLEN and I would be glad to have you if you can stay the four days". She obviously maintained contact with the Blathwayts and, in April 1910, at her request, Col Blathwayt sent her a hamper of plants, giving her both their Latin and common names, together with height and flowering details, to brighten her East-End garden.

Minnie Baldock carried on working for the WSPU until July 1911 when she became seriously ill and was operated on for cancer by "Dr Blake" (presumably Dr Louisa Aldrich-Blake) at the New Hospital for Women. She was visited in hospital by Christabel Pankhurst, an action that was mentioned in letters to her by other friends with something approaching reverence. She had worked tirelessly for the WSPU for nearly five years and it is not very far from Clement's Inn to Euston Road, but although Mabel TUKE said that she had tried to visit her, she did not actually quite manage it. She wrote, instead, "I am sure we can fix up a country visit for you when you come out of hospital with some kind member of the Union". In fact Minnie Baldock went to recuperate in Brighton with Minnie TURNER, who paid her expenses, and whom she obviously already knew. On some previous occasion Mrs Baldock had kept house for Minnie Turner, while the latter had a rest.

This brought an end to Mrs Baldock's main period of involvement with the WSPU, although in mid-1912 she was still receiving requests to speak at meetings from, for instance, Evelina HAVERFIELD and Gertrude Conolan. In 1912 she was a member of the CHURCH LEAGUE FOR WOMEN'S SUFFRAGE. By January 1913 she and her husband were living in Southampton and had previously been living in Birkenhead. It seems probable that it was her husband's search for work ("unrest in the labour world" was mentioned) that took them away from London. She did, however, subscribe to the WSPU in 1913. There is a gap of many years in Mrs Baldock's meticulously organized suffrage scrapbook. Then on 2 January 1928 Elsa GYE wrote to her saying how pleased she and Mrs How MARTYN were to trace her, in order to invite her to the final victory celebrations. Minnie Baldock was given a platform ticket for a meeting and told "You of all people must be on the platform as you were one of our earliest Prisoners . . . if you can come to the dinner you can sit at my table". Elsa Gye mentioned that it was Mrs Baldock who introduced her to her future husband, Will Bullock, in Nottingham in 1908. Mrs Baldock was then back in the fold. She carried a BANNER in the WSPU colours in front of the funeral cortege on the way to Mrs Pankhurt's burial in Brompton ceremony and at the unveiling of Mrs Pankhurst's statue in 1930. On 14 July 1947 she gave a talk to the SUFFRAGETTE FELLOWSHIP. In her will, from her tiny estate, she left bequests to the Women's Section of the Poole Labour Party, to the "Woman's Suffrage Fellowship" and to the "Garrett Anderson Hospital", doubtless in recognition of the care she had received there long before.

Address: (1906) 10 Eclipse Road, London E; (1954) 73 Lake Road, Hamworthy, Poole, Dorset.
Photograph: photograph by Ada Schofield (Museum of London); photograph of Minnie Baldock on her 90th birthday, wearing her "Holloway" brooch and looking very sprightly (Museum of London); by Col Blathwayt in B.M.W. Dobbie, *A Nest of Suffragettes in Somerset*, 1979; wearing her "Holloway" brooch in D. Atkinson, *Suffragettes in Pictures*, 1996.
Archival source: Suffragette Fellowship Collection, Museum of London.

BALFOUR, LADY FRANCES (1858–1931) Daughter of the 8th Duke of Argyll; her mother was a daughter of the 2nd Duke of Sutherland. She was brought up in a Liberal tradition; her father had served in the cabinets of Aberdeen and Palmerston, and was a close associate of Gladstone, her Sutherland grandmother had been a particularly fervent admirer of Garibaldi and a champion of Caroline Norton, and her immediate family was earnest in supporting the emancipation of slaves. Her eldest brother was married to one of Queen Victoria's daughters, Princess Louise. In 1879 Lady Frances Campbell married Eustace Balfour, an architect, the youngest brother of Arthur Balfour, the Conservative prime minister, and of Eleanor Sidgwick, the founder of Newnham. They had five children. In 1887 she became sister-in-law and a close friend to Lady Betty Balfour, sister of Lady Constance LYTTON. Lady Frances and her husband moved in comparatively bohemian circles; she became a close friend of Burne-Jones and his wife.

Lady Frances Balfour wrote in her memoirs, "I don't remember any date, in which I was not a passive believer in the rights of women to be recognised as full citizens in this country. No one ever spoke to me on the subject except as 'Shocking – Ridiculous', more often as an idea that was wicked, immodest and unwomanly." In the 1880s, feeling a need to be useful, she worked with Miss Jenner, an active suffragist, and Miss Dimock in the office of the Travellers' Aid Society, fighting the white slave traffic. She gained her practical political education as a member of the executive committee in the 1890s of the Liberal Unionist Women's Association. By 1896 she was president of the CENTRAL COMMITTEE OF THE NATIONAL SOCIETY FOR WOMEN'S SUFFRAGE and a member of the SPECIAL APPEAL COMMITTEE. In December 1902 she spoke at the first public meeting of the Glasgow and West of Scotland Suffrage Society. By 1904 she was president of the CENTRAL SOCIETY FOR WOMEN'S SUFFRAGE, still holding the position in 1914. In 1906, after the Liberal success in the general election, she was a member of a deputation to Campbell-Bannerman requesting that the question of women's enfranchisement be at the forefront of his government's programme. In 1906 she was a member of the WOMEN'S FRANCHISE DECLARATION COMMITTEE and is also recorded as giving one guinea to the WOMEN'S SOCIAL AND POLITICAL UNION. Rather than a membership subscription, this was probably a donation on the occasion of the Savoy banquet organized in December by Millicent FAWCETT to celebrate the release of the WSPU prisoners. In February 1907 Lady Frances took part, rather reluctantly ("I frankly hated this Appeal to the mob"), in the "Mud March" organized by the NATIONAL UNION OF WOMEN'S SUFFRAGE SOCIETIES. In 1907, at the Hardwicke Club, she debated against Christabel PANKHURST the motion "that the violent methods had put back the Cause". She wryly admits in her memoirs that "the honours of that debate remain with Christabel". Although she had been a close friend of Asquith, she became bitterly disillusioned by his intractable opposition to women's enfranchisement. Although she had been a member of the executive committee of the NUWSS from at least 1903, the CAMBRIDGE WOMEN'S SUFFRAGE ASSOCIATION minuted in 1911 that it would not vote for her re-election to the executive committee because she had so rarely attended the meetings. It did, however, note that if she were not re-elected she should be named a vice-president. She herself remarked in her memoirs that she was by no means one of the hardest workers in the cause, but that in the course of one of the autumns between 1910 and 1912 she had spoken at 60 meetings, and had only attended three golf matches. A traditional Liberal, she was initially hostile to the NUWSS Election Fighting Fund policy, but wrote that she came later to realize that it was the correct approach. Despite their differing political opinions she was very friendly with Ethel SNOWDEN. As she wrote in her memoirs, "My gifts, such as they were, lay in being a sort of liaison officer between Suffrage and the Houses of Parliament, and being possessed of a good platform voice."

She retained her interest in women-related institutions; in 1922 she was a vice-president of the Elizabeth Garrett Anderson Hospital and of the Edinburgh Hospital and Dispensary for Women and Children.

Address: (1879, 1907) 32 Addison Road, London W.
Photograph: photographs by Bassano, 1919 (National Portrait Gallery Archive).
Bibliography: Lady F. Balfour, *Ne Obliviscaris*, 1930.

BALGARNIE, FLORENCE (1856–1928) Born in Scarborough, where her father, Robert Balgarnie, was a Congregational minister. She noted that she first became a supporter of woman's suffrage when she was 17 and as soon as she left school was influenced by the work of Lydia BECKER and herself began petitioning for the suffrage cause and undertaking public speaking. The Misses Balgarnie (she had a younger sister, Mary) subscribed to the MANCHESTER NATIONAL SOCIETY FOR WOMEN'S SUFFRAGE in 1881–2. Florence Balgarnie was honorary secretary of the Scarborough branch of the University Extension Scheme and sat on the Scarborough School Board for two years. She probably went to live in London c. 1884, when she became secretary of the executive committee of the CENTRAL COMMITTEE OF THE NATIONAL SOCIETY FOR WOMEN'S SUFFRAGE, succeeding Lydia Becker. Even before she became secretary she had addressed meetings on behalf of the Society in numerous northern towns. She became an important speaker for the Central Committee; in 1887 she addressed the annual general meeting of the CAMBRIDGE WOMEN'S SUFFRAGE ASSOCIATION. The *Women's Penny Paper*, when interviewing her in the issue of 16 March 1889, remarked, "When the Committee elected Miss Balgarnie, they obtained not only an efficient Secretary and Organiser, but one of the most effective speakers of the day." Florence Balgarnie on this occasion noted, "I do not prefer speaking at drawing room meetings, I am more at home when addressing working people – especially working men." In a letter of resignation to the Central Committee in October 1888 she gave her reason for so doing as her inability to support the coverture clause in William Woodall's suffrage bill. She was asked to defer her resignation, which was then overtaken by the events of the Special General Meeting of 12 December. After the ensuing split in the societies, she became secretary of the society reconstituted under the new rules as the CENTRAL NATIONAL SOCIETY FOR WOMEN'S SUFFRAGE. She obviously found her position with the Central National difficult; she appears to have done a *volte face* at the 1889 AGM and given her support to the Woodall clause, apologizing for doing so to Jacob BRIGHT and Richard PANKHURST. She finally resigned her secretaryship in 1890. Helen BLACKBURN makes no mention of Florence Balgarnie in *Record of Women's Suffrage*, 1902, thereby giving the impression that Lydia Becker had continued as secretary of the Central Committee from 1884 to 1888. Florence Balgarnie was also an active member of the SOCIETY FOR PROMOTING THE RETURN OF WOMEN AS COUNTY COUNCILLORS. In January 1889 she spoke at meetings to support the campaign run by Jane Cobden (*see* Jane Cobden UNWIN), another stalwart of the Central National Society, for election to the London County Council. She subsequently wrote to Jane Cobden in November 1890 to sympathize with her on losing the case brought against her election by Walter de Souza and in the course of this letter wrote "What a hero the G.O.M. is." (The Grand Old Man was Gladstone.)

Always a staunch Liberal, in February 1894 she was a speaker at the WOMEN'S LIBERAL FEDERATION annual general meeting and by 1898 she was a member of the executive committee of that society; she was still a member in 1909. In 1889 she was a delegate to the Women's Rights Congress in Paris. In February 1902 she was a representative of the NATIONAL UNION OF WOMEN'S SUFFRAGE SOCIETIES at the International Conference on Women's Suffrage held in Washington. She spoke at the annual general meeting of the GLASGOW AND WEST OF SCOTLAND ASSOCIATION FOR WOMEN'S SUFFRAGE in 1904 and the next year undertook a suffrage speaking tour of Scotland. On 12 May 1905 she was present in the House of Commons when the women's suffrage bill was talked out. In February 1907 she took part in the NUWSS "Mud March". In the same year she contributed an essay "The Woman's Suffrage Movement in the Nineteenth Century" to Brougham Villiers (ed.), *The Case for Woman's Suffrage*, in which, incidentally, she only makes mention of Lydia Becker in a long list of other suffrage workers. On 24 January 1908, at the Women's Liberal Federation meeting in the Queen's Hall, she demanded that the Liberal government, to which she had pinned such hopes, must enfranchise women, and that women ought no longer to be patient. In February 1909 she was still a speaker for the NUWSS. Later that year she was a founder member of the executive committee of the PEOPLE'S SUFFRAGE FEDERATION and was still a member in 1912.

Florence Balgarnie was a member of the Personal Rights Association, in 1887 was a member of the Moral Reform Union, and in 1885 until at least 1888 was a member, as was Henrietta MULLER, whom she must have known, of Karl Pearson's radical élite, the Men and Women's Club. She was also a temperance worker, an active member of the British Women's Temperance Association; in 1906 Dora MONTEFIORE met her on board a ship in the Gothenburg canal after a visit she had made to Sweden to study the Gothenburg system for government control of alcohol. She died in a *pensione* in the centre of Florence, leaving her estate to her family and £1000 to endow a bed at Scarborough Hospital in memory of her parents.

Address: (1884) The Manse, Filey, Scarborough; (1901) Glenthorn, Muswell Road, Muswell Hill, London N; (1902) 51 Crouch Hall Road, London N; (1928) "Piggotts", Bardfield End Green, Thaxted, Essex.
Photograph: in E. Hill and O.F. Shafer, *Great Suffragists – and Why*, 1909.
Bibliography: E. Hill and O.F. Shafer, *Great Suffragists – and Why*, 1909; L. Bland, *Banishing the Beast*, 1995.

BALHAM (branch of London Society, NUWSS) Secretary (1913) Miss M. Powell, 82 Balham Park Road, London SW.

BALHAM AND TOOTING (WSPU) Secretary (1913) Mrs Cocksedge, 12 Foxbourne Road, Balham, London SW.

BANBURY (NUWSS) In 1913 the society was a member of the OXON, BERKS, BUCKS, AND BEDS FEDERATION OF THE NATIONAL UNION OF WOMEN'S SUFFRAGE SOCIETIES. Secretary (1913) Miss Penrose, 32 West Bar, Banbury and Miss Gillett, The Elms, Banbury, Oxfordshire.

BAND The WOMEN'S SOCIAL AND POLITICAL UNION formed a fife and drum band in 1909. By April the band had 20 members, and devoted three evenings a week to practice. George Bryer, 186a Queen's Road, Battersea, presumably father or brother to Constance BRYER, was band superintendant, Mary LEIGH was drum-major, and Miss Dallas was secretary. The band, wearing special uniforms in the colours, first appeared in public in May 1909 at the Women's Prince's Rink Exhibition. In the summer of 1909 they marched around Holloway daily "playing inspiring music" for the hunger-striking suffragettes inside. The band was filmed taking part in the "Prison to Citizenship" procession, 18 June 1910 (*see under* FILMS).

BANFF committee of the National Society for Women's Suffrage was in existence in 1872.

BANGOR (NUWSS) In 1913 the society was a member of the WEST LANCS, WEST CHESHIRE, AND NORTH WALES FEDERATION OF THE NATIONAL UNION OF WOMEN'S SUFFRAGE SOCIETIES. Secretary (1913) Mrs C. Price White, Rockleigh, Bangor.
Archival source: Minute Book of the Bangor and District Women's Suffrage Society, University College of North Wales, Bangor.

BANNERS Banners had been a feature of the rallies agitating for the reform of the electoral system in the 1860s but it was not until 1880 that a women's suffrage banner was displayed. On 4 November 1880 such a banner was carried at the "Grand Demonstration" held at the Colston Hall in Bristol. It had been designed and made at the office of the BRISTOL AND WEST OF ENGLAND SOCIETY FOR WOMEN'S SUFFRAGE at 69 Park Street, and is probably the "large white and gold banner made 25 years ago by the Bristol suffrage society, under the late Helen Blackburn" mentioned in the *Common Cause*, 1910, p. 385. However, there may have been an earlier banner, that was carried, albeit with difficulty, at the London "Grand Demonstration" held on 6 May 1880 in St James's Hall. It was noted that the women banner-bearers included some who worked at the Army Clothing factory (*see* Henrietta MULLER) and who presumably had access to the material and skill with which to make a banner. By 1884 banners were in abundance. A picture in the *Graphic*, 28 June 1884, shows that the women's suffrage meeting in St James's Hall was decorated with banners from Leeds, Edinburgh, Glasgow, Birmingham and Newcastle. The "Grand Demonstrations" did not lead to enfranchisement and when women were still excluded from the 1884 Reform Act, the campaign retreated to the parliamentary lobby and the drawing-room, spaces that did not lend themselves to banner waving. The first women's suffrage banner in the twentieth-century appears to have been made at home, with a slogan that included "Votes for Women", and taken by Christabel PANKHURST and Annie KENNEY to the Free Trade Hall on 13 October 1905. There is no mention of one having been produced at, for instance, the lobbying of parliament on 12 May 1905. Photographs of the first London WOMEN'S SOCIAL AND POLITICAL UNION march to Caxton Hall in February 1906 show the home-made banners carried by the East-End women.

Banners henceforward became an ever-developing feature of suffrage marches. The majority were worked by members of the suffrage movement, drawn either from the two artists' societies, the ARTISTS' SUFFRAGE LEAGUE and the SUFFRAGE ATELIER, or from the local society or branch. The majority of the banners were embroidered or appliquéd, skills which were synonymous with true womanhood and carried with them the resonances of service to a cause. The NATIONAL UNION OF WOMEN'S SUFFRAGE SOCIETIES organized a plethora of banners for the February 1907 "Mud March" and by June 1908 both the constitutional and the militant societies had perfected their design and production of banners. The Artists' Suffrage League, under the direction of Mary LOWNDES, produced a range of banners for the 13 June 1908 NUWSS procession. The *Scotsman* reported that "The most remarkable feature of the procession was the great display of banners and bannerettes. It was said there were as many as 800 of them, and the designs and mottoes which they bore appeared to be almost as numerous. Many of them were effective works of art, and bore striking inscriptions." Before the procession the banners were displayed in the Council Chamber of Caxton Hall. The *Daily Chronicle* remarked that "the beauty of the needlework... should convince the most sceptical that it is possible for a woman to use a needle even when she is also wanting a vote". *Votes for Women*, 25 June 1908, carried an article, "Unfurling the Banners", that gives a full description of many of those carried to Hyde Park on 21 June, with details of who made and who presented them.

Banners were not only symbols to be carried on the "high days" of the campaign, but could also be used to inspire sympathy and loyalty during quieter times. The Liverpool NUWSS banner, designed by a local artist and worked by local ladies, was displayed in the window of a shop that they rented for the purpose a week before it was taken to London to be carried in the 13 June procession.

The GLASGOW AND WEST OF SCOTLAND ASSOCIATION FOR WOMEN'S SUFFRAGE declined to display posters locally for the 13 June 1908 procession on the grounds that London was too far away for its members to be able to attend, but did suggest that the banners should be put on view in Glasgow in the autumn. The exhibition, held in the Fine Art Institute on 1 and 2 December 1908, was accompanied by tea, a small string band and a pianola. The GWSAWS bought 200 copies of the pamphlet describing the banners, which had been compiled by Helena SWANWICK. In 1908 the BIRMINGHAM NUWSS also held a Banner Exhibition, opened by Mrs FAWCETT one day, and by Margaret ASHTON the next.

Although the local societies clearly enjoyed devising their own motifs, NUWSS headquarters on occasion suggested that a harmonious image might be used to effect. For the NUWSS demonstration in Trafalgar Square on 9 July 1910 headquarters requested that the banners should carry the number of electors who signed the NUWSS petition at the January general election. The MANSFIELD society complied; its banner cost 5/9. The CAMBRIDGE ASSOCIATION made banners, "according to instructions from the National Union, bearing the numbers of voters who signed the Petition, in the borough and in East and West Cambridgeshire". In a similar vein Irene Dallas, as banner secretary for the June 1910 WSPU procession, had made a point of finding out from the local unions the colour and lettering of banners and standards that they were bringing to London in order to better co-ordinate them. For this procession the Suffrage Atelier contributed banners for the WOMEN'S FREEDOM LEAGUE sections. Newsreel films survive of both these June and July 1910 processions, showing how the women supported the swaying banners, swelling with the breeze. The designs and messages broadcast on the banners are easily decipherable (*see under* FILMS). The NUWSS also lent out banners from its headquarters. In March 1912 the BEDFORD SOCIETY held a party in St Cuthbert's Hall, which was decorated with suffrage banners lent by headquarters and "which made a splendid array". The NUWSS made a point of asking the individual societies to send in their banners to decorate the Queen's Hall victory celebration on 13 March 1918.

A description of the banners of individual societies and branches, where known, is included in their respective entries. *See also* COLOURS.

Archival source: The Fawcett Library Collection; The Suffragette Fellowship Collection, Museum of London.

Bibliography: L. Tickner, *The Spectacle of Women: Imagery of the Suffrage Campaign 1907–14*, 1987, which includes excellent descriptions of all the surviving banners, and illustrations of some.

BARGOED AND DISTRICT (NUWSS) In 1913 the society was a member of the SOUTH WALES AND MONMOUTH FEDERATION OF THE NATIONAL UNION OF WOMEN'S SUFFRAGE SOCIETIES. Secretary (1913) Mrs Iorwerth Clark, Caerdydd, Hillside Park, Bargoed.

BARMBY, [JOHN] GOODWYN (1820–81), **CATHERINE** (1817–54), and **ADA MARIANNE** (*c.* 1832–1911) Goodwyn Barmby and Catherine, his first wife, were Chartists, feminists and utopian socialists, founding members in 1841 of the Communist Church. They saw themselves as successors to Mary Wollstonecraft and Shelley, and were friends of Anne KNIGHT. In 1841 they published a *Declaration of Electoral Reform*, in which they demanded "unsexual Chartism". In 1843 Catherine Barmby published a *Demand for Emancipation*, encompassing the three spheres of political, domestic and "ecclesiastical", or spiritual, life. In the first she emphasized the points that were to form the main platform of all later claims for women's enfranchisement; that women had no control over the making of the laws to which they were subject and that women were taxed without being able to make their own choice of political representation. In the 1840s the Barmbys were associated with George HOLYOAKE in various attempts to found a feminist journal, although these came to nothing.

By 1866 Catherine Barmby had died and Goodwyn Barmby was a Unitarian minister, now married to Ada, the daughter of the governor of Wakefield prison. She signed the 1866 suffrage petition, as did Julia Barmby (*c.* 1827–93), sister to Goodwyn Barmby, and Maria Watkins, sister to Catherine. They all lived in Westgate in Wakefield. In 1867 Goodwyn Barmby organized a large demonstration in Wakefield in favour of mankind suffrage and in 1868 was in touch with Lydia BECKER.

The Rev. G. Barmby, Mrs Barmby and Miss Barmby were subscribers to the MANCHESTER SOCIETY FOR WOMEN'S SUFFRAGE from 1868 to 1871 and in 1872 Miss Julia Barmby was honorary secretary of the WAKEFIELD COMMITTEE OF THE NATIONAL SOCIETY FOR WOMEN'S SUFFRAGE.

Address: (1872) Westgate Parsonage, Westgate, Wakefield; (1888) Julia Barmby: Magnolia House, Yoxford, Suffolk; (1900) Ada Barmby: Mount Pleasant, Sidmouth, Devon.

Bibliography: J.M. Bellamy and J. Saville (eds), *Dictionary of Labour Biography*, 1972; B. Taylor, *Eve and the New Jerusalem*, 1983.

BARNARD CASTLE (NUWSS) The society was a member of the NORTH-EASTERN FEDERATION OF THE NATIONAL UNION OF WOMEN'S SUFFRAGE SOCIETIES. Secretary (1913) Miss Jane A. Barker, 20 Horse Market, Barnard Castle, Co. Durham.

BARNES (branch of the London Society (NUWSS)) Secretary (1913) Mrs M. Rackham, 20 Rodway Road, Roehampton, London SW.

BARNES (WSPU) In existence in 1908. Secretary: S.A. Wilson Horn.

BARNET (WSPU) Secretary (1913) Miss Mace, Selborne, Hadley Highstone, Barnet.

BARNSLEY Women's Suffrage Society Probably founded in 1902. Secretary (1908) Miss Celia Wray, Fairfield House, Barnsley, who, because she was leaving the town, finally resigned in October 1920, at which time the society transformed itself into the Barnsley Society for Equal Citizenship. In 1913 the society was a member of the WEST RIDING FEDERATION OF THE NATIONAL UNION OF WOMEN'S SUFFRAGE SOCIETIES. Only one of the society's minute books, dating from late 1913, survives. Records of meetings indicate that the society played an active part in the NATIONAL UNION OF WOMEN'S SUFFRAGE SOCIETIES. At a meeting held on 4 December it was decided to hold an important meeting "before Lent" and for Miss Wray to see if there was a suitable speaker in the Federation able to attend. Suggested names included those of Michael Sadler, Lord Lytton and Muriel MATTERS, an entertaining speaker who was always in demand. At this stage in the campaign the Barnsley Society followed NUWSS policy, working closely with Mr Roebuck, who represented the miners and the ILP, to see if he would arrange for a delegate to attend this meeting.

The Barnsley Society considered the FRIENDS OF WOMEN'S SUFFRAGE scheme and, although mildly interested, decided to make no definite campaign among working women. Particular notice was drawn to the fact that no-one who was a member of a militant society should be a member of the NUWSS. When on 14 March 1914 a letter received from Mrs HARLEY about the formation of the ACTIVE SERVICE LEAGUE was discussed, the Barnsley Society decided to take no particular action on this new, somewhat militaristic, method of campaigning. After the outbreak of war, the August meeting of the society agreed to "suspend ordinary political work and offer the services of members for relief of distress during the war". In November 1914 the Barnsley Society supported the MANCHESTER AND DISTRICT FEDERATION's call upon the NUWSS publicly to affirm its belief in conciliation and arbitration as opposed to war and in 1915 regretted that the NUWSS could not be represented at the International Council of Women at the Hague. The Barnsley Women's Suffrage Society's BANNER is now held in the Fawcett Library Collection.

Archival source: Minute book of the Barnsley Women's Suffrage Society, Sheffield Archives.

BARNSTAPLE (NUWSS)   In 1913 the society was a member of the SOUTH-WESTERN FEDERATION OF THE NATIONAL UNION OF WOMEN'S SUFFRAGE SOCIETIES. Secretary (1913) Miss C.L. Wodehouse, Bratton Fleming, R.S.O., North Devon.

BARNT GREEN (WSPU)   Secretary (1913) Mrs Kerwood, Watling House, Barnt Green, Worcestershire.

BARRETT, RACHEL (1875–1953)   Born in Carmarthen of Welsh-speaking parents. She was educated at a boarding-school in Stroud, won a scholarship to Aberystwyth College, graduated with an external London BSc degree in 1904, and became a science teacher at, successively, schools in Llangefni, Carmarthen and Penarth. In the autumn of 1906 she heard Mrs MARTEL speak on women's suffrage in Cardiff and signed a WOMEN'S SOCIAL AND POLITICAL UNION membership card at the end of the meeting. She then helped Adela PANKHURST in the spring of 1907 when the latter came to Cardiff as a WSPU ORGANIZER. In July 1907 Rachel Barrett resigned from her teaching post and enrolled as a student at the London School of Economics, intending to study economics and sociology, and to work for a DSc. During the summer she worked with Adela Pankhurst in Bradford and at her first by-election, at Bury St Edmunds, with Mrs PANKHURST, Mrs Martel, Gladice KEEVIL, Aeta LAMB and Elsa GYE. In the autumn she attended lectures at LSE, which was very convenient for WSPU activities in Clement's Inn. She helped the WSPU campaign at the Mid-Devon by-election during the Christmas vacation and on her return was asked by Christabel PANKHURST to become a full-time organizer. Although sorry to give up her studies she noted that "it was a definite call and I obeyed".

Rachel Barrett organized a campaign in Nottingham and then, in April 1908, helped at the by-elections in Dewsbury and Dundee, which she found very strenuous. In June 1908 she was chairman of one of the platforms at the WSPU Hyde Park Demonstration. Shortly after this she was forced to resign her position as organizer and spent the next year, including some time in a sanatorium, recuperating. In the autumn of 1909, having recovered, she went to work as a volunteer with Annie KENNEY in Bristol. She soon agreed to resume her position as a paid organizer and was sent to Newport in Monmouthshire. In January 1910 she ran the WSPU campaign in Bridgwater. In September 1910 during the Conciliation Bill truce she led a deputation of women from his constituency to Lloyd George and after two and a half hours left more convinced than ever of his opposition to the WSPU and of the insincerity of his support for the suffrage cause. Shortly after this she was appointed chief WSPU organizer for Wales, with headquarters in Cardiff, from where she organized a deputation of leading Welsh Liberal women to Lloyd George.

In early 1912, after the police raid on Clement's Inn and Christabel Pankhurst's escape to Paris, Rachel Barrett was chosen by Annie Kenney, with whom she had previously worked closely in the west of England, to help run the national WSPU campaign. Annie Kenney in her autobiography

Memories of a Militant, 1924, describes Rachel Barrett as "an exceptionally clever and highly educated woman. She was a devoted worker and had tremendous admiration for Christabel. She was learned, and I liked her". In the autumn of 1912 Rachel Barrett was put in charge of the new WSPU paper the *Suffragette*, "an appalling task as I knew nothing whatever of journalism". She often went to Paris to see Christabel and talked to her on the telephone and later mentioned that she could hear the click as Scotland Yard listened in. On 30 April 1913 she and other members of the paper's staff were arrested as they were making it up. The police seized all the materials for printing the paper, but Gerald Gould (*see* Barbara Ayrton GOULD) and the *Daily Herald* came to the rescue and the *Suffragette* appeared that week as usual, although in a rather attenuated form. At the end of the ensuing conspiracy trial Rachel Barrett was sentenced to nine months' imprisonment. She immediately began a hunger strike in Holloway and was then taken to Canterbury prison, where, in spite of her struggles, she was made to wear prison clothes until an order came from the Home Office that allowed her to wear her own. She particularly noted the indignity of having her fingerprints taken. After five days' hunger strike she was released under the "Cat and Mouse" Act and went to "Mouse Castle", the BRACKENBURYS' house. When she emerged after three weeks she was promptly rearrested, went on hunger strike for four days and was then again released to "Mouse Castle". After recovering she was smuggled out, spoke in disguise at meetings and was re-arrested on leaving one such on 17 July at the Memorial Hall in Farringdon Road. She then went on a hunger-and-thirst strike and was released after five days. She managed to elude the police watching "Mouse Castle" and escaped to an Edinburgh nursing home. She remained there until December 1913, was then smuggled into Lincoln's Inn House and lived there in a bedsitting room until May 1914, when, after she had gone on holiday, the office was raided. She visited Christabel Pankhurst in Paris and it was arranged that the *Suffragette* should be printed in Scotland, where printers were at less risk. Rachel Barrett, under the name of "Miss Ashworth", then lived in Edinburgh and brought out the paper until the last number appeared on the Friday after war was declared in August 1914.

In the 1920s Rachel Barrett was for a time the lover of Ida Wylie, novelist and short story writer, who had written for the *Suffragette* in 1913, and the two were close friends and literary advisers to Radclyffe Hall, particularly during the trial of *The Well of Loneliness*. In her will she left the residue of her estate to Ida Wylie. In her later years she was an active member of the SUFFRAGETTE FELLOWSHIP, remaining particularly friendly with Kitty Marshall, near whom she lived, and whose memoirs she offered in the late 1940s, unsuccessfully, for publication to Victor Gollancz. The fact that Harold Rubinstein, solicitor to Radclyffe Hall and himself a former suffragist, was a brother-in-law of Victor Gollancz doubtless influenced her choice of publisher approached.

Address: (1953) Lamb Cottage, Sible Hedingham, Essex.
Photograph: *Votes for Women*, 7 May 1908.
Archival source: Museum of London, Suffragette Fellowship Collection.
Bibliography: A. Kenney, *Memoirs of a Militant*, 1924; M. Baker, *Our Three Selves: A Life of Radclyffe Hall*, 1985; S. Cline, *Radclyffe Hall: A Woman Called John*, 1997.

BARROW-IN-FURNESS (NUWSS)   In 1913 the society was a member of the NORTH-WESTERN FEDERATION OF THE NATIONAL UNION OF WOMEN'S SUFFRAGE SOCIETIES. Secretary (1913) Mrs Warwick Bell, 42 Victoria Road, Barrow-in-Furness, Lancashire.

BARROW-IN-FURNESS (WSPU)   Organizer (1913) Miss Grew, 180 Blake St, Barrow-in-Furness, Lancashire.

BARRY (WFL)   Secretary (1913) Miss B. Ellis, 11 Gaen Street, Barry, Glamorgan.

BARRY (WSPU)   Secretary (1913) Mrs Jones, 259 Gladstone Road, Barry, Glamorgan.

BARRY, FLORENCE ANTOINETTE (1885–1965) Born in Birkenhead, a Roman Catholic of Persian descent, educated at a convent school, at a finishing school in Bruges, and at the School of Social Science attached to Liverpool University. In 1913 she was on the committee of the Birkenhead Women's Local Government Association. In 1911, after a brief period working with the WOMEN'S SOCIAL

AND POLITICAL UNION, she formed a branch of the newly-founded CATHOLIC WOMEN'S SUFFRAGE SOCIETY on Merseyside. In 1912 she worked for this society in Norwich, where the annual Catholic Congress was that year being held. In 1913 she became honorary secretary of the CWSS, succeeding its founder Gabrielle JEFFERY, and moved to London. She had a small private allowance that allowed her to undertake an unsalaried post and later took an interest in the Commission on the Status of Women set up by the United Nations. In 1934 she was a member of the executive committee of the Open Door Council and honorary secretary of the St Joan's Social and Political Alliance, the successor to the Catholic Women's Suffrage Society.

Address: (1912) 66 Park Road South, Birkenhead.
Bibliography: N.S. Parnell, *The Way of Florence Barry, 1885–1965*, 1973.

BARTELS, OLIVE, OBE (1889–1978) The daughter of an army contractor who died when she was five years old. The family was Protestant, Liberal, pro-Parnell and Home Rule. With her two sisters and brother she was brought up on little money by her mother who, born in Tipperary, had been one of the first nine Irishwomen to receive a university degree. When interviewed in 1976 Olive Bartels had a clear memory of her mother in 1903 attending the Houses of Parliament, dressed in her academic cap and gown, in order to petition for women's suffrage. Her mother and sisters became quietly active supporters of the WOMEN'S SOCIAL AND POLITICAL UNION, thereby putting themselves beyond the pale in suburban Dulwich. Olive Bartels was educated at Streatham High School and at art college until 1909, when she left, candidly admitting that she had little talent for art, in order to become a WSPU ORGANIZER. She campaigned with Grace ROE in the eastern counties and maintained a close friendship with her. In the period of active militancy, 1913–14, she worked "under cover" for the WSPU as "Margaret Cunningham". She was based first in Chelmsford and then in Cambridge. She was responsible for organizing the burning of a newly built house in Storey's Way in Cambridge. She bought and supplied the paraffin used but did not herself commit the actual act. She explained, when interviewed in 1976, that WSPU organizers were not allowed to perpetrate militant acts because if they were then caught it would be said that the WSPU had to rely on paid activists. In July 1913 she acted as a decoy to enable Mrs PANKHURST to elude the police and escape from a flat in Chelsea and in August she conducted the WSPU "Holiday Campaign", based in Lincoln's Inn. In March 1914 she organized the meeting to be addressed by Mrs Pankhurst, who was in hiding from the police, at St Andrew's Hall in Glasgow, barricading the platform with barbed wire concealed under flowers. Finally in June 1914, after the arrest of Grace Roe, Olive Bartels became the "third successor" to Christabel PANKHURST (the first being Annie KENNEY) as chief organizer in London. During this period she lived, disguised as a recently bereaved widow, in the Ivanhoe Hotel in Bloomsbury. She had no direct communication with the WSPU but kept in touch by "underground" methods, about which she has, unfortunately, left no explicit details apart from mentioning that messages were carried to and from her by "office girls".

In October 1914 she accompanied Christabel Pankhurst on a six months' tour of the USA and Canada. In 1915 she joined the War Office staff and was adamant that the authorities there knew nothing of her past suffragette activities. She was sent to Tours as an administrator of work of the WAAC (Women's Army Auxiliary Corps). By the end of the war she was a deputy assistant chief controller in charge of the Administrative Branch and was awarded the OBE for her war work in 1920.

After demobilization she worked, successively, on a small-holding in Guernsey, was secretary of the Anglo-American Clinic in Nice, was an organizer for the National Union of Women Teachers in 1934 and was Woman Advisory Officer of the Land Settlement Association. During the Second World War she was administrator of the London Region of the Women's Voluntary Service, becoming a close friend of Lady Reading. She then lived in Co. Mayo until returning to England *circa* 1960 to live near her sister. When interviewed in 1976 she spoke candidly and humorously of her militant activities, making it quite clear that she did not believe in hanging on to the past and had no desire to join "old girl associations". She remarked apropos the SUFFRAGETTE FELLOWSHIP that, with the passing

of time, "people take credit for things they didn't really do".
Address: (1910) 23 Acacia Grove, Dulwich, London SE; (1934) 39 Gordon Square, London WC1; (1976) The Witterings, Iden, near Rye, East Sussex.
Photograph: A. Raeburn, *The Militant Suffragettes*, 1973 (back end paper).
Archival source: Museum of London, Suffragette Fellowship Collection; B. Harrison, taped interview with Olive Bartels, 1976, Fawcett Library.
Bibliography: A. Raeburn, *The Militant Suffragettes*, 1973.

BARTLETT, FRANCES CLARA, MRS (1876–?) née Satterly Born in Newton Abbot, left school at the age of nine and worked in a dairy in Paignton, Devon. When she was 14 she came to London as a children's nurse. She married when she was 17 and by the time she was 21 had three children. She gradually became involved with working for her local church, then as a canvasser for the Liberal Party, and was elected to the executive committee of the Clapham Women's Liberal Association. Around 1906 she attended a Liberal Party meeting at which Christabel PANKHURST was heckled. Mrs Bartlett spoke up for her and after the meeting Christabel asked her to call at Clement's Inn. After that Mrs Bartlett resigned from the Liberal Party and devoted herself to the WOMEN'S SOCIAL AND POLITICAL UNION. At first she worked voluntarily, chalking pavements, selling *Votes for Women*, working at by-elections up and down the country, heckling cabinet ministers. She related how she was then told that she was an "ORGANIZER", although she was reluctant to become one because her husband worked in the Civil Service and she had three young children to care for. She was immediately, on 25 January 1909, sent on a deputation, driving into Downing Street with Mary CLARKE and Irene Dallas. She was arrested under her maiden name, Satterly, in order not to jeopardize her husband's position, and sentenced to one month's imprisonment. Her mother wrote to the Home Secretary a touchingly dignified letter appealing to him to reduce her sentence or to move her into the first division as a political offender.

Later Frances Bartlett worked for Dr Flora MURRAY at the nursing home where, she relates, all women who had been forcibly fed were brought. This is probably Nurse PINE's Pembridge Crescent nursing home: she noted that it was there that she nursed Mrs PANKHURST when Nurse Pine was not able to be with her. She also nursed Mrs Pankhurst at different houses after her hunger strikes and notes that they once stayed for three months at the country house of Dr Ede and Dr Amy Sheppard.

During the First World War she lived at Tower Cressy in Kensington, looking after the babies adopted by Mrs Pankhurst. Both her own sons were killed in the war. She may have helped keep house for Annie KENNEY after the latter's marriage in 1920.
Address: (her mother's, 1909) 24 Queen Street, Torquay, Devon.
Photograph: in Suffragette Fellowship Collection, Museum of London.
Archival source: Suffragette Fellowship Collection, Museum of London; Home Office Papers, Public Record Office.

BASINGSTOKE (NUWSS) In 1913 the society was a member of the SURREY, SUSSEX, AND HANTS FEDERATION OF THE NATIONAL UNION OF WOMEN'S SUFFRAGE SOCIETIES. Secretary (1909) Mrs E.N. Conran, Hackwood Road, Basingstoke, Hampshire; (1913) Miss Doman, Bramley Cottage, Winchester Road, Basingstoke and Miss Cicely Chadwick, Queen's Road, Basingstoke, Hampshire.

BATESON, ANNA, MRS (c. 1830–1918) Daughter of James Aikin of Liverpool, she married William Bateson, Master of St John's College, Cambridge. She and her three daughters (*see* Anna BATESON, Mary BATESON *and* Margaret HEITLAND) were all active workers for the suffrage cause. In 1884 Mrs Bateson was a founding member and secretary, until 1890, of the CAMBRIDGE WOMEN'S SUFFRAGE ASSOCIATION. She was still an active member in 1909. By 1885 she was a poor law guardian in Cambridge and she signed a petition to the House of Lords in support of the Woman's Suffrage Bill. In the 1888 split she supported the CENTRAL NATIONAL SOCIETY and was a member of its executive committee. In January 1889 the Cambridge Association withdrew its affiliation to the Central National Society and this may have been a factor in her resignation from the secretaryship of the Association, although in 1890 she did move out of Cambridge. She was a stalwart Liberal, president of the Cambridge Women's Liberal Association, and was one of the

vice-presidents of the WOMEN'S LIBERAL FEDERATION. She was an active speaker for the Federation; at the end of 1888 she spoke at the founding meeting of the Chatham branch. She was a member of the Ladies' Committee of the Home Rule Union. In 1905 she was a subscriber to the CENTRAL SOCIETY FOR WOMEN'S SUFFRAGE.
Address: (1885) 8 Harvey Road, Cambridge.
Archival source: Minutes of the Cambridge Association for Women's Suffrage, Cambridge Record Office.

BATESON, ANNA (1863–1928) Daughter of Mrs Anna BATESON, sister of Mary BATESON and Margaret HEITLAND. She grew up in Cambridge, spent one year at Karlsruhe and read natural sciences at Newnham, 1882–6. She worked as an assistant to Sir Francis Darwin in the University Botany Laboratory, 1886–90. With her mother she was a founding member of the CAMBRIDGE WOMEN'S SUFFRAGE ASSOCIATION in 1884 and represented the Association at the special general meeting of the CENTRAL COMMITTEE OF THE NATIONAL SOCIETY FOR WOMEN'S SUFFRAGE in London on 12 December 1888 and signified its general approval of the proposed new rules, thereby siding with those who formed the CENTRAL NATIONAL SOCIETY FOR WOMEN'S SUFFRAGE. In January 1889, however, the Association withdrew its affiliation to the Central National Society. She resigned from the executive committee of the Cambridge Association in November 1889.

In 1892 she moved to New Milton in Hampshire where she ran a market garden for the rest of her life. She was a poor law guardian, a school manager and a member of the Lymington District Council. She was secretary of the New Forest Suffrage Society (NUWSS), although in 1908–9 she gave £21 to the WOMEN'S SOCIAL AND POLITICAL UNION and in 1909 advertised her paeonies and michaelmas daisies in *Votes for Women*.
Address: (1912) Bashley Nursery, New Milton, Hampshire.

BATESON, MARY (1865–1906) Daughter of one Anna BATESON, sister of the other, and of Margaret HEITLAND. She was educated in Cambridge, at the Perse Girls' School and Newnham College, 1884–7, where she took a first-class degree in history. In the minutes of the CENTRAL COMMITTEE OF THE NATIONAL SOCIETY OF WOMEN'S SUFFRAGE, at a meeting dated 4 January 1888, approval was given to the employment of Miss M. Bateson of Cambridge until Easter as an ORGANIZER at the rate of one guinea and a half for each meeting, with, in addition, hotel expenses and second-class railway fares. She quickly arranged meetings in Bury St Edmunds, Great Yarmouth, Norwich, King's Lynn and Lowestoft. Later that year she took up at Newnham a lectureship which she held until her death; she published works on medieval history. She was elected to the executive committee of the CAMBRIDGE WOMEN'S SUFFRAGE ASSOCIATION in 1889 and was secretary from 1892 until 1898. In 1893 she was secretary of a sub-committee of the Cambridge Association that was formed to organize a house-to-house canvass for the SPECIAL APPEAL and in 1894 she was secretary of a sub-committee formed to promote women poor law guardian candidates. On 19 May 1906 she took part in the deputation to the Prime Minister, Sir Henry Campbell-Bannerman, representing "women who are doctors of letters, science and law in the universities of the United Kingdom and of the British colonies, in the universities also of Europe and the United States". She presented a petition signed by 1530 women graduates. In the *Suffragette*, 1911, Sylvia Pankhurst seems to have rolled a couple of Batesons together, and Mary Bateson appears in this deputation as "Mrs Mary Bateson".

Mary Bateson died suddenly later in 1906, leaving her entire estate to Newnham College, and was immortalized shortly afterwards in an entry in the *Dictionary of National Biography*. As so few women have been accorded this recognition it is worthwhile recording that Mary Bateson had herself been a contributor. Professor Tout, her biographer in the *DNB* and by 1913 a vice-president of the MEN'S LEAGUE FOR WOMEN'S SUFFRAGE, remarked that Mandall Creighton, Bishop of London, had attempted to persuade her not to dissipate her energies on the suffrage movement and "that her main business in life was 'to write true history' and pursue a scholar's career".
Address: (1893) 74 Huntingdon Road, Cambridge.
Archival source: Minutes of Cambridge Association for Women's Suffrage, Cambridge Record Office.

BATH Committee of the National Society for Women's Suffrage Formed in 1871. Clementia

TAYLOR had written to Anne and Lilias ASHWORTH (*see* Lilias Ashworth HALLETT) in July 1867, just after the formation of the LONDON NATIONAL SOCIETY FOR WOMEN'S SUFFRAGE, asking if they could form a committee of the society in Bath. This they agreed to do, but the intention may have been vitiated by their involvement in the fledgling BRISTOL AND WEST OF ENGLAND SOCIETY FOR WOMEN'S SUFFRAGE. In 1871 Lady Anna GORE LANGTON was president of the Bath committee and Anne Ashworth, Mrs Glover (wife of Rev. Josephus Glover, 17 Lansdown Crescent), Mrs Layton and Mrs Rawlinson were members of the committee. The honorary secretary was Emily SPENDER, the honorary treasurer was Miss A.B. Le Geyt, of Corston, near Bristol. The Bath society associated itself with the CENTRAL COMMITTEE OF THE NATIONAL SOCIETY FOR WOMEN'S SUFFRAGE in 1872. In 1884 the Bath committee amalgamated with the Bristol and West of England Society. The society continued in existence throughout the next 20 years, although at some point it apparently separated from the Bristol society because in March 1908 they re-amalgamated as the "Bristol, Bath & West of England Women's Suffrage Society". In 1907 Mary BLATHWAYT attended a drawing-room meeting at Mrs Long's house, 7 Great Bedford Street, and in October went to another meeting, at Sydney House, when Mr Phillips, JP "read out some letters and gave us tea after the meeting. Among the ladies present were Aethel and Grace TOLLEMACHE, Mrs Wheatcroft, Miss Johnson, Mrs Thomas and Grace Thomas." The committee, which in 1908 held its meetings at 2 Argyle Street in the lecture room of the Theosophical Society, consisted of Miss Whittaker, Mrs Ashworth Hallett, Miss Johnston, Miss Severs and Mary Blathwayt. In 1913 the society was a member of the SOUTH-WESTERN FEDERATION OF THE NATIONAL UNION OF WOMEN'S SUFFRAGE SOCIETIES.

Office (1910) 22a Broad St, Bath. Secretary (1909–13) Miss Wheelwright, (1909) 52 Sydney Buildings, Bath; (1913) 51 Pulteney Street, Bath. A rather disturbing figure, Miss Wheelwright had joined the WOMEN'S SOCIAL AND POLITICAL UNION in 1908, but like Mary Blathwayt had returned to the NUWSS fold. She was found unconscious in the canal in Bath in February 1913; the story put about, and recorded by Mary Blathwayt, was that she had fallen in while collecting water weed. A few days later Lilias Ashworth Hallett told Mary Blathwayt that Miss Wheelwright had gone into an asylum.

BATH (WSPU) Secretary/organizer (1910) Mrs MANSEL; (1913) The Misses TOLLEMACHE, 12 Walcot Street, Bath. Mary BLATHWAYT was an early member. The Bath WSPU office/shop opened in 1910 and a photograph of it appeared in *Votes for Women*, 6 October 1911.

Bibliography: B.M.W. Dobbie, *A Nest of Suffragettes in Somerset*, 1979.

BATTERSEA (branch of London Society, NUWSS) Secretary (1909) Battersea (South) Miss Neva Beaumont, 6 Elspeth Road, Lavender Hill, London SW; (1913) Mrs Rawlings, 74 York Mansions, Battersea Park, London SW.

BATTERSEA (WFL) Secretary (1910) Barbara Duval (*see* Emily DUVAL), 37 Park Road, St John's Hill, Battersea, London SW.

BATTERSEA (WSPU) Secretary (1906) Miss Fitzherbert, 9 Cambridge Mansions, London SW. Maud Fitzherbert left the WSPU in 1907 to join the WOMEN'S FREEDOM LEAGUE.

BEACONSFIELD AND DISTRICT (NUWSS) Formed in 1911. Chairman (1911) Mrs Commeline; secretary, Mrs Snow.

BEAMISH, [AGNES] OLIVE (1890–1978) Born in Cork, Ireland, into a family of Irish Protestant small landowners. The family moved to Bristol, in order that her brothers might attend Clifton College. Olive Beamish went to Clifton High School, wearing her "Votes for Women" badge to school after joining the WOMEN'S SOCIAL AND POLITICAL UNION when she was 16. She read mathematics and economics at Girton and as soon as she graduated in 1912 began to work for the WSPU in the East End of London. In April 1913, as "Phyllis Brady" she was arrested "on suspicion" with Elsie DUVAL ("Millicent Dean") after being found in Mitcham in the early hours of the morning in possession of paraffin and other incendiary materials. She was sent to Holloway, went on hunger strike, was forcibly fed both while on remand and after sentencing and was released under the "Cat and Mouse" Act on 28 April, one of the first prisoners to be so treated. The address to which she was sent in a cab, accompanied by a prison officer, was that of the Misses Kern, 199 Albany Street, Regent's Park (*see* Elizabeth Wolstenholme ELMY). Olive Beamish, as she related, then went "underground" and resumed her militancy. She was finally re-arrested, at Holborn Circus, having been followed by the police from an address they had under surveillance in King Henry's Road, Hampstead, in January 1914 and charged, again as "Phyllis Brady", with having set fire in March 1913 to Trevethan, the house of Lady White at Egham. There certainly had been a spate of arson incidents in Surrey at that time, just before Olive Beamish and Elsie Duval had been arrested, red-handed, in Mitcham. She was defended at her trial by Blanco White, but was found guilty and, after a plea for mercy from the jury, was sentenced to 18 months' hard labour. On 11 February she was released from remand, during which time she had been forcibly fed, in order to stand trial. Indeed, she had been one of the prisoners who had been the subject of the report undertaken by the Bishop of London into forcible feeding. In spite of his initial conclusion, a whitewash as it was deemed by the WSPU, that forcible feeding was performed "in the kindliest spirit", Dr Flora MURRAY claimed that tests showed that Olive Beamish had been given "large doses of bromide" in prison. When tested on 25 March, after she had been re-imprisoned and forcibly fed for 30 days, analysis of her urine disclosed the presence of bromine, a drug that had the effect of depressing the nervous system, reducing resistance. It is clear, however, from the daily Holloway medical reports, that during her imprisonment she had violently resisted every one of the twice-daily feedings, which had been effected at first by using a nasal tube and then, as she was able to expel this, by the oesophagal tube. On 24 March she was released from prison into the care of Dr Murray, her sentence remitted after she had given an undertaking that she would not in future break the law, or incite others to do so. A copy of the letter dated 26 March, in which Olive Beamish explained her reasons for giving the undertaking, sent from the Pembridge Gardens nursing home to Grace ROE, now lies in her Home Office file, having been seized by the police after the raid on Lincoln's Inn House in June 1914. In it she explained that, because she had to support herself, if she had kept up the hunger strike and had then been released as a "mouse", she would have rendered herself unemployable. One alternative would have been to have left the country, but she did not think that she could have obtained work abroad. This fact, coupled with the effect on her mother's health of her continuing imprisonment, meant that her only alternative was to give the undertaking. A month later, she had returned to her family home at Pucklechurch, outside Bristol, from where she was in touch with Kitty MARION, who it was averred had also undergone "chemical restraint".

From 1914 to 1919 Olive Beamish worked as an ORGANIZER with Sylvia PANKHURST in East London, first with the EAST LONDON FEDERATION OF SUFFRAGETTES and then with the Workers' Socialist Federation, supplementing her income working from home as a "typewriter". In 1919 she founded her own typewriting, duplicating and translating business in the City and in 1920 joined the Association of Women Clerks and Secretaries, becoming its vice-president. In 1940–41 she was a member of the national executive of the Clerical and Administrative Workers' Union. She retired to Suffolk in 1955 and by 1957 was minute secretary to the executive committee of the Ipswich Trades Council and a member of the executive committee of the Sudbury and Woodbridge Labour Party. In her will she left a legacy to Lillian LENTON and one to the Mary Macarthur Holiday Home for Working Women at Stanstead. She had actively supported the Republican side in the Spanish Civil War and amassed a collection of books on that subject and on the socialist movement.

Address: (1917) 85 Hoxton Street, London E; (1978) Primrose Hill, Hintlesham, Suffolk.
Photograph: as "Phyllis Brady" in Suffragette Fellowship Collection, Museum of London.
Archival source: Suffragette Fellowship Collection, Museum of London; Home Office Papers, Public Record Office.

BEARSDEN (WSPU)   Secretary (1913) Mrs Dickie, New Kilpatrick Manse, Bearsden, Dunbartonshire.

BEAULY (NUWSS)   In 1913 the society was a member of the NORTH OF SCOTLAND FEDERATION OF THE

NATIONAL UNION OF WOMEN'S SUFFRAGE SOCIETIES. Secretary (1913) Miss A. Munro, The School, Beauly, Invernesshire.

BECK, ELLEN (1845–1940) and **EDITH** (1847–1930) Quakers, their paternal grandmother worked for the emancipation of slaves and their great-aunt founded the Stoke Newington Invalid Asylum (still in existence in 1888). Their father's uncle, Joseph Lister, discovered the principle of the modern microscope. As early as 1870 Edith Beck was a supporter of the New Hospital for Women (later the Elizabeth Garrett Anderson Hospital) and in 1880 is recorded in its annual report as donating to it "old under linen". In 1889, with their mother, both sisters signed the Declaration in Favour of Women's Suffrage compiled by the CENTRAL COMMITTEE OF THE NATIONAL SOCIETY FOR WOMEN'S SUFFRAGE. The sisters subscribed to the WOMEN'S SOCIAL AND POLITICAL UNION in 1907; between them they gave over £90 in 1908–9 and £230 in 1909–10. With Katherine MARSHALL they ran the Farm Produce stall at the WSPU Prince's Rink Exhibition in May 1909. They offered up a promise of £100 at the "Great Indignation" WSPU Albert Hall rally in October 1909. Although they lived in Sussex the Beck sisters came up to London each week to attend WSPU meetings. Edith Beck was arrested on "Black Friday" in November 1910 after taking part in the deputation to Asquith, and, like so many other women, was charged with obstruction and then discharged. Both sisters went, again with Kitty Marshall, on the deputation from Caxton Hall to Parliament Square on 21 November 1911 but, unlike Mrs Marshall, were not arrested. They both took part, as did Kitty Marshall, in the Women's March from Edinburgh in September 1912. This event was organized by a Sussex neighbour, Florence DE FONBLANQUE. They continued to give money to the WSPU after the Pankhurst–Pethick-Lawrence split in 1912 and also took up the cause of passive resistance, refusing to pay their taxes. Harriet KERR recuperated in a cottage on their farm after her release from prison in 1913.

Both the Beck sisters were vegetarians and members of the International Franchise Club (*see under* CLUBS). In the 1930s they were members of the WOMEN'S FREEDOM LEAGUE and Ellen Beck was a life member of the Women's Farm and Garden Association. Their wills demonstrate their feminist-orientated interests. Besides bequests to their family, they left legacies to the New Sussex Hospital for Women; the Sussex Maternity and Women's Hospital; to an animal charity, Our Dumb Friends League; to Billinghurst Women's Institute; and to Christ's Hospital Girls' School to enable scholars to pursue further education. One of the trustees of Ellen Beck's will was Jean Ingelow Alexander, one of the children of William Cleverley Alexander, who in 1874 had bought Aubrey House from P.A. and Clementia TAYLOR. Jean Alexander, with another woman trustee, was requested in the will to divide the residue of the estate between "charities and charitable institutions for the benefit of women". The Beck sisters were typical of a large section of the WSPU membership. They keenly supported the cause of women's suffrage, were devoted to Mrs PANKHURST, involved themselves in fund-raising and conscience-raising activities, but stopped short of actual militancy.

Address: (1912, 1940) Duncans Farm, near Billinghurst, Sussex.

BECKENHAM (branch of the LONDON SOCIETY FOR WOMEN'S SUFFRAGE) Secretary (1909) Miss Hazlewood, 35 King's Hill Road, Beckenham, Kent.

BECKENHAM (WSPU) Secretary (1906) Mrs Kate Dice, 119 Newlands Park, Sydenham, London SE.

BECKER, LYDIA ERNESTINE (1827–90) Born in Manchester, the eldest of 15 children. Her father ran the family's bleaching works, which had been founded by her grandfather on coming to Lancashire from Germany in 1771. Not being very strong, she spent about a year from 1844 to 1845 living with relations who ran a hydropathic establishment in Thuringia. On her return, and especially after the death of her mother in 1855, she lived the life of a daughter-at-home, running the household and looking after her younger brothers and sisters, while at the same time developing an interest in politics and science. In 1862 she was awarded a gold medal by the Horticultural Society in an open competition for the best collection of dried plants made within a year. She had devised and built her own drying press. In 1864, as LEB, she wrote and had published by Remington of Rugby, *Botany for Novices*. She wrote a companion volume, *Astronomy for*

Novices, which was never published; the manuscript is now in the Fawcett Library. In 1865 the Becker family moved into central Manchester and in January 1867 Lydia founded, and was president of, the "Manchester Ladies Literary Society", which despite its name was intended as a society to study scientific matters. An indication that she always aimed high and did not underestimate her own worth may be gleaned from the fact that she solicited a paper from Charles Darwin, with whom she had previously been in correspondence about her own botanical discoveries, to be read at the inaugural meeting of her society.

In October 1866 she attended the meetings of the Social Science Association, held that year in Manchester. One of the papers she heard, and which inspired her to devote the rest of her life to the suffrage cause, was that given by Barbara BODICHON on "Reasons for the Enfranchisement of Women". It would appear that Lydia Becker had been unaware of the presence in Manchester of the Manchester Committee for the Enfranchisement of Women, which had been founded by Elizabeth Wolstenholme (*see* Elizabeth Wolstenholme ELMY) in the autumn of 1865, and it was presumably at the suggestion of Barbara Bodichon, as a first step to involvement in the suffrage movement, that Lydia Becker got in touch with Emily DAVIES in London. Sylvia PANKHURST in *The Suffragette Movement*, 1931, from information given her in 1906–7 by Elizabeth Wolstenholme Elmy, recorded that Lydia Becker, after hearing Barbara Bodichon's paper, wrote one of her own and sent it to Emily Davies, asking her to secure its publication in the *Contemporary Review*, the editor of which was Dean Alford, who had in 1866 become a member of the LONDON PROVISIONAL PETITION COMMITTEE. It is, however, clear that Lydia Becker had no specific publisher in mind when she wrote her article. Emily Davies had written to Helen TAYLOR on 15 December 1866 noting that Dean Alford had asked her to find someone to write an article on the question of women's enfranchisement for the *Contemporary Review;* Lydia Becker's article was, presumably, a fortuitous arrival. Elizabeth Wolstenholme Elmy, in a letter written in August 1900, long after the event, to Harriet MCILQUHAM noted that Emily Davies sent Lydia Becker's article to her, asking her opinion. "I begged her to do her utmost to get it accepted and then brought the matter before the Manchester Society for the Enfranchisement of Women, of which I was Hon. Sec., asking leave to call upon Miss Becker and, in their names, invite Miss B. to join us. She joined and I was only too glad to transfer my work in this post to her capable hands." Mrs Elmy repeated this account, virtually verbatim, in several letters to Sylvia Pankhurst over the course of the next few years. Lydia Becker's article was published as "Female Suffrage" in the March 1867 edition of the *Contemporary Review* and Elizabeth Wolstenholme induced the Manchester Committee to print 10 000 copies of it as a pamphlet.

In February 1867 Lydia Becker became honorary secretary of the Manchester Committee for Women's Suffrage, which had been relaunched the month before at a meeting which she did not attend. Emily Davies continued to correspond with her and advised her as to the most efficient method of collecting signatures and meeting deadlines for the submission of petitions. Two were presented from Manchester in April to give force to J.S. MILL's amendment to the Reform Bill. One was signed by 1605 women householders and the other was from 3000 members of the general public, men and women. On 30 June 1867 she sent to Helen Taylor for comment the draft constitution she had drawn up for "The Society for the Promotion of the Enfranchisement of Women", which finally became, in October/November, the MANCHESTER NATIONAL SOCIETY FOR WOMEN'S SUFFRAGE.

In July 1867 she went to Colchester as, in effect, the first women's suffrage ORGANIZER. The Colchester MP, Mr Karslake, had said during the course of the debate on Mill's amendment on 20 May that he opposed the motion because not a single woman in Essex had asked him to support the proposal. Helen Taylor, Frances Power COBBE and Clementia TAYLOR took up this challenge and devised the idea of collecting signatures in Colchester for a petition that Karslake could then present to parliament and in the process to set up there a suffrage committee. They had decided on Lydia Becker as a likely candidate for the post but were rather hesitant about asking her to undertake work involving journeying and staying away from home. Jessie BOUCHERETT ascertained, before Helen Taylor approached her directly, that Lydia Becker would be willing to go anywhere to help ladies set up a committee,

Portrait of Lydia Ernestine Becker, in its original state as painted by Susan Isabel Dacre *c.* 1886. By courtesy of The National Portrait Gallery, London

providing her travelling expenses were paid. Helen Taylor wrote to her at the end of June "I do not myself know anyone at Colchester, but we have obtained one or two introductions to some ladies; yet as these are not personal friends I suppose it would be necessary to take up your quarters at an hotel – do you see any objection to this? My plans at present are merely to go down with a few introductions and see what can be done according to your own judgement, staying as long as seems necessary to get a tolerable number of signatures, or to induce a few ladies to continue to carry on the work". Lydia Becker arranged to come to London and to meet Helen Taylor in the ladies' waiting room at Euston Station, noting, to aid recognition, that she would be wearing "a violet serge dress and jacket, black hat and spectacles". The episode was brought to a successful conclusion and on 25 July Mr Karslake presented a petition to parliament from 129 ladies resident in Colchester in favour of the proposed reform. In September 1867 Lydia Becker attended the meeting of the British Association for the Advancement of Science in Dundee and in a letter to Helen Taylor mentions that, when a botany question was being discussed, she found the opportunity to rise and make an observation. She remarks if "women will just quietly do what they feel they can do and make no fuss – they may do so with approval. But self consciousness, and artificial timidity stand in the way." At this time she was organizing an attempt, devised by Richard PANKHURST, to include women ratepayers on the electoral register and on 26 November personally conducted Lily MAXWELL, who happened to be a supporter of Jacob BRIGHT, to the polling booth at the Manchester by-election. Although the Manchester overseer refused to place women's names on the register, Lily Maxwell's being there by mistake, Lydia Becker had now broken the taboo against women appearing at the hustings and was preparing further breaches in the walls of propriety. Working towards the idea of holding a public meeting on the subject of women's suffrage she, with Alice Wilson, the owner of a baby linen warehouse and member of the Manchester Society, attended a meeting held by the National Reform Union in Manchester on 11 February. The Union had been founded in Manchester in 1864 by, among others, Richard Cobden, Henry Fawcett, James Stansfeld, P.A. Taylor and George Dawson, to campaign for household suffrage. Alice Wilson stood up at the meeting and made a pithy speech, which was subsequently lauded by the *Manchester Examiner* and paved the way for the first public meeting, and one at which women appeared on a public platform, of the Manchester National Society, which was held in the Assembly Room of the Free Trade Hall on 14 April 1868. In 1868 Lydia Becker wrote to Mary JOHNSON, secretary of the BIRMINGHAM SOCIETY FOR WOMEN'S SUFFRAGE, that the "one great object now is to make the public mind thoroughly familiar with the conception of women voters". This she saw as the main purpose behind all the public speaking and meetings. The remainder of 1868 was devoted to the campaign to persuade women householders to submit claims for inclusion on the electoral register, culminating in November in the case of *Chorlton v. Lings*, by which 5346 women householders were held to be debarred from registering as electors.

Lydia Becker read a paper on "Equality of Women" to the British Association meeting at Norwich in 1868. She was now much in demand as a speaker on women's suffrage in the north of England, although Mentia Taylor was doubtful about her platform appeal; she thought her injudicious, vulgar and foolish and likely to alienate potential supporters. For that reason Clementia Taylor was actually prepared to rule that there would be no women speakers at the LONDON NATIONAL SOCIETY's first public meeting in July 1869, if only to prevent Miss Becker appearing. Mrs FAWCETT and Caroline Ashurst BIGGS certainly did speak at the meeting; perhaps Miss Becker did not attend. Lydia Becker did not include diplomacy among her more obvious virtues. Her letters reveal a rather touching enthusiasm for people; certainly in the early days of her involvement in the suffrage movement she was very grateful for the attention she was shown by, for instance, Helen Taylor. However, this is tempered on occasion by her thoughtlessness or lack of consideration (see Philippine KYLLMAN). Indeed, one cannot imagine that she was doing anything other than speaking her mind, and could have had no intention of currying favour, when in 1868 she advised Elizabeth Wolstenholme, a past-mistress at inaugurating societies, not to be in too great haste to form a society to promote the Married Women's Property Bill and reminded her that forming societies was a very serious business. However, when the Married Women's Property Committee was indeed formed by Elizabeth Wolstenholme in 1868, Lydia Becker was a member of the executive committee from then until 1874, and served as its first treasurer.

She worked with Jacob Bright (she was then on visiting terms with the Brights) to secure the amendment in 1869 to the Municipal Franchise Bill which gave local voting rights to women ratepayers. In 1870, at the first School Board elections at which women were eligible to stand, she became the first woman in the country to be elected and then held her seat until her death. The Manchester elections were held five days before those in London at which Elizabeth Garrett (see Elizabeth Garrett ANDERSON) and Emily Davies were successful. In the 1870s Lydia Becker was at the forefront of the movement to repeal the Contagious Diseases Acts, despite the views of those, in particular members of the London National Society, who thought that the suffrage cause would be tainted by such involvement. She was also a founder member, with Josephine Butler and Elizabeth Wolstenholme, of the "Committee to Amend the law in points wherein it is Injurious to Women" and of its successor, the Vigilance Association for the Defence of Personal Rights.

Lydia Becker was the founder and editor of the *Journal of the Manchester National Society for Women's Suffrage*, which first appeared in March 1870. Needless to say, the journal did not receive unanimous approval. In June 1870 Mentia Taylor wrote to Helen Taylor that "We [the London National Society] have declined taking her Manchester Journal to the indignations of the M. & Edinburgh Committees – I will not be responsible for what Miss Becker writes – some of our committee were in favour of it – fortunately they were in a minority". Its purpose as a national journal, uniting all the suffrage societies, was made clearer when within a year its title was changed to the *Women's Suffrage Journal*, and it was no longer controlled by the Manchester National Society (see under NEWSPAPERS). The price of the journal was kept at 1d for the 20 years of its existence and Lydia Becker must have on occasion used her own funds to finance it. Certainly when the final, Memorial, issue of the journal was published in August 1890, a month after her death, it was necessary for Jessie Boucherett to guarantee the expense. Lydia Becker could not have entirely been *persona non grata* to Mentia Taylor because in 1873 A.J. Munby described meeting her at Aubrey House and related that she "I find, thinks as I do about female labour and respects the Lancashire pit girls and their work". Doubtless it was their right to employment that Lydia Becker respected rather than, like Munby, their biceps. She campaigned in the *Women's Suffrage Journal* against the imposition on women of restrictive employment legislation.

In 1874 she sided with those in the suffrage societies who were prepared, for political expediency, to promote a bill, first under William Forsyth and later under William Woodall, to enfranchise single women and widows only, thereby dividing herself from the Brights, Pankhursts and Elizabeth Wolstenholme Elmy. In 1877 she became parliamentary agent to the CENTRAL COMMITTEE OF THE NATIONAL SOCIETY FOR WOMEN'S SUFFRAGE. In 1881 Laura MCLAREN wrote to Lydia Becker on behalf of the Central Committee offering her the post of "responsible paid secretary" and continued "we thought that by the appointment of competent clerks to assist you in London and in Manchester you would be able to undertake the responsible work of both committees. With your intimate knowledge of the political work which lies before us, you will quickly see all the bearings of this proposal . . . It appears to us that there is a waste of force in having two centres of political action, and although the energy of Manchester is powerfully felt in the country, still, as all parliamentary business must be transacted in London, it is here we need the powerful head to act promptly in every turn of political affairs." Laura McLaren noted in the same letter "It [the suffrage movement] is your pet child which you have seen grow up from infancy and whose welfare is nearest your heart. I think it is now for you to decide whether you will extend your sphere of operation and knit the society together in one powerful organization." The question of money was, as usual, approached in a delicate manner: "The executive fully recognize that you offer your services as a free gift to the Cause, but in order to meet the expenses of your residence in London, and the cost of your journeys to and from Manchester, they place at your disposal the sum of £200 for this year." Thus Miss Becker became the secretary of the executive committee of the Central Committee, the accredited parliamentary agent of the National Society for Women's Suffrage, as well as honorary secretary of the Manchester National Society and editor of the *Women's Suffrage Journal*.

The years 1880 to 1884 were a time of optimism in the suffrage movement. It was thought that by developing a populist movement, holding overflowing, high-profile, public meetings in large provincial cities, women would demonstrate that they were in earnest in their desire to be included in the parliamentary reforms mooted for 1884. Helen BLACKBURN gives Lydia Becker the credit for formulating the idea of the demonstrations. Sandra Stanley Holton in *Suffrage and Beyond*, 1994, argues persuasively that the demonstrations emanated from the Radical Liberal wing of the women's movement, from the Brights and McLarens, and were originally to be held in spite of the opposition of Lydia Becker. The latter was always politically aware and, if initially reluctant, was, in the event, a leading speaker at eight of the nine demonstrations. In 1884 she was forced by the Manchester National Society to choose between her two secretarial positions; she chose to stay with Manchester, although remaining on the executive committee of the Central Committee and retaining her position as parliamentary agent. She was succeeded as secretary by Florence BALGARNIE. It may have been that, in the aftermath of the overwhelming defeat of Woodall's amendment in 1884, there was little heart for, or possibility of, direct political action in London. In the autumn of 1884 she took her only extended holiday, a visit with the British Association to Canada. Lilias Ashworth HALLETT, with whom she was in political sympathy, was one of her companions.

After the 1886 election had returned to parliament a greater number than ever before of sympathizers to the women's cause, Lydia Becker in 1887 was authorized by the Manchester Society, with the concurrence of the Central Committee, to call a meeting in London of members of parliament who were also members of their committees. Although she was the accredited parliamentary agent for the National Society for Women's Suffrage, Miss Becker was never admitted to the meetings of the Committee of the parliamentary supporters of the Franchise Bill that was founded at this meeting. After the 1888 split in the Central Committee she retained her position on the executive committee of the Central Committee of the National Society for Women's Suffrage, whose secretary was now Helen Blackburn. By the end of 1889 Lydia Becker's health was failing, she was no longer able to travel from Manchester to London, and, housebound, she was confined to editing the *Women's Suffrage Journal*. In early 1890 she arranged for Helen Blackburn to deputize as editor and went to Bath for treatment. Her physician was "Dr Spender", doubtless Dr John Kent Spender, surgeon to the Mineral Hospital and brother of Emily SPENDER. After a few months Lydia Becker set out for spa treatment at Aix-les-Bains. She contracted diphtheria and died on 21 July in Geneva.

Helen Blackburn, who as secretary to the Central Committee had access to the society's records, compiled a scrapbook which now forms part of the Blackburn Collection in Girton College Archives. This scrapbook contains the documentary evidence on which she based her *Record of Women's Suffrage* and, because its source is derived from material originating from Miss Becker, it quite naturally emphasizes the latter's part in the nineteenth-century suffrage movement. This documentary material, together with the collection of books known as the "Memorial" library, was given to Girton by Helen Blackburn in memory of Caroline Ashurst Biggs and of Lydia Becker.

Besides articles in the *Women's Suffrage Journal*, Miss Becker's published writings on women's suffrage are: "Female Suffrage" in *Contemporary Review*, vol. 4, January–April 1867; "The Equality of Women", a paper read before the British Association at Norwich, 1868; *Woman's Suffrage: Substance of a Lecture*, 1869; *The Political Disabilities of Women*, reprinted with permission from the *Westminster Review*, 1872; *Liberty, Equality and Fraternity. A Reply to Mr Fitzjames Stephen's Strictures on Mr J.S. Mill's Subjection of Women*, reprinted from the *Women's Suffrage Journal*, 1874; *A Reply to the Protest* which appeared in the *Nineteenth Century Review*, June 1889; *The Rights and Duties of Women in Local Government. A Paper*, 1879, which had been read at "the Conference on behalf of extending the Parliamentary Franchise to Women, held in the Victoria Rooms, Clifton, Bristol on 24 January 1879"; H. Blackburn selects *Words of a Leader. Being extracts from the writings of the late Miss L. Becker*, 1897.

Address: (1865) 10 Grove Street, Ardwick, Manchester; (1877) 155, Shrewsbury Street, Old Trafford, Manchester.
Portrait: by Susan DACRE in Manchester City Art Gallery. First exhibited in Manchester in 1886, after Lydia Becker's death the National Union of Women's Suffrage Societies raised money to purchase the portrait, and offered it to the National Portrait Gallery. It was, however, refused and only eventually accepted from the NUWSS by the Manchester City Art Gallery in 1920 after being cut down. There is no denying that a photograph, held in the National Portrait Gallery Archive, of the original portrait reveals that the hands were clumsily painted and they are, of course, excised from the remaining portion. For a discussion of the portrait see D. Cherry, *Painting Women*, 1993.
Photograph: in H. Blackburn, *Record of Women's Suffrage*, 1902.

Archival source: Women's Suffrage Collection, especially Lydia Becker's Letter Book, Manchester Central Library; Mill–Taylor Papers, London School of Economics; Elizabeth Wolstenholme Elmy Papers, British Library; Fawcett Library; Blackburn Collection, Girton College Archive.
Bibliography: H. Blackburn, *A Record of the Women's Suffrage Movement in the British Isles with Biographical Sketches of Miss Becker*, 1902; M. Holmes, *Lydia Becker: A Cameo Life-sketch*, no date (c. 1912 – published by the Women's Freedom League); D. Hudson, *Munby: Man of Two Worlds*, 1972; J. Liddington and J. Norris, *One Hand Tied Behind Us: The Rise of the Women's Suffrage Movement*, 1978; P. McHugh, *Prostitution and Social Reform*, 1980; D. Spender, *Women of Ideas and What Men Have Done to Them*, 1982; L. Holcombe, *Wives and Property: Reform of the Married Women's Property Law in Nineteenth-century England*, 1983; J. Lewis (ed.) *Before the Vote was Won*, 1987 (contains L.E. Becker, *The Political Disabilities of Women*, 1 January 1872 and *Liberty, Equality, Fraternity*, 1874); P. Levine, *Feminist Lives in Victorian England*, 1990; J. Parker, "Lydia Becker: Pioneer Orator of the Women's Movement", *Manchester Region History Review*, 5, 2, 1991–2; A. Kelly, *Lydia Becker and The Cause*, 1992.

BEDDOE, AGNES MONTGOMERIE, MRS (c. 1832–1914) Daughter of Rev. A. Christison, she married in 1858 Dr John Beddoe, a physician, anthropologist and fellow of the Royal Society. She signed the 1866 petition, which was presented to Parliament by J.S. MILL. She was a member of the first committee of the Bristol and Clifton Branch of the National Society for Women's Suffrage (*see* BRISTOL AND WEST OF ENGLAND SOCIETY FOR WOMEN'S SUFFRAGE) and has left a description of the first meeting, called in 1868 by the father of Florence and Rosamond Davenport HILL, in her brief memoir *The Early Years of the Women's Suffrage Movement*, 1911. She remained on the executive committee of the Bristol society for most of the rest of her life. In the campaigns of the 1880s she spoke at many meetings around the country, from Glasgow to Malmesbury, and presided over the "Grand Demonstration" held at the Colston Hall in Bristol in 1880, at which Jessie CRAIGEN was, according to Mrs Beddoe, "our most eloquent and moving orator". She supported the CENTRAL COMMITTEE OF THE NATIONAL SOCIETY after the split in the central societies in 1888. In 1899 she became a member of the executive committee of the NATIONAL UNION OF WOMEN'S SUFFRAGE SOCIETIES.

Agnes Beddoe was involved in the campaign to promote the Married Women's Property Act and in

1881, while living in Clifton, she lent her drawing-room to Frances Power COBBE in order that the latter might deliver her course of lectures on "The Duties of Women" to the ladies of Bristol. She was a member of the Bristol Women's Liberal Association. In 1889 she founded Mrs Beddoe's Working Women's Dwelling, 20 Bishop Street, Portland Square, in Bristol. She furnished this house and let it to 16 lodgers at a rent of 1/6 each. By 1896 she was a poor law guardian. Her husband, who died in 1911, was a vice-president of the Central Society, subscribed to the WOMEN'S SOCIAL AND POLITICAL UNION in 1907, and was a vice-president of the BRISTOL MEN'S LEAGUE FOR WOMEN'S SUFFRAGE. Mrs Beddoe was present on 19 March 1908 at a small dinner given at the Albemarle Club (*see under* CLUBS) in London by Lilias Ashworth HALLETT for Bath sympathizers, including Mary BLATHWAYT, who had earlier in the day attended the breakfast for released WSPU prisoners. Mrs Beddoe herself gave a small donation to the WSPU in 1909 and in April 1910, sitting in the front row, attended a WSPU meeting in Bath at which Annie KENNEY, Mrs PANKHURST, and H.W. NEVINSON were the main speakers. Her name is first in the alphabetical list, with Mary Carpenter, Frances Power Cobbe, Lilias Ashworth Hallett, Adelaide Manning, and Harriet Martineau, on a banner that is now in the Fawcett Library.

Address: (1900) Chantry House, Bradford-on-Avon, Wiltshire.

Photograph: by Sir Benjamin Stone, 1899, National Portrait Gallery Archive; in H. Blackburn, *Record of Women's Suffrage*, 1902.

Bibliography: A.M. Beddoe, *The Early Years of the Women's Suffrage Movement*, 1911; S.J. Tanner, *How the Women's Suffrage Movement began in Bristol Fifty Years Ago*, 1918; E. Malos, "Bristol Women in Action, 1839–1919: The Right to Vote and the Need to Earn a Living", in *Bristol's Other History*, 1983.

BEDFORD SOCIETY FOR WOMEN'S SUFFRAGE A committee was formed in 1873, with Miss Helen Coombs, Mill Street, Bedford, as honorary secretary. It was reconstituted in 1889 as a branch of the CENTRAL NATIONAL SOCIETY FOR WOMEN'S SUFFRAGE, inaugurated at a meeting held by Florence BALGARNIE. The honorary secretary, Mrs E. Ransom of 24 Ashburnham Road, Bedford, who was present at the annual general meeting of the Central National Society in 1891, is also mentioned in the 1890s by Elizabeth Wolstenholme ELMY as being "heart and soul with us [the WOMEN'S FRANCHISE LEAGUE] in feeling". Mrs Ransom was still an active member of the Bedford Society in 1911. In November 1891 Laura Morgan-BROWNE spoke at a meeting of what was then known as the Bedford and North Beds Women's Suffrage Society. This society presumably lost momentum and was refounded in 1908 by Amy WALMSLEY, after Margaret HEITLAND had come over from Cambridge on 4 December and addressed a drawing-room meeting at the home of Dr Ethel STACY, 34 Kimbolton Road, Bedford. The latter became the society's secretary. One of the other founding members was Miss Margaret Stansfield, who was a gymnastics teacher at Miss Walmsley's College and later founded the Bedford College of Physical Education. Marjorie STRACHEY spent a week with the society as an ORGANIZER in March/April 1909 but the Bedford Society did not affiliate to the NATIONAL UNION OF WOMEN'S SUFFRAGE SOCIETIES until it joined the EASTERN COUNTIES FEDERATION OF THE NATIONAL UNION OF WOMEN'S SUFFRAGE SOCIETIES, c. May 1911. It did, however, invite to its meetings many speakers from the NUWSS, including, in January 1911, Mrs FAWCETT. Demonstrating that they were in no way misanthropic, in 1911 members suggested, perhaps in deliberate contrast to WOMEN'S SOCIAL AND POLITICAL UNION policy, that a special appeal should be made to men to join the Bedford Society. However, it is not until April 1912, presumably as the result of a suggestion from headquarters, that there is any mention in the minutes of the society that more could be done to involve local working women in the movement. Margaret Heitland addressed the Bedford Society on the NUWSS's proposal to support the Labour Party but the society unanimously opposed all the resolutions proposed by the NUWSS, its argument being that it saw no point in alienating Conservatives and Liberals in order to conciliate a party which was already in favour of women's suffrage and pledged to its support. Even after Margaret Heitland outlined all the reasons for the NUWSS policy, the Bedford Society still opposed the proposals. However, the report of the society's annual general meeting in the *Bedfordshire Times* of 17 October 1913 noted that several trade unionists were in attendance. In December 1912 the Bedford Society left the Eastern Counties Federation and joined the OXON, BERKS AND BUCKS FEDERATION OF THE NATIONAL UNION OF WOMEN'S SUFFRAGE SOCIETIES. In 1913 Dora MASON was based in Bedford as organizer, on occasion being subjected to public hostility. A lengthy report in the *Bedford Record*, 24 June 1913, of a meeting held in the Market Place by the Bedford NUWSS described the efforts of "a gang of young 'nuts'" to capture the BANNER "Law Abiding Suffragists" that had been hoisted at the beginning of the meeting. It was torn from its pole and flung into the crowd. "The banner was actually torn up by three young women." By 1915 the society had been presented with a new banner by its president, Mrs Prothero. On 1 March 1918 NUWSS headquarters asked for it to be lent for the display of banners that accompanied the celebration in the Queen's Hall on 13 March. The Bedford Society dissolved itself on 14 March. The minutes of its final meeting proposed that the banner should be given or lent to the newly formed Women's Citizen Association.

Office: (1913) 39 St Peter's Street, Bedford.

Archival source: Documents relating to the Bedford Society for Women's Suffrage, Bedfordshire Record Office.

Bibliography: *Bedford Politics 1900–1924*, Bedfordshire Record Office: Background Papers No 2, 1986.

BEDFORD (WSPU)   Secretary (1913) Miss Smelt, 22 Goldington Avenue, Bedford.

Bibliography: *Bedford Politics 1900–1924*, Bedfordshire Record Office: Background Papers No. 2, 1986.

BELL, FLORENCE NIGHTINGALE HARRISON, MRS (1865–1948) School teacher. Her husband was secretary of the National Amalgamated Union of Labour. She was the first woman member of the Independent Labour Party's national administrative council and was replaced in 1898 by Emmeline PANKHURST. In 1902 she was director of the Newcastle Co-operative Society and was first secretary of the Newcastle Labour Representation Committee. In 1907 she organized women for the Women's Trade Union League. She was a member of the North-East Society for Women's Suffrage (NUWSS) (*see* NEWCASTLE AND DISTRICT SOCIETY) of which she was secretary until October 1909. From 1910 she was secretary of the Newcastle branch of the Women's Labour League. At the Women's Labour League conference, held in January 1911, at which she was the delegate from Newcastle, she moved a resolution in favour of adult suffrage (*see also* Dr Ethel BENTHAM). She was a member of the executive committee of the Women's Labour League in 1913 and chairman of the Standing Joint Committee of Industrial Women's Organizations in 1923, of which Ethel Bentham was one of the vice-presidents.

Address: (1910) 6 Hotspur Street, Heaton, Newcastle; (1923) Lady Somerset Road, Kentish Town, London NW; (1948) 121 Windsor Road, East Ham, London E6.

Bibliography: C. Collette, *For Labour and For Women: The Women's Labour League, 1906–18*, 1989; D. Neville, *To Make Their Mark: The Women's Suffrage Movement in the North East of England 1900–1914*, 1997.

BENETT, SARAH (1850–1924) Spent her youth in a village in the New Forest in Hampshire. From an early age she had a desire to reform society and to this end started a co-operative society in her village. After the death of her mother, she went to live in Burslem, and started in Hanley another co-operative society, which ran a general store, of which she was the manager. She was active in the campaign to improve the health of the pottery workers by banning the use of lead glaze in pottery. She joined the WOMEN'S SOCIAL AND POLITICAL UNION and was arrested in March 1907 after taking part in the deputation to the House of Commons, sentenced to 14 days' imprisonment in lieu of a 20s fine. In July 1907 Christabel PANKHURST stayed with her while campaigning in the Potteries. Within three months Sarah Benett had joined the newly formed WOMEN'S FREEDOM LEAGUE and in 1908 was one of its representatives at the Amsterdam conference of the INTERNATIONAL WOMAN SUFFRAGE ALLIANCE. By 1909 and until she resigned in June 1910, she was the WFL's treasurer. During this period she attended the founding meeting of the TAX RESISTANCE LEAGUE and was herself a tax resister. In 1910 she subscribed to the NEW CONSTITUTIONAL SOCIETY FOR WOMEN'S SUFFRAGE. She appears to have rejoined the WSPU; she was arrested on "Black Friday" in November 1910. She was arrested again in November 1911, for window smashing, and at her trial remarked that she remembered the days when she "walked her shoes off trying to get signatures to a petition; now she was at the forefront of the militant movement which was absolutely necessary". She caused considerable amusement in the Home Office by having the temerity, at her age, to request that gymnastic appliances, such as skipping ropes and balls, should be made available in Holloway in order that the suffragette prisoners might keep fit. Sarah Benett was a speaker at the dinner held in celebration of the release of the prisoners in February 1912. She was friendly with Emily Wilding DAVISON, who, through an intermediary, asked her to smuggle a watch into Holloway for her; in June 1916 she organized the annual memorial pilgrimage to Emily Wilding Davison's grave in Morpeth. Sarah Benett took part in the WSPU's second window-smashing campaign in March 1912 and was sentenced to three months' imprisonment. She was released on 13 April after hunger striking. In November 1912 she campaigned for George LANSBURY at the Bow by-election. In February 1913, after the government's proposed Franchise Bill had been withdrawn, she was arrested after breaking the windows of Selfridge's in Oxford Street and was sentenced to six months' imprisonment. Her name is not included in the lists of prisoners, published in *Votes for Women*, in the following weeks, and she may have quickly been released after hunger striking. In 1916 she sent a donation to Maud Arncliffe SENNETT, with whom she had worked in the WFL and who in her autobiography is scathing about her, in order that Gladys Evans, previously a member of the WSPU, could be employed as an organizer by the NORTHERN MEN'S FEDERATION FOR WOMEN'S SUFFRAGE. Sarah Benett's association with the Tax Resistance League continued until her death; one of her executors was Dr Elizabeth WILKS. Among her bequests she left £25 to Edith GARRUD and £1000 and the residue of her estate to the Elizabeth Garrett Anderson Hospital.

Address: (1907) 196 Waterloo Road, Burslem, Staffordshire; (1910) 25 Ferncroft Avenue, Hampstead, London NW; (1923) 24 Village Road, Finchley, Middlesex.
Photograph: by Lena Connell in the *Vote*, 5 March 1910.
Bibliography: The *Vote*, 5 March 1910; *Votes for Women*, 26 April 1912.

BENNETT, ETHEL SEYMOUR (1877–1956)   Educated at the Frances Mary Buss School, Camden Town, North London Collegiate School, and Newnham College, Cambridge (1896–1900). She was parliamentary secretary for the CONSERVATIVE AND UNIONIST WOMEN'S FRANCHISE ASSOCIATION, 1911–19, and was a member of the executive committee of the British Empire Union from 1919.

BENSUSAN, INEZ (?–?)   Born in Sydney, Australia. She acted professionally in Australasia, South Africa and England. She was a member of the ACTRESSES' FRANCHISE LEAGUE and in 1909 was organizing secretary of a department set up to commission PLAYS suitable for delivering the suffrage message. In May 1909 she was in charge of all the dramatic presentations which were such a feature of the WOMEN'S SOCIAL AND POLITICAL UNION exhibition held at the Prince's Skating Rink. She then organized performances of the plays and sketches to suffrage societies all over the country. She herself wrote a play, *The Apple*, published by the AFL in 1911. In 1912 Inez Bensusan wrote *True Womanhood*, in which she played the principal character when it was made into a film by Barker's Motion Photography (*see* FILMS). Decima MOORE had a supporting role. In 1913 Inez Bensusan set up the Women's Theatre Company, run entirely by women, the aim of which was "to widen the sphere of propaganda still further by establishing a permanent season for the presentation of dramatic works dealing with the Women's Movement". Its first, and only, season was a success; its second was pre-empted by the outbreak of war. In 1913 she was also a member of the council of the Royal Court Theatre. She was also a member of the WOMEN WRITERS' SUFFRAGE LEAGUE and a member of the executive committee of the JEWISH LEAGUE FOR WOMEN'S SUFFRAGE after it was founded in 1912. In 1948 she was a member of the committee of the 1930s Players, one of the Little Theatres that abounded then in London.

Address: (1912) 8 Lansdowne Road, Holland Park, London W; (1934) c/o 6a Blomfield Road, Maida Vale, London W9.
Photograph: *Votes for Women*, 23 May 1913.
Bibliography: J. Holledge, *Innocent Flowers*, 1981.

BENTHAM, ETHEL, DR (1861–1931)   A Quaker, she received her medical training in Brussels, Dublin (1894) and Edinburgh. She was in practice in

Newcastle with Dr Ethel WILLIAMS. Ethel Bentham joined the Labour party in 1902, was a member of the Fabian Society from 1907 until her death, a member of the FABIAN WOMEN'S GROUP and a leading member of the Women's Labour League. In 1900 she was a member of the executive committee of the Newcastle branch of the NATIONAL UNION OF WOMEN'S SUFFRAGE SOCIETIES. In 1907 she stood as a Labour candidate in a municipal by-election in Westgate South Ward in Newcastle and from then took an active role in exploring the possibility of NUWSS support for a joint Labour–Suffrage parliamentary candidate. This policy culminated in 1912 in the formation of the Election Fighting Fund. However, in January 1911 she had resigned from the executive council of the NUWSS, apparently critical of the setting up of federations. In 1911 she announced her conversion to adult suffrage. In 1908 she attended the INTERNATIONAL WOMAN SUFFRAGE ALLIANCE Conference in Amsterdam.

In 1909 Ethel Bentham moved to London, established a baby clinic in North Kensington and was a member of Kensington Borough Council from 1913, and of the Metropolitan Asylums Board. She was a member of the national executive of the Labour party, 1918–20, 1921–6, 1928–31, vice-chairman of the joint committee of Industrial Women's Organization in 1923, and Labour MP for East Islington from 1929 until her death.

Address: (1903) 46 Walker Terrace, Gateshead; (1916) 61 Lansdowne Road, Holland Park, London W.
Bibliography: P. Brookes, *Women at Westminster*, 1967; S.S. Holton, *Feminism and Democracy: Women's Suffrage and Reform Politics in Britain, 1900–1918*, 1986.

BENTINCK, RUTH MARY CAVENDISH-, MRS (1867–1953) Born in Tangier, the great-niece of Caroline Norton, and the illegitimate daughter of Ferdinand St Maur, the elder son of the 12th Duke of Somerset and a half-gipsy kitchen maid. After her father's death she was brought up by the Duke and Duchess of Somerset. She was married in 1887 to Frederick Cavendish-Bentinck. Influenced by the writings of William Morris, she became a socialist. She joined the WOMEN'S SOCIAL AND POLITICAL UNION in 1909, was a member of the FABIAN WOMEN'S GROUP in 1910 and was elected to its Suffrage Section in 1912. In July 1912 she used her influence with George Bernard Shaw to lobby for the release of Gladys Evans from imprisonment in Dublin. With Florence DE FONBLANQUE, she was one of the organizers of the "Women's March" from Edinburgh to London in September 1912 and became secretary of the QUI VIVE CORPS which was formed in 1912, probably as a result of the success of the "Women's March". In 1912 she also gave a donation to the NEW CONSTITUTIONAL SOCIETY FOR WOMEN'S SUFFRAGE which incidentally shared an address in Knightsbridge with the Qui Vive Corps. In 1912, having transferred her allegiance from the WSPU, she was a member of the first Election Fighting Fund Committee, formed by the NATIONAL UNION OF WOMEN'S SUFFRAGE SOCIETIES to back Labour party candidates at by-elections. In January 1913 she was asked by the Suffrage Section of the Fabian Women's Group to urge the Qui Vive Corps to start a propaganda campaign among the miners of Staffordshire and Derbyshire. In the summer of 1913 she became an organizer for the NORTHERN MEN'S FEDERATION FOR WOMEN'S SUFFRAGE. In 1914 she contributed articles to Sylvia PANKHURST's *Woman's Dreadnought* and by 1917 was a member of the executive committee of the UNITED SUFFRAGISTS.

In 1909 Ruth Cavendish-Bentinck began forming a library of feminist literature, the "Cavendish-Bentinck Library", from which those interested in the suffrage cause were able to borrow books (*see under* LIBRARIES). The Library contained a section of antiquarian books, printed in the sixteenth and seventeenth centuries, as well as contemporary studies, and was first housed in the International Women's Suffrage Club (*see under* CLUBS). By 1923 it had been given to the NATIONAL UNION OF SOCIETIES FOR EQUAL CITIZENSHIP, and by 1933 was housed by the LONDON NATIONAL SOCIETY FOR WOMEN'S SERVICE, of which Ruth Cavendish-Bentinck became a vice-president, in Women's Service House in Marsham Street where it was managed by a trained librarian. It was combined with the Edward Wright Library (*see* Lady WRIGHT) and was eventually given to the Fawcett Library, of which it now forms an important part.

Address: (1913) 78 Harley Street, London W; (1950) 36 Harley House, Marylebone Road, London W.
Photograph: in J. Colville, *Strange Inheritance*, 1983; in Fawcett Library.
Bibliography: J. Colville, *Strange Inheritance*, 1983.

BERKHAMSTED (NUWSS) In 1913 the society was a member of the OXON, BERKS, BUCKS, AND BEDS FEDERATION OF THE NATIONAL UNION OF WOMEN'S SUFFRAGE SOCIETIES. Secretary (1913) Mrs Richards, Downage, Berkhamsted, Hertfordshire.

BERKS (NORTH) (NUWSS) In 1913 the society was a member of the OXON, BERKS, BUCKS, AND BEDS FEDERATION OF THE NATIONAL UNION OF WOMEN'S SUFFRAGE SOCIETIES. Secretary (1913) Mrs Cross, Aston Tirrold Manor, Wallingford, Berkshire.

BERWICKSHIRE (NUWSS) In 1913 the society was a member of the SCOTTISH FEDERATION OF THE NATIONAL UNION OF WOMEN'S SUFFRAGE SOCIETIES. Secretary (1909, 1913) Mrs Hope, Sunwick, Berwick-on-Tweed, Berwickshire.

BETHESDA AND DISTRICT (NUWSS) In 1913 the society was a member of the WEST LANCS, WEST CHESHIRE AND NORTH WALES FEDERATION OF THE NATIONAL UNION OF WOMEN'S SUFFRAGE SOCIETIES. Secretary (1913) Miss Agnes Huws, 17 Ogwen Terrace, Bethesda, Wales.

BEVERLEY (NUWSS) Secretary (1910) Miss F. Andrews, Holland House, Beverley, Yorkshire.

BEXHILL (NUWSS) Secretary (1913) Miss Norton, Dalhousie, Buckhurst Road, Bexhill-on-Sea, Sussex.

BEXHILL (WSPU) Was in existence in 1910 In 1913 it was a member of the SURREY, SUSSEX, AND HANTS FEDERATION OF THE NATIONAL UNION OF WOMEN'S SUFFRAGE SOCIETIES. Honorary secretary (1913) Miss Young, "Berbico", Sea Road, Bexhill-on-Sea, Sussex.

BIGGLESWADE (NUWSS) In 1913 the society was a member of the OXON, BERKS, BUCKS, AND BEDS FEDERATION OF THE NATIONAL UNION OF WOMEN'S SUFFRAGE SOCIETIES. Secretary (1913) Mrs Aggias, Leigham, Drove Road, Biggleswade, Bedfordshire.

BIGGS, CAROLINE ASHURST (1840–89) Daughter of Matilda Ashurst BIGGS and Joseph Biggs. After her mother's death, the family moved from Kent to Notting Hill. In 1867 Caroline Ashurst Biggs gave a donation to the Society for the Promotion of the Employment of Women for its Apprenticeship Fund. She was elected to the executive committee of the LONDON NATIONAL SOCIETY FOR WOMEN'S SUFFRAGE in November 1867, replacing Frances Power COBBE. Clementia TAYLOR, who with her husband, the MP for Leicester, was a near neighbour and an old friend, described her then as "very clever and energetic, and thoroughly at one with us. She lives in Notting Hill Square – and will give me assistance whenever needed – so that a paid secretary is not needed". Caroline Ashurst Biggs became joint honorary secretary of the London National Society and spoke in July 1869 at the first public meeting held by the society, although Jessie BOUCHERETT reported that she was thought to be rather indistinct. In 1870 Caroline Biggs also subscribed to the MANCHESTER NATIONAL SOCIETY and seconded a resolution at its 1871 annual general meeting. Her father was treasurer of the London National Society in 1871 but she, like Mentia Taylor, resigned as secretary after it became clear that their support of the movement to repeal the Contagious Diseases Acts was anathema to John Stuart MILL and Helen TAYLOR. Mill, who described her in a letter of 20 September 1871 as having been "thrust in" to the London National Society by Mrs Taylor, went so far as to ensure that a vote of censure was passed on Caroline Ashurst Biggs, giving her no option but resignation. She then became the first secretary of the CENTRAL COMMITTEE OF THE NATIONAL SOCIETY FOR WOMEN'S SUFFRAGE when it was formed in 1872. She held this post jointly with Agnes GARRETT until August 1873, and then kept her membership of the executive committee until her death. She was one of the Central Committee's most active speakers at a time when it was still unusual for a woman to speak in public. In 1872 she accompanied Lilias Ashworth (see Lilias Ashworth HALLETT) on her speaking tour of South Wales. In 1875 she organized the campaign to elect Martha Merington, who had been one of the signatories to the 1866 suffrage petition, as a poor law guardian in London. In 1881, she was the founder, with Eva Muller (see McLAREN), of the SOCIETY FOR PROMOTING THE RETURN OF WOMEN AS POOR LAW GUARDIANS. In 1886 she was involved with Annie Leigh BROWNE in forming the Local Electors Association, and was one of the first London members of the WOMEN'S LIBERAL UNIONIST ASSOCIATION. She strongly supported the Central Committee of the National Society for Women's Suffrage, led by Millicent Garrett FAWCETT, after the 1888 split in the central society.

Caroline Ashurst Biggs became editor of the *Englishwoman's Review* in 1871 and held the position until her death. In 1882 she edited *Suffrage Stories*, a series of pamphlets published by the National Society. In 1884 she was entrusted with editing the *Women's Suffrage Journal* for two months while Lydia BECKER was in Canada. She contributed a very useful chapter on the suffrage movement in Great Britain to Vol. III of *History of Women's Suffrage*, edited by Elizabeth Cady Stanton, Susan B. Anthony and Matilda Joslyn Gage, published in 1886. She also wrote *Ought Women to Have Votes for Members of Parliament?* in a four-page pamphlet, 1879; *Women as Poor Law Guardians* reprinted from the *Englishwomen's Review*, 1887; and in 1889 the Central Committee published, posthumously, her pamphlet, *A Letter from an Englishwoman to Englishwomen*. In addition, when young, she wrote a novel, *The Master of Winbourne*. After her death the "Caroline Ashurst Biggs Memorial Loan Fund" was set up in order to lend money to deserving women students. Helen BLACKBURN united her name with that of Lydia Becker when forming the "Memorial" library that she gave to Girton College.

Address: (1867) 19 Notting Hill Square, London W.
Photograph: in Blackburn College, Girton College, Cambridge, reproduced in H. Blackburn, *Record of Women's Suffrage*, 1902.
Archival source: Blackburn Collection, Girton College, Cambridge; Mill–Taylor Collection, London School of Economics and Political Science.
Bibliography: obituary by Jessie Boucherett in the *Englishwoman's Review*, 14 September 1889; P. Hollis, *Ladies Elect: Women in English Local Government, 1865–1914*, 1987.

BIGGS, MATILDA ASHURST (1818–66)   Unitarian, daughter of William Ashurst, who was a solicitor, a member, with P.A. Taylor, of the National Association for the Promoting of the Political and Social Improvement of the People, patron of Robert Owen, Garibaldi, George HOLYOAKE, and all radical causes of the mid-nineteenth century. She was the sister of Emilie VENTURI and of Caroline STANSFELD. She married, c. 1840, Joseph Biggs, a Unitarian from Leicester, another radical, who was proposed as a member of the National Association in 1845 by James Stansfeld and William Lovett. They had three daughters, Caroline (*see* Caroline Ashurst BIGGS), Elizabeth and Maude, who was to carry on the family tradition by supporting, throughout her life, the cause of Polish nationalism. In 1840 Matilda Biggs attended the Anti-Slavery Convention in London and entertained the visiting American abolitionists; after their return to America she began a correspondence with William Lloyd Garrison and Lucretia Mott. In the 1840s she was, like the rest of her family, at the centre of the group supporting the Italian cause, friend of Garibaldi, Mazzini and Margaret Fuller. With her sister Emilie Venturi she established a rescue mission for "fallen women" in Leicester. In 1847 Matilda Ashurst Biggs was, Helen BLACKBURN related, sent a leaflet by Anne KNIGHT, advocating universal suffrage. The family moved to Italy for a year, 1850–51, on account of Matilda's ill health and on their return settled in Kent. In 1859 she wrote to the Northern Reform Society, founded in Newcastle with universal suffrage as its aim, asking to join. She was told that, although many of its members were in favour of "woman suffrage", the society only contemplated asking for suffrage for men. It would, however, "be very glad of women's subscriptions". She gave a donation to the Society for the Promotion of Employment of Women in 1865, signed the 1866 women's suffrage petition and was a subscriber to the ENFRANCHISEMENT OF WOMEN COMMITTEE in 1866.

Address: (1866) Barden Park, Tunbridge Wells, Kent.
Bibliography: C.A. Biggs, "Great Britain", in E.C. Stanton, S.B. Anthony and M.J. Gage (eds), *History of Women's Suffrage*, Vol. III, 1886; H. Blackburn, *Record of Women's Suffrage*, 1902; E.A. Daniels, *Jessie White Mario: Risorgimento Revolutionary*, 1972; C. Midgeley, *Women Against Slavery: The British Campaigns, 1780–1870*, 1992; K. Gleadle, *The Early Feminists: Radical Unitarians and the Emergence of the Women's Rights Movement, 1831–51*, 1995.

BILLINGHURST, [ROSA] MAY (1875–1953)   Born in Lewisham, known to her contemporaries as the "cripple suffragette"; she had suffered from "total paralysis as a child". She worked among the inmates of a workhouse in Greenwich, taught in Sunday School and for the Band of Hope. Her sister was a "rescue worker" on the streets of London. May

Billinghurst had been a member of the Women's Liberal Association but joined the WOMEN'S SOCIAL AND POLITICAL UNION in 1907, having realized the importance of the vote for women as a result of her social work experiences. On her invalid tricycle she took part in the 13 June 1908 National Union of Women's Suffrage Societies' march to the Albert Hall, using the occasion to distribute leaflets advertising the next week's WSPU Hyde Park demonstration. For the occasion she had billeted at her house two French suffrage workers, one of whom was Madeleine Pelletier. In July 1908 May Billinghurst helped in the successful WSPU campaign at the Haggerston by-election. Among her other activities she trained 200 children to sing "the Suffragist ditty, the greatest line of which is 'And Keep the Liberal Out'". In July 1910 she founded and became the secretary of the Greenwich branch of the WSPU. She took part in the "Black Friday" demonstration in November 1910 and was thrown out of her tricycle. She was arrested again in Parliament Square in November 1911 and this time was sentenced to five days' imprisonment for obstructing the police. In March 1912 she was sentenced to one month's hard labour after taking part in the WSPU window-smashing campaign. In December 1912 she was arrested on suspicion of having damaged letter boxes in Deptford and, having made a long political speech from the dock, was sentenced to eight months' imprisonment. She immediately went on hunger strike and was forcibly fed. A description of this experience and of her speech are held in the archives of the Fawcett Library. She was released after two weeks on order of the Home Secretary. It is interesting to note just how much agitation went on behind the scenes on these occasions. Mrs PANKHURST had interceded for her with a friend of the Home Secretary and on 14 January 1913 Isabel SEYMOUR of the WSPU had written to her sister to say that she was hoping that a question concerning May Billinghurst's case would be asked the next day in the House of Commons. On 15 January Keir HARDIE replied to a letter from May Billinghurst's brother, suggesting that he should write directly to the Home Office giving details of his sister's medical condition. She was sufficiently recovered from her experience to speak at a meeting in West Hampstead in March 1913. On 14 June 1913 she took part, dressed in white, in her invalid car, in the funeral procession for Emily Wilding DAVISON. On 21 May 1914, according to her own memoir, she chained herself, in her wheelchair, to the railings at Buckingham Palace as part of the WSPU demonstration. Charlotte DRAKE, as reported by Sylvia PANKHURST in *The Suffragette Movement*, 1931, wrote that she remembered May Billinghurst on this occasion being thrown out of her wheelchair by two policemen, but then lost sight of her. May Billinghurst remained loyal to the Pankhursts. In 1918 she gave active support in Smethwick to Christabel PANKHURST's election campaign and in 1925 wrote to Emmeline Pankhurst, inviting herself to tea. May Billinghurst later joined the WOMEN'S FREEDOM LEAGUE and then the SUFFRAGETTE FELLOWSHIP. Because she propelled herself in an invalid car, she attracted considerable attention at the WSPU demonstrations. This raised her profile in news coverage of such events, but did lay her open, from at least one fellow member of the WSPU, to the charge that she played upon her physical infirmity. The "Suffragette Spirit" was not immune from petty rivalries.

Address: (1910) 7 Oakcroft Road, Lewisham, London SE.
Archival source: R.M. Billinghurst Papers, Fawcett Library.
Bibliography: I. Dove, *Yours in the Cause: Suffragettes in Lewisham, Greenwich and Woolwich*, 1988.

BILLINGTON-GREIG, TERESA, MRS (1877–1964) Born in Preston, brought up in Blackburn, Lancashire, destined to follow the family trade, drapery, she left home and, with no qualifications, managed to obtain a post as an assistant teacher in a Roman Catholic school in Manchester. Recognizing that she had become an agnostic, she renounced her Catholic upbringing and moved into the Municipal Education School Service, teaching, in 1901, with Alice Schofield (*see* Alice Schofield COATES) in a school in Lower Crumpsall. She ran into conflict with the educational authorities because she refused to give the prescribed religious instruction to her pupils and, in 1903, thus met Emmeline PANKHURST, who was a member of the Education Committee. The matter was resolved by finding a position for Teresa Billington at a Jewish school, where the problem did not arise. In April 1904 she founded and was first honorary secretary of the Manchester branch of the Equal Pay League, which was the first feminist pressure group within the National Union of Teachers. She was also honorary secretary of the Associates of Ancoats University Settlement, where she learned public speaking at the "Fawcett" debating society and came in contact with Eva GORE-BOOTH and Esther ROPER. Teresa Billington joined the WOMEN'S SOCIAL AND POLITICAL UNION just after it was founded, either in December 1903 or January 1904, speaking at Labour and radical societies (Socialist Sunday Schools, Socialist Churches, Ethical and philosophical groups, Socialist Democratic Federation, and trade unions) around Manchester, attempting to raise support for the women's equal suffrage bill. In the spring of 1905 she was asked by Emmeline Pankhurst and Keir HARDIE to become a full-time ORGANIZER, only the second to be appointed, and the first woman, for the Independent Labour Party, of which she had been a member since 1903. There is a hint of resentment in her memoir, "I gave up my teaching, my Equal Pay [League] work and my activity at the Manchester University Settlement and sacrificed my chance of a science degree to forward the woman's cause through the ILP". She obviously worked hard. Elizabeth Wolstenholme ELMY wrote on 30 January 1906 that "It is to Miss Billington, more than to any other person or persons that the great labour victories [parliamentary] in the Potteries are due. That was her last field of work." In October 1905 she orchestrated the publicity resulting from the imprisonment of Christabel PANKHURST and Annie KENNEY after their disruption of Sir Edward Grey's meeting at the Free Trade Hall in Manchester. She was in London at the end of the year, taking part in the heckling of Asquith and Campbell-Bannerman, and on 22 December was a member of a deputation to the latter at his home, requesting an interview. At Easter 1906, again at Mrs Pankhurst's request, she became a paid organizer for the WSPU, working with Annie Kenney to build up a national headquarters in London. She stayed with Sylvia PANKHURST in her lodgings in Park Walk, Chelsea. Sylvia Pankhurst in *The Suffragette*, 1911, notes that Teresa Billington was employed as an organizer specifically in order to ensure that the WSPU's first public demonstration, in Trafalgar Square on 19 May 1906 after the deputation to Campbell-Bannerman, was a success and in no way overshadowed by anything planned for the occasion by the NATIONAL UNION OF WOMEN'S SUFFRAGE SOCIETIES.

On 19 June 1906 Teresa Billington led a deputation of women from the East End to Asquith's house in Cavendish Square, was involved in a fracas with the police, was arrested and subsequently sentenced to a fine or two months' imprisonment in Holloway. Minnie BALDOCK has left among her papers an eye-witness account of the confrontation in Cavendish Square. An anonymous reader of the *Daily Mirror* paid Teresa Billington's fine and she was quickly released. Her status as the first suffragette prisoner in Holloway to become a member of the WOMEN'S FREEDOM LEAGUE was commemorated when, in June 1910, she walked at the head of the WFL "Prisoners" section, carrying a special BANNER, in the Coronation Procession. This marks the end of the first period in the life of the WSPU. Later in June Mrs Pankhurst and Christabel, who had recently graduated from Manchester University, came to London and broke up the original team. Sylvia, according to Teresa Billington, was "sent into a form of retirement to write a suffragette history, five great cases of her father's and mother's accumulated papers at her disposal. Annie Kenney was despatched to organise the West of England [she did not go until mid 1907], and I myself given the like job in Scotland". Certainly in October 1906 a member of the GLASGOW AND WEST OF SCOTLAND ASSOCIATION FOR WOMEN'S SUFFRAGE noted that she had heard Miss Billington of the WSPU speak and urged the society to invite her to speak to them; characteristically it refused. Later in October 1906 she returned to London to take part in a WSPU demonstration at the opening of parliament and, with Annie Cobden SANDERSON, Minnie Baldock and Annie Kenney, among others, was arrested and sentenced to two months in Holloway.

On 8 February 1907 in Glasgow, from the home of Isabella Bream Pearce, who wrote as "Lily Bell" for the *Labour Leader* and was a friend of Elizabeth Wolstenholme Elmy, Teresa Billington married Frederick Lewis Greig. By June 1907 her differences with the Pankhursts had become such that she resigned as a paid organizer, though she continued to work for the WSPU on an honorary basis. In October 1907, although Mrs Pankhurst had torn up the draft constitution and appointed herself "dictator" of the WSPU, Teresa Billington-Greig held the "Annual General Conference of the WSPU" on the date that had already been arranged, and, with Charlotte DESPARD, formed the Women's Freedom League. Her political and tactical philosophies are contained in a range of essays she published over the next few years while working as national honorary organizing secretary of the WFL. In 1908 she was one of the WFL's representatives at the Amsterdam conference of the INTERNATIONAL WOMAN SUFFRAGE ALLIANCE. She resigned from the WFL in December 1910, horrified by the renewal of militancy after the "torpedoing" of the Conciliation Bill.

Over the next few years, besides writing *The Militant Suffrage Movement*, 1911, perhaps her most important work, she offered her sevices as a freelance "Lecturer and Debater on a wide range of subjects – Literary, Philosophical, Economic, Political, feminist, Ethical, and Rationalist". Topics included "The Rights of the Child" and "Can Women Be Saved by the Vote Alone" and her charge was two guineas with railway expenses and hospitality, which could be reduced to one guinea for poor or small propaganda societies. An article, "The Truth About White Slavery", that she published in the *English Review* in June 1913 gives a clear indication of the rationality that she brought to the women's cause, in contrast to the hysteria whipped up by some elements in the WSPU. In this article she described the making of an urban myth and exposed the lack of any hard evidence to underpin the panic. By this time she had become disillusioned with the efficacy of all reforming organizations, including the Labour party. Her only child, a daughter, was born in 1915. Both during and after the war she worked for her husband's billiard table firm and in the 1920s founded the Women's Billiards Association. From 1927 to 1930 she was honorary secretary of the Sports Fellowship, which aimed to interest underprivileged girls in athletics. In 1934 she was honorary director of the Women's Billiards Centre. In 1937 she resumed her association with the WFL, working for its Women's Electoral Committee, which after the Second World War became Women for Westminster. In 1947–51 she took part in the Conference on the Feminine Point of View, which was organized by Olwen Campbell (daughter of Mary WARD) and included, among many others, Margery Corbett ASHBY. After 1958 she was involved with the Six Point Group. She was concerned that a history of the suffrage movement more objective than any that had appeared in her lifetime should be written. She had little time for the prison-orientated autobiographical writings and speeches, without historical or political background, which emanated from members of the SUFFRAGETTE FELLOWSHIP. Ironically, a WFL banner embroidered with her name and "Holloway" is now in the Fawcett Library Collection.

Address: (1913) The Myth, High Possil, Glasgow; (1934) Women's Billiards Centre, 16 Soho Square, London W1; (1938) 32 Carnaby St, London W1; (1957) 146 Dora Road, Wimbledon, London SW19.
Photograph: in the Suffragette Fellowship Collection, Museum of London.
Archival source: Billington-Greig Papers, Fawcett Library; B. Harrison, taped interviews with Fiona Billington-Greig (daughter of Teresa Billington-Greig), 24 August, 19 September, 1974, and with Mrs Blackman (niece of Teresa Billington-Greig) 19 September 1974, Fawcett Library; Elizabeth Wolstenholme Elmy Papers, British Library; Minnie Baldock Papers, Museum of London.
Bibliography: C. McPhee and A. FitzGerald (eds), *The Non-Violent Militant: Selected Writings of Teresa Billington-Greig*, 1987; B. Harrison, *Prudent Revolutionaries*, 1987.

BINGLEY (NUWSS) In 1913 the society was a member of the WEST RIDING FEDERATION OF THE NATIONAL UNION OF WOMEN'S SUFFRAGE SOCIETIES. Secretary (1913) Miss Moulden, 100 Main Street, Bingley, Yorkshire.

BINGLEY (WSPU) Organizer (1906) Miss Nellie Kenney, 14 Leonard's Place, Bingley, Yorkshire.

BIRKENHEAD AND WIRRAL WOMEN'S SUFFRAGE SOCIETY A Birkenhead committee of the NATIONAL SOCIETY FOR WOMEN'S SUFFRAGE was formed in 1873, honorary secretary Mrs Y.G. O'Brien, Fern Nook, Birkenhead. The society was refounded in 1895, affiliated to the CENTRAL NATIONAL SOCIETY FOR WOMEN'S SUFFRAGE and then, in 1898, to the NATIONAL UNION OF WOMEN'S SUFFRAGE SOCIETIES. In 1913 the society was a member of the WEST LANCS, WEST CHESHIRE AND NORTH WALES FEDERATION. Secretary (1900, 1913) Miss A. Wyse, 4 Mather Road, Oxton, Birkenhead.

BIRMINGHAM branch of the FRIENDS' LEAGUE FOR WOMEN'S SUFFRAGE   Founded by 1913. Honorary secretary, Miss Joyce, 12 Frederick Road, Edgbaston (which was across the road from the home of Eliza Sturge, secretary of the BIRMINGHAM WOMEN'S SUFFRAGE SOCIETY more than 40 years before).

BIRMINGHAM branch of the MEN'S LEAGUE FOR WOMEN'S SUFFRAGE   Founded in 1909. Honorary secretary Mr A.W. Evans. Among the members of the Committee was Julian Osler, son of Catherine OSLER.
Address: (1909) 382 Moseley Road, Birmingham.

BIRMINGHAM branch of the MEN'S POLITICAL UNION FOR WOMEN'S ENFRANCHISEMENT   Founded on 21 April 1910.

BIRMINGHAM branch of the UNITED SUFFRAGISTS   Formed in February 1915 at the instigation of Bertha Brewster, formerly a militant member of the WOMEN'S SOCIAL AND POLITICAL UNION who had undergone hunger strikes and forcible feeding. Honorary secretary (1915) Miss Margaret Haly, 59 County Buildings, Corporation Street; (1917) Julia Green. Organizer (1915) Elizabeth Jenkins, 13 Suffolk Street, Birmingham. Office (July 1915) 19 New Street, Birmingham.

BIRMINGHAM (WSPU)   Organizer (1908–end 1909) Gladice KEEVIL; (1910–13) Miss Dorothy EVANS, 97 John Bright Street, Birmingham. Office (1910) 33 Paradise Street, Birmingham.

BIRMINGHAM AND DISTRICT branch of the WOMEN'S EMANCIPATION UNION   Honorary secretary (1895) Miss Julia Smith (*see* Caroline SMITH), 19 Carpenter Road, Edgbaston, Birmingham.

BIRMINGHAM SOCIETY FOR WOMEN'S SUFFRAGE
Founded, as a committee of the NATIONAL SOCIETY FOR WOMEN'S SUFFRAGE, at "A Public Meeting on Women's Suffrage" held at the Exchange Rooms, New Street, on 8 May 1868. Its first secretary, Mary JOHNSON (later Mrs Robert Feast), gave Clementia TAYLOR the credit for being "the Parent of the Birmingham Committee". William and Caroline TAYLOR, brother and sister-in-law of P.A. and Clementia Taylor, were, from the first, members of the Birmingham executive committee and in 1871 Caroline Taylor was treasurer. Another large public meeting organized by the society was held on 5 December 1871 and was fully reported in the *Women's Suffrage Journal*. In 1872 the Birmingham Society associated itself with the new CENTRAL COMMITTEE OF THE NATIONAL SOCIETY FOR WOMEN'S SUFFRAGE. At this time the treasurer of the Birmingham Society was Mrs Ashford, of Speedwell Road, Birmingham, and the honorary secretary was Eliza STURGE, 17 Frederick Road, Edgbaston. Among the members of the executive committee were Mrs Feast (the former Miss Johnson), Rev. and Mrs H.W. CROSSKEY, Mr and Mrs William Taylor, and Mrs Dawson, whose husband George Dawson (1821–76) was an independent nonconformist minister, the promoter of a "civic gospel", a member of the Reform League, of the Birmingham Sunday League, of the Freehold Land Society, of the Birmingham Liberal Association and of the Birmingham Educational Society. He had been a Chartist. A letter, unfortunately without a year date, from him to Anne KNIGHT survives among her papers. In it he writes, "The subject, dear friend, on which you write is of the highest importance. About it I have thought much, but have not yet altogether gained that clear vision on the matter which I always require before I speak. With Woman's present position no one can be satisfied and I am not sure that the strenuous efforts to educate men, without corresponding ones on behalf of women have not rendered the position worse by making a gulf of separation between the somewhat educated man and the non-educated woman. At present little has been done here by the Committee of the Whittington Club but the preparation of rules etc. All the privileges of the club will be open to women with this difference only, that the women's subscription is lower." This letter presumably predates the disbanding of the Birmingham Whittington Club in 1848. Bessie Rayner PARKES had attended lectures given by Dawson in Birmingham *c*. 1848 and had written for the *Birmingham Journal* of which Dawson was editor. Dawson married into a Unitarian family and Mrs George Dawson signed the Declaration in Favour of Women's Suffrage organized by the Central Committee of the National Society in 1889.

In January 1874 the National Society for Women's Suffrage held a conference in Birmingham which resulted in the presentation of a Memorial to Gladstone (although Disraeli had become prime minister by the time it was presented) and in April 1877 the city was again the venue for another of the National Society's conferences. From 1885 Catherine OSLER was secretary of the BWSS, her sister Edith was treasurer, and her father William Taylor was still a member of the executive committee. In October 1900 the minutes of the society record that one of its best ever drawing-room meetings had just been held in a private house, at which 100 ladies were present, an interesting discussion was held and 26 new members were enrolled. By 1901 Catherine Osler had become president of the BWSS and, with help from ORGANIZERS from the NATIONAL UNION OF WOMEN'S SUFFRAGE SOCIETIES, had supervised the opening of new branches in 1903–4 at Coventry, Warwick, Leamington and Redditch. The BWSS was very active during the winter of 1906–7 organizing support for Clementina BLACK's Women's Franchise Declaration (see WOMEN'S FRANCHISE DECLARATION COMMITTEE), employing an organizer for three weeks specifically for this purpose. The BWSS held 30 meetings in Birmingham and the surrounding district during 1907 and in 1908–9 drew in £8 6s 3d in subscriptions, making it, therefore, the second largest society; the London Society's total was £32 0s 9d. In 1908 more than 150 members of the BWSS went to London to take part in the 13 June NUWSS procession. The society worked assiduously at making a success of its frequent meetings and keeping all sections of the populace happy; complimentary tickets were regularly given to working-women's associations, to the secretary of the local Women's Social and Political Union, the chief of police and the head of the Fire Station. Dr Mary Sturge, niece of Eliza Sturge, and Dr Annie Clark (1844–1924), sister-in-law of Helen Bright CLARK and one of the signatories of the 1866 women's suffrage petition, a member of the BWSS and a tax resister, were also both among those regularly in receipt of platform tickets for meetings.

As early as 1903 the BWSS thought it advisable to undertake some work among working women, on the lines of that being done among the textile workers of Lancashire and the North. They began with the women chain-makers of Cradley. A Miss Rowton came down from the NORTH OF ENGLAND SOCIETY FOR WOMEN'S SUFFRAGE to start the work, and was then succeeded by a Mrs Green. They went from yard to yard, talking to the women, and held cottage meetings. Esther ROPER and Constance GORE-BOOTH, the pioneers from the north, spoke in Birmingham on 22 October 1903 (two days after the reception given to Christabel PANKHURST and Annie KENNEY in the Free Trade Hall in Manchester). In early 1904 the BWSS continued the work in Cradley, now among the nail makers, who in March joined with women from Leicestershire and Lancashire to present a suffrage petition to Sir Charles McLaren, son of Priscilla Bright MCLAREN. By 1913 the BWSS had enrolled 1600 FRIENDS OF WOMEN'S SUFFRAGE and had opened a branch at Bourneville for workers there. The society suggested founding Study Circles at which working women could meet in each other's homes and discuss such texts as "Why Women Need the Vote" (a 4d pamphlet written by Catherine Osler), *The Feminist Movement* by Ethel SNOWDEN, and J.S. MILL's *The Subjection of Women*. The society also founded a Franchise Club, which operated from its Easy Row office and was for those who were willing to be more active than merely subscribe. For instance, in 1910 the Franchise Club organized a Speakers' Class. The BWSS supported the NUWSS Election Fighting Fund policy in 1912, at which time Julia VARLEY was a member of the society. In 1909 Catherine Osler left the Liberal party, which had such a strong tradition in Birmingham and with which her family had for so long been associated, and also, as an individual, supported the Election Fighting Fund. By 1912 the BWSS had 700 members. By 1913 the society was a member of the MIDLAND (WEST) FEDERATION OF THE NATIONAL UNION OF WOMEN'S SUFFRAGE SOCIETIES. In 1918 the BWSS became the Birmingham Society for Equal Citizenship.

Office (1877) 4 Broad Street Corner, Birmingham; (1909) 10 Easy Row, Birmingham. Secretary (1909, 1913) Mrs Ring, 10 Easy Row, Birmingham. Secretaries of branches (1910) Miss G. Johnstone, Bindire, Four Oaks; Mrs Shrimpton, Eversleigh, Redditch; Miss Wright, Sutton Lodge, Solihull. Organizer (1910) Miss E.M. Gardner, 10 Easy Row, Birmingham.

Archival source: Papers of the Birmingham Women's Suffrage Society, Birmingham Archives and Local History Library; Anne Knight Papers, Friends' Library, London.

BLACK, CLEMENTINA (1853–1922)   Born in Brighton, sister of Constance Garnett, the translator of Tolstoy. Clementina Black joined the Fabian Society and in 1886 was appointed secretary of the Women's Protective and Provident League (later the Women's Trade Union and Provident League) until resigning in 1889 to join the newly formed Women's Trade Union Association (which by 1897 had merged with the Women's Industrial Council of which she became president). She was succeeded as secretary of the WPPL by Emilie Holyoake, daughter of George HOLYOAKE. One of Clementina Black's fellow workers on the WIC was Mrs Amie HICKS and by 1908 the Council certainly included among its aims that of educating working women about the importance of women's suffrage. Clementina Black was also a member of the executive committee, and by 1913 was a vice-president of the LONDON SOCIETY FOR WOMEN'S SUFFRAGE, and was from 1911 a vice-president of the NATIONAL UNION OF WOMEN'S SUFFRAGE SOCIETIES. In 1906 she drew up the Suffrage Declaration, which was signed by 257 000 professional and other women, and was honorary secretary to the WOMEN'S FRANCHISE DECLARATION COMMITTEE. She spoke at meetings of suffrage societies, both militant and constitutional. For example, in 1907 she addressed a meeting organized by the MANSFIELD WOMEN'S SUFFRAGE SOCIETY (NUWSS) on the subject of women ratepayers and the municipal elections. From 1912 to 1913 she was acting editor of the *Common Cause*.

Clementina Black is particularly remembered for her writings on women and work, sweated industries, trade boards, and, finally on that feminist chimera, co-operative housekeeping. She was also a prolific journalist, novelist and biographer. Her adopted daughter married H.W. Massingham, a journalist working on such Liberal newpapers as the *Daily News* and the *Manchester Guardian* and who in 1907 became the editor of the *Nation*.

Address: (1901) 70 Marylands Road, London W; (1913) Pilgrim's Place House, Hampstead, London NW; (1916) 10 Priory Gardens, Highgate, London NW; (1920) 22 Westmoreland Road, Barnes, London SW.
Photograph: in *Common Cause*, 1912.

Bibliography: L. Glage, *Clementina Black: A Study in Social History and Literature*, 1981, which includes a bibliography of all her writing; E. Mappen, *Helping Women At Work: The Women's Industrial Council, 1889–1914*, 1985; B.C. Johnson (ed.), *Tea and Anarchy!: The Bloomsbury Diary of Olive Garnett, 1890–1893*, 1989.

BLACKBURN branch of the MANCHESTER NATIONAL SOCIETY FOR WOMEN'S SUFFRAGE   In existence in the 1870s. By 1912 the society had joined the MANCHESTER AND DISTRICT FEDERATION OF THE NATIONAL UNION OF WOMEN'S SUFFRAGE SOCIETIES. Secretary (1913) Mrs Foxcroft, 6 St James's Road, Blackburn, Lancashire.

BLACKBURN (WSPU)   Secretary (1906) Mrs A. Duxbury, 7 Langham Road, Blackburn, Lancashire.

BLACKBURN, HELEN (1842–1903)   Born on Valentia Island, off the south-west coast of Ireland, where her father worked as a civil engineer. Little is known of her early life except that she had been interested in water-colour painting but by the age of 21 had to give it up as her eyesight deteriorated. In the scrapbook compiled, presumably by her, now in the Girton College archive, there is an invitation, filed under the year 1872, for Miss and Mr Blackburn to attend a meeting at 9 Berners Street on 30 April of the recently formed CENTRAL COMMITTEE OF THE NATIONAL SOCIETY FOR WOMEN'S SUFFRAGE. "Mr Blackburn" may have been her brother Alexander, or her father. In due course she contributed a few papers to the *Englishwoman's Review* and in 1874 became secretary *pro tem* of the executive committee of the Central Committee, succeeding Emma PATERSON. She herself was succeeded by Kate Thornbury in 1877, while remaining a member of the executive committee. In 1875 Helen Blackburn attended, as did Eliza ORME, Mr Hunter's class in Roman Law at University College, London. In 1877 she was treasurer of the Berners Club for Ladies (*see* CLUBS), which was based at the same address as the offices of the Central Committee, and which in the 1890s was at 22 Berners Street, which by then, presumably by no coincidence, was the address of the *Englishwoman's Review*, of which Helen Blackburn was editor. In 1880 she became secretary to the BRISTOL AND WEST OF ENGLAND SUFFRAGE SOCIETY and in that year organized the suffrage demonstrations held in London and Bristol. The 1881 census shows her living as a lodger in the house of a confectioner, his wife and two young children; her room, or rooms, also acted as the office for the Bristol and West of England Suffrage Society. In 1883 she was the representative from Bristol on the committee of the SOCIETY FOR PROMOTING THE RETURN OF WOMEN AS POOR LAW GUARDIANS. From 1886 to 1888 Helen Blackburn attended classes at University College, Bristol. At the end of 1888 she was asked, after the split in the Central Society, to combine temporarily the secretaryship of the Bristol Society with that of the Central Committee under Mrs FAWCETT. This "temporary" situation lasted for seven years until, in 1895, she retired in order to care for her aged father. She remained as honorary secretary while being succeeded in the paid position by Edith PALLISER. She had been very friendly in Bristol with the PRIESTMAN sisters, who were adherents to the rival faction, the CENTRAL NATIONAL SOCIETY. It is clear from Miss Priestman's sentiments, as quoted by Lilias Ashworth HALLETT, that friendship bridged political divides. In 1894 Helen Blackburn was a member of the SPECIAL APPEAL COMMITTEE, drawn from women of all parties and societies, that organized the collection of nearly a quarter of a million names of women who supported women's enfranchisement. In 1897 she was a member of the parliamentary committee formed by the newly constituted NATIONAL UNION OF WOMEN'S SUFFRAGE SOCIETIES and in 1900 she was a member of the executive committee of the newly formed CENTRAL SOCIETY FOR WOMEN'S SUFFRAGE.

Lady Frances Balfour has left a deft sketch of Helen Blackburn's manner of living. In her autobiography she wrote:

> The small Suffrage Committtee met at that time [1887] in her house in Great College Street, Westminster. I am not sure whether the house was hers, or belonged to the Suffrage committee, any way, Miss Blackburn lived there, and her personality pervaded the place. It was a small panelled room stacked with endless files of Suffrage papers. There was a sofa couch, which was her bed, and I used to see a frugal meal unnoticed on the hob. On the table amid her work was a small glass, in which stood a single flower, or sprig of green, and not infrequently a little bit of shamrock, in strange outward contrast to the large uncouth figure of Miss Blackburn, her shortsighted eyes always close to the papers she was working at, and no one ever saw her without "documentary evidence". Her face was greatly marred by long illness, most patiently borne, but through its plainness there shone the countenance of a great soul. I learnt to connect her with that single flower so daintily arranged, and knew that whatever it meant to her, that it was a true type of herself. Miss Blackburn was a born chronicler and antiquarian, particularly in one line of research, what she used to call "the spindle side." In her lighter moments she would draw up "trees" and diagrams showing the progress of women through the ages. Any position conceded or won by them she would tabulate, and rejoice over as the heralds of coming events. Sometimes in her work in Committee, she would seem to spend almost too much time in recording what we felt minute progresses. Or, she would have some plan that the rest of us did not think a hopeful line. Then, she would throw back her large head, and laugh with a childlike mirth, and in another minute she was "wondering" whether we could scale this height, or plumb this depth. Her knowledge and experience was at everyone's disposal. She would spend hours tramping the streets, looking up someone who might help the Cause, and the lobby of the House was familiar ground to her.

Her rooms in the house at 10 Great College Street were rented, as were those in the same house used by the Central Committee. In 1898 both the CENTRAL AND EAST OF ENGLAND SOCIETY, as the Central Committee had become, and Helen Blackburn had to find new premises when the houseowner wanted to relet her property furnished.

Helen Blackburn edited the *Englishwoman's Review* from 1889 to 1902. From 1886 to 1899 she edited *The Woman's Suffrage Calendar*. Among the articles and pamphlets she wrote were "Relation of Women to the State in Olden Time" published in the *National Review* in November 1886; *Because: being reasons from Fifty Women Workers why it is of national importance that the Parliamentary Franchise be no longer denied to Women as Women*, 1888; *Supporters* of the Women's Suffrage Movement, 1897; Women's Suffrage in the Light of the Second Reading of 1897, 1898; and the chapter "Great Britain" in vol. IV of Susan B. Anthony and Ida Husted (eds), The History of Women's Suffrage, 1902.

Helen Blackburn was a strenuous opponent of legislative restrictions on the labour of women, and contended that what women wanted were more and not fewer opportunities of earning their living. With Jessie BOUCHERETT she founded the Freedom of Labour Defence Association to protect workers, especially women workers, from restrictive legislation. In 1885 she organized in Bristol a Loan Exhibition of Women's Industries. The first rule in the catalogue to the Exhibition stated "That all the work in the Exhibition is done by women who made a profession of their pursuit. No work is shown done for recreation or amusement only". One feature of the Exhibition was a room devoted to a consciousness-raising display of portraits of women who led the way in opening new fields for the employment of women, or who had shown special excellence in work already done by women. Included among these were Florence Nightingale, Mrs Nassau Senior, Mary Carpenter, Elizabeth Garrett ANDERSON, Mary Somerville, Millicent Garrett Fawcett, Lydia BECKER, Barbara BODICHON, and Clementia TAYLOR. After being shown at the Exhibition, they were on display at the offices of the Central Committee, and then in the Woman's Building at the World's Columbian Exposition held in Chicago in 1893. On its return in 1894 she gave the collection, this monument to "the spindle side", to Bristol University to decorate its women's reading room. Many portraits were included by Helen Blagg, a member of the Fabian Society, in a Loan Exhibition held at Grosvenor House in May 1905 to benefit the Girls' Friendly Society. Unfortunately Bristol University has now no knowledge of what would be a very interesting visual realization of Helen Blackburn's feminist philosophy. A "Detailed Catalogue", printed by the Women's Printing Society, of the "Collection of Portraits of Eminent British Women as Exhibited at Chicago in 1893" is held in the Blackburn Collection. A parallel collection, the "Memorial Library", has survived – perhaps because books are considered more cerebral, less ephemeral, than pictures, and certainly because Helen Blackburn gave clear instructions about the gift to Girton College in her will. The library has a strong international perspective, containing books and pamphlets from 11 countries, in English, Dutch, French, German and Italian, and covering women's education, employment, temperance, suffrage, and social and domestic duties. Each book in the collection bears a bookplate, designed by Edith Mendham and printed by the Women's Printing Society; some of the bookplates have handwritten ink annotations, noting the source of the gift. From these one can see that the donors included, for example, Helen Blackburn herself, the Englishwoman's Review and Jessie Boucherett. Many of the books had been presented either to the Central Committee or to its secretaries, but some had obviously been carefully chosen second-hand purchases. The collection was held in bookcases, dated 1897, decorated with portraits by Elizabeth Guinness of Lydia Becker and Caroline Ashurst BIGGS, Helen Blackburn's predecessors in the secretaryship of the Central Committee, to whose memory the Library was dedicated. Elizabeth Guinness, who had studied at the Royal Academy Schools in 1872 and who lived with her friend and fellow artist Flora Reid, was a member of the Primrose League, a suffragist and a friend of Caroline Ashurst Biggs. Elizabeth Guinness, with Edith Mendham, had copied some otherwise inaccessible original works to fill out the Collection of Portraits. In her will, which was witnessed by Antoinette Mackenzie, her successor as editor of the Englishwoman's Review, and by Nora Vynne, Helen Blackburn described it as the "'Memorial Library' of books on women's questions" and directed her brother as her sole executor to deliver the bookcases and all the contents to Girton College. Included with the books is a very interesting archive from which she drew the material that constituted the basis of her history of the suffrage movement, Women's Suffrage: A Record of the Women's Suffrage Movement in the British Isles with Biographical Sketches of Miss Becker, 1902. The originals of most of the photographs that appear in this book are still in the archive.

Among Helen Blackburn's other published works are two pamphlets, Some of the Facts of the Women's Suffrage Question and Comments on the Opposition to Women's Suffrage, both published in 1878; A Handbook *for Women Engaged in Social and Political Work*, 1881; *A Handy-Book of Reference for Irishwomen*, published at the Irish Exhibition, Olympia, 1888; with Jessie Boucherett, *The Condition of Working Women*, 1896; and, with Nora Vynne, *Women Under the Factory Act*, 1903.

Address: (1874) 14 Victoria Road, Kensington, London W; (1881) 20 Park Street, Bristol; (1889–98) 10 Great College Street, Westminster, London SW; (1901) 18 Grey Coat Gardens, Westminster, London W.

Portrait: by Elizabeth Guinness, commissioned on Helen Blackburn's retirement from the secretaryship of the Bristol and West of England Suffrage Society, given, with her portrait collection, to University Hall, Bristol. The original is now lost but a photograph appears in the *Englishwoman's Review*, 15 April 1903.

Archival source: Blackburn Collection, Girton College Archive.

Bibliography: obituaries in the *Englishwoman's Review*, 15 January and 15 April 1903; *Memorials of Some Notable Women*: catalogue of loan exhibition, Grosvenor House, 1905; S.J. Tanner, *How the Suffrage Movement Began in Bristol Fifty Years Ago*, 1918; Lady F. Balfour, *Ne Obliviscaris*, 1930; J. Lewis (ed.) *Before The Vote was Won*, 1987 (contains H. Blackburn, *Some of the Facts of the Women's Suffrage Question*, 1878; *Comments on the Opposition to Women's Suffrage*, 1878).

BLACKHEATH (branch of LONDON SOCIETY FOR WOMEN'S SUFFRAGE) Secretary (1909) Miss J. Duckham, The Red House, Dartmouth Grove, Blackheath, London SE; (1913) Miss M. Peppercorn, 97 Blackheath Park, London SE.

BLACKHILL AND CONSETT (NUWSS) In 1913 the society was a member of the NORTH-EASTERN FEDERATION OF THE NATIONAL UNION OF WOMEN'S SUFFRAGE SOCIETIES. Secretary (1913) Miss Trotter, Oakleigh, Woodlands Road, Shotley Bridge, Co. Durham.

BLACKPOOL AND FYLDE (NUWSS) Founded in 1904. In 1913 the society was a member of the WEST LANCS, WEST CHESHIRE, AND NORTH WALES FEDERATION OF THE NATIONAL UNION OF WOMEN'S SUFFRAGE SOCIETIES. The society's BANNER is now held in the Fawcett Library Collection. Secretary (1913) Mrs M.E. Edwards, 125 Hornby Road, Blackpool, and Mrs Bamford Tomlinson, 16 Clevedon Road, Blackpool, Lancashire.

BLAIRMORE (NUWSS) In 1913 the society was a member of the SCOTTISH FEDERATION OF THE NATIONAL UNION OF WOMEN'S SUFFRAGE SOCIETIES. Secretary (1913) Mrs Leggat, Duart Tower, Blairmore, Argyllshire.

BLAND, VIOLET ANN (1863–1940) Began work as a kitchen maid at Dudmaston Hall near Bridgnorth, now owned by the National Trust, and by the turn of the century was head of a Ladies' College of Domestic Science in Bristol, of which she appears to have been sole owner. She advertised in *Votes for Women* on, for instance, 14 May 1909, offering to receive paying guests: "Henley Grove is a fine old mansion, standing in 15 acres of park-like grounds" with "tennis, croquet, badminton, Swedish gymnasium . . .". She became an active member of the WOMEN'S SOCIAL AND POLITICAL UNION in Bristol, providing (paid) hospitality for such WSPU activists as Annie KENNEY, Lettice FLOYD, Elsie HOWEY, Vera WENTWORTH and Mary PHILLIPS. In August 1909 she gave her garden, "lavishly decorated", for the reception to Mrs DOVE-WILLCOX and Mary ALLEN on their release from prison, although Mary BLATHWAYT's diary reveals that the guests paid 1/– each for the tea.

In 1910 Violet Bland moved to London where she was the proprietress until 1935 of a guest house in the heart of the West End. She was arrested on "Black Friday" in November 1910 but, as was usual on that occasion, was discharged. On 4 March 1912 she was arrested, having broken a window in Northumberland Avenue. At her trial she said that she "had paid rates and taxes to the tune of nearly £1 a week for 20 years, and she had been working for her citizenship for a number of years". She was sentenced to four months' imprisonment, which she spent at Aylesbury. She was visited there by the Rev. Frederick HANKINSON, in his capacity as a Unitarian minister, who read letters to her. The conversation was conducted in whispers but, even so, Hankinson was reprimanded by the governor of the prison and the regulation about not communicating news from friends or family to prisoners was reread to him. Violet Bland joined in the hunger strike and gave a description, in *Votes for Women*, 5 July 1912, of her experience of being forcibly fed.

In 1915, after the death of her younger sister, she fostered four very young children, while carrying on with the running of her guest house. In 1917 the Hon Evelina HAVERFIELD's and Sergt-Major Flora Sandes' Fund for Providing Comforts for Serbian Soldiers and Prisoners was based at the same address as Violet Bland. A signed photograph of Evelina Haverfield held in the Suffragette Fellowship Collection is annotated on the reverse, by an unknown hand, as having been received from Violet Bland in 1938, which suggests that the location of the Haverfield Fund was not fortuitous.

Address: (1909) Henley Grove, Henleaze, Bristol; (1910) 22 Old Burlington Street, London W.
Photograph: in Suffragette Fellowship Collection, Museum of London.
Archival source: information compiled for Bayston Hall Library by Allan Bland.

BLATCH, HARRIOT STANTON (1856–1940) Born at Seneca Falls, New York, daughter of Elizabeth Cady Stanton. She graduated from Vassar, spent some time as a tutor to Americans in Germany and in 1880 was studying in France. She returned to the US in 1881 and helped her mother to prepare the last chapter of the second volume of *The History of Women's Suffrage*. They sailed together to France in May 1882, where Harriot was studying French in Toulouse and where her brother Theodore was gathering material for *The Woman Question in Europe*. Mr Blatch, an Englishman whom she had met on board ship to America the previous year, visited the Stantons there and he and Harriot were married at the end of the year by William Henry Channing at the Unitarian Chapel in Little Portland Street. Harriot Stanton Blatch spent the next 20 years in England. A daughter, Nora, named for the Ibsen heroine who had given her name to *Nora*, as translated by Frances LORD, friend of both Harriot and her mother, was born by the end of 1883. In 1885 Harriot Stanton Blatch agreed to speak at the first public meeting held by the CAMBRIDGE WOMEN'S SUFFRAGE ASSOCIATION. In October 1887 she attended the meeting in London at which it was decided to form a WOMEN'S LIBERAL FEDERATION and became a member of her local branch. Her mother did not approve of women dissipating their efforts by offering their services to political parties and wrote "the whole movement was an insult to women". Harriot Stanton Blatch was a member of the SOCIETY FOR PROMOTING THE RETURN OF WOMEN AS COUNTY COUNCILLORS and in 1889 spoke at a public meeting to support the candidature of Lady SANDHURST for the County Council election in Brixton. In 1890 she left the CENTRAL NATIONAL SOCIETY FOR WOMEN'S SUFFRAGE in order to join the WOMEN'S FRANCHISE LEAGUE. In the 1890s she was very friendly with Richard and Emmeline PANKHURST; Christabel and Sylvia went as children to stay with her family in Basingstoke. In 1893 she attended the World's Congress of Representative Women at Chicago and gave a paper on "The Progress of Society Dependent on the Emancipation of Woman". She left the Women's Franchise League, according to Ursula BRIGHT in a letter to Emmeline Pankhurst, "because her name was attached to the Gladstone address in which she thought the street women [prostitutes] were not sufficiently respectfully spoken of". In 1895 she was a member of the WOMEN'S EMANCIPATION UNION; she was very friendly with Elizabeth Wolstenholme ELMY and at Christmas 1896 contributed £2 towards a gift for her. In 1896 her second daughter Helen, aged four, died; Esther Bright, daugher of Ursula, played the violin at the funeral. In the late 1890s Harriot Stanton Blatch was a speaker at the Pioneer Club (*see under* CLUBS); was a member of the Fabian Society, which she joined in 1891 or 1892, becoming a member of its executive committee in 1894–5; and in 1898 was a member of the executive committee of the UNION OF PRACTICAL SUFFRAGISTS. In February 1902 she was a delegate from the NATIONAL UNION OF WOMEN'S SUFFRAGE SOCIETIES at the International Conference on Women's Suffrage held at Washington. She and her family finally returned to the US in 1902, where she became a founder and president of the Equality League of Self-Supporting Women (later the Women's Political Union), which adopted the purple, white, and green colours of the WOMEN'S SOCIAL AND POLITICAL UNION, and supported the militant methods that the suffragettes used in Britain, although not necessarily advocating their use in the US. Her daughter, now Nora Blatch de Forest (later Barney, d. 1971) who in 1905 was the first woman in the US to graduate with a degree in civil engineering, was a committee member of the

Equality League and contributed to the WSPU in 1908. In September 1907 Harriot Stanton Blatch arranged meetings for Mrs Pankhurst on her visit to New York, and at the end of the same year for Annie Cobden SANDERSON. In 1909 she persuaded the US immigration authorities to put no obstacles in Mrs Pankhurst's way, despite her British prison conviction, when she landed again in New York. She then organized the first meeting, which proved to be the largest suffrage meeting yet held in the US, of Mrs Pankhurst's subsequent tour. She also organized a lecture tour given by Sylvia PANKHURST in 1912 and another by Mrs Pankhurst in the autumn of 1913.

Address: (1890) The Mount, Basingstoke, Hampshire.
Photograph: in E.C. Stanton, *Eighty Years and More: Reminiscences of Elizabeth Cady Stanton*, 1898.
Archival source: Elizabeth Wolstenholme Elmy Papers, British Library; Correspondence between Ursula Bright and Emmeline Pankhurst in The Papers of Sylvia Pankhurst, Internationaal Instituut voor Sociale Geschiedenis, Amsterdam.
Bibliography: E.C. Stanton, *Eighty Years and More: Reminiscences of Elizabeth Cady Stanton*, 1898; H.S. Blatch and A. Lutz, *Challenging Years; The Memoirs of Harriot Stanton Blatch*, 1940; E.C. DuBois, *Harriot Stanton Blatch and the Winning of Woman Suffrage*, 1997.

BLATHWAYT FAMILY Col Linley Blathwayt (1839–1919) retired army colonel, naturalist, and photographer; Mrs Emily Marion Blathwayt (*c.* 1852–1940), his wife; Mary Blathwayt (1879–1962), his daughter, who joined the WOMEN'S SOCIAL AND POLITICAL UNION in July 1906, noting in her diary "Have also sent 3/– to Mrs F.W. Pethwick Lawrence [*sic*] Hon Treasurer of the 'Women's Social & Political Union's Campaign Fund' I sent it to 87 Clement's Inn, London." Mary led the safe but monotonous life of a "daughter-at-home", tending her hens and noting the births, marriages and deaths of all acquaintances, and there is nothing in her diary up until then to show that she was interested in feminism or women's suffrage. She subscribed to a number of causes and she and her friends were regular attenders at lectures on a wide range of subjects – from "Ants" to "Cooperative Production" – both in Bath and at summer schools in Oxford and Cambridge. There is little evidence in Mary Blathwayt's diaries that these were of more than a momentary interest, a way of filling in the time. Among her friends, Aethel and Grace TOLLEMACHE also became active suffrage workers. Mrs PETHICK-LAWRENCE immediately sent Mary some "Votes for Women Leaflets" and was sent the reply that "she may enroll my name on their Membership List". Mary spent from October 1906 until early May 1907 in Germany with her brother but within two weeks of her return attended a NATIONAL UNION FOR WOMEN'S SUFFRAGE SOCIETY drawing-room meeting at which Frances STERLING was the speaker. Mary Blathwayt then paid 1/– to join the "Bath branch of the N.U. of Women's Suffrage Societies". In June she renewed her subscription to the WSPU and in July sent £1 towards their "£20 000 Fund". In July 1907 she was sent "a new paper '*Women's Franchise*'" and agreed to subscribe to it for three months; she later renewed this for a further six months. She passed one of the first copies she received on to a friend and later put a copy each week into the Bath and Counties Ladies' Club (*see under* CLUBS), of which she was a member, and into Bath Reference Library, although permission for the latter copy was quickly rescinded by the Town Clerk. On 6 October she received the first copy of *Votes for Women* and immediately took out a year's subscription. In November 1907 Mary Blathwayt attended, with the Blathwayts' maid, Ellen Morgan, a Miss Johnson and Aethel Tollemache, a WSPU meeting in Bristol and for the first time met Annie KENNEY, Emmeline Pethick-Lawrence, and Christabel PANKHURST. This meeting sparked off, in the context of Mary Blathwayt's life, a considerable degree of proselytizing activity. She wrote twice within the next few days to Clement's Inn for pamphlets, leaflets and postcards and sent copies of *Women's Franchise* to several friends. She herself set about distributing leaflets through the letterboxes of Bath, in the station ladies' waiting room and at factory gates. In December she renewed her subscription to the Bath NUWSS society for another year and found, to her surprise, that she had been elected onto its executive committee. She was soon joint honorary secretary. In January 1908 she was lent a copy of Helen Blackburn, *Record of Women's Suffrage*, 1902 (she does not record whether or not she actually read it; she certainly makes no comment on its contents) and then passed it on to Aethel Tollemache. At her first Bath NUWSS executive committee meeting she gave away copies of *Taxation without Representation is Tyranny* and a copy of the *Woman's Franchise* to other committee members. In February 1908 she went to London to take part in the Women's Parliament in Caxton Hall. The day after her return she wore her "Votes for Women" badge for the first time, and chalked "Votes for Women" on a wall in Batheaston and on the wall surrounding Eagle House. She also wrote to Lilias Ashworth HALLETT to say that she had been asked by Aeta LAMB to organize a WSPU meeting in Bath on 1 April and "don't see how I can work for two Suffrage Societies at the same time". But that is just what she did do. She was joint honorary secretary of the Bath branch of the NUWSS and carried on distributing posters for a NUWSS meeting on 9 March, while organizing the WSPU meeting. At the NUWSS meeting Mrs Ashworth Hallett was in the chair and the speakers were Millicent Garrett FAWCETT and Alice CLARK. Aeta Lamb and the Misses CODD, all from the WSPU, assisted on the night. For distribution at this meeting Mary had ordered 400 copies of *Women's Franchise* (of which 127 were sold) and 700 leaflets from the NUWSS. Prior to the meeting Mrs Ashworth Hallett had invited Mary Blathwayt and other suffrage sympathizers to Claverton Lodge to meet Miss Clark and Mrs Fawcett. In her diary Mary wrote, "I have never been to the house before, it is a beautiful place. Mrs Hallett is most kind. I could not believe I was looking at Mrs Fawcett, she looks so young. I believe she has been working for Votes for Women for 40 years". In March Mary went up to London with Mrs Ashworth Hallett, although the latter travelled first-class and Mary third, to attend the release of the WSPU prisoners from Holloway, the celebratory breakfast at the Eustace Miles Restaurant organized by Millicent Fawcett and a meeting at the Albert Hall. Mary's organization of the WSPU April meeting proved satisfactory; Nellie CROCKER and Annie Kenney were the speakers. Later that month she organized another meeting for the Bath NUWSS, at which Frances SWINEY was the main attraction. That, however, was Mary's last for that society; she resigned her secretaryship and became treasurer of the newly founded Bath WSPU. Throughout the summer and autumn of 1908 and through 1909 she went with Annie Kenney campaigning in the west country at successive by-elections. She spoke from dogcarts at open-air meetings, chalked pavements and sold pamphlets. She lived in rented rooms and was, of course, unpaid. She felt, however, unable to take part in any militancy and in June 1909 refused a written request from Mrs Pankhurst to join a deputation at the end of the month which carried with it the virtual certainty of a prison sentence. The reason for her refusal was "Father would not like it." She did also note in her diary "Annie Kenney does not wish me to go."

After Annie Kenney had paid a visit in May 1908, the first of many, to the Blathwayts' home she was taken under the family's wing. Col Blathwayt practised one of his hobbies on the suffragettes, photographing them, framing and getting the sitters to sign the result, and donating the pictures for sale at WSPU bazaars. By April 1909 he was developing another hobby, a suffragette arboretum in a field adjacent to his house. Visiting suffragettes were offered rest and recuperation both at the house and in the "Suffragette Rest", a summerhouse Col Blathwayt built in the grounds, and were invited to plant a tree to commemorate their prison sentences and hunger strikes. Among over 60 tree planters were Lady Constance LYTTON, Clara Codd, Elsie HOWEY, Jessie KENNEY, the BRACKENBURY sisters, Clara MORDAN, Lilias Ashworth Hallett, Helen WATTS and Gladice KEEVIL. Col Blathwayt photographed many of the planting ceremonies. Many other suffrage workers visited, without necessarily planting a tree. For example on 5 April 1910 Col Blathwayt wrote to Minnie BALDOCK, sending her a hamper of plants; they had met when she was campaigning with Annie Kenney in Bristol. At the January 1910 election Col Blathwayt voted for the Liberal Unionist candidate; he was unable, as he would previously have done, to support the Liberal.

Much as the Blathwayts were devoted to individual suffragettes and although they kept in touch with, for instance, Annie and Jessie Kenney, they were unable to condone the increasing militancy. Mrs Blathwayt resigned from the WSPU in September 1909 and Mary Blathwayt in June 1913. Militancy had eventually come too close to home; a local house had been burned and Aethel and

Grace Tollemache, disguised as "market women", had interrupted a government minister's meeting in Trowbridge. Mary rejoined the NUWSS but still supported the WSPU in what might be called a "domestic" manner, buying from their shop and attending their meetings and garden parties. In 1914 she read aloud Christabel Pankhurst's *Great Scourge* to her maiden aunt. As soon as war was declared Mary made herself several "Red X aprons", brought fruit to Belgian refugees and devoted herself to the new cause. In the ensuing years, "Annie's Arboretum", the "Suffragette Rest" and the "Pankhurst Ponds" became neglected and overgrown, and Mary's suffragette uniform was sold for three shillings after her death. Some of the plaques commemorating the tree planting, their associated photographs and Blathwayt diaries of the period have survived. These latter give a vivid and unrivalled picture of the minutiae of the suffragette daily round. Mary's diaries are suffocatingly naïve. The Mr Pooter of the suffrage movement, she is revealed as the diligent, kind, uninspiring helper who provides the fuel for all causes. She followed faithfully all the publicity-seeking strategies that poured out of Clement's Inn, beginning by badge-wearing and ending up parading the streets of Bath with an advertising sandwich board. She wore the correct uniform on all occasions, bought all the WSPU haberdashery, games and tea (although she did have to return a bag that was "off" to the WSPU Bath shop) but was unable to become involved personally in anything as socially unacceptable as stone-throwing. There must have been many hundreds such as Mary, but they have not left us their diaries. Her mother reveals rather more political awareness in her diary entries, although equally delighted by Annie Kenney and many other of the visiting suffragettes. The Blathwayt diaries give an excellent worm's-eye view of the WSPU at work.

Address: (1906) Eagle House, Batheaston, Bath, Somerset.
Photographs: in B.M.W. Dobbie, *A Nest of Suffragettes in Somerset*, 1979.
Archival source: Blathwayt Diaries, Dyrham Park (The National Trust), Avon.
Bibliography: B.M.W. Dobbie, *A Nest of Suffragettes in Somerset*, 1979.

BODICHON, BARBARA LEIGH SMITH, MADAME

(1827–91) Unitarian, daughter of Benjamin Leigh Smith, a Radical Liberal MP and his common-law wife, Anne Longden. The irregularity of her parents' liaison resulted in ostracism from branches of her extended family; she was a cousin of Florence Nightingale but they never met. Barbara Leigh Smith was educated at home and, briefly in 1849, at art life-classes organized by the new college founded in Bedford Square. Her aunt Julia Smith was a close friend of Elizabeth Reid, the founder of Bedford College, and had in 1840, with her, Anne KNIGHT and Elizabeth PEASE, attended the anti-slavery convention in London. Barbara Leigh Smith was a gifted artist, a close friend of Bessie Rayner PARKES and George Eliot, and her own woman. In 1854 she opened a secular school in rooms at the Portman Hall, with Elizabeth Whitehead (*see* Elizabeth MALLESON) and Octavia Hill among its teachers. In the ten years of its existence the school numbered Garibaldi's son among its pupils. In 1854, with assistance from Matthew Davenport Hill (*see* Florence and Rosamond Davenport HILL), she wrote and published a pamphlet, *A Brief Summary in Plain Language of the Most Important Laws of England Concerning Women.* The clarity of her analysis, particularly that part outlining the law as it affected married women, and the coincident publication of two pamphlets by Caroline Norton, led to a demand for action. In early 1856 she induced the Law Amendment Society, which had been founded in 1844 and which included among its members Matthew Davenport Hill and Benjamin Leigh Smith, to consider the question of the position of married women, and they reported in May. At the same time a ladies' committee was formed, which included among its members Bessie Rayner Parkes, Barbara Leigh Smith, Anna Jameson, Mrs Bridell Fox and Mary Howitt, who acted as secretary (a task later undertaken by Maria Rye), to organize a petition to be presented to parliament. Barbara Leigh Smith drafted the petition, of which there were 70 copies circulated. One signed by 3000 women and others, from throughout the country, signed by 26 000 men and women, were presented to both houses of parliament in March 1856. The resulting parliamentary motion failed but that committee, the first to be composed entirely of women and formed to discuss their own rights, was extremely important in establishing a feminist network, at its nucleus the Langham Place Group, to support subsequent campaigns. These included the founding of the Victoria Printing Press, the Society of Female Artists, the *English Woman's Journal,* the Society for Promoting the Employment of Women, and the women's suffrage movement.

After their marriage at the Unitarian Chapel in Little Portland Street, London in 1857 Barbara Leigh Smith and her French husband, Eugène Bodichon, went on an extensive tour of America, seeing slavery in action and meeting Lucretia Mott, "who showed me a mass of Woman's Right literature and I made my pick for the benefit of B.R.P. [Bessie Rayner Parkes] and M.H. [Mary Howitt]".

In July 1865 John Stuart MILL was elected to Parliament as the member for Westminster; Barbara Bodichon, Isa CRAIG, Emily DAVIES and Bessie Rayner Parkes enthusiastically supported his campaign. The enfranchisement of women, which idea Mill's wife had publicly, if anonymously, advocated 14 years before, was now considered a subject meriting serious attention. In November 1865 Barbara Bodichon, who was in Algiers, wrote a paper for the KENSINGTON SOCIETY in reply to the set question, "Is the extension of the Parliamentary suffrage to women desirable, and if so, under what conditions?" Helen TAYLOR, who with Mill was wintering in Avignon beside her mother's grave, also sent in a paper, with which Emily Davies expressed herself rather disappointed. At the meeting a resolution in favour of women's suffrage was carried by a large majority. On 14 November Emily Davies had written to H.R. Tompkinson, with whom she was involved in her work on opening the Cambridge local examinations to girls, "She [Barbara Bodichon] thinks (and so do I) that more women care for the suffrage than is supposed, and that more still would care if they thought about it." Although Barbara Bodichon wanted to form a women's suffrage committee immediately, Emily Davies urged caution. It was a meeting on 25 April 1866 between J.S. Mill, Helen Taylor and Emily Davies that convinced the latter that the time, while discussion of the Reform Bill was underway in Parliament, was indeed ripe for action. In a letter to Helen Taylor dated 9 May 1866 Barbara Bodichon, from the offices of the Society for the Promotion of Employment for Women, wrote:

My dear Madam, I am very anxious to have some conversation with you about the possibility of doing something immediately towards getting women votes. I should not like to start a petition or make any movement without knowing what you and Mr J.S. Mill thought expedient at this time. I have only just arrived in London from Algiers but I have already seen many ladies who are willing to take some steps for this cause. Miss BOUCHERETT who is here puts down £25 at once for expenses. I shall be every day this week at this office at 3 here. Could you write a petition – which you could bring with you. I myself should propose to try simply for what we were most likely to get.

In a reply drafted the same day (so speedy were the posts then) Helen Taylor wrote:

I think that while a Reform bill is under discussion and petitions are being presented to parliament from various causes – asking for representation or protesting against disfranchisement, it is very desirable that women who wish for political enfranchisement should say so, and that women [she means "not" – has scored out some words and left "women" but not "not"] saying so now will be used against them in the future and delay the time of their enfranchisement ... this is no reason why women should not ask for what they will never obtain till they have asked for it very long, and I think the most important thing is to make a demand and commence the first humble beginnings of an agitation for which reasons can be given that are in harmony with the political ideas of English people in general. No idea is so universally acceptable in England as that taxation and representation ought to go together, and people in general will be much more willing to listen to the assertion that single women and widows of property have been (unfairly [?]) overlooked and left out from privileges to which their property entitles them, than to the much more startling general proposition that sex is not a proper ground for distinction in political rights. It seems to me therefore that a petition asking for the admission to the franchise of all women holding the requisite property qualification would be highly desirable now, quite independently of any immediate results to follow from it. The only doubt is whether enough signatures could be got to prevent it from being insignificant as a demonstration on the part of women themselves. I do not think that less than one hundred would be enough, anything more than that would seem to me very satisfactory. I see no reason why the signatures should be confined to those who would profit by the plan if carried out; it would be perfectly reasonable for all women to ask for the franchise for those among them who can fullfill [sic] the conditions at present demanded of all men, just as men who are not £7 [?] householders petition in favour of the present reform bill. We should only be petitioning for the omission of the word *male* or *men* from the present act.

As regards myself I will do my best to preface a sketch of a petition for your consideration but it will take me some days to think over what seem the best heads to put down. Probably the petition finally should be drawn up from the suggestions of many. I am afraid we cannot expect to get many influential names but this would not be of much importance if numbers could be got.

If a tolerably numerously signed petition can be got up my father will gladly undertake to present it and will consider whether it might be made the occasion for anything further. He could at least move for the return of the number of householders disqualified on account of sex, which could be useful to us in many ways if it could be got.

I shall be very glad to subscribe £20 towards expenses and may perhaps be able to call at 19 Langham Place on Friday or Saturday at the time you mention . . .

Barbara Bodichon replied on 11 May:

As soon as you send us the petition which I have no doubt we shall all approve we can begin to collect signatures. I have no doubt that we can get 100 names of ladies of property and education easily. I do not think we shall have any expenses for the petition nevertheless we thank you very much for your donation which will be wanted if we begin any agitation on this subject. Miss Davies, Miss Parkes, Miss Boucherett, Miss Garrett, Miss Jane Crow and myself will begin at once to get signatures. I believe Miss Isa Craig would be our Secretary – but she could not be asked at present as she is otherwise engaged . . .

(She was due to be married on 17 May.) Barbara Bodichon wrote to Helen Taylor from 20 Upper Berkeley Street, Elizabeth Garrett's (see Elizabeth Garrett ANDERSON) address, on a letter without date, presumably a few days later:

We received your letter and petition at 19 Langham Place yesterday. Miss Parkes, Miss Davies, Miss Boucherett and I myself, later we saw Miss Garrett and Miss Crow. We carefully considered the petition and came to the conclusion that it would be better to make it as short as possible & to state as few reasons as possible for what we want, everyone has something to say against the reasons.

We have left a very bare sharp statement, which I send you, do you think it will do? The fact that we do petition is the great matter and as Miss Davies thinks this is the best manner of proceeding, we were all very much decided by her, as she has managed so admirably the educational movement.

None of the 5 ladies I have named would consent to be secretary and they insisted on my accepting this post pro tem. On my return to France in the autumn I believe Miss Craig will be willing to be permanent secretary. I am not a good secretary I am well aware, being legally a Frenchwoman and having a French name, but I could not refuse under present circumstances.

Last evening I called on Mrs Peter Taylor, who is willing to do all in her power. Miss Garrett has lent us the Drawingroom of this house for our meetings, and will allow all letters to be addressed here – & Miss Crowe will help me. Next Thursday at 3pm we shall have a meeting here, and we shall be very glad if you can attend . . .

On 23 May A.J. Munby noted that he met at the P.A. Taylors' "buxom Mme Bodichon, fresh from Algiers, who was in great request & earnest about a petition to Parliament to grant votes to women; & let them vote by all means, if they will also *work*". Among the 1499 signatures finally appended to the petition were those of many workers, including a clutch of women shopkeepers, or the wives of shopkeepers, as well as Rebecca Fisher, the wife of the station master from Battle, close to Barbara

Bodichon's country home. One can imagine the canvassing of the High Streets. Barbara Bodichon certainly seems to us now to have been the driving force in the matter of the petition although, after it was all over, on 21 August Jessie Boucherett remarked in a letter to Helen Taylor, "When I think how narrowly we escaped moving in this matter [the franchise] I rejoice. If your letter had not been so strong Mme Bodichon would not have moved." Barbara Bodichon was ill on 7 June 1866 and was unable to accompany the petition when it was handed over to John Stuart Mill. During the summer she rewrote her Kensington Society paper as *Objections to the Enfranchisement of Women Considered* and asked Helen Taylor for her comments on it. The resulting article was published as a pamphlet. An article on the same subject was turned down by the *Cornhill*, the *Fortnightly* and *Macmillan's* as too radical even for those conduits of advanced Liberalism, so Barbara Bodichon decided to present a paper, "Reasons for the Enfranchisement of Women", to the Social Science Congress being held that autumn in Manchester. There was no immediately obvious result of her succinct argument; only a brief extract was given in Society's *Transactions*. However, she received many letters of congratulation and support from women and, most importantly for future developments, among her audience on this occasion was Lydia BECKER. A little later Barbara Bodichon, in a letter to Helen Taylor, reported that Emily Davies, in Manchester on educational business, had written that "a Miss Wolstenholme her friend there is at work, [and asks] for 3000 copies of my paper [that given by her at the Social Science Congress meeting] on thin paper to send round to 3000 female householders in Manchester with the petitions and her letter gives the evidence of great interest with the matter" (*see* Elizabeth Wolstenholme ELMY). A slightly rewritten version of Barbara Bodichon's Manchester paper appeared in Jessie Boucherett's new journal, the *Englishwoman's Review*, 1 January 1867, as "Authorities and Precedents for Giving the Suffrage to Qualified Women".

Barbara Bodichon did not support the view held by Mill and Helen Taylor that the committee of any society for women's enfranchisement should consist only of women. She was a subscriber in 1866–7 to the ENFRANCHISEMENT OF WOMEN COMMITTEE and from February 1867 her name appeared, without her knowledge and in her absence abroad, as secretary after the unexpected death of Louisa SMITH. Although recovering from a serious bout of typhoid, she did make an effort to fulfil her role until June 1867 when organizational and philosophical differences within the Committee broke it apart. Barbara Bodichon, Emily Davies and Elizabeth Garrett comprised the less radical or, as they termed it, "the quiet section", which bowed out of direct involvement in the suffrage movement, concentrating instead on the educational and medical aspects of the women's movement. Barbara Bodichon was, however, present at the first public meeting held by the LONDON NATIONAL SOCIETY FOR WOMEN'S SUFFRAGE in July 1869 and was particularly pleased to notice that women of all classes had attended. In 1869 she published the third edition of *Laws Concerning Women*, and this time concentrated attention on the necessity of women having the vote if they were to acquire full citizenship. In 1873 she wrote for the *Englishwoman's Review* an article, "A Conversation on the Enfranchisement of Female Freeholders and Householders", an ironic comment on the response to women's petitions. It had taken nearly 20 years for the gradual accretion of ideas, and of people willing to implement them, to have brought the movement for women's suffrage this far. Working with Emily Davies, Barbara Bodichon devoted the rest of her life to the founding and expansion of Girton College. As she remarked in a letter to William Allingham in 1862 she was "more enterprising for boar-hunts or painting excursions, than for long sojourns in stifling rooms with miserable people". Barbara Bodichon was an innovator and inspirer, not a committee woman, and left the seed she had sown to be cultivated by others.

Address: (1866) 5 Blandford Square, London NW; Scalands, Robertsbridge, Sussex.
Portrait: by Emily Mary Osborn, 1888, now in Girton College, Cambridge. For a discussion of this and an earlier (*c.* 1884), now untraced, portrait (now known only by a photograph in H. Blackburn, *Record of Women's Suffrage*, 1902) by the same artist see D. Cherry, *Painting Women*, 1993. Another, 1868, by Eliza Bridell-Fox, daughter of W. Johnson Fox, now untraced.
Photograph: an ambrotype taken on 7 October 1863 by Silas A. Holmes of New York, presented to the National Portrait Gallery in 1912 by Elizabeth Malleson.

Archival source: Mill-Taylor Collection, London School of Economics and Political Science.
Bibliography: Obituary by Mme Belloc in the *Englishwoman's Review*, 15 July 1891; B. Stephen, *Emily Davies and Girton College*, 1927; H. Burton, *Barbara Bodichon*, 1949; J.R. Reed Jr, *Barbara Leigh Smith Bodichon: An American Diary, 1857–8*, 1972; D. Hudson, *Munby, Man of Two Worlds: The Life and Diaries of Arthur J. Munby 1828–1910*, 1974; L. Holcombe, *Wives and Property: Reform of the Married Women's Property Law in Nineteenth-century England*, 1983; J. Matthews, "Barbara Bodichon: integrity in diversity", in D. Spender (ed.), *Feminist Theorists*, 1983; S.R. Herstein, *A Mid-Victorian Feminist, Barbara Leigh Smith Bodichon*, 1985; Jane Rendall, "'A moral engine'?: feminism, Liberalism and the *English Woman's Journal*", in J. Rendall (ed.), *Equal or Different*, 1987; C.A. Lacey (ed.), *Barbara Leigh Smith Bodichon and the Langham Place Group*, 1987 (which contains the text of all her pamphlets and articles mentioned); P. Hirsch, *Barbara Leigh Smith Bodichon: Feminist, Artist, and Rebel*, 1998.

BOLTON branch of the UNITED SUFFRAGISTS Founded in 1914. President Mrs J. Almond, Farnworth; honorary secretary and treasurer, Mrs S.W. Holden, 3 Lowerfold, Harwood, Bolton-le-Moors, Lancashire.

BOLTON Women's Suffrage Society (NUWSS) Founded as a branch of the NORTH OF ENGLAND SOCIETY on 17 March 1908 with Mrs Mildred HASLAM as its president, with her daughter then acting as honorary secretary. As a result of a meeting addressed by Helena SWANWICK in June sufficient money was collected to send five delegates to London to join the 13 June procession organized by the NATIONAL UNION OF WOMEN'S SUFFRAGE SOCIETIES. Later that year there was a procession in Manchester by which time members of the Bolton Society were able to display the BANNER of a heraldic design which had been executed for them by the ARTISTS' SUFFRAGE LEAGUE. In 1909 both Mrs FAWCETT and Margaret ASHTON addressed meetings of the society. These meetings were sometimes held in "the vegetarian restaurant" and were conscientiously advertised by means of posters, notices in the town's trams and, on the days of meetings, by sandwich men, and by the distribution of leaflets and posters. In the January 1910 general election a shop was taken at 131 Deansgate and with help from members of the LANCASHIRE AND CHESHIRE WOMEN TEXTILE AND OTHER WORKERS' REPRESENTATION COMMITTEE and from the MEN'S LEAGUE FOR WOMEN'S SUFFRAGE 2657 signatures for a petition in favour of women's enfranchisement were gathered from men electors. At meetings audiences needed to be reassured that the Bolton Society was intent on advocating only that women ratepayers, or those possessing the qualifications that enfranchised men, would be enfranchised and that they did not belong to the militant party. In 1910 the Bolton Society joined the MANCHESTER AND DISTRICT FEDERATION OF THE NATIONAL UNION OF WOMEN'S SUFFRAGE SOCIETIES.

In 1910 a meeting held in Bolton to explain the Conciliation Bill drew an audience of 400. Twenty-four members of the Bolton Society joined a special train from Manchester to take part in the demonstration in support of the bill in Trafalgar Square. In June 1911, 28 members of the Bolton Society went to London to take part in the Coronation suffrage procession. The Bolton Society, in its turn, gave support to the Lancashire and Cheshire Women Textile and Other Worker's Representation Committee in its agitation in resisting protective legislation aimed at restricting the right to work of pit-brow women. By 1912 the Bolton press, which had always been favourable to the Bolton Women's Suffrage Society, was willing regularly to accept paragraphs of suffrage news supplied to them. In 1912 the Bolton Society doubled its membership and by 1913 had over 300 members.

Although the pro-Liberal committee of the Bolton Society minuted in May 1912 doubts about being bulldozed into accepting the NUWSS Election Fighting Fund policy, the rank and file entered with some gusto into the FRIENDS OF WOMEN'S SUFFRAGE scheme. Forty-two members of the Bolton Society each formed a circle of "Friends" and after six months 334 Friends had been enrolled, some eventually becoming full members. In 1913 the Bolton Society recommended that no new member should be enrolled who was a member of any militant organization or who gave any active help to such an organization. Thirty members of the Bolton Society, with their BANNER, accompanied NUWSS Pilgrims from Bolton to Stockport in June and July 1913 (*see* PILGRIMAGE). One of their members, Mrs Mason, went all the way to London partly on foot and partly on bicycle. Mrs Haslam was convinced that it was the Pilgrimage and the power of the resulting meeting in Hyde Park that persuaded Asquith to meet a deputation. In 1913 the Bolton Society opened a shop and office, complete with sign board, "Bolton's Women's Suffrage Society" painted below the window in red, white and green (*see* SHOPS). By this time it also had a full-time ORGANIZER, Mrs Florence Blincoe (d. 1932), to whom in 1922 Mildred Haslam left a legacy.

During the First World War the Bolton Society raised money for the Scottish Women's Hospital and formed study circles; one of the books thus read was R.W. Seton-Watson, *War and Democracy*, 1914. Energy was diverted into other non-suffrage activity. Annot ROBINSON addressed a garden party given by Mrs F. Taylor for munition and other women workers and Florence Blincoe worked among members of the trade unions. In 1915 Mrs Haslam was asked to join the Manchester Society, but replied that she was too busy with that in Bolton, of which she was still president when women were partially enfranchised in 1918. Bolton sent delegates to a conference held in Manchester to discuss "The Future of the Women's Movement" and their organizer attended a conference in Hampstead on "Problems of Reconstruction". After 1918 it was decided that although the society should continue to work for further suffrage it should also interest itself in all other "reforms, economic, legislative, and social, as are necessary to secure a real equality of liberties, status and opportunities between men and women". In Bolton a meeting of 25 women's societies led to the inauguration of the Women's Citizens' Association, although it had originally been intended that the Suffrage Society should continue independently. However, by 1920 it was clear that the WCA had effectively monopolized all the activities with which the Suffrage Society had concerned itself and the Bolton Women's Suffrage Society was disbanded in July 1920.

Secretary (1908–12) Miss Haslam, White Bank, Bolton, Lancashire; (1913) Miss Bridson, Bridge House, Bolton, Lancashire.

Archival source: Bolton's Women's Suffrage Association Minute books, 1908–20; printed Annual Reports, 1909–19, Bolton Studies Library.
Bibliography: M.H. Haslam, *Women's Suffrage in Bolton, 1908–1920, c.* 1922.

BOLTON (WSPU) Organizer (1906) Mrs Waller, 139 Crescent Road, Bolton, Lancashire.

BORCHARDT, LOUIS, DR (1825–1905) Born in Prussia, which he left after the failure of the 1848 attempts at reform. Settling in Manchester he became physician to the Children's Hospital. He was a Liberal, a close friend of the STEINTHAL family, and it was at his house that the Manchester suffrage society (*see* MANCHESTER NATIONAL SOCIETY) was refounded in January 1867. Louis Borchardt was auditor to the Manchester National Society. One of his daughters, Helene, was a member of the Society in 1869, and another, Malvina, was a member in 1871–2 before going up to Girton in 1873, where she was a student in the same year as Henrietta MULLER. She later became headmistress of Devonport High School and in May 1884 signed the Letter from Ladies to Members of Parliament, asking that women heads of households should be included in the government's Franchise Bill.
Address: (1863) Swinton House, Wilmslow Road, Fallowfield, Manchester; (1864) 128 Rusholme Road, Rusholme, Manchester.

BOSTON (NUWSS) In 1913 the society was a member of the EASTERN COUNTIES FEDERATION OF THE NATIONAL UNION OF WOMEN'S SUFFRAGE SOCIETIES. Secretary (1913) Miss M.A. Cheavin, Sydney House, Spilsby Road, Boston, Lincolnshire.

BOUCHERETT, [EMILIA] JESSIE (1825–1905) Born in Lincolnshire, where her father Ayscogne Boucherett was high sheriff. Her mother was Louisa, daughter of Frederick John Pigou of Dartford, Kent and Jessie Boucherett was a cousin of both Florence Nightingale and Lady Knightley of Fawsley. She spent two years, 1840–42, at Avonbank, the school in Warwickshire which had numbered Elizabeth Gaskell among its pupils. The "story" of her introduction to the Langham Place Group was told by Helen BLACKBURN, who related that Miss Boucherett bought a copy of the *English Woman's Journal* at a railway bookstall (it is interesting that a new and rather serious journal should have been available from such a source) and was so impressed by the contents that she came to London in June 1859 to meet the editors. Having herself been from an early age concerned about the exclusion of women from sources of employment, and having been influenced by reading Harriet Martineau's article on "Female Industry" which appeared in the April 1859 issue of the *Edinburgh Review*, Jessie Boucherett joined with Adelaide Procter and Barbara BODICHON in founding that year the Society for Promoting the Employment of Women (SPEW), with offices at 19 Langham Place, just north of Oxford Circus. In 1866 she was a member of the first general committee of Elizabeth Garrett's (*see* Elizabeth Garrett ANDERSON) St Mary's Dispensary for Women and Children. In 1865 Jessie Boucherett was a member of the KENSINGTON SOCIETY and, indeed, it was at one of its meetings that she first met Elizabeth Wolstenholme (*see* Elizabeth Wolstenholme ELMY). Helen Blackburn noted that Jessie Boucherett was one of those who sent in a paper to the Society in response to the question "Is the extension of the Parliamentary franchise to women desirable, and if so, under what conditions?" In 1866 she was involved in the drafting of the suffrage petition, which was also signed by both her mother and her sister, Louisa. She was the subscriber of the largest amount (£25) to the ENFRANCHISEMENT OF WOMEN COMMITTEE in 1866–7 and was a member of the LONDON NATIONAL SOCIETY in 1867. Emily DAVIES had written to Helen TAYLOR on 9 June 1866 about arrangements for publicizing the petition in the press and noted that she had asked Miss Boucherett to call on Harriet Martineau to ask her to use her influence with the *Daily News*, for which she wrote. Much as Jessie Boucherett enjoyed hunting and other such country pursuits, she particularly relished being useful to the woman's cause. Barbara Bodichon noted how much Jessie Boucherett had gained in allying herself to "us". "She has a vivid interest in life which nothing in 'the society' she was born in could have given her." Elizabeth Wolstenholme Elmy remembered, in a letter to Harriet MCILQUHAM prompted by the death of Jessie Boucherett:

> She spent a fortnight with me at Moody Hall in /65 – driving out with her maid in a little pony carriage (in which she explored almost all England and Wales) in which she saw all our beautiful neighborhood, this whilst I was teaching – and the rest of the time we were concocting plans of work for the woman's cause. She was desperately anxious that I should give up teaching and devote myself to the legal work needed in connection with the woman's cause, and proposed, if I would do this, to settle on me £100 a year for my life so settled that it should be independent of her life or of any change in her views. I could not entertain the proposal, for I loved my work, and we were at the beginning of all our schemes for the higher education of girls and women. It was a time of living enthusiasm... One result of her visit was that I founded the Manchester Branch of the Society for Promoting the Employment of Women... and another the drafting of the memorial which we later presented to the (London Society) part of the Social Science Association, and so started the MWP [Married Women's Property] work. Later on she was hopelessly at variance about CDA [Contagious Diseases Acts], horribly shocked at our touching such matters – and later still, she went strenuously with Miss Becker, for the exclusion of married women from the Franchise.

Jessie Boucherett subscribed to the MANCHESTER NATIONAL SOCIETY in 1868, to the EDINBURGH NATIONAL SOCIETY in 1869 and to the BRISTOL AND WEST OF ENGLAND Branch of the National Society in 1873 (while living in Brighton with her sister). She was a member from its formation in 1871 of the CENTRAL COMMITTEE OF THE NATIONAL SOCIETY FOR WOMEN'S SUFFRAGE and from 1875 was a member of its executive committee, despite that society's support of the campaign to repeal the CDA acts. In 1888 she sided with Mrs FAWCETT's faction after the split in the central society and was a member of the executive committee of the reconstituted Central Committee of the National Society for Women's Suffrage. She did indeed, as Elizabeth Wolstenholme Elmy had intimated, sign the letter to MPs in support of William Woodall's amendment to the 1884 Representation of the People Bill, which called for only the inclusion of unmarried women and widows in any extension of the franchise. In August 1890 she guaranteed the expenses of producing the final issue of the *Women's Suffrage Journal*, which was published as a memorial to Lydia BECKER. Jessie Boucherett contributed articles to the *English Woman's Journal* and came to its financial rescue in 1866 by selling some of her diamonds. She was then, until 1870, editor of its successor, the *Englishwoman's Review*. Helen Taylor had told Emily Davies in the autumn of 1866 that Miss Boucherett was prepared to sell her diamonds in order to provide money to finance petition campaigns; she was certainly willing to dispose of her wealth for the good of the cause. In July 1869 she had written on "The Employment of Women" for *Nowadays*, a journal with which she was editorally involved, but which appears to have published only one issue and even that has disappeared without trace. In addition she wrote *Hints for Self Help for Young Women*, 1863; "How to Provide for Superfluous Women", in Josephine Butler (ed.), *Woman's Work and Woman's Culture*, 1869; *The Probable Use Women Would Make of the Political Franchise*, a paper given to the National Association for the Promotion of Social Science, 1870; "The Industrial Movement", in Theodore Stanton (ed.), *The Woman Question in Europe: A series of original essays*, 1884; and, with Helen Blackburn, *The Condition of Working Women and the Factory Acts*, 1896. Her obituarist in the *Englishwoman's Review* wrote that "She was the brain of all the various agencies she either started or joined; the other workers recognise this, and so simple and straightforward was she, that she never thought about herself as leading, she thought of her cause only". Her estate was assessed at over £39 000 and of this she left £2000 to SPEW, £2000 to the Freedom of Labour Defence Society (the aim of which was to protect women from protective labour legislation), £500 to the British Union for the Abolition of Vivisection, £200 personally to Antoinette Mackenzie, and £500 to her in her capacity as editor of the *Englishwoman's Review* to be devoted to the interests of the paper, £700 personally to Gertrude King, who was secretary of SPEW, and she left her dog "Rock" to Helen Ogle Moore.

Address: (1880s) 9 Upper Phillimore Gardens, London W; (1860–1905) Willingham Hall, Market Rasen, Lincolnshire.
Photograph: in H. Blackburn, *Record of Women's Suffrage*, 1902; by J. Owen, Bournemouth, c. 1891, in National Portrait Gallery archive.
Archival source: Mill–Taylor Collection, London School of Economics and Political Science; Elizabeth Wolstenholme Elmy Papers, British Library.
Bibliography: J. Mills, *From Tinder-Box to the "Larger" Light: Threads from the Life of John Mills, Banker . . . interwoven with some early century recollections by his wife*, 1899; H. Blackburn, *Record of Women's Suffrage*, 1902; *Englishwoman's Review*, January 1906; L. Holcombe, *Wives and Property: Reform of the Married Women's Property Law in Nineteenth-century England*, 1983; J. Rendall, "'A moral engine'?: feminism, Liberalism and the *English Woman's Journal*", in J. Rendall (ed.), *Equal or Different*, 1987.

BOURNE, ADELINE (1873–1965) Actress, honorary secretary of the ACTRESSES' FRANCHISE LEAGUE until she left for the United States in 1913; she resumed the position in the 1930s. She was a tax resister. During the First World War she was honorary organizing secretary of the British Women's Hospital. Adeline Bourne was a friend of Ada WRIGHT, who left her a picture in her will, and she read one of the lessons at the memorial service held for Christabel PANKHURST.
Address: (1913) 6a Blomfield Road, Maida Vale, London W.

BOURNEMOUTH branch of the MEN'S LEAGUE FOR WOMEN'S SUFFRAGE Founded in 1909.

BOURNEMOUTH (NUWSS) Was in existence in 1902. Secretary (1909, 1913) Mrs Warren, Calluna, West Cliff Road, Bournemouth, Hampshire.

BOURNEMOUTH (WFL) Secretary (1913) Miss Ford, Heather Cottage, Bengal Road, Winton, Bournemouth, Hampshire.

BOURNEMOUTH (WSPU) Secretary (1913) Miss B. Berry, 221 Old Christchurch Road, Bournemouth, Hampshire.

BOW AND POPLAR (WSPU) Secretary (1906) Mrs Corderey, 74 Devas Road, Bromley-by-Bow, London E.

BOWERMAN, ELSIE EDITH (1889–1973) Born in Tunbridge Wells, educated at Wycombe Abbey School 1901–7, in Paris, and then at Girton 1908–11, where she studied medieval and modern languages. In 1908 her mother Mrs Chibnall (a widow who had remarried) was a member of the WOMEN'S SOCIAL AND POLITICAL UNION, giving one of the BANNERS to be carried in the 21 June demonstration in Hyde Park. It was designed by Sylvia PANKHURST, showing a rose, thistle and shamrock, with the legend "Rebellion to tyrants is obedience to God" in gold on a violet ground. Elsie Bowerman joined the WSPU in 1909, founding a small group at Girton. In October 1910 she invited Margery Corbett (*see* Margery Corbett ASHBY), a member of the CAMBRIDGE ASSOCIATION FOR WOMEN'S SUFFRAGE, to Girton to "begin early on the Freshers". In the summer of 1910, while she was in France, she made sure that she was sent *Votes for Women* each week and very much regretted missing the Coronation procession in London. She sent a 5/– donation to Mrs PETHICK-LAWRENCE to ensure its success. In October 1910 she noted that the Girton authorities would not allow Lady Constance LYTTON to speak in the college so Miss Radcliffe (of Newnham) was going to try and hire a small hall in the town and have an "at home" for their visitor. Elsie Bowerman continued, "I don't think the Authorities can very well have any objection to that – as we shall get a married lady to act as hostess". The meeting was eventually arranged for 26 November. Her mother was one of the ten chosen to accompany Mrs PANKHURST on the deputation to the House of Commons on "Black Friday", 18 November 1910. Mrs Chibnall also went on the next deputation three days later and, although not arrested, was dealt a severe blow on the head and her coat was torn to pieces. Elsie Bowerman was happy to proselytize; she sent copies of the issue of *Votes for Women* that contained details of the "Black Friday" debacle to as many people as she could afford to and remarked in a letter, "I always wear my badge in as conspicuous a position as possible in lectures". After she left Girton she became an enthusiastic organizer for the WSPU in St Leonards. Her mother had set the pace, running the WSPU shop on the Grand Parade at Hastings during the December 1910 general election.

On 15 April 1912 Elsie Bowerman and her mother were passengers on the *Titanic* when it sank. First-class passengers, they both survived. During the First World War she took part in the Women's War Procession in July 1916 and was then asked by Evelina HAVERFIELD, with whom she had been friendly since at least 1910, to go out to Serbia as a hospital orderly to join Elsie INGLIS. She was there until 1917 and after her return took part in the Pankhurst campaign for industrial peace. She went to Sheffield and started work there, standing on stools, addressing meetings outside factory gates, preparing the way for the arrival of Flora DRUMMOND. She next organized a campaign for Mrs Pankhurst in Manchester and then worked for 18 months with Phyllis AYRTON in the west country and in South Wales, holding meetings for miners at the pit heads and up in the valleys. At the 1918 general election Elsie Bowerman was Christabel PANKHURST's agent in Smethwick and then was co-founder and honorary secretary, 1920–29, of the Women's Guild of Empire, the campaigns of which culminated in 1926 in a great procession in London and a meeting in the Albert Hall in an attempt to avert the General Strike. She edited the Guild's *Bulletin*. The Women's Guild of Empire was finally wound up in the 1930s, although a few branches struggled on.

Elsie Bowerman was called to the Bar as a member of the Middle Temple in 1924, and practised on the South-Eastern Circuit until 1938, when she joined Lady Reading in starting the Women's Voluntary Service (WVS). During the Second World War she was first based at the Ministry of Information, then at the BBC, where she was liaison officer of its North American Service, 1941–5. After the war she spent one year at the United Nations in New York, where she was in charge of the Status of Women section. She maintained chambers in the Temple until 1963 and, after retirement, wrote a history of Frances Dove and Wycombe Abbey School, *Stands There A School*, 1965. In her entries in *Women's Who's Who, 1934–5*, 1935, and in the *Girton Register*, 1948, she makes no mention at all of her involvement in the suffrage movement.

Address: (1934) 1 Temple Gardens, London EC4; (1973) Batchelors, Cowbeech Hill, Hailsham, Sussex.
Archival source: Elsie Bowerman Papers, Fawcett Library.

BOWES PARK (WSPU) Secretary (1906) Miss Todd, 34 Highworth Road, New Southgate, London N; (1913) Miss H. Gargett, 4 Stonard Road, Palmers Green, London N.

BOWKER, DOROTHY AGNES (1886–1973) Born in Bedford, she originally was opposed to the use of militant methods in the suffrage movement but joined the WOMEN'S SOCIAL AND POLITICAL UNION in 1909 after hearing Mrs PANKHURST speaking at a meeting in Torquay. She was soon working with Dorothy PETHICK, organizing the WSPU campaign in Cornwall. Still with Dorothy Pethick, she helped organize branches in Loughborough and Leicester. From the end of 1910 until 1912 she was WSPU organizer in Hastings and St Leonards. She took part in the March 1912 window-smashing campaign, breaking the windows of Swan and Edgar, and as a consequence spent three months in prison in Aylesbury. She joined in the hunger strike. In 1914 she joined the Women's Land Army and after the end of the war went to Canada and California. She returned to Lymington in Hampshire in 1934, and in 1938 was elected to the borough council there and served as a councillor and alderman for 19 years.

BOYLE, NINA [CONSTANCE ANTONINA] (1865–1943) A journalist in South Africa, on her return to Britain she joined the WOMEN'S FREEDOM LEAGUE, rapidly becoming one of its main speakers and a member of its executive committee. She was quite prepared to take part in militant action, was arrested on five occasions and imprisoned three times. In 1911 she took part in a tour organized by the SCOTTISH FEDERATION OF THE NATIONAL UNION OF WOMEN'S SUFFRAGE SOCIETIES and spoke to the GLASGOW AND WEST OF SCOTLAND ASSOCIATION FOR WOMEN'S SUFFRAGE. In 1911 she subscribed to the NEW CONSTITUTIONAL SOCIETY FOR WOMEN'S SUFFRAGE. On 5 May 1913, having been arrested with Anna MUNRO on a charge of obstruction, she received a sentence of 14 days' imprisonment. She protested against the conditions under which they were taken in a prison van to Holloway, particularly the fact that the van also contained men who "began to signal to us and to make obscene gestures, from the sight of which it was impossible to escape" (*Votes for Women*, 23 May 1913). The Home Office was forced to carry out a lengthy investigation into the allegations, involving affadavits from Charlotte DESPARD and Dr Elizabeth KNIGHT, who both swore on oath that the prison vans that conveyed them on separate occasions to Holloway had also contained men. By August a report had been produced for the Home Secretary that concluded that "the complaints made by three suffragettes as to their being exposed to annoyance by their fellow prisoners in the Vans are well-founded" and suggested improvements that could be made, which included the introduction of motor vans and the use of separate vehicles for women prisoners. Although the Home Office did get quotes for motor vans, matters had not improved sufficiently to satisfy Nina Boyle who, after a further arrest in July 1914, repeated her complaints.

On 19 August 1914 Nina Boyle founded and became chief of the Women Police Volunteers and was one of the first women to appear in police uniform. During the war she went to Serbia with a hospital unit. In early 1918, at the Keighley by-election, she was the first woman to be nominated as a parliamentary candidate. The Returning Officer reported to her that an election petition judge had ruled that she could not be nominated because, in common law, if a thing had not been, it could not be until a statute was passed enabling it to be. However, parliamentary law officers very quickly overcame this technicality, ruling that women, if now eligible to vote, were also eligible to stand for Parliament. In spite of this, a technical error was found in Nina Boyle's papers and she was barred from standing. She then worked in Russia for the "Save the Children Fund" in 1921, was a supporter of the "Never Again" Association and a champion of black women in South Africa. She wrote *Out of the Frying Pan, Nor All the Tears, Anna's, Treading on Eggs, The Late Unlamented, How Could They?* (the profits of which she left in her will to the Save the Children Fund), *My Lady's Bath* and *Good Old Potts*. The executors of her will were Eunice MURRAY, to whom she left "the two rings I wear on my hands", and Marian Reeves, the proprietor of the Minerva Club (*see under* CLUBS).
Address: (1934) 20 Talbot House, Great St Martin's Lane, London WC; (1943) 20 Oakley Street, Chelsea, London SW.
Photograph: in Suffragette Fellowship Collection, Museum of London.
Archival source: Home Office Papers, Public Record Office.
Bibliography: C. Hamilton, *Nina Boyle*, no date (1943).

BRACKENBURY, HILDA, MRS (1832–1918); **GEORGINA AGNES** (1865–1949); **MARIE [MARY] VENETIA CAROLINE** (1866–1946) The widow and daughters of an army general. Mrs Brackenbury had never previously been involved in the suffrage movement when she joined the WOMEN'S SOCIAL AND POLITICAL UNION in 1907. In March 1912, in her eightieth year, after five years of continuous involvement in the militant movement, she was arrested, and served eight days on remand and then a 14 days' prison sentence in Holloway. With a hammer she had broken two windows in the United Service Institution in Whitehall. She chose that particular building as her target in order to contrast her family's military involvement (two of her sons had died on active service) with her own lack of political enfranchisement. On her release in April 1912 she addressed a large audience at the London Pavilion.

Georgina Brackenbury had studied at the Slade from 1888 to 1900. In 1907 and 1908 she subscribed to the NATIONAL UNION OF WOMEN'S SUFFRAGE SOCIETIES, and joined the WSPU in March 1907. She was arrested in February 1908, after taking part in the "pantechnicon raid" on the House of Commons, and was sentenced to six weeks in Holloway. She was chairman of one of the platforms on the 21 June WSPU Demonstration in Hyde Park and in that year spoke at WSPU meetings all over Britain and to interested groups in Germany. In spring 1909 she was working with Vera WENTWORTH, Annie KENNEY, and Mary BLATHWAYT in the west country. In autumn 1910 she took over as ORGANIZER from Mary GAWTHORPE in Manchester. She was imprisoned for a month after taking part in the March 1912 window-smashing campaign. She was particularly friendly with Rose Lamartine YATES and was a regular speaker on Wimbledon Common. In 1927, commissioned by Katherine MARSHALL, Rosamund MASSY and Lady RHONDDA, she painted the portrait of Mrs PANKHURST that now hangs in the National Portrait Gallery. It is thought to have been painted from life, although there is in existence a photograph (reproduced as a postcard) of Mrs Pankhurst, wearing exactly the same clothes and jewellery as appear in her portrait. However, the position of the figure differs and doubtless by then Mrs Pankhurst's finances did not allow her an extensive wardrobe. Georgina Brackenbury was a pallbearer at Mrs Pankhurst's funeral in 1928.

Marie Brackenbury studied at the Slade and was a landscape painter. Like her sister, she also subscribed to the NUWSS in 1907 and 1908, and joined the WSPU in March 1907. She had been worried at what she might hear when she attended her first WSPU meeting at Caxton Hall, but was particularly impressed by Mrs Pankhurst's "womanliness". With her sister she took part in February 1908 in the "pantechnicon raid" on the House of Commons and was imprisoned in Holloway. She contributed a cartoon to *Woman's Franchise* and in June 1908 chaired one of the platforms at the Hyde Park Demonstration. In March 1912 she spent eight days on remand and then two weeks in Holloway, with her mother and sister, after causing a disturbance in New Palace Yard. At her trial she is quoted as saying "I am a soldier in this great Cause". Both sisters were active supporters of the TAX RESISTANCE LEAGUE and members of the International Women's Franchise Club (*see under* CLUBS). They were both vegetarians and interested in theosophy.

In the later years of the militant campaign the Brackenbury family house in Campden Hill Square was notorious as "Mouse Castle", where suffragettes released under the "Cat and Mouse" Act went to recuperate. Police, stationed outside, were unable to prevent the "mice" escaping. In June 1914 the WSPU made the house its temporary headquarters after their premises at 17 Tothill Street in Westminster were raided by the police. Georgina Brackenbury, as the last survivor of her immediate family, left the house to the "Over Thirties Association". As a memorial to the Brackenbury family, the SUFFRAGETTE FELLOWSHIP in 1950 commissioned from Ernestine MILLS a plaque to hang in the erstwhile "Mouse Castle". It was enamelled in the colours, cost £35, and is now on display in the Museum of London. As Mary THOMPSON wrote in a letter to Stella NEWSOME which accompanied her contribution towards the cost of the plaque, "The Brackenbury trio were so whole-hearted and helpful during all the early strenuous years of the militant suffrage movement. We remember them with honour."

Address: 2 Campden Hill Square, London W.
Photograph: of Georgina Brackenbury on postcard published by Verlag F. Kreuzer, Munich; of Georgina and Marie Brackenbury in A. Raeburn, *The Militant Suffragettes*, 1973.

BRACKNELL (NUWSS) In 1913 the society was a member of the OXON, BERKS, BUCKS, AND BEDS

Federation of the National Union of Women's Suffrage Societies. Secretary (1913) Miss F.G. Bradford, Fir Cottage, Bracknell, Berkshire.

BRADFORD branch of the Men's Political Union for Women's Enfranchisement   Founded in 1910.

BRADFORD Women's Suffrage Society   Founded sometime before 1888; in the division of the Central Committee for Women's Suffrage in that year it affiliated to the Central National Society for Women's Suffrage.; Eva McLaren was a notable personality locally. In 1905 its president was Mrs Margaret Illingworth. In 1913 the society was a member of the West Riding Federation of the National Union of Women's Suffrage Societies. Secretary (1909) Mrs Bauer, 20 Springwood Terrace, Bradford, Yorkshire; (1913) Mrs James Riley, 2 Hollings Mount, Bradford. Organizer (1913) Miss Hilston. Office (1913) 5 Eldon Place, Bradford, Yorkshire.

BRADFORD (WSPU)   Secretary (1906) Mrs Armitage, 81 Tivoli Place, Little Horton, Bradford; organizer (1910) Miss Mary Phillips; (1913) Miss Millar Wilson, 68 Manningham Lane, Bradford, Yorkshire. In the 21 June 1908 Hyde Park demonstration members of the Bradford branch of the Women's Social and Political Union carried a banner, designed by Sylvia Pankhurst, which bore the Bradford city arms and the motto: "Grant to womanhood the justice England should be proud to give", and is now in the Museum of London Collection.

BRAILSFORD, HENRY NOEL (1873–1958)   Radical journalist. While a student at Glasgow University he was on the committee of the University Fabian Society when it was founded in 1896. In 1901 he became leader writer for the *Echo*, the progressive London evening newspaper which had recently been rescued from financial failure by Frederick Pethick-Lawrence. Brailsford had married Jane Malloch (*see* Jane Brailsford) in 1897 and, although sympathizing with her interest in the woman's suffrage movement, did not put much faith in the efficacy of militant tactics as developed by the Women's Social and Political Union. He preferred to exert influence through his journalism for the *Nation* and the *Daily News*, although, with H.W. Nevinson, he resigned from the latter in 1909 because the paper refused to condemn the government's policy of forcible feeding. Although he was a founding member of the Men's League for Women's Suffrage, Brailsford did not have much faith in that society's ability to accomplish anything. In December 1909 the Scottish Women Graduates invited him to contest Dundee (Winston Churchill's seat) at the general election as a woman's suffrage candidate. In January 1910, after consultation with the leadership of the National Union of Women's Suffrage Societies, he had begun the process that resulted in the formation of a non-partisan Conciliation Committee, the president of which was Lord Lytton. The Committee eventually produced the Conciliation Bill, which proposed to extend the franchise to women house occupiers. This was supported by both Liberal and Labour parties because it enfranchised lodgers as well as house owners. If a married woman qualified on her own she would be able to vote, but most married women would be excluded because both husband and wife could not qualify on the basis of one occupancy. However, the bill eventually failed and the leadership of the WSPU regarded Brailsford as a traitor. He wrote a pamphlet, *Woman Suffrage: The Conciliation Bill, an explanation and defence*, 1910.

With Dr Jessie Murray, H.N. Brailsford gathered information and drafted a Memorandum, which was forwarded by the "Parliamentary Conciliation Committee for Woman Suffrage", accompanying a request for a public inquiry into the events of "Black Friday", 18 November 1910. He was nominated as a women's suffrage candidate, supported by the NUWSS, at South Salford in the December 1910 general election, but withdrew his nomination after the adoption of a Liberal candidate who supported women's suffrage. The Liberal's first choice, Hilaire Belloc, although the son of Bessie Rayner Parkes, was an arch-opponent of women's suffrage and had been hastily withdrawn.

In March 1912 Brailsford, acting on behalf of the NUWSS, began discussions with the Labour party that eventually led to the development of the Election Fighting Fund policy, whereby the NUWSS would promote and support Labour party

candidates at by-elections. He was a member of the first EFF Committee.
Address: (1911) 32 Well Walk, Hampstead, London NW; (1926) 87 Prince of Wales Mansions, Battersea, London SW11.
Portrait: by his second wife, E.M. Brailsford (photograph in National Portrait Gallery Archive).
Bibliography: C. Morrell, *"Black Friday": Violence against Women in the Suffragette Movement*, 1981; F.M. Leventhal, *The Last Dissenter: H.N. Brailsford and His World*, 1985; S.S. Holton, *Feminism and Democracy: Women's Suffrage and Reform Politics, 1900–1918*, 1986.

BRAILSFORD, JANE, MRS (1874–1937) née Malloch One of six children of a prosperous Renfrewshire cotton spinner, educated at Paisley Grammar School and, from 1893, Queen Margaret College, University of Glasgow. She studied Greek under Professor Gilbert Murray, and was a founder member of the Glasgow University Fabian Society. In 1897 she spent two terms at Somerville College, Oxford, and then in September married H.N. BRAILSFORD, cut short her education and went with him to Crete. She was a member of the NATIONAL UNION OF WOMEN'S SUFFRAGE SOCIETIES until she became impatient with lack of progress and joined the WOMEN'S SOCIAL AND POLITICAL UNION in July 1909. On 9 October 1909 she attacked a barricade with an axe at a meeting being held in Newcastle by Lloyd George. She was there with Lady Constance LYTTON, who was also arrested. Mrs Brailsford was sentenced to a month's imprisonment, went on hunger strike, but, because of her connection with the press, was released without having being forcibly fed. During the January 1910 general election campaign she was a speaker for the WSPU. On 21 November 1911 Mrs Brailsford was arrested for obstruction during the deputation to Parliament Square which followed on the "torpedoing" of the Conciliation Bill. A speech she gave at the London Pavilion on 18 December was published in the 29 December issue of *Votes for Women*. In 1912 she was shocked by the split between the PANKHURSTS and the PETHICK-LAWRENCES and resigned from the WSPU. According to her husband's biographer, "her disillusionment with the Pankhurst's leadership precipitated a breakdown, whose effects lasted well into 1914 and probably long after". In May 1913 she and Brailsford agreed to separate and F.M. Leventhal suggests that she was then well on the way to the alcoholism that eventually led to her death. In 1911 Col BLATHWAYT had noted when she stayed at Eagle House that "like so many Suffragettes [she was] a vegetarian, but she took Burgundy".
Address: (1911) 32 Well Walk, Hampstead, London NW.
Bibliography: F.M. Leventhal, *The Last Dissenter: H.N. Brailsford and His World*, 1985.

BRAMHALL (NUWSS) By 1912 the society had joined the MANCHESTER AND DISTRICT FEDERATION OF THE NATIONAL UNION OF WOMEN'S SUFFRAGE SOCIETIES. Secretary (1913) Miss A. Bell, Inglewood, Moss Lane, Bramhall, Stockport, Cheshire.

BRECHIN (NUWSS) In 1913 the society was a member of the SCOTTISH FEDERATION OF THE NATIONAL UNION OF WOMEN'S SUFFRAGE SOCIETIES. Secretary (1913) Miss Jeannie Duncan, 81 Southesk Street, Brechin, Angus.

BRECON AND DISTRICT (NUWSS) In 1913 the society was a member of the SOUTH WALES AND MONMOUTH FEDERATION OF THE NATIONAL UNION OF WOMEN'S SUFFRAGE SOCIETIES. Secretary (1913) Miss E.J. Edwards, 2 Camden Villas, Brecon.

BRIDGEND (NUWSS) In 1913 the society was a member of the SOUTH WALES AND MONMOUTH FEDERATION OF THE NATIONAL UNION OF WOMEN'S SUFFRAGE SOCIETIES. Secretary (1913) Mrs Fred Couth, The Hut, Park Street, Bridgend, Glamorganshire.

BRIDGWATER (NUWSS) In 1913 the society was a member of the WEST OF ENGLAND FEDERATION OF THE NATIONAL UNION OF WOMEN'S SUFFRAGE SOCIETIES. Secretary (1913) Mrs Alice Corder, Silver Birch, Northfield, Bridgwater, Somerset.

BRIDLINGTON branch of the MEN'S LEAGUE FOR WOMEN'S SUFFRAGE Founded in 1912.

BRIDLINGTON (NUWSS) In 1913 the society was a member of the NORTH AND EAST RIDINGS FEDERATION OF THE NATIONAL UNION OF WOMEN'S SUFFRAGE SOCIETIES. Secretary (1909) Mrs Overbury, 4 Ashbourne Avenue, Bridlington, Yorkshire; (1913) Moffat Ecob, Esq, Mow Cop, St John's Avenue, Bridlington, Yorkshire.

BRIDPORT Women's Suffrage Society   In 1890 was affiliated to the CENTRAL NATIONAL SOCIETY FOR WOMEN'S SUFFRAGE. The president and secretary was Mrs Russell Carpenter (*see also* WOMEN'S EMANCIPATION UNION).

BRIGHOUSE (WSPU)   Secretary (1906) Mrs Tordoff, 6 Old Lane, Brighouse, Yorkshire.

BRIGHT, JACOB (1821–99)   Quaker, Radical Liberal MP for Manchester, 1867–74 and 1876–85, and for the southern division, Manchester, 1886–95. He was the brother of John Bright, Priscilla Bright MCLAREN and Margaret Bright LUCAS, uncle to Anne ASHWORTH and Lilias Asworth HALLETT and husband of Ursula BRIGHT (*see* Appendix). He was a director of John Bright of Rochdale and of the Manchester Ship Canal. He was, according to Elizabeth Wolstenholme ELMY, present at the meeting held on 11 January 1867 at which the Manchester Suffrage Society (*see* MANCHESTER NATIONAL SOCIETY FOR WOMEN'S SUFFRAGE) was refounded. It is not clear if he was a member of the first incarnation of the society. In 1867 Lydia BECKER wrote to Helen TAYLOR, "Of Mr Jacob Bright's services to our cause, it is impossible to speak too highly. He deserves the hearty thanks of every one interested in it. His influence in Manchester is great, and he freely devotes it to our service." In 1869 he took over from J.S. MILL the parliamentary sponsorship of the women's suffrage movement and moved the amendment to the Municipal Corporation Bill that gave women the local government franchise. In 1870 he moved for a women's suffrage bill, extending the parliamentary franchise to women householders, to go to committee. It had passed its second reading by 124 votes to 91, but was defeated after pressure from the leaders of the Liberal party.

In 1870 Jacob Bright gave a speech to the EDINBURGH NATIONAL WOMEN'S SUFFRAGE SOCIETY, of which his sister Priscilla was president, and this was later published as a 12-page pamphlet. At this meeting the first resolution was passed supporting another bill "For the Removal of the Electoral Disabilities of Women" which Bright with Sir Charles Dilke introduced in 1870, and which was again outvoted. At a meeting held the next day at Aubrey House, the London home of P.A. and Clementia TAYLOR, it was resolved to reintroduce the bill the next year. In April 1871 a Women's Suffrage Conference was held at the Langham Hotel at which it was resolved to present a memorial to Gladstone signed by 2000 women, among them Florence Nightingale and Harriet Martineau, supporting Jacob Bright's bill. Despite hopes raised after the first reading of the bill, a Liberal whip ensured that the second reading was defeated.

In January 1872 Jacob Bright presided over the meeting at which the provincial suffrage committees signified their desire to associate themselves with the CENTRAL COMMITTEE OF THE NATIONAL SOCIETY, which had been formed at Bright's instigation at the end of 1871. He brought in another bill in May 1872 and next day was present at a Women's Suffrage Conference held at the Westminster Palace Hotel. At this the breach between those who supported a limited enfranchisement, unmarried women and widows only, and those who supported the inclusion of married women, became clear. Bright lost his seat at the general election in 1874 and was succeeded as the parliamentary supporter of women's suffrage by a Conservative, W. Forsyth. On his return to parliament Jacob Bright took charge again, in 1877, of the suffrage bill, which had dropped a couverture clause. This bill was lost in scenes of disorder of which Helen BLACKBURN wrote, "Truly the echoes of that afternoon ring even now in one's memory as the most painful experience of all those years". Jacob Bright's declining health led him to relinquish the support of future suffrage bills to Leonard Courtney, although in 1884 a move was made by some of his relations, but not Lilias Ashworth Hallett, to reinstate him. Being unable to support the couverture clause, which was backed by Lydia Becker and the moderate wing of the suffrage movement and introduced by William Woodall, he withdrew as a supporter of the bill. He was an active member of the Married Women's Property Committee for its whole life, 1868–82, and of the Vigilance Association for the Defence of Personal Rights. From 1870 he was a supporter of the campaign to repeal the Contagious Diseases Acts. He did not support the 1889 women's suffrage bill, which would have excluded married women, and although he was not involved from the very first in the WOMEN'S FRANCHISE LEAGUE, he was a member of its Council by 1890 when on 16 and 17 July he presided over the first sitting of an International Conference on the Position of Women in All Countries, held by the League at Westminster Town Hall. He retired from parliament in 1895 and was made a privy councillor.

His daughter Esther wrote of Jacob Bright that he was "a man of high moral courage, of fine ideals, . . . a passionate love of freedom, a hatred of any form of coercion. A splendid champion of women". Miss Horniman, founder of the Manchester Gaiety Theatre, wrote in the *Daily Herald*, 22 May 1912, "when I was a little girl playing with dolls I heard tell of a Bill by which women should have votes. The name mentioned in connection with it was Jacob Bright". The NATIONAL UNION OF WOMEN'S SUFFRAGE SOCIETIES sent a wreath costing £2.12.6 to Jacob Bright's funeral. His funeral card bore the legend "Born into the World of Shadows, May 26th, 1821/ Entered the Land of Light, November 7th, 1899."

Address: (1890) Alderley Edge, Cheshire; 31 St James's Place, London SW.
Photograph: photograph by Elliot and Fry in Blackburn Collection, Girton College (reproduced in H. Blackburn, *Record of Women's Suffrage*, 1902); photograph carte de visite in Josephine Butler Collection, Fawcett Library.
Bibliography: Mrs J. Bright (ed.), *Speeches of Jacob Bright*, 1885; H. Blackburn, *Record of Women's Suffrage*, 1902; E. Bright, *The Ancient One*, 1927; *Old Memories and Letters of Annie Besant*, 1936; J. Lewis (ed.), *Before the Vote Was Won: Arguments For and Against Women's Suffrage 1864–1896*, 1987 (contains a transcript of "The debate in the House of Commons on the Women's Disabilities Bill, 3 May 1871").

BRIGHT, URSULA, MRS (1835–1915) Daughter of Joseph Mellor, a merchant from Liverpool. Her mother was a daughter of John Pennington of Hindley, Lancashire, and among her uncles were Frederick PENNINGTON and Thomas THOMASSON (*see* Appendix), who had married another daughter of John Pennington. Her father and her brother, J.P. Mellor, were generous supporters of women's suffrage societies. Among her cousins were Martha Paulton, whose husband was at one time editor of the *Manchester Examiner and Times*, and Alice Hargreaves, whose husband William was a close friend of Cobden. Isabel Petrie Mills related how at the Bright family home in Rochdale she, Priscilla Bright (*see* Priscilla Bright MCLAREN) and Martha Mellor discussed women's suffrage 20 years before the movement actually began. Ursula Mellor married Jacob BRIGHT in 1855. They had two sons, one daughter, Esther, and two other sons who died in early childhood within a fortnight of each other, of diphtheria. Ursula Bright with her two cousins signed the 1866 suffrage petition and was a subscriber to the ENFRANCHISEMENT OF WOMEN COMMITTEE in 1866–7. In early 1867 she was a member of the Manchester suffrage society (*see* MANCHESTER NATIONAL SOCIETY FOR WOMEN'S SUFFRAGE) and in 1868, with Lydia BECKER, she attended the founding meeting of the BIRMINGHAM SOCIETY FOR WOMEN'S SUFFRAGE. Ursula Bright was not expected to take part in the proceedings; Esther was born in 1868. In April 1871 she attended a Women's Suffrage Conference held in London and in 1872 she was a founder member of the executive committee of the CENTRAL COMMITTEE OF THE NATIONAL SOCIETY FOR WOMEN'S SUFFRAGE. In 1874 she read a paper at the conference held by the National Society in Birmingham.

In 1870 Ursula and Jacob Bright were founder members of the Ladies' National Association, lobbying for the repeal of the Contagious Diseases Acts. Ursula Bright was a member of the executive committee of the Vigilance Association for the Defence of Personal Rights in the 1880s and of the Married Women's Property Committee for its entire duration (1868–82) and was its treasurer from 1874 to 1882. In *Speeches of Jacob Bright*, which she edited in 1885, she remarked, "Before the Married Women's Property Act, we did not ask for votes for married women, for the simple reason that they were not legal householders, had no property rights and paid no rates. Several attempts were made, however, by the weaker and more faithless members of the Women's Suffrage Association to add a clause to the Bill directly excluding married women from its operation, hoping by this means to catch the votes of certain less intelligent, or more timid members of Parliament . . . when Mr Woodall, who now has charge of the Bill, added a clause which expressly excludes all married women whatever property they may possess". By 1890 she was firmly aligned with those who supported the inclusion of married women in any suffrage bill and, with her husband, joined the committee of the WOMEN'S FRANCHISE

LEAGUE. Elizabeth Wolstenholme ELMY, the founder of the League, was wary of the Brights' obvious allegiance to the Liberal party; in the 1890s Ursula Bright was president of the Lancashire and Cheshire Union of Women's Liberal Associations. The appointment of Ursula Bright, through the influence of her old Manchester friends Richard and Emmeline PANKHURST, as the honorary secretary of the Women's Franchise League was a major contributory factor in Elizabeth Wolstenholme Elmy's departure from the League and to a complete break in their personal relations. Mrs Bright's work with the League resulted in the inclusion in the Local Government Act of 1894 of clauses conferring upon married women the right to all local franchises, confirming their eligibility for election as poor law guardians, and entitling them to election as parish and district councillors. In January 1893 she contributed an article, "The Laws Which Affect Women", to the *Young Woman*, in which she encourages her young readers to consider carefully the difficulties encountered by married women. In May 1893 Ursula Bright read a paper on "The origin and objects of the Women's Franchise League of Great Britain and Ireland" to the World's Congress of Representative Women in Chicago.

Elizabeth Wolstenholme Elmy was quite correct in assessing Mrs Bright's close attachment to the Liberal party; she was certainly a member of the executive committee of the WOMEN'S LIBERAL FEDERATION in 1898 and a member of the Ladies Committee of the Home Rule Union. However, she did not put party entirely before principle and around 1896 wrote a leaflet, "Shall we work for candidates who are against women's suffrage?", published by the UNION OF PRACTICAL SUFFRAGISTS with the WLF, and another in 1899, "One More Word!", about putting the suffrage test question to candidates. In this latter pamphlet she wrote, "We are expected to lay down at the command of Party wire-pullers our most cherished convictions concerning Reforms urgently needed for the cause of morality and justice (no less than for our own protection) in order to secure the return of any candidate the Liberal Party may find it convenient to support." Emmeline Pankhurst has recorded that when in 1894 she joined the Independent Labour Party, Ursula Bright offered to join with her. She was dissuaded as it would mean losing contact with so many old friends. After her husband's death in 1899 and the onset of osteoarthritis, Ursula Bright drifted away from the suffrage movement. She was, however, present at the banquet in December 1906 which was organized at the Savoy by Millicent FAWCETT to celebrate the release of the WOMEN'S SOCIAL AND POLITICAL UNION prisoners and did give a donation of £12 to the WSPU in 1907.

Ursula Bright was involved with many other of the radical Liberal campaigns. She was against compulsory vaccination (as were also, for instance, Peter Taylor and Walter McLaren) and in 1884 published as a pamphlet two letters inspired by the fourth annual meeting of the London Society for the Abolition of Compulsory Vaccination. She objected to compulsory vaccination "because it is an outrageous piece of class legislation. No one in easy circumstances, no one possessing the luxury of a family doctor, need have his child vaccinated . . . But the family doctor of the poor is the parish doctor. He is quite independent of his patients, and being paid by other people to vaccinate them, he not only vaccinates them against their will, but he does it *when* he likes and with *what* lymph he likes, irrespective of the feelings or opinions they may entertain." She was also a keen advocate of another of the Women's Franchise League platforms, the abolition of the House of Lords. Ursula Bright thought that parties of all "advanced" brands of opinion should at least unite on that one campaign.

In 1893 Ursula Bright, already a vegetarian, joined the Theosophical Society; she was sponsored by Annie Besant. Elizabeth Cady Stanton remembered that Ursula and Esther Bright had visited her at Bournemouth in 1890 and they had discussed theosophy. Ursula Bright was invited to be a member of the Revising Committee for Elizabeth Cady Stanton's *The Woman's Bible*. After Jacob Bright's death, Annie Besant, on her visits to London, lived with Ursula and Esther, as did, on occasion, Krishnamurti, thought by theosophists to be the reincarnation of "the Lord" and his brother, Niityanandm. Although Esther remarked that her mother did not always agree with Annie Besant, Ursula Bright was generous in her donations. In 1898 she gave £3000 towards the founding of a theosophical headquarters in the north of India.

She left her entire estate and all her papers to her daughter, Esther, noting that she had already, in her lifetime, given large sums to her sons. Esther Bright was a member of the WOMEN'S FREEDOM LEAGUE in the 1920s.

Address: (1860s) Alderley Edge, Cheshire; 31 St James's Place, London W; (1900s) 82 Drayton Gardens, London SW.

Archival source: Elizabeth Wolstenholme Elmy Papers, British Library.

Bibliography: U.M. Bright, *An Evil Law Unfairly Enforced*, 1884; Mrs J. Bright (ed.), *Speeches of Jacob Bright*, 1885; E.C. Stanton, S.B. Anthony and M.J. Gage (eds), *History of Woman Suffrage*, Vol. III, 1886; U. Bright, "Origins and objects of the Women's Franchise League of Great Britain and Ireland", in M.W. Sewall (ed.), *The World's Congress of Representative Women*, 1894; E. Bright, *The Ancient One*, 1927; *Old Memories and Letters of Annie Besant*, 1936.

BRIGHTON Committee of the NATIONAL SOCIETY FOR WOMEN'S SUFFRAGE Formed in 1872; members included Prof. Fawcett, MP for Brighton, and Mrs FAWCETT and Miss BOUCHERETT. The secretary was Mrs A.A. Ruxton, 5 Montpelier Crescent, Brighton. This society presumably lost impetus because in 1891 Margaret Harvey, a niece of Clementia TAYLOR, was in the process of setting up a women's suffrage society in Brighton when she died in a fire accident. In 1906 the Brighton society was refounded as a local committee of the LONDON SOCIETY FOR WOMEN'S SUFFRAGE. In 1913 the society was a member of the SURREY, SUSSEX, AND HANTS FEDERATION OF THE NATIONAL UNION OF WOMEN'S SUFFRAGE SOCIETIES. Secretary (NUWSS) (1909, 1913) Miss F. De G. Merrifield, 14 Clifton Terrace, Brighton.

BRIGHTON (WFL) Secretary (1913) Miss Mary HARE, 8 San Remo, Hove, Sussex.

BRIGHTON (WSPU) The Brighton branch was well established by October 1907, when 160 women attended a WOMEN'S SOCAL AND POLITICAL UNION meeting at which Mrs Louisa MARTINDALE spoke, in Hove Town Hall. Many members, such as the Misses Cobb (*see* Minnie BALDOCK), had defected from the NATIONAL UNION OF WOMEN'S SUFFRAGE SOCIETIES. Minnie TURNER's boarding-house "Sea View" proved a Brighton mecca for suffragettes seeking rest or recreation. Mary CLARKE, a very popular ORGANIZER in Brighton before her untimely death at the end of 1910, made "Sea View" her base. By October 1908 the Brighton WSPU had been given a BANNER, in the colours, designed by Miss F. White. Organizer (1907) Mrs McKEOWN, 209 Preston Drive, Brighton; (1910) Mary Clarke; (1913) Miss G. Allen, 8 North Street Quandrant, Brighton, Sussex.

BRISTOL branch of the MEN'S LEAGUE FOR WOMEN'S SUFFRAGE Founded by 1908 and was based at 5 Berkeley Square, Bristol. At one meeting that year it was addressed by speakers from both the NATIONAL UNION OF WOMEN'S SUFFRAGE SOCIETIES (Miss Tanner) and from the WOMEN'S SOCIAL AND POLITICAL UNION (Annie KENNEY). Honorary secretary (1910) F.W. Rogers, 2 Kensington Villas, Clifton. Vice-presidents included Dr John Beddoe (*see* Agnes BEDDOE) and Col Linley BLATHWAYT.

BRISTOL branch of the MEN'S POLITICAL UNION FOR WOMEN'S ENFRANCHISEMENT Founded in 1910.

BRISTOL (WSPU) Founded by Annie KENNEY in 1907. She arrived as ORGANIZER with no previous knowledge of the city, quickly made contact with the leading members of the BRISTOL and WEST OF ENGLAND (NUWSS) society; Aeta LAMB came from Clement's Inn to help her. Mary BLATHWAYT in her diary recorded in November 1907 details of the first WSPU meeting she attended in Bristol and in 1908, when she became more fully involved, gave day-to-day organizational minutiae. Volunteers came to help, particularly in the summer when rousing meetings were regularly held on the Downs. Among the transient helpers were Clara CODD, Lettice FLOYD, Annie WILLIAMS and Millicent Browne, who met her future husband, Reginald Price, when he, an undergraduate at the university, was defending suffragettes from abuse. The WSPU SHOP and office, then at 33 Queen's Road, was operating by September 1908, when a photograph of it appeared in the *Bristol Times and Mirror*. It moved in April 1909 to 37 Queen's Road; Mary Blathwayt was a conscientious shopkeeper for the cause. This shop was attacked and most efficiently smashed in October 1913 by university undergraduates, in retaliation for the destruction presumed to have been by the WSPU (the message "Businesss before pleasure. Hobhouse being responsible, will pay. Release Mary

Richardson" was found at the scene), of their sports pavilion at Coombe Dingle. The Colston Hall, where the BRISTOL AND WEST OF ENGLAND SOCIETY had held its "Grand Demonstration" in 1880, was the scene of such WSPU stunts as that perpetrated from the depths of the hall organ by Vera WENTWORTH and Elsie HOWEY on 2 May 1909, and the city's prison at Horfield housed suffragette prisoners, including Theresa GARNETT, who had accosted Winston Churchill with a whip at Temple Meads station.

Organizer (1906–1911) Annie Kenney; (1913) Miss Pridden, 37 Queen's Road, Clifton, Bristol.

BRISTOL AND WEST OF ENGLAND SOCIETY FOR WOMEN'S SUFFRAGE Formed in 1868, as the Bristol and Clifton branch of the National Society for Women's Suffrage, as a committee, the fourth in the country, of the NATIONAL SOCIETY FOR WOMEN'S SUFFRAGE. In 1869 its title was changed to the West of England branch. The first executive committee of the society comprised Agnes BEDDOE, Mrs Alfred Brittain, the Rev J. Estlin Carpenter, Mary ESTLIN, Florence Davenport HILL, Prof. F.W. NEWMAN and Mr J.F. Norris. Lilias Ashworth (*see* Lilias Ashworth HALLETT) had joined the committee by the end of the year and in 1870 was joined by Anna Maria PRIESTMAN and Miss Ramsey. Prof. Newman was the society's first honorary secretary. In 1872 Bristol associated itself with the new CENTRAL COMMITTEE OF THE NATIONAL SOCIETY FOR WOMEN'S SUFFRAGE. Until then the executive committee had included Mrs Mill Colman, the sister of J.S. MILL, who had signed the 1866 women's suffrage petition; she may have resigned in solidarity with her brother's opposition to the establishment of the Central Committee. In 1872 the president of the Bristol society was Viscountess AMBERLEY, the treasurer was Mary Estlin, joint honorary secretaries were Lilias Ashworth and Miss Ramsay, and the rest of the committee comprised Agnes Beddoe, Rev Urjiah Thomas, Prof. F.W. Newman, John F. Norris and Anna Maria Priestman. In 1874 Lady Anna GORE LANGTON succeeded as president after the death of Lady Amberley. The position of president remained vacant for some time after Lady Gore Langton's death in 1878; in 1890 it was held by the Countess of Portsmouth.

In 1873 the Bristol society opened an office at 3 Park St. with Miss Westland as an organizing secretary; by 1876 it had moved to 16 Park St. with, as secretary, Mrs Turner, who was replaced after her departure for Australia in 1877 by Mrs Birt. She, in turn, was replaced in 1880 by Helen BLACKBURN. Maria Colby was employed as an ORGANIZER. In 1875 the committee was enlarged to 20, reflecting the increase of support that the work of the society was receiving. After the launch of the *Women's Suffrage Journal* in 1870 the society took care of its distribution to correspondents in the west of England, sent it to all the newspapers in its area and to MPs in the west of England and South Wales. In the 1870s the society was active in campaigning in its area; speaking tours were undertaken by Mrs Fawcett, Lilias Ashworth, Helen Bright CLARK, Emily Sturge and Rhoda and Agnes GARRETT. Two of the earliest suffrage NOVELS emanated from the Bristol society; one, by Emily Spender, was dedicated to Lilias Ashworth and the other, by Miss Ramsay, to Lady Anna Gore Langton.

The society's first public meeting, at which none of the speakers was a woman, was held in January 1870 in support of the "Women's Disabilities Bill". The culmination of the campaign in the 1870s was the "Grand Demonstration" held on 4 November 1880 in the Colston Hall, the 3000 seating capacity of which could not contain the meeting, which overflowed into another hall in the building. The meeting was preceded by a large procession of women with a suffrage BANNER, one of the earliest sightings of the phenomenon that was to become so closely associated with the suffrage movement. The meeting was addressed by eight speakers, Lydia BECKER, Helena DOWNING, Jessie CRAIGEN, Alice SCATCHERD, Eliza STURGE, Henrietta MULLER, Helena Richardson and Emily Sturge (*see* STURGE SISTERS); all women. Two resolutions were passed at the meeting. The first was the adoption of a Memorial, protesting against the exclusion of women ratepayers from the franchise, to Gladstone, who had just been returned to office at the 1880 election. The second resolution appointed a deputation, to consist of representatives from all the provincial societies together with the parliamentary supporters, to wait on the prime minister. This latter resolution eventually came to nothing; in view of the "expressed unwillingness of ministers to receive the deputation" it was indefintely postponed. Bristol was the cradle of the attempt to reform from within the Liberal party's policy on women's enfranchisement. Anna Maria Priestman and Emily Sturge, two of the most active members of the Bristol and West of England Women's Suffrage Society, founded the first Women's Liberal Association in the country, hoping through it to make suffrage a test question for parliamentary candidates. When the suffrage movement was revived in the twentieth century, Anna Maria Priestman was still a member of the executive committee of the Bristol and West of England Society for Women's Suffrage, noted by Annie KENNEY as offering help when she arrived in Bristol as WOMEN'S SOCIAL AND POLITICAL UNION organizer in the west of England in 1907. Lilias Ashworth Hallett, treasurer of the Bristol society, was initially very sympathetic to the WSPU. The Bristol society continued active as part of the NATIONAL UNION OF WOMEN'S SUFFRAGE SOCIETIES, which it had joined in 1898, being a member of the WEST OF ENGLAND FEDERATION; in 1912 a separate society was formed in East Bristol, supporting, under the Election Fighting Fund policy, a Labour party candidate. When the NUWSS EFF policy was adopted in 1912, three members of the Bristol society had resigned, it always having been a Liberal stronghold. The society sent a contingent led by Mrs W.H.C. Cross on the PILGRIMAGE in June/July 1913. She was probably the Mrs Cross who resigned from the NUWSS executive with Eleanor RATHBONE and Margery Corbett ASHBY in April 1914, no longer able to support the EFF policy. After the outbreak of the First World War, the society put agitation for the suffrage to one side, and undertook all the activities supported by the NUWSS, such as the Scottish Women's Hospital and the opening of clubs for women and schools for mothers.

Secretaries (1903) Miss Danger; (1906) Miss A.E. Wright; (1907–9) Miss G. Williams; (1909–18) Mrs H.T. Willis.

Offices (1880) 20 Park Street (this was, in fact, Helen Blackburn's lodgings, afterwards renumbered 69 Park Street); (1905) 19 Berkeley Square; (1909) 49 Whiteladies Road, office and shop; (1910) 111a Whiteladies Road, office and shop; (1913) 40 Park Street.

Archival source: Bristol and West of England Society AGM Report 1890; 1899–1900, Fawcett Library.
Bibliography: A.M. Beddoe, *The Early Years of the Women's Suffrage Movement*, 1911; S.J. Tanner, *How the Women's Suffrage Movement began in Bristol Fifty Years Ago*, 1918; E. Malos, "Bristol women in action, 1839–1919: the right to vote and the need to earn a living", in I. Bild (ed.), *Bristol's Other History*, 1983.

BRITISH DOMINIONS WOMAN SUFFRAGE UNION Founded in New Zealand in 1913 in the course of a lecture tour undertaken by Margaret Hodge and Harriet Newcomb and was then constituted in London at a conference held over the course of a week in July 1914. The scheme received support from New Zealand, every state of Australia, in South Africa, and in Canada. The Union held interesting conferences in London in 1916 and 1918, giving opportunities for delegates from a wide range of suffrage societies to meet. Even in the middle of the war the public meeting devoted to a discussion of women's suffrage attracted an audience of 1000. The Union also held regular luncheons and lectures at the Minerva Café attached to the office of the WOMEN'S FREEDOM LEAGUE. The Union's advisory committee in 1915–16 included Emmeline PETHICK-LAWRENCE, Millicent FAWCETT, Adeline CHAPMAN, Maud Arncliffe SENNETT, Catherine MARSHALL and Sylvia PANKHURST. By 1918 the society was renamed the British Dominions Women Citizens' Union, when its secretary for literature was Daisy SOLOMON, 64 Pattison Road, London NW2, and its treasurer was Dorothy PETHICK, 39 Meadway Court, London NW4. The Union took part in the NATIONAL UNION OF WOMEN'S SUFFRAGE SOCIETIES victory celebration held in the Queen's Hall on 13 March 1918 and held its biennial conference over three days in June. At its "At Home" held in Caxton Hall on 3 June, the tea was served by Mrs Fisher of the Minerva Café, "kindly assisted by Miss Stella Miles Franklin (Australia)"; its session on International Government was addressed by Leonard Woolf. Although optimistic of growth in 1918 and opening an office at 19 Buckingham Street, Strand, in the post-war, post-enfranchisement years the Union could not maintain its momentum and in early 1922 amalgamated its work with that of the British Overseas Committee of the INTERNATIONAL WOMAN SUFFRAGE ALLIANCE.

Archival source: Reports of the British Dominions Woman Suffrage/Women Citizens Union, 1914–22.

BRIXTON (branch of London Society, NUWSS) Secretary (1913) Miss Downs, 2 Acre Lane, Brixton, London SW.

BRIXTON AND STREATHAM (WSPU) Secretary (1906) Mrs McArthur, 21 Akerman Road, Brixton, London SW.

BROCKHAM AND BETCHWORTH (NUWSS) In 1913 the society was a member of the SURREY, SUSSEX, AND HANTS FEDERATION OF THE NATIONAL UNION OF WOMEN'S SUFFRAGE SOCIETIES. Secretary (1913) Miss Paquerette Forrester, Red Gables, Brockham Green, Betchworth, Surrey.

BROMLEY, BECKENHAM, AND SHORTLAND'S SUFFRAGE SOCIETY Formed in 1882, as a branch committee of the NATIONAL SOCIETY FOR WOMEN'S SUFFRAGE. Mrs Daniel Harrison, who was a sister of Mary Howitt, had been a member of the LONDON NATIONAL SOCIETY in 1867, and was a founding member of the Bromley Society. One of her daughters, Lucy Harrison, read a paper written by Mrs John Macdonell (who was, I think, a sister) to the society in March 1883. Eliza ORME was a member of the society's general committee in 1882. In 1882 the society issued a paper read by Mrs E. Lynch, "Upon the Claims of Women-Ratepayers to the Parliamentary Vote", which had been printed in the *Victoria Magazine*. Mrs Ashton DILKE was a speaker at a meeting of the society in Beckenham in April 1892. The society was still active in 1907 (when Miss Heppel, headmistress of Bromley High School (GPDST) was present at a meeting) but appears to have disappeared before 1913.

BROMSGROVE AND DISTRICT (NUWSS) In 1913 the society was a member of the MIDLAND (WEST) FEDERATION OF THE NATIONAL UNION OF WOMEN'S SUFFRAGE SOCIETIES. Secretary (1913) Mrs F. Horton, Coombe Cottage, Finstall, Bromsgrove, Worcestershire.

BROWN, MYRA ELEANOR SADD, MRS (1872–1938) Mother of three daughters and a son, a poor law guardian for Hackney in 1898 and honorary secretary of the North Hackney Women's Liberal Association. She subscribed to the CENTRAL SOCIETY FOR WOMEN'S SUFFRAGE from 1902 and to its successor the LONDON SOCIETY FOR WOMEN'S SUFFRAGE in 1906–7, and to the WOMEN'S SOCIAL AND POLITICAL UNION in 1907. In 1908 she also gave a donation to the WOMEN'S FREEDOM LEAGUE and, after it was founded in 1910, was a member of the FREE CHURCH LEAGUE FOR WOMAN SUFFRAGE. She was on the committee of the TAX RESISTANCE LEAGUE in 1911. In March 1912 Myra Sadd Brown was sentenced to two months' hard labour after taking part in the WSPU window-smashing campaign. She joined in the hunger strike and was fed by means of a nasal tube even though she had, in the past, suffered a broken nose and had had an operation on both her nose and her throat. During 1914–15 she helped to raise money for the EAST LONDON FEDERATION OF SUFFRAGETTES and by 1916 was a member of the UNITED SUFFRAGISTS. In 1920 she was a shareholder in the Emerson Club (*see under* CLUBS). From 1933 until her death in Hong Kong she was a member of the national executive of the WFL. The Sadd-Brown Collection of Commonwealth Literature held in the Fawcett Library commemorates her involvement with the women's movement.
Address: (1912, 1938) 2 Chesterfield Gardens, London NW.
Photograph: in Fawcett Library Collection.

BROWNE, ANNIE LEIGH (1851–1936) Unitarian, she grew up in Clifton in Bristol, where her father Samuel Woolcot Browne carried out works of philanthropy. In an interview she gave to the *Woman's Herald* she noted that "I am tired of being told to wait patiently and help the Liberal party, seeing that it is 25 years since I attended for the first time a Woman's Suffrage meeting at the house of Dr and Mrs BEDDOE in Bristol. . . . When the question of Women's Suffrage was first discussed there, my mother joined in the movement. The social reformers, Miss Carpenter, Mr Matthew Davenport Hill and Miss Frances Power COBBE were their friends. I did not have the advantage of going to Girton or Newnham, but when we came to London I attended various courses of lectures". She remarked that the writers who most influenced her thinking were Theodore Parker, William Henry

Channing, and Dr Martineau, all Unitarians. In 1882 with her sister, Lady Lockyer, Mary Kilgour, and also, according to Barbara Stephens in *Emily Davies and Girton College*, 1927, Henrietta MULLER, she founded College Hall for Women Students in Byng Place in Bloomsbury. This was particularly attractive as a residence for women medical students; Annie Leigh Browne was also a governor of the London School of Medicine for Women. She was the founder and honorary secretary of the SOCIETY FOR PROMOTING THE RETURN OF WOMEN AS COUNTY COUNCILLORS (which later became the WOMEN'S LOCAL GOVERNMENT SOCIETY) from 1888 until retiring in 1921, honorary secretary of the Paddington Women's Liberal Association in 1892 and a member of the Pioneer Club in the 1890s (*see under* CLUBS). In 1888/9 she and her society sponsored the election of Jane Cobden (see Jane Cobden UNWIN) and Lady SANDHURST to the London County Council. They chose George LANSBURY to run Jane Cobden's campaign. In 1898 Annie Leigh Browne was a member of the executive committee of the UNION OF PRACTICAL SUFFRAGISTS. In 1905 she was a member of the CENTRAL SOCIETY FOR WOMEN'S SUFFRAGE and of its successor, the LONDON SOCIETY FOR WOMEN'S SUFFRAGE, 1906–7. She took part in the "Mud March" organized by the NATIONAL UNION OF WOMEN'S SUFFRAGE SOCIETIES in February 1907 and in 1913 was a vice-president of the FREE CHURCH LEAGUE FOR WOMEN SUFFRAGE.

Annie Leigh Browne founded a Cottage Hospital in Sidmouth, from where her mother's family came. In 1934 she was a life member of the Women's Farm and Garden Association and in her will left land she owned in Salcombe Regis to the National Trust and £5000 to "my beloved friend Miss Mary Stewart Kilgour".

Address: (1913) 58 Porchester Terrace, London W.
Photograph: in Jane Cobden Unwin Papers, University of Bristol.
Archival source: Papers of Jane Cobden Unwin, Bristol University Library.
Bibliography: The *Woman's Herald*, 4 February 1893; obituary in *The Times*, 14 March 1936.

BROWNE, LAURA ELIZABETH MORGAN-, MRS (*c*. 1843–1942) In 1892 she was a member of the committee of the Healthy and Artistic Dress Union and then, still in 1896, of the executive committee of the CENTRAL NATIONAL SOCIETY FOR WOMEN'S SUFFRAGE. Her husband also addressed suffrage meetings organized by this society and her two daughters were members. In 1891 she wrote a leaflet, "The Census and Women's Suffrage", that was published by the Central National Society. In 1893 she was a member of the executive committee of the WOMEN'S LIBERAL FEDERATION and wrote for it a leaflet, *Reasons Why Women Want the Vote*. In 1894 she was a member of the WOMEN'S FRANCHISE LEAGUE and in that year also supported the WOMEN'S EMANCIPATION UNION. In 1898 she gave a talk to the Weymouth Women's Liberal Association, in 1899 attended the International Congress of Women in London, and in 1898 and in 1900 was a member of the executive committee of the UNION OF PRACTICAL SUFFRAGISTS. Throughout the 1890s she was a regular contributor to *Shafts*. After the formation of the CENTRAL SOCIETY FOR WOMEN'S SUFFRAGE in 1900 she was a member of its executive committee and honorary secretary of its Ealing branch. In 1908 she subscribed to the WOMEN'S SOCIAL AND POLITICAL UNION and was the author of "The Purple, White, and Green", a song to be sung to the tune of "The Wearing of the Green", the chorus of which runs "For it is the grandest movement the world has ever seen,/ And we'll win the Vote for Women, wearing purple, white and green." In 1913, with Mrs Ennis Richmond, she organized the WSPU campaign in Scarborough.

Address: (1899) 7 rue de Bruxelles, Paris; (1900) 9 Blakesley Avenue, Ealing, London W; (1934) 67 Church Road, Richmond, Surrey; (1942) Quarrycot, 49 Quarry Road, Headington, Oxfordshire.
Photograph: in *Portrait Album of Who's Who at the International Congress of Women*, 1899.
Bibliography: L.E. Morgan-Browne, "The census and women's suffrage", in J. Lewis (ed.), *Before The Vote was Won*, 1987.

BRYER, CONSTANCE (1870–1952) A violinist who gave up her study to work for the cause of women's suffrage. A male member of her family accompanied one of the bands in the procession on WOMEN'S SOCIAL AND POLITICAL UNION'S "Women's Sunday" in June 1908. She appears to have come from a family of musicians; Bryer's Band met Patricia WOODLOCK when she was released from Holloway in June 1909 (*see* BAND). Constance

Bryer was a member of the CHURCH LEAGUE FOR WOMEN'S SUFFRAGE and was secretary of the Islington North branch of the WSPU, 1911–13. She was arrested, charged with obstruction and discharged after "Black Friday" in November 1910. In November 1911 she was sentenced to five days' imprisonment after taking part in the WSPU protest against the "torpedoing" of the Conciliation Bill and in March 1912 was sentenced to four months after breaking windows in Regent Street as part of the organized WSPU campaign. She served that sentence in Winson Green Prison, Birmingham, with, among others, Olive WHARRY, for whose will in 1946 she acted as an executor. Her own hunger-strike medal, together with that of Olive Wharry, who left it to her, is now in a private collection. At the time of her death she was in possession of some of Olive Wharry's etchings and books.
Address: (1911) 49 Tufnell Park, London N; (1946) 70 Alexandra Road, Hampstead.

BUCKS (MID) (NUWSS) In 1913 the society was a member of the OXON, BERKS, BUCKS, AND BEDS FEDERATION OF THE NATIONAL UNION OF WOMEN'S SUFFRAGE SOCIETIES. Secretary (1913) Mrs Sichel, Lindholm, Wendover, Buckinghamshire.

BUDLEIGH SALTERTON (NUWSS) In 1913 the society was a member of the SOUTH-WESTERN FEDERATION OF THE NATIONAL UNION OF WOMEN'S SUFFRAGE SOCIETIES. Secretary (1913) Miss Mathieson, Otterbourne, Budleigh Salterton, Devon.

BURBURY, CHARLOTTE AMY MAY, MRS (c. 1832–95) Sister of Professor Kennedy of Cambridge, who was himself a member of the LONDON NATIONAL SOCIETY in 1867. His daughters Jean and Marion, Mrs Burbury's nieces, were later particularly active members of the CAMBRIDGE WOMEN'S SUFFRAGE ASSOCIATION. Charlotte Burbury was a member of the executive committee of the London National Society from May 1868 and probably became honorary secretary of that society in 1871/2 after the resignation of Caroline Ashurst BIGGS and Clementia TAYLOR. She certainly held that position by 1874 but did not do so when the society rejoined with the CENTRAL COMMITTEE OF THE NATIONAL SOCIETY FOR WOMEN'S SUFFRAGE in 1877. Helen BLACKBURN makes no mention of her in *The Record of Women's Suffrage*, 1902.

Charlotte Burbury was a member of the Society for Promoting the Employment of Women from 1870 and was a member of its managing committee from 1871 until her death. In 1876 she canvassed for Helen TAYLOR's election to the London School Board and, with her, was a member of the Sunday Society, part of the "rational recreation" movement that lobbied for the Sunday opening of museums and art galleries. In 1877 she was a member of the governing council of the London School of Medicine for Women and subscribed regularly to the New Hospital for Women (later the Elizaeth Garrett Anderson Hospital).
Address: (1872) 15 St George's Terrace, Queensgate, London W; (1895) 36 Oxford Terrace, Hyde Park, London W.

BURKITT, [EVELYN] HILDA (1876–1955) (later Mrs Mitchener) A secretary from Sparkbrook in Birmingham. She joined the WOMEN'S SOCIAL AND POLITICAL UNION in 1907 and in the autumn of 1908, when a regional office was opened in Birmingham, took charge of publicity in the Midlands campaign. She was arrested four times in 1909 and on the final occasion, in October, was sentenced to one month's imprisonment for causing disruption during Asquith's visit to Birmingham. When she, Mabel CAPPER, Ellen Barnwell, Laura AINSWORTH, Mary LEIGH and Patricia WOODLOCK arrived at Winson Green Prison, according to the Prison Visitors' Committee minutes, "on alighting from prison van [they] started singing, shewed defiance, threatened to assault prison officials, and said they would not go in cells or undress until they were placed in the First Division". They all then went on hunger strike and were forcibly fed. Hilda Burkitt was the first suffragette prisoner to be so treated. According to the minutes of the Winson Green Prison Visiting Committee she was tube fed and afterwards agreed to eat.

In 1912 she was sentenced to four months' imprisonment for window smashing and was released on medical grounds after hunger striking. She was arrested again in Leeds in November 1913, charged with attempting to set fire to a grandstand at the Leeds Football Ground. She went on hunger strike and was released on 3 December 1913, to the care of Mrs Whitehead, 297 Killinghall Road, Bradford, under the "Cat and Mouse" Act. She escaped recapture until, with Florence Tunks, she was tried at Felixstowe in May 1914 for burning two wheat stacks, the Pier at Great Yarmouth, and the Bath Hotel, Felixstowe. The damage to the latter, which had been fully furnished but unoccupied, was estimated at £30 000 and Hilda Burkitt was sentenced to two years' imprisonment. One of the witnesses against the two women was a retired naval officer who had, while they were out walking in Felixstowe, asked them the time and then tried on another occasion again to talk to them. The two suffragettes took great exception to him and are recorded as saying, "Such men as he ought not to be allowed to give evidence against women who are fighting for the purity of the country". While on remand in Ipswich prison Hilda Burkitt went on hunger-and-thirst strike and was forcibly fed. She was released from prison on 1 September 1914, having voluntarily given an undertaking to no longer be involved in militancy; she had been forcibly fed 292 times. The prison reports record that she vomited after most of the feedings. It is not clear why she was not released on 10 August, as were other suffrage prisoners under the amnesty. During the militant period Hilda Burkitt on occasion went under the alias "Byron".

Address: (1910) 214 Wellington Road, Perry Bar, Birmingham; (1955) 48 South Road, Morecambe, Lancashire.

Archival source: Suffragette Fellowship Collection, Museum of London; Visiting Committee of HM Prison Winson Green, Birmingham Archives and Local History Library; Home Office Papers, Public Record Office.

BURNAGE (WFL)   Secretary (1913) Mrs Brickhill, 33 South Avenue, Garden Village, Levenshulme, Manchester.

BURNHAM (NUWSS)   In 1913 the society was a member of the WEST OF ENGLAND FEDERATION OF THE NATIONAL UNION OF WOMEN'S SUFFRAGE SOCIETIES. Secretary (1913) Miss M.A. Greswell, The Colony, Burnham, Somerset.

BURNLEY (NUWSS)   Formed in 1911 and by 1912 had joined the MANCHESTER AND DISTRICT FEDERATION OF THE NATIONAL UNION OF WOMEN'S SUFFRAGE SOCIETIES. In 1912 Lady Ottoline Morrell, whose husband was the local MP, was president of the society. Secretary (1913) Miss Lee, Thorn Hill, Burnley, Lancashire.

BURNS, LUCY (1879–1966)   Born in Brooklyn, New York, graduated from Packer Institute in 1899 and from Vassar College in 1902, studied at Yale 1902–3, at the University of Berlin, 1906–8, and read modern languages at the University of Bonn 1908–9. She joined the WOMEN'S SOCIAL AND POLITICAL UNION in 1909 while on holiday in London, and was arrested while taking part in her first demonstration – the 29 June deputation to the House of Commons. While being held at Cannon Row police station after her arrest she met Alice PAUL for the first time. She was imprisoned, went on hunger strike and was released. With Alice Paul, she was arrested in July 1909 for interrupting a meeting being held by Lloyd George at Limehouse, was sent to Holloway, hunger struck and was again released. After they had recovered, the two Americans set off for Scotland by car with Mrs PANKHURST to assist with the WSPU campaign in Scotland. They and Edith NEW were arrested in September after interrupting a meeting held by Herbert Samuel in Dundee. They were released from prison after going on hunger strike for four days, without having been force fed. Adela PANKHURST, who was then a local WSPU ORGANIZER, noted that the prison officials were very kind to them, and understood exactly the meaning of their protest. Once free they were welcomed at a meeting presided over by the Lord Mayor. Lucy Burns helped organize the October 1909 WSPU pageant and procession in Edinburgh and then, in November, took over as organizer there from Florence MACAULAY. Life as an organizer was not easy. Christabel PANKHURST in a letter from Paris to Janie ALLAN dated 26 May 1914 wrote, "Miss Lucy Burns was virtually driven away from Edinburgh, so unhappy was she because of a few members. The ostensible reason of the trouble was the stand she made with regard to a certain Miss Gorrie, who does not now seem to possess the confidence of the very people who were her champions at the time in question. I doubt whether there is any person living who, as an organiser, would entirely satisfy some people!" Lucy Burns returned to America in the summer of 1912 and with Alice Paul founded there the Woman's Party, in which they employed many of the tactics developed by the WSPU.

Photograph: in M. MacKenzie, *Shoulder to Shoulder*, 1975; I.H. Irwin, *The Story of Alice Paul and the National Women's Party*, 1977.

Archival source: Janie Allan Papers, National Library of Scotland.

Bibliography: I.H. Irwin, *The Story of Alice Paul and the National Women's Party*, 1977; L. Leneman, *A Guid Cause: The Woman's Suffrage Movement in Scotland*, 1991.

BURTON-ON-TRENT (NUWSS) In 1913 the society was a member of the MIDLANDS (EAST) FEDERATION OF THE NATIONAL UNION OF WOMEN'S SUFFRAGE SOCIETIES. Secretary (1913) Mrs P.H. Mellor, Woodville, Burton-on-Trent, Staffordshire.

BURY (NUWSS) Formed in 1911. Joint secretaries (1911) Miss M. Ashworth and Mrs Maddox, Bury, Lancashire.

BUXTON (NUWSS) By 1912 the society had joined the MANCHESTER AND DISTRICT FEDERATION OF THE NATIONAL UNION OF WOMEN'S SUFFRAGE SOCIETIES; it had lapsed by 1917. Secretary (1913) Mrs Ashwell Cooke, Brackendale, Lightwood Road, Buxton, Derbyshire.

C

CAIRD, [ALICE] MONA HENRYSON, MRS (1854–1932) Feminist essayist and novelist, married James Henryson-Caird in 1877 and had one son, born in 1884. She subscribed to the CENTRAL COMMITTEE OF THE NATIONAL SOCIETY FOR WOMEN'S SUFFRAGE in 1878. In the 1880s she attended meetings of Karl Pearson's Men and Women's Club, although she was never a formal member. In 1890 she was a member of the WOMEN'S FRANCHISE LEAGUE and Elizabeth Wolstenholme ELMY thought that Mona Caird certainly (and possibly her father-in-law Sir James Caird) would give drawing-room meetings for the League. Later that year, while wintering in Italy, Mona Caird gave Ben Elmy advice towards the writing of a paper, for private circulation only, on the "Physical Emancipation of Women". In 1891, loyal to Elizabeth Wolstenholme Elmy, Mona Caird became a member of council of the WOMEN'S EMANCIPATION UNION and in that year an article by her on "The Position of Women", published in the *Manchester Guardian*, 7 July, was reissued as the WEU's second leaflet. In 1892 a paper by Mona Caird, "Why Women Want the Franchise", was read at the Union's conference in Birmingham. In 1904 she joined the Theosophical Society, resigning in 1909. In May 1906 Elizabeth Wolstenholme Elmy, while in London to take part in the WOMEN'S SOCIAL AND POLITICAL UNION deputation to Campbell-Bannerman, had lunch with Mona Caird and Frances ROWE. In October 1907 Mona Caird gave £20 to the WSPU, in November gave her support to its new paper, *Votes for Women*, and in June 1908 took part in the Hyde Park Demonstration. She was a member of the LONDON SOCIETY FOR WOMEN'S SUFFRAGE from 1909 to 1913. Of her essays those that have most direct bearing on the suffrage issue are "A Defence of the 'Wild Women'", *Nineteenth Century*, 1892; "Phases of Human Development", *Westminster Review*, 1894; "Militant Tactics and Women's Suffrage", *Westminster Review*, 1910; "The Lot of Women", *Westminster Review*, 1910. In 1888 an article by her, "Marriage", published in the *Westminster Review*, caused a furore and sparked off a succession of "New Woman" essays and novels. A collection of her essays, comprising a very forceful attack on marriage, was published as *The Morality of Marriage* in 1907.
Address: (1896) 7 Kensington Court Gardens, London W; (1932) 34 Woronzow Road, St John's Wood, London NW; Cassencary, near Creetown, Dumfries and Galloway.
Portrait: reproduced in A. Heilmann, "Mona Caird", in *Women's History Review*, 5, 1, 1996; a portrait of her by Millais (whose wife, Effie Gray, was aunt to Mona Caird's husband) was shown at the Grosvenor Gallery, 1880.
Photograph: by H.S. Mendelssohn in the *Review of Reviews*, 10, 1894.
Bibliography: A. Heilmann, "Mona Caird", *Women's History Review*, 5, 1, 1996, which includes a complete bibliography of her work.

CAMBERLEY AND DISTRICT (NUWSS) In 1913 the society was a member of the SURREY, SUSSEX, AND HANTS FEDERATION OF THE NATIONAL UNION OF WOMEN'S SUFFRAGE SOCIETIES. Secretary (1913) Miss Evelyn Atkinson, Portesbery Hill, Camberley, Surrey.

CAMBERWELL (branch of the London Society, NUWSS) Secretary (1909) Mrs Dines, 3 Orchard House, County Grove, Camberwell, London SE; (1913) Mrs Harvey, 46, The Gardens, East Dulwich, London SE.

CAMBERWELL AND DULWICH (WFL) Secretary (1913) Nurse Evans, 404 Old Kent Road, London SE.

CAMBRIDGE (WSPU) Organizer (1913) Miss Olive BARTELS, 11 New Square, Cambridge.

CAMBRIDGE WOMEN'S SUFFRAGE ASSOCIATION Founded in 1884, and affiliated to the NATIONAL

SOCIETY FOR WOMEN'S SUFFRAGE. Its founding members included Mrs Anna BATESON, Mr Brambley, Mr B.E. Hammond, Mr Piggott, Mr Rae, Mr Roberts, Mr C. Turner, Mr Evelyn Shuckburgh, Miss Anna BATESON, Mrs Dale, Mrs FAWCETT, Mrs Peile (wife of the Master of Christ's College), Mrs Tillyard, Miss Eliza Rhodes (the auditor of the CWSA's accounts), Hon Mrs A.T. Lyttleton (wife of the Master of Selwyn College) and Dr Venn. The society's first move was to ask the CENTRAL COMMITTEE OF THE NATIONAL SOCIETY how it should go about sending a petition to the House of Lords. In 1886 the CWSA supported the Woodall amendment, which excluded married women from the proposed franchise bill, while regretting the necessity for so doing. In March 1886 Miss Jeanette Wilkinson (a former upholsteress, now a peripatetic lecturer, who died later that year) gave a lecture to the society on the "Social and Political Position of Women". One of the men members of the executive committee undertook to ask his friends at the Working Men's Club to act as stewards for the occasion. Mrs Bateson was invited to ask a gentleman to act as chairman at the meeting. This appears to have been the convention; invariably the master of a college presided over the society's annual general meeting.

In 1886 the society sent two petitions requesting the enfranchisement of women to parliament, one from graduate members of the university and one from women householders. In 1888 the father of John Maynard Keynes, J.N. Keynes, who was a close friend of Henry FAWCETT and a close neighbour of the Bateson family, was the society's auditor. After the First World War his wife became a magistrate in Cambridge, in 1930 was the president of the National Council of Women of Great Britain, in 1931 was a Cambridge alderman, and in 1932 mayor.

Miss Anna Bateson represented the CWSA at the special general meeting of the CENTRAL NATIONAL SOCIETY in London on 12 December 1888 and signified the Cambridge society's general approval of the proposed new rules. However, in the event, in January 1889 the Association withdrew its affiliation from the Central National Society. Miss Anna Bateson had retired from the committee of the CWSA in November 1889 on the grounds that she was leaving Cambridge and her mother gave up her position as secretary the following June. She was succeeded by Mrs Archer-Hinde. Blanche Athena CLOUGH was a member of the CWSA at this time. The society does not appear to have been very active, holding few meetings apart from its AGM in 1890, 1891 and 1892. At the 1891 AGM Emily DAVIES gave an address on the best means of furthering the cause of women's suffrage. At the 1892 AGM Mary BATESON was elected secretary to succeed Mrs Archer-Hinde.

Mary Bateson, Miss Fawcett, Mrs Fordham, Mrs Bethune-Baker, Miss Marion Kennedy (niece of Charlotte BURBURY), Mrs Tillyard and Mrs Peile were delegates to the conference held in Birmingham on 16 October 1896 to discuss the proposal that all the societies for women's suffrage should present a common front. This resulted in the formation of the NATIONAL UNION OF WOMEN'S SUFFRAGE SOCIETIES. As a consequence the Cambridge Association agreed in 1897 to affiliate to the CENTRAL AND EASTERN SOCIETY FOR WOMEN'S SUFFRAGE and in October agreed to join the NUWSS.

In 1901 the CWSA agreed to donate three guineas to the NUWSS towards the cost of collecting signatures to the Factory Workers' Petition but, for an unspecified reason, the offer was withdrawn in December. Miss Hardcastle, the secretary of the CWSA, was the society's representative on the NUWSS executive committee in 1903. Cambridge had previously been represented by Mrs Shaw, but she had only attended 4 out of a possible 14 meetings, and it was agreed that in future the secretary should herself attend "in order to enable the Cambridge Committee to keep in close touch with the other provincial and London committees". She was granted two guineas towards her travelling expenses. The Association was mainly Liberal in its sympathy. Margaret HEITLAND took the chair at the AGM in 1903. The CWSA fully supported Mr Hubert Sweeney as the candidate for the LANCASHIRE AND CHESHIRE WOMEN TEXTILE AND OTHER WORKERS at Wigan, felt that his candidature should be supported in every possible way by the NUWSS, and contributed 1 guinea for this purpose. In February 1904 Miss Hardcastle reported that she had held an informal meeting at Girton College under the auspices of the Oratorical Club; about 60 students had attended and had seemed very interested in the cause of women's suffrage.

In 1905 the Association thought it would circularize "certain official representative persons in the town and county of Cambridge on the question of women's suffrage" and would consider the replies received, with a view to asking the NUWSS for the services of an ORGANIZER. Miss Hardcastle resigned as secretary in 1905 and it was agreed to start a fund to pay for secretarial services, to which Miss Hardcastle donated £5 and Mrs Heitland £3. Although membership of the CWSA was increasing in the city, the society did not proceed with the suggested campaign in the county. The CWSA asked Alison GARLAND to speak at the 1905 AGM and at NEWNHAM and at GIRTON, defraying her travelling expenses.

The CWSA Minutes for 1906–8 are missing. By 1909 meetings were held at the home of Mrs Mary WARD and plans were much more ambitious. An important women's suffrage meeting was planned for 5 May at the Corn Exchange and the CWSA hoped that about 50 leading members of the community would appear on the platform; arrangements were made for university men in favour of women's suffrage to be asked to attend and Lady Darwin, Miss Constance Jones, mistress of Girton, and Mrs Sidgwick, of Newnham, were to be asked for their involvement. The Corn Exchange was engaged for the day previous to the meeting in order to allow time for it to be suitably decorated. Six people were to be secured to take a collection at the doors and the same number were to distribute leaflets in the street to people standing in queues. Advertisements of the meeting were to be put in the weekly local papers and the *Cambridge Daily News* was to have a display advertisement every day from 28 April to 5 May, the editors being asked to call attention to the meetings in a paragraph. Two trollies with porters were to be sent around the streets of Cambridge on 4 and 5 May, and sandwich men were to patrol, advertising the meeting. Red and white rosettes were to be made for the stewards. Tickets and handbills were to be sent out to college secretaries. In March a "second handsome BANNER" had been purchased by Mrs Wright. As the meeting was planned to take part during the period in which the quinquennial congress of the INTERNATIONAL WOMAN SUFFRAGE ALLIANCE was taking place in London, delegates from that were to be entertained in Cambridge, for example Margaret Heitland was prepared to be hostess to eight delegates, Miss Kennedy to four (preferably French) and Mary Ward to eight. The Cambridge meeting was a great success, attended by about 2000 people, and hundreds had to be turned away. Alice ABADAM and Frances STERLING were among the speakers. The meeting cost about £42 to stage (of which 10/– was sent to the Police Orphan Fund as thanks for police services, and 5/– to the Corn Exchange caretaker in recognition of his helpfulness). Receipts amounted to £62.

In 1909 it was agreed that, for the first time, members should each take over a small neighbourhood and visit it, collecting subscriptions, distributing leaflets, notices of meetings "and stirring up in various ways, an interest in the suffrage in that area". Mrs Ramsey organized a CWSA stall to be set up in the Market Place. During May Week it was "to be gaily decorated – the banners put up & picture postcards, brooches and fresh literature provided". By now many more meetings of the CWSA were being held (16 in 1909) and it was agreed that the members should meet regularly once a month, on the second Thursday, interim meetings being held when necessary. In July 1909 a "Garden Meeting" for 200 elementary and higher grade schoolmasters and mistresses was held, with help from the MEN's LEAGUE FOR WOMEN'S SUFFRAGE, at The Lodge, Mill Road. In 1909 the CWSA also ordered a few copies of Lady McLAREN's "Women's Charter" and supported the NUWSS resolution put forward at the council meeting held in Cardiff, "That the NU of WSS strongly condemns the use of violence in political propaganda and authorizes the executive committee to sign a letter to be sent to the press. And further that the Council urges all the Societies to circulate the letter in their local press signed in addition by the officers of their societies." Margaret Heitland was the CWSA delegate to this council meeting. Blanche Athena Clough was among the members elected to the executive committee in 1909, Margery Corbett (*see* Margery Corbett ASHBY) was co-opted, and an organizer, Miss Joseph, was employed at a salary of 30/– a week and with £1 for board, when hospitality was not obtainable, travelling and other expenses to be additional. She was to canvass for signatures in the centre of town for the Voters' Petition, to act as secretary of the Petition Committee, and to send a report of her work to each committee meeting.

In December the CWSA agreed to oppose the running of suffrage candidates by the National Union. By December 1909 the society had £100 in donations towards its election campaign in Cambridge. Two of the Liberal parliamentary candidates (Buckmaster and Montagu) could not agree to both the test questions on women's suffrage devised by the National Union. These were: (1) Will you in your election address declare yourself to be a supporter of the enfranchisement of women, and will you do everything in your power to press its urgency upon your party leader? (2) Will you oppose the enactment of any measure for extending the franchise to men which does not include women? Buckmaster and Montagu could answer "yes" to the first question but not to the second. Two members of the executive committee of the CWSA therefore withdrew for the election period (one of these was Julia Kennedy, who was an honorary secretary of the Cambridge and County Liberal Association). Sir Charles Rose, who had answered satisfactorily both the test questions, actually asked (or at least his agent did) that some members of the CWSA should speak at some of his meetings. The CWSA hired premises at 41 Green Street to act as their committee rooms during the election campaign; their flags were broken off and removed from outside the building. During the January election campaign the CWSA organized meetings throughout the county, both in village halls and in the open air, undertaking journeys to evening meetings by wagonette, and making three motor-car journeys into different parts of the county, each trip starting at 6 pm and taking about three hours. Blanche Athena Clough gave hospitality to the organizer for a few days during the campaign. Meetings were very well attended; one in Ely had an audience of 600, with another 200 accommodated in an overflow hall. On polling day members of the CWSA collected names of 2148 voters for their petition.

In April 1910 the CWSA discussed the proposed divisional federations of the NUWSS and decided to ask Wisbech, Bedford, Woburn Sands, Southwold, Huntingdon, Harleston and Norwich to join in an EASTERN COUNTIES FEDERATION. The CWSA carried out a vigorous campaign for the December election, hiring a committee room in Rose Crescent, which Miss Denson was employed to run for three weeks at a salary of 15/– a week. At the beginning of 1911 the CWSA opened a permanent committee rooms and SHOP at 2 Benet Street, decided henceforward to hold two meetings a month, and to organize a young people's suffrage society, aimed at shop assistants and elementary school teachers. Throughout the summer they held drawing-room meetings, garden-party meetings, and open-air meetings both in Cambridge and in the surrounding districts. In the early summer they ordered stuff with which Mrs Kellett was to make banners to carry in the Coronation procession in London in June. Slings were to be provided for the banner bearers and bamboo sliding poles were to be ordered from the NUWSS for "the big blue Cambridge banner".

In January 1912 the CWSA's secretary Mary Ward was asked to write to the Independent Labour Party, expressing the Association's sympathy with the ILP's views on the women suffrage question and "our gratification at the strong line some of them had taken in declaring that they would oppose a Reform Bill which did not include women, and our earnest hope that they would persevere in their policy". The CWSA was prepared to back, with very few amendments, the NUWSS's Election Fighting Fund policy. By 11 March 1912 a number of members of the CWSA had sent in their resignations "because of militants"; the executive committee resolved that the resigners were "to be called on and reasoned with". In 1912 Miss Bagnall, 3 Justice Walk, Chelsea, was asked to come to Cambridge in July as an organizer for three weeks, to work officially for the formation of East and West Cambs Societies, and was to get up the garden meeting at Newmarket. By 1912 the CWSA had a press secretary, Miss Fanny Johnson. By 1913 the CWSA had 519 members. In 1913 several members of the Association, including Jean Kennedy, who were also members of the executive of the Women's Liberal Association, resigned from the WLA in consequence of the "illiberal" action of the government. Mary Ward resigned as an ordinary member of the WLA.

The CWSA was very active during the First World War; Fanny Johnson remained press officer and kept the suffrage question alive in the local papers. In

1919 the CWSA became the Cambridge Association for the Political Equality of Women, becoming in 1920 the local standing committee of the National Union of Societies for Equal Citizenship, with Mrs Bethune-Baker, who in 1923 was elected a member of the town council, as chairman. Membership of this committee, which included Mary Ward, had, in fact, changed very little from that of the pre-war CWSA.

Secretary (1898) Mary Bateson, 74 Huntingdon Road, Cambridge; (1902) Miss F. Hardcastle, 14 Huntingdon Road, Cambridge; (1905–15) Mrs Mary Ward, 6 Selwyn Gardens, Cambridge.

Archival source: Records of the Cambridge Association for Women's Suffrage, County Record Office, Cambridge.

CAMBRIDGE UNIVERSITY branch of the MEN'S LEAGUE FOR WOMEN'S SUFFRAGE Founded in 1909.

CAMBRIDGE UNIVERSITY WOMEN'S SUFFRAGE SOCIETY Formed in 1908 by the amalgamation of the NEWNHAM and GIRTON suffrage clubs and then affiliated to the NATIONAL UNION OF WOMEN'S SUFFRAGE SOCIETIES. Three hundred members of the CUWSS marched in the June 1908 NUWSS procession and by August 1908 membership of the society, drawn from present and past members of the colleges, was 425, rising to 632 in 1909. In the summer of 1908 the society organized a CARAVAN tour through the Lake District and into Scotland. Ray Costelloe (see STRACHEY FAMILY) was one of the caravanners. In 1910, however, the college magazine, *Thersites,* noted that a meeting organized in Newnham by the society was very poorly attended. But a meeting in October 1910 noted that Ray Costelloe's address to the society on women's suffrage was well attended "and a good deal of literature was sold after the meeting". In November 1910 there was a debate between Helena SWANWICK and Mabel Smith of the Anti-Suffrage Society, at which the motion in favour of women's suffrage was carried by a large majority. Mary Lilias Mackenzie (1888–1953) was president of the CUWSS in 1911, went on to become assistant secretary to the NUWSS, 1911–15, and was registrar of Royal Archives at Windsor Castle, 1929–53. In 1912 Isabella FORD addressed a well-attended meeting of the society at which she explained the FRIENDS OF WOMEN'S SUFFRAGE scheme, which the NUWSS was initiating in order to distribute suffrage literature to working women in their own homes. In November 1912 Lady Frances BALFOUR spoke to a very well attended meeting of the CUWSS and a successful sale of literature and badges was held at the door. In the Michaelmas term 1913 Muriel MATTERS addressed the society on the subject of women's suffrage from what the College Letter referred to as "a somewhat idealistic and poetical point of view".

The society's BANNER, designed by Mary LOWNDES and carried in the June 1908 NUWSS procession, is now held by Newnham College. It bears the motto "Better Is Wisdom Than Weapons of War" and is stencilled with the daisies of Newnham and the irises of Girton.

Secretary (1908–9) F. Elinor RENDEL; (1909) Miss M. Leon, Newnham College, Cambridge; (1913) Miss Curwen, Newnham College, Cambridge.

Archival source: Newnham College Archive.

CAMBS (East and West) (NUWSS) Both societies were by 1913 members of the EASTERN COUNTIES FEDERATION OF THE NATIONAL UNION OF WOMEN'S SUFFRAGE SOCIETIES. Secretary (1913) Miss N.M. Gray, 9 Station Road, Cambridge.

CANNING TOWN (branch of the London Society, NUWSS) Secretary (1913) Mrs Taylor, 17 Crosby Road, Forest Gate, London E. Office: 348 Barking Road, London E.

CANNING TOWN (WSPU) A group known as the "Unemployed Women of South-West Ham" was formed on 29 January 1906 and was refounded, as the first branch of the WOMEN'S SOCIAL AND POLITICAL UNION in London, at a meeting on 27 February 1906, eight days after the WSPU had held its first public rally, attended by many of the Canning Town women, in Caxton Hall. Minnie BALDOCK was elected chairman, and the 27 February meeting was addressed by Mrs PANKHURST and Annie KENNEY. Meetings were held at the ILP Club, 11 Swanscomb Street, Canning Town. By 9 March the branch had 40 members. Subsequent speakers over the next 18 months included Flora DRUMMOND, Dora MONTEFIORE, Irene MILLER, Selina COOPER, Teresa Billington (*see* Teresa BILLINGTON-GREIG) and Marie NAYLOR, but there were also disappointing occasions when such expected speakers as Mrs PETHICK-LAWRENCE failed to arrive. In the early days meetings sometimes began with the Lord's Prayer and closed with a hymn; after Adelaide KNIGHT became involved meetings were more likely to end with the singing of the "Red Flag". Mrs Knight resigned from the branch in April 1907, taking Mrs Montefiore's part in a disagreement with the WSPU Central Committee. From this point, and as Mrs Baldock became increasingly involved in her work as a peripatetic ORGANIZER for the WSPU, it becomes clear that the Canning Town branch was consigned to a backwater. The later entries in the minute book make sad reading in comparison with the enthusiasm of the earlier ones. By December 1907 the minutes record that the members were dissatisfied with the paucity of speakers willing to attend their meetings; it is clear from previous enthusiastic entries how much they had enjoyed hearing talks on Florence Nightingale and on the role of women through the ages. Some splendid teas were recorded, but in the winter months meetings must have been uncomfortable for both members and speaker. Marie Naylor sent the branch half-a-crown in November 1907 to pay for coals for a fire in the club room. The minute book ends with the entry for 3 December 1907, the meeting resolved to write to Mrs Baldock to "know why the Canning Town branch was neglected". It is not clear whether there were any further meetings.

After 1913 Sylvia PANKHURST moved suffrage work into the East End and both before and during the First World War the EAST LONDON FEDERATION OF SUFFRAGETTES had a base in Canning Town, organized, until she fell out with Daisy PARSONS, by Olive BEAMISH.

Secretary (1906) Minnie Baldock, 10 Eclipse Road, London E; (1907) Adelaide Knight, New City Road, Plaistow, London E.

Archival source: Minute book of Canning Town branch of the WSPU, 1906–7, Museum of London.

CANTERBURY (WSPU) Organizer (1910) Miss F.E.M. MACAULAY, "Trevarra", 30 Bouverie Road West, Folkestone, Kent; Secretary (1913) Miss Burch, St Sepulchre's, Canterbury, Kent; organizer, Miss Billing, 6 St George's Place, Canterbury, Kent. In July 1910 an erstwhile independent suffrage society, the Thanet Women's Suffrage Society, dissolved in order that its members might join the Canterbury and Thanet WSPU.

CAPPER, MABEL HENRIETTA (1886–1966) (later Mrs Chisholm) Born in Manchester, she joined the WOMEN'S SOCIAL AND POLITICAL UNION in the early part of 1907 and "gave all her time as a voluntary 'soldier' until 1913". Her mother was a member of the WSPU, as was one of her aunts, who had formerly been a president of a Women's Liberal Association. Her father was honorary secretary of the MANCHESTER BRANCH OF THE MEN'S LEAGUE FOR WOMEN'S SUFFRAGE. Mabel Capper worked at first as an ORGANIZER in Manchester, being succeeded there by Mary GAWTHORPE. She later took part in by-election and protest campaigns throughout the country and in most of the WSPU deputations to the House of Commons. She was first imprisoned, for a month, in October 1908 for having taken part in the attempted "rush" on the House of Commons. At the end of July 1909 she was arrested with Alice PAUL, Lucy BURNS and Emily Wilding DAVISON after taking part in a protest outside a meeting Lloyd George was holding in Limehouse, and was sentenced to three weeks' imprisonment. She was released after hunger-striking for six days. In September 1909 she was arrested with Mary LEIGH, Laura AINSWORTH and Hilda BURKITT in Birmingham after disrupting Asquith's meeting at the Bingley Hall, and this time was force fed for a week. The minutes of the Winson Green Prison Visiting Committee record that she "like Ainsworth takes the food through the tube without force". On her release she made a formal complaint about the use on her of a stomach pump. In all, she was imprisoned six times and forcibly fed. After it was founded in 1909 she was a member of the CHURCH LEAGUE FOR WOMEN'S SUFFRAGE. In August 1912 she was arrested with Mary Leigh in Dublin, tried and acquitted. In October 1912 a play she had written, *The Betrothal of No. 13*, was produced at the Royal Court Theatre.

During the First World War Mabel Capper at first worked as a VAD nurse, but then became involved with the pacificst and socialist movements. She became a journalist and was on the editorial staff of the *Daily Herald* from 1919 until 1922. In 1921 she married Cecil Chisholm.

Address: (1913) 21 Oxford Road, Manchester; (1966) 63 Pevensey Road, St Leonards-on-Sea, Sussex.

Photograph: in *Votes for Women*, 27 August 1909; in Fawcett Library Collection.

Archival source: Suffragette Fellowship Collection, Museum of London; Visiting Committee of HM Prison Winson Green, Birmingham Archives and Local History Library.

CARAVANS AND CARS Political caravanning by women had nineteenth-century precedents. As early as 1892 the Primrose League Ladies' Grand Council Touring Van had undertaken a journey through Bedfordshire and Buckinghamshire, during the course of which its occupants had distributed leaflets and made speeches. In 1896 the Independent Labour Party launched its Clarion Van on the road and in 1898 Dora MONTEFIORE joined it for a tour of the Midlands, a journey that had its repercussions. By the summer of 1908 the women's suffrage societies had begun caravanning for the cause. In August Helen FRASER, who had recently defected from the WOMEN'S SOCIAL AND POLITICAL UNION to become an ORGANIZER with the NATIONAL UNION OF WOMEN'S SUFFRAGE SOCIETIES, travelled from Selkirk to Tynemouth in a caravan. During the same summer members of the Newnham NUWSS society, Ray Costelloe (*see* STRACHEY FAMILY), Elinor RENDEL, Gwen Williams and two others, undertook a caravan tour from Scotland through the Lake District, where they were given hospitality by Catherine MARSHALL and her family, travelling as far south as Oxford. This was probably in a caravan, "Curlew", that belonged to Louisa Lumsden, the founder of St Leonards School at St Andrews. Louisa Lumsden in her autobiography described how she had had the caravan built and that "although comfortable, [it] was not luxuriously fitted up like motor caravans today. It was so light as to be easily drawn by our big grey horse, Jock". Certainly Ray Costelloe's caravan was drawn by a "very large" horse called Jock and the driver was a "silent Scotchman". The Newnham College Club: Newnham College Letter 1908, told that:

> Our first excitement was to explore the van: it looked very elegant and comfortable with its three berths, one of which was also a linen chest, its art nouveau curtains, and its green canvas walls; there were also tables and chairs, a stove, a locker, a china cupboard, a minute bookcase, one or two shelves and a row of hooks. We carried with us also a tent and two camp-beds. Our clothes were stowed away in various boxes and baskets; we unpacked a large hamper of jam, sardines, tinned fruits etc and stored them in a meat safe at the back of the van; the shelves were piled high with patience cards, penknives, string and other useless property.... At Keswick we were welcomed by the local Women's Suffrage Society. Meetings were arranged for us in the Market Place, and on Derwent Island.... In spite of the rain and cold weather, we spoke to large audiences who came and listened, and bought badges and pamphlets, and gave their pennies generously.... In Derby we had four meetings, and at the first one, which was in the market place, over 1000 people came to hear.... From there we went south to Oxford, where we held our last meeting and parted.... The audiences were mostly working men. In the front row children in clogs, generally rather noisy, and behind them the men, two, three or four hundred. Some women came to hear us and sometimes a passing tourist. The police always came.... We always began by saying what we wanted and to what society we belonged. Four of us spoke and the whole meeting lasted about an hour and a quarter. While one answered questions, the others went round collecting money in a hat, distributing pamphlets, selling post-cards and badges, and exchanging remarks. We always had a good collection, and we sold a great number of brooches.

"Curlew" was also used by Helen Fraser for a Scottish tour in the autumn of 1909; photographs of "The Curlew and her Crew" appeared in the *Common Cause*, 14 October, and in 1910 by Frances PARKER and the SCOTTISH UNIVERSITY WOMEN'S SUFFRAGE UNION for a tour in Aberdeenshire and Banffshire. In her autobiography Louisa Lumsden noted that, a strong suffragist, she had been "furious" when Whitekirk was burned; one can speculate as to whether she ever knew that "Curlew" had been under the command of a future church arsonist. In September 1908 Emilie Gardner and

Margaret Robertson toured for the NUWSS through Yorkshire in a caravan of a rather more sophisticated and comfortable appearance than "Curlew".

The WOMEN'S FREEDOM LEAGUE entered with gusto into caravanning for the cause. In May 1908 a specially built WFL caravan, with "Women's Freedom League", "Votes for Women" and "Women's Suffrage" boldly painted on its sides, set forth from Oxshott on its travels; the horse that pulled it was called "Asquith". Lilian HICKS and Muriel MATTERS were in charge for the first three months; in August Mrs DESPARD with, first, Alison NEILANS and then Marguerite SIDLEY, took over until October. Marguerite Sidley, whose delicate health benefited from the open-air life, spent the next three summers touring the country in the WFL caravan, accompanied by Miss Henderson, Annie Roff, or Violet Tillard.

The WSPU seems to have been less keen than the other societies on caravanning. In the summer of 1909 Mrs Howey (*see* Elsie HOWEY) gave the Midlands branch of the WSPU a caravan "decorated gaily in purple, white, and green" to tour through the locality. There is no record of the WSPU's other branches emulating this initiative; it did not prevent Ernest Ibbetson, the illustrator of a delightful comic postcard, adding purple, white and green, rather than the colours of the NUWSS or the WFL, to the depiction of a suffrage caravan being brought to an ignominious halt.

While enjoying the benefits of this healthy open-air form of propaganda, the women's suffrage campaign was not slow to adopt the benefits offered by a more speedy form of twentieth-century transport. In 1905 the NUWSS gave a grant of £30 to the LANCASHIRE AND CHESHIRE WOMEN TEXTILE AND OTHER WORKERS' REPRESENTATION COMMITTEE towards the cost of the purchase of a motor car for the special outdoor campaign. Elizabeth Wolstenholme ELMY was well acquainted with this car, describing how it was used during the celebrations at the Free Trade Hall on the night of 20 October 1905. In early 1906 the Pethick-Lawrences' car, nicknamed "La Suffragette", was used to carry WSPU propaganda placards. In April 1909 the WSPU presented Mrs PETHICK-LAWRENCE on her release from prison with a new car, registration "W.S. 95". It was an Austin, painted and upholstered in the colours, with white wheels and a green body lined with a narrow purple stripe. Mrs Pethick-Lawrence dedicated the car to the general use of the WSPU and it was often used to take Mrs PANKHURST on her country-wide tours, driven by the WSPU chauffeur, at first Muriel Thompson, later succeeded by Vera HOLME. In 1911, very suitably, Mary Dodge, heiress to the automobile fortune and friend of the Countess DE LA WARR, gave a Wolseley to the WSPU. Aileen Preston, the first woman to qualify for the Automobile Association Certificate in Driving, was employed as its chauffeur. By February 1913 it is clear from Home Office files that the police had a WSPU car, registration LF-4587, under surveillance. It was sometimes kept at the Avenue Garage, Princes Road, Holland Park, sometimes at the Church Street Garage, Notting Hill, and was suspected of being used by Norah Smyth and Olive HOCKIN when they set out on their arson attacks.

Photograph: several caravan photographs are held in the Fawcett Library collection.

CARDIFF committee of the NATIONAL SOCIETY FOR WOMEN'S SUFFRAGE Formed in 1873, when its honorary secretary was Miss Jenner, Nenvoe Cottage. This society presumably failed; the Cardiff and District Women's Suffrage Society was refounded in July 1908. Its president was a Conservative, Mrs Henry Lewis of Tongwynlais, and its vice-president was Mrs Millicent Mackenzie, wife of the professor of philosophy at Cardiff University. Ivor Guest, the Cardiff Liberal MP, an anti-suffragist, was the cousin of Mrs Mildred MANSEL, an active member of the WOMEN'S SOCIAL AND POLITICAL UNION. By 1910 Cardiff had a thriving women's suffrage society, affiliated to the NATIONAL UNION OF WOMEN'S SUFFRAGE SOCIETIES, campaigning over much of south-east Wales. The society was sufficiently large for a group in PENARTH to be able to break away from it, with the aim of existing as an independent society; they re-amalgamated in 1913. During 1912–13 the Cardiff and District Women's Suffrage Society was the largest outside London. In that year it raised over £355, organized, or its members addressed, 46 meetings, and by 1914 had 1200 members. By 1913 the society was a member of the SOUTH WALES AND MONMOUTH FEDERATION OF THE NATIONAL UNION OF WOMEN'S SUFFRAGE SOCIETIES. New, larger office premises were opened in Queen Street. Although it had initially been opposed to the Election Fighting Fund policy, the society had by 1913 been won over and cultivated links with the Labour movement. Although the Cardiff society continued in existence during the First World War, it concentrated on war work, such as staging a Patriotic Housekeeping and Child Welfare Exhibition, decorated in red, white and green, in 1915, putting its political activities to one side.

The Cardiff and District Women's Suffrage Society was active again by January 1919, keen to encourarge women to stand as poor law guardians, urban district councillors, and for the education committee. In 1921 the society reconstituted itself as the Cardiff and District Women's Citizenship Association and in 1923 Helen FRASER addressed its members on "The Future of the Women's Movement".

Secretary (1909, 1910) Miss Marietta Jones, 23a Newport Road, Cardiff; (1913) Miss Howell. Office: (1913) 35 Windsor Place, Cardiff; (1914) Queen Street, Cardiff.

Archival source: Minutes of the Cardiff and District Women's Suffrage Society, Glamorgan Record Office.

Bibliography: K. Cook and N. Evans, "'The petty antics of the bell-ringing boisterous band'? The woman's suffrage movement in Wales, 1890–1918", in A.V. John (ed.), *Our Mothers' Land: Chapters in Welsh Women's History 1830–1939*, 1991.

CARDIFF (WFL)   Founded at the end of 1909. Secretary (1913) Mrs Keating Hill, 98 Diana Street, Roath, Cardiff.

CARDIFF (WSPU)   Organizer (1906) Mrs Hill, 98 Diana Street, Roath, Cardiff; (1913) Miss Annie WILLIAMS, 27 Charles Street, Cardiff.

CARLISLE branch of the NATIONAL SOCIETY FOR WOMEN'S SUFFRAGE   Founded in April 1869 after Lydia BECKER gave a lecture in the town. In 1872 the branch affiliated with the new CENTRAL COMMITTEE OF THE NATIONAL SOCIETY FOR WOMEN'S SUFFRAGE. The first secretary was Miss Smith of 8 Finkle St., Carlisle. In 1913 the society was a member of the NORTH-WESTERN FEDERATION OF THE NATIONAL UNION OF WOMEN'S SUFFRAGE SOCIETIES. Secretary (1913) Mrs Campbell, 22 Warwick Square, Carlisle, Cumberland.

CARLISLE, ROSALIND FRANCES HOWARD, COUNTESS OF (1845–1921)   Daughter of Lord and Lady Stanley of Alderley, and sister of Lady AMBERLEY. In 1864 she married George Howard, who became a Liberal Unionist and MP in two parliaments, the second being between 1881 and 1885. Between 1865 and 1884 she had 11 children; her relationship with most of them makes distressing reading. She and her husband led increasingly separate lives as her politics became more radical. By 1899 until 1915 she was president of the WOMEN'S LIBERAL FEDERATION and a strong supporter of women's enfranchisement, although she did not support the wing, led by Laura McLAREN, that wished the "Test Question" (that is whether or not they supported women's suffrage) to be put to Liberal candidates. Lady Carlisle subscribed to the CENTRAL NATIONAL SOCIETY FOR WOMEN'S SUFFRAGE in 1890 and took part in the NATIONAL UNION OF WOMEN'S SUFFRAGE SOCIETIES "Mud March" in 1907. Besides the suffrage campaign, her other main concern was temperance and she was president for many years of the National British Women's Temperance Association. A house reputedly owned by her, "The Elms" at Hampton-on-Thames, was set on fire by Mary RICHARDSON and Rachel Peace in October 1913. In her will, besides bequests to the temperance movement, Lady Carlisle left £20 000 to Girton.

Address: Castle Howard, York and Naworth Castle, Carlisle.

Photograph: in D. Henley, *Rosalind Howard, Countess of Carlisle*, 1958.

Bibliography: D. Henley, *Rosalind Howard, Countess of Carlisle*, 1958.

CARMARTHEN (NUWSS)   Founded on 4 November 1911, when among those elected to serve on its executive committee was Miss Morris of Brynmyrddin, niece of Alice ABADAM. The society distributed suffrage leaflets printed in Welsh. In 1913 the society was a member of the SOUTH WALES AND MONMOUTH FEDERATION OF THE NATIONAL UNION OF WOMEN'S SUFFRAGE SOCIETIES. Secretary (1913) Miss Alice Evans, Greenhill, Carmarthen, Carmarthenshire; treasurer (1913) Miss B.A. Holme.

Archival source: Minutes of the Carmarthen Women's Suffrage Society, The Record Office, County Hall, Carmarthen.

CARMARTHEN (WSPU) Secretary (1913) Nurse Rose, The Infirmary, Carmarthen, Carmarthenshire.

CARNARVON (NUWSS) In 1913 the society was a member of the WEST LANCS, WEST CHESHIRE, AND NORTH WALES FEDERATION OF THE NATIONAL UNION OF WOMEN'S SUFFRAGE SOCIETIES. Secretary (1913) Mrs D.O. Evans, Brynafon, Carnarvon, and Miss Ryle Davies, Cartrefle, Segontium Road, South Carnarvon.

CARNFORTH (NUWSS) In 1913 the society was a member of the NORTH-WESTERN FEDERATION OF THE NATIONAL UNION OF WOMEN'S SUFFRAGE SOCIETIES. Secretary (1913) Miss Edith Willis, Ormonde House, Carnforth, Lancashire.

CARWIN, SARAH (1863–1933) Born in Bolton, went with her family to live in Russia, where her father had business, in 1866. She returned to England in 1873, but when she was 18 went back as a nursery governess to a family in St Petersburg. After four years she returned to England and for a time undertook social work with the West London Mission. She then started a co-operative dressmaking business in order to help seamstresses who were turned away from conventional businesses in the slack season. This was apparently a financial success, but she became dissatisfied and found employment at Great Ormond Street Children's Hospital. After three years' training she began a Babies' Home for illegitimate children and in 1897 joined with a friend in a similar, larger, undertaking. Throughout this period she had taken any opportunity to travel, had accompanied a small child on a journey to Ecuador and had returned several times to Russia. At the turn of the century she was nurse-in-charge of the Invalid Children's Special School founded by Mrs Humphry Ward at the Passmore Edwards Settlement.

Sarah Carwin joined the WOMEN'S SOCIAL AND POLITICAL UNION, which she saw as "a crusade against injustice", and was devoted to Mrs PANKHURST. She was arrested in February 1909 in Old Palace Yard, Westminster, and imprisoned for one month with, among others, Mary THOMPSON, who described her as a "tall, interesting-looking woman". She was again arrested after breaking the windows of a government building during the deputation of 29 June 1909 to the House of Commons. She was taken to Holloway, where she broke every pane in her cell window, was put in a basement cell as a punishment for insubordination, went on hunger strike and was then released. In September she was sent one of the WSPU's "stone-throwers" brooches (*see* JEWELLERY) and a letter from Emmeline Pankhurst which eulogized: "Women have reason to be grateful that you and others have the courage to play the soldier's part in the war we are waging in the political freedom of women". Sarah Carwin was arrested on several other occasions, but always released, until in March 1912 she broke 12 windows in Regent Street during the WSPU window-smashing campaign. She was then sentenced to six months' imprisonment, spent in Winson Green Prison where she went on hunger strike, was forcibly fed until, after four months, the deterioration in her physical condition led to her release.

After this Sarah Carwin took no further active part in the WSPU campaign. She "lived in the country with a devoted friend" until the friend died. She then went to live abroad, living in the south of France and Italy for the last ten years of her life. Her executrix Frances Mabelle Unwin wrote the short biography of her that is contained in the Suffragette Fellowship Collection. Mabelle Unwin had been a childhood friend of Emmeline PETHICK-LAWRENCE and it was her father, Mark Guy Pearse, who had influenced Emmeline to join the Sisterhood of the West London Mission and embark on her career in social work. It is not clear if Sarah Carwin's time at the Mission coincided with that of Emmeline Pethick but they clearly moved in the same circles and it is likely that the expulsion of the Pethick-Lawrences from the WSPU may have influenced Sarah Carwin's own departure at about the same time. Mrs Unwin noted that Sarah Carwin had always been a feminist and had been particularly influenced by the works of Olive Schreiner. Sarah Carwin in her will left her property, which included houses in Letchworth, to her niece, with directions that it was to be passed on after her death to a female relative on her mother's side – feminism in action.

Address: (1913) 11 Tavistock Mansions, London WC; (1933) 3 The Crescent, Sandgate, Kent.

Photograph: in Suffragette Fellowship Collection, Museum of London.
Archival source: Suffragette Fellowship Collection, Museum of London.
Bibliography: M.E and M.D. Thompson, *They Couldn't Stop Us! Experiences of Two (usually Law-abiding) Women in the Years 1909–1913*, 1957.

CASEY, EILEEN (1886–alive 1963) Born in New South Wales, Australia, moving to England with her family when she was nine years old. In 1911 she joined the WOMEN'S SOCIAL AND POLITICAL UNION and gave a donation to the MEN'S POLITICAL UNION. She was sentenced to four months' imprisonment in Holloway in March 1912 having, with Olive WALTON, smashed the windows of Marshall and Snelgrove's shop in Oxford Street. She joined in the hunger strike and was forcibly fed. In 1913 Kitty MARION and Clara (Betty) Giveen were staying with the Casey family at Kew when they set fire to Hurst Park stadium. Police had been detailed to watch the house, presumably on account of the Caseys' suffragette connections, and Kitty Marion and Betty Giveen were arrested on their return from committing arson. At the ensuing trial great astonishment was expressed that the Caseys had been prepared to have as guests two women of whom they knew nothing, except that they were suffragettes. Eileen Casey was arrested, as "Eleanor Cleary", in March 1913 for what she described as "pillar-box work", was sentenced to two months' imprisonment, but soon released when her fine was paid. In October 1913 she was arrested, as "Irene Casey", in Bradford on a similar charge, was sentenced to three months' imprisonment in Leeds prison and went on hunger strike. When released under the "Cat and Mouse" Act she escaped dressed in men's clothes, while her mother impersonated her. She then wandered around England for eight months until she was arrested on a charge of possessing explosives in Nottingham in June 1914, at a time when a visit was about to be made by the King and Queen. From circumstantial evidence the police suspected that she might have been involved in the recent arson of Breadsall church in Derbyshire and might have been planning to set fire to Southwell Cathedral. She was held on remand until 8 July in Holloway, where she went on hunger strike and was forcibly fed. When, immediately after her arrest, she had been on hunger strike in Nottingham prison the medical officer there had advised that, because of her frail physical condition, she should not be forcibly fed. This lack of will may explain her transfer to Holloway; the Home Office was adamant that she should not be released under the "Cat and Mouse" Act. After a hearing on 8 July at Nottingham, at which she was committed for trial, she was transferred to Winson Green Prison, Birmingham, where she continued with a hunger-and-thirst strike. On 28 July she was sentenced to 15 months' imprisonment, to be released soon after under the general amnesty granted to suffragette prisoners at the outbreak of war.

During the First World War Eileen Casey worked as a landgirl and then trained as a gardener at Kew Gardens. In 1923 she went as a teacher to Japan, where she stayed until 1940. During the Second World War she was a translator for the Board of Censors in Australia. *Calling All Women*, 1968, revealed that she had a "working knowledge of most European languages, as well as Russian, Japanese and Esperanto". She was an active member of the Australian branch of the SUFFRAGETTE FELLOWSHIP and, when living in Melbourne in 1949, was in touch with Jennie BAINES. In 1951 she returned to England and by 1956 was a member of the committee of *Calling All Women*. She was connected with the theosophist movement.

Address: (1913) 25 West Park Road, Kew, Surrey.
Archival source: Suffragette Fellowship Collection, Museum of London; Home Office Papers, Public Record Office.

CATHOLIC WOMEN'S SUFFRAGE SOCIETY Founded by Miss Gabrielle JEFFERY, who was the society's secretary, and Miss Kendall in June 1911 in order "To band together Catholics of both sexes in order to secure for women the Parliamentary Vote on the same terms as it is, or may be, granted to men". The society's methods were non-party and constitutional, educating those in the Catholic Church in the needs for women's enfranchisement. Immediately after the society was founded it took part, as a society, in the June 1911 Coronation procession. Branches were established in Liverpool, Brighton and West Sussex, and Hastings and East Sussex. In 1912 the society affiliated to the FEDERATED COUNCIL OF SUFFRAGE SOCIETIES; it later became the St Joan's Social and Political Alliance. On 13 March 1918 the society participated in the NATIONAL UNION OF WOMEN'S SUFFRAGE SOCIETIES victory celebration held in the Queen's Hall. By 1923 the society had five branches, was affiliated to the INTERNATIONAL WOMAN SUFFRAGE ALLIANCE, and its secretary was Florence BARRY. Among the society's publications were pamphlets by Leonora de Alberti, *Woman Suffrage and Pious Opponents*, 1913, and Elizabeth Christich, *A Word on Women's Suffrage*, 1913.

In 1912 the society was presented with two BANNERS. One was designed, worked, and presented by Beatrice Gadsby, the other was designed by Edith CRAIG, represented Joan of Arc, and was given by Christopher ST JOHN. One of the society's banners, although it is not clear if it is one of these, is held in the Fawcett Library Collection.

Honorary secretary (1912) Beatrice Gadsby; (1913) Florence Barry; honorary treasurer (1912) Monica WHATELY.

Address: (1912) 51 Blandford Street, Baker Street, London W; (1913, 1923) 55 Berners Street, London W.

Archival source: Catholic Women's Suffrage Society, 1st Report, 1912; 2nd Report 1913, Fawcett Library.

CENTRAL AND EAST OF ENGLAND SOCIETY FOR WOMEN'S SUFFRAGE From 1897 this was the new name of the erstwhile CENTRAL COMMITTEE OF THE NATIONAL SOCIETY FOR WOMEN'S SUFFRAGE, reorganized to raise awareness of the cause for women's enfranchisement in the middle and eastern counties of England. It was affiliated to the NATIONAL UNION OF WOMEN'S SUFFRAGE SOCIETIES. By 1900 it had a fund "For Enrolling Local Associates", by which scheme it hoped to increase the spread of its membership through all the constituencies in its area. "Associates" did not pay a subscription and the society, therefore, was able to draw the attention of poorer women to its work. In 1900 this society merged with the CENTRAL AND WESTERN SOCIETY FOR WOMEN'S SUFFRAGE to form the CENTRAL SOCIETY FOR WOMEN'S SUFFRAGE.

President (1897–1900) Lady Frances BALFOUR; honorary treasurer (1897–1900) Mrs Bertha STERLING; honorary secretaries (1897–1900) Mrs Millicent FAWCETT and Helen BLACKBURN; secretary (1897–1900) Edith PALLISER; assistant secretary (1897–1900) Miss Torrance.

Address: (1897) 10 Great College Street, Westminster, London SW; (1898–1900) 20 Great College Street, Westminster, London SW; (October 1900) 28 Millbank Street, Westminster, London SW.

Archival source: Annual reports of the Central and East of England Society for Women's Suffrage 1898, 1899, Fawcett Library.

CENTRAL AND WESTERN SOCIETY Based on the former CENTRAL NATIONAL SOCIETY FOR WOMEN'S SUFFRAGE. It was formed in 1897 to increase membership of suffrage societies from Dorset to Wales and was affiliated to the NATIONAL UNION OF WOMEN'S SUFFRAGE SOCIETIES. In 1900 it merged with the CENTRAL AND EASTERN SOCIETY FOR WOMEN'S SUFFRAGE to become the CENTRAL SOCIETY FOR WOMEN'S SUFFRAGE.

Treasurer (1900) Mrs Russell Cooke (see Maye DILKE); secretary (1900) Miss Delia Wilkin.

Address: (1897) 39 Victoria Street, London SW.

Archival source: Annual reports of the Central and Western Society for Women's Suffrage, 1898–1900, Fawcett Library.

CENTRAL COMMITTEE OF THE NATIONAL SOCIETY FOR WOMEN'S SUFFRAGE Formed after Jacob BRIGHT, who was at that time promoting the Women's Disabilities Bill, expressed the view at the annual general meeting of the MANCHESTER NATIONAL SOCIETY FOR WOMEN'S SUFFRAGE in November 1871 that greater pressure could be made among MPs if there was a standing central committee in London representing all the suffrage societies. The Central Committee of the National Society for Women's Suffrage was not to be synonymous with the existing LONDON NATIONAL SOCIETY. Indeed some members of the latter society took strong objection to the Central Committee; it was seen to contain too large a proportion of members from provincial committees, many of whom (for example Jacob and Ursula Bright, and Lydia BECKER) were also working for the repeal of the Contagious Diseases Acts. J.S. MILL was adamant that the CDA campaign should not be associated with the suffrage campaign. The matter had been simmering since early 1871 but by the end of the year it was decided that the two societies should co-exist in London. In 1871 Mrs Frederick Pennington (*see* PENNINGTON FAMILY), Professor Sheldon AMOS and Mr Charles Hopwood acted as honorary secretaries *pro tem*. The Central Committee of the National Society for Women's Suffrage held its first meeting on 17 January 1872. The first executive committee consisted of: Prof. Sheldon Amos, Mrs Sarah Amos, Mr and Mrs Arthur Arnold, Mr Ashurst, Mr Edwin Arnold, Miss Caroline Biggs, Mrs Jacob Bright, Mr Percy Bunting, Mrs Chesson, Miss Courtenay, Miss Frances Power Cobbe, Miss Agnes Garrett, Miss Rhoda Garrett, Miss Katherine Hill, Mr Frederic Hill, Mr James Heywood, Mr Henry Hoare, Mrs Priscilla Bright McLaren, Mr and Mrs William Malleson, Mrs Frederick Pennington, Mr Edwin Pears, Mrs Agnes Pochin, Mr Peter Rylands, Dr Humphrey Sandwith, Mrs Caroline Stansfeld, Mrs Emilie Venturi and Miss Williams. Mrs Fawcett had remained with London National, but became exasperated and in 1874 joined the Central Committee.

In 1874 the Central Committee instituted a "Shilling League for Women's Suffrage" whereby, by subscribing a shilling yearly, supporters would be entitled to free admission to all meetings. Otherwise a "subscription of any amount constitutes membership of the society". The society numbered among its members Florence Nightingale and Harriet Martineau.

In 1874 the Central Committee accepted, reluctantly, the alteration by W. Forsyth (the Conservative MP for Marylebone who had taken over the handling of the suffrage question in the House of Commons, Jacob Bright having lost his seat in the general election) of the wording of the bill to remove the electoral disabilities of women, to explicitly exclude married women. Some members left the Central Committee in protest. In 1877 the two London societies (the Central Committee and the London National Society for Women's Suffrage) joined together as the Central Committee of the National Society for Women's Suffrage and Lydia Becker, although still based in Manchester, became the Central Committee's parliamentary agent.

In a letter dated 17 February 1881 Laura McLaren wrote to Lydia Becker that "we feel that the position of the Central Committee is now satisfactory. It was established (if I understand rightly) to be a means by which all local committees could concert their plans and harmonize their policy. Instead of this it has become a local committee only, for London and the south-east district. While *you* remain in Manchester it can never have proper authority to manage the political business of the movement as it should be qualified to do by its situation in London and its representative character." Lydia Becker accepted the position of secretary to the Central Committee.

In 1885 the executive committee of the Central Committee of the National Society for Women's Suffrage comprised: Mrs Ashford (Birmingham), Miss Lydia Becker (Manchester), Alfred W. Bennett, Miss Caroline Ashurst Biggs, Miss Helen Blackburn, Miss Jessie Boucherett, Hon Emmeline Canning, Miss Frances Power Cobbe, Miss Jane Cobden (*see* Jane Cobden Unwin), Miss Courtenay, Leonard Courtney, MP (who was then in charge of the women's cause in the House of Commons), Mrs Cowen (Nottingham), Miss Mabel Sharman Crawford, Mrs Ashton Dilke, Mrs Maurice Drummond (Hampstead), Mrs Millicent G. Fawcett, Miss Agnes Garrett, Rev C. Green (Birmingham), Mrs Ashworth Hallett (Bristol), Viscountess Harberton, Thomas Hare, Mrs Ann Maria Haslam (Dublin), Frederick Hill, Mrs John Holland, Mrs Frank Morrison, C.H. Hopwood, MP, Mrs John Hullah, Coleridge Kennard, MP, Mrs Margaret Bright Lucas, Mrs E.M. Lynch, Robert Main, Mrs Laura McLaren, Mrs Eva McLaren (Bradford), Mrs Priscilla Bright McLaren (Edinburgh), Henrietta Muller, Frederick Pennington, MP, Mrs F. Pennington, Miss Reeves, Mrs Saville, Miss Lillie Stacpole, Rev S.A. Steinthal (Manchester), J.S. Symon, Miss Helen Taylor, Sir Richard Temple, J.P. Thomasson, MP, Mrs Katherine Thomasson (Bolton), Miss Isabella Tod (Belfast), Miss Williams and William Woodall, MP.

In 1888 the Central Committee split into two factions over the issue of political affiliation. Mrs Fawcett, Lydia Becker and their adherents did not wish the new women's societies associated with the two political parties to affiliate, in order to keep the suffrage movement above party politics. The gloss was that this group, labelled by the *Women's Penny Paper* as Liberal Unionists, tended to favour the Conservatives, whose Primrose Leagues were forbidden by their constitutions to affiliate with other organizations, and they did not wish to see the Central Committee swamped by members of the Women's Liberal Associations. The Central

Committee remained committed to a formulation of the franchise that expressly excluded married women. This group retained the name Central Committee of the National Society for Women's Suffrage; the breakaway group became the CENTRAL NATIONAL SOCIETY FOR WOMEN'S SUFFRAGE. Confusingly, although retaining the name, the Central Committee was the society that moved to new premises. The post-1888 Central Committee was known to contemporaries as the "Great College Street Society"; its address came to embody its philosophy. The Provisional Committee of the reconstructed Central Committee in 1888 included: Col Cotton MP, Lady Harberton, Lady GOLDSMID, Miss Tod (Belfast), Caroline Biggs, Miss Courtenay, Miss Becker, Miss Agnes Garrett, The Misses Davenport HILL, Miss Reeves, Mr T.W. Russell, MP, Mrs Fawcett, Mr and Mrs Ashworth Hallett, Mrs Haslam (Dublin), Jessie Boucherett, Mrs Ashford (Birmingham), Miss Blackburn, Mr Frederic Hill, Miss MORDAN and Mr Thomas Hare. Mrs Fawcett was appointed acting honorary secretary and honorary treasurer, with Helen Blackburn as permanent (paid) secretary. By 1896 the executive committee included Clara Mordan, Mrs STERLING, Miss Holland, Miss Gray Allen, Helen Blackburn, Mrs Spring Rice, Emily DAVIES, Lilias Ashworth Hallett, Miss Blackham, Miss Vernon, Lady Frances BALFOUR, Hon. Mrs Alfred Lyttleton, Mrs Arthur Francis, Isabella FORD and Mrs E. Mylne. By 1896 the Central Committee was undertaking many joint projects, both social (for example a *conversazione* on 18 May 1896) and political (for example the SPECIAL APPEAL COMMITTEE), with the Central National Society. In October 1896, after a conference of all the suffrage societies held in Birmingham at which it was agreed that the country should be divided into areas between each of the main societies, the Central Committee agreed to concentrate on the central and eastern counties of England, changing its name in September 1897 to reflect this, to the CENTRAL AND EAST OF ENGLAND SOCIETY FOR WOMEN'S SUFFRAGE. Honorary secretaries: (1872–August 1873) Caroline Ashurst Biggs and Agnes Garrett; (1888) Millicent Fawcett; (1896) re-elected, joint honorary secretaries Millicent Fawcett and Helen Blackburn.
Secretary (1873–4) Emma Smith (*see* Emma PATERSON); (1874) Mary Dowling (who died suddenly); (1874–early 1877) Helen Blackburn; (1877–c. April 1881) Kate Thornbury; (1881–4) Lydia Becker; (1884–end 1888) Florence BALGARNIE; (1888–95) Helen Blackburn; (1895–7) Edith PALLISER (at a salary in 1896 of £110 per annum).
Parliamentary secretary (1884–8) Lydia Becker.
Assistant secretary (1885–8, 1892–7) Miss Torrance; Organizing agent (1885) Miss Moore; Treasurer (1885) Mrs Laura McLaren. Miss Torrance joined the Central National Society when the central society split at the end of 1888, but rejoined the Central Committee as the assistant secretary in 1892.

Address: (January 1872) 17 Hyde Park Terrace, London W (address of Mr and Mrs Frederick Pennington); (June 1872–4) 9 Berners Street (which also housed the Berners Club, *see under* CLUBS) London W; (1874) 294 Regent Street (Langham Place), London W; (1875) 64 Berners Street, London W (Regent Street having proved too expensive); (1885–end 1888) 29 Parliament Street, Westminster, London SW; (1889–97) 10 Great College Street, Westminster, London SW.

Archival source: Annual reports of the Central Committee of the National Society for Women's Suffrage, 1872–88, 1889–97, Fawcett Library; Minute Book of the Central Committee of the National Society for Women's Suffrage, 1896–8, Camellia PLC.

Bibliography: *Englishwoman's Review*, April 1872; *The Work of the Central Committee*, published by the National Society for Women's Suffrage (Great College St.), 1893; B. Caine, *Feminism, Suffrage and the 19th-century Englishwomen's Movement*, Women's Studies International Forum 5, 1982.

CENTRAL NATIONAL SOCIETY FOR WOMEN'S SUFFRAGE The name given to the rump of the CENTRAL COMMITTEE OF THE NATIONAL SOCIETY FOR WOMEN'S SUFFRAGE after the Mrs FAWCETT-led faction had broken away in 1888. This latter group, confusingly, retained the name "The Central Committee", while the Central National Society retained the premises. The Central National was known to *aficionados* as "The Parliament Street Society", but, beware, it moved to Victoria Street in 1896. The Central National's 1889 annual report explained, "In the early days of the struggle a small self-centred body might direct the movement for the enfranchisement of women; political women were few and far between and the Women's Suffrage Committee was the rallying ground for these scattered units; now women are banded together in political and social organizations of all shades of opinion. The individual having been largely merged in the organization, it is by the co-operation of organizations as well as of individuals that the Suffrage movement will be advanced." The Central National's position was that it was prepared to accept affiliation from other organizations, whose aim was not primarily to obtain women's enfranchisement, but whose policy supported it. It affiliated many Women's Liberal Associations in the provinces, placing its faith in the belief that women's enfranchisement would be granted by a Liberal government. The Central National Society was less committed than the Central Committee to excluding married women from any franchise bill. However, because it would not expressly include them, it lost its ultra-radical wing to the WOMEN'S FRANCHISE LEAGUE in 1889. Its income remained at a steady £1000 per year. The Central National Society was dominated by such radical liberals as the McLaren family, in all its ramifications (although Walter and Eva McLAREN were members of the Central Committee as well as the Central National), Jane Cobden (*see* Jane Cobden UNWIN), Anna Maria PRIESTMAN, Laura Ormiston CHANT, Mr Woodall, Mrs Mary BATESON, Mr and Mrs J.P. THOMASSON, Mrs Sheldon AMOS, Mrs PENNINGTON and Mrs Ashton DILKE. In 1894 the executive committee included: Mrs Bateson, Laura Ormiston Chant, Mrs Russell Cooke (the erstwhile Mrs Ashton DILKE), Priscilla Bright McLAREN, Laura McLAREN, Eva McLaren, Dr Kate Mitchell, Mrs Morgan-BROWNE, Mrs M.H. Muller (mother of Henrietta MULLER), Anna Maria Priestman, Mrs D.A. Thomas (*see* Lady RHONDDA), Jane Cobden Unwin and William Woodall.

In 1895–6 the Central National worked with the Central Committee on the SPECIAL APPEAL COMMITTEE and on a joint sub-committee to lobby for support for Mr Faithfull Begg's women's suffrage bill. This co-operation paved the way for the formation of the NATIONAL UNION OF WOMEN'S SUFFRAGE SOCIETIES in 1897. Between 1888 and 1896 the Central National was most active in the west country. At the conference held with the Central Committee in Birmingham in October 1896 this fact was recognized; the Central National's territory was designated henceforward to comprise Wales, Stafford, Shropshire, Worcester, Monmouth, Oxfordshire, Berkshire, Wiltshire, Hampshire and Dorset. In 1897 the society changed its name to the CENTRAL AND WESTERN SOCIETY FOR WOMEN'S SUFFRAGE.

Secretary (1888–90) Florence BALGARNIE; (February 1891–4, when she resigned on her marriage) Cicely Philipps, daughter of the Rev. Sir James Philipps, Bart, Vicar of Warminster, Wilts; (1894–7) Miss Gertrude Stewart (who had in 1893 attended the conference organized by the WOMEN'S EMANCIPATION UNION); (1897) Mrs Charles Baxter.

Assistant secretary (1889–92, when she resigned to accept a similar post with the Central Committee of the National Society for Women's Suffrage) Miss Torrance; (1893) Edith Clinton.

Organizing agent (1890–92) Caroline Fothergill; (1896) Miss Cameron.

Address: (1888–95) 29 Parliament Street, London SW. This was the original office of the Central Committee of the National Society for Women's Suffrage and the Central National took advantage of the change to undertake some interior decorating. The *Women's Penny Paper* reported in June 1889 of 29 Parliament Street that "The walls have been tinted a delicate blue, the floors and even the staircase handsomely carpeted, and the whole now forms a cheerful and artistic interior". (January–April 1896) 47 Victoria Street, London SW; (1896) 39 Victoria Street, London SW.

Archival source: Annual reports of the Central National Society for Women's Suffrage 1889–1897, Fawcett Library; Minutes of the Central National Committee, 1896–April 1897 (miscatalogued as minutes of the Women's Franchise League), in The Papers of Sylvia Pankhurst, Internationaal Instituut voor Sociale Geschiedenis, Amsterdam.

Bibliography: *Women's Penny Paper*, 15 December 1888, gives a report of the Special General Meeting at which the reasons for wishing to change the rules of the Central Committee of the National Society for Women's Suffrage, which led to the forming of the Central National Society, were discussed.

CENTRAL SOCIETY FOR WOMEN'S SUFFRAGE

Formed in 1900 by the amalgamation of the CENTRAL AND WESTERN SOCIETY FOR WOMEN'S SUFFRAGE and the CENTRAL AND EAST OF ENGLAND SOCIETY FOR WOMEN'S SUFFRAGE. The Central and Western no longer attached importance to the affiliation of societies which had objects other than obtaining the parliamentary suffrage for women. In 1907 the Central Society became the LONDON SOCIETY FOR WOMEN'S SUFFRAGE.

President: Lady Frances BALFOUR; chairman: Mrs Millicent FAWCETT; treasurer: Mrs Bertha STERLING; secretary: Edith PALLISER.; assistant secretary: Delia Wilkin.
Address: (1900–1903) 28 Millbank Street, Westminster, London SW; (1903–7) 25 Victoria Street, Westminster, London SW.
Archival source: Annual reports of the Central Society, 1901–6, Fawcett Library.

CHANT, LAURA ORMISTON, MRS (1848–1923) née Dibdin A Congregationalist, born in Chepstow, married in 1876 (her husband, a doctor, died in 1913), had one son and three daughters, one of whom in 1907–8 gave lectures for the Women's Industrial Council. Laura Dibdin was educated at home, became an Associate of Arts, Apothecaries' Hall, and before her marriage taught in schools, nursed in hospitals, including the London Hospital, where she was known as "Sister Sophia", and was the assistant manager of a private lunatic asylum. With Caroline Ashurst BIGGS and Eva MULLER (*see* Eva McLAREN), she was one of the founders in 1881 of the SOCIETY FOR PROMOTING THE RETURN OF WOMEN AS POOR LAW GUARDIANS. In 1884, with her husband, she was a member of the Vigilance Association for the Defence of Personal Rights. She was a member of the general committee of the CENTRAL COMMITTEE OF THE NATIONAL SOCIETY FOR WOMEN'S SUFFRAGE in 1883. In March 1888 she went as a delegate to the first International Council of Women held in Washington. She was a delegate from the EDINBURGH NATIONAL SOCIETY FOR WOMEN'S SUFFRAGE to the meeting held in November 1888 at which the CENTRAL COMMITTEE OF THE NATIONAL SOCIETY split. A Liberal (she was a member of the executive committee of the WOMEN'S LIBERAL FEDERATION) she joined the CENTRAL NATIONAL SOCIETY and from 1889 to 1896 was a member of its executive committee. In 1893, with Jane Cobden UNWIN and Mrs Fenwick MILLER, she attended the World's Congress of Representative Women in Chicago, as a representative of the Central National Society, of the British section of the World's Christian Temperance Union and of the Woman's Anti-Opium Urgency Committee. She reported to the World's Congress on the activities of the Central National Society, on the Anti-Opium Committee, and took part in a discussion on "The Ethics of Dress". In 1906 she was a vice-president of the CENTRAL SOCIETY FOR WOMEN'S SUFFRAGE.

Mrs Ormiston Chant was a vigorous social purist. Although she had been a member of the Ladies' National Association for the Repeal of the Contagious Diseases Act, she was editor in the late 1880s of the *Vigilance Record*, the journal of the National Vigilance Association and was renowned for her supervision of music-hall morals. Among her writings are: "In Memoriam of Henry Fawcett", a poem published in *Verona and Other Poems*, 1887; *Words to Christian Women on Religion and Politics*, a pamphlet published in 1891; and "Woman as an Athlete: A reply to Dr Arabella Kenealy", in *Nineteenth Century*, 1899.
Address: (1903) 49 Gower Street, London WC; (1913) 2 Sutton Place, Hackney, London NE; (1916) Wenlock Barn, Prince of Wales Road, Carshalton, Surrey; (1920) The Homestead, Pinvin, Pershore, Worcestershire.
Portrait: in *Punch* cartoon, 27 October 1894.
Bibliography: L. Bland, *Banishing the Beast: English Feminism and Sexual Morality, 1885–1914*, 1995.

CHAPMAN, ADELINE MARY, MRS (1847–1931) Married in 1900, as her second husband, Cecil Chapman, Metropolitan police magistrate, also a supporter of women's suffrage, who was based at Tower Bridge Police Court. From 1901 she was a member of the CENTRAL SOCIETY FOR WOMEN'S SUFFRAGE. Mildred MANSEL, her daughter from her first marriage, became WOMEN'S SOCIAL AND POLITICAL UNION organizer in Bath. The Rev. Hugh Chapman of the CHURCH LEAGUE FOR WOMEN'S SUFFRAGE and incumbent at the Savoy Chapel, was a relation. In 1909, horrified by the forcible feeding of suffragette prisoners, Adeline Chapman resigned her membership of the Ladies' Free Trade Committee in order to devote herself to working for non-party suffrage societies. In December 1909 she gave £5 to the WSPU general election fund and in 1910 became president of the newly founded NEW CONSTITUTIONAL SOCIETY FOR WOMEN'S SUFFRAGE. She was a member of the TAX RESISTANCE LEAGUE and in 1913 had her goods distrained in lieu of non-payment of tax. In 1913 Mrs Chapman was a supporter of the NATIONAL POLITICAL LEAGUE and a member of the general purposes committee of the FEDERATED COUNCIL OF SUFFRAGE SOCIETIES. She was later a member of the committee that ran Ruth Cavendish-BENTICK's feminist library (*see* LIBRARIES).

Address: (1912) 24 Buckingham Gate, London SW (which was also the address of the Children's League of Kindness for South London of which she was honorary secretary) and The Cottage, Roehampton, London SW.
Photograph: *Votes for Women*, 6 June 1913.

CHATHAM branch of NATIONAL SOCIETY FOR WOMEN'S SUFFRAGE Was in existence in 1871 and in 1872 associated itself with the new CENTRAL COMMITTEE OF THE NATIONAL SOCIETY FOR WOMEN'S SUFFRAGE. Honorary secretary was Miss Annie Young, Luton Road, Chatham, Kent.

CHELMSFORD (NUWSS) In 1913 the society was a member of the EASTERN COUNTIES FEDERATION OF THE NATIONAL UNION OF WOMEN'S SUFFRAGE SOCIETIES. Secretary (1909, 1913) Miss Richenda Christy, Orchards, Broomfield, Chelmsford, Essex.

CHELSEA (branch of LONDON SOCIETY FOR WOMEN'S SUFFRAGE) Secretary (1909) Mrs Bertram, 38 Palace Mansions, Addison Bridge, London W; (1913) Mrs Cecil Hunt, Mallord House, Church Street, Chelsea, London SW (mother of Violet Hunt).

CHELSEA (WFL) The first branch formed after the split with the WSPU in November 1907. Secretary (1907) Cicely HAMILTON, 28 Glebe Place, Chelsea, London SW.

CHELSEA (WSPU) Secretary (1906) Miss Cicely HAMILTON, 28 Glebe Place, Chelsea; (1913) Miss Florence HAIG; (September 1913) Miss B. Edwards, 308 King's Road, Chelsea, London SW. By 1911 the branch had a SHOP at 308 King's Road where all the local outdoor meetings were organized, *Votes for Women* was sold and distributed, and poster parades were sent out into the neighbourhood. These parades were used to advertise local meetings, which were usually held twice a week, on Friday at 12 noon in Sloane Square and one in the evening at World's End. The branch's writing paper had a small picture of "Chimneys" drawn by Janet Stratton, a Chelsea artist. There was a lending library at the shop, for which Zoe PROCTER and a Miss Keith were responsible. This branch included many writers and artists among its members and, fittingly, ran the Art Stall at the 1909 Prince's Rink Exhibition; many BANNERS and symbolic devices were designed and executed in the shop's basement.

In 1911 Maud JOACHIM and Zoe Procter spent days there preparing and colouring the bannerets which were carried in Coronation procession. The Chelsea branch was also very much involved in the organization and implementation of the window-smashing campaigns of November 1911 and March 1912. During the First World War the Chelsea shop remained open and a certain amount of suffrage propaganda was quietly carried on there. Dorothea ROCK and Zoe Procter were allowed by Florence Haig, until she became too nervous of official sanction and closed the shop, to sell there the toys made by Sylvia PANKHURST's factory.

Chelsea's banner, designed by Hermann Ross for the 21 June 1908 Hyde Park demonstration, shows two burly policemen standing either side of a representation of Holloway, from one of the barred windows of which a woman waves a flag, "Votes for Women". The banner is now held in the collection of the Museum of London.
Bibliography: Z. Procter, *Life and Yesterday*, 1960.

CHELSEA, WESTMINSTER AND ST GEORGE'S branch of the NEW CONSTITUTIONAL SOCIETY FOR WOMEN'S SUFFRAGE Chairman (1913) Lady Muir Mackenzie, 22 Draycott Place, London SW.

CHELTENHAM branch of the NATIONAL SOCIETY FOR WOMEN'S SUFFRAGE Founded in 1871, with Mrs Griffiths of Clan Tavi House, Montpellier Grove, as secretary. The Cheltenham society associated itself with the new CENTRAL COMMITTEE OF THE NATIONAL SOCIETY FOR WOMEN'S SUFFRAGE in 1872. The Cheltenham Society for Women's Suffrage was refounded in 1896 and in 1898 joined the NATIONAL UNION OF WOMEN'S SUFFRAGE SOCIETIES. In 1913 the society was a member of the WEST OF ENGLAND FEDERATION OF THE NATIONAL UNION OF WOMEN'S SUFFRAGE SOCIETIES.
President (1896, 1913) Mrs Frances SWINEY. Secretary (1898) Miss Platt, Toseville, Hewlett Road, Cheltenham; (c. 1902, 1913) Theodora MILLS, Lowmandale, Leckhampton, Cheltenham, Gloucestershire.

CHELTENHAM (WFL) The society's banner is now held in the Fawcett Library Collection. Secretary (1913) Mme Borovikowsky, Mostyn Villas, Hales Road, Cheltenham, Gloucestershire.

CHELTENHAM (WSPU) Secretary (1906) Mrs Florence EARENGEY, BA, 3 Wellington Square, Cheltenham; (1913) Miss E.L. Andrews, 2 Vittoria Walk, Cheltenham, Gloucestershire.

CHEPSTOW (NUWSS) In 1913 the society was a member of the SOUTH WALES AND MONMOUTH FEDERATION OF THE NATIONAL UNION OF WOMEN'S SUFFRAGE SOCIETIES. Secretary (1913) Miss Edith Smith, 28a High St, Chepstow, Monmouthshire.

CHESTER (NUWSS) In 1913 the society was a member of the WEST LANCS, WEST CHESHIRE, AND NORTH WALES FEDERATION OF THE NATIONAL UNION OF WOMEN'S SUFFRAGE SOCIETIES. Secretary (1913) Miss Annie Adams, Shirley House, Liverpool Road, Chester, Cheshire.

CHESTER (WFL) Secretary (1913) Miss Woodall, 13 Abbey Square, Chester, Cheshire.

CHESTER-LE-STREET (NUWSS) In 1913 the society was a member of the NORTH-EASTERN FEDERATION OF THE NATIONAL UNION OF WOMEN'S SUFFRAGE SOCIETIES. Secretary (1913) Miss Isa Faulkner, 14 Hilda Terrace, South Pelaw, Chester-le-Street, Durham, Co Durham.

CHEW, ADA NIELD, MRS (1870–1945) Socialist and suffragist, born, one of 13 children, on a small farm in north Staffordshire. She left school at the age of 11, spent time at home looking after her younger brothers, and between 1887 and 1896 worked in a shop in Nantwich and as a tailoress in a factory in Crewe. In 1894 she had published anonymously in the *Crewe Chronicle* a series of letters describing conditions in her factory. As a result of the publicity and her subsequent resignation, she joined the Independent Labour Party and was elected to the Nantwich Board of Guardians. In 1896 she spent several weeks travelling around the north-east in the Clarion van, holding meetings to publicize the policies of the ILP. She married George Chew, an ILP organizer, in 1897, and her only child, a daughter, was born in 1898. In 1900 Ada Nield Chew was appointed an organizer for the Women's Trade Union League, taking her daughter with her as she travelled around the country.

In December 1904 Ada Nield Chew conducted a correspondence with Christabel PANKHURST in the columns of the *Clarion* about the proposed limited franchise bill. At that stage she favoured adult suffrage but by about 1910 was an ardent supporter of women's suffrage, particularly influenced in her thinking, especially in the need for co-operative households, by the work of Charlotte Perkins Gilman, whom she heard speak in Rochdale. Ada Nield Chew was a vegetarian, entirely opposed to the use of militant methods, and became a member of the NATIONAL UNION OF WOMEN'S SUFFRAGE SOCIETIES. From 1911 to 1914 she was an ORGANIZER for the NUWSS, based in Rossendale. In May 1912, as a member of the FABIAN WOMEN'S GROUP, she offered her services as a paid organizer to its Suffrage Section, although in the event there proved to be insufficient funds to employ her. In the same month the NUWSS revealed its Election Fighting Fund policy and for the next two years Ada Nield Chew, with Selina COOPER and Annot ROBINSON, campaigned for it and the Labour candidates at by-elections. She was a regular contributor to the *Freewoman*, for which paper, with its uncertain finances, she was prepared to write without pay, the *Englishwoman* and the *Common Cause*, lacing vignettes of everyday working-class life with suffrage arguments. During the First World War, a practical pacifist, she was a member of the Manchester branch of the Women's International League for Peace and Freedom and Rochdale Trades Council representative on the Mayor's Central Relief Committee.

Address: (1903) The Greave, Rochdale, Lancashire.
Photograph: in D. Nield Chew, *Ada Nield Chew*, 1982.
Bibliography: J. Liddington and J. Norris, *One Hand Tied Behind Us: The Rise of the Women's Suffrage Movement*, 1978; D. Nield Chew, *Ada Nield Chew: The Life and Writings of a Working Woman*, 1982, which includes republication of many of Ada Nield Chew's letters, sketches, and stories.

CHINA AND SILVER British commemorative pottery has a long and interesting history; the nineteenth century witnessed its flowering. Daniel O'Connell and Catholic Emancipation, the campaign for the abolition of slavery, "Orator" Hunt and Peterloo, Grey, Russell, Brougham and the 1832 Reform Bill, Parnell and Home Rule, and, most popular of all, Cobden, Bright, and the Anti-Corn Law League were among the many political campaigns

Cup and saucer from one of the tea sets commissioned by the WSPU from the Diamond China Co. for use at the Scottish WSPU Exhibition, held in Glasgow in April 1910. The tea sets were afterwards sold. (Author's collection)

that featured on a plethora of jugs, mugs, plates and bowls. That it attracted neither transfer-printed admiration nor satire is a measure of the failure of the nineteenth-century women's suffrage campaign to capture the popular imagination. Although Lydia BECKER was mentioned in popular songs, unlike Amelia Bloomer she did not achieve a degree of attention sufficient for a Staffordshire pottery to render her as a free-standing figure.

No firm produced pottery and porcelain supportive of the women's suffrage campaign as a commercial venture; such pieces were commissioned from within the suffrage movement. The first order was placed, probably in early 1909, with Williamsons of Longton, Staffordshire, by the WOMEN'S SOCIAL AND POLITICAL UNION. The china was to be used in the refreshment room at the May 1909 Prince's Skating Rink Exhibition and was afterwards sold, made up in sets of 22 pieces. The white china has strikingly clean, straight lines and is rimmed in dark green with green handles. Each piece carries a single motif, the "angel of freedom" blowing her trumpet and flying the banner of "Freedom", designed by Sylvia PANKHURST specifically for the exhibition. In the background are the initials "WSPU" set against dark prison bars, surrounded by the thistle, shamrock, and rose, and dangling chains. This china was still being advertised for sale in 1911.

A Scottish version of the tea set was commissioned from the Diamond China Co. for use at the refreshment stall at the Scottish WSPU Exhibition, held in Glasgow at the end of April 1910. The "angel of freedom" is allied with the Scottish thistle, handpainted, in purple and green, inside transfer outlines, on white china. *Votes for Women*, 13 May 1910 noted that some of the china was still for sale: "a breakfast set for two, 11s; small tea set, 15s; whole tea set, £1; or pieces may be had singly". The only other china that can be specifically attributed to the WSPU was a bulb bowl rendered in "pretty leadless glaze in the colours", on sale in the WSPU shop in Lincoln's Inn House and advertised in the *Suffragette*, 12 September 1913.

Although Staffordshire had produced no figure of Lydia Becker, Edith DOWNING produced a small quantity of statuettes of Christabel PANKHURST and Annie KENNEY, for sale at the 1909 Prince's Skating Rink WSPU Exhibition. It is not clear if any of these still exist; there is not one in any of the known suffrage collections.

The WOMEN'S FREEDOM LEAGUE also produced a tea service, in white china with, as its sole decoration, the WFL shield, containing within it "Votes for Women" and "WFL" in gold, white and green, and "Dare to be Free" underneath. The china was likely to have been produced after 1910; pieces of the set bear the mark of the retailer, J. Abrahams, Pembroke House, 133 Oxford Street. Jacob Abrahams, china retailer, only moved from Westbourne Grove to that address in the course of 1910–11.

A variation of this WFL china was produced for use in the Minerva Club (*see under* CLUBS). The white glazed earthenware is decorated with a dark green stripe at the rim and decorated c. 15–45mm from the edge with a depiction of an oval medallion depending from a ribbon bow. The outlined border contains, printed in the same green as the rim stripe, the legend "Women's Freedom League: Minerva Club" and inside at the centre, on a yellow ground, is a depiction of Minerva, in profile, wearing a hat. This motif appears to be handpainted. The china was made by Pountney & Co. of Bristol.

The only other piece of china that can be documented as possibly supportive of the women's suffrage campaign is an enigmatic small dish, handpainted in purple, white and green, with "Vote for

Women" (sic) in its centre. It is marked "Copenhagen Denmark $-\frac{342}{387}$".

There is little documentary evidence about the makers of the modelled pieces that were produced to satirize the twentieth-century militant women's campaign. The images are very similar to those that appear on comic postcards and draw on a tradition of misogynist humour. The following is a list of those known to exist; there may well be others.

A porcelain matcholder in the shape of three white geese, orange beaks wide open, the chorus "We Want our Votes!" inscribed on the green base. The piece carries no mark and may have been made in Germany. Geese also appear as a recurring motif on comic suffrage postcards.

The combination of policemen and suffragettes, a potent source of humour on postcards, was also rendered in clay. In one piece a very tall policeman escorts a rotund little girl, who is waving an "I want a vote" banner. He is in a very blue uniform, she is in gold, with yellow hair. "Votes for Women" is repeated, inscribed on the front base.

Another piece shows a harridan in a green hat and purple dress, waving her umbrella, and trampling on a contorted policeman. She wears a large "Votes for Women" placard around her neck. The design, when registered on 26 August 1909, was laconically described as "Suffragette standing on a prostrate policeman".

As on postcards, the cat image was considered appropriate to associate with the suffragettes. One unattributed piece is modelled in the shape of an uncuddly bluish stoneware cat, mouth open, and is inscribed around its base "Votes for Women".

So effective was the WSPU's introduction of its "colours" that the addition of purple, white and green to a stock piece gave a topical twist to an old saw. One unmarked piece is in the shape of the head of a harridan with staring eyes and an open mouth. She wears in her hat a purple, white and green favour. The top of the hat/head is removable. Around the base is inscribed, "I say / Down with the trousers".

The harridan image is repeated as a match holder. She wears a green dress and sports a big purple bow, a "Votes for Women" sash, and "A Match for Any Man" inscribed around the base. The piece may have been made in Germany.

Doulton was the only well-established firm to make an allusion to the suffrage movement in its range of bibelots. It produced two inkwells modelled by Leslie Harradine, the designs registered between 21 and 24 July 1909. One is in the shape of an angry baby with "Votes for Women" inscribed on its blue/green bib. Its head tips back to reveal the ink. A companion piece is modelled as an angry old woman with folded arms, in blues, with her green apron inscribed "Votes for Women". She is hinged at the waist. In 1978 Doulton produced a sympathetic, graceful "Votes for Women" figure, designed by W.K. Harper. It was withdrawn from production in 1981. In 1997 the firm reissued the "virago" inkwell, remodelled by W.K. Harper as part of a condiment set.

Crested china was a by-product of the increasing ability of the working masses to holiday away from home and achieved, like the postcard, the zenith of its popularity in the years before the First World War. In the 1880s the firm of W.H. Goss pioneered the production of miniature china items, to which were added the coat of arms of the holiday resort in which it was sold, thereby providing returning holidaymakers with an appropriate memento of their visit. This idea, appealing to what was then termed the "Bazaar Trade", was taken up by other firms, several of whom, although not Goss, produced such items, linking the Edwardian suffrage movement with such places as Pwllheli, Eastbourne, Torquay and the Isle of Man. It appears that orders were executed to the order of the local outlet, shop, bazaar, hotel, chemist, restaurant, station bookstall, or local library, which would select its shape and slogan and have the town's coat of arms added. Crested china stalls were a feature of the Edwardian seaside promenade; the one at Brighton was at the entrance to the West Pier. In such holiday towns, while the local WSPU was organizing a poster parade along the promenade or holding a meeting on the sands, holidaymakers, having now been sufficiently educated as to the existence of the campaign, if not converted to the cause, were able to select from the wide range of miniature objects, including busts, buildings, animals, allusions to folklore, sport, ancient artefacts, transport, musical instruments, jugs, lifeboats and haystacks, all produced for this mass market. Some did choose the handbell or candle snuffer that appear to have been the most usual shapes linked to the suffrage cause; they can still occasionally be found on antique stalls or at auction, testament to a political campaign mediated through the holiday souvenir trade.

All the pieces of crested china depict women as two-faced, one side old and ugly, the other demure. The contrast recalls the report in *Votes for Women* of a meeting at Lewisham in 1908, at which a heckler observed that if the suffragettes generally were better looking they would be more likely to get the vote. The suffragette speaker smartly retorted that "If good looks are to be the basis of the franchise many of the gentlemen present would lose their vote, and most decidedly our friend".

The following pieces were known to have been made by the Arcadian China Co. of Stoke on Trent, the largest British producer of crested china, probably between 1910 and 1912.

A two-sided bust, one side a harridan, a blue band round her neck, carrying a vestigial umbrella. "Votes for women" is emblazoned across her hat and on her chest is a rather odd coat of arms. The top bannerette says "Woodnotes Wild". The coat of arms has a bird on a twig and underneath is a horn crossed with a walking stick and below that a tree. The bottom bannerette reads, "Better a Wee bush than nae Bield" and underneath that "Arms for Burns". The other side shows a gentle-faced woman, wearing a delicate pendant, with, across her chest, "This one shall have a Vote". There is a variation of this model, with on one side the sour old woman, minus her umbrella, inscribed at "chest" level "Votes for women". On the reverse is the pretty young girl, inscribed "This one shall have the vote". A smaller version exists with no colouring or inscription. The larger design also exists as a handbell and the smaller as a candle snuffer.

There is another version, as a handbell, with clapper, showing a harridan in a bonnet, with "Votes for Women" and the arms of the City of Exeter. On the other side is her *alter ego*, demure and smiling, and "This one shall have a Vote". The piece is marked with the name of the retailer, "W.A. Gardner, 12 & 13 High St Exeter".

Victoria China made similar pieces. A handbell, one side a harridan in cap with "Votes for Women" underlined and below that, "I can talk/ Ring the bell/ And be forcibly fed as well". The other side has a gentle smiling face with ringlets and across her bust "The lady shall have a vote". Underneath are the arms of Pwllheli. The same firm also produced a handbell inscribed "Votes for Women", the reverse a pretty young girl, inscribed "This one shall have a vote". This comes in two sizes, 72mm and 108mm.

A small two-sided hand bell, harridan on one side in bonnet with the arms of Eastbourne. The figure the other side is merely demure and carries no message. This shape is also found inscribed, "Nature has endowed woman with so much power that the law gives them very little. Dr Johnson".

Carlton China also produced a 100mm handbell inscribed "Votes for Women" and "She shall have votes" (*sic*).

Novelties that made allusion to the women's suffrage campaign were also made from silver. A mantel clock depicts, in relief, a comic suffragette and a policeman. Another piece, variously described as a pepperette or a caster, is in fact, the design registration document reveals, a muffineer. It is in the shape of a little lady in a bonnet (the top unscrews) carrying a sandwich board, one side saying, "We Can Make Things Hot for You" and the other, "Votes for Women". The piece, the design registered between 28 March and 7 April 1908, was made by Saunders & Shepherd Ltd of Fetter Lane, manufacturing gold and silversmiths, and carries a Chester hallmark.

Archival source: Fawcett Library; James Blewitt Collection; Design Registry, Public Record Office.

Bibliography: J. and J. May, *Commemorative Pottery, 1780–1900*, 1972; R. Dennis, *Catalogue of an Exhibition of Doulton Stoneware and Terracotta, 1870–1925*, 1971; S. Andrews, *Crested China: The History of Heraldic Souvenir Ware*, 1980; L. Hallinan, *British Commemoratives: Royalty, Politics, War and Sport*, 1995.

CHISWICK (WSPU) Secretary (1908) C.M.O. Coombes.

CHISWICK AND BEDFORD PARK (branch of LONDON SOCIETY FOR WOMEN'S SUFFRAGE) Secretary (1909, 1913) Miss Iles, 17 Lonsdale Road, Bedford Park, London W.

CHORLEY (NUWSS) In 1913 the society was a member of the WEST LANCS, WEST CHESHIRE, AND NORTH WALES FEDERATION OF THE NATIONAL UNION OF WOMEN'S SUFFRAGE SOCIETIES. Secretary (1913) Miss Annie A. Gauge, 5 Russell Square, Chorley, Lancashire.

CHORLEY WOOD (WSPU) Secretary (1913) Miss Thornbury, Chimes, Chorley Wood, Hertfordshire.

CHORLEY WOOD AND DISTRICT branch of the UNITED SUFFRAGISTS Formed in 1915. Honorary secretary (1915) Agnes Harben (*see* Henry HARBEN), Newland Park, Chalfont St Giles, Buckinghamshire; (from April 1915) Mrs Varcoe, Launceston, The Swillett, Chorley Wood.

CHURCH LEAGUE FOR WOMEN'S SUFFRAGE Founded in 1909 by the Rev. Claude and Mrs Hinscliffe in order to "band together, on a non-party basis, Suffragists of every shade of opinion who are Church people in order to secure for women the vote in Church and State, as it is or may be granted to men". "The methods of the League are Devotional and Educational" (*Suffrage Annual and Women's Who's Who*, 1913). The first Sunday of every month was observed by members of the CLWS as a day on which to make special intercession at Holy Communion for the objects of the League and its members. A committee of the CLWS was preparing draft recommendations for the revision of the Marriage Service in the Book of Common Prayer. By the end of 1913 the CLWS had 103 branches and 5080 members. In February 1914 the League rejected a motion, proposed by its Worcester branch, that it should declare itself opposed to militancy. As a result it lost a number of members, including the Bishop of Worcester. After the First World War it was retitled the League of the Church Militant and enlarged its horizons to include work for the ordination of women.

The CLWS produced a series of pamphlets, for example Ursula Roberts, *The Cause of Purity and Women's Suffrage*; Rev. Maurice Bell, *The Church and Women's Suffrage*; Dr Helen B. HANSON, *From East to West*; A. Maude ROYDEN, *May Mission Speeches*; as well as many leaflets. By 1912 the Church League had for its main BANNER a depiction of St Margaret of Antioch from a design by Oswald Fleuss and worked by the Audrey School of Needlework. The following branches of the League are known to have had banners: Oxford (given by Miss G.F.M. Hopkins), Brighton (Miss Newman), Southport, Bromley, Kensington, Bedford Park, Anerley and Crystal Palace, Birmingham, Hendon and Golders Green, Ilford, Islington, Manchester, Parkstone, Regent's Park, Sheffield, Worthing. The banner of the Hampstead branch of the CLWS designed by Laurence HOUSMAN and worked by the SUFFRAGE ATELIER (perhaps by Clemence HOUSMAN) is now in the Museum of London Collection.
Chairman (1910) Maude Royden; secretary (1910) Rev. Claude Hinscliffe.
Address: (1913) 11 St Mark's Crescent, Regent's Park, NW; (1914, 1917) 6 York Buildings, Adelphi, London W.
Archival source: Church League for Women's Suffrage annual reports 1–4, 1910–13, Fawcett Library.

CHURCH STRETTON (NUWSS) In 1913 the society was a member of the MIDLANDS (EAST) FEDERATION OF THE NATIONAL UNION OF WOMEN'S SUFFRAGE SOCIETIES. Secretary (1913) Miss Jasper Jones, Ashbrook Villa, Church Stretton, Shropshire.

CIRENCESTER branch of the NATIONAL SOCIETY FOR WOMEN'S SUFFRAGE Founded in 1871 and in 1872 associated itself with the new CENTRAL COMMITTEE OF THE NATIONAL SOCIETY FOR WOMEN'S SUFFRAGE. Its first secretary was Rev. Henry Austin, Pembroke Terrace, Cirencester, Gloucestershire. In 1913 the society was a member of the WEST OF ENGLAND FEDERATION OF THE NATIONAL UNION OF WOMEN'S SUFFRAGE SOCIETIES. Secretary (1913) Miss Grace Hadow, Foss Lodge, Cirencester, Gloucestershire.

CIVIL SERVICE WOMAN SUFFRAGE SOCIETY Founded in 1911. By 1913 it had a membership of about 600, consisting of women employed in the various Civil Service departments in London. It was intended that branches should be formed in Edinburgh and Glasgow. Its methods were educational and constitutional. It was not aligned with any other organization. The society's banner, featuring its colours, gold and blue, is now held in the Fawcett Collection.
Address: (1913) Manor Gardens, London N; (1914) 19 Sotheby Road, Highbury, London N; (1917) 56 Squire's Lane, Finchley, London N3.

CLACTON-ON-SEA (WSPU)   Secretary (1913) Miss Lilley, Holland House, Clacton-on-Sea, Essex. Office: 47 Rosemary Road, Clacton-on-Sea, Essex. The shop at that address was opened in 1911 (photograph in *Votes for Women*, 6 October 1911).

CLAPHAM (WFL)   Secretary (1913) Miss Florence Underwood, 1 Robert Street, Adelphi, London WC.

CLAPHAM (WSPU)   Secretary (1913) Mrs Strong, 84 Elspeth Road, Lavender Hill, London SW.

CLAPPERTON, JANE HUME (1832–1914)   Birth control pioneer, author of *Scientific Meliorism and the Evolution of Happiness*, 1885; *What Do Women Want?* c. 1900; in *Shafts*, 1893, on co-operative households; and a novel, *Margaret Dunmore: or A Socialist Home*, 1888, in which co-operative living is put into practice. In her will, dated 1913, she made clear that many copies of both *Scientific Meliorism* and *Margaret Dunmore* were still unsold, in store, which may explain why both titles are virtually unobtainable today. In the introduction to *Scientific Meliorism* she remarked that in her youth she was part of the circle that included Charles Bray and George Eliot, although she did not personally know the latter. She was then presumably living in the West Midlands; from 1840 Bray, a radical thinker and ribbon manufacturer, lived just outside Coventry.

Jane Hume Clapperton joined the EDINBURGH NATIONAL SOCIETY FOR WOMEN'S SUFFRAGE in 1871. She was an associate of the Men and Women's Club in the 1880s and a supporter of the anarchist Legitimation League. She subscribed to the CENTRAL NATIONAL SOCIETY FOR WOMEN'S SUFFRAGE in 1890 and to the WOMEN'S EMANCIPATION UNION in 1894 and 1896, was part of Elizabeth Wolstenholme ELMY's correspondence circle, and was influential on another member, Dora MONTEFIORE. She subscribed to the WOMEN'S SOCIAL AND POLITICAL UNION in 1907, influencing her niece Lettice FLOYD to do likewise. By 1908 she was a member of the WOMEN'S FREEDOM LEAGUE and in December 1909 was a hostess of one of the WFL "At Homes" at the Café Vegetaria in Edinburgh. But she did not entirely reject the WSPU, supplying in May 1909, Edinburgh rock and books for the Edinburgh stall at the WSPU Prince's Skating Rink Exhibition.

Address: (1905) 22 Drummond Place, Edinburgh.
Photograph: in *Portrait Album of Who's Who at the International Congress of Women*, 1899.
Bibliography: interview in the *Women's Penny Paper*, 22 June 1889.

CLARK, ALICE (1874–1934)   Quaker, born in Street, Somerset, daughter of Helen Bright CLARK and William S. Clark, owner of C. & J. Clark's shoe factory. In 1893 she left the Southport school she had attended for one year, took a course in housewifery in Bristol and then went to work in her father's factory. By 1904 she supervised the Machine Room, the Trimming Room, and the Turn Shoe department, and was also in charge of the Home Order office, carrying on correspondence with customers. She was in close touch with her Bristol aunts Anna Maria and Mary PRIESTMAN, and shared the family support of the women's suffrage movement (*see* Appendix). In 1890 Alice had been present at the formation of the Street Women's Liberal Association and was its secretary for 11 years. Like other members of her circle she became severely disillusioned by the lack of will to enfranchise women evinced by the Liberal party and in February 1907, with her mother's cousin Lilias Ashworth HALLETT, took part in the WOMEN'S SOCIAL AND POLITICAL UNION'S deputation from the Women's Parliament in Caxton Hall to the House of Commons. A member of the NATIONAL UNION OF WOMEN'S SUFFRAGE SOCIETIES, she never formally joined the WSPU, although she did subscribe to the WOMEN'S FREEDOM LEAGUE, and in 1907 took the historically legitimated Quaker course of tax resistance. Alice Clark was quite prepared to support passive resistance and civil disobedience, and after the failure of the Conciliation Bill in 1910, although unable through illness to take part herself, was willing to condone the window smashing of government buildings. In 1908 she attended the INTERNATIONAL WOMAN SUFFRAGE ALLIANCE Conference in Amsterdam. Between 1909 and 1912 she received treatment in a sanatorium for tuberculosis. On her return to England in 1912 after convalescing abroad, she moved to London, where she was given a fellowship established by Charlotte Townshend Shaw (the wife of G.B.S.) at the London School of Economics in order to pursue the research that culminated in the publication of *Working Life of Women in the 17th Century*, 1919.

In 1910 Alice Clark had expressed the wish that there was a suffrage society that stood between the WSPU and the NUWSS; apparently the WFL did not answer. By 1912, however, she approved of the way that the NUWSS had remoulded itself to accommodate the Election Fighting Fund policy. In June 1913 she was co-opted onto the NUWSS executive and the EFF committee as assistant to Catherine MARSHALL and, acting as assistant parliamentary secretary, conducted negotiations and consultations with MPs. For a time they lived in the same house in Westminster. In 1912, with her brother, Alice Clark founded and was honorary secretary of the FRIENDS' LEAGUE FOR WOMEN'S SUFFRAGE.

On the outbreak of war in 1914, as a Quaker, Alice Clark could not take part in any war work but did support some of the NUWSS enterprises. In 1915 she agreed with the necessity for NUWSS representation at the international congress of women to be held at the Hague. When the leadership of the NUWSS refused to sanction a NUWSS presence there, Alice Clark resigned from the executive committee. She remained a member of the committee of the Election Fighting Fund, urging the NUWSS to give continued support to the Labour party, until resigning, with Catherine Marshall, Isabella FORD and Margaret ASHTON, in 1916. She served in London on the Friends' Committee for the Relief of War Victims and for a time, from the end of 1916, in France. After the end of the war she completed her historical research and carried on administering the Quaker relief effort from London and in Vienna. She then returned to Street to work at the family factory, one of four people chiefly responsible for the daily administration of the business. Towards the end of her life she left the Society of Friends and joined the Christian Science Church.
Address: (1900) Mill Field, Street, Somerset; (1913) 1 Barton Street, Westminster, London SW.
Photograph: in S.S. Holton, *Suffrage Days*, 1996.
Bibliography: M.C. Gillett, *Alice Clark of C. & J. Clark Ltd, Street, Somerset,* (c. 1935); S.S. Holton, *Suffrage Days: Stories from the Women's Suffrage Movement,* 1996 (which draws on the private Clark archive).

CLARK, HELEN PRIESTMAN BRIGHT, MRS
(1840–1927) A Quaker, born in Rochdale, daughter of John Bright by his first wife Elizabeth Priestman, and, therefore, niece to Priscilla Bright MCLAREN, Margaret Bright LUCAS, Jacob and Ursula BRIGHT, Margaret TANNER, Anna Maria and Mary PRIESTMAN, and cousin to Anne ASHWORTH, Lilias Ashworth HALLETT and Katherine THOMASSON (*see* Appendix). Helen Bright's mother died very soon after her birth and she was cared for by Priscilla Bright, to whom she remained particularly close. She was educated at the Quaker school in Southport run by Hannah Wallis, at which, under Hannah's mother, Priscilla Bright herself had been a pupil. In the early 1860s Priscilla Bright McLaren intimated in a family letter that her stepson John McLaren might be taking a more than cousinly interest in Helen Bright; perhaps this was just a wish to make Helen even more of a daughter to her. Helen Bright was very friendly with her step-cousin, Agnes McLAREN, writing to her from One Ash, Rochdale in May 1861, "We have some of John Stuart Mill's Essays in the house – one on the enfranchisement of women [is] very good. Mill I am happy to say hopes that another century will not pass without women being admitted to the franchise. I'm afraid he is too sanguine. But how absurd to talk of representation and taxation going hand in hand, and all the while excluding wholly the one half of the population from the franchise. I will send you Papa's autograph with pleasure." As Helen Bright she signed the 1866 suffrage petition, as did her former teacher Hannah Wallis, and later that year married William S. Clark, a Quaker and the owner of the C. & J. Clark shoe factory in Street, Somerset. His sister and niece had also signed the 1866 petition. Helen Bright Clark subscribed to the ENFRANCHISEMENT OF WOMEN COMMITTEE in 1866–7 and was a member of the MANCHESTER NATIONAL SOCIETY FOR WOMEN'S SUFFRAGE in 1870. In 1872 she spoke at a public meeting in Taunton organized by the BRISTOL AND WEST OF ENGLAND NATIONAL SOCIETY FOR WOMEN'S SUFFRAGE, of which she was also a member. She said then that "they were told that though it was perfectly right for a woman to dance at a public ball, the moment she ventured upon a public platform to advocate public peace, morality and justice, she was stepping out of her sphere". In 1879 at Bristol she gave a suffrage speech that was then published as a four-page pamphlet and in 1881 she spoke at the Bradford Demonstration of Women. As

the delegate of one of the few Liberal Associations that then included women among its members, she attended in October 1883 the major Reform demonstration at Leeds, over which her father, who was opposed to women's enfranchisement, presided. She spoke in favour of the resolution to extend the parliamentary franchise to women on the same terms as it might be extended to men, which was presented by Rev. CROSSKEY and Walter MCLAREN. Susan B. Anthony was in the audience and, through Elizabeth Cady Stanton's *Reminiscences*, has left us the impression that Mrs Bright Clark's speech made on "that immense gathering of sixteen hundred delegates [which was] hushed into profound silence. For a daughter to speak thus . . . in opposition to her loved and honored father . . . was an act of heroism and fidelity to her own highest conviction". Only 30 of the delegates voted against the resolution. In May 1884 Helen Bright Clark supported the Lydia BECKER wing of the suffrage movement rather than the more radical section favoured by Priscilla Bright McLaren and Ursula Bright, and backed the Woodall couverture clause added to the Liberal Reform bill.

Helen Bright Clark was, according to Elizabeth Wolstenholme ELMY, responsible for persuading the governing body of the Society of Friends to sit together. Previous to her intervention men and women had held their discussions separately, the women then reporting to the men. A liberal in all senses, Helen Bright Clark had in the 1860s been active in the Freedman's Aid Society, in the mid-1880s was a founder member of the Society for the Futherance of Human Brotherhood, and in 1906, with Jane Cobden UNWIN and Helena DOWSON, was an active member of the Aborigines Protection Society. In 1914 she signed the Open Christmas letter to the Women of Germany and Austria and in 1915 supported the section of the NATIONAL UNION OF WOMEN'S SUFFRAGE SOCIETIES that favoured that society being represented at the international congress of women at the Hague.

Of her daughters Alice CLARK, Hilda Clark, Esther Bright CLOTHIER and Margaret Clark Gillett (1878–1962) were all active suffragists or sympathizers and her son Roger Clark was co-founder of the FRIENDS' LEAGUE FOR WOMEN'S SUFFRAGE. Her daughter-in-law Sarah Bancroft Clark (b. 1877–still alive 1963?), an American Quaker who had been a student at Newnham in the same year as Margaret Clark, subscribed to the WOMEN'S SOCIAL AND POLITICAL UNION in 1911, marched in the Coronation Procession, and by 1913 was a tax resister and honorary treasurer of the NUWSS WEST OF ENGLAND FEDERATION.

Address: (1900) Mill Field, Street, Somerset.
Photograph: carte de visite in Josephine Butler Collection, Fawcett Library.
Archival source: Priscilla Bright McLaren Papers, National Library of Scotland.
Bibliography: E.C. Stanton, *Eighty Years and More: Reminiscences of Elizabeth Cady Stanton*, 1898; H.B. Clark, "Speech at a meeting held in support of the bill to remove the electoral disabilities of women, at the Victoria Rooms, Clifton, Bristol, 9 March 1876" and "Speech at a woman's suffrage congress", Bristol 23 January 1879 reprinted in J. Lewis (ed.), *Before the Vote Was Won: Arguments For and Against Women's Suffrage 1864–1896*, 1987; S.S. Holton, *Suffrage Days: Stories from the Women's Suffrage Movement*, 1996.

CLARKE, MARY JANE, MRS (?1863–1910) Younger sister of Emmeline PANKHURST, one of ten children. Little is known of her early life in Salford, where her father was the managing director of a cotton-printing works, except that she was a keen artist and wanted to be an actress, an ambition that her parents refused to countenance. In the late 1870s Emmeline accompanied Mary when she attended the school in Paris, the Ecole Normale in the Avenue de Neuilly, that Emmeline had attended earlier. In the late 1880s Mary left her father's house and launched, with Emmeline, their shop, Emerson & Co., in Hampstead Road in London, living with Richard and Emmeline Pankhurst and their growing family first above the shop and then in Russell Square. Mary, the artistic one, helped with the decoration of the shop's stock of art-enamelled fancy goods; indeed, in the 1891 census she is described as a "decorative artist", and encouraged Sylvia PANKHURST's love of drawing. The Pankhursts moved back to Manchester in 1893 and Mary paid lengthy visits but was not then a permanent member of the household. She intended to qualify as a teacher of dress-cutting. In December 1895 Mary married John Clarke, described on his marriage certificate as a "clothier" from Old Trafford, about whom nothing else is known except that, according to Sylvia Pankhurst, "he had adopted a child of alien parentage". Immediately after Dr Pankhurst's death in 1898 Mary helped Emmeline Pankhurst relaunch Emerson's in Manchester. In 1904 Mary Clarke was living in what Sylvia Pankhurst, who used to visit her there, described as "a dreary southeast London suburb". There was a suggestion that her husband was cruel to her, certainly the marriage was unhappy, and Mary on at least one occasion left him, taking the child with her. She eventually left for good, although there is no information as to what happened to the child. In the early years of the WOMEN'S SOCIAL AND POLITICAL UNION Mary Clarke acted as Emmeline Pankhurst's deputy as registrar in Manchester; however, by February 1906 she was fully involved herself with the WSPU. She was present at the first London meeting held in February 1906 at Sylvia Pankhurst's lodgings in Park Walk, Chelsea, at which the Central London Committee of the WSPU was formed. She was an informal member of this first committee but in June 1906, when the organization was formalized after Emmeline and Christabel Pankhurst took up headquarters in London, was not listed on the printed note-paper. However, by March 1907 she was appointed a WSPU ORGANIZER and in January 1909 led a small deputation to the prime minister in Downing Street and as a result was sentenced to one month's imprisonment. Her sentence overlapped with that given, as a result of a different incident, to Lady Constance LYTTON, who mentions Mrs Clarke's presence in Holloway, describing her in *Prisons and Prisoners* as "exceptionally gentle and courteous in her manner, but her outward calm nevertheless suggested a reserve of inward force". Lady Constance only learned after Mrs Clarke had left prison that she was Mrs Pankhurst's sister.

In March 1909 Mary Clarke was speaking for the WSPU in Yorkshire. By the summer of 1909 she was the WSPU's organizer on the south coast, based in Brighton and apparently living in Minnie TURNER's guest house. In January 1910 she ran the WSPU's general election campaign in Brighton. In November 1910 she took part in the "Black Friday" deputation and was then arrested for breaking windows at the subsequent protest meeting. She was sentenced, for the third time, to a month's imprisonment, and died a few days after her release, on Christmas Day at the home of her brother Herbert Goulden, in Winchmore Hill. On 23 December she had attended and spoken at the Christmas luncheon for released prisoners held at the Criterion Restaurant. Emmeline PETHICK-LAWRENCE described her in the *Votes for Women* obituary as "the first woman martyr who has gone to death for this cause". However, the death of this "martyr", the sister of the leader of the WSPU, did not attract the publicity that was to be given to the death of Emily Wilding DAVISON. Mrs Pethick-Lawrence goes on to descibe how, because of the Christmas holiday, the funeral was very quiet "and but few were able to be present". Mary Clarke left £57 11s 11d and probate was granted to her husband.

Address: (1891) 8 Russell Square, London WC; (1895) 4 Buckingham Crescent, Victoria Park, Manchester; (1909) Sea View, 14 Victoria Road, Brighton.
Photograph: *Votes for Women*, 6 January 1911.
Bibliography: obituary by E. Pethick-Lawrence, *Votes for Women*, 6 January 1911; S. Pankhurst, *The Suffragette Movement*, 1931.

CLAYTON, EDWY GODWIN (1858–1936) Born in Lambeth, an analytical chemist, an authority on the manufacture of matches, with a laboratory at 23 Holborn Viaduct. His wife Clara, and daughter Hilda, were both very active members of the WOMEN'S SOCIAL AND POLITICAL UNION and the CHURCH LEAGUE FOR WOMEN'S SUFFRAGE, each being honorary secretary of one these societies in the Richmond and Kew district. Mr Clayton was a member of the MEN'S LEAGUE FOR WOMEN'S SUFFRAGE and the MEN'S POLITICAL UNION. At the end of April 1913 a letter and a memorandum from Edwy Clayton were found by the police during a raid on the flat shared by Jessie and Annie KENNEY in Mecklenburgh Square, Bloomsbury. According to Christabel PANKHURST, the papers were, very suitably, found within the pages of a book describing the Bristol franchise riots of 1831 and should have been destroyed by Jessie KENNEY. She, however, was ill, had been treated in Switzerland earlier that year for lung disease, and had obviously forgotten the existence of the incriminating evidence. The papers included a list of timber yards, government offices, cotton mills and other places suitable for attack and suggested that Clayton had carried out experiments with chemicals suitable for making explosives. He was tried, with Annie Kenney,

Harriet KERR, Beatrice SANDERS, Rachel BARRETT, Geraldine LENNOX and Agnes Lake, on charges of conspiracy, including that of inflicting damage on "houses, foods, and chattels belonging to divers subjects of the King", and sentenced to 21 months' imprisonment. He went on hunger strike, was released under the "Cat and Mouse" Act, and managed to elude re-arrest. He was directed to pay his share of the prosecution cost of his trial, and foreseeing this, had, on the advice of Mrs Ayres Purdie, financial adviser to the WSPU, before sentencing put a selection of his belongings into auction. The treasury solicitor went to some trouble to prevent him benefiting from the potential profit. Clayton became a member of the UNITED SUFFRAGISTS. In *The Suffragette Movement* Sylvia Pankhurst records that Edwy Clayton's business was ruined by his prosecution and he was eventually assisted by J.E. Francis of the Athenaeum Press (see PUBLISHERS AND PRINTERS), who "paid him a small wage".
Address: (1913) Glengariff, Kew Road, Richmond, Surrey.
Photograph: in the *Suffragette*, 20 June 1913.
Bibliography: C. Pankhurst, *Unshackled*, 1959.

CLEEVES, MARY MCLEOD, MRS (?–alive 1931) Her husband's family owned the Cleeves Anthracite coal-mining company in South Wales. She had been honorary secretary of the local Women's Liberal Association in Swansea and became honorary secretary of the Swansea branch of the WOMEN'S FREEDOM LEAGUE when it was founded in 1909. In 1910 she was a member of the national executive of the WFL and honorary organizer for Wales. In that year and in 1911, as a tax resister, she had goods distrained and auctioned. In 1931 she was chair of the local branch of the Women's Guild of Empire, which after the First World War had concentrated much of its campaigning in South Wales.
Address: (1909) Chez-Nous, Sketty, Glamorganshire.
Photograph: The *Vote*, 12 February 1910.
Bibliography: L. Dee and K. Keineg (eds), *Women in Wales*, 1987.

CLERKS' WOMEN'S SOCIAL AND POLITICAL UNION A branch of the WOMEN'S SOCIAL AND POLITICAL UNION, 62 Edith Road, West Kensington, formed for the purpose of involving women engaged in clerical and secretarial work in the suffrage movement. Honorary secretaries (1913) Phyllis AYRTON and Cynthia MAGUIRE.

CLEVEDON (NUWSS) In 1913 the society was a member of the WEST OF ENGLAND FEDERATION OF THE NATIONAL UNION OF WOMEN'S SUFFRAGE SOCIETIES. Secretary (1913) Miss Clayton, 2 Hallam Road, Clevedon, Somerset.

CLITHEROE (NUWSS) The society was originally founded in 1906 by Selina COOPER as the Nelson Women's Suffrage Society. It was renamed in 1909 when the societies were realigned to follow constituency boundaries. In 1910 the society became part of the MANCHESTER AND DISTRICT FEDERATION OF THE NATIONAL UNION OF WOMEN'S SUFFRAGE SOCIETIES. The society's BANNER, carried in the Coronation Procession, 1911, was donated by Mary Cooper, daughter of Selina Cooper, in whose house it was embroidered, to Towneley Hall Art Gallery, Burnley, Lancashire.
Secretary (1913) Miss Shimbles, 74 Carleton St, Nelson, Lancashire.

CLOTHIER, ESTHER BRIGHT, MRS (1873–1935) Quaker, born at Street, Somerset, daughter of Helen Bright CLARK, educated at the Mount School, York, 1888–91, and then at Armstrong College, Newcastle, where she met and became very friendly with Mabel, the daughter of Elizabeth Spence WATSON. In 1897 after completing her BLitt, she married Samuel Thompson Clothier, whose mother had been one of the signatories of the 1866 petition. They had one son. In June 1908 Annie KENNEY and Mary BLATHWAYT, in the course of a west-country tour, called on Esther Clothier who showed them the BANNER she was making for the 21 June WOMEN'S SOCIAL AND POLITICAL UNION Hyde Park Demonstration, which she subsequently attended. She does not appear to have maintained her association with the WSPU and by 1913 was the honorary secretary of the Street branch of the NATIONAL UNION OF WOMEN'S SUFFRAGE SOCIETIES and honorary treasurer of the WEST OF ENGLAND FEDERATION OF SUFFRAGE SOCIETIES. In 1914 she was involved with the newly formed NUWSS ACTIVE SERVICE LEAGUE and was a member of the FRIENDS' LEAGUE FOR WOMEN'S SUFFRAGE, of which her brother and sister,

Roger and Alice CLARK, were the honorary secretaries. During the First World War she was a member of the No-Conscription Fellowship.

Before marriage put her the wrong side of the marriage bar, Esther Clothier had aimed to be the headmistress of an elementary school. Instead she worked for education and was a member for ten years of the Somerset education committee, chairman of one of its sub-committees, and was a member of the BBC School Programme Committee. In 1934 she was a member of the Somerset County Council.

Address: (1913) Leigh Holt, Street, Somerset.
Archival source: Friends' Library.

CLOUGH, BLANCHE ATHENA (1861–1960) Cousin of Florence Nightingale and Barbara BODICHON, through her grandfather Samuel Smith. She was a student at Newnham between 1884 and 1888, but did not take a tripos. From 1888 to 1892 she was secretary to the Principal of Newnham, her aunt Anne Jemima Clough; from 1896 to 1920 she was herself vice-principal of Newnham; and from 1920 to 1923 principal. Given her position in the college, and Newnham's position in the university, she was unable to play a prominent part in the suffrage campaign, although by 1890 she was a member of the CAMBRIDGE WOMEN'S SUFFRAGE ASSOCIATION and during the January 1910 general election gave hospitality to the visiting NATIONAL UNION OF WOMEN'S SUFFRAGE SOCIETIES organizer for a few days. From its founding in 1908 the CAMBRIDGE UNIVERSITY WOMEN'S SUFFRAGE SOCIETY, formed by the amalgamation of the NEWNHAM and GIRTON societies, thrived and two Newnham protégées, Elinor Rendel and Ray Costelloe (see STRACHEY FAMILY), were later very active members of the NUWSS executive. In 1913, as a member of the SURREY, SUSSEX, AND HAMPSHIRE FEDERATION, rather than that of the Eastern Counties, Thena Clough spoke at the meeting held in Hyde Park at the end of the NUWSS PILGRIMAGE. In 1916 she was temporary acting secretary, working with Ray and Philippa Strachey, of the Women's Service Bureau, the organization dealing with women's employment run by the LONDON SOCIETY FOR WOMEN'S SUFFRAGE. By 1950 she was a vice-president of its successor, the LONDON AND NATIONAL SOCIETY FOR WOMEN'S SERVICE. She wrote the biography of her aunt, *Anne Jemima Clough*, 1897.

Address: (1888–1923) Newnham College, Cambridge; (1934) 22 Gerald Road, London SW1.
Portrait: by William Nicholson, 1924, at Newnham. Two by Ray Strachey, National Portrait Gallery Reserve Collection.

CLUBS In 1860 the novelty of the facility offered by the Ladies' Institute opened by Bessie Rayner PARKES and Barbara BODICHON was reflected by the spleen with which it was greeted by the press. Deep suspicion was accorded the idea of women meeting together in the centre of town in a space that was not regulated by the family. The Institute's prospectus mentioned that one of its purposes was to provide a wide range of reading material for its members; the reviewer in the *Saturday Review* could see no reason why they should wish to read anything other than cookery books. By 1898 E. Wills was able to write in the *Lady's Realm* that "The multiplying of women's clubs, and the accompanying facilities for social intercourse, is distinctly a latter-day feature of London society. Twenty years ago they were practically unknown: today they are to be met with on all sides. They are a sign of the times; women have awakened to the fact that they want something outside their domestic and home duties." Amy Levy made the point that it was only in her club that a woman could write letters and read, "undisturbed by the importunities of a family circle, which can never bring itself to regard feminine leisure and feminine solitude as things to be respected".

The upper- and middle-class women's clubs of the last quarter of the nineteenth century may be divided into those, such as the Alexandra and Empress, that provided "tea and shopping facilities" and those, such as the Pioneer and Berners, that offered a socially and politically radical educational programme alongside the creature comforts. In her novel *In Haste and at Leisure*, Eliza Lynn Linton, although abhorring the New Woman, in the process gives a vibrant description of life at the Excelsior Club, where women of advanced views, typifying the range of members attracted to such an institution, were united as one "on the great questions of the diabolical nature of husbands; the degrading institution of marriage; the shameful burden of maternity; women's claims to be a County Councillor, a voter, a lawyer, a judge, and M.P., ... and the right of the sex in general, married or single, to live like men in every particular, if they chose to do so". Florence Marryat, through her character Lady Phyllis Macnaughten, describes the fictional Pushahead Club in *At Heart a Rake*, as "a Hall of Freedom for Women" and dwells lovingly on the splendours of its smoking-room and dressing-rooms, and its restaurant, where meals could be had up to ten o'clock at night. In Dorothy Leighton's novel *Disillusion*, the Spade Club, housed like the Somerville Club in the two upper floors of a house in Oxford Street, was one such at which "the debates had grown more and more daring in subject, and freer and bolder in expression". In addition to these there were other clubs that aimed to provide facilities for the growing number of middle-class "professional" women, allowing them to entertain and socialize in a respectable public space. Similarly, attempts were made to provide public restaurants for lower middle-class and working women at which they could eat wholesome food at prices they could afford. The Dorothy Restaurant had been opened in Oxford Street in 1889, backed by Archibald Coats, the Paisley thread manufacturer, and the Women's Dining Rooms in Barrett Street, off Oxford Street, with Debenhams as a shareholder, in 1906. In the 1880s and 1890s restaurants in London such as Gattis set aside separate small dining-rooms, with a separate entrance, for women, but these were hardly the places in which a male friend or colleague might be entertained. The very fact that there were no public places in which a woman might host such a meal perpetuated the idea that such entertainments were intrinsically unnatural. The majority of women's clubs, in order to fulfil their function, were based in the West End of London, and the larger provincial cities also provided similar facilities in similarly central positions. Writing in 1909 the French commentator David Staars remarked on the rapid increase in women's clubs and described them as "the corollary of women's emancipation". One might also suggest that the existence of the clubs, in which like-minded women gathered together in drawing, dining and smoking rooms, were fertile seed beds in which the burgeoning suffrage campaign was nurtured. In 1899, when London hosted the International Congress of Women, Miss Kerr, secretary of the Somerville Club, Miss Johnson, secretary of the New Victorian Club, and Miss Routledge of the Writers' Club, were members of the hospitality sub-committee set up to organize the reception and entertainment of delegates drawn from all parts of Britain and the world. On this, and on later occasions when the suffrage societies staged processions and demonstrations, the London women's clubs were obvious gathering points for refreshment and the discussion of the exciting events of the day. In her novel *The Garden of Desire*, Ethel Hargrove described the fictional Minerva Club as "not merely a *pied-à-terre* for social functions and tea parties. The majority of its members were professional women, consequently Agnes [her heroine] had the opportunity of associating with many kindred spirits. She attended lectures, joined the Debating Society, and exhibited her last summer's Thames pictures in the picture gallery." Rather than watching the 1911 Women's Coronation Procession from the balcony of the Minerva Club, which was "in a good central position", Agnes, as a member of the Women Writers' Suffrage League, took part, wearing a large quill pen in her hat and "holding a black and gold banner embroidered with the badge of her Society". By 1910 the campaign was sufficiently central to social life as to generate two clubs specific to the suffrage movement. In the aftermath of the Edwardian campaign two more clubs, the Emily Wilding Davison and the Minerva, catered for the veterans, dying with them. All the following clubs were for women only, unless otherwise specified.

ALBEMARLE, 13 Albemarle Street, London W. A club for men and women founded by 1881 by, among others, Henry Holiday and Elizabeth MALLESON. Members included May SINCLAIR, Millicent FAWCETT, Mrs Mary HASLAM, Mrs Margaret PENNINGTON, Mrs Laura Stuart, president of the Norwich branch of the NUWSS, Mrs Katherine THOMASSON and Lilias Ashworth HALLETT who, in 1908, invited Mary BLATHWAYT when they were up in London on suffrage business to dine at the club with her. The club later moved to 37 Dover Street and was still in existence in 1923. Secretary (1909) Miss Sangster.
Bibliography: *Women's Penny Paper*, 8 November 1890.

ALEXANDRA CLUB, 12 Grosvenor Street, London W, was founded in 1884 as a convenient centre for ladies and a permanent London address for country members. Membership was restricted to those eligible to attend Court, a rule which Constance Smedley in her novel *Redwing* decoded as excluding divorcées. Men were not allowed to enter even as visitors, a rule that Amy Levy regretted. The club was large and extremely comfortable, residential for short visits only, but with accommodation for accompanying ladies' maids. Millicent FAWCETT had been made an honorary life-member of the club by 1899. The club was still in existence in 1928. Secretary (1909) Miss Boyd.

ALLIANCE, 61 Curzon Street and 37 Clarges Street, London W. A club for ladies interested in evangelical Christian work. Among its members in 1913 was Mrs Margaret Whidborne, member of the CONSERVATIVE AND UNIONIST WOMEN'S FRANCHISE ASSOCIATION, and vice-president of the East Grinstead branch of the NUWSS.

ARACHNE CLUB, 60 Russell Square, London WC, founded in 1905. Election to membership was based on social references. Secretary (1909) Mrs Armstrong.

BATH CLUB, 34 Dover Street and 16 Berkeley Street, London W, founded in 1894, open to ladies and gentlemen, although the ladies could only enter from Berkeley Street and could not make use of the residential accommodation. The club's main emphasis was on sport, especially, as its name might suggest, swimming.

BATH AND COUNTIES LADIES' CLUB, 43 Milsom Street, Bath. Mary BLATHWAYT was a member and gave copies of *Women's Franchise* and *Votes for Women* to the club's reading room. It was useful as a place where visiting WSPU speakers could change their dresses before meetings. Honorary secretary (1909) Miss Northey, Ashley Manor, Box, Wiltshire.

BEECHWOOD, 6 and 7 Oakley Street, Chelsea. A ladies-only residential club founded in 1895. Manageress (1909) Miss Lilias Eaton.

BERNERS CLUB FOR WOMEN was founded at 9 Berners Street, London W before 1871. It had formerly been called the Working Women's Club. From 1872 until 1874 it shared its address with the CENTRAL COMMITTEE OF THE NATIONAL SOCIETY FOR WOMEN'S SUFFRAGE, during the course of which time that society's secretaries included Emma Smith (*see* Emma PATERSON) and Helen BLACKBURN who was, in 1877, treasurer of the Berners Club. In 1874 the club's shareholders included Helen Blackburn, Lady Anna GORE LANGTON, Alexander Macmillan, the publisher, Emma Paterson, Margaret PENNINGTON, Augusta and Thomas WEBSTER, and Alice and John WESTLAKE. In the 1890s the club moved to 22 Berners Street, which from 1875 had also been the home of the Society for the Promotion of Employment of Women and from the 1880s of the *Englishwoman's Review*, of which, from 1889 Helen Blackburn was the editor. In 1871 the committee of the Berners Club included Frances Power COBBE and Barbara BODICHON. The club, to which the annual subscription was 10s, was open from 8 am until 10.30 pm on weekdays and from 9 am until 10.30 pm on Sundays. The club contained a reading room, supplied with newspapers and periodicals; a drawing room, for society and conversation; and a dining room. The club was strictly unsectarian, and was open to foreign as well as English members. The committee required each potential member to supply a reference as to respectability. The Berners Club was no longer in existence by 1898.

Archival source: Papers of Berners Club Ltd, Public Record Office.
Bibliography: *Daily News*, 2 February 1871; article by F.P. Cobbe in the *Echo*, 14 March 1871.

BRIGHTON LADIES' CLUB, 27 King's Road, Brighton. In 1906 Miss Watson, who was working as ORGANIZER for the NUWSS in the southern counties, was based at the club.

CLIFTON, BRISTOL, AND COUNTIES' LADIES CLUB, 45 Royal York Crescent, Clifton, Bristol, affiliated to the Bath and County Ladies' Club and the New County Club, Hanover Square, London. Honorary secretaries (1909) Mrs Gronow Davis and Miss E.H. Smith.

DENISON CLUB, 15 Buckingham Street, Strand, London WC, and then, by 1909, at Denison House, Vauxhall Bridge Road, London SW, for men and women. The object of the club, to which membership was by election, was "To afford to persons interested in charitable and social subjects a place of meeting and conference, a reading and writing room, and such of the ordinary conveniences of a club as may from time to time be possible". The club was non-residential.

EMERSON, 19 Buckingham Street, Strand, London WC, a club for men and women founded in 1911. In 1913 among the club's members were Amy HICKS, Mrs Jane Strickland, chairman of the committee of the FREE CHURCH LEAGUE FOR WOMEN'S SUFFRAGE, and Clementina BLACK. Sarah BENETT was an early shareholder in the club and maintained her interest until her death; Florence BALGARNIE was a shareholder by 1917. The club appears to have become rather popular in the 1920s when among its shareholders were Myra Sadd BROWN, Mary HANKINSON, Adela COIT, Harold Baillie-Weaver (see Gertrude Baillie-WEAVER), Margaret Bondfield, Sophy Sanger, Alison NEILANS, Elizabeth KNIGHT, as well as Emmeline Pankhurst's brother, Walter, and the mother and sister of Olive BARTELS. In 1923 the club was the address of the Woman's Group of the Ethical Movement. The Emerson moved to 14 Great George Street, Westminster, in 1925, and in 1927 to 1 Little George Street. It appears to have closed in 1928 and was formally wound up in 1931.

Archival source: Papers of the Emerson Club Co., Public Record Office

EMILY WILDING DAVISON CLUB, 144 High Holborn, London WC, was founded as the Emily Wilding Davison Lodge by Mary LEIGH in memory of her friend (see Emily Wilding DAVISON). The address was also that of the WOMEN'S FREEDOM LEAGUE and after 1915 of the SUFFRAGETTES OF THE WSPU. It was at the Emily Wilding Davison Club on 24 October 1915 that a farewell tea was held for Kitty MARION on the eve of her departure for America and it was there in 1925 that a reunion was held on one of her return visits to England. The Club was still in existence in 1940 when members of the WFL were informed that they might "find it convenient to know that they can get a good mid-day meal at the Emily Davison Club, 144 High Holborn, above the W.F.L. Office". In 1925 refreshment rooms run by Mrs Maud Helen Fisher had shared the address. The secretary of the Emily Wilding Davison Club was (1915) Mrs Alice Green, at whose address in Clapham Emily Davison had been living shortly before her death; (1922) Miss E. Frisby.

EMPRESS CLUB, Dover Street, London W, founded in 1897. The club's premises were purpose-built and boasted two drawing rooms, a dining room, a lounge, a smoking gallery and a smoking room, a library, a writing room, a tape machine for news, a telephone, a room in which servants could be interviewed, dressing rooms, and one of the best orchestras in London. In addition there was provided a sitting room for accompanying ladies' maids. Among the club's members in 1913 were Princess Sophia Duleep-SINGH, Viscountess Dillon, president of the Oxfordshire branch of the CONSERVATIVE AND UNIONIST WOMEN'S FRANCHISE ASSOCIATION, and Lady Leila Treacher, who was an active member of the WOMEN'S FREEDOM LEAGUE. The club was still in existence in 1952 but had closed by 1956. Secretary (1909) Otho Oliver (brother of Gilbert Oliver, founder of the New County Club).

ENTERPRISE CLUB, 57 and 58 Leadenhall Street, London EC, founded in 1899 to provide a convenient centre for rest and recreation for women over 18 years of age engaged in clerical work. The club ran a registry for lady clerks. Secretary (1909) Miss Freda Wale.

FORUM CLUB, 6 Grosvenor Place, London W, formed in 1919 as "The London Centre for Women's Institute Members", by, among others, Elizabeth ROBINS. In the 1920s Mary ALLEN and Sybil, Lady Rhondda (the former Mrs D.A. Thomas, see under Viscountess RHONDDA) were members of its executive committee. The club contained a library, a billiard room, a bridge room, a salon which could be hired by members for picture exhibitions, a darkroom for photographers, and a fully equipped hairdressing room. There was accommodation for members' personal maids.

GIVE AND TAKE CLUB, St James's Hotel, a luncheon club founded by Mary Cholmondeley in 1910. Among its members were Elizabeth ROBINS, Lady Florence Bell and Lady Brassey.

GREEN PARK CLUB, 10 Grafton Street, London W, founded in 1894, catering for those particularly interested in drama and music, but restricted to those who were eligible to be presented at Court. Louise Jopling ROWE was a member.

GROSVENOR CRESCENT CLUB, 15 Grosvenor Crescent, London SW, a residential club founded in July 1897 by Mrs Nora Wynford Philipps. After the death of Mrs MASSINGBERD in 1897 many members left the Pioneer Club, which she had founded, and joined the Grosvenor Crescent Club. It is not clear if there had been internal feuding or whether it was simply thought that after Mrs Massingberd's death the Pioneer would close. Many women were members of both clubs. Like the Pioneer Club, the Grosvenor Crescent offered a lower subscription rate to professional women. The Grosvenor Crescent was the parent body of the Women's Institute (see below). L.M. Hubbard, the editor of *The Englishwoman's Year Book*, gave the club as her address in 1902. Among its members in 1913 was Charlotte Moberly, principal of St Hugh's College, Oxford, and vice-president of the Oxford branch of the NUWSS.

Bibliography: *Shafts*, October 1897.

GROSVENOR GALLERY LIBRARY AND CLUB, 18 South Molton Street, London W, open to men and women, an addition to the progressive art gallery, which numbered among its exhibitors such supporters of the women's suffrage cause as Margaret Gillies, Emily Osborn (whose portrait of Barbara BODICHON was shown there in 1884, *see also* Jane Cobden UNWIN), Emily FORD and Annie SWYNNERTON. From 1880 the Grosvenor Gallery offered the use of a Ladies' Drawing Room, as a privilege of the two-guinea annual membership. In 1880 the Gallery formed a company to "establish and maintain in the West End of London a circulating library, and also reading and writing rooms and a reference library and to furnish the same respectively with books, reviews, magazines, newspapers and other publications, including instrumental and vocal music". Charlotte DESPARD, her husband Maximilian, and her sister Katherine HARLEY, were founding shareholders in the Grosvenor Gallery Library Company. By 1883 Eliza ORME is also listed among the shareholders. By 1885 the Gallery had opened Ladies' Reading Rooms and by 1889, shortly before it closed, offered a Ladies' Restaurant.

Archival source: Papers of the Grosvenor Gallery Library Company, Public Record Office.
Bibliography: S.P. Casteras and C. Denney, *The Grosvenor Gallery: A Palace of Art in Victorian England*, 1996.

HALCYON, 13 Cork Street, London W. A club for professional women. Among its members in 1913 were Beatrice HARRADEN, Maude ROYDEN, Mrs Victor Veley, member of the committee of the Marylebone and Paddington branches of both the CONSERVATIVE AND UNIONIST WOMEN'S FRANCHISE ASSOCIATION and the CHURCH LEAGUE FOR WOMEN'S SUFFRAGE, Marion Wallace-DUNLOP, Agnes Warburg, member of the council of the Conservative and Unionist Women's Franchise Association, Miss E.G. Wood, vice-chairman of the Hampstead branch of the Conservative and Unionist Women's Franchise Association, and Mrs Darent Harrison, founder and honorary secretary of the HASTINGS AND ST LEONARDS WOMEN'S SUFFRAGE PROPAGANDA LEAGUE. The club was still in existence in 1923.

ILCHESTER CLUB, Ilchester Gardens, Hyde Park, London W, was in existence in 1898, with the aim of bringing "all the comfort and refinement of a private house within the means of a slender income". It had sufficient sleeping accommodation for 40 members, a large dining room, a smoking room, a music room, a "silent" room and a drawing room.

THE INTERNATIONAL WOMEN'S FRANCHISE CLUB, for men and women supporters of women's enfranchisement, was opened in temporary premises at 66 Russell Square, London WC, by February 1910. Among its first directors were Lilian HICKS and several leading members of the MEN'S LEAGUE FOR WOMEN'S SUFFRAGE, including Malcolm Mitchell, Capt. C. Gonne, Charles Vansittart Conybeare, Herbert Jacobs and Goldfinch Bate, who acted as solicitor for the club. The chairman was Robert Cholmeley, headmaster of Owen's School in Islington, one of the founding members of the Men's League. By December 1910 the club had moved to 9 Grafton Street, London W. "The house consists of a good private entrance on the ground floor, with a hall leading to a fine staircase; on the first floor is a large drawing room with a silence room attached; the smoking rooms are on the second floor and on the third floor are the kitchen, offices, and rooms for the staff. Literature of all kinds bearing upon the Suffrage movement will be obtainable at the Club; there will eventually be a Library and an Information Bureau." The club welcomed men and women from all sections of the suffrage movement from all parts of the world. Not long after opening it had a membership of over 800. Meetings of the TAX RESISTANCE LEAGUE were held at the club in 1910 and in autumn 1911 the club organized a lecture series. In July 1914 the club's facilities were extended to delegates from overseas attending the formation of the BRITISH DOMINIONS WOMAN SUFFRAGE UNION.

The club was inexpensive to join, its subscription being one guinea per annum (Irish, Scottish and foreign members, 10/6). Non-members paid 5/6 per annum. Luncheons and dinners were available from 1s. The club eventually housed Ruth Cavendish-BENTINCK's feminist library, which acted as both a reference and lending LIBRARY and to which access was free to members. The club held an annual dinner which, on 26 February 1914, was held at the Criterion Restaurant at Piccadilly Circus. Among the club's members were Georgina and Maria BRACKENBURY, Charlotte DESPARD and her sister Katherine HARLEY, Victor DUVAL, J.E. Francis (publisher of *Women's Franchise*), Mary GAWTHORPE, Malcolm Mitchell, Hugh FRANKLIN and his aunt, the Hon. Mrs Henrietta Franklin, Elizabeth ABBOTT, Margery Corbett ASHBY, Adelaide CHAPMAN, Margaret ASHTON, Edwy CLAYTON, Anne Cobden SANDERSON, Ellen and Edith BECK, Mary HARE, Mrs Lowy, Mrs Marie CORBETT, Mrs DUVAL, Kathleen COURTNEY, Lady Dorothea Garrett Gibb (niece to Millicent Fawcett and Elizabeth Garrett Anderson), Helga Gill (NUWSS organizer in Oxford), the Rev. Claude and Mrs Hinscliff, co-founders of the CHURCH LEAGUE FOR WOMEN'S SUFFRAGE, Elsie Howey, Dr Elizabeth KNIGHT, Mrs Margaret Mackworth (later Lady RHONDDA), Chrystal MACMILLAN, Mrs Mildred MANSEL, Mrs Emilie Holyoake Marsh (*see* George HOLYOAKE), Mrs Kitty MARSHALL, Mrs Rosamund Massy, Rosaline MASSON, Winifred MAYO, Mary Milton, honorary secretary and treasurer of the Farnham and District branch of the NUWSS, Margaret NEVINSON, Mrs Robena Nicholson, president of the North Middlesex Women's Suffrage Society, Mrs Marie Nutt, a vice-president of the National Political League and proprietor of the radical publishing firm, David Nutt, Frances PARKER, Mrs Emily Pertwee, musical director of the ACTRESSES' FRANCHISE LEAGUE, Mrs Marjorie Rackham, honorary secretary of the Barnes branch of the NUWSS, Hermione Ramsden, member of the NUWSS and translator of feminist works by Laura Marholm Hansson, Frances ROWE, Mary Sargant FLORENCE, Sime SERUYA, Mrs Stephen Spring-Rice, Mrs Katherine THOMASSON, Mrs Rosa Tudor, member of the WOMEN'S FREEDOM LEAGUE, Marion Wallace-DUNLOP, Agnes Warburg, Eva Ward, sometime organizer for the EASTERN COUNTIES FEDERATION OF THE NUWSS, Mrs Wilkinson of York, Lady Marie Willoughby de Broke, president of the Warwickshire branch of the CONSERVATIVE AND UNIONIST WOMEN'S FRANCHISE ASSOCIATION, Alice Zimmern, author of *Women's Suffrage in Many Lands*, and Mrs Lilian Hicks.

The club appears to have had 1500 members by April 1911, 1700 by May 1916, and 2000 in July 1917. At this time its vice-presidents included Lady Betty Balfour, Lady Aberconway (*see* Laura McLAREN), Lena ASHWELL, Adela Stanton COIT, Charlotte Despard, Vida GOLDSTEIN, Laurence HOUSMAN, Olive Schreiner and Ethel SNOWDEN. Despite its impressive membership figures the club at this time faced financial difficulties that cast some doubt on whether it could continue in existence, but it stayed open, known from 1923 as the International Franchise Club, until 1924. In its final years its committee included Nina BOYLE, Vera Laughton (*see* Vera Laughton MATHEWS), Marie LAWSON and Lady Frances BALFOUR. Its honorary secretary was (1911) Cicely Dean Corbett, sister of Marjery Corbett Ashby; assistant secretary (1910) Rosalind Gray Hill, who remained as secretary into the 1920s; (1924) Miss M. Garlick.

Archival source: Papers of the International Women's Franchise Club Ltd, Public Record Office.
Bibliography: *Votes for Women*, 11 February 1910; 22 July 1910.

INVERNESS LADIES' CLUB, 2 Castle Tolmie, founded in 1899, with residential accommodation. Secretary (1909) Miss M.A. Knight.

KELVIN CLUB, 97 Buchanan Street, Glasgow, founded 1898 for wives and daughters of officers in the army or navy. Secretary (1909) Miss Mary Stewart Wright.

KENSINGTON LADIES' CLUB, 19 & 21 Penywern Road, SW, was in existence 1897 and in 1914.

LADIES' ARMY AND NAVY, 2 Burlington Gardens, London W. A large club with, in 1909, 3500 members, who had to be near relations to officers serving in the army or navy. The club was still in existence in 1924. Founder and secretary (1909) Mrs G.A. Dundas.

LADIES' ATHENAEUM, 31 Dover Street, London W, founded in 1913 by Mrs Jennie Cornwallis-West (the former Lady Randolph Churchill and mother of Winston) for ladies interested in politics, art, literature and music. The club was still in existence in 1924, but had disappeared by 1928. Secretary (1909) Mrs H. Fitzclarence.

LADIES' AUTOMOBILE, Brook Street, London W. Among the club's members in 1913 was Helena Auerbach, honorary treasurer of the NATIONAL UNION OF WOMEN'S SUFFRAGE SOCIETIES. The club was still in existence in 1924.

LADIES' CALEDONIAN, Edinburgh. Among the club's members in 1913 was Lisa Gordon, organizing secretary of the Edinburgh branch of the NUWSS, and Chrystal MACMILLAN.

LADIES' EMPIRE CLUB, 69 Grosvenor Street, London W, founded under the auspices of the Victoria League. Among its members in 1913 was Mrs Stephen Spring-Rice, member of the South Paddington committee of the LONDON SOCIETY FOR WOMEN'S SUFFRAGE, and Lady Willoughby de Broke. The club was still in existence in 1950. Secretary (1909) Miss F.M. Brooke-Alder.

LADIES' IMPERIAL, 17 and 18 Dover Street, London W, open to women members of the Conservative or Unionist parties and residential for visits. The club was still in existence, at 9 Arlington Street, in 1924. Secretary (1909) Mrs Elderton.

LADIES' INSTITUTE, 19 Langham Place, London W, opened there at the beginning of 1860 by Bessie Rayner PARKES and Barbara BODICHON. The club had originally been established in a room at 14a Princes Street, Cavendish Square, the office of, first, the *Waverley Journal* and then of the *English Woman's Journal,* for the double purpose of collecting together all those magazines and papers which women of cultivation but limited means wished to read but could not otherwise afford, and also to be a place of rest and recreation for London's many middle-class working women, such as daily governesses. In May 1857 Bessie Parkes had written to Barbara Bodichon, "If the Waverley can be got chiefly into friendly hand and brought to London . . . , we can have our own book shop, or the beginning of a club room for exhibiting pictures etc etc. . . . I shall try to have the shop in Oxford St and Isa Craig could be put into it as Locum General. My idea is to make the whole thing *respectable and practical*". In its early days the Institute had closed at 5 pm, but this proved to be too early to allow governesses to make use of its facilities and it then remained open to 10 pm, under the supervision of a respectable married servant, although apparently not that of Isa CRAIG. Seventy women subscribed to the club in its early days.

In 1860 the Institute moved to bigger premises, which now also housed the office of the *English Woman's Journal* and the registry office for woman's work (which excluded private tuition and domestic service) run by Jessie BOUCHERETT and the Society for Promoting the Employment of Women. The Institute comprised a Ladies' Reading Room, open from 11 am to 10 pm, in which were available the leading daily and weekly papers, magazines and reviews. For the convenience of members visiting the West End on shopping or other business, attached to the Reading Room was a Luncheon Room, and a room also for the reception of parcels. There was also available a committee room which could be hired by philanthropic societies for meetings. The subscription was one guinea a year and for two guineas members were enabled to bring to the Institute any (lady) non-member. Professional ladies (presumably those of the daily governess class) paid subscriptions at half price. By 1862 the secretary of the Institute was Sarah Lewin, niece of Harriet GROTE.

The novelty of the facilities that the Institute offered to middle-class women may be assessed by the degree of venom employed in an article in the *Saturday Review,* 7 January 1860:

What business, society will remark, have ladies with a reading-room and a luncheon-room? What is the reading in the morning-room of the Club which they cannot get at home? The Englishwoman's Magazine and the domestic manuals of Kitchener and Soyer are not so dear . . . We have our doubts about that reading room. And what of the luncheon department . . . Is the early-closing movement to extend to Langham-place? In the opera season is the Club to be open till two o'clock, am? . . . If, as we should judge from the scanty revelations of the advertisement, all that is meant is a lounge for the unprotected female, in which she can daily meet her like-minded and strong-minded sisterhood to discuss the Divorce court till half-past one, and then console the inner woman with sandwiches and sherry and the mutual confidences of the gynaecaeum til half-past six – and this is the simplest conception we can form of a Ladies' Reading-Room and a Ladies' Luncheon-Room – we can only hint to the ladies that this may be a mistake.

Bessie Parkes cut out this article and, together with a rather more generous one from the Liberal *Daily News*, 21 January, pasted it into her "On Women's Rights" scrapbook. The Ladies' Institute closed during the course of 1867 but its work and ethos was later developed by the Berners and Somerville clubs. Of its Langham Place premises Jessie Boucherett wrote, in her contribution to Theodore Stanton's *Woman Question in Europe*, 1884, "They have long passed into other hands and become a shop, but I shall always regard the place as classic ground".

Archival source: Parkes Papers, Girton College, Cambridge.
Bibliography: The *English Woman's Journal*, 1 January 1860; October 1860.

LADIES' INTERNATIONAL CLUB, 74 Prince's Square, Dawson Place, and 4 Prince's Terrace, Bayswater, London W. Secretary (1909) Mrs Dawson. The club was still in existence in 1947.

LADIES' PARK CLUB, Wilton House, 32 Knightsbridge, London SW, a residential club in which smoking and card-playing for money were not allowed. Among its members in 1913 were Gladys WRIGHT, Naomi Bassett Fox, honorary secretary of the Falmouth branch of the NUWSS and a member of the FRIENDS' LEAGUE FOR WOMEN'S SUFFRAGE, and her mother Mrs Ellen Fox. The club was still in existence in 1924. Secretary (1909), Miss Knollys, Perham House, Perham Road, West Kensington, London W.

LADIES' RESIDENTIAL CLUB, 19 and 21 Lexham Gardens, London W. Secretary (1897) Mrs Gordon Haynes.

LADIES' TOWN AND COUNTRY CLUB, 73 and 75 Mortimer Street, Cavendish Square, London W, a club open to gentlewomen for short residential visits. It was still in existence in 1924. Secretary (1909) Miss Jackson.

LADIES' VICTORIA, 145 Victoria Street, London SW, had been founded in 1891 in premises in Holles Street, Cavendish Square, London W.

LAUDERDALE CLUB, 138 Lauderdale Mansions, Maida Vale, London W, providing residential accommodation, either bed-sitting rooms or self-contained suites, for working gentlewomen in London. By 1914 its premises had spread to include 118–142 and 156 Lauderdale Mansions. The club was still in existence in 1923.

LEWISHAM WOMEN'S SUFFRAGE CLUB, 1 Lewis Grove, Lewisham, London SE, the address of Miss Campbell, secretary of the Lewisham branch of the WOMEN'S SOCIAL AND POLITICAL UNION. Among the club's members was Caroline TOWNSEND. The Club published *The Woman Teacher's Own Fault*, 1914.

LITERARY CLUB, Glasgow. Among its members in 1913 were Teresa BILLINGTON-GREIG and Miss MacFarlane Mary Park, president of the Glasgow branch of the CONSERVATIVE AND UNIONIST WOMEN'S FRANCHISE ASSOCIATION.

LIVERPOOL LADIES' CLUB, 58 Bold Street, Liverpool (1897). Founded in 1888, by 1909 the club had moved to 5 Slater Street, Liverpool. Honorary secretary (1909) Mrs H. Sutton Timmis.

LYCEUM CLUB, founded, as a breakaway group from the Writers' Club, on 6 June 1904. It obviously quickly advertised its existence because on 1 November 1904 Elizabeth Wolstenholme ELMY wrote from Congleton to Harriet McILQUHAM, "I shall not join 'The Lyceum Club' though it is a very interesting 'new departure' and may be very useful." The Lyceum was first housed at 128 Piccadilly, London W, the former premises of the Imperial Services Club, and later moved to 138 Piccadilly; it was the first woman's club to brave the male clubland of Piccadilly. Constance Smedley, its begetter, wrote that it was founded for ladies engaged with literature, journalism, art, science and medicine, who required "a substantial and dignified *milieu* where [they] could meet editors and other employers and discuss matters as men did in professional clubs: above all in surroundings that did not suggest poverty". She was concerned about the problems that faced middle-class girls, who had left home in order to work in London and were now living in boarding-houses and bed-sitting rooms. "A girl alone in those days missed that tacit chaperonage and sense of shelter and recognized the need of protecting her reputation: but this led to inevitable isolation and drove her into too feminine a world." The Lyceum had a library, an art gallery in which to display the work of members, 35 bedrooms and hairdressers, sewing maids and an American expert on chafing-dish suppers on its staff. From its inception the club had international aspirations, branches were soon formed in Berlin, Paris, Rome and Florence, and Lyceum members formed an interesting literary and artistic coterie. Monthly concerts were held at which new music was heard, a book gallery sold books written by members and once a week a club dinner was held. The membership of the Lyceum was defined as being confined to women who had published an original work in literature, journalism, science or music, who had university qualifications, or were the wives or daughters of distinguished men. Among its first shareholders were Annie Spong (*see* SPONG FAMILY), Christine MURRELL, the mistress of GIRTON, Penelope Lawrence, headmistress of Roedean, Walter Crane and Mabel Collins (*see under* PLAYS). The club's committee was chaired by Lady Frances BALFOUR and included Lady Lugard (Flora Shaw), Lucy Kemp-Welch, Mrs Stanley Boyd MD, and Mrs Oscar Beringer. Among the club's members in 1913 were Helena DOWSON, Sarah Grand, novelist and president of the Tunbridge Wells branch of the NUWSS, Beatrice HARRADEN, Mrs Darent Harrison, Ada Hines, co-founder of the MANCHESTER branch of the Women's Freedom League, Dr Louisa MARTINDALE, Constance Maud, author of the suffrage novel *No Surrender*, who belonged to the Paris branch, Mrs Clara Rackham, chairman of the EASTERN COUNTIES FEDERATION OF THE NUWSS, Edith and Florence Stoney, members of the LONDON SOCIETY FOR WOMEN'S SUFFRAGE, Lady STRACHEY, Mary Tait, Janie TERRERO, Mrs Katherine THOMASSON, Bettina Borrmann Wells, who was very active in the Women's Freedom League before moving to the United States, Mrs Wilkinson, president of the York branch of the NUWSS, Mrs Theodore Williams, chairman of the committee of the Women's Local Government Society, Mrs Dora Wingrove Cooke, honorary secretary of the Australian and New Zealand Women Voters' Association, Eleanor Woodgate, sometime president of Wisbech and District branch of the NUWSS, and Chrystal MACMILLAN. On 28 January 1918 Dora MONTEFIORE presided over a rather dramatic dinner held at the Lyceum Club to celebrate women's limited enfranchisement. Constance Smedley was the club's honorary secretary. The club was still in the same premises in 1924.

Bibliography: C. Smedley, *Redwing*, 1916; *Crusaders: the reminiscences of Constance Smedley*, 1929.

MANCHESTER LADIES' CLUB, 46 King Street, Manchester, founded in 1883 as a convenient centre for ladies visiting Manchester. It was non-residential. Secretary (1909) Miss Waddington.

MINERVA CLUB, 28a Brunswick Square, London WC, founded as a residential club by the WOMEN'S FREEDOM LEAGUE in 1920. The WFL had, during the war, run the Minerva Café at its Holborn headquarters, which was used for luncheons and lectures; a club would have been a natural progression. A very long lease on its premises on the west side of Brunswick Square, in a stretch of street that already included several ladies' hostels, was paid for by Dr Elizabeth KNIGHT, who also furnished the club. The Minerva was even supplied with purpose-designed CHINA. Although its prospectus stated that its membership was open to all men and women in sympathy with progressive thought, it may have been that the residential facilities were only available to women. The Minerva Club became a rallying point in the agitation for the extension of the franchise to women under 30; Elizabeth Knight ran the press and publicity campaign for the EQUAL POLITICAL RIGHTS CAMPAIGN COMMITTEE. The club attracted members from all branches of the erstwhile militant suffrage movement. The nexus between suffrage and vegetarianism was maintained; in 1923 the club's advertisements stressed that its restaurant supplied vegetarian dishes, guaranteed free of animal fat, prepared and cooked separately. In 1926 the first reunion dinner organized by the newly formed SUFFRAGETTE FELLOWSHIP was held at the Minerva Club. In the 1930s meetings of the WFL national executive committee were held at the Minerva although it was described by Mrs Juanita Frances as being, by 1938, a "shabby place" "run on a shoestring". Alice Schofield COATES arranged for her daughter Marion to live at the Minerva when she came to London University in the 1930s. In an interview she, now Mrs Marion Johnson, described the club as "tatty", the carpets threadbare, and the food indifferent, although not sufficiently bad as to dissuade E.M. Forster from breakfasting there. Mrs Johnson also remembered seeing Maud Gonne at the Minerva. She described, with the jaundiced eye of a young woman who would much have preferred not to be living in what she clearly thought were rather eccentric premises, the single bed-sitters, communal dining room, and common room, which was often let for meetings of other societies, such as those of spiritualists. Dr Knight had died in 1933, making no mention of the Minerva in her will, and without her financial support doubtless the club was not economically viable. The Minerva was at some point taken over by Marian Reeves. It was still used residentially after the Second World War; Theresa Garnett was living there in 1947, and the club did not finally disappear until 1962, when it was swept away in the development of what is now the Brunswick Centre.

Archival source: B. Harrison, taped interview with Mrs Juanita Frances, 1974; with Mrs Marion Johnson, 1975, Fawcett Library.

NEW CENTURY CLUB, Hay Hill, London W, was in existence by 1908. Among its members in 1913 was Lisa Gordon, organizing secretary of the Edinburgh branch of the NUWSS, and Leslie McMurdo, who was known to the WSPU as "Leslie Lawless". The club was still in existence in 1928.

NEW COUNTY CLUB, 21 Hanover Square and 84 Grosvenor Street, London W, founded in 1899, a successor to the Ladies' Tea and Shopping Club which had been launched in 1894. Among its members in 1913 were Amy Sharp, chairman of the committee of the Ambleside and District branch of the NUWSS, and M.A.R. Tuker, active member of the WSPU and the CATHOLIC WOMEN'S SUFFRAGE SOCIETY. The club closed during the course of 1923–4. Founder and secretary (1889, 1909) Mr Gilbert Oliver.

NEW ERA LADIES' CLUB, 67 Curzon Street, London W, a combined club and circulating library, affiliated to the Lady Artists' Club, Glasgow. By 1914 it had moved to 11 Curzon Street and by 1924 had closed. Secretary (1909) Mrs Christina McNab.

NEW FRANCES CLUB, 425 Strand, London WC. For an annual subscription of one guinea members had use of a cosy sitting room and dining room, piano, and circulating library.

NEW REFORM CLUB, Adelphi Terrace, London WC, a political club founded for men and women in 1899 as the Liberal Forward Club. Honorary secretary (1909) Holford Knight.

NEW VICTORIAN, 30a Sackville Street, Piccadilly, London W, was founded in 1893 as the Victorian Club for Gentlewomen. Evelyn SHARP, living independently, in her early 20s, moved into the club in 1897, shortly after it had been refounded as the New Victorian. In her autobiography she recorded that the club had a writing room and that the top floor was divided into bedrooms let off to professional women. An inventory of the furnishings of the club reveals that a top-floor bedroom contained 6′ × 9′ Brussels carpet, and iron bedstead, with hair cushions and a feather bed, pillows and bolster. There were three blankets, two bedspreads, an iron washstand, one toilet set, one china pail, a chest of drawers, a painted looking glass, one rush-bottomed chair, two cretonne, two muslin and two sateen curtains. In 1893 the first-floor bedrooms appear to have offered rather more comfort. This club does not appear to have had even an apology for a library. Among the members in 1913 was Gertrude Mosely, joint honorary secretary of the Tunbridge Wells branch of the NUWSS. The club was still in existence in 1928. Honorary secretary (1897) Miss Johnson; proprietress (1909) Mrs Smart.

Archival source: Papers of the Victorian Club for Gentlewomen, Public Record Office.

Bibliography: E. Sharp, *Unfinished Adventure*, 1933.

PIONEER CLUB, founded by Emily MASSINGBERD by 1892 as a home for women of advanced views, although men were invited as guests and as speakers; by 1909 the club is described as "mixed". The Pioneer was initially based at 180 Regent Street, London W, where it had a "Drawing Room, Reading Room, Tea Room, and Visitors' Room, also comfortable Bed Rooms for the use of Members at moderate charges. Annual subscription 2 guineas, entrance fee, 1 guinea". Following the tradition set by the Ladies' Institute, the Pioneer Club offered professional women a lower rate of subscription. By late 1893, by which time it had 320 members, the club had moved to Bruton Street. Its membership badge was a brooch in the shape of a silver axe. Members included Margaret Shurmer Sibthorpe, founder-editor of *Shafts*, Eleanor Marx Aveling,

Olive Schreiner, Dora MONTEFIORE, Harriot Stanton BLATCH, Sarah Grand, Mona CAIRD, and, by 1913, Margery Corbett ASHBY, Mrs Pelham, vice-president of the Newport and District branch of the NUWSS, Mrs Laura Stuart, and Mrs Sarah Smithson, chairman of the committee of the Hitchin, Stevenage and District branch of the NUWSS. The Pioneer encouraged women to discuss political and social questions and to learn how to "separate personal friendships from matters of principle". Debates were held each Thursday evening on such subjects as vivisection, the benefits of socialism for women, co-education and Ibsen's plays. Speakers included Millicent Garrett FAWCETT, Clementina BLACK, Amie HICKS and George Bernard Shaw. In 1893 Isabella FORD opened a Pioneer Club debate on "Why Should Not Women Vote". Dates of Pioneer Club lectures were advertised in *Shafts*, which also included reports of the meetings. The debates were preceded by a club dinner, to which members might bring a friend. Fittingly, as Mrs Massingberd was an earnest worker in the temperance cause, the consumption of alcohol was forbidden, although smoking was allowed. Pioneer members were shocked by the untimely death of Mrs Massingberd and sent to her funeral a floral *memento mori* in the shape of two hatchets crossed, tied together with white, black and grey silk streamers. Dissension among the Pioneers immediately after the death of the founder led to some members leaving in order to join the Grosvenor Crescent Club. The Pioneer moved to 5 Grafton Street, London W in 1898, then to 12 Cavendish Place, London W, and by 1914 was at 9 Park Place, London SW. It was still based at these premises in 1924 but it would seem that at some later point it amalgamated with the Sesame and Imperial clubs. Secretary (1909) Lady Hamilton.

Bibliography: *Shafts*, 3 November 1892; "The Story of the Pioneer Club", *Shafts*, January, February and April 1896. H. Friederichs, "A Peep at the Pioneer Club", *Young Woman*, 1896.

PORTMAN CLUB, 26 George Street, Hanover Street, London W, in existence in 1909.
QUEEN'S CLUB, Edinburgh, 7 Frederick Street, founded in 1897. Residential for visits. Secretary (1909) Miss Lena Meiklejohn. Among its members were Alice Low, a member of the executive committee of the Edinburgh branch of the NUWSS and of the Scottish Federation, and Mrs Florence MacAlister, vice-president of the Oban Suffrage Society (NUWSS).
QUEEN SQUARE CLUB, 9 Queen Square, Bloomsbury, London WC, for men and women, a meeting place for those of all political opinions. In 1906 the club invited the National Union of Women's Suffrage Societies to a debate to discuss the methods of Women's Social and Political Union. The NUWSS replied that as they had not expressed any opinion of the methods employed by the WSPU it could not take part in the discussion. On 21 May 1906 the Queen Square Club was represented, alongside the NUWSS, the WSPU and other organizations, in the deputation to the Prime Minister.
ST ANDREW'S HOUSE CLUB, Tavistock Place, WC, for women engaged in nursing and other professions. Among the club's members in 1913 was Mrs Georgina Foster, honorary treasurer of the Southwold branch of the NUWSS. Honorary secretary (1897) Miss Paddon, 18 Chenies St Chambers, WC; proprietor (1909) Edith Debenham.
SESAME CLUB, 29 Dover Street, founded in 1895 for men and women, by, among others, Lady Isabel MARGESSON. The club organized a literary and educational programme and offered a lower subscription to professional women, especially hoping to attract teachers. May SINCLAIR, Hermione Ramsden, Mrs Eleanor Osmaston, president of the Oxted and Limpsfield branch of the NUWSS, Una DUGDALE, Margaret Tuke, principal of Bedford College and vice-president of the North Herts branches of the NUWSS and of the Conservative and Unionist Women's Franchise Association, Lady Betty Balfour, Mona CAIRD, Catherine MARSHALL and her mother Mrs Caroline Marshall, and Kathleen COURTNEY were among the club's members in 1913. The club was still in existence in 1924. By 1963 the Sesame, Imperial and Pioneer Club (presumably the three had amalgamated) was based at 49 Grosvenor Street, London W. Secretary (1909) Mrs Plowden.
SHUTTLEWORTH CLUB, Fye Foot Lane, Queen Victoria Street, London EC, a social and literary club for men and women. Secretary (1909) H.C. Anning.
SLADE CLUB, The Constable Studios, 78 Charlotte Street, Fitzroy Square, London W, provided a rendezvous for past and present women members of

the Slade School of Fine Art. Honorary secretary and treasurer (1909) Olive Guthrie Ure.

SOCIETY OF LADY ARTISTS' CLUB, 5 Blythswood Square, Glasgow, founded in 1882 to promote art, music, literature, and to provide a convenient centre. Exhibitions of art and of decorative ware by members were held each year. Janie ALLAN used the club as a base while working for the WSPU. Honorary secretary (1909) Miss Smart.

Bibliography: D.L. Dewar, *History of the Glasgow Society of Lady Artists' Club*, 1950.

SOMERVILLE CLUB, founded in 1878, by 1888 was based at 231 Oxford Street, London W, in utilitarian premises above an ABC cafeteria. The club had developed out of the Ladies' Institute and aimed to act as a discussion and social centre across a wide social spectrum. Its subscription being kept low, it catered particularly for women who lived in cramped lodgings. It dissolved itself at the end of 1887 and then re-established itself as the New Somerville Club. By 1898 it was based at 19a Hanover Square, London W. In 1890 the SOCIETY FOR PROMOTING THE RETURN OF WOMEN AS COUNTY COUNCILLORS held a meeting at the club. It appears to have disappeared by 1908. Secretary (1898) Miss E.M. Kerr.

Bibliography: *Women's Gazette*, 25 May 1889.

THE SUFFRAGE CLUB, 3 York Street, London W, for men and women, although bedrooms and board were available to lady members only. Among its members in 1913 were Helen CRAGGS, Joan Dugdale, Lettice MacMunn, a member of the Hastings and St Leonards Women's Suffrage Propaganda League, the novelist Constance Maud, Charlotte Moberly, vice-president of the Oxford branch of the NUWSS, Sime SERUYA, Frances Sutcliffe, secretary of the Buxton branch of the Church League for Women's Suffrage, Olive WALTON, Miss E.G. Wood, and Lady Marie Muir-MacKenzie, who was a member of four suffrage societies and four social clubs. The club appears to have closed in the course of 1916–17.

TWENTIETH CENTURY CLUB, 24–29 Stanley Gardens, London W, a residential ladies' club, with 105 bedrooms. It was founded in 1902 "to provide furnished residential rooms and board at economical prices, for educated women workers engaged in professional, educational, literary, secretarial or other similar work" and to supply them with "attendance, light, coal, dining, library, and other sitting rooms". It was here that Ada FLATMAN was living when she joined the WSPU. Two of the three, male, directors of the company gave their profession as "rentier"; the club was presumably expected to make a profit. The club was still in existence in 1918, but had disappeared by 1924, and was wound up in 1937.

Archival source: Papers of the 20th Century Club Company, Public Record Office.

UNIVERSITY CLUB FOR LADIES, founded in 1887, at 31 New Bond Street, London W; by 1909 it had moved to 34 George Street, Hanover Square, London W, and it later moved to South Audley Street, London W. In 1921 it changed its name to the University Women's Club. Membership was restricted to 300 members, who were required to be university graduates or registered medical practitioners. When first founded, its premises in New Bond Street were described by Amy Levy as "a small but daintily-furnished set of rooms on the upper floor of a house". It was able to supply only simple meals; members requiring more luxurious fare were able to order meals to be sent over from the Grosvenor Gallery restaurant. Writing in 1888 Amy Levy described how the typical member, the "suburban high-school mistress, in town for a day's shopping or picture-seeing, exchanges here the discomfort of the pastrycook's or the costliness of the restaurant for the comforts of a quiet meal and a quiet read or chat in the cosy club precincts; the busy journalist rests here from her labours of 'private viewing,' strengthening herself with tea and newspapers before setting out for fresh lands to conquer". Among the members of the University Club for Ladies in 1913 were Mrs Bertha Johnson, principal of the Society of Oxford Home-Students (now St Anne's College) and vice-president of the Oxford Women Students' Society for Women's Suffrage, Constance Jones, mistress of Girton and member of the Cambridge University branch of the NUWSS and of the Conservative and Unionist Women's Franchise Association, Mrs Maude White, honorary organizing secretary of the Radlett branch of the WSPU, Eleanor Jourdain, vice-principal of St Hugh's College, Oxford, and a member of the NUWSS, Annie Rogers, member of the Oxford Women's Students Suffrage Society, Elizabeth MALLESON (who did not have the requisite formal educational qualifications), Mrs Laura Stuart, Mrs Agnes Suttill, honorary secretary of the West Dorset branch of the NUWSS, Helena SWANWICK, Mary Tait, member of the committee of the Dunfermline branch of the NUWSS, Margaret Tuke, Marian Verrall, chairman of the Brighton and Hove branch of the NUWSS, Alice Zimmern and Mary MacKenzie, who was parliamentary secretary to the NUWSS Election Fighting Fund. Of all the women's clubs of this period the University Woman's is the only one still in existence at the end of the twentieth century. Secretary (1909) Miss L. Brierley.

UNIVERSITY EXTENSION CLUB, Brighton, described in 1906 in the minutes of the Central Society for Women's Suffrage sub-committee on organizations, as "a small mixed club consisting of the most intellectual people in Brighton". This club held a meeting on 29 November 1906 to discuss aspects of the women's suffrage campaign.

VICTORIAN COMMEMORATION CLUB, Southampton Street, Strand, London W, which was in existence in 1898, specifically for the use of trained nurses and associated workers.

WEST RIDING LADIES' CLUB, 14 Park Row, Leeds.

WOMEN'S INSTITUTE, founded at 15 Grosvenor Crescent, London W, by Mrs Nora Wynford Philipps as a centre for women engaged in professional, educational, social and philanthropic work. Lady ABERDEEN was a member of its governing council. The Institute contained a library, a lecture department, a secretarial agency (which also trained typists), a general employment service for members, and various social and educational features. The Institute also ran an Information Bureau which undertook to supply information on general subjects and to do research work in the library of the British Museum. In 1898 the Women's Institute published a *Dictionary of Employments Open to Women*. By 1900 it had over 800 members, had established links with more than 45 societies and had largely succeeded in its aim of acting as an information centre and meeting place for women engaged in social and related work. According to Isabella Ford it "embraces an educational programme of appalling size, to the frivolous mind". The WSPU held a meeting on its premises in May 1907. In 1913 the Institute numbered among its members Rosabel Watson, the conductor of the Aeolian Ladies' Orchestra, which played at many suffrage gatherings. The Institute was still in existence in 1923 but had disappeared by 1928. Sometime after 1900 the Women's Institute moved to 92 Victoria Street, London SW, an address which throughout the first 30 years of the twentieth century housed a variety of feminist organizations, the Women's Pioneer Housing company, the Women's Sanitary Inspectors' and Health Visitors' Association, the National Women's Citizens' Associations, the Six Point Group, and the photographic studio of Madame Yevonde, as well as a society of interest to many women, the National Anti-Vivisection Society.

THE WRITERS' CLUB, Hastings House, 10 Norfolk Street, Strand, London WC, founded in 1892 by a woman journalist, Frances Low, to provide a social and working centre for women authors and journalists. The club, housed on the sub-ground floor of a building that gave shelter to many small businesses associated with publishing and journalism, comprised a reception room, a dining room, an occasional room, and a writing room, where silence was enforced in order that members might work if they so chose. Mrs Flora Annie Steel, a stalwart of the WOMEN WRITERS' SUFFRAGE LEAGUE, was at one time chairwoman of the club. Membership was limited to 300 members. Constance Smedley, who was for a time a member, described the club as "A cosy spot and greatly enjoyed by all of us, but all the same it was not an impressive environment." It was because the food was indifferent and the surroundings of the Writers' Club rather shabby that Constance Smedley led the initiative to found the Lyceum Club. She felt that as women developed their place in the artistic, literary and business worlds so they required surroundings that gave conviction to their established status. Isabella FORD was a member of the Writers' Club, as was Flora DRUMMOND, who invited Mr Baldock (*see* Minnie BALDOCK) to lunch with her there in December 1909. The club was still in existence in 1923. Honorary secretaries (1909) Miss G.M. Ireland Blackburne and Miss L. Mitchell.

Photographs: of Empress Club, Ilchester Club, Ladies' County Club, Pioneer Club, Sesame Club, and Writers' Club in *Lady's Realm*, 5, 1899.

Bibliography: A. Levy, "Women and club life", *Woman's World*, 1888; D. Leighton, *Disillusion*, 1894; E. Lynn Linton, *In Haste and at Leisure*, 1895; F. Marryat, *At Heart A Rake*, 1895; E. Wills, "Ladies' clubs in London", *Lady's Realm*, 5, 1899; Eve Anstruther, "Ladies' clubs", *Nineteenth Century*, 45, 1899; D. Staars, *The English Woman: Studies in her Psychic Revolution*, 1909; E.C. Hargrove, *The Garden of Desire*, 1916.

CLUNAS, LILA (1876–1968)

Born Maggie Clunas in Glasgow. Educated at Bell-Baxter School, Cupar, Fife, and as a teacher at Moray House in Edinburgh. She taught in Dundee and joined the WOMEN'S SOCIAL AND POLITICAL UNION there in 1906. After it was formed, she joined the WOMEN'S FREEDOM LEAGUE and was secretary of the Dundee branch from 1908 until 1912. In 1913 her sister Elsie, with whom she lived, was still treasurer of the branch and another sister, Jessie, was also a member. In 1909 Lila Clunas took part in the WFL picketing of the House of Commons and at the end of June was arrested in Downing Street, attempting to present a petition to Asquith, during the WSPU-organized deputation from the Women's Parliament in Caxton Hall. She was sentenced to three weeks' imprisonment but was released, as the Home Office explained, "on consideration of all the circumstances and as an act of clemency", before the end of her term. She was thereafter an active, if non-militant, suffragist, leading deputations to Winston Churchill, the Dundee MP, organizing meetings, and writing to the press. After the First World War she was a member of the Dundee Town Council, with a particular interest in education.

Address: (1913) 1 Blackness Crescent, Dundee.
Archival source: Home Office Papers, Public Record Office.
Bibliography: L. Leneman, *A Guid Cause: The Women's Suffrage Movement in Scotland*, 1991; N. Watson, *Daughters of Dundee*, 1997.

COATES, ALICE SCHOFIELD, MRS (1881–1975)

Born in Cleveland. She had three brothers and, her mother being unable to cope, Alice was sent to Manchester to be brought up by an uncle and aunt, of whom she was very fond. She gained a teacher-training certificate from Stockwell Training College and taught mathematics at the same school as Teresa Billington (*see* Teresa BILLINGTON-GREIG) in Lower Crumpsall, Manchester, in 1901. Influenced by Teresa Billington, she joined the WOMEN'S SOCIAL AND POLITICAL UNION at the end of 1903/beginning of 1904, very soon after it was formed. She remembered that in mid-1904 Susan B. Anthony, on her way back from the conference of the International Council of Women in Berlin, came to a small room at the top of a warehouse in Portland Street, Manchester, to talk to the embryonic WSPU. In 1907, with Teresa Billington, Alice Schofield left the WSPU to join the WOMEN'S FREEDOM LEAGUE, and from March 1908 was an ORGANIZER. In February 1909 she was sentenced to one month's imprisonment after taking part in the deputation from the Women's Parliament in Caxton Hall to the House of Commons. In old age she described prison as "dreary". In 1909 she was based in Middlesborough, working for the WFL in the north-east and in February 1910, the general election safely out of the way, she married there Charles Coates, who had come to her rescue when she was attacked at an open-air WFL meeting in Guisborough. He was a coal exporter who, until the mid-1920s, was comparatively wealthy. His sister Marion Coates-Hanson had also been an early member of the WSPU before joining the WFL. The Schofield Coates had two daughters and one son, who were brought up in a household of several servants, including a governess and nurse. Alice Schofield Coates later went to Scotland for periods of time in order to organize WFL election campaigns. Throughout the First World War Alice Schofield Coates was an active member of the WFL national executive, often travelling to London for its meetings. In 1920 she was a delegate for the WFL at the conference of the INTERNATIONAL WOMAN SUFFRAGE ALLIANCE in Geneva. In the 1930s she was a vice-president of the WFL. She had from childhood been a vegetarian and in the 1920s ran a health-food restaurant below the WFL office in Middlesborough. This venture, never money-making, was subsidized by her husband until he lost his money in 1924. For a short time after this she was an organizer for the National Union of Women Teachers in the Middlesborough area. She was a life-long member of the Labour party and became a JP. One of her daughters, when an undergraduate at London University, lived for a time in the Minerva Club (*see under* CLUBS).

Address: (1913) Wilstrop House, Roman Road, Linthorpe, Middlesborough; (1975) Levick House, Cambridge Road, Middlesborough.

Archival source: B. Harrison, taped interview with Alice Schofield Coates, 1975; with Mrs Marion Johnson, her elder daughter, 1975, Fawcett Library.

COATES, DORA MEESON, MRS (c. 1870–1955) Born in New Zealand, daughter of a barrister, John Meeson. An artist, in 1893 she studied at the Slade under Henry Tonks, at the National Art Gallery in Melbourne in 1895, and then in Paris, where she shared a studio with Constance Gore-Booth (later Countess Markievicz, the first woman to be elected to the British parliament, and sister of Eva GORE-BOOTH). She worked as a portrait, landscape figure and flower painter and exhibited at the Royal Academy and the Royal Institute of Oil Painters. In her will she left all her paintings and drawings to a great-nephew, although one of her canvases, *Members of the QMAAC at work in the cookhouse, RAF Camp, Charlton Park,* is in the collection of the Imperial War Museum. In 1903 Dora Meeson married in London an Australian artist, George Coates, and they lived in Chelsea at 9 Trafalgar Studios, whose previous tenant had been Augustus John. Dora Coates met and subsequently became very friendly with Mary Sargant FLORENCE, when the latter was looking for a suffrage meeting that was being held in a neighbouring studio. Although history does not record the fact, this studio was probably that belonging to Florence HAIG, who lived at no. 4 and also became a close friend. Certainly it was at a suffrage meeting at Florence's studio, at which Mrs PANKHURST was the principal speaker, that Dora Coates first met Cicely HAMILTON. In 1907 Dora Coates subscribed to the WSPU. She writes that "George and I threw ourselves heart and soul into the suffrage movement". George joined the MEN'S LEAGUE FOR WOMEN'S SUFFRAGE and "walked with me in the processions, which was a great ordeal for him – he hated publicity and crowds". Through the suffrage movement they made friends with Mary LOWNDES and, through her, Christiana HERRINGHAM, the founder of the Tempera Society, Annie SWYNNERTON and Emily FORD, with whom for a time Dora shared a studio. She wrote that she avoided doing anything really militant because her husband would have been upset if she had gone to prison. They did, however, at night, paste notices on public hoardings and pillar boxes in Chelsea. She mentioned that, unlike her husband, Chelsea men artists, always conservative, were not in general supporters of the women's suffrage movement.

Dora Meeson Coates was a member of the ARTISTS' SUFFRAGE LEAGUE and, a socialist, joined the WOMEN'S FREEDOM LEAGUE as soon as it was formed, a member of its Kensington branch. On one occasion she lent her studio to Mrs DESPARD in order to hold a suffrage meeting and in the summer of 1908, while they were on holiday on the south coast, the Coates met at Sandwich Mrs Despard, who was on a CARAVAN lecture tour, and, in breaks from sketching, chalked pavements for her and attended her outdoor meetings. In 1907 Dora Coates was the winner of a poster competition organized by the NUWSS and the Artists' Suffrage League ("Mrs John Bull: Now you greedy boys. I shall not give you any more until I have helped myself"). In 1909, with Mary Lowndes and C. Hedley Charlton, she contributed line drawings to *Beware! A Warning to Suffragists*, with words by Cicely Hamilton, and to *A.B.C. of Politics for Women Politicians*, delightful, now very scarce, examples of work published by the Artists' Suffrage League. She designed the "Commonwealth Australia" BANNER that was carried in the National Union of Women's Suffrage Societies procession of 13 June 1908 and she herself "was one of the four bearers who staggered under its weight when we passed a windy corner" in the 1911 Coronation procession. This banner is now in the Parliament House Collection in Canberra. On 30 September 1909 her full-page cartoon, "Miss Wales: 'Do justice to the women, David'", appeared in the *Common Cause*. In 1912 Dora Coates was a member of the London-based AUSTRALIAN AND NEW ZEALAND WOMEN VOTERS' COMMITTEE. Her husband was friendly with, and indeed painted the portrait of, Will Dyson, another Australian expatriate artist, who, with an excellent line in dramatically pro-suffrage images, became the *Daily Herald*'s cartoonist (*see under* NEWSPAPERS AND JOURNALS). George Coates also painted the portrait of Arthur Walker, the sculptor of the statue of Emmeline Pankhurst; a joint portrait of Cicely Hamilton and her sister, Evie Hammill, which was exhibited at the Royal Academy in 1913; a portrait of Kate Courtney, also exhibited at the Royal Academy in 1913; and one of her sister

Beatrice Webb, which now hangs in the London School of Economics. In her biography of her husband Dora Coates gives a complete list of all his major work; unfortunately no-one has done the same for her and it is not known if she herself painted any members of her circle. In 1930 she is described in *The Woman's Leader* as "well-known for her Thames pictures and studies of little children".

As soon as war was declared in August 1914 Dora Meeson Coates was one of the first to enrol in Miss Damer Dawson's newly formed Women's Police Force, becoming, by 1915, chief inspector. She was also during the war Australia's representative in London at meetings of the BRITISH DOMINIONS WOMAN SUFFRAGE UNION. In 1920, with other former members of the Artists' Suffrage League, she worked on a frieze illustrative of women's work during the war that decorated the hall of Danecourt, at Danehill near Brighton, the home of Mrs William Corbett. She mentions that in these post-war years she often met Mrs Jopling ROWE and Flora Lion, who painted the portrait of Flora DRUMMOND.

Address: (1913) 55 Glebe Place, Chelsea. London SW; (1952) 52 Glebe Place, Chelsea, London SW.
Portrait: watercolour, by George Coates, Print Room, Victoria and Albert Museum; photograph in D.M. Coates, *George Coates: His Art and Life*, 1937.
Bibliography: D.M. Coates, *George Coates: His Art and Life*, 1937; L. Tickner, *The Spectacle of Women: Imagery of the Suffrage Campaign, 1907–14*, 1987.

COBBE, FRANCES POWER (1822–1904) Feminist, campaigning journalist, and philanthropist. She was born in Newbridge, County Dublin, into an influential Anglo-Irish family, and received a typical education, of which she gives full damning details in her autobiography, for a girl of her class. Thereafter, as was expected of her, she remained at home although this fallow period allowed ample time to think, and (what was not expected) thinking led her into a full-blown agnosticism which eventually evolved, after her mother's death, into a religious position akin to Unitarianism. When she revealed to her father her rejection of Christianity she appears to have felt herself threatened with disinheritance, but eventually she settled down in the family home as her father's housekeeper. In 1857, after her father's death, her brother inherited the house and estate and Frances was left with an annuity of £200. After extensive travelling, meeting in Rome the circle of emancipated women that included Mary Somerville, Matilda Hays and Mary Lloyd, with whom she was eventually to spend the rest of her life, she went to Bristol to work at the Red Lodge reformatory with Mary Carpenter. During these years she, as she recorded, "turned out (as a painter would say) a great many *Pot-Boilers*", that is, articles on a wide range of subjects for British and Italian papers and journals. She then settled in London and turned her attention seriously to journalism, specializing in religious and social themes including "Women's Rights". Her articles on this subject included "Female Charity, Lay and Monastic" and "What Shall We Do With Our Old Maids?", both published in *Fraser's Magazine*, 1862, "Women in Italy in 1862", and "Social Science Congresses and Women's Part in Them". In 1862 she read a paper on "University Degrees for Women" at the annual meeting of the Social Science Association. She was one of the earliest members of the KENSINGTON SOCIETY, joining in March 1865. Emily DAVIES copied out, and thereby preserved, a paper Frances Power Cobbe wrote for the Kensington Society on "The Limits of Obedience of Daughters", a subject of particularly personal relevance. On 7 June 1866 A.J. Munby met Frances Power Cobbe at Clementia TAYLOR's house in Kensington in "a small party of women (Mr Shaen and I the only men, for Mr Taylor was at the House)". He described her as "round and fat as a Turkish sultana, with yellow hair, and face mature and pulpy, but keen and shrewd and pleasantly humorous, who sat talking lively unpretending talk to a circle of admirers. The women's petition, which she and Mme BODICHON and Mrs Taylor have got up, was presented tonight by J.S. MILL. They say it has 1500 signatures". Frances Power Cobbe and Mary Lloyd were present at the meeting in October 1866 at which the ENFRANCHISEMENT OF WOMEN COMMITTEE was formed, and Miss Cobbe became a subscriber until the Committee formally dissolved in July 1867. On 15 June 1867 Mentia Taylor wrote to Helen TAYLOR, who had been in France, "I am v pleased to have had the opportunity of introducing you and Miss Cobbe to each other – and though she is somewhat conservative – and differs from us in many points

– she is so earnest in our present work – and so straightforward – that I feel her cooperation will be of great value to us." Frances Power Cobbe had had discussions with Mentia Taylor in the previous month about forming a new women's suffrage society and, with Helen Taylor, the three were the force behind the founding of the LONDON NATIONAL SOCIETY FOR WOMEN'S SUFFRAGE. She wished the society to be called the London National Society for Woman Suffrage, according to Mentia Taylor (in a letter to Helen Taylor, 15 July 1867) "strongly objecting to the use of the genitive". J.S. Mill, the often invisible power behind Helen Taylor, revealed himself in favour of "Women's Suffrage" and thus it was. By October 1867 differences between Frances Power Cobbe and other members of the committee led to her resignation, along with that of her two supporters, Mary Lloyd and Miss Hampson. The ostensible reason for their resignation was that they did not care for the nature of the union of the London and Manchester societies and were worried that London might be held responsible for any, presumably too radical, actions of which they might not approve. Mentia Taylor thought that Frances Power Cobbe was influenced by Mary Lloyd's (inferior) mind. In a letter dated 4 December 1867 Frances Power Cobbe wrote to Helen Taylor, "But in truth the different ideas of radicals and conservatives as to which is advisable under a hundred circumstances are more various than I had imagined and I came to the conclusion that Miss Hampson and Miss Lloyd – and in many cases myself, would be mere obstructions to the action of the others, or else called on to yield successively every point of judgement". She developed the point that she had had strong misgivings about the amalgamation of the societies but had bowed to Helen Taylor's wishes. "It sounds very ungenerous to go on harping about the possibility of the Manchester ladies (who have hitherto done nothing but what is judicious and spirited), acting in a way to which we should not wish to commit ourselves. But this woman-question is precisely the one on which it is hardest and yet most imperative to preserve the strictest dignity and on which I could trust only those I know most thoroughly to take any step of importance. I would not for instance have found Miss Matilda Hays writing as Secretary for a society in which I had a prominent place for anything that could be named. I am sure you feel *quite* with me in this, though perhaps you would be more generally ready to run a risk for the good of a political cause than I would be." It is interesting to note that it was the unmarried members of the executive committee, Mary Lloyd and Frances Power Cobbe, who had themselves been part of the circle of emancipated women in Rome with Matilda Hays in the late 1850s, who, with Miss Hampson, should be the ones who feared most to be associated publicly with such strong-minded Manchester women as Lydia BECKER. There was no suggestion that Matilda Hays should be secretary of the society; the introduction of her name, which since the days in Rome had been tarnished by the suggestion of scandal, was presumably as a metaphor for that which was most reprehensible in the feminist cause. Frances Power Cobbe did remain a member of the general committee of the London National Society. In November 1868 she wrote to Helen Taylor, telling her that her name (presumably as "Francis") appeared on the electoral register in Chelsea, and asking for J.S. Mill's ruling on whether or not she should attempt to exercise this vote. She continues "Of course I would rather not incur the exceptional publicity of voting now all other women's claims have been refused – but the point is simply whether (supposing my claim to stand) I shall do good or harm to our cause". She was obviously not afraid to expose herself to the possibility of notoriety if Mill deemed it necessary. For the London National Society in 1869 she wrote "Why Women Desire the Franchise" (which was updated and reprinted for the Central Committee *c.* 1873) and in the early 1870s another pamphlet, "Our Policy: An Address to Women concerning the Suffrage". Always a Conservative, in the mid-1880s Frances Power Cobbe became a Dame of the PRIMROSE LEAGUE. As one might expect from one of her Anglo-Irish background, she abhorred Gladstone and Home Rule. Speaking at the Women's Suffrage Conference held at the Westminster Palace Hotel in May 1872 she observed that it was a Conservative principle that those who paid their taxes should have representation, and that it was most important that those who had the greatest interest in the peace and good government of the country should have the power, and not those "who were in the habit of turning the world topsy turvy". Time had overtaken whatever had been at the root of her resignation from the London National Society and in 1872 she became a member of the executive committee of the newly formed CENTRAL COMMITTEE OF THE NATIONAL SOCIETY FOR WOMEN'S SUFFRAGE, working alongside such Manchester radicals as Mr and Mrs Jacob BRIGHT. The intervening five years had obviously brought about a lessening of her apprehension about the judiciousness of their behaviour. She was still a member of this executive committee in 1888 and, when in that year the society split, wrote of the episode in her autobiography, "[I] naturally followed my fellow-Unionist, Mrs FAWCETT, when she reorganized the moiety of the society and established an office for it in College Street, Westminster". Frances Power Cobbe was, however, no longer a member of the executive committee. In her autobiography she dated the split to after Lydia Becker's death, although that did not occur until mid-1890, implying that if she had been alive it might not have taken place, and adding another mote to the Lydia Becker "myth". From 1871 until 1874 Frances Power Cobbe was a member of the executive committee of the Married Women's Property Committee, working alongside Lydia Becker, Jacob and Ursula Bright, Lilias (see Lilias Ashworth HALLETT) and Anne ASHWORTH, and Mentia Taylor on this other feminist cause, to which she contributed many books and articles, the most notorious of which was "Truth on Wife Torture", *Contemporary Review*, 1878. Her other great cause was that of anti-vivisection in which she took a leading part, being co-founder of the Victoria Street Society for the Protection of Animals liable to Vivisection and, by her own estimation, writing for that society over 400 pamphlets.

Address: (1866) 26 Hereford Square, London SW.
Photograph: in *Life of Frances Power Cobbe by Herself*, 1894.
Archival source: Mill–Taylor Papers, London School of Economics and Political Science; Emily Davies Papers, Girton College.
Bibliography: *Life of Frances Power Cobbe by Herself*, 1894; D. Hudson, *Munby, Man of Two Worlds: The Life and Diaries of Arthur J. Munby, 1828–1910*, 1974; L. Holcombe, *Wives and Property*, 1983; J. Lewis (ed.), *Before the Vote was Won*, 1987 (includes a reprint of F. Power Cobbe, "Our policy: an address to women concerning suffrage"; "Speech at the women's suffrage meeting, St George's Hall, 13 May 1876"); M.A. Elston, "Women and anti-vivisection", in N. Rupke (ed.), *Vivisection in Historical Perspective*, 1987; B. Caine, *Victorian Feminists*, 1992.

CODD, CLARA (1877–1971) The eldest of ten girls in a west-country Liberal family. Her father was an inspector of schools in Devon and Cornwall. After a time spent as a governess in Ireland, she returned home to Bath and in 1905 became a theosophist, as eventually did her entire family, and a member of the Social Democratic Federation. In 1907 she was asked by Aeta LAMB, who was organizing for the WOMEN'S SOCIAL AND POLITICAL UNION in the west country, to act as a steward at a meeting addressed by Christabel PANKHURST and Annie KENNEY. It was the latter who attracted Clara Codd and she immediately joined the WSPU. She was also in the spring of 1908 a member of the Bath branch of the NATIONAL UNION OF WOMEN'S SUFFRAGE SOCIETIES, helping at NUWSS meetings until resigning in April 1908 to become honorary secretary of the newly founded Bath WSPU. In the summer Clara Codd went to work for Annie Kenney in Bristol, eventually resigning her post as a governess. As she wrote, "Miss Kenney asked a wealthy woman sympathizer to give me 10/– a week for passing needs and I continued to share her big bed". She gave a description in her autobiography of life as an ORGANIZER in Bristol. She never mentioned by name Mary BLATHWAYT, Annie Kenney's other acolyte of this period, although Clara and her sisters feature in Mary's diary. On 5 July 1908 Mary noted, "Later I rested with Annie on her bed; Miss Douglas Smith in another bed in the same room." Obviously Annie's bed was a much contested trophy. In October 1908, clearly influenced by Annie Kenney who "flung her arms round my neck with joy", Clara Codd volunteered to take part in the "rush" on the House of Commons. She partnered Mabel CAPPER, was arrested and sentenced to one month's imprisonment. Her autobiography contains a detailed description of prison life. Christabel Pankhurst obviously spotted Clara Codd as suitable material as an organizer and she was offered a training in London under Flora DRUMMOND and a salary of £2 per week. However, Clara Codd turned down the offer and devoted the rest of her life to the THEOSOPHICAL SOCIETY. She may have

influenced Annie Kenney's thinking, although Annie did not formally join the Theosophists until 1912.
Address: (1908) 12 Springfield Place, Bath; (1971) Flat 3, Ways End, Beech Avenue, Camberley, Surrey.
Photograph: by Col Blathwayt in B.M. Willmott Dobbie, *A Nest of Suffragettes in Somerset*, 1959.
Bibliography: C. Codd, *So Rich A Life*, 1951.
Archival source: Blathwayt diaries, The National Trust, Dyrham Park, Avon.

COHEN, LEONORA, MRS (1873–1978) Born in Leeds, daughter of Canova Throp, a sculptor. She married Henry Cohen in 1898 and they had one son. She became a member of the Leeds branch of the WOMEN'S SOCIAL AND POLITICAL UNION and in November 1911 came to London, paying her own fare, as she noted, to take part in the demonstration in Parliament Square. She recorded that she was roughly handled there by the police and then decided to make a protest against this treatment by breaking the window of the Local Government Board office. She was sentenced to seven days' imprisonment in Holloway. She took part in the March 1912 window-smashing campaign but managed to evade arrest. At the end of January 1913, representing the tailoresses of Leeds, she was a member of a WSPU deputation of working women led by Flora DRUMMOND from a rally in the Horticultural Hall in Vincent Square to a meeting with Lloyd George, Sir Edward Grey and other members of the cabinet at the House of Commons. They received bland assurances that women would be included in the proposed government Franchise Bill and when a few days later this was withdrawn, Mrs Cohen took her part in the resulting protest by breaking the glass of a showcase displaying the Regalia of the Order of Merit in the Tower of London. She was arrested and tried, but after the jury was unable to reach a verdict, the case against her was dismissed. During this visit to London she stayed with Mrs Morrison, a sister of Professor Gilbert Murray. During 1913 she may have been imprisoned for a time in Armley Prison, Leeds. In 1914 Leonora Cohen joined the club-wielding bodyguard that attempted to protect Mrs Pankhurst from recapture by the police. Mrs Cohen noted that in 1913 she had already been a vegetarian for 22 years; she was to remain so for the rest of her life, spending her final years in a vegetarian old people's home. In June 1914 she ran her home in Harrogate as guest-house, advertising it in the *Suffragette* as "Pomona", a "Reform Food Establishment. Excellent catering by specialist in Reform diets. Late Dinners. Separate Tables". From 1909 she was a member of the THEOSOPHICAL SOCIETY and eventually became a member of the Ancient and Mystical Order of Rosae Crucis. She was a magistrate in Leeds for 30 years, the first woman in Leeds to serve on a prison visiting committee, and in 1928 was awarded the OBE in recognition of her social work. She was president of Leeds Trades Council and Leeds district organizer for the National Union of General and Municipal Workers. In the 1930s she was a member of the WOMEN'S FREEDOM LEAGUE. In 1966 a scrapbook she had kept detailing her suffrage activities was displayed at the Abbey House Museum in Leeds.
Address: (1914) "Pomona", Harlow Moor Drive, Harrogate; (1934) 2 Claremont Villas, Leeds 2.
Photograph: Suffragette Fellowship Collection, Museum of London.
Bibliography: A. Raeburn, *The Militant Suffragettes*, 1973.

COIT, ADELA STANTON, MRS (1863–1932) Born in Frankfurt-am-Main, Germany, married, as her second husband, Dr Stanton COIT in 1898. She had six children, three from each marriage. In 1904, with her husband, she attended the meeting in Berlin at which the INTERNATIONAL WOMAN SUFFRAGE ALLIANCE was founded. This was an aspect of the suffrage movement in which she was especially interested and in 1907 she became treasurer of the IWSA, working actively for the Alliance throughout the First World War. She subscribed to the WOMEN'S SOCIAL AND POLITICAL UNION in 1907. In 1911 she held a drawing-room meeting for the TAX RESISTANCE LEAGUE; in 1912, having transferred her allegiance from the WSPU, she was a member of the first Election Fighting Fund Committee of the NATIONAL UNION OF WOMEN'S SUFFRAGE SOCIETIES, still a member in 1917; and by 1913 she was a member of the executive committee of the LONDON SOCIETY FOR WOMEN'S SUFFRAGE.
Address: (1904) 30 Hyde Park Gate, London SW.
Photograph: in M. Bosch, *Politics and Friendship: Letters from the International Woman Suffrage Alliance, 1902–1942*, 1990.
Bibliography: M. Bosch, *Politics and Friendship: Letters from the International Woman Suffrage Alliance, 1902–1942*, 1990.

COIT, STANTON, DR (1857–1944) Born in Columbus, Ohio, educated at Amherst College, Columbia College and Berlin University, from where he received his doctorate. His mother was a friend of Susan B. Anthony. He founded the New York University settlements before becoming a minister of the Ethical Church. He came to London in 1888 and was eventually naturalized as a British subject. He assisted in founding 40 Ethical societies in Britain, becoming the leader of the country's Ethical movement. He succeeded, as minister of the South Place Chapel, Moncure D. Conway who had in turn followed in the footsteps of that early supporter of women's suffrage, William Johnson Fox. Stanton Coit was a member of the WOMEN'S FRANCHISE LEAGUE in 1890 and in 1891 proposed a vote of thanks at the annual general meeting of the CENTRAL NATIONAL SOCIETY. By 1899 he was involved with the Independent Labour Party. In 1901 he was a contributor to the "Grateful Fund" that gave a sum of money each year to Elizabeth Wolstenholme ELMY. She, however, rather regretted his involvement, writing in December, "I am a little sorry that Dr Stanton Coit is a contributor to the G.F.; I do not wish to be unfair, but I cannot trust him. He seems to me to be more anxious to found a new sect, of which he shall be pope, than to do real service to humanity – I should like to find myself mistaken". In 1903 he was a member of the executive committee of the CENTRAL SOCIETY FOR WOMEN'S SUFFRAGE. With his wife Adela (*see* Adela Stanton COIT), he was a delegate in 1904 to the conference in Berlin at which the INTERNATIONAL WOMEN'S SUFFRAGE ALLIANCE was founded. While there he met the American delegates and Elizabeth Wolstenholme Elmy reported in a letter to Harriet MCILQUHAM, 12 October 1904, that "Lucy and Susan Anthony and Anna Shaw have much the same opinion of Dr Coit as I have – that he is a pretty considerable *humbug* – working really for his own ends. They admire Mrs Coit very much indeed, and think *her* incomparably his superior in ability, industry and usefulness. The thing they count most to his credit . . . is that he has won and returns the love of such a woman – but – he does not half appreciate her". Elizabeth Wolstenholme Elmy had lent to Dr Stanton Coit her notes on the changes since 1869 in the law as it affected women for his use while preparing a new edition of J.S. MILL's *Subjection of Women* that was eventually published by Longmans in 1906. He does acknowledge her help, although Elizabeth Wolstenholme Elmy in her 1904 letter had been sure that "he will undoubtedly make a real hash of the whole matter . . . The misfortune – the horrid misfortune of our WS cause is that it is burdened with so many persons of this same calibre – who delay our progress, hampering and hindering in every way". Elizabeth Wolstenholme Elmy wrote for a time in 1904 and 1905 for Stanton Coit's journal *Ethics*, but fell out with him over what she termed "impertinent editing".

Stanton Coit spoke in April 1905 at the inaugural meeting of the Hammersmith committee of the Central Society and became treasurer of the MEN'S LEAGUE FOR WOMEN'S SUFFRAGE when it was formed in 1907 although, by 1913, he held no position within the League. In 1912 he subscribed to the NUWSS Election Fighting Fund and in 1913 supported the NATIONAL POLITICAL LEAGUE.

Address: (1904) 30 Hyde Park Gate, London W; (1944) The Birlings, Birling Gap, Eastbourne, Sussex
Photograph: in F.J. Gould, *The Pioneers of Johnson's Court*, 1929.

COLCHESTER (NUWSS) In 1913 the society was a member of the EASTERN COUNTIES FEDERATION OF THE NATIONAL UNION OF WOMEN'S SUFFRAGE SOCIETIES. Secretary (1913) was based at 16 North Hill, Colchester, Essex.

COLOURS Colours were first used to give identity to a women's suffrage society by the NATIONAL UNION OF WOMEN'S SUFFRAGE SOCIETIES, which had adopted red and white as early as 1906. Green had been added to these by November 1909, when an exhortation from Helen FRASER went out in the *Common Cause* to make these, as constitutional colours, as well known as their militant counterparts. One gloss given, in the *Common Cause,* 26 May 1910, to the use of these three colours was that red, white and green were the colours of the standard of the Italian Risorgimento, and therefore were used in memory of Garibaldi and Mazzini.

In its early days the WOMEN'S SOCIAL AND POLITICAL UNION's "Votes for Women" flags had been red and white, although it is unclear whether this was to show solidarity with socialism, with suffrage, or simply because it made a bright banner. Emmeline PETHICK-LAWRENCE in May 1908 introduced purple, white and green as the colours for the WSPU for use at the Hyde Park rally of 21 June. In her article, "The Political Importance of the Colours", *Votes for Women,* 7 May 1909, Christabel PANKHURST lauded the success of the use of the colours and heralded the coming WSPU Exhibition at the Prince's Skating Rink as a magnificent opportunity for purchasing the myriad of purple, white and green articles ingeniously devised by the Union. By so doing, and wearing the results, she wrote that "every member of the Union will become an advertiser for the Exhibition, and will bring to the Prince's Skating rink a dozen or a score, or an even larger number, of men and women of her acquaintance who, seeing for themselves, will appreciate for the first time the strength of the woman's movement". The programme of the Exhibition contained an article by Emmeline Pethick-Lawrence giving a soulful gloss to the colours (white for purity, green for hope, and purple for dignity). Other suffrage societies followed suit and adopted their own combination of colours by which they might be represented at meetings and in processions.

- ACTRESSES' FRANCHISE LEAGUE = pink and green
- CATHOLIC WOMEN'S SUFFRAGE SOCIETY = blue, white and gold
- CHURCH LEAGUE FOR WOMEN'S SUFFRAGE = yellow and white
- CIVIL SERVICE SUFFRAGE SOCIETY = gold and blue
- CONSERVATIVE AND UNIONIST WOMEN'S FRANCHISE ASSOCIATION = pale blue, white and gold
- EAST LONDON FEDERATION OF THE SUFFRAGETTES = purple, white, green and red
- FREE CHURCH LEAGUE FOR WOMEN'S SUFFRAGE = blue, green and white
- INTERNATIONAL WOMAN SUFFRAGE ALLIANCE = white and gold
- JEWISH LEAGUE FOR WOMAN SUFFRAGE = purple and celestial blue
- LONDON GRADUATES' UNION FOR WOMEN'S SUFFRAGE = black, white and green
- MEN'S LEAGUE FOR WOMEN'S SUFFRAGE = black and gold
- MEN'S POLITICAL UNION FOR WOMEN'S ENFRANCHISEMENT = purple, white and green
- MEN'S SOCIETY FOR WOMEN'S RIGHTS = violet and white
- NATIONAL UNION OF WOMEN'S SUFFRAGE SOCIETIES = red, white and green
- NEW CONSTITUTIONAL SOCIETY FOR WOMEN'S SUFFRAGE = green, white and silver
- NORTHERN MEN'S FEDERATION = red, white, gold and black
- SUFFRAGE ATELIER = blue, black and yellow
- TAX RESISTANCE LEAGUE = black, white and grey
- VOTES FOR WOMEN FELLOWSHIP = purple, white and red
- WOMEN WRITERS' SUFFRAGE LEAGUE = black, white and gold
- WOMEN'S FREEDOM LEAGUE = green, white and gold
- WOMEN'S SOCIAL AND POLITICAL UNION = purple, white and green
- YOUNGER SUFFRAGISTS = red, white and green

Bibliography: L. Tickner, *The Spectacle of Women: Imagery of the Suffrage Campaign 1907–14,* 1987.

COLWYN BAY (NUWSS) In 1913 the society was a member of the WEST LANCS, WEST CHESHIRE, AND NORTH WALES FEDERATION OF THE NATIONAL UNION OF WOMEN'S SUFFRAGE SOCIETIES. Secretary (1913) Miss M. Spencer, Farlands, Penrhyn Bay, nr Llandudno.

COMMITTEE FOR THE REPEAL OF THE PRISONERS' (Temporary Discharge for Ill-Health) ACT, 1913 Commonly called the "Cat and Mouse" Act. This committee included Ruth Cavendish-BENTINCK, Zelie Emerson, George LANSBURY, Charles and Edith MANSELL-MOULLIN, Margaret and Rachel McMillan, Flora MURRAY and Lady Sybil Smith.

CONGLETON AND MID-CHESHIRE committee of the NATIONAL SOCIETY FOR WOMEN'S SUFFRAGE Formed in 1872. Among its members were Mr B.J. Elmy, Buglawton and Miss Wolstenholme, Moody Hall, Congleton, Cheshire (*see* Elizabeth Wolstenholme ELMY).

CONISTON (NUWSS) In 1913 the society was a member of the NORTH-WESTERN FEDERATION OF THE NATIONAL UNION OF WOMEN'S SUFFRAGE SOCIETIES. Secretary (1913) Miss Mary Dixon, Haws Bank, Coniston, Lancashire.

CONOLAN, GERTRUDE (1872–?) Born in Cheshire, the grand-daughter of two MPs, one of whom was Sir Oswald Mosley, MP for Burton-on-Trent. She was educated at St Margaret's Convent, East Grinstead, at a Kindergarten Training College, and in Paris. She was a teacher at Highbury and Islington GPDST High School when she joined the WOMEN'S SOCIAL AND POLITICAL UNION in 1906. She became treasurer of the Kensington branch and had a platform at the Hyde Park Demonstration in June 1908. By October 1908 she had moved to Scotland, as WSPU ORGANIZER in Glasgow, where she remained until at least December 1910. She took part in the "Black Friday" demonstration in Parliament Square in November 1910. In 1911 Gertrude Conolan subscribed to the NEW CONSTITUTIONAL SOCIETY FOR WOMEN'S SUFFRAGE. In August 1911 she succeeded Joan Dugdale as secretary of the ACTRESSES' FRANCHISE LEAGUE and in November 1912, while retaining this position, also became honorary secretary of the newly formed FEDERATED COUNCIL OF SUFFRAGE SOCIETIES.
Photograph: *Votes for Women*, 7 May 1908.

CONSERVATIVE AND UNIONIST WOMEN'S FRANCHISE ASSOCIATION Founded in November 1908, "To form a bond of union between all Conservative and Unionists who are in favour of the removal of the sex disqualification and the extension of the franchise to all duly-qualified women. To work for women's enfranchisement by educative and constitutional methods consistent with Unionist principles. To maintain the principles of the Conservative and Unionist party with regard to the basis on which the franchise should rest, and to oppose manhood suffrage in any form. The Association, though pledging itself not to oppose any official Unionist candidate yet, will not work as an Association for any candidate who is opposed to Women's Franchise." In 1910 the Association published a pamphlet, "An Analysis of the debate in the House of Commons on the Woman's Franchise Bill, 11 and 12 July, 1910", written by Lady Betty Balfour, sister of Lady Constance LYTTON, and in 1912 Lady Julia Chance's, "Words to Working Women on Women's Suffrage". The first president of the Association was Lady KNIGHTLEY of Fawsley. Among the vice-presidents were Constance Jones, the Mistress of Girton; Lady STRACHEY; and Miss Tuke of Bedford College. The president (1913) was the Countess of Selborne. On 13 March 1918 the Association participated in the NATIONAL UNION OF WOMEN'S SUFFRAGE SOCIETIES' victory celebration held at the Queen's Hall.
Secretary (1909) Mrs Gilbert Samuel.
Address: (1909, 1917) 48 Dover Street, Mayfair, London.

COOK, HARRIET (1843–1869) Born at St Andrews, one of the daughters of John Cook, professor of ecclesiastical history at the University. In 1862 she met and became friendly with Elizabeth Garrett (*see* Elizabeth Garrett ANDERSON) when the latter lived for a time at St Andrews in order to attend medical classes. Harriet Cook at this time probably also met Emily DAVIES who visited Elizabeth Garrett at St Andrews. Harriet Cook was later a member of the KENSINGTON SOCIETY, often visited Elizabeth Garrett in London, and during one of these sojourns assisted with the mechanics of organizing the women's suffrage petition in May 1866. It was suggested, after the petition had been presented and when a committee was being set up, that Harriet Cook, for a salary at a rate of £60 for six months, might act as an assistant to Emily Davies so that the latter could carry on working for the franchise as well as for education. Harriet Cook does appear to have been appointed as assistant secretary, in the event to Louisa SMITH rather than to Emily Davies, of the ENFRANCHISEMENT OF WOMEN COMMITTEE for six months from 1 January 1867. The salary agreed on was rather less than that originally proposed, being at the rate of £50 a year. The accounts of the Enfranchisement of Women Committee, which run from October 1866 to July 1867 show that she actually received £25. Her name does not feature again in correspondence and it is likely that when Elizabeth Garrett (as a member of the "quiet section") retired in June 1867 from direct involvement in the suffrage campaign, Harriet Cook went also.

Harriet Cook certainly remained in close touch with Elizabeth Garrett because in 1868, while again staying with her, she was present during a discussion about the founding of a women's college at Hitchin. She mentioned that friends in St Andrews were interested in the proposal and thus it was that her younger sister Rachel (1848–1905, later Mrs

C.P. Scott, the wife of the editor of the *Manchester Guardian*) was one of the Girton Pioneers. An elder sister, Mrs Elizabeth Rodger (c. 1840–1916) was one of the founders of St Leonards School, St Andrews, of which yet another sister, Isabella (1841–1894), was for many years secretary. Harriet Cook was cut off before she was able to contribute any further to the woman's cause, dying of TB in London, after a three-month illness.

Address: (1866) Mansefield, St Andrews; (1869) 16 Cambridge Square, Paddington, London W.

Archival source: Mill–Taylor Papers, London School of Economics and Political Science.

COOKE, MRS RUSSELL See DILKE, [MARGARET MARY] MAYE, MRS.

COOPER, SELINA, MRS (1864–1946) Born in Cornwall but, after her father's early death, left with the remainder of her family for Lancashire, where, not yet 12 years old, she went to work in a cotton mill. Politically aware and outspoken, she became associated with the Social Democratic Federation, through which she probably met Robert Cooper, a cotton weaver, whom she married in 1896. In 1898 she founded a local branch of the Women's Co-operative Guild and in 1900, now living in Nelson where she was to spend the rest of her life, she collected 800 of the 29 359 signatures for the petition launched among the women cotton workers of Lancashire by Esther ROPER and Eva GORE-BOOTH of the NORTH OF ENGLAND SOCIETY FOR WOMEN'S SUFFRAGE. With 14 other suffragists, including Sarah REDDISH with whom she had worked for some time in the Women's Co-operative Guild, she went to London in March 1901 to take the petition to the House of Commons and was dined by members of the NATIONAL UNION OF WOMEN'S SUFFRAGE SOCIETIES, including Millicent Garrett FAWCETT, Lady Frances BALFOUR and Isabella FORD. In 1901, sponsored as a joint SDF–ILP candidate, Selina Cooper was elected as a representative for Nelson on the Burnley Board of Guardians. In 1902 she was involved in the campaign, sponsored by the Labour Representation Committee, to elect David Shackleton as the MP for Clitheroe. A levy on all trade unionists, women as well as men, to pay for the campaign, highlighted the anomaly that women were subsidizing the election of an MP for whom they could not vote, and gave impetus to the involvement of the North of England Society for Women's Suffrage. Esther Roper, Eva Gore-Booth, Sarah Reddish, Mrs PANKHURST, still a member of the ILP, and Christabel PANKHURST all took part in the campaign and pressed Shackleton for an assurance that he would take the fight for women's suffrage into the House of Commons. Although this was easily given it soon became clear that Shackleton, once in parliament, was not taking their cause seriously. The leaders of the North of England Society, who now included Selina Cooper, decided to sponsor their own suffrage candidate and, as a vehicle, formed the LANCASHIRE AND CHESHIRE WOMEN TEXTILE AND OTHER WORKERS' REPRESENTATION COMMITTEE which ran, without success, a women's suffrage candidate at the general election of January 1906.

In early 1905 Selina Cooper was the delegate from the Nelson ILP to the Labour Representation Committee Conference held that year at the Sun Hall, Liverpool. Soon after her return home she received a letter from Emmeline Pankhurst who wrote, "I hope you feel more cheerful than when we parted in Liverpool and ready to renew the fight. . . . I think that Mr Shackleton should be told that Mr Hardie means to reintroduce the Bill next session and should be asked to back it and ballot for a place. . . . If I can be of any use to you in getting the textile women to assert themselves let me know and I will do all I can". The reason for Selina Cooper's depression was the implacable opposition that had been shown by the Labour Representation Committee for anything other than adult suffrage; the conference rejected her assertion that a large body of "working-class" women would be emancipated under the existing property qualifications and insisted that this would only give the vote to "propertied women". The bill, introduced by Bamford Slack (Keir HARDIE had not been lucky in the ballot) was talked out. In October 1905 Christabel Pankhurst, replying to Selina Cooper who had obviously congratulated her on the stand she had taken at the Free Trade Hall in Manchester, wrote "The Oldham ILP is holding a meeting on Thursday next for Miss Kenney and myself to address. The Sheffield ILP will do the same. Could anything be done in your district? I am sure all the lady Liberals and Tories will be heckled when they speak in your neighbourhood. We shall soon be able to prove that there is a strong demand for the franchise for women. I want to see it in the King's Speech next Session and if we go on as we have begun – making meetings impossible – there will soon be heard from Liberal and Tories a fervent prayer for Women's Franchise. I shall stop at nothing and all the Manchester ILP women seem ready for prison or anything else." Selina Cooper and her suffrage society were still, with the NUWSS, working along constitutional lines and their next move was to organize, in May 1906, a deputation to the new Liberal prime minister, Campbell-Bannerman, which after an initial refusal he agreed to receive. Selina Cooper, representing the cotton workers of Lancashire, took part in this deputation. In May 1906 she wrote to congratulate Dora MONTEFIORE, whom she had apparently already met, on her dramatic tax resistance and in October, when Mrs Montefiore, with Minnie BALDOCK, Annie KENNEY and others, was arrested after the opening of parliament, signed an ILP manifesto of solidarity with the WSPU. However, at the Huddersfield by-election in November 1906 Selina Cooper campaigned for the Labour candidate and the Pankhursts, following their election strategy, were campaigning to keep the Liberal out, not positively to support Labour. At the 1907 Labour party conference Selina Cooper, at Ramsay MacDonald's suggestion, was an ILP delegate, pressing for a reversion of the previous adult suffragist resolution. This proved unsuccessful, in spite of Keir Hardie's threat of resignation. In 1907, while remaining a member of the ILP and attending its conferences, but, now that it was clear that it would not campaign for women's suffrage, no longer able actively to support it, Selina Cooper took on a full-time post as a NUWSS ORGANIZER. She spent the next years travelling around the country; in 1908, for instance, she took part in at least eight by-elections. When she was away from home the NUWSS paid the expense of a housekeeper to care for her daughter, who had been born in 1900. Selina Cooper's style was appreciated by those in the London headquarters and in March 1908 Philippa STRACHEY wrote to her, after the Peckham by-election, "I can't tell you what a difference it made when you came down and joined us, nor how much I admire your splendid energy and your convincing speaking". Besides speaking at the by-elections, Selina Cooper addressed societies of every persuasion. In 1911 Lady Betty Balfour invited her to speak at a Conservative suffrage meeting in Sussex, Norah O'SHEA arranged that she should spend a short time organizing the SURREY, SUSSEX AND HAMPSHIRE FEDERATION, and in June she was arranging the MANCHESTER AND DISTRICT FEDERATION contingent for the Coronation Procession in London.

By 1911 Selina Cooper was not alone as a radical suffragist in the NUWSS; among the full-time organizers were now Annot ROBINSON and Ada Nield CHEW. At its 1912 conference the Labour party reversed its support for adult suffrage and was prepared to support a partial measure that would include women. Selina Cooper attended the annual council meeting of the NUWSS in February 1912 at which the decision of the Labour party was welcomed, by May the NUWSS's new policy of supporting Labour candidates was revealed, and in May–June the Election Fighting Fund was established. Selina Cooper undertook the joint Labour/NUWSS campaign at the first by-election, at Holmfirth on 20 June, under the new policy. The Labour candidate came third in this three-cornered fight, but in the course of the next two-and-a-quarter years the EFF, with Selina Cooper's help, was responsible for four Liberal by-election losses. In 1913 Selina Cooper devoted her energies to lobbying among miners, a traditional bastion against the desire for women's suffrage, in order to gain support for the Election Fighting Fund policy in coalfield constituencies. By October the Miner's Federation agreed to support the women's cause.

After the outbreak of war Selina Cooper was retained by the EFF on a fee of £1 per week, although all suffrage activities were suspended. She and her husband were pacifists, members of the No-Conscription Fellowship. She maintained her support of the NUWSS through the war, organizing improvements in the care of mothers and babies and involving herself in the Nelson Women's Peace Crusade. In 1919 she was an organizer for the National Union of Societies for Equal Citizenship, which was headed by a close friend, Eleanor

Rathbone. By 1923, although carrying on lobbying for family allowances, she was no longer an employee of any society. She had been the longest-serving organizer with the National Union. She now became a birth-control campaigner, in 1924 a magistrate, and, with Monica WHATELY, sponsored by Women Against War and Fascism, went to Germany in October 1934 to investigate the treatment of women prisoners under the Nazi regime. On her return she spoke at meetings, attempting to alert women to the dangers of fascism. In 1940 her support of the People's Convention, an organization initiated by the Communist party which opposed the Second World War as an imperialist conflict, led to her forced resignation from the Labour party. She never rejoined. After her death her daughter received letters of condolence from, among others, Elizabeth ABBOTT and Kathleen COURTNEY. The latter wrote that Selina Cooper had been "a source of inspiration and comfort to very many – [a] combination of aggressiveness, kind heartedness and sense of humour".

Address: (1901) 27 St Mary's Street, Nelson, Lancashire.
Photograph: in J. Liddington, *The Life and Times of a Respectable Rebel: Selina Cooper, 1864–1946*, 1984.
Archival source: Papers of Selina Jane Cooper, JP, Lancashire Record Office.
Bibliography: J. Liddington and J. Norris, *One Hand Tied Behind Us: The Rise of the Women's Suffrage Movement*, 1978; J. Liddington, "Looking for Mrs Cooper", in *Women and the Labour Movement*, North West History Society Bulletin 7, 1980–81; J. Liddington, *The Life and Times of a Respectable Rebel: Selina Cooper, 1864–1946*, 1984.

CORBETT, MARIE, MRS (1859–1934), née Gray Wife of Charles Corbett, who was a supporter in parliament of the NATIONAL UNION OF WOMEN'S SUFFRAGE SOCIETIES from 1906 until 1910, when he was a Liberal MP for the hitherto traditionally Conservative East Grinstead seat. Marie Corbett was the mother of Margery Corbett ASHBY and Cicely Corbett, who became the first secretary of the International Franchise Club (*see under* CLUBS). Marie Corbett was one of the first women poor law guardians and was a rural district councillor in Uckfield, Sussex. She gradually removed all children from the local workhouse and boarded them out with foster families. She was a close friend of Louisa MARTINDALE and of Elizabeth Wolstenholme ELMY; in 1893 she was a supporter of the WOMEN'S FRANCHISE LEAGUE, and in 1896 of the WOMEN'S EMANCIPATION UNION. As befits the wife of a Liberal MP, in 1898 she was a member of the Burgess Hill Women's Liberal Association and from 1905 to 1909 was a member of the executive committee of the WOMEN'S LIBERAL FEDERATION. In 1906 she organized a temperance meeting in Horsted Keynes at which another Liberal suffragist, Florence BALGARNIE, was the main speaker. Marie Corbett subscribed in 1905 to the CENTRAL SOCIETY FOR WOMEN'S SUFFRAGE and took part in the NUWSS "Mud March" in February 1907. In early 1907 Mrs Corbett sent out a circular to poor law guardians throughout the country; a copy has survived in Selina COOPER's papers. In this circular she denounced a suggestion that emanated from the Pontypool Union to the effect that a married daughter with sufficient means should be equally liable with her brothers for the support of her parents. Mrs Corbett protested that women should not attract equal duties when they did not have equal rights. She urged poor law guardians to ask their MPs to support the Enfranchising Bill due to be debated in March. In October 1907 she gave a small donation to the WOMEN'S SOCIAL AND POLITICAL UNION but, although tempted, unlike her sister-in-law Catherine Corbett (*c.* 1870–1950), felt unable for her family's sake to risk going to prison. In October 1908 Marie Corbett became honorary secretary of the newly founded FORWARD SUFFRAGE UNION, a group she formed with Eva McLAREN and Frances Heron Maxwell to concentrate the effort of Liberal women within the Women's Liberal Federation on their own enfranchisement. As a delegate of the Forward Suffrage Union she attended the 1913 Budapest Congress of the INTERNATIONAL WOMAN SUFFRAGE ALLIANCE.

Address: (1906) Woodgate, Danehill, Sussex.
Photograph: in A. Whittick, *Woman Into Citizen*, 1979.
Bibliography: B. Harrison, *Prudent Revolutionaries: Portraits of British Feminists between the Wars*, 1987.

CORFIELD, EMMA ANN (*c.* 1836–1910) Daughter of Joseph Corfield (1809–1888), a Unitarian, who was a member of the South Place Institute and, with his wife Elizabeth, a member of the National Association for the Promoting of the Political and Social Improvement of the People, along with other middle-class reformers such as P.A. Taylor (*see*

Clementia TAYLOR) and William Ashurst (*see* Matilda Ashurst BIGGS). In 1844 Joseph Corfield presented the National Association's library with a copy of Burke's *French Revolution*. Emma Corfield and her mother both signed the 1866 suffrage petition. Emma Corfield was a subscriber to the CENTRAL COMMITTEE OF THE NATIONAL SOCIETY FOR WOMEN'S SUFFRAGE in 1873, contributed to the MANCHESTER NATIONAL SOCIETY Demonstration Fund in 1880, and was a member of the WOMEN'S EMANCIPATION UNION in 1894. In her will she left legacies to the woman with whom she lived, to the Working Men's College, the New Hospital for Women in the Euston Road (later the Elizabeth Garrett Anderson Hospital), the Chelsea Hospital for Women, and to the Sailors' Orphan Girls' School and Home in Hampstead.

In 1885 Joseph Corfield organized the erection of the Reformer's Memorial in the Dissenters' section of Kensal Green Cemetery. This obelisk has carved into it the names of men and women "who had defied custom and interest for the sake of conscience and public good". Among these names are Lady Noel Byron, Frances Wright, Harriet Martineau (who signed the 1866 petition), William Lovett (whose wife signed the 1866 petition), W.J. Fox and Richard Cobden (their wives and daughters signed the 1866 petition). In 1907 Emma Corfield arranged for more names to be added on a third side of the obelisk. Among these are Henry FAWCETT, Barbara BODICHON, Frances Power COBBE, Francis NEWMAN, Josephine Butler, George HOLYOAKE and Lydia BECKER. In subsequent years, on the fourth side, a few more names have been added. These include Margaret Llewelyn DAVIES and E.O. Greening, a friend of George Holyoake and Max Kyllmann (*see* Philippine KYLLMANN). Mrs Greening had also signed the 1866 petition. In 1925 the Co-Operative Union published W.H. Brown, *Pathfinders: Brief Records of 74 Adventurers, in clearing the Way for Free Public Opinion, whose names are inscribed on the Reformers' Memorial, Kensal Green, London*. The poem that brings the book to a conclusion is by V.H. FRIEDLANDER, who had been an active member of the WOMEN'S SOCIAL AND POLITICAL UNION. Because in the past it has not been their involvement in the women's movement that has been noted, one has to rechart the connections between the names in order to "read" the Memorial as silent witness to the desire for men and women throughout the nineteenth century to enfranchise women.

Address: (1866) 33 Gerrard Street, Islington; (1909) 23 St Mary's Road, Canonbury, Islington, London N.

CORNWALL (WSPU) Secretary (1913) Miss E. Williams, Glanafon, Devoran, Cornwall.

CORNWALL (EAST) (NUWSS)   In 1913 the society was a member of the SOUTH-WESTERN FEDERATION OF THE NATIONAL UNION OF WOMEN'S SUFFRAGE SOCIETIES. Secretary (1913) Miss Jessie Williams, Grove Park, Liskeard, Cornwall.

COURTAULD FAMILY   Unitarian silk manufacturers, business partners and intermarried through three generations with the Taylor family (*see* Appendix). Ellen Courtauld (Mrs Samuel Courtauld) signed the 1866 women's suffrage petition. She was the aunt twice over of P.A. Taylor, husband of Clementia TAYLOR – once as his father's sister and once as his mother's brother's wife. In 1850 she had been responsible for employing Mary MERRYWEATHER at the family mill as a teacher to the Courtauld employees. Her husband had in 1853, after years of refusing to pay the church rate, brought the test case on this issue to the House of Lords. His solicitor in this case was William Ashurst, father of Matilda Ashurst BIGGS, Caroline STANSFELD and Emilie VENTURI. In 1858 Samuel Courtauld and his wife read with approval a pamphlet written by Bessie Rayner PARKES and in 1859 Samuel attended the meeting of the National Association for the Promotion of the Social Sciences in Bradford at which she read a paper on educated female labour which made a great impression on him. He also heard "an exceedingly well-written paper that should have been read by its author" – George Hastings, the Secretary of the National Society had read Jessie BOUCHERETT's paper. Samuel Courtauld was one of the three founding male shareholders in the *English Woman's Journal* in 1858, in 1874 was a member of the MANCHESTER SOCIETY FOR WOMEN'S SUFFRAGE and in 1874 gave £20 to the CENTRAL COMMITTEE OF THE NATIONAL SOCIETY FOR WOMEN'S SUFFRAGE. His aunt Sophia Courtauld (1799–1887), who was a friend of Harriet Martineau, also signed the 1866 petition, subscribed to the ENFRANCHISEMENT OF WOMEN COMMITTEE in 1866–7, to the BRISTOL AND WEST OF ENGLAND SOCIETY in 1871 and was a member of the Central Committee of the National Society for Women's Suffrage in 1873. In 1879 Agnes MCLAREN stayed with Sophia Courtauld in Clifton, Bristol, where she was then living. The PRIESTMAN sisters had known Sophia Courtauld from at least 1861. Another Courtauld sister, Catherine Taylor (1795–1885), mother-in-law of Mentia Taylor, also signed the 1866 petition.

[Sydney] Renée Courtauld (1873–1962), was the niece of Samuel Courtauld and daughter of Sydney Courtauld and Sarah Lucy Sharpe, the latter in 1872 having been elected to the School Board in Braintree. Renée was sister of Samuel Courtauld (founder of the Courtauld Institute and Gallery) and of Catharine Courtauld (see below). She was educated at Roedean and Newnham 1892–4, but left without taking a tripos. She became a social work helper at the Women's University Settlement and with the Charity Organization Society. She was a member of the Braintree School Board 1902–3, a member of the CENTRAL SOCIETY in 1906, and of its successor the LONDON SOCIETY FOR WOMEN'S SUFFRAGE in 1906–7. In 1913 she was secretary of the North and East Essex branch of the NATIONAL UNION OF WOMEN'S SUFFRAGE SOCIETIES. She gave a donation to the National Society for Equal Citizenship in 1922 and, after her enfranchisement, used her vote to lobby her MP to support women's membership to Cambridge University. In 1934 she was a member of the Women's Farm and Garden Association. In her will Renée Courtauld left bequests to, among others, the Over-Forty Association, Hillcroft College and the British Federation of University Women.

Catharine Courtauld (1878–1972) (later Mrs Dowman) sister of Samuel and Renée Courtauld, was a member of the Central Society for Women's Suffrage in 1906 and later became a member of the SUFFRAGE ATELIER. Several of her designs, such as "The Anti-Suffrage Ostrich", *c.* 1909; "The Anti-Suffrage Society as Portrait Painter", *c.* 1912; "The Anti-Suffrage Society as Prophet", *c.* 1912; "The Anti-Suffrage Society as Dressmaker", *c.* 1912; "The Prehistoric Argument", 1912; "Waiting for a Living Wage", *c.* 1913, were produced as postcards. In the 1908 London Post Office Directory she is accorded the title "artist".

Address: (1866) Mrs S. Courtauld, Gosfield Hall, Essex; (1908) Catharine Courtauld, 4a Upper Baker Street, London NW; (1972) Wyke Lodge, 92 Buxton Road, Weymouth, Dorset; (1913) Miss (Renée) Courtauld, Colne Engaine, Earls Colne, RSO, Essex; (1934) Bocking, Little Heath, Berkhamsted, Herts; (1961) "The Beacon", Wyke Road, Weymouth, Dorset.

Bibliography: S.L. Courtauld, *The Huguenot Family of Courtauld*, 1957; L. Davidoff and C. Hall, *Family Fortunes: Men and Women of the English Middle Class 1780–1850*, 1987; L. Tickner, *The Spectacle of Women: Imagery of the Suffrage Campaign 1907–14*, 1987.

COURTNEY, KATHLEEN D'OLIER (1878–1974) DBE, 1952   Born in Chatham, one of seven children, the fifth daughter of a major in the Royal Engineers. She was brought up in Kensington, educated there at an Anglo-French school and then at Malvern, before spending a year at a boarding school in Dresden. In January 1897 she went up to Lady Margaret Hall, Oxford, where she read French and German, graduating in 1900 with second-class honours, and having commenced a life-long friendship with Maude ROYDEN. She worked first as a volunteer in the Daisy Club, a girls' club in Lambeth, before returning to Oxford as an administrator for the University Extension Delegacy. She never, throughout her long life, had of necessity to earn her own living, sharing in the income her father derived from Dublin property. However, in 1908 she did accept the position as paid secretary of the NORTH OF ENGLAND SOCIETY FOR WOMEN'S SUFFRAGE. She worked there in close co-operation with Helena SWANWICK, who revealed in her autobiography that Kathleen Courtney had arrived in Manchester armed "with a big reputation as an office organizer from Hudson Shaw", Maude Royden's close friend. Of her time in Manchester Kathleen Courtney later commented, "It taught me method and how to get on with subordinates". On 26 January 1911 she was elected honorary secretary of the NATIONAL UNION OF WOMEN'S SUFFRAGE SOCIETIES, replacing Edith Dimock. Her arrival at the London headquarters coincided with the implementation of the federation scheme and her organizational skills were much appreciated. She was a member of the first Election Fighting Fund Committee in 1912.

Kathleen Courtney was, with Catherine MARSHALL, one of those who went to the Hague in February 1915 to discuss the proposal for a Women's Peace Congress. The realization that the Congress would not have the backing of the NUWSS led to her resignation from the NUWSS on 25 February 1915, a week after Maude Royden, resigning as editor of the *Common Cause*, had been the first of the anti-war campaigners to make the break. In her letter of resignation Kathleen Courtney wrote, "I feel strongly that the most important thing at the present moment is to work, if possible on International lines for the right sort of peace settlement after the war. If I could have done this through the National Union, I need hardly say how infinitely I would have preferred it and for the sake of doing so I would gladly have sacrificed a great deal. But the Council made it quite clear that they did not wish the Union to work in this way." Mrs FAWCETT afterwards felt particularly bitter towards Kathleen Courtney, whom she felt had been intentionally and personally wounding, and refused to effect any reconciliation, relying, as she said, on time to erase the memory of this difficult period. With Chrystal MACMILLAN and Emmeline PETHICK-LAWRENCE, Kathleen Courtney was the only British woman, because of the exigencies of war, able in April to attend the Women's Peace Congress. In October she was one of the vice-chairmen of the Women's International League, the British section of the International Committee for Permanent Peace. In 1916 she went to Salonika and Baxtia with the Serbian Relief Fund. For the work she did there she was later decorated by the Serbian government.

Kathleen Courtney was, with James Middleton of the Independent Labour Party, joint secretary of the NATIONAL COUNCIL FOR ADULT SUFFRAGE when it was formed in 1916. She was re-elected to the NUWSS executive in March 1918, although she had not concurred with the NUWSS acceptance of the limited measure of enfranchisement for women that was contained in the Representation of the People Bill. She was later a member of the executive committee of the National Union of Societies for Equal Citizenship, in 1923 was chairman of the committee of the Family Endowment Council, of which she had been a member since it was set up by Eleanor Rathbone during the war, and a delegate from the NUSEC to the International Alliance of Women for Suffrage and Equal Citizenship in Paris in 1923. In the 1930s she was a vice-president of NUSEC.

After the end of the war she worked with Hilda Clark in the Friends' Relief Mission in Vienna. She became president of the British section of the Women's International League for Peace and Freedom. In 1926 she was the organizer of a Women's Pilgrimage for Peace, an idea derived from the 1913 suffrage PILGRIMAGE, which culminated in a rally in Hyde Park and a deputation to the foreign secretary. In 1928 she joined the executive of the League of Nations, becoming vice-chairman in 1939, and presented a petition signed by millions to the 1932 Disarmament Conference. In 1949 she became chairman of the executive of the United Nations Association.

Address: (1916) 51 Morpeth Mansions, London SW; (1923) 44 Upper Park Road, London NW2; (1974) 3 Elm Tree Court, London NW8 (a block originally built to provide accommodation at a moderate rent for professional women).
Photograph: in Kathleen Courtney Papers, Fawcett Library.
Archival source: Kathleen Courtney Papers, Fawcett Library; typescript biography of Kathleen Courtney by Francesca Wilson, Lady Margaret Hall, Oxford (copy in Fawcett Library).
Bibliography: S.S. Holton, *Feminism and Democracy: Women's Suffrage and Reform Politics in Britain, 1900–1918*, 1986; J. Alberti, *Beyond Suffrage: Feminists in War and Peace, 1914–28*, 1989; J. Vellacott, *From Liberal to Labour with Women's Suffrage: The Story of Catherine Marshall*, 1993.

COVENTRY (NUWSS)   In 1913 the society was a member of the MIDLANDS (EAST) FEDERATION OF THE NATIONAL UNION OF WOMEN'S SUFFRAGE SOCIETIES. Secretary (1913) *pro tem* Miss Wilks, 70 Holyhead Road, Coventry, Warwickshire.

COVENTRY branch of the WOMEN'S EMANCIPATION UNION   Honorary secretary (1895) Miss Amy Hurlstone.

COVENTRY (WSPU)   Was founded in May 1908. Secretary (1910) Miss Dawson, St Peter's Vicarage, Coventry; (1913) Miss C. Arnott, Beech Brae, Berry Street, Coventry, Warwickshire.

COWDENBEATH (WFL)   Branch was in existence in 1914.

COWDRAY, ANNIE PEARSON, LADY (1860–1932) Born in Bradford, daughter of Sir John Cass, a merchant, married Weetman Dickinson Pearson, a building contractor and oil magnate, who was created a baronet in 1894, became Liberal MP for Colchester in 1895 and was raised to the peerage in 1910. Walter Crane was commissioned to make a plaster frieze for the dining room of their first country house, Paddockhurst, near Crawley; very suitably, it describes the history of transport from primitive times, represented by such concepts as "The Genius of Mechanical Invention uniting Agriculture and Commerce" and the "Genius of Electricity uniting the Parts of the Earth". Lady Cowdray was the mother of three sons and one daughter. As Lady Denman, the latter became one of the founders of the Women's Institute movement in Britain. Lady Denman's biographer records that Lady Cowdray was "possessed of a driving social ambition, a determination, with her husband's wealth and achievements, to surmount Victorian and Edwardian barriers of caste, and, despite snubs and set-backs, to become a leading political and social hostess". Her grand-daughter, Lavinia Smiley, recorded that "everything was to be done for the advancement and advantage of her own immediate family". Lady Cowdray was an active member of the WOMEN'S LIBERAL FEDERATION, in 1910 gave £20 to the WOMEN'S SOCIAL AND POLITICAL UNION and in September 1911 held a magnificent reception at Dunecht, her Scottish house outside Aberdeen, for Mrs PANKHURST, then on speaking-tour of Scotland. By 1913 Lady Cowdray was a vice-president of the NATIONAL POLITICAL LEAGUE. In 1913 she subscribed to the QUI VIVE CORPS launched by Florence DE FONBLANQUE, and was a supporter of the NORTHERN MEN'S FEDERATION FOR WOMEN'S SUFFRAGE founded by Mrs de Fonblanque's sister Maud Arncliffe SENNETT, holding a luncheon for the NORTHERN MEN at her London home on 18 July 1913. However, she did not prove to be as generous a financial benefactor as Mrs Arncliffe Sennett had hoped. Quite tartly Lady Cowdray advised Mrs Arncliffe Sennett that members of deputations should not have their fares paid from Scotland, nor should the names of the women who organized such deputations be publicized, because she thought that by doing so it was revealed to the House of Commons just how few activists there really were. In August 1913 Lady Cowdray entertained Qui Vive marchers at Cowdray Park in Sussex. She was honorary treasurer of the London Committee of the Scottish Women's Hospitals when it was formed in 1915. In 1922 she was a vice-president of the South London Hospital for Women and continued to be a generous supporter of the London Society for Women's Service.

Address: (1913): 16 Carlton House Terrace, London SW; Cowdray Park, Midhurst, Sussex; Dunecht House, Aberdeenshire.

Photograph: in G. Huxley, *Lady Denman, GBE, 1884–1954*, 1961.

Bibliography: G. Huxley, *Lady Denman, GBE, 1884–1954*, 1961; L. Smiley, *A Nice Clean Plate: Recollections 1919–1931*, 1981.

COZENS, MARY ELIZABETH (1857–1920) Honorary secretary in 1892 of the WOMEN'S SUFFRAGE DEMONSTRATION COMMITTEE, a body which originated, under the aegis of the WOMEN'S FRANCHISE LEAGUE, with the idea of holding a rally in Hyde Park. She appears to have reneged from the Women's Franchise League and have been the organizer in 1882 of the "demonstration" held at St James's Hall in London as a joint meeting of suffrage societies, in support of Sir Albert Rollit's women's suffrage bill. In April Mary Cozens had written to Richard Pankhurst, "As you may have heard our committee has split up. Mr Burrows wanted us to hold our meeting in opposition to our own Enfranchisement. . . . Sir Albert Rollit's bill is a thoroughly good bill – it enfranchises four classes of married women". This meeting, which included among its speakers Lady Frances BALFOUR and Millicent Garrett FAWCETT, was so disturbed by protesting members of the WFL, among them Richard Pankhurst, that it had to be abandoned. Mary Cozens was also the honorary treasurer of the Committee, soliciting funds in order that the Committee might support women's suffrage candidates regardless of their political persuasion at the next general election. She wrote to the governor of New Zealand congratulating his legislature on being the first in the British Empire to recognize the citizenship of women.

Having left the WFL, Mary Cozens joined the WOMEN'S EMANCIPATION UNION. At the Union's 1892 conference in Birmingham she caused consternation by suggesting that dynamite might be used to further the cause and that "If they had a regiment of women who could shoot, they would have the franchise in a week" (*Personal Rights Journal*,

November 1892). The *Woman's Herald*, 12 November 1892, noted "The Chairman stated that Miss Cozens spoke only for herself; nevertheless, we have received letters and inquiries as to whether the WEU is responsible for a policy of physical force ... we trust that the matter will soon be forgotten, and that Miss Cozens will learn to regret the criminal folly of her language". In a letter to the *Woman's Herald*, 19 November 1892, a member of the WEU, Charles Beaumont, wrote, "It is perfectly true that if a large proportion of our women appealed to physical force, they could obtain the franchise and every other phase of Liberty, Equality, Fraternity enjoyed by man; and though I do not think the sex will debase their womanhood by resorting to dynamite, if they could not obtain emancipation in any other way they would be as justified in doing so, as any one is ever justified in an appeal to arms." In 1894 Mary Cozens was a member of the council of the WEU, but left after unsuccessfully attempting to remove Elizabeth Wolstenholme ELMY as secretary.

In December 1893 Mary Cozens founded the PARLIAMENTARY COMMITTEE FOR WOMAN SUFFRAGE, a body which operated without reference to the other suffrage organizations. Helen Blackburn in *Record of Women's Suffrage*, 1902, deals briefly with what she terms "this coterie" and does not dignify the organization with a title, although she does waspishly refer to such groups whose "magnificence of their titles seems disproportionate to their numbers". She carries on in the same vein to say that "when such coteries force themselves into the lobbies of the House panoplied with a self-confidence only to be equalled by their inexperience, then indeed the consequences are disastrous". Mary Cozens favoured the Conservatives as the party most likely to grant suffrage to women. In February 1895 Lady Frances Balfour wrote to Millicent Fawcett that she found Mary Cozens "Rather a pleasing woman", but denouncing her as a "little reptile" for promoting a parliamentary bill which clashed with the plans of the older societies. This was the bill proposed by Mr Macdona on 1 May; it failed. In 1896–7 Mary Cozens again put forward her own bill, which was introduced into the House of Lords by Lord Templetown, and lobbied leading politicians. In March 1897 Lady Frances Balfour criticized this bill in a letter to *The Times*. Mary Cozens replied in the same medium on 16 March writing, "The action of Lady Frances and her friends has been in the main confined to the atmosphere of drawing rooms: my society has striven, and so far with some measure of success, to secure the discussion of the question in Parliament and by the Press. I may add that both Bills before Parliament this Session emanated from this committee. It is well that these senseless jealousies and bickerings between rival societies should cease. They retard the movement, and in some degree justify the criticism that women are not sufficiently enlightened to exercise the franchise". In February 1907 a "Miss Mary Cuzens" is shown as a member of the WOMEN'S SOCIAL AND POLITICAL UNION and a Mary Cozens in 1909. Doubtless militancy appealed to this loose cannon.

In 1907 Mary Cozens joined the THEOSOPHICAL SOCIETY, resigning in July 1912. In her will she left a bequest to Mrs Gertrude Howey, the mother of Elsie HOWEY, who also, incidentally, became a theosophist. Mary Cozens also left a sum of money to the Brighton Animal Institute and the "Cozens Bequest" from the interest of which a yearly distribution was to be made to "necessitous women either widows or spinsters residing in the parish of Tetsworth", from which town her family originated. The Cozens Bequest is still in operation although, in these egalitarian days, it includes men as well as women. The feminist slant of her will is underlined by the clause in which, when requesting, as was often done, that after death and before cremation her jugular vein should be cut, Mary Cozens specifically requested that this operation should preferably be performed by a woman surgeon.

Address: (1894) 21 Earl's Court Gardens, London SW; (1901) 21 Abingdon Mansions, Kensington, London W; (1907–20) 74 Stanford Avenue, Brighton, Sussex.
Archival source: Papers of Sylvia Pankhurst, Internationaal Instituut voor Sociale Geschiedenis, Amsterdam.
Bibliography: D. Rubinstein, *Before the Suffragettes: Women's Emancipation in the 1890s*, 1986.

CRAGGS, HELEN MILLAR (1888–1969) (later Mrs McCombie, then Lady Pethick-Lawrence) One of eight children of Sir John Craggs, a chartered accountant, she was educated at Roedean, to which she returned after a short interval as a member of staff, teaching physics and chemistry, gymnastics and dancing. Her father refused to allow her to study medicine. As "Miss Millar", a slight pseudonym adopted to avoid embarrassing her father, and possibly in order not to jeopardize her teaching post, she campaigned for the WOMEN'S SOCIAL AND POLITICAL UNION, chalking announcements of meetings, ringing the bell to summon audiences and selling suffragette postcards, at the Peckham by-election in 1908. She then repeated the process, under the care of Flora DRUMMOND, at the Manchester by-election, where the intention was to prevent Churchill's election. Helen Craggs left Roedean to work fulltime for the WSPU and by 1910 was an ORGANIZER, paid 25/– a week, working at Clement's Inn and living in a rented room in Bloomsbury. She had met Emmeline PANKHURST's young son, Harry, while she was in Manchester; affection was heightened by his fatal illness and she was at his bedside during the last few weeks of his life; he died in January 1910. In February 1910 Helen Craggs took over from Grace ROE as organizer in Brixton and in March had moved to Hampstead to organize the WSPU campaign there. She was a friend of Ethel SMYTH, Evelyn SHARP and Beatrice HARRADEN. She was imprisoned in Holloway in March 1912 after taking part in the window-smashing campaign, and went on hunger strike. In July 1912 she was arrested, carrying all the paraphernalia for arson, while attempting to burn down Lewis Harcourt's country house at Nuneham Courtney in Oxfordshire. Although no fire was set, this was the first occasion on which a WSPU activist had attempted an act of serious damage to property. The leadership of the WSPU was careful to make clear that Helen Craggs was acting on her own initiative. She was released on bail of £1000, pending her trial. She obviously took pride in her notoriety, writing on 19 October 1912 to Hugh FRANKLIN from Oxford prison, the day after being sentenced to nine months' imprisonment, thanking him for getting photographs of Nuneham Courtney. She was transferred to Holloway, where she immediately went on hunger strike, was forcibly fed and, after 11 days, released. Within a year Lewis Harcourt had given £1000 to the funds of the National League for Opposing Women's Suffrage. Helen Craggs's family, although supporting women's enfranchisement, had been horrified by her association with militancy.

Her mother was a suffragist, a member of the CONSERVATIVE AND UNIONIST WOMEN'S FRANCHISE ASSOCIATION (a member of its central executive committee, its finance committee, and of the local Kensington Committee).

Helen Craggs then trained for midwifery at Rotunda Hospital in Dublin, and in 1914 married Alexander McCombie, a GP from Aberdeen, who was working in the East End of London. Her parents did not attend the wedding. She qualified as a pharmacist in order to act as her husband's dispenser. After her husband's early death she supported her two young children by running a business making jigsaw puzzles. After the Second World War she emigrated with her daughter to the US and then to Canada. She occasionally saw Christabel PANKHURST in Los Angeles. She married Frederick PETHICK-LAWRENCE as his second wife in 1957.

Address: (1930) Dilkhoosh, Chalfont St Peters, Buckinghamshire; (1950) 81 Belgrave Road, London SW; (1969) 3350 Woodburn Avenue, Victoria, British Columbia, Canada.
Archival source: S. Walker, Helen Pethick-Lawrence (typescript memoir by her daughter), c. 1983, Fawcett Library.

CRAIG, EDITH (1869–1947) Born without the benefit of clergy to Ellen Terry and the architect Edward Godwin. Edith (Edy) was given a theatrical education at the Lyceum by her mother and by Henry Irving. She studied piano at the Royal Academy of Music and in 1888 went to Berlin for a year in order to further her musical studies, but chronic rheumatism in her finger joints ended the possibility of music as a career. She did work as an actress, taking the surname "Craig", with the Lyceum company but in the 1890s moved more into the production side, particularly adept at devising costumes. In 1899 she began living with Christopher ST JOHN; they were together for the rest of her life.

Her brother, the theatrical designer Gordon Craig, noted that Edy was involved with the suffrage movement by 1903. In an interview in *Votes for Women*, 15 April 1910, she said that she had been a suffragist all her life; "When I was at school I lived in a house of Suffrage workers, and at regular periods the task of organising Suffrage petitions kept everybody busy". In this interview she remarked that she belonged to ten suffrage societies and sold *Votes for Women* from her pitch outside the Eustace Miles

Restaurant (*see under* HALLS AND RESTAURANTS). Cicely HAMILTON noted that although Edy Craig approved of militant tactics, she never took part in any law-breaking activities. Instead she put her designing skill to use in the suffrage cause when, for example, with the SUFFRAGE ATELIER, of which she was a member, she was responsible for staging the WOMEN FREEDOM LEAGUE contingent's part in the 18 June 1910 procession. The following month, with Laurence HOUSMAN, she designed the western section of the 23 July procession, choosing a Roman theme, flying pennants and laurel wreaths, in order to highlight women's claims for "Victory" and "Justice".

Edith Craig, as a very active member of the ACTRESSES' FRANCHISE LEAGUE, used her skills to create a political theatre. She produced *How the Vote Was Won* by Cicely Hamilton and Christopher St John for the WOMEN'S SOCIAL AND POLITICAL UNION's Prince's Skating Rink Exhibition in May 1909 and *A Pageant of Great Women*, also by Cicely Hamilton, at the Scala Theatre in November 1909. In the latter production she took the part of Rosa Bonheur. A letter dated 30 August 1909 from George Bernard Shaw to Bertha NEWCOMBE revealed that Edith Craig was planning to tour "villages and small places where they are giving performances in schoolrooms with fitups" with such propaganda plays as Shaw's *Press Cuttings*.

Perhaps considered rather arrogant, Edith Craig gained a reputation for brusqueness; this may have been a contributory factor in her break with the AFL. In 1911 she set up the Pioneer Players, "To produce plays dealing with all kinds of movements of interest at the moment". With Ellen Terry as president and Edy as managing director, the Pioneer Players treated a broader range of matters than the purely suffrage. Between 1911 and its final season in 1921, the advisory committee of the Players included Cicely Hamilton, Laurence Housman and Lena ASHWELL. The first season opened on 8 May 1911 at the Kingsway Theatre with a production of Cicely Hamilton's *Jack and Jill and a Friend*, followed by Margaret Wynne NEVINSON's *In the Workhouse* and Christopher St John's *The First Actress*. After the demise of the Pioneer Players, Edith Craig had difficulty, for unspecified reasons, in getting employment in the commercial theatre, and worked with the Little Theatre movement in provincial cities. After her mother's death she converted a barn next to Smallhythe into a theatre and staged annual Shakespeare productions, in which Vera HOLME, former suffragette and thespian, took part. Edith Craig's papers were destroyed at her death by Christopher St John.

Address: (1899) 7 Smith Square, Westminster, London SW; (1901) Priest's House, Smallhythe, Kent; (1906, 1913) 31–32 Bedford Street, London WC; (1928) Smallhythe, Tenterden, Kent.

Photograph: by Lena Connell, in National Portrait Gallery Archive; by Lena Connell of Edith Craig and Cicely Hamilton together, published at The Suffrage Shop (*see* SHOPS).

Bibliography: E. Adlard, *Edy: Recollections of Edith Craig*, 1949 (in particular the essay "Triumphant women" by Cicely Hamilton); M. Steen, *A Pride of Terrys: A Family Saga*, 1962; J. Melville, *Ellen and Edy*, 1987; J. Holledge, *Innocent Flowers: Women in the Edwardian Theatre*, 1981; L. Woolf, *Suffragettes of the Edwardian Theatre: Edith Craig and the Pioneer Players*, thesis, 1989, in Fawcett Library; S. Stowell, *A Stage of Their Own: Feminist Playwrights of the Suffrage Era*, 1992; C. Dymkowski, "Entertaining ideas: Edy Craig and the Pioneer Players", in V. Gardner and S. Rutherford (eds), *The New Woman and Her Sisters*, 1992; K. Cockin, *Edith Craig (1869–1947): Dramatic Lives*, 1998.

CRAIG, ISA [ISABELLA] (1831–1903) (later Mrs Knox) Born in Edinburgh, the only child of a hosier and glover; orphaned at an early age, she was brought up by her grandmother. She left school at the age of ten, although it is not known how she was then employed. In a letter to Helen TAYLOR, 21 February 1860, J.S. MILL wrote that he thought "Miss Craig got her living at Edinburgh as a needlewoman till Miss Parkes found her out". However, having contributed verses to the *Scotsman* over a period of years, Isa Craig was eventually given a post on the paper. It is not entirely clear how she came into the orbit of the Langham Place Group. Bessie Rayner PARKES appears to have known Isa Craig when she was in Edinburgh in October 1856. She mentions that, having noticed there the *Waverley Journal*, "a periodical professing to be edited by ladies", she and Isa Craig both contributed articles to it. Isa Craig came to London in the summer of 1857 in order to take up a post as assistant secretary and literary assistant to George Hastings of the National Association for the Promotion of Social Science. Mill made clear that Miss Craig's appointment, of which he thoroughly approved, was the result of "a most strenuous personal canvass by Miss Parkes & others". In 1859 Isa Craig joined the committee of the newly founded Ladies' Sanitary Association, founded herself, with Maria Rye, the Telegraph School in order to teach women to operate this new technology, and won a 50-guinea prize offered by the Crystal Palace Company for a poem to commemorate the centenary of Burns's birth (A.J. Munby, barrister and diarist, was one of the runners-up). She was already a contributor to the *English Woman's Journal*, although *The Times* in its account of the prize-giving chose to omit this from the biographical information furnished to them by Bessie Rayner Parkes's father. In 1862 Isa Craig was a member of the committee set up by Emily DAVIES to obtain the admission of women to university examinations. In 1863 a tract she wrote, *The Essence of Slavery*, which was extracted from Fanny Kemble's *A Journal of Residence on a Georgian Plantation*, was published by the Ladies' Emancipation Society and printed by Emily FAITHFULL. The latter's Victoria Press also published in 1865 *Poems: An Offering to Lancashire*, a collection of poems by, among others, Christina Rossetti, George MacDonald, Bessie Rayner Parkes, Mary Howitt and Isa Craig, the proceeds of which were destined for the relief of distress among Lancashire cotton operatives. In December of that year Isa Craig became, for a short time, the editor of Alexander Strahan's new monthly magazine the *Argosy*, attracting to it three contributions from her friend Christina Rossetti. Strahan had in 1864 published Isa Craig's verse drama *Duchess Agnes* (*see* PUBLISHERS AND PRINTERS).

In 1865 Isa Craig became a member of the managing committee of the newly formed KENSINGTON SOCIETY. On 17 May 1866, in the midst of the flurry to organize the women's suffrage petition (*see* WOMEN'S SUFFRAGE PETITION COMMITTEE), at St John's Church, Deptford, she married her cousin John Knox. He was described as an "iron merchant" and was seven years her junior. The couple were to have at least one child, a daughter Margaret, born in mid-1869. The witnesses to the marriage included George Hastings, Bessie Rayner Parkes, Emily Davies and Jane Crow. Later that month, as Isa Craig Knox, she, with Margaret Knox her mother-in-law, signed the suffrage petition and on 5 June 1866 Emily Davies wrote to Helen Taylor that she proposed going to see Mrs Knox to see whether she would be willing to take part in the continuing suffrage campaign. At "the acacia-tree party", as Clementia TAYLOR termed it, which was held at Aubrey House around 20 June 1866, it was decided to form the LONDON PROVISIONAL PETITION COMMITTEE, of which Mrs Knox was to be the secretary, although, for an undisclosed reason, she shrank from being involved with the Press and Emily Davies agreed to undertake this part of the work. After June discussions about forming the Committee meandered until, at the end of October, a more formal committee, the ENFRANCHISEMENT OF WOMEN COMMITTEE, with a membership different from that of the London Provisional Petition Committee, was proposed; Mrs Knox's position as secretary was the one constant. In the event she was a member of the Enfranchisement of Women Committee, but not the secretary. Her name does not appear in the membership lists of any of the later suffrage societies, although she did sign the Declaration in Favour of Women's Suffrage organized by the CENTRAL COMMITTEE OF THE NATIONAL SOCIETY FOR WOMEN'S SUFFRAGE in 1889. As Isa Craig-Knox she published novels, *Esther West*, 1870, and *Deepdale Vicarage*, 1884, a book of poems, *Songs of Consolation*, 1874, and several books for children, *Little Folks' History of England*, 1872, and *Tales on the Parables*, 1872.

Address: (1866) 14 Clyde Terrace, Brockley Road, New Cross, London.

Bibliography: F.E. Mineka and D.N. Lindley, *The Later Letters of John Stuart Mill 1849–1873*, 1972; C.A. Lacey, *Barbara Leigh Smith Bodichon and the Langham Place Group*, 1987.

CRAIGEN, JESSIE HANNAH (*c.* 1835–99) Suffrage speaker. Her father was a ship's captain, who died when she was a child, and her mother was an Italian actress. Young Jessie Craigen appeared on the stage, but left to take up temperance work and by 1870 was addressing suffrage meetings. Sandra Holton has suggested that Alice SCATCHERD introduced Jessie Craigen to suffrage speaking in northern England, but it is not clear when exactly she first made contact with the suffrage movement. She is first recorded speaking in July 1870 at an open-air gathering at Hebden Bridge at which a petition for women's suffrage was signed. In September 1870 she gave a lecture to a large audience in Bradford

on "The Rights and Wrongs of Women". In October and November 1870 she addressed public meetings in Haworth, Heaton, Idle, Worksop, Huddersfield and Longwood, and at all these petitions were circulated. In February 1871 she continued her progress through Burslem and Kidsgrove. In 1879, certainly, Alice Scatcherd deployed Jessie Craigen as a speaker at a large suffrage meeting in the Free Trade Hall, Manchester. Helen BLACKBURN wrote of Jessie Craigen, "With the power of her magnificent voice, she gathered audiences round and held them riveted". Her obituary in the *Englishwoman's Review* noted that "She would send a bell-ringer round with a few bills, then mount on a chair, a cart or a barrel, and begin . . . Every now and then she would send up a bundle of petitions, to Miss Ashworth or to Miss Becker from these meetings 'very genuine and very dirty', and ask for a little money to go on and get more." Her main supporters were the radical suffragists, Priscilla Bright MCLAREN, Lilias Ashworth HALLETT and the PRIESTMAN sisters, who as early as 1870 realized the necessity of gaining support from the working classes for the suffrage movement. It was in this area that Jessie Craigen's main strength lay. As Helen Blackburn continued, those that Jessie Craigen held riveted were "miners at the pit-bank in Northumberland or Durham, now fishers in Aberdeen or in Cornwall, or agricultural labourers in the market-place of country towns". She was also involved in campaigning for the Women's Protective and Provident League in 1874, setting up a women's union among Dundee's jute workers and, with support from the Aberdeen Trades Council, a women's union in Aberdeen. In February 1880 she addressed a meeting of the organized suffrage movement at the "Demonstration of Women" chaired by Priscilla Bright McLaren at the Free Trade Hall in Manchester. Her speech was considered a triumph. Helen Blackburn wrote that at the close of the meeting her voice "like a mighty melodious bell, rang out over that vast assemblage, electrifying the audience, who rose as one woman to their feet, cheering and waving their handkerchiefs". The speech she gave then was published as "On Women's Suffrage", reprinted from the *Women's Suffrage Journal*, 14 February 1880. A month later Jessie Craigen addressed a meeting of women Liberal party supporters at the Albert Hall in Leeds. The *Yorkshire Post* of 26 March gave a very full report of the meeting, which Alice Scatcherd mounted in her scrapbook and annotated as having been written by someone with a sense of humour. The report described how:
Presently the platform shook beneath the martial tread of Miss Craigen, and that lady proceeded to address "my sisters" in the deepest baritone voice that ever issued from the delicate throat of a woman. At first the effect was doubtful. The audience laughed, and evidently hardly knew what to make of this robust traveller, who said she came from Wales on purpose to attend the meeting, and had to make another journey immediately . . . If Mrs Scatcherd was fluent, Miss Craigen was dramatic. No subject from international policy to the price of cabbages but furnished a text for her withering scorn and fierce denunciation of the powers that be, and such a stalwart assailant was felt to be a mighty champion amongst the woman righters. Her speech was a real treat, and although at times she was rather short of breath, and the perspiration stood in beads upon her. massive features, the sound of her deep tones reverberating through the hall must have made the men outside believe that something awful was happening to the wives and sweethearts whom they waited for so patiently.

Jessie Craigen, as did Helena DOWNING, spoke at eight of the nine "Demonstrations". Of her speech at the one held in the Colston Hall in Bristol, November 1880, the *Englishwoman's Review* noted that she gave a "thrilling address, which moved some of her auditors in the great hall to tears". It was after attending this meeting that Anna Maria and Mary Priestman, leaders of the suffrage movement in Bristol, became particularly attached to Jessie Craigen. At some time in the winter of 1881–2 she appears to have been briefly imprisoned, the first suffrage prisoner, in Millbank in London, possibly for some disturbance resulting from her public speaking. Between 1880 and 1883 Jessie Craigen was also a paid speaker for the Ladies' National Association for the Repeal of the Contagious Diseases Act and was by now devoted to Helen TAYLOR and, influenced by her, spent some time campaigning for the Irish Land League, in Ireland as well as in England. Jessie Craigen, however devoted, was her own woman and managed without difficulty to offend Helen Taylor by denigrating Charles Stuart Parnell. Priscilla Bright McLaren, having arranged for Jessie Craigen to be re-employed by the LNA, wrote to Helen Taylor on 21 September 1882, "We have got Jessie Craigen into work – she is dreadfully upset about some disagreement between you and herself and we had some difficulty at first in persuading her to come – because she said she understood the W. Suffrage ladies had put you and her out of court and she was such a very humble individual that she could not think of being taken into favour unless you were – and unless I would tell you how her very life was bound up in your approbation of her/ having now performed my promise to her thus to write to you, which I hope you will receive in the spirit in which I perform it – tho' I confess I am a little amused at the duty imposed upon me . . .". The final suffrage "Demonstration" that Jessie Craigen addressed was held in Glasgow in November 1882.

Jessie Craigen published a "Letter to the Ladies of the Women's Suffrage Movement", in which she expressed astonishment that an attempt was being made to introduce a franchise bill excluding married women. The Letter bears no date, although from internal evidence this may be 1883 and, if so, may be based on a speech she gave that summer at a meeting in London which brought into the open the difference in thinking between the moderate section of the suffrage movement, led by Lydia BECKER, and that of the radical suffragists. There is no indication in Jessie Craigen's pamphlet of a backing society or publisher, but the printer is Pewtress & Co. who in the 1880s were printers of the *Journal of the Vigilance Association for the Defence of Personal Rights*, the organ of the Vigilance Association for the Defence of Personal Rights, a society supported by such radicals as Elizabeth Wolstenholme ELMY and P.A. Taylor. The *Personal Rights Journal* lobbied against bureaucratic encroachments such as compulsory vaccination, in which it was certainly supported by Jessie Craigen. As the suffrage movement fragmented after the failure to win any measure for women's enfranchisement in 1884, Jessie Craigen's position as a freelance speaker, with no income other than that given her by sponsors, became more difficult. The days of rousing demonstrations had now passed and Jessie Craigen's strength did not lie in the diplomacy and politicking now required as new pressure groups were formed. The Priestman sisters organized in 1886 the "Jessie Craigen Lecture Fund" which provided her with a small income. She does not appear to have been henceforward involved in the suffrage movement, although she did continue to appear as a public speaker. In 1895 she spoke at the annual general meeting held to commemorate 21 years of the Social Purity Alliance and in 1898 she spoke against vivisection in Bristol. She died in her lodgings in Ilford.

Archival source: Mill–Taylor Papers, London School of Economics; Scatcherd Collection, Morley Public Library.

Bibliography: H. Blackburn, *Woman's Suffrage; A Record of the Women's Suffrage Movement in the British Isles*, 1902; Mrs A.M. Beddoe, *The Early Years of the Woman's Suffrage Movement in Bristol*, 1911; J. Craigen, "On woman suffrage, 14 February 1880", in J. Lewis (ed.), *Before The Vote was Won*, 1987; S.S. Holton, *Suffrage Days: Stories from the Women's Suffrage Movement*, 1996; S.S. Holton, "Silk dresses and lavender kid gloves: the wayward career of Jessie Craigen, working suffragist", *Women's History Review*, 5, 1, 1996.

CRAWFURD, HELEN (1877–1954) Born in the Gorbals, Glasgow, the fourth child of a master baker. The family moved to Ipswich and Helen Jack was educated there, before returning to Scotland in 1894. In 1898 she married a clergyman, Alexander Montgomerie Crawfurd, who was considerably older than herself. She began training to be a missionary and became interested in the work of Josephine Butler. The first suffrage speaker she heard, when on holiday at Rothesay, was Helen FRASER. Helen Crawfurd joined the WOMEN'S SOCIAL AND POLITICAL UNION in 1910 after attending, with her sisters, a meeting in Rutherglen. Helen Fraser left the WSPU and joined the NATIONAL UNION OF WOMEN'S SUFFRAGE SOCIETIES in mid-1908 so Helen Crawfurd presumably either waited some time after this first exposure to the suffrage message, or, having heard both the case for the NUWSS and for the WSPU, decided to join the latter. In her memoir she remarked that the main advantage that she gained as a result of joining the women's suffrage movement was that she found it necesssary to study economic conditions in order to speak effectively in public. She noted that she was influenced by Charlotte Perkins Gilman's

Women and Economics, Olive Schreiner's *Woman and Labour* and August Bebel's *Woman and Socialism*. She also read socialist material supplied by Mrs Swann of the Reformers' Bookstall in Bothwell Street, Glasgow. In March 1912 Helen Crawfurd went to London with other women from Glasgow, including Mrs Swann, Margaret and Frances MCPHUN, and Janet Barrowman, to take part in the window-smashing raid organized by the WSPU. She broke the windows of the Ministry of Education, and was sentenced to a month in Holloway. In March 1914 Helen Crawfurd was a member of the bodyguard that attempted to protect Mrs PANKHURST when she spoke at St Andrew's Hall, Glasgow. She remarked that before that meeting she had inclined to be sceptical about the brutality of the police as reported on other occasions in the pages of the *Suffragette*. When Mrs Pankhurst was arrested at the meeting, despite the bodyguards' valiant efforts to prevent it, Helen Crawfurd as a protest broke two windows in the Army Recruiting Office in Glasgow. She was sentenced to ten days' imprisonment, went on hunger strike, was not forcibly fed, but was released under the "Cat and Mouse" Act. She went through a succession of recaptures and releases until finally picked up by the police on 10 July while picketing outside Perth prison, inside which suffragette prisoners were being force fed. She again went on hunger strike and was released for the last time on 15 July, her sentence having been deemed served. In her memoir Helen Crawfurd related how during this period she and Dr Mabel Jones went to London to speak to Emmeline and Christabel Pankhurst to protest against the removal of Janie ALLAN as WSPU ORGANIZER for the west of Scotland. Leah Leneman has noted that Helen Crawfurd's memoir, written long after the events described, is unreliable as to dates and particularly highlights the intrinsic unlikelihood of Helen Crawfurd and Dr Mabel Jones speaking to both Emmeline and Christabel PANKHURST in London. Helen Crawfurd was at this time "on the run" and Christabel was in Paris, although she did return to London on occasion.

In the months immediately prior to the outbreak of war in August 1914 Helen Crawfurd and the Glasgow WSPU had been working increasingly with the socialist *Daily Herald* League. After the suspension of WSPU activity, she began speaking for the Independent Labour Party and was elected a member of its Scottish Divisional Council. She was very disappointed by the pro-war attitudes of Flora DRUMMOND and Christabel Pankhurst. She was on friendly terms with Charlotte DESPARD, with whose socialist pacifist outlook she was firmly in agreement. In 1916 Helen Crawfurd was one of the founders of the Women's Peace Crusade. She formed and was secretary of a branch of the Women's International League for Peace and Freedom. With Isabella FORD and Ethel SNOWDEN, and with Helena SWANWICK as chairman, Helen Crawfurd spoke at a meeting in London on 15 October to report on the success of the Peace Crusade. Selina COOPER had been invited, but was unable to attend; Helen Crawfurd had spoken at a meeting of the Nelson Peace Crusade. In 1919 she was one of the British delegates to the Women's International Congress at Zurich, at which the Women's International League for Peace and Freedom was founded. In 1920 she left the ILP to join the Communist party, was elected to its executive and put in charge of the party's work among women. She later worked for the Workers' International Relief Organisation. She was honorary secretary of an anti-fascist committee in Renfrew in the 1930s and later moved to Dunoon, where she became the first woman town councillor.

Address: (1908) 17 Sutherland Street, Hillhead, Glasgow.
Photograph: in E. King, *The Thenew Factor: The Hidden History of Glasgow's Women*, 1993.
Archival source: Helen Crawfurd's unpublished autobiography, Marx Memorial Library.
Bibliography: L. Leneman, *A Guid Cause; The Women's Suffrage Movement in Scotland*, 1991; E. King, *The Thenew Factor: The Hidden History of Glasgow's Women*, 1993.

CREETOWN branch of the WOMEN'S EMANCIPATION UNION President (1895) Mrs Cliff; honorary secretary, Miss Eva Colvin; honorary treasurer, Miss Jane Colvin.

CREWE (NUWSS) Formed in 1911, becoming a member of the MANCHESTER AND DISTRICT FEDERATION OF THE NATIONAL UNION OF WOMEN'S SUFFRAGE SOCIETIES, although it had lapsed by 1917. Secretary (1913) Mrs Atherton, 7 Maxwell Street, Crewe, Cheshire.

CRICCIETH (NUWSS) In 1913 the society was a member of the WEST LANCS, WEST CHESHIRE, AND NORTH WALES FEDERATION OF THE NATIONAL UNION OF WOMEN'S SUFFRAGE SOCIETIES. Secretary (1913) Mrs Walter Jones, Emu, Criccieth.

CRICK (NUWSS) In 1913 the society was a member of the MIDLANDS (WEST) FEDERATION OF THE NATIONAL UNION OF WOMEN'S SUFFRAGE SOCIETIES. Secretary (1913) Mrs Roberts, Crick Rectory, Rugby, Warwickshire.

CRIEFF (NUWSS) In 1913 the society was a member of the SCOTTISH FEDERATION OF THE NATIONAL UNION OF WOMEN'S SUFFRAGE SOCIETIES. Secretary (1913) Miss Kinghorn, Mayfield, Crieff, Perthshire.

CROCKER, ELLEN (NELLIE) (1872–1962) Cousin of Emmeline PETHICK-LAWRENCE. She was honorary secretary of the Wellington, Somerset, Women's Liberal Association but resigned in the autumn of 1907 as a protest against the Liberal government's lack of support for women's enfranchisement, and joined the WOMEN'S SOCIAL AND POLITICAL UNION. Nellie Crocker was a speaker at the first meeting of the Bath WSPU, which was organized by Mary BLATHWAYT, and was the first suffragette to stay with the Blathwayts at Eagle House, Batheaston. She was the principal speaker on one of the platforms at the WSPU June 1908 Hyde Park demonstration. She became a WSPU ORGANIZER in Yorkshire and in April 1909 campaigned with Adela PANKHURST at the Sheffield by-election. From 1909 until 1912 she was mainly based in Nottingham. She was arrested after taking part in the 29 June 1909 deputation to the House of Commons and in September was arrested in Leicester after interrupting a meeting being held by Winston Churchill. On that Saturday afternoon she was arrested, sentenced and imprisoned within the space of two hours. She went on hunger strike and was released after four days. She was involved in the "Black Friday" demonstration in Parliament Square in November 1910 and when in March 1912 she was on trial for taking part in the WSPU's window-smashing campaign, she gave her reason for so doing as a protest against the way women had been treated on that previous occasion. Nellie Crocker was in Holloway from 4 March to 4 June 1912, went on hunger strike, and took the part of "Fear" in the production put on there of Vera WENTWORTH's *Allegory*. She wrote to Helen WATTS from Holloway on 23 March 1912, describing her situation and telling her that she was in the company of Louisa Garrett ANDERSON, Emmeline PANKHURST and Ethel SMYTH. Nellie Crocker's work as a WSPU organizer ended in 1912; presumably she resigned as a protest against the treatment of the Pethick-Lawrences. In her will she left the residue of her estate to the SUFFRAGETTE FELLOWSHIP.
Address: (1908) Venice House, Teignmouth, Devon; (1909) 8 East Circus Street, Nottingham; (1912) The Mount, Wellington, Somerset; (1913) 156 Castellain Mansions, Maida Vale, London W.
Photograph: *Votes for Women*, 7 May 1908.

CROMER AND DISTRICT (NUWSS) In 1913 the society was a member of the EASTERN COUNTIES FEDERATION OF THE NATIONAL UNION OF WOMEN'S SUFFRAGE SOCIETIES. Secretary (1913) Miss Foxall, Shamrock Villa, The Meadow, Cromer, Norfolk.

CRONDALL, CROOKHAM AND EMSHOTT (NUWSS) In 1913 the society was a member of the Surrey, Sussex, and Hants Federation of the NATIONAL UNION OF WOMEN'S SUFFRAGE SOCIETIES. Secretary (1913) Mrs Griffiths Baker, Kerisley, Reading Road, Fleet, Hampshire.

CROSSKEY, HENRY WILLIAM, REV. (1826–93) Unitarian minister. Before moving to Birmingham in 1868 he was a minister in Glasgow, where he numbered among his congregation, before her marriage, Ottilie McLaren, step-daughter-in-law of Priscilla Bright MCLAREN. He was an associate of James Martineau, George Dawson and George HOLYOAKE in the Young Italy Movement and a member of the executive committee of the National Education League. Louis Blanc, another associate of Holyoake, was a frequent visitor to the Crosskeys in Glasgow. As early as the 1850s Crosskey was friendly with S.A. STEINTHAL, a fellow Unitarian minister who was also, later, to be a stalwart supporter of the women's suffrage movement. In 1852 Crosskey married Hannah, the daughter of Richard Aspden of Derby. By 1870 Crosskey was a member of the executive committee of the BIRMINGHAM

SOCIETY FOR WOMEN'S SUFFRAGE. His wife presided over the "Demonstration of Women" held in Birmingham in 1881. At the conference held by the National Liberal Federation and the National Reform Union at Leeds in 1883 Crosskey moved a motion, "That in the opinion of this meeting, any measure for the extension of the suffrage should confer the franchise on women, who, possessing the qualifications which entitle men to vote, have now the right of voting in all matters of local government". In this he was seconded by Walter McLaren and supported by Jane Cobden (*see* Jane Cobden UNWIN) and Helen Bright CLARK. A few months before he died he and his wife went to Scotland to attend the wedding of Ottilie McLaren's daughter. His biographer particularly remarked, "He advocated Woman's Suffrage at a time when that great policy of justice was far more unpopular than it is to-day". One might add that it would not have been unusual, in 1895, for a biographer to entirely ignore this aspect of his subject's career.
Address: (1892) 117 Gough Road, Birmingham.
Bibliography: R.A. Armstrong, *Henry William Crosskey: His Life and Work*, 1895.

CROWBOROUGH (NUWSS) In 1913 the society was a member of the SURREY, SUSSEX, AND HANTS FEDERATION OF THE NATIONAL UNION OF WOMEN'S SUFFRAGE SOCIETIES. Secretary (1913) Mrs Rendel, Ghyllmead, Crowborough, Sussex.

CROWTHORNE (NUWSS) In 1913 the society was a member of the OXON, BERKS, BUCKS, AND BEDS FEDERATION OF THE NATIONAL UNION OF WOMEN'S SUFFRAGE SOCIETIES. Secretary (1913) Miss Ethel Fox, Woodleigh, Crowthorne, Berkshire.

CROYDON committee of the NATIONAL SOCIETY FOR WOMEN'S SUFFRAGE Formed in 1873 when among its members were Mr and Mrs William Malleson (see Elizabeth MALLESON). By 1906 Croydon had become a branch of the LONDON SOCIETY FOR WOMEN'S SUFFRAGE. Secretary (1909) Miss Crickmay, 7 St James's Park, Croydon, Surrey; (1913) Miss W.M. Hudson, 34 Birdhurst Road, Croydon, Surrey.

CROYDON (WFL) Secretary (1913) Mrs Terry, 9 Morland Avenue, Croydon, Surrey.

CROYDON (WSPU) One of the earliest London branches, formed in 1906. The office of the Croydon branch was raided by the police on 30 June 1914. Secretary (1906) Miss D. Arter, "Melrose", 38 Blenheim Park Road, South Croydon; (1913) Mrs Cameron Swan, 79 Mayfield Road, Sanderstead, Surrey. WSPU shop, 50 High Street, Croydon, Surrey.

CULLEN, LOUISE, MRS (1876–?, alive, in Australia, in 1958) In *Votes for Women*, 2 July 1909, noted that she joined the WOMEN'S SOCIAL AND POLITICAL UNION in 1906 after hearing Annie KENNEY speak. In a biographical piece that she wrote later, now in the Suffragette Fellowship Collection, Museum of London, she cited Dora MONTEFIORE's refusal to pay tax as bringing to her attention for the first time the way that law was unjustly applied to women. It may well have been that in 1909 it was not acceptable to draw attention to Dora Montefiore in the pages of *Votes for Women*, and that Annie Kenney was the approved role model, thereby adding another piece of evidence to Dora Montefiore's conspiracy theory. Louie Cullen had left school at 14 and since then had worked for her living. By 1906 she was married and her husband was in sympathy with her work for the WSPU. She joined the WSPU before it had any offices and noted that they first met in Emmeline PETHICK-LAWRENCE's flat in Clement's Inn. With the Misses Auld, Louie Cullen started a WSPU branch in Kensal Rise. In October 1906 Hannah MITCHELL stayed with Louie Cullen, who was then caretaker of a house in Kensington, when she came down to London and they both took part in the demonstration before the opening of parliament. In November 1906 Louie Cullen organized the meeting in Kensington Town Hall out of which grew the KENSINGTON WSPU. She also organized the HAMMERSMITH branch and was friendly with Frances ROWE, who invited her to Somerset in the summer of 1907 to undertake some propaganda work there with the village women. In July 1907 Louie Cullen wrote to Maud Arncliffe SENNETT asking her to address the Harrow Road branch of the WSPU. In February 1908 she was arrested after taking part in the "pantechnicon raid" on the House of Commons and sentenced to six weeks' imprisonment. She was a speaker at the

June 1908 Hyde Park demonstration. She was again arrested on 29 June 1909 after taking part in the deputation to the House of Commons but did not receive a sentence. Ill-health meant that she could not take any further part in the WSPU's increasingly militant campaign. With her husband she emigrated to Australia in 1911 and was an active member of the Australian branch of the SUFFRAGETTE FELLOWSHIP in Sydney in 1946.

Archival source: The Suffragette Fellowship Collection, Museum of London.

CUPAR (NUWSS) In 1913 the society was a member of the SCOTTISH FEDERATION OF THE NATIONAL UNION OF WOMEN'S SUFFRAGE SOCIETIES. Secretary (1913) Miss Davidson, Bonvil, Cupar, Fife.

CYMRIC SUFFRAGE UNION Founded by Edith MANSELL-MOULLIN at a meeting on 10 July 1911 in the aftermath of the suffrage Coronation Procession, in which a Welsh contingent, picturesquely attired in costumes designed by Mrs Mansell-Moullin, had been conspicuous. The Cymric Suffrage Union had, like the WOMEN'S SOCIAL AND POLITICAL UNION, of which Edith Mansell-Moullin was an active member, an anti-government policy and united Welsh men and women, their sympathizers and friends, in putting the enfranchisement of women before any other cause. The Union concentrated its campaign in London by handing out suffrage handbills written in Welsh at Welsh chapels in London and translating pamphlets on the Conciliation Bill into Welsh. The Union canvassed the traditionally Welsh milkshops in London, many of which were run by spinsters and widows. Meetings in Wales were addressed by the Union's secretary, speaking in both English and Welsh, and Welsh MPs were lobbied. After the failure of the Conciliation Bill Edith Mansell-Moullin, prepared to adopt a militant policy, took her supporters and set up the FORWARD CYMRIC SUFFRAGE UNION. The rump appears to have withered and disappeared.

President (1911) Mrs D.A. Thomas (*see* Lady RHONDDA); honorary secretary (1911) Mrs M.E. Davis, 57 Racton Road, Fulham, London SW; honorary treasurer (1911) Miss Norbury, 33 Morpeth Mansions, Westminster, London SW.

Bibliography: K. Cook and Neil Evans, "'The petty antics of the bell-ringing boisterous band'?: the women's suffrage movement in Wales", in Angela V. John (ed.), *Our Mothers' Land: Chapters in Welsh Women's History, 1830–1939*, 1991.

D

DACRE, SUSAN ISABEL (1844–1933) Born in Leamington, Warwickshire, educated at a convent school in Salford. Her portrait of her mother, painted *c*. 1884, is now in Manchester City Art Gallery. From 1858 to 1868 Susan Dacre lived in Paris, attending a school there first as a pupil and then as a governess. In 1869 she spent the winter in Italy, the following year she was caught in Paris during the Commune. She returned to England and lived in Manchester from 1871 until 1874, attending classes at the School of Art, from which she was awarded in 1875 the Queen's Prize. In 1874, with Annie Robinson (later SWYNNERTON) she went to Rome, where she stayed for two years. From 1877 to 1880, although still based in Manchester, Susan Dacre again studied art in Paris, where she was a fellow student of Marie Bashkirtseff. In 1879 she was one of the founders of and became president of the Manchester Society for Women Painters. After coming back to London she lived there with Annie Robinson from 1880 until 1883. After Annie Robinson's marriage in 1883 Susan Dacre returned to Manchester. She became friendly with Lydia BECKER, and was a member of the executive committee of the MANCHESTER NATIONAL SOCIETY FOR WOMEN'S SUFFRAGE from 1885 until at least 1895. There are no records for the Society available from then until 1899, by which time she was no longer a member of the committee. However, she signed the claim for women's suffrage published by the CENTRAL COMMITTEE OF THE NATIONAL SOCIETY FOR WOMEN'S SUFFRAGE in 1889 and the Women Householders' Declaration of 1889–90. Helena SWANWICK and C.P. Scott, editor of the *Manchester Guardian*, were included in her wide circle of friends in Manchester. C.P. Scott left to Manchester City Art Gallery a painting by Susan Dacre, a view of Assisi from Perugia.

In 1886 Susan Dacre painted the portrait of Lydia Becker that now hangs in Manchester City Art Gallery. Although she is wearing her usual spectacles and well-corseted dark dress, Lydia Becker is portrayed as both "womanly" and business-like. Looking at this portrait one realizes how powerful are the caricatures that were her usual lot. Susan Dacre has captured a rather rueful or quizzical look and softened her dress with a rose corsage and a collar of well-painted lace. When in 1892, after Miss Becker's death, the NATIONAL UNION OF WOMEN'S SUFFRAGE SOCIETIES, who had bought the painting, attempted to present it to the National Portrait Gallery it was rejected on the grounds that the Gallery could only immortalize those who had been dead for at least ten years, a rule that remained in place until 1969. There is, however, a photograph of the painting in its original state in the NPG archive collection (*see* p. 44). The final version, now in Manchester, is cut off at the sitter's waist; the City Gallery would only accept the portrait, when offered it by the NUWSS in 1920, if the painter did so alter it. There was doubtless no slight on Miss Becker, rather a recognition that, unlike the rest of the portrait, the hands were awkwardly painted. Susan Dacre also painted another member of the Manchester National Suffrage Society – her portrait of Agnes POCHIN now hangs at Bodnant. As there is no complete catalogue of Susan Dacre's work, it has not yet been possible to trace whether she painted portraits of any other suffragists. From 1904 she lived in London. In the Coronation Procession of June 1911, with Annie Swynnerton she headed the section representing Chelsea artists. She exhibited for the last time at the Royal Academy in 1929. In her will, made in 1931, witnessed by Annie Swynnerton, Susan Dacre left her entire estate to a younger fellow artist, Francis Dodd, RA, whom she had befriended in Manchester at the end of the nineteenth century and with whom in 1908 she shared her home in London.

Address: (1889) 31 Sibson Street, Sale; (studio) 10 South King Street, Manchester; (1908) 13 Fitzroy Street, London W; (1931) 20 St John's Park, Blackheath, London SE.

Portrait: by Annie Swynnerton, 1880, presented to Manchester City Art Gallery, 1932; at least three of her by Francis Dodd (one, 1925, in Ferens Art Gallery, Kingston-upon-Hull, and another, as "Signora Lotto", 1906, in Manchester City Art Gallery).
Bibliography: Catalogue of an Exhibition of Paintings of S. Isabel Dacre, with etchings by Francis Dodd and sculpture by F. Derwent, Manchester City Art Gallery, 1927; D. Cherry, *Painting Women: Victorian Women Artists*, 1993.

DALKEITH committee of the NATIONAL SOCIETY FOR WOMEN'S SUFFRAGE Was in existence in 1872 when its honorary secretary was Miss J. Harris.

DARLINGTON Women's Suffrage Society Probably founded in 1902. In 1904 the society joined the NATIONAL UNION OF WOMEN'S SUFFRAGE SOCIETIES and by 1913 was a member of the NORTH-WESTERN FEDERATION. Secretary (1909, 1913) Miss Swanson, 17 Waverley Terrace, Darlington, Co. Durham.

DARWEN (NUWSS) In 1910 the society joined the MANCHESTER AND DISTRICT FEDERATION OF THE NATIONAL UNION OF WOMEN'S SUFFRAGE SOCIETIES. Secretary (1913) Mrs Jepson, 15 Cleveland Terrace, Darwen, Lancashire.

DAVIES, [SARAH] EMILY (1830–1921) Born in Southampton, fourth child of Rev John Davies and his wife, Mary, daughter of John Hopkinson. In 1839 the family moved to Gateshead, where in 1848 Emily met Jane Crow, through whom, in 1854, she eventually made the acquaintance of Elizabeth Garrett (see Elizabeth Garrett ANDERSON). In 1856 Emily's brother Llewelyn became rector of Christ Church, Marylebone and through him she came into contact with London's social and educational reformers. In 1858, while accompanying another of her brothers on a futile trip to Algiers to allay the progress of his tuberculosis, she met and became friendly with Annie Leigh Smith and, through her, her sister Barbara BODICHON. These strands of friendship all met when in the spring of 1859 Emily Davies, while staying with her brother in Marylebone, went to tea, accompanied by Elizabeth Garrett, with the Leigh Smiths. On that occasion she met two other members of the Langham Place circle, Adelaide Procter and Bessie Rayner PARKES. In 1860 Jane Crow became secretary of the Society for Promoting the Employment of Women (SPEW) and Emily Davies, having returned home, established and became treasurer of a Northumberland and Durham branch of SPEW. In 1862 after her father's death she and her mother came to live in London and settled in Marylebone; her brother Llewelyn was now living in Blandford Square, a few doors from the Leigh Smiths. Emily Davies was an enthusiastic and effective supporter of Elizabeth Garrett's aim to acquire a medical education. In 1862 she wrote a paper on "Medicine as a Profession for Women" which was read to the National Association for the Promotion of Social Science, in September began a six-month stint as acting editor of the *English Woman's Journal* and in October constituted a committee to obtain the admission of women to University Local Examinations. As a result of the committee's campaigning, Cambridge University in 1865 agreed to admit women to its local examinations. In 1864 Emily Davies became, although she held the post for only a short time, editor of the *Victoria Magazine*, newly founded by Emily FAITHFULL and in the same year was a member of the committee of the Ladies' Emancipation Society. When the KENSINGTON SOCIETY was founded in early 1865, Emily Davies became its secretary. In May 1865 she, with Barbara Bodichon, Isa CRAIG and Bessie Rayner Parkes publicly supported J.S. MILL's election campaign in Westminster. After the Kensington Society discussed women's enfranchisement in November 1865 Emily Davies, although she had already achieved a measure of success in her education campaign, was not enthusiastic for forming a committee to further this new cause. She wrote "I don't see much use in talking about the Franchise till first principles have made more way", believing that the matter of women's education should come first, as a springboard for wider freedoms. She was, however, now much in the society of women such as Clementia TAYLOR, Lady AMBERLEY and Frances Power COBBE who were keen to capitalize on Mill's position in the House of Commons in order to bring attention in the Reform Bill debates to women's claim for enfranchisement. On 25 April 1866 Emily Davies paid a first visit to J.S. Mill and Helen TAYLOR at Blackheath. Two weeks later Barbara Bodichon wrote to Helen Taylor, asking her and Mill to support a petition for women's enfranchisement. Emily Davies then became a member of the small, informal committee that organized the 1866 petition (see WOMEN'S SUFFRAGE PETITION COMMITTEE). This document was handed over by Elizabeth Garrett and Emily Davies to J.S. Mill on 7 June and then presented by him to parliament. Emily Davies was very energetic in her efforts to publicize the petition. She organized its printing, with the list of 1499 names and addresses, and sent it to members of both houses of parliament and to newpapers. By 18 July Emily Davies was able to write to Helen Taylor that she had that day sent the petition to all the weekly papers of any consideration, "that in case they take any notice, they may know what they are commenting upon".

Even before the petition was actually presented there was an idea that the protest against women's disenfranchisement should continue. In letters from Emily Davies to Helen Taylor on 5 and 6 June she discussed the putative membership of a committee, and whether or not men could be included. In the flow of letters and personal discussions between the main protagonists Emily Davies revealed a slight hesitancy about joining any proposed committee, in case working with that should hamper in any way her mission to improve women's educational lot. However, by August, after much informal discussion, she was happy to be involved in the issuing of three further petitions, using the experience she had gained from directing her Education Committee to suggest that this should be done in "a semi-public, semi-private manner". From her letters it is clear that she was loath to be involved in a formal society, where she might be held responsible for the actions of others. On 20 October 1866 at a meeting at which it was proposed to form a "Provisional Committee for obtaining the abolition of the legal disabilities which at present prevent unqualified women as such from voting for members of Parliament", Emily Davies expressed her determination not to be involved, finding, as Barbara Bodichon wrote to Helen Taylor, "the educational movement as much as she could do". However, such was the opposition to her withdrawal that when the ENFRANCHISEMENT OF WOMEN COMMITTEE was formally constituted on 23 November 1866 Emily Davies was a member of its permanent committee. She was to be, in effect, secretary of the Committee, but to be protected behind the name of Louisa SMITH, Elizabeth Garrett's sister. Emily Davies wrote, "My name was to be kept out of sight, to avoid the risk of damaging my work in the education field by its being associated with the agitation for the franchise." She was also to be given secretarial assistance by Harriet COOK. However, although the petitions were successfully organized, the process of so doing brought to the surface differences of opinion and approach between the members of the committee that led, once Mill's amendment to the Reform Bill had been defeated in May 1867, to the dissolution of the Enfranchisement of Women Committee. Emily Davies was, with Barbara Bodichon, of the "quiet party". She naturally favoured a gradualist approach, prepared as an expedient measure to exclude married women from the franchise, and she was, unlike Mill and Helen Taylor, keen that men, with whom she had worked very successfully on her Education Committee, should be included on a franchise committee. She was now content to leave further agitation for the franchise to the radicals. A hint of the tact she found it necessary to employ in those brief months is given in a letter she wrote on 16 February 1867 to Lydia BECKER, the new secretary of the Manchester Enfranchisement of Women Committee. "It is I suppose a general rule that in all controversy, a tone of exaggerated courtesy to the other side is best, but I am sure it is so as regards women. People notice our manners more than our arguments, and the one thing they fear is that by descending into the arena, as they call it, women will get their polish rubbed off. Sarcasm, unless it is of the tenderest sort... will not be endured from women. I venture to make these very few remarks, because I think those who have not had experience in this controversy scarcely know how much depends on scrupulous avoidence of the slightest tinge of bitterness." When the LONDON NATIONAL SOCIETY was formed in the summer of 1867 Emily Davies declined to join.

In November 1870 Emily Davies was elected to the London School Board on which she remained until, overpowered by the work involved at a time when the college, Girton, that she had founded in Cambridge was going through a critical period, she declined to stand for re-election in 1873. By 1874, when the more radical members had left to join the CENTRAL COMMITTEE OF THE NATIONAL SOCIETY FOR WOMEN'S SUFFRAGE, Emily Davies rejoined the London National Society, becoming one of its vice-presidents. In 1889 she joined the London's general committee and in 1890 the executive committee. After the split in the Central Committee in 1888 she became a member of the executive committee of the new Central Committee and signed the Declaration in Favour of Women's Suffrage in 1889. On occasion she did speak in public on the issue of women's suffrage; in 1891 she addressed the annual general meeting of the CAMBRIDGE ASSOCIATION FOR WOMEN'S SUFFRAGE and in the same year took part in a small deputation, with Millicent FAWCETT, Helen BLACKBURN and Lady GOLDSMID to the First Lord of the Treasury. She was also involved in quieter, more domestic, propaganda; in 1889 she held a "suffrage drawing room" at 8 Harewood Square, Marylebone. From 1900 to 1906 Emily Davies was a member of the executive committee of the CENTRAL SOCIETY FOR WOMEN'S SUFFRAGE, a member of its literature subcommittee. For this in 1905 she wrote a pamphlet, *The Women's Suffrage Movement: I. Why Should We Care For It? II. How Can We Help it Further?* She then became a member of the executive committee of the Central's successor, the LONDON SOCIETY FOR WOMEN'S SUFFRAGE, and was a member of the executive committee of the NATIONAL UNION OF WOMEN'S SUFFRAGE SOCIETIES. Having resigned as honorary secretary and as a member of the executive committee of Girton in 1904 she was able to return more publicly to the suffrage cause. On 12 May 1905 she was present in the House of Commons when the women's suffrage bill was talked out. In 1906 she took part in the large deputation of women to the Prime Minister, Henry Campbell-Bannerman. She opened the proceedings, which were brought to a close by a speech from Mrs PANKHURST. In the same year Emily Davies also went, with Millicent Fawcett, to interview Asquith. By 1907 she was chairman of the Marylebone branch of the London Society for Women's Suffrage, took part in February in the NUWSS "Mud March", and on 13 June 1908 walked, wearing the robes denoting her honorary doctorate from Glasgow University, in the NUWSS march from the Embankment to the Albert Hall. A figure which may well be Emily Davies appears on film, wearing a frilled bonnet and leaning on a stick, walking in the "University Section" of the 18 June 1910 procession, which was organized by the WSPU, but in which many members of the NUWSS participated. After the NUWSS developed, in 1912, the Election Fighting Fund policy to support Labour candidates at elections, Emily Davies, a natural conservative, felt constrained to leave the London Society and joined the CONSERVATIVE AND UNIONIST WOMEN'S FRANCHISE ASSOCIATION, of which she became a vice-president. In 1918 she was able, aged 88, to cast her vote in the general election.

Most of Emily Davies's published writing relates to her work for women's education. An article she wrote in 1905 on "The woman's suffrage movement" for the *Girton Review* is contained in E. Davies, *Thoughts on Some Questions Relating to Women*, 1910.

Address: (1862) 17 Cunningham Place, London NW; (1899) 12 York Street, London W; (1907) 6R Montagu Mansions, Portman Square, London W; (1913) 17 Glenmore Road, Belsize Park, London NW.
Portrait: by Rudolf Lehmann, 1880, in Girton College, Cambridge; it had been exhibited at the Grosvenor Gallery in 1880 (*see under* CLUBS); photograph, 1901, in H. Blackburn, *Record of Women's Suffrage*, 1902.
Archival source: Emily Davies Papers, Girton College; Mill–Taylor Papers, London School of Economics.
Bibliography: M. Fawcett, *What I Remember*, 1924; B. Stephen, *Emily Davies and Girton College*, 1927; M. Forster, *Significant Sisters: The Grassroots of Active Feminism, 1839–1939*, 1985.

DAVISON, EMILY WILDING (1872–1913) Born at Blackheath, educated at Kensington High School (GPDST) and at Holloway College. Her father died a year before the end of her course, and the ensuing lack of funds meant that she had to leave Holloway and work as a resident governess. She saved sufficient money to pay for a term in residence at St Hugh's Hall, Oxford, before sitting her finals. She took a first-class degree. From 1893 until 1895 she probably worked as a governess. In 1895–6 she was employed by the Church of England College for Girls in Edgbaston, her first school appointment, and from 1896 to 1898 she taught at Seabury School, West Worthing. From 1900 until 1906 she remained as a governess with one family, living in Berkshire. Emily Davison joined the

WOMEN'S SOCIAL AND POLITICAL UNION in November 1906. Sylvia PANKHURST described her as "tall and slender, with unusually long arms, a small narrow head and red hair. Her illusive, whimsical green eyes and thin, half-smiling mouth, bore often the mocking expression of the Mona Lisa". For the WSPU procession on 21 June 1908 Emily Davison acted as chief steward at Marylebone Station, shepherding the arriving participants to Hyde Park. In March 1909 she was one of 21 women arrested after taking part in a deputation from Caxton Hall to see Asquith; she was sentenced to one month's imprisonment. After this experience she wrote in a letter to *Votes for Women*, 11 June 1909, "Through my humble work in this noblest of all causes I have come into a fulness of joy and an interest in living which I never before experienced". In July 1909, with Mary LEIGH, Alice PAUL and Lucy BURNS, she was arrested after interrupting a meeting being held by Lloyd George at Limehouse. This time she went on hunger strike, a weapon introduced by Marion Wallace-DUNLOP in the previous month to protest against the fact that suffragettes were not accorded the status of political prisoners. After five and a half days Emily Davison was released from a two-month sentence. On 4 September she was arrested, with, among others, Dora MARSDEN, having thrown iron balls, each weighing over three ounces and labelled "bomb", through a window during a meeting held by Birrell in Manchester. A letter published from her in the *Manchester Guardian*, 11 September, just after her release, makes it clear that, in her mind at least, the disruption of the meeting was "meant as a warning to the general public of the personal risk they run in future if they go to Cabinet Ministers' meetings anywhere". Charged with nothing more serious than damaging glass, she was sentenced to two months' imprisonment, in default of paying a fine, went on hunger strike and was released after two and a half days. During that short period of incarceration she broke five panes in her cell windows and as a result was forced into handcuffs, her hands held in front of her body. She was as surprised as the Home Office at the speed with which the prison governor discharged her and her companions. In early October she was again arrested, having accompanied Lady Constance LYTTON when the latter threw a stone at Sir Walter Runciman's car in Newcastle. Lady Constance was sentenced to one month's imprisonment, but Emily Davison was released. On 20 October she was arrested in Radcliffe, with Helen Gordon Liddle, after breaking windows to protest against the exclusion of women from a meeting being held there by the Chancellor of the Exchequer, Runciman. On that same day Helen Gordon Liddle had been a witness to Emily Davison's will which she made while staying at the home of Jane Ratcliffe, 19 Parkfield Street, Rusholme, Manchester, who was the treasurer of the Manchester branch of the WSPU. By this time Emily Davison had obviously given up paid employment; she could have hardly expected to be retained as a teacher or governess between prison sentences. She is described on this occasion in *Votes for Women* as "one of the most devoted voluntary workers in the Union" and was presumably not then receiving any pay as a WSPU ORGANIZER. She was sentenced to two months' hard labour, went on hunger strike, and this time was forcibly fed. Forcible feeding had been used for the first time on suffragette prisoners, including Emily Davison's friends, Mabel CAPPER and Mary Leigh, the previous month in Winson Green Prison. It was presumably a realization that this treatment, with its yet unknown pain, awaited her in Strangeways that prompted the writing of her will. The latter was a low-key, private document, by which she left her entire estate to her mother. It contained no messages of martyrdom. The very fact of its execution at that particular time gives an insight into the mind of a woman in the position of Emily Davison. She really did not know what might happen to her and was approaching this uncertainty in a sensible, matter-of-fact way. Perhaps she had planned to resist the feeding; in the event, having received one such treatment, she barricaded her cell door with the prison plank bed. A hose-pipe was put through the window of her cell and a jet of water streamed in for a quarter of an hour. As she still refused to open the door it was eventually broken down. She was then forcibly fed; she was released after she had served eight days of her sentence. In January 1910 she won a case against the Strangeways authorities in respect of the mistreatment they had inflicted on her by the use of the hose-pipe. By April 1910 she was a paid worker for the WSPU, contributing articles to *Votes for Women*. After her death the WSPU commented particularly on the "constitutional" work she had undertaken, citing her journalism and letters to the press. She was not arrested as a result of the "Black Friday" debacle of November 1910, although it would have been uncharacteristic if she had not been present. The next day, 19 November, to protest against the treatment of women on that occasion and against Asquith's side-stepping of the Conciliation Bill, she broke a window in the House of Commons. She was sentenced to one month's imprisonment, went on hunger strike, and was again forcibly fed. She was released after eight days. In 1910 and 1911 on three occasions she managed to evade security officers in the House of Commons and remain there, hidden, for some time. One of these nights was that of the census in April 1911. In December 1911 Emily Davison initiated a new form of militancy, and moved the stakes up a notch, when she set fire to a pillar box. Stone throwing, the previous militant weapon, had been first employed in 1908 by her close friend Mary Leigh, again without taking directions from the WSPU leadership. Emily Davison said at her trial that she acted entirely on her own responsibility. This time she was sentenced to six months' imprisonment. She did not go on hunger strike, but was deemed by the prison authorities to be taking insufficient nourishment and was forcibly fed from 29 February until 7 March. In June, by which time she had the company in Holloway of the many suffragette prisoners who had taken part in the March window-smashing campaign, Emily Davison did join in the hunger strike that resulted from the denial to the many the status of first-class treatment that had been accorded to their leaders. She then, on two successive occasions, threw herself over the landing railings in Holloway, the second time inflicting on herself some considerable damage. From the article she wrote shortly afterwards, which was only published in *Votes for Women* after her death, she makes clear that she acted thus in order to draw attention to the horrors of forcible feeding. She continued, despite her injuries, to be forcibly fed and was released into the care of Eleanor Penn GASKELL, on 28 June, only ten days before the end of her six-month sentence. A poem, "L'Envoi", she wrote at this time was included in *Holloway Jingles*, the volume of poems written by her fellow prisoners, edited by N.A. John and published by the Glasgow branch of the WSPU. At the end of November 1912 Emily Davison, using the alias "Mary Brown", was arrested in Aberdeen, accused of having taken a horsewhip to a man she thought, mistakenly, was Lloyd George. After sentence she spent four days in prison, on hunger strike, before her fine was paid anonymously.

Sylvia PANKHURST in *The Suffragette Movement* and Andrew Rosen in *Rise Up Women!*, presumably following Sylvia Pankhurst's lead, implicate Emily Davison in the bombing of Lloyd George's new house at Walton-on-the-Hill in Surrey on 18 February 1913. Liz Stanley and Ann Morley in *The Life and Death of Emily Wilding Davison* argue quite plausibly that this is unlikely. Emily Davison may or may not have been involved; other than Sylvia Pankhurst's statement there is no proof. Home Office papers indicate that the perpetrators were, in fact, Olive HOCKIN and Norah Smyth and make no mention whatsoever of Emily Davison. After 1909 all the acts of defiance for which Emily Davison was charged were enacted, on her own initiative, publicly. The stone throwing and pillar-box arson were so openly perpetrated that it seems unlikely that she was at the same time involved in other, more secret, activities. At this late stage it seems doubtful that she would have co-operated with others to organize a bombing raid, which would have both been secretly executed and, in effect, the responsibility of Christabel and Emmeline PANKHURST. Hindsight has marked Emily Davison as the epitome of the militant suffragette and to her has accrued all features of militancy. It is much more likely that, at the time, she was assessed by the WSPU leadership, if they thought of her at all, as an independent and as a liability. Much more characteristic was her final act, through which her whole life has been interpreted. On 4 June 1913 she rushed onto the Derby race course and attempted to hold the bridle of Anmer, the King's horse. She was seriously injured, never regained consciousness,

Derby Day, 4 June 1913. Emily Wilding Davison lies on the ground after being kicked by horses' hooves. The police attempt to staunch the wound with newspaper. (Author's collection)

and died on 8 June. Inside her coat were pinned two WSPU flags. Andrew Rosen in *Rise Up Women!* mentioned that Emily Davison was at the Derby with her "flat-mate". There is no suggestion in contemporary accounts that she was accompanied to Epsom. Even Mary RICHARDSON, who in her *post hoc* and self-serving memoir claims to have been an eye-witness at the Derby that day, does not go so far as to say that she accompanied Emily Davison there. On 14 June Emily Davison was accorded a martyr's funeral. The WSPU, WOMEN'S FREEDOM LEAGUE, NEW CONSTITUTIONAL SOCIETY, WOMEN WRITERS' LEAGUE, CHURCH LEAGUE FOR WOMEN'S SUFFRAGE and the ACTRESSES' FRANCHISE LEAGUE combined to achieve the spectacle, organized by Grace ROE, which has come to represent the suffrage movement in the popular imagination. The long, impressive procession, witnessed by a newsreel photographer (see under FILMS) made its way through the streets of London to St George's, in Hart Street (now New Oxford Street), Bloomsbury, where the funeral service was conducted by the vicar, Rev. C. Baumgarten, and the Rev. Claude Hinscliff, stalwarts of the Church League for Women's Suffrage. From there the coffin was taken to King's Cross, and on by train to the Davison family grave in Morpeth, Northumberland. This now contains three memorials. One is an obelisk recording family members, one in the shape of an open book was given by Emily Davison's "Loving Aberdeen Friend", whom Liz Stanley and Ann Morley have so patiently traced, and the third was, presumably, from the WSPU. Mary Leigh made a pilgrimage each year to the grave, bearing one of the flags that Emily Davison had taken to Epsom. On any visit to the grave one will still find flowers there, in "the colours", such is the power of the martyr and her myth.

The consensus of opinion is that Emily Davison acted as she did to draw attention yet again in as public a manner as possible to the sufferings of those involved in the militant struggle; that she probably did not intend to die, but was willing to accept the risk. The verdict at the time was "misadventure". Hindsight, through which we view her death, could not reveal to Emily Davison that Mrs Pankhurst, who was seriously ill after a succession of imprisonments and hunger strikes, and who had taken upon herself all responsibility for militant action, although suffering, would not die. At the time, as Rebecca West's article, "The Life of Emily Davison", published in the *Clarion*, 20 June 1913, makes clear, it was thought only too likely that Mrs Pankhurst might well succumb and this fear drove women such as Emily Davison and later Mary Richardson to desperate public acts. The "persecution" of Mrs Pankhurst was in no way lessened by Emily Davison's death; in fact she was re-arrested on her way to the funeral.

The enigma of Emily Davison and that of so many of her fellow campaigners is that, because at the time they measured out their achievements and identified themselves in terms of imprisonment and self-sacrifice, it is very difficult to comprehend their day-to-day reality. We do not know how Emily Davison supported herself in her last three years. Gertrude Colmore stressed that by 1912 she "had no settled work, and consequently no salary" and that her "position of free lance" activist was incompatible with employment by the WSPU, although Cecily HALE related that in 1913 Emily Davison did work in the WSPU office in Lincoln's Inn House. In February 1913 Harriet KERR wrote to H.G. Daniels at the *Manchester Guardian* office in Fleet Street, asking him to spare a few minutes to speak to Emily Davison who was "anxious to get some literary work" and would be grateful for his advice. In April Emily Davison inquired about the possibility of writing for the *Nursing Times,* and in a letter dated 2 June, only two days before the Derby, the secretary of the TAX RESISTANCE LEAGUE wrote to her regretting that the vacant position for which she had applied was only for a junior shorthand typist, rather than a secretary, and returning her, by now rather dog-eared, testimonials. An undated, possibly family, letter to her alludes to her workless state, encloses a postal order "to keep you going for a bit", and comments "I do think the Militants might remember your services & give you something". In an interview taped in 1974 Cecily Hale described Emily Davison as "a fanatic", as "smouldering" and as "always waiting for the next thing to do". She surmised that Emily Davison did not intend to die, but was prepared to take the risk. Emily Davison could have earned little through her journalism. Her estate was valued for probate at £186 1s 7d. We know very little about where and how she lived except that in 1913 her address was 133 Clapham Road, the home of Mrs Alice Green, a close friend who came to her bedside in Epsom Cottage Hospital. Emily Davison supported the Worker's Education Association and the Central Labour College, which was represented at her funeral, and attended classes on aspects of the labour movement. Liz Stanley and Ann Morley draw attention to Emily Davison's concern for the vote as a means to an end; her belief was that with the vote women would be able to effect social and moral reform. Emily Davison has left published articles in which she sets out her philosophy. However, with their rhetoric set in Edwardian amber, these shield rather than reveal the living woman. Despite the best efforts of Liz Stanley and Ann Morley, who have very successfully breathed life into her friends, it is difficult to understand the reality of Emily Davison. The fact that Elinor Penn GASKELL, Rose Lamartine YATES and Edith Mansell-MOULLIN all seem eminently sensible women and did not die for the cause makes them more easily comprehensible to our prosaic age. The manner of Emily Davison's death seemed then, as now, so bizarre, so public, her intention, if she did not mean to die, so naïve, that it has coloured all recountings of her life. Her death came at a time when militancy was reaching a crescendo. When Mary CLARKE, Mrs Pankhurst's sister, died at the end of 1910, immediately after release from prison after involvement in the protest against the "Black Friday" assaults, a case could have been made, if the WSPU had so chosen, to treat her as the first martyr to the cause. It was presumably not deemed expedient and she went very quietly to her grave. The contemporary interpretations of Emily Davison as comrade and martyr, recounted in numerous articles and in Gertrude Colmore's biography, depict her as living to make a martyr's death. Perhaps we should not be too prosaic; perhaps, given the heady atmosphere of the time, by June 1913 it may even have seemed like that to Emily Davison. Alive, she was subsequently able to explain her attempts at self-damage while in Holloway as intended to draw attention specifically to the pain and horror of forcible feeding. "In my mind was the thought that some desperate protest must be made to put a stop to the hideous torture which was now being our lot". Dead, she was, of course, unable to explain what she had intended to achieve at the Derby. Her memory was perpetuated both by popular culture and by her friends who founded the Emily Wilding Davison Club (*see under* CLUBS).

Address: (1913) Longhorsley, near Morpeth, Northumberland (the house bears a memorial plaque); 133 Clapham Road, London SW.

Archival source: B. Harrison, taped interview with Cecily Hale, 1974, Fawcett Library.

Bibliography: J. Marcus (ed.), *The Young Rebecca: Writings of Rebecca West 1911–1917*, 1982; L. Tickner, *The Spectacle of Women: Imagery of the Suffrage Campaign 1907–14*, 1987; A. Morley and L. Stanley, The Life and Death of Emily Wilding Davison, with Gertrude Colmore's *The Life of Emily Davison*, 1988; G. Norquay, *Voices and Votes: A Literary Anthology of the Women's Suffrage Campaign*, 1995.

DE FONBLANQUE, FLORENCE GERTRUDE, MRS

(1864–1949) Born in London, educated in Brussels

and Brighton, daughter of Amelia and Gaudente Sparagnapane, sister of Maud Arncliffe SENNETT. She records in her *Suffrage Annual* entry that her father, an Italian, was a friend of Garibaldi and Mazzini and that before her marriage she played leading parts on the stage. She was married in 1891 (on her marriage certificate giving her age as 21, although she was in fact 26) to Robert de Fonblanque (Marquise de Juliers, Comte de Hautserve, Comte de Fonblanque, who was 22), and her marriage certificate, while giving her husband's profession as "actor", accords to her no such complementary title. In 1906–7 she subscribed to the LONDON SOCIETY FOR WOMEN'S SUFFRAGE and to the WOMEN'S SOCIAL AND POLITICAL UNION in 1907. In 1909 Florence de Fonblanque was a member of the WOMEN'S FREEDOM LEAGUE and by 1912 she was a member of the NEW CONSTITUTIONAL SOCIETY FOR WOMEN'S SUFFRAGE and a member of the committee of the West Sussex branch of the CONSERVATIVE AND UNIONIST WOMEN'S FRANCHISE ASSOCIATION. In 1912 she originated the idea of the "Woman's March". "Inspired by the bravery of the militant women of the movement to organise a definite plan of activity on constitutional lines, she originally planned to march from London to Edinburgh, but was advised by more experienced friends to change the direction of the route, and make London the last, instead of the first stage of the journey" (*Suffrage Annual*). Maud Arncliffe Sennett wrote in her autobiography, *The Child*, "She dressed her little army in warm autumnal brown and bright emerald green brazzards and rossettes, and she secured a splendid Press, London as well as the provinces". Although invitations were sent in early September to all the suffrage societies, only six women, among them Sarah BENETT, set off from Edinburgh on 12 October. Katherine MARSHALL and her friends Edith and Ellen BECK, Ruth Cavendish-BENTICK, Alexandra and Gladys Wright (see WRIGHT SISTERS), the last three all associated with the New Constitutional Society, were among those who joined the march *en route*. The report in the *Suffrage Annual* remarked that the "character of the 'March' was distinctly more religious and spiritual than political" and that the suppression of sweated labour and of the white slave trade were of concern as well as the enfranchisement of women.

The marchers reached London on 16 November, having held as many as three meetings a day along the route. Maud Arncliffe Sennett co-ordinated the arrival into London of the women, who were accompanied at this stage by male suffragists such as Cecil Chapman and Israel ZANGWILL. A large meeting was held in Trafalgar Square at which Charlotte DESPARD was one of the speakers, and a petition, which had been a feature of the march, was presented by Florence de Fonblanque to a representative of the prime minister. "Mr Asquith promised to give it his consideration; and later, informed Mrs de Fonblanque that he had nothing to add to his previous statement." On the following Monday many of the marchers went to the East End to support George LANSBURY, who was then standing as suffrage candidate at Bromley and Bow.

Although the March achieved no political success it provided an outlet for active women who could not condone militancy. Florence de Fonblanque founded and became leader and honorary organizer of what was originally called the "Marchers 'Qui Vive' Corps", later the QUI VIVE CORPS. She still held that position in 1917. Maud Arncliffe Sennett remarked that Mrs Fawcett had not wished to associate herself and her society with the March. However, the NATIONAL UNION OF WOMEN'S SUFFRAGE SOCIETIES obviously recognized the value of the idea and shamelessly adopted it, organizing its own PILGRIMAGE the next year. The idea was used again in 1921 when Millicent Fawcett took part in a National Pilgrimage in support of the League of Nations. Florence de Fonblanque's gravestone in the tiny parish churchyard at Duncton carries the legend, "Originator and leader of the women's suffrage march from Edinburgh to London 1912", from which one might infer that her contribution to the suffrage cause represented the highlight of her life.

Address: (1891) 68 Southampton Row, London WC; (1913) Duncton, Petworth, Sussex.
Photograph: in *Votes for Women*, 22 November 1912.
Bibliography: *Suffrage Annual and Women's Who's Who*, 1913; M. Arncliffe Sennett, *The Child*, no date (1938).

DE LA WARR, MURIEL AGNES, COUNTESS (1873–1930) Daughter of Earl Brassey and his first wife Annie, author of *Voyage of the Sunbeam*, 1878. Muriel Brassey was married in 1891 to Earl de la Warr, had three children and divorced him in 1902. In 1910 she lived with the wealthy American Mary Dodge, heiress to the automobile millions. They were both introduced to the THEOSOPHICAL SOCIETY by Lady Emily Lutyens, who was the sister of Lady Constance LYTTON and of Lady Betty Balfour, and like them a supporter of the suffrage movement. Lady de la Warr and Mary Dodge lived a few doors away from Ursula Bright, who was also involved in the Theosophical Society. In 1912 Countess de la Warr and Mary Dodge sponsored Annie KENNEY when she joined the Theosophists. Countess de la Warr was originally a supporter of the WOMEN'S SOCIAL AND POLITICAL UNION but by 1912 was a member of the first Election Fighting Fund Committee, launched by the NATIONAL UNION OF WOMEN'S SUFFRAGE SOCIETIES to support Labour party candidates, from which she resigned, along with such others as Margaret ASHTON and Alice CLARK, only in 1916. In 1912 Lady de la Warr provided a car to aid the Labour candidate's campaign at the Midlothian by-election. There is reason to believe that her relationship with George LANSBURY may have been more than merely friendly. In 1913 Lady de la Warr was president of the East Grinstead Woman's Suffrage Society (NUWSS) and honorary treasurer of the NATIONAL POLITICAL LEAGUE, which was affiliated to the FEDERATED COUNCIL OF SUFFRAGE SOCIETIES, of which she was president. In mid-1913 she gave £100, of which £50 was paid in £5 notes, to Maud Arncliffe SENNETT in order to guarantee the work of the newly founded NORTHERN MEN'S FEDERATION FOR WOMEN'S SUFFRAGE, on the strict understanding that her gift was to be anonymous. She later joined the UNITED SUFFRAGISTS. Through the Theosophical Society Lady de la Warr was friendly with Gertrude Baillie-WEAVER, who wrote as Gertrude Colmore (see Emily Wilding DAVISON). During the First World War the Baillie-Weavers took over the care of Krishnamurti, thought by Theosophists to be Christ reborn, and his younger brother, in a house in Wimbledon rented for them by Countess de la Warr, who with Mary Dodge now lived nearby. Lady Emily Lutyens remarked in Candles in the Sun that Lady de la Warr "was rather fond of managing other people's lives". In the last year of her life Lady de la Warr was involved in an arbitration dispute with Mary Dodge. She lived just long enough to see her elder son become a junior minister in Ramsay MacDonald's second Labour government in 1929.

Address: (1908) 25 St James's Place, London SW; Old Lodge, Uckfield, Sussex; Sand Hill, Steeple Clayden, Berkshire; (1933) The White House, Wimbledon Common, Surrey.

Bibliography: Lady E. Lutyens, *Candles in the Sun*, 1957; A. Morley and L. Stanley, *The Life and Death of Emily Wilding Davison*, 1988.

DEAL AND SANDWICH committee of the NATIONAL SOCIETY FOR WOMEN'S SUFFRAGE was formed in 1873. Deal and Walmer society was in 1913 a member of the KENTISH FEDERATION OF THE NATIONAL UNION OF WOMEN'S SUFFRAGE SOCIETIES. Joint secretaries (1913) Mrs Clare Royse, 2 Herschell Road, Walmer, Kent and Miss Marsh, The Manor House, Upper Deal, Kent.

DEPTFORD (branch of London Society, NUWSS) Secretary (1913) Miss Goddard, 32 Stanwick Mansions, West Kensington, London W.

DERBY (NUWSS) In 1913 the society was a member of the MIDLANDS (EAST) FEDERATION OF THE NATIONAL UNION OF WOMEN'S SUFFRAGE SOCIETIES. Secretary (1909) Miss Annie Brewer, Mickleover, Derby and Miss Bridget Martin, Darley Abbey Vicarage, near Derby, Derbyshire; (1913) Mrs Sowler, Field House, Duffield, nr Derby, Derbyshire.

DESPARD, CHARLOTTE, MRS (1844–1939) Daughter of Capt. William French, of Irish descent, who had retired from naval service in 1836, and Margaret Eccles, a Scottish heiress. Her brother, later Field-Marshal Lord French, was a commander in the First World War and in 1918 lord-lieutenant of Ireland. One of her younger sisters, Katherine HARLEY, became a member of the NATIONAL UNION OF WOMEN'S SUFFRAGE SOCIETIES. Charlotte French, like so many suffragists of her generation, was an energetic supporter of the struggle for Italian independence, waiting at Dover to greet Garibaldi's arrival in England. Her father died in 1854 and her mother, committed to a lunatic asylum, died in 1860. In 1870 Charlotte French married Maximilian Despard, a wealthy radical liberal. Having had a negligible education, longing to be active, she embarked, once married, on a career of novel-writing.

She was the author of seven impossibly romantic three-decker novels. After her husband's death in 1890 she was persuaded out of the depression of bereavement by an Esher neighbour, the Duchess of Albany, who suggested that she devote some time to the Nine Elms Flower Mission in Battersea. At the end of that year Charlotte Despard bought a house in Wandsworth and in 1891 lived there, moving again, permanently, the next year to Nine Elms itself, a desperately poor area of Battersea. She was now wealthy and free to run her life as she wanted. She became a vegetarian. Shelley had long been an influence, and she embarked on a career of practical socialism, opening a welfare clinic for children and a boys' club. In 1894 she was elected a poor law guardian in Vauxhall, remaining on the board for nine years. At the same time she moved from radical liberalism to support the Social Democratic Federation and in 1896 attended the Congress of the Second International in London as an SDF delegate. She continued her association with the SDF until 1906 and also joined the Independent Labour Party. Charlotte Despard was by this time very much involved in the attempt to improve the social and economic position of the impoverished women with whom she was in daily contact and in 1901 joined, briefly, the UNION OF PRACTICAL SUFFRAGISTS, and then the Adult Suffrage Society, the only suffrage group advocating the vote for all classes of women. In 1898 she was friendly with Margaret Bondfield, then an active worker for the Adult Suffrage Society, who was a protégée of Louisa MARTINDALE, a founder of the Union of Practical Suffragists. Charlotte Despard must at this time have come into contact with Dora MONTEFIORE, who was a member of the Union of Practical Suffragists, and, also living in west London, was involved with setting up "Distress committees" to help the unemployed. In July 1905, with Anne Cobden SANDERSON and Julia SCURR, both also poor law guardians, Charlotte Despard spoke at Caxton Hall to women from the East End of London, a deputation organized by George LANSBURY to protest against the government's lack of progress in passing the Unemployment Relief Bill. Dora Montefiore took part in this march and Emmeline PANKHURST used the occasion to urge the audience to demand the vote for women. Charlotte Despard was by no means immediately convinced by WOMEN'S SOCIAL AND POLITICAL UNION policy. On 9 April 1906 she appeared on the platform at the first meeting of the Women's Labour League, a body formed by the Independent Labour Party in order to counter the burgeoning success of the WSPU. In a letter of 15 September 1907 Elizabeth Wolstenholme ELMY wrote to Harriet McILQUHAM, "The only time I have had any real talk with Mrs Despard was in May last year [on the occasion, 19 May 1906, of the deputation from the suffrage societies to the prime minister], at the House of Commons. She was unspeakably rough and rude to me – on the sole ground that I supported what she pleased to call the 'limited' bill instead of working for 'adult' suffrage, that I can well imagine her as a desperate person on a Committee whenever she failed to get her own way. She then regarded us of the WSPU as narrow-minded foolish people and the movement (W[omen's] S[uffrage] altogether) as worthless. Later events showed her its true vitality and then she joined the WSPU, to its great misfortune." It would appear that it was the commitment of Keir HARDIE, whom she much admired, together with the undeniable appeal and vitality of the WSPU workers that convinced Charlotte Despard that a "limited" bill was worth pursuing. By October 1906 Charlotte Despard was well acquainted with Annie KENNEY and Teresa Billington (see Teresa BILLINGTON-GREIG), both of whom had transferred to London their interest in bringing the campaign to working women. It was Teresa Billington, with her background as a Labour party ORGANIZER, who won Charlotte Despard over to the WSPU, apparently, appropriately, over a meal at the Eustace Miles vegetarian restaurant. When in the summer of 1906 Christabel and Emmeline Pankhurst arrived from Manchester to make the WSPU headquarters in London, Sylvia PANKHURST had just resigned as secretary and her place had been taken jointly by Charlotte Despard and Edith How MARTYN. After various attempts, Charlotte Despard managed to achieve the palm of imprisonment, arrested after taking part in the February 1907 deputation from the Women's Parliament in Caxton Hall to the House of Commons, and was sentenced to 21 days in Holloway. In 1908 she was to make capital out of her experience by including detailed description of the prison regime in a novel, *Outlawed*, that she wrote with a fellow Theosophist, Mabel Collins. Her spiritual affiliations, like her politics, had led her from group to group. Brought up in an atmosphere of oppressive Protestantism, after her husband's death she had succumbed to the *fin de siècle* interest in spiritualism, receiving messages in spirit-writing from Mazzini, had then joined the Roman Catholic church and by 1908 was a member of the Theosophical Society.

In April 1907, with Anne Cobden Sanderson and Edith How Martyn, Charlotte Despard sent a message to the ILP annual conference in which they made clear that they would not take part in any by-election at which a Labour party candidate was standing. It was becoming clear that the Pankhursts' policy of campaigning against a Liberal candidate meant that the WSPU was in effect giving support to Conservative candidates. In a three-cornered fight, when a Labour party candidate was standing he would not benefit over a Conservative in attracting WSPU support. Emmeline Pankhurst, who was present at the ILP conference, immediately repudiated this pledge and when in September at a meeting of the WSPU she cancelled the forthcoming annual general meeting and tore up the constitution, she gave as a reason the fact that some members of the WSPU were intent on chaining it to the Labour party. Sylvia Pankhurst puts the emphasis on the clash of strong personalities. Charlotte Despard and Teresa Billington-Greig organized a conference for the day originally fixed for the annual general meeting and elected a new committee. They continued calling their organization "the WSPU" until November 1907, when the name was changed to the WOMEN'S FREEDOM LEAGUE. Charlotte Despard guaranteed the League's first year's expenses and rent on its offices.

Charlotte Despard advocated, within the structure of a democratic organization, civil disobedience, militancy that broke no "moral law", and a need for an awareness of the reality of the social and economic ills that could be remedied if women were enfranchised. She devoted her time, money and energy to the League. In 1908 she spent five months touring around the country in the Women's Freedom League CARAVAN, on occasion being pelted with stones and earth. Always with an eye for

Charlotte Despard (1844–1939), president of the Women's Freedom League. (Author's collection)

the greater good, she was keen for the WFL to co-operate with other suffrage societies in conferences and rallies and was a member of the executive of the International Women's Franchise Club, which was open to men and women of all suffrage societies, after it was founded in 1910 (*see under* CLUBS).

In January 1909 Charlotte Despard was sentenced to her second prison term, having been arrested while leading a small deputation to Asquith. She was discharged on the grounds of ill health by the prison authorities after five days. In February she was elected president of the WFL. She was a keen supporter of tax resistance, a policy which the WFL, with its associated TAX RESISTANCE LEAGUE, made its own. However, as her income derived from trusts, income tax could be paid at source by her trustees and she, herself, was only able to refuse to pay house duty. This she did with the maximum of publicity. In 1908 she had met M.K. Ghandi, then a young lawyer and fellow member of the London Vegetarian Society (of which she was to become president in 1918), and with him discussed the merits of "spiritual resistance" or *satyagraha*. Civil disobedience was given a political edge, the impact of which historians of the suffrage movement have yet to feel, when Charlotte Despard devised a scheme put into effect by the WFL, by which women refused to give information for the census taken in April 1911. Charlotte Despard added the post of treasurer to that of president after Sarah BENETT resigned in 1910, and in 1911 she also became editor of the *Vote*. In addition she spoke at ILP meetings, attended meetings of women's trade unions and ran her clubs in Nine Elms. All this resulted in what Teresa Billington-Greig, when she resigned from the WFL, referred to as "lack of *grip*". In 1911 Charlotte Despard weathered one attempt to dislodge her from her position in the WFL and in 1912, after the defeat of the Conciliation Bill, when despondency allowed personal differences in the WFL to come to the surface, she was accused by the executive of being autocratic, incompetent and bad-tempered. The rank-and-file, however, gave her their support. She remained president and the seven members of the executive who had opposed her resigned. Among her friends elected onto the executive were Anna MUNRO, Nina BOYLE and Elizabeth KNIGHT.

In 1912, after the Labour party passed the resolution including women's suffrage in its programme, the WFL agreed to campaign for the Labour candidate in a three-cornered fight, a policy very dear to Charlotte Despard's heart. However, by 1913 the WFL was suffering from the backlash of anti-suffragette feeling whipped up by the increasing militancy of the WSPU and the League's help was rejected by the Labour party at the Keighley by-election. In the summer of 1913 Charlotte Despard represented the WFL at the Budapest Congress of the INTERNATIONAL WOMAN SUFFRAGE ALLIANCE. The disturbances in 1913 and 1914 caused by strikes and growing unrest in Ireland were rival concerns with the suffrage movement for Charlotte Despard's attention. On the outbreak of war she directed the WFL's policy of carrying on as before with the suffrage campaign, refusing to follow the path taken by the NUWSS and, to an even greater extreme, by the WSPU, of supporting the government's war efforts. She, like Sylvia Pankhurst in the East End, organized the distribution in Nine Elms of relief, which included vegetarian meals, to the women and children left behind by the new soldiers. In 1915 Charlotte Despard joined the Women's International League and after her brother's removal from command of the Western Front was able actively to support it and to join the No Conscription Fellowship, the National Council for Civil Liberties and the Women's Peace Crusade. In 1919 she was one of the British delegates to the Women's International Congress at Zurich, at which was founded the Women's International League for Peace and Freedom. With Dora Montefiore and Sylvia Pankhurst, Charlotte Despard attended the Convention in Leeds in 1917 at which British socialists welcomed the Russian Revolution, and was elected to the provisional committee of the Workers' Socialist Federation. In February 1918, after the victory conference to celebrate women's (limited) enfranchisement she resigned as president of the WFL, remaining as a member of the executive. In 1918 she was one of the first women to stand as a candidate at a general election – in Battersea as a representative of the extreme left wing of the Labour party. She was soundly defeated. From 1921 until her death she devoted her remarkable energies to the cause of Irish freedom and Irish socialism. In 1925 she moved to Ireland, living at first in the South, hoping to build there the Communist utopia she thought she had glimpsed on a visit to the USSR, and later in Belfast. She remained a figurehead for the Women's Freedom League, the only erstwhile suffrage society that maintained purely feminist aims, until her death, accruing a similar veneration, such as the ceremony of the birthday, that was accorded to Emmeline Pankhurst by her followers. Her 84th birthday, in 1928, was the occasion of the final victory celebration to mark women's achievement of the vote on equal terms with men. The pith of her approach to life was included in the speech she gave then: "I never believed that equal votes would come in my lifetime. But when an impossible dream comes true, we must go on to another".

Among Charlotte Despard's writings in support of women's enfranchisement are: *Women's Franchise and Industry*, pamphlet, 1908; *Economic Aspects of Woman's Suffrage*, 1908, which originated as a paper given to the National Liberal Club Political and Economic Circle; *Women in the Nation*, pamphlet, 1909; *Women in the New Era*, pamphlet, 1910; and *Theosophy and the Woman's Movement*, 1913.
Address: (1879) Courtlands, Esher, Surrey; (1890) 95 Wandsworth Road, Wandsworth, London SW; (1891) 2 Currie Street, Nine Elms, London SW – she held these properties simultaneously. After 1892 she gave up the main house at Courtlands, retaining Earnshaw Cottage on the estate.
Portrait: by Mary Edis, 1916, given by the artist to the National Portrait Gallery in 1974; another, attributed to Charles Horsfall, given to the National Portrait Gallery by Marie LAWSON in 1964.
Photograph: in the Suffragette Collection, Museum of London.
Bibliography: A. Linklater, *An Unhusbanded Life: Charlotte Despard: Suffragette, Socialist and Sinn Feiner*, 1980; M. Mulvihill, *Charlotte Despard: A Biography*, 1989.

DEWSBURY (NUWSS) In 1913 the society was a member of the WEST RIDING FEDERATION OF THE NATIONAL UNION OF WOMEN'S SUFFRAGE SOCIETIES. Joint secretaries (1913) The Misses Law and Pickersgill, The Wheelwright Grammar School, Dewsbury, Yorkshire.

DEWSBURY AND BATLEY (WSPU) Secretary (1906) Miss Turner, 73 Talbot St, Batley, Yorkshire.

DILKE, EMILIA FRANCIS, LADY (1840–1904) and **DILKE, CHARLES, SIR** (1843–1911) Francis Strong (she was known as "Francis" before becoming "Emilia" on her second marriage) was born in Devon, daughter of a retired Indian Army officer and his wife Emily Weedon. At the suggestion of Ruskin she studied at the new School of Art in South Kensington, leaving in 1861 and later that year marrying Mark Pattison, rector of Lincoln College, Oxford, 27 years her senior. She exhibited at the Society of Female Artists. Within a few years she became very friendly with George Eliot who may or may not have used the Pattisons' marriage as a model for that of the Casaubons in *Middlemarch*. Francis Pattison developed an interest in the women's movement; in 1871 she and her husband both subscribed to the newly founded CENTRAL COMMITTTEE OF THE NATIONAL SOCIETY FOR WOMEN'S SUFFRAGE and in 1872 she was honorary secretary of the Oxford branch of the National Society for Women's Suffrage. In that year she attended a women's suffrage meeting in the Albert Hall, sitting between Millicent FAWCETT and Harriet GROTE. She became interested in the Women's Protective and Provident League (later the Women's Trade Union League) which was founded in 1874 by Emma PATERSON to protect women's industrial interests. Francis Pattison inaugurated a branch in Oxford in 1881 and after Emma Paterson's death in 1886 became the League's leader. She attended every Trade Union Congress from 1889 until her death in 1904. Shortly before her death she left the Women's Liberal Association in order to join the Independent Labour Party.

In 1886, Mark Pattison having died, his widow married her long-time friend Sir Charles Dilke despite the scandal of a divorce case surrounding him. Sir Charles, a Radical Liberal, closely associated with J.S. MILL, P.A. TAYLOR and Thomas HARE, had in July 1869 spoken at the first public meeting of the LONDON SOCIETY FOR WOMEN'S SUFFRAGE, had in 1870, with Jacob BRIGHT, proposed the inclusion of women ratepayers in the municipal franchise and, in the same year, seconded Jacob Bright's women's suffrage bill. In 1884, despite being a member of the cabinet, he abstained from voting against William Woodall's women's suffrage amendment to the Reform Bill. In 1890 Sir Charles, who always insisted that married women should not be specifically excluded from enfranchisement, gave £10 to the WOMEN'S FRANCHISE LEAGUE. Later that year Dilke asked Dr Richard Pankhurst to draft a statement in support of Lady Dilke's inclusion on the roll of County Council electors in respect of their country house. Elizabeth Wolstenholme ELMY was very concerned that he, who was a close friend of the Pankhursts (*see* Richard and Emmeline PANKHURST), was to be "foisted" on the League. She was clearly not at all in sympathy with his unorthodox extra-marital history, probably much influenced by W.T. Stead who ran a campaign against Dilke in the *Pall Mall Gazette*. She felt that, by association, Dilke would harm the WFL. In addition she distrusted what she perceived as his personal ambition. In 1889 the *Women's Penny Paper* had published a statement signed by 1604 women protesting against the candidacy of Sir Charles Dilke as a London County Council alderman. Among those signing were Elizabeth Garrett ANDERSON, Millicent Garrett FAWCETT, Priscilla Bright McLAREN, Eva McLAREN, Laura Ormiston CHANT and Caroline Ashurst BIGGS. Elizabeth Wolstenholme Elmy was, therefore, not alone in her suspicion of him, which from the women suffragist point of view appeared to be justified by the support he gave in 1901 to a bill for adult suffrage. He, a party politician first and suffragist second, saw any limited enfranchisement of women as only benefiting the Conservative party.

See also under NEWSPAPERS AND JOURNALS.

Address: (1886) 76 Sloane Street, London SW.
Photograph: in B. Askwith, *Lady Dilke: A Biography*, 1969.
Archival source: Elizabeth Wolstenholme Elmy Papers, British Library.
Bibliography: S. Gwynn and G. Tuckwell, *The Life of the Rt. Hon. Sir Charles Dilke*, 1917; R. Jenkins, *Sir Charles Dilke: A Victorian Tragedy*, 1958; B. Askwith, *Lady Dilke: A Biography*, 1969.

DILKE, [MARGARET MARY] MAYE, MRS (1857–1914) Always known during her involvement in the suffrage campaign as Mrs Ashton Dilke, and later as Mrs Russell Cooke. Daughter of Eustace Smith, shipowner, shipbuilder, MP for Tynemouth and his wife Mary Dalrymple Smith. The latter, besides having nine children, was a patron of Walter Crane and Frederic Leighton, the mistress of Sir Charles DILKE, and in 1892 a member of the CENTRAL NATIONAL SOCIETY FOR WOMEN'S SUFFRAGE, from 1900 a member of the re-formed CENTRAL SOCIETY FOR WOMEN'S SUFFRAGE, and in 1907 a member of the LONDON SOCIETY FOR WOMEN'S SUFFRAGE. Maye Dilke's sister Virginia Crawford had also been Dilke's mistress, and it was the case in which her husband sued for divorce that brought about, in 1886, Dilke's political downfall. Maye Smith lived as a child in Gosforth House, the family home in Newcastle; it was, ironically, destroyed by suffragette arson in 1914. She was educated at Orleans and passed the public examinations for French schoolmistresses. She married in 1876 Dilke's younger brother, Ashton, had three children and was widowed in 1883. Her husband, who was MP for Newcastle-on-Tyne and a successful newspaper proprietor, had as early as 1870, when he was only 20 years old, been a member of the LONDON NATIONAL SOCIETY FOR WOMEN'S SUFFRAGE. By 1883 Mrs Ashton Dilke was a member of the executive committee of the CENTRAL COMMITTEE OF THE NATIONAL SOCIETY FOR WOMEN'S SUFFRAGE. In March 1888 she attended, with Alice SCATCHERD and Laura Ormiston CHANT, the International Council of Women at Washington. Helen Taylor, on learning that Maye Dilke was included in the mission to Washington, had refused to join. There is little doubt that the divorce scandal left no member of the Smith or Dilke family unscathed. Mrs Ashton Dilke travelled from Southampton to America with Elizabeth Cady Stanton, who particularly remarks on her kindness and generosity in serving others. The other two members of the party travelled from Liverpool. In November 1888 after the rupture in the Central Committee, Mrs Ashton Dilke became a member of the executive committee of the Central National Society, becoming, in 1896, the society's treasurer. In 1888 she successfully contested the Lambeth seat on the London School Board lost by Henrietta MULLER in 1885. She advocated a policy of free education before retiring from the Board in 1891. She was also a member of the Metropolitan Radical Federation, the Kensington Women's Liberal Association and, in 1890, the WOMEN'S FRANCHISE LEAGUE. By 1896 she was an active member of the WOMEN'S EMANCIPATION UNION, presiding over one of the meetings at its October conference. She wrote *Women's Suffrage*, published in 1885 with a foreword by William Woodall. In 1883 she became a trustee for the *Weekly Dispatch,* of which her husband had been owner and editor. She was married again, to William Russell Cooke, in 1891, and had two more children. The family was sufficiently friendly with its neighbours, the Leslie Stephens, for the nine-year-old Virginia Stephen to attend Sybil Dilke's birthday party in 1892, despite the fact that, in the eyes of Julia Stephen, Mrs Ashton Dilke (as she was still thought of) was "tainted" by her "connection with women's rights". In 1900, as Mrs Russell Cooke, she was treasurer of the CENTRAL AND WESTERN SOCIETY and, after the merger of that society with the CENTRAL AND EAST OF ENGLAND

SOCIETY, she was vice-chairman and a member of the executive committee of the CENTRAL SOCIETY FOR WOMEN'S SUFFRAGE and was a speaker for its successor, the LONDON SOCIETY FOR WOMEN'S SUFFRAGE. In 1899 Sybil Dilke was the honorary secretary in the Paddington area of the Associate scheme organized by the NATIONAL UNION OF WOMEN'S SUFFRAGE SOCIETIES to visit in their own homes women who would not otherwise attend suffrage meetings.

Address: (1876) 52 Princes Gate, London W; (1882) 1 Hyde Park Gate, London W; (1903) 87 Westbourne Terrace, London W; (1914) Bellcroft, Nr Newport, Isle of Wight.
Photograph: in R. Jenkins, *Sir Charles Dilke: A Victorian Tragedy*, 1958.
Bibliography: E.C. Stanton, *Eighty Years and More: The Reminiscences of Elizabeth Cady Stanton*, 1898; R. Jenkins, *Sir Charles Dilke: A Victorian Tragedy*, 1958; H. Lee, *Virginia Woolf*, 1996.

DINGWALL committee of the NATIONAL SOCIETY FOR WOMEN'S SUFFRAGE In existence in 1872, founded in the aftermath of the speaking tour undertaken by Agnes MCLAREN and Jane TAYLOUR. Its convenor then was Mr Dewar. In 1913 the society was a member of the SCOTTISH FEDERATION OF THE NATIONAL UNION OF WOMEN'S SUFFRAGE SOCIETIES. Secretary (1913) Miss Ledingham, High Street, Dingwall, Ross and Cromarty.

DOLGELLY (NUWSS) In 1913 the society was a member of the WEST LANCS, WEST CHESHIRE, AND NORTH WALES FEDERATION OF THE NATIONAL UNION OF WOMEN'S SUFFRAGE SOCIETIES. Joint secretaries (1913) Mrs John Jones, Wenallt, Springfield Street, Dolgelly, and Miss Gertrude Lewis, Dr Williams' School, Dolgelly.

DOLLAR committee of the NATIONAL SOCIETY FOR WOMEN'S SUFFRAGE Formed in 1872. In 1913 the society was a member of the SCOTTISH FEDERATION OF THE NATIONAL UNION OF WOMEN'S SUFFRAGE SOCIETIES. Secretary (1913) Mrs E. Miller, Institution Place, Dollar, Clackmannanshire.

DONCASTER (WSPU) Secretary (1913) Miss Brown, 61 Broxholme Lane, Doncaster, Yorkshire.

DORNOCH (NUWSS) In 1913 the society was a member of the SCOTTISH FEDERATION OF THE NATIONAL UNION OF WOMEN'S SUFFRAGE SOCIETIES. Secretary (1913) Miss M. Davidson, Oversteps, Dornoch, Sutherland.

DORSET (WEST) (NUWSS) Secretary (1913) Mrs Sutill, 24 West Street, Bridport, Dorset.

DOVER (NUWSS) Secretary (1909, 1910) Dr A. Brunyate, 4 Effingham Crescent, Dover, Kent.

DOVER branch of the NEW CONSTITUTIONAL SOCIETY FOR WOMEN'S SUFFRAGE Honorary treasurer (1913) Mrs Foster, 9 Guilford Lawn, Dover, Kent.

DOWNING, EDITH ELIZABETH (1857–1931) Born in Cardiff, a sculptor, studied at the South Kensington School under Lanteri, at the Slade School of Fine Art 1892–3, exhibited at the Royal Academy, the Society of Women Artists and elsewhere in London and in Paris, 1890–1912. She first exhibited at the Royal Academy in 1892, in 1898 she had two sculptures accepted (*Music Sent Up to God* and *There is a Silence that Says, Ah Me*), in 1899 *St Margaret*, in 1900 *Pompilia: Brownings "Ring and Book"*, in 1903 a miniature of *Miss Burton*, in 1904 a sculpture *Mrs G. Bishop*, and in 1911 *St Cecilia*. Her most important work was a marble altarpiece with 32 alabaster figures made for a church in Wormbridge, Herefordshire. In the same church are two memorial portrait busts by Mary Grant, the sculptor of the memorial to Henry Fawcett on the Embankment in London. There may be a connection which explains Edith Downing's commission.

Edith Downing subscribed to the CENTRAL SOCIETY FOR WOMEN'S SUFFRAGE in 1903, and to its successor the LONDON SOCIETY FOR WOMEN'S SUFFRAGE in 1906–7. She noted in *Votes for Women*, 25 November 1910, that "Learning the futility of quiet work, she joined the WSPU". This was in 1908 when, with her sister Caroline, she joined the Chelsea branch. Edith Downing sold a small statue of a cherub, dated 1907 and titled, over her signature, "A Sketch", in aid of suffragette funds, in November 1908 gave the proceeds (£5) of the sale of a statuette of "Peter Pan" to the WOMEN'S SOCIAL AND POLITICAL UNION and in 1909 developed the idea to its logical conclusion by making for sale at the Prince's Skating Rink WSPU Exhibition statuettes of Christabel PANKHURST and Annie KENNEY.

They were priced at 5 guineas and 2 guineas respectively. For the January 1910 general election she was WSPU ORGANIZER for the Kensal Town area of the Chelsea parliamentary division. For the 18 June 1910 joint WSPU and WFL "Prison to Citizenship" Procession Edith Downing with fellow-artist Marion Wallace-DUNLOP organiżed a 'Prisoners' Tableau". A contingent of girls (12–20-year-olds), dressed in white, accompanied a float on which was enthroned Mary Howey (see Elsie HOWEY), who represented all suffrage prisoners. After this, "working day and night", with Marion Wallace-Dunlop she designed further WSPU processions, including the East procession on 23 July 1910, and the Prisoners' Pageant, the Historical Pageant and the Pageant of Empire in the 17 June 1911 Coronation Procession. She and Marion Wallace-Dunlop also devised a little performance put on at the WSPU Christmas Fair in 1911.

Edith Downing was quite prepared to make a militant as well as an artistic contribution to the WSPU. On 18 November 1910 she was arrested after taking part in the "Black Friday" disturbance in Parliament Square, although like all the other prisoners she was released on that occasion without charge. On 21 November 1911 one group of WSPU volunteers, who were to take part in the deputation from Caxton Hall to the Houses of Parliament, were given instructions to meet beforehand at Edith Downing's studio. Exact directions to Tite Street were given and the women were particularly requested not to ask the way in the street. They apparently received from Edith Downing a supply of stones. On 23 November she was sentenced to seven days' imprisonment for throwing a stone through a window of Somerset House. On 1 March 1912 she was arrested while taking part in the WSPU window-smashing campaign, after breaking the windows of a fine art dealer in Regent Street, a delicately selected target. In a speech to the jury at her trial she referred to the brutality on "Black Friday" when she said she nearly lost her life. She regretted the fact that peaceable and law-abiding women should be forced to take such actions as window breaking. While in Holloway she took part in the mass hunger strike and was forcibly fed. She was released in the week of 26 June–3 July, before the end of her sentence. In the autumn of 1914 she designed and helped to make toys for Sylvia PANKHURST's East London Toy Factory, modelling the head for a doll which was then made up by a London manufacturer.

From 1896 Edith Downing lived with Ellen Sparks, who specialized in leather chasing and embossing, until Miss Sparks moved to Hampshire in 1910. In her will Edith Downing left her portrait of Ellen Sparks to one of Ellen's relatives and to Marion Wallace-Dunlop "a sketch she may choose. I should like her to have something she really likes".

Address: (1892) 40 Rossetti Mansions, Cheyne Walk, Chelsea, London SW; (1908) 30 Tite Street, Chelsea, London SW; (1931) Robins Rough, Peaslake, Surrey.

Photograph: working in her studio, in the Suffragette Fellowship Collection, Museum of London.

DOWNING, HELENA (c. 1845–85) (later Mrs Ronald Shearer) Niece of Mr McCarthy Downing, MP for Cork from 1868 to 1879. In 1875 she founded the North London Photographic and Fine Art Repository, a photographic studio run with an all-women staff. It was managed by her sister Martha Downing and appears to have had a short life, ceasing trading in 1878. Coincidentally, this business adjoined the premises of Beck Opticians (Lister Works), the family firm of Ellen and Edith BECK. In the 1870s, under the aegis of the CENTRAL COMMITTEE FOR WOMEN'S SUFFRAGE, Helena Downing became a speaker in the cause of women's suffrage. She was present at the meeting held by the Central Committee at the Hanover Rooms on 28 April 1873 and later in the year gave a series of lectures in Devon and Somerset at the invitation of the BRISTOL AND WEST OF ENGLAND SOCIETY. On 19 December 1878 she was a speaker with Helen TAYLOR at a suffrage meeting in Hertford. In 1879, with support from Helen Taylor, Helena Downing contested the Tower Hamlets seat at the elections to the London School Board. She was defeated and became instead a poor law guardian. Although now married, her marital home, which was her property qualification for holding the office of guardian, had been settled on her under the Married Women's Property (1870) Act. Despite this the Returning Officer cum Vestry Clerk refused to consider her, a married woman, the ratepayer, and sued her husband for the rates which he, on principle, refused to pay. She was then disqualified from standing for re-election to the Board of Guardians. From 1880 to 1882, doubtless fired by this injustice, she was a member of the executive committee of the Married Women's Property Committee. She was an energetic lecturer for the Vigilance Association for the Defence of Personal Rights and in 1882 was a member of its executive committee. In May of that year she spoke at a women's suffrage meeting at Beckenham; the *Bromley Record*, 1 May 1882, reported that "[she] is a successful speaker, and has already often, and brilliantly, advocated the Women's Suffrage cause". Between 1880 and 1882, with Jessie CRAIGEN, she spoke at all eight Grand Demonstrations of Women. By the time of the ninth, at Edinburgh in 1884, she was terminally ill, despite having undertaken a sea journey to New Zealand in an effort to stave off what was doubtless tuberculosis. After her death Helen BLACKBURN wrote of Helena Downing: "Her addresses were full of force and fire, mingled with pathos and humour; and this little bright-eyed Irishwoman never failed to win the sympathy of her hearers".

Address: (1875) North London Photographic and Fine Art Repository Co., 356a Holloway Road, Islington; (1882) 126 Hemingford Road, Barnsbury, London N.

Photograph: carte de visite (very suitably photographed by the North London Photo. Repository) in Josephine Butler Collection, Fawcett Library.

Bibliography: H. Blackburn, *Record of Women's Suffrage*, 1902.

DOWSON, HELENA BROWNSWORD, MRS (1866–1964) Unitarian, born in Nottingham, a member of a family involved through three generations in the women's suffrage cause. Her father, Anderson Brownsword, chaired the first women's suffrage meeting in Nottingham. In 1894 she married William Enfield Dowson, whose father was educated in the 1840s at Hove House School, owned and run on Unitarian principles by Elizabeth MALLESON's father-in-law. Helena Dowson's mother-in-law Alice Dowson (1844–1927) was the daughter of Samuel Greg of Styal Mill, Quarry Bank, Lancashire, now preserved by the National Trust. Alice Dowson, the mother of ten children, spoke, together with Helen TAYLOR, Caroline BIGGS, Helena DOWNING, Jessie CRAIGEN and Viscountess HARBERTON, at the "Grand Demonstration" held at Nottingham in November 1881 and in 1894 became the first honorary secretary of the NOTTINGHAM WOMEN'S SUFFRAGE SOCIETY. A supporter of Gladstone, she was a member of the local Women's Liberal Association. She attended a WOMEN'S SOCIAL AND POLITICAL UNION fund-raising rally in the Albert Hall in March 1908 and took part in the Women's Coronation Procession of 17 June 1911. Her daughter Maud (b. 1870) was by 1913 secretary of the MIDLANDS (EAST) FEDERATION OF THE NATIONAL UNION OF WOMEN'S SUFFRAGE SOCIETIES and her daughter-in-law Hilda (1889–1963) was also a member of the executive committee of the Nottingham branch of the NUWSS. Hilda was the daughter of another NUWSS activist Mrs Greg of Prestbury, Cheshire, and married her cousin Gerald Dowson (*see* PILGRIMAGE). It was her son who, in 1974, gave the Minute Book of the Nottingham Suffrage Society to the Nottingham Record Office. One of Alice Dowson's granddaughters, Alix, was to be one of the first women entrants to the Administrative Grade of the Civil Service and to marry, as his third wife, Sir Francis Meynell, who had himself been an active supporter of women's suffrage.

Helena Dowson records in her entry in *The Suffrage Annual* that she was converted to the cause of women's suffrage as a child "by finding that a married shopwoman had had her shop sold up by her husband who had deserted her years before, and that he was within the man-made law". From 1895 she became secretary of the Nottingham Women's Suffrage Society and a member of the CENTRAL NATIONAL SOCIETY FOR WOMEN'S SUFFRAGE. In 1899 she was a member of the executive committee of the National Union of Women's Suffrage Societies. By 1898 she was a leading member of the Nottingham Women's Liberal Association and in 1899 was honorary secretary to the Nottingham Society for the Abolition of State Regulation of Vice. In 1906, with Jane Cobden UNWIN and Helen Bright CLARK, she was a member of the Aborigines Protection Society. In June 1908, with other members of the Dowson family she took part in the WSPU's "Women's Sunday" in Hyde Park. Although non-militant, she endured considerable discomfort for the cause, being heckled and pelted with missiles while speaking at suffrage meetings. As well as organizing fund-raising activities at "Felixstowe" and running the Nottingham society's suffrage shop, she joined the THEOSOPHICAL SOCIETY in 1901, resigning in 1909. Perhaps not unrelated to this interest, she wrote *Love and Life*, 1902, a collection of essays, musings inspired by the paintings of G.F. Watts. She became a Nottingham city councillor and by 1922 was a justice of the peace. In 1918 she was given an illuminated address by the Nottingham Women's Suffrage Society "in recognition of her splendid services in the cause of the Enfranchisement of Womanhood". In her will she left to a niece "my small bronze statuette of a Girl presented to me in connection with my work for the Women's Suffrage Movement".

Address: Helena Dowson (Mrs W.E. Dowson) (1913) Felixstowe, The Park, Nottingham and (1961) North Field, Newby Bridge, Lancaster; (1913) Alice Dowson (Mrs B. Dowson) and Maud Dowson, Sulney Fields, Upper Broughton, Melton Mowbray.
Photograph: carte de visite of Mrs B. Dowson (Alice) in Josephine Butler Collection, Fawcett Library.
Archival source: Dowson Papers, Nottinghamshire Archives.
Bibliography: *Dame A. Meynell: Public Servant, Private Woman: An Autobiography*, 1988; Dame A. Meynell, *What Grandmother Said: The Life of Alice Dowson*, 1998.

DRAKE, CHARLOTTE, MRS (1883–1970) Described by Sylvia PANKHURST in *The Home Front* as "a fair Saxon type, bleached by the hardships of an East End mother, clear-eyed in serene tenderness for her children". Orphaned, she had, by working as a barmaid and sewing machinist, supported her younger brothers and sisters from the age of 16. She married a Canning Town factory worker and had five children. She joined the WOMEN'S SOCIAL AND POLITICAL UNION, probably in 1913, after hearing Mary PHILLIPS speaking outside a factory. She herself began speaking on the issue of women's suffrage in the East End. She distrusted Emmeline and Christabel, and loyally supported Sylvia Pankhurst. Mrs Drake was sent for by Sylvia, who was in hiding as a "mouse", and was asked if she would join the newly formed EAST LONDON FEDERATION OF SUFFRAGETTES. She became one of the ELFS's main speakers, quite happy to lobby MPs. While on ELFS business and away from home she was paid 30s a week to cover the cost of a housekeeper; her husband was very supportive. On 21 May 1914 she took part in the deputation to the King in Buckingham Palace and described the rough handling received by women from the police.

After the outbreak of war, in September 1914 Charlotte Drake was a member of a deputation to Walter Runciman, President of the Board of Trade, complaining of the sweated conditions endured by women employed on Army contracts, and of exorbitant food prices. She carried on campaigning for the ELFS, speaking in South Wales and the west country. In January 1915 she was elected a member of the General Committee of the ELFS and in April was a delegate to the Conference of Women's Organizations called by Runciman. She spoke strongly of the need to give women workers registered for war service equal pay with men and membership of the men's trade unions in order to stop exploitation. Lady Aberconway (*see* Laura McLAREN) and Eleanor RATHBONE were among the other delegates. In 1916 Charlotte Drake was a member of the party from Britain that attempted to attend the Women's Peace Congress at the Hague until thwarted by the government. In the same year she was a member of a deputation from ELFS to Robert Cecil, who was thought to be the most reliable supporter of women's suffrage in the cabinet, although likely to back only a limited enfranchisement of women with property qualifications. In July 1916 she addressed the biennial conference of the BRITISH DOMINIONS WOMAN SUFFRAGE UNION. She attended, this time without Sylvia Pankhurst, a meeting of women workers and suffragettes, who included Mrs Pankhurst, called by Lloyd George at 10 Downing Street at the end of 1917.

After the end of the war Charlotte Drake opened a general drapery store. She remained very friendly and supportive of Sylvia Pankhurst, both in her private life and as honorary secretary of the Socialist Workers' National Health Council. As late as July 1954 Sylvia Pankhurst was enlisting Charlotte Drake's support to protest against Violet Markham, an erstwhile anti-suffragist, whom she described as "that foul traitor", being given a seat on a royal commission and appearing so often on the radio!

Address: (1915) 20 Railway Street, Poplar, London E; (1918) 150 Butchers Road, Custom House, London E16.
Photograph: *Workers' Dreadnought*, Christmas, 1915.
Archival source: David Mitchell Papers, Museum of London.

Bibliography: S. Pankhurst, *The Home Front*, 1932; D. Mitchell, *The Fighting Pankhursts*, 1967; R. Taylor, *In Letters of Gold*, 1993.

DRIFFIELD (NUWSS) In 1913 the society was a member of the NORTH AND EAST RIDINGS FEDERATION OF THE NATIONAL UNION OF WOMEN'S SUFFRAGE SOCIETIES. Secretary (1913) Mrs William Blakeston, Aspen House, Beverley Road, Driffield, Yorkshire.

DRUMMERS' UNION A junior association, for girls and, rather surprisingly, for boys, under the age of 18, founded in February 1910 and attached to the WOMEN'S SOCIAL AND POLITICAL UNION. It was the idea of Janet and Irene McLeod (*for whom see* YOUNG, PURPLE, WHITE, AND GREEN CLUB *and* NOVELS). Honorary secretary (1910) 9 Fernshaw Mansions, Fernshaw Road, Chelsea, London SW; honorary treasurer, 2 Phillimore Terrace, London SW.

DRUMMOND, FLORA, MRS (1879–1949) née Gibson Born in Manchester, of Highland stock, she spent her childhood on the Isle of Arran. After leaving school at Pirnmill, she continued her education in Glasgow, taking business training courses and attending lectures on economics at the University. She had qualified to work as a post mistress for the Post Office, but was refused entry because she was too short; this rejection always rankled. She was married in 1898 and then lived in Manchester, where she and her husband were among the earliest members of the Independent Labour Party and of the Fabian Society. Flora Drummond was also a keen member of the local Clarion Club. She recorded in a later memoir that it was in order to acquire knowledge of the lives of working women, that she took employment in a mantle-finishing factory and in a baby-linen factory. She later explained her involvement in the women's suffrage movement by her experience at this time. She saw that women were paid such low wages that they were forced to engage in prostitution in order to live. Flora Drummond's husband, an upholsterer, was often out of work and it seems unlikely that she would have elected to take low-paid work if she could have been more gainfully employed. It is possible that she is giving a *post hoc* gloss to her experience at this time. She recorded that in her spare time she did voluntary social work in Ancoats and, if so, must then have known Teresa Billington (*see* Teresa BILLINGTON-GREIG). She was also involved in the co-operative movement and in the Women's Co-operative Guild. In *The Suffragette Movement*, Sylvia PANKHURST gave the impression that Flora Drummond joined the WOMEN'S SOCIAL AND POLITICAL UNION only as a result of the publicity that followed the arrest of Christabel PANKHURST and Annie KENNEY at the Free Trade Hall on 13 October 1905. However, Hannah MITCHELL in her autobiography mentioned that Flora Drummond was one of the speakers with her in the WSPU campaign to Lancashire towns in the summer of 1905 and Teresa Billington-Greig noted in 1960 that she and Flora Drummond went along with Christabel Pankhurst and Annie Kenney to the Free Trade Hall and witnessed the altercation that led to their arrests. Teresa Billington and Flora Drummond were in Manchester at the time; Sylvia Pankhurst was in London. The balance of probability would appear to lie with Hannah Mitchell and Teresa Billington. Mrs Drummond was working for the Oliver typewriting office in Manchester and had already put it at the disposal of the WSPU, which was now planning to take advantage of the publicity that imprisonment would entail. She was responsible for producing the hundreds of ensuing circulars and the embryonic WSPU organized five meetings within three weeks in order to capitalize on its newsworthiness. She devoted all her spare time in the following two years to secretarial and organizational work for the WSPU. Like the Pankhursts, she left the ILP, considering that it only paid lip-service to the women's cause.

In early 1906 Flora Drummond left Manchester for London in order to work there with Annie Kenney. On 9 March she, Irene Fenwick Miller and Annie Kenney led a demonstration to Downing Street, repeatedly knocking on the door of No. 10. The police were called, but Campbell-Bannerman desired that no charge should be made. At the end of 1906 Flora Drummond served her first term of imprisonment in Holloway, having been arrested inside the House of Commons. By 1908 she was in charge of the office at Clement's Inn and had also acquired the nickname "General" for riding at the head of WSPU processions dressed in epaulettes and a peaked cap. In June 1908 she manned the megaphone aboard a steam launch that paraded past the Terrace of the House of Commons, inviting MPs to attend the WSPU Hyde Park demonstration. In October she was arrested with Christabel and Emmeline Pankhurst, charged with being involved in the incitement to "rush the House of Commons" as advertised on a WSPU handbill. She was sentenced to three months' imprisonment but she was discharged after nine days, the prison authorities having discovered that she was pregnant. Her son was named Keir after Keir HARDIE. In all, Flora Drummond was imprisoned on nine occasions, and when, later, the hunger strike was employed as a weapon of retaliation she, while taking part, was never forcibly fed. Like Mrs Pankhurst, she was probably deemed too prominent a personality to be so treated.

In 1909 Flora Drummond moved to Glasgow as WSPU ORGANIZER there. On 20 December 1909 she wrote to Minnie BALDOCK's husband that "Joe [Mr Drummond] has gone to Australia for two or three years, Keir and Granny are with me in Glasgow". She organized there the WSPU campaign in the January 1910 general election and stayed to mastermind the Woman's Exhibition in April 1910. She then returned to London and in late 1911 was working from Clement's Inn, put in charge of the organization of the local WSPU unions throughout the country. Christabel Pankhurst, whose responsibility these had previously been, was now in Paris.

On 23 January 1913 Flora Drummond, with Annie Kenney, led the deputation of working women, which included Leonora COHEN and Jessie STEPHEN, to Lloyd George. According to Beatrice HARRADEN writing in *Votes for Women*, 31 January 1913, he complimented Mrs Drummond on her handling of the deputation. Four hours later, in the House of Commons, the Speaker indicated that it was likely that amendments to the bill would so alter it as to render it inadmissible. Sylvia Pankhurst in *The Suffragette Movement* dismisses Flora Drummond and Annie Kenney as being merely Christabel's spokeswomen.

After Mrs Pankhurst was arrested in February, Mrs Drummond and George LANSBURY were deemed the main speakers for the WSPU. On 15 April all WSPU meetings were prohibited in London and Flora Drummond was summoned to appear at Bow Street magistrate's court charged with being a disturber of the peace. She said that she would hunger strike if sent to prison and "She did not like the idea of hunger striking any more than the most normal human beings, but hunger strike she would if she were sent to gaol. She had experience of short commons while engaged on sociological work in the East End" (*Daily Herald*, 17 April 1913). The case against her was eventually withdrawn; apparently the police were satisfied that she was not engaged in militancy. It emerged during the trial that her salary was at that time £3 10s a week. On 13 August 1913 she joined the THEOSOPHICAL SOCIETY, sponsored by Countess DE LA WARR and Mary Dodge; she lapsed in 1916. In March 1914 she was present at the meeting in the St Andrew's Hall in Glasgow at which Mrs Pankhurst was re-arrested, spoke in Edinburgh the following day, and carried on the WSPU campaign, speaking at meetings throughout the country. She was arrested on several occasions in London while doing so, such meetings still, of course, being prohibited. Her final arrest was in May 1914.

On the outbreak of the First World War Flora Drummond returned to London from Arran, where she was recuperating, having been released from prison under the "Cat and Mouse" Act. She offered her services to the London County Council as a tram driver, but was turned down, considered "crazy". She became a star speaker in the WSPU's industrial campaign in South Wales, Clydeside, Leeds and Sheffield. In 1918 she campaigned for Christabel Pankhurst when she stood in Smethwick as a candidate at the general election. She then founded, with Elsie BOWERMAN, the Women's Guild of Empire, which in the 1920s at the peak of its success had more than 30 branches and a membership of 40 000. In April 1926 Flora Drummond led the "Great Prosperity March" of women in London, organized by the WGE to demand an end to the industrial unrest that was about to culminate in the General Strike. In 1927 she spent three months touring Canada with a group of Guild of Empire delegates. In the 1930s the influence of the WGE dwindled although Flora Drummond remained as controller, working, as late as 1945, from offices in

Dover Street, Mayfair. Mrs Juanita Frances, who for a time ran the North Kensington branch of the WGE, described Mrs Drummond at this time as "extremely confused politically". She also mentioned, rather apologetically, Mrs Drummond's "working-class accent" and that she "looked as she spoke" "rather like a charwoman", "rather shabby" and "a little unkempt". Ada WRIGHT in her will written in 1939 left £100 to Flora Drummond to carry on campaigning, under the aegis of the WGE, for the welfare of animals.

In 1924 Flora Drummond remarried, this time a cousin, Alan Simpson, an engineer from Glasgow, who was killed in an air raid in the Second World War. After this second marriage, Flora retained "Drummond" as her surname for professional purposes. In June 1928 she was a pallbearer at Mrs Pankhurst's funeral. In 1909 she had been a member of the Writers' Club, inviting Mr Baldock to meet her there for lunch (*see under* CLUBS). In later years she was on the executive committee of the Lyceum Club and was in the 1930s chairman of the Six Point Group and a member of the executive committee of Equal Rights International. In 1947 she was a patron of the Suffragette Museum and Record Room.
Address: (March 1906) 45 Park Walk, Chelsea, London SW (Sylvia Pankhurst's address); (1913) 21 Coram Street, London WC; (1934) 27 Princes Gardens, West Acton, London W3.
Portrait: by Flora Lion, 1936, was purchased by the Scottish National Portrait Gallery in 1974. The portrait was presented to Flora Drummond "in recognition of the services she rendered to her country in war and peace". It depicts her tub thumping, wearing her prison suffrage medal and a large pendant of purple, white and green stones.
Photograph: in Suffragette Fellowship Collection, Museum of London.
Archival source: Suffragette Fellowship Collection, Museum of London; B. Harrison, taped interview with Mrs Juanita Frances, 1974, Fawcett Library.
Bibliography: D. Mitchell, *The Fighting Pankhursts*, 1967.

DUGDALE, UNA HARRIET ELLA STRATFORD

(1880–1975) (later Mrs Duval) Daughter of Commander Edward Stratford Dugdale, who became a supporter of the MEN'S LEAGUE FOR WOMEN'S SUFFRAGE, and his wife, who also had suffrage inclinations. Una Dugdale was educated in Aberdeen, at Cheltenham Ladies' College, in Hanover and in Paris, where she studied singing. The Dugdales' London household is described in an advertisement for a "good Plain Cook" in *Votes for Women*, 18 February 1909 as "Five in family; five servants kept and between-maid". The family also had a house, Gordon Lodge in Aboyne, near Aberdeen, where they regularly spent the summer. Her nephew described Aboyne at this time as a "Scottish Weybridge". Una Dugdale remembered that she first consciously heard about "votes for women" from Frank RUTTER, who was later to be the founder of the MEN'S SOCIAL AND POLITICAL UNION. It was probably in the summer of 1907 while in London from Aberdeen for "The Season", that she first heard Christabel PANKHURST speak in Hyde Park. She then joined the WOMEN'S SOCIAL AND POLITICAL UNION (she certainly subscribed in 1907) and embarked on journeys around the country with Mrs PANKHURST; she was just the type of young woman whom the WSPU was hoping to attract by moving its headquarters to London. In 1908 she was working for the cause in Aberdeen; Helen FRASER, who had by then transferred allegiance from the WSPU to the NATIONAL UNION OF WOMEN'S SUFFRAGE SOCIETIES, noted that Una Dugdale asked her to speak at a meeting. For the 21 June 1908 WSPU demonstration in Hyde Park Una, with her sister Joan, gave a BANNER, sporting a golden sun on a white ground and the plea "Justice". On 2 February 1909 Una Dugdale organized a Woman Suffrage Ball in London for the WSPU. On 24 February she was arrested in Parliament Square following a "raid" on the House of Commons, and served one months' imprisonment. In April 1909 she was a guest at a dinner given on the occasion of the 5th INTERNATIONAL WOMAN SUFFRAGE ALLIANCE Convention and in the summer, with Joan, carried on a WSPU campaign in Brighton, living in Mary HARE's house. Joan Dugdale (later Mrs Cruickshank) was in 1909 banner-bearer in the WSPU Drum and Fife BAND, in 1911 was organizing secretary of the ACTRESSES' FRANCHISE LEAGUE and in 1913 wrote a suffrage propaganda play, *Clowning Street*. In 1910 and 1911 Una Dugdale accompanied Mrs Pankhurst on her two Scottish tours. In the course of the latter in September 1911, she helped organize a suffrage "At Home" at Lady COWDRAY's Scottish estate, Dunecht House. She met her future husband Victor DUVAL when he was best man at Frank Rutter's wedding. They were married in January 1912 at the Savoy Chapel and caused controversy when they insisted that "obey" should be removed from the wording of the marriage service. As Una Duval she wrote a pamphlet *Love and Honour – but not Obey*, which was published in 1912. Una Duval had two daughters and managed her husband's business during the First World War. She did not, apparently, encourage her daughters to develop careers. She was for many years treasurer of the SUFFRAGETTE FELLOWSHIP. She inherited the guardianship of the Suffrage Record Room and its contents from Rose Lamartine YATES and, thanks to her, the Suffragette Fellowship Collection is now in the care of the Museum of London. At the time of her death she owned the full-length portrait of Christabel PANKHURST by Ethel Wright. She had offered it to the National Portrait Gallery in 1966, but this offer was rejected.

Address: (1907) 13 Stanhope Place, Hyde Park, London W; (1938) The Old Manor, Sunningwell, Berkshire; (1975) 16 Harrington Court, Glendower Place, London SW7.
Portrait: by Frank Muller in a private collection.
Archival source: B. Harrison, taped interview with George Dugdale, her nephew, 1977, Fawcett Library.

DULWICH branch of the NEW CONSTITUTIONAL SOCIETY FOR WOMEN'S SUFFRAGE   Honorary secretary (1913) Mrs O'Mara, Dunlica, College Road, Sydenham Hill, London SE.

DUMBARTON (WSPU)   Secretary (1906) Mrs Annie R. Craig, 1 Roundriding Road, Dumbarton, Dumbartonshire.

DUMBARTONSHIRE branch of the WOMEN'S EMANCIPATION UNION   Honorary secretaries (1895) Mr and Mrs Hailes.

DUMFRIES committee of the NATIONAL SOCIETY FOR WOMEN'S SUFFRAGE   Formed in 1871 when the honorary secretary was Miss Harkness, 22 Castle St., Dumfries.

DUNBAR (NUWSS)   In 1913 the society was a member of the SCOTTISH FEDERATION OF THE NATIONAL UNION OF WOMEN'S SUFFRAGE SOCIETIES. Secretary (1913) Miss F. Melise Aspinwall, 4 Bowmont Terrace, Dunbar, Lothian.

DUNDEE branch of the MEN'S POLITICAL UNION FOR WOMEN'S ENFRANCHISEMENT   Was founded in 1910.

DUNDEE (NUWSS)   In 1913 the society was a member of the SCOTTISH FEDERATION OF THE NATIONAL UNION OF WOMEN'S SUFFRAGE SOCIETIES. Secretary (1913) Miss Henderson, 4 Camperdown Place, Broughty Ferry. Office: 12 Meadowside, Dundee, Angus.

DUNDEE (WFL)   Secretary (1913) Miss H. Wilkie, M.A., 280 Perth Road, Dundee (*see* Lila CLUNAS). In October 1913 the WOMEN'S FREEDOM LEAGUE branch joined with the local WOMEN'S SOCIAL AND POLITICAL UNION to demonstrate against forcible feeding.

DUNDEE (WSPU)   Organizer (1906) Miss Wilkie, 101 Rosebery St., Dundee; (1910) Miss McLean; (1913) Miss Frances PARKER, 61 Nethergate, Dundee, Angus.

DUNFERMLINE (NUWSS)   In 1913 the society was a member of the SCOTTISH FEDERATION OF THE NATIONAL UNION OF WOMEN'S SUFFRAGE SOCIETIES. Secretary (1909) Miss Margaret Duguid, 12 Maygate, Dunfermline; (1913) Miss Robertson, Benachie, Dunfermline, Fife.

DUNFERMLINE (WFL)   Secretary (1913) Miss McCallum, 72 Brucefield Avenue, Dunfermline, Fife.

DUNLOP, MARION WALLACE- (1865–1942)   Born in Scotland, daughter of Robert Wallace-Dunlop, CB. She studied at the Slade and in 1903, for the first time, exhibited at the Royal Academy, and again in 1905 and 1906. The first exhibit was a portrait of Miss C.W.D. – undoubtedly her sister, Constance. She also worked as an illustrator, publishing *Fairies, Elves, and Flower Babies*, 1899, and *The Magic Fruit Garden*, 1899. In 1900 and 1905 Marion Wallace-Dunlop subscribed to the CENTRAL SOCIETY FOR WOMEN'S SUFFRAGE and in 1906–7, as did her mother, to its successor the LONDON SOCIETY FOR WOMEN'S SUFFRAGE. She was a member from 1906–13 of the FABIAN WOMEN'S GROUP, as was another artist, Ernestine MILLS. In 1907 she was the hostess at a drawing-room meeting for the London Society; by July 1908 she was an active member of the WOMEN'S SOCIAL AND POLITICAL UNION, arrested and imprisoned for "obstruction". She was arrested again in November 1908 for leading a deputation to the House of Commons and again sentenced to one month's imprisonment. In June 1909 she was arrested for stencilling a notice advertising the 29 June deputation and the message, "It is the right of the subject to petition the King, and all commitments and prosecution for such petitions are illegal" on the wall of St Stephen's Hall in the House of Commons. This time when she was imprisoned she retaliated by initiating a hunger strike. As with all the weapons employed by the WSPU, its first use sprang directly from the decision of a sole protagonist; there was never any suggestion that the hunger strike was used on this first occasion by direction from Clement's Inn. Marion Wallace-Dunlop fasted for 91 hours and was then set free. During the hunger strike her mother appealed to Dr Elizabeth Garrett ANDERSON, who sent a message of sympathy. In *Votes for Women*, 16 July 1909, Mrs PETHICK-LAWRENCE referred to the ingenuity and magnificent resolution Miss Dunlop had shown "in finding a new way of insisting upon the proper status of political prisoners, and of the resourcefulness and energy in the face of difficulties that marked the true Suffragette". In January 1910 Marion Wallace-Dunlop was honorary secretary of the Weybridge branch of the WSPU. By February 1911 she had devised a new machine with which to stencil "Votes for Women This Session" outside 10 Downing Street. In 1910 and 1911, with Edith DOWNING, she designed many of the spectacular WSPU processions, including the Pageant of Empire in the Coronation Procession. She was one of the organizers of the window-smashing campaign in November 1911, arranging for WSPU members to receive suitable missiles. She herself was arrested for breaking windows in the Home Office and sentenced to three weeks' imprisonment. She remarked in court that she had worked for many years "and was now reduced to throwing stones".

Marion Wallace-Dunlop was a vegetarian and in June 1911 joined the THEOSOPHICAL SOCIETY, sponsored by Lady Emily Lutyens; she resigned in 1913. In 1928 she was a pallbearer at Mrs PANKHURST's funeral. After this, for a time, she took care of Mrs Pankhurst's adopted daughter Mary, in what was described as her "splendid Elizabethan house at Peaslake". She herself adopted a daughter, to whom she left her entire estate.

Address: (1907–12) Ellerslie Tower, Ealing, London W; (1905–11) 2 Studio, 53 Sussex Place, Kensington; (1941) Mackie's Hill, Peaslake, Surrey (this, presumably the "splendid Elizabethan house", in 1913 had been the address of another suffragette, Helen Gordon Liddle, who had commissioned from C.R. Ashbee alterations to the house and the addition of a studio, see L. Weaver, *Small Country Houses: Their Repair and Enlargement*, 1914).

Photograph: in C. Pankhurst, *Unshackled*, 1959; by Col Blathwayt in B.M. Willmott Dobbie, *A Nest of Suffragettes in Somerset*, 1979; in L. Tickner, *Spectacle of Women: Imagery of the Suffrage Campaign, 1907–14*, 1987.

Bibliography: L. Tickner, *Spectacle of Women: Imagery of the Suffrage Campaign, 1907–14*, 1987.

DUNSTABLE AND HOUGHTON REGIS (NUWSS) Formed in January 1914. President Mrs Lathbury; honorary secretary Mrs C.K. Garrett.

DURHAM (NUWSS) In 1913 the society was a member of the NORTH-EASTERN FEDERATION OF THE NATIONAL UNION OF WOMEN'S SUFFRAGE SOCIETIES. Secretary (1913) Miss Burgess, St Hilda's College, Durham, Co. Durham.

DUVAL, ELSIE (1892–1919) (later Mrs Franklin) Daughter of Ernest and Emily Diederichs DUVAL, one of six children, brought up in a household ardent for the cause of women's suffrage. She joined the WOMEN'S SOCIAL AND POLITICAL UNION in 1907, but was too young to take part in any militant activity. Instead, she worked for three years in the offices of the MEN'S POLITICAL UNION. She was arrested for the first time on 23 November 1911 on a charge of obstructing the police. She was discharged and immediately volunteered and was accepted by the WSPU for the next militant protest. If she took part in the March 1912 window-smashing campaign she was not arrested, but in July, after breaking a window in Clapham post office was sentenced to a month's imprisonment, having been remanded in custody for her "state of mind to be inquired into". During this sentence, spent in Holloway, she was forcibly fed nine times, by two doctors and nine warders on each occasion.

She was released on 3 August 1912. On 3 April 1913 she was arrested for "loitering with intent" with "Phyllis Brady" (Olive BEAMISH), was remanded for a week and then sentenced to one month's imprisonment. She was forcibly fed while on remand and then during her sentence. She recorded in her diary the heart pains she felt after the feeding, which she strenuously resisted, and which took place with her lying on the floor, her bed having been dismantled. Under the "Cat and Mouse" Act, on 28 April 1913 she was the first suffragette prisoner to be released from Holloway. During this term of imprisonment a charge was being prepared, apparently quite justifiably, against her for burning Lady White's house at Egham. Olive Beamish was actually so charged and received a sentence of five years' penal servitude. Before her arrest Elsie Duval had also, with Olive Beamish, been responsible for burning Sanderstead station and other, unnamed, targets.

In March 1913 Elsie Duval had become engaged to Hugh FRANKLIN but "the Cat and Mouse Act rendered our plans too unsettled to marry". After her release, and that of Hugh Franklin, under the "Cat and Mouse" Act in April 1913 they escaped to the Continent. Her licence of release from Holloway was only for 14 days but she did not return. Elsie Duval took the alias "Eveline Dukes" and received character references to assist her in obtaining work, from Eveline HAVERFIELD and from Frank RUTTER, who said that he had known her for six years, and her parents even longer, and that for a year in London she had assisted him with secretarial work. Another reference came from her brother Victor DUVAL, saying that in 1912–13 she had been in the employ of Valite Ltd, of which he was managing director. Armed with these testimonials, Elsie Duval spent ten months in Germany as a governess, three months in Brussels learning French and doing office work, and two months in Switzerland. In March 1914 she received a letter from Jessie KENNEY, writing as "C. Burrows" to say that "Miss Pankhurst thinks it would be better for you to stay where you are for the time being and until you get stronger." While in Dresden in May 1914 Elsie Duval spent some time in hospital. It was obviously a very lonely exile. She and Hugh Franklin had thought that they might travel together, but Winifred MAYO who had been consulted, advised that it would be too difficult for them both to find work. It was only the outbreak of war, and the amnesty for suffragettes, that allowed Elsie Duval to return to Britain.

At Christmas 1914 Elsie Duval gave Sylvia PANKHURST a blue velvet cap. She was, however, still committed to the other Pankhurst camp, keen to join the WSPU war effort campaign. In January 1915 she offered her services to the hospital in France run by Louisa Garrett ANDERSON and Flora MURRAY. She was apparently not accepted because in July 1915 she sold papers in London during the WSPU's Women's War Work Procession. In June 1915 she wrote to Mrs Pankhurst asking if she would be a witness at her wedding; in fact she and Hugh Franklin were prepared to time the date of the wedding to fit in with Mrs Pankhurst's plans. Mrs Pankhurst replied that she was going to be away at the end of July and all of August, giving the impression she was not enthusiastic and, certainly, when the wedding did take place at the West London Synagogue on 28 September 1915, she was not one of the two main witnesses. She may, of course, have been present at the wedding. Elsie Franklin loyally joined Mrs Pankhurst's Women's Party in 1917. Her brief though eventful life ended during the influenza epidemic on 1 January 1919 when she died from heart failure caused by septic pneumonia. It would seem only too likely that her heart had been weakened by the treatment she received in prison. The two illuminated scrolls that she received to commemorate her imprisonments are still in existence, in a private collection.

Address: (1907) 37 Park Road, Wandsworth Common, London SW; (1915) Chartridge Lodge, Chesham, Buckinghamshire.
Archival source: Duval Papers, Fawcett Library; Suffragette Fellowship Collection, Museum of London.

DUVAL, EMILY, MRS (1861–1924) Daughter of Thomas Hayes, in 1881 married Ernest Diederichs Duval, who is described as the manager of a factory, and who became a member of the MEN'S POLITICAL UNION. She and her husband were friends of longstanding of Frank RUTTER, a portrait of whom was given to them. Emily Duval joined the WOMEN'S SOCIAL AND POLITICAL UNION in 1906 but in 1907 left to join the WOMEN'S FREEDOM LEAGUE, being chairman of its Battersea branch for three years and a member of its national executive. In November 1907 she took part in the WFL campaign of protesting in police courts when women were in the dock. The argument was that women had no part in making the laws and they, therefore, would not obey them. In January 1908 she was sentenced to one month's imprisonment after taking part in a deputation to Asquith at his home in Cavendish Square and in October was arrested after being involved in the disturbances that occurred when Muriel MATTERS chained herself to the grille of the Ladies' Gallery in the House of Commons. One of her daughters, Barbara, was arrested at the same time, but was discharged on promising to abstain from further militancy until she was 21. In February 1909 Emily Duval was sentenced to six weeks' imprisonment in Holloway; Constance LYTTON in *Prisons and Prisoners* recorded her presence, and later wrote to Mrs Duval reminiscing about their experience. In November 1911, having left the WFL as insufficiently militant, she rejoined the WSPU and was sentenced to two weeks' imprisonment, having broken windows of the Local Government Board offices, and, while under arrest, smashing some more. On 20 December 1911 the Men's Political Union held a dinner in honour of the entire Duval family, at which Frederick PETHICK-LAWRENCE was the main speaker. In March 1912 Emily Duval was again sentenced to two weeks' imprisonment for window smashing and on 26 March 1912 received a six months' sentence, which was spent in Winson Green Prison, Birmingham. At the end of four months she joined in the hunger strike, was forcibly fed, and then released to be taken to a nursing home at the beginning of July. She has left a description of her experience of this time in prison, including that of being forcibly fed. This text, together with one of the scrolls she received from the WSPU to commemorate her imprisonment, is now held in a private collection.

In 1915, and probably before, Emily Duval was working for Sylvia PANKHURST's EAST LONDON FEDERATION OF SUFFRAGETTES and in 1916 was on the first committee of the SUFFRAGETTES OF THE WSPU, formed by members of the WSPU who wished, unlike the Pankhursts, to continue the suffrage campaign during the war. From 1918 to 1921 Emily Duval was a member of Battersea Borough Council. In 1922 she had obviously been ill for some time and received a letter of sympathy from Emmeline Pethick-Lawrence. Of her six children, four (Elsie, Victor, Norah, who in 1913 had been living for some time in Leeds with Frank Rutter and his wife, and Laura) went to prison for the cause. Three of her daughters did not live long enough to vote; Winifred died in April 1918, Elsie on 3 January 1919, and Barbara on 5 January 1919.
Address: (1908) 37 Park Road, Wandsworth Common, London SW.
Photograph: in the *Vote*, 14 November 1924; portrait of Barbara Duval by Cicely Hamilton, in a private collection.
Bibliography: Obituary by Margaret Wynne Nevinson in the *Vote*, 14 November 1924.

DUVAL, UNA, MRS see DUGDALE, Una.

DUVAL, VICTOR DIEDERICHS (1885–1945) Son of Emily and Ernest Diederichs Duval, brother of Elsie DUVAL, and, eventually, brother-in-law of Hugh FRANKLIN. Victor Duval was secretary of the Clapham League of Young Liberals, but resigned from it and became a suffragist after seeing a woman thrown out of one of John Burns's meetings. In 1909 he helped Marion Wallace-DUNLOP stencil her petition on the walls of St Stephen's Hall in the House of Commons and in 1910 was the founder of the MEN'S POLITICAL UNION FOR WOMEN'S ENFRANCHISEMENT. In October 1910 he was imprisoned for a week after a disturbance when he addressed Lloyd George outside the City Temple and in November 1911 received another sentence of five days. Victor Duval gave his support to the NEW CONSTITUTIONAL SOCIETY FOR WOMEN'S SUFFRAGE in 1910 and was on the committtee of the International Women's Franchise Club (*see under* CLUBS). He published two pamphlets, *An Appeal to Men*, 1910 and *Why I Went to Prison*, 1910. In January 1912 he married Una DUGDALE. He spent two years of the First World War at Salonika, serving with the Royal Engineers, and on his return rejoined the Liberal party. He stood as a Liberal, unsuccessfully, at three elections, including South Nottinghamshire in 1923 and North Camberwell in 1924.
Address: (1913) 18 Harrington Road, London SW.
Photograph: in A. Raeburn, *The Militant Suffragettes*, 1973.
Archival source: Duval Papers, Fawcett Library.

E

EALING (WSPU) Secretary (1913) Mrs Finlay, 35 Warwick Road, Ealing, London W.

EALING, ACTON AND BEDFORD PARK (branch of the LONDON SOCIETY FOR WOMEN'S SUFFRAGE) Secretary (1909) Mrs O'Regan, 18 Clovelly Road, Ealing, London W; (1913) Miss Debac, 37 Sandringham Gardens, Ealing, London W.

EARENGEY, FLORENCE, MRS (1877–1963) née How Sister of Edith How MARTYN, born in Kensington, a graduate of the University of London. Both she and Edith were married in Cheltenham in mid-1899. Florence married Dr William Earengey, who later became a judge, and by 1910 they had one daughter. In 1907 Florence Earengey was in charge of "literature" for the Cheltenham branch of the NATIONAL UNION OF WOMEN'S SUFFRAGE SOCIETIES. It would appear possible that she also subscribed to the WOMEN'S SOCIAL AND POLITICAL UNION in 1907. A "Mrs B.A. Earengey" is shown on the WSPU subscription list; no other Mrs Earengey features in the suffrage movement at any other time, and Florence, in those days when a woman graduate was a rare species, used to add "B.A." after her name. Anyway, by 1908 she had, like her sister, joined the WOMEN'S FREEDOM LEAGUE and by 1911 was honorary secretary of its Cheltenham branch. Her husband in the next few years chaired meetings for the WFL Cheltenham branch, but by 1913 was president of the Tewkesbury branch of the NUWSS and was a member of the MEN'S LEAGUE FOR WOMEN'S SUFFRAGE. In 1913 he wrote *Woman Under the Law*, which was published by the WFL. Florence Earengey eventually became a barrister, practising from the Temple, and a JP. In the 1930s she was chairman of Holloway Visiting Justices and chairman of Holloway Discharged Prisoners' Aid Society (London) Committee. In 1949 she wrote *The Legal and Economic Status of Women*, which was published by the National Council of Women.
Address: (1907) 3 Wellington Square, Cheltenham, Gloucestershire; (1913) Ashley Rise, Cheltenham, Gloucestershire; (1938) 1 Chesterford Gardens, Hampstead, London NW3; (1963) Ashley Rise, Brackendale Road, Camberley, Surrey.
Photograph: in the *Vote*, 7 May, 1910 – weighing her baby.

EAST DEREHAM branch of the NEW CONSTITUTIONAL SOCIETY FOR WOMEN'S SUFFRAGE Honorary secretary (1913) Violet Cory, Market Place, Dereham, Norfolk.

EAST GRINSTEAD branch of the MEN'S LEAGUE FOR WOMEN'S SUFFRAGE Founded in 1912.

EAST GRINSTEAD (NUWSS) In 1913 the society was a member of the SURREY, SUSSEX, AND HANTS FEDERATION OF THE NATIONAL UNION OF WOMEN'S SUFFRAGE SOCIETIES. Secretary (1913) Mrs CORBETT, Woodgate, Danehill, Sussex.

EAST LONDON FEDERATION OF SUFFRAGETTES Had its origins in the campaign undertaken in the East End of London in 1912 by Sylvia PANKHURST. This campaign represented Sylvia Pankhurst's reaction to the calls frequently made by Asquith, Herbert Gladstone, and most forcefully by C.E. Hobhouse in February 1912 for the women's movement to give proof that women wanted their own enfranchisement. Whereas Christabel PANKHURST had reacted by instituting a policy of militant damage and Emmeline PANKHURST by courting a charge of sedition, Sylvia Pankhurst "regarded that the rousing of the East End was of utmost importance". She felt that only a mass movement could bring presssure to bear on parliament and, as she explained in *The Suffragette Movement*, "the East End was the greatest homogeneous working-class area accessible to the House of Commons by popular demonstrations". She had, that summer, convinced local WOMEN'S SOCIAL AND POLITICAL UNION branches in London to hold large popular demonstrations in London's parks and open spaces – such as Wimbledon, Clapham and Streatham commons, Peckham Rye and Regent's Park – culminating in a mass demonstration in Hyde Park on 14 July, happily, by coincidence, the anniversary of both the fall of the Bastille and the birth of Emmeline Pankhurst.

In October 1912 WSPU headquarters agreed to rent a shop in Bow Road and Sylvia Pankhurst collected a body of voluntary workers, mainly, initially, drawn from the Kensington, Chelsea and Paddington branches of the WSPU. In November George LANSBURY, Labour MP for Bromley and Bow, resigned his seat in order to fight a by-election on the "Votes for Women" issue. This was a policy advocated by Emmeline and Christabel Pankhurst and resulted in his defeat. For the duration of the campaign Sylvia Pankhurst was required by the WSPU ORGANIZER, Grace ROE, to vacate the Bow Road office. After the ignominious outcome of the election Sylvia Pankhurst was ordered to close her East End operation. She managed to persuade Emmeline Pankhurst that this would be interpreteted as retreat and suggested that a deputation of working women from the East End might be sent to interview Lloyd George. Again, diplomacy indicated that it would be wise to let Flora DRUMMOND be the titular head of the deputation, which, sent to Lloyd George on 17 January 1913, included working-class women from all parts of the country. The subsequent ruling by the Speaker that the proposed amendment to introduce women into the Manhood Suffrage bill would invalidate the bill led the WSPU to renew its arson campaign. Christabel Pankhurst was obviously not interested in stimulating a popular campaign among the working classes and WSPU headquarters withdrew its financial aid and workers from the East End.

Sylvia Pankhurst and Lady Sybil Smith, her wealthy Tolstoyan supporter, were determined that the campaign should continue in the East End and in February 1913, with a few pounds that remained from the by-election fund, opened a permanent East End headquarters at 321 Roman Road. Branches were subsequently opened in Bow, Bromley, Stepney, Limehouse, Bethnal Green and Poplar. Sylvia Pankhurst's policy was to combine large-scale public demonstrations with public militancy, that is, window-smashing that attracted immediate arrest, rather than secret arson. She herself underwent a succession of arrests, hunger-and-thirst strikes and forcible feedings. The East End campaign proved very popular in its localities and a "Women's May Day" rally in Victoria Park was held on 25 May 1913. The East London Federation of the WSPU was formally instituted on 27 May in order to unite the local branches. The Federation, unlike its parent organization, had a democratic structure, its executive comprising honorary officers who were subject to re-election, and two representatives from each branch. Among those attending its first executive committee meeting were Florence HAIG, representing Limehouse, Amy HICKS and Mary LEIGH. At this time the Federation appointed its first organizer. On 29 June 1913 the East London Federation organized a procession to Trafalgar Square at which suffrage societies, trade unions, labour organizations and the Free Speech Defence League joined. One of the chief speakers from the latter society, which had been founded by Keir HARDIE, was Frank Smith, who in February 1906 had lent his support to the very first WSPU Caxton Hall meeting. Sylvia Pankhurst urged her audience to march on Downing Street and as a consequence was arrested a few days later under the the statute of Edward III that the Home Office was deploying against "disturbers of the peace". The arrest was effected at a large meeting at Bromley-by-Bow, in scenes of violence which engendered the required publicity. She went on hunger-and-thirst strike and was released under the "Cat and Mouse" Act. The East London Federation, with the aid of the MEN'S FEDERATION FOR WOMEN'S SUFFRAGE, organized another Trafalgar Square rally for 27 July, at which Sylvia Pankhurst, who had overrun her licence, appeared as a speaker, again urging the crowd to march on Downing Street. She was again arrested, but the crowd, men and women, who had rallied to her call, demonstrated by their numbers and enthusiastic support that there was now a popular movement based in the East End. In the course of the summer the ELF enrolled the services of Sir Francis Vane, who was also involved in training the Citizen Army in Dublin, to drill a People's Training Corps. Men and women of this organization took the pledge, "I promise to serve the common cause of Justice and my comrades under duly elected officers... I am a sincere believer in a Vote for every Woman and every Man." By March 1914 Sylvia Pankhurst was recommending members of the army to carry their weapons at all times both in order to impress and to be ready for action. In a letter written to Norah Smyth in November 1913 Sir Francis Vane recommended Evelina HAVERFIELD as someone able to keep the police in their place. He did not, however, continue his association with the People's Army, which eventually appears to have withered for want of training. Besides giving military training the ELF was keen to educate. Between 29 December 1913 and 11 January 1914 a suffrage school was held, organized jointly by the East London Federation and the Kensington WSPU, at which lectures were given on such subjects as the history of the franchise, the history of the women's movement and the industrial position of women by, among others, Dr Flora MURRAY, Dr Jessie Murray, Henry NEVINSON, Joseph Clayton and Theodora Bonwick. Rose LEO also came over to the East End to hold speakers' classes. The cracks between the East London Federation and Lincoln's Inn House were widening. On 1 November 1913 Sylvia Pankhurst had spoken at a meeting organized in the Albert Hall by the *Daily Herald* League, in support of Jim Larkin, the leader of the Dublin lock-out. Christabel Pankhurst immediately repudiated any association between the WSPU and the *Daily Herald* League, insisting that the WSPU was independent of this as of all men's parties and movements. She wrote to Sylvia on 7 November, "it is essential for the public to understand that you are working independently of us. As you have complete confidence in your own policy and way of doing things, this should suit you perfectly. There is room for everybody in the world, but conflicting views and divided counsels inside the WSPU there cannot be." A circular letter dated 25 November 1913 was sent by Annie KENNEY to all WSPU branches, repudiating another that had been sent a little earlier by Sylvia Pankhurst, in which she had drawn attention to the dearth of WSPU speakers and the lack of WSPU public meetings. The minutes of the ELF record that at a meeting held on 27 January 1914 Sylvia Pankhurst reported that she had been to Paris and had been asked by Christabel, in the presence of their mother, to change the name of the federation and to separate from the WSPU. The minute noted, "We had more faith in what could be done by stirring up working women than was felt at headquarters, while they had most faith in what could be done for the vote by people of means of influence." The new society's device was the red cap of liberty surrounded by the initials ELFS.

In March 1914 the ELFS launched its own paper, the *Women's Dreadnought*, the first issue of which was printed by J.E. Francis of the Athenaeum Press (*see* PUBLISHERS AND PRINTERS). Among the ELFS's most effective workers at this time were Charlotte DRAKE, Melvina Walker, Nellie Cressell and a young American woman, Zelie Emerson. On 5 May 1914 the ELFS opened new, bigger headquarters at 400 Old Ford Road. On 24 May, three days after the WSPU's deputation to the King and the re-arrest of Mrs Pankhurst and the day after the police raid on Lincoln's Inn House, the ELFS held its Women's May Day procession from Beckton to Victoria Park. Sylvia Pankhurst was re-arrested after a struggle with the police. After a series of rallies, at each of which the resolution taken was that the ELFS should ask the government for the vote for all women over 21, and tumultuous popular processions to parliament, Asquith eventually promised Sylvia Pankhurst, who weak from a series of hunger-and-thirst strikes was lying outside the House of Commons, that he would meet a small deputation of women from the ELFS. The deputation was led by Julia SCURR and included Daisy PARSONS. As a result of Asquith's reception of the deputation the *Labour Leader* deduced that "there seems to be a recognition that Women's Suffrage cannot be long delayed". This was a view not unsurprisingly promoted by Sylvia Pankhurst in *The Suffragette Movement*, vindicating as it did both her policy and the considerable physical hardships she had endured. Realistically, it is unlikely that Asquith would have been persuaded by the pleas of six working women, however heartfelt, and mass pressure, if he was at all perturbed by that, had not spread outside a small area of east London.

For the duration of the First World War the ELFS, from March 1916 renamed the Workers' Suffrage

Federation, besides undertaking humanitarian work in the East End, campaigned for "Human Suffrage". In January 1916 the WSF organized a Joint Suffrage Conference in Essex Hall with the hope of widening the franchise to all men and women over 21. The conference was acrimonious; the WSF could not induce the other societies to join it in asking for adult suffrage. In 1916 spearheaded by Jessie STEPHEN in Bradford, the WSF opened branches in the provinces and held rallies in large cities in order to impress its ideas on the Speaker's conference on electoral reform. It had already spread out of east London; branches had been opened in Holborn (with a bookshop attached) in 1915, in St Pancras in 1916 and in Holloway in 1917. At the end of 1916 the WSF organized a Women's Exhibition in Caxton Hall, to which both Charlotte Drake and Muriel MATTERS contributed. Lloyd George excluded the ELFS, knowing that they would press for adult suffrage, from a deputation of suffrage societies he received on 29 March 1917. From July 1917 the *Women's Dreadnought* was renamed the *Workers' Dreadnought* and, after the partial enfranchisement of women, in May 1918 the Workers' Suffrage Federation was renamed the Workers' Socialist Federation.

Honorary general secretary (1913–18) Sylvia Pankhurst; honorary treasurer (May 1913) Lady Sybil Smith; (December 1913) Mrs D.A. Thomas (*see* Lady RHONDDA); (April 1914) Evelina Haverfield; (early 1915) Edgar Lansbury; (1916?) Norah Smyth; honorary financial secretary (1913) Elsa Dalglish, 16 West Cromwell Road, London SW; (1914) Norah Smyth.

Address: (1912) 198 Bow Road, London E; (1913) 321 Roman Road, London E; (1914) 400 Old Ford Road, London E.

Archival source: Minute book of the ELFS, Papers of Sylvia Pankhurst, Internationaal Instituut voor Sociale Geschiedenis, Amsterdam.

Bibliography: S. Pankhurst, *The Suffragette Movement*, 1931; K. Weller, *"Don't be a Soldier!": The Radical Anti-war Movement in North London, 1914–1918*, 1985; R. Taylor, *In Letters of Gold: The Story of Sylvia Pankhurst and the East London Federation of the Suffragettes in Bow*, 1993; B. Winslow, *Sylvia Pankhurst: Sexual Politics and Political Activism*, 1996.

EAST MOLESEY (branch of LONDON SOCIETY FOR WOMEN'S SUFFRAGE) Secretary (1909) Mrs Burton, Homefield, The Park, East Molesey, Surrey.

EASTBOURNE branch of the MEN'S LEAGUE FOR WOMEN'S SUFFRAGE Founded in 1912.

EASTBOURNE (NUWSS) In 1913 the society was a member of the SURREY, SUSSEX, AND HANTS FEDERATION OF THE NATIONAL UNION OF WOMEN'S SUFFRAGE SOCIETIES. Secretary (1909) Miss Susan Gatliff, Fernholme, 91 Enys Road, Eastbourne, Sussex; (1913) Miss Peacey, Rydal Mount, Eastbourne, Sussex.

EASTBOURNE (WFL) Was in existence in 1910. Secretary A. Dilks, 39 Milton Road, Eastbourne, Sussex.

EASTERN COUNTIES FEDERATION OF THE NATIONAL UNION OF WOMEN'S SUFFRAGE SOCIETIES The societies at Cambridge, Wisbech, Southwold, Huntingdon, Harleston and Norwich joined together in a federation in 1910. In May 1910 it was agreed that the Federation should if possible also embrace North Herts (Hitchin), North Essex (Saffron Walden, Maldon, Harwich), North Beds (Woburn Sands and Bedford), Huntingdonshire, Norfolk and Suffolk. The GIRTON and NEWNHAM suffrage societies were also to be asked to join. When the Federation was finalized in January 1911 it comprised Norfolk, Suffolk, Cambridgeshire, Bedfordshire, Huntingdonshire, Essex (with the exception of Romford and Walthamstow) and Hertfordshire (with the exception of Watford), the Spalding division of Lincolnshire and the borough of Boston.

Secretary (1913) Mrs Kellett, 4 Belvoir Terrace, Cambridge, Cambridgeshire.

EASTLEIGH (NUWSS) In 1913 the society was a member of the SURREY, SUSSEX, AND HANTS FEDERATION OF THE NATIONAL UNION OF WOMEN'S SUFFRAGE SOCIETIES. Secretary (1913) Miss Mary Bugden, 48 Newton Road, Eastleigh, Hampshire.

EATES, LOUISE MARY, MRS (1877–1944) née Peters Born at Richmond, Yorkshire, and educated at Edinburgh Ladies' College. In 1901 she married, and was converted to the cause of women's suffrage by her husband, a GP. She was introduced to the Women's Industrial Council by Mrs Ramsay MacDonald in 1902 and acted as honorary secretary to the Investigation Committee of the Council 1902–6, being succeeded in this position by Edith MANSELL-MOULLIN. She assisted in the preparation of such reports as "Women in the Straw-Hat Trade" and "Women in the Artificial Flower Trade". In 1906–7 Louise Eates spoke at meetings held by the LONDON SOCIETY FOR WOMEN'S SUFFRAGE and in the course of that year was taken to the headquarters of the WOMEN'S SOCIAL AND POLITICAL UNION at Clement's Inn by Louie CULLEN of Kensal Rise and with her helped to form the Kensington branch of the WSPU, of which she was then secretary from 1906 to 1910. In its first year the branch raised £32 and in 1910 £804 and was one of the largest and most active of the unions. In one year the branch sold 25 927 copies of *Votes for Women* and its "Votes for Women" shop in Church Street, Kensington, was the first and one of the most imaginative of its kind (*see* SHOPS, OFFICES AND BAZAARS). Louise Eates ran election campaigns in North Kensington in January 1909 and in West St Pancras in December 1909. In May 1909 Harry Pankhurst, after being cared for by Dr Herbert Mills (*see* Ernestine MILLS) at Nurse PINE's nursing home, went to convalesce with Dr Eates. In January 1910 Louise Eates was the WSPU ORGANIZER for the Kensington (North) Division in the general election campaign. She was chief marshall of the two Kensington processions and spoke on a platform at Hyde Park in June 1908. Besides speaking at local meetings, she travelled in Wales and the Midlands to campaign for the WSPU nationally. In March 1909 she was arrested in Parliament Square while taking part in a deputation with Mrs PETHICK-LAWRENCE and was sentenced to a month's imprisonment in Holloway.

Louise Eates spent two years from 1910 living in India and Vienna. On their return in 1913 she and her husband settled in Marylebone and had a daughter, Margot, who later became an art historian of some repute. Louise Eates became a member of the UNITED SUFFRAGISTS. From 1917 until 1923 she was a member of the committee of the St John's Wood Infant Welfare Centre and Day Nursery and worked there regularly. She became a lecturer for the Workers' Educational Association. In 1924 Louise Eates went to live in Kent where she acted as secretary to her local Women's Institute for two years. In 1927 the family returned to London and Louise Eates was honorary secretary of the Acton Women's Citizen Association and, in 1930, its president.

Address: (1944) 135 Avenue Road, Acton, London W.
Portrait: drawing by Glen Hensham in the Suffragette Fellowhip Collection, Museum of London.
Archival source: Suffragette Fellowship Collection, Museum of London.

ECCLES (NUWSS)   Formed in 1911 and joined the MANCHESTER AND DISTRICT FEDERATION OF THE NATIONAL UNION OF WOMEN'S SUFFRAGE SOCIETIES. Secretary (1913) Mrs R.A. Norbury, West Leigh, Broad Oak Park, Worsley, Lancashire.

ECCLES (WFL)   Secretary (1913) Miss J. Heyes, Newholme, Hazelhurst, Worsley, Lancashire.

EDINBURGH branch of the UNITED SUFFRAGISTS   Founded in mid-1914.

EDINBURGH (WFL)   Secretary (1913) Miss Alexia JACK, 33 Forrest Road, Edinburgh. A WFL shop was opened at 33 Forrest Road, Edinburgh, in May 1910.

EDINBURGH (WSPU)   Organizer (1906) Mrs Grant, 108 George St., Edinburgh; (1909) Florence MACAULAY; (1909–13) Lucy BURNS, 8 Melville Place, Queensferry St., Edinburgh; (1913) Miss Macdonald, 27 Frederick St., Edinburgh; (1914) Miss Gorrie.

EDINBURGH AND DISTRICT branch of the WOMEN'S EMANCIPATION UNION   Honorary secretary (1895) Mrs Leslie Mackenzie.

EDINBURGH MEN'S POLITICAL UNION FOR WOMEN'S ENFRANCHISEMENT   Founded in 1910.

EDINBURGH NATIONAL SOCIETY FOR WOMEN'S SUFFRAGE   Founded on 6 November 1867, as the Edinburgh branch of the NATIONAL SOCIETY FOR WOMEN'S SUFFRAGE, working in conjunction with the LONDON NATIONAL SOCIETY and the MANCHESTER NATIONAL SOCIETY. Its first president was Priscilla Bright McLAREN, whose brother Jacob BRIGHT MP spoke at a public meeting of the society on 17 January 1870, comparing the position of married women with that of the "negro" before the presidency of Lincoln, in the southern states of America. Agnes MCLAREN, step-daughter to Priscilla Bright McLaren, and Eliza WIGHAM were the society's first joint secretaries. In the first months after its formation the Edinburgh society organized a petition, on the same lines as those submitted to parliament from the London and Manchester societies. On 12 January 1871 John Stuart MILL addressed a women's suffrage meeting in the Music Hall, organized by the society. The Edinburgh society associated itself with the new CENTRAL COMMITTEE OF THE NATIONAL SOCIETY FOR WOMEN'S SUFFRAGE in 1872. Agnes McLaren, with Jane TAYLOUR, was responsible for much of the society's missionary work, touring the Highlands and islands in 1871 and 1872, initiating suffrage committees in many small towns. The Edinburgh society was enthusiastic and successful. In 1875 16 678 signatures were collected for a petition which the society sent to parliament and in that year the Edinburgh society received an income of £228 19s 2d from donations. Between 1867 and 1876 it had been responsible for about two million of the signatures in support of women's enfranchisement that had been laid before parliament. By 1878, however, instead of monster petitions the society was concentrating its efforts on "selected important classes among the inhabitants of the city, and country at large, and has canvassed those as thoroughly as it was possible for them to do. This was done not by personal application, but by letters written and addressed by a sub-committee, meeting week by week for this purpose." As all this effort achieved nothing, the original optimism began to fade, as Priscilla McLaren wrote to Helen TAYLOR on 17 December 1879, "strictly *entre* nous, I am much discouraged – not as to ultimate success – as Mr Courtney says, tho' I cant see this, I can forsee it – it was a beautiful way of putting it. But our workers are almost nowhere. Our Committee women are growing too old to work, and such as are not, are invalid . . .".

The granting of the municipal franchise to women ratepayers in Scotland in 1881–2 gave fresh impetus to the work of the Edinburgh society. Jessie CRAIGEN held meetings around the country to educate those thus enfranchised in their duties and responsibilities. In 1884 a "Great Demonstration of Women" was held in Edinburgh. At this the speakers included Alice SCATCHERD, Flora STEVENSON, Eliza Wigham, Priscilla Bright McLaren, Florence BALGARNIE, Sarah Siddons MAIR and Laura Ormiston CHANT.

In 1888, when the Central Committee of the National Society split, the Edinburgh society, with its radical Liberal and Bright family associations, affiliated to the CENTRAL NATIONAL SOCIETY. In 1893 the society gave support to the four women candidates who were standing for parochial board elections; all were successful. In 1896 the Edinburgh Society affiliated to the Central Committee of the National Society and in 1897 to the new NATIONAL UNION OF WOMEN'S SUFFRAGE SOCIETIES and, with the prospect of an impending general election, had by 1905 formed new committees in many constituencies, from Stirlingshire to the Borders. Many of the women flocking to join the WOMEN'S SOCIAL AND POLITICAL UNION came from the ranks of the Edinburgh National Society; even its secretary, Jessie METHVEN, left to join the militants. However, there was initially an atmosphere of tolerance; the Edinburgh National Society co-operated with the WSPU over the staging of Scotland's first suffrage procession, held in Edinburgh on 5 October 1907.

In 1909 W.H. Lamond (*see* Elizabeth ABBOTT) was employed as an ORGANIZER by the Edinburgh society and the NUWSS, spreading the cause out to Orkney and Shetland. By 1910 the Edinburgh society had 854 members and an income of £858. In 1909–10 the SCOTTISH FEDERATION FOR WOMEN'S SUFFRAGE was established. Although the proposal had come from Glasgow the headquarters of the Federation was established in Edinburgh, with S.E.S. Mair as its president and Elsie INGLIS as its secretary. In November 1912 the Edinburgh society co-operated with the WOMEN'S FREEDOM LEAGUE and the WSPU in taking part in the Women's March instigated by Florence DE FONBLANQUE and helped to steward and sell tickets for a WFL meeting, at which Charlotte DESPARD was the star speaker. As WSPU militancy increased the Edinburgh society had to battle on two fronts, to convince the general public that not all suffragists were arsonists, while continuing the constitutional struggle. The Edinburgh society, unlike that in Glasgow, fully supported the NUWSS Election Fighting Fund policy.

During the First World War the Edinburgh society undertook relief work in the city, while supporting the Scottish Federation's grand gesture, the Scottish Women's Hospitals. In 1918 the Edinburgh National Society became the Edinburgh National Society for Equal Citizenship.

President (1867–1906) Priscilla Bright McLaren; (1906–18) S.E.S. Mair. Secretary (1867) Agnes McLaren and Eliza Wigham; (1890s) Jessie Methven; (1906) Elsie Inglis; (1909) Miss A.N. Balfour; (1913) Miss K.M. Loudon; secretary and office, Miss Lisa Gordon, 40 Shandwick Place, Edinburgh.

Archival source: Annual Reports of the Edinburgh National Society, Fawcett Library.
Bibliography: L. Leneman, *A Guid Cause: The Women's Suffrage Movement in Scotland*, 1991.

EDINBURGH UNIVERSITY WOMEN SUFFRAGE SOCIETY A member of the SCOTTISH UNIVERSITY WOMEN'S SUFFRAGE UNION. Secretary (1913) Miss E.M. Gorrie, The Women Students' Union, The University Edinburgh. Miss Gorrie had joined the WSPU c. 1908, played the prized part of Mary Queen of Scots in the WSPU procession held in Edinburgh in October 1909, and in 1914 been WSPU ORGANIZER in Edinburgh (*see* Lucy BURNS). Her photograph album, in its WSPU covers, is now in the collection of the National Library of Scotland.

EGHAM AND DISTRICT (NUWSS) Joint secretaries (1913) Miss A.M. Leake, South Tower, Royal Holloway College, Englefield Green, Surrey, and Mrs Holland, Glanty, Egham, Surrey.

ELGIN committee of the NATIONAL SOCIETY FOR WOMEN'S SUFFRAGE Was in existence in 1872 when its convenor was Ex-Provost Russell. In 1913 the society was a member of the NORTH OF SCOTLAND FEDERATION OF THE NATIONAL UNION OF WOMEN'S SUFFRAGE SOCIETIES. Joint secretaries (1913) Miss MacPherson, The Studio, 23 High St., Elgin, and Miss Forsyth, Dalquharran, Lossiemouth, Moray.

ELLAND (WSPU) Secretary (1906) Miss Holland, 1 Turnpike St, Elland Lane, Elland, Yorkshire.

ELMY, ELIZABETH CLARKE WOLSTENHOLME, MRS (1833–1918) Born at Cheetham Hill, Manchester, daughter of Joseph Wolstenholme, a Methodist minister from Eccles who died c. 1843. Her mother died when she was very young; she had a stepmother, Mary. She experienced radical sympathies from an early age, recalling 40 years later in a *Westminster Review* article how she watched "with deep emotion the great Manchester procession in celebration of the repeal of the Corn Laws". Her brother Joseph Wolstenholme (d. 1891) was a student at St John's College, Cambridge, and eventually became professor of mathematics at the Royal Indian Engineering College. As a fellow of Christ's College, Cambridge, he was one of three members of the MANCHESTER NATIONAL SOCIETY FOR WOMEN'S SUFFRAGE living in Cambridge in 1870. While at Cambridge he became a close friend of Leslie Stephen and, according to Quentin Bell, was to be the model for Augustus Carmichael in Virginia Woolf's *To the Lighthouse*. An orphan, Elizabeth Wolstenholme spent two years at the Moravian school at Fulneck, near Leeds, leaving when she was 16. Her desire to go on to Bedford College, then recently founded, was vetoed by her trustees. She spent the next two or three years in unassisted study, becoming, for instance, proficient in Latin, then worked for two years as a governess. Her guardians suggested that she invest her small inherited capital in opening a "high-class boarding school". For the next 18 years she conducted such a school, first at Worsley four miles to the west of Manchester, and then from about 1865 at Moody Hall, Congleton, Cheshire. She ran her first school in Boothstown Lane, Worsley, with help from an Irish cook and a housemaid. Her stepmother lived with her, but Elizabeth Wolstenholme was head of the household. In 1861 she had five pupils, all girls, whose ages ranged from 11 to 16, most of whom came from Manchester. In 1871, at Moody Hall, she ran the school with help from a cook, and with her stepmother as housekeeper. At the time of the census she had six pupils, aged between 12 and 17, who came from Worsley, Bacup, Burslem and Anlaby. There were no other teachers living in at either school. She later remarked that several of the headmistresses of public high schools had the advantage of her teaching. Frances ROWE was one of her pupils at Congleton.

Elizabeth Wolstenholme founded in 1865 the Manchester Schoolmistresses Association, assisted in the foundation of similar boards in other northern towns and, with Mrs Butler and Miss Clough, established in 1867 the North of England Council for Promoting the Education of Women. This popularized the Oxford and Cambridge Local Examinations, already opened to girls, and instituted a system of local lectures which led to the University Extension Movement. It also worked for the Higher Examinations for Women and for the giving of lectures to women students in Cambridge, which led to the foundation of Newnham. In 1869 she herself took the Higher Examination and attained "the Certificate with Honour". There is absolutely no doubt but that she had an excellent mind, clear and analytical, and a tenacious memory. Apparently she was offered "eminent educational and collegiate positions"; her lack of religious orthodoxy prevented their acceptance. In a letter written in September 1900 she noted that "If I *could* have feigned a theology, I might, 30 years ago, have had my choice as to the head-mistress-ship of almost any of the Schools on the enclosed list. A conscience is the most costly of all possessions, but it is the most precious."

Elizabeth Wolstenholme made the journey to London to be present in St James's Hall on 5 July 1865 when J.S. MILL addressed the Westminster electors. In that year she gave a paper titled "What better provision ought to be made for the education of girls of the upper and middle classes?", at the conference of the National Association for the Promotion of Social Science. She was obviously now in touch with members of the Langham Place group and became a corresponding member of the KENSINGTON SOCIETY. She attended at least one meeting at Mrs Manning's house in Phillimore Gardens and on this occasion met for the first time Jessie BOUCHERETT, who later in the year came to stay with her at Moody Hall, and who inspired her to found a Manchester branch of the Society for Promoting the Employment of Women. At around the same time, in October 1865, Elizabeth Wolstenholme was the honorary secretary and doubtless the instigator of a small committee that was founded in Manchester with the purpose of collecting signatures to a petition in support of women's enfranchisement (*see* MANCHESTER NATIONAL SOCIETY FOR WOMEN'S SUFFRAGE). In a letter written to Sylvia PANKHURST on 20 May 1908 she remarked, apropos the 1866 petition for which she was responsible for collecting 300 of the 1499 signatures, "Of course I could not have done this work had I not been working hard during the previous five years – from 1861 – with regards to the employment and education of women." This, she continued, had brought her into contact with those who were in a position to give effective help to the embryonic suffrage movement. It was through this work that she had been put in touch, by Emily DAVIES, with Josephine Butler, with whom she remained friends for life. The good offices of Emily Davies were again employed when in early 1867 Lydia BECKER was introduced to the Manchester suffrage committee. In her letter to Sylvia Pankhurst, 20 May 1908, Elizabeth Wolstenholme Elmy explained that "as I had just moved to Congleton and much further from Manchester, than I had been at Worsley, and being cruelly pressed with other work, I was too thankful to resign my secretaryship into her [Lydia Becker's] most capable hands". She must have maintained some position in the organized campaign, because it was to her in July 1867 that the publisher Trubner sent 200 copies of J.S. Mill's "Speech in the House of Commons". Lydia Becker received a further 200 copies a month later. To Sylvia Pankhurst in 1908, Elizabeth Wolstenholme Elmy also made the point that in 1867 she had handed to Lydia Becker the minute book of the first Manchester suffrage committee and assumed that it had now vanished; she was well aware that history can, either actively or passively, be rewritten when there is no documentary evidence to explain the exact sequence of events. Helen BLACKBURN, who had inherited Lydia Becker's papers, made no mention of the first Manchester committee in her scrapbook, now held by Girton, nor in her *Record of Women's Suffrage*, 1902. Elizabeth Wolstenholme Elmy on 1 July 1910 sent to Sylvia Pankhurst a copy of Helen Blackburn's book which, she explained, had belonged to her husband and which had only recently been returned to her, several years after his death. Noting, rather pointedly, that it contained two photographs of Lydia Becker, and one each of 22 other "pioneers" (among whom she is not included), she drew attention to the fact that "Miss Becker was not then associated with the movement. But although unknown to us she was an absolute suffragist".

In the spring of 1866 Elizabeth Wolstenholme gave evidence, as the Manchester representative of the North of England Council for the Higher Education of Women, to the Taunton Commission, the first Royal Commission to deal with secondary education as a whole. Emily Davies, Dorothea Beale and Frances Buss were others who gave evidence. Emily Davies spent some time in Manchester later that year, again involved in educational work. She was obviously in contact there with Elizabeth Wolstenholme, who was busy canvassing for the petitions from female householders. Elizabeth Wolstenholme subscribed to the ENFRANCHISEMENT OF WOMEN COMMITTEE, 1866–7.

She was still running her school when she embarked on another campaign, working in parallel with the suffrage movement, that to reform the law as it affected the property of married women. She became the secretary of the Married Women's Property Committee when it was formed in April 1868; Lydia Becker was treasurer, Josephine Butler and Richard PANKHURST were members of the executive committee. It was a distinctly Manchester enterprise, although in May 1868 Helen TAYLOR accepted Elizabeth Wolstenholme's invitation to join the general committee. In 1870 Jacob BRIGHT, a Manchester MP, introduced the Married Women's Property Bill in the House of Commons. In tandem with the suffrage and MPW campaigns Elizabeth Wolstenholme was a founder of the Ladies' National Association for the Repeal of the Contagious Diseases Acts, asking her friend Josephine Butler to head "the great crusade". By now she was also in correspondence with a Bristol circle of sympathizers – the PRIESTMAN SISTERS, Margaret TANNER and Mary ESTLIN. With Josephine Butler and Lydia Becker she founded in 1871, and became honorary secretary of, the Committee for Amending the Law in Points Injurious to Women (CALPIW), for which body she wrote *Infant Mortality, its Causes and Remedies*, 1871.

In 1872, having given up her school, she moved to London, where her assiduous attention to legislation in women's interests led, wrote Ben Elmy, to her nickname of "Parliamentary watch-dog". She worked for the Married Women's Property Committee for almost the entirety of its life, 1868–82, with a short, bitter interlude around the time of her precipitate marriage. While in London she also established in 1872, as an offshoot of CALPIW, the Vigilance Association for the Defence of Personal Rights, of which she was the first secretary, very well remunerated at £300 a year. She resigned her position after her marriage in 1874 and her return to Congleton, remained as a member of the executive committee throughout the 1880s, but had given up this position by 1892. From 1881, when it was launched, she became a prolific contributor to the *Journal of the Vigilance Association for the Defence of Personal Rights*. In the early 1870s she was also, apart from all her major campaigns, the first honorary secretary of an association formed to diffuse, as the *Women's Suffrage Review* explained, "amongst women accurate information as to the nature and working of the [Elementary Education] Act", took part in a deputation to W.E. Forster to press for the appointment of women school inspectors in 1870 (a cause which one of her later creations, the WOMEN'S EMANCIPATION UNION, was to reiterate in 1892 and 1896), and in 1872 was a member of the General Committee for Medical Education. She was also a regular attender at meetings of the Social Science Association.

In 1871 she was a member of the CENTRAL COMMITTEE OF THE NATIONAL SOCIETY; in 1872 both she and Ben Elmy, her Congleton neighbour, are listed as members, he being a delegate member to the executive committee. Ben Elmy (1838–1906) was born in Rochdale, had been a teacher, but in 1869 set up in business in Congleton as a manufacturer of silk-crape, an eminently Victorian material and one in many ways representing the antithesis of women's freedom. In 1871 he lived alone at Buglawton with his housekeeper, her husband, who acted as gardener, and their child. He was a "Fair Trader", had been a vice-president of the National Secular Society and became an "advanced socialist". Elizabeth Wolstenholme and Ben Elmy entered into a free union, in accord with their secular views and attitude to couverture, a relationship of which Josephine Butler, and presumably other of her associates, was cogniscent. By the autumn of 1874 it became clear that Elizabeth Wolstenholme, now 40, was pregnant. In *Baby Buds*, 1895, "Ellis Ethelmer" explained the general procedure: "We found in talking and writing to one another that our thoughts and desires and general wishes were so much the same, that we began to love each other. So, at last, we resolved to marry – that is to live together, for the sake of our own sweet companionship, and also to more readily do our duty, as tender parents, to any dear little child which our love might cause, and bring to life." In 1897 Elizabeth Wolstenholme Elmy stated, "The only absolute right I should claim for a woman as against a man is that she should never be made a mother against her will." Although this was an allusion to marital rape rather than to failed contraception, it must be hoped that she had intended to become a mother. In a letter written to Frances Rowe on 11 August 1901 Harriet McIlquham refers to Mrs Elmy's "unworldly enthusiasm". Working as she was for equality between men and women, alongside others she thought to be of a like mind, Elizabeth Wolstenholme may just have been sufficiently unworldly as to think that motherhood without marriage, as the logical outcome of her philosophy, would not detract from her political effectiveness. She was mistaken and it was apparently Ursula Bright who persuaded the couple to undergo an official form of marriage, in order that the honour of the women's movement should not be besmirched. The marriage took place by licence at Kensington Register Office on 12 October 1874. Emilie Ashurst Venturi, herself a divorcée and therefore something of a sexual renegade, was one of the two witnesses. At the time of the marriage Elizabeth Wolstenholme was living in a newly built house in Finborough Road, Kensington, the home, the Post Office directory reveals, of "Mrs Woolstenholme". Unfortunately the house had changed hands by the time of the 1881 census, and it is not possible to be certain that "Mrs Woolstenholme" was Elizabeth Wolstenholme's step-mother, although the balance of probability suggests that this might have been so. The Elmys' son Frank Wolstenholme was born in January 1875. The choice as a first name of "Frank" *tout court*, not a shortened form of "Francis", gives an indication of the character they hoped their son would develop. In *Baby Buds,* a boy, "Frank", features as an example, tall and true, to his young cousin "Nora", the young girl, with a name resonant to a "New Woman" readership to whom the book is addressed. Sadly, as Sylvia Pankhurst reveals in *The Suffragette Movement*, the real Frank, although a good son, fell far short of these ideals.

Elizabeth Wolstenholme Elmy's critics did not, however, consider a belated marriage sufficient to regularize the situation. Having returned briefly to the political arena, her position as secretary of the MWP Committee was put to the vote at the annual general meeting held in the autumn of 1875. There is little extant correspondence about the matter; Josephine Butler's accounts now seem inconsistent, although perhaps they did not at the time. She may have advised Elizabeth Wolstenholme Elmy to resign from her position with the MWP Committee; she was certainly weary of the matter by December 1875, writing "I must wash my hands of her *present & future* action". She had been with the Elmys when they had received an intemperate letter from Millicent Garret Fawcett, threatening if Elizabeth Wolstenholme Elmy did not resign from the MWP Committee to reveal her immoral conduct to the campaign's parliamentary supporters. One of the factors that persuaded Mrs Butler that Mrs Elmy should resign from the MPW Committee was the strain that the matter was causing her. Although in October there had been a suggestion that Ben Elmy might take over the editorship of the *Shield* from Emilie Venturi, by December Josephine Butler had received a letter signed by both Elmys, making it clear that they "desired to live out of sight at Congleton & cease to be spoken of". Twenty-five years later, on 11 August 1901, Harriet McIlquham wrote of the Elmys' married life to Frances Rowe, "Of this I feel sure that her life with Mr Elmy has been one of mixed happiness and sorrow – and that in her private life she has shown that loyal unselfishness which is so conspicuous in her public work. In many ways I believe he has been a great intellectual help to her – and in other ways a great tax on her energies – possessing a mixed character akin to our Coleridge; or the American Poet – E.A. Poe." This opaque allusion suggests a dark, or at least difficult, side to his character. Ben Elmy was frequently and severely ill. There are hints in letters between Mrs McIlquham and Mrs Rowe that this illness was more debilitating than one might expect from the bronchitis from which he was known to suffer. Esther Roper, in 1929 replying to Sylvia Pankhurst's request for information about the Elmys, wrote "I think the tales must have been true – poor thing. They came only from a friend. She was a most able brain – a dauntless spirit. I was always fond of her." Sylvia Pankhurst does then paint a very dark portrait of the Elmys' home life. No criticisms of her husband appear in Elizabeth Wolstenholme Elmy's letters; on the contrary she writes of him with love and with respect for his literary work in the woman's cause. When at the beginning of 1906 he was diagnosed to have cancer she wrote on 8 January 1906 to Mrs McIlquham, "I have often wished that people realised how much he has done for our woman's cause, how true and loyal he has been." When he died she wrote, 3 March 1906, "he died with my warm kiss on his lips". It is overly misanthropic to assume that the books on human physiology and sex-education written by "Ellis Ethelmer", because they are tender and domestic, could not have been written by a man. One might as well deduce that the works of "Ignota", because they are rational, analytical, revealing an enviable grasp of legal history and parliamentary procedure, could not have been written by a woman. All the books, with the exception of *Woman Free*, which was published by the Women's Emancipation Union, were printed as obtainable from "Mrs Wolstenholme Elmy". The British Library catalogue ascribes all "Ellis Ethelmer's" works to her. However, a study of Elizabeth Wolstenholme Elmy's extant correspondence gives no indication that she herself used the pseudonym "Ellis Ethelmer". She repeatedly mentions her husband's writings and does not assume in any way the persona of "Ellis Ethelmer". A card for the New Year/Century written by Elizabeth Wolstenholme Elmy to Harriet McIlquham comes from both "Ellis Ethelmer" and Elizabeth C.W. Elmy. In the obituary article she wrote in 1906 Elizabeth Wolstenholme Elmy explained that Ben Elmy wrote as "Ellis Ethelmer", a combination of his mother's maiden name Ellis, and an earlier form of his paternal surname, thinking that women would not trust his books on women and sex if they were obviously written by a man, "whilst other men were amusing in their scornful attitude towards a writer whom they insisted on assuming to be a woman". Sylvia PANKHURST who knew at firsthand, or from firsthand gossip, something of the background to the Elmys' life and work states that "together and severally" they produced their works on sex education for children. She specifically ascribes *The Human Flower*, 1894, to Mrs Elmy.

The reviewer of *The Human Flower* in *Shafts*, a paper to which Elizabeth Wolstenholme Elmy was then a contributor, referred to the book as probably written by a man. There can be little doubt that the Elmys shared ideas and reading. For instance, in 1898 Elizabeth Wolstenholme Elmy noted that one of the five books that had delighted her most in recent years was Richard Jefferies' *Story of My Heart*, a book referred to extensively in the notes to Ellis Ethelmer's *Woman Free*, 1893. These notes include a poem described as having been written by an anonymous woman, which, from other references, can almost certainly be ascribed to Elizabeth Wolstenholme Elmy. Although the poem is a plea for the removal of couverture, the poet is bound by romantic love, "Could I only stand/ Between the gray moor and gray sky,/ Where the winds and the plovers cry,/And no man is at hand/ And feel the free wind blow/ On my rain-wet face, and know/ I am free – not yours, but my own –/ Free and alone . . .".

It is not clear how matters over the impropriety attached to the Elmys' behaviour before their marriage were resolved; the passage of time doubtless blunted hurts on all sides. In 1881 it was as *de facto* secretary of the MWP Committee that Elizabeth Wolstenholme Elmy spent at least three months living as a lodger, with her young son, in the home of Thomas Hoade and his wife at 137 Chesterton Road, Notting Hill; she wrote later to Harriet McIlquham that "they were *very good* to me and to Frank". The boy was presumably left with the Hoades, who were retired domestic servants, while his mother attended the House of Commons, lobbying MPs, and enduring late-night sessions. On 8 July 1881 she wrote in a letter published in the *Journal of the Vigilance Association*, "it would need no violent dislocation of the arrangements of society to adapt Parliamentary hours to a more healthful and business-like mode of procedure", a *cri de coeur* echoed by women in parliament a hundred years later. In an article she wrote for the *Westminster Review*, August 1899, she described the central lobby of the House of Commons as "the dreariest of all dreary waiting-places". After the passing of the MWP Act she spent three years, 1883–6, campaigning for the maternal guardianship of children which led in 1886 to the passing of the Guardianship of Infants Act. This appears to have been a solo campaign, under the aegis of no society. In 1886 Elizabeth Wolstenholme Elmy published *The Infants Act: A Record of Three Years' Work for Legislative Reforms with its Results*, in which she related that she had distributed in this campaign nearly half a million leaflets and over 40 000 pamphlets. Alice SCATCHERD and Agnes SUNLEY were particularly singled out for thanks and among those listed as contributing money towards the modest cost of the campaign were Mona TAYLOR, Jessie Boucherett, Ursula Bright, Caroline Ashurst BIGGS, Helen CLARK, Charlotte BURBURY, Frances Power COBBE, Emma CORFIELD, Lady GOLDSMID, Harriet McIlquham, Dr Julia Mitchell, Dorinda NELIGAN, Mrs PENNINGTON, Mary Priestman, J.P. THOMASSON and William Michael Rossetti. As an adjunct to this report, published separately in order not to embarrass any of her "friends and helpers who do not yet feel prepared for the acceptance of the full programme to which its appearance as a part of this report might seem to commit them", she set out a claim in *The Emancipation of Women* for "equality with men in every respect before the law", which concentrated on the revived threat of contagious diseases legislation, on the horror of marital rape, and appealed for the removal of couverture. This report provided the springboard for her next campaign.

On 21 February 1889 Elizabeth Wolstenholme Elmy led a deputation to Jacob Bright, asking him "to bring in a genuine Women's Suffrage Bill". By "genuine" she meant one that did not specifically exclude married women, as did the one that was proposed by William Woodall and backed by both the Central Committee and the CENTRAL NATIONAL SOCIETY. When it became clear at a March annual general meeting that the Central National, which had been less firmly committed to the Woodall clause, would indeed support it, Elizabeth Wolstenholme Elmy and other Manchester radicals such as Alice Cliff Scatcherd and the Pankhursts formed the WOMEN'S FRANCHISE LEAGUE, of which she became secretary. In June 1889 she described in a letter to Harriet McIlquham how, "In addition to my household work, and to all this public work for the League, the Divorce Bill, Fair Trade, and the C.D. agitation, I have been working at the mill – . . . over 50 hours each of the last 2 weeks – I shall have much the same work each week till the middle or end of September. We have been finishing off all goods (crape finishing work) and Mr Elmy and I do with our own hands, with the help of one man and one woman what, before the scattering of our people in consequence of the frightfully bad trade and low prices . . . was the work of eight distinct and carefully trained persons." The Elmys were winding up the business, apparently unable to compete with imports from northern Italy, and considering emigration to America, taking the crape machinery with them. In July 1889 Elizabeth Wolstenholme wrote to Alice Scatcherd, proposing a visit to London for committee meetings, which were held at the Pankhursts' house, and an evening and afternoon at the House of Commons meeting MPs, "I want to be prepared to announce on the 25th at our own meeting that 3 Bills will be introduced next session on behalf of our League. 1. I present our Franchise Bill. 2. The Divorce Bill, equalizing the law between husband and wife. 3. Then Devolution of Estates Bill which will give equal rights of inheritance to females as with males. This would be a grand programme – and would sufficiently mark the differences between us and the other Societies . . . The Bills are all ready . . . but I want the sanction of the committee for my plans". While in London she stayed at a lodging house at 6 Upper Bedford Place, convenient for Russell Square. As in all societies, discordancies lurked. On 20 July she wrote to Mrs McIlquham, "What are we to do with our unbusiness-like Treasurer? She is not much better than Mrs Jacob Bright and that is saying a great deal. Better as to business faculty I mean – for she is undoubtedly more willing to work hard and take suggestions from those who know, than the other lady." Alice Scatcherd had been slow at paying in cheques to the bank. In the *Illustrated London News*, 31 August 1889, Elizabeth Wolstenholme Elmy received a graceful tribute from Florence Fenwick MILLER, describing her "directing soul and . . . statesmanlike brain" and as "a woman who works so quietly and with such complete self-abnegation that nine-tenths even of those interested in some degree in the women's movement have not heard her name. But Members of Parliament who have helped (or tried to hinder) the legal reforms for women of the last quarter of a century know Mrs

Wolstenholme-Elmy." Discussing the Custody of Infants Act she continued, "Mrs Elmy's labour in altering that law was superhuman. Yet nobody outside the circle who worked with her know of it." She quoted Elizabeth Wolstenholme Elmy as saying:

> There is no force in the universe so powerful as moral enthusiasm. Nothing has astonished and delighted me more than the rapid growth of opinion in our favour during the last seven years. All over the country friends are springing up, accepting to the full our principles as the basis of the higher domestic and social morality yet to be; and even in the House of Commons, the last place in the world to be influenced by this new current of thought and feeling, there are now men, many men, especially amongst the younger members of the House, who regard these questions as earnestly, as seriously, and with almost as much of passionate conviction as ourselves, and who, not only for the sake of justice to women but also for the resultant justice to all mankind, are determined to spare no effort to set right these inequalities.

Ironically it was the author of this article who was, Mrs Elmy later believed, her nemesis. By October the hand finishing work at the mill had more or less been completed and she wrote thanking Harriet McIlquham for sending her home produce: "Frank has keenly appreciated the apples and pears, and we have all enjoyed the beautiful tomatoes." When planning a visit to London in November for a second round of League meetings, again to be held at the Pankhursts' house, she wrote to Mrs McIlquham, "I wish it were possible for *us* to stay somewhere together, way from Mrs Scatcherd". Elizabeth Wolstenholme Elmy's main complaint seems to have concerned Alice Scatcherd's behaviour to Agnes Sunley and the fact that she had not guaranteed £50 a year for five years to the League as she had appeared to promise at the beginning. She continued, "She is a broken reed, not to be counted on for a moment. Well, it is sad, but she is only like others, *who have never worked* and have money they do not know how to use rationally." There was doubtless an all too human bitterness towards one whose material life was so very much more comfortable. Although most of Elizabeth Wolstenholme Elmy's letters concentrate on social, political and strategic matters, her correspondent knew only too well the condition of her home life. On 15 January 1890 Elizabeth Wolstenholme Elmy wrote to Harriet McIlquham, "I had a huge wash yesterday, having been obliged to put it off by my poor right arm and I was so tired after being at work from 4.30 am to 6 pm." In response to this Mrs McIlquham sent her a "combination", Mrs Elmy replying, "I will certainly, for your sake, try the 'combination', which arrived yesterday, but I have never yet been able to bear wool next the skin, though I have never tried repeatedly, and have never worn any thing close or tight fitting since I was 12 years old, not even corsets!!" Her life was further aggravated by a summons against her taken out by "Helena Beatrice Temple" for the sum of two pounds, alleged to be due to her for a report and 500 copies of newspapers ordered. She knew that "Helena Beatrice Temple" was the pseudonym of Henrietta MULLER as editor of the *Women's Penny Paper*. Hurt and indignant, Elizabeth Wolstenholme Elmy paid the £2 "simply to prevent further waste of time, money, temper and effort that ought to be put to better use". On 20 February 1890, planning further League business in London, she wrote to Mrs McIlquham, "I want . . . to choose a *decent*, but not costly, bonnet and mantle – I cannot be the scarecrow of the League at the forthcoming meetings. Can you recommend me a good place and could you go with me to select them? . . . Please, dear, bring with you, . . . your letter to W[omen's] P[enny] P[aper]. . . . People like Dr Pankhurst, devoted to our cause as he is, find it difficult to believe that women can so monstrously try to hurt each other." She was present, perhaps in a new bonnet and mantle, at a drawing-room meeting held by the WFL towards the end of March in the Pankhursts' house at which, so Alice Scatcherd wrote in a letter to Harriet McIlquham on 31 March, "Elmy excelled herself". However, she resigned from her post as secretary to the Women's Franchise League in May 1890. The exact reason is veiled by time and innuendo, but appears to have been the result of a personality clash with Florence Fenwick Miller and a suspicion that Ursula Bright intended to supplant her as secretary. Her resignation may also have been connected with the interest Sir Charles and Lady DILKE, encouraged as she thought by the Pankhursts, were taking in the WFL. A letter to Mrs McIlquham of 5 June 1890 contains the gist of the story. In July 1890 she and Mrs Cady Stanton spoke at a meeting in Oxford; Elizabeth Wolstenholme Elmy was staying in Basingstoke with Mrs Cady Stanton and her daughter, Harriot Stanton BLATCH. She was still working for the League, arranging the International Conference, but later that month, after a committee meeting at which she failed to gain support, felt compelled to resign, according to "Ellis Ethelmer" in the *Westminster Review*, "owing to the reversion of the majority of the committee to the policy and complexion of political partnership". It was always Elizabeth Wolstenholme Elmy's fear that politics would divide the women's movement.

Bitterly she wrote to Harriet McIlquham, "I do not intend ever again to take any part whatever in political action on behalf of women. I have done my part and more ... When any one of the women who so insulted and wronged me can show such a record, I may begin to believe in her zeal for the causes of womanhood." Irrepressible, she resolved to take up "free trade work ... The American tariff legislation, the falling in of so many of our commercial treaties in 1892, the urgent need of federation of the Empire, all make the next 2 years most important and critical. I shall write regularly for the Free Trade journal now, and shall probably be speaking in many places during the winter." In November 1890 Ben Elmy was writing a paper, for private circulation only, on the "Physical Emancipation of Women". He solicited advice from both Mona CAIRD, who was wintering in Italy, and Dr Julia Mitchell. Albion Mill was closed, but was not sold until September 1891. The Elmys then had, on Mrs Elmy's estimation, their freehold home, furniture (including a valuable library), some valuable works of art and £400 to £500. In November she thanked Mrs McIlquham for a hamper of duck, chicken, jams and apples: "We greatly enjoyed ... your perfect fowl. Was it a Cochin China? We thought so – Anyhow it was a beauty".

Elizabeth Wolstenholme Elmy was at this time setting up the WOMEN'S EMANCIPATION UNION, her successor to the Women's Franchise League. She was in correspondence with H.N. Mozley, a barrister and fellow of King's College, Cambridge, who wrote for the *Journal for the Vigilance Association for the Defence of Personal Rights*, and was a nephew of Professor NEWMAN. He had contributed an essay on "Property Disabilities of a Married Woman, and other legal effects of Marriage" to *Woman's Work and Woman's Culture*, 1869, which had been edited by Josephine Butler, for which Elizabeth Wolstenholme had contributed "The Education of Girls, its Present and its Future". She made visits even in the depth of winter to the Manchester Law Library on occasion to check up references.

In 1892 she published as a leaflet a letter she had written to the *Manchester Guardian* in which she took to task a previous correspondent who had urged Liberals to vote against Sir Albert Rollit's women's enfranchisement bill on the grounds that it did not expressly include married women. This named correspondent was Isabel Mills, who, as Isabel Petrie, had cared for the three-year-old Elizabeth Wolstenholme on the day of Queen Victoria's coronation. Isabel Petrie had been then a friend of the Brights and now supported the policy of the Women's Franchise League in opposing Rollit's bill. Mrs Elmy, more politically sophisticated, eschewed the absolutist position, recognizing that the bill did not expressly exclude married women and being convinced that in law their right to enfranchisement would not be disputed if the bill was successful. In October 1892 she attended the WEU conference in Birmingham, staying for the occasion, together with Mrs McIlquham, at the home in Edgbaston of Caroline SMITH, sister of George HOLYOAKE. Mrs Smith's daughter, Julia, had been responsible for many of the arrangements for the conference. In March 1893 the WEU held another conference, this time in London, at which Mrs Wolstenholme Elmy spoke on "Women in the Civil Service". In August 1893 she wrote to Mrs McIlquham that she was working 14 hours a day. She did not want to take any salary from the Union, feeling that to be a "paid agent" made her position insecure. Her contention was that it was because of this vulnerability that Mrs Fenwick Miller had been able to edge her out of the Women's Franchise League. By 1894 Elizabeth and Ben Elmy had mortgaged their house so that she could carry on working unpaid for the Union. After Mrs McIlquham's insistence that she must be paid met with no acceptance, in 1895 a few of Mrs Elmy's friends launched a "Grateful Fund" to provide for her £1 a week. Harriet McIlquham and Louisa MARTINDALE were trustees of the fund, which by 1901 was paying Elizabeth Wolstenholme Elmy at the rate of 25s a week. At Christmas 1894 she received £9 as a gift from a group of friends, who included Harriot Stanton Blatch and Harriet McIlquham, who wrote that it was *"to spend on yourself therefore none on any account must be put to the funds of the Union"*. By December 1901 subscribers to the Grateful Fund included Emily FORD and Dr Stanton COIT. At the end of 1903 Harriet McIlquham, Anna Priestman, Julia Smith and Louisa Martindale organized a fund to pay Mrs Elmy a weekly sum throughout 1904.

From September 1893 Elizabeth Wolstenholme Elmy contributed regularly to *Shafts* a column titled "Practical Work for Women Workers: Bills before Parliament" and a series, "Progress at Home and Abroad", drawing on information from a wide range of newspapers and journals, both from Britain and overseas. Her careful analysis of bills before parliament and the progress of legislation concerning women is something of a contrast to the more ethereal writing of the rest of the journal. She stood as a candidate for election as a poor law guardian in 1894, but, although defeated, was delighted that so many more women guardians had been returned as the result of the removal of property qualifications. In 1895 and 1896 she was involved in the movement to organize the SPECIAL APPEAL and in May 1896 came to London to speak at meetings at the Somerville Club, the Pioneer Club (*see under* CLUBS), at various drawing-room meetings, including one at the home of Mrs Haweis, and appeared with Millicent Garrett Fawcett and Helen Blackburn at Westminster Hall to present to Parliament the petition, with 257 000 signatures. Elizabeth Wolstenholme Elmy commented in a letter to Harriet McIlquham a few months later on "The number of Women's Suffrage Meetings and discussions being far greater than I have ever before known it", thereby contradicting, as one at the heart of it, the idea that the women's suffrage movement suffered a decline in the 1890s. All this effort sat alongside the daily chores; on 9 December 1896 she began a letter to Harriet McIlquham,

"Dear Friend, I would have written yesterday but unfortunately it was washing day" before going on to discuss the Liberal Party's attitude to women and county councils.

Elizabeth Wolstenholme Elmy had a fine sense of history and was intent on putting women's future emancipation in the context of the philosophies of past thinkers and workers. In 1896 she asked Harriet McIlquham to search in the British Museum library for a copy of William Thompson's *Appeal*, with an introductory letter to Mrs Wheeler, "and try if you can at the Museum to come upon any other trace of this lady, of whom we can learn nothing, though she seems to have been one of the most advanced thinkers of the day. There is also, amongst minor publications, a little tractate of still earlier date, also on the woman question, by 'Sophia, a person of quality'. Can any other trace be found of any writings of this lady? I have a MS copy of the tract in the Museum, but cannot just now put my hands on it." She presumably enthused Harriet McIlquham, whose article on "Sophia" appeared in the November 1898 issue of the *Westminster Review* and who subsequently contributed other essays on women "workers" of the past, while Elizabeth Wolstenholme Elmy's articles in that journal tackled current political issues. In October 1897 she published as "Ignota", "Woman's Suffrage", a history of the women's question in England. In July, September and October 1898 she wrote, again as "Ignota", "The Part of Women in Local Administration", which was continued in the next year's February and March issues. She contributed to the same journal in August another article, "Privilege vs Justice to Women".

Elizabeth Wolstenholme Elmy's work for the Women's Emancipation Union demanded public appearances as well as pamphleteering. On 4 January 1897, preparing for the year's campaign, she sent Mrs McIlquham "the best fitting old bodice that I have. Though made 14 years ago it fits perfectly today, except that the sleeves should be half an inch longer. Length of skirt; front 35 in, back 37 in. This would comfortably clear the ground in walking." The pattern was successfully and very speedily copied, for on 15 January she wrote "The two parcels arrived this morning in perfect condition. The cloak is delightful and the gown fits perfectly.

Thank you for all care and trouble and kindness for my comfort, including the bonnet. I will sew on the pretty collarette and cuffs received from Mrs Martindale as you wish." A new dress was doubtless a treat; she was sometimes given cast-off dresses by well-wishers but, because she was so small, they invariably had to be altered to fit. The Women's Emancipation Union dissolved in 1899, unable to attract sufficient funding to continue, but holding a final conference, printing a full report of its achievements, and meeting its end with dignity. The final conference was timed to coincide with the London meeting of the Women's International Congress, to which Elizabeth Wolstenholme Elmy contributed a paper on "the Marriage Law of England". The Women's Emancipation Union was Elizabeth Wolstenholme Elmy's last solo creation, although she was doubtless the *éminence grise* behind the MALE ELECTORS' LEAGUE, which had been founded c. 1897 by her husband and which continued, after Ben Elmy's death in 1906, fronted by their son, long enough to memorialize, in the time-honoured way, Campbell-Bannerman.

Elizabeth Wolstenholme Elmy was heartened by the new life stirring through the NORTH OF ENGLAND SOCIETY FOR WOMEN'S SUFFRAGE, often visiting Esther Roper and Eva GORE-BOOTH at their house in Manchester, and very much approving of their suffrage work among the textile workers. Although living in such a retired position, through her indefatigable correspondence she was an information centre, putting the different sections of the women's movement in touch with each other. It was probably through Louisa Martindale, a long-time friend, that she came into contact with Dora MONTEFIORE, whom she in turn introduced to Frances Rowe. Mrs Elmy was present with Louisa Martindale at the International Congress of Women in 1899; disgrace overtook Dora Montefiore and she was unable to attend, although billed to appear. When in July 1903 W.T. Stead, another of her correspondents, organized a meeting at Mowbray House in Norfolk Street, Strand, his London office, to discuss plans for an autumn suffrage campaign, she stayed for the occasion with Dora Montefiore. In September she was again in London, to attend a NATIONAL UNION OF WOMEN'S SUFFRAGE SOCIETIES meeting to discuss the forthcoming convention that had been the outcome of the July meeting. She travelled to London in the company of Esther Roper and stayed this time with Hilda Martindale in her Westminster flat. It was, in the main, as a result of Mrs Elmy's persistence that the National Convention for the Civic Rights of Women was held on 16–17 October 1903 in Holborn Town Hall. It was backed by W.T. Stead, sponsored by the National Union of Women's Suffrage Societies and financially supported by J.P. Thomasson and his wife Katherine, who had long been associated with Elizabeth Wolstenholme Elmy. This convention, which was attended by 200 delegates, marked a revitalizing of NUWSS activity; Elizabeth Wolstenholme Elmy pressed for the raising of a fund to finance a mass suffrage campaign in the run-up to the next general election. It was in the course of one of her 1903 London visits that she attended a Fabian supper, writing to Mrs McIlquham that she had "had some very interesting talk with [HG Wells] on the woman question about which he is 'thinking, thinking' – and I am sending him material for further thought. He is certain to go far. He is as simple as a child, and quite flushed with pleasure when I thanked him in a very few words for his 'Mankind in the Making' . . . Unspoiled yet, anyway." In 1903 Anne Cobden SANDERSON gave Elizabeth Wolstenholme Elmy a copy of *The Life and Work of Susan B. Anthony*, published by her brother-in-law's firm T. Fisher Unwin, and Ben Elmy received acknowledgement from Queen Alexandra for a copy of the Danish edition of *Baby Buds*.

Elizabeth Wolstenholme Elmy had first mentioned Christabel PANKHURST in her correspondence in April 1902 and in December 1903 wrote glowingly to Harriet McIlquham of a letter Christabel had published in the *Manchester Guardian*. Mrs Elmy was associated with the WOMEN'S SOCIAL AND POLITICAL UNION very soon after its formation in the autumn of 1903. Now 70 years old she was revitalized by contact with the "new wave" of the suffrage movement, prepared to bury past differences with Emmeline Pankhurst, particularly pleased, in a letter of 30 March 1904, to report to Harriet McIlquham her comment, in response to a plea from Dilke for the women's movement to work for adult suffrage, "that 'the only service Dilke can render the women's cause is to leave it alone'. Fancy that from her, of all people in the world." She was also willing to put aside a lifetime's aversion to party politics and joined the Manchester Central branch of the Independent Labour Party, of which Mrs Pankhurst was a founder member. In July 1904 she met again "our beautiful souled Susan Anthony. . . . – clear-headed, warm-hearted, great-souled" and with her stayed for a few days at Katherine THOMASSON's home near Bolton. Although the meetings with Susan Anthony were enjoyable Mrs Elmy learned later that Susan Anthony had been given the idea that she was unable "to work in harmony with others" and immediately suspected Ursula Bright as being the source of this calumny; time would not heal all past dissensions. Her hopes for a renewed NUWSS campaign had not been fulfilled. In October 1904 she wrote that "they have not troubled to send papers to the 300 names and addresses I sent them, names which included many capital workers". She thought that the work being done by the LANCASHIRE AND CHESHIRE WOMEN TEXTILE AND OTHER WORKERS' REPRESENTATION COMMITTEE, outside the NUWSS, "is of more value to our cause than all the work of the N.U. put together". She did, however, attend the NUWSS conference in London in November 1904.

At New Year 1905–6 Elizabeth Wolstenholme Elmy sent out 300 leaflets she had had specially printed, asking for support for a bill for the Enfranchisement of Women, drafted by Keir Hardie. By this means she hoped to get at least 300 MPs written to by their personal friends and constituents. In February, to her great regret, Mrs Elmy was too unwell to travel to London and, with Mrs Pankhurst, Sylvia Pankhurst, Mrs McIlquham and others, to lobby MPs in order to persuade one who had been successful in the ballot for private members bills to give the place to women's suffrage. She did, however, prime MPs, such as Sir Wilfred Lawson (who had been a member of the first parliamentary committee of supporters of women's suffrage in 1887) and Mr J.G. Weir, to give every help, sent the lobbyists lengthy written details about the procedures to follow and in a letter to Mrs McIlquham dated 9 February, such advice as "After dinner, 9 to 11 or 12 will be the best time on Tuesday to see M.P.s." From Congleton she followed daily the details of the lobbying and was in correspondence on 17 and 18 February with the MP, Bamford Slack, who eventually gave his ballot place to the suffrage bill. At her suggestion the lobbyists sent a cable from the House of Commons to Susan Anthony on 15 February, her last birthday. All this activity on Mrs Elmy's part rather belies Sylvia Pankhurst's suggestion, in *The Suffragette Movement*, that she and her mother were alone and friendless at the House of Commons. In the event the second reading of the WSPU-favoured bill, which was introduced on 12 May by Bamford Slack, was, as Mrs Elmy feared, "talked out". She had been in London for days previously, staying at Mrs Martindale's flat in Westminster Mansions, lobbying for the enfranchisement bill to be given a more prominent position in the parliamentary day, and distributing Male Electors' League leaflets. She wrote to Harriet McIlquham that "I shall be at the House of C. from 3 to 7 each afternoon till Friday, then from noon to 5.30". In the same letter she commented on the recalcitrance of the Liberal party; the annual general meeting of the Women's Liberal Federation was about to take place and would, she knew, undo "all the works of the Practical Suffragists. . . . Oh! these Liberals – which are worse – the men or the women – on this great question". In a letter written on 7 October 1907 to Sylvia Pankhurst, who was then seeking information for the articles on the history of the women's suffrage movement that she was preparing for publication in *Votes for Women*, Elizabeth Wolstenholme Elmy gave a description of the scenes at the House of Commons on 12 May 1905 when the bill was talked out, commenting "This day began the fusion of classes – for women [who] have left the wash-tub to come to the House walked hand in hand, side by side with fashionably dressed ladies. There were in the House that day 170 women of the W.C. [Women's Co-operative] Guild." She described how, when they learned the bill had been talked out, the women began a protest "but the police interfered and we had not then formulated the policy of defiant resistance. However they were very kind and sympathetic and volunteered to find us a safer meeting place". Hers was the first signature to a resolution condemning the procedure of the House of Commons, which Keir Hardie duly presented. Writing as "Ignota" she gave a description of the day's events in an article, "The Enfranchisement of Women" published in the July 1905 issue of the *Westminster Review*. Emmeline Pankhurst commented in her autobiography, *My Own Story*, that this protest constituted "the first militant act of the WSPU". It was fitting that Elizabeth Wolstenholme Elmy was present; she revealed in the 7 October 1907 letter to Sylvia Pankhurst that she had hoped to go to prison that day and that she did not now believe that women would be enfranchised until they suffered imprisonment "and even death itself, for the sake of our great Common Cause".

In July Elizabeth Wolstenholme Elmy addressed, at the home of Esther Roper and Eva Gore-Booth, a meeting of women textile workers, among whom was Annie KENNEY, who impressed her by asking very relevant questions. On 20 October she attended the meeting organized by the Manchester Central Branch of the ILP to welcome Christabel Pankhurst and Annie Kenney on their release from prison. She stayed for the night with Esther Roper and Eva Gore-Booth. To Harriet McIlquham three days later she described the scene in breathless detail:

> After the meeting was over, our little group found each other and went down to the front door of the Hall to find our vehicle. But nothing and nobody was there, only the side street was *crowded* with people. We waited a few minutes and at last the policeman on duty came up and said "Are you looking for the motor car?" "Yes" "I had to tell them to take it round the corner, because I may not allow a crowd here." And started to escort us. But there was no need for his help. The moment we appeared, a lane through the crowds opened out and we passed through a silent, most respectful throng, most of the men taking off their hats or caps. They stood thus whilst we took our seats and arranged matters, and as we started off, raised a ringing cheer, which we heard sustained long after we were out of sight. For the car was the famous Women's Suffrage motor car, which has done such splendid service for W.S. during the last six months in the villages and towns of East and South-West Lancashire and North Cheshire; amongst its five occupants were 2 of the women speakers of the evening, one of whom, Mrs Dickenson, Sec of the Women's Trades and Labour Council, was driving. The people, many hundreds of them, had only waited to give us a joyous "send off". I tell you these things as signs of the temper of the people with regard to our great question.

In another letter written the same day she wrote:

> It is the beginning of the end – no such magnificent demonstration for W.S. has ever before been made in England as was made in the Manchester Free Trade Hall last Friday night.... I say, our meeting – for naturally I was there to stand by my beloved Christabel, and her faithful co-agitator, Annie Kenny [*sic*] ... The greater part of us who were in the ante-room went on the platform early, the Hall being so densely crowded and the people so eager half an hour before the advertised time of opening the meeting and then cheering. There was enough to have satisfied a very hungry appetite. But when the speakers entered and last the two convicts, the whole vast audience rose and cheered and cheered – women waving their hand-kerchiefs.

Elizabeth Wolstenholme Elmy explained the "spitting incident", for which Christabel Pankhurst had been arrested, as:

> "spitting" in the severest technical sense only – for as a sensible doctor said "No one in a state of such tense excitement could have had moisture enough in the mouth to spare for that purpose". But she did, admittedly, make a "puf, pouf" such as we might have done on some slight occasion to express disapproval, or objection, and did make it as contemptuous as, under the circumstances, she could and was, moreover, under the belief that these plain clothes policemen were only another batch of her previous Liberal assailants, who had come off the platform to assault two young women.... Could you let your sister, as well as dear Mrs Martindale and Miss Priestman see this. I have neither time nor strength to write to all I wish to do.

In December she paid several visits to Manchester, one day "concocting plans with the Women's Textile Workers and the Women's Social and Political Union", and on 14 December spending three hours with Christabel and Annie Kenney. In the same issue (29 December 1905) that the *Labour Leader* printed a report of the disruption caused by Annie Kenney and others at Campbell-Bannerman's Liberal rally at the Albert Hall on 21 December 1905, it also published a letter from Mrs Elmy appealing for each ILP candidate in the forthcoming general election "to give special prominence in his election address and speeches to the enfranchisement of women; and for every comrade in the ILP to work for no candidate who is either opposed to or careless of this gravest of all social and political issues". She then analysed the voting history, as regards women's enfranchisement, of each member of the cabinet and warned against the "dead wall of 'manhood suffrage'" that might follow if a Liberal government were to introduce its mooted electoral reform. Her husband's illness (he was dying, desperate to finish his last piece of work for the women's cause, his translation of Tennyson's "The Princess" into Esperanto) prevented her from travelling to London to attend the Woman's Parliament at the Caxton Hall on 19 February. Shortly after the meeting she used a photographic postcard of the London procession to give Mrs McIlquham news of Ben Elmy. He died on 3 March 1906; his cremation was attended by Eva Gore-Booth, Esther Roper and Christabel Pankhurst, the latter two giving an address. Elizabeth Wolstenholme Elmy's obituary of her husband, "Pioneers, O Pioneers", appeared in the April 1906 issue of the *Westminster Review*. A month later she came to London, stayed with Dora Montefiore in Hammersmith, and on 19 May took part, alongside Emily Davies, Eva McLaren, Margaret Ashton and Eva Gore Booth, in the deputation to Campbell-Bannerman. Although her name had not been formally placed in the list of speakers, she did not hesitate to address the prime minister, recalling her long involvement in the cause. Afterwards she walked in the WSPU procession, with Mrs Pankhurst, Teresa Billington, Annie Kenney and Keir Hardie, to Trafalgar Square, where she spoke to the assembled crowd.

On 30 June she attended, with Esther Roper, Christabel Pankhurst's graduation ceremony at Owen's College in Manchester. In the course of the visit she met, with Esther and Eva Gore-Booth, "the splendid women (working women all) of the newly formed Bolton Committee of the Lancashire and Cheshire WS Society". Later in the month she returned to Manchester to spend a day in the reference library before meeting Esther Roper and Sarah Reddish to hear from them of the deputation of textile workers to Lloyd George. She then met Mrs Pankhurst and addressed, as she explained to Harriet McIlquham in a letter dated 31 July, "some of the most cultured women of the Manchester District . . . who had hitherto been 'shocked' by the 'insurgent' policy. They know better now." She was hoping to spread the gospel of insurgency further than Manchester, using her world-wide correspondence to bring the policy to the notice of the INTERNATIONAL WOMAN SUFFRAGE ALLIANCE and the American Women's Suffrage Association.

Elizabeth Wolstenholme Elmy was in London for the opening of parliament and attendant demonstrations on 23 October 1906. Accompanied by Frank, she stayed for eight days with Amelia and Mary Kern, 199 Albany St., Regent's Park. The Misses Kern later advertised in 1908 issues of *Votes for Women*, "a bed-sitting room; terms very moderate". Amelia Kern was to be imprisoned in February 1908, after taking part in the disturbances surrounding the Women's Parliament at Caxton Hall. Mrs Elmy and Frank were met at Euston by Dora Montefiore and went with her to see W.T. Stead at the *Review of Reviews* office. They then went to Clement's Inn where, as she wrote to Harriet McIlquham on 3 November, "we met a host of friends and helped in settling the arrangements for Saturday's Conference and meetings. Saturday was a crowded and most important day. The morning and afternoon were spent in absorbing the Constitution and Rules of the WSPU of which as finally approved, I enclose a copy. I believe I spoke some 6 times, but only for a minute or so each time – to make some slight practical suggestions, which were in each case accepted – 64 delegates from branches were present and Mrs Pankhurst made an ideal chairman, practical, clear, business-like, firm yet gentle all through." The next day she went to Hackney with Mrs Montefiore, who was to chair a WSPU meeting in Victoria Park. Among the other speakers were Annie Kenney, Teresa Billington (*see* Teresa BILLINGTON-GREIG), Irene Fenwick Miller, Mrs SBARBORO and Mrs BALDOCK. Elizabeth Wolstenhome Elmy, in a letter, gives an excellent description of the Caxton Hall meeting held to accompany the opening of parliament on 23 October, particularly mentioning all the "poor, dear Poplar women". She did not reiterate her disappointment at not being arrested.

Elizabeth Wolstenholme Elmy was upset not only by what she perceived as the change in Mrs Montefiore but also, back in Manchester, by the attitude of Esther Roper and Eva Gore-Booth towards the WSPU. She passed on her lifetime's experience of parliamentary procedure to the WSPU, explaining to Harriet McIlquham on 14 January 1907 [misdated 1906 on the letter] that "I have advised our friends, in case WS is not named in the King's Speech, to appeal at once from the Convention by letter to the Speaker, to be heard at the Bar on behalf of WS. This will probably force a discussion and division for the presence of Keir Hardie and the Labour Party in the House will make unanimous refusal impossible. If a hearing is granted our case can be effectively stated, if refused, stronger action will be justified". This rider was borne out by the arrests on 19 February. In the same letter she revealed that "During the past three years I have written over 300 begging letters – either for them (WSPU) or for the Women Textile Workers' Committee – but I have now told them I can write no more, and have sent them all the names and addresses of those I think likely to help, so that they may write themselves." In May 1907 Annie Kenney, now briefly back in Manchester, and Alice Milne visited Mrs Elmy to discuss the progress of the campaign and in the same month a WSPU-nominated photographer called at her home to take three photographs of her; one of the images then appeared as a WSPU postcard, captioned as a member of the National Committee of the WSPU. Her name was also included on the committee list on the WSPU's printed notepaper. On 8 June she spoke in Manchester at a WSPU reception for Elizabeth ROBINS, Mrs Pankhurst, Mrs PETHICK-LAWRENCE, Mrs DESPARD, and Annie Kenney and in July Flora DRUMMOND and Jessie KENNEY cycled over to see her from the mining district of north-west Staffordshire, where they were working at a by-election. In November she spoke at another meeting of the Manchester WSPU and sent a message of support to the new venture *Votes for Women*. During the course of 1907 the Independent Labour Party published Mrs Elmy's pamphlet, *Woman's Franchise: The Need of the Hour*, in which she describes the WSPU as being "an active offshoot of the ILP". At least 15 thousand copies of the pamphlet were printed and it went into a third edition.

Throughout 1907 Elizabeth Wolstenholme Elmy was attempting to sort out the mass of papers that she had accumulated during the previous 40 years. In April she mentioned to Harriet McIlquham that she was thinking of "utilizing some of them as a permanent record – for they are richly worth it (by arranging them in order of date, in a form available for reference), and making over the volume – when complete – to the Manchester branch of the WSPU who, I know, will prize it". Later in the year she adds, apropos the proposed volume, "In the British Museum it would be almost as useless as in the hands of a private uninterested person". By October 1907 Elizabeth Wolstenholme Elmy was supplying Sylvia Pankhurst, who had been deputed to write a history of the women's suffrage movement for *Votes for Women*, with both memories and documents. In November she sent to Sylvia her bound volume of annual reports of the Manchester National Society, adding "Kindly return *to me* as soon as you can as I should like to take some notes". In May 1908 she wrote "I used to possess the pamphlet you want but fear it has gone the way of so many hundreds of other valuable papers, been lent and lent and *finally not returned*". In July 1908 she wrote to Harriet McIlquham that "The Editor of the Westminster Review wanted me to write for the August number an article on 'The History of Women's Suffrage in England', but it was impossible – Sylvia Pankhurst has all my papers". A little later in the year she wrote, "Sylvia Pankhurst spent Saturday afternoon here, talking over the early history of the woman movement in the UK – and I was able to give her a mass of information, oral and printed, for use in her articles for 'Votes for Women'". Elizabeth Wolstenholme Elmy had, amongst all other activity, still been contributing to the *Westminster Review*. Two of the articles, in March 1904 and May 1906 had been devoted to Susan B. Anthony, the second article an obituary. In July and November 1905 she had written two articles on "The Enfranchisement of Women", and in November 1906 one on "The Case for the

HYDE PARK DEMONSTRATION, SUNDAY, JUNE 21, 1908:
MRS. PANKHURST, MRS. WOLSTENHOLME ELMY.

In Hyde Park on "Woman's Sunday", 21 June 1908, Elizabeth Wolstenholme Elmy, wearing a "Votes for Women" sash and carrying her bouquet of ferns, purple lilies, and lilies of the valley, stands with Mrs Pankhurst in front of the latter's personal banner ("Famed Far for Deeds of Daring Rectitude"), which had been donated by Emmeline Pethick-Lawrence. (Author's collection)

Immediate Enfranchisement of the Women of the United Kingdom". These had all been published under her pseudonym "Ignota". From September and October 1907, when she contributed two more articles on "The Enfranchisement of Women", she wrote under her own name. In January 1908 she published "Justice Between the Sexes", and finally, in July, "Party Politicians and Justice to Women".

In June 1908 Elizabeth Wolstenholme Elmy took a prominent part in the WSPU Hyde Park rally. Describing the experience, she wrote to Harriet McIlquham on 26 June:

> You probably know that Mrs Pankhurst and I headed the Euston Road procession – walking between the band and the great banner. We were the "North Country" procession, Lancashire lasses mainly and North London. The Bradford 600 women ought to have been with us; but their train was an hour late, so after waiting a little beyond the advertised time of arrival, 1.30pm, we started without them and they formed a procession by themselves an hour later, though how they got into the Park and found standing room I do not know. When Miss Kern [with whom she was again staying] and I went down to the Euston Road at 11 a.m. we found the side-walks filled with spectators. I carried a lovely huge bouquet of ferns, huge purple lilies and lilies of the valley.

She describes the procession, accompanied by a band and a thronging crowd, as "a thrilling hour or more". She sat with Charlotte Carmichael STOPES on one of the platforms, probably that led by Mrs Pankhurst, and wrote that "I can never forget the wonderful beauty of the spectacle, looked at from my point of vantage ... As a mere picture it was beyond expression beautiful, when one thought of all it expressed and symbolised!!! It was an hour of glorious life. The Queen's Hall Meeting was very fine. I received what people call an 'ovation'." Mary BLATHWAYT noted of the Queen's Hall meeting that "a very old lady who has worked for the Suffrage all her life, Mrs Elmey [sic][spoke]. We could not hear all she said." The WSPU subsequently published as a postcard a photograph, taken on the Hyde Park platform, of Mrs Pankhurst and Mrs Wolstenholme Elmy, the latter still holding her bouquet.

Back to real life in Manchester, Elizabeth Wolstenholme Elmy noted in July that Mary GAWTHORPE was consulting her about the continuing campaign in Lancashire and the north of England and that she had spoken at the WSPU demonstration in Manchester on 19 July. In October she went to Scotland, stayed with her friend "Lily Bell", Isabella Bream Pearce, and interviewed H.Y. Stanger, the Liberal MP whose Women's Enfranchisement Bill had been blocked at its second reading in February. She was able to report, "He seems now to realize the immense importance of our case – and to be more in earnest than he was." She stayed with her friend Mrs Hunter at Bridge of Allan and "had long talks with Lady Steele, Miss METHVEN and Miss Chrystal MACMILLAN" remarking "it is delightful to have come thus fully into touch with the younger workers in the North. Helen FRASER has begun the work." She paid another visit to Glasgow in October 1909.

Back in Manchester in the autumn of 1908 she took part in a WSPU demonstration and then went to London, where she attended a meeting in the Albert Hall. While in London she went with Mrs Rowe to the office of the WOMEN'S FREEDOM LEAGUE where she met "that charming Mrs How-MARTYN". Elizabeth Wolstenholme Elmy had strongly supported Mrs Pankhurst against what she termed, in a letter to Sylvia Pankhurst of 11 October 1907, the "Separatists". However, by the autumn of 1908 she was able to write to Harriet McIlquham that "I regard the WSPU and the WFL as only two wings of the one great army whose true leader is invisible". They then went to see W.T. Stead, "with whom we had a long talk", to the "National Union of WSS where the Sec, Margery Corbett & Mrs Rowe fraternized as daughters of Newnham College ought to do", and then to the office of the Women's Liberal Federation. Still at the heart of things, she reported to Harriet McIlquham on 9 December 1908, "I fancy Sir C. and Lady McLAREN are now playing for a Peerage, which they think themselves rich enough to deserve. I have no faith whatever in either of them, though I owe to Charles my chance of addressing C-B [Campbell-Bannerman] on the day of our WS deputation [19 May 1906]. You will remember that Lady McLaren wrote to me 2 or 3 months ago, sending me what she called a Woman's Charter and wanting me to draft for her Bills dealing with each several point. I wrote back that should I live to see women enfranchised, I should be delighted". She travelled to London again for the International Women Suffrage Alliance meeting held on 27 April in the Albert Hall, but was too ill to attend. Her intended presence was advertised as an attraction at a WSPU meeting in the same hall on 29 April, but it is not clear if she recovered sufficiently to attend. A pioneer was still honoured, even though vigour and physical militancy increasingly became the hallmark of the WSPU. In the course of the same visit to London she did appear at a WSPU meeting at the Queen's Hall, was introduced by Christabel Pankhurst, and gave a short speech.

From 1907 Elizabeth Wolstenholme Elmy had been planning to write a series of books of reminiscences. In May 1908 she wrote to Sylvia Pankhurst that "There are two books I am desperately anxious to write – one of 'Memories', the other of 'Hopes' but every day brings me so much work and unexpected work that I begin to despair. Every post brings claims for help or information – not from the WSPU, who are most lovingly considerate in the main, but from women workers all the world over . . . My writing day begins at 3 a.m. & lasts as long as I am *too tired to do more*". As an example of the work she undertook it is worth recording that she copied out for Dr Louisa Martindale, daughter of her old friend, the whole of the 1866 Contagious Diseases Act bill. She very much approved of Dr Martindale's book on venereal disease, *Under the Surface*, describing it as "most delicately written" and suggesting that it "will be of immense service to the woman's cause". In March 1909 Elizabeth Wolstenholme Elmy wrote to Mrs McIlquham that she was still working hard at her book "which I propose to call 'Some Memories of a Happy Life'. I have promised the Mss to Stead, who will look after its publication. I want to do justice to so many of the early workers – especially the men who helped me". In 1910 she gave all her letters from Josephine Butler to Helen Fraser who was, she believed, selling them for the benefit of the NUWSS and she intended to give all her letters from Lydia Becker to the WSPU for the same purpose. She was still in the process of preparing for the WSPU what she described as the "monster album", containing many letters which she thought would prove "most interesting to the younger workers who do not and cannot till they know the facts realize how much they owe to the patient toil of the early workers". In October 1909 she had been moved to remark that "The one fault I find with our WSPU friends is that so many of them seem to think that nobody worked for W[omen's] S[uffrage] till they came on the scene."

It is doubtful if, a few years earlier, she would have been prepared to give any financial support to the NUWSS, believing then that they were wasteful of money; she had presumably revised her opinion as the organization became increasingly active and better managed. However, at this time her support for the WSPU's policy was unchanged, publicly endorsing it in a letter published in *Votes for Women* in March 1910. She was expected to take part in the 18 June 1910 WSPU Procession, but with the death of Harriet McIlquham the major source of information about Mrs Elmy's daily movements comes to an end, and it is not clear if she did in fact go to London on that occasion. From now on we can only catch glimpses of her, nearing her eighties, and still active. On 13 July 1910 she wrote to Sylvia Pankhurst that "I wrote a fortnight ago to every member of the Ministry whom I personally know (and it fortunately happens that I know more members of this Ministry than of any in my life-time since Gladstone's Second Administration) urging each to do his utmost with Mr Asquith and elsewhere to secure the passage of our W.S. Bill *this session* – and I *telegraphed* the day before yesterday to 21 professed friends in the Commons urging each to do also his utmost to secure the passing into law this session of our W.S. Bill and so, tho' I have no longer strength to make journeys . . . I am still trying to help as much as I can." In early 1911 she wrote in the *New Age* that "In my opinion the militant methods have been most effective in rousing the attention of the people at large to this grave question – far more so than all our previous quiet and peaceful agitation of forty-five years". She found the strength to travel to London to take the salute, standing on a balcony of a building in St James's Street, as the 17 June 1911 Coronation Procession marched past and then to take her place on the platform of the Albert Hall that evening. The 17 November 1911 issue of *Votes for Women* carried her response to the torpedoing of the Conciliation Bill and the hope that she might be in London to take part in the demonstration in London on 21 November. She wrote that unless the manhood suffrage bill was exchanged for a "sound and wise Adult Suffrage Bill . . . it will be the duty of all justice loving men and women to resist to the death the present unwise and unjust proposal and the Ministry responsible for it". Sometime between January and April 1912 she responded to a survey on women's suffrage and militancy, published as *Women's Suffrage and Militancy*, edited by Huntly Carter, by still firmly holding the view that militant methods "have been more effective in rousing the attention of the people at large to this grave question – far more so than all our previous quiet and peaceful agitation of forty-five years". She also intimated that she was still a member of the executive of the WSPU. However, a few months later, her attitude to militancy had undergone a dramatic change. She signed, the only member or former member of the WSPU to do so, alongside Millicent Garrett Fawcett, Eleanor RATHBONE, Margaret ASHTON and Sarah LEES, a public letter of protest against militancy that appeared in *The Times* on 23 July 1912. The ground of the protest was that a renewal of militancy would jeopardize the amendments proposed for an enfranchisement bill. It would seem that Elizabeth Wolstenholme Elmy, in spite of the emotion she had invested in the WSPU in the previous years, had come to the conclusion that matters had now come to a point where only constitutional methods would bring success. As a corollary it must be presumed that at this time she resigned from the WSPU's committee, although, living in Manchester, she can hardly ever have attended meetings even in the days when they had been convened. It is very likely that she was won over by the Election Fighting Fund policy, with which the others who signed the letter were associated. It represented a political tactic that would have appealed to her; she was, however, too old to be included on committees and too poor to contribute funds, thereby excluding herself from documented history. She was definitely a vice-president of the Tax Resistance League in 1913 and in July played a token part in the NUWSS Suffrage PILGRIMAGE, leading the procession of Pilgrims into Congleton. Margaret Greg, of Lee Hall, Prestbury, Cheshire, who described the scene in a letter to her sister Mrs Hilda M. DowsoN, secretary of the Nottingham Branch of the NUWSS, obviously held Mrs Elmy in high regard, and related that "Vixen [her pony] had the great honour of conveying her home".

It does not appear that Mrs Elmy derived any financial benefit from her involvement with the WSPU. Apart from the "Grateful Fund" operated by Harriet McIlquham and Louisa Martindale, she received no income from her political activity. Indeed since 1904 she had increased the number of her visits out of Congleton and incurred travelling and lodging expenses. During 1906 she had sold some of her library in order to raise money. However, in February 1907 Frank was appointed assistant overseer and rate collector for the urban district council, with a salary of £52 per annum, bringing an improvement to the Elmys' financial position. After Harriet McIlquham's death in early 1910, Mrs Martindale arranged for the wife of George Holyoake to be her co-trustee of the fund. It is more than likely that the fund had depended to a considerable degree on Mrs McIlquham's financial generosity; by August 1910 Mrs Martindale was organizing a Testimonial Fund for Elizabeth Wolstenholme Elmy. This apparently amounted to £500 and was presented to her in December 1910.

Elizabeth Wolstenholme Elmy died on 12 March 1918 at a Manchester nursing home run by Miss C.M. Macneary, as a result of falling down stairs and injuring her head. This was six days after the royal assent was given to the Representation of the People Act; one sincerely hopes that she had been able to savour the moment. A notice of her death, inserted in the "Deaths" column of the *Manchester Guardian*, appears on the same page as the news that the Solicitors (Qualification of Women) Bill had passed through its committee stage in the House of Commons, opening to women a career for which Elizabeth Wolstenholme Elmy would have been eminently fitted. Despite her close association over the years with C.P. Scott, editor and owner of the *Manchester Guardian*, the paper gave her no obituary. Short notices did appear in the *Common Cause* on 15 March, accompanied by a photograph of her in what must have been a very characteristic position, seated at a writing table, and on 22 March, and in the *Workers' Dreadnought*, 23 March. The latter, accorded a front-page position, was presumably written by Sylvia Pankhurst and recorded the inspiration which the younger generation of women "derived from her selfless devotion to principle and keen, vigorous, and never-pausing industry in the cause. Even in her extreme old age she rose during the small hours of the morning in order that all her house work and cooking for the day might be finished before nine a.m. in order that she might devote the rest of her time to toiling for the cause of women and progress". Elizabeth Wolstenholme Elmy's lifetime's accumulation of papers including, presumably, the "monster album" and the manuscript of her reminiscences, were apparently sacrificed to a "paper drive" during the First World War and her library was dispersed. Apart from an interesting sketch of her life given by Sylvia Pankhurst in *The Suffragette Movement*, 1931, it is only in the past ten years that Elizabeth Wolstenholme Elmy has been written back into the history of the women's movement. Even Richard Pankhurst, in *Sylvia Pankhurst Artist and Crusader*, 1979, identified "Ignota" incorrectly as Sylvia Pankhurst.

Elizabeth Wolstenholme Elmy was the author of: "The Education of Girls: Its Present and Its Future", in J. Butler (ed.), *Woman's Work and Woman's Culture*, 1869, reprinted in D. Spender, Education Papers; *The Enfranchisement of Women*, 1892; and *A Woman's Plea to Woman. A Paper reprinted from the Macclesfield Courier*, 1886. Her pamphlets include *Woman's Franchise: The Need of the Hour*, ILP, no date.

Address: (1865) The Grange, Boothstown, Manchester; (1871) Moody Hall, Congleton, Cheshire; (1883) The Low, Congleton; (1896) Buxton House, Buglawton, Congleton, Cheshire; (1918) 231 Upper Brook Street, Manchester.
Photograph: in the Suffragette Fellowhip Collection, Museum of London, one of several photographs taken of her by Taylor of Glasgow in May 1907, showing that she is wearing a "Votes for Women" button badge.
Archival source: Papers of Elizabeth Wolstenholme Elmy, Manuscripts Department, British Library; A Collection of Pamphlets and Leaflets Relating to the Guardianship of Infants for the most part written or published by E.C.W. Elmy, 1883–1886, British Library; Women's Emancipation

Union Papers, British Library and John Johnson Collection, Bodleian Library, Oxford; Correspondence between Ursula Bright and Emmeline Pankhurst in the Papers of Sylvia Pankhurst, Internationaal Instituut voor Sociale Geschiedenis, Amsterdam; Josephine Butler Collection, Fawcett Library.

Bibliography: D. Beale (ed.), *Reports Issued by the Schools' Inquiry Commission, on the Education of Girls*, no date, *c.* 1870; E. Ethelmer, "A woman emancipator: a biographical sketch", *Westminster Review*, 1896; S. Jeffreys, *The Spinster and Her Enemies: Feminism and Sexuality 1880–1930*, 1985; S.K. Kent, *Sex and Suffrage in Britain, 1860–1914*, 1987; M.L. Shanley, *Feminism, Marriage, and the Law in Victorian England, 1850–1895*, 1989; L. Bland, *Banishing the Beast: English Feminism and Sexual Morality 1885–1914*, 1995; S.S. Holton, *Suffrage Days*, 1997.

ENFIELD (branch of LONDON SOCIETY FOR WOMEN'S SUFFRAGE, NUWSS)   Secretary (1913) Mrs Nicholson, Copthorne, Village Road, Enfield, Middlesex. The society's BANNER is now in the Museum of London.

ENFRANCHISEMENT OF WOMEN COMMITTEE

Formally founded by the personnel of the LONDON PROVISIONAL PETITION COMMITTEE at a meeting held in London on 23 November 1866, although its accounting period begins in October 1866. The hesitancy involved in its creation is echoed in the uncertainty about the name by which the society, if indeed it was to be a society, was to be called. Only a month before, on 22 October, Clementia TAYLOR, one of its begetters, was referring to it as "The Extension of the Suffrage to Women Society", a descriptive if not a beguiling title. Further, Emily DAVIES informed Lydia BECKER in a letter dated 6 April 1867 that the committee had decided in late February to use the society's full title on its headed notepaper, in order that there might not be any mistake as to its exact aim. This, as now printed, gave the title "Enfranchisement of Unmarried Women and Widows, Possessing the Due Property Qualification", an honest description, if not pithy. Doubtless there had been much discussion to arrive at this exactitude.

The committee had "for its object the abolition of the legal disability which at present disqualifies women as such from voting for Members of Parliament". The committee hoped to achieve this aim by presenting further petitions to parliament in order to demonstrate the earnestness of women in this matter. The members of the committee were Dean Alford, Jessie BOUCHERETT, Prof. Cairnes, the Rev. W.L. Clay, Emily Davies, Lady GOLDSMID, George W. Hastings, James Heywood, Mrs Knox (Isa CRAIG), Miss Manning and, as treasurer, Clementia Taylor. Louisa SMITH was, until her untimely death, honorary secretary. Harriet COOK was to be assistant secretary for six months from 1 January 1867 at a salary at the rate of £60 a year. The society attracted, in its short existence, 88 members, most of whom, drawn from the radical section of the middle class, had been signatories to the May 1866 petition.

The work of the committee appears not to have proceeded smoothly, although the evidence is somewhat biased. The main source of information is the correspondence of Helen TAYLOR and although she was not a member of the society, she was not a disinterested observer. She had objected, in letters written to Barbara BODICHON and Mentia Taylor between 21 and 29 October 1866, to the inclusion of men on the committee. J.S. MILL had agreed with her that it would be educationally useful to have an exclusively female woman's movement. Clementia Taylor and Barbara Bodichon disagreed, the latter citing her experience of meeting in America the leaders of the women's movement, who had "frightened" her; she said she came home of the opinion that the women there had wasted their energy by trying to do too much at once, by not working with men and by being too sentimental. She thought that having a woman as secretary and a woman as treasurer gave a sufficiently decided female character to the committee. Mentia Taylor wrote to Helen Taylor on 29 October:

I read, which I had forgotten – your objection to a mixed committee of men and women. Now my experience bears testimony to the practical benefit resulting from the combined efforts of men and women – we gain advantage from the more logical and from the more practical qualities of men – and men gain from women more earnestness of purpose – more subtle views of questions – I believe so strongly in the reciprocal benefit of both I would from the earliest age have boys and girls educated together – associated together in all the higher purposes of life and believe that morally as well as mentally the world would gain much – but to our committee I deeply grieve that we are not at one upon this question, it was not without due thought and consideration that we determined upon the mixed working committee... I have been on committees formed of women only and upon more – men and women together – the latter certainly acted more effectively and I believe that the committees of men only would be less effective than if women were associated with them...

Helen Taylor was unable to contemplate remaining a member of the committee if men were included among its members. In November she wrote to Mentia Taylor that she did not intend to subscribe, wishing to retain an independent voice. She had handed over all responsibility for the petitions to the committee. After Louisa Smith's death in February 1867, Emily Davies acted as temporary secretary, while Barbara Bodichon was abroad, it still being thought advisable for the society to be fronted by a married woman. Miss Hensleigh Wedgwood was added to the committee. As early as 4 March Mentia Taylor wrote to Helen Taylor that after the presentation of the petitions "there should be a large meeting of the earnest friends of the cause to decide upon future work, organisation etc *and* form a new committee – have a paid Secretary – officials – such a Committee as *you* will be induced to join – and in which I shall not feel myself as a Pariah". Helen Blackburn's scrapbook contains a copy of the draft, dated 23 November 1866, of the petition to enfranchise women householders, which could be signed by unmarried women and widows, of full age, holding the legal qualification for voting in either counties or boroughs. The presentation of this petition on 8 April did not, however, engender the atmosphere of euphoria that had accompanied the one laid before parliament by J.S. Mill in June 1866. Comparison was drawn between the work of the London Enfranchisement of Women Committee and of that in Manchester. Jessie Boucherett wrote to Helen Taylor on 9 April, "Now however I perceive that Miss Davies knows so little of what is going on, that there cannot be much communication between you, perhaps there is none at all". Certainly there are no letters in Helen Taylor's surviving correspondence from Emily Davies on suffrage matters between 15 December 1866 and 24 June 1867. An indication of the confusion that resulted from this lack of co-operation can be gleaned from Mill's correspondence. On 24 May 1867 Mill revealed in a letter to Herbert Spencer that Helen Taylor planned that Trubner should reprint a series of papers on the representation of women. Included in this series was to be a reprint of the speech Mill had given in the House of Commons four days before, on 20 May. By 1 June Mill had been informed by Trubner that the "Society for the Extension of Suffrage to Women" had, without his knowledge, ordered this speech to be reprinted. Jessie Boucherett's 9 April letter to Helen Taylor continued:

Our affairs have been very ill managed. I wrote to the Committee begging them to make arrangements to have all the Petitions presented on the same day. They replied however through Miss Davies that they did not think there would be any advantage in so doing, which is to say the least was extremely stupid on their part.

The consequence is that our chief petition has been wasted, for though I hear it has been presented it must have been done in such a way as to attract no attention, as Mrs Taylor is the only person I know of who saw the account of its presentation, and I now take four newspapers and have read the petitions every day for a fortnight in all of them.... it seems to me that we want a head Committee, a central Committee rather, composed partly of persons appointed by the regular Committees and partly of independent persons, such as yourself, to regulate when the petitions should be presented. I am of course supposing we do not win this year. Most certainly some reform is needed if we are to go on another year. The London Committee is I believe too jealous of the other Committees to co-operate with them.

There may be some reasonable explanation of the failure of our petition but I am inclined to think it is all the Committee's fault in not arranging to have as many petitions presented at once as could be got together.

How well the Manchester petition has been managed. It is wonderful that Miss BECKER should have got so many signatures in so short a time.

The Edinburgh Petition is numerously signed also... There is room enough in England for a dozen or rather 100 franchise Committees for women.

Why should you not set one up on yr own principles?

The present committee whether reformed or not will never do things on a sufficiently large scale to please me. I thought all along that yr plan of a large general Committee of a hundred members was much the best, but as you live so much abroad I feared you would not be able to manage it, and I thought Miss Davies being on the spot would be able to do better than you could at a distance.

I believe I was mistaken, but at any rate, two Committees would do more work than one. The present Committee might be called the North London and the new one the South London Committee or the Westminster Committee.

At the moment we are wasting power and influence. There are numbers of distinguished people who would join a general Committee of a hundred and so give us the moral support of their names, whose influence we are now making very little use of. The small size of the present Committee composed as it almost entirely is of undistinguished people (no one but the Dean of Canterbury being at all remarkable) prevents it from having any weight, and consequently in order to get signatures it is necessary to send round the names of persons who have already signed for the sake of their moral influence. There would be no necessity for so doing if we had the names of a hundred persons of good position, on the list of the Committee . . .

If I cannot get the Committee reformed I shall leave it, and I doubt Mrs Taylor and I having sufficient power to get it reformed, with Mrs Bodichon's assistance we could, but it is not certain she will take our view, nor is it certain she will be well enough to attend to business as she is most seriously ill; I'm not sure whether I shall be well enough to go to town at all.

I would therefore beg you to consider whether (if we do not win in Parliament this year) you would not do well to organize a second committee. The MPs who vote for us would be a capital foundation for the general Committee and there is no reason the General Comm should only [be] 100.

If by good fortune the government was beat and there was a delay of a year before the Reform Bill is passed, I feel sure we should succeed then, if there was a numerous and influential Women's Franchise Committee to work during the interval.

I'm afraid however there is no chance of that and that the government bill is sure to be carried.

Helen Taylor obviously replied that she was unable to form another Committee and Jessie Boucherett wrote to her on 12 May "We must trust to the forlorn hope of Mrs P.A. Taylor being able to reform the present Committee."

On 7 June 1867 Jessie Boucherett wrote to Helen Taylor:

I suspect (but don't know) that Mrs P. Taylor's feeling with regard to joining the Manchester Central Committee is like mine. I feel that London ought to be a centre, though I don't at all object to Manchester's being one too, and it would suit me far better to belong to the London Central Committee than to the Manchester one . . . What I should like would be to have three central Committees, London, Manchester & Edinburgh, & perhaps ultimately one at Dublin. There is no harm, but good in a little emulation between the various Committees. I should like to have on the London Centre yourself, Mrs P. Taylor, Miss Cobbe, myself and half a dozen or a dozen more, active zealous persons. . . . I dare say all this will prove impracticable, and in that case I should probably wish to join the Manchester Centre, or rather Mrs P. Taylor's local London Committee . . .

Between 7 and 18 June the idea of forming a new London Society to work in conjunction with Manchester had taken shape. Emily Davies wrote, with a measure of abruptness, to Helen Taylor on 24 June:

You may probably have heard that the Committee formed last autumn for the enfranchisement of women, has been dissolved. At the last meeting of the Committee it was agreed to place the "property", consisting chiefly of pamphlets and stationery, at Mrs Bodichon's disposal. I intend transferring to her also, as soon as she is able to receive them, the letters and other papers which are at present in my hands, and as I shall no longer be in any official sense a depository of documents on this subject, I ask you to discontinue the magazines which I have hitherto received from you according to the agreement of last year.

Emily Davies, with Barbara Bodichon, wished to take a gradualist approach to enfranchisement, whereas Helen Taylor, Jessie Boucherett and Mentia Taylor (who since the previous August had obviously changed her mind) were convinced that suitably qualified married women should not be excluded. The petition presented by the Manchester Enfranchisement of Women Committee (*see* MANCHESTER NATIONAL SOCIETY) in 1867 did not exclude married women. The final accounts (October 1866–July 1867) for the Enfranchisement of Women Committee were drawn up. They read: "Income: (from subscriptions) £225 9/6; Receipts (for pamphlets) £6/11. Expenditure: Postage and stationery £101/19/9; Printing and Pamphlets £94/4/6; Newspapers £7 2/11; Advertisements £5 6/6; Salary of assistant secretary £25; Petty expenses £4; 150 balance sheets 10/6." The committee was formally dissolved on 17 July 1867 and relaunched as the LONDON NATIONAL SOCIETY FOR WOMEN'S SUFFRAGE.

Secretary (October 1866–February 1867) Louisa Smith; (February 1867–July 1867) Barbara Bodichon, for public purposes, with the work done by Emily Davies. Address of the society (October 1866) Aubrey House, Campden Hill, Kensington, London W (Clementia Taylor's home); (February 1867) 5 Blandford Square, London NW (Barbara Bodichon's home).

Archival source: Mill–Taylor Correspondence, London School of Economics and Political Science; Helen Blackburn Collection, Girton College Archive.

Bibliography: H. Blackburn, *Women's Suffrage: A Record of the Women's Suffrage Movement in the British Isles*, 1902; F.E. Mineka and D.N. Lindley, *The Later Letters of John Stuart Mill, 1849–1873*, 1972.

EPSOM AND DISTRICT (branch of the LONDON SOCIETY FOR WOMEN'S SUFFRAGE, NUWSS) Secretary (1913) Mrs Garrido, Ewell, Surrey.

EQUAL POLITICAL RIGHTS CAMPAIGN COMMITTEE Founded in 1926 to unite all feminist organizations, under the chairmanship of Lady RHONDDA, in a campaign to reduce the voting age for women to 21. The campaign was satisfactorily concluded by the passing of the Representation of the People (Equal Franchise) Act in 1928.

ESHER AND EAST MOLESEY (branch of the LONDON SOCIETY FOR WOMEN'S SUFFRAGE, NUWSS) Secretary (1913) Miss Mildred Martineau, Littleworth, Esher, Surrey.

ESSEX (N. AND E.) (NUWSS) In 1913 the society was a member of the EASTERN COUNTIES FEDERATION OF THE NATIONAL UNION OF WOMEN'S SUFFRAGE SOCIETIES. Secretary (1909, 1913) Miss S.R. COURTAULD, Colne Engaine, Earl's Colne, Essex.

ESTLIN, MARY ANNE (*c.* 1820–1902) Unitarian, daughter of Dr John Bishop Estlin, a pioneering ophthalmologist and abolitionist. From 1851 she was the leader of the Bristol and Clifton Ladies' Anti-Slavery Society and an important activist, associated with Eliza WIGHAM in the national abolitionist campaign. In 1863 she was a member of the executive committee of the Ladies' London Emancipation Society, the first national female anti-slavery society, formed by Clementia TAYLOR. Mary Estlin was a committee member of the BRISTOL AND WEST OF ENGLAND branch of the Women's Suffrage Society when it was founded in 1868 and in 1870 was its treasurer. In 1868 she visited America and met such like-minded women as Lucretia Mott, Elizabeth Cady Stanton, and Susan B. Anthony. She was involved in a transatlantic correspondence with Maria Weston Chapman, the editor of the *Life of Harriet Martineau*. By 1870 Mary Estlin was also a member, together with, for instance, Margaret TANNER, Margaret Bright LUCAS and Priscilla Bright MCLAREN, of the executive committee of the Ladies' National Association for the Repeal of the Contagious Diseases Acts. She was in correspondence with Elizabeth Wolstenholme ELMY by 1869 and in 1870 they were both present, together with Anna Maria PRIESTMAN, at the 1870 Social Science Congress in Newcastle. In 1871 the Priestman sisters were living in Bristol at the same address as Mary Estlin. They were all active in the mid-1870s in forming in Bristol the National Union of Women Workers. After the split in the CENTRAL COMMITTEE OF THE NATIONAL SOCIETY FOR WOMEN'S SUFFRAGE in 1888 Mary Estlin became a member of the CENTRAL NATIONAL SOCIETY. In 1890 she was joint secretary, with Anna Maria Priestman, of the Bristol Women's Liberal Association; in 1898 she was the Association's treasurer. In her will she left provision for rooms in her houses (she also owned 37 Upper Belgrave Road) to be put at the disposal of "Lady Teachers in need of rest", with the proviso that "the hours of meals to be adhered to and the house locked up at 10.30 p.m."

Address: (1871) 37 Durdham Park Road, Redland, Bristol; (1902) 36 Upper Belgrave Road, Clifton, Bristol.
Photograph: carte de visite in Josephine Butler Collection, Fawcett Library.

EVANS, DOROTHY ELIZABETH (1889–1944) Born in London, the daughter of a successful "London Welsh" builder, educated at the North London Collegiate School, trained as a gymnastic teacher at Chelsea Physical Training College and, while there, in July 1907 joined the WOMEN'S SOCIAL AND POLITICAL UNION. In October 1909, while employed as a physical culture mistress at the Batley Girls' School in Yorkshire, she was arrested after protesting at a meeting being held by Walter Runciman. As *Votes for Women*, 29 October 1909, reported "she risked her professional position for the sake of the cause she believes in so wholeheartedly". She was sentenced to a fine or ten days' imprisonment. Against her will, her fine was paid by her father. By early 1910 she had resigned as a teacher and was WSPU ORGANIZER of the Birmingham and Midlands branch, succeeding Gladice KEEVIL. Bertha RYLAND, one of her fellow organizers in Birmingham at this time, paid tribute to her in the memorial published by the Six Point Group after her death. In 1910 Dorothy Evans served seven days in Winson Green Prison for failing to pay a dog tax. She took part in London in the "Black Friday" demonstration in November 1910 and in 1911 was arrested for holding a prohibited meeting in the Bull Ring in Birmingham; on both occasions she was not charged. She took part in the window-smashing campaign in the West End of London and was sentenced to four months' imprisonment. She spent her prison term, March to July 1912, in the Feeble-Minded Inebriate block at Aylesbury prison. During this time she took part in two hunger strikes and endured two periods of forcible feeding.

In 1913, after the raid on the WSPU headquarters and the arrest of the leaders, Dorothy Evans was actively concerned in organizing the continuing campaign. She was wanted in connection with the distribution of the "Raided" number of the *Suffragette*. The type was broken up by the police just as the issue was going to press and the original copy was confiscated. Gerald Gould (*see* Barbara Ayton GOULD), Dorothy Evans, Grace ROE and Cicely HALE, working from Maud JOACHIM's flat, were mainly responsible for putting together the complete issue in a few hours and distributing it directly to retailers all over the country. Dorothy Evans recorded that on a visit to Paris to confer with Christabel PANKHURST, she heard that an innocent Mrs Dorothy Evans had been arrested in mistake for her. Rather than returning and giving herself up, she donned disguise and spent six months travelling around Britain, leaving, as Monica WHATELY in her memoir delicately puts it, "evidence for the public to read of the determination of the women to be governed with their consent or not at all". One can only assume that the "evidence" was that effected by arson. She was then sent to organize for the WSPU first in Bristol and then in northern Ireland. In March 1913 she led a deputation of women from northern Ireland to see Sir Edward Carson, leader of the Ulster Volunteers. In April 1913, after an attempt had been made to burn Lisburne Castle, Dorothy Evans was charged with "conspiracy". Her case was adjourned, she was not given bail, she went on hunger-and-thirst strike and was released after six days. She was again arrested in 1913, the case was again delayed, and while on remand she went on hunger-and-thirst strike, and was sent to prison in Tullamore in southern Ireland. A second conspiracy charge had meanwhile been preferred against her and Muriel Muir (Florence Macfarlane) and in 1914 she was arrested, again kept in custody, went on hunger-and-thirst strike and was released. She was again arrested in 1914 and was still in prison when war broke out. Irish political prisoners were not released under the suffragette amnesty and she had to endure a further hunger-and-thirst strike in order to be set free. The cases against her proceeded, but she was not sentenced.

Despite her "record", Dorothy Evans did obtain a position as gymnastics and mathematics mistress at Shrewsbury County School, but left it in order to campaign as a pacifist. In 1915 she was one of the women who waited at Dover, hoping to be able to travel to the International Women's Congress at the Hague. She had been associated with Anstey College of Physical Education from January to July 1915. In 1916 she was a member of the INDEPENDENT WSPU and in 1917 she organized a holiday campaign in the north-east for the WOMEN'S FREEDOM LEAGUE. At the end of the war she went to America on a Peace Campaign and in 1921 was the secretary of the Women's League for Peace and Freedom. She was now a committed socialist, a member of the Standing Joint Committee on Industrial Women's Organizations. For many years she was chairman of the Six Point Group, founded by Lady RHONDDA in 1918.

Dorothy Evans was sufficiently unconventional and strong-minded to put into action her conviction that women should have the freedom to have a child out of wedlock if they were able and prepared to care for it. She did have a partner, Emil Davies, a LCC councillor, and according to Monica Whately "saved up for three years to have her baby". She and Davies had also co-operated in the writing of *Land Nationalisation, the Key to Social Reform*, published by Leonard Parsons in 1921. Her daughter Lyndal, named for Olive Schreiner's heroine in *Story of an African Farm*, was at the time of her mother's death a member of the executive committee of the Six Point Group. In her will Dorothy Evans left to Monica Whately "the coat which she embroidered for me" and to Lilian Metge (of 79 Pembroke Road, Dublin), an erstwhile Irish suffragette, a gold watch that she had been given in 1915 as a presentation by a few Belfast suffragette friends.

Address: (1915) Clyde Villa, Brook Street, Shrewsbury, Shropshire; (1943) Redcap, Greenstreet Green, Farnborough, Kent.
Photograph: in M. Whately, *Dorothy Evans and the Six Point Group*, 1945.
Archival source: Suffragette Fellowship Collection; Museum of London; B. Harrison, taped interview with Lyndal Evans, 1975, Fawcett Library.
Bibliography: M. Whately, *Dorothy Evans and the Six Point Group*, 1945; I.M. Webb, *History of Chelsea College of Physical Education*, 1998.

EXETER (NUWSS) In 1913 the society was a member of the SOUTH-WESTERN FEDERATION OF THE NATIONAL UNION OF WOMEN'S SUFFRAGE SOCIETIES. Secretary (1909, 1910) Miss Jessie Montgomery, 10 Baring Crescent, Exeter, Devon; (1913) Mrs Fletcher, 48 Polsloe Road, Exeter, Devon.

EXETER (WSPU) Secretary (1913) Mrs Montague, Penton, Crediton, Devon.

EXMOUTH (NUWSS) In 1913 the society was a member of the SOUTH-WESTERN FEDERATION OF THE NATIONAL UNION OF WOMEN'S SUFFRAGE SOCIETIES. Secretary (1913) Miss Joan Retallack, Chypraze, Exmouth, Devon.

F

FABIAN WOMEN'S GROUP Founded in 1908; the "Provisional Committee of the Fabian Women's Group Suffrage Section" met for the first time on 19 October 1911. Mabel ATKINSON was appointed chairman, Elspeth Carr, treasurer, and Miss Berry, secretary. The Suffrage Section was established in order to lobby Labour MPs, asking them to support the Conciliation Bill as the only practical means of obtaining for women full practical rights and of securing, in the future, adult and not merely manhood suffrage. The Committee invited co-operation and subscriptions from men members of the Fabian Society and remained neutral on the subject of militant tactics. Members of the Suffrage Section intended to concentrate on the constituencies of Deptford and Greenwich, but the intention was to employ a paid ORGANIZER for those in Wales, the Midlands and Yorkshire. H.N. BRAILSFORD recommended Annot ROBINSON as a potential organizer (her quoted fee was £2 2s a week plus expenses). Mabel Atkinson and Elspeth Carr undertook to arrange work in Newcastle and West Durham. By February 1913 the Section was deploring what it considered the anti-suffrage conspiracy that resulted in the withdrawal of the Franchise Bill and calling on the Labour party to put pressure on the government by opposing any extension or alteration of the franchise that did not include women.

In May 1913 the Section joined the WOMEN'S SOCIAL AND POLITICAL UNION in a demonstration in Victoria Park in Hackney. The last meeting of the Section before the war was held in March 1914; it was decided that in view of the political situation it was not possible for the Section to take any particular action and to wait and see what happened. It was agreed at a meeting in January 1917 that the Section should affiliate to the National Council for Adult Suffrage and disband its own work.

Archival source: Fabian Society Archive, London School of Economics and Political Science.

FAHEY, [CHARLOTTE EMILY] CAPRINA, MRS (c. 1883–still alive 1933) (later Mrs Knight) Daughter of Alfred Gilbert, RA, the sculptor of the statue of Eros in Piccadilly Circus, of the memorial in Westminster Abbey to Henry Fawcett (see Millicent Garrett FAWCETT), and, incidentally, of the statue of John Howard in the Market Place in Bedford at the base of which Dora MASON and other members of the BEDFORD SOCIETY FOR WOMEN'S SUFFRAGE were attacked by a mob while holding a meeting in June 1913. Caprina Gilbert married Alfred Edward Fahey, a painter, in 1901 and in 1905 had a son. Her husband died in 1907. She was a trained masseuse ("Attendance at Ladies' own Homes, from 5s per Visit") and joined the WOMEN'S SOCIAL AND POLITICAL UNION at the Hyde Park Demonstration in June 1908. In 1908 she shared an address with Vera WENTWORTH. They lived in the house of Robert Wyatt and on 12 November 1908 a drawing-room meeting for the WSPU was held there "at Mrs Wyatt's kind invitation". Mrs Wyatt in 1911 was the honorary WSPU organizer for Hendon and Golders Green. Caprina Fahey took part in the deputation from the Women's Parliament in Caxton Hall to the Houses of Parliament on 24 February 1909 and was arrested and received one month's imprisonment. In September she was in correspondence with Helen WATTS with whom she had been in Holloway.

For the January 1910 general election Caprina Fahey was the WSPU organizer for the Middlesex (Harrow) Parliamentary Division. In November 1910 she was sentenced to two weeks' imprisonment for stone throwing following the "Black Friday" demonstration. In June 1913 she was one of the "group captains" at the funeral of Emily Wilding DAVISON. Sir Alfred Gilbert made no mention of his daughter, or her son, in his will.

Address: (1908) Derby House, Parson Street, Hendon; (1911) working as a masseuse from 18 New Street, Dorset Square, London NW.

FAITHFULL, EMILY (1835–95) The youngest daughter of the rector of Headley, Surrey, she attended a Kensington boarding school and was presented at court. She was one of the founding members in 1859, with Jessie BOUCHERETT, Barbara BODICHON and Bessie Rayner PARKES, of the Society for Promoting the Employment of Women, of which she became secretary. By 1859/60 she was a member, with Bessie Rayner Parkes, Isa CRAIG and Jessie Boucherett, of the committee of the National Association for the Promotion of Social Science. In 1860, having been taught the rudiments of typesetting by Austin Holyoake, brother of George HOLYOAKE, Emily Faithfull set up a printing office, the Victoria Press, in which all the compositors were women. In 1863 she founded the *Victoria Magazine*, of which she was editor, although Emily DAVIES held the post for a short time in 1864. This may have been during a period when Emily Faithfull was involved, tangentially and damagingly, in a divorce case. The *Victoria Magazine* published the annual reports of SPEW and the Victoria Press printed the papers and tracts of the Ladies' London Emancipation Society. Emily Faithfull was not, however, a member of the KENSINGTON SOCIETY and did not sign the 1866 suffrage petition. It may well be that her involvement in the divorce case made her unacceptable to suffragists concerned that no taint of the unconventional should jeopardize their cause. In an interview she gave to the *Women's Penny Paper*, 2 August 1890, she remarked that she was the first to give a lecture on subjects of interest to "the woman's movement" and that "no one interested in the woman's movement had ventured on giving a public address until after I had broken the ice by a lecture in the Hanover Square Rooms, in 1868 the subject was 'The Claim of Women'". On the subject of women's suffrage she said "I am strongly in favour of it, but I do not give it the enormous prominence some do. I do not believe it is the end and aim of all things. In politics I am a Conservative... I am not in favour of Socialists or Revolutionists, nor do I wish to see the Empire dismembered". These were very suitable sentiments from one who had been Printer and Publisher in Ordinary to Her Majesty.

Although not active in the suffrage movement, Emily Faithfull was involved alongside suffragists in other concerns. She was, in 1875, a member of the Women's Trade Union League founded by Emma PATERSON, acted as treasurer to a girls' club in Lamb's Conduit Street in Bloomsbury and, after moving to Manchester, conducted the Manchester branch of Mrs Blanchard's Colonial Emigration Society. She wrote for many years for the *Lady's Pictorial*, both under her own name and as "The Lancashire Witch". Rutland Barrington, who was later to sing in a Gilbert and Sullivan production with Vera HOLME, and Mr Faithfull Begg, the Conservative MP, who in 1897 introduced a suffrage bill and who, from 1899 to 1900 was parliamentary adviser to the NATIONAL UNION OF WOMEN'S SUFFRAGE SOCIETIES, were both nephews. In her will Emily Faithfull singled the latter out as her favourite nephew and left him "any political volumes likely to be acceptable". In an interview given to the *Woman's Signal*, 1 March 1894, she gave a description of her life in Manchester with Charlotte Robinson, "Home Art Decorator to Her Majesty", with whom she had then lived for ten years. In her will she described Charlotte Robinson as her "beloved friend" and drew attention to her "affectionate tenderness and care which made the last few years of my life the happiest I ever spent".
Address: (1872) 50 Norfolk Square, Hyde Park, London W; (1895) 10 Plymouth Grove, Manchester.
Photograph: Fawcett Library Collection.

FAKENHAM (NUWSS) In 1913 the society was a member of the EASTERN COUNTIES FEDERATION OF THE NATIONAL UNION OF WOMEN'S SUFFRAGE SOCIETIES. Secretary (1913) Mrs King, Market Square, Fakenham, Norfolk.

FALKIRK (NUWSS) In 1913 the society was a member of the SCOTTISH FEDERATION OF THE NATIONAL UNION OF WOMEN'S SUFFRAGE SOCIETIES. Secretary (1913) Mrs Robb, Laurieston Manse, Falkirk, Stirlingshire.

FALMOUTH committee of the NATIONAL SOCIETY FOR WOMEN'S SUFFRAGE Formed in 1871 when its secretary was Mrs Howard Fox. In 1913 the society was a member of the SOUTH-WESTERN FEDERATION OF THE NATIONAL UNION OF WOMEN'S SUFFRAGE SOCIETIES. Secretary (1913) Miss Naomi Bassett Fox, Grove Hill, Falmouth, Cornwall.

FALMOUTH AND DISTRICT (WSPU) Secretary (1913) Mrs Pascoe, 37 Marlborough Road, Falmouth, Cornwall.

FARMERS DISTRICT (NUWSS) In 1913 the society was a member of the SOUTH WALES AND MONMOUTH FEDERATION OF THE NATIONAL UNION OF WOMEN'S SUFFRAGE SOCIETIES. Secretary (1913) Miss Bessie Williams, Bedwellty, Farmers, Llanwrda, Carmarthen, Carmarthenshire.

FARNHAM AND DISTRICT (NUWSS) In 1913 the society was a member of the SURREY, SUSSEX, AND HANTS FEDERATION OF THE NATIONAL UNION OF WOMEN'S SUFFRAGE SOCIETIES. Secretary (1909, 1913) Miss Milton, Fernlea, Lower Bourne, Farnham, Surrey.

FARNWORTH (NUWSS) In 1913 the society was a member of the MANCHESTER AND DISTRICT FEDERATION OF THE NATIONAL UNION OF WOMEN'S SUFFRAGE SOCIETIES. Secretary (1913) *pro tem* Mrs Harold Barnes, 40 Bolton Road, Moses Gate, Farnworth, Lancashire.

FAWCETT, MILLICENT GARRETT, MRS (1847–1929) DBE, 1925   Born at Aldeburgh, one of the younger daughters of Newson and Louisa Garrett, sister of Agnes GARRETT and Elizabeth Garrett ANDERSON, educated, like her sisters, at Miss Browning's school at Blackheath. She left school at the age of 15 and thereafter educated herself at home. The younger generation of Garretts were firm supporters of the Liberal party, although their father had favoured the Conservatives before family pressure resulted in his conversion to liberalism. The Garrett family was fiercely interested in the political questions of the day and in July 1865 Millicent and Agnes, paying a visit in London to their married sister Louisa SMITH, were taken to hear John Stuart MILL address one of his few election meetings. Millicent Fawcett later wrote "This meeting kindled tenfold my enthusiasm for women's suffrage". Two months earlier, in April, on the day in which news of the assassination of Abraham Lincoln reached England (probably 27 April), she met at one of Clementia TAYLOR's Aubrey House parties, Henry Fawcett, who, despite his blindness, was professor of political economy at Cambridge and the Radical Liberal MP for Brighton. He had, as it were, an "eye" for strong women of independent mind, having unsuccessfully proposed in the past to, among others, Bessie Rayner PARKES and Millicent's own sister Elizabeth. Two years after their meeting in the radical salon, on 23 April 1867 Millicent Garrett married Henry Fawcett. A year later their only child, Philippa (d. 1948) was born. In the same month as she gave birth Millicent Fawcett's first published article, "The education of women of the middle and upper classes", appeared in *Macmillan's Magazine*. She gave her fee, £7, to John Stuart Mill's ill-fated re-election campaign fund. She was herself one of the principal founders and supporters of Newnham College, at which her daughter was later to achieve a very significant success.

Apparently considered too young to sign the petition in favour of women's suffrage that John Stuart Mill presented to parliament in 1866, Millicent Fawcett, now a married woman, was present in the Ladies' Gallery on 20 May 1867 during the debate on Mill's amendment to the Representation of the People Bill. Two months later, in July 1867, Millicent Fawcett joined the first executive committee of the newly founded LONDON NATIONAL SOCIETY FOR WOMEN'S SUFFRAGE, attending its first meeting at Aubrey House. On 17 July 1869 she was one of the speakers at the first public meeting of the London National Society and then at the second, on 26 March 1870, in the Hanover Rooms. In the same month she gave a lecture on women's suffrage to her husband's Liberal association in Brighton, and in 1871 undertook a speaking tour organized in the west country by Lilias Ashworth (*see* Lilias Ashworth HALLETT). The lecture, "Electoral Disabilities of Women", that she delivered in the course of this tour on 11 March 1871 at the New Hall, Tavistock, was published for the London National Society by Trubner, and is reprinted in J. Lewis, *Before the Vote was Won*, 1987. Millicent Fawcett quickly acquired the assured and formidable platform manner that stood her in good stead for the next 60 years.

Millicent Fawcett supported in principle the campaign to repeal the Contagious Diseases Acts, although she was clear that it should be kept quite separate from the suffrage movement. In this she was in agreement with John Stuart Mill and, unlike

MRS. HENRY FAWCETT L.L.D.
PRESIDENT OF THE NATIONAL UNION OF WOMEN'S SUFFRAGE SOCIETIES

Mrs Millicent Garrett Fawcett, president of the National Union of Women's Suffrage Societies. (Author's collection)

Agnes and Rhoda GARRETT, did not join the CENTRAL COMMITTEE FOR WOMEN'S SUFFRAGE when it was formed in 1871. However, becoming progressively disenchanted with the London National Society, in 1874, after Mill's death, she resigned from its executive committee and joined the Central Committee. After the two societies merged in 1877, Millicent Fawcett the next year joined the executive committee of the Central Committee. A gradualist by nature, Millicent Fawcett, unlike her husband, was prepared to exclude married women from any franchise measure if thereby the sex bar against women might to any degree be removed. She was therefore a keen supporter of William Woodall's amendment to the 1884 Reform Bill. Henry Fawcett, by now a cabinet minister, defied Gladstone and abstained from voting in the division. Although he did retain his ministerial position, he died suddenly later that year.

After nearly ten years' absence from provincial platforms, by 1886 Millicent Fawcett had resumed a position as a touring speaker in the suffrage cause. By 1888, when dissension grew within the Central Committee as to the issue of whether or not to allow other women's organizations to affiliate, she was the leader of the faction that wished to maintain the *status quo*. Her attitude to this question was influenced by her relationship with the Liberal party. A fierce opponent of Gladstone, after the 1886 split in the Liberal party over Home Rule she became a Liberal Unionist and a member of the executive committee of the WOMEN'S LIBERAL UNIONIST ASSOCIATION. She therefore had no desire for the Central Committee to be influenced by members of the Women's Liberal Federation, who would be the most likely beneficiaries of any change in the rules. She became honorary secretary and, for a time, honorary treasurer of the rump of the Central Committee after the majority, which wished for the change of the rules, departed to reconstitute itself as the CENTRAL NATIONAL SOCIETY. In 1893 she was president of the SPECIAL APPEAL COMMITTEE that represented a concerted effort by the suffrage societies to put their differences aside and work towards a common goal. Philippa Fawcett was in 1893 a member of the Special Appeal sub-committee of the CAMBRIDGE ASSOCIATION FOR WOMEN'S SUFFRAGE. In this period, after Lydia BECKER's death, Millicent Fawcett gravitated naturally to the forefront of the suffrage movement. On 16 October 1896 she was chosen to preside at the meeting of the suffrage societies that resulted in the territorial reorganization that led in 1897 to the setting up of the NATIONAL UNION OF WOMEN'S SUFFRAGE SOCIETIES and the renaming of the old societies as the CENTRAL WESTERN SOCIETY FOR WOMEN'S SUFFRAGE and the CENTRAL AND EASTERN SOCIETY, of which she was honorary secretary. As a representative of the Central and Eastern Society she was merely a member of the parliamentary committee of the NUWSS. It was only after the reorganization in 1907 that she became its president. She remained chairman of the LONDON SOCIETY until 1909. Philippa Fawcett was in 1913 honorary secretary of their local, St Pancras (South), branch of the London Society.

In 1904 Millicent Fawcett resigned from the Women's Liberal Unionist Association in protest against Liberal Unionist rejection of free trade in favour of tariff reform. With the return of a Liberal government in January 1906 her lack of direct party affiliation accorded well with her subsequent position as president of the NUWSS, for which to be at least superficially neutral was a strength. Her tendency towards what would now be termed the right of the Liberal party provided a useful corrective to the radical Liberal elements in the NUWSS. In January 1906 she refused to condemn the mild militancy of the WOMEN'S SOCIAL POLITICAL UNION, although acknowledging that its tactics would not be adopted by the NUWSS. She was concerned then and later, even though sorely tried by the damage she felt the WSPU was doing to the cause, that those working for the women's cause should not turn against each other. She visited Anne Cobden SANDERSON in Holloway and was instrumental in organizing the banquet held on 11 December 1906 at the Savoy to welcome the members of the WSPU who had been recently released from Holloway. Her idea of staging a protest demonstration against their imprisonment had not been favourably received by the NUWSS committee. In February 1907 she was one of the leaders of the "Mud March" through London that had been organized by the CENTRAL SOCIETY (renamed the London Society by the time it took place). Lady Frances BALFOUR noted in her autobiography that "Mrs Fawcett thoroughly enjoyed it, and pirouetted through her part as leader with the step of a girl of seventeen". She was to march again, attired in the doctor's robes to which she was entitled by virtue of an honorary degree from St Andrews University, on 13 June 1908 in the NUWSS procession from the Embankment to the Albert Hall and to enjoy the Coronation Procession in June 1911, to stage which the NUWSS co-operated with the WSPU. She was able to bring an adaptable mind to both NUWSS policies and to the changing conditions as constitutional suffrage speakers, undifferentiated by the general public from the militants, endured heckling and incipient violence. She matched Mrs PANKHURST in the number and variety of the speaking engagements she undertook, roving the country, always certain to attract a good audience and put heart into the local suffrage workers. There the similarity between the two suffrage leaders ended. Mrs Fawcett's contribution to the cause was a flair for conciliation, spiced with a dry wit, rather than charisma. The impressive development of the NUWSS as a political machine between 1907 and 1914 is a tribute to her success as a leader. An excellent tactician, she realized the advantage to the NUWSS in working with the Labour party and in 1912 was a member of the first Election Fighting Fund Committee. In the summer of 1913, now 66 years old, she took a very active part in the PILGRIMAGE, walking with the East Anglian pilgrims between speaking engagements on the other routes. Asquith, in reply to her request for him to receive a deputation on behalf of those who took part in the Pilgrimage, wrote "I quite recognise that the request which you put forward, after the recent law-abiding demonstration of your Societies, has a special claim on my consideration and stands upon another footing from similar demands proceeding from other quarters, where a different method and spirit is predominant", but added that he doubted that he would be able to give them any indication of any change in government policy. Although on leaving Downing Street after the interview Millicent Fawcett felt that there had been "a notable improvement in his attitude and language", she put no faith in release from deadlock while the Liberal government remained in office.

On 4 August 1914 Mrs Fawcett presided at a meeting in the Kingsway Hall that, too late, called on the government to "leave untried no method of conciliation and arbitration". Once war was declared she supported the NUWSS in suspending its political work and turning itself into an organization available to aid the war effort by alleviating distress. She was in her quiet and determined way passionate in her patriotism, as she had demonstrated during the Boer War. In 1902 she had been elected second vice-president of the INTERNATIONAL WOMAN SUFFRAGE ALLIANCE at its inaugural meeting in Washington. She had not attended that meeting, but was at Copenhagen in 1906 and at

Amsterdam in 1908. In 1909 at the IWSA meeting in London she was elected first vice-president, and again in 1913 when she attended the Budapest congress. Despite this close association with the international suffrage movement she could not support the majority of her NUWSS executive committee who in 1915 wished to attend the Women's Peace Congress at the Hague. As a result all the officers of the NUWSS except Mrs Fawcett and Mrs Auerbach, the treasurer, resigned in April, along with ten members of the executive committee. Although those who supported the anti-war movement were in the majority, there was no attempt to oust Mrs Fawcett from her presidency. She was, however, deeply hurt by remarks made at the time, perhaps unintentionally, by Kathleen COURTNEY and Catherine MARSHALL and, unwilling to forgive them, hoped only that time would erase the memory of the episode. In June at a special NUWSS council meeting in Birmingham Mrs Fawcett was accorded a vote of confidence and an ovation. In August she moved quickly to warn member societies of the NUWSS against affiliating with the Union of Democratic Control, whose founder, E.D. Morel, had made this suggestion and with which Helena SWANWICK, another erstwhile member of the NUWSS, was closely associated.

In March 1917 Millicent Fawcett led a deputation that included representatives of 24 women's suffrage societies and ten other organizations to the new Prime Minister, Lloyd George and on 10 January 1918 was present to witness the debate in the House of Lords that resulted in a majority for the women's suffrage clause to the Representation of the People Bill. On 13 March she took the chair at the NUWSS Celebration in the Queen's Hall. Millicent Fawcett retired from the presidency of the NUWSS in March 1919, when it became the NATIONAL UNION OF SOCIETIES FOR EQUAL CITIZENSHIP, making way, as she said, for a younger woman who, in the event, was Eleanor RATHBONE. In 1920 Millicent Fawcett was chairman of the board of the *Woman's Leader*, successor to the *Common Cause*, retaining this position until 1925. She remained the IWSA first vice-president until 1920 and was elected a vice-president of the League of Nations in 1918. In June 1926 she was one of the principal speakers at the rally in Hyde Park to mark the end of the Women's Peace Pilgrimage, of which Kathleen Courtney was the organizer. In 1925 she was created a Dame of the British Empire and, shortly afterwards, resigned as a member of NUSEC and from the board of the *Woman's Leader*, having been defeated over a move to block NUSEC's advocacy of family allowances. There was, however, this time no bitterness over the split in the ranks. In July 1925 NUSEC held for her a garden party in the grounds of Aubrey House, in which house she had attended 58 years previously the first meeting of the London National Society for Women's Suffrage.

Among Millicent Fawcett's works on women's suffrage are: *Mrs Fawcett on Women's Suffrage*, c. 1872; *A Reply to the Letter of Mr Samuel Smith, M.P. on Women's Suffrage*, Central Committee of the National Society for Women's Suffrage; *Men are men and women are women*, NUWSS, 1910; *Extracts from various articles and speeches by Mrs Henry Fawcett LL.D. on women's suffrage*, NUWSS, 1909; *Home and Politics: an address delivered at Toynbee Hall and elsewhere*, London Society for Women's Suffrage, no date; *Women's Suffrage: A Short History of a Great Movement*, 1912; *The Women's Victory – and After: Personal Reminiscences, 1911–1918*, 1920. In 1884 she contributed the essay on "The Women's Suffrage Movement in England" to Theodore Stanton's *The Woman Question in Europe*; in 1891 she wrote a foreword to a reissue, the first since 1844, of Mary Wollstonecraft's *Vindication of the Rights of Woman*, which was published by T. Fisher Unwin; and in 1912 supplied an introduction to the Oxford University Press's World Classics edition of J.S. Mill, *On Liberty, Representative Government*, and *The Subjection of Women*.

Address: (1867) Bessborough Gardens, Pimlico, London SW; (1874) 51, The Lawn, South Lambeth Road, London SW; (1874) 18 Brookside, Cambridge; (1885) 2 Gower Street, London WC.

Portrait: portrait in oils of Millicent Garrett Fawcett with Henry Fawcett, by Ford Maddox Brown, 1872, was bequeathed to the National Portrait Gallery by Sir Charles DILKE. It is now held at the NPG outpost at Bodelwyddan Castle in North Wales. In 1930 a portrait painted by Annie SWYNNERTON of Millicent Fawcett, dressed in academic robes, was bought by the Chantrey Bequest and is now held at the Tate Gallery. Another portrait by Annie Swynnerton, perhaps a slightly smaller copy, was sold in London in 1972 (photograph in National Portrait Gallery Archive).

A memorial to Henry Fawcett from "faithful countrywomen", a drinking fountain with a bronze medallion portrait of him by Mary Grant, was unveiled in the gardens to the east of Charing Cross in 1886. Plaster medallion portrait by Mary Grant, 1886, National Portrait Gallery. Memorials were commissioned from Sir Alfred Gilbert (see Caprina FAHEY) to be set in Westminster Abbey and in Aldeburgh Church. A posthumous portrait of him, 1886, by Harold Rathbone was offered to the National Portrait Gallery by Philippa Fawcett (National Portrait Gallery Archive). Portrait by Sir Hubert von Herkomer, Fitzwilliam Museum, Cambridge. A terracotta statue of Henry Fawcett, made by one of the workers at the Doulton factory was given by Sir Henry Doulton and unveiled in Vauxhall Park, 1897, destroyed c. 1955, photograph of it in National Portrait Gallery Archive.
Archival source: Millicent Garrett Fawcett Collection, Fawcett Library; Papers of Millicent Garrett Fawcett, Manchester Central Library.
Bibliography: M.G. Fawcett, *The Women's Victory – and After: Personal Reminiscences, 1911–1918*, 1920; M.G. Fawcett, *What I Remember*, 1924; R. Strachey, *Millicent Garrett Fawcett*, 1931; A. Oakley, "Millicent Garrett Fawcett: duty and determination", in D. Spender (ed.), *Feminist Theorists: Three Centuries of Women's Intellectual Traditions*, 1983; D. Rubinstein, *A Different World for Women: The Life of Millicent Garrett Fawcett*, 1991 (which includes a full bibliography of her writings).

FEDERATED COUNCIL OF SUFFRAGE SOCIETIES Founded in November 1912 "to determine a united policy and action which all the constitutional societies might adopt". By 1916 the Council had 22 affiliated societies, among which were the LONDON GRADUATES' UNION FOR WOMEN'S SUFFRAGE, the NEW CONSTITUTIONAL SOCIETY, the TAX RESISTANCE LEAGUE, the ACTRESSES' FRANCHISE LEAGUE, the WOMEN WRITERS' SUFFRAGE LEAGUE, the UNITED SUFFRAGISTS, the FREE CHURCH LEAGUE FOR WOMEN'S SUFFRAGE; the JEWISH LEAGUE FOR WOMEN'S SUFFRAGE, the CATHOLIC WOMEN'S SUFFRAGE SOCIETY and the MEN'S LEAGUE FOR WOMEN'S SUFFRAGE. Among the members of the society's general purposes committee in 1913 were Adelaide CHAPMAN and Mary HANKINSON. The Federated Council was known as "The middle party of the movement". It did not actively support the war effort during the First World War.
President (1912) Muriel, Countess DE LA WARR. Chairman (1912) Miss M.A. Broadhurst, (1916) Alice ABADAM; honorary secretary (1912) Gertrude CONOLAN, (1916) Edith Quinlan; honorary treasurer (1913) Dr Adelaide Roberts, (1916) Lady Sybil Smith.
Address: (1913) Lloyds' Bank Buildings, 16, St James's Street, London, SW; (1914) 31 Alfred Place, Tottenham Court Road, London W.

FELIXSTOWE (WSPU) Secretary (1913) Miss E. LOWY, Woodcroft, Bath Road, Felixstowe, Suffolk.

FELIXSTOWE, WALTON AND DISTRICT (NUWSS) In 1913 the society was a member of the EASTERN COUNTIES FEDERATION OF THE NATIONAL UNION OF WOMEN'S SUFFRAGE SOCIETIES. Secretary (1913) Miss Edith Place, 34 Quilter Road, Felixstowe, Suffolk.

FILEY branch of the MEN'S LEAGUE FOR WOMEN'S SUFFRAGE Founded in 1912.

FILEY (NUWSS) In 1913 the society was a member of the NORTH AND EAST RIDINGS FEDERATION OF THE NATIONAL UNION OF WOMEN'S SUFFRAGE SOCIETIES. Secretary (1913) Miss Hankes, 11 Southdene, Filey, Yorkshire.

FILM The renaissance of the women's suffrage campaign at the beginning of the twentieth century coincided with the birth of the film industry. The extant films may be categorized, in the same manner as suffrage postcards, as either comic features, which take "suffragettes" to represent a range of stereotypical harridans or unwomanly women, or as moving images of a reality, of occasions to which the cumbersome cameras of the day were attracted. Newsreel was particularly geared to spectacle, the camera remaining static as the procession passed by. Indeed the camera was often so close to the scene that individual participants can be recognized. The films are an excellent source of information on dress and demeanour, BANNERS, policing and the numbers and attitudes of bystanders, as well as placing the men and women of the first decade of the century in a real world of streets, buildings, advertisements, cars, smoke, sun and wind. Of all the extant newsreels, the capturing on camera of Emily Wilding DAVISON's dash onto the Derby racecourse alone stands out as being the product of chance. The camera was not there for the purpose of recording an action now considered "historic", as it was, for instance, at the Women's Coronation Procession in 1911.

From 1908 the French company Pathé, which dominated the filming and distribution of news before the First World War, assembled its "topical" news items into regular issues, which were sent either once or twice weekly to be shown as a prelude to feature films in the new purpose-built cinemas that were opened following the passing of the 1909 Cinematograph Act. The WOMEN'S SOCIAL AND POLITICAL UNION was quick to adopt the new medium of communication, in 1908 using cinematograph advertisements, projected onto sheets in its shop windows, to invite people to demonstrations and showing short scenes from the suffragette campaign. On 18 June 1908 the Graphic Cinematographic Co., of 154 Charing Cross Road (next door to the offices of George Allen and Unwin and the shop that the WSPU was to open two years later) wrote to Minnie BALDOCK, confirming arrangements they had made to "cinematograph" her meeting the next day during the "dinner hour" at Waterlows printing works in Shoreditch. There may well have been many more such relatively informal scenes filmed that, because they were not dramatic set pieces, have not survived. Because there is so little extant film material relating to the constitutional campaign, the popular history of the suffrage campaign has been dominated by the shots of militant demonstrations and spectacles that have subsequently been woven into compilations and re-screened throughout the century.

NEWSREELS   Copies of the following films are held by the British Film Institute; some can be viewed.

Scenes from suffrage demonstration at Newcastle, 8 October 1909, showing a procession of women carrying banners headed by a band. (Production company probably Warwick)

Scenes from the "Prison to Citizenship" procession, 18 June 1910 (Pathé). Flora DRUMMOND, Evelina HAVERFIELD, Vera HOLME, Dora MARSDEN, Maud JOACHIM and Mary LEIGH, who is walking backwards conducting the WSPU fife and drum BAND, are all there and Emily DAVIES, leaning on a stick, can be seen walking under the BANNER of the "University Section".

Mass meeting of NATIONAL UNION OF WOMEN'S SUFFRAGE SOCIETIES supporters in Trafalgar Square; women standing with placards showing the numerical support given by (male) voters to the NUWSS petitions at the January 1910 general election. 9 July 1910. (Pathé)

"Black Friday" disturbances in Parliament Square, 18 November 1910. (Pathé)

Women's Coronation Procession in London, 17 June 1911. (Pathé). *Votes for Women* noted that the film was shown by Oswald Stoll at the Coliseum Bioscope.

George LANSBURY after he had declared that he would fight the Bow by-election on a women's suffrage platform, November 1912. (Pathé)

Suffragists addressing mill-girls during the course of the Bolton by-election campaign, 23 November 1912. (Pathé)

Scenes outside the House of Commons on the day after the Speaker announced that the Reform Bill was not capable of being amended to include women, 28 January 1913. (Warwick Bioscope Chronicle)

The burned-out house belonging to Lady White at Egham (*see* Olive BEAMISH *and* Elsie DUVAL), 20 March 1913. (Pathé)

Levetleigh, St Leonards, Sussex, the home of Arthur du Cros destroyed by fire, 13 April 1913 (*see* Kitty MARION). (Pathé)

St Catherine's Church, Hatcham, completely destroyed by suffragette arson, 6 May 1913. (Williamson)

Emily Wilding DAVISON under the horse's hooves at Tattenham Corner during the Derby, 4 June 1913. (Gaumont Graphic)

Emily Wilding DAVISON's funeral, 14 June 1913. (Pathé)

NUWSS rally in Hyde Park at the end of the PILGRIMAGE, July 1913. (Pathé)

Mrs DRUMMOND picketing the home of Sir Edward Carson, 1913.

Sylvia PANKHURST arrested in the course of a meeting organized by the Free Speech Defence Committee in Trafalgar Square on 10 August 1913. (Pathé)

Yarmouth Pier destroyed by suffragette arson on night of 17 April 1914. (Eclair 18 April)

WSPU May Day Pageant procession in London on 1 May 1914, organized to promote sales of the *Suffragette*. It looks very impressive. The next week's issue of the *Suffragette* emphasized that the procession had been arranged at very short notice and that, because it would have been refused, police permission had not been sought. The WSPU had, however, alerted Pathé.

WSPU deputation to the King, scenes outside Buckingham Palace, 21 May 1914. (Pathé)

Christabel PANKHURST returns to London from France, August 1914. (Topical Budget)

Women's War Work Procession, 17 July 1915, organized by the WSPU at the suggestion of Lloyd George in order to promote the right of women to undertake war work. (Topical Budget, 21 July)

EAST LONDON FEDERATION OF SUFFRAGETTES march from Bow to Portman Rooms, Baker Street, on Registration Sunday, 15 August 1915, to protest against conscription and ask for control of food supplies, equal pay and votes for women. They were joined by the UNITED SUFFRAGISTS, WOMEN WRITERS' SUFFRAGE LEAGUE and the FORWARD CYMRIC SUFFRAGE UNION. (Topical Budget, 18 August)

Meeting at the Queen's Hall to found the WOMEN'S PARTY, 1917.

Bonar Law holds a meeting for women only at the Drury Lane Theatre, 6 November 1922. (Gaumont Graphic)

INTERNATIONAL WOMAN SUFFRAGE ALLIANCE meeting at Rome, 1923.

Susan Lawrence becomes MP for East Ham, 6 December 1923. (Topical Budget)

Lady Astor re-elected as Conservative MP for Plymouth, 6 December 1923. (Topical Budget)

Mrs Wintringham re-elected as Liberal MP for Louth, 6 December 1923. (Topical Budget)

Unveiling of Mrs PANKHURST's statue in Victoria Tower Gardens, 1930. (Movietone News)

Mrs How-MARTYN and Inspector Jarvis attend a suffragette reunion dinner, 1936.

Suffragette reunion at Emmeline PANKHURST's statue, 14 July 1947. (Directed by W. Macquitty)

Former suffragettes lay flowers at the foot of Mrs PANKHURST's statue, 14 July 1950. (BBC Television newsreel)

Votes for Women – compilation, including a contemporary reunion at Caxton Hall, 1955. (Movietone)

Fifty Years On – Suffragettes. Compilation of Pathé newsreel items, including Emily Wilding DAVISON's dash onto the Derby course and her funeral, made in the 1960s. (Pathé)

Fanatics: a history of the suffragettes made up from still photographs, 12 December 1962. (Granada)

FEATURE FILMS The following were known to have been made; many may no longer exist.

The Voter's Guide, produced by Hepworth, directed by Lewin Fitzhamon, January 1906. Comedy with scenes illustrating Tariff Reform, Free Trade and Workman's Friend. The film was produced to coincide with the January 1906 election. The fact that it did not include any stereotypical scenes relating to women's suffrage is a measure of the lack of importance hitherto devoted to the campaign by popular media.

If Women Were Policewomen, Clarendon Films, directed Percy Stow, May 1908. Comedy, militant suffragettes take over the police force.

When Women Vote, Hepworth, directed Lewin Fitzhamon, May 1908. Suffragettes make man don skirts and take over fire station.

Suffering Suffragettes, produced by Wrench, September 1908. "Topical comedy, screamingly funny throughout".

Scroggins Puts Up for Blankshire, Cricks and Martin, directed A.E. Coleby, January 1910. Comedy, suffragettes pelt candidate and he wins by six votes. Produced to coincide with the January 1910 general election. In the four years since the previous general election the WSPU had made such an impact on popular politics that the maker of a comedy short could not ignore its campaign.

The Suffragettes and the Hobble Skirt, Kineto, directed by Theo Bourmeester, August 1910. Persecuted man gives women hobble skirts and they are jailed.

The Suffragette's Downfall, or Who Said "Rats", Acme Films, directed and starring Fred Rains, January 1911. Comedy, henpecked husband sets rats on golfing wife.

Scroggins Takes the Census, Cricks and Martin, directed Dave Aylott, March 1911. Comedy, census taker interviews spinster, tough farmer, and suffragette. Again illustrates the central position that the suffragettes, however stereotypical, had taken in the popular imagination.

True Womanhood, Barker's Motion Photography Company, 1911. Based on the play written by Inez BENSUSAN, who with Decima MOORE, Auriol Lee and Ben Webster appeared in the film. It was shown at such venues as the Cinematograph Theatre, Wood Green; Romilly Hall, Barry; and the St James's Picture Hall, Kingston-on-Thames (*Votes for Women*, 7 July 1911). In *Innocent Flowers*, 1982, Julia Holledge, notes that no copies of the film now exist.

The Elusive Miss Pinkhurst, Warwick Trading Co., March 1912. Trick photography, cabinet minister tries to catch suffragette. Again demonstrates how quickly a film company could pick up an idea and develop it; Christabel PANKHURST had fled to France on 6 March.

A Suffragette Inspite of Himself, Edison Films, directed by Ashley Miller, 1912. Comedy, man arrested while posing as a woman and is saved by a suffragette.

How They Got the Vote, Edison, directed by Ashley Miller, March 1913. Suffragette's suitor forces prime minister to accept suffrage by causing chaos in London. Cast includes a magician and a suffragette.

The Child of a Suffragette, Kineto, directed by F. Martin Thornton, April 1913. Drama, child trails suffragette mother and extinguishes her bomb.

Suffragettes in the Bud, Clarendon Films, directed by Percy Stow, April 1913. Comedy, schoolgirls play tricks on mistress.

The Suffragette, Britannia Films (Pathé), November 1913. Crime film, disowned schoolmistress's uncle destroys father's amended will.

Two Sides of a Boat, British and Colonial Kinematograph Co., November 1913. Comedy, pursued suffragette hides and thinks sailors intend to tar her.

What 80 Million Women Want, a US film made in New York, in which Mrs PANKHURST, on a lecture tour of America in October 1913, featured as a *dea ex machina*, playing herself. As Kevin Brownlow explains, "The plot is essentially a detective story, exposing the system of machine politics. The sleuth is female, and the remedy is votes for women". (US, Uneek Film Company, 1913)

Milling the Militants: A Comic Absurdity, Clarendon, 1913. The dreams of a man who has a suffragette wife.

Die Suffragette, a German film about the British suffrage movement, written and directed by a Dane, Urban Grad, and featuring his wife, Asta Nielsen, September 1913. The leader of the suffragettes is Mrs Panburne, and the leading politician is Lord Ascue. The film was certainly shown in America, but may not have been screened in Britain, perhaps because it contained violent scenes and the authorities and theatre owners may not have wished to be thought to be condoning suffragette activities.

The Militant Imp, 1914, directed by William Robert Daly. A US film, but based on the activities of the British militant suffrage movement.

The militant suffrage campaign was also depicted in the film version of Howard Spring's *Fame is the Spur* (1947), and by the screenwriters of the 1964 film of *Mary Poppins*; there was no suggestion that the mother in P.L. Travers' original story was a suffragette!

Archival source: British Film Institute, where many of the newsreels may be viewed; British Universities Film & Video Council/Slade Film History Register/British Universities Newsreel Project.

Bibliography: J. Ballantyne (ed.), *Researcher's Guide to British Newsreels*, 1983; D. Gifford, *The British Film Catalogue, 1895–1985: A Reference Guide*, 1986; K. Brownlow, *Behind the Mask of Innocence: Sex, Violence, Prejudice, Crime: Films of Social Conscience in the Silent Era*, 1990.

FINCHLEY (WFL) Secretary (1913) Mrs Tinkler, 3 Stanley Road, E. Finchley, London N.

FLATMAN, [SUSAN] ADA (1876–1952) Born in Suffolk. While travelling in Australia and Ceylon in 1907 she heard about suffrage activity back in Britain and on her return, when living in a residential club in London, she went to several drawing-room meetings held by the NATIONAL UNION OF WOMEN'S SUFFRAGE SOCIETIES, but was not impressed. After hearing Christabel PANKHURST speak at the Horticultural Hall, Westminster, she joined the WOMEN'S SOCIAL AND POLITICAL UNION, sending a cheque for £6.3.3. By July 1908 she was acting as a WSPU ORGANIZER, helping run the Pembroke by-election campaign, for which she was personally thanked by Mrs PANKHURST. At the end of September 1908 she was in Bristol, where she helped Mary BLATHWAYT in the WSPU shop. After taking part in the 13 October 1908 "raid" on the House of Commons, she received a sentence of one month's imprisonment. In early 1909 she was sent to Aberdeen to assist Sylvia PANKHURST cope with animosity from Caroline PHILLIPS and the original Aberdonian WSPU workers. At the end of April 1909 Ada

Flatman took over as organizer in the Midlands while Gladice KEEVIL was campaigning at the Stratford by-election. By May 1909 she was WSPU organizer in Liverpool and, with Patricia WOODLOCK, conducted the local holiday campaign on the Isle of Man. She was ambitious and did not always keep in step with Clement's Inn. In September she opened the first "Votes for Women" shop in Liverpool and in April 1911 wished to move premises. Mrs PETHICK-LAWRENCE, as the WSPU's treasurer, was not convinced that this plan made financial sense but, after Ada Flatman had organized a large fund-raising meeting, reluctantly gave her consent, writing, "I have confidence in your sense of responsibility ... I shall watch the result very carefully". The new shop was a success and Ada Flatman then wrote to ask Mrs Pethick-Lawrence if there was any opening for her in the London shop. She was told very firmly that it would be "an immense mistake for you to change your work. You have just got hold of Liverpool, you have got your position there, the members are beginning to understand you and rally round you. You have made the campaign there a signal success. A great deal of this would be thrown away if you were now to change the sphere of your work. For the year which ended on Feb. 28th 1910 Liverpool takes the prize with regard to the financial side of the work. During the year, £465 was expended on the Liverpool campaign and £592 raised". However, by February 1911, Ada Flatman had moved on from Liverpool to Cheltenham, where she was appointed WSPU organizer. Zealous, she immediately set about inviting the stars of the WSPU to appear at her meetings, writing to Beatrice HARRADEN asking her to come and read *Lady Geraldine's Speech* and booking Mrs Pankhurst for several days. Her requests were not always successful; Elizabeth ROBINS refused an invitation, saying that she was not a speaker, and in October Annie KENNEY declined, pointing out that two important speakers had already been booked for the meeting at which she was invited to speak. One of Ada Flatman's many drawing-room meetings (obviously a style suited to Cheltenham) was hosted by Mrs Frances SWINEY. Perhaps as a result of the WSPU's campaign, the Liberals lost their seat at the Cheltenham by-election.

In March 1912 Ada Flatman visited in Holloway Dr Alice KER, whom she had known from her days in Liverpool. She took fruit to the prisoner and was vociferous in her condemnation of "The National" [the NUWSS]. By April 1912 she was organizer in Hereford, in June she was in charge of the Ilkeston by-election campaign, where the Liberal majority was reduced by 3000, and in July was organizer at the Crewe by-election where the Liberal was defeated. However, this involvement all came to an end when, for undisclosed reasons, Ada Flatman resigned from organizing for the WSPU on 20 July 1912.

It would appear, from a letter to her written by Lena ASHWELL, that in October 1914 Ada Flatman was due to move to Southport, to work for the Women's Emergency Corps. Then, in 1915, she went to the USA to work for the *Suffragist*, the paper of the Congressional Union for Women's Suffrage, which was edited by Rheta Childe Dorr who had ghosted Mrs Pankhurst's autobiography, and to which one of the main contributors was Lucy BURNS. Ada Flatman appears to have been given the job of raising more advertising for the paper. During her sojourn in the USA and Canada, which lasted until mid-1917, she took the opportunity of writing for the *Suffragette*, c. November 1915, a description of one of the American suffrage parades. After the end of the war and the end of suffrage campaigning Ada Flatman had considerable difficulty in finding employment and involvement. In June 1921 she wrote to Alice PAUL in the USA to ask if there was a salaried position for her with the National Woman's Party; there was not. In January 1922 she returned from Poland, where she had been involved in relief work for Russian refugees and then wrote to the Secretary of the Immigration Department in Ottawa, offering her services to the Canadian government to raise funds for the Russian famine relief fund or any other charitable work. In this letter she wrote, "I have been an organiser for many years and as I am of middle age and commanding appearance, am quite capable of filling any responsible post ... If your Government could offer organising work I should be happy to come to Canada at once but I have not the means to come out on the chance of securing an appointment ... I am British but should prefer work in the Colonies as I like colonial life and sunshine." This candid approach did not persuade the Canadian authorities and in October 1922 Ada Flatman was enjoying the sunshine of Cape Town. There, capitalizing on her *curriculum vitae*, she wrote to the Women's Enfranchisement League, offering to set up for them a suffrage movement relying on militant tactics, but was rebuffed. She did, however, attempt to start there an organization, The Star in the East, which appears to have been a suffrage society. Ada Flatman may still have been in South Africa in 1928, but by 1936 she was settled in Eastbourne. In that year she had some correspondence with Christabel Pankhurst who, when she was in Eastbourne meeting with local clergy, did briefly visit her. Ada Flatman said that she supported Christabel Pankhurst's Second Adventist beliefs. It might be cynical to pry too closely into her motives for this avowal. In 1937 Ada Flatman wrote to Ruth Fry suggesting that they should set up a Woman's Peace Party. Ruth Fry replied that, as a Quaker, she believed in men and women working together and felt it better that energy should be put into the existing Peace Pledge Union rather than founding a separate woman-only party. Ada Flatman was very persistent and Ruth Fry had to write yet again, declining to be involved. In 1943 Ada Flatman was asked by Dorothy EVANS to support the Equal Citizenship (Blanket) Bill and was offered a seat on the platform of an associated meeting. In 1946 she reminisced about her suffragette activities on the BBC Home Service (*see under* RADIO, TELEVISION, RECORDINGS AND RECORDS). Her attachment to the memory of the WSPU continued to the end; in her will she especially mentioned that she would like the "charming young Congregational minister who took the service of my dear old suffrage militant friend of forty years, Miss TURNER late of 14 Victoria Road, Brighton", to conduct her own funeral and she left one-tenth of her estate, a sum which in the event amounted to £25, to the SUFFRAGETTE FELLOWSHIP.

Address: (1910) 65 Canning Street, Liverpool; (1913) 36 Richmond Mansions, London SW; (1952) 11 Upperton Road, Eastbourne, Sussex.
Photograph: *Votes for Women*, 22 July 1910; in D. Atkinson, *The Suffragettes in Pictures*, 1996.
Archival source: Suffragette Fellowship Collection, Museum of London.

FLEET (NUWSS) In 1913 the society was a member of the SURREY, SUSSEX, AND HANTS FEDERATION OF THE NATIONAL UNION OF WOMEN'S SUFFRAGE SOCIETIES. Secretary (1909, 1913) Mrs Kayser, The Garth, Fleet, Hampshire.

FLORENCE, MARY SARGANT, MRS (1858–1954) Daughter of Henry and Catherine Sargant, painter in watercolour, tempera and of decorative murals in fresco, she was educated privately, and then at the Slade and in Paris. In 1888 she exhibited several works at the first showing of the Arts and Crafts Exhibition Society and in the same year married an American musician, Henry Smythe Florence. She became the mother of a son, Philip, and a daughter, Alix, who was to marry James Strachey, brother of Lytton, Philippa and Marjorie STRACHEY. Her husband died in 1892 and, with her children, Mary Sargant Florence returned to England. In 1905 she subscribed to the CENTRAL SOCIETY FOR WOMEN'S SUFFRAGE. On 11 December 1906 she was present at the banquet organized at the Savoy by Mrs FAWCETT to celebrate the release of the WOMEN'S SOCIAL AND POLITICAL UNION prisoners. In 1907 she subscribed both to the NATIONAL UNION OF WOMEN'S SUFFRAGE SOCIETIES and to the WSPU and in 1908 gave £4 to the WOMEN'S FREEDOM LEAGUE. In 1907 Annie KENNEY and Teresa BILLINGTON-GREIG enjoyed weekend rests with her at her country home near Marlow, for which she had been her own architect. Her sister Ethel Sargant stayed faithful to the NUWSS and was actively involved in the TUNBRIDGE WELLS SUFFRAGE SOCIETY. Around 1908 Mary Sargant Florence designed the "Dare to be Free" BANNER for the WFL and her design "What's Sauce for the Gander is Sauce for the Goose" was printed as a poster by the ARTISTS' SUFFRAGE LEAGUE. She was a founder member and on the committee of the TAX RESISTANCE LEAGUE, for which she designed a badge and designed and donated a banner. The device was also used on a postcard published by the Tax Resistance League. In 1912 and 1914 she put principle into practice, refused to pay taxes, and her goods were distrained. In 1913 she was a supporter of the NATIONAL POLITICAL LEAGUE.

In 1909–10 Mary Sargant Florence reapplied for British nationality, which she had forfeited on her marriage. Among those supplying her with character references were Annie Leigh BROWNE and Emily FORD (later her neighbour in Glebe Place). Although the Home Office instigated a routine report as to her suitability, Mary Sargant Florence's suffrage affiliations did not call this into question. The Buckinghamshire police inspector reported that, "Applicant is able to speak, read and write English well . . . I should say (from my own knowledge) she is a lady by birth and education, her associates being persons of high character and position". Her solicitor Goldfinch Bates was a leading member of the MEN'S LEAGUE FOR WOMEN'S SUFFRAGE. In 1915 she was a member of the British general committee for the Women's International Congress at the Hague and, with C.K. Ogden, she wrote *Militarism versus Feminism*, an anti-war pamphlet. It has been suggested that "Daphne Sandomir", the enthusiastic, energetic and organizing mother (of "Alix") in Rose Macaulay's novel *Non-Combatants*, 1916, was based on Mary Sargant Florence, although Mary Sheepshanks and Maude ROYDEN have also been cited as possible progenitors.

In 1912, having won a competition, Mary Sargant Florence decorated in tempera the "Literature" panel in Chelsea Town Hall and in 1912–13 completed a series of murals at Bourneville for the Cadbury family. She also executed frescoes at the Old School, Oakham, Rutland, where one of her brothers was headmaster. She was in 1928 editor of the second edition of *Papers of the Society of Painters in Tempera, Vol. 1, 1901–1907*, to which Christiana HERRINGHAM had originally written the Introduction, was editor of *Papers of the Society of Painters in Tempera, Vol. 3, 1925–1935*, and published *Colour Co-ordination* in 1940. She was very friendly with a fellow suffragist artist, Dora Meeson COATES, and in July 1930 they were both members of the organizing committee for an exhibition, opened by Mrs Philip SNOWDEN, which was held at the Whitechapel Gallery by the Society of Tempera Painters. Dora Meeson Coates described Mary Sargant Florence as "one of our dearest friends", "one of England's finest decorators – an original, intellectual and profound artist". In her will Mary Sargant Florence left a painting to Dora Meeson Coates.

Address: (1908) Smollett Studios, Cheyne Row, London SW; (later) 43 Glebe Place, Chelsea, London SW; (1913) Lord's Wood, Marlow, Buckinghamshire.
Archival source: Sargant Florence Papers, Birmingham City Archives; Home Office Papers, Public Record Office.
Bibliography: D.M. Coates, *George Coates: His Art and Life*, 1937; M. Sargant Florence and C.K. Ogden, *Militarism versus Feminism*, in M. Kamester and J. Vellacott, *Militarism versus Feminism: Writings on Women and War*, 1987; L. Tickner, *The Spectacle of Women: Imagery of the Suffrage Campaign 1907–14*, 1987.

FLOYD, LETTICE ANNIE (1865–1934) Niece of Jane Hume CLAPPERTON. In 1907 Lettice Floyd and her sister Mary subscribed to the BIRMINGHAM WOMEN'S SUFFRAGE SOCIETY and instituted the Berkswell branch of the Society. Lettice was treasurer and Mary, the elder sister, was honorary secretary. However, this association was short-lived; the Annual Report of the Birmingham Women's Suffrage Society for 1908 notes that the "Berkswell branch is dissolved as its leading members have joined the WSPU". Lettice had become dissatisfied with the slow progress being made by the constitutional society and took the dramatic step, at the age of 42, of leaving home and becoming a full-time ORGANIZER for the WOMEN'S SOCIAL AND POLITICAL UNION. In August 1908 she was in Bristol, working alongside Mary BLATHWAYT and Annie KENNEY. There she met Annie WILLIAMS, who during the summer holidays had come there from Cornwall to help the WSPU campaign. The two were to become life-long companions. Lettice Floyd by September returned to Berkswell and sent from there purple and white flowers to decorate a WSPU "At Home" and to Annie Kenney a birthday cake with "Votes for Women" in purple and green decorating the white sugar top. In October 1908 Lettice Floyd was sentenced to a month's imprisonment after taking part in the "rush" on the House of Commons. In November, while she was imprisoned, a letter from Annie Williams was returned by the Governor of Holloway because she was not entitled to receive it. In July 1909 she returned to Bristol and in July gave £20 to the WSPU's Legal Defence Fund; Annie Williams had been among those arrested while on the deputation to the House of Commons at the end of June. In 1911 Lettice Floyd gave a donation to the MEN'S POLITICAL UNION. When Annie Williams became organizer in Newcastle in early 1910 Lettice Floyd joined her there, as "Literature Secretary" and gave a print of G.F. Watts's *Woman* to decorate the new WSPU shop. In March 1912 she was in Holloway, with Annie Williams, having taken part in the WSPU window-smashing campaign. She took part in the hunger strike and was forcibly fed. In November 1912 both Lettice and Mary Floyd contributed to George LANSBURY's expenses when he stood as a suffrage candidate at the Bow by-election.

After the First World War Lettice Floyd was a member of the National Council of Women, the Women's International League, and the Women's Institute. In the 1920s she noted that the peace movement and an improvement in the status of women were the issues she considered to be most important. In her will she left a legacy to the Rachel McMillan Training Centre, and £3000 and an annuity of £300 to Annie Williams.

Address: (1934) Hesper, Balsall Common, Warwickshire.
Photograph: in the Suffragette Fellowship Collection, Museum of London.
Archival source: Suffragette Fellowship Collection, Museum of London.

FOLKESTONE (NUWSS) In 1913 the society was a member of the KENTISH FEDERATION OF THE NATIONAL UNION OF WOMEN'S SUFFRAGE SOCIETIES. Secretary (1913) Mrs Napier Stuart, The Priory, Folkestone, Kent.

FOLKESTONE branch of the NEW CONSTITUTIONAL SOCIETY FOR WOMEN'S SUFFRAGE President (1913) Mrs Kenny, 63 Bouverie Road West, Folkestone, Kent.

FORD, EMILY SUSAN (1850–1930) Born in Leeds, into a Quaker family, sister of Isabella FORD. A landscape and figure painter, she attended the Slade from 1875 and had her own studio in London. In 1885 a chalk drawing by her, *The North Wind* was shown at the Exhibition of Women's Industries organized by Helen BLACKBURN in Bristol. The *Pall Mall Gazette*, 26 February 1885, singled it out: "It is a female figure, grand and stern, which gives the impression in its rapid movement of uncontrollable and pitiless power. As a work of imagination, there is nothing in the exhibition to compare with this". In 1889 Emily Ford exhibited a painting, *Life*, at the summer exhibition of the Grosvenor Gallery. In the late 1870s and early 1880s she was a member of the Society for Psychical Research and introduced her cousin Edward Pease to the Society and its then secretary, Frank Podmore. The two men went on to found the Fabian Society, the first meeting of which was attended by Emily and Isabella Ford. Emily eventually converted from Quakerism to Anglicanism and was baptized in 1890 at the church of All Souls in Leeds, for the font of which she later painted eight panels. She also painted altar panels for several churches in London and in 1902 held a one-woman show, "Devotional Art", at the Continental Gallery. Emily Ford, with her sisters and her mother, was a member of the Ladies' National Association for the Repeal of the Contagious Diseases Acts; Josephine Butler was a family friend. In 1908 Emily Ford attended a conference in Geneva on the state regulation of prostitution and its effect on the white slave trade. Emily Ford's portrait of Josephine Butler was presented to the Leeds City Art Gallery by R.B. Nisbet in 1924.

In 1886 Emily Ford was a member of the MANCHESTER SOCIETY FOR WOMEN'S SUFFRAGE and in 1889–90 signed the Women Householders' Declaration in favour of women's suffrage. She was a vice-president of the LEEDS SUFFRAGE SOCIETY and designed its membership card. In 1905 she was that society's delegate to the NATIONAL UNION OF WOMEN'S SUFFRAGE SOCIETIES' annual convention and in 1906–7 subscribed to the LONDON SOCIETY FOR WOMEN'S SUFFRAGE. She took an active part in the work of the Leeds Society, chairing outdoor meetings in spite of suffering from rowdy and threatening audiences. In 1892 she wrote *Rejected Addresses*, a one-act play with a suffrage content, as well as *A Perfect Character: A Sketch*. She also wrote and performed monologues, *Character Sketches from Yorkshire Life*, to suffrage societies. In 1913 she offered to perform the monologues to the CAMBRIDGE ASSOCIATION FOR WOMEN'S SUFFRAGE, an invitation which was duly accepted. The *Cambridge Independent Press* reported that "She succeeded in holding the interest of her hearers, an achievement of which any actress who gives an afternoon's entertainment alone, has every reason to feel proud".

Emily Ford also put her artistic abilities at the service of the suffrage movement. She was vice-chairman of the ARTISTS' SUFFRAGE LEAGUE and in

1908 designed "Factory Acts" ("They've a Cheek"), produced as a poster and a postcard, a commentary on protective legislation passed on women's behalf, without their acquiesence. She offered to make the 80 shield-shaped BANNERS on which were displayed the names of town councils which had passed resolutions in favour of the Conciliation Bill, which were carried in the Coronation Procession of 17 June 1911. Dora Meeson COATES, fellow artist, near neighbour and close friend wrote that Emily Ford's London studio "was a meeting-ground for artists, suffragists, people who *did* things. She had been a great beauty and, though no longer young . . . was still full of charm, with a wondrous energy for life and work". She also commented that "Emily had learnt much from Burne-Jones and her symbolic figures are strongly reminiscent of his work". Emily Ford's *Towards the Dawn*, described at the time as a "feminist painting", was given in 1890 to Newnham College by Millicent FAWCETT, an old friend, to celebrate her daughter's success in the tripos. Unfortunately this picture has now disappeared. Emily Ford exhibited regularly at the Leeds Arts Club, encouraged by Frank RUTTER, and designed several stained-glass windows with Mary LOWNDES. In her will Emily Ford left a small legacy to Dora Meeson Coates.

Address: Adel Grange, near Leeds; (from 1870s) 3L Hyde Park Mansions, Marylebone Road, London NW; studio at 44 Glebe Place, Chelsea, London SW; (1921) Adel Willows, near Leeds.
Photograph: in J. Hannam, *Isabella Ford*, 1989.
Bibliography: D.M. Coates, *George Coates: His Art and Life*, 1937; L. Tickner, *The Spectacle of Women: Imagery of the Suffrage Campaign 1907–14*, 1987; J. Hannam, *Isabella Ford*, 1989.

FORD, ISABELLA ORMSTON (1855–1924) Born in Leeds, into a Quaker family, sister of Emily FORD. Alfred Waterhouse, a fellow Quaker, in 1864 was the architect of the family home, Adel Grange. Their mother Hannah was a cousin of Elizabeth Pease NICHOL, and was involved in the planning of the early stages of the campaign conducted by the Ladies' National Society for the Repeal of the Contagious Diseases Acts. The family was part of the mid-nineteenth-century radical liberal network. Mazzini, John Bright and Stepniak were all friends of the family and in 1883 Susan B. Anthony stayed with the Fords, although both Emily and Isabella were away from home at the time. Isabella Ford, together with her mother and sister, was in 1886 a member of the MANCHESTER NATIONAL SOCIETY FOR WOMEN'S SUFFRAGE. They were, of course, long-time and most active members of the LEEDS SUFFRAGE SOCIETY. From her youth Isabella Ford was a friend of Millicent FAWCETT and of Josephine Butler and, from the 1880s, of Olive Schreiner. In 1888 Isabella Ford supported the Fawcett faction and remained a member of the CENTRAL COMMITTEE OF THE NATIONAL SOCIETY FOR WOMEN'S SUFFRAGE, but by 1895 she was a member of the executive committee of the CENTRAL NATIONAL SOCIETY FOR WOMEN'S SUFFRAGE. She was an active supporter of the Women's Trade Union League and, although a Liberal in the 1880s, by the early 1890s she had become involved with the Leeds Socialist League. In the early 1890s she was intent on organizing the women textile workers of the West Riding of Yorkshire and in 1896 was a delegate from the Tailoresses' Union to the Trades Union Congress. In the 1890s Isabella Ford was a member of the WOMEN'S EMANCIPATION UNION. She was an activist in the radical suffragist movement to involve working women in the cause. Elizabeth Wolstenholme ELMY remarked in a letter to Harriet McILQUHAM, 21 February 1902, that "Isabella Ford told me they were getting on splendidly with the Yorkshire working women eager to sign. So the Yorkshire and Cheshire sig[nature]s exceed those sent up from Lancashire last year". Sarah REDDISH, who had organized the Lancashire petition in 1901, had followed it up by instituting a similar campaign in Yorkshire and Cheshire and Isabella Ford had undertaken a major share of the work, finally accompanying a few of the women, and the petition, to present it to the House of Commons. Keir HARDIE arranged a meeting in Chelsea to publicize the petition at which Isabella Ford was one of the speakers. She stressed that the fact that suffrage bills had until then served only to enfranchise middle-class women was due merely to tactical necessity and that the socialist movement should not use this as an excuse to avoid taking seriously the women's suffrage movement. By 1903 Isabella Ford was elected to the National Administrative Council of the Independent Labour Party and she used this position to stress the interdependence of the interests of women and labour. In November 1903 Isabella Ford, speaking for the NATIONAL UNION OF WOMEN'S SUFFRAGE SOCIETIES, and Christabel Pankhurst, speaking for the newly formed WOMEN'S SOCIAL AND POLITICAL UNION appeared together at a meeting in Sheffield to persuade working women to join the SHEFFIELD SUFFRAGE SOCIETY. In 1904 Isabella Ford appeared, advocating a limited suffrage for women, in a debate organized by Sylvia PANKHURST for the Fulham ILP. Margaret Bondfield, speaking for an adult suffrage measure, was her opponent. In 1905 Isabella Ford attended the conference of the Labour Representation Committee, supporting Selina COOPER who failed to persuade the delegates to back a limited measure of suffrage for women. In the following years Isabella Ford maintained the pressure on the Labour party, attempting to persuade it to commit itself to women's suffrage. In May 1905 she was in the House of Commons, along with Mrs PANKHURST, Elizabeth Wolstenholme Elmy, Nellie Alma MARTEL and members of 28 branches of the Women's Co-operative Guild and heard Bamford Slack's suffrage bill talked out. In 1905 Isabella Ford was a delegate from Leeds to the NUWSS annual convention and in February 1906 gave £25 towards the costs of the first "women's parliament" organized by the WSPU in London at the Caxton Hall. She was present on the day and wrote a report of the occasion for the *Labour Leader*, 2 March. In 1906 she was a member of the WOMEN'S FRANCHISE DECLARATION COMMITTEE, vice-president of the CENTRAL SOCIETY FOR WOMEN'S SUFFRAGE and in the same year subscribed both to its successor, the LONDON SOCIETY FOR WOMEN'S SUFFRAGE, and to the WSPU. On 11 December 1906 she was present at the banquet at the Savoy organized by Mrs Fawcett to celebrate the release of the WSPU prisoners. In 1907, still committed to the Labour party, she was forced to disassociate herself from the WSPU, or, to be more accurate, the WSPU disassociated itself from suffragists, including Isabella Ford, who supported the Labour party. She then concentrated on working for the suffrage cause through the NUWSS, to the executive committee of which she was elected in 1907, and did not seek re-election to the National Administrative Council of the ILP. Over the next few years she continued working to persuade the Labour party of the necessity of supporting women's suffrage and to persuade the NUWSS to align itself with the Labour party, which was, she said, the natural supporter of working women and it was they who would most benefit from the social ameliorations that would follow from women's enfranchisement. In 1912 her hopes were justified when the NUWSS instituted the Election Fighting Fund to support Labour party candidates at elections. With Annot ROBINSON and Ada Nield CHEW she immediately went to campaign at Holmfirth, at the first by-election to be held under the new policy. Until the outbreak of war she covered the country, speaking at an immense number and wide range of suffrage meetings, and, for the first time for several years, attending the ILP annual conference.

In June 1908 Isabella Ford had attended the congress of the INTERNATIONAL WOMAN SUFFRAGE ALLIANCE in Amsterdam, in 1909 that held in London, and in 1913 went to Budapest for what was to prove the final meeting before the war. Fluent in French and German, and with an international outlook, Isabella Ford was adamant for peace and, with such other executive committee members as Helena SWANWICK and Catherine MARSHALL, was concerned that the NUWSS should support a peace campaign. Isabella Ford joined the Union of Democratic Control and in April 1915, with Margaret ASHTON, Kathleen COURTNEY and Catherine Marshall, resigned from the executive committee of the NUWSS when it refused to support a delegation to the International Women's Peace Congress to be held at the Hague. She was one of the 24 women who were prevented from attending the Congress when the government suspended all cross-Channel shipping. In 1919 Isabella Ford was one of the British delegates to the Women's International Congress at which was founded the Women's International League for Peace and Freedom. She was then one of the first members of the organizing committee of the British section of the Women's International League and continued to support it, both in spirit and financially, until her death.

By 1904 Isabella Ford was a member of the management committee of the Leeds Arts Club and associated through this with a wide range of artists and writers, including G.B. Shaw W.B. Yeats and

Thomas Cobden-Sanderson. Mary GAWTHORPE was a fellow member. Isabella Ford published three novels replete with social realism: *Miss Blake of Monkshalton*, 1890, *On the Threshold*, 1895, and *Mr Elliott*, 1901, as well as many articles over the course of 30 years for such journals as the *Labour League* and the *Common Cause*. Her pamphlet *Women and Socialism*, in which she considered the relationship between class and sex oppression, was published by the ILP in 1904.

Address: Adel Grange, near Leeds; (from 1870s) 3L Hyde Park Mansions, Marylebone Road, London NW; (1921) Adel Willows, near Leeds.
Photograph: in J. Hannam, *Isabella Ford*, 1989.
Bibliography: J. Hannam, *Isabella Ford*, 1989.

FOREST OF DEAN (NUWSS) In 1913 the society was a member of the WEST OF ENGLAND FEDERATION OF THE NATIONAL UNION OF WOMEN'S SUFFRAGE SOCIETIES. Secretary (1913) Mrs Price, Mount Pleasant, Yorkley, Lydney, Gloucestershire.

FORRES committee of the NATIONAL SOCIETY FOR WOMEN'S SUFFRAGE Was in existence in 1872 when its convenor was Mr Miller of the *Forres Gazette*. In 1913 the society was a member of the NORTH OF SCOTLAND FEDERATION OF THE NATIONAL UNION OF WOMEN'S SUFFRAGE SOCIETIES. Secretary (1913) Miss Jessie Hay, 91 High St., Forres, Morayshire.

FORTROSE (NUWSS) In 1913 the society was a member of the NORTH OF SCOTLAND FEDERATION OF THE NATIONAL UNION OF WOMEN'S SUFFRAGE SOCIETIES. Secretary (1913) Mrs S.J. Haldane, St Catherine's, Fortrose, Ross and Cromarty.

FORWARD CYMRIC SUFFRAGE UNION A breakaway group from, and the greater part of, the CYMRIC SUFFRAGE UNION. After the failure of the Conciliation Bill Edith MANSELL-MOULLIN and the majority of the members of the Cymric Suffrage Union pledged themselves to militant methods and broke away from the society and reformed, in October 1912, as the Forward Cymric Suffrage Union, pledged to work for no political party and to oppose any government that refused women the vote. It attracted members from Wales as well as continuing its campaign among the Welsh in London. Members of the FCSU sported a red dragon badge and a motto "O Iesu, n'ad gamwaith" (O Jesus, do not allow unfairness). In June 1914 the FCSU gave its support to Sylvia PANKHURST's EAST LONDON FEDERATION OF THE SUFFRAGETTES. Edith Mansell-Moullin, ill, resigned from her position with the Union in 1916.

Founder and honorary organizer (1913, 1916) Edith Mansell-Moullin, 69 Wimpole Street, London; honorary secretary (1913) Mrs M.E. Davies, 53 Wandsworth Bridge Road, London SW; honorary treasurer (1913) Miss Norbury, 33 Morpeth Mansions, Westminster, London SW.

Bibliography: K. Cook and Neil Evans, "'The petty antics of the bell-ringing boisterous band'?: the women's suffrage movement in Wales", in Angela V. John (ed.), *Our Mothers' Land: Chapters in Welsh Women's History, 1830–1939*, 1991.

FORWARD SUFFRAGE UNION Founded in September 1907 by Eva MCLAREN, Marie CORBETT and Frances Heron Maxwell, in order to concentrate the activities of Liberal women belonging to the Women's Liberal Associations affiliated to the WOMEN'S LIBERAL FEDERATION, on their own enfranchisement. Its formation acknowledged that the dissolution of the UNION OF PRACTICAL SUFFRAGISTS on the passing of a resolution in favour of women's suffrage by the Women's Liberal Federation in 1903 had been premature. On 17 November 1911 the Forward Suffrage Union was represented by Alison GARLAND in the deputation to Asquith and Lloyd George that attempted to resolve the crisis over the fate of the Conciliation Bill.

President (1908) Lady GROVE; honorary secretary (1908) Mrs Corbett, Woodgate, Danehill, Sussex, with (1909) Miss G. Hutcheson, 58 Leigh Road, Highbury, London N; honorary treasurer (1908) Mrs Harriette Raphael, Wild Hatch, Hendon, London NW.

Address: (1910) 75 Victoria Street, London SW.

FRANKLIN, HUGH (1889–1962) Brought up in a Jewish family, in 1909 he lost his religious faith. His father, Arthur Franklin, was a senior partner in the banking firm, A. Keyser & Co.; he also acquired the publishers George Routledge (later Routledge and Kegan Paul – *see under* PUBLISHERS AND PRINTERS) and was associated with the Notting Hill Electric Light Company. His mother Caroline Franklin had been educated at Bedford College, was a very active philanthropist, a member of the CENTRAL AND WEST OF ENGLAND SOCIETY FOR WOMEN'S SUFFRAGE in 1899 and a member of the executive committee of the JEWISH LEAGUE FOR WOMAN SUFFRAGE in 1913. Herbert Samuel, a member of the Liberal Cabinet, was an uncle. One of Franklin's sisters, Alice, was a socialist and honorary secretary of a group of young intellectuals who called themselves "The Utopians". She later became honorary secretary and treasurer of the Townswomen's Guild. Another sister, Helen, also a socialist, married Norman Bentwich; Eva Hubback was a cousin. Another cousin, Ruth Franklin, was honorary secretary of the Jewish League for Woman Suffrage and honorary secretary of the North Kensington branch of the LONDON SOCIETY FOR WOMEN'S SUFFRAGE. His aunt, Henrietta ("Netta") Franklin was in 1913 a member of the executive committee of the Jewish League for Woman Suffrage, from 1916 to 1917 chairman of the NATIONAL UNION OF WOMEN'S SUFFRAGE SOCIETIES, and from 1925 to 1927 president of the National Council of Women.

Hugh Franklin was educated at Clifton College and in 1908 went to Caius College, Cambridge, to read Engineering. In 1909 he attended a suffrage meeting in London at the Queen's Hall which was addressed by Christabel PANKHURST, Mrs PANKHURST and Mrs PETHICK-LAWRENCE; this was his first contact with the militants and he was impressed. During the summer he took part in the campaign by chalking pavements and selling *Votes for Women*, both in London and near his family's country home at Chesham in Buckinghamshire. In October 1909, already a member of the Independent Labour Party and of the Fabian Society, he changed his Cambridge course from Engineering to Economics and Sociology. He joined the Cambridge branch of the MEN'S LEAGUE FOR WOMEN'S SUFFRAGE, organizing meetings there for both Mrs FAWCETT and Lady McLAREN; he resigned in November 1911. In 1910 he had joined the newly-formed MEN'S POLITICAL UNION FOR WOMEN'S ENFRANCHISEMENT. His father appears to have offered Victor DUVAL, the founder of the MPU and later to be Hugh Franklin's brother-in-law, a monetary inducement to persuade his son to leave the MPU. The offer was spurned and Hugh Franklin became a member of the committee of the MPU and an assistant organizer. He missed most of his Cambridge final examinations because he was helping to organize the WSPU "From Prison to Citizenship" procession held on 18 June 1910. He reluctantly accepted an offer from Sir Matthew Nathan, Secretary to the Post Office, to be his private secretary; Herbert Samuel was Postmaster-General at the time.

Hugh Franklin was arrested during the "Black Friday" debacle in Parliament Square on 18 November 1910, but, as was the general experience that day, was not charged. Later, in February 1911 Mrs BRAILSFORD wrote to him asking if he could identify the woman whom he had seen struck in the face by a policeman and for any general account he could give of his experience of taking part in WSPU deputations. On 26 November 1910 Franklin took a whip to Winston Churchill, whom, as Home Secretary, he held responsible for the police brutality. According to Sylvia Pankhurst in *The Suffragette Movement*, Hugh Franklin was particularly incensed by Churchill's insulting attitude to Anne Cobden SANDERSON, when he had encountered her, a family friend, in the fray. Franklin was sentenced to six weeks' imprisonment. His father wrote to the Chief Rabbi to discuss his son's disgrace and received the reply, "Pray do not worry about your son. Hugh's act was foolish, but happily there was nothing dishonourable. We *have* reason for anxiety, as our only son is still very ill". Franklin went on hunger strike in Pentonville but served the whole sentence. Needless to say he was dismissed from his post as Sir Nathan's secretary. In February 1911 Hugh Franklin was enrolled in the YOUNG PURPLE WHITE AND GREEN CLUB, possibly in recognition of his suffering for the cause; he was obviously a good sport. Two months later, on 8 March 1911, he was arrested after trying to smash Churchill's windows in Eccleston Square, was sentenced to a month's imprisonment, went on hunger strike and was forcibly fed. On his release the Pethick-Lawrences arranged for him to go on holiday with them to Cornwall. He then became a peripatetic speaker, attending WSPU meetings throughout the country. On one occasion he stayed with the LOWYS. In February 1912 he wrote to his uncle Herbert Samuel to protest against the forcible feeding of William Ball. In February 1913, after two months spent in hiding above Henderson's book shop, known as the "Bombshop", at 66 Charing Cross Road, Hugh Franklin was arrested for setting fire to an empty train at Harrow. Apparently he was recognized while committing the act, because the railway line was that used regularly by his family as they travelled to their country home near Chesham. He was forcibly fed while on remand, was sentenced to nine months' imprisonment, went on hunger strike and was forcibly fed over 100 times until he was released under the "Cat and Mouse" Act. He did not return to prison but, under the alias of "Henry Forster", in April escaped to the Continent, where he stayed in Brussels until the outbreak of war.

During the war he served as a clerical officer at the Ordnance Factories at Woolwich and in 1915 married Elsie DUVAL, to whom he had been engaged since 1913. Although they were married in the West London Synagogue and his mother was a witness to the wedding, his father disinherited him for "marrying out" of the Jewish faith and never saw him again. Hugh Franklin was an admirer of Kathleen COURTNEY and the anti-war campagin, and supported Sylvia PANKHURST's *Workers' Dreadnought*; she even sought to borrow his bound volumes of the paper in 1920. In 1919 his wife Elsie died in the influenza epidemic and in 1921 he was married again, to Elsie Constance Tuke. After the war he entered the timber trade. In 1931 he rejoined the Labour party and contested, unsuccessfully, elections in 1931 and 1935. He did win a seat on the Middlesex County Council in 1946 and held office in the New Fabian Research Bureau, the National Executive of the Labour party, and was honorary treasurer of the National Council for Civil Liberties from 1934 to 1939.

Address: (1910) 29 Pembridge Gardens, London W; Chartridge Lodge, Chesham, Buckinghamshire; (1915) 38 Smith Street, Chelsea, London SW.

Photograph: on postcard, describing him as "Member of the Men's Political Union for Women's Enfranchisement", John Johnson Collection, Bodleian Library, Oxford, and in Fawcett Library Collection.

Archival source: Suffragette Fellowship Collection, Museum of London; B. Harrison, taped interview with Colin Franklin, nephew to Hugh Franklin, 1977, Fawcett Library.

Bibliography: H. Bentwich, *If I Forget Thee: Some Chapters of Autobiography, 1912–1920*, 1973; A.V. John and C. Eustance (eds), *The Men's Share?: Masculinities, Male Support and Women's Suffrage in Britain, 1890–1920*, 1997.

FRASER, HELEN (1881–alive 1964 in Australia) (later Mrs Moyes) Born in Yorkshire, to Scottish parents, educated at Higher Grade School, Queen's Park, Glasgow, and then opened a studio in Glasgow, specializing in black and white illustration work and embroidery. She joined the WOMEN's SOCIAL AND POLITICAL UNION in the autumn of 1906 after hearing Teresa Billington (*see* Teresa BILLINGTON-GREIG) speaking in Glasgow and, soon after, her father took the chair at a meeting at which Mrs PANKHURST and Annie KENNEY spoke. Helen Fraser then went to England to help the WSPU campaign at the Huddersfield by-election and on her return was asked to become treasurer of the Glasgow WSPU and an ORGANIZER in Scotland for the WSPU. In November, in this capacity, she wrote to the committee of the GLASGOW AND WEST OF SCOTLAND SUFFRAGE ASSOCIATION (NUWSS) to ask them "to afford her (and Mrs Pearce) [Isabella Bream Pearce, friend of Elizabeth Wolstenholme ELMY, who had written as 'Lily Bell' in the *Labour Leader*] an opportunity to address a meeting". She and Mrs Pearce were asked to meet the committee "with a view of ascertaining the lines on which their Union intend to prosecute their work and to receive suggestions from them regarding a proposal contained in Miss Fraser's letter that we should find some means of working along the same lines". In the event there was, of course, never any chance of the two societies being able to work together.

In early 1907 Helen Fraser went to Aberdeen to organize the WSPU campaign at the Aberdeen South by-election. Adela PANKHURST came up to help and Helen Fraser recalled that "It was winter and v. cold. I met her at the station and was horrified at her breathing (we were both v. young). I took her to lodgings and sent for the doctor, who, like me, was v. critical of her being allowed to travel. She had pneumonia. I asked if her mother had seen her before she left London and she said 'yes'." This lack of care, which Helen Fraser remembered 50 years after the event, may well have sown the seed of her disillusionment with the WSPU. However, Adela recovered, the WSPU campaign engendered much interest and the Liberal majority was reduced from 4000 to under 400. Helen Fraser was one of the speakers at the June 1908 Hyde Park Demonstration but soon after left the WSPU because she did not agree with "violent tactics". In July 1908 she wrote to Isabel SEYMOUR that she did not like Mary LEIGH's action in breaking Asquith's window; "that seemed to me a bad blunder". She also thought it "simply wicked" to have allowed Florence HAIG and Maud JOACHIM to commit violence, for which they received three months' imprisonment. There is also a suggestion that she fell foul of internal politicking in the WSPU. She hinted that, as a result of the publicity she received after campaigning at Hexham, including a very favourable article about her in the *Daily Mail*, she was asked not to take part in any other election campaign. With hindsight she had come to the conclusion that this was because Mrs Pankhurst was always fearful of any challenge to Christabel's supremacy. There may be some truth in this explanation; Helen Fraser had in the early months of 1908 extended and consolidated the WSPU operation in Scotland, setting up, as the SCOTTISH WOMEN'S SOCIAL AND POLITICAL UNION, a headquarters in Glasgow and apparently planning to publish a Scottish version of *Votes for Women* (see under NEWSPAPERS AND JOURNALS). Helen Fraser resigned from the Glasgow WSPU, describing, in the same letter to Isabel Seymour, how "it was utterly impossible to work with my Committee – I stood it as long as I could but I got to the stage where the thought of them made me feel hysterical".

Almost immediately Helen Fraser was approached by the NATIONAL UNION OF WOMEN'S SUFFRAGE SOCIETIES and asked if she would work for them. She accepted and on 20 August 1908 wrote to Caroline PHILLIPS that she had been "caravanning for the Cause" (see CARAVANS AND CARS). She had begun her journey at Selkirk and had travelled down as far as Tynemouth. In this letter she comments that "I had a very worrying time before I resigned and felt very tired and ill when I did. I still could do with more rest but feel much better and as if I saw things clearer. It doesn't seem true even yet that I am no longer connected with you all".

Committees, as usual, created problems. That of the Glasgow and West of Scotland Association for Women's Suffrage took exception to Helen Fraser's appointment, which they said was made without consulting the Scottish societies, and "that it was not an acceptable appointment and that we suggest that she should be employed in England and that the N.U. [National Union] should make us a grant towards the expenses of an organizer to be appointed by us". When in October 1908 Helen Fraser wrote to the GWSAWS to say that Louisa Lumsden, the renowned educationist (and owner of the caravan she had used on her travels), was willing to come and address them, the Association replied curtly that a meeting could not be arranged at such short notice. Helen Fraser was herself a very effective speaker and in the year 1908–9 the sums collected for the NUWSS at her meetings amounted to £56.19.10. She spoke all over the country, not only in Scotland. For instance, in 1912 she addressed a meeting organized by the CAMBRIDGE WOMEN'S SUFFRAGE ASSOCIATION held during a course of Extension Lectures. In 1915 Helen Fraser seems to have acted as temporary honorary secretary of the PENARTH WOMEN'S SUFFRAGE SOCIETY for a few weeks in the summer. She was a member of the executive committee of the NUWSS for 14 years.

During the First World War she worked for a time for the National War Savings Committee, was lent to the Board of Agriculture in a mission to persuade women to work on the land and in 1917, at the suggestion of Mrs FAWCETT, was sent to the USA in order to speak there about Britain's war effort. She returned in the summer of 1918 and her book *Women and War Work* was published as a result of this lengthy tour, during the course of which, travelling through 40 states, she spoke 332 times in 312 days.

At the end of the war Helen Fraser turned her attention to the campaign to elect women as members of parliament. She spoke, for instance in Cardiff, on behalf of the Joint Committee for Getting Women into Parliament. She herself was the first woman to be adopted in Scotland as a parliamentary candidate and fought, unsuccessfully, as a National Liberal, Glasgow (Govan) in 1922, Lanark in 1923 and Hamilton in 1924. In 1923 she attended as a delegate from the NUWSS the conference of the International Alliance of Women for Suffrage and Equal Citizenship in Paris (see INTERNATIONAL

WOMAN SUFFRAGE ALLIANCE). She married and in 1939 emigrated to Sydney, Australia, where she was in touch with Adela Pankhurst.

Address: (1923) 6 Kensington Park Gardens, London W11.
Photograph: in Suffragette Fellowship Collection, Museum of London.
Archival source: Suffragette Fellowship Collection, Museum of London.
Bibliography: H. Fraser, *Women and War Work*, 1918; H. Moyes, *A Woman in a Man's World*, 1971.

FREE CHURCH LEAGUE FOR WOMEN SUFFRAGE

Founded in 1910 by Mrs Strickland, the Rev. Hatty Baker and Miss L.E. Turquand. The object of the League was:

> the advocacy of the enfranchisement of women on the same basis that men are or shall be enfranchised. The methods of the F.C.L. are religious and educational... All men and women of Free Church principles of whatever denomination are accepted as members... Meetings are often held in Free Church Schoolrooms, even in the Churches themselves; sometimes with the Minister speaking or presiding... The key-note of the F.C.L. may be said to be the Puritan idea of respect for personality. The League consists of a Central Branch composed of members from all parts of Great Britain, and of Local Branches. Branches make their own rules, which must be in accordance with the general principles of the League. An Annual Meeting is held in May, to which all branches send representatives in proportion to their membership. The Governing Body consists of an Executive of not less than 21 members (two-thirds of which must be women), and is elected annually. (*Suffrage Annual and Women's Who's Who*, 1913).

The League's BANNER, with its motto "It is the Dawn" "Arise and Hear What the Spirit saith unto the Churches", was carried in the procession of 18 June 1910. In 1912 the League affiliated to the FEDERATED COUNCIL OF SUFFRAGE SOCIETIES. From 1913 to 1915 the League published the *Free Church Suffrage Times*, which between 1916 and 1920 continued as the *Coming Day*. Among the League's vice-presidents were Lady Aberconway (*see* Laura McLAREN), Annie Leigh BROWNE, Mrs Henry Holiday, Mr and Mrs PETHICK-LAWRENCE, Margaret McMillan, Mrs Saul SOLOMON, Albert Dawson, editor of the *Christian Commonwealth*, and Mrs Cobden UNWIN. On 13 May 1918 the League was represented at the NATIONAL UNION OF WOMEN'S SUFFRAGE SOCIETIES' celebrations in the Queen's Hall to mark the passing of the bill granting a limited enfranchisement to women.

President (1913) Rev. Dr J. Clifford; president of executive (1913) Mrs Strickland, "Halsteads", Hastings; honorary general secretary (1913) Rev. Fleming Williams; honorary treasurer (1913) Mrs S.H. Holman, 55 Talbot Road, Highgate, London N; honorary press secretary (1913) Miss L.E. Turquand, 73 Tremaine Road, Highgate, London N; secretary (1911, 1913) Mrs Fleming Williams, 2 Holmbury View, Springfield, Clapton, London NE; (1917) Miss Beatrice C.M. Brown.

Address: (1913) 2 Holmbury View, Springfield, Clapton, London, NE; (1914, 1917) 13 Bream's Buildings, Chancery Lane, London WC.

FRIEDLANDER, [VIOLET] HELEN (c. 1879–1950) Poet and novelist. She joined the WOMEN'S SOCIAL AND POLITICAL UNION in 1908 and her poem, "The Women's Army", sung to the tune of "Marching Through Georgia", appeared in *Votes for Women*, 5 March 1909. That summer, with her mother (both her parents and her brother were very supportive of the WSPU), she organized the WSPU summer campaign in Lowestoft. Lady WRIGHT helped by paying for half the cost of a WSPU poster at the railway station. In January 1910 V.H. Friedlander (as she always appears) was honorary secretary of the Forest Gate WSPU and was ORGANIZER in West Ham during the general election campaign. It was probably at this time that she and her brother helped to make the BANNER for the WSPU West Ham society, which is now in the collection of the Museum of London. Her literary credentials gained her the job of selecting the mottoes for the 1911 WSPU Calendar. In March 1912 she took part in the window-smashing campaign and was sentenced to four months' imprisonment, which was spent in Winson Green Prison. A novel she published in 1922, *Mainspring*, although not concerned with the suffrage movement, does contain a very realistic description of the journey in a Black Maria and the subsequent sojourn in a woman's prison. The very atmospheric description of a prison cell even includes mention of the text-book on *The Home*, the presence of which so many of the suffragettes remarked. Poems by V.H. Friedlander were published in the 1920s and 1930s in a range of magazines, including *Country Life*, and in 1931 a collection was published as *Mirrors & Angels*. She contributed the poem, "The Master Joy", which concludes *Pathfinders*, a description by W.H. Brown of the Reformers' Memorial (*see* Emma CORFIELD).

Address: (1910) 129 Earlham Grove, Forest Gate, London E; (1950) Byfield, 16 Laughton Way, Buckhurst Hill, Essex.

FRIENDS' LEAGUE FOR WOMEN'S SUFFRAGE The League's aim was "To secure for women the Parliamentary Franchise on the same terms as it is or may be granted to men." The honorary secretaries were Roger Clark and his sister Alice CLARK; the president was Mrs Guilema Crosfield, of Cambridge. In 1912 the League affiliated to the FEDERATED COUNCIL OF SUFFRAGE SOCIETIES. The secretary of the Bristol branch was Helen Sturge, sister of Emily and Elizabeth Sturge (*see* STURGE SISTERS). In 1933 Helen Sturge wrote to an inquirer to report that she could find no trace of any papers about the Friends' League, saying that she had moved house in 1927 and "cleared away things that seemed to be done with". She wrote that she could not remember exactly when the League was founded, but that it was probably two or three years before 1912. It may be that this is the same body as the "Friends' Council for Woman Suffrage" (honorary secretary Miss Sophia Seekings, 8 Brookfield, West Hill, Highgate, London N), which was founded *c.* Jan 1911. In 1912 the Yearly Meeting of the Society of Friends was held in Manchester and Helen Sturge remembered that a number of women Friends representing the League took the opportunity of discussing the question of women's suffrage. They gave her the responsibility of bringing the subject before Yearly Meeting which, although the Clerks were rather unwilling, she did. After that meetings were held in various places and she spoke at several of them. The League was still in existence in 1917. Joint honorary secretaries (1913) Roger Clark and Alice Clark, Mill Field, Street, Somerset, (1914) corresponding address of society, Walden, Gloucestershire, (1917) Mrs A.J. Crosfield, 5 Madingly Road, Cambridge.

Archival source: Friends' Library, London.

FRIENDS OF WOMEN'S SUFFRAGE A scheme implemented by the NATIONAL UNION OF WOMEN'S SUFFRAGE SOCIETIES at a special council meeting held in London on 14 May 1912; at the same council meeting the NUWSS ratified its adoption of the Election Fighting Fund policy. The idea was to build up working-class support for the NUWSS by visiting women in their own homes and giving them suitable reading material. It was received with varying degrees of warmth by district societies. In its first year the MANCHESTER SOCIETY reported that the scheme was thoroughly successful; it had established seven "Friends of Women's Suffrage" committees in its area, and 58 visitors had enrolled 230 Friends. In Bolton 42 members of the BOLTON SOCIETY each had a circle of Friends, with 334 of the latter enrolled after six months. The idea of Friends of Women's Suffrage was discussed at a meeting of the CAMBRIDGE ASSOCIATION on 25 April and by the end of May the Association had agreed to procure "Cards for the signatures of 'Friends of W. Suff.' [which were] used at all meetings and taken round with the distribution of leaflets." By April 1913, 277 Friends had been enrolled by the Association and were being visited. At a meeting on 16 April 1912 the BEDFORD SOCIETY made its first appeal to working women. Between 20 and 30 women joined as Associates paying 1d and receiving a badge. This was not the same as the "Friends of Women's Suffrage scheme" which was discussed at a meeting on 21 June 1912. Only full members, paying a subscription of not less than 1s a year, could vote at the annual general meeting, thus excluding Friends and Associates. In contrast, as soon as the proposal was made in May 1912, the SOUTHAMPTON BRANCH, always conservative, decided that it could not support the Friends of Women's Suffrage. By 1913 the NUWSS had enrolled 46 662 Friends and produced for them a four-page newsletter, *The Friend of Women's Suffrage* (no. 1, July 1913) to which Ida O'MALLEY was a contributor. One of the objectives of the ACTIVE SERVICE LEAGUE, formed in early 1914, was to recruit many new "Friends of Women's Suffrage".

Archival source: Minutes of the Cambridge Association for Women's Suffrage; minutes of the Bolton Society; annual report of the Manchester Society; National Union of Women's Suffrage Societies, Southampton branch Minute Book, 1911–1914.

FRODSHAM AND EDDISBURY (NUWSS)   In 1913 the society was a member of the WEST LANCS, WEST CHESHIRE, AND NORTH WALES FEDERATION OF THE NATIONAL UNION OF WOMEN'S SUFFRAGE SOCIETIES. Secretary (1913) *pro tem* Mrs Dutton, Brackenhurst, Helsby, Cheshire.

FULHAM (branch of the LONDON SOCIETY FOR WOMEN'S SUFFRAGE)   Secretary (1909) Miss Jenner, 25 Warwick Gardens, London, W; (1913) Miss M.J. Smith, 20 Talgarth Road, West Kensington, London W.

FULHAM (WSPU)   Secretary (1906) Miss I. Gardiner, 44 Brookeville Road, Fulham, London W.

G

GALASHIELS (NUWSS) In 1913 the society was a member of the SCOTTISH FEDERATION OF THE NATIONAL UNION OF WOMEN'S SUFFRAGE SOCIETIES. Secretary (1913) Miss Jessie Tod, 187 Magdala Terrace, Galashiels, Selkirk.

GALLOWAY branch of the National Society for Women's Suffrage Founded in 1870. Secretary (1872) Miss Dalziel, Glenluce, Wigtonshire. The Galloway society associated itself with the new CENTRAL COMMITTEE OF THE NATIONAL SOCIETY FOR WOMEN'S SUFFRAGE in 1872.

GAMES AND TOYS The translation of the mechanics of the women's suffrage campaign into board and card games was a masterstroke that originated from within the WOMEN'S SOCIAL AND POLITICAL UNION. Not only were funds raised, but the message of the cause was brought into domestic circles where more rabid propaganda might not have been welcomed. Novelty manufacturers clearly thought that the campaign had commercial appeal, launching several games to rival those of the WSPU. There is no evidence that donations were made from their profits to any of the suffrage societies. The many bazaars organized by the WSPU and the WOMEN'S FREEDOM LEAGUE attracted donations from members of dolls attired in suffragette costume. In December 1908 the Manchester Doll Show could boast a "Suffragette Exhibit"; there is no evidence that commercial manufacturers produced such consciousness-raising items. Rather, as with CHINA, FILM and POSTCARDS, "novelty" toys equalled "comic". Still extant are such novelties as a chess set which pits suffragettes against policemen, and a jack-in-the-box springing a "fright" of a caricature suffragette, but it is not clear if these were the result of commercial manufacture or one-off productions by amateurs. There are doubtless more such toys and games awaiting discovery. The following games were known to have been marketed.

SUFFRAGETTE, a card game invented by the KENSINGTON branch of the WSPU, probably in the late summer of 1907. The game is described in *Votes for Women*, November 1907.
RUSHING THE HOUSE, "Illustrating an Historical Event. An amusing game for young and old", Novelty Co., 6 High Street, Hampstead. It was launched in 1908, possibly in time for Christmas, inspired by the events of that October, when Christabel PANKHURST was charged with inciting onlookers to "Rush the House of Commons".
"HOLLOWAY", or VOTES FOR WOMEN. This appears to have been issued by November 1908 and to be a slighly more complicated version of "Panko".
THE LADIES PUZZLE, also known as THE SUFFRAGETTE PUZZLE, "To get the Women's Suffrage Bill through the Houses of Parliament", F.H. Ayres Ltd, 111 Aldersgate Street, London, launched in 1908. An advertisement for it ran, "buy the suffragette puzzle and see how it can be done".
PANK-A-SQUITH, a board game, first advertised in *Votes for Women*, 22 October 1909. Mary BLATHWAYT bought the game in December 1909. She and Annie KENNEY played "Pank-a-squith" and the card game "Panko" to pass an anxious time while Jennie Kenney was being operated on at Eagle House, Batheaston, in July 1910.
PANKO, a card game, launched by Messrs Peter Gurney Ltd. The cards were designed by E.T. Reed, a *Punch* cartoonist. The game is first mentioned in *Votes for Women*, 10 December 1909. The advertisement for the game claimed, "Not only is each picture in itself an interesting memento, but the game produces intense excitement without the slightest taint of bitterness." Mary BLATHWAYT gave a set of "Panko" to her mother for Christmas 1909.
SUFFRAGETTO, "an original and interesting game of skill for two players", available by May 1909. The game was played with a squared board and coloured pieces. "The object of the Suffragette is

to pass through the lines of the Police and to effect an entry into the House of Commons: and while doing so to prevent the Police from entering Albert Hall. The duty of the Police is to break up a meeting of the Suffragettes which is being held in Albert Hall, and to keep the Suffragettes out of the House of Commons".

SUFFRAGETTES IN AND OUT OF PRISON or HOW TO GET OUT OF GAOL, a penny board game, manufactured by Whitworth Hird Ltd, Norwich and London. It was described as "Game and Puzzle – Find the way out of Gaol". Holloway is at the heart of the labyrinth. The game's packaging carries an advertisement for the *Morning Leader*.

In his autobiography, *The Wharncliffe Gardens Story: Life in a London Village* (c. 1979), J. Ronald Andrew (b. 1904) wrote, "I remember the colours of the suffragettes, they were purple, white and green. I remember this especially as we had a game at home, run on similar lines to snakes and ladders, with a dice, numbered squares, and pictures of banner-carrying suffragettes, with the slogan 'Votes for Women'. Square one on the board showed a picture of the committee rooms of the Women's Social and Political Union at the inaugural meeting at Mrs Pankhurst's house, 62 Nelson St, Manchester, and the last picture arrival at the Houses of Parliament. The ladders being the advances made by the WSPU and the snakes being the setbacks including the imprisonment of various members." None of the public collections appear to hold this game.

PLAYING CARDS were devised by the WSPU, sporting conventional suits, but with a reverse design of prison arrows in purple, white and green.

ELUSIVE CHRISTABEL, an optical toy produced by the Flashograph Co. in 1912, an allusion to Christabel Pankhurst's escape to France. Monica WHATELY possessed one of these toys, now in the Fawcett Library collection. The mystery of Christabel's whereabouts provoked a more technically sophisticated response, as *The Elusive Miss Pinkhurst*, a short film, incorporating trick photography (see under FILM).

SUFFRAGETTE, a tin toy, probably German, circa 1908. Figure of a woman with a grey and black painted skirt, red, cream and green bodice (the red may have originally been more purple, or perhaps it was a misrendering of the WSPU colours) with painted striped ribbon, and ribboned bonnet. A clockwork mechanism causes her to move in circles and ring her bell, which is in her right hand, while she holds a "Votes for Women" pamphlet in her left. WSPU speakers at street meetings used to ring hand bells to announce their presence.

Archival source: (Games) British Library; Fawcett Library; (Andrew) Westminster City Archives; (Suffragette tin toy) Sotheby's Catalogue, 1 October 1985.

GARLAND, ALISON VICKERS (1862–1939) Born in Birkenhead. In 1897, as a Liberal, she spoke at meetings in Devon and Cornwall of the CENTRAL AND WEST OF ENGLAND SOCIETY FOR WOMEN'S SUFFRAGE. In 1898 she was a member of the executive committee of the UNION OF PRACTICAL SUFFRAGISTS and in 1899 was elected president of the Devon Union of the Women's Liberal Associations. She was the delegate sent by the British Indian Parliamentary Committee to the Indian National Congress held in Lucknow in December 1899, and, as such, was the first woman to address it. She took part in the NATIONAL UNION OF WOMEN'S SUFFRAGE SOCIETIES' "Mud March" in February 1907 and on 17 November took part, representing the FORWARD SUFFRAGE UNION, in the deputation to Asquith and Lloyd George. On this occasion, rather than, as other speakers did, asking the government to proceed with the Conciliation Bill, she asked that the government itself should introduce an amendment to include women in their proposed manhood suffrage bill. In 1913 Alison Garland, who had published novels at the end of the nineteenth century (see under PUBLISHERS AND PRINTERS) wrote a suffrage play, *The Better Half*, which received glowing reviews in the daily press. Copies of the play were to be had from Miss E.A. Garland, Pengwerne Terrace, New Brighton. Alison Garland was a member of the executive committee of the WOMEN'S LIBERAL FEDERATION by 1905 and stood, unsuccessfully, as the Liberal candidate at Portsmouth South in 1918 and at Dartford, Kent, in 1922. She left the WLF, of which she had been president, 1936–9, £50 in her will.

Address: (1906) Dousland Grange, Yelverton, Devon; (1933) 7 Pengwerne Terrace, Wallasey, Cheshire; (1936) 21 Ferndale, Tunbridge Wells, Kent.

GARNETT, [FRANCES] THERESA (1888–1966) Born in Leeds, educated at a convent school, and was for some time a teacher. In 1907 she heard Adela

PANKHURST speak and was inspired to join the WOMEN'S SOCIAL AND POLITICAL UNION. In April 1909, with four others including Mrs Bertrand Russell, Theresa Garnett chained herself to a statue in the Central Lobby of the Houses of Parliament to protest against the so-called "Brawling Bill", which was intended to penalize anyone found guilty of disorderly conduct within the confines of the Palace of Westminster while parliament was in session. There were no repercussions from this stunt. On 28 June she was provided with a ticket, a "husband" and suitable attire to attend a government reception at which she managed to harangue the guests on the subject of "Votes for Women" until she was conducted from the premises. Again, she was not charged but the next day was arrested after being a member of the deputation from Caxton Hall to the Houses of Parliament and then having taken part in the ensuing stone throwing in Whitehall. She was sentenced to a month's imprisonment during the course of which she went on hunger strike and was, in addition, charged with biting and kicking a wardress in Holloway. Her defence was that she had not bitten but that the wardress may have been scratched by her "portcullis" brooch (see JEWELLERY AND BADGES). She was found guilty of assault, sentenced to a further term of imprisonment, again went on hunger strike, and was released within a few days. In August 1909, as "Annie O'Sullivan", Theresa Garnett was sentenced with, among others, Mary LEIGH, after taking part in the demonstration on the roof of the Sun Hall in Liverpool. She was imprisoned in Walton Jail, went on hunger strike and was released on 26 August. In Bristol in November 1909, wearing a "Merry Widow" hat, she accosted Churchill with a whip in her hand. The account in *Votes for Women*, 19 November 1909, mentions that she struck him several times but in an interview she recorded in 1964, Theresa Garnett says that she did not touch him. She was, in the end, charged with disturbing the peace, sentenced to a month's imprisonment in Horfield Gaol and went on hunger strike. As a protest against being forcibly fed she set fire to her cell, and was then placed in a punishment cell, in solitary confinement, for 11 of the 15 remaining days of her sentence. After being found unconscious, she spent the rest of her sentence in a hospital ward. In February 1910 she was WSPU ORGANIZER in Camberwell but, when the level of militancy increased at the end of the year, she left the WSPU and did not join any other suffrage group, although she obviously kept in touch with her erstwhile comrades. She was a Sister at the London Hospital and nursed at the Front Line during the First World War. She was an active member of the SUFFRAGETTE FELLOWSHIP after the Second World War, living in 1947 at the Minerva Club (see CLUBS) and in 1960 was honorary editor of the WOMEN'S FREEDOM LEAGUE *Bulletin*. In 1962 she gave a wooden head of Frederick PETHICK-LAWRENCE, sculpted by Albert Moroder in 1949, to the National Portrait Gallery. She was herself left a bequest in the will of Charlotte MARSH, who had been with her in the 1930s a fellow member of the Six Point Group, but was almost penniless when she died.

Address: (1960) 152 Makepeace Mansions, Makepeace Avenue, Highgate, London N.
Photograph: *Votes for Women*, 6 August 1909; by Col Blathwayt in B.M. Willmott Dobbie, *A Nest of Suffragettes in Somerset*, 1979.
Archival source: interview, 1964, contained in *Blaze of the Day* CD.

GARRETT, AGNES (1845–1935) Sister of Elizabeth Garrett ANDERSON and Millicent Garrett FAWCETT, educated, like them, at Miss Browning's school at Blackheath. From an early age she struck up a devoted friendship with her cousin Rhoda GARRETT and in 1871 joined her in an architectural apprenticeship, with the aim of setting up a business together. They worked for a short time in the office of Daniel Cottier, who had originally been a glass-painter in Glasgow but who, around 1860, came to London and attended classes given by Ruskin and Ford Maddox Ford at the Working Men's College. After brief sojourns back in Glasgow and then in Edinburgh Cottier in 1867 opened a London office at 2 Langham Place and it was there, in the neighbourhood at the centre of the feminist network, that the Garretts prepared to receive their first instruction. Apparently, however, Cottier took their fees and taught them nothing and they quickly moved to the practice of J.M. Brydon, who had been a pupil of J.J. Stevenson, brother of Flora and Louisa STEVENSON, and who was for a time in partnership with Cottier. It is more than likely that by this time the Garretts were acquainted with the Stevenson family who had earlier lived in South Shields, near to Emily DAVIES at Gateshead, and to whom they were destined to become even closer when Elizabeth Garrett married a cousin of the Stevensons. He, J.G.S. Anderson, was a business adviser to Rhoda and Agnes Garrett. J.M. Brydon was to become the architect in 1888 of Elizabeth Garrett Anderson's New Hospital for Women in the Euston Road and of the original Chelsea Town Hall, which was later to be decorated by Mary Sargant FLORENCE.

Moncure Conway, who besides being the predecessor of Stanton COIT as the incumbent of the South Place Chapel, was the author of *Travels in South Kensington*, 1882, wrote of the Garrett cousins:

> They have arrived at conclusions concerning their sex which forbid them to emulate the butterflies ... The architect who had been connected with this glass-painting firm separated from it, and having begun a business of his own, accepted the Misses Garrett to become his apprentices. They were formally articled for 18 months, during which they punctually fulfilled their engagement, working from 10 to 5 each day ... When the apprenticeship reached its last summer they went on a tour throughout England, sketching the interior and furniture of the best houses, which were freely thrown open to them. They are now an independent firm, with extensive business, and have gained fame, not only by their successful decoration of many private houses, but by their admirable treatment of the new female colleges connected with the English Universities ... They tell me that they have recognised it as a want that a beautiful decoration should be brought within the reach of the middle-class families ... they believe that with care they are able to make beautiful interiors that shall not be too costly for persons of moderate means.

Thus, after their apprenticeship, in 1875 Agnes and Rhoda Garrett set up their own "Art Decoration" business and were certainly among the very first women interior designers. They were proponents of the "Queen Anne" style of architecture and furnishing associated with J.J. Stevenson and Norman Shaw. Perhaps not surprisingly one of their first commissions was to decorate the house at 20 Upper Berkeley Street leased by Elizabeth Garrett, in which much of the organization of the 1866 suffrage petition had taken place. Among their other clients were the composer Hubert Parry and his wife. The Garretts, whom they held in great affection, decorated both the Parrys' Kensington home and the country house, designed by Norman Shaw, which they built at Rustington, where they also found a cottage for Rhoda and Agnes. Lady Maud Parry signed the Declaration in Favour of Women's Suffrage compiled by the CENTRAL COMMITTEE OF THE NATIONAL SOCIETY FOR WOMEN'S SUFFRAGE in 1889, was by 1913 president of the Brighton and Hove branch of the NUWSS, and it was Sir Hubert Parry's specially composed setting of "Jerusalem" that was sung at the NATIONAL UNION OF WOMEN'S SUFFRAGE SOCIETIES party, held in March 1918 at the Queen's Hall to celebrate the granting of the limited franchise to women. Parry first met Ethel SMYTH in 1881 at the Garretts' Rustington cottage.

The Garretts jointly wrote *House Decoration*, 1877, which was published in the *Art at Home* series edited by W.J. Loftie, who had been one of Elizabeth Garrett's supporters when she contested the seat for the London School Board and who was married to one of J.G.S. Anderson's many cousins. One of the rooms at the Exhibition of Women's Industries organized in Bristol in 1885 by Helen BLACKBURN was devoted to Agnes Garrett's furniture and decoration. It included a carpet made entirely by women. In 1888 work by the firm "Rhoda and Agnes Garrett" was included in the first showing by the Arts and Crafts Exhibition Society, among the guarantors of which were Dr and Mrs PANKHURST. In the late 1880s Agnes was, with Christiana HERRINGHAM, a founding director of the Ladies' Residential Co., which was one of the first to build and manage blocks of flats intended mainly for such professional women as doctors, high-school teachers, artists and secretaries. J.M. Brydon was the architect of the company's first project, the Chenies Street Chambers. Agnes Garrett was responsible for designing and supplying some of the fittings and furniture for "York Street Chambers", for which the company employed as architects Thackeray Turner, Christiana Herringham's brother-in-law, and Capt. Eustace Balfour, husband of Lady Frances BALFOUR. It was to Agnes Garret that all matters pertaining to the upkeep of the two buildings were referred. Agnes Garrett also did the interior decoration for Brydon's

New Hospital and some work at Adel Grange, Leeds, the home of Isabella and Emily FORD. She retired as a house decorator in 1905.

Although too young to have signed the 1866 suffrage petition Agnes Garrett was, like all her family, an enthusiast for women's suffrage. In 1872, together with Rhoda, Agnes went on a suffrage speaking tour with Lilias Ashworth (see Lilias Ashworth HALLETT) in Gloucestershire and Herefordshire. She was a member of the executive committee of the Central Committee of the National Society for Women's Suffrage when it was formed in 1872 and until 1873 was, with Caroline Ashurst BIGGS, its secretary. Needless to say she remained with the Central Committee for Women's Suffrage, the faction led by her sister Millicent Garrett Fawcett, when the Society ruptured in 1888. Agnes Garrett was in charge of the arrangements for the banquet given by Millicent Fawcett at the Savoy on 11 December 1906 to celebrate the release of the WOMEN'S SOCIAL AND POLITICAL UNION prisoners. Perhaps she was responsible for the "emblematic picture of Queen Boadicea driving in a chariot waving a flag 'Votes for Women'" that press reports describe as having been given to each guest. In 1906–7 she subscribed to the LONDON SOCIETY FOR WOMEN'S SUFFRAGE and in 1912 subscribed to the NUWSS Election Fighting Fund. In June 1913 Agnes Garrett attended the INTERNATIONAL WOMAN SUFFRAGE ALLIANCE Conference in Budapest as a representative from the National Union of Women Workers. In 1882 she had been elected a poor law guardian in Holborn. In 1934 she was a vice-president of the National Council for Women of Great Britain and of the National Council for Equal Citizenship. After the deaths of Rhoda Garrett and Henry Fawcett, Agnes Garrett lived with her sister Millicent. In her will she left bequests to the secretary and the superintendent of the Ladies' Residential Chambers, Chenies Street.

Address: (1878–99) The Firs, Rustington, Sussex: 2 Gower Street, London WC; the "Garrett Warehouse", Morwell Street, Bedford Square, London WC.
Portrait: of Agnes Garrett, painted in Sussex by Annie SWYNNERTON, was included in an exhibition *Paintings by Mrs Swynnerton*, Manchester City Art Gallery, 1923.
Photograph: with Rhoda Garrett in R. Strachey, *Women's Suffrage and Women's Service: The History of the London and National Society for Women's Service*, 1927.

Archival source: Papers of the Ladies' Residential Chambers Co., Westminster City Archives.
Bibliography: M.D. Conway, *Travels in South Kensington*, 1882; M. Vince, "Agnes Garrett: pioneer of women house decorators", in the *Woman's Leader*, 11 September 1925; C.L. Graves, *Hubert Parry: His Life and Works*, 1926; B. Gould, *Daniel Cottier*, 1969; M. Girouard, *Sweetness and Light*, 1990.

GARRETT, RHODA (1841–82)   Born in Derbyshire, cousin of the Suffolk Garretts. Destined to be a governess, at the instigation of Louisa Garrett SMITH she was sent to continue her education first in Alsace and then to Miss Browning's school at Blackheath, at which Millicent and Agnes GARRETT were pupils. However, a strong-minded woman, she had decided that she wished to become an architect and in 1868 went to London to pursue this course. There were, however, no architectural practices willing to take a "lady pupil" until, having combined with her cousin Agnes, the two proved acceptable as apprentices to, first, Daniel Cottier and then John Brydon. Rhoda Garrett's ensuing career as an interior decorator proved very successful. Her obituarist in the *Englishwoman's Review* wrote, "Many delicate harmonies and beautiful forms adapted to household comfort are due to her taste and talents. If this useful and congenial pursuit is in future open to women, it is due in large measure to her courage and enterprise". She was also a member of the Royal Archaeological Institute and, from its founding, a member of the Society for the Preservation of Ancient Buildings.

Rhoda Garrett was involved with both the campaign for the Repeal of the Contagious Diseases Acts and the suffrage movement. In this she was at odds with her cousins; Elizabeth Garrett (*see* Elizabeth Garrett ANDERSON) thought the Contagious Diseases Acts necessary and Millicent Garrett FAWCETT thought that harm would be done to the suffrage campaign by supporting the crusade to repeal them. In 1871 Rhoda Garrett addressed a public meeting on women's suffrage in Ipswich and the *Woman's Suffrage Review* commented on "her quiet unaffected style of delivery at once gaining the sympathy of the audience". With Agnes Garrett, she spoke at other suffrage meetings in Leeds and Newark in June 1871. She was a member of the executive committee of the CENTRAL COMMITTEE of the NATIONAL SOCIETY FOR WOMEN'S SUFFRAGE when it was formed in 1872. In February 1872 she spoke at a suffrage meeting in Rochdale, together with Lilias Ashworth (*see* Lilias Ashworth HALLETT) and Eliza M. STURGE. On a tour organized by Lilias Ashworth, Rhoda Garrett gave a lecture on "The Electoral Disabilities of Women" at Cheltenham Corn Exchange in April 1872. This was published by the *Telegraph* Office, Cheltenham, and gives an excellent summary of the disadvantages endured by women, particularly the "prejudice against them working at all, which is all the more formidable inasmuch as it is unreasonable, and therefore *inconvinceable*". She considers the educational, economic and political disadvantages to women. "We only ask that women who fulfil the same conditions as men – who are householders, who pay taxes, and are rated to the relief of the poor, shall be admitted to the franchise. More than this we do not ask – at present." She was one of the main speakers at a meeting organized by the Central Committee in London on 29 May 1875 in St George's Hall, at which ladies were enabled to reply to speeches given on the latest suffrage bill in Parliament, and at the Grand Demonstration held at St James's Hall in London on 6 May 1880. Rhoda Garrett was much admired by Ethel SMYTH. In a letter written to Harriet MCILQUHAM on 30 November 1898, in the course of refuting a suggestion that Emily FAITHFULL "wore cropped hair and dressed in a mannish fashion" (though she certainly had short hair), Elizabeth Wolstenholme ELMY commented that "The person who really was somewhat of a nuisance to us in this direction was Rhoda Garrett, cousin of the other Garretts. Unfortunately she really did ape some of the smallest and meanest ways of men. But even she did good work. She and Agnes established the first woman's house-decorating firm which Agnes still carried on under the old name 'Agnes and Rhoda Garrett' though Rhoda died some years ago. Emily Faithfull on the other hand was essentially in appearance 'a womanly woman'." Hubert Parry, playing Bach in Rustington to Agnes on the evening after Rhoda's funeral, commented in his diary that "Her strength and bravery and brightness seem to throw her desolateness and the severance of that beautiful connexion between them into stronger relief."

Address: (1878–82) The Firs, Rustington, Sussex; 2 Gower Street, London WC.
Photograph: in E. Smyth, *Impressions That Remained*, vol. 2, 1919.
Bibliography: E. Smyth, *Impressions That Remained*, 1919; C.L. Graves, *Hubert Parry: His Life and Works*, 1926; R. Strachey, *Millicent Garrett Fawcett*, 1931; J. Lewis (ed.), *Before the Vote was Won*, 1987 (includes a reprint of R. Garrett, "Electoral Disabilities of Women").

GARRUD, EDITH MARGARET, MRS (1872–1971)

Born in Bath, née Williams, with her husband she ran a ju-jitsu school, first in Argyll Place, at Oxford Circus, and then in Golden Square, in London. Her husband's book, *The Complete Jujitsuan*, first published in 1914, became a standard work on the subject. The Garruds had at least two children, a son who was killed in the Second World War, and a daughter. In 1908 Edith Garrud was described as organizer of the women athletes' branch of the WOMEN'S FREEDOM LEAGUE. She was 4ft 11in tall and on one occasion demonstrated her skill by throwing a policeman weighing 13 stone. She gave a public demonstration of ju-jitsu at the WOMEN'S SOCIAL AND POLITICAL UNION Prince's Skating Rink Exhibition in 1909 and in December advertised in *Votes for Women* a "Suffragettes' Self-Defence Club, Tuesday and Thursday evening, from 7, 5s 6d per month". The address given for this "club" is Leighton Lodge, Edwardes Square, Kensington. In June 1910 Mrs Garrud headed the WFL "Athletes" section in the Coronation Procession. In March 1912 her gymnasium at Argyll Place was used as a bolt-hole to which at least six suffragettes dashed after smashing their allotted windows and Mrs Garrud then claimed that they were members of her ju-jitsu class. In 1913 she gave instruction to the bodyguard that was formed to protect Mrs PANKHURST from re-arrest by the police; they learned to swing their Indian clubs with considerable effect. Mrs Garrud was left a small bequest in the will of Sarah BENETT. At the age of 93, in the course of an interview, she regaled the journalist Godfrey Winn, who brought her a birthday cake (the recipe accompanies the interview), with tales of her suffrage days and showed him her suffrage scrapbook.

Address: (1923) 68 Church Street, London N16.
Photograph: in *Woman*, 19 June 1965; in M. MacKenzie, *Shoulder to Shoulder*, 1971.
Bibliography: interview by Godfrey Winn in *Woman*, 19 June 1965.

GASKELL, ELEANOR CHARLOTTE PENN, MRS (c. 1861–1937) née Lindsay   Married to George Penn Gaskell, who was secretary of the National Society for Epileptics; they did not have any children. She had been involved in social work and was a member of the council of the Royal Society for the Prevention of Cruelty to Animals. In 1906 she offered to organize a meeting for the NATIONAL UNION OF WOMEN'S SUFFRAGE SOCIETIES in Willesden, by 1907 she was honorary secretary of the Willesden branch of the LONDON SOCIETY FOR WOMEN'S SUFFRAGE, and then, with her husband, subscribed to the WOMEN'S SOCIAL AND POLITICAL UNION in 1908. Towards the end of 1908 Eleanor Penn Gaskell became a speaker for the WSPU and over the next few years was one of its most active in the London area. Although herself willing to take part in deputations and other types of "militancy", she appears to have been constrained by her husband from so doing. She was arrested on one occasion only, on 19 October 1908 in Piccadilly Circus, while distributing handbills for a WSPU meeting to be held at the Queen's Hall. She was bound over to keep the peace for six months, on her own recognizance of £10; she refused to pay the due fee, but was released, protesting that she had caused no obstruction. Her husband kept up a lengthy correspondence with the Home Office about the conditions under which she had had to wait at Marlborough Police Court before being charged and a question about the case was asked in the House of Commons on 4 November 1908. She and her husband gave handsome donations, towards the cost of an extra organizer, to WSPU funds in lieu of her active engagement. In 1911 her husband was a member of the MEN'S POLITICAL UNION. By January 1910 Eleanor Penn Gaskell was the honorary secretary of the North-West London branch of the WSPU and in July 1910 chaired a platform at the Hyde Park demonstration. Ann Morley and Liz Stanley have identified that Eleanor Penn Gaskell was part of a circle of friends that included Rose Lamartine YATES and Emily Wilding DAVISON. It was at the Penn Gaskells' house that the latter was nursed back to health in June 1912 after she had been on hunger strike, been forcibly fed, and injured herself in Holloway. Eleanor Penn Gaskell supported Maud Arncliffe SENNETT's NORTHERN MEN'S FEDERATION FOR WOMEN'S SUFFRAGE, the formation of which had been directly inspired by Emily Wilding Davison's death. Eleanor Penn Gaskell continued working in Kilburn for the WSPU until 1915 when, with such other long-time and active members as Rose Lamartine Yates, she protested against the way in which the Pankhursts had dropped campaigning for the vote in favour of "other purposes outside the scope of the Union". She was, indeed, until then listed, with Florence HAIG and Daisy SOLOMON, as one of the secretaries of the WSPU. On 25 November 1915 she chaired a meeting in Brondesbury at which a manifesto was issued to protest against the name "Women's Social and Political Union" being used for purposes other than for which it had originally been intended and against the fact that the accounts of the WSPU had not been made public since 1914. Eleanor Penn Gaskell then became a member of the SUFFRAGETTES OF THE WSPU. She certainly contributed towards the expenses of a meeting organized in 1915 by the Emily Wilding Davison Lodge (see under CLUBS).
Address: (1907) 10 Nicholl Road, Willesden, London NW; (1937) 14 Mapesbury Road, Cricklewood, Middlesex.
Photograph: in *Votes for Women*, 22 July 1910.
Archival source: Home Office Papers, Public Record Office.
Bibliography: M. Richardson, *Laugh a Defiance*, 1953; A. Morley with L. Stanley, *The Life and Death of Emily Wilding Davison*, 1988.

GATESHEAD-ON-TYNE (NUWSS).   In 1913 the society was a member of the NORTH-EASTERN FEDERATION OF THE NATIONAL UNION OF WOMEN'S SUFFRAGE SOCIETIES. Secretary (1909) Miss Hope Emley, 5 Carlton Terrace, Low Fell, Gateshead, Co. Durham, and Mrs Pitt, 46 & 48 Askew Road, Gateshead, Co. Durham; (1913) Miss Hope Emley.

GATTY, KATHERINE, MRS (1870–1952) (later Mrs Gatty Gillett)   Described in *Votes for Women* as a journalist and lecturer, she was a delegate to the International Congress of Women at Amsterdam in 1908. A member of the WOMEN'S SOCIAL AND POLITICAL UNION, she was imprisoned in Holloway from 19 February to 10 March 1909. In 1911 she was a member of the TAX RESISTANCE LEAGUE and was appointed at a salary of £2 per week to mind its office in London in the absence of Mrs Kineton PARKES. Katherine Gatty took part in the window smashing that resulted from the "torpedoing" of the Conciliation Bill in November 1911 and spent two weeks in Holloway. In January 1912 she was arrested for causing a disturbance after protesting at the exclusion of women during the trial of Emily Wilding DAVISON but was discharged. Emily Davison was obviously a close friend and was invited to tea on 28 May 1913, a couple of weeks before her death. In March 1912 Katherine Gatty took part in the WSPU window-breaking campaign, was sentenced to six months' imprisonment after smashing glass worth £42 and in June took part in the hunger strike. When Maud Arncliffe SENNETT tried to visit Mrs Gatty she was told that because she was in the prison hospital she was not entitled to a visit. Towards the end of August she was again arrested, this time in Abergavenny, for breaking a window in the post office. At her trial Katherine Gatty stated that the day on which she broke the window was the last day for the inclusion of names on the electoral register and that she was protesting against the exclusion of women from such lists. She was sentenced to a month's imprisonment with hard labour, went on hunger strike and was brought back to Holloway in a weakened state. She asked for a visit there from Frederick HANKINSON, the Unitarian chaplain and on her release Anne Cobden SANDERSON came to visit her at her home. According to *Votes for Women*, 13 December 1912, Mrs Gatty had by then become secretary of the SUFFRAGE ATELIER. In November 1913 she was national woman organizer of the National Amalgamated Union of Shop Assistants, Warehousemen and Clerks, based in Glasgow. In 1947, long remarried, she emigrated to Australia, where she died.

Address: (1911) 96 Churchfield Road, Acton, London W; (1912) 9 Alfred Road, Acton, London W.

GAWTHORPE, MARY ELEANOR (1881–1973) (later Mrs Sanders) Born in Leeds, where her father worked in a tannery and was honorary secretary of the local Conservative party. When she was 13 she was apprenticed as a pupil-teacher; one of her classmates was Ethel Annakin (*see* Ethel SNOWDEN). She passed the Government Teachers' Certificate with a first-class degree, teaching by day and studying at night, and when she was 20 won a scholarship in singing (she was a mezzo-soprano) at Leeds School of Music and took honours in the examinations of Trinity College of Music, London. She played the piano, a skill she put to good use at the early suffrage rallies. At this time she was engaged to be married to T.B. Garrs, a compositor on the *Yorkshire Post*, an active supporter of the Independent Labour Party and in 1904, with him, she joined the Leeds Arts Club, of which Isabella FORD was a member of the management committee. It was here that she was first encouraged to speak in public and here, too, with the local Fabian Society and Theosophical Lodge based in the same rooms, that she was exposed to new influences of art, philosophy and spirituality. Influenced by Garrs she joined the ILP, organizing lectures, and by 1906 had become vice-president of the Leeds branch. She also became a speaker at the Labour Church, edited the woman's page of the local *Labour News* and was active in the local National Union of Teachers. She later remembered that it was while she was a member of the Lord Mayor's Committee for Feeding School Children that she first saw the necessity of votes for women. She was nominated by Isabella Ford to the executive committee of the LEEDS SUFFRAGE SOCIETY (NUWSS).

Mary Gawthorpe first came into contact with the precursors of the WOMEN'S SOCIAL and POLITICAL UNION when she read Frederick PETHICK-LAWRENCE's *Labour Record* and then entertained Mr and Mrs Pethick-Lawrence when they visited Leeds. When Christabel PANKHURST, whom she had previously heard speak at the Leeds Labour Church, was imprisoned in October 1905, Mary Gawthorpe was impressed and wrote to her in Strangeways. In an article in the *Labour Leader,* 26 January 1906, Mary Gawthorpe dated the "Votes for Women" campaign in Leeds to 6 November 1905 when Herbert Gladstone was questioned at a public meeting in Stanningley as to his attitude to women's suffrage. She gives details of the way in which all local candidates were inteviewed by "ardent women suffragists" during the general election.

In the spring of 1906 Mary Gawthorpe resigned her teaching post and, as secretary of Leeds Women's Labour League, went to London for the first time to take part in discussions at the Board of Trade about school meals, and, while there, attended one of Margaret MacDonald's "At Homes" at her house in Lincoln's Inn Fields. Annie KENNEY in her autobiography mentions that Mary Gawthorpe worked in the WSPU cause with her in London in the early part of 1906. During the summer she campaigned with Mrs PANKHURST in Wales but at the Cockermouth by-election in the autumn of 1906, although already very sympathetic towards the WSPU, as an organizer of the Women's Labour League she campaigned for the Labour Party and was therefore excluded from the WSPU platform. After this, having spent a week in London as a guest of the Pethick-Lawrences, she took the decision to join the WSPU, becoming an official ORGANIZER and member of the Committee. She was very soon involved in the effects of the WSPU's militant policy, was arrested in October after taking part in the demonstration outside parliament during its opening session and was sentenced to two months' imprisonment with, among others, Minnie BALDOCK and Dora MONTEFIORE. Her mother came down from Leeds to visit her in Holloway and stayed for the occasion with Charlotte DESPARD. Garrs also visited her; the engagement was later broken. She attended the banquet for the released prisoners organized at the Savoy by Mrs FAWCETT and was taken into dinner by Sir John Cockburn. By February 1907 she was making her mark. Elizabeth Wolstenholme ELMY wrote to tell Harriet McILQUHAM that "Mary Gawthorpe ... is a splendid speaker, full of humour, brilliant and lucid". She spoke up and down England, Scotland and Wales and went to Ireland. Her "big 'fog-and-frost'" voice, so described by Helena SWANWICK, became overstrained and in her entry in *The Suffrage Annual and Women's Who's Who*, 1913, she gives her recreation as "Sleeping, not talking". She was often ill; after her arrest during the demonstrations surrounding the first Women's Parliament on 13 February 1907 the case against her was adjourned *sine die* on the grounds of her ill health. She was operated on by Louisa Garrett ANDERSON for appendicitis after returning from a campaign later that year and spent her convalescence at the Pethick-Lawrences' Surrey cottage and on a holiday in Italy with them and Annie Kenney.

Mary Gawthorpe wrote a pamphlet, *Votes for Men: How They Were Won*, which was published by the WSPU, and was one of the main speakers at the June 1908 Hyde Park Demonstration. Immediately after this she went to Manchester to implement there a WSPU decision to hold large meetings in the principal cities in order to capitalize on the publicity and success of Hyde Park. She stayed as chief organizer for the WSPU in Lancashire until ill-health forced her to retire at the end of September 1910. A year later she resigned from the WSPU and in November 1911 became co-editor with Dora MARSDEN of the *Freewoman,* a *Weekly Feminist Review,* a journal advocating social change, whose contributors included Teresa BILLINGTON-GREIG, Rebecca West, Ada Nield CHEW and H.G. Wells. Her relationship with Dora Marsden, although loving, was always stormy and, after Dora had written articles critical of the Pankhursts' revival of militancy, Mary Gawthorpe resigned her co-editorship in the spring of 1912. She makes no mention of this association with the *Freewoman* in the entry she supplied to *The Suffrage Annual and Women's Who's Who* in 1913. In February 1912 she was arrested after breaking a window at the Home Office to protest against the forcible feeding of William Ball, a member of the MEN'S POLITICAL UNION, who had subsequently been sent to the Colney Hatch Lunatic Asylum as the result of his treatment. She was remanded for a week and taken to Holloway where she went on a hunger-and-thirst strike. She was released after 36 hours into the care of Dr Flora MURRAY. In the summer Mary Gawthorpe organized a public petition against the forcible feeding of Mary LEIGH and Gladys Evans in Mountjoy Prison in Dublin and at the end of December 1912 she wrote in the *Daily Herald* to propose a National Hunger Strike of Women if the government did not carry out its promised amendment to the Manhood Suffrage Bill. This suggestion did not bear any fruit. She was a member of the organizing committee of the International Women's Franchise Club (*see under* CLUBS). In May 1913 an appeal, one of whose sponsors was Mrs LOWY, was launched for money to give Mary Gawthorpe treatment in a nursing home.

Mary Gawthorpe went with her mother to the United States in 1916 and there joined the staff of the New York State Woman Party. By November 1917 she was in charge of its publicity; a month later she was appointed State Press Chairman. Once the vote for women was secured she renewed her interest in the cause of labour. In 1918 she was involved with the National Consumers League and in 1919 was campaigning for a Minimum Wage Bill and working with the Cook County Labor Party in Illinois. In 1920 she became first educational director for the Amalgamated Clothing Workers of America. In 1921 she was executive secretary of the League for Mutual Aid, apparently on a meagre salary, but in 1922 had to resign, again through ill-health. In 1921 she married an American, John Sanders, and thereby became an American citizen.

For the rest of their lives she kept in touch with erstwhile suffrage comrades, particularly Rose Lamartine YATES. Although in the 1930s she had helped publicize Sylvia PANKHURST's *The Suffragette Movement* in the USA, she had been concerned that her own part had been eroded; in over 600 pages she merits five brief mentions and a rather dismissive footnote. In 1962 she published, with a very limited circulation, *Uphill to Holloway*, a memoir of her early life and first involvement with the WSPU.

Address: (1921) 40 West 9th Street, New York; (1930, 1960) 160–25 10th Avenue, Queens, New York, USA.
Photograph: in Fawcett Library Collection.
Portrait: a bust of her, sculpted by Jessie Russell, a Manchester teacher, was displayed at the Prince's Rink Exhibition in May 1909. Rose Lamartine Yates attempted to raise the money to buy it for the WSPU to present to Mary Gawthorpe, but there appears now to be no trace of it. Portrait in oils in Fawcett Library collection, given by Rose Lamartine Yates, possibly originally in the Suffragette Fellowship Record Room collection.
Archival source: Suffragette Fellowship Collection, Museum of London.
Bibliography: T. Steele, *Alfred Orage and the Leeds Arts Club, 1893–1923*, 1990; L. Garner, *A Brave and Beautiful Spirit: Dora Marsden, 1882–1960*, 1990; S.S. Holton, *Suffrage Days: Stories from the Women's Suffrage Movement*, 1996.

GERRARD'S CROSS (NUWSS) In 1913 the society was a member of the OXON, BERKS, BUCKS, AND BEDS FEDERATION OF THE NATIONAL UNION OF WOMEN'S SUFFRAGE SOCIETIES. Secretary (1913) Mrs Bernard Davis, Brantfell, Austenwood Common, Gerrard's Cross, Buckinghamshire.

GILCHRIST, MARION, DR (1863–1952) Born at Bothwell Park Farm, educated at Bothwell School, Hamilton Academy, St Andrews (LLA), and St Margaret's College, Glasgow University, where she qualified in medicine in 1894, becoming the first woman to do so from a Scottish university, and one of Glasgow's first women doctors. She was one of the founders of the GLASGOW AND WEST OF SCOTLAND ASSOCIATION FOR WOMEN'S SUFFRAGE in 1902 and a member of its executive committee. She, together with Janie ALLAN, backed a motion in January 1907 that regretted that no officials of the Association had appeared on a WOMEN'S SOCIAL AND POLITICAL UNION platform and that the Association was not achieving as much success as it might. Soon after this she resigned from the executive and finance committees, joined the WSPU, and in January 1908 opened its new headquarters in Glasgow. In March 1909 she gave a talk on "The Militant Woman". One male member of the audience, unconverted to the cause, described her in a letter to Evelyn SHARP, who had also spoken at the meeting, as "a really nice lady, a trifle nervous, but quite prepared to see the thing through". She contributed articles to the *Glasgow Herald* and to the medical press. In 1922 she was president of the Glasgow and West Scotland Association of the Medical Women's Federation and in the 1930s she was the eye surgeon at Redland Hospital for Women in Glagow and a member of the General Council of the Scottish Council for Women's Trade and Careers.

Address: (1913) 5 Buckingham Terrace, Glasgow.
Photograph: in E. King, *The Hidden History of Glasgow's Women*, 1993.
Archival source: Minutes of the Glasgow and West of Scotland Association for Woman's Suffrage, Mitchell Library, Glasgow; Evelyn Sharp Papers, Bodleian Library, Oxford.
Bibliography: L. Leneman, *A Guid Cause: The Women's Suffrage Movement in Scotland*, 1991; E. King, *The Hidden History of Glasgow's Women*, 1993.

GIRTON COLLEGE Had a suffrage society by 1907 and in 1908 it amalgamated with that of NEWNHAM to form the CAMBRIDGE UNIVERSITY WOMEN'S SUFFRAGE SOCIETY. In 1909 the 97 members of the CUWS from Girton included all the members of staff.

GIRVAN, Ayrshire, committee of the NATIONAL SOCIETY FOR WOMEN'S SUFFRAGE Formed in 1873.

GLASGOW branch of the MEN'S POLITICAL UNION FOR WOMEN'S SUFFRAGE Founded in 1910.

GLASGOW branch of the SCOTTISH UNIVERSITY WOMEN'S SUFFRAGE UNION   Secretary (1913) Miss M.L. Arthur, 24 Royal Crescent, Glasgow W.

GLASGOW branch of the UNITED SUFFRAGISTS Founded in 1915. Honorary secretary: Mrs Kelsall, 20 Queensborough Gardens, Glasgow.

GLASGOW branch of the WOMEN'S EMANCIPATION UNION   Honorary secretary (1895) Miss Anna Young.

GLASGOW (WFL)   Organizers (1909) Miss Anna MUNRO and Miss Olive Robertson, 30 Gordon Street, Glasgow. Secretary (1913) Miss Bunten, 70 St George's Road, Glasgow. Office and SHOP (1910) The Suffrage Centre, 302 Sauchiehall Street, Glasgow. In 1910 the Glasgow Central branch had 207 members.

GLASGOW (WSPU)   The Glasgow branch of the WOMEN'S SOCIAL AND POLITICAL UNION was formed by March 1906. In April 1910 it organized, in collaboration with the Edinburgh WSPU, a Scottish WSPU Exhibition held in the Charing Cross Halls. This was Scotland's answer to the one held in London the previous April. Edith CRAIG and Decima MOORE were in charge of entertainments. Special CHINA, featuring Sylvia PANKHURST's "WSPU angel device" and the Scottish thistle, was offered for sale. The Glasgow branch published, probably in 1913, *Holloway Jingles,* edited by Mrs N. John, a collection of prison poetry. Many of its leading members, such as the McPHUN sisters and Helen CRAWFURD, were socialists and in the months before the outbreak of war in 1914 the Union was working increasingly closely in co-operation with the *Daily Herald* League.

By October 1909 the Glasgow WSPU had been presented with a BANNER designed by Ann Macbeth and worked, under her direction, at the Glasgow School of Art.
Organizer (1906) Mrs Elizabeth Pollok, 152 Broomfield, Springburn, Glasgow; (1910) Miss Barbara WYLIE; (1913) Miss Underwood, 502 Sauchiehall Street, Glasgow.

GLASGOW MEN'S LEAGUE FOR WOMEN'S SUFFRAGE   Founded, as the West of Scotland Men's League for Women's Suffrage, in 1907 by Graham Moffat, the novelist and dramatist. His wife Maggie was a delegate from the Glasgow WOMEN'S SOCIAL AND POLITICAL UNION to the Women's Parliament at Caxton Hall in February 1907 and was arrested after taking part in the ensuing demonstration and imprisoned, "the second Scottish suffragist to go to prison for the cause" according to her husband. The League took part in the Edinburgh WSPU Demonstration in October 1909 and, the night before, held a large meeting, at which Mrs PANKHURST spoke and which made a profit of £80, at St Andrew's Hall in Glasgow. The BANNER the League carried in the procession bore the legend, "Men's League for Women's Suffrage. Scots wha hae votes: men. Scots wha haena: women". Graham Moffat marched in the procession beside Ethel SNOWDEN. The League also took part in a demonstration organized on Glasgow Green by the WOMEN'S FREEDOM LEAGUE in September 1909; Maggie Moffat left the WSPU for the WFL when "extremely militant methods" were adopted. The League gave an "At Home" for members of the WFL (Central Branch) on 6 November 1909 at which Graham Moffat and Miss Kate Moffat presented his suffrage propaganda PLAY *The Maid and the Magistrate.* Selina COOPER saw another of his plays, the popular and successful *Bunty Pulls the Strings: a Scottish Comedy in Three Acts,* when she was in London in spring 1912.
Bibliography: G. Moffat, *Join Me in Remembering,* 1955.

GLASGOW AND WEST OF SCOTLAND ASSOCIATION FOR WOMEN'S SUFFRAGE   The Glasgow branch of the NATIONAL SOCIETY FOR WOMEN'S SUFFRAGE was founded in 1870, with Mrs John Smith as president, succeeded in 1871 by Mrs Neilson of 42 Dalhousie Street, Glasgow. The society associated itself with the new CENTRAL COMMITTEE OF THE NATIONAL SOCIETY FOR WOMEN'S SUFFRAGE in 1872. A Scottish National Demonstration of Women in favour of Women's Suffrage, at which Priscilla Bright MCLAREN presided, was held at the St Andrew's Hall in Glasgow on 3 November 1882. The speakers at this meeting included Lydia BECKER, Caroline Ashurst BIGGS, Helena DOWNING, Jessie CRAIGEN, Agnes BEDDOE, Flora STEVENSON, Eliza WIGHAM and Laura MCLAREN.

The society was refounded, at the home of a former president of the Glasgow Women's Liberal Association, Mrs Greig, as the Glasgow and West of Scotland Association for Women's Suffrage in 1902 by, among others, Dr Marion GILCHRIST, Margaret IRWIN and Janie ALLAN. Andrew Ballantyne was chairman of the GWSAWS, the only man who regularly (and assiduously) attended meetings, and was still a member of the association's successor, the Glasgow Society for Equal Citizenship, in 1929. Mrs Ballantyne became a member of the committee in 1912. The society affiliated with the NATIONAL UNION OF WOMEN'S SUFFRAGE SOCIETIES in 1903 and by 1905 had set up branches in Castle Douglas, Dumfries, Motherwell, Paisley, Ayr and Greenock. In 1906 the GWSAWS refused to invite Teresa Billington (see Teresa BILLINGTON-GREIG) to address one of its meetings, perhaps worried by her connection with the Independent Labour Party, but did cooperate with the WOMEN'S SOCIAL AND POLITICAL UNION over the staging of the suffrage procession in Edinburgh in October 1907. Some members of the executive committee, however, including Marion Gilchrist and Janie Allan, and the ORGANIZER, Mary PHILLIPS, left the Association in order to join the WSPU. In 1909 the GWSAWS took the leading role in proposing the formation of a SCOTTISH FEDERATION, of which Andrew Ballantyne became chairman, within the NUWSS. In 1912 the GWSAWS, strongly Liberal, voted against the NUWSS's proposed Election Fighting Fund policy and on the outbreak of war in August 1914 suspended all political activity.

The minutes of GWSAWS, 31 May 1911, reveal that it had been decided "to get a BANNER for the [Coronation] Procession in London and the matter was remitted to a small committee". On 28 June 1911 "It was reported that a Banner for the Procession in London had been designed and carried out by Miss Dewar for the very moderate cost of 30/–. The Banner which was on view was greatly admired and it was agreed to send Miss Dewar a vote of thanks." De Courcy Lethwaite Dewar was a leading member of the Glasgow Society of Lady Artists' Club, and a member of the executive committee of the GWSAWS. This banner, "Let Glasgow Flourish", together with that of the Partick branch, is now held in the collection of the People's Palace, Glasgow.

Secretary (1909) Mrs J.T. Hunter, 11 Burnbank Terrace, Glasgow; (1913) Miss Lindsay, 202 Hope Street, Glasgow.
Office: (1909) 58 Renfield Street; (1911) 202 Hope Street, Glasgow.
Archival source: Minutes of the Glasgow and West of Scotland Association for Women's Suffrage, Department of Rare Books and Manuscripts, Mitchell Library, Glasgow.

GLASGOW UNIVERSITY The Queen Margaret College Suffrage Society was a member of the SCOTTISH UNIVERSITY WOMEN'S SUFFRAGE UNION. Margaret Milne Farquharson, who had been president of the society in 1909, became secretary of the NATIONAL POLITICAL LEAGUE. Secretary (1913) Miss E.A. Davidson, Queen Margaret College Suffrage Society, Queen Margaret College, Glasgow.

GLENFARG (NUWSS) In 1913 the society was a member of the SCOTTISH FEDERATION OF THE NATIONAL UNION OF WOMEN'S SUFFRAGE SOCIETIES. Secretary (1913) Miss Jessie Seaton, Green Bank, Glenfarg.

GLOSSOP (branch of the MANCHESTER SOCIETY, NUWSS) Secretary (1909) Miss Goldthorpe, 5 Lord Street, Glossop, Derbyshire.

GLOUCESTER branch of the NATIONAL SOCIETY FOR WOMEN'S SUFFRAGE Founded in 1871 when the secretary was Miss Rawlings, Wellington Villa, London Road, Gloucester. The society associated itself with the new CENTRAL COMMITTEE OF THE NATIONAL SOCIETY FOR WOMEN'S SUFFRAGE in 1872. In 1913 the society was a member of the WEST OF ENGLAND FEDERATION OF THE NATIONAL UNION OF WOMEN'S SUFFRAGE SOCIETIES. NUWSS secretary (1909, 1913) Miss Walrond, Cathedral House, Gloucester, Gloucestershire.

GLOUCESTER (WSPU) Joint secretaries (1906) Miss Thompson, 19 St James' St, Gloucester; Miss Mabel Prosser, 29 Ryecroft St, Gloucester, Gloucestershire.

GLOYN, ELIZABETH, MRS (?–?) Principal of a ladies' school in Manchester, president of the Manchester Board of Schoolmistresses, and in 1867 was, with Elizabeth Wolstenholme (see Elizabeth Wolstenholme ELMY), a founding member of the North of England Council for Promoting the Higher Education of Women. She signed the 1866 women's suffrage petition and on 11 January 1867 was present at the meeting at which the MANCHESTER NATIONAL SOCIETY FOR WOMEN'S SUFFRAGE was refounded. In December 1867, with Elizabeth Wolstenholme, Josephine Butler and Jessie BOUCHERETT she asked the Social Science Association to take up the cause of married women's property law reform.

Address: (1866) Acomb House, Greenheys, Manchester.

GODALMING (NUWSS) In 1913 the society was a member of the SURREY, SUSSEX, AND HANTS FEDERATION OF THE NATIONAL UNION OF WOMEN'S SUFFRAGE SOCIETIES. Secretary (1913) Miss T.W. Powell, Munstead Rough, Godalming, Surrey.

GOLDSMID, LOUISA SOPHIA, LADY (1819–1908) Married to her cousin Francis Henry Goldsmid, whose father was the first Jew in England to be created a baronet. Both men had been actively involved in the emancipation of Jews in Britain and were founders of the West London Synagogue, England's first Reform congregation. Sir Francis Goldsmid was the first Jew to become a barrister, and in 1860 was elected Liberal MP for Reading. In 1860 he was a member of the committee of the Society for Promoting the Employment of Women and on 20 May 1867 he voted in support of J.S. MILL's amendment to the Representation of the People Bill. In the summer of 1862 Lady Goldsmid was treasurer of a fund organized by Emily DAVIES to provide "incidental expenses connected with the effort to obtain for women admission to University Examinations in Arts and Medicine" and in October became treasurer of a committee for obtaining the admission of women to University Examinations. She was to prove a very generous benefactor to the movement for opening higher education to women and to Girton College in particular. Society and committee work intermingled; in February 1862 the Dissenting diarist Henry Crabb Robinson met Adelaide Procter, a member of the Langham Place set, in Lady Goldsmid's drawing room. In 1866 Lady Goldsmid was a member of the first general committee of Elizabeth Garrett's (*see* Elizabeth Garrett ANDERSON) St Mary's Dispensary for Women and Children. Lady Goldsmid, together with her husband's sister Anna Maria Goldsmid, signed the 1866 women's suffrage petition. She was a member of the LONDON PROVISIONAL PETITION COMMITTEE and became treasurer, a position she was often given, her wealth being a guarantee against a deficit, as Emily Davies candidly commented to Helen TAYLOR in a letter of 5 June 1866. She subscribed £20 to the ENFRANCHISEMENT OF WOMEN COMMITTEE, 1866–7, but in October became aware of the divisions possible in the women's suffrage movement when she opposed Helen Taylor's proposed wording of one of the petitions they were organizing. Lady Goldsmid was of the view that the words "unmarried women and widows" should be inserted; Helen Taylor wanted to leave the wording vague. By June 1867 Lady Goldsmid was, with Emily Davies and Elizabeth Garrett, one of the "quiet section" which decided to withdraw from the suffrage campaign and concentrate on that for women's education. After the campaign had settled down she did, in the 1870s, rejoin the MANCHESTER NATIONAL SOCIETY FOR WOMEN'S SUFFRAGE, to which she had subscribed in 1867, and by 1874 was vice-president of the LONDON NATIONAL SOCIETY FOR WOMEN'S SUFFRAGE. From 1881 to 1882 she was a member of the executive committee of the Married Women's Property Committee. In May 1884 she signed the Letter from Ladies to Members of Parliament asking that women heads of households should be included in the government's Franchise Bill. In 1885, with Millicent Garrett FAWCETT, she led a delegation, sponsored by the Women's Protective and Provident League, of women pit workers to protest to the Home Office about unfair wages. In 1887 she paid the expenses of a deputation of women nail and chain makers from Cradley Heath and went with them and Mrs Fawcett to protest to the Home Secretary against proposed protective legislation. In 1900 Lady Goldsmid was a member of the CENTRAL SOCIETY FOR WOMEN'S SUFFRAGE and in 1906–7 subscribed to its successor, the LONDON SOCIETY FOR WOMEN'S SUFFRAGE.

Address: (1908) 13 Portman Square, London, London W, and Red Lodge, Eastbourne, Sussex.
Photograph: in Girton College.

Archival source: Mill–Taylor Papers, London School of Economics and Political Science.
Bibliography: D.W. Marks and Rev. A. Lowy (eds), *Memoir of Sir Francis Henry Goldsmid* with a preface by Louisa Goldsmid, 1879; L.G. Kuzmack, *Woman's Cause: The Jewish Woman's Movement in England and the United States, 1881–1933*, 1990.

GOLDSTEIN, VIDA (1869–1949) Born at Portland, Victoria, New South Wales, brought up as a Unitarian, moved with her family to Melbourne in 1877, and attended the Ladies' Presbyterian College. After a decline in the family's financial fortunes Vida and her sisters, who had always been encouraged by their father to be economically independent, opened a co-educational preparatory school. In 1890 Vida Goldstein helped her mother, a staunch suffragist, collect names for a large Woman Suffrage Petition. By 1899 Vida, as well as being actively involved in several social welfare societies, was leader of the United Council for Women's Suffrage and closed down her school in order to devote herself to the cause. In that year she wrote to the NATIONAL UNION OF WOMEN'S SUFFRAGE SOCIETIES in London to ask if her Council could be affiliated. This move led to co-operation between the NUWSS and not only her Council but other colonial suffrage societies. In 1900 Vida Goldstein founded the *Australian Women's Sphere*, which she both owned and edited. After women in Victoria were enfranchised in 1908 Vida Goldstein founded another journal, *Woman Voter*. She was also the founder and president of the Women's Federal Political Association of Victoria, which later became the Woman's Political Association.

In 1902 she attended the conference in Washington at which the INTERNATIONAL WOMAN SUFFRAGE ALLIANCE, of which she was elected secretary, was founded and spoke at a hearing before the Committee on the Judiciary of the House of Representatives at which Carrie Chapman Catt asked that the House should appoint a committee to investigate the results of woman suffrage in operation. In 1903 Vida Goldstein stood as Woman's candidate in the first Australian Federal Elections, the first woman candidate in the British Empire ever to stand for parliament. Although unsuccessful, she polled 51 497 votes. She tried again, always unsuccessful, in 1910, 1913, 1914 and 1917. In 1911, a powerful role model, she visited Britain for eight months and did much to encourage the WOMEN'S SOCIAL AND POLITICAL UNION, writing several articles for *Votes for Women* and *Woman Suffrage in Australia* which was published by the Woman's Press, and representing Australia in the 17 June Coronation Procession. The MEN'S LEAGUE FOR WOMEN'S SUFFRAGE gave a dinner in her honour in May at which were represented all sides of the suffrage movement; Mrs FAWCETT, Christabel PANKHURST, Mrs DESPARD and Laurence HOUSMAN were all present. While in Britain she, with others, founded the AUSTRALIAN AND NEW ZEALAND VOTERS' ASSOCIATION, through which expatriates could support the British campaign. It was she who gave Adela PANKHURST the opportunity to emigrate to Australia and become an organizer of the Woman's Political Association there. During the First World War the two helped found the Australian Women's Peace Army. At the end of the war Vida Goldstein represented Australian women at the Women's Peace Conference in Zurich. She spent her remaining years lobbying for such social reforms as birth control and for disarmament.

Photograph: *Votes for Women*, 1 April 1910; by Col Blathwayt in B.M. Willmott Dobbie, *A Nest of Suffragettes in Somerset*, 1959.
Archival source: Vida Goldstein Papers, Fawcett Library; Suffragette Fellowship Collection, Museum of London.
Bibliography: V. Goldstein, "The political woman in Australia", *Nineteenth Century*, July 1904; A. Oldfield, *Woman Suffrage in Australia: A Gift or a Struggle?*, 1992.

GOOLE (NUWSS) In 1913 the society was a member of the WEST RIDING FEDERATION OF THE NATIONAL UNION OF WOMEN'S SUFFRAGE SOCIETIES. Secretary (1913) Mrs Parker, Fountayne Street, Goole, Yorkshire.

GORDON, VERA CONWAY (1874–1955) Born in India, where her father was Director General of Railways. In 1890 the family returned to Rochester and she attended Rochester Girls' Grammar School. She became honorary secretary of the Rochester, Kent, branch of the NATIONAL UNION OF WOMEN'S SUFFRAGE SOCIETIES when it was formed in 1912; the first meeting was held on 27 January. By March there were 42 members of the branch and Lady Frances BALFOUR spoke at a meeting held in the

Corn Exchange. The branch grew until in 1914 it had 159 members. Vera Conway Gordon was Rochester's delegate to the 1912 NUWSS Annual Council meeting and in June 1913 was present in Rochester Cathedral at the service held for the NUWSS Pilgrims (*see* PILGRIMAGE). She published her first novel, *Ordeal By Marriage*, in 1911. It was a denunciation of loveless and arranged marriages and was akin in thinking to that deployed by Cicely HAMILTON in *Marriage as a Trade*, 1909. Vera Conway Gordon published a second novel, *The Celibacy of Maurice Kane*, in 1913, and a third, *The Crown of Humanity*, in 1921. During the First World War the Rochester branch followed the advice that emanated from headquarters and put aside the campaign for the vote, concentrating instead on helping women and children. Mrs FAWCETT spoke to the branch in 1915 on "Women's Work in Wartime". In the late 1920s Vera Conway Gordon moved to Tankerton, Kent, where for some time she kept a shop, although by the time she died she was almost destitute.

Address: (1913) Longley House, Rochester, Kent.
Photograph: in Rochester upon Medway Studies Centre.
Archival source: Exhibition held at Rochester upon Medway Studies Centre, 1995.

GORE-BOOTH, EVA (1870–1926) Mystical poet and radical suffragist, influenced by both Unitarianism and theosophy, born in Co. Sligo, one of five children of Sir Henry Gore-Booth, landowner and Arctic explorer. Her sister Constance later became Countess Markievicz, Irish nationalist, suffragist, and the first woman to be elected to the British House of Commons, although, imprisoned at the time, unable to take her seat. In 1896, threatened by consumption, Eva Gore-Booth went to Italy and there met Esther ROPER at the home of George McDonald, mystical novelist, friend of William Morris and husband to one of the signatories of the 1866 women's suffrage petition. Shared concerns, including that of women's enfranchisement, led to a life-long friendship and Eva Gore-Booth moved to Manchester to live with Esther Roper, who had for four years been the secretary of the MANCHESTER NATIONAL SOCIETY FOR WOMEN'S SUFFRAGE. In 1899 Eva Gore-Booth was a member of the executive committee of the NATIONAL UNION OF WOMEN'S SUFFRAGE SOCIETIES. Both she and Esther Roper worked at the Ancoats Settlement and in 1900 Eva became, with Sarah Dickenson, co-secretary of the Manchester and Salford Women's Trade Union Council, of which one of the members of the Council was Rev. S. STEINTHAL. In the summer of 1902 Eva Gore-Booth campaigned at the Clitheroe by-election campaign, for David Shackleton, the Labour candidate, who had promised to support women's enfranchisement. Although he was elected, he did nothing to forward the suffrage movement and Eva Gore-Booth, Esther Roper, Sarah REDDISH and Sarah Dickenson took matters into their own hands and founded the LANCASHIRE AND CHESHIRE WOMEN TEXTILE AND OTHER WORKERS' REPRESENTATION COMMITTEE to support the election of an independent suffrage candidate.

On 11 October 1900 Christabel PANKHURST, although not yet a member of the College, attended a lecture on "The Politics of the Poets" at the Owen's College Women's Students' Debating Society, just round the corner from her home in Nelson Street. She spoke to some effect during the ensuing question-time and attracted the attention of Esther Roper, who took her home afterwards to meet Eva Gore-Booth. Christabel then attended Eva's Poetry Circle at the Ancoats Settlement and there met Teresa Billington (see Teresa BILLINGTON-GREIG). Christabel joined both the NORTH OF ENGLAND WOMEN'S SUFFRAGE SOCIETY, and the Women's Trade Union Council, and joined Eva and Esther on a holiday in Venice. Christabel's friendship with Eva was eventually eroded after she caused both the WTUC and the NEWSS to splinter. In 1904 Christabel brought about a rupture in the WTUC, of which she had been a committee member since 1901, by trying to force the Council to make women's suffrage one of its aims. The Council refused and Eva Gore-Booth and Sarah Dickenson, Christabel's friends if not supporters, felt constrained to resign. Together they set up a new organization, the Manchester and Salford Women's Trade and Labour Council. Although Mrs Pankhurst had founded the WOMEN'S SOCIAL AND POLITICAL UNION in the autumn of 1903 Christabel remained on the committee of the NEWSS. However, it was not with the Society's support that she made her demonstration at the Free Trade Hall in October

1905 and, although she was welcomed at the gates of Strangeways by Esther Roper and Eva Gore-Booth, they were pacifists and would have cared little for violence, however mild. In addition, Teresa Billington-Greig records that Eva Gore-Booth, intolerant of liars, heard Christabel give a version of the "spitting incident" at variance with the one first published. However, both Eva Gore-Booth and Esther Roper were among the members of the committee who, together with Christabel, resigned from the NEWSS at the end of 1905. Elizabeth Wolstenholme ELMY spent 13 December 1905 gathering information in Manchester and then explained the situation to Harriet MCILQUHAM in her inimitable way, "The North of England Society for WS has been captured by a Liberal gang . . . Esther and Eva, and dear old Mr Steinthal, at whose house in /65 the original Committee was formed, and who has ever since been connected with it, have all resigned, and will henceforth work through the Women's Trades and Labour Council – which happily is full of the most vivid life, and which Mrs THOMASSON is now helping liberally. Yet Esther and Eva have to do relatively far more out of their small means, besides losing (Eva £80) Esther £100 a year – of salary."

Thus Eva Gore-Booth and the other radical suffragists did not join the WSPU but concentrated their efforts on constitutional methods of campaigning. At the general election of January 1906 they fielded their own candidate, Thorley Smith, at Wigan, with no backing from the Wigan Trades Council or from the NESWS. Dora MONTEFIORE came up from London to help in the campaign. Although Smith was defeated, the radical suffragists were delighted at having beaten the Liberal into third place. In February Eva Gore-Booth and Esther Roper, the day after the first WSPU demonstration in Caxton Hall, at which they were presumably present, attended a meeting of what was the next week to become the CANNING TOWN BRANCH OF THE WSPU. The minutes of the meeting disclose that it was decided that a demonstration, "to claim the rights of women's suffrage", should be held in Hyde Park about the end of May. In May 1906 Eva Gore-Booth was present in the suffrage deputation to Campbell-Bannerman, speaking as the representative "of the Lancashire Working Women's Societies, the Trade Unions and Labour Societies in Lancashire", alongside Mrs PANKHURST, Elizabeth Wolstenholme Elmy and Margaret ASHTON of the NESWS who was representing the Women's Liberal Association. Eva Gore-Booth felt keenly the failure of this deputation and wrote two poems, "Women's Trades on the Embankment" and "A Lost Opportunity", that encapsulate her feeling of helplessness. In February 1907 she took part in the "Mud March" organized by the NUWSS and at the meeting, which was the culmination of the march, held at the Exeter Hall seconded the resolution calling on the government to pass a measure dealing with women's suffrage during the coming session. In 1907 she contributed an essay "The Women's Suffrage Movement Among Trade Unionists" to *The Case for Women's Suffrage* edited by Brougham Villiers. In this she ably and eloquently summarizes the reasons for and methods of the LCWTOW campaign to gain the vote for working women. The precise effect on wages of women's political disability was clearly stated. In 1908 she was a delegate to the Labour Party Conference at Hull and proposed a motion in favour of women's suffrage which was, as Selina COOPER's had been the year before, defeated in favour of one for adult suffrage. At the end of 1909 Eva helped run the radical suffragist general election campaign at Rossendale, where they put up their own candidate against Lewis Harcourt, a Liberal member of the cabinet vociferously opposed to women's enfranchisement, and were soundly defeated. In 1910 she gave support to the NEW CONSTITUTIONAL SOCIETY FOR WOMEN'S SUFFRAGE and in February 1911 with Esther Roper and Sarah Dickenson, attended as a visitor a meeting in London of the FABIAN WOMEN'S GROUP. On 17 November 1911 she was a member of the deputation, representing the working women of the north of England, which called on Asquith and Lloyd George not to drop the Conciliation Bill. Both Eva Gore-Booth and Esther Roper were committed to improving the lot of working women and to this end opposed all attempts at protective legislation. In 1906 Eva Gore-Booth wrote a pamphlet, *Women's Right to Work*, in 1907 supported bar-maids in their claim to be able to work after 8 pm, and in the next few years campaigned to prevent protective legislation interfering with the right to work of women at the pit brow. At Easter 1911 Eva worked for a short time as a pit-brow lass to sample the conditions for herself. Miss King May, a Manchester physical education teacher and treasurer of the GYMNASTIC TEACHERS' SUFFRAGE SOCIETY, had also undertaken a similar investigation and joined in the campaign. In 1913 fears for Eva's health necessitated a move to London. At this time her sister Constance was involved with the Workers' Lock-Out in Ireland and bailed from prison Dora Montefiore who was arrested on a charge of kidnapping after she had attempted to organize the movement of strikers' children from Dublin to England. On the outbreak of war Eva and Esther took up welfare work among German women and children in England, in December signed the "Open Christmas Letter" to women of Germany and Austria, in 1915 joined the Women's Peace Crusade, and in 1916 the No-Conscription Fellowship. After the Easter Rebellion in Dublin in 1916 Constance Markievicz was first sentenced to death and then reprieved. She was eventually sent to Holloway to serve the first of her prison sentences and was there helped in many ways by Anne Cobden SANDERSON, who had also seen the inside of Holloway and who was described by Esther Roper as "a wonderful friend to all in trouble". While in prison Constance Markievicz's name was put forward as the Sinn Fein candidate for the St Patrick's Division in Dublin at the 1918 general election and she was elected to the House of Commons. For the rest of her life Eva Gore-Booth continued working for peace, for the League for the Abolition of Capital Punishment, for the anti-vivisectionists, writing poetry, and for a privately circulated journal, *Urania*. In 1928 a stained-glass window, which had been commissioned by Esther Roper from Sarah Purser's studio in Dublin and made by Ethel Rhind, to commemorate Eva Gore-Booth, was installed in the Round House, the home of the Ancoats Settlement. The building was demolished in 1986, by which time the window had been stolen or destroyed.

Address: (1900) 83 Heald Place, Manchester; (1921) 14 Frognal Gardens, Hampstead, London NW.
Photograph: in G. Lewis, *Eva Gore-Booth and Esther Roper: A Biography*, 1988.
Bibliography: E. Gore-Booth, "Women's wages and the franchise and certain legislative proposals", 1906; E. Gore-Booth, "Women and politics: a reply", in *Nineteenth Century*, March 1907; Brougham Villiers (ed.), *The Case for Women's Suffrage*, 1907; E. Gore-Booth, "Women and suffrage: a reply to Lady Lovat and Mrs Humphry Ward", in *Nineteenth Century and After*, September 1908; E. Roper, Biographical Introduction to *Poems of Eva Gore-Booth*, 1929; J. Liddington and J. Norris, *One Hand Tied Behind Us: The Rise of the Women's Suffrage Movement*, 1978; A. Sebestyn, introduction to *Prison Letters of Countess Markievicz*, 1987.

GORE LANGTON, ANNA ELIZA MARY, LADY (*c.* 1820–79) Daughter of the 2nd Duke of Buckingham, signed the 1866 women's suffrage petition. In 1846 she married William Gore Langton, MP for West Somerset, who in May 1867 supported John Stuart MILL's amendment to the Representation of the People Bill and in 1873 presented to Disraeli a Memorial, signed by 11 000 women, in favour of women's enfranchisement. After the death in 1874 of Viscountess AMBERLEY, Lady Anna Gore Langton became president of the BRISTOL AND WEST OF ENGLAND branch of the National Society for Women's Suffrage. She had been president of the BATH committee since at least 1871, had given £50 to the MANCHESTER NATIONAL SOCIETY in 1872 and had spoken at the Public Meeting on Women's Suffrage organized by the CENTRAL COMMITTEE OF THE NATIONAL SOCIETY FOR WOMEN'S SUFFRAGE at the Hanover Square Rooms in London in April 1873. Helen BLACKBURN wrote that "her speaking was thoroughly practical, and carried with it great earnestness and conviction – perhaps it was all the more convincing because it was quiet and unassuming. Her fine presence and noble face lent great dignity to all she said." In June 1877 Lady Anna Gore Langton was a member of a deputation to the Chancellor of the Exchequer and sought his support in favour of the women's suffrage bill that Jacob BRIGHT was due to introduce to the House of Commons the next day. Despite having received promises of support, the bill was lost amid uproar in the House. Lady Anna Gore Langton called a meeting of suffrage workers at her London town-house five days later to discuss the position. At this meeting Maria Grey made a strong speech in favour of women's suffrage, deploring the comments made in parliament to the effect that supporters of the cause of women's education (supporters of Girton College had been particularly singled out) were not "friends to Women's Suffrage". In her will Lady

Anna Gore Langton left £1000 to Girton College. She was also a director of the Women's Printing Society and a supporter of the London Hospital for Women.

Address: (1866) Newton Park, Newton St Loe, Bath; (1877) Langton House, George Street, Hanover Square, London W.

Photograph: in H. Blackburn, *Record of Women's Suffrage*, 1902.

Bibliography: H. Blackburn, *Record of Women's Suffrage*, 1902

GOSFORTH AND BENTON (NUWSS) In 1913 the society was a member of the NORTH-EASTERN FEDERATION OF THE NATIONAL UNION OF WOMEN'S SUFFRAGE SOCIETIES. Secretary (1913) Mrs Angus Wilkinson, Claremont, Westerhope, Northumberland.

GOULD, BARBARA BODICHON AYRTON, MRS (1886–1950) Daughter of Hertha AYRTON and Professor William Ayrton, and half-sister of Edith ZANGWILL. She was educated at Notting Hill High School and University College, London, where she studied chemistry and physiology. She joined the WOMEN'S SOCIAL AND POLITICAL UNION, while a student, in 1906 and in the summer of 1908 gave up her post-graduate research in order to work full-time as an ORGANIZER. In November 1909 Barbara Ayrton played the part of "Grace Darling" in the first production of Cicely Hamilton's *A Pageant of Great Women*, which was held at the Scala Theatre in London. In January 1910 she was WSPU organizer of the general election campaign at Manchester (Salford West). In July 1910 she married Gerald Gould and, after her honeymoon, returned to her work as a WSPU organizer. Gould wrote a pamphlet, *The Democratic Plea*, published by the MEN'S POLITICAL UNION FOR WOMEN'S ENFRANCHISEMENT. In March 1912 Barbara Ayrton Gould was arrested for breaking windows in Regent Street, was remanded in Holloway and was subsequently bound over. In 1913, having been directly involved in militant activities, she escaped to France, disguised as a schoolgirl, and spent seven weeks in exile. Alienated by Christabel PANKHURST's continuing absence and increasing autocracy and disillusioned with what she saw as the wrecking of the WSPU, Barbara Ayrton Gould, together with her husband, H.M. NEVINSON and Evelyn SHARP, founded a new society, the UNITED SUFFRAGISTS, of which she was the first organizing secretary.

During the First World War she worked to keep the suffrage issue alive. The Goulds' son, who became the distinguished sculptor and designer Michael Ayrton, was born in 1921. After the First World War Barbara Ayrton Gould stood unsuccessfully as a Labour candidate for parliament on four occasions. In 1945, on the fifth attempt, she was elected for North Hendon. She had been a member of the executive committee of the Labour Party for nearly 20 years, was vice-chairman from 1938 to 1939 and chairman from 1939 to 1940. She had also, until 1930, been publicity manager of the *Daily Herald*, honorary secretary of the Women's International League for Peace and Freedom, and a JP in Marylebone.

Address: (1924) 1 Hamilton Terrace, St John's Wood, London NW; (1950) Philbeach Gardens, London SW.

Portrait: a portrait of her by her mother's cousin, Helena Darmesteter, who was also a member of the WSPU, was exhibited at the Salon in 1911.

Bibliography: E. Sharp, *Hertha Ayrton*, 1926; J.M. Bellamy and J. Saville (eds), *Dictionary of Labour Biography*, Vol. VII, 1984.

GOUROCK (NUWSS) In 1913 the society was a member of the SCOTTISH FEDERATION OF THE NATIONAL UNION OF WOMEN'S SUFFRAGE SOCIETIES. Secretary (1913) Miss M. Leitch, Redcliff, Gourock, Renfrewshire.

GRANTHAM (NUWSS) In 1913 the society was a member of the MIDLAND (WEST) FEDERATION OF THE NATIONAL UNION OF WOMEN'S SUFFRAGE SOCIETIES. Secretary (1913) Miss A.M. Medlock, 3 Church Trees, Grantham, Lincolnshire.

GRAYS (WFL) Secretary (1913) Mrs Tunstall, 3 Heath Road, Chadwell-St-Mary, near Grays, Essex.

GREENOCK (branch of the GLASGOW AND WEST OF SCOTLAND ASSOCIATION FOR WOMEN'S SUFFRAGE, NUWSS) Formed in 1907. In 1913 the society was a member of the SCOTTISH FEDERATION OF THE NATIONAL UNION OF WOMEN'S SUFFRAGE SOCIETIES. Secretary (1907, 1913) Mrs Laurie, Red House, 38 Ardgowan Street, Greenock, Renfrewshire.

GREENWICH AND DEPTFORD (WSPU) Secretary (1913) Miss May BILLINGHURST, 7 Oakcroft Road, Blackheath, London SE.

GRIMSBY committee of the NATIONAL SOCIETY FOR WOMEN'S SUFFRAGE Formed in 1873. In 1913 the society was a member of the WEST RIDING FEDERATION OF THE NATIONAL UNION OF WOMEN'S SUFFRAGE SOCIETIES. Secretary (1913) Mrs C. Kitching, Newlands, Park Avenue, Grimsby, and Miss D. Stephenson, 124 Hainton Avenue, Grimsby, Lincolnshire.

GROTE, HARRIET, MRS (1792–1879) Writer and radical liberal, married to George Grote, who was elected to parliament as a reformer in 1832 and was one of the founders of London University, of which he was treasurer in 1860 and president in 1868. Harriet Grote was a close friend of John Stuart MILL, Anna Jameson and Jenny Lind the singer, at whose house in Wimbledon Emma and Anne Shaen, sisters to William Shaen, solicitor to many women's causes, were staying when they signed the 1866 women's suffrage petition. Harriet Grote was also a signatory. With Jenny Lind, Harriet Grote was one of the founders of the Society of Female Artists, and it was perhaps not a coincidence that it was at the Architectural Association, then in Conduit Street, where the SFA had its headquarters for which George Grote stood guarantee for the rent, that the first public meeting organized by the LONDON NATIONAL SOCIETY FOR WOMEN'S SUFFRAGE was held in 1869. Harriet Grote, who was a member of the Society, was one of the speakers at this meeting. On 20 March 1870 she addressed another crowded meeting organized by the London National Society, presided over by Clementia TAYLOR, at the Hanover Square Rooms in London and, as Helen BLACKBURN reported her, said that "she had never been engaged in any work in which her feelings were more completely seconded by her reason . . . She had always felt that the arguments against women's franchise were so feeble and limited and ineffective, that it was a wonder they were ever put forth". Harriet Grote was very fond of Lady AMBERLEY, whom she adopted as an unofficial niece and was god-mother to the Amberleys' son, John Francis Russell. Lord Amberley described dining at Mrs Grote's house as "the pleasantest form of entertainment I have ever experienced". A friend of the Langham Place group, Harriet Grote was a supporter of the Society for the Promotion of the Employment of Women, of which her niece, Sarah Lewin, was for a time secretary.
Address: (1865) 12 Savile Row, London W; (1865) Ridgeway, near Shere, Surrey.
Bibliography: Lady Eastlake, *Mrs Grote: A Sketch*, 1880; H. Blackburn (ed.), *Record of Women's Suffrage*, 1902; T.H. Lewin (ed.), *The Lewin Letters*, 1909; B. and P. Russell (eds), *The Amberley Papers: The Diaries and Letters of Lord and Lady Amberley*, 1937; K. Deepwell, "A history of the Society of Women Artists", in *The Society of Women Artists Exhibitors 1855–1996*, 1996.

GROVE, AGNES GERALDINE, LADY (1863–1926) Daughter of Major-General Augustus Fox-Pitt-Rivers and Alice, a daughter of Lady Stanley of Alderley. Agnes Grove was, therefore, a niece of both Lady AMBERLEY and Rosalind Howard, Countess of CARLISLE. She was educated at Oxford High School and in 1882 married Sir Walter Grove and had five children. By 1898 she was a member of the executive committee of the WOMEN'S LIBERAL FEDERATION and in the same year, and still in 1900, was on the executive committee of the UNION OF PRACTICAL SUFFRAGISTS. In 1898 she was a member of the executive committee of the CENTRAL AND WESTERN SOCIETY FOR WOMEN'S SUFFRAGE, becoming, in 1900, a member of the executive committee of its successor, the CENTRAL SOCIETY FOR WOMEN'S SUFFRAGE. In 1907 she gave a drawing-room meeting for its successor, the LONDON SOCIETY FOR WOMEN'S SUFFRAGE. In 1907 one of her daughters was honorary secretary of the Holborn branch of the London Society. In February 1907 Lady Grove also subscribed to the WOMEN'S SOCIAL AND POLITICAL UNION. She was president of the FORWARD SUFFRAGE UNION, with Marie CORBETT as her honorary secretary, when that society was formed in 1908 with the aim of gingering up the Women's Liberal Federation. In that year Lady Grove published *The Human Woman*, a collection of essays described by M.L. Franklin, a contemporary American academic, as "the best of all recent books dealing with woman suffrage. It is extremely witty, full of ingenious examples and parallels, good-tempered, admirably written". She also wrote *Objections to Woman Suffrage*

Considered. In 1909 Lady Grove was present at the dinner given in London by the NATIONAL UNION OF WOMEN'S SUFFRAGE SOCIETIES for the Fifth International Convention of the INTERNATIONAL WOMAN SUFFRAGE ALLIANCE. In that year she also played the part of "Justice" in the first performance of Cicely HAMILTON's *Pageant of Great Women*.
Address: (1901) Sedgehill Manor, Shaftesbury, Dorset; (1913) 51 Bedford Square, London WC.
Bibliography: D. Hawkins (ed.), *The Grove Diaries*, 1995.

GUILDFORD (NUWSS) In 1913 the society was a member of the SURREY, SUSSEX, AND HANTS FEDERATION OF THE NATIONAL UNION OF WOMEN'S SUFFRAGE SOCIETIES. Secretary (1913) Miss Noeline Baker, Warren House, Guildford, Surrey.

GYE, ELSA, MRS (1881–1943) Born in London, educated at Croydon High School, and then studied violin and singing at the Guildhall School of Music, intending to follow a musical career, but gave this up after being converted to the cause of women's suffrage at a meeting in London in March 1907. She immediately subscribed to the WOMEN'S SOCIAL AND POLITICAL UNION and in February 1908 took part in the "pantechnicon raid" on the House of Commons. In April 1908 she was campaigning for the WSPU with Mary GAWTHORPE at first the Kincardineshire and then the Dundee by-elections and in July she was in Haverfordwest with Mary BLATHWAYT, Annie KENNEY, Mrs PANKHURST and Nellie MARTEL. On 24 February 1909 Elsa Gye was arrested following the "raid" on the House of Commons to which she had been summoned to partner and assist Lady Constance LYTTON. In September 1909 she organized the protest at the Bingley Hall in Birmingham, at which Charlotte MARSH and Mary LEIGH disrupted Asquith's meeting by sitting on the roof of a house beside the hall and throwing down a shower of slates; she was not arrested. In February 1910 she went as WSPU ORGANIZER to Derby, leaving there for London in April to work as the organizer in Camberwell.

In *Prisons and Prisoners* Lady Constance Lytton described Elsa Gye as "a delightful girl, young and fresh-looking" and mentioned that she had recently become engaged to be married. She was married in 1911 and eventually had three sons. In a letter of 2 January 1928 written to Minnie BALDOCK, Elsa Gye reminisced: "It was you who first introduced me to my husband, Will Bullock – as he was then – in Nottingham when we were there together in 1908. 8 years ago he took my name and is now Dr Gye and I retook my maiden name – which was very nice." Will Bullock's sister Daisy was also an active member of the WSPU. Elsa Gye was one of the organizers of the dinner in 1928 to celebrate universal womanhood suffrage, became secretary of the SUFFRAGETTE FELLOWSHIP, and in the 1930s was behind the idea of keeping a record of the militant suffrage movement, which led to the creation of the Record Room. Unfortunately she had not thought to include a photograph of herself in the collection, and after her death her husband was reluctant to part with one, with the result that no image of her can be traced.
Address: (1909) 25 Bishop's Mansions, Fulham, London SW; (1928) Adsett, The Ridgeway, Mill Hill, London NW7.
Archival source: The Suffragette Fellowship Collection, Museum of London.

GYMNASTIC TEACHERS' SUFFRAGE SOCIETY Founded in 1908 "to advocate the extension of the franchise to women on the same lines as it is or may be granted to men; to find out the numerical strength of the supporters of the Women's Suffrage Movement in the profession, and to protect the profession from restrictive legislation" (*Suffrage Annual and Women's Who's Who*, 1913). The society took part in the WOMEN'S SOCIAL AND POLITICAL UNION procession of 18 June 1910; the *Daily Telegraph* reported, "The Women Gymnasts, lithe and active, and keeping perfect step, attracted a great deal of attention." Members of the society wore a uniform of a navy blue short walking skirt, a white blouse, and a plain hat. Badges, medals, or suffrage emblems were to be worn on the left breast. The gymnasts carried a banner made in dark blue and silver and, in recognition of the source of their drill, sported the Swedish colours both on the banner and, carrying yellow and blue irises, in their hands. Rhoda Anstey, a committed theosophist, vegetarian, tax resister, and the founder of the Anstey College of Physical Education, which advertised regularly in *Votes for Women*, had enthused her students and staff in the cause of women's suffrage. A contingent from the College had joined the Birmingham excursion train to London on 18 June and over the next few years contributed to the WSPU money raised during self-denial weeks. The gymnasts' training made them an excellent choice as marshalls for processions, able to drill their charges in order to produce a splendid spectacle. In 1912 the Gymnastic Teachers' Suffrage Society affiliated to the FEDERATED COUNCIL OF SUFFRAGE SOCIETIES and by 1913 it had 97 members. The final annual general meeting of the society appears to have been held in 1915. President: Mary HANKINSON, 67 Shaftesbury Road, Crouch Hill, London N; honorary treasurer: Miss King May, who was a lecturer on Physical Training to the Women Students of the Educational Department of Manchester University. In 1906 Elizabeth Wolstenholme ELMY referred to Miss King May as "the finest teacher in Manchester of physical education and a splendidly developed woman. . . . She spent her last Easter holidays working as a pit brow girl at Wigan to test herself the life. She greatly enjoyed the work and was deeply interested in the girl and women workers." Honorary secretary was Miss E. Sharman.

Address: (1913) 2 York Place, Oxford Road, Manchester (address of Miss King May and Miss E. Sharman).
Archival source: Elizabeth Wolstenholme Elmy Papers, British Library.
Bibliography: C. Crunden, *A History of Anstey College of Physical Education 1897–1972*, 1974.

H

HACKNEY (WFL) Secretary (1913) Mrs Pierotti, 31 Walsingham Road, Clapton, London E.

HACKNEY (WSPU) Secretary (1906) Miss R. Scriven, 131 Homeleigh Road, Stamford Hill, London N; (1913) Mrs Jones, 39 Pembury Road, Clapton, London, E.

HACKNEY (NORTH) (branch of the LONDON SOCIETY FOR WOMEN'S SUFFRAGE, NUWSS) Secretary (1909) Mrs Croft Handley, 154 Stoke Newington Road, London N; (1913) Miss I. Hancock, BA, 85 Digby Road, Green Lanes, London N.

HACKNEY (SOUTH) (branch of the LONDON SOCIETY FOR WOMEN'S SUFFRAGE) Secretary (1909) Mrs Elliott, 37 St Thomas' Road, South Hackney, London E.

HADDINGTON committee of the NATIONAL SOCIETY FOR WOMEN'S SUFFRAGE In existence in 1872 when its honorary secretary was Miss Rachel Brown. In 1913 the society was a member of the SCOTTISH FEDERATION OF THE NATIONAL UNION OF WOMEN'S SUFFRAGE SOCIETIES. Secretary (1913) Miss Jennie Riddell, Oaklands, Haddington, Lothian.

HADLEIGH (WFL) Secretary (1913) Miss Matthews, 21 Fir Tree Terrace, Hadleigh, Suffolk.

HAIG, CECILIA WOLSELEY (c. 1862–1912) From Berwickshire, Scotland, sister of Evelyn and Florence HAIG and cousin of Margaret Thomas, later Lady RHONDDA. Her parents were both in favour of women's suffrage. She spent many years involved in social work and in 1898 was a member of the Edinburgh Ladies' Debating Society. She was a member of the CENTRAL NATIONAL SOCIETY FOR WOMEN'S SUFFRAGE from 1892 until 1899. Cecilia Haig was influenced to join the WOMEN'S SOCIAL AND POLITICAL UNION by the example of her sister, Florence, and was also a member of the TAX RESISTANCE LEAGUE, of the CHURCH LEAGUE FOR WOMEN'S SUFFRAGE, and gave a donation to the MEN'S POLITICAL UNION in 1911. In November 1911 she was severely assaulted and trampled on during the "Black Friday" debacle in Parliament Square. She died just a year afterwards, having been nursed in her illness by Florence Haig. A writer in *Votes for Women*, 5 January 1912, had no hesitation in blaming the treatment she received on "Black Friday" as the reason for her death. On 14 January 1912 Annie KENNEY planted a tree in her memory in the Blathwayts' arboretum at Eagle House, Batheaston.
Address: (1895) 87 Comely Bank Avenue, Edinburgh.

HAIG, (LOUISA) EVELYN COTTON (1863–1954) Born in Edinburgh, sister of Cecilia and Florence HAIG and cousin of Margaret Thomas, later Lady RHONDDA. She was an artist, specializing in miniatures, studied in Paris and exhibited at the Paris Salon and at the Royal Academy. She was a member of the Edinburgh Ladies' Debating Society in 1901. She was brought into the women's suffrage movement by her sister Florence, subscribed to the WOMEN'S SOCIAL AND POLITICAL UNION in 1907 and was one of the founding members in 1908 of the Edinburgh WSPU. She took part in the "Black Friday" demonstration in 1910 during which her sister, Cecilia, was injured, and in January 1913 was arrested, charged with obstruction and sentenced to one month's imprisonment after taking part in the protest outside the House of Commons against the withdrawal of the Franchise Bill after the Speaker had ruled that amendments to include women would necessitate a new bill. She served the whole sentence.
Address: (1901) 87 Comely Bank Avenue, Edinburgh.

HAIG, FLORENCE ELIZA (1856–1952) Daughter of James Haig, a barrister, from Berwickshire, sister of Cecilia and Evelyn HAIG and cousin of Margaret Thomas, later Lady RHONDDA. In 1901 and again in 1907 she donated £1 to the LONDON SOCIETY FOR WOMEN'S SUFFRAGE. On 13 February 1907, with a group of friends who belonged to the NATIONAL UNION OF WOMEN'S SUFFRAGE SOCIETIES, she attended the WOMEN'S SOCIAL AND POLITICAL UNION's Women's Parliament in Caxton Hall. After this experience she joined the WSPU and with her sister Evelyn helped found a branch in Edinburgh, then moved from there to London. In February 1908 Florence Haig was arrested after having taken part in the "pantechnicon raid" with her fellow artists the BRACKENBURYS, on the House of Commons, and was sentenced to six weeks' imprisonment. In the report in *Votes for Women* she is described as a "portrait cleaner" but she was by now an established artist, having first exhibited in 1886 and continuing to do so until 1929. For instance she had exhibited, with 12 other women artists, at the Doré Gallery in March 1906. She had a studio in Chelsea, at 4 Trafalgar Studios and was a neighbour of Dora Meeson COATES, who lived at number 9 and described her as "hospitable and sincere, like the true Scotswoman she is, and George [Coates] had great admiration for her good portraiture. He said she could paint a better portrait than a great many men, which was high praise in those days, when there were not so many fine artists." After she came out of prison she was invited to Wales to recuperate with Margaret Haig Thomas and her parents. As a result of her visit, Margaret Thomas determined to walk in the Suffage Procession to Hyde Park on 21 June. On 30 June 1908, with other women from Chelsea, Florence Haig took part in a deputation from Caxton Hall to the Houses of Parliament, and this time was sentenced to three months' imprisonment. Zoe PROCTOR recounts how "Miss Haig, whose hair nearly reach[ed] her ankles, told me she had been given a small comb for use [in prison] which was, of course, entirely inadequate." Throughout 1908, when out of prison, and in 1909 she spoke at WSPU meetings around London. In 1910 she was the WSPU organizer in Chelsea for the January 1910 general election campaign and became honorary secretary of the CHELSEA BRANCH. Interestingly, there is no evidence of her involvement in either of the suffrage artist societies, although doubtless she helped Edith DOWNING and Marion Wallace-DUNLOP with the preparations for the suffrage processions, the design of which was the responsibility of the Chelsea branch. In 1910 Florence Haig paid a visit with Marion Wallace-Dunlop to the BLATHWAYTS at Batheaston and Mrs Blathwayt noted that they were both vegetarians. In 1910 Florence Haig subscribed to the NEW CONSTITUTIONAL SOCIETY FOR WOMEN'S SUFFRAGE and in 1911 gave a donation to the MEN'S POLITICAL UNION. She nursed her sister Cecilia from the beginning of 1911 until her death in January 1912. On 1 March 1912 Florence Haig was arrested after breaking the windows of D.H. Evans in Oxford Street during the WSPU window-smashing campaign, was sentenced to four months' imprisonment, joined in the June hunger strike and was released after several days without being forcibly fed. On 27 May 1913 she was one of the 13 women present at the meeting held to form the EAST LONDON FEDERATION OF THE WSPU. However, in the early years of the First World War, until 1916, she is listed as one of the secretaries of the WSPU, working with Mrs PANKHURST, Mabel TUKE, and Annie KENNEY. In 1928 she was one of the pallbearers at Mrs Pankhurst's funeral. In 1934 she was a member, with Ernestine MILLS, of the Society of Women Artists. Her hunger-strike medal and prison diaries are now held by the Museum of London. Among her papers are handwritten notes that she used to accompany 109 lantern slides, giving details of the history of the WSPU, and explaining the policy of militancy.

Address: (1908) 4 Trafalgar Studios, Manresa Road, Chelsea, London SW; (1915) 8 Vale Terrace, Kings Road, Chelsea, London SW; (1951) Stafford House, Maida Avenue, London W2.
Archival source: Papers of Florence Haig, Suffragette Fellowship Collection, Museum of London.
Photograph: in Fawcett Library Collection.
Bibliography: D.M. Coates, *George Coates: His Art and Life*, 1937; Z. Proctor, *Today and Yesterday*, 1960.

HALE, CICELY BERTHA (1884–1981) Born in Paddington, the youngest daughter of a GP. After being, as she later related, inadequately educated at home by governesses, she trained as a secretary. She first heard Christabel and Mrs PANKHURST speaking in Hyde Park in the summer of 1908 and was immediately attracted to the idea of "votes for women". She and her sister (who later married Harry Ricardo, a cousin of Elinor RENDEL) attended the weekly meetings held by the WOMEN'S SOCIAL AND POLITICAL UNION at the Portman Rooms and took part in "Women's Sunday" in Hyde Park in June. Cicely Hale related that as she and her sister gained confidence they were encouraged by Grace ROE to campaign at by-elections and in the autumn she was employed part-time (10/– for a three-day week) by the WSPU in the Information Department at Clement's Inn, as an assistant to Mary Home. In her memoir she describes scanning the papers to select suffrage material and then checking facts and supplying concise information to speakers. She describes how as both militancy and police surveillance increased she helped to typeset the *Suffragette* in secret locations around London, moving from place to place each week. Another of her jobs at this time was to organize the stewards at the weekly WSPU meetings at the London Pavilion. In 1912 she took over the Information Department, which consisted of Aeta LAMB, a typist and an office girl, after Mary Home left, and was present in Lincoln's Inn House on 30 April 1913 when it was raided by the police. In her memoir she gives a vivid picture of this event and how the Information Department was allowed by Dr Schütze, husband of "Henrietta Leslie" (*see* Gladys SCHÜTZE), to use his house in Glebe Place, Chelsea, as a base until they were raided there. She then moved to live in the home in Maida Vale of the Stack family. Mollie Stack later founded the League of Health and Beauty. Cicely Hale continued as a typesetter on the *Suffragette* and its successor *Britannia* until 1916, when she left, partly because her salary was so low and partly because she "was not very keen on the kind of war propaganda the Union was carrying on". She did, however, help prepare the cots for Mrs Pankhurst's war-babies orphanage. Cicely Hale then trained as a health visitor, working for a short time, when funds ran low, as secretary to Dr Christine MURRELL. She worked as a health visitor and as a journalist specializing in child-care for the rest of her working life and then devoted 20 years to the Guide movement. She lived first with a fellow WSPU worker, Elizabeth Gordon, and then with a "pioneer policewoman". Her memoir, published in her 89th year, was typed by Esther Knowles, who had been a Clement's Inn office junior and then became Frederick PETHICK-LAWRENCE's secretary until his retirement in 1959.

Address: (1973) 10 Southlands Court, Littlehampton, Sussex.
Photograph: in C.B. Hale, *A Good Long Time*, 1973.
Archival source: B. Harrison, taped interview with Cicely Hale, 1974, Fawcett Library.
Bibliography: C.B. Hale, *A Good Long Time*, 1973.

HALIFAX branch of the MANCHESTER NATIONAL SOCIETY FOR WOMEN'S SUFFRAGE Was in existence in the 1870s and by 1894 was associated with the CENTRAL COMMITTEE OF THE NATIONAL SOCIETY FOR WOMEN'S SUFFRAGE. The Halifax Women's Suffrage Society affiliated to the NORTH OF ENGLAND SOCIETY FOR WOMEN'S SUFFRAGE in 1897 and to the NATIONAL UNION OF WOMEN'S SUFFRAGE SOCIETIES in 1898. It may have been reconstituted in 1904, and no longer appears to have been in existence in 1913.
Secretary (1898) Miss Tillotson, Heath Avenue, Halifax, Yorkshire.

HALIFAX (WSPU) Secretary (1906) Mrs Wilson, 111 Watkinson Road, Ovenden; (1913) Dr Helena Jones, 3 Rhodesia Avenue, Halifax, Yorkshire.

HALL, NELLIE (1895–?) (later Mrs Hall Humpherson) Daughter of Martha Alice (known as "Pattie" (c. 1866–1946)) and Leonard Hall, who in the 1890s were friends and associates in Manchester of Richard and Emmeline PANKHURST. The Halls joined the Manchester Central branch of the Independent Labour Party, to which the Pankhursts belonged, the families became close friends, and in 1887 Emmeline Pankhurst was godmother to Nellie Hall's sister, named Emmeline for her. In 1896 Leonard Hall was one of the ILP speakers imprisoned in Manchester for addressing a crowd at Boggart Hole Clough, a piece of open ground taken over by the Council and barred to members of the ILP. Mrs Pankhurst gave her active support to him and his family at this time and Leonard Hall was one of three men (Keir HARDIE and John Harker, whom Dr Pankhurst had defended in court in the Boggart Clough affair, were the others) who spoke on the platform at a meeting organized by the Manchester Central branch of the ILP, held on 20 October 1905 to welcome Christabel PANKHURST after her release from prison following her interruption of Sir Edward Grey's Liberal meeting at the Free Trade Hall. Nellie Hall noted in an article in *Calling All Women*, the magazine of the SUFFRAGETTE FELLOWSHIP, that her mother was one of the original six women who formed the nucleus of the WOMEN'S SOCIAL AND POLITICAL UNION in 1903 and took part in deputations organized by the WSPU. In September 1909 Nellie Hall, still a schoolgirl, joined a parade around Winson Green Prison in Birmingham each night at the time when the first of the forcible feedings were taking place inside. In November her mother was sentenced to two weeks' imprisonment after taking part in the stone throwing that resulted from the disgust felt by WSPU members at the debacle in Parliament Square on "Black Friday". From mid-1911 until 1913 Nellie Hall worked in a voluntary capacity in the Birmingham WSPU office. She was arrested on 21 July 1913 in Birmingham when she threw a brick through the window of Asquith's car, and was charged on suspicion of being involved in the arson of a house in Selly Park, Birmingham and other incidents planned to coincide with the prime minister's visit. She was sentenced to three weeks' imprisonment, went on hunger strike and was released after eight days, with mumps, under the "Cat and Mouse" Act. She escaped to London as "Marie Roberts" and started work as Prisoners' Secretary, at a salary of £2 a week, at Lincoln's Inn House. On 21 May 1914, the day of the WSPU deputation to the King at Buckingham Palace, Nellie Hall, with her mother, sister, and two other women, was arrested at their flat in Lauderdale Mansions, Maida Vale. The police uncovered what was described as a small arsenal – a haul of beach pebbles and window-smashing equipment. Nellie Hall was held on remand for six weeks before receiving a three-months' prison sentence. She went on hunger strike, was forcibly fed and was only released on 10 August, under the amnesty after the outbreak of war.

During the First World War Nellie Hall joined the Post Office in Birmingham as the first mail sorter for the British Expeditionary Force, took part in the WSPU-organized "War Work" procession on 17 July 1915 and later became a welfare officer in a munitions plant. She married in 1920 and by 1928, when Flora DRUMMOND put her back in touch with Mrs Pankhurst, was living in Warwickshire with her schoolmaster husband and two children. However, despite the domestic difficulties it entailed, she agreed to become secretary and liaison officer to Mrs Pankhurst when she stood in London as Conservative candidate for the St George in the East constituency and then, after that defeat, helped care for her in her final illness. She played a prominent role at Mrs Pankhurst's funeral and, having failed to gain employment at Conservative Central Office, in 1929 emigrated to Canada with her family.
Address: (1914) Lauderdale Mansions, Maida Vale, London W; Kingscoat Road, Edgbaston, Birmingham.
Photograph: in the *Suffragette*, 26 June 1914.
Archival source: Nellie Hall's "Votes for Women Sash", hunger-strike medal (dated 21 July 1913), portcullis "prisoners" badge, WSPU testimonial, photocopied typescript of "A Personal Experience of the Beginning's of Women's Liberation", a collection of newpaper articles and other suffrage ephemera kept by her, are all on permanent loan to Birmingham Museum and Art Gallery; Mitchell Collection, Museum of London.
Bibliography: *Canadian Weekly*, October 1963; D. Mitchell, *The Fighting Pankhursts*, 1967.

HALLETT, LILIAS SOPHIA ASHWORTH, MRS (1844–1922) Quaker, daughter of Thomas Ashworth and Sophia Bright, who was the sister of John and Jacob BRIGHT, Priscilla Bright MCLAREN and Margaret Bright LUCAS (*see* Appendix). Sophia Hallett died 16 days after Lilias was born. Lilias and her sister Anne (*see* Anne ASHWORTH) were the only children of Thomas Ashworth to reach adulthood; a daughter of his second marriage to Alicia Nicholls died aged 16 in 1865. Lilias Ashworth signed the 1866 women's suffrage petition, was a subscriber to the ENFRANCHISEMENT OF WOMEN COMMITTEE 1866–7, joined the LONDON NATIONAL SOCIETY in 1867 and the committee of the BRISTOL AND WEST OF ENGLAND SOCIETY when it was formed in 1868. In April 1868 she was present at the first public meeting of the MANCHESTER NATIONAL SOCIETY held at Manchester Town Hall and there, for the first time, met Lydia BECKER. She was also present, and seconded a resolution moved by Dr PANKHURST, at the Annual General Meeting of the Manchester Society in December 1869. In 1871 she organized

Mrs Fawcett's tour of the west of England and, in 1872, one with Rhoda Garrett in Gloucestershire and Herefordshire, and another with Caroline Ashurst Biggs in South Wales. She was herself a valuable and busy speaker for the suffrage cause. It required considerable courage then for a woman to sit on a public platform and actually to speak from one was regarded as almost indecent. Mrs Ashworth Hallett wrote that "when we appeared in our quiet black dresses it was amusing to note the sudden change in the faces of the crowd who had come to look at us". In the 1890s Lord Selborne said of her, "she possesses the oratorical power of her uncle [presumably John Bright], both for argument, pathos and satire". In December 1871 Lilias Ashworth spoke to an enthusiastic audience of the Birmingham Women's Suffrage Society. In February 1872 she addressed both the annual meeting of the Bristol and West of England Society and a suffrage meeting in Rochdale. The *Women's Suffrage Journal* noted that she was always received with considerable applause. From 1870 to 1895 she was honorary secretary of the Bristol and West of England Society, in 1899 she was its treasurer, and became a member of the executive committee of the Central Committee of the National Society when it was formed in London in 1872. She and her sister together gave £100 to the Central Committee in 1873. In addition Lilias Ashworth subscribed to the Ladies' National Association in 1871 and was on the executive committee of the Married Women's Property Committee, 1873–4.

Lilias Ashworth Hallett and her sister were comparatively wealthy women. When she attended the women's suffrage conference in London in April 1871, in seconding a motion she remarked that she was the owner of property which if she were a man would entitle her to a vote in seven constituencies. She and her sister gave generously to the main suffrage societies, both to those in England and to the Edinburgh National Society (£60 to the latter in 1872). In addition she gave £50 towards the cost of the suffrage meeting at which Millicent Fawcett and Rhoda Garrett spoke, held in St George's Hall in London on 29 May 1875. Also in 1875 she offered to pay the expenses of suffrage propaganda meetings in Grantham and Nottingham. She and her sister, after the death of their father, were ostensibly under the control of trustees. However, there is little doubt that they were both strong-minded women and as their aunt Priscilla Bright McLaren wrote in a letter to her stepson in July 1870, "they have no notion of being tied down by any trustees". On this occasion they had, as their aunt wrote, "fixed to go to St Moritz but Mr Bower their trustee was dead against it". They "engaged a first-rate courier" and, encouraged by Duncan McLaren and Jacob Bright, defied the trustees.

In 1877, at a Quaker ceremony, Lilias Ashworth married Professor Thomas George Palmer Hallett of Bristol University. He was born in 1840 in Martock, Somerset, and the 1891 census describes him as a barrister. He published pamphlets on two subjects of Liberal concern, Free Trade and Ireland. At her wedding Lilias Ashworth Hallett was given, very suitably, a silver inkstand by fellow suffrage workers, and her uncle Jacob Bright is reported in the *Women's Suffrage Journal* as saying "that he believed that the homes where women were politically instructed, were happier homes than those where women were politically ignorant". She had no children and carried on with her suffrage activities. In 1884 Lilias Ashworth Hallett, with Lydia Becker and a few other women members, joined a visit of the British Association to Canada and sent an address of thanks to the Canadian prime minister for introducing provisions for women's suffrage into a bill before the Dominion parliament.

By 1884 Lilias Ashworth Hallett had, with Millicent Fawcett, moved towards a position of supporting an enfranchisement bill for unmarried women and widows only and, with Lydia Becker, worked to forestall the reinstatement of Jacob Bright as parliamentary leader of the women's suffrage movement. By so doing she moved out of sympathy with such radical suffragists as the Priestman sisters, her relations by marriage who were also active in the suffrage movement in the west of England. In 1888 she stayed with the Central Committee of the National Society after the societies diverged, and was a member of its executive committee. In 1886, when the Liberal party split over the Irish Question, she, like Millicent Fawcett, became a Liberal Unionist, thereby finding herself at odds with the more radical members of her family.

In 1897 Lilias Ashworth Hallett was present in the Ladies' Gallery during the second reading of Mr Faithfull Begg's bill and was sure that success was imminent. She wrote, "Women have become necessary to the success of party organizations, and to deny them the power of quietly going into a polling booth to record a vote is no longer rationally possible...". Perhaps it was the ensuing disappointment that led her to subscribe that year to the WOMEN'S EMANCIPATION UNION. In July 1903 she attended the independent suffrage conference to discuss plans for an autumn campaign, organized by W.T. Stead in association with Elizabeth Wolstenholme ELMY at his London office, Mowbray House. By 1903 she was a member of the executive committee of the NATIONAL UNION OF WOMEN'S SUFFRAGE SOCIETIES, in 1906 she was a vice-president of the CENTRAL SOCIETY and in 1906–7 she subscribed to the LONDON SOCIETY. She was still a vice-president of that society in 1913.

Lilias Ashworth Hallett was a supporter of the WOMEN'S SOCIAL AND POLITICAL UNION until their tactics became too overtly militant. She gave at least £165 to WSPU funds (£75 in 1907, £90 in 1908). In 1906 she was, with Millicent Fawcett, on the organizing committee for the banquet at the Savoy to celebrate the release from Holloway of the WSPU prisoners. On 13 February 1907 she joined with the WSPU in the deputation from the Women's Parliament in Caxton Hall to the House of Commons. On 14 February in a letter to The Times she wrote that she

> attended yesterday, for the first time, a meeting called by the Women's Social and Political Union. I walked with the only two ladies in the procession I happened to know. My astonishment was great when I found we were suddenly encompassed by police on foot and horse-back, and our courage rose in proportion to the indignation we felt. Police blocked the footway. They laughed and jeered... I was twice arrested, and when I found the hands of the police upon me I pointed to the Houses of Parliament, and said, "If you don't take your hands off me there are men in that house who will know the reason why." They then dropped me. They were not sure who I might be. If I had seemed more like a Lancashire mill-hand, I should doubtless be in Holloway this morning.

She had apparently meant to attend the 1908 Women's Parliament but an accident prevented her and her ticket was taken by Aethel TOLLEMACHE. Mary BLATHWAYT noted that when she attended a meeting in 1908 of the Bath branch of the NUWSS, Mrs Ashworth Hallett wore a (WSPU) "Votes for Women" badge. In March 1908 Lilias Ashworth Hallett attended the breakfast in the Eustace Miles Restaurant for released WSPU prisoners. When Annie KENNEY was sent to Bristol in 1907 she was certainly in touch with Lilias Ashworth Hallett, who then, in May 1908 chaired a meeting at a garden party held by the Blathwayts at Eagle House at which Annie Kenney was the principal speaker. In March 1910 Mary Blathwayt reported in her diary that Mrs Ashworth Hallett told her "that the Militant methods of the Suffragettes... made her quite ill". However, according to Mrs BLATHWAYT, in 1911 Lilias Ashworth Hallett remarked that "she and her friends worked hard for suffrage for years, but there would never have been a chance for it without the new Militants".

In her will, dated 1914, Lilias Ashworth Hallett left £1000 to Bristol University to found a scholarship for girls and the same sum to Girton for the same purpose. Bertha Mason in *The Story of the Woman's Suffrage Movement* cites for special thanks Lilias Ashworth Hallett and "her collection of Women's Suffrage records and photographs". Some of the photographs are reproduced in that book. Although in her will Lilias Ashworth Hallett stipulated that all her books on the Women's Question should be given to Girton, the College can find no trace of such a bequest having been received. In 1903 she had undertaken the binding of a portion of the pamphlets in the collection left to Girton by Helen BLACKBURN. In her obituary of Helen Blackburn in the *Englishwoman's Review*, April 1903, Lilias Ashworth Hallett remarked that she thought it would be of interest to readers if there were to be compiled a catalogue of the books and pamphlets of this "Memorial Library". Similarly, she wrote to the College Bursar that she thought it worth binding the annual reports of the main Women's Suffrage committees "for they have lists of all the early workers and early subscriptions and I believe that these will be of lasting interest. There will always be a few women who will look back through the years with interest and gratitude to the struggles of the early workers." In view of her foresight and obvious interest in the sources of history it is a pity that there appears to be no trace now of any of her manuscript material or photographs. A copy of one book only with her ownership inscription, significantly Helen Blackburn's *Record of Women's Suffrage*, is known to be in a private collection. Her name is, however, visibly commemorated, embroidered on a BANNER with, among others, that of another west of England suffragist, Agnes BEDDOE. The banner is now in the Fawcett Library Collection.

Address: Claverton Lodge, 24 Bathwick Hill, Bath.
Photograph: carte de visite in Josephine Butler Collection, Fawcett Library; in H. Blackburn, *Record of Women's Suffrage*, 1902; by Col Blathwayt in B.M. Willmott Dobbie, *A Nest of Suffragettes in Somerset*, 1979.
Bibliography: Mrs A.M. Beddoe, *The Early Years of the Woman's Suffrage Movement*, 1911; B. Mason, *The Story of the Women's Suffrage Movement*, 1912.

HALLS AND RESTAURANTS Occasions need to be placed in their contexts: pressure groups build up their pressure within a variety of public buildings. Over the course of the women's suffrage campaign the myriad societies followed each other in and out of public halls across the country. Many of the London buildings to which both local activists and those from the provinces made their way for rallies and meetings have been demolished or are now defunct and require repositioning on the mental map.

ALAN'S TEA ROOMS, run by Alan Liddle, at 263 Oxford Street, on the south side, just west of Oxford Circus. The tea rooms advertised regularly in *Votes for Women* that they had available a large room that could be engaged for meetings, with no charge to members of the WOMEN'S SOCIAL AND POLITICAL UNION; doubtless Mr Liddle's profit came from the accompanying tea and buns. The TAX RESISTANCE LEAGUE held its first members' conference here on 14 November 1910, the CATHOLIC WOMEN'S SUFFRAGE SOCIETY its large inauguration meeting in March 1911, and on 26 July 1913 after the excitements of the Hyde Park rally at the end of the NUWSS PILGRIMAGE, Margory LEES and her companions went to Alan's for dinner.

CAXTON HALL, Caxton Street, Westminster, just round the corner from St James's Park Tube Station, was built in 1878, in French château style, as Westminster Town Hall; its halls were let out for concerts and public meetings. Caxton Hall was used in 1902 by the CENTRAL SOCIETY FOR WOMEN'S SUFFRAGE for its annual general meeting and in February 1906 was hired by Annie KENNEY and Sylvia PANKHURST for the first London meeting of the the WSPU, a straightforward journey on the District Line for the women from the East End. It was subsequently the scene of the WSPU's many Women's Parliaments from which deputations set forth along Victoria Street to the Houses of Parliament. Caxton Hall's centrality to the militant suffrage movement is now commemorated by a bronzed scroll that stands in the public gardens outside it, placed there in 1970 by the efforts of the SUFFRAGETTE FELLOWSHIP. Although still standing the Hall is now (1999) shrouded in scaffolding and netting.

ESSEX HALL, Essex Street, on the other side of Fleet Street from Clement's Inn, was the scene of the meeting on 10 September 1907 at which Mrs PANKHURST explained that the WSPU was no longer to have a constitution, prompting many to break away to found the WOMEN'S FREEDOM LEAGUE. It was here in July 1912 that the WOMEN TEACHERS' FRANCHISE LEAGUE held its inaugural meeting. Essex Hall was the head church of the Unitarian movement.

EUSTACE MILES RESTAURANT, run by Eustace Miles, the keep-fit expert, and his wife, Hallie, was at 40 Chandos Street, off the east side of Trafalgar Square, close to Charing Cross. The restaurant, with a ground and a gallery floor, supplied only "meatless", that is vegetarian, meals. It had lecture rooms for hire, boasting "ozonized air"; in one of these in February 1912 Vera HOLME operated the lantern slide to accompany a talk by Miss Hoskyns-Abrahall on "The Religion of the Great Mother". At 9.30 am on 6 March 1907 the breakfast to celebrate the release of the prisoners who had taken part in the deputation from the WSPU's first Women's Parliament was held here; the women had been met at 8 am at the gates of Holloway. Similar breakfast celebrations were held here for another batch of prisoners on 3 April and again a year later, in March 1908, for those who had taken part in the "pantechnicon" raid. The restaurant remained a favourite with many suffrage groups; it witnessed the inaugural meeting of the MEN'S POLITICAL UNION FOR WOMEN'S ENFRANCHISEMENT on 13 January 1910 and committee meetings of the UNITED SUFFRAGISTS in October 1914. Edy CRAIG chose the road outside the restaurant as her newspaper-selling pitch; the bohemian vegetarian clientele were naturals for suffrage "literature". The restaurant flourished throughout the First World War, when "meatless cookery" came of necessity into its own. The building was much later occupied by the publishing firm, Chatto & Windus.

EXETER HALL, on the north side of the Strand, opposite the Savoy, had been built, in classical style, in 1831, as a non-sectarian hall for religious and scientific gatherings. The meetings of the Anti-Slavery Convention were held there in 1840. It was to here that the women's deputation, comprising both constitutionalists and militants, repaired on 19 May 1906 after the disappointing interview with Campbell-Bannerman at the Foreign Office. The next year Exeter Hall was the culminating venue of the NATIONAL UNION OF WOMEN'S SUFFRAGE SOCIETIES' "Mud March" in February 1907, and a week later housed the overflow meeting of the WSPU's first Women's Parliament. It was demolished later that year; on its site now stands the Strand Palace Hotel.

HANOVER SQUARE ROOMS, on the east side of Hanover Square, had been opened in 1774 and was run as a concert hall, the scene of performances by J.C. Bach, Haydn and Liszt, until 1875 when the building became a private club. In March 1870 the Hanover Square Rooms was the scene of the second public meeting organized by the LONDON NATIONAL SOCIETY FOR WOMEN'S SUFFRAGE, at which the speakers included Helen TAYLOR, Harriet Grote and Millicent FAWCETT. The society's first meeting had been held close by in Conduit Street (*see* Harriet GROTE).

HOLBORN RESTAURANT, on the corner of High Holborn and the west side of Kingsway (almost next door to the office of Mrs Ayres Purdie, financial adviser to the militant suffrage movement) had a history of political breakfasting, having for hire a host of different sized rooms suitable for gatherings of all sizes. In 1891 the National Liberal Federation held a breakfast here, at which Gladstone spoke; the restaurant was in the early twentieth century the scene of many WSPU "release" breakfasts.

INNS OF COURT HOTEL, on the south side of Holborn, north of Lincoln's Inn Fields, was Emmeline PANKHURST's London base for much of the pre-war WSPU campaign. The hotel was the setting for the celebratory breakfast after the release of her sister Mary CLARKE and other WSPU prisoners in January 1909 and of that for Patricia WOODLOCK a few months later, in June. Amongst the Suffragette Fellowship Collection of photographs in the Museum of London is an interior shot of the January 1909 breakfast.

HOTEL CECIL was built by 1896 to the west side of the Savoy, now the site of Shell-Mex House. It had 1000 rooms, was lavish with Doulton tiles and palms, and was reputed to be the biggest hotel in the world. It was here in these opulent surroundings that the TAX RESISTANCE LEAGUE chose to hold its "John Hampden Dinner" on 12 December 1911, and the ACTRESSES' FRANCHISE LEAGUE and WOMEN WRITERS' SUFFRAGE LEAGUE their entertaining "Costume Dinner" on 29 June 1914, the last pre-war consciousness-raising suffrage "occasion".

PORTMAN ROOMS, 58 Baker Street, sited between the photographers Elliot and Fry and Hoppé, were used by the WSPU for its weekly "At Homes", when, around February 1908, these grew too large to be accommodated in Clement's Inn; the Women's Freedom League, for a time, also held its "At Homes" here. The Portman Rooms were the scene of the WSPU's themed and costumed "Christmas Fair" in December 1911.

PRINCE'S SKATING RINK, scene of the extravagant success of the WSPU's Exhibition in May 1909, was on the west side of Trevor Place, off the south side of Knightsbridge.

QUEEN'S HALL, Langham Place, on the east side, just to the south of All Soul's Church, was from its earliest days the setting for many a suffrage meeting. It was opened in 1893, its classical exterior based on the Parthenon, its interior florid Victorian red and gold. There were in fact two halls, one large and one small. It was probably only the smaller that was required for the meeting of the WOMEN'S FRANCHISE LEAGUE held there in 1894; the larger would have been necessary to accommodate the meeting of the International Congress of Women in 1899. It was here on 19 December 1905 that the WSPU made its first strike in London when Annie KENNEY and others interrupted Asquith's Liberal rally. Conscripted to its own use, the WSPU subsequently made the Queen's Hall a regular base for WSPU "At Homes", once they outgrew the Portman Rooms, and for eloquent rallies. It was also used by the NUWSS; it was here on 8 December 1911 that they held a special Council meeting and in March 1918 the "victory" celebrations.

ST GEORGE'S HALL, Langham Place, was adjacent and to the south of the "small" Queen's Hall. It was opened in 1867 as a concert hall and from 1874 appears to have been what might be termed a middle-class music-hall. Rhoda GARRETT spoke here at a meeting organised by the Central Committee on 29 May 1875.

ST JAMES'S HALL, on the north side of Piccadilly, close to Piccadilly Circus, was built as London's principal concert hall in 1858, with Owen Jones as its architect. It was the scene of London's "Grand Demonstration of Women" in 1880 and it was here, in its Venetian Gothic splendour, that in April 1892 members of the WOMEN'S FRANCHISE LEAGUE stormed the platform during the intemperate meeting held to discuss Sir Albert Rollit's Franchise bill. The St James's Hall was demolished in 1905.

ST JAMES'S HALL, Great Portland Street, on the corner of Langham Street, just north of the Queen's Hall, was much favoured by the WSPU as a venue for lectures, "At Homes" and, on 16 September 1909, as the scene of the first presentation of "Holloway" brooches (*see* JEWELLERY)

TEA CUP INN, which advertised in *Votes for Women* and the *Vote* that it was entirely staffed and managed by women, opened in January 1910 in Bank Buildings, on the corner of Kingsway and Portugal Street, close to Clement's Inn and, after 1912, to Lincoln's Inn House. The manageress was Mrs Alice Hawell, who was apparently a member of the WSPU. Vegetarian dishes were a speciality. W.T. Stead's *Review of Reviews* moved into the same building.

Bibliography: K. Baedeker, *London and Its Environs*, 1881; C.E. Pascoe, *London of To-day: An Illustrated Handbook for the Season*, 1888; L. Eustace Miles, *Untold Tales of War-Time London*, 1930; H. Hobhouse, *Lost London*, 1971; B. Weinreb and C. Hibbert, *The London Encyclopaedia*, 1983.

HAMILTON, CICELY MARY (1872–1952) née Hammill Born in London, the eldest of four children of a captain in the Gordon Highlanders. Her mother disappeared early from her family's life; whether this was due to death, elopement, or mental illness is not recorded. While her father was fighting in the Egyptian campaign in the 1880s, his children were most unhappily boarded out in Clapham. After his return he took them to live in Bournemouth with his sisters and Cicely went to boarding school at Malvern, followed by a period as a pupil-teacher at a German school at Bad Homburg. On her return in 1890 she reluctantly took up a position as a pupil-teacher at a school in the Midlands until, a year later, after her father's death, she changed her name to "Hamilton" and went to London to become an actress. For the next ten years persistence was rewarded with parts in touring plays, working with several different companies, travelling the country, living in digs, earning a pittance. When it became apparent that she was not going to achieve the desired success on the London stage she turned her hand to hack writing, while planning a new career as a dramatist. Her first play, *The Sixth Commandment*, was staged at Wyndham's Theatre in 1906.

Cicely Hamilton took part in the NATIONAL UNION OF WOMEN'S SUFFRAGE SOCIETIES "Mud March" in February 1907 and later that year subscribed to the WOMEN'S SOCIAL AND POLITICAL UNION. She was described by her friend Dora Meeson COATES at this time as "a fair-haired, Celtic-looking woman, with a strong, handsome face". Her independent feminist mind, honed by years of self-sufficiency, did not make her particularly sympathetic to organized militancy. She remarks in her autobiography that temperamentally she was probably more suited to the constitutional branch of the suffrage movement, but having found the PANKHURSTS too autocratic, and doubting the morality of militancy, it was the WOMEN'S FREEDOM LEAGUE that she joined. In November 1907 she was secretary of the Chelsea branch of the WFL, the first branch formed directly under its auspices after the break with the WSPU. At the beginning of 1908 Cicely Hamilton had achieved acclaim for her play *Diana of Dobson's*, starring, and staged by, Lena ASHWELL at the Kingsway Theatre. Cicely Hamilton's fame increased her attraction in the eyes of the suffrage movement and she was much in demand as a speaker. In 1908, with Bessie HATTON, who had been inspired by hearing her speak at a suffrage meeting, she founded the WOMEN WRITERS' SUFFRAGE LEAGUE, with the intention of fighting for the suffrage with her pen rather than by breaking windows. In March/April 1908 "Miss Hamilton's 'Waxworks'" was performed at a WFL bazaar. The exact nature of the "Waxworks" appears to be irrecoverable. It seems to have been a one-woman show, apparently using puppets; there is no evidence that an accompanying script was ever published, although 25 lines of verse from it did appear in the *Herald of Wales* on the occasion of the WFL Pageant in Swansea in 1910 (*see* PLAYS). A notice of the "Waxworks" in the *Common Cause*, 11 November 1909, explained that they "are designed to personify every argument against the suffrage, so as to render future Anti-Suffrage meetings superfluous. The characters are as follows: – 'The Truly Womanly Woman' (who, among other domestic occupations, is reading a novel by Mrs Humphry Ward), the 'Early Victorian Lady' (who faints at the mention of the atrocities committed by the Suffragette), 'Queen Elizabeth' (a salient feature of whose character, as the showwoman remarked, was her feminine deference to the opinion of her ministers), 'the Policeman', 'the Objector' (the one speaking figure) and 'the Suffragette'." The "Waxworks" proved very popular in the following years, being performed to suffrage societies of all persuasions throughout the country, included in the programme for the WSPU Prince's Skating Rink Exhibition in May 1909 and at an entertainment given by the NEW CONSTITUTIONAL SOCIETY in April 1910. Miss Smith of the NUWSS SCOTTISH FEDERATION suggested to the GLASGOW AND WEST OF SCOTLAND ASSOCIATION FOR WOMEN'S SUFFRAGE in 1911 that when Cicely Hamilton was in Scotland in December she would be willing to give her "Waxworks".

On 13 June 1908 Cicely Hamilton took turns with Evelyn SHARP and Sarah Grand in carrying the WWSL banner during the NUWSS-organized march to the demonstration in Hyde Park and in December, again with Evelyn Sharp, she spoke at the inaugural meeting of the ACTRESSES' FRANCHISE LEAGUE, of which she then became a member of the executive committee. It was through her work with the AFL that she met and became a lifelong friend of Edith CRAIG and Christopher ST JOHN.

The AFL's first dramatic success resulted from a collaboration between the latter and Cicely Hamilton. Christopher St John took a story written by Cicely Hamilton which had been published in pamphlet form with illustrations by C. Hedley Charlton, and turned it into an eponymous play, *How The Vote Was Won*, which had its first performance, directed by Edith Craig, at the Royalty Theatre on 13 April 1909. It then provided entertainment to audiences at the WSPU Exhibition in May. Its success led Edith Craig to suggest to Cicely Hamilton the idea for the *Pageant of Great Women*, a device to involve, with minimal professional support, large numbers of suffragists in the staging of artistic propaganda. The play took as its theme the painting by W.H. Margetson, depicting Woman being torn from the presence of blind Justice by (male) Prejudice; this was the device used as their icon by the WWSL. In the *Pageant* representative women of the past are called up to plead Woman's cause, giving ample scope for a large cast and imaginative costuming. The first performance of the *Pageant*, at the Scala Theatre in November 1909, in which Cicely Hamilton herself played the part of Christian Davies, a woman who had fought in Marlborough's army, proved a great success and repeat stagings were played to suffrage societies throughout the country. In 1910 Cicely Hamilton appeared in the leading part of "Woman" in performances in Swansea, Beckenham, Middlesborough, Sunderland and Ipswich. The *Pageant of Great Women*, including photographs and giving the cast list of the first performance, was in 1910 the first publication of the Suffrage Shop (*see* SHOPS). In addition to the *Pageant* Cicely Hamilton also wrote, again with Christopher St John, another suffrage propaganda play, a one-acter, *The Pot and the Kettle*, which opened on the same bill. It was through the *Pageant* that Cicely Hamilton achieved her original aim of acting on the London stage. In 1911 Lillah MCCARTHY, who had played the part of "Woman" at suffrage matinées, encouraged her husband Granville Barker to offer Cicely Hamilton the part of Margaret Knox, mother of the heroine, in George Bernard Shaw's *Fanny's First Play*, that he was directing at the Little Theatre. Cicely Hamilton described the play as a "truly obstinate success" and as a consequence was offered other parts in the commercial theatre.

Besides her plays, Cicely Hamilton's writings explicitly for the suffrage movement included *Beware! A Warning to Suffragists*, a delightful booklet in which her ironic rhymes accompany illustrations by Dora Meeson Coates, Mary LOWNDES, and C. Hedley Charlton, published c. 1909 by the ARTISTS' SUFFRAGE LEAGUE; the words, which she herself described as "workable doggerel", for Ethel Smyth's "March of the Women", 1911; and numerous articles in the *Vote* and the *English Review*. Cicely Hamilton was a member of the editorial board of the *Englishwoman* when it was founded in 1909. Her feminist polemic *Marriage as a Trade* was published by Chapman and Hall in 1909 and *Just To Get Married*, which translated the theme into novel form, was published by the same firm two years later and, dramatized, was directed by Gertrude Kingston, a member of the AFL, at the Little Theatre in November 1910. In *Marriage As A Trade* Cicely Hamilton's thesis was that marriage was for women, in a patriarchal society, the means by which most earned their keep. The consequent socialization of girls, with the aim of trapping a man, was to their detriment; women could only gain independence by working for their own living. In 1909, as an independent professional woman, she took a leading role in the founding of the TAX RESISTANCE LEAGUE and refused to pay her income tax. Her worldly goods were, apparently, so few that the Inland Revenue never distrained.

What Cicely Hamilton herself described as her "suffrage novel", *William an Englishman*, although written in 1918 and published in 1919, originated in her observations of the militant suffrage movement before the First World War. Her musings then on how the militants would feel if caught up in real warfare were given depth by her wartime experiences. She spent two and a half years with the Scottish Women's Hospitals Unit at Royaumont and then joined Lena Ashwell's "Concerts at the Front", based around Abbeville; her younger brother was killed in the last months of the war. She particularly remarked that when, in Abbeville, she heard the news of the passing of the bill granting women partial enfranchisement she was too busy worrying about the likelihood of imminent death to care about voting. However, 25 years later in a radio broadcast she did acknowledge the continuous improvement in the position of women since the granting of the vote and presumably considered her efforts for the cause not in vain.

In 1920 Cicely Hamilton, at the request of Elizabeth ABBOTT, who became a close friend, acted as press secretary at the meeting in Geneva of the conference of the INTERNATIONAL WOMAN SUFFRAGE ALLIANCE. After returning to England she devoted herself to writing – some plays and novels, but mainly journalism. She wrote for mainstream newspapers such as the *Daily Mail* and the *Daily Sketch*, as well as for such feminist enterprises as Lady RHONDDA's *Time and Tide*. Cicely Hamilton was treasurer of the Women's Election Committee, was a member of the Six Point Group until the 1930s, and of the Open Door Council until her death. She was also an active campaigner for birth control, a vice-president of the New Generation League (the successor to the Malthusian League) throughout the 1920s. Between 1931 and 1950 she published nine books on contemporary Europe, the material for which she gathered on her travels. In 1947 she was a patron of the Suffragette Record Room (*see* SUFFRAGETTE FELLOWSHIP). In her will she made a point of recording her appreciation for kindness shown to her by Lady Rhondda and left to Elizabeth Abbott copyright in all her literary work.

Address: (1908): 28 Glebe Place, Chelsea, London SW; (1952) 44 Glebe Place, Chelsea, London SW (which had once been the home of Emily FORD).

Portrait: by Miss A.E. Hope Joseph (who had been a member of the SUFFRAGE ATELIER), offered to the National Portrait Gallery in 1955. It was rejected, although a photograph of it remains in the NPG archive. Portrait of Cicely and Evelyn Hammill (her sister, with whom she lived until 1929) by George Coates was exhibited at the Royal Academy in 1913, whereabouts now unknown. Portrait of Cicely Hamilton by Thomas Lowinsky, 1926, Sheffield City Art Galleries. Portrait of Cicely Hamilton by Edmund Kapp, 1931, in Barber Institute, Birmingham.

Photograph: by Mrs Albert Broom, of Cicely Hamilton with Edith Craig, 18 June 1910; two photographs by Lena Connell (National Portrait Gallery Archive and Fawcett Library); by Marie Leon in C. Hamilton, *Pageant of Great Women*, 1910; in C. Hamilton, *Life Errant*, 1935.

Bibliography: C. Hamilton, *Life Errant*, 1935; D.M. Coates, *George Coates: His Life and Work*, 1937; C. Hamilton, *Marriage as a Trade*, 1909, reprint with introduction by Jane Lewis, 1981; J. Holledge, *Innocent Flowers: Women in the Edwardian Theatre*, 1981; L. Whitelaw, *The Life and Rebellious Times of Cicely Hamilton*, 1990; S. Stowell, *A Stage Of Their Own: Feminist Playwrights of the Suffrage Era*, 1992.

HAMMERSMITH (branch of LONDON SOCIETY FOR WOMEN'S SUFFRAGE, NUWSS) Founded in December 1905. In January 1907 Mrs Frances ROWE, its honorary secretary, called a meeting of the society's executive committee to discuss the advisability of dissolving the society and reforming it as a branch of the WOMEN'S SOCIAL AND POLITICAL UNION. At a vote, the resolution was lost and Mrs Rowe split off to found a Hammersmith branch of the WSPU. Secretary (1909) Miss West, Cambridge House, St Stephen's Avenue, Shepherd's Bush, London W; (1913) Mrs Arthur Wallis, 94 Percy Road, Shepherd's Bush, London.

HAMMERSMITH (WSPU) Founded in February 1907 by Frances ROWE and other former members of the Hammersmith branch of the National Union of Women's Suffrage Societies. Dora MONTEFIORE was a member and treasurer for a short time. Secretary (1906) Mrs Frances Rowe, 15 Hammersmith Terrace, London W, and Miss E.F. Haarbleicher, 32 Phoenix Lodge Mansions, Brook Green; (1913) Miss Carson, 905 The Grove, Hammersmith, London W. The society's banner is now held in the Museum of London.
Archival source: Hammersmith and Fulham Archives and Local History Centre.

HAMPSTEAD (branch of the LONDON SOCIETY FOR WOMEN'S SUFFRAGE, NUWSS) Originally formed in 1872 as a branch of the LONDON NATIONAL SOCIETY FOR WOMEN'S SUFFRAGE. President then was Emily DAVIES, honorary secretary was Mrs Fox Bourne, 14 King Henry's Road, NW. Secretaries (1909) Mrs John Osler, 4 Akenside Road, Hampstead, London NW, and Mrs Hartley, 168 Adelaide Road, London NW; (1913) Miss Boyd.

HAMPSTEAD branch of the NEW CONSTITUTIONAL SOCIETY FOR WOMEN'S SUFFRAGE Organizer (1913) Mrs Hartley, 168 Adelaide Road, London NW, who had left the Hampstead branch of the London Society.

HAMPSTEAD branch of the UNITED SUFFRAGISTS Formed in 1915. Honorary secretary, Mrs Lilian HICKS, 33 Downside Crescent, London NW. By June 1916 it had become the Hampstead and Golders Green branch. Joint secretaries: Daisy SOLOMON, 64 Pattison Road, London NW; Dorothy PETHICK, 39 Meadway Court, Golders Green, London NW.

HAMPSTEAD (WFL) Secretary (1913) Mrs Spiller, 63 South Hill Park, Hampstead, London NW. Mrs Lilian HICKS was until late 1910 a leading member of this branch, before moving to that of the WOMEN'S SOCIAL AND POLITICAL UNION. Louisa Thompson-Price, a suffragist of long standing and contributor to the *Vote*, chaired meetings of the branch. Two of the society's banners are now held in the Museum of London.

HAMPSTEAD (WSPU) Secretaries (1906) Miss Venning, 54 Park Hill Road, Hampstead and Miss Ballam, 68 Belsize Road, Hampstead; (1913) Miss Daisy SOLOMON, 178 Finchley Road, London NW.

HAMPSTEAD (WEST) (WFL) Secretary (1913) Mrs van Raalte, 23 Pandora Road, West Hampstead, London NW.

HANKINSON, FREDERICK, REVEREND (1875–1960) Unitarian minister, born in Altrincham, one of a family of 11 children, brought up in what he later described as a Unitarian atmosphere. In the family equality between men and women was discussed and the works of women such as Lydia BECKER, Elizabeth Blackwell, Mary Somerville, Anna Swanwick, Frances Power COBBE, Mary Carpenter, Florence Nightingale, Octavia Hill, Harriet Martineau and Mrs Barbauld were held up for emulation. He remembered that as a child he was used to thinking of women as bread winners, saw women sitting on committees and heard them speak at meetings. He attended Owen's College in Manchester, where on occasion he spoke up for the right of women students to attend certain social events, and then went on to train as a minister at the Unitarian Church's Manchester College. He attended what he described as "mild drawing-room meetings", presumably organized by the NORTH OF ENGLAND SOCIETY FOR WOMEN'S SUFFRAGE, but after the treatment of Christabel PANKHURST and Annie KENNEY at the Free Trade Hall meeting in October 1905 felt more strongly drawn towards the suffrage movement. Hankinson had for some time been a friend of Frederick PETHICK-LAWRENCE and joined the MEN'S LEAGUE FOR WOMEN'S SUFFRAGE after it was formed in 1907, carrying a banner in one of the marches. In 1908 he met another Unitarian minister and his four daughters, who were all members of the WOMEN'S FREEDOM LEAGUE, and decided to make his contribution to the suffrage cause by visiting, in his capacity as Unitarian minister, suffrage prisoners in Holloway, Brixton and Aylesbury. Helen WATTS noted that Hankinson read her letters to her when she was in Holloway in February 1909. When Marion Wallace-DUNLOP was imprisoned in Holloway in June 1909 and had begun the first hunger strike, she applied to see Hankinson, at Christabel PANKHURST's express wish. She remembered later that she felt rather mean doing this as she was "what people call a Free Thinker". It is likely that Christabel wished to use Hankinson as a conduit for information and as a means of monitoring the efficacy of this new tactic. In March/April 1912 Dr Alice KER explained in a letter to her daughter Margaret that the Unitarian minister, Mr Hankinson, was sent in twice a week from outside "and sees Unitarians, . . . Theosophists and all the queer sects. I have applied to see him, and when I do, you can write to him, and he will read me your letters. As he is our spiritual adviser, the wardress sits outside the glass door during his visit. He is the brickiest of brick of anybody yet – gives any amount of time and trouble to us." Among the other suffragettes visited by Hankinson were Muriel MATTERS (1908), Sime SERUYA (1909), Arabella and Muriel SCOTT (1909), Amy HICKS (1912) and Katherine GATTY (1912). Maud JOACHIM was refused a visit from Hankinson and had to content herself with the Church of England chaplain because she had given her denomination as "C. of E." when she arrived at Maidstone prison in 1912. Hankinson was presumably a source of information and comfort not only from friends, but also from WSPU activists on the outside. Olive WALTON mentioned in the diary she kept while in Aylesbury prison in 1912 that the Unitarian minister was visiting some of the prisoners. Two of these were Violet BLAND and Charlotte MARSH to whom Hankinson read letters. On this occasion he was reprimanded by the authorities for whispering and forced to give an undertaking to observe the prison regulations.

The Secretary of the Prison Commission asked him, in a letter dated 19 April 1912, why he passed public information to the two prisoners when he visited them in Aylesbury and in a further letter deemed Hankinson's explanation as unsatisfactory and stated that he had gone beyond his ministerial duties. His offer to supply Holloway and Aylesbury with a selection of Unitarian devotional books was accepted. However, by mid-1912 the Home Office debarred him from continuing as Unitarian chaplain to the prisons. When Mrs PETHICK-LAWRENCE was in prison in the summer of 1912 and asked to see Hankinson, she was told that he had "abandoned his visits". She expressed great surprise and only found out later that he had actually been prevented from visiting. He was never openly accused of breaking prison regulations, the Prison Commision merely appointed another chaplain, Mr Gow. In her autobiography, Emmeline Pethick-Lawrence expressly denied that Hankinson had ever discussed political matters with suffrage prisoners. Hankinson did retain as a memento of his prison-visiting a list giving full names of "Suffragette prisoners I visited", a list of all prisoners (giving initials and denomination only) visited by him between "1907 (or 8) and August 1913", and an autograph album containing the signatures of 27 suffragette prisoners collected in 1912. In addition to his work in the prisons Hankinson was the minister of the Free Christian Church in Clarence Road, Kentish Town, and advertised in the 14 May 1909 edition of *Votes for Women* that his church was playing host to an American woman minister and added "that he is delighted to be free to throw open his pulpit to a woman worker in the same cause as himself". After it was founded in 1914 Frederick Hankinson became a member of the UNITED SUFFRAGISTS. During the First World War he was an agent of the Society of Friends for providing relief work in Hungary and in the 1920s worked there as a delegate on behalf of the Unitarian Women's League in America. He remained for the rest of his life a close friend of Frederick Pethick-Lawrence, with whom for many years he went on holiday and who eventually wrote an obituary letter about him for publication in *The Times*. Hankinson kept up his suffrage association until the end, attending a WFL meeting at the Minerva Club in the year of his death.

Address: (1913) 60 Haverstock Hill, Hampstead, London NW.
Portrait: by a Hungarian painter (?), 1922, in a private collection.
Archival source: a private collection; letter of Dr Alice Ker, Fawcett Library.
Bibliography: E. Pethick-Lawrence, *My Part in a Changing World*, 1938; letter from Lord Pethick-Lawrence, *The Times*, 16 November 1960.

HANKINSON, MARY (1868–1952) Unitarian, born in Altrincham, eldest sister of Frederick HANKINSON. She began her training at Mme Osterberg's Physical Training College when she was over 30 and later founded the Ling Association (which became the Ling Physical Education Association). Margaret Cole, in *Growing Up Into Revolution*, described Mary Hankinson as "a short square woman with a bright red face and a determined manner". In 1910 she gave a donation to the WOMEN'S FREEDOM LEAGUE and played the part of Mrs PANKHURST in a play she had written called *How We Won the Vote*. Mary Hankinson was a member of the general purposes committee of the FEDERATED COUNCIL OF SUFFRAGE SOCIETIES in 1912 and was president of the GYMNASTIC TEACHERS' SUFFRAGE SOCIETY in 1913. She was a member of the Fabian Society from 1905 to 1948 and was a member of the executive committee of the FABIAN WOMEN'S GROUP when it was founded in 1908. In 1907 she was hired to give instruction in Swedish drill and to give a country dancing course to those attending the first Fabian Society Summer School. She then became general manager of all subsequent Summer Schools until 1938, when she retired after disapproving of a relaxation in some rules of behaviour. She was a close friend of Beatrice and Sidney Webb, and of George Bernard Shaw. The latter gave her a copy of his play *Saint Joan*, with the dedication "To Mary Hankinson, the only woman I know who does not believe she was a model for Joan, but also the only woman who actually was", dated 21 June 1924. Mary Hankinson later became hostess at the Co-operative Holiday Association hostels. The Physical Education Association set up a Mary Hankinson Memorial Lecture in her honour.
Address: (1913) 67 Shaftesbury Road, Crouch Hill, London N.
Bibliography: M. Cole, *Growing Up in to Revolution*, 1949; P. Pugh, *Educate, Agitate, Organize: 100 Years of Fabian Socialism*, 1984.

HANSON, HELEN, DR (1874–1926) Graduated from the School of Medicine for Women in London in 1901 and in 1905 went to India as a medical missionary, based at Kinnaird Hospital in Lucknow, returning in 1909, travelling steerage class in order to donate the money thus saved, 108 shillings, to the WOMEN'S SOCIAL AND POLITICAL UNION. She was employed as a medical assistant in the Public Health Department of the London County Council and, like so many other doctors, became a member of the TAX RESISTANCE LEAGUE. Helen Hanson was a member of the WOMEN'S FREEDOM LEAGUE and of the LONDON GRADUATES' UNION FOR WOMEN'S SUFFRAGE as well as being, in 1910, a member of the executive committee of the CHURCH LEAGUE FOR WOMEN'S SUFFRAGE, having joined that society as soon as it was founded. In 1910 she published a pamphlet, *From East to West: Women's Suffrage in Relation to Foreign Missions*. She gave a donation to the MEN'S POLITICAL UNION in 1911 and that April took part in the WFL Census Protest. Helen Hanson took part in a deputation to the House of Commons on 28 November 1911, was arrested, and sentenced, as "Helen Rice", to five days' imprisonment. She presumably did not want to jeopardize her job by going to prison under her own name. During the First World War she worked in Serbia, Malta and Constantinople with the Scottish Women's Hospitals Unit. After the war she became honorary secretary and then treasurer of the League of the Church Militant, as the CLWS was retitled.
Address: (1925) 28 Circus Road Mansions, London NW8.
Bibliography: E.L. Acres, *Helen Hanson: A Memoir*, 1928.

HARBEN, HENRY DEVENISH (1874–1967) Educated at Eton and Magdalen College, Oxford, grandson of the chairman of the Prudential Insurance Company, he trained as a barrister, and ran his Berkshire estate with the interests of his workers in mind. He stood as a Conservative candidate in 1900, by 1902 he was a Liberal, and in the 1906 general election he stood unsuccessfully as a Liberal candidate. In 1912 he resigned, rather dramatically in the middle of a by-election campaign, from the Liberal Party because of its attitude towards women's emancipation and particularly because of what he saw as its persecution of the suffragettes. He had, moreover, published a Fabian Society pamphlet, *The Endowment* *of Motherhood,* in 1910 and joined the executive committee of the Society in 1911, remaining a member until 1920. In 1913 he was a justice of the peace and honorary treasurer of the MEN'S POLITICAL UNION FOR WOMEN'S ENFRANCHISEMENT. In 1912 he joined the board of the *Daily Herald.* Lady DE LA WARR, with whom he shared an interest in theosophy, had introduced him to George LANSBURY. He was in close touch with the PANKHURSTS at the height of militant action in 1913 and 1914 and gave assistance in many ways, not the least by making the present of a bedjacket to Emmeline PANKHURST. In January 1913 she wrote to thank him for his offer to suffragettes of sanctuary at Newlands Park after their imprisonment and mentioned that Mrs DRUMMOND was due to be released the next day. Annie KENNEY certainly took up the invitation. In the same month he gave £25 to the WOMEN'S SOCIAL AND POLITICAL UNION and was asked by the Suffrage Section of the FABIAN WOMEN'S GROUP, to which he donated money, to exert pressure on the *Daily Citizen* to improve its attitude on the suffrage question. In February he offered £50 a year for three years to Sylvia PANKHURST and the EAST LONDON FEDERATION OF SUFFRAGETTES and to act as guarantor for the renting of premises for them in the East End. In the same month he stood surety for Hugh FRANKLIN, was ejected from the gallery of the House of Commons for protesting aginst forcible feeding, and was also dealing with the aftermath of May BILLINGHURST's imprisonment, including obtaining doctors' reports on the state of her health after she left prison. On 14 February 1913 Henry Harben wrote to Emmeline Pankhurst reporting that the *Daily Herald* had, the day before, seemed moribund and that "It would have been a disaster if the only daily paper which has furiously championed militancy in both the women's and the labour movements, had been allowed to die, and I was at work till after eleven last night to avert this. Happily, the miracle has now happened; we shall live after all . . . I had a good meeting with George Lansbury at Oxford on Tuesday and in spite of musical instruments and mice he held brainless and athletic undergraduates interested till half-past-ten". Sylvia Pankhurst noted that Harben donated the money to the *Daily Herald* that enabled it to acquire the Victoria House Printing Press and thereby stay in business.

In June 1913 both Harben and his wife Agnes were delegates to the INTERNATIONAL WOMAN SUFFRAGE ALLIANCE Conference in Budapest, he representing the Men's Political Union for Women's Enfranchisement and she the Fabian Women's Group. On 13 October 1913 Harben and Francis Meynell (*see* Helena DOWSON) were named in a Settlement made by Mary RICHARDSON after her previous term of imprisonment. Because Mary Richardson had no male relatives in Britain the Settlement included a clause throwing the onus onto Harben and Meynell of securing for her proper medical examination, medical attendance and care in the event of illness. It was thought that if the government knew that men of some importance were interested in her she might not be forcibly fed. In 1913 Harben bought, with attendant publicity, the licences given under the "Cat and Mouse" Act to Geraldine LENNOX, Mary Richardson, Sylvia Pankhurst and Emmeline Pankhurst. The money realized went towards WSPU funds. Harben visited Christabel PANKHURST several times in Paris, on one occasion travelling there with Harold Laski, who was also a member of the MPU. At the end of January 1914 Christabel Pankhurst asked Harben to come to see her in Paris but he put off his proposed visit until 9 February, hinting to her that something was about to happen, although giving no details. On 6 February the UNITED SUFFRAGISTS, of which his wife Agnes was a committee member, was formed as a breakaway group from the WSPU. It is likely that Harben wished to delay his proposed visit to Paris until after the announcement of the group's formation. In any event he did not go to see Christabel then and instead wrote to her, presumably as a way of explaining the necessity for the new group, criticizing, as one outside the WSPU, the way matters were being conducted inside the organization. He specifically instanced the way that Lincoln's Inn House was dealing with local branches – "turning people out neck and crop" – and thought that the quality of their following was not what it had been. He implied that Christabel was isolated but assured her that she could always rely on him financially. His letter is astonishingly similar in its critique to that written to Christabel by Beatrice HARRADEN the previous month. He did eventually visit Christabel in March

1914. In November 1913 Harben spoke at a meeting organized by the NORTHERN MEN'S FEDERATION in Edinburgh. He had been treasurer of the Men's Political Union and president of its Oxford branch but resigned in February 1914, telling Victor DUVAL that he intended to act on his own initiative for a while. Later that month he appeared at Bow Street with H.W. NEVINSON and Laurence HOUSMAN after being involved in a demonstration in Westminster. Harben did not immediately join the United Suffragists, although he did address a meeting held by them at Kingsway Hall on 7 July 1914.

During the First World War Mrs Harben was one of the founders, with George and Bessie LANSBURY, of the League of Rights for Soldiers' and Sailors' Wives and Relatives and H.D. Harben bought the Hotel Majestic in Paris to turn it into an English hospital. In 1920 he stood, and was defeated, as the Labour candidate for Woodbridge. He kept in touch with Sylvia Pankhurst and helped to pay for her son's education at the London School of Economics under Harold Laski.

Address: (1912) Newlands Park, Chalfont St Giles, Buckinghamshire.
Photograph: with his wife in *Votes for Women*, 14 February 1912.
Archival source: Museum of London Collection; Harben Papers, British Library.
Bibliography: A. Rosen, *Rise Up Women!: The Militant Campaign of the Women's Social and Political Union 1903–1914*, 1974; B. Harrison, *Prudent Revolutionaries: British Feminists Between the Wars*, 1987.

HARBERTON, FLORENCE, VISCOUNTESS (*c.* 1844–1911) Daughter of William Wallace Legge of Co. Antrim, married in 1861, and had two sons and one daughter. In 1878 she wrote an article, "Individual Liberty for Women: a remonstrance", which was published in *Macmillan's Magazine*. In the 1880s she was a member of the Vigilance Association for the Defence of Personal Rights. In 1882 she wrote "Observations on Women's Suffrage" which was printed as a pamphlet by the CENTRAL COMMITTEE OF THE NATIONAL SOCIETY FOR WOMEN'S SUFFRAGE. Viscountess Harberton was a member of the executive committee of the Central Committee in 1883 and presided over the Demonstrations of Women held in London (1880), Sheffield (1882) and Edinburgh (1884) as part of the campaign to show mass support for the inclusion of the enfranchisement of women in the 1884 Reform Bill. She sided with Millicent Garrett FAWCETT's faction when the Central Committee split in 1888 and became a member of the executive committee of the realigned Central Committee of the National Society for Women's Suffrage. In 1889 she subscribed to the MANCHESTER SOCIETY FOR WOMEN'S SUFFRAGE and in 1907 to the WOMEN'S SOCIAL AND POLITICAL UNION. On 11 December 1906 Viscountess Harberton was present at the banquet given by Mrs Fawcett at the Savoy to celebrate the release of the WSPU prisoners. In March 1907 she volunteered to lead a WSPU deputation to present a petition from the second Women's Parliament in Caxton Hall to the House of Commons and in June she presided at a meeting of the Hammersmith branch of the WSPU. In 1908 she gave £3 to the newly-founded WOMEN'S FREEDOM LEAGUE and was speaking at their meetings in 1909. In October 1909 she was present at the founding meeting of the TAX RESISTANCE LEAGUE.

In 1881 Viscountess Harberton was one of the co-founders, and president, of the Rational Dress Society, which attempted to introduce a new style of dress in which, as Elizabeth Cady Stanton observed when she saw Laura MCLAREN wearing the garment at a suffrage meeting, "all the garments are bifurcated but so skilfully adjusted in generous plaits and folds, that the casual observer is ignorant of the innovation". One of the recommended styles of garment, for which patterns were available from the Society, was called the "Harberton". Viscountess Harberton was a regular speaker at the Pioneer Club (*see under* CLUBS). She continued her interest in simplifying clothing from beyond the grave and specifically requested in her will that "no one who professes to have any affection for me shall wear mourning or make the smallest alteration in their clothing on account of my death".

Address: (1901) 198 Cromwell Road, London SW.
Bibliography: S.M. Newton, *Health, Art & Reason: Dress Reformers of the 19th Century*, 1974.

HARDIE, [JAMES] KEIR (1856–1915) Born James Keir in Lanarkshire, the illegitimate son of a farm servant. When his mother later married he added his stepfather's name to his own. Between the ages of 10 and 23 he worked as a miner in eastern

Lanarkshire. Brought up an agnostic, in 1877 Hardie converted to evangelical Christianity, became a lecturer in the temperance movement and in 1878 an agent for a miners' union. After a failed strike he was forced to leave the pit and for the next few years earned a competency as a journalist until in 1886 he became, still a Liberal, secretary of the Ayrshire Miners' Union. After defeat as an independent candidate at the Mid-Lanark by-election in 1888, Hardie was eventually returned to parliament in 1892 as the Labour MP for West Ham South. Immediately after his success at the poll (until 1918 elections were not all held on the same day, but spread out over a fortnight), he travelled across East London to Bow to help the Liberal candidate there, for whom George LANSBURY was acting as agent. In 1894 Hardie campaigned for Lansbury himself who was standing as a candidate, backed by the Social Democratic Federation, at the Walworth by-election. Richard and Emmeline PANKHURST, then living in Manchester, also came to help at Walworth and were already friendly with Hardie, whom they had met at both the International Labour Conference held in London in 1888 and at the International Socialist Congress, which launched the Second Socialist International, held in Paris in 1889. In January 1893 the Independent Labour Party was formed in Bradford, with Richard Pankhurst as one of its founding members, and in 1894 Hardie was elected its chairman, only to lose his parliamentary seat at the 1895 general election. In 1894 Hardie was thanked by the WOMEN'S EMANCIPATION UNION for his support and on 24 October 1896 Isabella Bream Pearce, a close friend of Elizabeth Wolstenholme ELMY and a regular contributor, as "Lily Bell", to Hardie's paper the *Labour Leader*, gave a most favourable report of the Women's Emancipation Union conference in her column. Earlier in 1896 Keir Hardie had supported the Pankhursts and other members of the Manchester ILP in their fight to speak at Boggart Hole Clough and the 11 July edition of the *Labour Leader* had included sketches of Emmeline, Christabel and Sylvia Pankhurst. In 1899 he came into contact with Dora MONTEFIORE when he acted as an arbiter in the case of libel brought by an ILP organizer, George Belt, against Mrs Ramsay MacDonald. In 1900 Hardie was returned again to parliament, as Labour member for Merthyr Tydfil, with the backing of the Liberal D.A. Thomas (father of the future Lady RHONDDA), who wanted to keep out a rival Liberal candidate. At the Easter 1901 ILP Conference Hardie was keen that Christabel PANKHURST, barely 21 years old, should speak; she and Sylvia Pankhurst attended and Christabel took part in a debate, opposing Mrs Ramsay MacDonald. In the same year Hardie organized a meeting in Chelsea at which Isabella FORD publicized the suffrage petition signed by the working women of Yorkshire and Cheshire that she had brought to the House of Commons.

The founding of the WOMEN'S SOCIAL AND POLITICAL UNION late in 1903 attracted no immediate mention in the *Labour Leader*, but Hardie was prepared to be an active worker in the suffrage cause. In 1904 after Mrs Pankhurst had been elected to the National Administrative Council of the ILP and had, after a struggle, been successful in overcoming opposition from the adult suffragist element on the NAC in order to press for a limited measure of women's enfranchisement, Hardie instructed the NAC to send out a questionnaire to ILP branches asking for a breakdown by class of women on each municipal register who were eligible to vote. The statistics thus realized were hopelessly untenable, although subsequently much trumpeted by the WSPU, but Hardie had at least tried to obtain information to support the WSPU's policy of pursuing the limited claim for women before that of adult suffrage. In 1905, although unsuccessful himself in obtaining a place in the parliamentary timetable for a private member's bill to extend the existing franchise to women, he, Elizabeth Wolstenholme ELMY and Mrs Pankhurst did eventually persuade another MP, Bamford Slack, to introduce the bill. On 12 May, after this bill had been talked out, Keir Hardie went, as Sylvia Pankhurst described, "hand in hand with old Mrs Elmy", together with the many other disappointed suffragists, to hold a meeting just outside the House of Commons at which they aired their grievances against the government and, as Isabella Ford, who was there, wrote in the *Labour Leader*, "cheered Mr Hardie". In the spring of 1905 Hardie had, at Mrs Pankhurst's suggestion, given Teresa Billington (*see* Teresa BILLINGTON-GREIG) a position as a full-time organizer for the ILP. Later that year Hardie asked, on Sylvia

Pankhurst's behalf, a question in the House of Commons about the disproportionate number of prizes and scholarships given to men by the Royal College of Art, where she was then studying. Hardie and Sylvia Pankhurst were at this time and for some years to come very close friends; the estimation of the exact degree of closeness gives ample scope to the interpretive skills of biographers. The importance of the affair to those concerned and to the politics of the day seems not to be in doubt; Kenneth Morgan, Hardie's biographer, concluded that it lent "a powerful personal dimension to Hardie's advocacy of women's suffrage" and "reinforced the pressure that the women's movement was bringing to bear on the Labour Party".

On 20 October 1905 Keir Hardie addressed the meeting held at the Free Trade Hall to celebrate and publicize the release from prison of Christabel Pankhurst and Annie KENNEY and in December 1905 it was through his influence that Annie Kenney and Minnie BALDOCK gained access to a box at the Albert Hall, from which they were able to heckle Campbell-Bannerman at a Liberal Party rally. In January 1906 Mrs Pankhurst and Annie Kenney campaigned for Keir Hardie in Merthyr Tydfil, alongside Mary Macarthur and Margaret Bondfield, in order to ensure his re-election; his election manifesto contained no mention of women's enfranchisement. He then asked Annie Kenney to stay behind there for a short time to carry on speaking to working women about the Labour Party. In February 1906 it was on his advice that Sylvia Pankhurst and Annie Kenney, who had now been sent from Manchester to "rouse London", hired Caxton Hall in which to hold a WSPU meeting to coincide with the opening of the new parliament. He had also, apparently, from an unnamed source raised £300 to finance the WSPU efforts. In the same month he gave Mrs Pankhurst an introduction to Emmeline PETHICK-LAWRENCE with the suggestion that she would be a suitable person to be treasurer to the WSPU. In April Hardie presented in the House of Commons a Resolution "That, in the opinion of this house, it is desirable that sex should cease to be a bar to the exercise of the Parliamentary franchise", which, when it was talked out, evoked an uproar from 12 WSPU members, who were then cleared from the Ladies' Gallery. Hardie was displeased by the uproar and the consequent failure of his Resolution to make it to a division. On 19 May he participated in the deputation of members from all the suffrage societies to Campbell-Bannerman and, responding to the Prime Minister's plea for patience, replied that "patience can be carried to excess". He was a speaker at the meeting that followed in Trafalgar Square.

Throughout 1906 Hardie spoke out in parliament as the WSPU campaign gathered momentum and women, including Teresa Billington and Sylvia Pankhurst, were sent to prison. Hardie published, with the imprimatur of the ILP, *The Citizenship of Women: a Plea for Women's Suffrage,* which had first been published by W.T. Stead in 1905. However, his relationship with the Labour Party, already strained by the strength of his attachment to women's suffrage, was damaged by WSPU tactics in August at the Cockermouth by-election, at which Christabel's policy of supporting the candidate most likely to unseat a Liberal meant that the WSPU was more likely to be urging the electorate to vote for a Unionist than a Labour candidate. At the January 1907 Labour Party conference a resolution to extend the franchise to women "on the same conditions as men" was defeated and Keir Hardie threatened to resign from the parliamentary party. However the parliamentary Labour Party agreed to allow its members to vote as they wished on the Women's Enfranchisement Bill and Hardie was elected party chairman. In February he spoke at the meeting held in Exeter Hall at the culmination of the "Mud March" organized by the NATIONAL UNION OF WOMEN'S SUFFRAGE SOCIETIES and, while urging suffragists to put the principle of enfranchisement before party considerations, was hissed by Liberal ladies on the platform. At the ILP Conference at Easter 1907 Hardie urged the party to support a resolution to extend the franchise to women on the same terms as it existed for men; this time the resolution was carried. In addition a resolution of congratulation to suffragette prisoners was proposed and carried by the conference. In 1907 Hardie wrote an article, "Socialism and the Woman Question", which was included in *From Serfdom to Socialism,* and "Women and Politics", which was published in Brougham Villiers (ed.), *The Case for Women's Suffrage.* In 1907 Hardie's wife, whom he had married in 1879 and who lived, apparently forgotten and apolitical, with their three children in Ayrshire, is shown as a subscriber to the WSPU. From July 1907 until April 1908 Hardie, who had been ill, undertook a world tour, sponsored by the Salvation Army and Joseph Fels.

Soon after his return to England, on 21 June 1908, Hardie travelled in a carriage at the head of one of the processions to Hyde Park on "Woman's Sunday". As the level of WSPU militancy increased and forcible feeding was introduced, Keir Hardie was vociferous in the House of Commons in his condemnation of the Liberal government's treatment of suffrage prisoners. In 1909 he persuaded the Home Secretary to accompany him, together with two Liberal MPs and Mary ALLEN, who had by then experienced imprisonment, to see for themselves conditions in Holloway. By 1912, after the failure of the Conciliation Bill, Hardie was prepared only to work for adult suffrage for both men and women. He was a member of the Labour Party subcommittee that on 30 April met with officers of the NUWSS who wished to seek clarification of the party's policy on votes for women. Hardie alone of the Labour Party members was clear that he would vote against a reform bill that did not include women. In 1912 the National Labour Press published his pamphlet, *Radicals and Reform*, in which he stressed that it could only be a question of "when?" not "whether?" women should be enfranchised. On 14 July 1912 Hardie spoke, dressed in a white suit and a red plaid tie and surrounded by the red caps of liberty carried by women dressed in white, at the rally in Hyde Park organized by Sylvia Pankhurst. In 1913 Hardie founded the Free Speech Defence Committee in retaliation for the government's ban on meetings held by the WSPU and the WOMEN'S FREEDOM LEAGUE, attended the INTERNATIONAL WOMAN SUFFRAGE CONFERENCE in Budapest, and was a supporter of the NATIONAL POLITICAL LEAGUE. A dedicated pacifist, he and Ramsay MacDonald alone of members of parliament opposed the government on the declaration of war. Hardie's health failed rapidly and he died in September 1915, mourned by Sylvia Pankhurst in the *Woman's Dreadnought*.

Address: (1902) 14 Nevill's Court, Fetter Lane, London WC; (1911) 10 Nevill's Court, Fetter Lane, London WC.

Portrait: by Sylvia Pankhurst in the National Portrait Gallery; by H.J. Dobson (1893) presented to the Scottish National Portrait Gallery by Hardie's son-in-law Emrys Hughes.

Bibliography: S. Pankhurst, *The Suffragette Movement*, 1931; S. Pankhurst, *The Home Front*, 1932; K.O. Morgan, *Keir Hardie: Radical and Socialist*, 1975; C. Benn, *Keir Hardie*, 1997.

HARE, MARY ADELAIDE (*c.* 1860–1945) Born in London, in 1883 she opened a small school for deaf and dumb children. Her view was that such children did not need protection in "asylums", but rather an education. By 1906 she had moved to Brighton and established there a co-education Private Oral School for Deaf Children. In March 1910 she was elected vice-chairman of the National Association of the Teachers of the Deaf and by 1916 her school, now called Dene Hollow Oral School for the Deaf, was regarded as one of the best schools for deaf children in the country. By her will she created a trust in order that the school, now established at Newbury as the Mary Hare Grammar School for the Deaf, should continue along the lines she had instituted.

She had been a member of the Brighton Women's Liberal Association and in 1906 subscribed to the WOMEN'S SOCIAL AND POLITICAL UNION, took part in the February 1907 "Mud March" organized by the NATIONAL UNION OF WOMEN'S SUFFRAGE SOCIETIES, later that year signed the Declaration organized by the Brighton branch of the WOMEN'S FRANCHISE DECLARATION COMMITTEE, in 1908 chaired WSPU meetings in Brighton and in March went to London in order to attend the breakfast given to celebrate the release of suffrage prisoners. In 1909 Una and Joan DUGDALE rented her house in order to carry on a WSPU holiday campaign in Brighton. Mary Hare left the WSPU and by 1913 was honorary secretary of the Brighton branch of the WOMEN'S FREEDOM LEAGUE and a member of the CHURCH LEAGUE FOR WOMEN'S SUFFRAGE. During the First World War she was active in running the Brighton branch of the Women Police Volunteers. She was also president of the Brighton branch of the Women's Co-operative Guild, a theosophist, founder of the Brighton Lodge of the Universal Co-Freemasonary, a vegetarian and a member of the International Women's Franchise Club (*see under* CLUBS).

Address: (1907) Oral School for the Deaf, Goldsmid Road, Brighton; (1909) Oral School for the Deaf, 8 San Remo, Hove, Sussex.

HARE FAMILY Thomas Hare (1806–91) was a political reformer, a Chancery barrister, and from 1853 an inspector of charities. He was the author of *Election of Representatives*, 1859, which set out a proposal for proportional representation. His scheme was supported by both John Stuart MILL and Henry Fawcett. Both his daughters, Katherine Hare (1843–1933) and Alice WESTLAKE, signed the 1866 women's suffrage petition. Katherine Hare in 1864 was interested in the movement led by Emily DAVIES to extend the Local Examination system to girls and was a member of the KENSINGTON SOCIETY. She and her father were friendly with Philippine KYLLMANN and entertained Lydia BECKER at Gosbury Hall in July 1867. Katherine Hare was, from 1867, a member of the executive committee of the LONDON NATIONAL SOCIETY FOR WOMEN'S SUFFRAGE and was one of the speakers, at Helen TAYLOR's behest, at the women's suffrage meeting, open to the public, held at the Hanover Square Rooms in March 1870. After Katherine Hare's marriage in 1872 to Lewis Clayton, who later became bishop of Leicester and assistant bishop of Peterborough, she disappears for some time from the suffrage movement. She had four children, was later awarded an OBE and made a freeman of the borough for her social work in Peterborough. In 1896 she signed a memorial to Balfour, asking him to ensure that government time was allowed to discuss the Parliamentary Franchise (Extension to Women) Bill. Glimpses of Katherine Clayton may be caught in the memoir of Louise Creighton, wife of the bishop of Peterborough. In 1891 she wrote to a friend, "I like the Claytons; they are very ugly, but they are quite a good sort." Katherine Clayton was secretary of the branch of the Mothers' Union founded by Mrs Creighton in Peterborough. The Claytons maintained a close friendship with Mrs Kyllmann; one of their granddaughters, born in 1919, was named Philippine. Thomas Hare was a member of the National Association for the Promotion of Social Science and a member of the committee of the Society for Promoting the Employment of Women from 1867 until his death. In 1867 he gave Lydia Becker advice on the drafting of the early suffrage petitions and subscribed to the MANCHESTER NATIONAL SOCIETY FOR WOMEN'S SUFFRAGE in 1868. Hare was an influential member of the LONDON NATIONAL SOCIETY FOR WOMEN'S SUFFRAGE, spoke in July 1869 at the first public suffrage meeting held in London and became president after the death of John Stuart Mill, remaining with the London Society after others broke away to found the Central Committee. After the societies merged in 1877 he became a member of the CENTRAL COMMITTEE OF THE NATIONAL SOCIETY FOR WOMEN'S SUFFRAGE and stayed with Millicent Garrett FAWCETT's faction after the 1888 split.
Address: (1866) Gosbury Hall, Hook, Surbiton, Surrey.
Portrait: of Thomas Hare by L. Dickenson, 1867, given to National Portrait Gallery by Alice Westlake in 1918; pencil drawing, *c.* 1885, by Alice Westlake, National Portrait Gallery.
Bibliography: K. Clayton, *Memoir of Bishop Clayton: Some Personal Reminiscences Written in 1917*, 1927; F.H. Clayton, *The Claytons Since 1800 A.D.*, 1959; J.T. Covert (ed.), *Memoir of a Victorian Woman: Reflections of Louise Creighton, 1850–1936*, 1994.

HARLEY, KATHERINE MARY, MRS (1855–1917) Sister of Charlotte DESPARD and of Sir John French, married with two daughters and a son; her husband died during the Boer War. She was a poor law guardian in Shropshire, was honorary treasurer of the Midland Region of the NATIONAL UNION OF WOMEN'S SUFFRAGE SOCIETIES in 1910 and by 1913 she was president of the Shropshire Society of the NUWSS and chairman of the (WEST) MIDLAND FEDERATION. She was also an active member of the CHURCH LEAGUE FOR WOMEN'S SUFFRAGE. Katherine Harley appears to have been the originator of the NUWSS Suffrage PILGRIMAGE in 1913, presumably recognizing the propaganda appeal of such a demonstration after the success, on a smaller scale, of the Women's March in 1912 organized by Florence DE FONBLANQUE. She and her daughter Edith travelled the Watling Street Route of the Pilgrimage. Mrs Harley was present at the NUWSS Suffrage Summer Camp held at Weymouth in 1914. The ACTIVE SERVICE LEAGUE set up by the NUWSS in 1913–14 was probably also her idea.

Having introduced sub-military organization to these fringes of the NUWSS, Katherine Harley was a natural to join, in December 1914, the first unit of the Scottish Women's Hospitals. In 1915, having resigned from the executive committee of the NUWSS, she originated the idea of a "flying column", headed by herself, to transport the wounded to hospital. She worked both in France and Serbia. Not an easy colleague, and not one happy to take orders, she was killed by a shell at Monastir, where, as one woman doctor laconically noted, she had no need to be.

Address: (1913) Condover House, near Shrewsbury, Shropshire.

HARRADEN, BEATRICE (1864–1936) Educated at Cheltenham Ladies' College, Queen's College, Bedford College, London, and at Dresden. In an interview for the *Young Woman* in 1897 she was described as "a pronounced Suffragist", influenced by the work of Shelley and Ibsen. Her writing was encouraged by Eliza Lynn Linton although, as she noted in the same interview, "I am everything which my friend Mrs Lynn Linton hates, and yet she loves me". Beatrice Harraden subscribed to the WOMEN'S SOCIAL AND POLITICAL UNION in 1906, was present, placed between Annie KENNEY and Minnie BALDOCK, at the banquet given at the Savoy on 11 December by Mrs FAWCETT to celebrate the release of the WSPU prisoners, and gave a message of support after the first issue of *Votes for Women* in 1907. She gave £3 to the WOMEN'S FREEDOM LEAGUE as well as £25 to the WSPU in 1908. She was one of the first members of the WOMEN WRITERS' SUFFRAGE LEAGUE after it was formed in 1908 and later became one of its 12 vice-presidents. She read a chapter from her most successful novel, *Ships That Pass in the Night*, at a WSPU concert in March 1908. Beatrice Harraden wrote *Lady Geraldine's Speech*, a short pro-suffrage play that was published in *Votes for Women* on 2 April 1909 and performed on 24 May 1909 at the WSPU Exhibition at the Prince's Skating Rink. She was one of the "celebrities" chosen to open the Exhibition each day, her turn coming on 15 May, and she gave two copies of each of her books, autographed, and the manuscript of *Lady Geraldine's Speech*, bound in green leather, to be sold at the WSPU stall. In March 1910 Beatrice Harraden was one of the first speakers, with Christabel PANKHURST, at the newly founded Hampstead branch of the WSPU and said on that occasion that the years she had been a member of the WSPU had been the happiest of her life. She was a committee member of the Hampstead branch in 1912–13. She wrote further articles for *Votes for Women*, including one about Miss Beale, 18 August 1911, and a rather trite story published in the issue of 8 November 1912.

In 1910 Beatrice Harraden subscribed to the NEW CONSTITUTIONAL SOCIETY FOR WOMEN'S SUFFRAGE, was a member of the LONDON GRADUATES' UNION FOR WOMEN'S SUFFRAGE and was a supporter of the TAX RESISTANCE LEAGUE, refusing to pay her tax in 1913. The 2 May 1913 edition of *Votes for Women* contains a report of a speech in which she gave her reasons for so doing. In the 16 May edition she reported on her visit to America and noted how much more sympathetic was the treatment given to women's suffrage by journalists there. She herself reported on Emily Wilding DAVISON's funeral in the *Daily Chronicle* on 17 June 1913. In July 1913 Beatrice Harraden was one of the signatories to a petition organized by the London Graduates' Union for Women's Suffrage and in that year was also a supporter of the NATIONAL POLITICAL LEAGUE. In January 1914 she wrote to Christabel PANKHURST remonstrating with her for allowing Mrs PANKHURST to carry on with her hunger strikes. She wrote, "I cannot think you sanction it without an agony of mind which must indeed be 'too huge for human tongue or pen of scribe'. Or if indeed you sanction it at all, it must only be because you have lost your way, lost the trail, lost the vision of the distant scene. And it would seem as if you had done so." She carries on to say that Christabel is alienating all the old workers and that the suffragette "mice" are not given sufficient care and "your exile prevents you from being in real touch with facts as they are over here". Beatrice Harraden was referring particularly to the case of Olive BEAMISH and Lilian LENTON, who had been re-arrested after WSPU mismanagement. Christabel Pankhurst in her reply refuted, needless to say, all such accusations. Beatrice Harraden left the WSPU and joined the PETHICK-LAWRENCES' VOTES FOR WOMEN FELLOWSHIP. From 1915 until the end of the First World War she was librarian at the military hospital run by Dr Flora MURRAY and Dr Louisa Garrett ANDERSON at Endell Street in London. In the 1930s she was a vice-president of the Six Point Group.

Address: (1901) 5 Cannon Place, Hampstead, London NW; (1914) 3 Fitzjohn's Mansions, Netherhall Gardens, Hampstead, London NW; (1926) South Bank, Belgrave Road, Torquay, Devonshire; (1928) 40 Belsize Square, London NW3; (1936) Greengates, Barton Court Avenue, Barton-on-Sea, Hampshire.
Photograph: in the *Vote*, 11 November 1909; *Votes for Women*, 25 April 1913.
Archival source: Janie Allan Papers, National Library of Scotland.

HARROGATE (NUWSS) Founded in 1904. In 1913 the society was a member of the NORTH AND EAST RIDINGS FEDERATION OF THE NATIONAL UNION OF WOMEN'S SUFFRAGE SOCIETIES. Secretary (1913) Miss Taunton, Ladies' College, Clarence Drive, Harrogate, Yorkshire.

HARROGATE (WSPU) In 1910 was a branch in the Bradford and District area. Organizer (1910) Miss Mary PHILLIPS, 109 Valley Drive, Harrogate; (1913) Miss Hughes, 18a King's Road, Harrogate, Yorkshire.

HARROW (branch of the LONDON SOCIETY FOR WOMEN'S SUFFRAGE, NUWSS) Secretary (1913) Miss Blake, 37 Staverton Road, Willesden Green, London NW.

HARROW (WFL) Secretary (1913) Mrs Hunstman, Rions, Northwick Park Road, Harrow, Middlesex.

HARROW (WSPU) Secretary (1913) Miss Wright, 15 Sheepcote Road, Wealdstone, Middlesex.

HARTLEPOOL (NUWSS) In 1913 the society was a member of the NORTH-EASTERN FEDERATION OF THE NATIONAL UNION OF WOMEN'S SUFFRAGE SOCIETIES. Secretary (1913) Mrs Ainslie, 17 Clifton Ave, West Hartlepool, Co. Durham.

HARTLEPOOL (WEST) (WFL) Secretary (1913) Mrs English, 23 Carlton Street, West Hartlepool, Co. Durham.

HARWICH AND DISTRICT (NUWSS) In 1913 the society was a member of the EASTERN COUNTIES FEDERATION OF THE NATIONAL UNION OF WOMEN'S SUFFRAGE SOCIETIES. Secretary (1913) Mrs W.H. Coysh, Rose Bank, Dovercourt, Essex.

HASLAM, ETHEL CLARICE (?1887–?) Member of the Romford Board of Guardians, secretary of the Ilford branch of the WOMEN'S SOCIAL AND POLITICAL UNION from June 1909 until the WSPU ceased activity. She was also an active member of the CHURCH LEAGUE FOR WOMEN'S SUFFRAGE. Ethel Haslam went on a WSPU deputation to the House of Commons on 16 November 1909, was arrested and then released the next day. She was arrested on "Black Friday", 18 November 1910, but released without charge. She then joined the protest on 22 November, threw a stone at a window of John Burns's house in Battersea, and was sentenced to 14 days in Holloway. In April 1911 she took part in the Census protest. In March 1912 she joined in the WSPU window-smashing campaign, her chosen target being in Coventry Street, and received a sentence of two months' imprisonment. She joined in the Holloway hunger strike. In 1913 Ethel Haslam was arrested and found guilty of the heinous crime of fixing an advertisement for the WSPU Self-Denial Week to a letterbox. Her fine was paid by friends, after she said that she would rather go to prison than pay it. In June 1914 the windows of her own house were broken after speakers at an open-air suffrage meeting took refuge there from tomatoes and other missiles.
Address: (1913) 68 Cranbrook Road, Ilford, Essex.

HASLAM, MARY HEYWOOD, MRS (1852–1922) Unitarian, born in Bolton, daughter of R. Heywood, manufacturer and local philanthropist. When she was still in her teens she paid a subscription to "the Society for Women's Suffrage" (possibly the Manchester Society) out of her first dress allowance. She was the first woman poor law guardian in Bolton and was president of the local branch of the SOCIETY FOR PROMOTING THE RETURN OF WOMEN AS POOR LAW GUARDIANS when it was founded in Bolton in May 1897. She was president of the BOLTON WOMEN'S SUFFRAGE SOCIETY, a branch of the NORTH OF ENGLAND SOCIETY FOR WOMEN'S SUFFRAGE, when it was formed on 17 March 1908. Her daughter was appointed secretary, remaining as such until her marriage in 1912, and immediately addressed meetings of the Horwich Unitarian Church Women's Society, the Darcy Lever Weslyan Young Men's Society and local Women's Liberal

Associations. To mark the end of the first year of the Bolton Suffrage Society Mrs Haslam presided over a meeting attended by 2000 people. In 1913 she supported the NATIONAL POLITICAL LEAGUE. In 1915 she was asked to join the Manchester Society, but replied that she was too busy running the Bolton Society, the minute books of which indeed show how very active she was. Mrs Haslam was still president of the Woman's Suffrage Society when it disbanded in 1920 and was president of its successor, the Women Citizens' Association. A brief appreciation of her work, published after her death, particularly singled out for comment the fact that "she consistently kept aloof from all the petty jealousies that so often beset the path of public life". She had the foresight to compile *Women's Suffrage in Bolton, 1908–1920*, which gives a concise history of the activity of the National Union of Women's Suffrage Societies in the area. In her will Mary Haslam left legacies to Sarah REDDISH and to the Bolton Womens' Citizens Association.

Address: (1910) White Bank, Bolton, Lancashire; (1922) 4 Kensington Palace Gardens, London W.
Bibliography: M.H. Haslam, *Women's Suffrage in Bolton, 1908–1920*.
Archival source: Minute Books of Bolton Women's Local Government Association, 1897–1918, Bolton Studies Library; Minute Books and Annual Reports of Bolton Women's Suffrage Association, Bolton Studies' Library.

HASLEMERE (NUWSS) In 1913 the society was a member of the SURREY, SUSSEX, AND HANTS FEDERATION OF THE NATIONAL UNION OF WOMEN'S SUFFRAGE SOCIETIES. Secretary (1909) Mrs Marshall, Tweenways, Hindhead, Haslemere, Surrey; (1913) Miss Rees, By the Way, Hindhead, Haslemere, Surrey

HASLINGDEN (NUWSS) By 1912 the society was a member of the MANCHESTER AND DISTRICT FEDERATION OF THE NATIONAL UNION OF WOMEN'S SUFFRAGE SOCIETIES, although it had lapsed by 1917. Secretary (1913) *pro tem* Mrs Darlington, 14 Kenwood Road, Stretford, Manchester.

HASTINGS (WSPU) Organizer (1913) Miss Mary ALLEN, 8 Claremont, Hastings, Sussex.

HASTINGS AND ST LEONARDS Women's Suffrage Society Founded in 1883 as a branch of the NATIONAL SOCIETY FOR WOMEN'S SUFFRAGE with as its honorary secretaries Mrs W. W. Fawcett, Hollington Park, Hastings and Mr E. J. Hawkes, 74 High Street, Hastings. In 1906 the Hastings society was still a branch of the LONDON SOCIETY FOR WOMEN'S SUFFRAGE. In 1913, as the Hastings, St Leonards, and East Sussex society it was a member of the SURREY, SUSSEX, AND HANTS FEDERATION OF THE NATIONAL UNION OF WOMEN'S SUFFRAGE SOCIETIES. Secretary (1913) Miss A. Kate Rance, 21 Boscobel Road, St Leonards-on-Sea, Sussex.

HASTINGS AND ST LEONARDS WOMEN'S SUFFRAGE PROPAGANDA LEAGUE Formed in 1910. Honorary secretary (1913, 1917) Mrs Darent Harrison; honorary treasurer, Mrs MacMunn, 1 St Paul's Place, St Leonards-on-Sea, Sussex. The League was founded in 1909 and affliated to the NEW CONSTITUTIONAL SOCIETY FOR WOMEN'S SUFFRAGE when the latter was founded in 1910. In 1909 the society was invited by Philippa STRACHEY to become a constituent member of the NATIONAL UNION OF WOMEN'S SUFFRAGE SOCIETIES, but appears to have refused. Its policy was to oppose the government by constitutional methods – tax and other forms of passive resistance. It was not aligned with any party. Elsie BOWERMAN's mother, Mrs Chibnall, was an active member of the League by 1911. On 13 March 1918 the League participated in the NUWSS victory celebrations held at the Queen's Hall.
Photograph: of 1 St Paul's Place decorated with posters, Suffragette Fellowship Collection, Museum of London.

HATTON, BESSIE (?–?) Daughter of Joseph Hatton, who was an author, playwright and journalist. She was the writer of romantic novels, including *The Village of Youth and Other Fairy Tales*, 1895, which was illustrated by her brother-in-law W.H. Margetson. In 1909 she wrote a one-act play, *Before Sunrise*, that was performed at the WOMEN'S FREEDOM LEAGUE's Yuletide Festival. In June 1908 she and Cicely HAMILTON founded the WOMEN WRITERS' SUFFRAGE LEAGUE. Bessie Hatton had heard Cicely Hamilton speaking on suffrage at "the Dramatic Debaters" and wrote congratulating her on her speech. Cicely Hamilton replied suggesting that a league of women writers should be formed, "if only someone would undertake the secretaryship".

Bessie Hatton agreed to perform that role and was still secretary in 1913. Her sister's husband, the painter W.H. Margetson, designed the image of "Justice and Prejudice" that was used on the League's postcard and on a banner carried by members of the League in the 1911 Coronation procession. In 1889 he had exhibited a portrait of Ellen Terry at the Grosvenor Gallery summer exhibition. During the First World War Bessie Hatton was honorary organizer and secretary of amusements at the Endell Street hospital run by Dr Flora MURRAY and Dr Louisa Garrett ANDERSON.

Address: (1909) 15 Sandringham Court, Maida Vale, London W.
Photograph: in the *Vote*, 23 December 1909.
Bibliography: The *Vote*, 23 December 1909.

HAVERFIELD, EVELINA, HON. MRS (1867–1920) Born in Scotland, youngest daughter of William Frederick Scarlett, 3rd Baron Abinger. Her mother was the daughter of a commodore in the US navy. In the 1880s Frances Power COBBE wrote to Lydia BECKER to give her Lady Abinger's address, noting that "she is a member of our Victorian Committee [the anti-vivisection society] and is a very sensible – rather silent – woman". Evelina Scarlett was a keen sportswoman, especially adept as a rider, habitually riding astride. She married Major Henry Haverfield in 1887, aged 19, moved to Dorset, and had two sons (John who was killed in 1915 and Brook who emigrated to Canada). Her husband died in 1895; in 1899 she remarried another Royal Artillery major, John Blaguy, but reassumed the name "Haverfield" by deed poll within a month of the marriage. She was in South Africa with her husband for two years during the Boer War and formed a retirement camp for horses left to die on the veldt. Her sister Ella qualified as a doctor and was in South Africa as a member of the commission, headed by Millicent FAWCETT, that investigated conditions in the British concentration camps. After her return Evelina Haverfield was overseer of the parish of Caundle Marsh in Dorset and was a co-opted member of the local Old-Age Pensions Committee. She had probably been a member of the Sherborne branch of the NATIONAL UNION OF WOMEN'S SUFFRAGE SOCIETIES since the 1890s and on 19 March 1908 transferred her allegiance to the WOMEN'S SOCIAL AND POLITICAL UNION after attending the large and successful rally held in the Albert Hall. In a letter to Minnie BALDOCK written in 1910 she remarks that Mrs Baldock was the first WSPU speaker she ever heard and she joined immediately. Evelina Haverfield was to prove a very generous benefactor to the WSPU. During 1909 she helped Annie KENNEY with the campaign in the west country and in March 1909 was the organizer of a meeting in Sherborne at which a WSPU branch was formed and of which she became honorary secretary. Throughout her involvement with the WSPU she appeared regularly as a speaker with Mrs Mildred MANSEL, sharing not only a west-country but also a similar family background. In May 1909 Evelina Haverfield provided a stall for the WSPU Exhibition at the Prince's Skating Rink. In June she took part in a NUWSS "caravan campaign" in Yorkshire, with, among others, Isabella Ford and Ray COSTELLOE (*see* STRACHEY FAMILY). Her horsemanship proved invaluable in dealing with the carthorses. After her return to London she was arrested on 29 June 1909 after taking part in the WSPU deputation from Caxton Hall to the House of Commons and was defended at the subsequent trial by Lord Robert Cecil, who claimed that she had been wrongfully arrested in the exercise of a constitutional right. Her case and that of Mrs PANKHURST were treated as test cases; they were found guilty and fined. The case went to appeal, was heard and dismissed in December, and the fine was upheld. It was paid without her consent.

In January 1910 Evelina Haverfield campaigned in Dundee, Churchill's constituency, during the general election. By May 1910 she was ORGANIZER of the Paddington branch, with which she was to remain associated until she left the WSPU. With Vera HOLME, with whom she was to share a very close relationship, Evelina Haverfield was a mounted marshal for the WSPU procession on 18 June 1910 and with Vera Holme and Maud JOACHIM she rode in the West Procession of 22 July. She was arrested on "Black Friday", 18 November 1910, and charged with assault. She had struck a policeman in the mouth and when charged was reported to have said, "It was not hard enough. Next time I will bring a revolver". When this was read out as part of a statement in court Mrs Haverfield, from the dock, commented "Quite right" and when her previous conviction was mentioned added, "I was wrongfully accused then. This time I thought I would have a run for my money". She put her knowledge of horses to use for the cause and perfected a technique of forcing police horses to sit down, by hitting them hard near the joint of their hind legs. She was sentenced to a fine or a month's imprisonment; again her fine was paid without her consent. On 21 November 1911 Evelina Haverfield concentrated on horses rather than men or glass, attempting to break through a police cordon by leading the horses out of their ranks during the outbreak of window smashing that followed the "torpedoing" of the Conciliation Bill. She was sentenced to two weeks' imprisonment. With the admirable flexibility that marks the suffrage cause, on her release from Holloway she ran the "Cushions and Mats" stall at the WSPU Christmas bazaar in the Portman Rooms. In 1910 she was a member of the TAX RESISTANCE LEAGUE and gave a donation to the NEW CONSTITUTIONAL SOCIETY FOR WOMEN'S SUFFRAGE. In 1911 she gave a donation to the MEN'S POLITICAL UNION. She starred in a series of advertisements for "Omne Tempus" raincoats in *Votes for Women* in 1912. Sylvia Pankhurst described her as habitually wearing a hunting stock and small black riding hat and continued, "When she first joined the Suffragette movement her expression was cold and proud . . . I was repelled when she told me she felt no affection for her children. During her years in the Suffrage movement her sympathies so broadened that she seemed to have undergone a rebirth."

By April 1914 Evelina Haverfield had left the main WSPU to join Sylvia PANKHURST's EAST LONDON FEDERATION OF THE WSPU, becoming honorary treasurer in succession to Mrs D.A. Thomas (*see* Lady RHONDDA). In 1914 she joined the UNITED SUFFRAGISTS, becoming a vice-president. In July 1914 Evelina Haverfield wrote a "character" for Elsie DUVAL, who, as a "mouse" on the run from the police, was escaping to the Continent. On 23 March 1918 Evelina Haverfield was a speaker, with Mrs Fawcett, at the "Women's Suffrage Celebrations" held at the Royal West of England Academy in Bristol.

At the outbreak of war Evelina Haverfield helped to launch the Women's Emergency Corps and then founded the Women's Volunteer Reserve, of which she became commandant. It was based in Old Bedford College, off Baker Street, and was the most militaristic of organizations, with khaki uniforms and felt hats. Christopher ST JOHN in *Christine Murrell*, 1935, described Evelina Haverfield at this time as looking "every inch a soldier in her khaki uniform, in spite of the short skirt which she had to wear over her well-cut riding-breeches in public". In late 1914 Evelina Haverfield served briefly as commander-in-chief of the Women's Reserve Ambulance (Green Cross Corps) which was one of the founding units of the future WAAC. In May 1915 she joined Dr Elsie INGLIS and went to Serbia. She spent the next two years in Serbia and Russia, in charge of a transport column, of which Vera Holme was a member. When matters were so unsettled that she was forced to stay in England, Evelina Haverfield promoted the Serbian cause there. With Flora Sandes she founded the Hon. Evelina Haverfield's and Sergt-Major Flora Sandes' Fund for Promoting Comforts for Serbian Soldiers and Prisoners, on the committee of which in 1918 were Nina BOYLE, Vera Holme and Edith CRAIG. The Fund's address was that shared by Violet BLAND. Evelina Haverfield spoke Serbian fluently, if ungrammatically, and returned to Serbia after the Armistice in 1918 in order to establish an orphanage. She founded the Hon. Evelina Haverfield's Fund for Serbian Children and shortly afterwards died of pneumonia. She was buried in Bajina Bashta, where in 1929 a new Health Centre was dedicated to her and a street named after her. The main bequest in her will left Vera Holme £50 a year for life.

Address: (1880) Inverlochy Castle, Kingussie; (1887) 46 Cornwall Gardens, London W; (1899) Marsh Court, Caundle Marsh, Dorset; (1910) Peace Cottage, Brendon, North Devon.
Photograph: in *Votes for Women*, 9 July 1909.
Archival source: typescript biography by Vera Holme in Suffragette Fellowship Collection, Museum of London.
Bibliography: L. Leneman, *In the Service of Life: The Story of Elsie Inglis and the Scottish Women's Hospitals*, 1994; B. Gaddes, *Evelina: Outward Bound from Inverlochy*, 1995.

HAWICK (NUWSS) In 1913 the society was a member of the SCOTTISH FEDERATION OF THE NATIONAL UNION OF WOMEN'S SUFFRAGE SOCIETIES. Secretary (1913) Miss Williamson, 18 Buccleuch Street, Hawick, Roxburghshire.

HAWKESHEAD (NUWSS) In 1913 the society was a member of the NORTH-WESTERN FEDERATION OF THE NATIONAL UNION OF WOMEN'S SUFFRAGE SOCIETIES. Secretary (1913) Miss E.G. Satterthwaite, Beckside, Hawkeshead, Lancashire.

HAWKINS, ALICE, MRS (1863–1947) Born at Stafford, moved to Leicester in her early youth and began work in 1876, aged 13, in the newly founded co-operative boot and shoe factory, the Equity. In 1884 she married Alfred Hawkins and they had seven children, five of whom were living in 1913. In 1892 Alice Hawkins joined the Independent Labour Party. In 1896 her factory formed its own Women's Co-operative Guild and through it she was introduced to the work of such socialist thinkers as Tom Mann. She had become interested in women's enfranchisement as early as 1895 and, in 1906, to promote the cause joined the Women's Labour League. She left the ILP because of its negative attitude to women's suffrage and in 1907 became the first secretary of the Leicester branch of the WOMEN'S SOCIAL AND POLITICAL UNION. She had met the PANKHURSTS, through her ILP involvement, in the 1890s and in 1907, when Sylvia PANKHURST came to Leicester to record the lives of working women, put her in touch with the Equity boot and shoe factory, supplied her with data for her articles and arranged for her to address suffrage meetings in the evenings. Sylvia Pankhurst was joined by Mary GAWTHORPE and the two remained in Leicester during the summer helping Alice Hawkins and other Leicester women organize their local branch. By 1913 Alice Hawkins had been in prison on five occasions. The first was a sentence of two weeks for obstructing the police in London during the demonstrations surrounding the first Women's Parliament in February 1907. Then in September 1909 she was imprisoned in Leicester for five days for trying to gain entry to a meeting held by Churchill. On this occasion, with Helen WATTS, she went on hunger strike. In November 1910, after "Black Friday", she received 14 days' imprisonment for breaking the windows of Lewis Harcourt's house, although her fine was paid by Mrs Pankhurst in order that she might return to Leicester to look after her children, her husband having had his leg broken while she was in prison. In November 1911 Alice Hawkins was again in Holloway for three weeks after breaking a window in the Home Office and in 1913 was arrested for pouring black ink into pillar boxes in Leicester. She was sentenced to five days' imprisonment, went on hunger strike, but gave up on the advice of family and friends.

Alice Hawkins also shared in WSPU spectacle, attending suffrage processions in London and speaking on one of the platforms at the June 1908 Hyde Park demonstration. In January 1913 she took part in the Deputation of Working Women to Lloyd George. In 1911 she founded the Independent National Union of Women Boot and Shoe Workers and by 1913 had twice served upon the executive of the Leicester Trades Council. In her entry in the *Suffrage Annual and Women's Who's Who*, 1913, she writes that she was "still working with might and main for votes for women". Ephemera relating to her involvement with the WSPU is still held by members of her family.

Alfred Hawkins was a member of the MEN'S POLITICAL UNION FOR WOMEN'S ENFRANCHISEMENT and was on several occasions ejected from meetings being held by cabinet ministers. While his wife was in prison in November 1910 he sustained a double fracture of the knee after being beaten by stewards at a meeting being held by Churchill. He spent a month in hospital and was unable to work for four months. In October 1911 he was awarded £100 in damages in a case brought against the stewards of this Liberal Party meeting.
Address: (1913) 181 Western Road, Leicester.

HAYES AND SOUTHALL (WFL) Secretary (1913) Mrs Cunningham, Oakdene, Hayes, Middlesex.

HEATHFIELD AND DISTRICT (NUWSS) In 1913 the society was a member of the SURREY, SUSSEX, AND HANTS FEDERATION OF THE NATIONAL UNION OF WOMEN'S SUFFRAGE SOCIETIES. Secretary (1913) Mrs Cunliffe, Little London, Horeham Road, East Sussex.

HEBDEN BRIDGE (WSPU) Joint secretaries (1906) Miss Louie Cobbe, 32 Industrial St., Hebden Bridge, Yorkshire and Miss Edith Berkeley, 2 Bank Side, Hebden Bridge, Yorkshire.

HEITLAND, MARGARET, MRS (1860–1938) Daughter of the Master of St John's College, Cambridge and Mrs Anna BATESON, and sister of Anna and Mary BATESON. She was honorary assistant secretary of the CAMBRIDGE WOMEN'S SUFFRAGE ASSOCIATION when it was founded in 1884. In 1886 Margaret Bateson started work as a journalist and from 1888 was associated with the *Queen,* and in 1913 was editor of the Public Work and Women's Employment Department of that journal. In 1898 she gave a talk on "Journalism" to the Grosvenor Crescent Club (*see under* CLUBS). She was author/editor of *Professional Women Upon Their Professions,* 1895, organizer and honorary secretary from 1908 to 1910, and then vice-president, of the Central Bureau for the Employment of Women, which she helped to found, and a fellow of the Institute of Journalists.

Margaret Bateson was married in 1901 and was elected to the executive committee of the Cambridge Association of Women's Suffrage in 1902. In 1905 she agreed to defray personally for seven months the expenses of a new secretary for the Cambridge Association. In December 1908 Margaret Heitland went to Bedford to speak at a drawing-room meeting that led to the founding of the BEDFORD SOCIETY FOR WOMEN'S SUFFRAGE. In 1911 she agreed to present the Cambridge suffrage shop with copies of the *Standard* and the *Manchester Guardian* for three months. In 1911 the wish was expressed by the Cambridge Association's executive committee that she should one day stand for the Town Council. In 1912 she addressed members of the Bedford Society on the NATIONAL UNION OF WOMEN'S SUFFRAGE SOCIETIES' proposal that support should be given to the Labour Party; Bedford was not impressed by the argument. Margaret Heitland herself subscribed to the NUWSS Election Fighting Fund, writing in a letter to Maud Arncliffe SENNETT that "this policy I believe to be the right one, since in the main our movement is a workers' movement. We want it to be possible for people of both sexes to live under better conditions than they do now." In the same letter she wrote of

> a lifelong determination about women's enfranchisement, never lost sight of since early girlhood. ...With your criticism about the stagnation into which the movement had lapsed during the 'nineties I wholly concur...our leaders at that time were few, were somewhat disheartened by constant defeats, and *they had not yet learnt how to organise political work among women on a large scale.* Also they were apt to be afraid lest anyone should say they appealed too much to the emotions of the public. For some of these reasons some us [sic] (including myself) were, though, steadily supporting Suffrage societies, trying to get political equality via economic, professional and social equality.

In 1920 Margaret Heitland was a member of the standing committee of the Cambridge branch of the National Union of Societies for Equal Citizenship. She left the residue of her estate to Newnham College.

Address: 4 Vernon Chambers, Theobalds Road, London WC; (1913) Carmefield, Wordsworth Grove, Newnham, Cambridge.

Archival source: Arncliffe Sennett Papers, British Library; Minutes of the Bedford Women's Suffrage Society, Bedford Record Office; Records of the Cambridge Association for Women's Suffrage, County Record Office, Cambridge.

HELENSBURGH, Dunbartonshire, committee of the NATIONAL SOCIETY FOR WOMEN'S SUFFRAGE Formed in 1873.

HENDON AND GOLDERS GREEN (WSPU) Founded in June 1908. Secretary (1913) Mrs Morris, 26b The Parade, Golders Green, London NW.

HENDON WOMEN'S FRANCHISE SOCIETY Affiliated to the UNITED SUFFRAGISTS in 1917. Honorary secretary: Mrs McCabe, 49 Bridge Lane, Hendon, London NW.

HEREFORD (NUWSS) In 1913 the society was a member of the MIDLAND (WEST) FEDERATION OF THE NATIONAL UNION OF WOMEN'S SUFFRAGE SOCIETIES. Secretary (1913) Mrs Bettington, Westwood, Hereford, Herefordshire.

HEREFORDSHIRE (WSPU) Secretary (1913) Mrs G.H. Davies, 7 The Cloisters, Hereford, Herefordshire.

HERNE HILL (WFL) Secretary (1913) Miss B. Spencer, 32 Geneva Road, Brixton, London SW.

HERRINGHAM, CHRISTIANA JANE, MRS (1852–1929) (later Lady Herringham)   Daughter of Thomas Wilde Powell, a wealthy stockbroker and patron of the Arts and Crafts movement. She married Wilmot Herringham in 1880 and had two sons, who, as children, were painted by Annie SWYNNERTON. Christiana Herringham was an artist, translator of Cennino Cennini's manual for painters in tempera and fresco, *Il libro dell' arte o trattato della pittura*, and one of the founders in 1901 of the Society of Painters in Tempera. In 1888 she was one of the founding directors, with Agnes GARRETT, of the Ladies' Residential Chambers Co., resigning, with regret, in 1890. Her brother-in-law Thackeray Turner, in partnership with Eustace Balfour, husband of Lady Frances BALFOUR, was architect for the company's second venture, the York Street Chambers. In 1903 Christiana Herringham was the originator of the National Art Collections Fund, which made its first purchase amid considerable publicity in 1906. Ironically the painting thus bought for the nation was the *Rokeby Venus* by Velázquez, which in 1914 was badly damaged by Mary RICHARDSON. In 1906 Christiana Herringham was the only director and sole managing director of the Women's Tribune Co. (*see under* NEWSPAPERS AND JOURNALS). In 1906 and again in 1911 she visited the caves of Ajanta in India, on the second occasion making copies of the Buddhist wall paintings that were then in a deteriorating condition. She was a generous benefactor to Newnham College at the turn of the century and was a close friend of Mary BATESON. In 1889 Christiana Herringham was a member of the general committee of the CENTRAL COMMITTEE OF THE NATIONAL SOCIETY FOR WOMEN'S SUFFRAGE, from 1901 subscribed to the re-formed CENTRAL SOCIETY FOR WOMEN'S SUFFRAGE and in 1907 subscribed to the WOMEN'S SOCIAL AND POLITICAL UNION. She supported the ARTISTS' SUFFRAGE LEAGUE, being its representative, with Mary LOWNDES, on the committee of the NATIONAL UNION OF WOMEN'S SUFFRAGE SOCIETIES that organized the 13 June 1908 Demonstration. For this she helped to embroider the ASL's BANNER "Alliance Not Defiance", now in the Museum of London, supplying silks that she had brought back from India. She gave a pale blue silk, presumably from the same source, to make a banner for Cambridge; it is now lost but was used to decorate the Queen's Hall for the NUWSS victory celebrations on 13 March 1918 and is described by the *Common Cause*'s commentator. For the 13 June 1908 demonstration Christiana Herringham also worked, from a design by Mary Lowndes, the banner of the WOMEN WRITERS' SUFFRAGE LEAGUE, appliquéd in black and cream velvet and depicting a black crow surmounted by a quill and "Writers". She was associated with Bertha NEWCOMBE; the two wrote a joint letter from Christiana Herringham's address in 1908. She was presumably the Mrs Herringham (no other person of that name features elsewhere in association with the suffrage movement) who, with a Miss Hodgson (probably Caroline Hodgson who was, with Edith How-Martyn, one of the founders of the WOMEN'S FREEDOM LEAGUE), wrote a duologue, "Granny's Decision", which was performed at a WFL bazaar in March/April 1908. In 1908 Christiana Herringham was a supporter of the *Women's Franchise* (*see under* NEWSPAPERS AND JOURNALS). In 1909 she gave financial help to launch the *Englishwoman*, which was, after the first six months of its life, edited by her friend Mary Lowndes. A copy of Cicely HAMILTON's *Pageant of Great Women*, 1910, was among her books given to Bedford College. Christiana Herringham was a supporter of the TAX RESISTANCE LEAGUE in 1910. In July 1911, soon after suffering from delusions of persecution and being committed to a private asylum, in which such institutions she was to spend the rest of her life, she asked her family to sell "three valuable rugs" and to give the proceeds to the suffrage movement through Mary Lowndes. Christiana Herringham's husband, Wilmot, became vice-chancellor of the University of London, a governor of Bedford College in 1913 and was knighted in 1914. He left their art collection and many of his wife's paintings and copies to Bedford and Newnham colleges.

Address: 40 Wimpole Street, London W.
Photograph: in M. Lago, *Christiana Herringham and the Edwardian Art Scene*, 1996.
Bibliography: Catalogue of the Herringham Collection, The Archives, Royal Holloway College; M. Lago, *Christiana Herringham and the Edwardian Art Scene*, 1996.

HERTS (EAST) (NUWSS)   In 1913 the society was a member of the EASTERN COUNTIES FEDERATION OF THE NATIONAL UNION OF WOMEN'S SUFFRAGE

SOCIETIES. Secretary (1913) Miss L. Puller, Youngsbury, Ware, Hertfordshire.

HERTS (WEST) (NUWSS) In 1913 the society was a member of the OXON, BERKS, BUCKS, AND BEDS FEDERATION OF THE NATIONAL UNION OF WOMEN'S SUFFRAGE SOCIETIES. Secretary (1913) Mrs Robinson, 6 The Parade, High Street, Watford, Hertfordshire.

HEXHAM (NUWSS) In 1913 the society was a member of the NORTH-EASTERN FEDERATION OF THE NATIONAL UNION OF WOMEN'S SUFFRAGE SOCIETIES. Secretary (1913) Mrs Walton, Ingleholme, Stocksfield, Northumberland.

HEYWOOD (NUWSS) Formed in 1911 and joined the MANCHESTER AND DISTRICT FEDERATION OF THE NATIONAL UNION OF WOMEN'S SUFFRAGE SOCIETIES. Secretary (1913) Mrs Tozer, Hopwood Vicarage, Heywood, Lancashire.

HICKS, [AMELIA JANE] AMIE, MRS (*c.* 1839–1917) Her father was a Chartist and, according to an interview in the *Woman's Signal*, her mother was the descendant of a North American Indian chief. She was brought up until she was 14 in the home of her uncle, the painter Thomas Dicksee. His children, Margaret (1858–1903), who signed the 1889 Declaration in Favour of Women's Suffrage, and Frank Dicksee, were also artists; they both taught drawing at Queen's College in Harley Street. When she was 14 Amie returned home and helped her father with his business. She married young, and, aged 25, with three children, emigrated with her husband, a cabinet maker, to New Zealand. However, the family experienced considerable difficulties there and returned to England. In 1883, with her husband and her daughter Margaretta, she joined the Social Democratic Federation and from 1884 to 1885 was a member of its executive council. From within the SDF she was adamant in her concern that women's suffrage should be considered as implicit in adult suffrage. In 1885 Amie Hicks was involved in the campaign to repeal the Contagious Diseases Acts. In 1885 and 1888 she stood, unsuccessfully, as a Labour candidate, sponsored by the SDF, for the London School Board. By 1889 she was organizing women ropemakers and was for ten years the secretary of their small but active union. She was a member of the National Union of Women Workers. In 1892 she addressed the annual general meeting of the CENTRAL NATIONAL SOCIETY FOR WOMEN'S SUFFRAGE and in 1896 was a supporter of the WOMEN'S EMANCIPATION UNION. In that year she became very friendly with Charlotte Perkins Gilman, who was in England on a lecture tour. She herself travelled round the country speaking at meetings; in 1898, for instance, she addressed the Pontefract Women's Liberal Association. From 1894 until 1908 Amie Hicks was a member of the Women's Industrial Council, friendly with one of its other activists, Margaret Macdonald, and in 1899 attended the International Congress of Women in London. By 1903 she was president of the Clubs' Industrial Association and in 1913 was vice-president of the National Organisation of Girls' Clubs.

Address: (1901) 3 Wilmot Place, Camden Town, London NW; (1913) 21 Rochester Square, Camden Road, London NW.
Photograph: *Woman's Signal*, 29 March 1894.
Bibliography: *Woman's Signal*, 29 March 1894; O. Banks, *The Biographical Dictionary of British Feminists*, vol. 1, 1985.

HICKS, AMY MAUD (1877–1953) (later Mrs Bull, MBE) and **HICKS, LILIAN MARTHA, MRS** (1853–1924) Lilian Hicks, mother of Amy, as well as of another daughter and a son, was born in Colchester to a father who "was a great believer in woman's capability, and trained both his daughters to manage their own affairs and depend on their own judgment just as carefully and thoroughly as he trained his sons". She worked for many years with the Charity Organization Society and as a school manager, both in East Anglia and then in North St Pancras, and for the suffrage cause from the early 1880s. During these early years she organized a number of meetings in East Anglia, at one of which Mrs FAWCETT had come to speak. In an interview in the *Vote* in 1910 Mrs Hicks remarked that "I cannot help sometimes contrasting the present suffrage agitation with the one that was supposed to sweep the country for the agricultural labourers' vote [in 1884]. I helped in that, too. My husband was extremely interested in it, and he and I organised and spoke at many meetings in our neighbourhood."

Lilian Hicks mentioned in this interview that she and her daughter joined the WOMEN'S SOCIAL AND

Political Union "at the dinner that was given to the Lobby demonstrators when they came out of prison some three and a half years ago", that is, the banquet given by Mrs Fawcett at the Savoy on 11 December 1906, and that they had then moved to the WOMEN'S FREEDOM LEAGUE as soon as it was formed. They had both previously, since 1902, been members of the CENTRAL SOCIETY FOR WOMEN'S SUFFRAGE. In the summer of 1908 Mrs Hicks travelled with Margaret Wynne NEVINSON in the WFL caravan through Surrey, Sussex and East Anglia. In 1910 she rejoined the WSPU and from the autumn of 1911 until 1913 she was honorary secretary of the Hampstead branch. She also supported the NEW CONSTITUTIONAL SOCIETY FOR WOMEN'S SUFFRAGE and the CHURCH LEAGUE FOR WOMEN'S SUFFRAGE. She was present in 1909 at the founding meeting of the TAX RESISTANCE LEAGUE, by 1913 was its honorary treasurer, and had twice had her goods distrained in lieu of tax. In November 1912 she contributed to the expenses of George LANSBURY when he stood as a suffrage candidate. By 1913 she had twice been arrested and charged with obstruction and once for window smashing, but each time was acquitted. In 1913 she was a member of the advisory committee of the International Suffrage Shop (*see* SHOPS) and in July became London organizer for the NORTHERN MEN'S FEDERATION FOR WOMEN'S SUFFRAGE. When it was founded in 1915 Lilian Hicks became honorary secretary of the Hampstead branch of the UNITED SUFFRAGISTS. Her only son was killed in the First World War. In 1918 she was a member of the SUFFRAGETTES OF THE WSPU.

Amy Hicks studied at Girton, taking the classical tripos, at London University, and then held a fellowship in Greek at Bryn Mawr in 1904–5. She then returned to England to teach classics and devote herself to the suffrage cause. She subscribed to the Central Society for Women's Suffrage and then, with her mother, to the WSPU in 1906–7. When the WFL was formed she broke from the WSPU to join that society, becoming its literary secretary by 1909. In July 1909 she was imprisoned for three weeks on a charge of obstruction. In 1910 she gave support to the New Constitutional Society for Women's Suffrage and rejoined the WSPU. She was arrested, with her mother, on "Black Friday" in November 1910. In 1910 Amy Hicks was a member of the committee of the Tax Resistance League. In March 1912 she was imprisoned for four months for window smashing. She spent time both in Holloway and Aylesbury, for a period in solitary confinement, went on hunger strike and was forcibly fed. She was considered by the Home Office to be, with Charlotte Marsh, the ringleader of the hunger strike at Aylesbury. Before being moved to Aylesbury she was visited in Holloway by the Rev Frederick HANKINSON. On 27 May 1913 Amy Hicks was one of the 13 women present at the meeting held to found the EAST LONDON FEDERATION OF THE WSPU. With her mother, Amy Hicks later became a member of the UNITED SUFFRAGISTS. Amy Hicks married in 1927, was a rural district councillor in Chelmsford from 1927 to 1930 and lectured to Women's Institutes on the production and preservation of home-grown food.

Address: (1880s) Great Holland, Essex; (1913) 33 Downside Crescent, Hampstead, London NW; (1924) Runsell Green Danbury, Essex; (Mrs Bull, 1948) The General's Orchard, Little Baddow, Chelmsford, Essex.
Photograph: of both mother and daughter, spring-cleaning together, in the *Vote*, 16 April 1910.
Bibliography: interview with Mrs Hicks in the *Vote*, 2 April 1910.

HIGH WYCOMBE (NUWSS) In 1913 the society was a member of the OXON, BERKS, BUCKS, AND BEDS FEDERATION OF THE NATIONAL UNION OF WOMEN'S SUFFRAGE SOCIETIES. Secretary (1913) Mrs R.H. Berney, Ulverscoft, High Wycombe, Buckinghamshire.

HIGHBURY (WFL) Secretary (1913) Miss John, 65 Marquess Road, Canonbury, London N.

HIGHGATE AND NORTH ST PANCRAS (branch of the LONDON SOCIETY FOR WOMEN'S SUFFRAGE, NUWSS) Joint secretaries (1909) Mrs Ernest Harrington, 3 Holly Terrace, West Hill, Highgate, London N, and Miss H.D. Thomson, Baveno, Broadlands Road, Highgate, London N; (1913) Mrs Ernest Harrington, and Mrs Bowman, 30 West Hill, Highgate, London N.

HILL, FLORENCE MARGARET DAVENPORT (*c.* 1829–1919) Unitarian, niece of Rowland Hill, deviser of the penny post, and daughter of Matthew Davenport Hill, who in 1832 had publicly endorsed female suffrage to enthusiastic mixed-sex audiences during his successful election campaign in Hull. In 1844 he was one of the originators of the Law Amendment Society which later merged with the National Association for the Advancement of Social Science. In 1856 he helped Barbara BODICHON draft *A Brief Summary in Plain Language of the Most Important Laws of England Concerning Women*. From 1851 the family lived in Bristol, where in 1853 Florence arranged a meeting at which Caroline Chisholm spoke on her scheme for women's emigration to Australia. In 1872 Florence and her sister, Rosamond, went themselves on a visit to Australia where their cousin, Miss Clark, worked in the interests of children. This area of social work was one in which Florence Davenport Hill and her sisters, Joanna and Rosamond, also took a keen interest. In 1868 Florence Davenport Hill published *Children of the State* and before going to Australia had attended, with Catherine Winkworth and Mary Carpenter, a Congress of Women Workers at Darmstadt arranged by Queen Victoria's daughter, the Grand Duchess of Hesse.

In 1866 Florence Davenport Hill signed the 1866 suffrage petition and in 1866–7 subscribed to the ENFRANCHISEMENT OF WOMEN COMMITTEE. In January 1868 a circular was sent out, from Matthew Davenport Hill, permitting "his daughter to invite so many as his drawing-room would hold to meet there on 24th January 1868, at 3p.m. with a view to forming a society to promote women's suffrage". Florence Davenport Hill was a member of the resulting Committee of the BRISTOL AND WEST OF ENGLAND SOCIETY FOR WOMEN'S SUFFRAGE. She was a member of the CENTRAL COMMITTEE OF THE NATIONAL SOCIETY FOR WOMEN'S SUFFRAGE and after the split in the society in 1888 stayed with Millicent Garrett FAWCETT's faction. By 1893 Florence Davenport Hill was a member of the executive committee of the Central Committee. She and her sister, Rosamond, had moved to London and Florence was elected for the first time in 1881 and, in 1884 for the fourth time, as a poor law guardian in St Pancras. In 1889 she took over her uncle's seat in Hampstead. In 1895 she presided at a conference held at Westminster Town Hall (Caxton Hall) to consider a plan for an appeal to the House of Commons from women from all over the United Kingdom (*see* SPECIAL APPEAL COMMITTEE). The idea was to convince the country in a more emphatic manner than was possible by the petitions, memorials and demonstrations that had already been tried so many times. This resulted in the collection of 257 796 signatures, which were presented on 19 May 1896 in Westminster Hall, and had as little effect as all previous efforts. In 1905 Florence Davenport Hill subscribed to the CENTRAL SOCIETY FOR WOMEN'S SUFFRAGE and in 1906–7 to its successor the LONDON SOCIETY FOR WOMEN'S SUFFRAGE. In 1913 the Watling Street branch of the NATIONAL UNION OF WOMEN'S SUFFRAGE SOCIETIES PILGRIMAGE was routed through the gardens of her house outside Oxford, in order that she might give the pilgrims her support. In her will she left bequests to "my friend Matilda Betham Edwards", the National Society for the Prevention of Cruelty to Children, the WOMEN'S LOCAL GOVERNMENT SOCIETY, the London Medical School for Women, the [Elizabeth Garrett Anderson] Hospital for Women and to the Rev. Booker T. Washington. She also left an annuity to the adopted daughter of Mary Carpenter and provision for young women who, as children, had been taken care of by her sister Joanna, with whom she had campaigned to ensure that children were fostered rather than incarcerated in workhouses.

Address: (1866) Heath House, Stapleton, Bristol; (1868) 3 The Mall, Clifton, Bristol; (1889) 25 Belsize Avenue, London NW; (1901) Hillstone, Headington Road, Oxford.
Photograph: in S.J. Tanner, *How The Suffrage Movement Began in Bristol Fifty Years Ago*, 1918.
Bibliography: R. and F. Davenport Hill, *A Memoir of Matthew Davenport Hill*, 1878; S.J. Tanner, *How The Suffrage Movement Began in Bristol Fifty Years Ago*, 1918; D. Gorham, "Victorian reform as a family business: the Hill family", in A. Wohl (ed.), The *Victorian Family*, 1978.

HILL, ROSAMOND DAVENPORT (1825–1902) Unitarian, daughter of Matthew Davenport Hill and sister of Florence Davenport HILL, in the 1850s she worked in Bristol with Mary Carpenter. She was a contributor to the *Victoria Magazine*. In 1879, having moved to London, Rosamond Davenport Hill was elected, her campaign managed by Elizabeth Garrett ANDERSON and her husband, as the member for the City of London on the London School Board.

She held her seat, an extremely active and effective member, working closely with Alice WESTLAKE, until her retirement in 1897. She was succeeded in her seat on the LSB by Ellen MCKEE. After the split in the Central Committee in 1888 Rosamond Davenport Hill was a member of the executive committee of the CENTRAL COMMITTEE OF THE NATIONAL SOCIETY FOR WOMEN'S SUFFRAGE led by Millicent Garrett FAWCETT. In 1896 she published *Women on School Boards*.

Address: (1852) Heath House, Stapleton, Bristol; (1901) Hillstone, Headington Road, Oxford.
Photograph: in E. Metcalfe, *Memoir of Rosamond Davenport Hill*, 1904.
Bibliography: E. Metcalfe, *Memoir of Rosamond Davenport Hill*, 1904.

HITCHIN (WSPU) Organizer (1913) Miss Garrett, Cleveland House, Benslow, Hitchin, Hertfordshire.

HITCHIN AND DISTRICT (NUWSS) In 1913 the society was a member of the EASTERN COUNTIES FEDERATION OF THE NATIONAL UNION OF WOMEN'S SUFFRAGE SOCIETIES. Secretary (1909, 1913) Miss Annie Villiers, 11 Julians Road, Stevenage, Hertfordshire.

HOCKIN, OLIVE (1881–1936) (later Mrs Leared) Artist, studied at the Slade, taking a mixture of full- and part-time courses between 1901 and 1904 and a part-time fine art course 1910–11. She exhibited at the Society of Women Artists, at the Walker Gallery, and until 1915 at the Royal Academy. She was a contributor to *Orpheus*, the journal of the Art Movement of the THEOSOPHICAL SOCIETY, which was printed by the Women's Printing Society. The editorial of the journal stated, "We are a group of artists who revolt against the materialism of most contemporary art. We are adherents of that ancient philosophic idealism which is known to our times as theosophy." Issue 16, October 1911, includes a reproduction of a painting by Olive Hockin, *The Blue Closet*, which has underneath it a text from William Morris, "And ever the great hall overhead/ Boom'd in the wind a knell for the dead, though no-one toll'd it, a knell for the dead". Issue 17, January 1912, included a reproduction of *A Phantast* by Olive Hockin and in issue 18, April 1912, she contributed an article, "Impressions of the Italian Futurist Painters". In issue 19, July 1912, she wrote the Art Notices, and particularly welcomed Epstein's controversial design for Oscar Wilde's tomb in Père la Chaise cemetery in Paris. That appears to have been her last contribution and the journal closed with the issue of April 1914. Fellow contributors had included Clifford Bax, Edward Thomas and Herbert and Eleanor Farjeon.

In July 1912, described by Sylvia PANKHURST in *Votes for Women* (19 July issue) as "a new worker in our movement", Olive Hockin helped to prepare the BANNERS for the Hyde Park "Bastille Day" rally. In March 1913 the police raided Olive Hockin's flat after a copy of the *Daily Herald* and of the *Suffragette*, which had been left at the scene of the crime after an arson attack on Roehampton Golf Club, were found to have her name and address pencilled on them. Her caretaker later identified the handwriting as that of their local newsagent. Olive Hockin's studio flat was described in the press as a "suffragette arsenal"; the police found wire cutters, a new hammer, a gallon tin of paraffin, a bag of stones, a false car licence plate and bottles of corrosive liquid. She was then charged with conspiring to set fire to a pavilion at Roehampton Golf Club, damaging the orchid house at Kew and pouring corrosive liquid into a letter box. She was also suspected by the police, although not charged, with the attack on Lloyd George's house at Walton Heath on 19 February, for which Mrs PANKHURST was awaiting trial for incitement to commit arson. It is clear from the New Scotland Yard reports of their investigation that Olive Hockin's address had been under surveillance. Her absence from home, the manner of her departure and the time of her return are all noted in the police report. The Criminal Record Office circulated her photograph, taken while she was exercising in the Holloway Prison yard, and a brief description (5' 3", brown hair, brown eyes), describing her as a "Known Militant Suffragette". The police suspected her fellow arsonist at Walton Heath to be Norah Smyth. In a speech given at her trial, fully reported in the 11 April issue of the *Suffragette*, Olive Hockin explained that she had been drawn into the militant suffrage movement after she had become aware of the evils of prostitution. She related that she had been told by Mr Coote of the National Vigilance Association that laws would never be passed to deal with it until women had equal political power with men. Olive Hockin was sentenced to four months' imprisonment and ordered to pay half the costs of the prosecution. In an attempt to thwart the latter order, Olive Hockin's mother and a friend, Vere Donnithorne, claimed that most of the property in her flat belonged to them. In order to supply information to the treasury solicitor, who was determined to pursue the order for costs, the police obtained from Mrs Hall, the Campden Gardens caretaker, a detailed inventory of Olive Hockin's studio. This reveals that among the contents were several books of theosophy, a print of G.F. Watts's *Love and Death*, the two-volume edition of Burne-Jones's biography and a print of his *The Golden Staircase*. When Olive Hockin threatened to hunger strike she was moved into the first division and agreed to serve the whole of her sentence if she was allowed to carry on her profession as an artist. In Portsmouth Record Office, in a box of material that emanated from the local NATIONAL UNION OF WOMEN'S SUFFRAGE SOCIETIES branch, are several copies of a mounted sketch by Olive Hockin of a prison cell, which carries as a caption a quote from W.E. Gladstone, "You have made of your prisons a temple of honour". There is no record, however, that Olive Hockin was a member of either of the suffrage artists' societies, although she designed the front page of the double summer number of *Votes for Women*, 26 June 1914. During the First World War Olive Hockin became a land girl and published *Two Girls on the Land: Wartime on a Dartmoor Farm*, 1918. In the summer of 1922 she married John Leared, the proprietor of a Cheltenham polo-pony training school, and became the mother of two sons.

Address: (1901, 1914) c/o Mrs Kirkwood, Burghfield Common, Mortimer, Berkshire; (1902–3) 32 de Vere Gardens, Kensington, London W; (1903–4) 20 Craven Hill, London W; (1908) 5 Edwardes Square Studios, Kensington; (1910–11) 60a Kenway Road, London SW; (1913) 28 Campden Hill Gardens, Notting Hill Gate, London W; (1932) Colmones, Elmstone Hardwicke, Cheltenham, Gloucestershire.
Photograph: issued by the Criminal Record Office, Public Record Office.
Archival source: Home Office Papers, Public Record Office.

HOCKWOLD AND BRANDON (NUWSS) In 1913 the society was a member of the EASTERN COUNTIES FEDERATION OF THE NATIONAL UNION OF WOMEN'S SUFFRAGE SOCIETIES. Secretary (1913) Mrs Tennant, Hockwold Rectory, Brandon, Norfolk.

HOLBORN (branch of the LONDON SOCIETY FOR WOMEN'S SUFFRAGE, NUWSS) Secretary (1909) Miss Agnes GARRETT, 2 Gower Street, London WC, and Miss H. Grove, 51 Bedford Square, London WC (see Lady GROVE); (1913) Mrs Bertram.

HOLME, VERA LOUISE (1881–1969) Born in Birkdale, Lancashire, the daughter of Richard Holme, a timber merchant and his wife, Mary Louisa Holme (née Crowe). Nothing is known for certain of her education; she may have spent some of her youth in a convent school in France. She was an accomplished violinist and singer and by 1908 was a member of the chorus of the D'Oyly Carte Company. Vera Holme joined the ACTRESSES' FRANCHISE LEAGUE in 1908. It is possible that it was through a connection with the Esperance Club that she joined the WOMEN'S SOCIAL AND POLITICAL UNION. In a letter of 17 October 1908 Lady Constance LYTTON related that another WSPU member, "who sings in the Gilbert and Sullivan Operas in the D'Oyly Carte Co" was also "one of my Littlehampton friends". Vera Holme is the only suffragette who has ever been mentioned as a member of the D'Oyly Carte; "Littlehampton" for Lady Constance was synonymous with the Green Lady Hostel, the holiday home of the Esperance Girls' Club run by Mary NEAL and Emmeline PETHICK-LAWRENCE. Sylvia PANKHURST in *The Suffragette Movement* described Vera Holme as "a noisy, explosive young person, frequently rebuked by her elders for lack of dignity". Although contemporary reports do not include mention of her, Vera Holme was probably campaigning at the Newcastle by-election in September 1908. A copy of *Women Under the Law* by W.G. EARENGEY now in the Fawcett Library is inscribed "Vera L. Holme, Newcastle Bye Election Sept 1908". *Diana of Dobson's*, the play by Cicely HAMILTON, was playing at the local theatre during the campaign, and one report in *Votes for Women*, "From Our Special Correspondent", dwells on WSPU activity taking place around the theatre. In October 1908 Vera Holme was in Bristol, where she showed lantern slides, and in that month she gave £1 to the WSPU. On 26 March 1909 she was one of the nine women riders, arrayed in WSPU regalia, who met 26 suffragette prisoners as they were released from Holloway. *Votes for Women* of 7 May 1909 contained a poem, "An organ record", written by Vera Holme to commemorate her escapade on 2 May with Elsie Howey; they had hidden after an evening concert inside the organ in the Colston Hall, Bristol, in order to call out "Votes for Women" during the course of the following evening when Mr Birrell was chairing a meeting of the League for the Taxation of Land Values. They were very proud that it had taken officials seven minutes to locate them. Vera Holme gave a lantern show in Bath in May 1909, probably staying with the Blathwayts at Eagle House, where on 9 May she planted a tree in "Annie's Arboretum". Mrs Blathwayt recorded in her diary that Vera Holme "is a splendid woman and interested in all L's [that is the Colonel's] subjects and she took up M[ary]'s violin and was very clever with it. She has a beautiful singing voice and we sang after washing up." On 10 June Vera Holme was a mounted marshal in the WSPU Hyde Park demonstration and on 29 June, again on horseback, she carried a letter to Asquith to let him know that the suffrage deputation was on its way to see him. By 20 August 1909 she was chauffeur to Mrs Pankhurst and Mrs Pethick-Lawrence, making her debut in this role by driving Mrs Pankhurst in Scotland. She wore a striking uniform in the WSPU colours, with a smart peaked cap, decorated with her RAC badge of efficiency, atop her decidedly short hair. In a photograph in *Votes for Women*, 20 August 1909, she sits in the WSPU car with Mrs Pankhurst and Edith Craig. In November 1909 she appeared as Hannah Snell, the woman who went to war disguised as a soldier, in Cicely Hamilton's *Pageant of Great Women*. In November 1911 Vera Holme was sentenced to five days' imprisonment on a charge of stone throwing; this appears to have been her only prison sentence and she never went on hunger strike.

In *The Life and Death of Emily Wilding Davison*, Ann Morley and Liz Stanley have suggested that Vera Holme may have been a close friend of Emily Davison. Certainly, as a Young Hot Blood, Vera Holme shared a similar approach to militancy, although, if she carried out acts of terrorism in the later years, she was never caught. No new evidence has come to light to link her directly to Emily Wilding Davison. She most definitely was, however, a very close friend of the Hon. Evelina Haverfield, with whom she lived in Devon from 1911. In January 1912 Vera Holme took part in a musical evening at the opening of new premises of the Paddington branch of the WSPU, of which Mrs Haverfield was the organizer. In a will made at this time Vera Holme left everything she had to Evelina Haverfield. Among their joint possessions was a bed which had "E.H. & V.H." carved on the sides. In the event Evelina Haverfield died first and left Vera Holme an annuity of £50. Vera Holme wrote the biography of Evelina Haverfield that is now part of the Suffragette Fellowship Collection in the Museum of London.

On the outbreak of war Vera Holme joined the Women's Volunteer Reserve, being commissioned a major on 1 October 1914 by Mrs Charlesworth. She served in the Transport Unit of the Scottish Women's Hospital from 1915 to 1916, in charge of horses and trucks, working with Mrs Haverfield. Elsie Bowerman knew Vera Holme at this time and has left a record of a fancy dress party held in September 1916, somewhere in Serbia, to which Vera Holme went "as a most realistic motor mechanic". The "Young Hot Blood" spirit resurfaces in references to Vera Holme's war work. In October 1917 it was she who, with another member of the SWH who memorized the report, was entrusted by Elsie Inglis to carry a scrap of paper containing its main headings back to England and instructed to present the full report of the situation of the Serb army on the Rumanian Front in person to Lord Robert Cecil of the Foreign Office and Lord Derby, the secretary of state for war. In interim periods spent in England and Scotland, Vera Holme went on lecture tours; in 1917–18 she gave her "Russian Lecture with lantern slide" in Bearsden, Biggar, Girvan, Castle Douglas, Pollokshields, Largs and Paisley. After the end of the war and the death of Evelina Haverfield, Vera Holme was the administrator of the Haverfield Fund for Serbian Children. At this time she became part of the "Greengates" artistic coterie in Kirkcudbrightshire which centred on Jessie M. King, who designed for her a most appropriate book plate. Laurence Housman was also a friend of Jessie M. King. Dorothy Johnstone, another member of this circle, painted Vera Holme's portrait at least three times, twice in oils and once in black chalk heightened with white. One of the oils is a head and shoulders in SWH uniform and in the other, very dashing, she wears a long cloak, a "Sandeman Port" hat, and is carrying a bunch of tulips. This portrait, dated June 1919, was exhibited as *Lady in Black with Tulips* in the Edinburgh Group Exhibition of 1919 and is now in Australia. When it was last exhibited in London in 1983 Vera Holme is described in the catalogue as a "fellow artist". She was certainly a good photographer, presumably having plenty of practice in the process of compiling her lantern shows, but there does not seem any evidence that she was a painter. She appears, wearing a mannish suit, with a long jacket, and a cravat alongside Dorothy Johnstone and a fellow painter, May Browne, who are, by contrast, both wearing flowing dresses, in a photograph in this catalogue.

After the war, and the death of Evelina Haverfield, Vera Holme lived with Margaret Greenless and Margaret Ker, who had both also served in Serbia, both with the SWH and in Mrs Haverfield's orphanage in Bajina Bashta. They supported the Women's Rural Institute when it was formed in Lochearnhead in 1923. Vera Holme had been an acting member of the Pioneer Players, 1914–15 and 1917–20, and remained a life-long friend of Edith Craig. Vera Holme put on drama productions both in Lochearnhead and at the annual Ellen Terry Memorial performance, which was organized by Edith Craig in the Barn Theatre at Smallhythe in Kent. In 1935 and 1936 certainly, and perhaps in other years, Vera Holme's August birthday was celebrated at the Barn Theatre. In 1932 she gave her lantern lecture "Serbia in Wartime" at the Barn Theatre; Edith Craig reciprocated and came to give a talk to the Lochearnhead WRI on "How to Trim Hats". Vera Holme kept in close touch with Serbian friends and visited the country again in 1934. On 25 May 1941 she broadcast, on the Home Service, a ten-minute talk, "I Knew – Elsie Inglis", recorded in the Edinburgh studio of the BBC; no recording survives.

Address: (1881) 6 Lulworth Road, Birkdale, Lancashire; (1923) Allt-Grainach, Lochearnhead.
Portrait: by Dorothy Johnstone in E.S. McLaren, *The History of the Scottish Women's Hospitals*, 1919; by Dorothy Johnstone in *Catalogue of Exhibition of Works by Dorothy Johnstone A.R.S.A., 1892–1980*, Fine Arts Society, 1983; with Edith Craig in the Barn Theatre, Smallhythe, by Clare Atwood in E. Adlard (ed.), *Edy: Recollections of Edith Craig*, 1949; photograph in *Votes for Women*, 20 August 1909.
Archival source: Papers of Vera L. Holme in the Fawcett Library.
Bibliography: C. White, "The bookplate designs of Jessie M. King", in the *Bookplate Journal*, March 1995 (in this interesting article Colin White makes the quite natural assumption that the "Vera L. Holme" for whom Jessie M. King designed a bookplate must be the sister of C. Geoffrey Holme, for whom she designed another. This would have meant that Vera Holme was the daughter of Charles Holme, the founder of the *Studio*. Unfortunately for the neatness theory of networks, she was not.); L. Leneman, *In the Service of Life: The Story of Elsie Inglis and the Scottish Women's Hospitals*, 1994.

HOLMES, MARION EMMA, MRS (?–?1943) Born in Retford, Nottinghamshire, married in 1888, and had two daughters. She moved to Margate c. 1895 and there co-founded, with Mrs M. Woolls, the Margate Pioneer Society in order to promote among women "the better education of women in laws pertaining to their sex, to instil a feeling of comradeship among women and to endeavour to ameliorate class distinction". Debates were conducted on a wide range of social matters, including social eugenics, female suffrage, socialism and the white slave traffic. The Margate Pioneer Society closed only in 1997. Marion Holmes was also a member of the Margate Art School Committee, and, for a time, of the Fabian Society, until she eventually gave up membership of all other societies in order to concentrate on her work for the suffrage cause.

In 1907 Marion Holmes was president of the Croydon branch of the WOMEN's SOCIAL AND POLITICAL UNION and as such chaired a meeting of released suffragettes in Croydon. The *Croydon Times* described her on this occasion as of "ample, almost Junoesque proportions – a singularly attractive personality. Her face is somewhat of the Ellen Terry type, but stronger, and more combative – tastefully, charmingly attired." In February 1907 Marion Holmes took part in the first deputation from Caxton Hall to the House of Commons, led by Charlotte DESPARD, was arrested and sentenced to two weeks' imprisonment, in the first division, in Holloway and was present at the breakfast held at the Eustace Miles restaurant to celebrate the release of all the prisoners. Christabel PANKHURST and Emmeline PETHICK-LAWRENCE were both present at a meeting held in Croydon on 5 March to welcome Mrs Holmes, who had received a mass of letters and telegrams of support from both individuals and other suffrage societies, back from prison. However, at the end of 1907 the whole Croydon branch moved over to join the newly formed WOMEN'S FREEDOM LEAGUE and Mrs Holmes, who was very attached to Charlotte Despard, became a member of the national executive of the WFL. Mrs Holmes was editor of the WFL columns in *Women's Franchise* from 1907 and then, with Cicely HAMILTON, was joint editor of the *Vote* when it was launched in 1909. She conducted many of the interviews with suffrage personalities that appeared in that paper. Like other suffrage workers, and despite her family commitments, she travelled around the country campaigning at by-elections. One of the WFL's principal speakers, she was at Dewsbury in April 1908 and with Emma SPROSON attempted to nominate a woman candidate. In May 1908 she was in Wolverhampton for the by-election, at which the WFL and the NATIONAL UNION OF WOMEN'S SUFFRAGE SOCIETIES supported the Conservative against the Liberal. In October 1908 Mrs Holmes travelled in Scotland with Charlotte Despard and Emma Sproson, visiting both Glasgow and Edinburgh, and on her return was arrested after being present at the demonstration in the House of Commons during which Muriel MATTERS and Helen Fox chained themselves to the grille of the Ladies' Gallery. Marion Holmes did not take part in the demonstration, but was sentenced and would have opted for prison, but her fine was paid and she was released from Holloway. In December 1908 Mrs Holmes was present at a meeting of the WFL at St James's Hall in London at which Mrs Despard presented to Mrs DUVAL and Muriel Matters silver "Holloway" brooches (*see* JEWELLERY AND BADGES). In January 1909 she was a speaker at a WFL meeting in the Queen's Hall at which the main speaker was Dr Thekla Hultin of Finland, who was supported by speeches from Mdme Aino Malmberg, Countess Russell, Ethel SNOWDEN, Cicely Hamilton, Charlotte Despard, Edith ZANGWILL, Anne Cobden SANDERSON and Muriel Matters. In May 1909 Marion Holmes addressed a meeting of the CONSERVATIVE AND UNIONIST WOMEN'S FRANCHISE ASSOCIATION, speaking on the industrial aspect of the suffrage movement, and in the same month was permitted by an auctioneer in Ipswich to take the rostrum at the sale of goods belonging to a WFL member who had refused to pay inhabited house duty. She spent the remainder of 1909 and all of 1910 travelling around the country for the WFL. In 1911 the Literature Department of the WFL published brief, consciousness-raising, biographical studies written by Marion Holmes on *Florence Nightingale, Josephine Butler, Elizabeth Fry, Frances Mary Buss* and *Lydia Becker*. She also wrote a "powerful dramatic sketch", *A Child of the Mutiny*, which was performed by members of the WFL, and the *ABC of Votes for Women*. She was present at the dinner given jointly by the ACTRESSES' FRANCHISE LEAGUE and the WOMEN WRITERS' SUFFRAGE LEAGUE at the Hotel Cecil on 29 June 1914 and, finally, at the Victory dinner held at the Economy Restaurant, 316 Regent Street, on 22 February 1918. In April 1918 Marion Holmes acted as agent for Nina BOYLE when she attempted to stand for Parliament.

Address: (1913) 327 Brighton Road, South Croydon, Surrey.

Photograph: in Suffragette Fellowship Collection, Museum of London.

Archival source: Marion Holmes' suffrage scrapbook contained in the Suffragette Fellowship Collection, Museum of London; Records of the Margate Pioneer Society, East Kent Archives Service.

HOLYOAKE, GEORGE JACOB (1817–1906) Born in Birmingham, a self-improved artisan, radical and follower of Robert Owen. In 1847 he attended classes given by Francis NEWMAN and William de Morgan at University College in London; his fees were paid by William Ashurst, with help from W.J. Fox and others including John Stuart MILL, who did so at the behest of Harriet TAYLOR. In the same year with William Lovett and others, Holyoake formed the "Friends of All Nations". He was a freethinker and creator of the Secularist movement in the 1850s, a member of the last executive committee of the National Charter Association in 1851 and secretary of the Garibaldi Committee in 1861. He met Garibaldi at the home of Caroline and James STANSFELD and named his daughter, Emilie Ashurst Holyoake, after Mrs Stansfeld's sister Emilie Ashurst VENTURI. He was involved with James Stansfeld in the 1850s in the Newspaper Stamp Abolition Committee. In the Social Reform League in the 1850s he worked with George Dawson, who was later to be closely involved with the BIRMINGHAM WOMEN'S SUFFRAGE SOCIETY. Holyoake worked with John Stuart Mill and Francis Newman in the London Association for Promoting Co-operation and was involved with, among others, Dr Richard PANKHURST in the National Association for the Promotion of Social Science. In June 1865 Isa CRAIG wrote to Holyoake, asking him to call at the NAPSS office; he was obviously very well known to her. His interest in the cause of women's suffrage was a legacy from his involvement in the Owenite movement, strengthened by his acquaintance with John Stuart Mill and Harriet Martineau, with whom he discussed Comte in 1851 and with whom in 1853, when in the Lake District, he visited Ruskin and William Linton, a leading republican. In that year when he visited Glasgow he had tea with the Rev. H.W. CROSSKEY. In 1857 he stood as a candidate at Tower Hamlets and, before withdrawing in favour of Acton Smee Ayrton (*see* Hertha AYRTON), he issued a full electoral programme which included provision for securing to married women rights over their own property. Ten years previously he had written an article on the woman question in the *Free Press*, and suggested a programme that even his supporters thought ambitious. In 1856 Holyoake had reprinted Harriet Taylor's 1851 *Westminster Review* article as a pamphlet titled "Are Women Fit for Politics? Are Politics fit for Women?" Unfortunately he had failed to ask permission to do so, earning himself a rebuke from Mill. Holyoake urged women to "take their own affairs into their own hands" and form a "fifth-estate". He suggested that they should hold women-only meetings with women speakers and "draw up a list of their legal disabilities, and take the usual constitutional moves of obtaining redress" and that they should publish a journal for women run by women. In 1858 his suggestion bore fruit in the publication of the *English Woman's Journal*. Among the women with whom he corresponded and to whom he suggested these ideas were Harriet Martineau, Emilie Venturi, Barbara Leigh Smith BODICHON, Bessie Rayner PARKES and Caroline Stansfeld. He published articles by Barbara Bodichon and Bessie Rayner Parkes and was also in touch with Goodwyn BARMBY. In 1859 Holyoake & Co. published Eugène Bodichon's *On Humanity*. The 1866 women's suffrage petition contains the names of many women in his radical, free-thinking circles. These included Louisa Farrah, whose husband Frederick, a radical bookseller and publisher, published work by George Holyoake in 1863 and 1864 as well as the *Journal of Human Rights*, and Jeanette Williams of 17 Johnsons Court, off Fleet Street, the address of George's brother Austin Holyoake, the printer who trained Emily FAITHFULL, and who was himself taught by the first printer of the Unitarian journal *The Reasoner*. However, George's wife Ellen (Eleanor) Holyoake, for whatever reason, did not sign the petition.

In the 1860s Holyoake was a regular attender at Clementia TAYLOR's Wednesday evening parties at Aubrey House. It was there in 1861 that he met for the first time Moncure Conway, successor to W.J. Fox at the South Place Chapel. On this occasion Holyoake was accompanied by his daughter, Evelina, whose wedding five years later was to be conducted at the South Place Chapel by Conway. At that time Holyoake was particularly friendly with Major Evans Bell (*see* Ernestine MILLS) who, with his future wife Miss Magnus, features regularly in Holyoake's diary. There is a hint in 1865 that Evans Bell might have been disappointed to learn of Evelina's engagement. In 1875 Major Evans Bell launched an appeal for subscriptions in order that an annuity might be purchased for Holyoake. In 1863 when visiting Manchester, Holyoake stayed with Max and Philippine KYLLMANN and there met, for the first time, E.O. Greening. In 1882 Elizabeth Cady Stanton met Holyoake at Barn Elms, the London home of Laura McLAREN. In 1884 he offered help to Helen TAYLOR when she stood for election to parliament in North Camberwell. Holyoake maintained his interest in women's suffrage; in 1894 he is noted as a supporter of the WOMEN'S EMANCIPATION UNION. His sister Caroline SMITH lived in Edgbaston in Birmingham and was a close friend of Elizabeth Wolstenholme ELMY. In 1892 her daughter Julia organized the conference of the WEU in Birmingham. In 1902 Holyoake wrote the preface for Lady Florence Dixie's *Isola: or, The Disinherited*, a drama in verse attacking laws unjust to women. Lady Florence was one of the WEU's main financial supporters. At the turn of the century Holyoake's second wife was a member of the executive committee of the Brighton Women's Liberal Association, of which Jane Cobden UNWIN was president. In 1904 he was invited by Mrs Unwin to a Cobden Centenary celebration, but was too disabled to attend. The *Independent Review*, 1906, published his "Woman Suffrage: A Suggestion". In 1909 *Votes for Women* headlined an extract from *The Life & Letters of George Jacob Holyoake*, edited by Joseph MacCabe (whose wife was a member of the WOMEN'S FREEDOM LEAGUE), as "A Parallel Case: The Fight for a Free Press". In his will, Holyoake left his portrait, painted by his brother William, to Birmingham Art Gallery (on the condition that the Gallery was open on a Sunday, another of the radical causes) and all his papers to his daughter Emilie Ashurst Marsh. The latter, carrying on her family's involvement in the woman's cause, was for five years before her marriage secretary to the Women's Trade Union League, was a member of the central committee of the Women's Co-operative Guild from 1888 to 1891 and again in 1893, and in 1913 was a member of the executive committee of the HIGHGATE BRANCH OF THE NATIONAL UNION OF WOMEN'S SUFFRAGE SOCIETIES.

Address: (1854) 17 Woburn Buildings, 1 Tavistock Square, London WC; (1866) Dymoke Lodge, Oval Road, Regent's Park, London NW; (1904) Eastern Lodge, 36 Camelford Street, Brighton, Sussex.

Portrait: by his brother, William Holyoake, Birmingham Art Gallery. Holyoake mentioned in his 1849 diary that he sat for his portrait to Henry Merrit, who was a very close friend; in 1853 he sat for his portrait to Matthias Robinson, and in 1856–7 to Emilie Ashurst Venturi. Walter Sickert exhibited a portrait of George Holyoake in the New English Art Club exhibition, 1893.

Archival source: diaries of George Jacob Holyoake in Bishopsgate Institute Reference Library.

Bibliography: J. MacCabe (ed.), *Life & Letters of George Holyoake*, 1908.

HORNSEY (WSPU) Founded in September 1908. Secretary (1908, 1913) Miss Bonwick, BA, 28 Weston Park, Crouch End, London N.

HORSHAM (NUWSS) In 1913 the society was a member of the SURREY, SUSSEX, AND HANTS FEDERATION OF THE NATIONAL UNION OF WOMEN'S SUFFRAGE SOCIETIES. Joint secretaries (1913) Miss Churchman, Middle St, Horsham and Mrs Blackburn, 35 Gladstone Road, Horsham, Sussex.

HOUSMAN, CLEMENCE ANNIE (1861–1955) Born at Bromsgrove (her birth registered, nameless, as "Female"), an artist and writer, sister of Laurence HOUSMAN. Having been left a small legacy, in 1883 she went to London and trained at the City and Guilds South London Technical Art School at Kennington, which included wood engraving, in which she was especially interested, among its subjects, and at the Millers' Lane City and Guilds School in South Lambeth. Laurence Housman records that it was only in order to look after him in London that she was "released from the Victorian bonds of home" and, indeed, after a year away, was very nearly sucked back into providing domestic support. She did, however, "claim a return to freedom" and began a career as a wood engraver. At first she provided illustrations for weekly illustrated papers such as the *Graphic*, but as wood engraving was superseded by photo-mechanical "process" engraving for commercial work, she began to work for fine private presses such as C.R. Ashbee's Essex House Press. She also published three novels, *The Werewolf*, 1896, *The Unknown Sea*, 1898 and *The Life of Aqlovale de Galis*, 1905. In 1908 Clemence Housman subscribed to the WOMEN'S SOCIAL AND POLITICAL UNION and in 1909 was a co-founder of the SUFFRAGE ATELIER, although no individual image created by the Atelier has been identified as her work. Laurence Housman described her as "chief banner-maker to the Suffrage between the years 1908–1914" and the studio in the Housmans' garden was a centre of such activity. Lisa Tickner has detailed that Clemence Housman worked on three BANNERS designed by her brother: the "Prison to Citizenship" banner for the Kensington WSPU in 1908, that for the Hampstead branch of the CHURCH LEAGUE FOR WOMEN'S SUFFRAGE that is now in the Museum of London and that for the UNITED SUFFRAGISTS in 1914. She also made a banner, now lost, for the CONSERVATIVE AND UNIONIST WOMEN'S FRANCHISE ASSOCIATION, and may have worked on those of the Oxford Graduates and the ACTRESSES' FRANCHISE LEAGUE.

In 1910 Clemence Housman was a member of the committee of the TAX RESISTANCE LEAGUE. She went to considerable lengths to merit imprisonment. If a woman refused to pay tax, goods were merely distrained to the value of the amount owed. Clemence Housman, therefore, went to the trouble of renting a holiday cottage and stocking it with furniture not her own. She stayed in it on occasion and when the inhabited house duty, for 4s 2d, was levied, refused to pay. As costs were added to the original amount, she continued with her refusal, until arrest and imprisonment were threatened. It took 18 months to achieve her goal, one week in Holloway, and the attendant publicity. Her arrest, on 30 September 1911, was photographed in the *Evening Standard* and the Tax Resistance League organized a procession and demonstration to protest against her imprisonment. She was released with no reason given, and did not pay her debt until after 1918. She remained loyal to the WSPU, even as militancy increased, and after the unveiling of Mrs PANKHURST's statue in Victoria Gardens, was assiduous for many years in supplying it with flowers. She and her brother were close friends of Roger and Sarah Bancroft Clark (see Helen Bright CLARK) and in the 1920s moved to Street, building a house in the Clarks' orchard.

Address: (1908) 1 Pembroke Cottages, Kensington, London W; (1927) Longmeadow, Street, Somerset.
Portrait: by Adrian Graham in Street Library, Somerset.
Archival source: Housman Papers, Street Public Library, Street, Somerset.
Bibliography: L. Housman, *The Unexpected Years*, 1937; L. Tickner, *The Spectacle of Women: Imagery of the Suffrage Campaign 1907–14*, 1987; S.S. Holton, *Suffrage Days: Stories from the Women's Suffrage Movement*, 1996.

HOUSMAN, LAURENCE (1865–1959) Born at Bromsgrove, brother of Clemence HOUSMAN and the poet A.E. Housman, brought up in a Conservative household. In 1883, with Clemence, he moved to London to study art at the City and Guilds South London Technical Art School at Kennington, Miller's Lane School of Art in South Lambeth, and then at South Kensington. He worked as an illustrator for such *fin de siècle* publishers as John Lane, contributing to the *Yellow Book*. He also wrote poetry, plays and, with considerable commercial success, in 1900 *An Englishwoman's Love-Letters*. He was friendly with George Bernard Shaw and John Masefield, both of whom supported the women's suffrage movement. A married sister of Laurence and Clemence Housman, Mrs Symons, lived in Bath and was in touch there with Mary BLATHWAYT. Housman in 1907 remarked in a letter to Evelyn SHARP that he was "not an enthusiast for the cause because I am not an enthusiast for man's suffrage, but you have a perfect right to it". However, he gave a donation to the WOMEN'S SOCIAL AND POLITICAL UNION in 1908 and in that year designed the "Prison to Citizenship" BANNER for the Kensington branch of the WSPU to carry in the "Woman's Sunday" procession to Hyde Park on 21 June and, later in the year, the WSPU's Christmas card. In 1909 he was a co-founder of the SUFFRAGE ATELIER and took the chair at its first public meeting in June. The Atelier used Laurence and Clemence Housman's garden studio for meetings and as a workshop.

Besides providing artistic sustenance to the suffrage cause, Housman also contributed the works of his pen. In January 1910 his "Women This, and Woman That", subtitled "Echo of a Barrack-Room Ballad, with acknowledgements to Mr Rudyard Kipling", was printed by the WSPU as an election leaflet and was to prove a mainstay of many a suffragette recital. In 1910 he wrote *The "Physical Force" Fallacy*, which was published by the Woman's Press. His other campaigning works include a pamphlet, *The Bawling Brotherhood*; *Articles of Faith in the Freedom of Women*, 1910; a "clever and up-to-date paraphrase of Aristophanes' *Lysistrata*", as it was advertised in *Votes for Women* on 17 March 1911; *Alice in Ganderland*, which was staged at the Lyceum by the ACTRESSES' FRANCHISE LEAGUE in October 1911; and *Pains and Penalties*, based on the marital difficulties of Queen Caroline, which was eventually staged by Edith CRAIG's Pioneer Players, having been banned by the Lord Chamberlain, and reviewed by Emily Wilding DAVISON in *Votes for Women* on 1 December 1911. In 1911 he compiled the delightful *Anti-Suffrage Alphabet* which was printed by hand by Leonora TYSON.

In 1911 Housman was the originator of an idea for resistance to the Census, a plan which he first offered to the WSPU, which rejected it, and then to the WOMEN'S FREEDOM LEAGUE, "who had already, I found, started a similar scheme of their own". He obviously enjoyed his part in this scheme of passive resistance. He was a member of both the MEN'S

Political Union for Women's Enfranchisement and of the Men's League for Women's Suffrage, being a member of the executive committee of the latter. Still a supporter of the WSPU, he was invited to join the first committee of the Election Fighting Fund, formed by the National Union of Women's Suffrage Societies to support Labour candidates at by-elections. This perceived treachery to the WSPU, which resulted in his being prevented from speaking at WSPU meetings, coincided with the spiralling of militancy to a level he felt unable to tolerate, and he felt himself "obliged to cease subscribing to WSPU funds". In 1913 he took part in the NUWSS Pilgrimage, was a supporter of the National Political League, and in 1914 joined the United Suffragists, for whom he then designed a banner. For Frederick and Emmeline Pethick-Lawrence he had also, rather earlier, designed a book plate. In 1914 Housman began writing for the *Daily Herald*, under the editorship of George Lansbury. He explained that he did not seek imprisonment because he felt that the fact that he actually did qualify to vote "seems to confuse the issue". On the only occasion that he was arrested, he, with other male demonstrators, was held for only a few hours and then released, which as he made clear, would not have been the fate of a woman in the same position at that time. Housman did not start the war as a pacifist, but became one, writing for Sylvia Pankhurst's *Workers' Dreadnought* and in 1919 joining the ILP. A homosexual, he was a supporter of the British Society for the Study of Sex Psychology, which was founded in 1914 to campaign for changes in attitudes to sexuality. He and his sister remained close friends with Roger and Sarah Bancroft Clark (*see* Helen Bright Clark), moving to Street in Somerset in the 1920s and building a new home in the Clarks' orchard. In the 1950s Housman was a supporter of the Campaign for Nuclear Disarmament and became a member of the Society of Friends.

Address: (1908) 1 Pembroke Cottages, Edwardes Square, Kensington, London W; (1927) Longmeadow, Street, Somerset.
Archival source: Housman Papers, Street Public Library, Street, Somerset.
Bibliography: L. Housman, *The Unexpected Years*, 1937; L. Tickner, *The Spectacle of Women: Imagery of the Suffrage Campaign 1907–14*, 1987; S.S. Holton, *Suffrage Days: Stories from the Women's Suffrage Movement*, 1996; A.V. John and C. Eustance (eds), *The Men's Share?: Masculinities, Male Support and Women's Suffrage in Britain, 1890–1920*, 1997.

HOWEY, [ROSE] ELSIE [NEVILLE] (1884–1963) Daughter of Gertrude and Thomas Howey, rector of Finningley in Nottinghamshire. After his death the family moved to Worcestershire. Elsie Howey spent 1902–4 studying at St Andrews University. In 1902 she matriculated as a first year arts student, unqualified, that is, not having passed the prelim examination and not entitled to a class certificate, attending "ordinary English" and "ordinary German" classes. In her second year she attended classes in "ordinary French" and "ordinary German". She then went to Germany where, as she reported in *Votes for Women* on 18 June 1908, "she had first occasion to realise woman's position". She was a member of the Women's Social and Political Union by February 1908 when she was arrested after taking part in the "pantechnicon raid" on parliament. She was sentenced to six weeks' imprisonment and when released on 18 March enjoyed the celebration breakfast organized for the prisoners at the Eustace Miles Restaurant. In May she was working for the WSPU at a by-election in Shropshire; Mary Blathwayt and Annie Kenney came from Bristol to help. In late May Elsie Howey, with Gladice Keevil, was holding meetings in Worcester to drum up support for the forthcoming "Women's Sunday" demonstration in Hyde Park and on 15 June, with Florence Macaulay, she repeated the performance in Malvern. Elsie Howey was a speaker on Platform 6 in the demonstration in Hyde Park on 21 June and was arrested for the second time on 30 June for her part in the disturbances that occurred when, Asquith having refused to take notice of the resolution taken by the thousands of women in Hyde Park, the WSPU resolved to fill "the streets with people from Westminster to Charing Cross" as John Bright had advised men to do when agitating for the 1832 Reform Bill. Elsie Howey, in her entry in the *Suffrage Annual and Women's Who's Who*, gave the reason for her arrest as "visiting Parliament Square and speaking to the people". As she put it elsewhere, although charged with obstructing the police, in reality the police obstructed her. She was sentenced to three months' imprisonment and on her release, together with Florence HAIG, Maud JOACHIM and Vera WENTWORTH, on 16 September was met at the gates of Holloway and then drawn by 50 women on a carriage from Holloway to the Queen's Hall. Full WSPU uniform was worn by the women, the traces attached to the carriage were stamped with "Votes for Women" and the "horses" were supplied with handkerchiefs in the colours, which they waved as a greeting to sympathizers in the crowd. Elsie Howey and her companions had served the longest and most severe sentences that then had been meted out to suffragettes. At the Queen's Hall they were escorted by a band, addressed by Emmeline PETHICK-LAWRENCE, and presented with bouquets in the colours and with illuminated scrolls designed by Sylvia Pankhurst to commemorate their imprisonment. Evelyn SHARP, who had been one of the "horses", described the occasion in Votes for Women, 24 September 1908. Elsie Howey was imprisoned for a total of 18 weeks in 1908. From the Queen's Hall Elsie Howey and her companions went directly to Newcastle, where the WSPU was actively campaigning against the Liberals at a by-election. The ex-prisoners were used as propaganda to illustrate the illiberality of the government. In early November Elsie Howey went to the west country as an unpaid organizer. She stayed with Annie Kenney and was very active raising funds, arranging meetings, both drawing-room and public, "At Homes" in the Corn Exchange and Guildhall in Plymouth as well as open-air meetings at the dock gates. Emily BLATHWAYT noted in her diary that "Elsie is a wonderful speaker". Mary Howey, her elder sister, was also working in the west-country campaign, based at Tregenna House in Penzance, and both she and Elsie planted trees in the Blathwayts' arboretum at Batheaston and were photographed by Col Blathwayt. In March 1909 Elsie became organizer in Paignton and Torquay, opening a WSPU shop in Torquay. She changed address frequently and must have travelled light. In that month she and Vera Wentworth accosted Mr Birrell, cabinet minister and Bristol MP, at Bristol Station and "informed him that women were determined to get the vote this session" to which he replied with an aggravating, "Tut tut". On 16 April Elsie Howey rode as Joan of Arc at the head of the procession to welcome Mrs Pethick-Lawrence on her release from Holloway. Flora DRUMMOND had requested in Votes for Women on 5 March for a body of horsewomen to volunteer for such processions and the issue of 23 April features a photograph of Elsie Howey in her symbolic role. On 2 May, with Vera Wentworth, she hid in the organ of the Colston Hall in Bristol in order to interrupt a meeting held by Mr Birrell. She later sent a postcard to her sister Mary, of the Colston Hall, with an inked "x" marking the spot where they had hidden. In May Gertrude Howey, Elsie's mother, contributed a pottery (leadless glaze only) stall to the WSPU Prince's Skating Rink Exhibition and in the summer enabled the Midland branch of the WSPU to run a CARAVAN tour, lending them a caravan decorated in the colours, while she herself spoke at meetings in Cornwall. Gertrude Howey's association with the suffrage movement may have predated the WSPU; she was sufficiently close to Mary COZENS, a very independent suffragist, to receive a legacy in the latter's will.

On 30 July 1909 Elsie Howey was sentenced to seven days' imprisonment in the third division, together with Vera Wentworth and Mary PHILLIPS, who was then ORGANIZER in Penzance, for demonstrating at a meeting being held in Exeter by Lord Carrington. She went on hunger strike and said that she and Vera Wentworth felt it their duty to disobey prison regulations and refuse food until they were moved to the first division and given political prisoner status. Elsie Howey said that they were treated with the utmost consideration and after they had caused considerable disruption were placed in the second division. They continued with their protest and were threatened with forcible feeding, the doctor telling them that he would have them certified insane if necessary. Elsie Howey fasted for 144 hours, spent several days recuperating with the Blathwayts, and at a reception in Torquay to celebrate her release was presented by the local WSPU with a travelling clock. She, Vera Wentworth and Jessie KENNEY hounded Asquith on 5 September in Lympne, where he was spending the weekend, knocking him as he left church and then cornering him and Herbert Gladstone on the golf course. They then planned a night assault on Lympne Castle and Elsie Howey was raised up to the window while Asquith was dining and shouted and threw stones. She certainly followed the WSPU precept of "Deeds Not Words"; Mrs Blathwayt in her diary entry for 7 September described Elsie and Vera Wentworth, rather affectionately, as "the two Hooligans we know". Herbert Gladstone was obviously disturbed by the incident. On 9 September he wrote in a memo to Sir Edward Troup, "Where did the Lympne gang come from? Who housed and cooperated with them at Hythe? It is not enough to deal with these people if and when they come. We ought to know what they are up to locally and all the more dangerous should be known". Elsie Howey continued working during the autumn and winter in the west of England and in January 1910 moved to Liverpool to campaign there at the general election. She was arrested on 14 January, together with Lady Constance LYTTON in her disguise as "Jane Warton", for breaking a window of the governor's house at Walton prison in protest at the treatment of Selina Martin, and was sentenced to six weeks' hard labour. On this occasion *Votes for Women* describes her as "a devoted honorary organiser who gives the whole of her services and the whole of her life to the cause. She is a beautiful, refined, and charming girl. She is a qualified woman voter." After hunger striking Elsie Howey was released early from her sentence into the care of a nursing home in St James's Road, Liverpool. A medical certificate of her condition on release was signed by Dr Alice KER. On 18 March, dressed in white and wearing her WSPU regalia, Elsie Howey was presented with the WSPU's medal of valour, "The Holloway medal", by Mrs PANKHURST at a meeting in the Albert Hall in London, and then resumed her campaigning in the west country for the rest of the spring and summer.

Elsie Howey disappears from view during the course of 1911; there is no trace of her in the pages of *Votes for Women* nor does the surviving collection of her suffragette memorabilia contain any letters or cards covering this period, until she surfaces again, speaking in Walthamstow in February 1912. Whatever she had been doing in the interim had not diminished her ardour for the cause and in March 1912 she took part in the WSPU window-smashing campaign, breaking two of Liberty's windows in Regent Street, was sentenced to four months' imprisonment and held at Aylesbury, where she was visited by the Rev Frederick HANKINSON. She was imprisoned again, this time in Holloway for two months, at the end of 1912 for setting off a fire alarm. She went on hunger strike and was forcibly fed. Mrs Howey in a letter written in 1928 to Elsa GYE noted that Elsie almost became dumb for life from the injuries inflicted on her throat by forcible feeding which took four months of treatment to recover, and "her beautiful voice was quite ruined". In June 1913 Elsie Howey rode as "Joan of Arc" beside Emily Wilding DAVISON's coffin in the procession through London. In November 1913 she sent to her mother a postcard, a photograph of Emily Davison's funeral car at Morpeth, saying "Dear Camerado ... Be of good cheer. All will be well!!!" Elsie Howey became a theosophist in 1923 and, after various bequests, left the remainder of her estate to the English Theosophical Trust. There is no record that she ever held any position of paid employment.

Address: (1913) Holly Lodge, Cradley, Malvern, Worcestershire; (1923) The Caravan, Cradley, Malvern, Worcestershire; (1958) Ashcroft, Upper Welland, Malvern, Worcestershire.
Portrait: by Col Blathwayt in B.M. Willmott Dobbie, *A Nest of Suffragettes in Somerset*, 1979.
Archival source: Suffragette Fellowship Collection (which includes a suffrage scrapbook kept by Mary Howey); Blathwayt Diaries, The National Trust, Dyrham Park, Avon; Home Office Papers, Public Record Office; Elsie Howey suffragette memorabilia in a private collection.
Bibliography: B.M. Willmott Dobbie, *A Nest of Suffragettes in Somerset*, 1979; A. Morley and L. Stanley, *The Life and Death of Emily Wilding Davison*, 1988.

HUCKNALL (NUWSS) In 1913 the society was a member of the MIDLANDS (EAST) FEDERATION OF THE NATIONAL UNION OF WOMEN'S SUFFRAGE SOCIETIES. Secretary (1913) Mrs S.B. Merrick, The Knoll, Hucknall Torkard, Nottinghamshire.

HUDDERSFIELD branch of the MANCHESTER NATIONAL SOCIETY FOR WOMEN'S SUFFRAGE Was in existence in the 1870s. The Huddersfield Women's Suffrage Society was refounded in 1904 and in 1913 was a member of the WEST RIDING FEDERATION OF THE NATIONAL UNION OF WOMEN'S SUFFRAGE SOCIETIES. Secretary (1909, 1913) Mrs J. Studdard, 44 Springwood Street, Huddersfield, Yorkshire.

HUDDERSFIELD (WSPU) Secretary (1906) Mrs Key, Regent Place, Bradford Road, Huddersfield, Yorkshire; (1913) Miss Lowenthal, The Grange, Huddersfield, Yorkshire.

HULL (NUWSS) Founded in 1904 by Dr Mary MURDOCH and in 1913 was a member of the NORTH-EASTERN FEDERATION OF THE NATIONAL UNION OF WOMEN'S SUFFRAGE SOCIETIES. Secretary (1909) Mrs H.W. Kirk, 152 Park Avenue, Hull, Yorkshire; (1913) Miss Hyde, Rosemont, The Park, Hull, Yorkshire; assistant secretary, Miss Coward, 67 Springbank, Hull, Yorkshire.

HULL branch of the UNITED SUFFRAGISTS Formed in 1915. Honorary secretary: Mrs E.M. Holmes, 9 Salisbury Street, Hull.

HULL (WSPU) Was in existence by May 1908. Organizer (1910) Mrs Jennie BAINES, c/o Miss Harrison, 14 Welbeck Street, Hull; Secretary (1913) Miss Little, 85 Park Street, Hull, Yorkshire.

HUNSTANTON (NUWSS) In 1913 the society was a member of the EASTERN COUNTIES FEDERATION OF THE NATIONAL UNION OF WOMEN'S SUFFRAGE SOCIETIES. Secretary (1913) Miss Caulton, Park Road, Hunstanton, Norfolk.

HUNTINGDON (NUWSS) Founded in 1911 and in 1913 was a member of the EASTERN COUNTIES FEDERATION OF THE NATIONAL UNION OF WOMEN'S SUFFRAGE SOCIETIES. Secretary (1911, 1913) Blanche Staley, Rose Cottage, Huntingdon Abbots, Huntingdonshire.

HYDE (NUWSS) In 1910 joined the MANCHESTER AND DISTRICT FEDERATION OF THE NATIONAL UNION OF WOMEN'S SUFFRAGE SOCIETIES. Secretary (1913) Miss A. Quayle, 12 Silver Hill Road, Hyde, Cheshire.

HYTHE branch of the NEW CONSTITUTIONAL SOCIETY FOR WOMEN'S SUFFRAGE Honorary secretary (1913) Miss Lewis Cravenhurst, Napier Gardens, Hythe, Kent.

I

ILFORD (WSPU) Secretary (1913) Miss HASLAM, 68 Cranbrook Road, Ilford, Essex. The banner of the Ilford WSPU is now in the National Museum of Labour History, Manchester.

ILFRACOMBE (WSPU) Secretary (1910) Mrs Du Sautoy Newby, St Mary's, Broad Park Avenue, Ilfracombe, Devonshire.

ILKESTON (NUWSS) In 1913 the society was a member of the MIDLANDS (EAST) FEDERATION OF THE NATIONAL UNION OF WOMEN'S SUFFRAGE SOCIETIES. Secretary (1913) Miss N.C. Hague, 12 Drummond Road, Ilkeston, Derbyshire.

ILLINGWORTH, MARGARET HOLDEN, MRS (1842–1919) Born in Yorkshire, the daughter of Sir Isaac Holden, married in 1866 to Alfred Illingworth, mother of six sons. By 1895 she was a member of the WOMEN'S FRANCHISE LEAGUE and in November 1896 sent £20 to the WOMEN'S EMANCIPATION UNION. In a letter to Harriet McIlquham, who had solicited the gift, Elizabeth Wolstenholme ELMY rather grudgingly comments on this generosity, "and she is rich enough for one not to feel that one is in any way hurting her". In 1899 Elizabeth Wolstenholme Elmy wrote that she had very much enjoyed meeting Mrs Illingworth and reported to Harriet McIlquham that she was "anxious to interest her more actively than hitherto in the woman question, as she is rich, intelligent, and kind hearted. She is quite able, if we could only stir her up to the point, to do great things financially for the woman's cause, since I suppose she has somewhat over half a million at her own disposal." She added that, rather to her surprise, Mr Illingworth, "though a stout Radical", was not in favour of the enfranchisement of married women. He had supported the Married Women's Property Act and it had made a very substantial change to his wife's financial position, presumably not to his own benefit. In 1910 Mrs Illingworth was, not surprisingly, a supporter of the TAX RESISTANCE LEAGUE. By 1913 she was president of the BRADFORD WOMEN'S SUFFRAGE SOCIETY and a vice-president of both the NATIONAL UNION OF WOMEN'S SUFFRAGE SOCIETIES and the LONDON SOCIETY FOR WOMEN'S SUFFRAGE.
Address: (1913) Daisy Bank, Bradford, Yorkshire; Queen Anne's Mansions, St James's Park, London SW1.
Archival source: Elizabeth Wolstenholme Elmy Papers, British Library.

INDEPENDENT WSPU Was, like the SUFFRAGETTES OF THE WSPU, a group that during the First World War broke away from the WOMEN'S SOCIAL AND POLITICAL UNION, which, although still led by Emmeline and Christabel PANKHURST, no longer addressed itself to the suffrage issue. The new society was formed on 21 March 1916 with Charlotte MARSH as its honorary secretary, Gladys SCHÜTZE its honorary treasurer, Dorothea ROCK its assistant honorary secretary and Dorothy EVANS its honorary provincial organizer. The group was represented in Preston by Edith RIGBY and in Glasgow by Janet Barrowman. Zoe PROCTER was a member. In 1916 and 1917 the group issued a paper, the *Independent Suffragette*.
Address: (1917) 30 Chester Terrace, Chelsea, London SW; (1918) 3 Duke Street, Adelphi, London WC2 (address of the International Suffrage Shop – *see* SHOPS).

INGLIS, ELSIE MAUD (1864–1917) Born in India, with her family settled in Edinburgh in 1875, was educated there and in Paris and then trained to be a doctor at Sophia Jex-Blake's Edinburgh School of Medicine for Women. In 1889, after disagreements with Dr Jex-Blake, Elsie Inglis, backed by her father and his influential friends, opened a rival medical school, the Scottish Association for the Medical Education for Women, where she herself continued her training, completing it first in Glasgow and then at the New Hospital for Women, opened by Elizabeth Garrett ANDERSON in 1890 in the Euston Road in London. Elsie Inglis had signed the Declaration in Favour of Women's Suffrage compiled by the CENTRAL COMMITTEE OF THE NATIONAL SOCIETY FOR WOMEN'S SUFFRAGE in 1889, but it was when she moved to London to take up position as house-surgeon in 1892 that she became an active suffrage worker, her first action being to obtain a sheet of signatures for a vote of thanks to MPs who had voted for the Rollit Suffrage Bill in 1892. Elsie Inglis was a supporter of Gladstone's policy of home rule for Ireland, and was a member of the WOMEN's LIBERAL FEDERATION, although disagreeing with any suggestion that party should be placed before the principle of women's enfranchisement. Soon after Elsie Inglis's arrival in London Elizabeth Wolstenholme ELMY asked her to write an article on women's medical education. Being so recently qualified, Elsie Inglis felt unable to accept the invitation, but when Mrs Wolstenholme Elmy then asked her to speak at a drawing-room meeting on women's suffrage, she felt obliged to accept. Elsie Inglis's suffrage debut was a success and Elizabeth Wolstenholme Elmy described her in a letter to Harriet MCILQUHAM as "very sweet and charming".

In 1894 Elsie Inglis returned to Edinburgh, graduated MB, CM, set up in practice with Dr Jessie MacGregor and in 1898 opened a hall of residence for women medical students. In 1899 Elsie Inglis was appointed lecturer in gynaecology at the Medical College for Women and in the same year opened a small hospital for women, at first in George Square and then in the High Street. In addition to her medical work, from 1900 she was a very active suffrage campaigner in Scotland, speaking at up to four meetings a week, travelling the length and breadth of the country. In 1906 she was one of the five women graduates, including Chrystal MACMILLAN, who applied, as full members of the General Councils of the Scottish universities, to vote for the two university MPs. Elizabeth Wolstenholme Elmy took a great interest in the case which was, in the end, unsuccessful. From 1909 Elsie Inglis, who was already honorary secretary of the EDINBURGH NATIONAL SUFFRAGE SOCIETY, became secretary of the newly-formed FEDERATION OF SCOTTISH SUFFRAGE SOCIETIES (NUWSS). She resigned from the Liberal party and by 1914, always a pragmatist, supported the NUWSS Election Fighting Fund policy. She was always adamant against militancy and in 1912 signed, with Elizabeth Garrett Anderson and Elizabeth Wolstenholme Elmy, the public letter of protest against WOMEN's SOCIAL AND POLITICAL UNION activity which appeared in *Votes for Women* on 26 July 1912. In November 1913 she sat on the platform at a meeting held in the Synod Hall in Edinburgh of the NORTHERN MEN'S FEDERATION FOR WOMEN'S SUFFRAGE. On the outbreak of war Elsie Inglis applied to Louisa Garrett ANDERSON for a place in the Women's Hospital Corps, but was told that the team was already complete. Having then been told, when she volunteered her services to the War Office, "My good lady, go home and sit still", she, with the backing of the Scottish Federation of Suffrage Societies, offered a fully equipped hospital unit staffed by women to an ally, either Serbia or France. This became the Scottish Women's Hospital Unit, the committee of which was mainly formed by members of the Scottish Federation executive committee, and for which many members of both the NUWSS and the WSPU worked throughout the war, as doctors, nurses and orderlies, in France, Serbia, Russia, Salonica and Macedonia. Elsie Inglis died of cancer in 1917, a day or so after travelling by ship from Archangel to Newcastle, where she was seen on her deathbed by Dr Ethel WILLIAMS.

Address: (1906) 8 Walker Street, Edinburgh.
Portrait: bronze bust by Ivan Mestrovic in Imperial War Museum.
Photograph: in L. Leneman, *In The Service of Life*, 1994.
Bibliography: Lady F. Balfour, *Dr Elsie Inglis*, c. 1919; M. Lawrence, *Shadow of Swords: A Biography of Elsie Inglis*, 1971; L. Leneman, *A Guid Cause: The Women's Suffrage Movement in Scotland*, 1991; L. Leneman, *In the Service of Life: The Story of Elsie Inglis and the Scottish Women's Hospitals*, 1994.

INNERLEITHEN committee of the NATIONAL SOCIETY FOR WOMEN'S SUFFRAGE Formed in 1872 and in 1913 the society was a member of the SCOTTISH FEDERATION OF THE NATIONAL UNION OF WOMEN'S SUFFRAGE SOCIETIES. Secretary (1913) Miss Newlands, 55 Traquair Road, Innerleithen, Peeblesshire.

INSTOW (NUWSS) In 1913 the society was a member of the SOUTH-WESTERN FEDERATION OF THE

NATIONAL UNION OF WOMEN'S SUFFRAGE SOCIETIES. Secretary (1913) Miss Joanna Preston-Whyte, The Bungalow, Instow, N. Devonshire.

INTERNATIONAL WOMAN SUFFRAGE ALLIANCE
Founded at a conference organized as a part of the annual convention of the National American Woman Suffrage Association at Washington in February 1902. Its purpose was to act as an international body to stimulate individual national women's associations to achieve enfranchisement. Susan B. Anthony presided and, among the delegates, Australia was represented by Vida GOLDSTEIN and Britain by Florence Fenwick MILLER, who became treasurer of what was at that stage called the International Woman Suffrage Committee. Millicent Garrett FAWCETT, although not present, was elected second vice-president of the Committee. The second International Woman Suffrage Conference was held in Berlin in June 1904; at this Adela Stanton COIT succeeded Florence Fenwick Miller as treasurer. Delegations attended from the USA, Britain (led by Millicent Fawcett), Germany, the Netherlands, Norway, Sweden and Denmark. The next conference was held in Copenhagen in August 1906; the WOMEN'S SOCIAL AND POLITICAL UNION was represented there by Dora MONTEFIORE. The fourth congress took place in Amsterdam in June 1908 and the fifth in London in April/May 1909. This occasion was used by both the militant and the constitutional societies to stage spectacular displays of sisterly solidarity. By the time of the sixth congress, held in Stockholm in June 1911, 24 associations were affiliated to the Alliance. The seventh congress, the last before internationalism was put to the test, was held in Budapest in the summer of 1913. Twelve delegates, including Millicent Fawcett, by now first vice-president, Helena SWANWICK, Kathleen COURTNEY, Chrystal MACMILLAN, Maude ROYDEN, Marie CORBETT and her daughter Cicely (now married and Mrs Corbett Fisher) attended from Britain. Despite a manifesto from the International Woman Suffrage Alliance, signed by Millicent Fawcett and Chrystal MacMillan, delivered to the Foreign Office and foreign embassies on 31 July 1914, and pointing out that "the fate of Europe depends on decisions which women have no power to shape", war was not averted. The IWSA continued to publish its journal, *Jus Suffragii*; an emergency committee, including Millicent Fawcett and Chrystal MacMillan, met monthly in London; and the Alliance reconstituted itself for the duration as the International Women's Relief Association.

In February 1919 a conference of delegates of the Allied countries affiliated to the IWSA was held in the Lyceum Club (*see under* CLUBS) in Paris to press for women to be represented at the Peace Conference. Margery Corbett ASHBY held the position of president of the IWSA (its name being changed in 1926 to International Alliance of Women for Suffrage and Equal Citizenship) from 1923 until 1946, during which time the Alliance pressed for, among other concerns, equal pay for women, equal educational rights and new legislation to safeguard the nationality rights of married women.

Archival source: Congress reports, Fawcett Library.
Bibliography: A. Whittick, *Woman Into Citizen*, 1979; J. Liddington, *The Long Road to Greenham: Feminism and Anti-militarism in Britain since 1820*, 1989.

INVERARY committee of the NATIONAL SOCIETY FOR WOMEN'S SUFFRAGE Formed in 1872.

INVERGORDON committee of the NATIONAL SOCIETY FOR WOMEN'S SUFFRAGE Was in existence in 1872 when its convenor was Mr James McKillichan of the *Invergordon Times*.

INVERNESS committee of the NATIONAL SOCIETY FOR WOMEN'S SUFFRAGE Formed in 1871 when its convenor was the Provost of Inverness. In 1913 the society was a member of the NORTH OF SCOTLAND FEDERATION OF THE NATIONAL UNION OF WOMEN'S SUFFRAGE SOCIETIES. Secretary (1909) Miss Jessie Munro, Nessmount, Inverness, Invernesshire; (1913) Mrs James Fraser, 19 Old Edinburgh Road, Inverness, Invernesshire.

IPSWICH committee of the NATIONAL SOCIETY FOR WOMEN'S SUFFRAGE Founded in 1871 when its secretary was Miss Grimwade, Norton House, who was succeeded in 1872 by Mrs Pickford, Butter Market, Ipswich. In 1906 the Ipswich society was still a branch of the LONDON SOCIETY FOR WOMEN'S SUFFRAGE but by 1913 it was a separate society and a member of the EASTERN COUNTIES FEDERATION OF THE NATIONAL UNION OF WOMEN'S SUFFRAGE

Societies. Secretary (1913) Miss Gardner, 73 Foxhall Road, Ipswich, Suffolk.

IPSWICH (WFL) Secretary (1913) Mrs Pratt, 160 Norwich Road, Ipswich, Suffolk.

IPSWICH (WSPU) Organizer (1910) Grace Roe, 19 Silent Street, Ipswich; (1913) Miss King, WSPU Shop, Dial Lane, Ipswich, Suffolk.

IRWIN, MARGARET HARDINGE (1858–1940) CBE. Born at Broughty Ferry, Forfars, educated privately, by 1892 was organizer for the Scottish branch of the Women's Trade Union League, in 1892 became a lady assistant commissioner to the Royal Commission on Labour, and in 1895 was appointed secretary of the Scottish Council for Women's Trades. In 1899 she attended the International Congress of Women in London. She was the author of *Women's Industries in Scotland*, 1896, *Women Shop Assistants: How They Live and Work*, 1901, and *The Problem of Home Work*, 2nd edn, 1903.

In 1902 Margaret Irwin was a founding member of the executive committee of the Glasgow and West of Scotland Association for Women's Suffrage. In 1906 she urged, to no avail, the committee of the Association to invite Teresa Billington (*see* Teresa Billington-Greig), who had recently arrived in Glasgow as the representative there of the Women's Social and Political Union, to address them. In October 1907 Margaret Irwin was a member of a sub-committee formed to liaise with the WSPU over the procession it was organizing in Edinburgh. She then resigned from the Association, unable to support its election policy and became a speaker for the Women's Freedom League, specializing in the economic position of working women. After the First World War she served on many government committees, organized a scheme whereby over 2600 unemployed girls were placed in domestic work in Scotland, was a member of the executive committee of the Glasgow Women Citizens' Association and a member of the Glasgow branch of the National Council of Women. She owned a fruit farm in Perthshire and employed men and women university students there during the harvest.

Address: (1913) 58 Renfield Street, Glasgow; (1934) 61 Kersland Street, Hillhead, Glasgow; Sholah Fruit Farm, Blairgowrie, Perthshire.

ISLINGTON (branch of the London Society for Women's Suffrage, NUWSS) Secretary (1909) Mrs Bartram, Fern Lea, Kelross Road, London N; (1913) Miss M.B. Brown, 39 Tollington Road, Holloway, London N.

ISLINGTON (WSPU) Secretary (1913) Miss Casserley, 39 Church Crescent, Muswell Hill, London N.

ISLINGTON branch of the Women's Emancipation Union Honorary secretaries (1895) Mrs Gomme and Miss Leah Anson.

ISLINGTON (NORTH) (WSPU) Secretary (1913) Miss Constance Bryer, 19 Thomas Road, Finsbury Park, London NE.

J

JACK, ALEXIA BUTTER (1863–1949) A teacher, she was first a pupil-teacher in Aberdeen before going to work and live in Edinbugh. By 1913 she held the position of "second master" in an elementary school, one of only three women to have achieved this level of promotion in Edinburgh. In 1907 she became the first honorary secretary of the Edinburgh branch of the WOMEN'S FREEDOM LEAGUE, remaining in that post certainly until 1915. She was also honorary secretary and treasurer of the Scottish Council of the WFL and was a Scottish representative on the national executive of the WFL in 1912. During the First World War, under the aegis of the WFL she worked to look after the interests of women engaged in agriculture until in 1915 she suffered a breakdown in health. After the partial enfranchisement of women in 1918 Alexia Jack became the first honorary secretary and a vice-president of the Edinburgh Women Citizens' Association. In her will, among other charitable bequests, she left £100 to the Edinburgh Women Citizens' Association, £100 to the WFL, and £100 to the Scottish Council of Women Citizens.
Address: (1908) 4 Fountainhall Road, Edinburgh; (1949) 46 Great King Street, Edinburgh.
Bibliography: L. Leneman, *A Guid Cause: The Women's Suffrage Movement in Scotland*, 1991.

JAMIESON, CHRISTINA (*c.* 1864–1942) Born at Cruisdale, Sandness, Shetland, the second child and elder daughter of Robert Jamieson, the local schoolmaster. After the death of her father, at the turn of the century the family moved to Lerwick. Christina Jamieson contributed articles to the *People's Journal*, the *Scotsman* and the *Weekly Scotsman*. As her obituarist in the *Shetland News*, 4 June 1942, recorded, "Keenly interested in public affairs, she could not abide the inferior position in their conduct accorded in her time to women" and in order to help change this state of affairs she founded and became secretary of the SHETLAND SUFFRAGE SOCIETY, a member of the NATIONAL UNION OF WOMEN'S SUFFRAGE SOCIETIES. She was the co-designer of the Orkney and Shetland BANNER and carried it in the suffrage Coronation procession in London on 21 June 1911. In 1909 she published, as *Sketch of Votes for Women Movement*, a brief history of the women's suffrage cause, the text of which she had delivered as a lecture to a packed meeting of the Lerwick Literary and Debating Society. A radical in politics, Christina Jamieson invited Ethel SNOWDEN to Lerwick to persuade Shetlanders of the justness of the case for women's suffrage. In 1916 Christina Jamieson was elected to the Lerwick School Board, the first woman to serve on any public body in Shetland. In 1935 she emigrated to New Zealand to spend her final years with one of her brothers.
Address: Twagios, Lerwick, Shetland.

JARROW (NUWSS) In 1913 the society was a member of the NORTH-EASTERN FEDERATION OF THE NATIONAL UNION OF WOMEN'S SUFFRAGE SOCIETIES. Secretary (1913) Miss Isabel Fletcher, Oaklands, Jarrow-on-Tyne, Co. Durham.

JEFFERY, GABRIELLE VIOLET (1886–1940) Born in Devon, she joined the WOMEN'S SOCIAL AND POLITICAL UNION in 1909. Mary BLATHWAYT noted in her diary that Gabrielle Jeffery arrived in Newport from Bristol on 6 September 1909 in order to be WSPU ORGANIZER there. Gabrielle Jeffery still held this position there in early 1910 and then in June, at Kensington Town Hall, founded the CATHOLIC WOMEN'S SUFFRAGE SOCIETY (which later became St Joan's Social and Political Alliance).
Address: (1913) 55 Berners Street, London W1; (1940) 5 Holly Place, Hampstead, London NW.

JEWELLERY AND BADGES At the end of the nineteenth century the concept of a badge to identify the wearer with a political campaign was not novel. Apart from those mentioned in the ditty below, in the 1840s the Anti-Corn Law League had produced a "Corn Law ribbon", which featured a wheat-ear pattern, and in 1889 a "Home Rule badge", sporting the profile of Gladstone, was advertised "for sleeve-links or button-hole". However, Laura Morgan-BROWNE's "Franchise Ballad III", published in the *Woman's Herald*, 20 February 1892, suggested for the first time the attraction of a badge for suffrage campaigners. The first verse runs:

> Who'll wear a badge? Come buy a badge
> None fairer can be seen,
> I've primrose pale for Primrose dame,
> I've rose for Liberal queen;
> I've ribbon blue for Temperance lass,
> I've leeks of valiant Wales,
> I've shamrock green for Ireland's cause
> I've thistles from Scotch dales,
> I've ambulance cross and silver signs
> Of mystical Theosophy.
> I've a badge of those who speak no ill,
> And owlets for Philosophy –
> But best of all there is a badge,
> I'd sell to English women,
> Who're staunch and true to battle through
> Our fight 'gainst Freedom's foemen.
> A little badge, a simple badge,
> With a magic word upon it,
> To bravely wear upon the breast,
> Or decorate a bonnet,
> Or ring oneself with cherished bond,
> Or tie it round the throat;
> A badge – in any shape you please
> With superscription *Vote!*

Her suggestion was taken up by the writer of a letter in the *Woman's Herald*, 26 March: "It would be useful, when one meets women who are strangers, to know, by a little brooch fastened somewhere about the dress, that there was one topic at least on which one could talk with them from a common point of view. I believe it would be useful also in showing that there are more women in favour of it than is generally supposed".

Nothing seems to have come of the suggestion and it appears that it was not until 1904 that the idea was again seriously mooted. A proposal from the NATIONAL UNION OF WOMEN'S SUFFRAGE SOCIETIES that a sketch or specimen for a badge should be circulated met with a rebuff from the GLASGOW AND WEST OF SCOTLAND ASSOCIATION FOR WOMEN'S SUFFRAGE who minuted in June that they did not want a badge. Again, it is not clear if any badge materialized at this time. The commonly found NUWSS celluloid badge is circular, red at the top, green at the bottom, with a white band across the middle. The use of all three colours probably dates it to 1909; in October of that year the minutes of the CAMBRIDGE ASSOCIATION mention that badges in the new colours were soon to be procured and offered for sale at a meeting at which Mrs Fawcett was expected to attend. One of the NUWSS enamelled badges has, on a red background, five green art nouveau tendrils radiating out from "NU" at the centre, linked by cartouches containing each of the words "National Union Women's Suffrage Societies". Another NUWSS enamel badge, a five-petalled red rose, with white petal surrounds and five pale green stamens, all superimposed on a dark green five-petalled rose with white petal surrounds, was made by W. Mark of Campden, Gloucestershire who was a member of Ashbee's Guild of Handicraft. Other of their enamel badges were made by Partridge of 72 Dean Street, Soho, and W.O. Lewis of Birmingham. To their organizers and organizing secretaries the NUWSS issued a badge that featured the bugler, designed by Caroline Watts for a poster to advertise the 13 June 1908 demonstration; it is probable that the badge was intended for use on this occasion. In 1914 the NUWSS issued badges for members of its ACTIVE SERVICE LEAGUE. These were paper-covered metal disks, a green circle with, in white, "Pilgrimage. 1913" and a white stylized palm bough, surrounded by a red circle bearing the legend in white "Active Service League NUWSS". In 1912 a badge was issued for "Associates". The Fawcett Library holds a variety of NUWSS badges, commissioned from several different makers, and badges issued for stewards to wear at meetings. There were doubtless many more varieties of NUWSS badges, uncatalogued and unremarked.

By 1909 members of the WOMEN'S SOCIAL AND POLITICAL UNION could choose to buy, from a wide selection, badges, brooches (distinguished from badges only by being devoid of a slogan), pendants, pins and hatpins that affirmed membership of their chosen society. They might also receive as reward for deeds done or hardships endured a number of specially commissioned brooches and medals. Many of the brooches and badges were made for the WSPU by Toye of 57 Theobalds Road, London.

Marie BRACKENBURY noted in 1908 that "the button badge nowadays, was even a passport to civility and attention"; the first WSPU badges, buttons stamped "Votes for Women", were on sale in July 1908. New badges and items of WSPU jewellery were issued throughout 1909 and 1910. The wearing of the colours, whether regalia or badges, was deemed compulsory for those attending the Coronation Procession in June 1911, but after the resumption of militancy, as attention moved from the masses to focus on the heroics of individuals in courtroom and prison, little further publicity was given to merchandising in the pages of *Votes for Women*, although the WSPU Christmas Fair in the Portman Rooms would have carried such items.

BADGES ISSUED BY THE WSPU
Badge, circular, enamel, with initials "WSPU", in purple, white and green, c. 1908.
Celluloid photo button of Mrs PANKHURST, Mrs PETHICK-LAWRENCE, and Christabel PANKHURST.
Badge, silver and glass, circular with portrait of Mrs Pankhurst, with purple, white and green ribbons. Mary Leigh is wearing one of these in a photograph issued as a postcard by the WSPU, probably in 1908.
Badge, square, in enamel and silver, with "Votes for Women" in purple, white and green.
Badge, shield-shaped, in enamel, with "Votes for Women – WSPU" in purple, white and green.
Badge, green centre with WSPU in white between celtic knots, and mauve border with legend "Votes for Women" in white.
Badge, circular in tin, with Sylvia PANKHURST's design of a woman in white, stepping over heavy chains, carrying a "Votes for Women" streamer, purple, white and green.
Badge, with angel blowing trumpet with scroll at her feet saying "Votes for Women". She is standing in front of a mauve enamelled globe, labelled "WSPU". With four-linked chain, a shamrock, a rose and a thistle.
Pin, shield-shaped, in enamel, with "Votes for Women", purple, white and green.

In December 1909, just before the general election, the WSPU was selling coloured ribbons, woven with "Votes for Women"; white buttons printed with "Votes for Women" in black; or the same message on a button in the colours.

JEWELLERY MADE FOR AND SOLD BY THE WSPU
In July 1908 one of the first purpose-made jewellery pieces that the WSPU commissioned was a plated brass belt buckle, using the "Haunted House" design that had appeared on the cover of the first issue of *Votes for Women*. "Boadicea" brooches were advertised in *Votes for Women* on 19 November 1908; Annie KENNEY gave one, with "To Bay from Annie with Love" cut onto the back, to Mary BLATHWAYT on 10 December; she wears it in the photograph of her, taken by her father, that appears in Willmott Dobbie, *A Nest of Suffragettes in Somerset*, 1979. Mrs Pankhurst is wearing a "Boadicea" brooch in a photograph taken by Elliott and Fry published as a postcard by J. Beagles & Co. Ltd.; Elsie HOWEY is wearing one in a photograph taken by Durrant of Torquay; and Ada FLATMAN is wearing one, together with a ribbon in the colours and her "Holloway" brooch, in a photograph published in Van Helmond, *Votes for Women*, 1992.

In 1909 the WSPU had for sale, besides the "Boadicea" brooch, one in the shape of a bow, one in enamelled silver in the shape of a flag (waving "Votes for Women"), a shamrock, and a broad (convict) arrow (either in silver or silver-plated). The latter symbol also featured as a silver hatpin, advertised in 1909. In February 1909 Annie Kenney gave Mrs Blathwayt an unspecified "Union brooch" for her birthday. The WSPU also issued an oval purple, white, and green brooch in enamel and silver. In December 1909 its Kensington shop, always adventurous and commercial, advertised "Votes for Women" badges, either in enamel or set with precious stones, and "the exhibition angel set in pendant". This would appear to be a silver pendant enamelled in purple, white and green, with the angel blowing a trumpet, facing left, that Sylvia Pankhurst had designed for the May 1908 WSPU Prince's Skating Rink Exhibition. The piece is hallmarked 1908 and was made by the Birmingham firm of Joseph Fray (*see* cover illustration).

The WSPU's "Holloway" badge, designed by Sylvia Pankhurst. (Author's collection)

MEDALS AND BROOCHES PRESENTED BY THE WSPU
In April 1909 the "New Union" presented Mrs TYSON, her sister Mrs Petre, and her daughter Diana Tyson, with a silvered badge bearing their Holloway convict letters and numbers. They were also presented with a flat gold bar, to be used for pinning on the colours, and on which was inscribed "February 24 – March 24, 1909" (*Votes for Women*, 9 April 1909). Leonora Tyson was given a similar one by the Streatham WSPU after serving her prison sentence in 1912. The Tysons' badges are now held in the Suffragette Fellowship Collection, Museum of London.

The "Holloway" brooch, designed by Sylvia Pankhurst, is first mentioned in the next week's issue of *Votes for Women*, 16 April 1909. It was described as "the Victoria Cross of the Union" and was presented in addition to the illuminated addresses, also designed by Sylvia Pankhurst, that had since September 1908 been awarded to released WSPU prisoners. The WSPU was organizing a mass demonstration in the Albert Hall for 29 April, to coincide with the meeting in London of the International Woman Suffrage Alliance and the presence on the platform of all ex-prisoners and the presentation of the brooches was designed to make an international impression. The design of the brooch is of the portcullis symbol of the House of Commons, the gate and hanging chains are in silver, and the superimposed broad arrow is in purple, white and green enamel. Some of the brooches, but not all, were inscribed with dates of imprisonment.

Ideas for commemorating milestones of militancy flowed apace. In the 30 July 1909 issue of *Votes for Women* mention is made by Emmeline Pethick-Lawrence of a proposal for "gold safety-pin brooches, with a bit of flint stone set in gold", to be presented by Mrs Pankhurst to the 14 stone-throwers who had broken windows in Whitehall after the 29 June deputation. Contributions towards their cost were invited and it was apparently intended to present the brooches at a meeting in St James's Hall (in Great Portland Street, not to be confused with the St James's Hall that had been in Piccadilly) on 16 September. The meeting certainly took place and the released hunger-striking prisoners were presented with "Holloway" brooches, but no mention was made of the "flint stone" ones. However, such brooches were at some point made and presented; one was included in the sale at Christie's in 1981 of the effects of Gladys Roberts, an ex-suffragette.

Hunger-strike medals were first presented, in St James's Hall, in early August 1909. They comprised a silver pin bar engraved "For Valour", a hanging length of ribbon in the colours, and either a silver or a striped enamel bar, from which depended a silver circle with the name of the presentee one side and "Hunger Striker" on the other. If the ribbon terminates in a silver bar, this is engraved with a date denoting the day of the owner's arrest. It is likely that these were given to women when they had been on hunger strike but had not been forcibly fed (see, for example, the medal given to Georgina Healiss, featured on the back cover of Van Helmond, *Votes for Women*, 1992). The enamelled purple, white and green bars are engraved on the reverse, for example "Fed by Force 1/3/12" (from Edith DOWNING's medal, the date of her imprisonment that resulted in hunger strike and forcible feeding). Some of the medals, for example that belonging to Maud JOACHIM, end in a metal bar but have an additional enamel bar, denoting that during her first hunger strike she was not forcibly fed, but that she was during a subsequent imprisonment. Some medals, for example that belonging to Olive

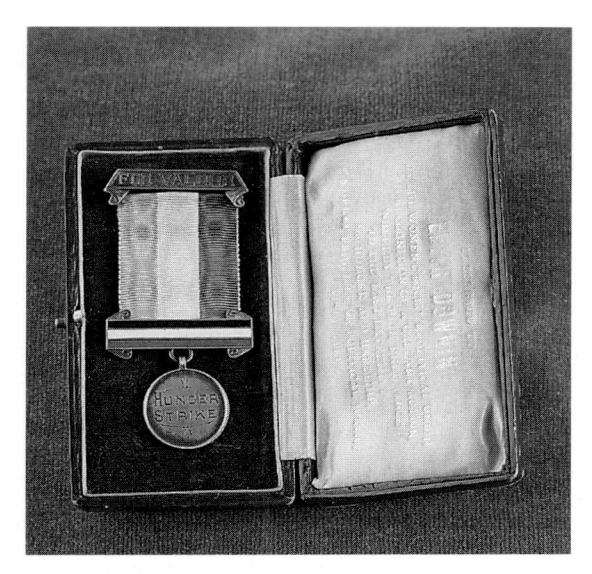

WSPU hunger strike medal, presented to Edith Downing. (Author's collection)

WHARRY, have two enamelled bars (Fed by Force 1/3/12 and Fed by Force 21/2/13). Once released from prison women were actually reminded by headquarters to return their medals in order that extra bars might be added after each hunger strike. It would appear that imprisonment stripes were also added retrospectively. Florence HAIG's medal in the Museum of London collection sports three bars, recording three dates, only one of which, in 1912, could have involved hunger striking, let alone forcible feeding. Each medal was presented in a purple box, with a green velvet lining. Printed in gold on white silk on the inside of the lid is: "Presented to [name] by the Women's Social and Political Union in recognition of a gallant action, whereby through endurance to the last extremity of hunger and hardship a great principle of political justice was vindicated". These medals were made by Toye and cost the WSPU £1 each. It is not clear if the WSPU organization, harried as it was by the police, was forced to abandon its award scheme. Such was the importance subsequently placed both by those inside and those outside the movement that the wearing of medals at post-First World War suffragette gatherings was de rigeur.

A silver "hammer" brooch was in 1912 presented to those who had broken windows for the cause.

The detail involved in WSPU organization is reflected in a few relics such as the textile "NWSPU Deputation" badge, dating from 1910, now held in the Fawcett Library collection, and the gilt metal crown brooch that tied a purple moire scarf printed with silver lettering "Section B Marshal", that is held amongst Mary PHILLIPS' effects and probably was issued to her before she joined Section B for the June 1908 Hyde Park demonstration.

WOMEN'S FREEDOM LEAGUE BADGES

The style of WOMEN'S FREEDOM LEAGUE badges and jewellery was, unsurprisingly, very similar to that of the WSPU. In November 1909 the *Vote* carried advertisements for WFL ribbon badges, a WFL badge and flag brooches in the colours. WFL badges included:

Badge, circular, of yellow metal and enamelled, with a white circle in the middle with "Votes for Women" surrounded by green circle with legend "Women's Freedom League". Made by Toye.

Badge, circular, golden shield on a sage-green background. To the left a white background with "Votes for Women", a green vertical bar in the middle, and "WFL" on a gold background to the right. The lettering is in green.

The WFL also apparently produced badges proclaiming "No Vote/No Census/Census Resisted" and one claiming for them the right to petition parliament.

The "flag" brooch advertised in 1909 is made of metal and enamel in the form of a flag with pole to the left, flag waving in the breeze, divided into three horizontal bands, with lettering "Votes" on green, "For" in gold and "Women" in white.

To celebrate the final enfranchisement of women in 1928 the WFL issued a circular badge, a black and white photograph of Charlotte DESPARD and Dr Elizabeth KNIGHT. This was produced for them, as had been others during the campaign, by the Merchant Portrait Co. of Camden Town.

As the WSPU, so the WFL issued a reward for imprisonment, in the form of a silver brooch depicting in relief a stylized Holloway. The result is not dissimilar to Holloway as outlined on a banner designed by Herman Ross for the Chelsea WSPU in 1908. These "Holloway" badges, inscribed on the back with the name of the prisoner and the date of arrest, were presented to Muriel MATTERS and Emily DUVAL by Mrs Despard at St James's Hall in December 1908, and therefore predated the WSPU version by at least four months. A "picketers" badge was given to those who maintained a vigil outside the House of Commons from July to November 1909, but it is not clear what form this took.

OTHER ORGANIZATIONS' BADGES

The ACTRESSES' FRANCHISE LEAGUE produced a button badge, c. 1908. It has a grass-green background with a five-sided shield with straight edges in the middle, outlined with a thin blade and green stripe. The shield is divided diagonally from top left to bottom right. The upper half is coloured eau-de-nil with "AFL" and lower half cream with "Votes for Women" in black art nouveau style lettering. It was made for the AFL by the Merchants' Portrait Co.

A badge was produced for the ARTISTS' SUFFRAGE LEAGUE in 1910. It is in the form of a Tudor rose, the silver ground represented white, the centre red, and the interstices between the petals were green.

The CATHOLIC WOMEN'S SUFFRAGE SOCIETY badge, designed by Gabrielle JEFFERY, is silver-coloured metal with a gold trim and fleur de lys motif in the centre, set on a saxe-blue background. The lettering of "Catholic Women's Suffrage Society" is blue on white, encircled by a gold border.

The CHURCH LEAGUE FOR WOMEN'S SUFFRAGE had three designs of large badges and two designs of small ones. One, 23mm in diameter, is a gold circle, quartered, with "CLWS", one letter to each quarter.

The INTERNATIONAL WOMAN SUFFRAGE ALLIANCE had a circular bronze-coloured metal badge, stamped with the figure of Justice in front of a rising sun. "Jus" is to the left of the figure, "Suffragii" to the right.

The JEWISH LEAGUE FOR WOMAN SUFFRAGE had a badge in purple and blue, bearing the shield of David and a quotation from Proverbs, "It is the Joy of the Righteous to do Justice".

The MEN'S LEAGUE FOR WOMEN'S SUFFRAGE badge was black, a three-petalled flower with sepals, "Men's League for Women's Suffrage" in black lettering around the edge. It was made by the Merchant Portrait Co. They also had another, plainer, badge in yellow with the name of the society printed in black.

The MEN'S POLITICAL UNION produced a photo button badge of Victor DUVAL.

The SUFFRAGE ATELIER had a badge showing their device, "Coin of Athens".

A badge was designed for the TAX RESISTANCE LEAGUE by Mary Sargant FLORENCE. In brown, black and cream, the centre circle contains a boat in full sail on swirling waters in black and white with a brown sky. A brown and black check line surrounds the picture. A band round the edge has the legend "No Vote * No Tax *" She designed another badge for the TRL to commemorate the census protest in 1911. She was not very happy with the finished sample, but it was produced despite her doubts.

The VOTES FOR WOMEN FELLOWSHIP issued "dog tag" membership badges, in brown passe partout, depending from an orange/rust knotted cord, and printed in silver "* Votes for Women * Fellowship Membership 1914".

The WOMEN WRITERS' SUFFRAGE LEAGUE had a button badge, with a white/cream background featuring a shield design outlined in black. It is quartered, the two small top quarters are white, the lower, larger, two are black. The monogram "WWSL" is superimposed on the lower edge of the top quarters. The lettering is gold outlined in black. Horizontal lines on the shield are wavy, and the vertical dividing line is white outlined in black. It was produced by the Merchants' Portrait Co.

"SUFFRAGETTE JEWELLERY"

Something of a mythology has gathered around the concept of "suffragette jewellery", fostered by auction houses and dealers in second-hand jewellery who like to claim that interesting association for any piece in which the colours purple, white and green feature. At the height of the WSPU campaign there certainly were such pieces manufactured, both by commercial and craft jewellers, but it is now very difficult to identify them with any certainty as "suffragette"; amethysts, pearls and demantoid garnets or emeralds were very commonly used in Edwardian jewellery. Some pieces of jewellery can, by association, be deemed to have been made and bought with the WSPU in mind. For instance, amongst Caroline Phillips' collection in Aberdeen is a bar pin with a prince of wales feather effect highlighted by purple, white and green stones. When seen alongside her photo buttons of Emmeline Pethick-Lawrence, and Emmeline and Christabel Pankhurst one has no doubt in labelling this piece "suffragette". The firm of Mappin and Webb certainly issued in December 1909 a catalogue of "Suffragette Jewellery". Their pieces are described as "in enamels and gems". Five designs are illustrated in the advertisement, mainly gold pieces set with amethysts, pearls and emeralds. No other commercial firms advertised such jewellery in *Votes for Women*. As it would have been an obvious place to have done so, one is tempted to conclude that little more was commercially manufactured. Craft workers, however, did advertise their colour co-ordinated wares. As there were so many women attempting to make a precarious living out of craft work, it would have been natural for them to recognize the market available among the supporters of women's suffrage. There must have been many women who enjoyed demonstrating links of friendship by giving as presents items associated with the common cause. The numerous fund-raising bazaars clearly afforded splendid opportunities for purchasing items of jewellery associated with the movement. Jewellery items were either made for them, for example in 1909 Miss Myers was contributing bead necklaces (surely "the colours" would have been involved) to the Birmingham stall at the WSPU Prince's Skating Rink exhibition, or bought from craft workers by others to donate. Since the founding of the Vittoria Street School for Jewellery and Silversmiths in the first years of the century, Birmingham had become one of the country's centres of inexpensive silverwork and jewellery, with many ex-pupils setting up as craft workers. In 1909 Annie Steen, Woodfield Cottage, Woodfield Road, King's Heath, Birmingham, advertised regularly in *Votes for Women* her "Jewellery, hand wrought in gold and silver, set with stones in the colours". It would seem, from the Birmingham WSPU's reports, that items made by Annie Steen were given for their stall at the exhibition by one of their members. Ernestine MILLS certainly donated enamel jewellery to the WSPU in 1908, although as this was in February, before the proclamation of the colours, the pieces can never be recovered as "suffragette". However, the work that she supplied for the Chelsea stall at the 1909 Prince's Skating Rink exhibition may well have included such a coded reference.

Charlotte Gere and Geoffrey Munn have attributed the brooch worn by Christabel Pankhurst in a postcard photograph to a design by C.R. Ashbee. Their published colour photograph of the spiralling gem-set brooch reveals, although the significance is not remarked, that the centre stone is green, encircled by pearls, and that the outer circle comprises seven amethysts. The coincidence of the colouring (purple, white and green) cannot be ignored and would presumably date the piece to not before May 1908. Ashbee's Guild of Handicraft disbanded in 1908, although some work continued to be worked by Guildsmen. In 1908 Ashbee designed for Helen Gordon Liddle (*see* Emily Wilding DAVISON) a new studio for her house in Chelsea (although it was apparently not built) but did build for her a studio for her country cottage at Peaslake, subsequently the home of Marion Wallace-DUNLOP. It is therefore possible that, through this association, Ashbee was commissioned to design the brooch, probably as a gift, for Christabel Pankhurst.

Jewellery certainly was commissioned to honour the movement's leaders. Mention is made in *Votes for Women*, 17 December 1908, of a "necklace and pendant wrought in gold with amethysts, pearls, and green agates" to be given to Mrs Pankhurst on her release from prison; unfortunately the jeweller is not named. The presentation took place on 14 January 1909. As Aylmer Vallance noted in the *Studio* special number on modern jewellery, enamelling, which had enjoyed a revival at the turn of the century, "offers abundant opportunities for the exercise of the decorator's skill and fancy". Suffrage iconography certainly lent itself to such a medium. Sylvia Pankhurst's silver enamelled "angel of freedom" pendant is delightful, the colours subtle. In May 1909 Ernestine Mills was commissioned by the Chelsea WSPU to make for Louise EATES, to celebrate her release from prison, a pendant in silver enamel, representing the winged figure of Hope singing outside the prison bars. This was held by a chain with stones of purple, white and green. A jewel was a natural medium of symbolism. In 1909/10 Emmeline Pethick-Lawrence was presented by her mother and sisters with a gold pendant set with opals, made by K.C. Price. A woman with arms outstretched, forms its central motif (see Studio, 1910). It was not, however, only the militant society that enjoyed commissioning pieces in its colours. In June 1913 the BOLTON SUFFRAGE SOCIETY presented its honorary secretary, Miss Haslam, with an enamelled pendant in the NUWSS colours of red, white and green, when she married in June 1913. There were doubtless many more such presentations; Flora DRUMMOND was painted by Flora Lion wearing her hunger strike medal and a large pendant of purple, white and green stones. This latter was presumably given to her at some time as a recognition of her services to the WSPU.

As with all the cultural manifestations of the women's suffrage movement, there was, alongside the uplifting iconography, a more comic rendering. A small advertisement appeared in *Votes for Women*, 27 January 1911, for a "Dainty Electric Pin; shows words 'Votes for Women' when flashed on. Complete with battery two shillings post free." In the early years of the First World War Moorhouse Ltd, of Padiham, Lancashire, stocked a "novel electric buttonhole", a "'Votes for Women' mask", a viragotype, with "Votes for Women" written in her open mouth. Buyers were promised "endless fun amongst your friends and particularly at political meetings. Inside the mask is an electrical bulb connected by insulated wire to a flash lamp and battery, which can be carried and controlled inside the jacket pocket. Just press the flash lamp switch and the mask becomes instantly illuminated."

Bibliography: C. Holme (ed.), "Modern Design in Jewellery and Fans", the *Studio*, 1902; A. Crawford, *C.R. Ashbee: Architect, Designer and Romantic Socialist*, 1985; C. Gere and G.C. Munn, *Artists' Jewellery: Pre-Raphaelite to Arts and Crafts*, 1989.

JEWISH LEAGUE FOR WOMAN SUFFRAGE
Founded in November 1912. In 1913 the League's entry in the *Suffrage Annual and Women's Who's Who* stated that "it was felt by a great number that a Jewish League should be formed to unite Jewish Suffragists of all shades of opinions, and that many would join a Jewish League where, otherwise, they would hesitate to join a purely political society". The League was non-party and its objective was "to demand the Parliamentary Franchise for women, on the same terms as it is, or may be, granted to men".

The League was open to both men and women and its intention was to carry on propaganda on constitutional lines, in the same manner as did the Church, Catholic, Free Church and Friends' Leagues. In 1913 the membership was over 300 and the executive committee included Inez BENSUSAN and Caroline Franklin (see Hugh FRANKLIN). In 1912 the League affiliated with the FEDERATED COUNCIL OF WOMEN'S SUFFRAGE. In 1913 the League signed the suffrage petition presented by the ACTRESSES' FRANCHISE LEAGUE to the House of Commons in April and in the summer sent representatives to the INTERNATIONAL WOMAN SUFFRAGE ALLIANCE congress at Budapest. In May 1913 the League opened an East End branch in London to gain supporters from among the Jewish immigrants. On Yom Kippur in 1913 three women members of the League interrupted the service in a synagogue in order to berate the two Jewish members of the cabinet, Herbert Samuel and Rufus Isaacs, for supporting the forcible feeding of suffragettes. On 13 March 1918 the League participated in the NATIONAL UNION OF WOMEN'S SUFFRAGE SOCIETIES' victory celebrations at the Queen's Hall. In 1913 the Jewish League for Woman Suffrage had a banner, designed by Mrs Robert Solomon and embroidered by Mrs Herbert Cohen.

Honorary treasurer (1913) Mrs Herbert Cohen, 2 Orme Court, London W; honorary secretaries, Miss Ruth Franklin and Miss Ansell, 32 Hyde Park Gardens, London W.

Address: (1913, 1917) 32 Hyde Park Gardens, London W.
Archival source: First Annual Report of the Jewish League for Woman Suffrage, 1913–14, Fawcett Library.
Bibliography: L. G. Kuzmack, *Woman's Cause: The Jewish Woman's Movement in England and the United States 1881–1933*, 1990.

JOACHIM, MAUD AMALIA FANNY (1869–1947) Daughter of a wool merchant and the niece of Joseph Joachim, the violinist and composer (and friend of Ursula BRIGHT), she read the Moral Science Tripos at Girton, 1890–93, being a contemporary there with a niece of Laura and Eva McLAREN and with a niece of Louisa and Flora STEVENSON. She joined the WOMEN'S SOCIAL AND POLITICAL UNION in 1907, was arrested in February 1908 after taking part in the "pantechnicon raid" on the House of Commons and was sentenced to six weeks' imprisonment. In *Votes for Women*, April 1908, she wrote, as a "Message of Encouragement to Women", "What one finds on joining the N.W.S.P.U. is, that one is brought into contact with a great number of people whose ideals are the same as one's own, and that the isolation and the reproach are things of the past". She was arrested again on 30 June after taking part in the deputation from Caxton Hall to the House of Commons and this time was sentenced to three months' imprisonment. The 1 October 1908 issue of *Votes for Women* contains an article by Maud Joachim on "My Life in Holloway Gaol" in which she mentions that "the ranks of militant suffragettes are mostly recruited from the mild vegetarians, and the authorities have allowed us a special vegetarian diet".

In February 1909 Maud Joachim was working in Aberdeen with Ada FLATMAN in the wake of Sylvia PANKHURST's displacement of Caroline PHILLIPS. In October 1909, with four others including Helen ARCHDALE and Adela PANKHURST, she was arrested in Dundee after interrupting a meeting being held by the local MP, Winston Churchill, refused to pay a fine and was sentenced to ten days' imprisonment. Following the lead that had now been set by suffrage prisoners in England, they went on hunger strike, the first time this weapon had been used in Scotland. Although forcible feeding had been used in Winson Green Prison a month earlier, Maud Joachim and the others were released by the authorities in Dundee without being so treated. In November she was speaking for the WSPU at the by-election in Portsmouth. Maud Joachim was in the thick of the "Black Friday" disturbance in November 1910, was arrested and, like most of the other women held that day, not charged. She was back in prison again for three weeks in December 1911 after taking part in the disturbances to protest against the "torpedoing" of the Conciliation Bill. After taking part in the window-smashing campaign in March 1912 she was sentenced to six months' imprisonment. She was transferred to Maidstone Prison because, the Home Office reported, "she is a person of some influence with the others and is fomenting trouble at Holloway". She clearly continued this work at Maidstone where, towards the end of June, the suffragette prisoners joined in the hunger strike for political status that had been started at Holloway. Maud Joachim was forcibly fed for two days and then released.

Maud Joachim took part in many by-election campaigns, advertising WSPU meetings from horseback, although, unlike Elsie HOWEY and Vera HOLME, she rode sidesaddle. In 1910 she subscribed to the NEW CONSTITUTIONAL SOCIETY FOR WOMEN'S SUFFRAGE and in 1914 joined the EAST LONDON FEDERATION OF THE SUFFRAGETTES. In August, when war was declared, she was with Sylvia Pankhurst in Dublin. They returned to London immediately and Maud Joachim became secretary of an unemployment bureau set up by the ELFS, appealing for work for the local unemployed, and was also manager of the ELFS toy factory until edged out by a more dominant personality. Sylvia Pankhurst described Maud Joachim, who continued working with her in her anti-fascist, pro-Ethiopian campaign, as "self-effacing". In her will Maud Joachim left a legacy to a fellow WSPU worker, Katherine Douglas-Smith. Girton College, the Women's University Settlement, and Sylvia Pankhurst received both specific legacies and a share in the residue of her estate.

Address: (1909) 118 Cheyne Walk, Chelsea, London SW; (1947) "Mouse Cottage", Steyning, Sussex.
Photograph: by Col Blathwayt in B.M. Wilmott Dobbie, *A Nest of Suffragettes in Somerset*, 1979.
Archival source: Home Office Papers, Public Record Office.

JOHN O' GROATS (NUWSS) In 1913 the society was a member of the SCOTTISH FEDERATION OF THE NATIONAL UNION OF WOMEN'S SUFFRAGE SOCIETIES. Secretary (1913) Mrs Begg, Brims, Thurso, Caithness.

JOHNSON, MARY (*c*. 1840–74) (later Mrs Feast) A member of the LONDON NATIONAL SOCIETY FOR WOMEN'S SUFFRAGE in 1867, she was the first secretary of the BIRMINGHAM SUFFRAGE SOCIETY when it was founded in 1868. Lydia BECKER was her mentor in these early days and wrote of her that she "is not at all rich, is very public-spirited, energetic – and having a small sum of money she determined to donate half of it to the 'woman question'." She was a teacher and, as Lydia Becker was at pains to make clear to her correspondent, was "not absolutely *obliged* to work – she does so – partly to help herself, and partly for occupation". Her mother Mrs G.B. Johnson of Wheeleys Road, Birmingham, was also a member of the first committee of the

Birmingham Suffrage Society. In 1868 Mary Johnson moved a resolution, unanimously passed, at the Social Science Association meeting in Birmingham, after three papers on married women's property law had been presented, calling on the council of the SSA to continue to pressure for parliamentary reform. After her marriage to Robert Bonner Feast in Ely in 1871 she was obliged to leave Birmingham and was succeeded as secretary of the Birmingham Suffrage Society by Eliza STURGE.

Archival source: Lydia Becker Papers, Women's Suffrage Collection, Manchester Central Library.

JOINT-COMMITTEE FOR SECURING THE ENFRANCHISEMENT OF WOMEN ON BROAD AND DEMOCRATIC LINES Probably founded in 1912. It was also known as the "Joint Campaign Committee" and "Women's Suffrage Campaign". It comprised representatives of the Fabian Society, the MEN's LEAGUE FOR WOMEN'S SUFFRAGE, the NATIONAL INDUSTRIAL AND PROFESSIONAL WOMEN'S SUFFRAGE SOCIETY, the National Women's Labour League, the Women's Co-operative Guild, the WOMEN'S FREEDOM LEAGUE, the Scottish Women's Freedom League, the NATIONAL UNION OF WOMEN'S SUFFRAGE SOCIETIES, and the PEOPLE'S SUFFRAGE FEDERATION, as well as MPs. The purpose of the Committee was obstensibly to obviate overlapping in lobbying but it also facilitated a greater transparency of tactics and goals. The composition of the Committee indicates that societies the aim of which was to work for women's enfranchisement were by this time prepared to co-operate with those directed to achieving adult suffrage. Honorary secretary: Walter R. Rea, MP, 30 Queen Anne's Chambers, Tothill Street, London SW.

K

KEEVIL, [GEORGINA] GLADICE (1884–1959) (later Mrs Rickford) Educated at the Frances Mary Buss School in Camden and then at Lambeth Art School. She worked as a governess for 18 months in France and the United States and on her return to England joined the WOMEN'S SOCIAL AND POLITICAL UNION, donating 1/– in September 1907. In February 1908 Gladice Keevil was one of the women arrested, with Mrs PANKHURST, as they took part in the protest against the imprisonment of the deputation from the "Women's Parliament" in Caxton Hall to the House of Commons. She then spent six weeks in Holloway and after her release was appointed a WSPU ORGANIZER and entrusted with a platform at the Hyde Park "Women's Sunday" rally on 21 June. The *Daily News* singled her out, reporting that "Miss Keevil was a particularly striking figure. Robed in flowing white muslin, her lithe figure swayed to every changing expression, and the animated face that smiled and scolded by turns beneath the black straw hat and waving white ostrich feather, was the centre of one of the densest crowds". In September 1908 she was appointed National Organizer of the Midlands, setting up a new regional office in Birmingham. She remained there until the end of 1909 when she left to organize the WSPU general election campaign in Exeter. She returned to the Midlands, where she had been succeeded by Dorothy EVANS, for a short time in February 1910. She visited Batheaston in the course of the year and Mrs BLATHWAYT noted that she was "a very nice girl... I taught her to crochet the shawls I make as she took a fancy to them". She was then a speaker in the summer campaign that year in Ireland. A member of the audience at an open-air meeting in Queen's Park, Belfast at the end of August or beginning of September sent a postcard photograph of Gladice Keevil to a friend saying, "Clever speaker and knows her subject". After that she disappears from the scene; a newspaper report in 1912 suggests that she had been on a long sea voyage after a breakdown in health. By 28 November 1912 she was back, chairing a WSPU meeting for Mrs Pankhurst. She married in Hendon in September 1913 and became the mother of three sons.

Address: (1959) The Wall Cottage, Burpham, Arundel, Sussex.
Photograph: by Col Blathwayt in B.M. Willmott Dobbie, *A Nest of Suffragettes in Somerset*, 1979.

KEIGHLEY (WSPU)   Secretary (1906) Miss Minnie Glyde, 6 Bronte Street, Keighley, Yorkshire.

KEITH, Banffshire, committee of the NATIONAL SOCIETY FOR WOMEN'S SUFFRAGE   Was in existence in 1872 when its convenor was Rev. Mr Nairn.

KELSO (NUWSS)   In 1913 the society was a member of the SCOTTISH FEDERATION OF THE NATIONAL UNION OF WOMEN'S SUFFRAGE SOCIETIES. Secretary (1913) Mrs Fleming, Abbey Row, Kelso, Roxburghshire.

KENDAL AND DISTRICT (NUWSS)   In 1913 the society was a member of the NORTH-WESTERN FEDERATION OF THE NATIONAL UNION OF WOMEN'S SUFFRAGE SOCIETIES. Secretary (1913) Miss Harrison, Hill Cote, Kendal, Westmorland.

KENNEY, [ANN] ANNIE (1879–1953) (later Mrs Taylor)   Fifth of 11 children of Ann (née Wood) and Horatio Kenney, born at Springhead, Saddleworth, in Lancashire. Annie Kenney began work as a half-timer at the local mill at the age of ten. Teresa BILLINGTON-GREIG later wrote that "at one time the propagandists of the [suffrage] movement made much publicity on 'Annie Kenney, The Suffragette Mill Girl' lines which she deeply disliked. Yet she bore it with patience for many years. I always believed she was right to object, for it presented her origin in a false aspect. Her factory work was a very temporary affair when like many families of those days, circumstances depressed them into poverty, but the Kenney family came from a home where there was a basis of culture and the ideals of a cultivated life, and in addition to Annie herself the stock bred daughters and sons of outstanding ability". Of the family, besides Annie, three of her sisters, Jessie, Jane (Jenny) and Nell were involved with the WSPU. Jenny and another sister, Kitty, were later trained as teachers by Maria Montessori, and after the First World War opened a school outside New York teaching, for instance, Caruso's daughter. Of her two brothers one became a business man in Manchester and the other, Rowland (b. 1882), was the first editor of the *Daily Herald* in 1912, a Guild Socialist during the war, Reuter's correspondent in Oslo, 1917–18, "the only genuine working-man ever to get into the Foreign Office" (Margaret Cole in *Growing Up Into Revolution*), 1920–38, press attaché in Oslo, 1939–40, and adviser to the Royal Norwegian government in London, 1941–5. He took a view of the WOMEN'S SOCIAL AND POLITICAL UNION very different to that of his sisters. He held to the Labour principles of their youth and in December 1912 wrote an article, "Women's Suffrage: the militant movement in ruins", for the *English Review*, in which he claimed that the movement's downfall was due to its having lost touch with its original supporters and to its wooing of the middle- and upper-class women in order to swell the WSPU's funds. He wrote that in mills and workshops "you will find that the subject [the suffrage] bores them, or is merely a peg for jokes. They have noted the spectacular side of the movement, they have apprehended the clever advertising which has carried it along, but they detect no warm spirit of appreciation and understanding of their own lives and difficulties in its present propaganda." Gail Braybon in *Women Workers of the First World War*, 1981, although making no connection with his sister, noted Rowland Kenney's writing in the *New Age* as being "peculiarly anti-feminist". He and his sisters were part of a family that discussed Spencer, Darwin and Haeckel around the tea table. Annie Kenney's husband, when interviewed in 1974, also stressed the extraordinary breadth and depth of the education received within the Kenney family. Annie Kenney recorded how, soon after her confirmation by the Bishop of Manchester, she was reading Voltaire in the Oldham Public Library.

Annie Kenney's mother died in early 1905 and as Annie wrote in her memoir, "the cement of love that kept the home life together disappeared. We felt more like individuals in a big world than a family group". Through a friend made in the Oldham Clarion Vocal Union, Annie Kenney, with her sisters Jessie and Jenny, was invited in the spring to a meeting of Oldham Trades Council which was addressed on the subject of women's suffrage by Christabel PANKHURST and Teresa Billington. Although she admitted in her memoir that she had never previously given a thought to the question of enfranchisement she was charmed by Christabel, promised to "work-up" a meeting for her among the factory women of Oldham and Lees, and was very quickly involved in travelling around Lancashire addressing meetings at the Wakes – "I had to speak at every meeting, and I had to start by telling them I was a factory-girl and a Trade Unionist." She was the first woman to be elected to the local committee of her union, that of the card and blowing-room operatives. She recorded in her memoir that she enrolled for a Ruskin College correspondence class in order to study the history of trade unionism. Sylvia PANKHURST revealed disparagingly, in *The Suffragette Movement*, that "the project fell through; she was no student". Annie Kenney was present at a meeting in July of the Women's Trades and Labour Council which was addressed by Elizabeth Wolstenholme ELMY who later remembered her as a "charming young woman who earnestly plied me with questions as to the best ways and means of working [for women's suffrage]". On 13 October, with Christabel Pankhurst, Annie Kenney went to a Liberal meeting held by Winston Churchill and Sir Edward Grey in the Free Trade Hall in Manchester. It was Annie Kenney who put the question, "If you are elected, will you do your best to make Woman Suffrage a Government Measure?", which received no answer except the forcible removal of the two women from the meeting. After a scuffle, she and Christabel were charged with obstruction, and capitalized on the publicity they received by refusing to pay a fine and incurring a short prison sentence, in Annie's case of three days. On 20 October Annie Kenney spoke at the meeting organized by the Manchester Central branch of the Independent Labour Party held at the Free Trade Hall to welcome her and Christabel Pankhurst from prison. Elizabeth Wolstenholme Elmy who reported enthusiastically on this meeting quoted Annie Kenney as saying, "There is not a woman on this platform who would not gladly go to prison, to win freedom for her sisters".

Annie Kenney had so quickly made the transition from factory girl to WSPU activist that she was selected to go to London with Teresa Billington to put there the question that had failed to elicit a reply from Sir Edward Grey in Manchester. The money to pay Annie Kenney's fare was raised by raffling a picture by Sylvia Pankhurst and from the proceeds of a social gathering organized by the Manchester Labour Party. On 19 December she was seated at the back of the platform at the Queen's Hall, from where she asked Asquith when he would give woman the vote. Teresa Billington and others were seated in the main body of the hall. She, Dora Montefiore, Teresa Billington and Minnie Baldock had seats in John Burns's private box at the Liberal rally in the Albert Hall on 21 December when, having received no reply to a request that Campbell-Bannerman should make a statement on the Liberal Party's attitude to women's suffrage, Annie Kenney interrupted his speech to ask "whether the Liberals, if elected, would give Votes to Women". The three women were evicted from the Albert Hall and afterwards went to see Keir Hardie at Nevill's Court. The next day Annie Kenney, with Teresa Billington and Minnie Baldock called at Campbell-Bannerman's house; he told them that he would be addressing the matter of women's suffrage sometime in the future. In January 1906 during the general election Annie Kenney went with Mrs Pankhurst, Mary Macarthur and Margaret Bondfield to campaign for Keir Hardie at Merthyr Tydfil and stayed behind for a short time to encourage support for Labour among the local women.

After returning briefly to Manchester, Annie Kenney was then sent to London. As she put it in her memoir, "London was to be roused, and I had been chosen by Christabel and Mrs Pankhurst to rouse it." Both Sylvia Pankhurst and Dora Montefiore claim that Annie Kenney stayed with them when she arrived in London and she may also have lived for a short time in the East End with Minnie Baldock. She approached Keir Hardie, W.T. Stead (who lent her a room at his house in Smith Square to which she could retire after lobbying at the House of Commons and who was, perhaps, a little too affectionate) and Isabella Ford for help and with Sylvia and Emmeline Pankhurst and Flora Drummond hired the Caxton Hall in order to hold there the WSPU's first London meeting. Both Lady Carlisle and Clara Mordan were won over on this occasion by Annie Kenney's appeal, as, shortly after, was Emmeline Pethick-Lawrence, who became treasurer of the WSPU. Annie Kenney spent some of the next two or three weeks campaigning among the laundresses of Battersea, holding open-air meetings and canvassing women in their homes. On 9 March, with Irene Fenwick Miller and Flora Drummond, Annie Kenney led a large group of women, which included Minnie Baldock, to 10 Downing Street where they demanded to see the prime minister, clinging to the door knocker and the railings. Although the police were called and arrested the women, Campbell-Bannerman refused to press charges. On 19 May 1906, dressed as the stereotypical "mill girl" in clogs and shawl, Annie Kenney took part in the futile deputation to the prime minister, Campbell-Bannerman, at the Foreign Office. A "Character Sketch" that W.T. Stead published in *Review of Reviews* at this time compared Annie Kenney to Joan of Arc and Josephine Butler and described her as "a woman of refinement and of delicacy of manner and of speech. Her physique is slender, and she is intensively nervous and high strung. She vibrates like a harpstring to every story of oppression." Annie Kenney was also profiled in the April issue of *Labour Record and Review*, in an article written by Frederick Pethick-Lawrence. In June she led the deputation that included Adelaide Knight and Minnie Baldock to Asquith's house in Cavendish Square, was arrested and sentenced to six weeks' imprisonment. As she observed in her memoir, her second imprisonment made her a greater attraction than ever before and after her release she set out on a lecture tour of Yorkshire and Lancashire and then joined Teresa

Billington in East Fife, Asquith's constituency. On 22 September she sent to Minnie Baldock from Markinch a postcard of Falkland Palace. In October she was again arrested after taking part in a demonstration in the House of Commons and was sentenced to two months' imprisonment, but was released some time before her sentence expired. In Holloway on this occasion she was put in the first division because, she said, women of greater social prominence, such as Anne Cobden SANDERSON and Emmeline Pethick-Lawrence, had been sentenced with her. She went into the dinner at the Savoy organized by Mrs FAWCETT to celebrate the release of the prisoners on the arm of Beatrice HARRADEN. She recorded that "Mrs Lawrence bought me a very pretty green silk Liberty dress for the occasion, and I wore a piece of real lace. I was so pleased with them both." She wrote *Prison Faces*, which was published by the Woman's Press, as a result of her experience of imprisonment. During the remainder of the year she organized the WSPU campaign at by-elections in Huddersfield, Bristol, North Staffordshire and in Somerset.

After the perceived success of the first Woman's Parliament in February 1907, Annie Kenney went with Adela PANKHURST back to Lancashire and Yorkshire to mobilize interest in the WSPU among the textile workers. Many of these women then came to London to take part in the second Women's Parliament on 20 March and then were invited by Christabel Pankhurst to take their deputation to the House of Commons, which, led by Viscountess HARBERTON, they did. Seventy-five women were arrested. Shortly afterwards Frederick and Emmeline Pethick-Lawrence took Christabel Pankhurst, Mary GAWTHORPE and Annie Kenney on holiday to Bordighera. This was the first time Annie had been abroad. Sylvia Pankhurst in *The Suffragette Movement* remarked apropos Annie Kenney, "Movements for liberation bring with them, to some, opportunities of personal advancement and release from uncongenial drudgery." In September Annie travelled abroad once more, again in the company of Emmeline Pethick-Lawrence, invited to speak at a conference held at Frankfurt by the German Women's Suffrage Society. Elizabeth Wolstenholme Elmy wrote to Harriet MCILQUHAM on 2 October to tell her that Annie was with her for six hours the day before, calling in on her way from London to Manchester "and she gave me a glowing account of the magnificent meeting of German women at Frankfurt, which Mrs Pethick Lawrence and Annie, by special invitation, addressed last Thursday". At Christmas 1907 the Pethick-Lawrences took Annie Kenney on holiday to Switzerland and in 1910, with Sylvia Pankhurst, to see the Passion Play at Oberammergau.

In 1907 Annie Kenney was appointed WSPU ORGANIZER, at a salary of £2 a week, in the west of England, based in Bristol, where she was to remain until October 1911. On her arrival she was helped by the PRIESTMAN SISTERS and Lilias Ashworth HALLETT, women who had been involved since 1866 in the suffrage cause. On 1 April 1908 Annie Kenney spoke at the first WSPU meeting in Bath; it was organized by Mary BLATHWAYT who had fallen under her spell and gave her a rose. Annie Kenney was introduced to the Blathwayt family, often staying at Eagle House, Batheaston, where, for the first time, she began to learn French, to play tennis, to swim, to ride and to drive. In December 1909 it was while staying at Eagle House that she wrote a touching and articulate 11-page letter to A.J. Balfour, the Conservative leader, in which she told him of her life and how having the vote would improve the lives of working women. She was at pains to assure him that the leaders of the WSPU did not know that she was writing to him. She felt his response to her letter was "cold", but thought that if she could only see him she could put her case more forcefully. A few months later, accompanied by Lady Constance Lytton she had her desired interview with Balfour.

In March 1910 as she and Christabel Pankhurst set off on holiday together to Guernsey, Annie Kenney sent her dirty clothes to the Blathwayts to be washed in her absence. Mrs Blathwayt noted in her diary, "Annie gets a wonderful influence over people". Teresa Billington-Greig in the 1950s commented on Annie Kenney's influence over Emmeline Pethick-Lawrence, a strong attraction "so emotional and so openly paraded that it frightened me as I saw it as something unbalanced and primitive and possibly dangerous to the movement". Teresa Billington-Greig claimed that, in turn, Annie was "emotionally possessed by Christabel". Mary

MRS. PANKHURST, MISS ANNIE KENNY, & MRS. PETHICK LAWRENCE.

With their hats prepared for motoring, Mrs Pankhurst and Annie Kenney sit in the back of the WSPU car. Mrs Pethick-Lawrence, to whom the car was presented in 1909, stands alongside. (Author's collection)

Blathwayt was Annie's devoted follower and in her diary gives a picture of her life at this time. There was some rivalry for Annie's attentions. Mary Blathwayt proudly noted in July 1908 that she shared a bed, while resting in the afternoon, with Annie, and then in August noted "Miss Browne is sleeping in Annie's Room now." Clara CODD in her autobiography talks of sharing a bed with Annie Kenney and this is confirmed by Mary Blathwayt, who on 7 September particularly noted that "Miss Codd has come to stay, she is sleeping with Annie." In May and June 1908 Mary and Annie travelled round the west country, speaking at open-air meetings and visiting people they thought might be sympathetic to the cause. On this occasion Mary mentioned that they called, unannounced, in Exeter on a Unitarian family and on the secretary of the local branch of the THEOSOPHICAL SOCIETY and in Bristol on the Anti-Vivisection Society Office, an indication of the communities from which they expected that support might be drawn. On 17 June Annie bought at Liberty's a hat costing £1/2/6 to wear on 21 June, "Woman's Sunday", in Hyde Park at which she chaired a platform. In Bristol she lived in a series of digs until in 1910, tired of a nomadic life, she moved into a flat in Clifton with Mrs Louie Hatfield to act as her housekeeper. Mary Blathwayt did not approve of flat living, which for her carried connotations of immorality, felt unable to visit Annie there, and returned home to live at Batheaston.

Although based in Bristol, Annie Kenney did travel out of the west country to take part in by-election campaigns around the country and was one of the WSPU's most popular speakers and charismatic figures. She was arrested again in February 1908 while taking part in a deputation, with Mrs Pankhurst, to the House of Commons and was sentenced to one month's imprisonment. On her release she spoke at the Albert Hall at a rally of which she afterwards wrote, "We all seemed charged with Suffragette electricity."

In 1912, after the window-smashing campaign, warrants were issued for the arrest of the leaders of the WSPU. The Pethick-Lawrences were arrested, Mrs Pankhurst and Mabel TUKE were already in prison, and Christabel Pankhurst escaped to Paris, summoning Annie Kenney to visit her there to take instruction as her successor. Annie Kenney described how, with Rachel BARRETT, she ensured that the policy of militancy, as conceived by Christabel, was carried out and that a scheme for a more constitutional approach devised by the Pethick-Lawrences was rebutted. She asked Elizabeth ROBINS to witness the letter that Christabel had sent her in which she was given control of the WSPU in London. Annie and Jessie Kenney and Rachel Barrett shared a flat, again with Mrs Hatfield as housekeeper. For a year, from March 1912 until she was arrested in April 1913, Annie Kenney ran the WSPU to Christabel's dictation, travelling, as she described in her memoir, every weekend to Paris. After the Pethick-Lawrences were ousted from the WSPU in October 1912 Annie Kenney was also required to act as treasurer or, as she terms it, "money-raiser". She had been very close to the Pethick-Lawrences, had every reason to be very grateful to them and was troubled by the testing of her loyalty, but had no doubt that she would always "Follow Christabel". On 14 July 1912, sponsored by the Countess DE LA WARR and Mary Dodge, Annie Kenney joined the Theosophical Society, but was forced by Christabel to resign in May 1914.

In January 1913 Annie Kenney took a leading part, with Flora Drummond, in the deputation of working women to Lloyd George. She described the episode in great detail in her memoir; Lloyd George obviously made a deep impression. She also recounted how, having had an afternoon meeting with Lloyd George, she and Flora Drummond caught the night train and boat to Paris, consulted Christabel, and then caught the early morning train and boat back in order to return to Downing Street the next day equipped with Christabel's arguments. Grace ROE was called to London from East Anglia to be trained as successor in the event of Annie Kenney's arrest. This occurred on 8 April 1913, when Annie was charged with inciting riot, and then released on bail, which was secured by her own surety of £200 and by one from Henry HARBEN. She immediately went to Paris to take instructions for the trial from Christabel and was re-arrested at Folkestone on her return. Annie Kenney was defended at her trial, at which she was charged with conspiracy to inflict damage to property, by Arthur Marshall, found guilty and sentenced to three years' imprisonment. An incidental piece of information that emerged at her trial revealed that she now received a salary of £4 4s a week. She was sent to Maidstone prison, went on hunger-and-thirst strike, was released under the "Cat and Mouse" Act three days later and taken into the care of the BRACKENBURYS at "Mouse Castle". She was eventually re-arrested and sent to Holloway, again went on hunger strike and was released after three days. Thus began a series of evasions, public appearances at suffragette meetings, re-arrests, all described in breathless detail in her memoir. She was never forcibly fed.

In August 1913 Annie Kenney met Christabel at Deauville, and then stayed at a small coastal village with, among others, her sister Jessie and Mary RICHARDSON. After her return to London she was re-arrested, went on hunger-and-thirst strike, but was not released until very ill. The propaganda value of her frailty could not be ignored. She appeared at large WSPU meetings, carried in on a stretcher, and was obviously too ill to be re-arrested. In December 1913 she went to Locarno in Switzerland for three months to recuperate. After returning she managed to evade recapture until asked by Christabel to go to Lambeth Palace and very publicly seek sanctuary with the Archbishop of Canterbury "until the Vote was won". He, of course, prevaricated and called in Scotland Yard, who sent Annie Kenney back to Holloway. After six days' hunger strike she was released and returned in an ambulance to Lambeth Palace. The police took her from there to a workhouse infirmary, from where she was at length returned to "Mouse Castle". The next day she tried the sanctuary tactic on the Bishop of London, but he pleaded that as a bachelor it would not be suitable for him to accommodate a single lady. From then until the outbreak of war Annie Kenney, in a variety of disguises, managed to evade the police and spoke at WSPU meetings around the country, raising money for the cause.

After the outbreak of war, on Christabel's instruction and with a berth provided through Janie ALLAN's shipping connection, Annie Kenney set sail for America in order to help the suffrage cause there and to be out of harm's way in case Germany invaded England. She carried on a suffrage campaign in North Dakota, Montana and Nevada, visited California, and then returned to New York to meet Christabel. By this time Annie was feeling homesick and was allowed to return to Britain, instructed "to organize a campaign explaining the Balkan situation to the people". She knew nothing of the Balkans but, provided with a small library on the subject by Grace Roe, spent two weeks mastering its history, geography and politics before launching her campaign in Huddersfield. In addition she was brought by Mrs Pankhurst into the campaign to introduce women to munition work and was then sent to Australia, at Christabel's behest, to persuade the prime minister, W.M. Hughes, to come to England to join the War Council. On her return she joined in Christabel's "Anti-Bolshevist Campaign" aimed at preventing munition, coal and dockyard strikes. In 1918 Annie Kenney worked behind the scenes at the election campaign at Smethwick, where Christabel was standing as an Independent, backed by the Coalition. In September Annie wrote to Col Blathwayt asking him to send a telegram to Major Thompson, the approved Unionist and Coalition candidate, requesting him to stand down in Smethwick to leave the field free for Christabel. As a result of such lobbying and with pressure from Lloyd George and Bonar Law, Thompson did withdraw his candidature. Annie Kenney also interviewed Lord Northcliffe, who agreed that the *Daily Mail* would give its support to Christabel. After the election, and Christabel's defeat, Annie Kenney withdrew from further involvement in Pankhurst campaigns.

After the war Annie Kenney lived in St Leonards with Grace Roe and they studied theosophy together. In 1918, while staying with her sister Jessie and Grace Roe on the Isle of Arran, at a hotel which had been much used by suffragette "mice" before the war, she met James Taylor, a Londoner, whom on 24 April 1920 she married at Lytham Parish Church. Grace Roe is noted by Mrs Blathwayt as writing that Mr Taylor "is quite simple like Annie and has a divine singing voice". Mary Blathwayt wrote in her diary, "Mr Taylor I was told used to come and see Annie at her flat". The passing years and a world war had not diminished for her the horror of flat-living. Annie was given away at the wedding by her brother Reginald, and a snapshot of the wedding party, slipped between the pages of Mary Blathwayt's diary and annotated by her, shows that those present included Jessie Kenney, Grace Roe and Mrs BARTLETT. The honeymoon was spent on the Isle of Arran. Annie Kenney became the mother of a son, Warwick Kenney Taylor, born on 4 February 1921, wrote her transparent (or *faux naif*) autobiography, and disappeared from the suffrage scene. Her husband has recorded how she henceforward lived a quiet domestic life in Letchworth, devoted to her son. She corresponded with Grace Roe and Christabel Pankhurst, both then living in the USA. James Taylor remembered that Christabel and Annie "idolized each other". Although Annie Kenney is recorded as having given some material to the SUFFRAGETTE FELLOWSHIP collection in 1951, most of her papers were apparently destroyed in the tidying up after her death. She joined the Order of the Rosicrucians, reaching their highest level of study. Her husband recorded that she never really recovered from her hunger strikes and, after a long, steady decline, she died of diabetes. Her ashes were scattered in a Lancashire valley.

Address: (March 1906) 45 Park Walk, Chelsea (Sylvia Pankhurst's address); (1907) Neville House, Whiteladies Road, Bristol; (1909) Downe House, Clifton, Bristol; (1910) 23 Gordon Road, Clifton, Bristol; (1910) 16 Arlington Villas, Clifton; (1912) 60 Clovelly Mansions, Grays Inn Road, London WC; (1913) 19 Mecklenburgh Square, London WC; (1953) 1 Camper's Road, Letchworth, Hertfordshire.
Photograph: in A. Kenney, *Memoirs of a Militant*, 1924; Suffragette Fellowship Collection, Museum of London.
Archival source: Suffragette Fellowship Collection, Museum of London; Blathwayt Diaries, The National Trust, Dyrham Park; B. Harrison, taped interview with James Taylor, widower of Annie Kenney, 1974, Fawcett Library.
Bibliography: W.T. Stead, "Miss Annie Kenney", *Review of Reviews*, June 1906; A. Kenney, *Memoirs of a Militant*, 1924.

KENNEY, JESSIE (1887–1985) Born at Lees, near Oldham, Lancashire, younger sister of Annie KENNEY. From the age of 13 she worked in a local cotton mill, at the same time attending evening classes, and with her siblings taught in a Sunday School. When she was 16 she took a typing course. In the spring of 1905 Jessie went, with Annie and another sister, Jenny, to hear Christabel PANKHURST and Teresa Billington (see Teresa BILLINGTON-GREIG) address the Oldham Trades Council, a meeting which was to have such an effect on all their lives. In 1906, soon after Annie Kenney was sent to "rouse London", Jessie followed her and, although only 19, became Mrs PETHICK-LAWRENCE's private secretary. By the time she was 21 she was the WOMEN'S SOCIAL AND POLITICAL UNION's youngest ORGANIZER, working from Clement's Inn, arranging meetings, publicity stunts, interruptions of cabinet ministers' meetings and, as time passed, acts of militancy. Sylvia PANKHURST described her in *The Suffragette Movement* as "eager in manner as her sister Annie, with more system and less pathos, and without any gift of platform speech". Jessie Kenney recorded how she took some of the pressure off Christabel by seeing relatives, who called at Clement's Inn, worried about their imprisoned daughters. On 30 June 1908 she herself was arrested after having taken part in the disturbances in Parliament Square and was sentenced to a month's imprisonment. In May 1909 she stayed with the BLATHWAYTS at Batheaston and, having been a prisoner, was entitled to plant a tree in "Annie's Arboretum". On another visit in August she had her first riding lesson. On this occasion two of her sisters, Kitty and Jenny, came over from Bristol to meet the Blathwayts. Jenny was later to spend a considerable period of time at Eagle House, convalescing from one operation before another was actually carried out on her there. In early 1910 Jessie Kenney was taken on holiday to Switzerland by Emmeline Pethick-Lawrence. On her return she carried on working at Clement's Inn. In October 1910 she was WSPU organizer at the Walthamstow and in May 1912 at the South Hackney by-election. In early 1913 she was sent to Switzerland with what was called at the time "a breakdown" but which Mary Blathwayt identifies as a threatening lung condition. Christabel Pankhurst in *Unshackled* recorded that it was because she was ill that Jessie Kenney failed to dispose of papers found in the flat she shared with Annie that incriminated Edwy CLAYTON in the WSPU arson campaign. She was in Switzerland for about four months and then in early 1914 went to live with Christabel in Paris, where she was known as "Constance Burrows". From May to August she travelled every week to Glasgow, where she was known as "Mary Fordyce", in order to see the *Suffragette* through the press in the cellar where it was printed. Christabel had ascertained that the government could not take action against a private printer in Scotland. For security Jessie Kenney posted Christabel's copy for the next week's paper at a post box near the Gare du Nord before setting out on her weekly journey. Jessie Kenney, like her sisters, remained loyal to the Pankhursts during the First World War. She went to the USA in 1915 to prepare the way there for Mrs Pankhurst's Serbian Mission. In 1916, back in London, she helped organize the July War-Work Procession, and in 1917 went to Russia with Mrs Pankhurst for three or four months, meeting Kerensky and other leading members of the Duma, reviewing women battalions, and talking to women in the factories. The typescript diary of her Russian visit, *The Price of Liberty*, is now in the Fawcett Library. Jessie Kenney wrote that throughout the war 10 Downing Street was open to the nucleus of the WSPU, "Yet we gained nothing by our patriotism. No money, no lasting position. By Armistice we were tired out, no homes, no jobs, no money, no cause. Forgotten." In 1919 Jessie Kenney was listed as the honorary parliamentary secretary of the WOMEN'S PARTY, as the WSPU was renamed.

After the war Jessie Kenney lived in St Cloud for a time, working in Paris for the American Red Cross. She became the first woman to qualify as a ship's Radio Officer (1st class certificate in wireless operating) but, being a woman, was not allowed to practise. In the 1930s she travelled all over the world, working as a steward on cruise liners. She joined the Rosicrucian Order in 1923, introduced by Annie, and was ensured a warm welcome from members of the Order when she landed in Australia or America. Until 1940 she was based, when in England, in Letchworth with Annie and her family. By 1947 Jessie Kenney was actively involved with the London chapter of the Rosicrucians and in 1958 became Master of the Francis Bacon Chapter in London and is remembered as being quiet and unassuming. After the Second World War she became administrative secretary, in Battersea, of one of London's first comprehensive schools.

Address: (1913) 19 Mecklenburgh Square, London WC; (1969) 49 Larkhall Rise, London SW4.

Photograph: Suffragette Fellowship Collection, Museum of London.
Archival source: Suffragette Fellowship Collection, Museum of London.

KENSAL RISE (WSPU)   Secretary (1906) Mrs Louie CULLEN, 1 Halstow Road, Kensal Green, London W.

KENSINGTON branch of the NEW CONSTITUTIONAL SOCIETY FOR WOMEN'S SUFFRAGE   Organizer (1913) Mrs Tite, 26 Bolton Gardens, Kensington, London W.

KENSINGTON branch of the UNITED SUFFRAGISTS   Formed in May 1915. Honorary secretary was first given as Mary RICHARDSON, but her name was quickly superseded by that of Miss Postlethwaite, erstwhile secretary of the Kensington WSPU. The branch opened an office and shop at 47 Earl's Court Road, London SW.

KENSINGTON (WFL)   Secretary (1913) Miss Reeves, 16 Bracewell Road, North Kensington, London W.

KENSINGTON (WSPU)   Secretary (1906) Mrs Louise EATES; (1911) Evelyn SHARP, 24 Mount Carmel Chambers, Duke's Lane, Kensington; (until July 1913) Miss Postlethwaite, 143 Church Street, Kensington, London W, which was the address of the WSPU shop and office. In July 1913 there was a rupture in the society, which had been co-operating with Sylvia PANKHURST's work in the East End of London. Many long-established committee members, such as Dr Louisa Garrett ANDERSON, Barbara WYLIE and Miss Postlethwaite resigned to be replaced by Sylvia Pankhurst, who was for a short time honorary secretary, before handing over to Elsa Dalglish. Among those co-opted were Norah Smyth and one of the Miss LOWYs. From the known affiliations of the various personalities, it would appear that the cause of the dissension might have been the close association being fostered between the East End branches and socialist organizations and the consequent impending breach with WSPU headquarters.

The Kensington BANNER, designed by Laurence HOUSMAN for the 21 June 1908 Hyde Park demonstration, and worked by members of the branch, showed the symbolic figure of Woman with broken fetters in her hand, and the words "From Prison to Citizenship". The figure is in white on a purple ground, across which are trailing green leaves, thereby using the WSPU colours devised by Emmeline PETHICK-LAWRENCE for the occasion of that demonstration.

KENSINGTON (NORTH) (branch of the LONDON SOCIETY FOR WOMEN'S SUFFRAGE, NUWSS)   Secretary (1909) Miss F. Gladys WRIGHT, 10 Linden Gardens, London W; (1913) Miss Ruth Franklin (see Hugh FRANKLIN), 32 Hyde Park Gardens, London W.

KENSINGTON (SOUTH) (branch of the LONDON SOCIETY FOR WOMEN'S SUFFRAGE, NUWSS)   Secretary (1909) Miss G. Bompas, 4 Phillimore Gardens, London W; (1913) Miss Boyd.

KENSINGTON SOCIETY   Something of a novelty when it was formed in 1865 with the objective of meeting informally to discuss all subjects related to the position of women. At its core was the group of women who had pressed for the local educational examinations to be opened to girls. The name of the society derived simply from the fact that its president, Mrs Charlotte Manning, lived in Kensington, at 44 Phillimore Gardens. The managing committee also included Isa CRAIG and Emily DAVIES, who was the secretary. Among the members of the society were Barbara BODICHON, Helen TAYLOR, Jessie BOUCHERETT, Elizabeth Garrett (see Elizabeth Garrett ANDERSON), Louisa SMITH, Alice WESTLAKE, Katherine HARE, Harriet COOK and Mme RONNIGER. Elizabeth Wolstenholme (see Elizabeth Wolstenholme ELMY), living in Manchester, was a corresponding member. In a letter to Harriet McILQUHAM of 31 October 1905, occasioned by the death of Jessie Boucherett, she reminisced, "I first met her at Mrs Manning's, at a meeting of the Kensington Society (the first Women's Debating Society in England).... It was really a London Society, but admitted two or three country members – besides Jessie and myself. We were seldom at the meetings, for she never lived in London, only coming for a few days or weeks at a time, but all papers were sent to us." Members of the society did not necessarily know each other before they were invited to join. In her letter of invitation of 18 March 1865, Alice Westlake wrote to Helen Taylor that "none but intellectual women are admitted and therefore it is not likely to become a merely puerile and gossipping Society, and the questions which will probably be asked will be some of those, I think which you have especially studied". Alice Westlake gave Helen Taylor more information in a letter of 28 March writing, "there are very few of the members whom you will know by name... the object of the Society is chiefly to serve as a sort of link, though a slight one, between persons, above the average of thoughtfulness and intelligence who are interested in common subjects, but who had not many opportunities of mutual intercourse". Women's suffrage was sufficiently high on the agenda for it to be the subject discussed at the society's second meeting, held on 21 November 1865. The question was, "Is the extension of the Parliamentary suffrage to women desirable, and if so, under what conditions?" and both Barbara Bodichon and Helen Taylor sent in a paper on the subject. Of Barbara Bodichon's paper Emily Davies remarked, "there are 2 or 3 expressions she would like to have altered e.g. I don't think it quite does to call the arguments on the other side 'foolish'. Of course they *are*, but it does not seem quite polite to say so." The resolution was carried by a large majority.

A year later, on 26 November 1866, Emily Davies reported in a letter to Helen Taylor that because the Mannings were in ill health and Mrs Knox (Isa Craig) was unable to work they had decided "to let the Kensington Society go to sleep for a little while. We shall not hold any discussions at present, and the new set of questions will not be [ready?] until after Christmas. By that time I hope we may be able to resume work, having simply skipped a term." The society did continue until March 1868. Emily Davies sent Helen Taylor a question for discussion on 22 January 1868, telling her that it would be the last because "I find it very difficult to spare the time for the Secretary's work, which owing to the universal forgetfulness and inaccuracy of mankind, is much more burdensome than might have been expected, and the Society does not seem now to be so much wanted as when we began. During the last 3 years, the Suffrage Committees, Schoolmistresses' Associations and other organizations, have come into existence, which supply links between our members and also consume their time and energy, so that they have less to spare for writing papers".

There can be no doubt that the Kensington Society proved a catalyst for the birth of the suffrage movement. Most of the members of the society were not only themselves signatories to the petition presented to parliament by J.S. MILL on 7 June 1866 but also organized the canvassing of friends and relations, spinning a web of connections across the country, that resulted in the creditable total of 1499 women's signatures achieved in under a month.

Archival source: Membership list of the Kensington Society, Fawcett Library; Mill–Taylor Papers, London School of Economics and Political Science; Elizabeth Wolstenholme Elmy Papers, British Library.

KENTISH FEDERATION OF THE NATIONAL UNION OF WOMEN'S SUFFRAGE SOCIETIES
Honorary secretary (1912) Dr Brunyate, 4 Effingham Crescent, Dover, Kent.

KER, ALICE J., DR (1853–1943) Unitarian, eldest of nine children of Edward Stewart Ker, a Free Church minister in Banffshire, she qualified as a doctor as a licentiate of the King's and Queen's College of Physicians, Dublin, and was the thirteenth woman to be included on the British Medical Register. She was a niece of Flora and Louisa STEVENSON, who paid for her to spend a year studying medicine at Berne University. Her younger sister Margaret Stewart Ker, while a student at GIRTON was very friendly with Hertha AYRTON and from 1904 to 1913 was a member of Glasgow Parish Council. In 1883 Alice Ker was medical officer at the Mill Street Dispensary in Leeds and in 1888 married her cousin Edward Ker, settled in Birkenhead, had two daughters and became a general medical practitioner and was honorary physician to the Wirral Hospital for Sick Children. In 1891 she published *Motherhood: A Book for Every Woman*. She was a supporter of the Temperance movement and of the Society for the Prevention of Cruelty to Animals, and by 1893 was an active member of the BIRKENHEAD AND WIRRAL WOMEN'S SUFFRAGE SOCIETY, becoming its chairman. Her husband died in 1907 and by 1909, when she took part in the reception of Patricia Woodlock after her release from Walton Gaol, Alice Ker, with her daughter Margaret (b. 1892), had become involved with the local WOMEN'S SOCIAL AND POLITICAL UNION. Henceforward Alice Ker dropped her association with the suffragist society. In November 1909 Lady Constance LYTTON stayed with Alice Ker when she came to speak in Liverpool and did so again in January 1910 the day before she was arrested as "Jane Warton". Alice Ker took an active part in propaganda work for the WSPU in Liverpool and came to London in June 1911 to take part in the suffrage Coronation Procession. She was back again in London in November and observed the militancy that ensued from the "torpedoing" of the Conciliation Bill. In March 1912 she returned to London, coming this time especially to break Harrods' windows as part of the WSPU militancy campaign. She was sentenced to three months' imprisonment in Holloway, but was released early, on 10 May, having either become ill or after having been forcibly fed. As a doctor she soon afterwards protested against forcible feeding, although she does not actually mention that she herself was so treated. She stated that the procedure was used as punishment not, as claimed, as medical treatment, and she complained of the inadequacy or total lack of sterilization of the equipment used. While in Holloway she was visited by the Unitarian chaplain, Frederick HANKINSON. In April 1911 she had joined the THEOSOPHICAL SOCIETY, sponsored by Lisa Ker. Alice Ker wrote a poem for *Holloway Jingles*, the collection of work by women who had been together in Holloway that was published by the Glasgow branch of the WSPU later in 1912 or in 1913.

On her release from prison Alice Ker faced the distinct possibility, because of her imprisonment, of losing patients. The Birkenhead Rescue Home, to which she was honorary physician, asked her to resign, but she refused. She continued to work for the WSPU, moving from Birkenhead to Liverpool in 1914, and acting as hostess for Sylvia Pankhurst when in 1916 she came there to speak at a conference on women and sweated labour. In 1916 Dr Ker moved to London, and was still in practice, in Golders Green, in 1923. Her younger daughter Mary was a student at Girton, 1915–18. Alice Ker's elder daughter Margaret, a student at Liverpool University, joined the WSPU with her mother in 1909 and in October 1912 was caught setting fire to a pillar box in Liverpool. She was sentenced to three months' imprisonment and was threatened with expulsion from the university. After the intervention of the vice-chancellor she was allowed to continue her studies, although she lost a bursary worth £30 a year from the Birkenhead Education Society. She worked in the War Office during the First World War and was a member of the Theosophical Society and the Women's International League for Peace and Freedom.

Address: (1897) 44 Grange Mount, Birkenhead, Liverpool; (1903) 6 Devonshire Road, Birkenhead; (1912) "Skene House", 6 James Street, Birkenhead; (1943) 28 Hill Top, Finchley, London N.
Photograph: in M. Van Helmond, *Votes for Women: The Events on Merseyside 1870–1928*, 1992.
Bibliography: M. Van Helmond, *Votes for Women: The Events on Merseyside 1870–1928*, 1992.

KERR, HARRIET ROBERTA (1859–1940) Born at West Ham, the daughter of an architect, "of whom", as Sylvia Pankhurst put it in *The Suffragette Movement*, "she had forgotten all save his acerbity, the memory of which, reaching down from her youth, had predisposed her to be a suffragette". He had been, in fact, professor of Architecture at King's College, London, and the author of *The English Gentleman's House*, 1864. This latter, the acme of Victorian house design, lays great stress on the gender of space. The dining room is masculine, the drawing room "to be entirely ladylike", "a Boudoir", "which may be somewhat retired in situation", should be provided for "the lady of the house", and separate cloak-rooms "for ladies and gentlemen" are to be provided "for the use of company". These should not be placed opposite each other in the entrance hall, "an error, as respects both good taste and convenience"; the "Ladies' Cloak-room ought to open from within the family boundary" whereas the gentlemens' should be near the entrance. Kerr also made clear that "the main part of the house must be relieved from the more immediate occupation of the Children". Harriet Kerr was five years old when this work was published; presumably her father put his preaching into practice. Neither does she appear to have been made for life in the boudoir. When interviewed in 1974, Cecily Hale remembered Harriet Kerr as "a bit masculine", very downright, a very good organizer, and with a good sense of humour. In 1908 Harriet Kerr ran a business as a "typewriter" in the City, listed as such in the London Commercial Directory, although the biography compiled for the Suffragette Fellowship Collection recounts how in September 1906, at the suggestion of the PETHICK-LAWRENCES, whom she knew through E.V. Lucas, she gave up her own secretarial business and became general manager of the office newly established at the WOMEN'S SOCIAL AND POLITICAL UNION headquarters in Clement's Inn.

It was Harriet Kerr who selected the quotes from Shelley that embellish the WSPU 1909 calendar. In 1908 she appeared at the head of a march, a photograph of which was captioned by the World's Graphic Press as "Miss Kerr leads suffragette march". All the women are in prison dress although Harriet Kerr had not by then been to prison. She carries a purple, white and green flag. She later stated that she "never desired or intended to go to prison for the Cause and could never have made up my mind to be militant". However, by 1912, as militancy increased she "could not desert WSPU in its hour of need – Mrs PANKHURST in prison, Mrs TUKE ill and on a voyage to South Africa – and Christabel in Paris". Still at her post, she was arrested with the other heads of the WSPU departments at Lincoln's Inn House on 30 April 1913 and charged with conspiracy to cause damage to property. She was found guilty and sentenced in June to 12 months' imprisonment, to be followed by 12 months' police supervision. She was sent to Holloway, went on hunger strike and was released on the eighth day under the "Cat and Mouse" Act. She then visited Christabel in Paris to discuss plans for the WSPU Summer Festival which was held in June. A petition to the Home Secretary on her behalf, organized at the Lyceum Club (see under CLUBS), was signed in July by, among others, Marie Belloc Lowndes, E.V. Lucas, H.W. Massingham, Eva Moore, William de Morgan and G.B. Shaw. She was re-arrested, after a struggle, outside the WSPU offices in Kingsway in October, went on hunger strike and was again released. She recounted how she then found the "friend with whom she had lived for 16 years 'broken down in health'" and was allowed by the police to take her to the country. After five weeks she was recalled to Holloway but, because her friend was incapacitated, Mrs Pankhurst and Christabel allowed her to give an undertaking never again to be involved in militancy and so secured her freedom. After her release she stayed first with Janie TERRERO in Pinner and then at a cottage on the Misses BECKS' farm at Billingshurst. She then retired from the WSPU and the suffrage cause, although in 1928 she was treasurer, and collector, of a fund to raise money to support Emmeline Pankhurst in her last illness. She left her entire estate to her niece.

Address: (1908) 13 Copthall Ave., London EC; (1913) Hook Cottage, Duncans Farm, Billingshurst, Sussex; (1929) 73 Fellowes Road, London NW; (1937) 41 Mall Chambers, Kensington, London W8; (1940) Rowlands Castle, Hampshire.
Photograph: Suffragette Fellowship Collection, Museum of London.
Archival source: Suffragette Fellowship Collection, Museum of London; B. Harrison, taped interview with Cicely Hale, 1974, Fawcett Library.
Bibliography: R. Kerr, *The Gentleman's House; or, How to Plan English Residences from the Parsonage to the Palace*, 1864.

KESWICK branch of the MEN'S LEAGUE FOR WOMEN'S SUFFRAGE Founded in January 1909 at a meeting chaired by Frank Marshall, father of Catherine MARSHALL.

KESWICK (NUWSS) Founded in May 1908 by Catherine MARSHALL and her mother Mrs Caroline Marshall; at the end of its first year it had 250 members. In 1913 the society was a member of the NORTH-WESTERN FEDERATION OF THE NATIONAL UNION OF WOMEN'S SUFFRAGE SOCIETIES. Secretary (1909) Miss Broatch, Allison House, Keswick, Cumberland; (1913) Miss Knight, 123 Main Street, Keswick and Mrs Marshall, Hawse End, Keswick, Cumberland.

KETTERING (NUWSS) In 1913 the society was a member of the MIDLANDS (EAST) FEDERATION OF THE NATIONAL UNION OF WOMEN'S SUFFRAGE SOCIETIES. Secretary (1913) Miss Plumbridge, 53 St Peter's Avenue, Kettering, Northamptonshire.

KIDDERMINSTER (NUWSS)   In 1913 the society was a member of the MIDLANDS (WEST) FEDERATION OF THE NATIONAL UNION OF WOMEN'S SUFFRAGE SOCIETIES. Secretary (1913) Mrs Ellis Talbot, Summermount, Kidderminster, Worcestershire.

KIDWELLY AND FERRYSIDE (NUWSS)   In 1913 the society was a member of the SOUTH WALES AND MONMOUTH FEDERATION OF THE NATIONAL UNION OF WOMEN'S SUFFRAGE SOCIETIES. Secretary (1913) Miss E.M. Meredith, Brynhyfryd, Kidwelly, Wales.

KILMALCOLM (NUWSS)   In 1913 the society was a member of the SCOTTISH FEDERATION OF THE NATIONAL UNION OF WOMEN'S SUFFRAGE SOCIETIES. Secretary (1909, 1913) Mrs Wood, Barclaven, Kilmalcolm, Renfrewshire.

KILMARNOCK (WFL)   Secretary (1913) Miss J.L. Waddell, 8 Douglas Street, Kilmarnock, Ayrshire.

KING'S LYNN a committee of the LONDON NATIONAL SOCIETY FOR WOMEN'S SUFFRAGE   Founded in 1871 when the secretary was Miss S.A. Pung of North Wootton. In 1872 the society associated itself with the new CENTRAL COMMITTEE OF THE NATIONAL SOCIETY FOR WOMEN'S SUFFRAGE. King's Lynn and District society was by 1913 a member of the EASTERN COUNTIES FEDERATION OF THE NATIONAL UNION OF WOMEN'S SUFFRAGE SOCIETIES. Secretary (1913) Miss Hovell, 21 Guanock Terrace, King's Lynn, Norfolk.

KING'S SUTTON (NUWSS)   In 1913 the society was a member of the OXON, BERKS, BUCKS, AND BEDS FEDERATION OF THE NATIONAL UNION OF WOMEN'S SUFFRAGE SOCIETIES. Joint secretaries (1913) Miss D. Browne, Greycourt, Astrop, Banbury, and Miss Harman, King's Sutton, Banbury, Oxfordshire.

KINGSTON-ON-THAMES (WSPU)   Secretary (1913) Mrs Dacre Fox, 3 The Parade, Claygate, Surrey.

KINGSTON AND SURBITON (branch of the LONDON SOCIETY FOR WOMEN'S SUFFRAGE, NUWSS) Secretary (1909) Miss V.G. Handley, The Limes, Kingston-on-Thames, Surrey; (1913) Miss Fanner, Melrose, Angelsea Road, Kingston-on-Thames, Surrey.

KINROSS (NUWSS)   In 1913 the society was a member of the SCOTTISH FEDERATION OF THE NATIONAL UNION OF WOMEN'S SUFFRAGE SOCIETIES. Secretary (1913) Miss Elizabeth Ross, Restenet, Kinross, Kinrossshire.

KIRKCALDY committee of the NATIONAL SOCIETY FOR WOMEN'S SUFFRAGE   Formed in 1872. In 1913 the society was a member of the SCOTTISH FEDERATION OF THE NATIONAL UNION OF WOMEN'S SUFFRAGE SOCIETIES. Secretary (1913) Mrs Honeyman, Sauchendene, Kirkcaldy, Fife.

KIRKINTILLOCH (WFL)   Secretary (1913) Miss McIntyre, Woodhead Avenue, Kirkintilloch, Dunbartonshire.

KIRKWALL committee of the EDINBURGH SOCIETY FOR WOMEN SUFFRAGE   Founded in 1871 as a result of the speaking tour undertaken by Agnes MCLAREN and Jane TAYLOUR. Its convenor was Mr Walls.

KNEBWORTH (WSPU)   Secretary (1913) Miss Avery, The School House, Knebworth, Hertfordshire.

KNIGHT, ADELAIDE ELIZA, MRS (1871–?)   Born in Bethnal Green, severely crippled in childhood, she spent much time in hospital, read and studied, and developed a love of elocution, poetry, music and history. In *Memories of a Militant*, Annie KENNEY described her as "extraordinarily clever". She was a keen supporter of the Temperance movement; her alcoholic father, a hairdresser, committed suicide. In 1894, at the parish church of Ramsay in Essex, she married a black seaman, a quartermaster, Donald Adolphus Brown. Most unusually for the time he adopted her surname "Knight" for general use (this is his name as it appears on their marriage certificate) although he kept his original name when at sea. She and her husband were very idealistic, longing to remedy the social ills that surrounded them. They joined first the Social Democratic Federation and then the Independent Labour Party. In 1906 Mrs Knight was a member of the CANNING TOWN branch of the WOMEN'S SOCIAL AND POLITICAL UNION, first as literature secretary and later as secretary. On 21 June she was arrested, with Annie Kenney, Mrs SBARBORO and Teresa Billington (*see* Teresa BILLINGTON-GREIG), while taking part in a deputation to Asquith's house in Cavendish Square. She was charged with disturbing the peace and, having refused to be bound over, was sent to Holloway for six weeks. She wrote from there to her husband, "equal taxation demands equal representation, and I am determined to continue the fight for progress" and that she sang the "Red Flag" night and morning. Her husband looked after their children, of whom the youngest was under two years old at the time. In *From a Victorian to a Modern*, Dora MONTEFIORE wrote that when Mrs Knight went to prison, it was a far worse experience for East End women than for their West End sisters. In the East End neighbours "had no notion of the idealism which inspired all of us militant women and they were only too ready with gibe and pointed finger to point out the 'jail birds' or to persecute the children of these women".

Dora Montefiore was very protective of her associates in Canning Town and on 15 December 1906, herself disillusioned with both the NATIONAL UNION OF WOMEN'S SUFFRAGE SOCIETIES and the WSPU, wrote to Mrs Knight:

> If the working women remain sound I do not mind; but my dear friend I greatly fear the working women are being betrayed. I want you, who are leader among them, and have good judgement to understand the position . . . the Tories . . . will only give the franchise to *women who will pay taxes directly*, they will *not* give it on the same terms as men now exercise it. The Tory women know this and that is why they are hastening to banquet and flatter the women who have "pulled the chestnuts out of the fire" for them . . . From the moment those women from the old Suffrage Society began to patronise you I knew that there was trouble ahead. I have worked with them in the past and know their methods and have denounced them. It was perhaps foolish to believe that the W.S. & Pol. Union was *really* democratic, but is governed by a clique, and that clique will allow no inside criticism, so that any one that criticises, even in the best spirit, must go.

Mrs Montefiore was astute in her analysis and Mrs Knight, whether influenced by this or having made her own observations, clearly became suspicious of the WSPU.

P. Hodgson wrote from Clement's Inn to Mrs Knight on 15 March 1907 to say that the WSPU would gladly pay the fares of 20 to 30 East End women (a 30/– postal order was sent) in order that they might take part in the deputation to the House of Commons from the second Women's Parliament in Caxton Hall on 20 March. She added that the WSPU realized that working women could not afford to be arrested. Mrs Knight reported to her branch that Clement's Inn had asked women from the East End to keep in the background, and interpreted this as a comment on the fact that the branch did not pay an affiliation fee. She resigned as secretary of the Canning Town branch on 26 March 1907. The next week the members did give a vote of confidence to Minnie Baldock, but shortly afterwards must have expressed dissatisfaction with the lack of democracy in the WSPU and wrote to Keir HARDIE to ask for his support in their demands for a more democratic organization. Christabel PANKHURST then visited the branch and is reputed to have said that she was present when Keir Hardie read the letter and that he had "wept bitter tears when he saw how misguided you poor souls were". Mrs Knight, who clearly had an eye for hypocrisy, described how she was able to produce the letter written to Keir Hardie, still in its sealed and unfranked envelope. A cousin, entrusted to post it, had forgotten to do so. However, the minutes of the Canning Town branch do not record any visit by Christabel Pankhurst at this time, or, indeed, at any time since 16 October 1906.

After leaving the WSPU, Mrs Knight maintained her contact with the SDF and Dora Montefiore, whom in 1908 she showed around homes in Canning Town in order to highlight the plight of sweated workers. In the same year Dora Montefiore took Mrs Knight to Paris to address French suffragists. From 1908 to 1910 Mrs Knight served on the West Ham Board of Guardians. In March 1909 she was forced by ill health to resign from the secretaryship of the Canning Town branch of the Adult Suffrage Society, of which Dora Montefiore was then general secretary. In 1920 Adelaide Knight, with Dora Montefiore, became a foundation member of the Communist Party of Great Britain.

Address: (1906) New City Road, Plaistow, London E.
Archival source: biographical notes on Mrs Knight by her daughter in Museum of London.

KNIGHT, ANNE (1786–1862) Quaker, born in Chelmsford, daughter of a prosperous grocer, by 1824 she had travelled widely in Europe and by 1830 was involved in the anti-slavery campaign. She was a friend of Elizabeth Pease (see Elizabeth Pease NICHOLL) and of Julia Smith, aunt of Barbara Leigh Smith BODICHON. Anne Knight was present at the World Anti-Slavery Convention held in London in 1840 and there met Lucretia Mott, who described her as "a singular-looking woman – very pleasant and polite". The exclusion of women from the proceedings prompted Anne Knight, as it did the other women involved, to work seriously for women's rights. She had doubtless met at the Convention Mrs Hugo REID and when it was published by William Tait in Edinburgh in 1843, acquired a copy of *A Plea for Woman* that is now in the Friends' Library. She annotated the title page thus: under the title she wrote "excellent with the exception of a great folly at page 146 – some other pages noted". The "great folly" was the suggestion that women would not wish to sit as representatives in parliament, although, if they did wish so, no artificial barriers should be set in their way. Anne Knight, in lengthy marginal annotations, refutes this: "What natural barriers? She has none but those placed equally before men. How stupid these sentimentalisms!" A pressed daisy lies in this page. Her copy of the book is extended by extra tracts and exhortations. Under the motto on the title page, "Can man be free, if woman be a slave?" she has written "No! Emancipate them!" Anne Knight took an active part in the Anti-Corn Law League and with Elizabeth Pease was a supporter of the Peace Movement. According to Elizabeth MALLESON, Anne Knight issued leaflets on the subject of peace in 1847. In 1848 she was a contributor to *La Voix des Femmes*, a journal influenced by the revolution in France, which called for women to be recognized as citizens. She attended the 1849 peace congress in Paris and on 13 August 1850 wrote a memorable letter to "Richard Cobden M.P." in which she protested "let us not be urged to prick our fingers to the bone in '*sewing circles*' for vanity fair, peace bazaars ... amassing names for petitions to men". She thought that the influence of women, if they were enfranchised, would bring about peace. She asked to attend the 1851 peace congress as a delegate, with a voice, but was refused; women did not speak in public, despite the tradition of preaching amongst women Quakers.

In 1847 Anne Knight was in correspondence with Matilda Ashurst BIGGS, writing to her that "I wish that talented philanthropists in England would come forward in this critical juncture of our nation's affairs and insist on the right of suffrage for all men and women unstained by crime". In the autumn of 1851 she spoke in Edinburgh and Glasgow advocating universal suffrage and urging that a memorial should be sent to Lord John Russell, calling upon him to grant equality of political rights in the proposed Reform Bill. That year she helped to form the SHEFFIELD FEMALE POLITICAL ASSOCIATION, based at 84 Pond Street, which published an "Address to the Women of England", the first demanding women's suffrage, and followed this with a petition to the House of Lords. In 1852 she was a member of the Women's Elevation League based in Camden Town, the object of which was the "Social, Moral, Professional, Pecuniary, Political Elevation of Women". In *Letter to Robert Bartlett, 8mo, 6 1852*, published by Johnson & Co., she invoked the age-old cry of "Taxation without Representation being tyranny" in respect of being "forbidden to vote for the man who inflicts the laws I am compelled to obey – the taxes I am compelled to pay". Anne Knight's manuscript book containing articles, predominately on the rights of women, written both by her (some in code) and by others, is now in the Friends' Library.

For much of the last 20 years of her life Anne Knight lived in France, moving in the last two years to Waldersbach, a village to the south-west of Strasbourg. Like all radicals of her day she took a keen interest in the politics of Italy, always able to draw lessons from the situation there that might be applied to the position of women. In a letter to her brother, 23 November 1860, she commented on the fact that Victor Emmanuel had been voted for by women "& if they vote for a King what thinken thou of the case of refusing the right of voting for a legislator?" She was dead by the time the suffrage movement in Britain began seriously to organize itself. One letter, preserved among her papers, bridges the gulf between the pre- and post-1866 worlds. It is addressed to Anne Knight from Lydia BECKER, dated 31 January 1868 and, sent as it was uninvited, gives us an idea of how the founders of the suffrage movement attempted to recruit members. Lydia Becker wrote, "Having heard from Mr Goodwyn BARMBY of Wakefield that you take an interest in the question of women's suffrage, I send you a circular of our Society and hope you will be willing to join us on the terms indicated". Anne Knight had been in contact with Barmby and his first wife, Catherine, but he had obviously lost touch with her and had not known that she had died.

Address: (1840) Quiet House, Chelmsford, Essex.
Portrait: as part of the group in *The Great Meeting of Delegates, held at the Freemasons Tavern, June 1840, for the abolition of slavery and the slave trade throughout the world,* painting by Benjamin Robert Haydon in the National Portrait Gallery.
Photograph: of Anne Knight, bearing a placard, "By tortured millions/ By our Divine redeemer/ Enfranchise Humanity/ Bid the Outraged World/ BE FREE", taken in Paris, in Fawcett Library.
Archival source: Anne Knight Papers, Friends' Library; Essex County Record Office; John Johnson Collection, Bodleian Library, Oxford.
Bibliography: F.B. Tolles (ed.), *Slavery and "The Woman Question": Lucretia Mott's Diary, 1840,* 1952; C. Midgley, *Women Against Slavery: The British campaigns 1780–1870,* 1992.

KNIGHT, ELIZABETH, DR (1869–1933) Quaker, born at Northfleet, Kent, educated at Kensington High School and Newnham, 1888–91, where she read classics but did not take a degree. From 1892 to 1904 she trained at the London School of Medicine for Women at the same time as Louisa Garrett ANDERSON. She practised medicine in London from 1904 until her death, with a brief interlude, 1912–13, when she returned to Cambridge to study for the Diploma in Public Health. She was introduced to the WOMEN'S FREEDOM LEAGUE by Octavia LEWIN and by 1913 was its honorary treasurer, remaining so until her death. As usual in such societies the treasureship went to one who was considered able to make up, if necessary, any shortfall in the accounts. Elizabeth Knight had inherited a sizeable fortune from her father, a cement manufacturer, partner in the firm of Knight, Bevan, and Sturge, who had died in 1880. Elizabeth Knight was imprisoned in 1908 after calling at 10 Downing Street to ask Asquith why he had promised manhood suffrage in answer to a demand for votes for women. As a result of this experience she wrote in 1908 *Social and Sanitary Conditions of Prison Life.* She took an active part in the 1911 Census Protest, was prosecuted on several occasions for refusing to pay taxes, and was twice imprisoned. In January 1913 she was, with Charlotte DESPARD, arrested while leading a march to Westminster, protesting against the Speaker's ruling that a women's suffrage amendment to the proposed franchise bill was inadmissable.

During the First World War Elizabeth Knight opposed the 40D Regulation, which involved the compulsory examination of women suspected of having transmitted venereal disease to a member of the Forces. In 1923 she attended the conference of the International Alliance of Women for Suffrage and Equal Citizenship in Paris. In 1920 she helped to found the Minerva Club (*see under* CLUBS) and supported it financially during her lifetime. In 1926 she ran the press and publicity campaign for the EQUAL POLITICAL RIGHTS CAMPAIGN COMMITTEE, working to equalize the franchise. She had an adopted daughter, Elsie Glover Knight. In her will, although she left no money to the Women's Freedom League, or to the Minerva Club, or to the *Vote,* which she had heavily subsidized, she did leave £3000 to Florence Underwood, who had been secretary of the WFL. After being injured in a street accident in Brighton, Dr Knight died at the home of Minnie TURNER, who was a sufficiently close friend to be appointed administrator of a small trust set up for a relative in Dr Knight's will.

Address: (1933) 7 Gainsborough Gardens, Hampstead, London NW.
Bibliography: S. Newsome, *The Women's Freedom League, 1907–1957,* 1957.

KNIGHTLEY OF FAWSLEY, LOUISA MARY, LADY (1842–1913) Daughter of Sir Edward Bowater, she was a cousin of Jessie BOUCHERETT, and in 1869 married Sir Rainald Knightley, who in 1892 was created a baron. She was on the committee of the Society for Promoting the Employment of Women

from 1875 to 1902, was a member of the general committee of the CENTRAL SOCIETY FOR WOMEN'S SUFFRAGE in 1893 and was the first president of the CONSERVATIVE AND UNIONIST WOMEN'S FRANCHISE ASSOCIATION. In 1896 she was a member of the SPECIAL APPEAL COMMITTEE and in 1906 of the WOMEN'S FRANCHISE DECLARATION COMMITTEE. Her pamphlets include *Woman and the Vote*, published by the CUWFA.
Address: Fawsley Park, Daventry.

KNUTSFORD (NUWSS) Formed in 1907 and in 1910 joined the MANCHESTER AND DISTRICT FEDERATION OF THE NATIONAL UNION OF WOMEN'S SUFFRAGE SOCIETIES. Secretary (1909) Mrs Helena SWANWICK, Annandale, Knutsford and Miss D. Hoffman, Hazelhurst, Knutsford, Cheshire; (1913) Miss D. Hoffman.

KYLLMANN, PHILIPPINE, MRS (*c.* 1834–1916) Signed the 1866 women's suffrage petition. Philippine Baret, who was probably French, married in 1864 Max Kyllmann, a wealthy young German who had settled in Manchester. Louis BORCHARDT was one of the witnesses to the wedding, which was conducted in the Registrar Office in Chorlton. After their marriage the Kyllmanns moved into Barcombe Cottage, the house in Fallowfield that Alfred Waterhouse, soon to be architect of Manchester Town Hall and Girton College had built for himself in 1858. Kyllmann was interested in co-operative matters and George HOLYOAKE stayed with him while lecturing in Manchester in 1863 and was introduced to E.O. Greening. Kyllmann provided the capital for a mill established in Manchester by Holyoake and Greening on a profit-sharing basis; the mill quickly failed. Max and Philippine Kyllmann were members of the first committee working for women's suffrage, which was founded in Manchester in October 1865, and Max Kyllmann was one of those present on 11 January 1867 at the meeting at which the MANCHESTER SOCIETY FOR WOMEN'S SUFFRAGE was refounded. Max Kyllmann died, aged 34, in May 1867. There was a rumour that he had committed suicide, but Katherine HARE wrote that he had suffered from cancer. Lydia BECKER wrote in a letter that he was "liable to brain disease", used to retire to an asylum, and had suffered one of these recurring attacks. Thomas Hare and his daughter Katherine stayed with Philippine for the funeral, in order to comfort her. J.S. MILL wrote both to Hare and to Edward Kyllmann, Max's brother, expressing regret that the critical Reform Bill debates prevented him from attending the funeral. Philippine Kyllmann was left with two young daughters and an uncertain financial position.

After the passing of the Reform Bill it was thought that Lord Romilly's Act, which provided "that all words importing the masculine gender shall be deemed and taken to include females, unless the contrary is expressly provided", might be used to reinterpret an old free-holding franchise (8 Henry VI) which stated that "Elections of knights of the shire shall be made in each county by people dwelling and resident therein of whom each has free-hold to the value of £40 by the year." Philippine Kyllmann, who was in correspondence with Helen TAYLOR, brought a case under this act, which was heard at the Court of Common Pleas on 7 November 1868. The case was argued by Thomas Chorlton, legal adviser to the Manchester Society for Women's Suffrage. He retained as counsel Sir John Coleridge and Dr Richard PANKHURST. The claim was rejected. Helen BLACKBURN in *Record of Women's Suffrage*, 1902, mentions the case but does not name the "lady" who brought it, although she does include "Mrs Max Kyllmann" in her list of "Supporters of the Movement". Philippine Kyllmann did, in fact, resign from the Manchester Society around the time that the case was heard, unable to tolerate Lydia Becker's methods of management. She had been appalled to discover that cheques of £25 and £35 sent to her from Helen Taylor and John Stuart Mill respectively were not, as she had assumed, spontaneous donations towards the costs of bringing her case, but resulted from a direct approach, asking for money, made to them by Lydia Becker. Philippine Kyllmann was mortified and returned the cheques. Helen Taylor did not hide from Mrs Kyllmann her annoyance with Lydia Becker's methods of fund-raising. It was clear that this was not the first time that she and Mill had been so approached and it also emerged that such requests had not beeen authorized by the committee of the Manchester Society. Mrs Kyllmann insisted that Lydia Becker should henceforward not write any letters without the sanction of the committee. Lydia Becker thought that this was an unreasonable requirement and threatened to resign. Philippine Kyllmann, noting that Lydia Becker was supported in everything she did by Ursula BRIGHT, then herself resigned from both the committee and the Manchester Society. She had been sufficiently important to the Society to have chaired its first annual general meeting on 30 October. Because she did not wish her name associated with Lydia Becker in any way she also resigned from the recently founded Married Women's Property Committee. She remained very friendly with Katherine Hare (later Mrs Clayton) and the two families spent a month together at Dieppe in 1888.

Mathilde Kyllmann, married to Max Kyllmann's brother Edward, had also signed the 1866 women's suffrage petition and resigned as treasurer of the Manchester Society in support of Philippine, but remained for a time a member of the Married Women's Property Committee.

Address: (1866) Barcombe Cottage, Fallowfield, Manchester; (1869) Mererela Villa, Parsonage Road, Withington, Manchester; (1905) 52 Stanhope Gardens, Kensington, London W; (1916) Chambon-sur-Vaueize, France.

Archival source: Mill–Taylor Papers, London School of Economics and Political Science.

L

LAMB, AETA ADELAIDE (1886–1928) Born in Demerara, where her father was a botanist; she was named Aeta after a palm he had discovered there. Her father died when she was about five years old and the family returned to England. She educated herself, except for a period when, aged around 12, she spent 18 unhappy months at Notting Hill High School. She joined the WOMEN'S SOCIAL AND POLITICAL UNION in 1906 and as her biographer Vera Douie recorded, "was frightfully thin and looked much older than her 20 years". Vera Douie noted that Aeta Lamb had "the very highest opinion of women and of their ultimate power and capabilities" and that "Being absolutely sexless herself – men for her did not exist – they really did not count. That they were there to do a certain amount of necessary work in the world she admitted but she mostly saw them as Oppressors of Women." Aeta Lamb was remembered as being very eloquent and Mary LEIGH stated that she wrote some of Christabel PANKHURST's speeches. Sylvia PANKHURST in *The Suffragette Movement* described her as "flitt[ing] about like a disembodied spirit; for her paleness and shyness seldom appreciated at her worth".

Aeta Lamb took part in the October 1906 WSPU deputation to the House of Commons and was arrested, but released after her mother paid her fine. Her biographer wrote, "To have faced a Deputation with all its horrors of close personal contact with unspeakable crowds of some 10 000 mostly composed of men of a most undesirable type – must have been a tremendous effort for such a fastidious person as Aeta, who hated to be touched by anyone." Despite her aversion to crowds, Aeta Lamb took part, in February and March 1907 and in October 1908, in two other deputations to the House of Commons. As a result of these she served terms of between one week and a one month in Holloway.

In 1907 Aeta Lamb campaigned for the WSPU, alongside Annie KENNEY, at the North-West Staffordshire by-election and by early 1908 was appointed a WSPU ORGANIZER, under Annie, in Bristol. Her biographer recalled that "she failed utterly to organise". Mrs BLATHWAYT, however, records in her diary that for a WSPU meeting in Bristol, which it was expected that medical students would attempt to disrupt, Aeta Lamb "hired six professional boxers to keep order". This would appear quite a coup for a gently-brought-up middle-class young woman. Aeta Lamb introduced Clara CODD to Annie Kenney and helped Mary Blathwayt to organize, on 1 April, the first WSPU meeting in Bath. At the end of that month she was in Scotland, helping Elsa GYE and Mary GAWTHORPE in the WSPU campaign at the Kincardineshire by-election. She then went on to work at the by-election campaign in Dundee but became ill. She was, however, working in Leeds in June, presumably at the Pudsey by-election. She then returned to London to work at the WSPU headquarters in London, where she remained until the outbreak of war. Although Mrs Blathwayt noted in her diary in November 1912 that "people like Miss Lamb do not at all like Mrs Pankhurst's present policy", Aeta Lamb stayed loyal to the WSPU, giving a small amount of money in 1913. Her final task was to compile a book of names of all the suffrage prisoners; this was removed from Lincoln's Inn House during a police raid and disappeared.

During the First World War Aeta Lamb worked in War Depots and afterwards found it very difficult to find work. Although she learned shorthand and typing, "her low vitality and her inability to adapt herself to new places and uncongenial people proved great obstacles in her way". Her end was sad. Having identified that cooks were always in demand, she borrowed money to take a cookery course, and was eventually told by the principal of the college that she was entirely unsuited to domestic work. Desperate, she then developed cancer, and died in the Elizabeth Garrett Anderson Hospital.

Photograph: in B.M. Willmott Dobbie, *A Nest of Suffragettes in Somerset*, 1979.

Archival source: biography by Vera Douie in The Suffragette Fellowship Collection, Museum of London.

LAMBETH (branch of the LONDON SOCIETY FOR WOMEN'S SUFFRAGE, NUWSS) Secretary (1909) Miss Packer, 65 Brixton Hill, London SW; (1913) Miss Deverell, 49 Hilldrop Road, London N.

LAMPETER (NUWSS) In 1913 the society was a member of the SOUTH WALES AND MONMOUTH FEDERATION OF THE NATIONAL UNION OF WOMEN'S SUFFRAGE SOCIETIES. Secretary (1913) Miss Minnie C. Davies, Velindre House, Lampeter, Wales.

LANCASHIRE AND CHESHIRE WOMEN TEXTILE AND OTHER WORKERS' REPRESENTATION COMMITTEE Formed in summer 1903 by Sarah REDDISH, Selina COOPER, Sarah Dickenson, Esther ROPER and Eva GORE-BOOTH with the aim of sponsoring an election candidate pledged to support women's suffrage. They had been disappointed by the performance in the House of Commons of David Shackleton, the Labour MP for whom they had campaigned at the Clitheroe by-election in 1902. Elizabeth Wolstenholme ELMY was immediately impressed by their circulars and was privy to their deliberations, writing to Harriet McILQUHAM in December 1903, "The Women Textile Workers will ask Balfour to receive a deputation from them. This is private yet, please." Although no deputation appears to have taken place, the committee was obviously prepared to aim high. LCWTOWRC published a manifesto in July 1904 stating that "a Committee has been formed . . . to select a suitable and zealous candidate, and . . . to collect and be responsible for the spending of £500, which is the amount absolutely necessary for one candidate's election expenses". Wigan was chosen as the seat to be contested, a traditionally Tory seat, without the complication of a Labour candidate. At a time of slump in the cotton trade, LCWTOWRC had great difficulty in raising the necessary £500. It had financial support from neither the NORTH OF ENGLAND SOCIETY FOR WOMEN'S SUFFRAGE nor from the Wigan Trades Council. In June 1904 Esther Roper wrote a plea for funds to each of those women who had signed the graduates' petition in 1902. In October 1904, not long after her husband's death, Katherine THOMASSON turned down a request to support LCWTOWRC's work, although money she later gave to Esther Roper and Eva Gore-Booth may well have been used for this cause. Elizabeth Wolstenholme Elmy was prepared to ask W.T. Stead to make an appeal for Funds for them: "As I hold that what is being done amongst the women workers of the North is of more value to our cause than all the work of the N.U. [NATIONAL UNION OF WOMEN'S SUFFRAGE SOCIETIES] put together, and as it works outside the N.U. the latter of course cannot finance, even if they wished to, which they do not." Priscilla Bright McLAREN was impressed by the enthusiasm of the Lancashire women textile workers and some funds may have been channelled through her; LCWTOWRC was represented at her funeral in 1906. In early 1905 a suffrage meeting at the Free Trade Hall in Manchester heard speeches by Sarah Dickenson, Sarah Reddish and Eva Gore-Booth, as well as from Keir HARDIE and Philip Snowden. By 1905 the LCWTOWRC had 29 members and had attracted considerable support from the Women's Co-operative Guilds.

The first LCWTOWRC candidate chosen to contest Wigan was Hubert Sweeney, a London teacher, a barrister in training, with no connection with Wigan. However, shortly before the January 1906 general election Hubert Sweeney withdrew and Thorley Smith, a local councillor and chairman of the local Labour Representation Committee took his place. His election manifesto contained a plea for the enfranchisement of working women. In the event he was defeated by the Conservative candidate, but beat the Liberal into third place. The LCWTOWRC was quite prepared to bring its cause to London. On 21 May 1906 its members, including Sarah Reddish and Selina Cooper, in London to support the delegation to Campbell-Bannerman, joined in a demonstration in Hyde Park with women from the CANNING TOWN branch of the WSPU. Such a rally had been suggested when Eva Gore-Booth and Esther Roper addressed a February meeting in Canning Town. On 3 November 1906 LCWTOWRC was back in London, holding a demonstration jointly with the Manchester and Salford Women's Trade and Labour Council and the CENTRAL SOCIETY FOR WOMEN'S SUFFRAGE, in Trafalgar Square. Among the speakers on this occasion were Sarah Reddish, Sarah Dickenson, Selina Cooper, Eva Gore-Booth and Esther Roper. The LCWTOWRC was back in London in July 1909, holding a meeting at the Queen's Hall. In the January 1910 general election the LCWTOWRC combined with the INDUSTRIAL AND PROFESSIONAL WOMEN'S SUFFRAGE SOCIETY to field a candidate at Rossendale, a staunchly Liberal stronghold, seat of the anti-suffragist Lewis Harcourt. Their candidate, Arthur Bulley, came bottom of the poll. During the course of the general election members of LCWTOWRC also helped the BOLTON WOMEN'S SUFFRAGE SOCIETY gather signatures at polling stations for the petition from men voters. LCWTOWRC was also involved in the struggle to prevent protective legislation removing the livelihood of pit-brow women, working both separately and under the umbrella of the Industrial and Professional Women's Suffrage Society.

Address: (1913) 5 John Dalton Street, Manchester.
Archival source: Papers of Elizabeth Wolstenholme Elmy, British Library.
Bibliography: J. Liddington and J. Norris, *One Hand Tied Behind Us: The Rise of the Women's Suffrage Movement*, 1978.

LANCASTER (NUWSS)　In 1913 the society was a member of the NORTH-WESTERN FEDERATION OF THE NATIONAL UNION OF WOMEN'S SUFFRAGE SOCIETIES. Secretary (1913) Mrs Croft Helme, Castramont, Lancaster, Lancashire.

LANGPORT (NUWSS)　In 1913 the society was a member of the WEST OF ENGLAND FEDERATION OF THE NATIONAL UNION OF WOMEN'S SUFFRAGE SOCIETIES. Secretary (1913) Mrs George Wedd, Eastdon House, Langport, Somerset.

LANSBURY, GEORGE (1859–1940)　Born in Suffolk, the son of a railway "navvy", by 1868 his family had settled in East London. In 1880 he married Elizabeth (Bessie) Brine, his childhood sweetheart, and eventually became the father of 12 children. For a year, 1884–5, he, with his wife, three children, and a younger brother, emigrated to Australia, to discover that only unemployment awaited. Penniless, they were able to return only after his father-in-law sent money for the voyage home. Lansbury was henceforward employed in the Brine saw-mill in Bow. Lansbury first attracted political attention by attacking the fraud, to which he had fallen prey, perpetrated on emigrants to Australia. By 1886 he was general secretary to the Bow and Bromley Liberal Association. In December 1888 he ran, under its auspices, Jane Cobden's (*see* Jane Cobden UNWIN) campaign for election to the London County Council. The campaign was sponsored by Annie Leigh BROWNE and the SOCIETY FOR PROMOTING THE RETURN OF WOMEN AS COUNTY COUNCILLORS and it was agreed that Lansbury should receive a fee of £20. Annie Leigh Browne said of Lansbury, "no money can really pay for his devotion", but there proved to be some difficulty about the fee, Lansbury's honesty was doubted and there was a measure of ill-feeling. Despite this, after Jane Cobden was unseated, Lansbury was approached by a group of Liberals and asked to stand in her stead. However, inspired by H.M. Hyndman and the propaganda of the Social Democratic Federation, Lansbury in 1892 left the Liberal Party and became a socialist. In 1894, sponsored by the SDF, he stood twice, unsuccessfully, as the parliamentary candidate in Walworth. Among those who came to campaign for him were Richard and Emmeline PANKHURST. By 1903, having recovered an interest in the Church of England, he left the SDF for the Labour Representation Committee. In June 1905, with Keir HARDIE and Dora MONTEFIORE, Lansbury was involved in arranging the march of 1000 destitute women from the East End to Westminster. Sylvia PANKHURST took Annie KENNEY, shortly after she came to London in early 1906, to see the Lansburys at their home at Bow. In 1906–7 Lansbury donated money to the WOMEN'S SOCIAL AND POLITICAL UNION and Bessie became a member. In 1910 he was a member of the CHURCH LEAGUE FOR WOMEN'S SUFFRAGE. In March 1910 he was elected an "Independent Labour" member of the London County Council and in December as Labour MP for Bow and Bromley. Throughout his parliamentary career Lansbury was a staunch supporter of women's enfranchisement. After becoming an MP he became a regular contributor to *Votes for Women*.

In June 1912 he created uproar in the House of Commons by attacking Asquith for allowing women to be forcibly fed. Hereafter, advised by Christabel and Emmeline Pankhurst, he pursued a policy that would have involved the parliamentary Labour Party voting against every government bill until an official measure for women's suffrage was introduced. This was not a tactic suggested by either H.N. BRAILSFORD or Keir Hardie, the WSPU's other Labour Party advisers. The parliamentary Labour Party required Lansbury to conform to party policy, but instead he went to France to consult with Christabel Pankhurst, who suggested to him that he should resign and stand for re-election as a suffrage candidate. This he did, and was defeated. Sylvia Pankhurst in *The Suffragette Movement* is scathing of the WSPU's arrogance in riding roughshod over the needs of the East End electorate and of ignoring the hard work of the Labour Party volunteers who had been responsible for Lansbury's election in 1910. She wrote, "Suffragists of all sorts, united in nothing save the demand for some sort of franchise for women, and otherwise differing from Marxism to the most extreme Conservatism, flooded the constituency." She particularly castigated the young WSPU ORGANIZER (who, although she does not name her, was Grace ROE), who had no experience in conducting a campaign which involved supporting a candidate and who reportedly refused to take any directions or help from men. The National Union of Women's Suffrage Societies gave support to Lansbury's campaign, although because he was not an official Labour candidate, the money to finance this was not drawn from their Election Fighting Fund.

Lansbury continued his support for the WSPU and after a particularly vociferous speech at the Albert Hall on 10 April 1913 he was arrested, with Flora DRUMMOND, the chairman of the meeting, and prosecuted under a Statute of Edward III. Annie Kenney had been held under the same statute a few days earlier. Lansbury refused to be bound over and was sentenced to three months' imprisonment. He was taken to Pentonville and went on hunger-and-thirst strike. He was quickly released under the "Cat and Mouse" Act and was never sent back to prison. The government did not need the publicity engendered by a hunger-striking ex-MP.

Lansbury then turned his attention to the *Daily Herald*, the first Labour daily paper, becoming editor in 1913. Annie Kenney's brother Rowland had been the first editor. The paper's writers included Gerald Gould (*see* Barbara Ayrton GOULD) and, aged 19, for two weeks Rebecca West was "Woman's Editor". A page was put at the disposal of supporters of women's suffrage and Will Dyson (*see* Dora Meeson COATES) was the paper's cartoonist. Lady DE LA WARR and Mary Dodge gave generous donations to the paper; Lansbury joined the THEOSOPHICAL SOCIETY. There was a suggestion that Lady de la Warr and Lansbury may have been more than close friends. Francis Meynell (*see* Helena DOWSON) wrote for the paper and may have helped select its new typefaces. The paper's printer, Mr Drew, manager of the Victoria House Printing Company, was prosecuted and imprisoned for printing the suppressed *Suffragette*. When the UNITED SUFFRAGISTS was formed in February 1914, George Lansbury was a member, becoming, with his wife, one of its vice-presidents. He addressed the newly formed United Suffragist branches in Stroud and Amersham in May 1914. The United Suffragists and Sylvia Pankhurst's EAST LONDON FEDERATION OF SUFFRAGETTES worked together at the Poplar by-election in February 1914. Many members of the extensive Lansbury family were involved in supporting Sylvia Pankhurst and the East London Federation of Suffragettes. On 5 May 1914 they helped hoist the Suffragette flag on the roof of the Women's Hall, newly opened at 400 Old Ford Road, Bow, and Sylvia Pankhurst on occasion used the Lansbury family home as a place of refuge. By August 1914 Lloyd George had begun negotiations with Sylvia Pankhurst and Lansbury, understanding that they and their associated groups were likely to array themselves with the constitutional side of the movement. Christabel Pankhurst repudiated any suggestion that the WSPU might call a truce. The outbreak of war led to the discontinuance of the Liberal Party's negotiation, and Lloyd George's "promise to give a public pledge... to decline to enter any Government after the next general election that did not make Women's Suffrage the first plank in its legislative programme" was not put to the test. In any case, Sylvia Pankhurst's version of the interview with Lloyd George differed from that of Lansbury. Despite a widening gap in ideology between Lansbury and Sylvia Pankhurst, his timber yard supplied the wood for her Toy Factory as well as the furniture for the "Mother's Arms", of which, in April 1915, Bessie Lansbury became a director. In 1916 Lansbury was a member of the executive of the NATIONAL COUNCIL FOR ADULT SUFFRAGE, formed by democratic suffragists to press their case at the Speaker's conference called in 1916 to discuss the suffrage issue.

Address: (1913) 103 St Stephens Road, Bow, London E.
Photograph: in R. Postgate, *George Lansbury*, 1951.
Bibliography: R. Postgate, *George Lansbury*, 1951.

LARGS committee of the NATIONAL SOCIETY FOR WOMEN'S SUFFRAGE Formed in 1872 and in 1913 the society was a member of the SCOTTISH FEDERATION OF THE NATIONAL UNION OF WOMEN'S SUFFRAGE SOCIETIES. Secretary (1913) Miss Margaret Paton, Mansfield, Largs, Ayrshire.

LAURENCEKIRK, Kincardineshire, committee of the NATIONAL SOCIETY FOR WOMEN'S SUFFRAGE Formed in 1872.

LAWSON, [MARIAN ADELINE] MARIE (1881–1975) Born in Sunderland, one of six children of a solicitor. The family was Liberal, her mother was president of the local Women's Liberal Association, and politics was a staple topic of conversation at the lunch table. She was (badly) educated at home by a daily governess, attended Milton House School (later the High School) in Sunderland, and after coming to London at the age of 16, on her father's retirement, attended classes in mathematics at the University Tutorial College, where one of the tutors was H.G. Wells, and in law at the London School of Economics. Law being a profession then closed to women, Marie Lawson learned to type and found employment as a clerk in an engineering firm, the Sheridan Machinery Company, with which she remained for 50 years, for much of the time as chairman and owner. Unusually for the time, she left the family home in Dulwich when she was 21 and took a flat on her own in Guilford Street in Bloomsbury, then considered a rather disreputable area. As she remarked when interviewed, it was thought "very forward" to live in such a manner. She joined the WOMEN'S SOCIAL AND POLITICAL UNION in London in 1907, and was present at the meeting at the Essex Hall in the Strand when Mrs PANKHURST revealed that the WSPU was no longer to be a democratic body with a constitution. Marie Lawson was shocked that women were not to be considered worthy of a vote in their own society and had no hesitation in leaving the WSPU and joining the WOMEN'S FREEDOM LEAGUE. She was elected to the national executive committee of the WFL in 1908 and took part in the main WFL activities, such as sandwich board parades, picketing of the House of Commons and census resistance. In 1909, in order to produce the *Vote*, she formed the Minerva Publishing Company and became its managing director until 1910 when, in the furtherance of her business career, she left for the USA. The engineering company for which she worked produced printing and binding machinery and her expertise in this area was of use to the WFL. In 1909 Marie Lawson refused to pay income tax and in December some of her jewellery was distrained and sold in lieu; in 1910 she joined the newly founded TAX RESISTANCE LEAGUE. Although not a member of the WSPU, at some point between 1912 and 1914 she went to Paris to take instruction from Christabel PANKHURST about the *Suffragette*. In 1913 she was a member of the advisory committee of the International Suffrage Shop (*see* SHOPS).

In 1920–23 Marie Lawson was vice-president and honorary organizer of the Women's Election Committee and was a member of the committee of the International Women's Franchise Club (*see under* CLUBS). She was made a freeman of the City of London in 1928. In 1947 she was a member of the committee that organized the Record Room for the SUFFRAGETTE FELLOWSHIP, having donated £50 towards the cost of its establishment. In her will she left, after specific bequests, two-thirds of her estate to the Christine MURRELL Fellowship of the Medical Women's Federation "which commemorates the work of my dear friend Christine Murrell M.D." From 1922 Marie Lawson had shared "a common life" with Honor Bone and Christine Murrell, from 1930 living with them in a *ménage à trois*. Christine Murrell, to whom she was greatly attached, had guaranteed the money that allowed

her to buy the Sheridan Company. Marie Lawson died at Menton, in the south of France, where she had enjoyed the food, wine and casinos.
Address: (1921) 27 Gordon Square, London WC; (1930) 21 North Gate, Regents Park, London NW; (1947) High Holborn House, 52/54 High Holborn, London WC1; (1974) 44 Mount Street, London W.
Photograph: in the *Vote*, 12 March 1909.
Archival source: B. Harrison, taped interviews with Marie Lawson, 1974, and with Mrs Anne Blake, her companion, 1975, Fawcett Library.
Bibliography: C. St John, *Christine Murrell*, 1935.

LEAGUE OF JUSTICE Advertised in the *Suffragette* in 1913 that it ran a "Programme of uncompromising militancy without violence or law-breaking to win the Vote and break up unjust monopolies".
Address: (1913) 2 Lyndale, Hampstead, London N.

LEAMINGTON (WSPU) Was in existence in 1910 when its organizers were Miss Bertha RYLAND and Miss M. Bull, Ashton House, Leamington. It appears no longer to have been in existence in 1913.

LEEDS Committee of the NATIONAL SOCIETY FOR WOMEN'S SUFFRAGE Founded in 1871 as a branch of the MANCHESTER NATIONAL SOCIETY FOR WOMEN'S SUFFRAGE. The secretary was Mrs Buckton, 1 Moorland Terrace, Leeds. In 1872 meetings averaged 100 or so, mainly of the working class and on each occasion a petition for the suffrage was signed by the women voters present. In 1872 the Leeds society associated itself with the new CENTRAL COMMITTEE OF THE NATIONAL SOCIETY FOR WOMEN'S SUFFRAGE.

The society was refounded in 1889 as the Leeds Women's Suffrage Society; Isabella and Emily FORD were among its most active members. In 1898 the society joined the NATIONAL UNION OF WOMEN'S SUFFRAGE SOCIETIES. In 1913 the society was a member of the WEST RIDING FEDERATION OF THE NATIONAL UNION OF WOMEN'S SUFFRAGE SOCIETIES. Secretary (1891) F.L. Barber, 34 Mount Preston, Leeds; (1898) Mrs Gray Heald, The Red House, East Street, Leeds; (1909) Miss Foster, Oakwood Nook, Roundhay, Leeds; (1913) Mrs Thornton, Bramdean, Buckingham Road, Headingley, Leeds. Treasurer (1900) Mrs Rawlinson Ford, Quarrydene, Weetwood, Leeds. Office (1913) 9 Park Lane, Leeds.

LEEDS branch of the UNITED SUFFRAGISTS Formed in 1915. Honorary secretary: Mrs J.E. Thornton, Bramdean, Headingley, Leeds.

LEEDS AND DISTRICT (WSPU) Secretary (1906) Miss Rhys Davids, 40 Cliff Road, Hyde Park, Leeds, (1913) Mrs Leonora COHEN, 3 Cookridge Street, Leeds. Meetings were often held at the Leeds Arts Club.

LEEDS AND YORKSHIRE branch of the WOMEN'S EMANCIPATION UNION Honorary secretary (1895) Mrs Agnes SUNLEY, 15 Castleton Place, Armley, Leeds.

LEES, MARGORY (1878–1970) Younger daughter of Charles and Sarah LEES, she was secretary of the Oldham branch of the National Union of Women Workers which had been founded by her mother, was secretary of the local Charity Organization Society and of the Guild of Help, was a member of the board of governors of Oldham Royal Infirmary and, from 1904 to 1930, a poor law guardian. In 1907 she forwarded to the prime minister a resolution on the subject of the qualification of women to serve on all governing bodies. When it was formed in 1910 she became president of the OLDHAM WOMEN'S SUFFRAGE SOCIETY, a branch of the NATIONAL UNION OF WOMEN'S SUFFRAGE SOCIETIES. In 1911 Margory Lees sent a resolution, under the auspices of the Oldham Suffrage Society, to the government, drawing attention to the difficulty of finding suitable woman candidates for county and borough councils "owing to the fact that women of leisure and experience are for the most part not electors, but are living at home as wives or daughters of electors". In 1911, under the auspices of the NUWW she sent a resolution to the government protesting against the proposed protective legislation to prevent women working at the pit brow, claiming that their work was not too hard, nor in any way unsuitable for women. Margory Lees was a tax resister. In 1912 she wrote *An Account of the Women's Suffrage Movement* for the Oldham District Teachers' Association and was a member of the first Election Fighting Fund Committee formed by the NUWSS to support Labour Party candidates at by-elections. On 5 October 1912 she organized an "Oldham's

Woman Suffrage Demonstration" in the grounds of her home, Werneth Park. In June 1913 she may have attended the VII International Woman Suffrage Congress in Budapest; a menu of the farewell supper is among her papers. In July 1913 she certainly joined the Oldham contingent on the NUWSS PILGRIMAGE and has left a full diary description of the event. It made such an impression on her that she listed her involvement in *Hutchinson's Woman's Who's Who* in 1934.

After 1918 Margory Lees became president of the Oldham Women Citizens' Association and of the local branch of the National Council of Women. She was also honorary secretary of the Oldham Council of Social Welfare and a vice-president of the Canning Town Women's Settlement Hospital in London. After her mother's retirement from Oldham Town Council in 1919, Margory Lees took over her seat, remaining a member for 15 years. In 1934 she was president of the Oldham branch of the National Council of Women and in her will, amongst numerous charitable bequests, left £1000 to the NCW.

Address: (1910) Werneth Park, Oldham; (1933) Westholme, Werneth, Oldham.
Archival source: Lees Papers, Oldham Local Studies Library.

LEES, SARAH ANNE, MRS (1842–1935), DBE Born at Carr Hall, Mossley, daughter of John Buckley, she married in 1874 Charles Lees and had two daughters. Her husband, who died in 1894, was a spinning and textile manufacturer, an art collector who gave many pictures to Oldham Art Gallery. Sarah Lees was a wealthy woman with a social conscience, a generous benefactor to Oldham. In 1903 she founded the Beautiful Oldham Society and planned a garden suburb for the town, modelled on Ebenezer' Howard's Letchworth. A co-operative building society was formed among mill-workers and 150 houses were built. In 1897 she founded and became president of the the Oldham branch of the National Union of Women Workers. From 1902 she was a member of the local education authority. In 1907 she was elected as a Liberal to the Oldham Town Council, in one of the first elections in which women were eligible to stand. The following year she was returned unopposed, having been nominated by both the Conservatives and the Liberals. In October 1910 she became mayor of Oldham, one of the first women mayors in the country. She pointed out the irony of the fact that as mayor she was also returning officer and, in the event of a tie between parliamentary candidates at an election, would have had the casting vote. Her seat on the Town Council was never again challenged and in 1919 when she retired was taken by her daughter, Margory LEES.

Sarah Lees was a founding member of the OLDHAM WOMEN'S SUFFRAGE SOCIETY (NUWSS), of which her daughter was president, and was a vice-president of the FREE CHURCH LEAGUE FOR WOMEN'S SUFFRAGE. A progressive Liberal, a feminist, and a suffragist, she signed the public protest against militancy that was printed in *Votes for Women*, 26 July 1912, and in July 1913 signed a memorial to the prime minister as one of the prominent Manchester citizens protesting against the "Cat and Mouse" Act. By 1934 she was a vice-president of the British Federation of University Women and had received an honorary doctorate from Manchester University. A memorial to her was set up in Wernerth Park, the house and land for which her daughter gave to Oldham Borough Council.

Address: Werneth Park, Oldham.
Photograph: in P. Hollis, *Ladies Elect: Women in English Local Government, 1865–1914*, 1987.
Archival source: Lees Papers, Oldham Local Studies Library.
Bibliography: P. Hollis, *Ladies Elect: Women in English Local Government, 1865–1914*, 1987.

LEICESTER branch of the LONDON NATIONAL SOCIETY FOR WOMEN'S SUFFRAGE Founded in 1871 when its secretary was Rev. A.F. MacDonald. It was refounded in 1880 and in 1891, when its honorary secretary was Miss Gittins, it affiliated to the CENTRAL NATIONAL SOCIETY FOR WOMEN'S SUFFRAGE. The Leicester Women's Suffrage Society affiliated to the NATIONAL UNION OF WOMEN'S SUFFRAGE SOCIETIES in 1898. By 1913 it was a member of the MIDLANDS (EAST) FEDERATION. Honorary secretary (1898) Mrs W. Evans, 6 St Martin's, Leicester; (1909) Miss Evelyn Carryer, Rough Close, St John's Road, Leicester; (1913) Miss Sloan, MA, 13 Welford Road, Leicester. Office and secretary (1913) Miss Elgood, 90 New Walk, Leicester.

LEICESTER branch of the MEN'S POLITICAL UNION FOR WOMEN'S ENFRANCHISEMENT   Founded in 1910.

LEICESTER (WSPU)   Secretary (1907) Mrs Alice HAWKINS, 181 Western Road, Leicester. Organizer (1906) Miss N. Sherriff, 83 Friday Street, Leicester; (1910) Dorothy PETHICK, Dorothy BOWKER; (1913) Miss G. Hazel, 14 Bowling Green Street, Leicester.

LEIGH (NUWSS)   In 1910 the society joined the MANCHESTER AND DISTRICT FEDERATION OF THE NATIONAL UNION OF WOMEN'S SUFFRAGE SOCIETIES. Secretary (1913) Miss L. Cook, 13 Railway Road, Leigh, Lancashire.

LEIGH, MARY, MRS (1885–?, alive 1978) (later known as Mrs Mary Brown)   Born in Manchester, was a teacher until her marriage. Her husband was described as a quiet man, a builder. By March 1907, when she was sentenced to a month's imprisonment after taking part in the deputation to the House of Commons, she was in London and a member of the WOMEN'S SOCIAL AND POLITICAL UNION. The fact that she unfurled a WSPU flag and waved it in the court so annoyed the magistrate that he commented that he did not think it "a decent thing to wave a flag in a court of justice". On 30 June 1908, after she and Edith NEW had watched "violence and indecency" perpetrated by the police against crowds of women protesting in Parliament Square, they went to 10 Downing Street and threw stones at a window. This was the first act of physical militancy carried out by suffragettes; it had not been suggested by the leadership but was a spontaneous response by individuals. Mary Leigh was sentenced to two months' imprisonment. She and Edith New were welcomed on their release from Holloway by a team of women, dressed in the WSPU regulation white dresses and regalia, who drew their carriage to Clement's Inn. On 13 October she took part in the "rush" on the House of Commons from the Women's Parliament in Caxton Hall, attempted to seize the bridle of a police horse, and was sentenced to three months' imprisonment. She spent more than six months of 1908 in prison.

In May 1909 Mary Leigh was drum-major of the newly-founded WSPU drum and fife BAND which was introduced to publicize the Women's Exhibition at the Prince's Skating Rink. In July 1909, after disturbances at Lloyd George's meeting at Limehouse, Mary Leigh, with Emily Wilding DAVISON, Lucy BURNS and Alice PAUL, was arrested, went on hunger strike and was released. In August she sat on the roof of a house near the Sun Hall in Liverpool, in which Haldane was holding a meeting, tore off the slates and threw them to the ground. She was arrested, imprisoned pending trial, went on hunger strike after sentencing and was released, to a nursing home, on 26 August. The government had expressly taken the decision not forcibly to feed the suffragette prisoners held in Walton Gaol.

In September, with Charlotte MARSH, Mary Leigh repeated the exercise, sitting on the roof of the Bingley Hall in Birmingham, in which Asquith was speaking, and throwing slates to the ground. She and her companions, who included Mabel CAPPER, were arrested and taken to Winson Green Prison. Mary Leigh, as a repeat offender, was sentenced to four months' hard labour. She afterwards reported that she was handcuffed for more than 30 hours, her hands were fastened behind during the day and in front, with palms outward, at night. All the suffragettes again went on hunger strike; this time they were not released, but were forcibly fed. Thus Mary Leigh was one of the first members of the WSPU to be so treated. The Winson Green Prison Visiting Committee reported that she was at first fed by spoon, then, as she resisted, a nasal tube had to be applied; by the end of September she was taking food from a feeding cup. Mary Leigh applied to be made a political prisoner, which would have involved a move to the first division. The WSPU brought a case on her behalf against the Home Secretary and the Governor of the prison, to the effect that a prisoner had a right to refuse such "treatment" as feeding, which could not, anyway, be performed without the prisoner's consent. The action was held on 9 December before the Lord Chief Justice, who ruled that it was the duty of a prison medical officer to prevent prisoners committing suicide. A statement made by Mary Leigh, "Forcible Feeding in Prison", based on her experience in Winson Green, was published by the WSPU. A copy of it is included in the Scottish Office prison file on the suffragette prisoners who were held in Dundee in October 1909. The Governor of Dundee

The WSPU fife and drum band prepares to march to advertise the May 1909 Exhibition at the Prince's Skating Rink. Mary Leigh, the drum-major, stands to the right of the foreground. (Author's collection)

prison and the Secretary for Scotland avoided using forcible feeding on this occasion, but obviously read all the literature applicable to the case.

In November 1910 Mary Leigh was one of the many arrested after taking part in the "Black Friday" struggle, but, like the others, was discharged. In March 1911, however, she was back in prison – for not paying her dog tax. She was arrested again in November 1911 and sentenced to two months' imprisonment. Lady Constance LYTTON, who had received only a 14-day sentence for what she thought was a greater crime, wrote to the Home Secretary accusing the government of differentiating in its treatment between those with influential friends and "working-class women & women who can count on no supporters in political circles". On 18 July 1912, while Asquith visited Dublin, Mary Leigh, Gladys Evans, who had been a drummer in the WSPU band, Mabel Capper and Jennie BAINES took the WSPU protest over to him. Mary Leigh threw a hatchet, wrapped with the message, "This symbol of the extinction of the Liberal Party for evermore", into the carriage in which Asquith was riding with John Redmond. She escaped into the crowd and later, with Gladys Evans, made a spectacular appearance at the Theatre Royal, setting fire to a theatre box. She was defended on this charge by Tim Healy and remanded to Mountjoy Gaol. She was sentenced to five years' penal servitude. Mary Leigh went on hunger strike and was forcibly fed. Grace ROE was sent over to Dublin to look after Mary Leigh's interest; there were rumours that she might be certified and committed to a lunatic asylum. After a prolonged campaign Mary Leigh was released on a "ticket of leave" on 21 September. After a period of enforced house arrest, a second trial on the case of throwing the hatchet was eventually dropped, and she was able to return to England. The judge at this second trial had called her "a clever, earnest, and in her own way a good woman". In November 1912 Mary Leigh was sentenced to two months' imprisonment after taking part in the WSPU window-smashing campaign; she was charged with assaulting a policeman. The court report gives a good idea of Mary Leigh's fiery nature.

On 13 October 1913 Mary Leigh was present at Bow Baths Hall when the police attempted to arrest Sylvia PANKHURST; she was knocked unconscious. Twice towards the end of the campaign Mary Leigh went to France to see Christabel PANKHURST. Although one of the militants who created the image of the WSPU she, like Emily Wilding DAVISON, was a "free-lance" activist and not one who took orders.

In June 1913, with Rose Lamartine YATES, Mary Leigh went to the bedside of the dying Emily Wilding Davison in Epsom Cottage Hospital. In her memory Mary Leigh founded the Emily Wilding Davison Club (later the Emily Wilding Davison Lodge, *see under* CLUBS) and for the rest of her life arranged for a Morpeth florist to provide flowers for Emily Davison's grave. This she visited every year, accompanied by the flag which Emily Davison had pinned inside her coat at the Derby and which also Mary Leigh later carried when she went on the first Aldermaston "Ban the Bomb" march.

At the outbreak of the First World War, Mary Leigh offered her services to the war effort but, with a record of being a "trouble-maker", was turned down. She reverted to her maiden name (Brown) and underwent a special course of instruction as an ambulance driver. She then worked with the New Zealand Expeditionary Force hospital in Surrey.

Address: (1907) Houghton Place, Camden Town, London N; (1930s) Sunbury-on-Thames; (1965) West Ealing, London.
Photograph: Suffragette Fellowship Collection, Museum of London.
Archival source: Suffragette Fellowship Collection and the David Mitchell Collection, Museum of London; Visiting Committee of HM Prison Winson Green, Birmingham Archives and Local History Library; Home Office Papers, Public Record Office.
Bibliography: A. Morley and L. Stanley, *The Life and Death of Emily Wilding Davison*, with Gertrude Colmore's, *The Life of Emily Davison*, 1988.

LEIGHTON BUZZARD AND DISTRICT (NUWSS) In 1913 the society was a member of the OXON, BERKS, BUCKS, AND BEDS FEDERATION OF THE NATIONAL UNION OF WOMEN'S SUFFRAGE SOCIETIES. Secretary *pro tem* (1913) Mrs Burditt, 47 Wellington Street, Luton, Bedfordshire.

LEITH (WSPU) Secretary (1906) Miss Cairns, 37 Lower Broughton Road, Edinburgh, Midlothian.

LEITH HILL AND DORKING (NUWSS) In 1913 the society was a member of the SURREY, SUSSEX, AND HANTS FEDERATION OF THE NATIONAL UNION OF WOMEN'S SUFFRAGE SOCIETIES. Secretary (1913) Miss Rawlings, 7 Rose Hill, Dorking, Surrey.

LENNOX, [LAURA] GERALDINE (1883–1958) Born in Bantry, Co. Cork, educated at Trinity Church School, Cork. She joined the WOMEN'S SOCIAL AND POLITICAL UNION on 30 June 1909, inspired by the example of those who had taken part in the deputation to the House of Commons the day before. She had secretarial experience and was based in Clement's Inn. She organized the Irish contingent in the WSPU of 18 June 1910. A "Deputation 1910" badge, with "Lennox" written on the reverse, now preserved in the Fawcett Library, would suggest that Geraldine Lennox took part in at least one of the deputations that year although, because she was never arrested, there is no corroborating evidence. She was on the staff of *Votes for Women* and, in 1912 after the Pankhurst/Pethick-Lawrence split, became sub-editor of the *Suffragette*. On 30 April 1913 she was arrested, with the other heads of department in Lincoln's Inn House, the WSPU headquarters. After trial on a charge of conspiracy she was sentenced to six months' imprisonment, taken to Horfield Prison in Bristol, went on hunger strike and was released on licence, under the "Cat and Mouse" Act. She was recaptured in Shirehampton, again went on hunger strike and this time, in disguise, evaded re-arrest. In November H.D. HARBEN, with whom she was obviously friendly, paid £15 for her "licence", which money she used towards the expenses of setting up a WSPU office in Cork. It appears clear from a letter to Harben that she had borrowed money from him previously. She wrote that "Two detectives were on the look out for me in Dublin but I evaded them and got home by the midnight train". She remained in Ireland working for the WSPU until the outbreak of war. During the First World War Geraldine Lennox worked with a hospital unit in France. After the war she ran a Secretarial and Service Bureau, was a member of the committee of management of the

Women's Pioneer Housing Association, of the Six Point Group and of the Women's Auxiliary Service. In 1932 she wrote a pamphlet *The Suffragette Spirit*. In 1934 she wrote that she "earned her living by helping people to live within their incomes, by keeping accounts, checking bills, and knowing the cost of necessities". She was at that time the Custodian to the SUFFRAGETTE FELLOWSHIP but was not, however, a member of the committee that set up the Fellowship's Record Room in 1947.

Address: (1913) 43 Kempsford Gardens, South Kensington, London SW; (1923) 18 Victoria Street, London SW1; (1934) 12 St George's Mansions, Vauxhall Bridge Road, London SW1; (1958) Room 502, Block 5, Albert Hall Mansions, Westminster and 8 Adelaide Place, St Luke's, Cork, Eire.

Photograph: in the *Suffragette*, 20 June 1913; *Daily Sketch*, 28 October 1933.

LENTON, LILIAN IDA (1891–1972) Joined the WOMEN'S SOCIAL AND POLITICAL UNION when she was 21, having waited until she gained qualifications. She was, according to Mrs Marion Johnson, a professional dancer. As "Ida Inkley" she was sentenced to two months' imprisonment after taking part in the WSPU window-smashing campaign in March 1912. After the resumption of militancy at the beginning of 1913 Lilian Lenton resolved to commit arson and, with Olive WHARRY, who had the same idea, she embarked on a series of terrorist acts. She was arrested in February 1913, suspected of having set fire to the tea pavilion in Kew Gardens. After hunger striking for two days she was forcibly fed, and then quickly released from prison seriously ill, suffering from pleurisy after food had entered her lungs. The case caused a furore, not least because the Home Secretary attempted to deny that she had been forcibly fed and suggested that her illness was due to the effects of her hunger strike. The Home Office papers make it quite clear that she had been fed once, by nasal tube, on 23 February. Two hours later the prison doctor was summoned and found her "in a very collapsed condition". She then, as the doctor reported, "remained for about two hours in a very critical condition". She was sent, accompanied by a doctor and hospital officer, to friends at 34 Harrington Square. Once she had recovered she managed to evade recapture, although for some of the time the police certainly knew her whereabouts, until in June she was arrested in Doncaster and charged, as "May Dennis", with being on the premises of "Westfield", an unoccupied house at Balby, which had been set on fire. She was released from Armley Prison, Leeds, after several days' hunger strike, there being no attempt this time forcibly to feed her. Her accomplice in the arson attack was Harry Johnson, a local reporter, who was sentenced to 12 months' hard labour in Wakefield Gaol. Lilian Lenton sheltered in Frank RUTTER's house in Leeds and, with the aid of Leonora COHEN and Norah DUVAL, evaded the Leeds police, who on 20 June filed a report to the Home Office giving in breathless detail the manner in which they had been outmanoeuvred. In July Lilian Lenton escaped in disguise to France on a private yacht. At this time the Criminal Record Office issued a "wanted" photograph of her, in which she looks very pretty, with her hair loose. She is described as 5' 2" with brown eyes and brown hair. Lilian Lenton has stated that her aim was to burn two buildings a week, in order to create such a condition in the country that it would prove impossible to govern without the consent of the governed. She was re-arrested in October 1913, while reclaiming a bicycle from the left-luggage office of Paddington Station. She went on hunger-and-thirst strike while on remand and was forcibly fed, although her condition caused some alarm and she was eventually released under the "Cat and Mouse" Act on 15 October, on licence for five days, to the care of Mrs Diplock, The Limes, Putney Park Avenue, London SW. Lilian Lenton was eventually recaptured on 22 December, arrested on a charge of setting fire to a house in Cheltenham. She was identified from police photographs, went on hunger-and-thirst strike, and was released at 11 am on Christmas Day to the care of Mrs Impey, Cropthorne, Middletonhall Road, King's Norton, Birmingham. She evaded the police until early May 1914 when she was re-arrested in Birkenhead. She was then remanded, to await trial on the Doncaster charge at the Leeds Assizes, to Leeds prison where she again went on hunger-and-thirst strike until she was released on 12 May. Lilian Lenton had not been recaptured by the time that the WSPU brought an end to militancy in August 1914. She revealed in the course of a BBC documentary (*see under* RADIO,

TELEVISION, RECORDS AND RECORDINGS) that she had been unimpressed by the terms on which the vote was won, that is to women householders, or the wives of householders, over the age of 30, saying, "Personally I didn't vote for a very long time, because I hadn't either a husband or furniture, although I was over 30".

During the First World War Lilian Lenton worked in Serbia with the Scottish Women's Hospitals Unit and later worked for the British Embassy in Stockholm. She became a speaker for the Save the Children Fund and then, from 1924 to 1933, was travelling organizer and speaker for the WOMEN'S FREEDOM LEAGUE. During this period she often stayed with Alice Schofield COATES in Middlesbrough. Lilian Lenton, like Mrs Schofield Coates, was a vegetarian. Then, after a period working in Scotland on behalf of animal welfare, she became, until 1953, financial secretary of the National Union of Women Teachers. In addition, for over 11 years she was editor of the WFL *Bulletin*. In 1970, as treasurer of the SUFFRAGETTE FELLOWSHIP, she unveiled, in Christchurch Gardens, Westminster, opposite Caxton Hall, a memorial to the women who fought for the vote.

Address: (1968) 66 Thames Eyot, Twickenham, Middlesex.
Photograph: issued by Criminal Record Office, Public Record Office.
Archival source: Home Office papers, Public Record Office; The Suffragette Fellowship Collection, Museum of London; B. Harrison, taped interview with Mrs Marion Johnson, 1975, Fawcett Library.
Bibliography: The *Listener*, 8 February 1968.

LENZIE (NUWSS)   In 1913 the society was a member of the SCOTTISH FEDERATION OF THE NATIONAL UNION OF WOMEN'S SUFFRAGE SOCIETIES. Secretary (1913) Miss M.H. Kerr, Clunaline, Lenzie.

LEO, ROSA EMMA LOUISA (1862–?) Born in Islington, cousin of Hertha AYRTON. Her mother Hannah Leo, sister to Hertha Ayrton's mother, was the co-owner of the school at which both Rosa Leo and Sarah Marks (as Hertha Ayrton then was) were educated. Her father Louis Leo was a musician. Rosa Leo joined the WOMEN'S SOCIAL AND POLITICAL UNION in 1909 and was a member of the ACTRESSES' FRANCHISE LEAGUE. She was "Honorary Instructor in Voice Production" to the WSPU Speakers' Class, which was for a time held in Hertha Ayrton's house in Norfolk Square, at which she instructed women in the skills of outdoor speaking. Both Israel ZANGWILL, Hertha Ayrton's stepson-in-law, and her daughter Barbara Ayrton (see Barbara Ayrton GOULD) gave endorsements, in advertisements in *Votes for Women*, to Rosa Leo's skill in training public speakers. By 1911 Rosa Leo was also holding speakers' classes for the MEN'S POLITICAL UNION and after 1913 she did the same service for the EAST LONDON FEDERATION OF SUFFRAGETTES. An annuity left to Mrs Leo in Hertha Ayrton's will was, after her death, to be inherited by Rosa.

Address: (1909, 1923) 45 Ashworth Mansions, Elgin Avenue, London W.
Photograph: on postcard, 1911, John Johnson Collection, Bodleian Library, Oxford.

LETCHWORTH branch of the MEN'S LEAGUE FOR WOMEN'S SUFFRAGE   Founded in 1912. Its president was Ebenezer Howard, the designer of the garden city.

LETCHWORTH (NUWSS)   In 1913 the society was a member of the EASTERN COUNTIES FEDERATION OF THE NATIONAL UNION OF WOMEN'S SUFFRAGE SOCIETIES. Secretary (1913) Miss E. Wilkinson, Brightcot, Meadow Way, Letchworth. Organizing secretary Miss Sugden, Fircroft, Letchworth, Hertfordshire.

LETCHWORTH branch of the UNITED SUFFRAGISTS   Formed in 1915. Honorary secretary: Ruth Pym, 2 Meadow Way, Letchworth, Hertfordshire.

LETCHWORTH (WFL)   Secretary (1913) Miss Lee, 2 Norton Way North, Letchworth, Hertfordshire.

LETCHWORTH (WSPU)   Secretary (1913) Mrs Goodliffe, Elm Tree House, Letchworth Lane, Letchworth, Hertfordshire.

LEVEN (NUWSS)   In 1913 the society was a member of the SCOTTISH FEDERATION OF THE NATIONAL UNION OF WOMEN'S SUFFRAGE SOCIETIES. Secretary (1913) Mrs Galloway, Kinellan, Leven, Fife.

LEWES (NUWSS)   In 1913 the society was a member of the SURREY, SUSSEX, AND HANTS FEDERATION of the NATIONAL UNION OF WOMEN'S SUFFRAGE SOCIETIES. Secretary (1913) Miss Vallance, Pontisbright, Lewes, Sussex.

LEWIN, OCTAVIA MARGARET SOPHIA, DR (1869–1955) Born in Hertfordshire, educated privately by a German governess, and then at Frances Holland School, Queen's College, Harley Street, and Girton, 1888–91, where she read the Natural Sciences Tripos. She then qualified as a doctor at the London School of Medicine for Women and the Royal Free Hospital. She was assistant physician at the Homeopathic Hospital when she joined the WOMEN'S SOCIAL AND POLITICAL UNION in 1906. In 1907 Octavia Lewin became a founder member of the WOMEN'S FREEDOM LEAGUE. She was a supporter of the TAX RESISTANCE LEAGUE, the second annual meeting of which was held at her house. She refused to pay the levy on armorial bearings, that being the only tax that she was then in a position to withstand. During the First World War she was aural surgeon to the Women's Hospital Corps at the Endell Street Military Hospital run by Louisa Garrett ANDERSON and Flora MURRAY. In the 1930s she was a member of the council of management of Bedford College.
Address: (1911) 25 Wimpole Street, London W; (1948) 8 Manchester Square, London W.

LEWISHAM (branch of the LONDON SOCIETY FOR WOMEN'S SUFFRAGE) Was in existence in 1906 when its honorary secretary was Mrs Wollersent, Gloucester Lodge, Lawrie Park Road, Sydenham, London SE.

LEWISHAM (WSPU) Secretary (1913) Miss Campbell, 1 Lewis Grove, Lewisham, London SE. The society's banner, probably dating from 1910, is now held in the Museum of London.

LIBERAL WOMEN'S SUFFRAGE UNION Formed in 1913 after the withdrawal of the Liberal government's Reform bill and the defeat, at the annual conference of the WOMEN'S LIBERAL FEDERATION, of a motion to the effect that only local associations who would put the "test question" (i.e. whether or not he would support women's enfranchisement) to candidates should be affiliated. The Liberal Women's Suffrage Union was the latest in a series of societies formed by women Liberals to put pressure on their party, having been preceded by the UNION OF PRACTICAL SUFFRAGISTS and the FORWARD SUFFRAGE UNION. Since the adoption by the NATIONAL UNION OF WOMEN'S SUFFRAGE SOCIETIES of its Election Fighting Fund policy and its active support for Labour candidates, it was felt necessary for women suffragist Liberals to have their own society, through which they could put pressure on their party to ensure that anti-suffragist candidates were not selected. Eleanor Acland, a close friend of Catherine MARSHALL, the NUWSS' parliamentary secretary, was the society's driving force; she and her husband Francis Acland, the Liberal MP, were already members of the executive committee of the PEOPLE'S SUFFRAGE FEDERATION. The LWSU's first public meeting was held in London in March 1914. Honorary secretary (1916) Mrs May, Cabra, Hadley Wood, Barnet, Hertfordshire; secretary (1914, 1917) Miss M. Stonestreet.
Address: (1914, 1917) Denison House, 296 Vauxhall Bridge Road, London SW.

LIBRARIES The power of the written word and fear of its effect was implicit in the remarks made in the *Saturday Review*, 7 January 1860, on the reading room proposed by the founders of the Ladies' Institute (*see under* CLUBS): "What is the reading in the morning-room of the Club which they cannot get at home? The Englishwoman's Magazine and the domestic manuals of Kitchener and Soyer are not so dear.... We have our doubts about that reading room." These doubts were well founded. By furnishing reading rooms and libraries with material that would not be found in most homes, activists broadened women's knowledge of and interest in issues that affected them, the necessity for enfranchisement being the most powerful. In the late 1850s there was as yet no public library system. Books could be borrowed from proprietory or subscription libraries, such as the London Library, or from commercial circulating libraries run by booksellers. The women who founded the Ladies' Institute were well acquainted with the material that could be found in existing libraries. In 1849 Bessie Rayner PARKES borrowed books from the British Library (a few doors away from the British Hotel and not to be confused with the British

Museum library), run by a bookseller, Mrs Maria Cawthorn, at 24 Cockspur Street, near Charing Cross. The fact that her chosen bookseller/librarian was a woman may be worth remarking, although she was by no means the only one running such a business at the time. Neither Bessie Parkes nor her co-workers have left complaints of any difficulty that they themselves encountered in finding the material that they wished to read; they presumably took pleasure in the thought of making such books and journals available to others less fortunate.

The concept of reading room and lending library was dear to those raised in the tradition of rational recreation; for instance, the P.A. Taylors (*see* Clementia TAYLOR) had formed a lending library and reading room in their Aubrey Institute, donating to it 500 volumes, the titles unfortunately uncatalogued and lost to us. Many of the leaders of the nineteenth-century suffrage campaign were well acquainted with the historiography of the women's movement and had built up interesting collections of books. Of one of the scarcest tracts, *Woman Not Inferior To Man* written by "Sophia" in 1739, Mentia and P.A. Taylor possessed a copy and Elizabeth Wolstenholme ELMY had the text, transcribed by hand from the copy in the British Museum library. It is clear from Lilias Ashworth HALLETT's will that she had intended that the collection of books, manuscript material and photographs on "the woman question" that she had formed should be given to Girton, presumably to supplement Helen BLACKBURN's library, with which she had been associated in such practical ways as organizing the binding of its pamphlets. Alone of the nineteenth-century libraries, Helen Blackburn's still stands as a memorial to her enthusiasm for books on the "distaff" side. Although it comprises much contemporary work, including gifts from authors, she had clearly bought copies of antiquarian books to fill out the history of her subject. She possessed a copy of *An Essay in Defence of the Female Sex*, 1696 (which in the nineteenth century was thought to have been by Mary Astell and has now been reattributed to Judith Drake) and of *Education of Daughters*, one of Mary Wollstonecraft's scarcest works. It is likely that this library was, in Helen Blackburn's lifetime, available for consultation by members of the CENTRAL COMMITTEE OF THE NATIONAL SOCIETY FOR WOMEN'S SUFFRAGE. The rival CENTRAL NATIONAL SOCIETY certainly had a library in 1891, for which it ordered six copies of the new edition of Mary Wollstonecraft's *Vindication of the Rights of Women*, with an introduction by Millicent Fawcett.

In the 1870s the Berners Club contained, according to the *Englishwoman's Review*, a reading room supplied with newspapers, periodicals and books. The women's clubs of the 1890s housed small libraries; six copies of Mrs Meredith's suffrage novel *A Woman's Crusade* were sent by the publisher to "clubs". Although there is no firm evidence, one imagines that, for instance, the Pioneer Club and the Grosvenor Crescent would have maintained good feminist libraries. By 1893 the WOMEN'S PROGRESSIVE SOCIETY had opened a "book club" bearing on all questions relating to woman; her social, economic, political and legal status, in the past and in the future. The terms to join were 5/– yearly or 2/– a quarter. From 1900 the Margate Pioneer Society, which concerned itself with economic and social matters affecting women, had a reading room and library. Near their home in Horsted Keynes, Louisa MARTINDALE and her daughters opened, in the early years of the new century, a reading room in which feminist material, including a complete set of the *Transactions of the International Congress of Women*, 1900, might be consulted. Activists were, therefore, as the suffrage campaign moved into its most active phase, fully conscious of the power of literature to educate and convert. Alongside their publishing programmes, the women's suffrage societies were careful to maintain a tradition of lending books to their members.

In 1908 it appears that the WOMEN'S SOCIAL AND POLITICAL UNION ran a library in Clement's Inn. This may have been mainly for the use of ORGANIZERS; it is not clear if it actually lent out the books. At this time Elizabeth Wolstenholme Elmy sent, by carrier, to Sylvia PANKHURST a large quantity of material to aid her in writing, initially for publication in *Votes for Women*, the history of the suffrage movement. With each consignment Mrs Elmy insisted that the books must, after Sylvia had used them, be passed to the WSPU library. Among the items specifically mentioned were the first annual report of the Manchester Society, early women's suffrage pamphlets, bound volumes of the *Englishwoman's Review* (an incomplete set; others, Mrs Elmy mentioned, had been borrowed and not returned); volumes of the *Women's Suffrage Journal* and a copy of Helen Blackburn's *Record of Women's Suffrage*. No trace remains of the library; perhaps, as with so much else, it was packed into the police pantechnicon in April 1913. In 1909 the Kensington branch of the WSPU housed a library of reference books at its shop at 143 Kensington Church Street; the enrolment fee was 1s, and books could be borrowed at 2d per volume per week. For this library the Kensington branch particularly wanted to acquire the "best speeches by Burke, Bright etc" and Sydney Low's *Governance of England*. In 1912–13 the Hampstead branch of the WSPU also had a lending library attached to its shop. Although Hampstead and Kensington might, numbering so many authors amongst their members, have been atypical, it is likely that many other WSPU branches also ran small libraries; the Fulham one certainly did. Minnie TURNER, whose Brighton guesthouse gave material rest and comfort to so many suffragettes, also provided for them food for thought – a small lending library of suffrage books. By July 1910 the WOMEN'S FREEDOM LEAGUE had a suffrage library at its office in Robert Street. It was free; Miss Chapin was the librarian.

The branches of the NATIONAL UNION OF WOMEN'S SUFFRAGE SOCIETIES appear, from around 1912, to have made a determined effort to run suffrage lending libraries. This development coincided with the move to woo working women to the cause and, on a practical level, with the opening of permanent SHOPS. The BOLTON WOMEN'S SUFFRAGE SOCIETY opened a lending library in its new shop in October 1913. The BEDFORD WOMEN'S SUFFRAGE SOCIETY from 1913 ran a lending library in the club room above its shop; books could be removed from the library at the cost of 1d each a week, and had to be renewed weekly. A sub-committee was set up to select and buy books and supervise the library. Mrs FAWCETT donated some books; it was decided to put one in the library and sell the others. The minutes unfortunately do not record the titles of these unsuitable tomes. The GLASGOW AND WEST OF SCOTLAND WOMEN'S SUFFRAGE ASSOCIATION, although it did not open a shop, in 1913 ran a lending library from its office, charging what appears to be the standard 1d a book per week. By 1914 the BRISTOL SUFFRAGE SOCIETY had a lending library, from which it lent books out to its satellite branches. It was probably by following a similar scheme that the SOUTHAMPTON branch had acquired in June 1913 three lists of books that could be obtained on loan by members. They included plays and pamphlets useful for reference and study. The lists may have been of books held by the Portsmouth branch; Norah O'SHEA was in charge of both. The remnants of the Portsmouth lending library exist, held in the Portsmouth Record Office. Some books carry labels, "Women's Suffrage Society Portsmouth Branch, 36 Stanley St, Southsea/ 2 Kent Road/ 20 Highland Road." The majority of the books were probably given by Norah O'Shea. The ones that remain are: A.B. and M. Wallis Chapman, *The Status of Women Under the English Law, 1066–1909*; C.C. Stopes, *British Freewomen* [no. 21, Lent for 14 days]; Olive Christian Malvery, *The Soul Market* [no. 11]; H. Blackburn, *Record of Women's Suffrage*; Jane Addams, *The Spirit of Youth and the City Streets*; Jane Addams, *A New Conscience and an Ancient Evil*; Clementina Black, *Sweated Industry and the Minimum Wage*; Mary Higgs, *Glimpses Into the Abyss*; Immanuel Kant, *Perpetual Peace*; W. Lyon Blease, *The Emancipation of English Women*; Olive Schreiner, *Woman and Labour*; Emily Davies, *Questions Relating to Women*. Also included is a copy of Sylvia Pankhurst, *Soviet Russia As I Saw It*, and several copies of her prison poems, *Writ on Cold Slate*, both of which were published after the First World War and therefore would not have formed part of the original suffrage society library.

The CAMBRIDGE ASSOCIATION FOR WOMEN'S SUFFRAGE proposed starting a small lending library of more expensive books in its suffrage shop. These were to be lent at 2d each. However by 1912 this library still had not materialized and in May, it was recorded in the society's minutes, Lady WRIGHT gave £2 to provide "a small 'pass it on' library of suffrage books. She had also presented the apparatus for stamping the books." The NOTTINGHAM WOMEN'S SUFFRAGE SOCIETY lent books at 1d a week. Its library, the best documented, although no trace of the books remain, comprised: Arnold Harris, *Women's Suffrage*; *Debate in Parliament*; Brougham Villiers (ed.), *The Case for Women's Suffrage*; Louisa

Martindale, *Under the Surface*; *Life of Josephine Butler*; John Stuart Mill, *Subjection of Women*; Emily Davies, *Questions Relating to Women*; Laurence Housman, *Articles of Faith*; Mrs C.C. Stopes, *Sphere of Man*; Lyon Blease, *Emancipation of Women*; Josephine Butler, *Personal Reminiscences*; Miss Cobbe, *Duties of Women*; Ibsen, *The Lady of the Sea*; Cicely Hamilton, *Marriage as a Trade*; Lady McLaren, *Charter*; and Olive Schreiner, *Women and Labour*.

In 1913, as soon as she opened her EAST LONDON FEDERATION OF THE SUFFRAGETTES shop in the Roman Road, Sylvia Pankhurst instituted in it a lending library. The London headquarters of the CHURCH LEAGUE FOR WOMEN'S SUFFRAGE received from an anonymous donor a bookcase and a library of more than 60 volumes and by 1913 the League's Edinburgh branch had also started a lending library at its office at 34 St Andrews Square. The Kensington branch of the League had its own lending library at 21 Lexham Gardens, home of Miss Amabel Ransom. The International Suffrage Shop (*see under* SHOPS) opened a lending library in 1913. The Amersham branch of the United Suffragists maintained the tradition and had formed a library for use of local members by August 1915.

Ruth Cavendish-BENTINCK, in the tradition of Helen Blackburn, built up a feminist library which was eventually housed in the International Women's Franchise Club. Many of these books would probably have been bought, but some pamphlets are stamped "Group Library, 4 Clement's Inn" and may have come from the library of the FABIAN WOMEN'S GROUP, of which she was a member. The Cavendish-Bentinck Library was given an accolade by Lady RHONDDA in her autobiography, describing how the library was "supplying all the young women in the suffrage movement with the books they could not procure in the ordinary way". She mentioned specifically that one such work she had borrowed from the library, and which otherwise she might not have been able to read, was Havelock Ellis's *Psychology of Sex*, which "opened up a whole new world of thought to me". By 1922 the Cavendish-Bentinck Library had merged, still housed in the International Women's Franchise Club, with that formed by Lady Wright and named "The Edward Wright Library" in memory of her son. The two libraries were given to the National Union of Societies for Equal Citizenship, which, because it had no room to house it, lent it to the LONDON SOCIETY FOR WOMEN'S SERVICE. In 1925 the latter advertised in the *Woman's Leader* that the two libraries contained some 3000 volumes, including sections on current political, economic and social matters of special interest to women as citizens, as well as an historical section of the women's movement. Boxes containing approximately 20 books were available on loan to societies and study circles. The fees charged were 10/6 per annum for two volumes at a time or 4d per volume per week. The Cavendish-Bentinck library was given, on the division of NUSEC's assets, to the Townswomen's Guild. This was not what Ruth Cavendish-Bentinck wished and, under a new trust deed, in 1931 she gave the library permanently to the LONDON AND NATIONAL SOCIETY FOR WOMEN'S SERVICE. The 1951 annual report of the latter society described how "It has grown from a shelf or two of books to a Library of some 10 000 bound volumes, 300 government publications, and countless pamphlets, leaflets, reports and newscuttings. Based on the valuable Cavendish-Bentinck Library, it has an antique collection which is its pride and joy, and which has attracted visitors from all over the world. It has lent approaching 30 000 books and has answered nearly 2500 enquiries. It has achieved something of a reputation in its own modest field. Its books have travelled to four continents, and it has been used by men and women from over 40 countries." The Cavendish-Bentinck and Edward Wright libraries are now at the heart of the Fawcett Library.

Alongside the development of specialist suffrage libraries, the women's cause by the beginning of the First World War had made a real impact on the public library system. A random selection of library catalogues (Brighton, Victoria Lending Library, 1890; Battersea Public Libraries, 1897; Ewart Library, Dumfries, 1904; Birmingham Central Library, 1906 and 1910; Gravesend Public Library, 1906; Woodside District Library, Glasgow, 1910; Islington Public Libraries, 1910; Bolton Public Libraries, 1914) reveals that the classification "Woman", used in the earlier catalogues, was refined in the majority of the later ones to provide sections on "Women's Rights", or "Suffrage", or "Woman's Position and Treatment", proof, on the basis that a concept exists if one can give it a name, of the general growth in awareness of the women's suffrage campaign in the first years of the twentieth century. In the earliest catalogue, that for Brighton, 1890, the only book that could be classified as pertaining to women's suffrage was J.S. Mill, *Subjection of Women*. In 1897 Battersea stocked Mill, plus Mrs Craik, *A Woman's Thoughts on Woman*; the 1891 edition of Mary Wollstonecraft, *Vindication of the Rights of Women*; and Mrs Ashton Dilke, *Women's Suffrage*. Birkenhead in 1898 could offer only Mill and Mrs Ashton Dilke. In 1904 the Ewart Library (Dumfries) stocked Mill; Craik, Wollstonecraft (1891); Charlotte Perkins Stetson, *Women and Economics*; T.W. Higginson, *Common Sense About Women*, 1897; and Charlotte Carmichael Stopes, *British Freewomen*, 1894. Gravesend Library in 1906 stocked under "Women and the Women Question" only Craik and Stopes. In the same year Birmingham Central Library could offer Mill; Ostrogorski, *Rights of Women*, 1893; and *Words of Weight on the Women Question*, 1871. By 1910 Birmingham had added to these Crepaz, *Emancipation of Women*; Higginson; and Stopes. In 1910 the Woodside District Library, Glasgow, stocked two copies of Craik; two copies of Crepaz; Wollstonecraft (1891); Ostrogorski; two copies of the 1906 edition of Stetson (by now Gilman); Higginson; Stopes; Mary Taylor, *The First Duty of Women*, 1870; and Brougham Villiers (ed.), *The Case of Women's Suffrage*, 1907. In the same year Islington libraries stocked Gilman, Craik; Mill; Ostrogorski; Wollstonecraft (1891); Stopes; Villiers; Helen Blackburn, *A Handbook for Women Engaged in Social and Political Work*, 1895; Annette Meakin, *Women in Transition*, 1907; David Staars, *The English Woman*, 1909; Chapman and Chapman, *The Status of Women under English Law*, 1909; Helen Blackburn, *Women's Suffrage*, 1902; Lady Grove, *The Human Woman*, 1908; the *Englishwoman's Year Book and Directory*, 1906 to date; and the *Englishwoman's Review*. In 1912 Reading library could offer Gilman; Stopes; Villiers; Higginson; Mill (1870 edition); Craik; Crepaz; Mrs Ashton Dilke; Bessie Parkes, *Essays on Woman's Work*, 1865; *The Law in Relation to Women*, 1888; Millicent Fawcett, *Home and Politics*, 1888; Hart, *Women's Suffrage and National Danger*, 1889 (anti-suffrage); and Sylvia Pankhurst, *The Suffragette*, 1911. By 1914 Bolton Library offered *Words of Weight*; Mill; Ostrogorski; Helen Blackburn, *Woman's Suffrage*; Lady Grove; Villiers; Higginson, Stetson; Crepaz; Staars; Pankhurst; Teresa Billington-Greig, *The Militant Movement: Emancipation in a Hurry*, 1911; S. (M.E.) *Mixed Herbs: A Working Woman's Remonstrance Against the Suffrage Agitation*, 1908; Josephine Butler, *Woman's Work and Woman's Culture*, 1869; Mrs Caplin, *Women in the Reign of Queen Victoria*, 1876; Densmore, *Sex Equality*, 1907; the *Englishwoman's Year Book*, current year; Hartley, *The Truth About Women*, 1913; Eliza Lynn Linton, *The Girl of the Period*, 1883; Belfort Bax, *Fraud of Feminism*, 1913; Laura Marholm, *The Psychology of Woman*, 1899; Stanton, *the Woman Question in Europe*, 1884; Elizabeth Robins, *Way Stations*, 1913; and even the *Suffrage Annual and Women's Who's Who*, 1913.

From this brief survey it is clear that the public library system was receptive to the growing women's movement, prepared to add appropriate books to their shelves as they were published. Presumably it was in response to a real demand from readers, as well as to the blandishments of publishers, that libraries selected their purchases. It may be significant to note that the Islington library, the only one to stock a run of the *Englishwoman's Year Book*, dated the beginning of this run from 1906. Unless previous volumes had been put into storage, it would appear that the library's willingness to stock this useful directory had coincided with the increasing interest in the women's movement engendered by the start of militancy. It may be that even the vestigial reflection of the nineteenth-century suffrage movement in the library system is in fact a chimera. Of the earlier books stocked, Mill, *The Subjection of Women*, would doubtless have had its entrée to the library system secured by the author's reputation, whatever its subject; the other two most commonly featured titles, by Higginson and Mrs Ashton Dilke, were published in (separate) series, for which libraries probably had standing orders and were not necessarily titles individually selected by the librarian. Swan Sonneschein and Fisher Unwin (*see under* PUBLISHERS AND PRINTERS), the publishers of Stopes, Ostrogorski, the 1891 edition of Wollstonecraft, and Crepaz, clearly had effective relationships with library suppliers; all these titles were included in virtually all the twentieth-century catalogues studied. However, by 1914 there was a very marked increase in the range of titles, from a variety of publishers, on library shelves, reaching its apogee in the purchase of the newly published *Suffrage Annual and Women's Who's Who* for consultation by readers in Bolton. It may be no coincidence to note that Bolton was a town with a large, well organized NUWSS society.

Although we can piece together the details of these lending libraries, there is no real evidence of how they were used. Ironically it was imprisonment and the preservation of so much of the associated correspondence, both in Home Office files and in those of the SUFFRAGETTE FELLOWSHIP, that has provided information about the type of books that women involved in the militant suffrage movement read. Suffrage prisoners were not impressed by the books left for them in their cells. Mary Anne Rawle noted that in Holloway in 1907 the authorities had provided her with "The Bible, Hymn Book, Prayer Book, *A Healthy Home*, and *The Narrow Way*". The last named was still a feature in prison cells five years later; Zoe PROCTER noted its presence in her cell in March 1912. *A Healthy Home* provided the prisoners with grim amusement, Florence SPONG in 1909 giving as a reason for breaking her cell glass that this book, provided by the prison authorities, recommended plenty of fresh air. There is no doubt that the imprisonment of so many literate women left its mark on the prison library system. Before being granted of a degree of privilege under Rule 243A, suffrage prisoners in the second-class division were not entitled to receive books sent in from outside. This was one of the most keenly felt differences between the treatment of first-class (political) and second-class prisoners. In November 1906, after she had been moved into the First Division, Minnie BALDOCK mentioned in a letter to her husband that Dr Stanton COIT had sent her a copy of *Women and Economics* (by Charlotte Perkins Gilman), remarking "it is very good indeed. I was glad to get it". When she was in prison a few months earlier Mrs SBARBORO had read *Temple Bar*, a popular fiction magazine, probably obtained from the prison library because as a second-class prisoner she was not entitled to any other literature, even if she had wanted it. Moreover during the first month of their sentence second-class prisoners were not permitted to read novels from the prison library, although Shakespeare was allowed. In April 1912, when the prison was full with WSPU window-smashers, the Winson Green, Birmingham, Prison Visiting Committee noted that "the Prisoners were specially allowed to have books to read, although some of them asked for classical books not in the Prison library. Prison Rules 67, 70 & 299 deal with the provision of books and papers for circulation among the prisoners. A list was produced by the Governor of books which had been recently asked for by him for use in connection with the Prisoners' library, and such books would shortly be in the prison." Unfortunately this interesting catalogue no longer appears to exist. In March 1909 the Home Office had written in reply to a query about what books and magazines could be sent to suffragette prisoners, that approved books might be sent upon condition that they were added to the prison library. A list of any to be sent had first to be approved by the prison governor. It is clear from Home Office notes that books had been sent into Holloway in such large numbers that a suggestion had been made that if the library became too full books might be distributed around the libraries of other prisons.

The library in Holloway was, apparently, administered by the (Church of England) prison chaplain. In 1910 Mrs Chapin said she read J.S. Mill, *On Liberty*, in prison, recommended to her by the librarian. In 1912, in Holloway, Rose Lamartine YATES read both *On Liberty* and *Subjection of Women*. At the same time Dr Alice KER was reading from the prison library *Pride and Prejudice* (the edition with Brock's illustrations), a book on Joan of Arc, *Corleone*, "A Tale of Sicily" by Marion Crawford, *Hypatia* by Charles Kingsley, and Ruskin's *Seven Lamps of Architecture* and the first *Book of Modern Painters* ("there are some good books in the prison library"). She also had time to read *Brethren* by Rider Haggard, the *Bhagavad-Gita*, *Beauchamp's Career*, which she remarked was "by one of our members" (George Meredith). Miss Armour sent in to her *The Inner Life* (a theosophical work by C.W. Leadbetter) and Lady Constance LYTTON sent a copy of Sylvia Pankhurst's *The Suffragette*, presumably sanctioned by the prison governor. Alice Ker also asked for an Esperanto grammar to be sent in and mentioned that "Votes [for Women] came in once, cut into strips, wrapped in oiled paper, in the stuffing of a roast chicken." Florence HAIG in Holloway in the spring of 1912 also selected a book about Joan of Arc, perhaps the same copy as that read by Alice Ker. Her prison diary records it as *Jeanne d'Arc*, edited by T. Douglas Murray, and also mentions that she read *Romola*, *Middlemarch*, and *Felix Holt*, by George Eliot, and *Uncle Tom's Cabin* by Harriet Beecher Stowe. In Aylesbury prison in 1912 Olive WALTON tried to read Annie Besant, *Riddle of Life* ("but fear it is greatly beyond me"); Israel Zangwill, *Mantle of Elijah*; R.W. Kauffman, *The Daughters of Ishmael* ("it is truly terrible"); Kropotkin, *Memoirs of a Revolutionist* ("an ideal book for a rebel in prison"); Tolstoy's *Essays*; and Elizabeth Robins, *The Open Question*. Janie TERRERO read *Barnaby Rudge* in Holloway ("what a solace Dickens was in prison"). Mary THOMPSON was also of the same opinion, although she chose *Little Dorrit* ("seems appropriate"), as well as reading a pamphlet by Bernard Shaw on Religion (which was also read by Mrs PANKHURST during the same period of imprisonment in 1912), a book about the Indian Mutiny, and Tennyson's "Ulysses", which she learnt by heart. When in Holloway Leonora TYSON wanted to read a Tauchnitz edition of *Helen of the High Hand* by Arnold Bennett, which she had at home. However, it could not be found and she had to make do with *Cashel Byron's Profession* by George Bernard Shaw. Emily DUVAL made good use of her time in Winson Green in 1912, reading Mathilde Blind's biography of *Madame Roland* (in W.H. Allen's "Eminent Women" series), Mary E. Coleridge's *Gathered Leaves*, and Thomas Wentworth Higginson, *Common Sense About Women*. Her daughter Norah read William Morris, *News from Nowhere*. The heroes of the Italian Risorgimento provided uplifting prison reading. In 1912 a Miss Collier read the life of Mazzini (doubtless that edited by Emilie Ashurst VENTURI), because he, too, had been in prison, and Emmeline PETHICK-LAWRENCE remarked that she always advised suffragists to read "Trevelyan's Garibaldi Books" (G.M. Trevelyan's *Garibaldi and the Making of Italy* had been published in 1911). The cult of the "hero" clearly appealed to those conscious of their role in history; in Holloway in March 1912 Winifred MAYO was reading *Frederick the Great* by Thomas Carlyle. It is doubtful if many of these books, apart from those noted, were in the prison library when the suffrage prisoners arrived; they certainly were when they left. It would be interesting to know if this more extensive range of available material had any effect on the reading of non-suffrage prisoners. In any event the prison authorities, along with civic library committees, were in the twentieth century forced to take note of the burgeoning literature of the women's suffrage campaign.

Archival source: Parkes Papers, Girton College; Elizabeth Wolstenholme Elmy Papers, British Library; Papers of Bolton Women's Suffrage Society, Bolton Studies Library; documents relating to the Bedford Society for Women's Suffrage, Bedfordshire Record Office; Minutes of Portishead Women's Suffrage Society, private collection; National Union of Women's Suffrage Societies, Southampton branch Minute Book, 1911–14, Southampton Archives Service; Records of the Cambridge Women's Suffrage Association, County Record Office, Cambridge; Minute Books of the Nottingham Women's Suffrage Society, 1909–24, Nottinghamshire Archives; Suffragette Fellowship, Museum of London; Home Office files, Public Record Office.

Bibliography: K. Flint, *The Woman Reader, 1837–1914*, 1993.

LIMEHOUSE (WSPU) Secretary (1906) Mrs Bennett, 218 Rhodeswell Road, London E.

LINCOLN (NUWSS) In 1913 the society was a member of the MIDLAND (EAST) FEDERATION OF THE NATIONAL UNION OF WOMEN'S SUFFRAGE SOCIETIES. Secretary (1913) Miss K.C. Huddleston, 185 Monks Road, Lincoln, Lincolnshire.

LITTLEHAMPTON (NUWSS) In 1913 the society was a member of the SURREY, SUSSEX, AND HANTS FEDERATION OF THE NATIONAL UNION OF WOMEN'S SUFFRAGE SOCIETIES. Secretary (1913) Miss Arnett, Pellew House, Littlehampton, Sussex.

LIVERPOOL branch of the MEN'S LEAGUE FOR WOMEN'S SUFFRAGE Founded in 1908. Its first president was W. Lyon Blease.

LIVERPOOL committee of NATIONAL SOCIETY FOR WOMEN'S SUFFRAGE Formed in 1871. The Rev. George Butler and his wife Josephine Butler were members of its executive committee and Mrs Mactaggart of Ivy House, Aigburth, nr Liverpool was its honorary secretary. In 1872 the Liverpool committee affiliated with the new CENTRAL COMMITTEE OF THE NATIONAL SOCIETY FOR WOMEN'S SUFFRAGE. The society was refounded in 1894 and in 1896 affiliated to the CENTRAL NATIONAL SOCIETY FOR WOMEN'S SUFFRAGE. In 1898 it joined the NATIONAL UNION OF WOMEN'S SUFFRAGE SOCIETIES and in 1913 was a member of the WEST LANCS, WEST CHESHIRE, AND NORTH WALES FEDERATION OF THE NATIONAL UNION OF WOMEN'S SUFFRAGE SOCIETIES. Secretaries (1895) Mrs Bright, Gorse Hey, West Derby, Liverpool; (1898) Miss Eleanor RATHBONE, Greenbank, Liverpool; (1913) Miss E.E. Deakin, 9 Alexandra Drive, Liverpool and Miss Eleanor Rathbone.

LIVERPOOL branch of the UNITED SUFFRAGISTS Founded in mid-1914. Honorary secretary: Isabel Buxton, 11 Queen's Road, Liverpool.

LIVERPOOL (WFL) Secretary (1913) Mrs Evans, 49 Kimberley Drive, Great Crosby, Liverpool. In 1910 the organizers were Miss M.A. Broadhurst and Miss M.M. Farquharson. In 1911 Miss Broadhurst founded the NATIONAL POLITICAL LEAGUE, for which Miss Farquharson became an organizer.

LIVERPOOL (WSPU) Organizer (1906) Miss Labouchere, 281 Upper Parliament Street, Liverpool; (1910) Miss Ada FLATMAN, 28 Berry Street, Liverpool; (1913) Miss Jollie, Canning Chambers, 2 South John Street, Liverpool. This was one of the WSPU's earliest branches.

LIVERPOOL UNIVERSITY (NUWSS) Secretary (1909) Miss Madge S. Workman, The University of Liverpool, Liverpool; (1913) Miss A.D.B. Harvey, The University of Liverpool, Liverpool.

LLANDUDNO (NUWSS) In 1913 the society was a member of the WEST LANCS, WEST CHESHIRE, AND NORTH WALES FEDERATION OF THE NATIONAL UNION OF WOMEN'S SUFFRAGE SOCIETIES. Secretary (1909) Miss Walton Evans, 4 Abbey Road, Llandudno; (1913) Miss Wright, Preswylfa, Abbey Road, Llandudno, Wales.

LLANELLY (NUWSS) In 1913 the society was a member of the SOUTH WALES AND MONMOUTH FEDERATION OF THE NATIONAL UNION OF WOMEN'S SUFFRAGE SOCIETIES. Secretary (1913) Miss Smith, 9 Mina Street, Llanelly, Wales.

LLANGOLLEN (NUWSS) In 1913 the society was a member of the WEST LANCS, WEST CHESHIRE, AND NORTH WALES FEDERATION OF THE NATIONAL UNION OF WOMEN'S SUFFRAGE SOCIETIES. Secretary (1913) Miss B. Stewart, Hafod-y-Coed, Llangollen, Wales.

Archival source: Minutes of the Llangollen branch NUWSS, 1914–18, National Library of Wales.

LOCHGELLY (WFL) Was in existence in 1914.

LONDON AND NATIONAL SOCIETY FOR WOMEN'S SERVICE The name taken by the LONDON SOCIETY FOR WOMEN'S SERVICE in 1926 in order to reflect the broadening field of its activities. Although still actively campaigning for women's complete enfranchisement, its main work was to improve employment opportunities for women throughout the country. In 1926 a trust fund, established by an anonymous gift, ensured the survival of the society, which in 1953 became the Fawcett Society.
Secretary: (1926–51) Philippa STRACHEY.

Address: (1926–50) (although evacuated during the Second World War) Women's Service House, 35–37 Marsham Street, London SW; (1950–June 1950) 40 Broadway Chambers, Westminster, London SW; (June 1950–53) 50 Tufton Street, Westminster, London SW.
Bibliography: R. Strachey, *Women's Suffrage and Women's Service*, 1927.

LONDON GRADUATES' UNION FOR WOMEN'S SUFFRAGE Founded in 1909, affiliated to the NATIONAL UNION OF WOMEN'S SUFFRAGE SOCIETIES, in order to promote "by means befitting a University Association, the extension of the franchise to women on the same terms as it is, or may be, granted to men". Membership was open to both men and women graduates of the University of London and to those closely associated with the university in a teaching capacity or otherwise. Twenty-nine local centres, often based in training colleges or high schools, had been set up in various parts of the country by the end of 1912, by which time the membership of the society was over 850. In 1912 the society affiliated to the FEDERATED COUNCIL OF SUFFRAGE SOCIETIES and in July 1913 it presented a

petition in favour of women's suffrage signed by 474 graduates and teachers. Among the society's vice-presidents were Elizabeth Garrett ANDERSON, Israel ZANGWILL and Sir John Cockburn. In 1913 the executive committee included Mary Adelaide Broadhurst (see NATIONAL POLITICAL LEAGUE).
Chairman: (1913, 1918) Dr Helen Gwynne-Vaughan (by 1918 she was chief controller of the WAAC); honorary treasurer (1913, 1918) Lady Busk (her husband was chairman of convocation, University of London, and in 1909 she had given a contribution to the WSPU). The society's banner, designed by Mary LOWNDES, is now in the Museum of London Collection.
Address: (1913, 1917) Chester Gate, Ealing, London W.
Archival source: London Graduates' Union for Women's Suffrage Report, May 1918, Fawcett Library.
Bibliography: *Suffrage Annual and Women's Who's Who*, 1913.

LONDON NATIONAL SOCIETY FOR WOMEN'S SUFFRAGE

Succeeded the ENFRANCHISEMENT OF WOMEN COMMITTEE, after the latter's dissolution in July 1867. Plans for its formation had been under discussion by, among others, Helen TAYLOR, Clementia TAYLOR and Frances Power COBBE in May and June. From the outset it was intended that this new society in London was to be part of a federated scheme. On 12 June Mentia Taylor wrote to Helen Taylor that she was willing "to undertake the secretary-ship (and to join at once 'The National Society') of the 'London Central Committee' – the centres all to be affiliated together and in constant correspondence with each other so that no work shall be repeated. I think different centres will be necessary for local actions – but no centre to take any important step without reference to all the other centres". On 18 June Mentia Taylor was waiting to hear the decision of the Manchester Society about the possibility of co-operation. She received a positive response, c. 28 June, from Jacob BRIGHT. Mentia Taylor had in the meantime spoken to Priscilla McLAREN, then in London, who with her step-daughter Agnes McLAREN was quite prepared to establish a similar centre in Edinburgh.

The next stumbling-block came over the title of the society. In a letter of 20 June to Helen Taylor, Mentia Taylor reported that it was proposed to call the society "The London Woman Suffrage Society" in co-operation with the Manchester Society for the Enfranchisement of Women. By 11 July this had changed to "The London National Society for Woman Suffrage" and it was with this heading that notepaper was printed. It quickly became apparent that this phraseology was not acceptable to J.S. MILL and Helen Taylor, who threatened to resign if the title did not include the term "Women's Suffrage". Mentia Taylor, as mediator, wrote to Helen Taylor on 15 July to explain that Frances Power Cobbe preferred "Woman Suffrage", "strongly objecting to the use of the genitive". The connotations that distinguished the two phrases are now somewhat obscure, indeed both P.A. Taylor and Moncure Conway expressed themselves mystified by the distinction at the time. It would appear that Helen Taylor and Mill thought that "Woman Suffrage" implied that of only unmarried women and widows. By 23 July Mentia Taylor was able to report to Helen Taylor that the committee had agreed to Mr Mill's title, "The London National Society for Women's Suffrage". However, the subject was so delicate that, when writing to Helen Taylor on 8 August, Mentia Taylor altered the printed heading by hand, feeling it necessary to explain that she had been doing this on every letter until new paper arrived. In August, Mentia Taylor wrote to ask Lydia BECKER if the Manchester Society had adopted the same phraseology in its title as had London. "The Edinburgh will do so and I suppose we may then consider ourselves as parts of our National Society – united yet independent." The first executive committee of the London National Society comprised only women and was put together by Mentia Taylor, probably at the suggestion of Helen Taylor who, backed by Mill, had insisted on the exclusion of men. Its members were: Frances Power Cobbe, Millicent Garrett FAWCETT, Miss Hampson (a friend of Frances Power Cobbe), Mary Lloyd (companion of Frances Power Cobbe), Margaret Bright LUCAS, Caroline STANSFELD and Mentia Taylor. Frances Power Cobbe, Miss Lloyd and Miss Hampson resigned in October 1867, and Caroline Ashurst BIGGS was added to the committee. In *The History of Woman Suffrage*, Vol. III, Caroline Ashurst Biggs includes Katherine HARE as a member of this committee. Besides being treasurer, Mentia Taylor was also, with Caroline Ashurst Biggs, joint secretary of the society until 1871. Although Caroline Ashurst Biggs undertook most of the administrative work, Mill was adamant that the society should be represented to the world by a married secretary.

On 15 July 1867 Mentia Taylor had written to Helen Taylor that "Our present course of action is the dissemination of information throughout the kingdom and it seems to me, we cannot apply our pounds to better purpose than by the publication of good papers". The London National Society reprinted as a pamphlet in 1868 Harriet TAYLOR's article "The Enfranchisement of Women", and distributed Helen Taylor's pamphlet *The Claims of Englishwomen to the Suffrage Constitutionally Considered*. Both these tracts were published on commission for the Society by Trubner (see under PRINTERS AND PUBLISHERS). Emily DAVIES had passed over to the new society the remainder of the copies of the speech made by Mill when he moved the amendment to the Reform Bill on 20 May 1867, which had been published by the Enfranchisement of Women Committee, and Barbara BODICHON had bequeathed them her pamphlets. The London National Society received a measure of publicity from a pamphlet written by a youthful Anna Kingsford, *An Essay on the Admission of Women to the Parliamentary Franchise*, which was published by Trubner in early 1868. She was aware that her readers might not have realized that such a society had been formed and urged those interested to get in touch with either herself or Mrs P.A. Taylor. The latter was particularly keen that working men and women should not be excluded from the London National Society and subscribers of less than 1/– annually were to be enrolled as members and were to be entitled to receive all circulars and publications of the society. Subscribers of 1 guinea annually were entitled to be members of the General Committee. Jessie BOUCHERETT, in particular, had thought it necessary that the society should have a large General Committee, packed with influential names and in August 1867 Mill had invited a number of the great and the good, including Mary Carpenter, Florence Nightingale and Lord Brougham to join it.

The first public meeting organized by the London National Society was held in the Gallery of the Architectural Society in Conduit Street (see Harriet GROTE) on 17 July 1869. The chair was taken by Mentia Taylor and the audience heard for the first time women speak from a London platform in the furtherance of their cause. The next year, on 26 March 1870, another meeting was held, this time in the Hanover Square Rooms, again with Mrs Taylor presiding. Among the speakers were Mill, Harriet Grote, Millicent Garrett Fawcett, Lord Amberley, Katherine Hare, Helen Taylor and Sir Charles Dilke.

In 1871 leading members of the Manchester National Society pressed for the formation of a new London-based central committee, the more effectively to lobby parliament. The London National Society, firmly directed by their president J.S. Mill, objected to this new venture on two grounds. The main objection was set out in a published leaflet. "We hold it to be important that no person conspicuously engaged, whether as an officer or as lecturer, in some other agitations now proceeding, to which we will not further allude, should hold any conspicuous place in the movement for Women's Suffrage. In this opinion the founders of the new Committee totally disagree, in proof of which we have merely to refer to the name of its Honorary Secretaries." The "agitations" alluded to were those against the Contagious Diseases Acts and the "honorary secretaries" were Mrs Margaret PENNINGTON and Professor Sheldon AMOS. The second, rather less substantial ground for the London Society's objection was that the new Central Committee would bring to prominence members of the provincial societies. After the split in November 1871, when some members of the London National Society, including Clementia Taylor and Caroline Ashurst Biggs, did leave to join the CENTRAL COMMITTEE OF THE NATIONAL SOCIETY FOR WOMEN'S SUFFRAGE, the London National continued as a smaller society. Relations between it and the Manchester National Society were strained. In a letter to Helen Taylor, 18 February 1872, Prof. Croom Robertson, a member of the London National's executive committee, refers sarcastically to Lydia Becker as "the fountain of all enlightenment". After Mill's death in 1873, Thomas HARE succeeded as president. Mill's influence lingered, his strategy continually invoked by Helen Taylor. As Mill had written in a letter to Croom Robertson, 4 December 1871, "I look upon it that the important thing for your Committee is much more to *be* than to *do*". This policy was one of avoiding the unseemly methods of campaigning adopted by the Manchester Society and the Central Committee and of doing very little until after a dissolution and election of a new House of Commons, by which time it was hoped that the circumstances would be so altered as to give reasonable cause for the adoption of a new plan of action. When Charlotte BURBURY, the London National's secretary asked Helen Taylor in January 1874, a month before the general election, to speak at a large public meeting to be organized by the society later in the spring, she replied that a successful meeting would take far longer than they were allowing to arrange, and that she would pay £50 for them not to have a meeting. She continues, "One year's patience is all that is required to carry out Mr Mill's repeated and urgent advice". Helen Taylor thought that the London National should not do anything precipitate, but should carry on lecturing, distributing tracts, petitioning and working on public opinion.

In the year 1875–6 the London National Society appears to have held three public meetings, four at working mens' clubs, and 13 drawing-room meetings. At one of the meetings held at St Pancras it was made quite clear that "the object of the society is to obtain the Parliamentary franchise for widows and spinsters on the same conditions as those on which it is granted to men"; Helen Taylor, Eliza ORME, Miss Buss and Charlotte Burbury were among those present. In 1877, after Jacob Bright, who had been so strongly identified with the CDA agitation, had retired through illness from his position as parliamentary spokesman for the suffrage campaign, he was succeeded by Leonard Courtney, who reformulated the demand for the vote in terms of those women who had achieved the local government vote in the previous decade, that is, widows and spinsters only, but with no attempt, as Forsyth had done, specifically to exclude married women. As Helen BLACKBURN put it, "the objections of its members having disappeared with the lapse of time", the London National Society now felt able to join with the Central Committee as the Central Committee of the National Society for Women's Suffrage.

Secretaries (1867–71) Clementia Taylor and Caroline Ashurst Biggs; (1871–2) Eliza Orme; (1872–c. 1877) Charlotte Burbury. Address: (1867–71) Aubrey House, Campden Hill, Kensington, London W; (1871–2) 81 Avenue Road, Regent's Park, London; (1872–c. 1877) 15 St George's Terrace, Queensgate, London W. Unlike the Manchester National Society, the London National operated in a domestic atmosphere and never established a formal office.

Archival source: Mill–Taylor Collection, London School of Economics and Political Science.

LONDON PROVISIONAL PETITION COMMITTEE

It is clear that even before John Stuart MILL presented to parliament the petition prepared by the WOMEN'S SUFFRAGE PETITION COMMITTEE on 7 June 1866, members of that committee intended that their work should continue. It did, however, take from June until the end of November for the project to take shape, and for much of that time the group of workers did not conceive of themselves as a committee. They had no headed notepaper, nor formal officers, although, by default, Clementia TAYLOR appears to have acted as treasurer. The name "London Provisional Petition Committee" is merely descriptive of their objective (to petition for women's enfranchisement), the uncertainty of their existence, and their geographical location.

Barbara BODICHON wrote to Helen TAYLOR, c. 4/5 June 1866, "I wish very much to speak to you about forming the Association" and Emily DAVIES wrote to Helen Taylor on 5 June 1866 that she proposed going to see Mrs Knox (see Isa CRAIG) to find out whether she was able to take part in the "approaching campaign". She followed up this letter with another on 6 June 1866:

It occurred to me that we might have two Secretaries, one of whom should be unmarried, and that Miss Manning would make an admirable second to Mrs Knox, being in many ways *complementary*. I will find out whether she is willing. If it is worth while to have a Treasurer, which would be a merely nominal office, I should be inclined to propose Lady GOLDSMID, who has resources to fall back upon in case of deficit. If all our officers are women, do you not think we might then have men on the Committee? Some of those who are on our Examinations Committee would I am sure join us, if asked, and they have been of real use on that Committee.

Both points raised by Emily Davies, that of having a married woman as a secretary, in order that the public face of the society should be irrefutably respectable, and that of including men in the committee, were to bedevil the London suffrage society for some time. Helen Taylor obviously ruled against two secretaries and Emily Davies concurred, saying that Mrs Knox would do admirably and that she had not spoken to Miss Manning about it. Helen Taylor wrote to Barbara Bodichon during the course of the week following Friday, 8 June:

> I have been talking with my father [i.e. John Stuart Mill] over some of the points you suggested on Friday, and among others, how far we can be responsible for the sort of people who join us. He recommends that we should have a very numerous general Committee, including all the best and most unimpeachable names of men and women who are willing to join us. This seems to me to be an excellent idea. The society would then consist of three parts – the executive committee, willing and able to do all the practical work; the general committee giving their names and support, and a moderate regular subscription; and the members consisting of all who voluntarily choose to join us. What should you say to having a general committee of one hundred and given an annual subscription of £1? Of course this would not prevent larger donations from individuals among them.
>
> It seems to be very important that the plan should not be talked of until it is quite complete, until indeed we have ourselves made out the list of the whole general committee (supposing this to be decided upon), else we may have people offering to be on it who may embarrass us.
>
> Another point too on which I think I did not properly explain my own idea, was the part that men should take.
>
> In the petition it seemed to me desirable that we should not even consult them, in order that Mr Mill might be able to say that it was entirely women's doing. Now although I know that no man suggested one word of the petition . . . yet you see the Spectator today insinuate that it was written by a man. . . . In our new plan I do not see the same reason not to consult men. . . . But to admit men into the governing body is merely to give over the whole credit into their hands – all the women concerned will merely be considered to take their usual and proper subordinate position. The greatest thing, to my mind, that this society can do for many years to come is to present the example of women quietly and steadily occupied with purely political work. For this reason I am anxious that we should take no part whatever in any social or even legal question; that the object of the society should be solely to obtain the right of voting in the election of members of parliament, for those women who already by the law of England possess all the other rights of citizens. I think we should disclaim any intention of interfering in any of the other questions.

In the meantime, on 9 June, Helen Taylor wrote to Barbara Bodichon, "It seems to me that if Miss Davies does not herself think that being on our committee will be injurious to her own special work of education, she would be the best fifth person. Mr Mill thinks your idea of 5 members very good, to me also it seems exactly the right number." Barbara Bodichon replied to Helen Taylor on 10 June, "I have thought much of your reasons for wishing to have women exclusively on the Committee and I do not think they are good. I believe it will be better to have men and women. I do not think that men will get the credit for the movement and I do not think the educational ability of an exclusively woman's movement would be of much value. Women do manage things now and after all what we aim at is getting the suffrage and I think we shall get it 10 years quicker by working the association with a small committee composed of men and women."

At a meeting held between herself, Emily Davies, Helen Taylor, Barbara Bodichon and Isa Craig Knox at Aubrey House, *c.* 20 June, referred to by Clementia Taylor as the "acacia-tree party", it appears to have been decided not, in fact, to form a society but merely to press ahead with the gathering and presentation of further petitions. It is likely that Helen Taylor, to whom, backed as she was by J.S. Mill, the others tended to defer, took the view that she did not wish to be held responsible for the action of any other member of a putative society. Such a society was, at that time, unthinkable without her involvement. It is interesting to note just how hesitant were the beginnings of what was to become such a powerful cause.

However, barely six weeks later, as a result of directly experiencing the complications of organizing further petitions, Emily Davies wrote to Helen Taylor, 6 August:

> I have been thinking lately that the time has come for those of us who met at Mrs Taylor – to *call* ourselves a Committee. We are at present labouring under the disadvantage that there is no one person, and not even any definite body, to take the general direction of affairs, and we shall feel the inconvenience of this more and more as we go on. Mrs Knox says she is made Secretary, after all, by taking the direction of the Petitions, and so we have come in fact to a part of your original proposal, i.e. a Managing Committee of five ladies, with Mrs Knox as Sec, with only this difference, that my taking the Press department relieves Mrs Knox of the particular kind of responsibility that she shrank from. . . . If you will kindly let me know your opinion, I will get those of Mrs Taylor, Mrs Bodichon and Mrs Knox, and if we all agree in thinking it desirable to constitute ourselves a Committee, we can do so without meeting again. There need be no publication of names, but we shall be able to say that there *is* a Committee at the centre of affairs, and we can say who compose it, to any one that cares to know . . .

A letter from Emily Davies to Helen Taylor, dated 28 August, makes clear the care required to handle those, necessarily strong-minded women, involved in the cause. She explains what she understood to have taken place at the meeting at Mrs Taylor's, "I think it now distinctly understood when we met at Mrs Taylor's that all idea of forming a *Society* was abandoned. The new idea, which has now called up by new circumstances, is different except as to the object and the proposed personnel." By this she meant that those continuing the suffrage campaign had no rules and no fixed methods of working, only their object, the people prepared to work for it and the unwritten law of committees for their guidance. Their aim would be to keep the number involved few, but with the possibility of adding new people to the committee from time to time. Emily Davies continues, drawing a parallel with the work of her Education Committee:

> We do not consider ourselves responsible to anybody but ourselves. The money is either offered or privately asked for. It seems to me that we might work for the Franchise for the present in a similarly semi-public, semi-private manner i.e. with an object (the extension of the suffrage to women), personnel, and a fund collected privately, the manner of working being decided upon from time to time as occasions arise. If we could have met again, it would of course have been more satisfactory, but as that was impossible for many months, I thought we might arrange it by writing, to constitute ourselves, if it was agreed to be desirable, without a formal meeting. I saw Mrs Taylor and consulted her, and then saw Mrs Knox, tho' I knew beforehand that she wished for this kind of organization, as she had said so some weeks ago. I also wrote about the same time to you and Mrs Bodichon. . . . I think that a permanent committee for the general object would do better than one limited to the preparation of a single petition. It has already been proposed to have two Petitions: one from "qualified" women besides the general one; and we are pretty sure to be asked for help and guidance by the promoters of the local Petitions.

The proposed petition was probably drafted by Helen Taylor. In a letter of 8 August Mentia Taylor had written to her, suggesting that it should expressly exclude married women, in order that the suffrage campaigners should work their way by careful stages to universal enfranchisement. As she wrote, "we women have many stumbling blocks because of man-made laws". The question of whether or not to include married women was one that was to exercise workers for the cause on many occasions over subsequent years.

On 28 September Emily Davies reassured Helen Taylor, "With regard to the Committee, nothing is fixed. We propose to meet as soon as we can after we get back to Town. The first thing will be to settle whether to have a Committee at all. If that is decided in the affirmative, we must then pass some formal Resolutions, constituting ourselves, and we can then transmit what business there may be on hand. In the meantime I think we may consider Mrs Knox as our Sec., as she undertook before the

Committee was proposed at all, to act as sec to these two petitions."

A month later matters had progressed and on 21 October, Barbara Bodichon informed Helen Taylor, who was in Avignon, that:

> We had a meeting yesterday and we proposed "That the ladies present form a Provisional Committee for obtaining the abolition of the legal disabilities which at present prevent unqualified women as such from voting for members of Parliament."
>
> The ladies present were: Miss BOUCHERETT, Miss COBBE, Mrs P.A. Taylor, Mrs Knox, Miss Lloyd, Miss Garrett [see Elizabeth Garrett ANDERSON], Miss Davies, Mme Bodichon, Miss PARKES. Miss Davies read some letters re Manchester [i.e. letters in response to the paper, "Reasons for the Enfranchisement of Women", that Barbara Bodichon had read to the Social Science Congress in Manchester]. Very gratifying. She then expressed her determination to withdraw altogether from the work finding the educational movement as much as she could do – every one was against her withdrawing and all proposed to her to have a sec. to do some of both work so that she might direct both works. Miss COOK was proposed and in the end Miss Davies consented to go on working at both if a sec. could be found. Mme Bodichon withdrew her name . . . (I cannot be on a committee as I am only in London 2 months or so of the year.) The permanent committee was proposed.

Mrs Taylor Treasurer (Accepted)
Mrs Knox Hon Sec pro tem (with an assistant sec)
Mr Hastings
Mr Clay
The Dean of Canterbury [Mr Alford]
Mr Russell Gurney
Lady Goldsmid
Miss Manning
Miss Boucherett
Professor Cairnes
Miss Davies
Mr Heywood
Mr Westlake [see Alice WESTLAKE]

On 2 November Helen Taylor wrote to Mentia Taylor mentioning that she understood

> that you have succeeded in establishing a "society for the extension of the Suffrage to Women". I rejoice to hear that you have established it on so good a footing, and have obtained so many good names that by it work can now be undertaken which no individuals can so fitly take charge of, and from which therefore I shall now gladly retire. From the moment there is a society in existence for extending the suffrage to women, it is on it and not on me that the charge of the petitions properly devolves, and therefore I will place the sketch I have prepared in your hands at once without any further delay.

The more formal successor to the London Provisional Petition Committee, the ENFRANCHISEMENT OF WOMEN COMMITTEE, was founded at a meeting held on 23 November 1866.

Archival source: Mill–Taylor Collection, London School of Economics and Political Science; Barbara McCrimmon/Barbara Leigh Smith Bodichon Collection, Fawcett Library.

LONDON SOCIETY FOR WOMEN'S SERVICE The name taken by the LONDON SOCIETY FOR WOMEN'S SUFFRAGE in 1919. It was now working not only for the enfranchisement of women between the ages of 21 and 30, but also for greater opportunities for women's employment. In 1926 it changed its name to the LONDON AND NATIONAL SOCIETY FOR WOMEN'S SERVICE.

Secretary: (1919–26) Philippa STRACHEY.

Address: (1919–23) 58 Victoria Street, London SW; (1923–4) Buckingham Gate, London SW; (1924–6) Women's Service House, 35–37 Marsham Street, London SW1.

Bibliography: R. Strachey, *Women's Suffrage and Women's Service*, 1927.

LONDON SOCIETY FOR WOMEN'S SUFFRAGE The new name given to the CENTRAL SOCIETY FOR WOMEN'S SUFFRAGE when the NATIONAL UNION OF WOMEN'S SUFFRAGE SOCIETIES was reorganized in 1907. The London Society had 62 member branches in London and its suburbs and increased its membership to 4000 by 1912. The London Society also concentrated its efforts on obtaining "Friends of Women's Suffrage", non-paying members, of whom they had 20 000 by 1912. The London Society was responsible for organizing the first large-scale women's suffrage demonstration, the "Mud March" in February 1907, and for the final two-day demonstration at the end of the PILGRIMAGE in 1913, as well as a myriad of smaller meetings and public displays. In 1909 the London Society was forced to repel, at its annual general meeting, an attempt by militants to capture it and thereafter was firmly "Non-Party and Constitutional". The London Society was not subject to the reorganization into federations that took place throughout the rest of the NUWSS in 1910 and at the end of 1913 a plan to adopt a moderate reform led to dissension. The perception was that the LSWS was less democratic and less open to the interests of the non-middle class than the rest of the NUWSS. A compromise was eventually reached in February 1914 whereby the London Society was given the status of a federation, with all its rights and responsibilities, but did not adopt the federation rules.

During the First World War the London Society opened the Women's Service Bureau, using the organizational skills developed for the cause, to place women in employment in order to release men for the front. The London Society also supported the London Units of the Scottish Women's Hospitals. In 1917 the London Society played an active part in the final campaign to ensure that at least some women were included in the categories enfranchised by the Representation of the People Act. Between 1918 and 1928 the society kept up the pressure to gain the vote for all women on the same terms as it was granted to men. In 1919 the title of the society was changed to the LONDON SOCIETY FOR WOMEN'S SERVICE, in order to reflect its desire to concentrate on questions relating to women's employment as well as women's suffrage.

President (1907) Lady Frances BALFOUR; (1919) Philippa Fawcett; secretary Philippa STRACHEY; chairman of the executive committee (1914) Edith PALLISER; treasurer, Hon. Mrs Spencer Graves. Millicent FAWCETT remained chairman of the London Society until 1909. In 1914 the executive committee included Mary LOWNDES, Ida O'MALLEY, Mrs Stanton COIT, Bertha NEWCOMBE, Maude ROYDEN. Its vice-presidents included Lilias Ashworth HALLETT, Clementina BLACK, Lord COURTNEY of Penwith, Millicent Fawcett, the Countess of Selborne, Mrs Cobden UNWIN, Mrs D.A. Thomas (*see* Lady RHONDDA).

Address: (1907) 25 Victoria Street, London SW; (1910) 58 Victoria Street, London SW.
Archival source: Annual reports, 1907–14, Fawcett Library.

Bibliography: R. Strachey, *Women's Suffrage and Women's Service: The History of the London and National Society for Women's Service*, 1927.

LONG EATON (WSPU) Secretary (1906) Miss Bullock (*see* Elsa GYE), Adsett Cottage, College St., Long Eaton, Derbyshire.

LORD, [HENRIETTA] FRANCES (1848–1923) (later Mrs Williams) Born in London, daughter of James Lord, a barrister. Having passed the University of London General Examination of Women in 1872, she attended Girton for two terms in 1876, a contemporary there of Hertha AYRTON and Henrietta MULLER, with whom she became very friendly. She apparently discontinued her studies, according to College records, "owing to the serious illness of her grandmother". By 1881 Frances Lord was a member of the MANCHESTER NATIONAL SOCIETY FOR WOMEN'S SUFFRAGE, and in 1882 she was elected a poor law guardian in Lambeth. At the time of the 1881 census she was living as a boarder in a house in Norland Square, her income noted as "from mortgages". In 1882 Frances Lord became the first translator of Ibsen's 1879 play, using the title *Nora*, because she thought "The Doll's House" would be thought a children's book. Her translation of *Ghosts* in 1885 also predated that of William Archer. Ibsen's biographer, Koht, wrote in 1931 that it was Ibsen's radicalism that had induced Miss Lord to make her translations, but that they did not prove successful. With her sister Emily, who was the principal of Miss Lord's Kindergarten School (9/10 Norland Place, Notting Hill), which functioned as the "prep" school for Notting Hill and Ealing High School, she translated *Mothers' Songs* by Froebel. Frances Lord subscribed to the CENTRAL COMMITTEE FOR WOMEN'S SUFFRAGE from 1884 to 1886, and in 1890, 1894, and 1895.

By 1883 Frances Lord had become a theosophist and inspired Elizabeth Cady Stanton and her daughter, Harriot Stanton BLATCH, to study Madame Blavatsky and Anna Kingsford. In 1886 she was invited by Mrs Cady Stanton and her daughter to visit America to help them create *The Woman's Bible*. However, after a time Frances Lord became more interested in psychical research and lost interest in the scheme. It was when she was in

America, 1887–8, that she discovered the Christian Science movement. She became the owner of the *Woman's World*, a journal based in Chicago. She was involved in a dispute with the similarly named, the *Lady's World*, edited by Oscar Wilde, which began US publication in 1887. After her return to England, Frances Lord was a member of the Moral Reform Union in 1889 and in the same year spoke at a meeting for the SOCIETY FOR PROMOTING THE RETURN OF WOMEN AS COUNTY COUNCILLORS. In 1897 Frances Lord was president and honorary secretary of the General Bond of Union among Workers for the Common Good, which met at the Pioneer Club (*see under* CLUBS), and entertained representatives from the NATIONAL UNION OF WOMEN'S SUFFRAGE SOCIETIES, one of whom was Clara MORDAN, and from the WOMEN'S LOCAL GOVERNMENT SOCIETY. In 1903 she spoke at meetings organized by the CENTRAL SOCIETY FOR WOMEN'S SUFFRAGE. In 1904, despite having in earlier years been sympathetic to Henrietta Muller's ideas on *The Future of Single Women*, Frances Lord, at the Registry Office in Wandsworth, married Edward Aldred Williams, the author of two works on French and Italian pronunciation.

Address: (1848) 31 Bedford Square, London WC; (1881) 47 Norland Square, London W; (1904) 11 Bolingbroke Grove, Battersea, London SW; (1923) Malling Place, West Malling, Kent; 3 Field Row, Bognor, Sussex.

Bibliography: F. Lord, *Christian Science Healing: Principles and Practice with Full Explanations for Home Students*, 1888; E.C. Stanton, *Eighty Years and More (1815–1897)*, 1898.

LOUGHBOROUGH (WSPU) Secretary (1913) Miss Corcoran, Castledine Street, Loughborough, Leicestershire.

LOUTH (NUWSS) In 1913 the society was a member of the NORTH AND EAST RIDINGS FEDERATION OF THE NATIONAL UNION OF WOMEN'S SUFFRAGE SOCIETIES. Secretary (1913) Miss K. Jackson, Carlton Lodge, Louth, Lancashire.

LOWNDES, MARY (1857–1929) One of eight children of the rector of Sturminster Newton, Dorset. She was a painter and stained-glass artist, trained as a cartoon-maker with Henry Holiday (with his wife and daughter, long a supporter of the suffrage movement) and exhibited between 1884 and 1888 at the Royal Society of British Artists, the Society of Women Artists, Manchester City Art Gallery and the Walker Art Gallery. She became the co-founder in 1897 of Lowndes and Drury, a firm making stained glass, which until 1906 was based at 35 Park Walk, Chelsea, a few doors away from the house where Sylvia PANKHURST was living and where the first London meetings of the WOMEN'S SOCIAL AND POLITICAL UNION were held. In 1899 Mary Lowndes attended the International Congress of Women in London. In January 1907 she was a founder of the ARTISTS' SUFFRAGE LEAGUE and became its chairman. Her companion, Barbara Forbes, was the League's secretary. In 1907 Mary Lowndes subscribed to the WSPU and in 1907–8 designed a "Holloway" BANNER for the WOMEN'S FREEDOM LEAGUE. She was, however, henceforward associated with the NATIONAL UNION OF WOMEN'S SUFFRAGE SOCIETIES as a member of the LONDON SOCIETY FOR WOMEN'S SUFFRAGE, of which, by 1913, she sat on the executive committee.

Her album of designs identifies Mary Lowndes and the Artists' Suffrage League with many of the banners carried in the 13 June 1908 NUWSS procession and it is with these that suffrage pageantry made its first real impact. The banners included those representing "Susan B. Anthony", "Mary Moser", "Boadicea", "Cambridge Alumnae" ("Better is Wisdom Than Weapons of War"), and the WRITERS' SUFFRAGE LEAGUE. Mary Lowndes was responsible for the "corporate image" of the Pageant of Women's Trades and Professions, which on 27 April 1909 processed from Eaton Square to the Albert Hall to mark the Quinquennial Congress of the INTERNATIONAL WOMAN SUFFRAGE ALLIANCE, and was assisted in the execution of the myriad of emblem designs by Mabel Esplin (1874–1921).

In 1910 for a meeting in the Albert Hall Mary Lowndes devised heraldic shields for 50 NUWSS branches and as the branches proliferated and were divided between federations she produced yet more designs. She was, however, doubtful about the ethics of taking part in a public display with the WSPU, doubtful about the physical possibility of creating a procession on the scale envisaged, and cited the pressure of her own work to avoid participation in the arrangements for the Coronation Procession in June 1911. She was, however, a member of the committee that arranged the Oriental Fete and Bazaar, held at the Empress Rooms in the Royal Palace Hotel in Kensington in 1912, in order to raise funds for the LSWS.

Mary Lowndes was a member of the committee of the *Englishwoman* when it was published in 1909 and contributed to it regularly throughout its life. One of her earliest articles, published in September 1909, was "On Banners and Banner-Making". She contributed illustrations to *Beware! A Warning to Suffragists,* a rhyme book written by Cicely HAMILTON and published, probably about 1909, by the Artists' Suffrage League and wrote *A.B.C. of Politics for Women Politicians*, another rhyme book published, probably a little later, by the ASL and illustrated by C. Hedley Charlton and Dora Meeson COATES.

During the First World War Mary Lowndes set up in Notting Hill, under the aegis of the LSWS, a school to train women in oxy-acetelyne welding, a skill with which her stained-glass work made her peculiarly acquainted. In co-operation with Emily FORD, who was her vice-chairman in the Artists' Suffrage League, Mary Lowndes designed at least three church windows, including one at St Mark's, Marylebone. In her will she left Barbara Forbes, besides a sum of money, all her pictures, prints, cartoons, studio effects and, although they could not have been worth much by then, her shares in the Englishwoman Ltd.

Address: (1907) Brittany Studios, 259 King's Road, Chelsea, London SW; (1929) 27 Trafalgar Studios, Chelsea, London SW.

Archival source: Mary Lowndes's album in Fawcett Library; Papers of the Artists' Suffrage League in Fawcett Library.

Bibliography: P. McCormack, *Women Stained Glass Artists of the Arts and Crafts Movement,* 1985; L. Tickner, *The Spectacle of Women; Imagery of the Suffrage Campaign 1907–14,* 1987 (Appendix 4 gives a list of all surviving suffrage banners, many of which can be attributed to Mary Lowndes).

LOWY FAMILY Jewish. Mrs Henrietta Lowy (1866–1953) née Solomon. Mrs Lowy was not a dogmatic feminist, but troubled by inequality. In 1908 she was living in Holland Park and with one of her daughters joined the WOMEN'S SOCIAL AND POLITICAL UNION after hearing Mrs PANKHURST speak at a meeting held at the Paddington Baths. She held a drawing-room entertainment at her home for the Kensington WSPU at which two suffrage plays were performed. In May 1909, with her daughters and Una DUGDALE, she helped run the Tea Stall at the Prince's Rink WSPU Exhibition. In December 1909 a subscription dance, organized by the Misses Dugdale, was held at her house to raise money for WSPU funds. She and her husband Ernest were generous in their donations to the WSPU; they each gave £50 in June 1910. Mrs Lowy was sentenced to one month's imprisonment in November 1910, having taken part in the stone-throwing retaliation for the indignities of "Black Friday". She was again convicted after breaking a window at Lewis Harcourt's house during the March 1912 demonstrations. Mrs Lowy was a tax resister and became a member of the JEWISH LEAGUE FOR WOMAN SUFFRAGE after it was founded in 1912. She became increasingly attracted to the radical wing of the suffrage movement and as late as 1918 was a supporter of Sylvia PANKHURST's EAST LONDON FEDERATION OF THE SUFFRAGETTES. Her husband was a generous supporter of the MEN'S POLITICAL UNION, of which his son Albert was also a member, and on occasion stood bail for suffragettes. In 1939 Ada WRIGHT appointed Ernest Lowy and his son-in-law Harold Rubinstein as two of the executors of her will.

Four of the Lowys' daughters were actively involved with the WSPU. In November 1911 Ethel (b. 1890, later Mrs Harris, died in Israel) was sentenced to a week's imprisonment after breaking a window in the Strand. In 1910 she had bought a picture for three guineas from Sylvia Pankhurst and asked her, "Do let me know when you have done a sketch of your mother". By 1912 she was honorary secretary of the WSPU branch in Felixstowe and in 1913 was group captain of Section C at the funeral of Emily Wilding DAVISON. In 1915 Ethel Lowy contributed to the fund organized by the East London Federation of the Suffragettes to provide milk and help to alleviate distress in the East End.

In March 1912 Gertrude Lowy (1887–1982, later Mrs Salaman) was sentenced to two month's hard labour after having taken part in the WSPU window-smashing raid. In June 1913 she ran the Photography stall at the WSPU's Summer Fair. Lina Lowy (1889–1939, later Mrs Rubinstein) was also involved in militant activity, reputed to have set fire to a haystack. In the early summer of 1914, with her brother Albert she was studying in Dresden at the Eurhythmics School of Jacques-Dalcroze. Her future husband, the solicitor Harold Rubinstein, was an active supporter of the militant campaign, contributing a PLAY to the cause; in 1928 he acted for Radclyffe Hall in the *Well of Loneliness* case. A younger Lowy sister, Ruth (1892–1973), who later married the publisher Victor Gollancz, acted as an usherette at WSPU meetings in the Albert Hall. She took part in the deputation to Buckingham Palace in May 1914 but lost interest in the WSPU at the outbreak of the First World War. Being a pacifist she was unable to accept the PANKHURSTS' support of the war. In 1958 she was, however, a member of the committee formed to organize a memorial to Christabel PANKHURST.

Address: (1908) 76 Holland Park, London W; (1939) 12 Ladbroke Terrace, Notting Hill Gate, London W; (1952) 37 Buckingham Court, Kensington Park Road, London W11.
Portrait: of *Ruth and Ethel* by Mrs Lily Delissa Joseph exhibited at the Society of Women Artists in 1905, and of Mrs Lowy by the same artist, exhibited at the Royal Academy in 1931. Mrs Delissa Joseph, who was Henrietta Lowy's sister, was sentenced to a month's imprisonment in March 1912, having taken part in the window-smashing campaign. Despite a plea to the Home Secretary from the Jewish chaplain to Holloway, she was not let out of prison a day before the end of her sentence in order to allow her to take part in the first day of Passover (*see also under* Frank RUTTER).

LUCAS, MARGARET BRIGHT, MRS (1818–90) Quaker, sister of John and Jacob BRIGHT and of Priscilla Bright McLAREN (*see* Appendix). She married, *c*. 1838, her cousin Samuel Lucas, editor of the *Morning Star* and friend of John Bright and Richard Cobden. She wrote, "My first political work was with the Anti-Corn Law League, when so many ladies both worked for the great bazaars, and raised money by canvassing from house to house, and I well remember how the doors were sometimes slammed in my face when people learned my errand". In 1843 she worked with her sister Priscilla at the great Anti-Corn Law bazaar at the Covent Garden theatre and was involved with the anti-slavery movement. After moving to London *c*. 1850 she was a member of the London Ladies' Emancipation Society. Margaret Bright Lucas signed the 1866 women's suffrage petition and subscribed in 1866–7 to the ENFRANCHISEMENT OF WOMEN COMMITTEE. She was proposed as a member of the committee of the LONDON NATIONAL SOCIETY FOR WOMEN'S SUFFRAGE when it was formed in June 1867. Clementia TAYLOR described her at this time as "a very practical business-like woman – good common sense and untiring energy". In 1868 the London National Society brought a case in her name, as a free-holder, using the same legal arguments as were used in the case brought by the Manchester Society in the name of Philippine KYLLMANN.

In 1872 Margaret Bright Lucas was enlisted into the Temperance movement and in 1877 became president of the British Women's Temperance Association. She was also a member of the committee of the Ladies' National Association for the Repeal of the Contagious Diseases Acts but continued with her interest in the suffrage movement. In 1874 she attended suffrage meetings in Birmingham, North Wales, Nottingham, Northampton, Leicester, Chelmsford, Maldon and Sheffield. She presided over the overflow meeting of the Grand Demonstration held in Manchester in February 1880, while her sister Priscilla Bright McLaren presided over the main meeting in the Free Trade Hall and was a member of the platform party at the Grand Demonstration held in Sheffield in February 1882. She was president of the Bloomsbury branch of the Women's Liberal Association. Margaret Bright Lucas was a friend of Elizabeth Cady Stanton and was a member of the committee that prepared *The Women's Bible*.

Address: (1887) 10 Charlotte Street, Bedford Square, London WC.
Photograph: carte de visite in Josephine Butler Collection, Fawcett Library.
Bibliography: H.J.B. Heath, *Margaret Bright Lucas*, 1890.

LUTON committee of the NATIONAL SOCIETY FOR WOMEN'S SUFFRAGE Formed in 1873, honorary secretary, Mrs Wright, St John's College. It was refounded as the Luton Women's Suffrage Society in 1889, affiliated with the CENTRAL COMMITTEE OF THE NATIONAL SOCIETY FOR WOMEN'S SUFFRAGE, and joined the NATIONAL UNION OF WOMEN'S SUFFRAGE SOCIETIES in 1898, but seemed to disappear in 1901. It was refounded as an NUWSS society and in 1913 was a member of the OXON, BERKS,

Bucks, and Beds Federation of the National Union of Women's Suffrage Societies. Secretary (1898) Louisa Bigg, Lyndhurst, Luton; (1913) Mrs I.M. Burditt, 47 Wellington Street, Luton, Bedfordshire.

LYTTON, LADY CONSTANCE GEORGINA (1869–1923) Second daughter of Robert, afterwards first Earl Lytton, and his wife, Edith Villiers. Her father's grandmother was Anna Wheeler, feminist, supporter of the early co-operative movement, and credited by William Thompson in helping him write *Appeal of One-half the Human Race, Women, Against the Pretensions of the Other Half, Men*, 1825. Earl Lytton was viceroy of India and Constance lived there until she was 11 years old. Apart from a further period of four years spent in Paris, she afterwards lived with her family in London and in Hertfordshire. After her father's death in 1892 her mother was appointed a lady-in-waiting to Queen Victoria. In 1906 Lady Constance was in touch with the Espérance Girls' Club, bringing members to teach folk dances to village girls in Knebworth. In 1908 she visited the Green Lady Hostel run by the Espérance at Littlehampton and there met Emmeline Pethick-Lawrence and Annie and Jessie Kenney. Enthused by them with an interest in women's suffrage, she joined the Women's Social and Political Union in January 1909. She had obviously been studying the literature of the subject and on 12 February 1909 A.C. Fifield published her 32-page pamphlet, *"No Votes for Women": A Reply to Some Recent Anti-Suffrage Publications*. Lady Constance immediately offered herself as a member of a deputation, joining that of 24 February. She was arrested and, having refused to be bound over, was sentenced to a month's imprisonment. She spent most of this time in the hospital ward in Holloway, aware that she was being accorded special treatment on account of her family background and known heart condition. She did lobby to be treated as the other suffragette prisoners and was eventually placed in a prison cell. In October 1909, inspired by the example of Laura Ainsworth, whom Mrs Pankhurst had taken her to see as she recovered from having been forcibly fed in Birmingham's Winson Green Prison, Lady Constance resolved on a further act of militancy. In Newcastle with Emily Wilding Davison she threw a stone at a car she thought was carrying Lloyd George and, after a trial at which every effort was made on the part of the authorities not to convict her, she was, after reiterating that she had intended to be disorderly, eventually sentenced to a month's imprisonment. She immediately took part in the hunger strike but, after the prison doctors had been alerted of her heart condition, was released. Mrs Brailsford, who had taken part in the same demonstration and whose name was also well known, was released at the same time. Lady Constance was deeply ashamed of having been given preferential treatment and resolved to disguise herself when continuing with her militant campaign.

She was working for the WSPU's general election campaign in Liverpool in January 1910 and was moved to protest against the treatment of the suffragette prisoners in Walton Gaol. She disguised herself as "Jane Warton", making herself as ugly as possible for "I had noticed several times while I was in prison that prisoners of unprepossessing appearance obtained least favour", and, at the end of a meeting held by Ada Flatman and Jennie Baines outside the Gaol, led the crowd to the governor's house, demanding the release of the suffragette prisoners. She was arrested, together with Elsie Howey, and as a "first offender" was sentenced to two weeks' imprisonment in the third division. She went on hunger strike and, as Jane Warton, was not tested for any heart disease before being forcibly fed. The process was repeated on seven subsequent occasions and she describes the brutality with which it was accomplished in considerable detail in *Prisons and Prisoners*. She was eventually released, on medical grounds, after rumour that she was imprisoned under an assumed name reached the Press Association. The medical grounds were based on her loss of weight; there was never any attempt to test her heart.

On 12 June 1910 Lady Constance was appointed a paid organizer of the WSPU with a salary of £2 a week, backdated six months, and then helped organize the Musicians' contingent of the 18 June 1910 WSPU procession. The salary enabled her to take a small flat, very close to that of Mary Neal, opposite Euston Station. In 1911 she was a member of the Church League for Women's Suffrage and gave a donation to the MEN'S POLITICAL UNION. In the same year T. Fisher Unwin published Olive Schreiner's *Woman and Labour*, which is dedicated to Constance Lytton. The two women had first met in 1892 when Constance Lytton visited South Africa with her mother.

Lady Constance worked hard to promote the Conciliation Bill; her brother, the Earl of Lytton, a Conservative, was chairman of the Conciliation Committee. In November 1911, after the failure of the Bill, Lady Constance, despite having suffered a slight stroke a year earlier, resumed her militancy, joining in the window-smashing campaign. She returned to Holloway and noted the great improvements that had taken place in the treatment since her first incarceration there nearly three years previously. She was, however, quickly released after her fine was paid anonymously. She suffered another stroke in May 1912 which affected her right side, paralyzing her arm, and to a lesser degree affecting her right foot and leg. Although this put an end to her direct involvement in the militant suffrage campaign, she wrote, with her left hand, of her philosophy and experiences in *Prisons and Prisoners*, published by William Heinemann in 1914. She and her book proved to have a charismatic effect on other members of the WSPU. As Ethel SMYTH wrote to Betty Balfour, Lady Constance's sister, on 6 March 1912, "The adoration of Suffragettes for 'Lady Conny' is a thing to see, not tho' to wonder at." She remained an invalid for the rest of her comparatively short life.

Address: (1902) "Homewood", Knebworth, Hertfordshire; (1910) 15 Somerset Terrace, Duke's Road, Euston Road, London NW.
Photograph: Suffragette Fellowship Collection, Museum of London.
Bibliography: C. Lytton, *Prisons and Prisoners: Some Personal Experiences by Constance Lytton and Jane Warton, Spinster*, 1914; B. Balfour (ed.), *Letters of Constance Lytton*, 1925; C. Lytton, *I, Constance Lytton*, 1987.

M

MACAULAY, FLORENCE ELIZABETH MARY (1862–1945) Daughter of a Reading bookseller, she went to SOMERVILLE COLLEGE, Oxford, on a Samuel Morley Exhibition only to have to leave after two terms, her father having died. Her first teaching post on leaving was at Miss Buckland's School in Reading. She was subsequently a teacher at St John School, Hamilton Place in St John's Wood in London (at a salary of £60 a year with board and lodging), and in 1887 became assistant mistress at the Orphanage of Mercy at Kilburn. In 1886 she returned to Somerville on a further exhibition of £25, but was obliged to leave after a term, having exhausted her funds. She taught for the next 20 years, including a period of six years at Great Yarmouth High School. By 26 February 1907, when she addressed a meeting of the Canning Town branch, she was a member of the WOMEN'S SOCIAL AND POLITICAL UNION and became one of its peripatetic ORGANIZERS. She was speaking for the WSPU in Brighton in 1907, in Bristol in October 1908 and in the Midlands in January 1909. She was WSPU organizer in Edinburgh for much of 1909. From February 1910 until late 1912 Florence Macaulay was organizer in Canterbury and Thanet and in 1913 was addressing meetings in Scotland. In 1913 she was present on the platform at the meeting at the Essex Hall, London, which resulted in the arrest of Annie KENNEY for incitement to riot. In 1909 F.E.M. Macaulay was the author of "The Women's Marseillaise", "Arise, ye daughters of a land/ That vaunts its liberty!", a marching SONG published by the WSPU.
Address: (1910) "Trevarra", 30 Bouverie Road West, Folkestone; (1945) 38 Howard Road, Newbury, Berkshire.

MACCLESFIELD Had a branch of the MEN'S LEAGUE FOR WOMEN'S SUFFRAGE; its BANNER is now held in the Manchester Central Library Archives.

MACCLESFIELD (NUWSS) Founded in 1908, in 1910 the society joined the MANCHESTER AND DISTRICT FEDERATION OF THE NATIONAL UNION OF WOMEN'S SUFFRAGE SOCIETIES. Secretary (1913) Miss Annie Ryle Wright, Upton Mount, Macclesfield, Cheshire. The society's BANNER, which was probably designed by Mary LOWNDES, is now in Manchester Central Library Archives.

MACCLESFIELD Had a branch of the UNITED SUFFRAGISTS; its BANNER is now held in Manchester Central Library Archives.

MACMILLAN, [JESSIE] CHRYSTAL (1871–1937) Born in Edinburgh, the only daughter, with eight brothers, of a stockbroker. She was educated in Edinburgh and at St Leonards School, St Andrews. Having rejected a proferred scholarship at Girton, Chrystal MacMillan matriculated at Edinburgh University in 1892, the first year in which it was open to women, and in 1896 took a first-class degree in Mathematics and Natural Philosophy and in 1900 a second-class MA in Mental and Moral Philosophy. She attended Berlin University for a period in 1900. In 1902 she was a member of the Edinburgh Ladies' Debating Society, in 1908 seconding a proposal in support of uncontributory old-age pensions. She became honorary secretary and treasurer of the Committee of Women Graduates of the Scottish Universities (Parliamentary Franchise) when it was formed in 1906. Chrystal MacMillan, Elsie INGLIS, Frances Simson, Frances Melville and Margaret Nairn, all graduates and full members of the General Council of Edinburgh University, were refused voting papers for the University seat at the election and attempted to bring an action against the University Courts and the Chancellors, Vice-Chancellors and Registrars. They argued that the universities had no legal right to withold their voting papers and that the 1868 act specified "person" rather than "man". Chrystal MacMillan wrote to Elizabeth Wolstenholme ELMY on 9 March 1906 asking her, as the author of the pamphlet *The Enfranchisement of Women,* if she could help by giving information on the ancient rights of women. She ended her request by writing, "I formed my beliefs on your pamphlet". Elizabeth Wolstenhome Elmy gave her all the help she could and also advised her to approach Charlotte Carmichael STOPES. In 1907 the case was lost and an appeal was brought, which confirmed the finding of the lower court. Undeterred, the Committee determined to take the case to the House of Lords, raising the £1000 necessary to do so. Chrystal MacMillan, backed by Frances Simson, appeared at the bar of the House of Lords in November 1908. By arguing the case through the whole gamut of the justice system she and her fellow graduates hoped to draw attention to women's capabilities and highlight the absurdity of denying the vote to such women as themselves.

Chrystal MacMillan had been a member of the NATIONAL UNION OF WOMEN'S SUFFRAGE SOCIETIES from the early years of the century, becoming a member of its executive committee and a vice-president of the Edinburgh Society. A lecture she gave on 16 February 1909, the day of the opening of parliament, was published as a pamphlet by the WOMEN'S SOCIAL AND POLITICAL UNION; she must have agreed to this association. Indeed in 1909 she gave a donation to the WSPU. By 1913 Chrystal MacMillan was a member of both the NORTH-EASTERN and the SCOTTISH FEDERATIONS OF THE NUWSS, by 1915 becoming chairman of the Scottish Federation. She also became honorary secretary of the SCOTTISH UNIVERSITY WOMEN'S SUFFRAGE ASSOCIATION, embarking on a speaking tour of northern Scotland for that society in the late summer of 1909, travelling as far as Orkney and Shetland. She had undertaken a CARAVAN tour with Eunice MURRAY of the WOMEN'S FREEDOM LEAGUE in 1908. Although a Liberal and clear that NUWSS election support for the Labour Party should be based only on suffrage grounds, she did subscribe to the NUWSS Election Fighting Fund in 1912. Always a watchdog of constitutions, she defended the right, on the grounds that minorities should be represented, of Andrew Ballantyne, the Liberal chairman of the GLASGOW AND WEST OF SCOTLAND ASSOCIATION FOR WOMEN'S SUFFRAGE, to membership of the Scottish EFF Committee in the face of opposition from the NUWSS executive. In 1913 she was defeated by Catherine MARSHALL in the election to succeed Edith PALLISER in the post of honorary parliamentary secretary of the NUWSS. In that year she was Scottish chairman of the NUWSS PILGRIMAGE. She remained a member of the NUWSS executive committee throughout the First World War. In 1909 Chrystal MacMillan wrote *The Struggle for Political Life,* published by the Woman's Press; in 1914, *Facts versus Fancies on Women's Suffrage,* published by the NUWSS; and, after the war, *Woman Suffrage in Practice, 1913-1923.*

In June 1911 Chrystal MacMillan attended the sixth Congress of the INTERNATIONAL WOMAN SUFFRAGE ALLIANCE held in Stockholm, as proxy for Millicent Garrett FAWCETT and in 1913 was a delegate to the seventh Congress in Budapest. She was honorary secretary and vice-president of the International Woman Suffrage Alliance from 1913 to 1923. It was at Chrystal MacMillan's suggestion that the International Peace Conference was held at the Hague in 1915. She was one of only three British women (Kathleen COURTNEY and Emmeline PETHICK-LAWRENCE were the others) who were able to be present at the Conference. Chrystal MacMillan was appointed secretary of the Committee of Women for Permanent Peace that was formed as a result of the Conference and was one of the envoys who visited countries then neutral to the war, including Russia, in an attempt to persuade them to mediate a peace. She arrived in America in September 1915 and then went to Canada to set up, with Ethel SNOWDEN, a peace group there. In 1919 Chrystal MacMillan was honorary secretary of the Zurich Women's International Congress, at which was founded the Women's International League for Peace and Freedom. She remained an active member of the WILPF and, after being called to the English Bar, practised as a barrister, specializing in the nationality laws of married women. In 1923 she was a founder member of the Open Door Council, working for equal employment opportunities of women, and in 1929 was a founder member and president of Open Door International. In 1934 she was also a committee member of the National Union of Societies for Equal Citizenship, an honorary vice-president of the Edinburgh Equal Citizenship Society and a vice president of the Association of Moral and Social Hygiene. In 1935 she stood, unsuccessfully, as a Liberal candidate in Edinburgh at the general election. She appointed Elizabeth ABBOTT one of the executors of her will.

Address: (1902) Costorphine Hill House, Costorphine Road, Edinburgh; (1913) The Ladies' Caledonian Club, 39 Charlotte Square, Edinburgh; (1915) 46 Cranley Gardens, London SW; (1923) 71 Harcourt Terrace, London SW10; (1934) 4 Pump Court, Temple, London EC4.
Photograph: in A. Wiltsher, *Most Dangerous Women: Feminist Peace Campaigners of the Great War*, 1985.
Archival source: Elizabeth Wolstenholme Elmy Papers, British Library.
Bibliography: A. Whittick, *Woman into Citizen*, 1979; A. Wiltshire, *Most Dangerous Women: Feminist Peace Campaigners of the Great War*, 1985; S.S. Holton, *Feminism and Democracy: Women's Suffrage and Reform Politics in Britain, 1900–1918*, 1986; L. Leneman, *A Guid Cause: The Women's Suffrage Movement in Scotland*, 1991.

MAGUIRE, CYNTHIA HELEN ADELAIDE (1889–1966) Born in London, founding member, with Phyllis AYRTON, and honorary secretary of the CLERKS' WOMEN'S SOCIAL AND POLITICAL UNION. In 1907 she was one of the team of women that pulled Edith NEW and Mary LEIGH through the streets from Holloway to Holborn. In July 1910 she was in charge of the "Chalking Brigade" advertising the WSPU Procession to be held on 23 July and in 1913 she was a group captain in charge of Section G at Emily Wilding DAVISON's funeral. During the First World War Cynthia Maguire worked for the Pankhursts' WOMAN'S PARTY. She died in Chichester.
Address: (1913) 39 Priory Road, West Hampstead; (1956) Welherden Rectory, Stowmarket, Suffolk.

MAIDENHEAD (NUWSS) In 1913 the society was a member of the OXON, BERKS, BUCKS, AND BEDS FEDERATION OF THE NATIONAL UNION OF WOMEN'S SUFFRAGE SOCIETIES. Secretary (1913) Miss Duncan, Abbotsleigh, Cookham Road, Maidenhead, Berkshire.

MAIDSTONE (NUWSS) In 1913 the society was a member of the KENTISH FEDERATION OF THE NATIONAL UNION OF WOMEN'S SUFFRAGE SOCIETIES. Secretary (1913) Mrs Blackett, Hill View, St Philip's Avenue, Maidstone, Kent.

MAIR, SARAH ELIZABETH SIDDONS (1846–1941) DBE Born in Edinburgh, great-granddaughter of Sarah Siddons, her mother was a friend of Lady Noel Byron. At the age of 18, S.E.S. Mair founded the Edinburgh Essay Society (from 1869 renamed the Ladies' Edinburgh Literary Society and after 1880 known as the Ladies' Edinburgh Debating Society). She was president during the entire life of the Society, from 1865 to 1935. The first debate to touch on the question of women's suffrage was held by the Society in 1866, perhaps prompted by discussion surrounding the women's suffrage petition, although none of the founding members of the Society were signatories to it. The motion was resoundly defeated, by 15 votes to 5. In March 1872 when the motion, seconded by S.E.S. Mair, "Should women be admitted to the Parliamentary franchise?" was again debated, it was defeated by three votes. The matter was next debated in 1884, the motion again being seconded by Miss Mair, and this time was carried by 13 votes to 8. In 1891 the motion, led by Miss Mair, "Should Political Associations for Women make Female Suffrage a primary object?" was carried by 11 votes to 3. The matter was not again debated until November 1905, perhaps significantly, very soon after the arrest of Christabel PANKHURST and Annie KENNEY at the Free Trade Hall in Manchester had given fresh publicity to the question. Miss Mair on this occasion again seconded the motion in favour of extending the suffrage to women and it was carried by 27 votes to 6. In 1914, 42 years after the first suffrage debate, Miss Mair proposed the motion, "Is it desirable that women should have the parliamentary vote?", and this was carried by 29 votes to 9, with two women abstaining. In 1869 Miss Mair had reviewed, in the Society's magazine *The Attempt*, the collection of essays edited by Josephine Butler, *Women's Work and Women's Culture,* and had singled out for commendation the essay on "Female Suffrage" by Julia Wedgwood.

In 1867, with Mary Crudelius, who had signed the 1866 women's suffrage petition, S.E.S. Mair was one of the founders of the Edinburgh Association for the University Education of Women. In 1889 the Edinburgh branch of the Northern United Registry for Governesses was run from Miss Mair's address. She was an early member of the EDINBURGH

National Society for Women's Suffrage and was one of the main speakers at the Grand Demonstration held in Edinburgh in March 1884. In 1889 she signed the Declaration in Favour of Women's Suffrage compiled by the Central Committee of the National Society for Women's Suffrage. In 1899 she was a member of the executive committee of the National Union of Women's Suffrage Societies. She succeeded as president of the Edinburgh society after the death of Priscilla Bright McLaren in 1906, in addition becoming president of the Scottish Federation of the NUWSS after its formation in 1910. In October 1913 the monthly meeting of the newly formed Northern Men's Federation for Women's Suffrage was held in S.E.S. Mair's house. Immediately after the outbreak of war in 1914 she, with Elsie Inglis, proposed that the Federation should equip a hospital to be staffed entirely by women, a scheme that developed into the Scottish Women's Hospitals. Miss Mair was president of the Scottish Women's Hospital Committee for the duration of the war and contributed the chapter "Our Chief", a biographical essay on Elsie Inglis, to Eva Shaw McLaren's *A History of the Scottish Women's Hospitals*, 1919. At the end of the war she was made a member of the Order of St Sava (Serbia), Class IV. She was also made a Dame of the British Empire and given an honorary doctorate by Edinburgh University. In 1934 she was honorary president of the Edinburgh National Society for Equal Citizenship and a vice-president of the National Council for Equal Citizenship. However, a small bequest she had left to the Edinburgh society in her will made in 1934 was, for whatever reason, retracted in a codicil of 1937.

Address: (1867) 29 Abercromby Place, Edinburgh; (1880) 5 Chester Street, Edinburgh.
Photograph: in L. Milne Rae, *Ladies in Debate: Being a History of the Ladies' Edinburgh Debating Society, 1865–1935*, 1936.
Bibliography: L. Milne Rae, *Ladies in Debate: Being a History of the Ladies' Edinburgh Debating Society, 1865–1935*, 1936; E. Shaw McLaren, *A History of the Scottish Women's Hospitals*, 1919; L. Leneman, *A Guid Cause: The Women's Suffrage Movement in Scotland*, 1991; L. Leneman, *In the Service of Life: The Story of Elsie Inglis and the Scottish Women's Hospitals*, 1993.

MALE ELECTORS' LEAGUE FOR WOMEN'S SUFFRAGE

Probably the first men's society in support of women's suffrage, formed before mid-1897 by Ben Elmy (*see* Elizabeth Wolstenholme Elmy). Charles Pearce, the husband of Isabella Bream Pearce, who wrote as "Lily Bell" for the *Labour Leader* and was a close friend of Elizabeth Wolstenholme Elmy, was a member of the society's executive committee until his death in 1905. By 1904 Frank Elmy's name had been substituted, by hand, for that of his father (d. 1906) on the society's printed notepaper. This paper was headed by a quote from Tennyson much favoured by the Elmys, "THE Woman's cause is Man's: they rise or sink/ Together; dwarf'd or godlike, bond or free." Frank, ever helpful, distributed MEL leaflets at a meeting held by Anna Maria Priestman in Bristol in 1903. In October 1904 Women's Social and Political Union and MEL leaflets were being distributed together at meetings of the Lancashire and Cheshire Women and Other Workers' Representation Committee and MEL leaflets were handed out at the Manchester Free Trade Hall meeting to welcome Christabel Pankhurst's release from prison in October 1905. In 1906 the MEL sent a memorial about the proposed redistribution of parliamentary seats to Henry Campbell-Bannerman, and in 1907 gained a new member in Bayard Simmons, who became the first man to go to prison for the cause.

Archival source: Elizabeth Wolstenholme Elmy Papers, British Library.

MALLESON, ELIZABETH WHITEHEAD, MRS (1828–1916)

Unitarian, daughter of Henry and Frances Whitehead, the eldest of 11 children, she was inadequately educated, as she related, at home and at a Unitarian school in Clapton. Her mother worked at the 1845 Anti-Corn Law Bazaar at the Covent Garden theatre and her father worked alongside Peter Taylor Snr, the future father-in-law of Clementia Taylor, in the Anti-Corn Law League. Elizabeth Whitehead and her siblings became friendly with P.A. Taylor and his family (*see* Appendix). Her family was also intimate with William Johnson Fox, minister of the South Place Chapel and through him she became acquainted with Miranda and Octavia Hill. It was Fox who in 1853 told Elizabeth Whitehead of Barbara Leigh Smith's (*see* Barbara Bodichon) plan to establish an elementary school on the principles and methods she had conceived essential for a "people's school" and that she was seeking a teacher for it. Elizabeth Whitehead arranged to qualify herself for this new kind of teaching (she was already giving lessons to one child) by attending Mr Shields' Birkbeck school at Peckham. Portman Hall School, which was attended by, among other children, Garibaldi's sons and Barbara Leigh Smith's nieces, opened in November 1854. After a year of strenuous activity Elizabeth Malleson's health broke down and she went to recuperate at the home of P.A. Taylor's mother.

In 1857 Elizabeth Whitehead married Frank Malleson, whose father ran a Unitarian boys' school in Hove. The service, at which the word "obey" was omitted, was conducted by Frank's father in the Little Portland Street Chapel, of which James Martineau, Harriet's brother, was the minister. The Mallesons were to become the parents of three daughters and a son. Elizabeth Whitehead had worked in the "Friends of Italy" movement with Frank Malleson, who was cousin and brother-in-law (so interconnected are these Unitarian families) of P.A. Taylor. Her own sister married P.A. Taylor's uncle. Frank's brother William Malleson married P.A. Taylor's sister, who as Mrs W.T. Malleson was in 1866–7 to be a subscriber to the ENFRANCHISEMENT OF WOMEN COMMITTEE and in 1871 to publish "Mrs W.T. Malleson's Reply to Miss Garrett's letter on the Contagious Diseases Acts in the *Pall Mall Gazette*". William Malleson presided at the meeting at which J.S. MILL first spoke to Westminster electors in June 1865.

Together the Mallesons opened, in October 1864 at 29 Queen's Square in Bloomsbury, the College for Working Women, based on the idea of the Working Men's College, which had been founded ten years earlier by F.D. Maurice. As Elizabeth Malleson wrote in her memoir, the College was founded "to meet the needs of the several classes of women who are at work during the day ... The coffee-room, provided with periodicals and newspapers, etc, will open every evening from 7 to 10, and will be made as far as possible the centre of the social life of the college". William Morris, a neighbour in Queen Square, lent a series of Burne-Jones's cartoons to decorate this coffee room. The College was supported by Barbara Bodichon, J.S. Mill, George Eliot and Harriet Martineau and among its earliest teachers were Octavia Hill, Elizabeth Garrett (*see* Elizabeth Garrett ANDERSON), Frances Power COBBE, A.J. Munby (who in his diary entry of 5 February 1864 describes Elizabeth Malleson, at the meeting convened to discuss the idea for the college, as "gentle & womanly as well as energetic and earnest") and George MacDonald, the novelist, whose wife Louisa was in 1866 a signatory to the women's suffrage petition. Eventually Elizabeth Malleson came to doubt the wisdom of educating men and women separately, citing the desire to "see the relations of men and women purified and ennobled by common educational intercourse". The College was open to men in 1874, becoming the Men and Women's College. Elizabeth Malleson was secretary of the College and her husband the treasurer until they retired in 1882. The College was finally closed in 1901. After moving to Gloucestershire in the early 1880s Elizabeth Malleson apparently oversaw the education of a few pupils, Edith CRAIG being one of them.

Elizabeth Malleson joined the Ladies' London Emancipation Society in 1864 as its honorary auditor. Mentia Taylor was its honorary secretary, E.A. Manning was its treasurer and its tracts were published by Emily FAITHFULL. Elizabeth Malleson was a member of the Society for Promoting the Employment of Women in 1867, a member of the Westminster Committee for the Repeal of the Contagious Diseases Acts and honorary secretary of the Ladies' National Association when it was formed in 1870. She signed the "Protest" against the CD Acts that appeared in the *Daily News* on 1 January 1870. In 1889 she founded the Rural Nursing Association, the precursor of district nursing, and wrote a paper on the philanthropic aspect of nursing which was read at the Chicago Exhibition of 1893–4.

Elizabeth Malleson, who, with Barbara Bodichon, had discussed the question of women's enfranchisement since they were both in their twenties, signed the 1866 women's suffrage petition and subscribed to the Enfranchisement of Women Committee in 1866–7. She joined the LONDON NATIONAL SOCIETY FOR WOMEN'S SUFFRAGE in 1867 and became a member of its executive committee around December 1868. In 1871, being a strong supporter of the campaign against the Contagious Diseases Act, she joined the CENTRAL COMMITTEE, leaving the London National Society, the committee of which objected to any member engaging in the CDA agitation. She was not a good public speaker and so did not take a very active part in the suffrage movement, but gave it her support, for instance signing the Declaration in Favour of Women's Suffrage compiled by the Central Committee in 1889. After moving to Gloucestershire in 1882 she arranged drawing-room meetings and invited speakers to interest her neighbours in the suffrage cause. In 1889–90 she and her husband were members of the council of the WOMEN'S FRANCHISE LEAGUE. Her daughter Hope joined the WOMEN'S SOCIAL AND POLITICAL UNION in 1909 but Elizabeth, although sympathetic to the WSPU's aims, could not support their methods. In 1913 she was active in the anti-White Slave Trade agitation of 1913 and founded a Gloucestershire branch of the National Vigilance Association.

Address: (1828) Whitehead's Grove, Chelsea, London; (1882) Dixton Manor House, Winchcombe, Gloucestershire.
Photograph: in Josephine Butler Collection, Fawcett Library.
Bibliography: E. Malleson, *Notes on the Early Training of Children*, 1885; H. Malleson (ed.), *Elizabeth Malleson 1828–1916: Autobiographical Notes and Letters, with a Memoir by Hope Malleson*, 1926; J.F.C. Harrison, *A History of the Working Men's College 1854–1954*, 1954; D. Hudson, *Munby: Man of Two Worlds*, 1972.

MALTON AND DISTRICT (NUWSS) In 1913 the society was a member of the NORTH AND EAST RIDINGS FEDERATION OF THE NATIONAL UNION OF WOMEN'S SUFFRAGE SOCIETIES. Secretary (1913) Miss Janet Brooke, Slingsby Rectory, Malton, Yorkshire.

MALVERN (NUWSS) In 1913 the society was a member of the MIDLAND (WEST) FEDERATION OF THE NATIONAL UNION OF WOMEN'S SUFFRAGE SOCIETIES. Secretary (1913) Miss Dawson, Broadmeadow, Gt. Malvern, Worcestershire.

MANCHESTER branch of the MEN'S LEAGUE FOR WOMEN'S SUFFRAGE Formed in 1908. In 1914 it was presented with a new black and gold BANNER by Professor and Mrs Merrick. Honorary secretary (1910) W. Bently Capper (see Mabel CAPPER), 21 Oxford Road, Manchester; (1915) J. Beanland, 52 Parsonage Road, Withington, Cheshire.

Archival source: Manchester Men's League for Women's Suffrage Annual Report 1914–15, Fawcett Library.

MANCHESTER branch of the MEN'S POLITICAL UNION FOR WOMEN'S SUFFRAGE Founded in 1910.

MANCHESTER branch of the UNITED SUFFRAGISTS Founded in March 1915. Honorary secretary (1915) Mrs L.E. Smith, Highfield, Wellington Road North, Heaton Norris, Stockport; (end of 1915) Miss Hope Hampson, Trevena, Bowden.

MANCHESTER (WFL) Honorary organizer (1910) Miss Manning, Harper Hill, Sale, Cheshire; Secretary (1913) Miss A.E. Hordern, 478 Stockport Road, Longsight, Manchester, Lancashire.

MANCHESTER (WSPU) Elizabeth Wolstenholme ELMY referred to this as the "mother branch" of the WOMEN'S SOCIAL AND POLITICAL UNION, which was founded by Mrs PANKHURST at her home at 62 Nelson Street on 10 October 1903. Even after 1907, by which time the entire Pankhurst family had moved to London, Manchester remained an important centre. Secretary (1906) Miss Alice Milne, 116 Portland Street, Manchester. Significantly, by 1910, Alice Milne was a member of the WOMEN'S FREEDOM LEAGUE. Organizers (1910) Miss Mary GAWTHORPE and Miss Rona Robinson, 164 Oxford Road, Manchester; (1913) Miss K. Wallwork, 32 King Street West, Manchester, Lancashire.

MANCHESTER AND DISTRICT FEDERATION OF THE NATIONAL UNION OF WOMEN'S SUFFRAGE SOCIETIES Formed in 1910. Previously the branches of the NORTH OF ENGLAND SOCIETY FOR WOMEN'S SUFFRAGE had been represented on its committee but they were not individually affiliated to the NATIONAL UNION OF WOMEN'S SUFFRAGE SOCIETIES. With the formation of the federation the branches became societies affiliated to the NUWSS. In 1910–11 the federation consisted of the women's suffrage societies at: ALTRINCHAM, ASHTON-UNDER-LYNE, BOLTON, CLITHEROE, CREWE, DARWEN, ECCLES, HEYWOOD, HYDE, KNUTSFORD, LEIGH, MACCLESFIELD, MANCHESTER, MARPLE, NORTHWICH, OLDHAM, ROMILEY, RADCLIFFE-CUM-FARNWORTH, STOCKPORT,

Whaley Bridge, Wigan, Wilmslow, Alderley Edge and Styal. By 1912 the following societies had been added: Blackburn, Bramhall, Burnley, Buxton, Haslingden, Marple Bridge, Middleton, Rawtenstall, Sale, and Winsford.

On 12 November 1914 the Manchester and District Federation called upon the NUWSS publicly "1) to affirm its belief in conciliation and arbitration as opposed to War. 2) to demand that all diplomacy should be subject to democratic control, and that the word democratic be defined as including the representation of all classes of the community irrespective of sex. The NUWSS calls upon the organised women of the world to combine in agitation for political freedom in the belief that no tribunal for international arbitration can secure universal peace until the opinions of womanhood are rendered effective by the grant of political power". Secretary (1913) Mrs Barnes, Grosvenor Chambers, 16 Deansgate, Manchester.

MANCHESTER AND SALFORD WOMEN'S TRADE AND LABOUR COUNCIL Founded in 1904 after Christabel Pankhurst effected a rupture in the Manchester and Salford Women's Trade Union Council, of which she had been a committee member since 1901, by trying to force the Council, whose first allegiance was to trade unionism, to make women's suffrage one of its aims. The Council refused and Eva Gore-Booth and Sarah Dickenson, Christabel's friends, if not supporters, felt constrained to resign, taking with them seven unions and 2000 members. "The Women's Council has a political department for Suffrage work and for watching industrial legislation on behalf of women workers" (*Suffrage Annual and Women's Who's Who*, 1913). The Women's Trade and Labour Council was described as primarily a federation of Lancashire trade unions and, besides campaigning for women's suffrage and against protective legislation, formed a Women's Insurance Society, after the passing of the National Insurance Act, which was run by women officials to secure the maximum benefit for women and, through their representatives on the National Advisory Committee, to uphold the interests of women. The Council worked both separately and under the aegis of the National Industrial and Professional Women's Suffrage Society.

Honorary secretaries (1913) Eva Gore-Booth and Sarah Dickenson; treasurer (1913) Nellie Keenan, a member of the Weavers' Union who was, until resigning in 1905, a member of the executive committee of the North of England Women's Suffrage Society.
Address: (1913) 5 John Dalton Street, Manchester.
Bibliography: J. Liddington and J. Norris, *One Hand Tied Behind Us: The Rise of the Women's Suffrage Movement*, 1978.

MANCHESTER NATIONAL SOCIETY FOR WOMEN'S SUFFRAGE Elizabeth Wolstenholme Elmy maintained that she founded, in October 1865, the initially nameless group that became, first, the Manchester Committee for the Enfranchisement of Women, and then the Manchester National Society for Women's Suffrage. The members of the earliest group included the Rev. S.A. Steinthal and his wife (at whose house the first meeting was held), Max and Philippine Kyllmann, Jacob and Ursula Bright, Dr Richard Pankhurst, Elizabeth Gloyn (president of the Manchester Board of Schoolmistresses, then in the process of formation) and Alice Wilson, with Elizabeth Wolstenholme acting as honorary secretary. In letters written to Harriet McIlquham in 1902 and to Sylvia Pankhurst in 1907–10, Elizabeth Wolstenholme Elmy explained the formation of the first committee as being for the express purpose of working for the women's suffrage petition presented to parliament by John Stuart Mill in 1866. Knowing that the correspondence that explains the formation of the Women's Suffrage Petition Committee dates the decision to present a petition to 12 May 1866, one might conclude that, by now an old woman, Mrs Elmy had, excusably, elided events that had taken place nearly 50 years previously. However Mrs Elmy's sense of historical truth is not to be discounted; she was present in St James's Hall in London in the summer of 1865 when J.S. Mill addressed the Westminster electors and, as she wrote, "made it the occasion of a most powerful plea for the Enfranchisement of Women". It is entirely possible that in informal conversations with like-minded women, in all probability Emily Davies and other members of the Kensington Society, the suggestion was made that committees might be formed and a petition presented. Elizabeth Wolstenholme Elmy, ever an earnest worker, in October put the suggestion into practice in Manchester, while in London the Kensington Society members were still dithering in November and did not galvanize themselves into action until the following May. Mrs Elmy specifically wrote, in a 1903 letter to Mrs McIlquham, "It was, I believe, in October that I began to collect signatures to the Petition. I was just then very busy with the negotiations which ended in the formation of the Manchester Board of Schoolmistresses, and the first & best suffrage workers were found amongst the friends I had thus made." Elizabeth Wolstenholme was responsible for canvassing 300 of the names that appeared in May 1866 on the historic petition.

In October 1866 Barbara BODICHON reported that she had heard from Emily DAVIES, who was in Manchester, that "a Miss Wolstenholme her friend there is at work, she writes to ask for 3000 copies of my paper [that given by her at the Social Science Congress meeting] on thin paper to send round to 3000 female householders in Manchester with the petitions and her letter gives the evidence of great interest with the matter." The Manchester society was formally refounded on 11 January 1867 at a meeting held at Louis BORCHARDT's house. The purpose of the society was by now to canvass women householders in Manchester to encourage them to sign further petitions to parliament. This society was, therefore, doing in Manchester what the ENFRANCHISEMENT OF WOMEN COMMITTEE was doing at that time in London. According to Helen BLACKBURN the meeting was chaired by Jacob Bright; according to Elizabeth Wolstenholme Elmy he and Ursula Bright were not present at this meeting, attending only the second meeting of the committee. Elizabeth Wolstenholme was present at the 11 January meeting, as were Louis Borchardt, the Rev. S.A. Steinthal, Mrs Gloyn and Max Kyllmann. According to Helen Blackburn the second meeting was held on 13 February; she does not include the Brights among those present. At this meeting Elizabeth Wolstenholme handed over the secretaryship to Lydia BECKER, who had been made known to her by Emily Davies. On 4 June 1867 Jessie BOUCHERETT wrote to Helen TAYLOR that Miss Becker had told her that "the Manchester Committee is trying to set up an Enfranchisement Society". On 30 June 1867 Lydia Becker wrote to Helen Taylor on notepaper headed "Enfranchisement Of Women", from her own address, 10 Grove Street, Ardwick, Manchester, sending a draft copy of the rules for the new society for comment. A subsequent printing of notepaper was headed "Manchester Committee for the Enfranchisement of Women" and the names given on the paper as members of the committee were: Josephine Butler, Mrs Elizabeth Gloyn, Mrs Edmund Grundy, Philippine Kyllmann, Sarah Miall (who with her sisters ran a ladies' school in Manchester), Mrs Rebecca Moore (the owner of a kindergarten and Pestalozzian school), Mrs W. Hume Rothery, Mrs S. Alfred Steinthal, Mrs Winkworth (daughter of Thomas THOMASSON), Miss Wilson (with her sisters the owner of a baby linen warehouse), Elizabeth Wolstenholme, Rev. B. Glover, Rev. John Fox, Rev. S. Alfred Steinthal, Jacob Bright, T.H. Genn, Professsor Greenbank and Max Kyllmann.

On 4 July 1867, as the London Enfranchisement of Women Committee was dissolving and plans were underway to set up there a new society to work in co-operation with the societies in Manchester, Edinburgh and Dublin, Lydia Becker wrote to Helen Taylor:

> I shall be very glad to have the opportunity of consulting with you as to the course of action to be taken by our committee. No doubt the four centres should each work independently collecting their own funds and through their own general and executive committees. But I do not quite understand from your note what is the bond of union you propose between the different centres. It should be one which, while securing the advantage of concert and co-operation and mutual communication – should leave each centre free to work in the mode best adopted to the locality in which they are engaged. Should we form four independent societies? Or a National Society with four centres? If the latter should there be a general central committee? All these details want arranging.

In a letter to Helen Taylor of 30 July 1867 she mentions that she hopes to meet "our committee in Manchester next week to formally constitute our new Society and to set earnestly to work to extend our organisation and operations."

By September 1867 the Manchester society was employing an ORGANIZER, Miss Knott, to canvass in Liverpool and Bolton for names for the petitions that they were preparing. Lydia Becker contrasted this plan of efficient working with that of the London Committee who canvassed by letter, incurring considerably greater expense. Even as early as August 1867 there can be no doubt but that Lydia Becker was introducing a spirit of competition into the affairs of the two societies. When writing to Helen Taylor, asking for a donation, Lydia Becker commented that, because the London committee was so rich in comparison with that in Manchester, and because she thought Manchester was much more efficient, should not people give money to the society that used the money most effectively? Manchester's energy did not go unremarked. Jessie Boucherett wrote to Helen Taylor in November 1867 that the Manchester committee was setting up committees in other towns and could she not stir up London to do the same.

In November 1867 the Manchester Society joined in a loose federation, the NATIONAL SOCIETY FOR WOMEN'S SUFFRAGE, with the societies in London and Edinburgh. The decision to unite in this way had not been taken without difficulty. Lydia Becker had written to Helen Taylor on 12 October 1867, following a committee meeting of the Manchester society:

> there seemed an inability to perceive the advantages of a corporate union with the London and Edinburgh societies, and a strong disposition to let the bond between them consist wholly in working together for a common object, and in affording all possible mutual help and encouragement. When I endeavoured to explain the prospect of uniting all the committees, I was met by the inquiry "What shall we gain by it?" Unless I can answer this question by shewing some very great advantage from union with the other centres I am sure the committee will not accede to the proposal. If therefore the plan we thought of at your house is to be carried out, it will be needful to have a distinct proposal to lay before the committee – a Constitution for the proposed national Society in which the position of each committee shall be clearly defined. It is a fair question whether such a course is advisable.

> The Manchester Society is perfectly satisfied with its own independent position. It does not seek union with London – at the same time it is quite willing to listen to any such proposal, and to adopt what can be proved to be advantageous. If you think it would be a good thing to unite the committees in the way you proposed when I was at your house will you be so kind as to draw up a form of proposal which I can lay before the committee at our next meeting and accompany it by a letter stating the advantages you expect may accrue from adopting it.

Lydia Becker also wrote, at the same time, to Clementia TAYLOR of the LONDON NATIONAL SOCIETY, explaining her committee's reluctance to federate. It is clear from these exchanges that the idea for federation had been hammered out at a meeting at Mill's house in Blackheath and that the proposal had probably come from Mill and Helen Taylor. On 27 October Lydia Becker wrote, on notepaper with the heading already printed as "Manchester National Society for Women's Suffrage", to Helen Taylor, thanking her for her proposal for the National Society and saying she could find no fault with it and would lay it before her committee. The reluctance of the Manchester committee was overcome and at a meeting held on 6 November 1867 Manchester agreed to join the National Society for Women's Suffrage, as the Manchester National Society for Women's Suffage.

However, real differences between Manchester and London as to the strategy to be employed soon emerged. In Manchester the Rev. S.A. Steinthal, in particular, took a strong stand in October 1867 against petitioning, thinking it a waste of time to promote petitions unless they were in support of a motion to be brought before parliament. No such motion was likely to be brought in that parliamentary session. In addition, because the Manchester society was hopeful that their test case, eventually brought by Philippine Kyllmann in November 1868, would prove that the law as it stood did allow women to vote, it would be impolitic to agitate for a change. This difference in opinion as to the value of petitioning was discussed in correspondence. The Manchester society decided in early January 1868 to discontinue collecting signatures for petitions in order to direct attention to increasing the number of members of the society, and thereby raise funds to enable them to continue testing the existing state of the law. In the Manchester area in 1868 Lydia Becker's dynamism encouraged around 6000 women to attempt to register as voters. Helen Taylor, doubtless encouraged by Mill, directed the London National Society to concentrate on petitioning. The Manchester society was the first, on 14 April 1868, to hold a public meeting, devoted to a discussion of women's enfranchisement at which women spoke from the platform.

Animosity between the Manchester and London societies was increasing. A letter, in the Mill–Taylor archive, from Lydia Becker to Helen Taylor, dated only "23 October", in which this may be detected has, I believe, been miscatalogued as though written in 1867. From internal evidence the true year date is more likely to be 1868; the move to register women as voters took place in the autumn of 1868, not 1867. Lily MAXWELL did attempt to vote in November 1867, but that was only because her name was by accident on the register. In this particular letter Lydia Becker asked for a contribution (Mill and Helen Taylor had promised £100) towards the cost of the appeals to register women as voters. Lydia Becker rather abrasively puts forward the claim of Manchester to receive donations and in a draft reply Helen Taylor asks tetchily why, as Manchester had stopped petitioning work and as it had just as many rich members of its committee as London, it was appealing to the London Committee for funds. This was, in fact, a misunderstanding; it transpired that Lydia Becker was appealing to her and Mill in their private capacity (*see* Philippine Kyllmann). Helen Taylor continued, "it is much to be regretted as it must cripple the exertions of the Manchester Committee, since it cannot be expected that the London will be willing often to contribute much towards work in the direction of which it is permitted no voices. If the London committee is to take upon itself the pecuniary burdens of a mother-committee I imagine it will wish also to have the weight and influence of one." Lydia Becker, supported by Jacob and Ursula Bright, was able to withstand this threat; Mill, Helen Taylor and Philippine Kyllmann resigned from the Manchester society. As the latter wrote to Helen Taylor on 8 December 1868, "I long feared that the great latitude left to our Secretary would bring us some day into trouble". In 1872 the new CENTRAL COMMITTEE OF THE NATIONAL SOCIETY FOR WOMEN'S SUFFRAGE was formed, based in London, the idea for it having been put forward in November 1871 by Jacob Bright at the annual general meeting of the Manchester National Society. The Manchester society's influence was from now on in the ascendant, as that of London waned.

At the Manchester society's first annual general meeting on 30 October 1868, chaired, before her resignation, by Philippine Kyllmann, the following executive committee was appointed: Jacob Bright, Ursula Bright, Lydia Becker, Josephine Butler, Thomas Chorlton (the society's legal adviser), Prof. T.K. Greenbank, Mathilde Kyllmann, Philippine Kyllmann, Sarah Miall, Rebecca Moore, Dr Pankhurst, R.D. Rusden, Esq., Rev. S.A. Steinthal, Katherine THOMASSON, Alice Wilson, Miss M. Wilson and Elizabeth Wolstenholme. The personnel of the executive committee of the Manchester National Society remained remarkably constant over the next 18 years. Elizabeth Wolstenholme left the committee in 1871, Alice SCATCHERD joined in 1876, Mrs Joseph Cross (Anne ASHWORTH) in 1877, and Walter and Eva MCLAREN in 1883. From 1886 the committee ballooned, swollen by an influx of eight MPs, a number which in 1889 increased to eleven. After Lydia Becker's death in 1890 the Manchester society lost direction until Esther ROPER took it in hand after being appointed secretary in 1893. There do not appear to have been any annual general meetings or reports in 1891 and 1892. From 1893 the committees were rationalized, the MPs joining a newly created general committee, leaving a smaller executive committee which included Thomas Chorlton, Rev. S.A. Steinthal, Isabel DACRE, Walter McLaren, Alice Scatcherd and, making her first appearance, Emmeline PANKHURST. In 1894 Bertha MASON joined the executive committee and in 1895 the Manchester society affiliated with the CENTRAL NATIONAL SOCIETY. In 1897, along with 500 other suffrage societies, Manchester joined the NATIONAL UNION OF WOMEN'S SUFFRAGE SOCIETIES, as the NORTH OF ENGLAND SOCIETY FOR WOMEN'S SUFFRAGE.

From 1877 the Manchester Society employed an organizer, Mrs McCormick, who travelled all over the north of England, arranging public meetings for the society. In 1877 she accompanied Alice Scatcherd to Grimsby and north Northamptonshire to campaign at parliamentary elections and to attend deputations to the candidates. In that year she devoted 156 days to office and other work in Manchester. She remained as organizer for the Manchester Society until 1885; in 1886 Alice Scatcherd tried to arrange an annuity for her. In 1893 the society's new secretary, Esther Roper, launched a campaign among textile workers in support of the Special Appeal (see SPECIAL APPEAL COMMITTEE) that was to demonstrate to parliament the widespread grass-roots support from women for their own enfranchisement. On 5 June 1896 a conference of all the northern suffrage societies (Birmingham, Manchester, Liverpool, Leeds, Southport and Birkenhead) was held in Manchester at which it was agreed to employ an organizer to conduct the campaign in the northern and midland counties.

Secretary (1865–7) Elizabeth Wolstenholme; (1867–90) Lydia Becker; (1890–3) Miss Atkinson; (1893–7) Esther Roper. Treasurer (1867–84, 1894–5) Rev. S.A. Steinthal; (1885, 1890, 1893) Thomas Dale; (1886–9) Prof. Adamson. Assistant secretary (1881–90) Miss Backhouse. Her services were dispensed with that year; apparently the society could no longer afford to employ her. In 1874 the society's income had been c. £1415 and £617 had been spent on management. Organizer (1881–5) Mrs McCormick.

Address: (1868–87) 28 Jackson's Row, Albert Square, Manchester; (1887–97) Queen's Chambers, 5 John Dalton Street, Manchester.

Archival source: Elizabeth Wolstenholme Papers, British Library; Mill–Taylor Papers, London School of Economics and Political Science; Papers of Manchester National Society for Women's Suffrage (including annual reports, 1868–95), Manchester Central Library.

MANCHESTER SOCIETY FOR WOMEN'S SUFFRAGE

The name given in 1911 to the NORTH OF ENGLAND SOCIETY FOR WOMEN'S SUFFRAGE, when it became a constituent society of the MANCHESTER AND DISTRICT FEDERATION OF THE NATIONAL UNION OF WOMEN'S SUFFRAGE SOCIETIES. It continued forming "branches", which were now called "working committees". Most members of the executive committee had held similar positions with the North of England Society. In 1911 the executive committee comprised: Mrs d'Auquier, Mrs Barnes, Rev. A.L. Bradbury, Miss Lucy Cox, Miss Caroline Herford, Mrs Forrest Hewit, Frank Leigh, Mrs Norbury, C.W. Pidduck, Mrs Prestwick, Miss Vernon, Mrs Muter Wilson and Mrs T.M. Young. In 1912, after the introduction of the Election Fighting Fund policy, Annot ROBINSON joined the executive committee and in 1913 there were three joint meetings between the Manchester Society and ILP Manchester Central branch, at which the speakers were Helena SWANWICK, Annot Robinson and Margaret ASHTON. In 1915 the Manchester society which, under Margaret Ashton, had backed the anti-war faction within the NUWSS, revoked this policy. The society dissolved in January 1919 after the passing of the Representation of the People Act that enfranchised women over the age of 30.

Chairman: (1911–15) Margaret Ashton. Honorary secretary (1911–12) Helena Swanwick; (1912–14) Mrs Hillyer. Honorary treasurer (1912–14) Miss M.G. Taylor.

Secretary: (1909) Kathleen COURTNEY, 85 Deansgate Arcade, Manchester; (1913) Miss Darlington, Grosvenor Chambers, 16 Deansgate, Manchester.

MANNERS, EMILY, MRS (1857–1934) Quaker, née Barringer, born in Wakefield, educated at the Quaker Ackworth School, 1867–71 and later at Lewes. Her family moved to Mansfield in Nottinghamshire where, in 1881, she married Charles Manners of Croydon. They had two children. In 1901 Emily Manners was elected a poor law guardian in Mansfield and at the time of her death she was a justice of the peace for Nottinghamshire.

Emily Manners became honorary secretary of the MANSFIELD WOMEN'S SUFFRAGE SOCIETY when it was founded in 1893 and remained in this position until the Society disbanded in 1919. By 1903 she was a member of the executive committee of the NATIONAL UNION OF WOMEN'S SUFFRAGE SOCIETIES, representing the Mansfield Society. In October of that year she attended the National Convention for the Civic Rights of Women held, mainly at the instigation of Elizabeth Wolstenholme ELMY, at Holborn Town Hall. In May 1906 Emily Manners was present at a demonstration held at the Exeter Hall in London by members of the NUWSS after the disappointment earlier that day of the deputation to the Prime Minister, Campbell-Bannerman.

In April 1908 she travelled to Sheffield to help the NUWSS campaign at the by-election. In August she reported on the open-air meetings held in the market place in Mansfield by Mrs DOWSON and Cicely Dean Corbett, "Very able addresses were given to large and appreciative audiences... and literature and badges were sold". She herself was an active public speaker, being prepared to address the cause of women's suffrage from Liberal, Conservative and Labour platforms. In 1911 she became president of a junior branch of the Mansfield Society and took part in the Coronation Procession in London on 17 June. In 1913 she accompanied the NUWSS PILGRIMAGE from Chesterfield, where she had been speaking, and was met at Pleasley by Mrs FAWCETT. During her speech on this occasion in Mansfield market place, Mrs Manners particularly noted, "I am glad to say that a number of working women of the country are with us. Possibly in Mansfield our society is regarded as a middle-class one, but I can tell you it is composed largely of working women". In 1913 she attended the Suffrage Summer School in Oxford. In 1919 Mrs Manners was presented with a silver rosebowl, suitably inscribed, in honour of her 26 years' work for the Mansfield Suffrage Society. The bowl survives, in a private collection.

In 1910 Emily Manners signed a petition from women Friends asking that women's suffrage should be discussed at the next Yearly Meeting of the Society of Friends and by 1913 was secretary of the Mansfield branch of the FRIENDS' LEAGUE FOR WOMEN'S SUFFRAGE. In 1914 she published a monograph, *Elizabeth Hooton: First Quaker Woman Preacher (1600–1672)*.

Address: (1893) Edenbank, Mansfield, Nottinghamshire.
Photograph: in *The Friend*, 1935.
Archival source: Minutes of Mansfield Women's Suffrage Society, 1893–1918, Nottinghamshire Record Office; Friends' Library, London.

MANSEL, MILDRED ELLA, MRS (1868–1942) Daughter of Adeline CHAPMAN, by her first marriage to Arthur Guest. She was, therefore, granddaughter of Lady Charlotte Guest (later Schreiber), niece of the Lord Wimborne, and cousin of Ivor Guest, at one time the Liberal Chief Whip and an anti-suffragist. She married Col J.D. Mansel of Smedmore, Corfe Castle in 1888 and had two daughters and a son. Mrs Mansel joined the WOMEN'S SOCIAL AND POLITICAL UNION, was arrested when taking part in the deputation from Caxton Hall to the House of Commons on 29 June 1909 and in 1910 became the local ORGANIZER in Bath. In 1911 she rented 12 Lansdowne Crescent in Bath in order that suffrage protesters might spend the night of 2 April there and thereby evade the census. She planted a tree in Col BLATHWAYT's arboretum. On 21 November she broke two windows in the War Office in London and was sentenced to seven days' imprisonment in Holloway from 23 to 29 November. Mildred Mansel was an active public speaker on behalf of the WSPU both in the west country and in London and was a particular friend of Lady Constance LYTTON. Grace ROE noted that, as cousin to the Liberal Chief Whip, Mrs Mansel was virtually immune from arrest and provided a vital link between the commander in exile and the chief organizer in London. In 1913 Mrs Mansel visited Christabel PANKHURST in Paris and received orders to find a safe flat in London for Grace Roe. Eventually she rented for this purpose an upstairs flat in a house in Earls Court. Mrs Mansel was much to the fore as a WSPU organizer in 1914; she presided over a large meeting in Holland Park Hall and her London flat was raided by the police looking for "mice". By 1934 Mrs Mansel had founded the Mid-Somerset Musical Competitive Festival and was honorary secretary of the British Confederation of the Arts.

Address: (1913) Bayford Lodge, Wincanton, Somerset; (1940) 33 Lower Belgrave Street, London SW1.
Photograph: by Goodfellow, Wincanton, on postcard published by the WSPU, John Johnson Collection, Bodleian Library, Oxford; in C. Pankhurst, *Unshackled*, 1959.

MANSELL-MOULLIN, EDITH RUTH, MRS (c. 1859–1941) née Thomas After she left school she went to work in the slums of Bethnal Green. She joined the Anti-Sweating League and worked in a soup kitchen at the dock gates during the London Dock Strike and witnessed Annie Besant leading the Match Girls' Strike. After her marriage to Charles Mansell-Moullin, who became an eminent surgeon, and the birth of her son, she carried on her involvement with settlement work, only giving it up when she joined the WOMEN'S SOCIAL AND POLITICAL UNION, probably in 1907. She remained, however, involved with the Women's Industrial Council and succeeded Louise EATES as secretary of its Investigating Committee. Edith Mansell-Moullin was the first treasurer of the CHURCH LEAGUE FOR WOMEN'S SUFFRAGE and then became a regular contributor to WSPU funds, a regular visitor to the KENSINGTON branch of the WSPU, shared a platform with Mrs PANKHURST at the 1910 Hyde Park Demonstration, and was imprisoned in November 1911 after taking part in a deputation to the House of Commons. She also took part in the deputation on "Black Friday" in November 1910. She was the organizer of the Welsh contingent in the 1911 Coronation Procession and, as a result, founded the CYMRIC SUFFRAGE UNION and then, in 1912, the FORWARD CYMRIC SUFFRAGE UNION. She held many suffrage meetings in both Wales and London. Edith Mansell-Moullin was a close friend of Emily Wilding DAVISON, who was operated on by Charles Mansell-Moullin after she had been taken unconscious from the Derby race track in June 1913. He, by now a vice-president of the Royal College of Surgeons as well as an active member of the MEN'S LEAGUE FOR WOMEN'S SUFFRAGE, had since 1909 vociferously condemned the practice of forcibly feeding suffrage prisoners. In May 1913 Edith Mansell-Moullin was the honorary secretary of the committee formed by Sylvia PANKHURST to lobby for the repeal of the "Cat and Mouse" Act. Later in 1913 Edith Mansell-Moullin left the WSPU, but was a supporter of the NATIONAL POLITICAL LEAGUE, and continued working with the Forward Cymric Suffrage Union until she retired, owing to ill health, in 1916. Both husband and wife were present at the Costume Dinner organized by the ACTRESSES' FRANCHISE LEAGUE and the WOMEN WRITERS' SUFFRAGE LEAGUE at the Hotel Cecil on 29 June 1914. Edith Mansell-Moullin supported pacifism during the First World War and worked for the blind at St Dunstan's.

Address: (1913) 69 Wimpole Street, London W.
Photograph: on postcard published by the Church Socialist League, 1912, John Johnson Collection, Bodleian Library, Oxford; in A. Morley and L. Stanley, *The Life and Death of Emily Wilding Davison*, 1988; D. Atkinson, *The Suffragettes in Pictures*, 1996.
Archival source: The Suffragette Fellowship Collection, Museum of London.
Bibliography: A. Morley and L. Stanley, *The Life and Death of Emily Wilding Davison*, 1988.

MANSFIELD WOMEN'S SUFFRAGE SOCIETY Founded in 1893, with Mrs Emily MANNERS as honorary secretary. The society immediately resolved to send a donation of 1 guinea to the CENTRAL COMMITTEE OF THE NATIONAL SOCIETY FOR WOMEN'S SUFFRAGE. The branch sent two delegates to the women's suffrage conference held in Birmingham in 1896 at which the proposal for forming the NATIONAL UNION OF WOMEN'S SUFFRAGE SOCIETIES was discussed. In 1896 the Mansfield society resolved to pay a fee of 2 guineas to the MANCHESTER NATIONAL SOCIETY FOR WOMEN'S SUFFRAGE, to pay for which an extra subscription was required from members. In 1898 the society agreed to affiliate to the NUWSS. In 1900 Mrs FAWCETT addressed a public meeting at the Town Hall, Mansfield; there was only a small attendance. There is a resolution, dated January 1904, in the minute book of the Mansfield society to the effect that the society was in sympathy with the effort of the Lancashire and Cheshire Textile Workers to return a parliamentary representative pledged to work for their interests. In 1904 the Mansfield Women's Suffrage Society forwarded an affiliation fee of 1 guinea to the CENTRAL SOCIETY OF WOMEN'S SUFFRAGE and 1 guinea to the Campaign Fund. By the January 1910 general election the society had taken a SHOP, where posters were displayed, which attracted a good deal of attention. The electors' petition could be signed there; 1374 signatures were obtained. The Mansfield society backed the National Union in not accepting the WOMEN'S SOCIAL AND POLITICAL UNION's invitation to join in their demonstration in the Albert Hall on 28 May 1910. In 1913 the Mansfield society was a member of the MIDLANDS (EAST) FEDERATION OF THE NATIONAL UNION OF WOMEN'S SUFFRAGE SOCIETIES and raised £20 to donate to the costs of the NUWSS PILGRIMAGE.

Secretary (1893–1918) Mrs Emily Manners, Edenbank, Mansfield, Nottinghamshire.

Archival source: Minutes of the Mansfield Women's Suffrage Society, 1893–1918, Nottinghamshire Archives.
Bibliography: C. Weir, *Women's History in the Nottinghamshire Archives Office 1550–1950*, 1989.

MARGESSON, ISABEL AUGUSTA, LADY (1863–1946) Daughter of Lord Hobart, sister of the Earl of Buckinghamshire, and a proud descendant of

John Hampden. She married in 1886 Sir Mortimer Margesson and became the mother of two sons and one daughter. In 1894 she was honorary secretary of the Belgravia branch of the Parents' National Educational Union, but resigned, disagreeing over plans for its future. In 1895 she was one of the founders of the Sesame Club (*see under* CLUBS), becoming a member of its executive committee. She was a member of the NATIONAL UNION OF WOMEN'S SUFFRAGE SOCIETIES, president in 1904 of the newly opened branch at Redditch, but resigned in 1906–7 to join the WOMEN'S SOCIAL AND POLITICAL UNION. By February 1909 she was a very active speaker for the WSPU and, despite this, was one of the people that the Birmingham NUWSS regularly asked to appear on its platforms. In April 1914 Lady Isabel took the chair at the meeting held in St Andrew's Hall, Glasgow, at which Mrs PANKHURST was re-arrested among scenes of riot. In 1917–18 Lady Isabel was a member of the preliminary central committee of management of the newly founded Women's Institute movement and in later years she was a justice of the peace in Worcestershire. Her daughter Catherine was based in Reading as WSPU organizer from February 1910 and by 1919 was Secretary for Industries of the National Federation of Women's Institutes.

Address: (1916) Barnet Green House, nr Worcester; (1934) 147 Victoria Street, London SW1; (1944) 135 Marsham Court, London SW1.

"MARION, KITTY" (1871–1944) Adopted name of Katherina Maria Schafer. Born in Westphalia, Germany, her mother died when she was two years old, and she came to England in 1886 to stay with an aunt. She was intent on going on the stage, taught herself English, had dancing lessons and, by 1889, had been engaged for the pantomime season in Glasgow. She seems to have been constantly in work, touring up and down the country, working in variety and music hall, billed as "Refined Vocal Comedienne". In 1899 she appeared at the Prince of Wales Theatre in Liverpool, on the same bill as Vesta Tilley. Kitty Marion appears to have joined the WOMEN'S SOCIAL AND POLITICAL UNION in June 1908 and quickly volunteered to join deputations from Caxton Hall to the House of Commons. She records that plain-clothes policemen infiltrated the crowd to break the suffrage ranks and that she was mauled by the police but not arrested. She also sold *Votes for Women* in the street and comments, "What a lesson in self-denial, self-abnegation, self-discipline!"

Kitty Marion joined the ACTRESSES' FRANCHISE LEAGUE as soon as it was formed and on 13 April 1909 helped carry the AFL BANNER in a procession from Marble Arch to Aldwych to celebrate Mrs PETHICK-LAWRENCE's release from Holloway. On 29 June 1909 she was arrested for the first time, while taking part in the WSPU deputation to the House of Commons. Kitty Marion records that it was at the instigation of Christabel PANKHURST, who urged her to follow the lead of Marion Wallace-DUNLOP (who had just initiated the use of the hunger strike as a weapon against authority) and "to do deeds not words", that she went to Newcastle, knowing that Lloyd George was to be there, and, in the company of Dorothy PETHICK, threw a stone through a government (post office) window. She was sentenced to a month's imprisonment, went on hunger strike, was forcibly fed and set fire to her cell. She received a WSPU hunger strike medal in a ceremony at the Albert Hall on 9 December and then went on to do the Christmas pantomime season.

Besides her involvement in the suffrage movement, Kitty Marion was at the fore of the Variety Artists' Federation agitation against theatrical agents and in February 1910 broke the windows of the office of the Moss Empire to draw attention to this grievance. The suggestion was that some theatrical employment agencies were fronts for "white slave traders" and in the course of 1910 agents were at last, as the result of the campaign, required to be licensed. In 1910 Kitty Marion took part in the WSPU processions of 18 June and 23 July, in between appearing at the Hippodrome, Hastings, at the end of June and at the Royal County Theatre, Reading, on 14 July. She took part in the "Black Friday" debacle in November 1910, was arrested then and again three days later during the further protest, but was discharged on both occasions. In 1911 Kitty Marion appeared, as "Music Hall Artiste and Militant Suffragette" at the annual meeting of the Colchester Liberal Unionist Association and the resulting report notes that "The awe experienced by the audience was quickly succeeded by delight, for the lady proved a charming vocalist." In November 1911 she was again arrested after taking part in the protest following the "torpedoing" of the Conciliation Bill, and was sentenced to 21 days' imprisonment. Kitty Marion records how, on 1 March 1912, the WSPU having determined on its window-smashing campaign, she was given a hammer and told to break windows at 5.45 pm, in the twilight as shoppers were going home. She broke the windows of the Silversmiths' Association and of Sainsbury's at 134 Regent Street. She was sentenced to six months' imprisonment and was taken, with 23 others, to Winson Green Prison in Birmingham, Holloway being full. She went on hunger strike and records that the wardresses were in tears, having already performed 20 such "operations" before they came to her. Helen ARCHDALE, the prisoners' secretary, arrived the next day from Clement's Inn with instructions that there should be no further hunger strike until Mrs Pankhurst and Mr and Mrs Pethick-Lawrence were sentenced, imprisoned and, if denied the status of political prisoners, had themselves gone on hunger strike, in which case all other suffragette prisoners should join in sympathy. When this eventuality occurred, Kitty Marion did as directed, went on hunger strike and was released after 10 days. On 5 September she went to the Welsh National Eisteddfod at Wrexham (seat 338 in Row 11 Block C, price 5/–) and heckled Lloyd George. She was set upon by the crowd and "received blows and abuse from every side, my hat being torn off and hair pulled down". The occasion is vividly reported in *Votes for Women*, 13 September 1912. A month later, on 17 October, Kitty Marion was present at the meeting in the Albert Hall at which the Pethick-Lawrences' departure from the WSPU was announced. She mentions that she had noted with surprise Mr Pethick-Lawrence's absence from the platform – "he had always been there at previous meetings to show the audience, with a counting machine, how the contributions were flowing into the militant 'war chest'". At the end of the year she was again arrested, after breaking a fire alarm near Bow Street as a protest against the way the new Insurance Act affected women. She was at the time working as housekeeper to three WSPU members and had refused to pay insurance. She was sentenced to a month's imprisonment, petitioned to be given the status of a political offender, and when this was refused went on hunger strike and was forcibly fed until her sentence expired.

Kitty Marion records that in 1913 the edict went out, presumably from Christabel Pankhurst, "to do all the damage possible without being caught". She herself was certainly responsible for burning down "Levetleigh" at St Leonards in Sussex, the home of the local MP, Arthur du Cros, on 13 April and probably for a large furze fire near the Royal Pavilion at Aldershot. She also committed, undetected, two other acts of arson. Her fifth success did, however, lead to her arrest. After Emily Wilding DAVISON's death at Epsom, it was suggested to Kitty Marion and Clara (Betty) Giveen that the Grand Stand at the Hurst Park racecourse "would make a most appropriate beacon". In her memoir Kitty Marion gives a detailed description of how they carried out the arson, remarking, "We both regretted that there was no movie camera to immortalise the comedy of it." They walked back, dodging police patrols, to the house in Kew at which they were staying with the family of Eileen CASEY, another WSPU member. A police constable from Richmond, who had been detailed to watch the house, saw the two women return and during the course of the next morning they were arrested. Kitty Marion and Betty Giveen were both bailed on their own sureties of £1000 each and two sureties of a like amount, which were given by two wealthy WSPU supporters, Mrs Williams and Mrs Potts. During the course of the trial, which was held at Guildford on 3 July, it became clear that the Caseys only knew Betty Giveen through her suffragette activities and had never before met Kitty Marion. The latter records that "there was great astonishment at the Freemasonary among suffragettes, for one to trust a mere acquaintance who had never previously been to her house, with a latch key and to bring another, an utter stranger. Neither court nor counsels could grasp the idea. . . . 'She was a Suffragette', said Mrs Casey, 'that was quite good enough for us. We trust anyone who is a Suffragette'." Kitty Marion was sentenced to three years' penal servitude, went on hunger-and-thirst strike, and was not forcibly fed. She was visited by the WSPU solicitor, Arthur Marshall, and was then told that she would be released for five days under the "Cat and Mouse"

Act. She was taken to the WSPU nursing home, into the care of Dr Flora MURRAY. On 12 July, influenced, so she records, by the injustice of the Piccadilly Flat Case, in which a woman was sentenced for running a brothel but the names of prominent men involved were suppressed, which had just been tried, and was given considerable prominence in the pages of the *Suffragette*, she threw a stone, wrapped in suitable quotations, through a window of the Home Office. She was taken back to Holloway, went another four and a half days without food or drink, and was again released to the nursing home. She escaped to a rendezvous in Surrey with Betty Giveen. She then went in August to Bristol and then to Liverpool, where, she records, she had a most interesting and busy time. Her scrapbook contains cuttings relating to the fire at Seafield House, Seaforth, Liverpool, which caused £30 000 worth of damage, and to an unexploded bomb left in the Sefton Park Palm House. It also contains the cryptic comment "No record of Lynton". "Hollerday", a large house at Lynton, was destroyed on 4 August. She also paid visits from Liverpool to "work" in Manchester (Alexandra Park House was destroyed there on 11 November) and, also in November, to Leeds to help there with a "reception" given to Asquith. After spending Christmas with friends on the east coast, on her return to London she was recognized by a detective at Charing Cross station. She was returned to Holloway, where fingerprints were now taken to ease future identification. She went on hunger strike and was forcibly fed twice a day. She was visited in prison by the Bishop of London, who regretted that the suffragettes had not continued with their "beautiful processions". She was released under the "Cat and Mouse" Act on 16 April, having been forcibly fed 232 times in the course of 14 weeks and two days, and was again taken to the nursing home run by Dr Flora Murray and Nurse PINE. The day before her licence expired Kitty Marion was taken in a taxi, followed by CID men, to the house of a WSPU member, from which she escaped. She was taken to Folkestone to recuperate at a boarding house, "Trevarra", which had been the address of Florence MACAULAY when she was WSPU organizer in the area. Beatrice HARRADEN was a fellow guest on this occasion. On 31 May Kitty Marion was taken to Paris by, among others, Dr Violet Jones, Mrs Alice Green and Mary LEIGH, to show Christabel Pankhurst the result of the government's treatment of her.

After the declaration of war on 4 August 1914 there was a period of uncertainty as to the position of "mice" who were in hiding. Suffragette prisoners were given an amnesty but the Home Secretary wanted those on the run to return to prison to go there through the red tape of release. It is clear that Kitty Marion, a German by birth, was upset by the ease and gusto with which the Pankhursts had dropped the suffrage cause in order to concentrate on war propaganda. As she was regarded as an invalid after her prison treatment, she did receive maintenance from WSPU funds for a short time, but by October she was back on the stage, appearing in *The Sphinx* by Janette Steer at the Court Theatre. In December, with Mary Leigh, she formed a choir and sang carols in the streets to raise money for Sylvia PANKHURST's East End children. As the war continued, and anti-German feeling increased, Kitty Marion became worried about being suspected as a German spy. When the time came when Germans were required to register, she knew that her suffragette past would count against her. She wrote, "Everything that friends could do was done to keep me in England but the Home Secretary decreed that I should be deported to Germany." She was, eventually, allowed to go instead to America. The money for her fare was raised by, among others, Mrs Alice Green, Emmeline Pethick-Lawrence, Lady Constance LYTTON, Rose Lamartine YATES and Ada WRIGHT. On 24 October she was given a farewell tea at the Emily Wilding Davison Club (*see under* CLUBS) in High Holborn.

Kitty Marion spent most of the rest of her life in America, working there for Margaret Sanger and the birth-control movement, attracting another prison sentence, this time for disseminating birth-control literature. She returned to England in March 1930 for the unveiling of Mrs Pankhurst's statue, despite having been "cut" in the street by Mrs Pankhurst and Nurse Pine when in 1915 their paths had crossed in New York. She was advised by Margaret Sanger not to return to the US as there was no work for her there, but was, instead, offered work in London with the Birth Control International Information Centre, of which Edith How MARTYN was the director. Kitty Marion did eventually return to New York where she was, rather grudgingly, found some basic office work by Margaret Sanger. She wrote her autobiography, which was never published, and died in the Margaret Sanger Home in New York.

Photograph: in Suffragette Fellowship Collection, Museum of London.
Archival source: Kitty Marion's typescript autobiography and scrapbook in the Suffragette Fellowship Collection, Museum of London.
Bibliography: M. Sanger, *An Autobiography*, 1939; G.D. and J. Heath, *The Women's Suffrage Movement In and Around Richmond and Twickenham*, 1968.

MARLOW (WFL) Secretary (1913) Miss Hayes, "Drifts", Bovingdon, Marlow, Buckinghamshire.

MARPLE (NUWSS) In 1910 the society joined the MANCHESTER AND DISTRICT FEDERATION OF THE WOMEN'S SUFFRAGE SOCIETIES. Secretary (1909) Mrs Ashwell Cooke, Manor Hill, Marple, and Mrs Leonard, Eversley, Marple, Cheshire; (1913) Miss Sinclair, Green Bank, Marple, Cheshire.

MARPLE BRIDGE (NUWSS) By 1912 the society was a member of the MANCHESTER AND DISTRICT FEDERATION OF THE NATIONAL UNION OF WOMEN'S SUFFRAGE SOCIETIES. Secretary (1909, 1913) Mrs T.A. Leonard, Waldon, Townscliffe Lane, Marple Bridge, Cheshire.

MARSDEN (WSPU) Secretary (1906) Miss A. Pitcher, Marsden, Nr Huddersfield, Yorkshire.

MARSDEN, DORA (1882–1960) Born in Marsden, a village near Huddersfield, Yorkshire, one of five children of a "woollen waste dealer". Her father's business proved so precarious that in 1890 he left his family to attempt to improve his fortunes in the USA; they never saw him again. At the age of 13 Dora Marsden became first a probationer and then a pupil-teacher at the local school. In 1900 she entered Owen's College, Manchester, on a Queen's Scholarship, which paid for her tuition fees and maintenance on condition that she taught for five years after graduation. This she did, first in Leeds, then in Colchester, before returning to Manchester in 1905. She already knew many of the women who comprised the Manchester base of the WOMEN'S SOCIAL AND POLITICAL UNION, in particular Mary GAWTHORPE and Teresa Billington (*see* Teresa BILLINGTON-GREIG) and was soon speaking on behalf of the society. By 1908 she was a volunteer organizer of WSPU demonstrations around Manchester, sharing a platform with Emmeline PETHICK-LAWRENCE and Christabel PANKHURST. In September she wrote a report for *Votes for Women* of a rally in Huddersfield that had attracted an audience of 50 000. In December 1908 when Mary Gawthorpe was ill, Dora Marsden temporarily took over her role as ORGANIZER.

At the end of March 1909 Dora Marsden volunteered to join a WSPU deputation, which was to comprise mainly Lancashire women, to the House of Commons from the seventh Women's Parliament in Caxton Hall. To do so she resigned from her post as headmistress of the Altrincham Pupil-Teacher Centre. Carrying a WSPU banner, she was arrested and was sentenced to a month's imprisonment. After her release she became a paid organizer for the WSPU, in June spending a short time in Fulham and Putney, preparing the ground for the deputation to Parliament planned for 29 June. She then returned north as organizer of the WSPU's North-West Lancashire Campaign. On 4 September 1909 with, among others, Emily Wilding DAVISON, she was arrested after breaking the windows of a hall at the White City, Old Trafford, Manchester, in which Birrell was holding a meeting and was sentenced on 6 September to two months' imprisonment in Strangeways. She violently resisted the routine prison medical examination and, with the others, went on hunger strike and was released within two days. Dora Marsden refused to wear prison clothing and spent her time in prison naked, stripping off her clothes each time an attempt was made to dress her. At one point she was put in "the canvas dress" (a strait jacket) because "as she was 'not well' [a euphemism for menstruating?] at the time it might have been dangerous to allow her to remain in that state", but she managed to wriggle out of it, being, as the governor reported, "a very small woman". During her time in Strangeways she petitioned the Home Secretary to be given the status of a political prisoner. In October, with Mary Gawthorpe, in order to draw attention to the force feeding of suffragettes in Winson Green Prison, Birmingham, she interrupted a meeting being held by the Chancellor of Manchester University. They were thrown out of the meeting but were not prosecuted. Photographs of Dora Marsden, a tiny figure attired in her academic gown, manhandled by policemen, appeared in the press and she received praise from the WSPU leadership.

During the January 1910 general election campaign Dora Marsden was WSPU organizer in Southport, an active if not a particularly efficient worker. She apparently was dissuaded by Emmeline Pethick-Lawrence from carrying out any militant acts that might entail imprisonment, both in order not to endanger her health and because it was considered advisable for organizers to stay at their posts. However, in December Dora Marsden interrupted in a spectacular fashion a meeting being held by Winston Churchill. With two companions she had the night before entered the roof space of the Empire Hall in order to heckle the speaker. Magistrates dismissed all charges against them and, although the incident engendered its own publicity, Dora Marsden was not able to martyr herself, as she had apparently hoped, by going on hunger strike and being force fed. Her relations with Clement's Inn became increasingly difficult; she did not provide Beatrice SANDERS with balanced accounts and other requested statistical information and was unwilling to follow policy instructions. Her grandiose plan for a Southport WSPU bazaar to rival the 1909 Prince's Skating Rink exhibition, although absorbing a great deal of time and energy, proved a chimera and was finally prohibited by headquarters. Dora Marsden resigned as a WSPU organizer on 27 January 1911. She then negotiated with the WOMEN'S FREEDOM LEAGUE, but no agreement as to her future role in the WLF could be reached.

Encouraged by Teresa Billington-Greig, who had recently resigned from the WFL, Dora Marsden determined to found a paper to provide a radical feminist platform removed from the constraints of the militant suffrage campaign. She moved to London, apparently living on small amounts of money given to her by Mary Gawthorpe, and attempted to raise the funds necessary to start the paper. Charles Grenville, owner of the radical publishers Stephen Swift, eventually agreed to back her and the first issue of the *Freewoman*, edited by Dora Marsden, was published on 23 November 1911, at the very moment that the WSPU campaign entered into its final militant stage. The *Freewoman* lasted only 11 months and in its short life attracted both love and hatred. Radical suffragists such as Ada Nield CHEW were ardent supporters and constitutional suffragists such as Millicent FAWCETT thought it objectionable. Among its contributors were Teresa Billington-Greig, H.G. Wells, Rebecca West and Stella Browne and articles ranged way beyond the suffrage issue to encompass feminism in all its manifestations. Before the end of 1911 the *Freewoman* launched an attack on the WSPU and the Pankhursts, fiercely condemning the resumption of militant tactics, and doubtless alienating much of its potential readership. Hertha AYRTON was one who felt that the paper had betrayed the trust of those supporters who had assumed that it would be sympathetic to the WSPU and the suffrage movement. In March 1912 Mary Gawthorpe resigned, in anger, from her association with the paper; Dora Marsden was not an easy colleague. In April 1912, at a meeting held in the International Women's Suffrage Shop (*see* SHOPS), "The Freewoman Discussion Circle" was launched, inspired by the wish of readers to have a forum to debate issues raised in the paper. It was agreed to organize similar groups in the provinces and Scotland. The London group proved very popular and successful; eugenics, birth-control, anarchy, prostitution and divorce were among the topics covered. As the *Freewoman* became even more radical, W.H. Smith refused to stock it; the final issue, by now "A Weekly Humanist Review", appeared on 10 October 1912. However, with the help of Harriet Shaw Weaver, later to be the patron of James Joyce, it was relaunched as The *New Freewoman* in June 1913. In the second issue Dora Marsden emphasized that "*The New Freewoman* has no Cause... *The New Freewoman* is not for the advancement of Woman, but for the empowering of individuals – men and women". She continued her attack on the Pankhursts, using the death of Emily Wilding Davison to highlight her conviction that they were prepared to make use of dedicated individuals, who otherwise were considered as trouble-makers, only when it suited them. The paper became progressively more literary; Ezra

Pound joined the editorial staff, Rebecca West resigned in October, and the final issue of the *New Freewoman* appeared on 15 December 1913. It was relaunched in January 1914, still backed by Harriet Shaw Weaver, as the *Egoist* and, although Dora Marsden was a contributer, it is as the vehicle for the work of Richard Aldington, H.D. (Hilda Doolittle), Ezra Pound and James Joyce that the journal is remembered. Dora Marsden carried on her anti-Pankhurst vendetta, attacking in the *Egoist* (2 February 1914) Christabel Pankhurst's *The Great Scourge and How to End It* as hysterical. In mid-1914 Harriet Shaw Weaver took over as editor of the *Egoist* and Dora Marsden became a contributing editor, remaining, to some extent, associated with the journal until its demise at the end of 1919. She devoted herself to philosophy, developing her own egoistic analysis.

After the First World War Dora Marsden settled with her mother at Seldom Seen, a remote cottage on the lower slopes of Hellvellyn in the Lake District, her physical and mental health declining as she struggled to realize her amibition of writing a multi-volume philosophical work. Harriet Weaver and Sylvia Beach, of Shakespeare and Co., the Parisian bookshop, supplied her with a wide range of research material and Harriet Weaver funded the publication of *The Definition of the Godhead*, 1928, and *The Mysteries of Christianity*, 1930. From 1935 until her death Dora Marsden, suffering from severe psychotic depression, was a patient at the Crichton Royal Hospital in Dumfries, her fees there paid by Harriet Weaver.

Address: (1909) 141 Chorlton Road, Manchester; (1912) 22 Grove Place, Christchurch Road, Hampstead, London NW; (1913) 9 Hatfield Road, Ainsdale, Southport, Lancashire; (1920) Seldom Seen, near Glenridding, Ullswater, Cumberland.

Photograph: on cover of L. Garner, *A Brave and Beautiful Spirit: Dora Marsden 1882–1960*, 1990.

Archival source: Home Office Papers, Public Record Office.

Bibliography: L. Garner, *A Brave and Beautiful Spirit: Dora Marsden 1882–1960*, 1990.

MARSH, CHARLOTTE AUGUSTA LEOPOLDINE

(1887–1961) Born, one of five sisters, in Newcastle, where her father, Arthur Hardwick Marsh, was an artist. She joined the WOMEN'S SOCIAL AND POLITICAL UNION, inspired, in March 1907, by meeting Edith RIGBY, but because her family was anxious that she should finish her training as a sanitary inspector, she refrained from taking an active part in the militant campaign until she had completed her examinations. On 3 March 1908, her training finished and just 21, she volunteered to join a WSPU deputation. On 30 June she went with Elsie HOWEY to Parliament Square and was arrested on a charge of obstructing the police. She was sentenced to a month's imprisonment in Holloway. In January 1909 she was a WSPU ORGANIZER in Yorkshire. In September 1909 she took part, with Mary LEIGH, in the rooftop protest while Asquith was speaking at the Bingley Hall in Birmingham. She was sentenced to three months' imprisonment in Winson Green Prison. After taking part in the hunger strike in the attempt to achieve the status of a political prisoner, Charlotte Marsh was one of the first suffragette prisoners to be forcibly fed. The Prison Visiting Committee reported that at first she had to be fed by placing food in the mouth and holding the nostrils, but that she later took food from a feeding cup. *Votes for Women*, on her release, reported that she had been fed by tube 139 times. Although the prison authorities knew her father to be seriously ill, she was not released from prison until 9 December (if granted the usual remissions she could have been released on 7 December) and she arrived back in Newcastle just before her father, by then unconscious, died.

In February 1910 Charlotte Marsh was WSPU organizer in Oxford and in the summer was in charge of the "Civil Servants, Stenographers and Clerks" section of the 18 June WSPU Procession, herself carrying the banner at the head of the cavalcade. In September 1910 she conducted a WSPU holiday campaign in Southsea and stayed until March 1912 as WSPU organizer at Portsmouth. Lancelot Surry, whose mother was active in the local WSPU, described her as "a tall young woman, of quiet, resolute bearing. She was supposed to have been a sanitary inspector before she became an advocate of the WSPU. Her photograph used to hang in our home. It bore an inscription to the effect that for the sake of women's rights she had undergone imprisonment in Holloway Gaol."

In March 1911 Charlotte Marsh planted a tree in the arboretum at Eagle House, Batheaston.

Mrs BLATHWAYT noted in her diary on 5 March, "She greatly dislikes her first name Charlotte and all her friends call her Charlie . . . (She also goes by the name Calm). We liked her very much what we saw of her. She is very fair with light hair and a pretty face. She is very tall . . . She has a wonderful constitution and seems very well after all she has gone through. She has begun the late custom of not taking meat or chicken." After taking part in the window-smashing campaign in March 1912, during which she broke at least nine windows in the Strand, Charlotte Marsh was sentenced to six months' imprisonment, spent in Aylesbury, Holloway being full. She joined in the hunger strike and was forcibly fed. On her release she went, with Ada WRIGHT and two other ex-prisoners, to Switzerland to recuperate. From 1913 until the beginning of the First World War she was WSPU organizer in Nottingham although she was often in London, in disguise, working alongside Grace ROE. In June 1913 she was the Standard Bearer at the funeral of her close friend, Emily Wilding DAVISON.

After the outbreak of war Charlotte Marsh worked as a motor mechanic, as chauffeuse to Lloyd George, and then as a land girl. By 1916 she had broken away from the Pankhursts to become honorary secretary of the the INDEPENDENT WSPU. In 1919 she worked with the Women's International League for Peace and Freedom. She then spent some time with the Department of Social Work in San Francisco and then with the Overseas Settlement League. By 1934 she was working with the Public Assistance Department of the London County Council and was a member, with Theresa GARNETT, to whom she later left a bequest in her will, of the executive council of the Six Point Group. She herself was left a bequest in the will of Emmeline PETHICK-LAWRENCE.

Address: (1934) 132 Cheyne Walk, London SW; (1960) 514 Chelsea Cloisters, London SW.
Photograph: in Suffragette Fellowship Collection, Museum of London. A portrait bust of her, by Mrs D. Russell, was offered to the London Museum in 1961; whereabouts now unknown.
Archival source: Birmingham Archives (Visiting Committee of HM Prison Winson Green); Blathwayt Diaries, Dyrham Park (The National Trust), Avon.
Bibliography: M. Lawson, *Memories of Charlotte Marsh*, 1961; A. Morley and L. Stanley, *The Life and Death of Emily Wilding Davison*, 1988.

MARSHALL, CATHERINE ELIZABETH (1880–1961) Daughter of Caroline and Frank Marshall, mathematics master at Harrow School. Educated first at a small private school run by her aunts, from the age of 16 she was a boarder at St Leonards School at St Andrews. Once she left school she continued educating herself, particularly in economics. She was brought up a Liberal and her first political speech, soon after leaving school, was in defence of free trade. She was the secretary and her mother president of the local Women's Liberal Association in Harrow. In 1904 her father retired from Harrow and the family moved to live permanently at Hawse End, their house on the edge of Derwentwater. Catherine Marshall campaigned in Cumberland for the Liberal cause at the general election in January 1906 and in May 1908, with her mother, formed at Keswick a branch of the NATIONAL UNION OF WOMEN'S SUFFRAGE SOCIETY. Catherine Marshall took part in the NUWSS procession organized in London on 13 June 1908 and in July played host to the CAMBRIDGE UNIVERSITY WOMEN'S SUFFRAGE SOCIETY CARAVAN as, with Ray Costelloe (see STRACHEY FAMILY) in charge, it travelled through Keswick. Catherine Marshall's initiative of setting up a stall in Keswick marketplace from which to sell suffrage literature was one that was soon emulated by other NUWSS societies. She was full of energy in campaigning across Westmoreland and Cumberland, organizing there a model campaign for the general election in January 1910. She arranged the printing of a leaflet, "Election Campaign in Cumberland", which set out the NUWSS's objects and methods, and very efficiently included a tear-off sheet instructing the recipient to indicate their proposed degree of involvement in the campaign, ranging from a donation, through canvassing for signatures, to supplying board and lodging for helpers. By December 1909 Catherine Marshall had been elected a member of the NUWSS committee set up to reform its structure. The federated structure that resulted was based on an idea that she had suggested to the National Union at a council meeting in July 1909.

Since 1904 Catherine Marshall had returned to London frequently for lengthy visits and was a member of the LONDON SOCIETY FOR WOMEN'S SUFFRAGE. After 1910 the time spent in London increased. She was enthusiastic for the Conciliation Bill and, through the NORTH-WESTERN FEDERATION OF SUFFRAGE SOCIETIES, of which she was chairman, lobbied MPs to support it. After January 1911, when Kathleen COURTNEY was elected honorary secretary, Catherine Marshall became part of the influential group at the heart of the NUWSS. She soon became honorary secretary of the press department, with the aim of increasing coverage of suffrage issues in the daily papers. In June 1911 she attended the INTERNATIONAL WOMAN SUFFRAGE ALLIANCE meeting in Stockholm. Although dismayed by Asquith's announcement in November of the proposed introduction of a Manhood Suffrage bill, open to an amendment to include women, she, with the rest of the NUWSS executive, was satisfied that he had promised in good faith to give facilities for such an amendment and to grant time for the Conciliation Bill. At this important period, January 1912, Catherine Marshall agreed to deputize, as honorary assistant parliamentary secretary, for Edith PALLISER, who was ill. Catherine Marshall proved exceptionally adept at the political manoeuvring that marked this stage of the suffrage campaign, working both at keeping local societies concentrated on lobbying their MPs and herself bringing influence to bear on the political leaders at Westminster. Edith Palliser returned in early March and Catherine Marshall resumed her work with the press department. On 21 March she was confirmed as honorary assistant parliamentary secretary of the NUWSS, with a seat on the executive. After the defeat of the second reading of the Conciliation Bill on 28 March she returned to Keswick. When she came back to London it was to live in a room rented from Mary Sheepshanks at 1 Barton Street, Westminster. She had previously stayed with friends; the inference may be drawn that she intended, whatever her family thought, henceforward to centre her work in London. She broke her holiday for a few days in early May in order to attend a special NUWSS council meeting and give her support to the Election Fighting Fund policy that would draw the NUWSS close to the Labour Party. Catherine Marshall became honorary secretary of the EFF, with primary responsibility for winning over the mainly Liberal members of the NUWSS to this new initiative. The policy was soon tested at by-elections at Holmfirth and Ilkeston and at others throughout the summer. By September 1912 she was convinced that the EFF policy would bring the required degree of pressure to bear on the political machine. In addition to her chairmanship of the EFF, after Edith Palliser's resignation, she was appointed honorary parliamentary secretary of the NUWSS. She had already resigned her position with the North-Western Federation in order to concentrate on her work in London.

After the defeat of the Conciliation Bill, NUWSS politicking concentrated on the proposed Reform bill. Catherine Marshall and Kathleen Courtney bore the brunt of this work, with the aid of the parliamentary committee. On 23 January 1913 the Speaker intimated that the proposed amendment to include women was likely to be ruled out of order. Asquith refused to receive an NUWSS deputation. It was left to Lloyd George to meet Millicent FAWCETT, Kathleen Courtney and Catherine Marshall, who left him in no doubt that it was their view that the only way in which Asquith could redeem his pledge was by granting facilities for a government measure for women's enfranchisement. It was clear that this was an unlikely outcome and the NUWSS realized that it would have to concentrate its EFF policy on by-elections while waiting for the next general election. The policy might at first have been seen by the NUWSS as a way of convincing the Liberal Party that it was in earnest. However, as no real change in Liberal policy was forthcoming by the end of 1913, the EFF was progressively considered as a means of unseating the Liberals.

In February 1913 Catherine Marshall was re-elected to her position as honorary parliamentary secretary, defeating Chrystal MACMILLAN, who had contested the position. Besides all her other work she was an active member of the committee organizing the rally to mark the culmination of the NUWSS PILGRIMAGE in Hyde Park on 26 July. Delicate manoeuvring resulted in a meeting on 8 August with Asquith, who had long refused to receive any suffrage deputation. Asquith was apparently considerably impressed by the Pilgrimage and by the information that the NUWSS officers gave to him of the state of working-class public opinion on the suffrage question. Catherine Marshall and her companions, although pleased with the deputation, placed no unrealistic expectations on

Asquith's interest. A year later Sylvia PANKHURST was prepared to invest rather more belief in a similar reception he gave her deputation of working women. Catherine Marshall was, in fact, distinctly disillusioned by the lack of support given by cabinet ministers, such as Lloyd George and Sir Edward Grey, who professed to support their cause while doing so little, even that which was within their power, to bring it to fruition. As a corollary she was finding the Labour Party increasingly sympathetic. In an article she wrote for the *Englishwoman*, August 1913, she concluded that the best hope for women's enfranchisement would be a general election resulting in a small majority for the Liberal Party, with a strong Labour Party, with women's suffrage as one of its platforms, waiting in the wings.

From mid-August 1913 until February 1914 parliament was in recess. Catherine Marshall spent the time back home in Keswick, corresponding from there with politicians of all parties whom she thought would prove most useful to the cause. Among her correspondents were Lord Robert Cecil, a longstanding Conservative supporter, his sister Lady Selborne, president of the CONSERVATIVE AND UNIONIST WOMEN'S SUFFRAGE ASSOCIATION, who gave valuable insights into likely future Conservative moves on women's suffrage, and Ramsay MacDonald, chairman of the parliamentary Labour Party. On 15 December she had a very interesting private meeting with Sir Edward Grey, in which she set out for him the likely electoral outcome of a hardline implementation of the EFF policy, the implication of a closer alliance between the interests of women and labour and the similarities in the struggle for freedom being pursued by women and "subject races" throughout the world. Apart from parliamentary politicking, during 1914 she was occupied with internal NUWSS dissension, including criticism of the the EFF policy both within the SCOTTISH FEDERATION and from individual members of the NUWSS executive, resulting in the resignation of four members, led by Eleanor RATHBONE.

In February 1915 Catherine Marshall was one of those who attended the informal meeting in Holland that laid the foundations for the Women's Peace Congress and, an internationalist, was a leader of the faction in the NUWSS that wanted to work for peace. In March she resigned both her position as honorary parliamentary secretary and her seat on the NUWSS executive committee. She later appeared to be rather bitter and angry with Mrs Fawcett and the rump of the NUWSS. In the same month she gave a talk, "Women and War", denouncing militarism. In September 1915 she was elected honorary secretary of the Women's International League, the British section of the International Committee of Women for Permanent Peace. In 1916 she was working with Bertrand Russell in running the No-Conscription Fellowship and in September resigned her position with the WIL. She was at this time also a member of the executive committee of the National Council for Adult Suffrage. A year later she suffered a breakdown for which she was still receiving treatment when the war ended. However, she had recovered by May 1919 when she attended the Women's International Congress at Zurich. She continued to work for peace between the wars and gave refuge to German and Austrian Jews at Hawse End.

Address: (1900, 1956) Hawse End, Keswick, Cumberland; (1913) 1 Barton Street, Westminster, London SW; (1961) 2 Linnell Drive, Hampstead Way, London NW11.
Photograph: in J. Vellacott, *From Liberal to Labour with Women's Suffrage: The Story of Catherine Marshall*, 1993.
Bibliography: A. Wiltsher, *Most Dangerous Women: Feminist Peace Campaigners of the Great War*, 1985; S.S. Holton, *Feminism and Democracy: Women's Suffrage and Reform Politics in Britain, 1900–1918*, 1986; M. Kamester and J. Vellacott, *Militarism versus Feminism: Writings on Women and War*, 1987; J. Alberti, *Beyond Suffrage: Feminists in War and Peace, 1914–28*, 1989; J. Vellacott, *From Liberal to Labour with Women's Suffrage: The Story of Catherine Marshall*, 1993.

MARSHALL, KITTY [EMILY KATHERINE WILLOUGHBY], MRS (1871–1947) Daughter of Canon Kinton Jaques, dean of Leyland, Lancashire. In 1904 she married Arthur Marshall, a partner in the firm of solicitors Bisgood and Marshall of 5 Moorgate Street Buildings, London EC. There do not appear to have been any children of the marriage. She was an artist, exhibiting at the Royal Academy, 1927, and was a weaver and a woodcarver. On 11 December 1906 she attended the banquet given at the Savoy by Mrs FAWCETT to celebrate the release of the WOMEN'S SOCIAL AND POLITICAL UNION prisoners. By 1907 she was attending meetings of the WSPU at Clement's Inn and on 29 June 1909 she volunteered to take part in the deputation to Asquith. She, with Mrs PANKHURST and Evelina

HAVERFIELD, was charged with obstructing the police. Her husband acted as solicitor for the WSPU, from conviction and sympathy rather than for any financial gain. As Ethel SMYTH noted in *Female Pipings in Eden*, not only did he give his time generously to the WSPU but, by so doing, he risked incurring professional censure. Among the many prisoners for whom he acted were Laura AINSWORTH when she was forcibly fed in 1909, Hugh FRANKLIN in 1910 and May BILLINGHURST in 1913.

In May 1909, with Edith and Ellen BECK, Kitty Marshall ran the Farm and Produce stall at the Prince's Rink WSPU Exhibition. In November 1910 she was arrested twice, once on "Black Friday" and a few days later while protesting against forcible feeding of suffrage prisoners. On this occasion she was sentenced to 14 days' imprisonment for throwing a potato at the fanlight over the front door of the Home Secretary, Churchill. In her suffrage memoir she gives a clear description of prison life, particularly remarking how the sheets had holes in the centre where the acid used to mark on prison arrows had burned through the cloth. In 1911 she delivered each week a copy of *Votes for Women* to 10 Downing Street, braving the six policemen guarding the door. On 21 November 1911 she was arrested after taking part in a deputation to the House of Commons. She was reported to have shouted "Charge" – which resulted in 10 days' imprisonment. By late December Kitty Marshall was organizing hampers for suffrage prisoners. On 1 March 1912 she took Mrs Pankhurst and Mabel TUKE in a motor car to 10 Downing Street and threw five stones, carrying such messages as "We demand the Vote", through a window and, after her arrest, the sixth through the window of the India Office. She was arrested, remanded in custody to Holloway, and after a three-day trial was given two sentences, one of two months and one of three weeks, to run consecutively, for conspiring and inciting others to do damage. She describes the turmoil occasioned by holding over 200 suffrage prisoners in Holloway – the banging on doors and the singing of the WSPU Marseillaise. She broke the panes of glass in her cell, was taken before a board of visiting magistrates and ordered to spend five days in solitary confinement in an underground cell. On 22 July 1913 she was charged with assaulting a police inspector after a fracas during the re-arrest of Mrs Pankhurst at the London Pavilion.

In 1919, Kitty Marshall and her husband, who had remained close to Emmeline Pankhurst, opened a Pankhurst Testimonial Fund, which purchased for her a house in Devon. The house was hardly lived in before the Pankhursts left for America and was sold at a loss. The Marshalls remained faithful and at Easter 1927 took Emmeline Pankhurst on a cruise to Gibraltar in an attempt to restore her to health. Ethel Smyth records, in *Female Pipings in Eden*, that at this time Emmeline Pankhurst had no more devoted friends than the Marshalls and that their home was her refuge. Kitty Marshall was godmother to Enid Goulden Bach, Mrs Pankhurst's niece, and was a pallbearer at Mrs Pankhurst's funeral. With Mrs MASSY she was joint honorary secretary of the Mrs Pankhurst Memorial, which was to consist of a headstone, designed by a woman sculptor, for the grave in Brompton Cemetery, a portrait by Georgina BRACKENBURY, and a statue. Kitty Marshall was determined on the latter and was prepared to demolish one of two freehold sites that she and her husband held in Westminster if she could not obtain for the statue a position close to parliament. She organized the unveiling ceremony in March 1930 and was herself at about the same time presented by the SUFFRAGETTE FELLOWSHIP with a replica of the statue. With £200 left over from the subscription for the statue, new choir stalls, copies of ones Mrs Marshall had admired in Liverpool Cathedral, with the addition of "EP" carved on the seats, were given to Ongar Church. Shortly before she died she wrote a memoir of her suffragette exploits, which Rachel BARRETT, her close neighbour, undertook to bring to the attention of the publisher, Victor Gollancz. It was not published. Christabel Pankhurst attended Kitty Marshall's funeral in Sible Hedingham Church.

Address: (1913) Turpin House, York Street, Buckingham Gate, London SW and Theydon Bois, Essex; (1947) The Bridge House, Sible Hedingham, Essex.
Archival source: E.K.W. Marshall, "Suffragette Escapes and Adventures", in The Suffragette Fellowship Collection, Museum of London.
Bibliography: E. Smyth, *Female Pipings in Eden*, 1933.

MARTEL, NELLIE ALMA, MRS (?1855–1940) Born in Cornwall, the daughter of a blacksmith, emigrated to Sydney, Australia, in the early 1890s, in the footsteps of at least two of her brothers. One of these, David Morley Charleston, had been associated with the labour movement in England and in 1891 was elected to the South Australian upper house as a member of the United Labor party. By 1894 Nellie Martel was a member of the council of the Womanhood Suffrage League of New South Wales, which had been founded in 1891 by Dora MONTEFIORE. By 1901 Nellie Martel was protesting against the lack of autonomy afforded to the branches of the League and, although remaining a member of the League, formed and became president of the Women's Progressive Association, which conducted a more vigorous campaign in the final year before the vote was granted. She became president of the Women's Liberal and Reform Association of New South Wales, which was formed as soon as women were enfranchised. Although defeated, she received 20 000 votes in the election of December 1903 in which she stood as a New South Wales candidate for the Senate. In November 1904 Mrs Martel arrived back in England, with her husband who was ill, intending only to stay a short time. She records that she went to the headquarters of the NATIONAL UNION OF WOMEN'S SUFFRAGE SOCIETIES to inquire how women's suffrage was progressing in Britain "and learned that drawing-room meetings, petitions, and pledges were what they chiefly depended upon". She was moved by the condition of the women of West Ham, whose plight was dominating the newspapers and, wasting no time, made her first public speech, on this subject, in north London on 4 December 1904. Nellie Martel immediately began speaking at public meetings, particularly for the Women's Co-operative Guild whose theme of study for 1905 was "The Citizenship of Women". On 12 May 1905 she was accompanied by members of the Guild when she attended the House of Commons, only to hear the women's suffrage bill talked out. She afterwards took part in a protest, together with Elizabeth Wolstenholme ELMY, Dora Montefiore and Mrs PANKHURST, outside the Commons. Mrs Wolstenholme Elmy had already referred to Nellie Martel in her correspondence, presumably having been told about her by Dora Montefiore. In July 1905, at the invitation of Mrs Pankhurst, Nellie Martel went to speak in Manchester and attended there a meeting of the WOMEN'S SOCIAL AND POLITICAL UNION, noting that its membership then was less than 30. Hannah MITCHELL mentions in her autobiography that Mrs Martel was one of the speakers in the WSPU summer 1905 Lancashire campaign.

Nellie Martel was back in Manchester to attend the dinner given on 20 October 1905 to celebrate the release from prison of Annie KENNEY and Christabel PANKHURST. A photograph shows her, in gaudy splendour, sitting next to Annie Kenney; she is not shown in the version of the photograph that appears in Sylvia Pankhurst's *The Suffragette*, 1911. In February 1906 she was present at the meeting at Sylvia PANKHURST's lodgings at which the London committee of the WSPU was formed and "attired in a large picture-hat and yellow satin blouse", as the *Daily Mirror* reporter chose to notice, was one of the speakers at the first WSPU Caxton Hall meeting on 19 February. In May 1906 she, with Annie Kenney and Teresa Billington (*see* Teresa BILLINGTON-GREIG), demonstrated outside Dora Montefiore's besieged house at Hammersmith. On 3 October 1906 Mrs Martel was arrested, with Anne Cobden SANDERSON and Minnie BALDOCK, after taking part in a protest in the Lobby of the House of Commons and was sentenced to two months' imprisonment. She was present at the dinner at the Savoy on 11 December given by Mrs FAWCETT to celebrate the release of the prisoners. In late 1906 she spoke at a meeting in Cardiff, and was influential in persuading Rachel BARRETT to join the WSPU. In 1906 the Woman's Press published a pamphlet by Mrs Martel on *The Women's Vote in Australia* and in 1907 she contributed an essay, "Women's Votes in New Zealand and Australia", to Brougham Villiers (ed.), *The Case for Women's Suffrage*. By 1907 Nellie Martel was an official ORGANIZER for the WSPU. At the end of June 1907 she was in Jarrow campaigning at the by-election. Jessie STEPHENSON, who was also there, recorded that "malice mongers" said Mrs Martel dare not go to prison for fear of what would become of the wonderful auburn tint of her hair. Sylvia Pankhurst in *The Suffragette Movement* described Mrs Martel as "golden-haired and bejewelled".

In January 1908 Nellie Martel was present at Newton Abbott when the result of the by-election, revealing the defeat of the Liberals, was declared and, with Mrs Pankhurst, was badly beaten by a mob. She chaired a platform in the WSPU Hyde Park rally of 18 June 1908. Minnie Baldock, with whom she had been working in the East End, appeared on her platform. By late 1908 she appears to have been out of favour with WSPU headquarters. In 1910 she subscribed to the NEW CONSTITUTIONAL SOCIETY FOR WOMEN'S SUFFRAGE. She was present at a reunion dinner given by Dora Montefiore in the Minerva Club (*see under* CLUBS) in the early 1920s.

Address: (1940) 18 Ladbroke Gardens, Notting Hill, London W.

Photograph: in *Votes for Women*, 7 May 1908; E. Hill and O.F. Shafer, *Great Suffragists – and Why*, 1909; D. Atkinson, *The Suffragettes in Pictures*, 1996.

Bibliography: E. Hill and O.F. Shafer, *Great Suffragists – and Why*, 1909; A. Oldfield, *Woman Suffrage in Australia*, 1992.

MARTINDALE, LOUISA, MRS (1839–1914) née Spicer Congregationalist. Two of her sisters married brothers of T. Fisher Unwin, and she was, therefore, related by marriage to Jane Cobden UNWIN. She had become interested in women's suffrage between 1867 and 1871 and appeared to have heard of both Mrs Wolstenholme ELMY and the MANCHESTER SOCIETY FOR WOMEN'S SUFFRAGE at the same time. She married William Martindale in 1871 and had three daughters, one of whom died the day before her husband's death and one, Hilda, who was born six months later. Having lived abroad for a time she came back to England with her daughters and settled first in Lewes, 1880–85, and then in Brighton. She worked for the Brighton Women's Liberal Association after its formation in 1891; at the turn of the century Jane Cobden Unwin was president of the branch and George HOLYOAKE's wife was a member of its executive committee. In 1894 Louisa Martindale was an active member of the CENTRAL NATIONAL SOCIETY FOR WOMEN'S SUFFRAGE, joined the UNION OF PRACTICAL SUFFRAGISTS within the WLF in 1896 and by 1898 was a member of the executive committee of the WOMEN'S LIBERAL FEDERATION. In this year she was also a member of the Women's Co-operative Movement and of the WOMEN'S EMANCIPATION UNION. She was a member of the WEU by 1895 and at the Union's conference held in London on 15 October 1896 read a paper on "Women in India, and the duty of their English sisters", which was subsequently published as a pamphlet by the WEU. When the WEU was wound up in 1899, Louisa Martindale was one of those who cleared up its debts. In 1897 Elizabeth Wolstenholme Elmy wrote of her, "Think Mrs Martindale one of the sweetest and best women *all through* that I have ever met." In this year Louisa Martindale was in correspondence with Mrs Elmy about a set of lectures she had written on the Rights of Women. In the spring of 1898 she worked with Dora MONTEFIORE in Sussex in an attempt to increase the number of women parish councillors elected in the local elections. One of the women whose interest she engaged in this endeavour was Mrs Marie CORBETT of Danehill. Louisa Martindale's brother Albert Spicer, Liberal MP for Monmouth, in the mid-1890s was in charge of a bill for admitting women to sit on county councils. In 1896 he supported the WEU and from 1906 to 1913 was a vice-president of the CENTRAL SOCIETY FOR WOMEN'S SUFFRAGE and its successor the LONDON SOCIETY FOR WOMEN'S SUFFRAGE.

In 1904 Louisa Martindale went with her daughter Hilda and Dora Montefiore to the International Congress of Women in Berlin. Mrs Wolstenholme Elmy encouraged her to meet Susan B. Anthony while she was there. In 1905 Louisa Martindale was a member of the executive committee of the NATIONAL UNION OF WOMEN'S SUFFRAGE SOCIETIES and in 1906 was a vice-president of the Central Society. In October 1907 she spoke at a WOMEN'S SOCIAL AND POLITICAL UNION meeting at Hove at which Christabel PANKHURST was the main speaker and in 1911 is recorded as giving £5 to the WSPU. In 1912 she was a member of the FREE CHURCH LEAGUE FOR WOMEN'S SUFFRAGE and in 1913 was one of its vice-presidents, as was her sister-in-law Lady Spicer.

In the 1880s Louisa Martindale kept open house on alternate Saturdays for Brighton shopgirls and in this way met and took under her wing Margaret Bondfield, then 16 years old and a shop assistant but later to be Britain's first woman member of the cabinet. Louisa Martindale was very interested in co-operative housekeeping and in 1899 gave a lecture on "The Scientific Treatment of Domestic Service". She rented a series of mansion flats in order to take care of her daughters while they were studying in London. Her elder daughter Louisa (1872–1966) was educated at Royal Holloway College, 1890–93, and then became a doctor, working for a time with Mary MURDOCH in Hull. On her return to Brighton she founded the New Sussex Hospital for Women. In 1913 she published *Under the Surface*, dealing with prostitution and the futility of the system of regulation. She was a member of the Brighton and Hove branch of the NUWSS, of the LONDON GRADUATES' UNION FOR WOMEN'S SUFFRAGE, of the Royal Holloway College Suffrage Society, and was a supporter of the NATIONAL POLITICAL LEAGUE. After the First World War she was a member of the executive committee of the Association for Moral and Social Hygiene and in 1934 she was president of the Brighton and Hove branch of the National Council of Women.

Louisa Martindale's younger daughter Hilda (1875–1952) was active in the Women's Liberal Federation in 1898, became a senior lady inspector of factories and was the author of *Women Servants of the State*, 1938.

Address: (1896) 5M Hyde Park Mansions, Marylebone Road, London NW; (1902) 16 Westminster Mansions, London SW; (1905) Church House, Lancaster Road, Brighton; (1910) Cheeleys, Horsted Keynes, Sussex.

Photograph: in H. Martindale, *From One Generation to the Other*, 1944.

Archival source: Elizabeth Wolstenholme Elmy Papers, British Library; Dr Louisa Martindale Papers, Wellcome Institute, London.

Bibliography: H. Martindale, *From One Generation to the Other*, 1944.

MARTYN, EDITH HOW, MRS (1875–1954) Born in London, née How, sister of Florence EARENGEY, educated at North London Collegiate School and University College, Aberystwyth. She was the first woman to take the Associateship in Physics and Mathematics. She took her BSc degree after her marriage, which took place in Cheltenham in mid-1899, to George Martyn. She was a member of the Independent Labour Party and became an early member of the WOMEN'S SOCIAL AND POLITICAL UNION, having been attracted to a meeting at Clement's Inn by an advertisement in the *Labour Leader*. In May 1906 Edith How Martyn gave her first public speech at one of the meetings held outside Dora MONTEFIORE's besieged house. She took part in the deputation to Asquith on 21 June 1906, in the course of which Teresa BILLINGTON-GREIG was arrested. In summer 1906 she was, with Charlotte DESPARD, appointed joint honorary secretary of the WSPU. Edith How Martyn gave up her post as lecturer in mathematics at Westfield College in the University of London in order to devote herself full time to the suffrage movement and in October 1906 she was one of the women arrested in a struggle with the police in the Lobby of the House of Commons. She received a two-month prison sentence, but was released after serving one month. In 1907, with Mrs Despard, she broke away from the WSPU to found the WOMEN'S FREEDOM LEAGUE. She believed that violent militancy made the passing of any suffrage bill impossible, but that militancy in the form of passive resistance impressed both parliament and the public. She also felt that, although the parliamentary vote should be the chief object of the women's movement, they should also work for the removal of all the other artificial disabilities imposed on women. Edith How Martyn was honorary secretary of the WFL from October 1907 until January 1911 and was then head of the WFL's Political and Militant department until April 1912, when she resigned, ostensibly through illness, but very disappointed by the results achieved by the League.

In the 1918 general election Edith How Martyn stood, unsuccessfully, as an independent candidate in Hendon. In 1919 she became the first woman member of the Middlesex County Council and was its first woman chairman. From at least 1915, when she met Margaret Sanger, she was actively involved in the birth-control movement and became honorary director of the Birth Control International Information Centre. In 1926 she was founder and first president of the SUFFRAGETTE FELLOWSHIP; she also joined the LONDON SOCIETY FOR WOMEN'S SERVICE. Ironically, although she had been opposed to militancy as practised by the WSPU, it was she who devised the questionnaire, sent out to erstwhile suffragettes, that particularly asked for details of their imprisonments and, as a consequence, by making the information easily available to researchers, has concentrated a disproportionate amount of attention on this one aspect of the suffrage movement. After she and her husband emigrated, at the outbreak of the Second World War, to Australia, she organized

there a branch of the Fellowship, which by 1946 had about 100 members. She left the residue of her estate to the Suffragette Fellowship.
Address: (1913) 38 Hogarth Hill, London NW.
Photograph: in the *Vote*, 19 March 1910 and, making jam, in the issue of 26 March.
Archival source: Edith How Martyn Papers, Fawcett Library.
Bibliography: interview by M. Holmes in the *Vote*, 19 March 1910.

MARYLEBONE (branch of the LONDON SOCIETY FOR WOMEN'S SUFFRAGE, NUWSS)   Secretary (1906, 1913) Mrs Bertram, 35 Palace Mansions, Addison Bridge, London W. Emily DAVIES was chairman of the Marylebone committee in 1906.

MARYPORT (NUWSS)   In 1913 the society was a member of the NORTH-WESTERN FEDERATION OF THE NATIONAL UNION OF WOMEN'S SUFFRAGE SOCIETIES. Joint secretaries (1913) Miss Sybil Maughan, Hayborough, Maryport and Miss B. Ritson, Ridgemount, Maryport, Cumberland.

MASON, BERTHA (*c*. 1849–1939)   Elder daughter of Hugh Mason, a wealthy Liberal who in 1880, as MP for Ashton-under-Lyne, introduced a resolution in support of women's enfranchisement, and who, until he retired from parliament in 1883, was the MP responsible for helping the CENTRAL COMMITTEE FOR WOMEN'S SUFFRAGE with the parliamentary conduct of suffrage bills. He was still a member of the MANCHESTER SOCIETY FOR WOMEN'S SUFFRAGE in 1886, the year of his death. Bertha Mason records in *The Story of the Women Suffrage Movement* that she became a worker for the suffrage movement in 1890. She was a member of both the CENTRAL NATIONAL SOCIETY FOR WOMEN'S SUFFRAGE and of the executive committee of the Manchester National Society for Women's Suffrage in 1894. By 1899 she was chairman of the Manchester Society's reincarnation, the NORTH OF ENGLAND WOMEN'S SUFFRAGE SOCIETY, a position she held until 1903. She was also the first woman member of the Board of Guardians in Ashton-under-Lyne, president of the Lancashire Union of the British Women's Temperance Association, treasurer of the Lancashire and Cheshire Union of Women's Liberal Associations, and secretary of the Ashton-under-Lyne WLA.

Around 1900 Bertha Mason moved to London and in 1904 her place on the Ashton Board of Guardians was taken by Hannah MITCHELL. Bertha Mason became honorary secretary of the Women's Local Government Society, joined the CENTRAL SOCIETY FOR WOMEN'S SUFFRAGE, and by 1906 was a member of its executive committee. In 1902 she was a member of the executive committee of the NATIONAL UNION OF WOMEN'S SUFFRAGE SOCIETIES and a delegate from the NUWSS to the annual meeting of the National Union of Women Workers, held that year in Edinburgh. From 1902 to 1910 Bertha Mason was the honorary treasurer of the NUWSS and from at least 1909 until the annual council in 1911, parliamentary secretary. At this meeting, to her dismay, she lost her seat on the executive.

In February 1910 Bertha Mason gave, as a lecture to the Bath NUWSS society, an account, accompanied by lantern slides, of the forerunners of the contemporary suffrage movement. She also gave this "limelight lecture", which was described as "Pictures of unique interest of the forerunners of the movement, the advance guard, the parliamentary champions, the present day workers, election incidents", to members of the Croydon branch of the NUWSS and to the Mansfield Suffrage Society. It was eventually published in book form in 1912 and provides an interesting angle on the radical Liberal aspect of the early suffrage movement. Bertha Mason particularly thanks Lilias Ashworth HALLETT for allowing her to make use of her collection of women's suffrage records and photographs, some of which are reproduced, thereby giving us a tantalizing glimpse of a rich but vanished archive.

After the First World War Bertha Mason was chairman of the Women's Local Government Society and by 1934 was a vice-president of the National Council of Women of Great Britain, of which she had been for some years honorary parliamentary secretary, and a co-opted member of the Women's Advisory Council of the League of Nations Union.
Address: (1913) 9 Hyde Park Square, London W, and Ryecroft Hall, Audenshaw, near Manchester; (1934) 8 Basil Mansions, Knightsbridge, London SW; (1939) Brownlow House, Hindhead, Surrey.
Photograph: in Fawcett Library Collection.
Bibliography: B. Mason, *The Story of the Women's Suffrage Movement*, 1912.

MASON, DORA (1882–1978) Born at Bexleyheath, educated at Blackheath High School and Girton, 1900–1904, where she read Classics and Philosophy. Having been assistant lecturer in Classics at Royal Holloway College, 1904–5, and at Liverpool University, 1907–12, from 1912 until 1915 Dora Mason was head organizer of the OXON, BERKS AND BUCKS FEDERATION OF THE NATIONAL UNION OF WOMEN'S SUFFRAGE SOCIETIES. She travelled around the region during this period, addressing, for instance, in June 1913 the BEDFORD SOCIETY FOR WOMEN'S SUFFRAGE, the Women's Adult School, the Women's Co-operative Guild, a meeting for working women at the Kempston Temperance Hall, drawing-room meetings, and "dinner-hour meetings" at Allen's Works, Howard's Works and Grayton Works. After the outbreak of war she organized workroom and ambulance classes in Bedford, under the aegis of the Centres for Working Girls' Committee and then in High Wycombe as organizer for the Belgian Workroom Committee and for the Women's Employment Sub-Committee of the Mayor's Relief Committee. In 1915 she organized a suffrage summer school at St Andrews.

From 1915 to 1920 Dora Mason trained as a doctor at the Royal School of Medicine for Women, at the Royal Free Hospital and at St Mary's Hospital. From 1922 to 1936 she was in general practice in Bedford with Dr Ethel STACY and was medical officer to the Bedford Borough Maternity and Child Welfare Clinic. From 1930 to 1933 she was president of the Bedford branch of the National Council of Women, subsequently becoming its vice-president.
Address: (1948) 5 Linden Road, Bedford.

MASSINGBERD, EMILY, MRS (1847–97) A landowner, incensed that after the 1884 Reform Act her agricultural labourers had the vote while she did not, she became a member of the general committee of the SOCIETY FOR PROMOTING THE RETURN OF WOMEN AS COUNTY COUNCILLORS and stood, unsuccessfuly, as a candidate for the county council election in the Lindsey division of Lincolnshire in 1889. She was a member of the WOMEN'S FRANCHISE LEAGUE in 1890, a member of the executive committee of the CENTRAL NATIONAL SOCIETY FOR WOMEN'S SUFFRAGE in 1892, in 1893 a member of the executive committee of the Women's Liberal Association and in 1894 a member of the SPECIAL APPEALS COMMITTEE. She was a temperance worker and, most importantly, the founder of the Pioneer Club in London (*see under* CLUBS).
Address: Gunby Hall, Lincolnshire.
Bibliography: P. Hollis, *Ladies Elect*, 1987.

MASSON FAMILY David Masson (1822–1907) was a friend of J.S. MILL, the first secretary of The Society of the Friends of Italy and a member of the circle of radical thinkers who involved themselves in the early beginnings of the women's suffrage movement. When in 1853 he married [Emily] Rosaline Orme (*c.* 1835–1915), daughter of one Eliza ORME and sister of another, Mazzini was one of the guests. Rosaline Orme had been one of the first pupils of Bedford College. Ironically, her aunt Emily, her mother's sister, was the wife of Coventry Patmore and the model for the archetypal poem of Victorian feminine subjugation, *The Angel in the House*. From 1859 until 1868 Masson was editor of *Macmillan's Magazine*. The Massons moved to Edinburgh in 1865, where David Masson became professor of English Literature at the University, and where in 1866 Rosaline Masson signed the women's suffrage petition. Mrs Masson subscribed to the EDINBURGH NATIONAL SOCIETY FOR WOMEN'S SUFFRAGE in 1872, in 1874 was a member of its executive committee and in 1877 became, with Eliza WIGHAM, joint honorary secretary. David Masson spoke, in July 1869, at the first public meeting organized by the LONDON SOCIETY FOR WOMEN'S SUFFRAGE and was present on the platform on 17 January 1870 at the first public meeting in favour of women's suffrage to be held in Edinburgh and, a year later, at that addressed by J.S. Mill on the only occasion he spoke on women's suffrage outside London. David Masson was a champion of the higher education of women, giving, from its foundation in 1868, lectures to the Edinburgh Ladies' Education Association, of which Louisa STEVENSON later became honorary secretary. In 1870 he was a member of the election committee formed to support Elizabeth Garrett ANDERSON's candidacy for the London School Board. In 1877 he was a member of the governing council of the London School of Medicine for Women. One of his daughters, Flora (1856–1937) wrote on the subject of women's enfranchisement in the *Ladies' Edinburgh Journal*, 1876, and was, with her mother, a member of the Ladies' Edinburgh Debating Society in 1881 and the other, Rosaline (1867–1949), was a member of the Ladies' Edinburgh Debating Society in 1890, of the CONSERVATIVE AND UNIONIST WOMEN'S FRANCHISE ASSOCIATION in 1909, by 1913 honorary secretary of the Edinburgh branch, and also in 1912–13 spoke at meetings of the National Union of Women's Suffrage Societies. After the First World War she was honorary press secretary of the Edinburgh branch of the Edinburgh National Society for Equal Citizenship.

Address: (1866) 3 Rosebery Crescent, Edinburgh; (1881) 58 Great King Street, Edinburgh; (1913 and 1934) Rosaline and Flora Masson, 20 Ann Street, Edinburgh.
Portrait: of David Masson by Sir George Reid in Scottish National Portrait Gallery.
Bibliography: F. Masson, *Victorians All*, 1931; L. Leneman, *A Guid Cause: The Women's Suffrage Movement in Scotland*, 1991; I. Anstruther, *Coventry Patmore's Angel: A Study of Coventry Patmore, His Wife Emily and* The Angel in the House, 1992.

MASSY, ROSAMUND, MRS (1870–1947) Daughter of Lady Knyvett, who was herself a very active member of the WOMEN'S SOCIAL AND POLITICAL UNION. Rosamund Massy was married to a colonel in the Dragoon Guards, who gave her his full support, and had one daughter. She probably joined the WSPU in 1908 and in November 1909 was imprisoned for the first time. She had travelled as a WSPU ORGANIZER from London to Preston to help Edith RIGBY gate-crash a meeting to be held there by Churchill and in the course of a demonstration threw a stone through a window of the post office. She went on hunger strike but, after a week, her fine was paid by her mother and she was released. She was arrested on another three occasions but not again imprisoned until November 1910, when she served a one month's sentence in Holloway for breaking a window during the "Black Friday" debacle. Rosamund Massy was a veteran WSPU campaigner of between 25 and 30 by-elections, a very useful public speaker, prepared to take part in debates and drawing-room meetings, as well as the hustings. On 8 April 1913, with her mother, Mrs Massy sought an interview with Sir William Byrne at the Home Office, requesting information about Mrs PANKHURST's condition in Holloway. Mrs Massy told him that Mrs Pankhurst was the most-loved woman in England and that if she was allowed to die "bloodshed would follow at once". The Home Office report of the interview is annotated to the effect that Sir Casey Knyvett, now dead, had been chief clerk in the Home Office, that his widow was a kind-hearted old lady who gave to the WSPU money that should go to her grandchildren and that Mrs Massy was a fierce suffragette who had been imprisoned.

When Mrs Pankhurst stood for election in Whitechapel in 1928 Rosamund Massy, although she herself was not a Conservative, went weekly for several months to give support. It was Rosamund Massy's prison badge and hunger strike medal that was placed in a casket in the plinth of Mrs Pankhurst's statue when it was erected in Victoria Tower Gardens in 1930. In 1939 she was left £300 in the will of Ada WRIGHT.

Address: (1908) 56 Oakley Street, Chelsea, London SW; (1913) 48 Wetherby Mansions, London SW.
Photograph: by Rita Martin on postcard published by the WSPU, John Johnson Collection, Bodleian Library, Oxford.
Archival source: The Suffragette Fellowship Collection, Museum of London.

MATHEWS, VERA LAUGHTON, DAME (1888–1959) Educated at King's College, London. As Vera Laughton she was a sub-editor on the *Suffragette*, working on it in both London and Glasgow and becoming acting editor in August 1914. In the early part of the First World War she worked as a sub-editor on the *Ladies' Field*, before joining the newly formed Women's Royal Naval Service in November 1917. In 1921 she was a member of the committee of the International Women's Franchise Club (*see under* CLUBS). In 1928 she compiled, with Phyllis C. Challoner, *Towards Citizenship: A Handbook of Women's Emancipation*, to which Millicent Garrett FAWCETT added a foreword, while distancing herself from Mrs Laughton Mathews' support for militancy. During the Second World War Vera Laughton Mathews was the director of the WRNS. A Catholic, in 1932 she was chairman of the St Joan's Social and Political Alliance. In the late 1950s she was chairman of the Christabel Pankhurst Memorial Appeal.

Address: (1921) 11 Stanton Road, Wimbledon, London SW.
Bibliography: V. Laughton Mathews, *Blue Tapestry*, 1948.

MATTERS, MURIEL (1877–1969) (after 1914 Mrs Matters-Porter) Born in Adelaide, Australia, where she took a musical degree and became an actress and elocutionist. She later noted that her interest in women's suffrage was stimulated at the age of 14 by reading Ibsen's *The Doll's House*. She came to England, probably around the autumn of 1905, intent on furthering her musical career. She had an introduction to Prince Kropotkin the anarchist, and it was through meeting socialists and social reformers at his house that she became convinced that her personal career must give way to the larger cause. Within six weeks of her arrival in England she was attending WOMEN'S SOCIAL AND POLITICAL UNION meetings in Caxton Hall. She was particularly impressed by Charlotte DESPARD and joined her when she broke away from the WSPU in 1907 to found the WOMEN'S FREEDOM LEAGUE. In late October 1908 Muriel Matters received considerable publicity when, with Helen Fox, she padlocked herself to "that vile grille behind which women have had to sit in the House of Commons for so many years", the removal of which she saw as "a symbol of the breaking down of one of the barriers that are between us and liberty". She described how she put a "burglar proof chain around my waist and key down my back. They wrenched the grille away and marched down to 13 Committee Room carrying the grille behind. Quite a number of M.P.s collected there to meet me and inspect." The chain was there filed off and she was taken to the Westminster Bridge side entrance and pushed out. When she went round to the front of the House of Commons to find out where her friends were, she was arrested, charged with disorderly conduct and subsequently imprisoned. She said that if she had been arrested inside the House of Commons she would have had to be tried at the Bar of the House. Muriel Matters was awarded a special badge to commemorate this protest. At one time it formed part of the collection held by the SUFFRAGETTE FELLOWSHIP Record Room (*see* JEWELLERY AND BADGES).

In May, June and July 1908 Muriel Matters travelled in a CARAVAN through Kent, Surrey and Sussex on a WFL speaking tour. She later remembered that the crowds sometimes exceeded their expectations and they had to call for police protection. In Godalming they were set upon by a mob. The crowd sang, "They'd only been married for a week/ When underneath her thumb went Jim/ Isn't it a pity that the likes of her/ Should put upon the likes of him" and "Put me among the girls . . ." and Muriel Matters sang along with them. She was regarded as an entertaining speaker.

On 17 February 1909 Muriel Matters hired an airship, painted with "Votes for Women" and, with a pilot, flew from Welsh Harp, Hendon, sailing over the House of Commons on the day of the opening of parliament, as 21 members of the WFL were arrested for attempting to interview ministers in Downing Street and at the House of Commons. She noted later that she had been refused life insurance when she applied before the trip and that the dirigible reached a height of 3500 feet, landing eventually at Coulsdon. She did not think that the airship could have been seen as it flew over Westminster, but she dispensed about 6lbs of WFL leaflets, the trail of which was tracked by a car containing Edith How MARTYN and Edith CRAIG. This exploit spawned numerous cartoons and comic postcards.

In 1909 Muriel Matters was organizer for the WFL in South Wales and jointly with Violet Tillard, a Quaker who became a theosophist, founded at the end of the year a branch in Carmarthen. She conducted the WFL campaign in Lloyd George's constituency during the January 1910 general election. She returned to Australia for three months in 1910 and on her return, besides her continuing involvement in the WFL, she gave some support to the NEW CONSTITUTIONAL SOCIETY FOR WOMEN'S SUFFRAGE and to the CHURCH LEAGUE FOR WOMEN'S SUFFRAGE, speaking at the inaugural meeting of the Swansea branch of the latter society in 1913. In July 1911, again with Violet Tillard, she undertook a caravan campaign in Buckinghamshire ("John Hampden country") for the TAX RESISTANCE LEAGUE. In 1913 she was involved in helping to relieve the distress caused to the workers during the Dublin lock-out. In October 1913, speaking for the NATIONAL UNION OF WOMEN'S SUFFRAGE SOCIETIES (it would appear that she had recently left the WFL), she addressed the Miners' Federation, helping to persuade them to support women's suffrage (*see also* Selina COOPER). She addressed the Durham Miners' Gala on women's suffrage in July 1914. In October 1914 she spoke to the BEDFORD WOMEN'S SUFFRAGE SOCIETY on the industrial and economic position of women. The minutes of the Society record that "Miss Matters showed how the present crisis was playing into our hands if we could be adaptable and adjust ourselves to the new conditions."

Muriel Matters married in 1914, noting that her husband could not understand her commitment to the cause and that, having refused him for the previous three years, she would not have married him if war had not put an end to her suffrage activities. During the First World War she went to Spain to train under Maria Montessori and on her return ran Sylvia PANKHURST's model school for young children, based in The Mothers' Arms in Bow. In April 1915 she was organizing secretary of the British Committee of the International Council of Women, which was attempting to meet at the Hague. In July 1916, with Charlotte Despard, Muriel Matters-Porter was involved with the Women's Peace Crusade in Glasgow. During the war she was a member of the BRITISH DOMINIONS WOMAN SUFFRAGE UNION. After the war she spoke at meetings of the Glasgow branch of the Women's International League for Peace and Freedom and was in demand as a speaker for the National Union of Women Workers. In September 1924 she stood, unsuccessfully, as Labour candidate at Hastings. By 1934 she was a member of the committee of the Women's Guild of Empire. She died at Hastings.

Photograph: by Lena Connell in the *Vote*, 19 February 1910.
Archival source: The Suffragette Fellowship Collection, Museum of London; notes by Muriel Matters in private collection.
Bibliography: interview by Marion Holmes in the *Vote*, 19 February 1910.

MAXWELL, LILY (fl. 1867) Described by Lydia BECKER in a letter to Helen TAYLOR on 26 November 1867 as "an elderly woman who keeps a little shop for the sale of crockery, red herrings and suchlike merchandise. We could not have a better representative case – she is a poor working woman, maintaining herself by her own trade with no man to influence, or be influenced by, paying her own rates and taxes out of her own earning, and with decided political sentiments of her own." Lily Maxwell's name had, by accident, been included on the register for the city of Manchester and the newly founded MANCHESTER NATIONAL SOCIETY FOR WOMEN'S SUFFRAGE used this to their advantage. As Lydia Becker wrote "How her name came on the register no one knows, certainly we did not put it there, but finding it there, we made use of the chance." Susan B. Anthony wrote from America a letter of encouragement to Lily Maxwell and Lydia Becker took her to the polling station where she voted, as luck would have it, for Jacob BRIGHT. Lily Maxwell's name is listed as one of the members of the NATIONAL SOCIETY FOR WOMEN'S SUFFRAGE in a printed leaflet for 1868.

Archival source: Mill–Taylor Papers, London School of Economics and Political Science.

"MAYO, WINIFRED" Adopted name of Winifred Alice Monck-Mason (*c.* 1870–1967), an actress, born in India, although her family was associated with Bathwick in Somerset, educated privately in England and France. She trained as an actress at the Italia Conti Dramatic School. One of her cousins, Jessie Street, was to become one of Australia's leading twentieth-century feminists. Winifred Mayo joined the WOMEN'S SOCIAL AND POLITICAL UNION, as did her mother Mrs Alice Monck-Mason, who was actively involved with the KENSINGTON branch in 1908. In February 1908 Winifred Mayo was sentenced to six weeks' imprisonment for taking part in the demonstration surrounding the deputation from Caxton Hall to the House of Commons. Rather intriguingly, she does not mention this episode in her entry in the *Suffrage Annual and Women's Who's Who*, although she did write an article, describing her prison experiences, which appeared in the *Idler*, April 1908. She was arrested again in June 1909 and in November 1910, after the "Black Friday" demonstration in Parliament Square, but was both times discharged. In November 1911 she was imprisoned for three weeks after taking part in the window-smashing campaign. In March 1912 her mother was arrested on a similar charge, was remanded for four days and then acquitted.

Winifred Mayo put her stage skills at the service of the suffrage cause and in 1909 gave elocution lessons for WSPU speakers; often these classes were held in Florence HAIG's studio in Chelsea. On 7 October 1910 she appeared in *The Pot and the Kettle*, a suffrage propaganda play written by Cicely HAMILTON and Christopher ST JOHN, at a meeting of the Chiswick branch of the WSPU. Winifred Mayo was a founder member of the ACTRESSES' FRANCHISE LEAGUE, in 1912–13 was its organizing secretary, and was joint honorary treasurer in 1934. In 1913 she was a supporter of the NATIONAL POLITICAL LEAGUE. During the First World War she was a member of the advisory committee of the British Women's Hospital. From 1921 to 1926 she was organizing secretary of the Six Point Group, a vice-president in the 1930s, and was still a member in 1944–5. She was a member of the Open Door Council and honorary secretary of The Equal Rights International, 1930–4. She became chairman of the SUFFRAGETTE FELLOWSHIP.

Address: (1913) 93 Oakley Street, Chelsea, London SW; (1934) 1 Selwood Place, London SW7; (1947) Fir Tree Cottage, Hythe, Southampton.

MCCARTHY, LILLAH (1875–1960) (later Lady Keeble, OBE) Actress, a member of the Royal Court Theatre company, friend and leading lady of George Bernard Shaw. Mrs PANKHURST told Lillah McCarthy that her playing of "Ann Whitfield" in *Man and Superman* in 1906 had strengthened her resolution and fortified her courage. In November 1909 Lillah McCarthy played "Justice" in the first performance of Cicely HAMILTON's *Pageant of Great Women* which was directed by Edith CRAIG at the Scala Theatre in London. As a result of seeing Cicely Hamilton's own performance in the *Pageant* Lillah McCarthy gave her a part in Shaw's *Fanny's First Play* (see PLAYS) which she produced at the Little Theatre in 1911. Although she was a close friend of Asquith, he appears to have paid little heed to her arguments in favour of women's suffrage. She was also a vice-president and some-time treasurer of the ACTRESSES' FRANCHISE LEAGUE, taking part in many suffrage processions. She particularly remarks in her autobiography of her close friendship with Laurence HOUSMAN and their shared interest in the cause. In the late 1940s Lillah McCarthy took part in several BBC radio programmes reminiscing about her suffragette days (see under RADIO, TELEVISION, RECORDINGS AND RECORDS).

Address: (1960) Flat 6, Cranley Mansions, 100 Gloucester Road, London SW7.
Photograph: in L. McCarthy, *Myself and My Friends*, 1933.
Bibliography: L. McCarthy, *Myself and My Friends*, 1933; J. Holledge, *Innocent Flowers*, 1981; S. Stowell, *A Stage of Their Own: Feminist Playwrights of the Suffrage Era*, 1992.

MCILQUHAM, HARRIET, MRS (1837–1910) Born in London, where in her youth she attended lectures on social and political questions and was a reader of "advanced" literature. She married in 1858 and moved to Staverton, near Cheltenham; her husband was district county surveyor for Gloucestershire. She and her husband had four children and shared their home with his brother who had been deaf and partly dumb since childhood. By 1877 Harriet McIlquham was a member of the MANCHESTER NATIONAL SOCIETY FOR WOMEN'S SUFFRAGE and was also a member of the BRISTOL AND WEST OF ENGLAND SOCIETY FOR WOMEN'S SUFFRAGE. In 1880 she signed an endorsement for the delegate from Cheltenham to the Grand Demonstration of Women held at St James's Hall in London. In February 1881 she was, with Maria Colby, the organizer of the Birmingham Grand Demonstration and on 22 November was one of the speakers at that held in Bradford. She had long advocated that women should take part in local government and, to test the law with regard to women's right to be elected to public bodies, stood as a candidate in 1881 and became the first married woman to become a poor law guardian (for Boddington in the Tewkesbury Union). When the Local Government Board was appealed to in order to annul her election on the grounds that she was a married woman, a searching inquiry into the bona fides of her property qualification proved that it was entirely independent of her husband, and she was duly elected. On the 1891 census she described herself as "Farmer". She stood unsuccessfully for the county council election in Cheltenham in 1889.

Harriet McIlquham attended the annual general meeting of the CENTRAL NATIONAL SOCIETY on 21 March 1889 and seconded a vote of thanks to Jacob BRIGHT, which had been proposed by Alice SCATCHERD. In July 1889 Mrs McIlquham was proposed by Elizabeth Wolstenholme ELMY to be president of the newly founded WOMEN'S FRANCHISE LEAGUE, writing to her, "This will give you the *highest* official status, and there is no one else half so fit for the post, which ought by right to be held by a woman." It is not clear when exactly Harriet McIlquham first met Elizabeth Wolstenholme Elmy. Their preserved correspondence begins in 1889, although there may have been previous letters now lost. It appears, however, from the correspondence that the two had not met often before July 1889. In 1891 Harriet McIlquham followed Elizabeth Wolstenholme Elmy into the WOMEN'S EMANCIPATION UNION, becoming a member of its Council. Elizabeth Wolstenhome Elmy appreciated Harriet McIlquham's legal turn of mind and encouraged her to write articles and pamphlets. In early 1892 the Hansard Publishing Co. published her pamphlet *The Enfranchisement of Women: An Ancient Right, A Modern Need*, of which, by February, 2000 copies had been sent out by the Women's Emancipation Union. In 1904 Elizabeth Wolstenholme Elmy sent a copy to Christabel PANKHURST and a copy found its way into Susan B. Anthony's collection, now housed in the Library of Congress. In 1898 and 1898, encouraged by Elizabeth Wolstenholme Elmy, Harriet McIlquham published a series of articles in the *Westminster Review* on Mary Astell, "Sophia", and on Lady Mary Wortley Montagu, whom she attempts to identify with "Sophia". She had obviously closely studied the original works of these ladies and the articles are interesting now in revealing the source of historical and literary inspiration for late-nineteenth-century thinking on "women's rights" (which is described by Harriet McIlquham as "the somewhat objectionable term").

Mrs McIlquham was one of the overseers for the parish of Staverton, then a unique post for a woman to hold, and eventually became the first chairman of Staverton Parish Council and returning officer at the second parish council election. She also acted as rural district councillor for Boddington and sat for some years on Boddington and Staverton School Board and for five years after the Education Act of 1902 on the Board of Management. In February 1893 she spoke on "Women as Poor Law Guardians" at a meeting in East London and in 1894 gave a paper to the Women's Emancipation Union conference at Bedford, which was then published as a pamphlet, *Women's Work in Local Government*.

Harriet McIlquham was a member of the National Union of Women Workers, and became a member of the CHELTENHAM BRANCH OF THE NATIONAL UNION OF WOMEN'S SUFFRAGE SOCIETIES. She was associated early on with the WOMEN'S SOCIAL AND POLITICAL UNION, being present, along with Sylvia and Emmeline PANKHURST, to lobby MPs at the House of Commons on 21 February 1905, in an attempt to find a sponsor for a new women's suffrage bill. While in London on this occasion she stayed with Mrs Wood of 186 Highbury New Park Road, London N, who had also been a member of the Women's Emancipation Union. Harriet McIlquham was present at the first meeting of militant suffragists in Cheltenham, organized on 28 September 1906 under the auspices of the WSPU by Edith How MARTYN. She remarked that it was 50 years to the very day since she had attended her first meeting on the subject of women's suffrage, at which George HOLYOAKE had been the principal speaker. She gave a donation to the WSPU in 1908 and to the WOMEN'S FREEDOM LEAGUE in 1909.

Harriet McIlquham was one of the organizers of the "Grateful Fund" by which those who appreciated Elizabeth Wolstenholme Elmy's work for the women's movement showed their support in tangible form. Harriet McIlquham was not ill for long before she died, but in this time took the trouble to send to Louisa MARTINDALE the cheque book for the Fund. She had preserved all the letters she had received, over a period of about 21 years, from Elizabeth Wolstenholme Elmy and had mentioned to Mrs Martindale some time before she died that in that event she wished this correspondence to be donated to the British Museum. Her daughter held on to the letters with some tenacity, despite Mrs Wolstenholme Elmy's requests to borrow them. In the light of the complete disappearance of Mrs Elmy's own papers this was probably a wise decision. Frances ROWE was allowed to have the letters for some time, in order that copies of extracts might be made for Mrs Elmy; they were eventually returned to Miss McIlquham in 1913. She offered to lend Christabel PANKHURST, then in Paris, some of the papers. The offer was probably not accepted although Christabel wrote, "I remember

Mrs McIlquham very well, as I met her on various occasions with Mrs Wolstenholme Elmy. My mother, of course, knew her too. As one of the Suffrage pioneers, she had always my great admiration, and whenever we met she was always exceedingly kind". In 1908, when discussing the correspondence, Frances Rowe had written to Harriet McIlquham, "It is a most precious bundle and I hope that they will one day see the light. What a revelation they would make of the cooperation of two gifted earnest unselfish women in perhaps the greatest struggle for liberty there has ever been!"

Address: (1889) Staverton House, Staverton, Gloucestershire.
Photograph: in the *Vote*, 12 February 1910.
Archival source: Elizabeth Wolstenholme Elmy Papers, British Library; Harriet McIlquham Papers, Autograph Collection, Fawcett Library.
Bibliography: H. McIlquham, "Of women in assemblies: a reply", *Nineteenth Century*, November 1896; H. McIlquham, "Mary Astell: a seventeenth century advocate for women", *Westminster Review*, April 1898; H. McIlquham, "Sophia: a person of quality. The eighteenth century champion of women's rights", *Westminster Review*, November 1898; H. McIlquham, "Lady Mary Wortley Montagu and Mary Astell", *Westminster Review*, March 1899; H. McIlquham, "Some further eighteenth century advocates of justice for women", February 1903; H. McIlquaham, "Women's suffrage in the early nineteenth century", *Westminster Review*, November 1903; obituary in the *Vote*, 12 February 1910.

MCKEE, ELLEN COURTAULD (1844–1929) Unitarian, born in Tavistock, daughter of the Rev. McKee and his wife Louisa Jeffrey, who was a cousin of P.A. Taylor (*see* Clementia TAYLOR). In 1834 Louisa Jeffrey had been "a suitable, discreet and retiring . . . pleasant and intelligent companion" to Harriet Martineau on her travels to and around America. Miss Martineau, who paid for everything except Louisa Jeffrey's ticket, described her as "Not only well educated but remarkably clever, and above all, supremely rational, and with a faultless temper, she was an extraordinary boon as a companion." Ellen McKee and her mother both signed the 1866 women's suffrage petition and Ellen joined the LONDON NATIONAL SOCIETY FOR WOMEN'S SUFFRAGE in 1867. She was very friendly with the P.A. Taylors, indeed she was staying at Aubrey House when the 1871 census was taken and in 1922 she was able to afford Florence Gladstone, author of *Aubrey House*, information about the Taylors' part in its history. Ellen McKee was secretary of the suffrage society in her home town, Shrewsbury, subscribed to the CENTRAL COMMITTEE OF THE NATIONAL SOCIETY FOR WOMEN'S SUFFRAGE in 1872 and was still supporting it in 1887. From 1889 she was a member of the CENTRAL NATIONAL SOCIETY FOR WOMEN'S SUFFRAGE. By 1882 she had moved to London and in 1891 stood as a poor law guardian in Marylebone. Her brother S. Jeffrey McKee was solicitor to the SOCIETY FOR PROMOTING THE RETURN OF WOMEN AS POOR LAW GUARDIANS in the 1880s. In 1897 Ellen McKee succeeded to Rosamond Davenport Hill's City seat on the London School Board, giving her attention to the needs of physically disabled children. In 1903 she was a member of the executive committee of the CENTRAL SOCIETY FOR WOMEN'S SUFFRAGE, in 1906 was its honorary treasurer, and in the same year subscribed to the WOMEN'S SOCIAL AND POLITICAL UNION. This latter donation might not be unconnected with her presence at the banquet given by Mrs FAWCETT at the Savoy on 11 December 1906 to celebrate the release of the WSPU prisoners. She was present at the dinner given in 1908 by the NUWSS for the delegates to the fifth Convention of the INTERNATIONAL WOMAN SUFFRAGE ALLIANCE. Ellen McKee remained as treasurer to the LONDON SOCIETY FOR WOMEN'S SUFFRAGE (as the Central Society was renamed) until 1909 and in 1912 was still a member of the NUWSS. In her will she left legacies to the Elizabeth Garrett Anderson Hospital, of which she had been a supporter since 1882, to the South London Hospital for Women, to the London School of Medicine for Women, to the National Education Association, to the Association for Moral and Social Hygiene and to the Unitarian church in Shrewbury, where her father had been minister for 19 years.

Address: (1882) 26 St George's Square, Regent's Park, London NW; (1884) 22 Primrose Hill Road, London NW; (1901) 12 Tavistock Square, London WC; (1913) 14 Cleveland Gardens, Bayswater, London W; (1929) 6 Bentinck Mansions, Bentinck Street, Marylebone, London NW.
Bibliography: M.W. Chapman (ed.), *Harriet Martineau's Autobiography*, 1877; F.M. Gladstone, *Aubrey House*, 1922; P. Hollis, *Ladies Elect: Women in English Local Government 1865–1914*, 1987.

MCKEOWN, ISABELLA GREIG, MRS (*c.* 1858–1941) In 1906, probably a widow and certainly with one daughter, she was a member of the newly formed Brighton branch of the CENTRAL SOCIETY FOR WOMEN'S SUFFRAGE. In 1907 she was secretary of the WOMEN'S FRANCHISE DECLARATION COMMITTEE in Brighton. Later in 1907 Isabella McKeown left the NATIONAL UNION OF WOMEN'S SUFFRAGE SOCIETIES and joined the WOMEN'S SOCIAL AND POLITICAL UNION, becoming its ORGANIZER in Brighton. She remained in this position for some time and returned to it for a couple of months after the death of Mary CLARKE in December 1910. On 24 February 1909 Isabella McKeown took part in the deputation from Caxton Hall to the House of Commons. By the autumn of 1911 it would appear that she had moved to London and was then a member of the KENSINGTON WSPU. In 1912 she was an active WSPU speaker in London, appearing at meetings in Kilburn, Harlesden, Putney, New Barnet and on Wimbledon Common.

Address: (1908) 209 Preston Drive, Brighton, Sussex (this address was that of Mrs Wright, who in 1911 advertised in *Votes for Women* "Board-residence or Apartments, in home of Suffragette, W.S.P.U. Special care to those needing rest."; (1927) Arundel Gardens, Winchmore Hill, London N; (1941) "Chase Bank", Avenue Road, Southgate, London N.

MCLAREN, AGNES, DR (1837–1913) Daughter of Duncan McLaren by his second marriage and therefore stepdaughter of Priscilla Bright McLAREN (*see* Appendix). Agnes McLaren signed the 1866 women's suffrage petition and when the EDINBURGH NATIONAL SOCIETY FOR WOMEN'S SUFFRAGE was founded in November 1867, with her stepmother as president, Agnes McLaren became, with Eliza WIGHAM, joint secretary. In September 1871 she accompanied Jane TAYLOUR on a suffrage speaking tour of the Highlands, from Oban to Orkney. In late 1872 she and Miss Taylour held 18 meetings in two months in the west of Scotland. In 1875 she was a member of the executive committee of the CENTRAL COMMITTEE OF THE NATIONAL SOCIETY FOR WOMEN'S SUFFRAGE.

Agnes McLaren had for some years been a friend of Sophia Jex-Blake, whom Duncan McLaren had in 1869–70 supported in her attempt to enter the Edinburgh University medical school. However, when Agnes intimated that she too wished to study medicine she had to face opposition not only from her father but, to a lesser extent, from Priscilla Bright McLaren. Despite this, in 1876 she entered the school of medicine at the university at Montpellier, and eventually became the tenth woman in Britain to qualify as a doctor. In 1877 Agnes McLaren was a member of the governing council of the London School of Medicine for Women. By 1882 she was a fellow of the Royal College of Physicians at Dublin. She had set up practice in Cannes around 1879 and in 1884 was visiting physician at the Canongate Medical Mission Dispensary in Edinburgh. She spent from June to October in Edinburgh and the rest of the year in Cannes. In 1899 she joined the Catholic church and went to India, with a Catholic mission, as a doctor specializing in the treatment of women. She maintained her interest in women's suffrage and subscribed to the WOMEN'S SOCIAL AND POLITICAL UNION in 1909 and to the NATIONAL UNION OF WOMEN'S SUFFRAGE SOCIETIES' Election Fighting Fund in 1912. At the time of her death she was a member of the CATHOLIC WOMEN'S SUFFRAGE SOCIETY.

Address: (1866) Newington House, Edinburgh; (1913) Villa Ste Anne, Antibes, France.
Photograph: in Blackburn Collection, Girton Archives.
Bibliography: M.V. Ryan, *Dr Agnes McLaren*, 1915; K. Burton, *According to the Pattern: The Story of Dr Agnes McLaren and the Society of Catholic Medical Missionaries*, 1946.

MCLAREN, EVA MARIA, MRS (*c*. 1853–1921) Quaker, daughter of an emigré German businessman, William Muller, of Valparaiso, Chile and "Hillside", Shenley, Hertfordshire. By 1883 her father was a JP in Hertfordshire. Eva had at least three sisters, one of whom was Henrietta MULLER, and a brother (*see* Appendix). In 1883 at the new Westminster Meeting House in St Martin's Lane she married Walter Stowe Bright McLaren, younger son of Priscilla Bright MCLAREN. They had no children of their own but adopted a daughter, Mary Florence Campbell McLaren. Before her marriage Eva Muller was trained by Octavia Hill in housing management, by Agnes Jones in nursing at the Liverpool Workhouse Infirmary, and worked with Josephine Butler in the campaign to repeal the Contagious Diseases Acts. In 1881, with Caroline Ashurst BIGGS and Laura Ormiston CHANT, she was one of the founders of the SOCIETY FOR PROMOTING THE

Return of Women as Poor Law Guardians. Before her marriage, having bought a house to qualify as a ratepayer, she had been elected a poor law guardian in Lambeth and in 1884, after moving north with her husband, she was elected in Bradford. However, her advocacy of the Temperance movement proved unpopular there and she was quickly unseated. She was later a vice-president of the British Women's Temperance Association and, with her husband, was a prominent member of the Moral Reform Union, of which her sister's close friend Frances Lord was a member of the committee. Eva McLaren was the first honorary treasurer of the Society for Promoting the Return of Women as County Councillors and in 1889 spoke at meetings in support of the election of Jane Cobden (see Jane Cobden Unwin).

From its formation in 1886 Eva McLaren was national organizer and honorary treasurer of the Women's Liberal Federation. In 1888 at the conference of the WLF held at Birmingham she stressed that the WLF should put the enfranchisement of women before support for the Liberal Party, a view she was to modify in later years. In 1898, still working for suffrage from within the Liberal Party, she was a member of the executive committee of the Union of Practical Suffragists. She was also president of the Southport Women's Liberal Association, which had for two of its objectives women's suffrage and home rule for Ireland, in 1892 was honorary secretary of the Welsh Union of Women's Liberal Associations and in 1898 was president of the Cardiff Women's Liberal Association. In 1909 she was president of the Home Counties Union of the WLF.

In 1885 Eva McLaren was a member of the executive committee of the Central Committee of the National Society for Women's Suffrage and after the 1888 split was a member of both the Central National Society for Women's Suffrage and, from 1889 until 1897, of the general committee of the Central Committee. In 1894 she was a member of the Special Appeals Committee, formed from members of all the societies to organize the collection of nearly a quarter of a million names of women who supported women's enfranchisement. In partnership with her friend, Frances Heron Maxwell, Eva McLaren owned a piece of land at Newton Stewart in Galloway. In 1893 Mrs Heron Maxwell, who was also a member of the Women's Liberal Association and of the Central National Society and, by 1903, honorary secretary of the Rational Dress League, held a meeting of the Women's Emancipation Union in Newton Stewart and by 1896 a branch of the WEU was established in this rather remote outpost. It is unlikely Eva McLaren was actively involved in this ultraradical offshoot of the suffrage movement, but she would have been well aware of its existence. After its formation in 1896 Eva McLaren was a member of the executive committee of the National Union of Women's Suffrage Societies, representing the Central and West of England Society, in 1901 took over as representative of the Edinburgh Society on the committee and in 1903 was appointed treasurer of the NUWSS. In 1900 she became a member of the executive committee of the re-formed Central Society for Women's Suffrage. Representing the Women's Liberal Federation, she took part in the deputation to the prime minister at the Foreign Office on 19 May 1906.

Elizabeth Wolstenholme Elmy had long complained in her letters to Harriet McIlquham that women such as Eva McLaren always put party first. In February 1907 Eva McLaren's speech at the rally held at Exeter Hall after the NUWSS "Mud March" tackled this thorny subject. She said that Liberal women were being called upon to abandon their party and work for women's suffrage as women only and that, although she had once thought that way (presumably referring to the sentiments she had propounded in 1888) she had realized that if women were to obtain the franchise there must be a means, and the party was that means. Her husband presided over this meeting. Walter McLaren, who was elected Liberal MP for Crewe in 1886 and 1892, was a stalwart supporter of women's suffrage throughout his career. In October 1883 at the Liberal Conference held in Leeds to consider parliamentary reform, he seconded the proposal made by the Rev. Crosskey to extend the parliamentary franchise to women. In 1887 he was appointed the secretary representing the Liberal interest on the newly formed Committee of the Parliamentary newly formed Committee of the Parliamentary supporters of the Women's Franchise Bill and he wrote *The Political Emancipation of Women* which was published by the Central Committee of the National Society in 1888. In October 1908, with Marie CORBETT and Frances Heron Maxwell, Eva McLaren formed the FORWARD SUFFRAGE UNION which, while working from within the Liberal Party, aimed to concentrate the activities of Liberal women on their own enfranchisement. Eva McLaren wrote a 20-page pamphlet, *Civil Rights of Women*, published by the Central Committee of the National Society, probably in late in 1888; *The Election of Women on Parish and District Councils*, 1894; *The Duties and Opinions of Women with Reference to Parish and District Councils*, 1894; and *The History of the Women's Suffrage Movement in the Women's Liberal Federation*, 2nd edn, 1903.

Address: (1892) 3A Poets' Corner, London SW; (1901) 56 Ashley Gardens, London SW; (1921) 20 Ebury Street, London W1; Great Comp, Borough Green, Kent.

Photograph: as Eva Muller, carte de visite in Josephine Butler Collection, Fawcett Library; as Eva McLaren in the *Woman's Herald*, 4 February 1893.

Bibliography: E. McLaren, "The civil rights of women", reprinted in J. Lewis (ed.), *Before the Vote Was Won: Arguments For and Against Women's Suffrage 1864–1896*, 1987.

MCLAREN, LAURA ELIZABETH, MRS (1854–1933) (later Baroness Aberconway of Bodnant, CBE) Born in Salford, the only surviving daughter of Henry Davis Pochin, industrial chemist and Radical Liberal MP, and his wife Agnes POCHIN. Her father was a friend of Richard Cobden and of John and Jacob BRIGHT and in 1877 at the old Westminster Meeting House, with John Bright as the witness, Laura Pochin married Charles McLaren, elder son of Priscilla Bright MCLAREN (*see* Appendix). Four of their children survived infancy. Charles McLaren was a barrister at the time of their marriage, became a Liberal MP from 1880 to 1886 and was then re-elected for Bosworth in 1892. He was actively involved in running steel, iron and colliery undertakings, many linked with the Pochin inheritance which had passed to his wife rather than to her unsatisfactory elder brother. Although he was a Quaker, there is no evidence that Laura adopted his faith. His active lifelong support in parliament for women's suffrage culminated in his being one of the two signatures to the whip sent out on the suffragist side for the final debate in the House of Lords of the 1918 Representation of the People (Equal Franchise) Bill. His brother Walter was the husband of Eva MCLAREN, who was, therefore, Laura's sister-in-law.

In a letter to *The Times*, 17 April 1912, Laura McLaren remarked that she had attended the first women's suffrage meeting held in this country. This, presumably, was that held in Manchester in April 1868, of which her father was chairman and at which her mother was one of the speakers. In 1877 Laura McLaren became a member of the executive committee of the LONDON NATIONAL SOCIETY FOR WOMEN'S SUFFRAGE, joining the finance committee and by 1885 becoming treasurer. Later she was a member of the executive committee of the CENTRAL NATIONAL SOCIETY FOR WOMEN'S SUFFRAGE, was president of the South Kensington Women's Liberal Association and a member of the executive committee of the WOMEN'S LIBERAL FEDERATION. Laura McLaren was a member of the platform party at the Sheffield Grand Demonstration of Women in February 1882 and in November 1882 spoke in Glasgow at that city's Grand Demonstration, over which Priscilla Bright McLaren presided, and was observed by Elizabeth Cady Stanton to be wearing the dress reform outfit, with a divided skirt, advocated by Viscountess HARBERTON.

In 1908 Fisher Unwin published a pamphlet written by Lady McLaren (her husband was created a baronet in 1902 and a peer in 1911). In it she puts cogently the arguments that she and her fellow suffragists had broadcast for the previous 40 years. Responding to Herbert Gladstone's suggestion that women must get out to convert the electorate she writes:

men who suggest this spade-work do not know at what cost to women it is done. In the first place women are miserably poor; the wives of rich men have often nothing but their dress allowance; ... half the women of this country work for a wage which a Royal Commission declared to average not more than 1s a day; married women are busily occupied with their homes and with their children ... to do spadework – to carry on political agitation – needs a lifetime of leisure. ... How often have we tramped along the muddy lanes, how often have we gone round from door to door, often receiving rebuffs and unkindness. Well do we remember dreary railway stations at midnight, the last train gone, and snow upon the ground.

In 1909 Lady McLaren was the author of a very practical document, "The Woman's Charter of Rights and Liberties – Preliminary Draft", which was undertaken as the result of a decision, made at the 5th INTERNATIONAL WOMAN SUFFRAGE ALLIANCE Congress, to present simultaneously in 1910 to all the parliaments of the world a comprehensive statement or charter, detailing the legal injustices and legislative needs of women. Her obituarist in *The Times* noted that her husband introduced the nine bills of "The Woman's Charter" into parliament at her insistence. By 1913 Laura McLaren was a vice-president of the non-party NATIONAL POLITICAL LEAGUE for Men and Women and was a vice-president of the TAX RESISTANCE LEAGUE. On 15 May 1913, using Bodnant notepaper, presumably staying with the Aberconways while visiting his North Monmouth constituency, Reginald McKenna, the Home Secretary, made clear in a letter to his officials his worry that Mrs PANKHURST, then out of prison on licence, might avoid all further punishment. One would surmise from this close association with McKenna that the Aberconways were now quite out of sympathy with the militants. Lady Aberconway was, however, by now no longer a supporter of the Liberal government. In July 1914, with Eva McLaren, she protested in the short-lived *Liberal Women's Review* against the government's attitude to women's suffrage. On 29 June 1914 she was present at the Costume Dinner held at the Hotel Cecil organized by the ACTRESSES' FRANCHISE LEAGUE and the WOMEN WRITERS' SUFFRAGE LEAGUE, sitting at the same table as Dr and Mrs Stanton COIT and Dr Marie Stopes. During the First World War, in which one of her sons was killed, she ran a nursing home for officers in her London house, receiving a CBE for this work. By 1916, when she succeeded the Countess of CARLISLE as president of the Women's Liberal Federation, she had returned to the Liberal fold. In the 1920s Laura McLaren was a member of the Open Door Council and of the Society of Women Journalists, and a supporter of the Women's Institute. At Bodnant, the estate above the river Conway that she had inherited from her father, she developed the gardens that are now run by the National Trust.

Address: (1880) Barn Elms, Barnes, London; (1884) 45 Harrington Gardens, London SW; (1913) 43 Belgrave Square, London SW; Bodnant, Taly-Cafn, Wales.
Portrait: by Tissot, 1878; by Philip de László, 1920, both in a private collection (photographs of both in the National Portrait Gallery Archive).
Bibliography: "'Better and happier': an answer from the Ladies' Gallery to the speeches in opposition to the Women's Suffrage Bill, February 28, 1908", 1908; "The Women's Charter of Rights and Liberties", 1909; J. Travis Mills, *John Bright and the Quakers*, 1935; H.T. Milliken, *The Road to Bodnant*, 1975.

MCLAREN, PRISCILLA BRIGHT, MRS (1815–1906) Quaker, born in Rochdale, the fifth of 11 children, sister to John and Jacob BRIGHT and to Margaret Bright LUCAS, stepmother of Agnes McLAREN, mother-in-law of Laura and Eva McLAREN, and aunt of Anne ASHWORTH and Lilias Ashworth (*see* Lilias Ashworth HALLETT), of Katherine THOMASSON and of Helen Bright CLARK. Her stepson John McLaren married Ottilie Schwabe, whose mother, Matilda Schwabe of Victoria Park, Manchester had signed the 1866 women's suffrage petition. The Schwabes were Unitarians, members, when they lived in Glasgow, of Rev. H.W. CROSSKEY's congregation, and intimate friends of Cobden, John Bright and Mazzini. In 1854, in a letter to Margaret Bright Lucas, Priscilla Bright McLaren wrote that she "shd like to have my four nieces all together – Helen, Kate and the little Ashworths – I shd be quite set up – and Nurse *would* make a *fuss* over them". She kept up a round of family visits, as did all the other members of the clan (*see* Appendix), often staying with Margaret TANNER in Bristol. In 1864 she stayed with the Cobdens at Midhurst.

Around 1826 Priscilla Bright attended a Quaker school in South Parade, York, conducted by Hannah Wilson. She then, with her sister Esther, went to the school in Southport run by another Quaker, Mrs Johnson, whose daughter Hannah Wallis was to be a lifelong friend, a supporter of the women's suffrage movement and governess to Helen Bright. Priscilla Bright was at school in Southport in 1828 when she was summoned home to her mother's deathbed. It would appear that by about 1830 she was at school in London. Louisa Roberts in *Memories of a Quaker Childhood* records how her friendship with Priscilla Bright dated back to their schooldays in London. Louisa Roberts did attend for a short period S. and M. Palmer's school at Croydon, but it would seem more likely that it was when she was a pupil at Susanna Corder's Quaker School at Stoke Newington, which had the reputation of providing a better education for women than was common at the time, that she met Priscilla Bright. Back home in Rochdale Priscilla Bright, with her sisters, ran a school to teach reading, writing and sewing to her father's factory girls. After the death of John Bright's first wife Elizabeth, sister of Anna Maria and Mary PRIESTMAN and of Margaret Tanner, Priscilla Bright kept house for him and looked after his young daughter Helen, whom in her will she referred to lovingly as "eldest child". While living in Rochdale in the 1840s Priscilla Bright, with her sister Esther, her brother Jacob and Martha Mellor, are described by Isabel Petrie Mills as discussing the necessity of the vote for women. This same Isabel Petrie Mills had entertained the young Elizabeth Wolstenholme (*see* Elizabeth Wolstenholme ELMY) on the day of Queen Victoria's coronation in 1837. In 1842 Priscilla Bright met for the first time her future husband, Duncan McLaren, when he came to Rochdale from Edinburgh to see John Bright after attending a meeting of the British Association for the Advancement of Science in Manchester. In 1843 Priscilla Bright attended the first Anti-Corn Law meeting, held in Toad Lane, Rochdale, and in May 1845 ran the Rochdale stall at the Anti-Corn Law Bazaar held in the Covent Garden Theatre in London. Mrs Renton, one of Duncan McLaren's mothers-in-law (he was by then twice a widower) and Eliza WIGHAM were organizers of the Scottish stalls.

In 1848 Priscilla Bright and Duncan McLaren were married in a registrar's office; she was disowned by the Quakers for "marrying out". Despite this, she put her Quaker ideals into practice in her early married life; she was a determined influence on the move to close on Sundays public houses in Edinburgh, where her husband was Provost, and on the organizing of the 1853 Peace Conference. Duncan McLaren was a Liberal MP from 1865 until 1881. On 17 January 1870 he presided over the first public meeting in favour of women's suffrage to be held in Edinburgh and he introduced and carried the first Married Women's Property (Scotland) Act in 1881. Priscilla Bright McLaren was involved in a wide range of radical feminist movements during her lifetime. She was a member of the committee of the Edinburgh Ladies' Emancipation Society, a member of the executive committee of the Ladies' National Association for the Repeal of the Contagious Diseases Acts when it was formed in 1870, brought into the movement, she recorded, by Ursula BRIGHT. She also subscribed to the Married Women's Property Campaign and in 1869 actively supported the entrance of women to medical education in Edinburgh, where her stepdaughter Agnes was later to receive her training. In the 1890s Priscilla Bright McLaren was a member of the Revising Committee for Elizabeth Cady Stanton's *The Woman's Bible* and in 1893, when it was in financial difficulties, gave a donation to the progressive feminist paper *Shafts*.

With her two stepdaughters, Grant McLaren (daughter of Duncan McLaren by his first wife) and Agnes, Priscilla Bright McLaren signed the 1866 women's suffrage petition. As the wife of a member of parliament, during the parliamentary session she stayed in London and it was from there that, on 16 April 1866, she wrote to her stepson John McLaren, "I think thou would admire MILL's speech on Friday night – I doubt if there was a speech to equal it in the House of Commons. Papa says he was sometimes quite silent for about 3 minutes as tho' arranging a new sentence – yet perfectly calm and apparently unconscious of the pause – but the house cheered and manifested its impatience – I just missed being in the House. Sophy Sturge and Mary Priestman went. Papa has got a place for my sister [Margaret Bright Lucas?] and me tomorrow night." The "Friday night" speech was that of 13 April, when Mill defended the Reform Bill.

When it was founded on 6 November 1867 Priscilla Bright McLaren was president of the EDINBURGH NATIONAL SOCIETY FOR WOMEN'S SUFFRAGE. In June 1868 she wrote, again to John McLaren, that she and her husband

> were at Mr and Mrs P.A. TAYLOR's last evening and met Dr Elizabeth Garrett – who was most charming. What a brightness superior work gives to a woman! Really this woman's question in its various aspects is along with the Irish Church,

the question of the hour. We are writing to Miss Wigham to call a meeting of our women's committee to take a fresh action on our behalf – it is with a view to putting the names of householders on a Register and we have told her to ask thee to attend in order to help them how to proceed and explain the law of the case. I hope thou will help us in this interesting and important matter – the Englishwomen are working very zealously . . . it is likely John Stuart Mill will be strongly opposed by the richer parts of Westminster . . . so the women of England are combining to raise a fund to defray his election expenses – and Scotland will I hope contribute her measure. Mill seems quite proud of such grateful recognition.

John McLaren did indeed conduct the case brought by Scottish women householders to test the right, under the 1867 Reform Act, of women to be added to the electoral roll.

In May 1870 Priscilla Bright McLaren wrote to John McLaren from London that "tomorrow we have a long conference in London and Mrs Tanner, Miss Priestman and Kate Thomasson are coming to lodge here". The conference referred to was probably that held at Aubrey House to discuss the Second Reading of the Women's Disabilities Bill. Priscilla Bright McLaren was intending to take some of the ladies to the House of Commons.

In April 1871 both Priscilla Bright McLaren and her husband attended the Women's Suffrage Conference held in London and she moved the principal motion asking for Gladstone's support of the Women's Disabilities Bill. Her obituarist in *The Times* was later to note that she was "an excellent speaker – singularily free from egotism". In 1872 she was a member of the executive committee of the newly formed CENTRAL COMMITTEE OF THE NATIONAL SOCIETY. It was Priscilla Bright McLaren, perhaps inspired by her memories of the success of the Anti-Corn Law rallies, who suggested the idea of the Grand Demonstrations of Women as a means of showing to parliament, in the years leading up to the 1884 Reform Bill, the popular support for women's enfranchisement. In 1880 she presided over the first of these Demonstrations, held at the Free Trade Hall in Manchester, and in 1882 she took the chair at the Demonstrations in Glasgow and in Bradford. In 1888 she, in spite of favouring the Liberal Unionist cause, remained affiliated, as did the younger generation of McLarens, and the Edinburgh National Society, to the CENTRAL NATIONAL SOCIETY FOR WOMEN'S SUFFRAGE after the split in the Central Committee. In the 1890s Priscilla Bright McLaren was president of the Scottish branch of the SPECIAL APPEAL COMMITTEE, which by 1894 was responsible for collecting a total of 248 000 signatures in favour of women's suffrage with which it was hoped to impress parliament.

Even into her extreme old age Priscilla Bright McLaren continued to develop in step with the radical wing of the suffrage movement. In 1901 she strongly supported Esther ROPER's involvement of the Lancashire factory women in the suffrage cause. She wrote a birthday letter to her grandson, Duncan, son of John McLaren, on 20 March 1901 mentioning that "yesterday a Deputation of 16 factory women from Manchester took a Petition to the House of Commons signed by 30 000 Factory women – all their own getting up" and to Esther Roper on 26 March "I have been delighted with those Manchester women . . . I wish indeed some such action may arouse the London women to work./ Will you kindly tell me what Mr and Mrs Thomasson contribute now to your committee. We must go on with the workers, I wrote to John THOMASSON to say as he withdrew his subscription to the Cause because the women did not show themselves anxious for suffrage, I hoped now he would help to get up the needful money to carry on this work in Cheshire and Yorkshire." She herself in the financial year 1901–2 gave £100 to the Special Organising Fund of the NORTH OF ENGLAND SOCIETY and collected money for it from Agnes POCHIN, Lucy Priestman, Mary Curry, Lilias Ashworth HALLETT, Mrs Muller (mother of Eva McLaren and Henrietta Muller), Anna Maria Priestman and Laura McLaren. In 1902 while writing again to her grandson she mentioned that "there is a very important Deputation of Women graduates, going up to London to present a Petition today, in favour of Women's Suffrage – 1800 names – there are about 2000 graduates – but many of these are spread over the Globe, but have sent letters warmly approving it. About

66000 Textile weavers presented a like Petition last month. These Petitions are very educational – and the women will help to raise the men to see that justice ought to be extended to women and this would be well also for men." On 20 March 1905, again in a birthday letter to young Duncan McLaren, she wrote, "There was a very splendid Women's Suffrage meeting in London last Tuesday – Uncle Walter had much to do in getting it up – but the papers to please the men of the nation gave a very poor account of it and of its great size and enthusiasm." Just before she died Priscilla Bright McLaren dictated on 3 November 1906 a letter from her sickbed addressed to the WOMEN'S SOCIAL AND POLITICAL UNION women, who included Anne Cobden SANDERSON and Minnie BALDOCK, who had been arrested and imprisoned in October. Using the headed paper of the Edinburgh Society for Women's Suffrage she wrote, "We send you our heartfelt sympathy in the trying circumstances in which you are placed. We offer you, too, our warm admiration for the noble courage and self-sacrifice which you have manifested in your earnest efforts to improve the conditions of the women of your country. These efforts we feel assured, will bear fruit at a very early date in the passing of real measures of pure justice for which so many of us have now for nearly half a century, by every constitutional mean, strived in vain". Her funeral, *The Times* noted, was well attended by members of the NATIONAL UNION OF WOMEN'S SUFFRAGE SOCIETIES, of which she had been a member of the executive committee, by representatives from the Edinburgh Society for Women's Suffrage, the Lancashire and Cheshire Women's Suffrage Society, Lancashire and Cheshire Women Textile Workers' Committee, Edinburgh Women's Liberal Association, Edinburgh University Graduates, Women Workers' Union, British Women's Temperance Association, and the Women's Co-operative Guild. The executive committee of the CENTRAL SOCIETY FOR WOMEN'S SUFFRAGE suggested, just after her death, that a memorial service should be held in St Margaret's, Westminster, and this was attended by Mrs FAWCETT, Lady and Miss STRACHEY, Keir HARDIE, Florence BALGARNIE, representatives of the WOMEN'S LIBERAL FEDERATION, Bertha MASON representing the North of England Suffrage Society and the Women's Temperance Society, Edith PALLISER representing the Central Society, Mrs Thomasson, Emily DAVIES, Mrs Cobden SICKERT, Mr and Mrs Fisher UNWIN, Mr Cobden Sanderson (his wife was still in prison), Frances STERLING, Emily FORD and Miss Pennington. An appreciation of Priscilla McLaren appeared in the December 1906 edition of the *Westminster Review*. Elizabeth Wolstenholme ELMY, thinking that it was to be written by Jessie METHVEN, had sent her facts about Priscilla Bright McLaren's early life. In the event the author of the article was J.B. Mackie, biographer of Duncan McLaren, who reveals no interesting new facts, citing instead that "she became the devoted and cherished wife of one of the most heroic and patriotic Scotsman . . .".

Priscilla Bright McLaren's will is a model of clarity and caring – of both the possessions with which she was surrounded in her life and of the members of her family to whom she chose to leave them. Among the objects she catalogues are "the seven carved oak chairs with owls upon them which I bought at the Anti-Corn Law League Bazaar and which I greatly prize"; "Thirteen portraits of Members of the Anti-Corn Law League"; "Mahogany work table – bought with £5 – the sale of a pig my father had given me – very proud of it when young"; "Portraits of Cowper, Hannah More, Dr John Brown"; "Mirror in leather frame given by Annie and Lilly Ashworth"; "Elizabeth Fry reading to prisoners on Staircase"; "Portrait of my dear brother John Bright his gift on my marriage"; "Portrait of my dear brother Jacob Bright – his gift"; "Portrait of my dear nieces Annie and Lilly Ashworth" by Duval, and left to Anne Ashworth's son, Guy Cross; "Ugly portrait of myself by Lewis [Lowes] Dickenson"; "Picture of Bonchurch Isle of Wight purchased at Manchester Anti-Corn Law Bazaar"; "Plain wood cupboard with shelves bought at the Women's Suffrage Stall at the Exhibition"; "Roman cameo (pendant) bought for me by Papa [Duncan McLaren] at Avignon thinking I should prize it as connected with John Stuart Mill and our visit there – always valuable to me", left to Agnes McLaren; "my much valued portrait of John Stuart Mill a remembrance of his generous assistance to the cause of Women's Suffrage and my deep interest in it", which had been given to her by Oliver Scatcherd, husband of Alice SCATCHERD, and which she left to Katherine Thomasson; and "The beautiful worked chair given as a marriage present by my dear friends Margaret, Anna Maria, and Mary Priestman", left to Helen Bright Clark.

Address: (1840) Green Bank, Rochdale; (1848) Newington House, Edinburgh.
Portrait: by Lowes Dickinson, 1874 (one of the papers, by her right hand, on the table at which she is sitting, is headed "Woman Suffrage", in a private collection (photograph in National Portrait Gallery Archive).
Photograph: in Blackburn Collection, Girton College; carte de visite in Josephine Butler Collection, Fawcett Library.
Archival source: Priscilla Bright McLaren Papers, National Library of Scotland.
Bibliography: J.B. Mackie, *The Life and Work of Duncan McLaren*, 1888; I. Petrie Mills, *From Tinder-Box to the "Larger" Light. Threads from the life of John Mills . . . interwoven with some early century recollections by his wife*, 1899; E. Roberts (ed.), *Louisa: Memories of a Quaker Childhood*, 1970.

MCPHUN, FRANCES MARY (1880–1940)   Daughter of John McPhun, timber merchant, the police magistrate of the City of Glasgow, and one of the founders of the People's Palace. She was the sister of Margaret MCPHUN. Frances McPhun was the holder of an MA degree in Political Economy from Glasgow University and a winner of prizes in English Literature, Moral Philosophy and Political Economy. She worked in the Queen Margaret College Settlement in Glasgow before joining the WOMEN'S SOCIAL AND POLITICAL UNION in 1909. She helped organize the "Pageant of Famous Scottish Women" for the Edinburgh procession held in that year, was joint organizer of the WSPU Exhibition held in Glasgow in 1910 and was honorary secretary of the Glasgow WSPU, 1911–12. She was imprisoned in Holloway from 5 March to 29 April 1912, and was forcibly fed, after taking part in the WSPU window-smashing campaign in London. The letters written from prison by Frances McPhun, together with her hunger strike medal, and that of her sister, are still in the possession of their family. Helen CRAWFURD, with whom she and her sister undertook a WSPU tour of Lanarkshire, described Frances McPhun as "a beautiful woman, and [one who] had a real sense of humour".

Address: (1909) 19 Doune Terrace, Hillhead, Glasgow.
Photograph: in E. King, *The Thenew Factor: The Hidden History of Glasgow's Women*, 1993.
Archival source: People's Palace Collection, Glasgow; Suffragette Fellowship Collection, Museum of London.
Bibliography: L. Leneman, *A Guid Cause: The Women's Suffrage Movement in Scotland*, 1991; E. King, *The Thenew Factor: The Hidden History of Glasgow's Women*, 1993.

MCPHUN, MARGARET POLLOCK (1876–1960)   Sister of Frances MCPHUN, educated for a time at the Girls' High School in Hanover, Germany, and then graduated with an MA degree in Psychology from Glasgow University, winning university prizes in Psychology, Logic and Metaphysics. Like her sister, Margaret McPhun worked at the Queen Margaret College Settlement and also in connection with an East End Medical Mission. From 1906 to 1908 she was honorary treasurer of the North Kelvinside and Maryhill Liberal Association. She was Glasgow convenor of the Scottish University Women's Suffrage Union before joining the WOMEN'S SOCIAL AND POLITICAL UNION in 1909. She was press secretary for the Scottish WSPU from 1912 to 1914 and, with her sister, was imprisoned in Holloway in March 1912 after taking part in the WSPU window-smashing campaign. During this incarceration she wrote a poem, dedicated to Janie ALLAN, that was included in *Holloway Jingles*, published by the Glasgow branch of the WSPU in 1913. She was a contributor to *Votes for Women*, the *Suffragette* and, her politics having apparently moved to the left, to the Scottish Socialist journal *Forward*, 1911–13. She later wrote for Lady RHONDDA's *Time and Tide*. After the First World War Margaret McPhun was secretary of the Scottish Council of Women's Citizens' Association and a member of the Glasgow Women Citizens' Association. She was an active member of the League for Prohibition of Cruel Sports, a member of the Open Door Council and, with Marion GILCHRIST and Eunice MURRAY, a member of the general council of the Scottish Council for Women's Trades and Careers. In the 1930s, with her sister, she gave a large house in Callender to the Glasgow Guild of Aid, to be used as a holiday home for the disadvantaged.

Address: (1909) 19 Doune Terrace, Hillhead, Glasgow; (1934) Fairholme, 23 Monteith Road, Glasgow S3.
Photograph: in E. King, *The Thenew Factor: The Hidden History of Glasgow's Women*, 1993.
Archival source: People's Palace Collection, Glasgow; Suffragette Fellowship Collection, Museum of London.

Bibliography: L. Leneman, *A Guid Cause: The Women's Suffrage Movement in Scotland*, 1991; E. King, *The Thenew Factor: The Hidden History of Glasgow's Women*, 1993.

MELROSE (NUWSS) In 1913 the society was a member of the SCOTTISH FEDERATION OF THE NATIONAL UNION OF WOMEN'S SUFFRAGE SOCIETIES. Secretary (1913) Miss Riddell, The Cloisters, Melrose, Roxburghshire.

MELTON MOWBRAY (NUWSS) In 1913 the society was a member of the MIDLANDS (EAST) FEDERATION OF THE NATIONAL UNION OF WOMEN'S SUFFRAGE SOCIETIES. Secretary (1913) *pro tem* Miss A.M. Dowson (*see* Helena DOWSON), Sulney Fields, Upper Broughton, Melton Mowbray, Leicestershire.

MEN'S COMMITTEE FOR JUSTICE TO WOMEN Founded in January 1909 after WOMEN'S FREEDOM LEAGUE delegates to the House of Commons had been arrested and imprisoned. The committee charged itself to watch cases in which women were prosecuted in connection with their suffrage work. Its members on occasion placed special information at the disposal of the Home Office. The Men's Committee gave every support to the Conciliation Committee after its formation in 1910. Capt. Gonne was one of its leading members.
Chairman (1909) Mr Albert Dawson, editor of the *Christian Commonwealth*. Dawson later became a member of the UNITED SUFFRAGISTS.
Address: (1911) Strathleven, Oakleigh Park, London N.

MEN'S DECLARATION COMMITTEE Appears to have been formed in 1909 for the purpose of collecting the signatures of men prominent in their profession or community to a declaration in favour of women's suffrage. The GLASGOW AND WEST OF SCOTLAND ASSOCIATION FOR WOMEN'S SUFFRAGE agreed to send to the committee lists of local men who might be approached. Secretary Miss Newcombe.

MEN'S FEDERATION FOR WOMEN'S SUFFRAGE Founded *c.* 1912. The Federation members spoke at open-air meetings and sold suffragist papers and the *Daily Herald*. They also attended suffrage meetings in Hyde Park to "see that women get fair play". In July 1913 the Federation was working closely with the EAST LONDON FEDERATION OF SUFFRAGETTES, for instance obtaining police permission for a demonstration in Trafalgar Square that would have been denied to the ELFS.
Honorary secretary: Victor Prout, who had, in December 1909, written to Christabel PANKHURST, putting his vote at the disposal of the WOMEN'S SOCIAL AND POLITICAL UNION.
Address: (1913) 34 & 35 Ludgate Chambers, Ludgate Hill, London EC4; (1914) temporary address, 19 Buckingham Street, Strand, London WC.

MEN'S INTERNATIONAL ALLIANCE FOR WOMAN SUFFRAGE Founded *c.* 1912, comprising, from Britain, the MEN'S LEAGUE FOR WOMEN'S SUFFRAGE, the MEN'S POLITICAL UNION FOR WOMEN'S ENFRANCHISEMENT, and the MEN'S FEDERATION FOR WOMEN'S SUFFRAGE, together with societies from Holland, France, Hungary, the United States, Sweden, Germany and Denmark. In 1912 the Alliance held its first congress in London, the British delegates including Victor DUVAL, Laurence HOUSMAN and its president Sir John Cockburn.
Honorary secretary (1913) Lt Col W. Mansfeldt, Dillensburgstaat 19, Utrecht, Holland; honorary treasurer (1913) F.W. Kehrer, Gorinchem, Holland.

MEN'S LEAGUE FOR WOMEN'S SUFFRAGE Founded in 1907 "with the object of bringing to bear upon the movement the electoral power of men . . . To obtain for women the vote on the same terms as those on which it is now, or may in the future, be granted to men" (*Suffrage Annual and Women's Who's Who*, 1913). The League had no political party affiliation, was non-militant in its methods, but supported both the WOMEN'S SOCIAL AND POLITICAL UNION and the WOMEN'S FREEDOM LEAGUE. The founder of the Men's League was Herbert Jacobs, who later stood as a woman's suffrage candidate in East St Pancras; Charles Mansell-Moullin, husband of Edith MANSELL-MOULLIN, was one of the League's most active speakers. The League concentrated on "propagandist work", bringing pressure to bear upon MPs and parliamentary candidates through their constituents, by letter and deputation. It was itself prepared to field parliamentary candidates. On 18 June 1910 members of the CAMBRIDGE UNIVERSITY MEN'S LEAGUE walked in the WSPU procession, "some in slouched hats and smoking pipes, some in cap and gown, some with their hands in their pockets and wearing a diffident air" (*Vote*, 25 June 1910). Between 1907 and 1911 the League's affairs were reported each week in the *Women's Franchise*. It later founded its own paper, *The Men's League Monthly Paper*, the subscribers to which in August–September 1913 included the artist Lucien Pissarro, Rev. HANKINSON, G. Penn Gaskell (*see* Eleanor Penn GASKELL), Silvester Sparrow and Joseph Fels; Mrs CORBETT (more probably Catherine, rather than Marie) and Janie ALLAN gave donations. In 1912 the League issued the *Handbook on Women's Suffrage*, which gave a comprehensive exposition of the state of the suffrage question. By 1910 the League had ten branches; it eventually had an overseas branch in the United States. In 1911 the University of Cambridge branch asked the CAMBRIDGE ASSOCIATION FOR WOMEN'S SUFFRAGE for advice about how to set about organizing a large meeting; they were advised, for the novelty value, to confine it to "men only". The BANNER of the Manchester branch is now in the collection of Manchester Central Library Archive. Other branches were founded in Birmingham, Sussex and Edinburgh. It was suggested in 1913 by the SOUTHAMPTON BRANCH OF THE NATIONAL UNION OF WOMEN'S SUFFRAGE SOCIETIES, usually very unadventurous, that a branch of the Men's League should be formed in their city. In 1912 the League affiliated to the FEDERATED COUNCIL OF SUFFRAGE SOCIETIES.

A Declaration of Representative Men in Favour of Women's Suffrage, issued by the League in 1909, contains a list of prominent men in favour of women's suffrage; included are 83 officeholders, past and present, in the Liberal and Conservative parties, 49 church leaders, 24 high-ranking army and navy officers, 86 academics and such writers as E.M. Forster, Thomas Hardy, H.G. Wells, John Masefield and Arthur Pinero. In 1913 its vice-presidents included the Bishop of Lincoln, Sir John Cockburn, William de Morgan, Prof. T.F. Tout, Sir J. Forbes Robertson, D.A. Thomas (*see* Lady RHONDDA), Philip Snowden and Israel ZANGWILL. By 1916 the Rt Hon. W.H. Dickenson, MP had been added to the list. In 1913 the League's executive committee included H.N. BRAILSFORD, Dr F.A. Bather (of the WIMBLEDON WSPU), R.F. Cholmeley (headmaster of the Alice Owen's School, Islington), Laurence HOUSMAN and Silvester Sparrow. On 13 March 1918 the League took part in the NATIONAL UNION OF WOMEN'S SUFFRAGE SOCIETIES victory celebrations at the Queen's Hall.

President (1913) the Earl of Lytton; honorary treasurer (1907) Stanton COIT, (1913) Reginald Potts; honorary political secretary (1913) J. Malcolm Mitchell; honorary secretary (1913) C.V. Drysdale (whose pamphlet *Why Men Should Work for Women's Suffrage* was published by the League, c. 1912).

Address: (1908) 38 Museum Street, London WC; (1910) 40 Museum Street, London WC; (1913, 1916) 136 St Stephen's House, Westminster, London SW.

Bibliography: S. Strauss, *"Traitors to the Masculine Cause": The Men's Campaigns for Women's Rights*, 1982.

MEN'S POLITICAL UNION FOR WOMEN'S ENFRANCHISEMENT Founded in 1910, as a militant society, the male counterpart of the WOMEN'S SOCIAL AND POLITICAL UNION, by Victor DUVAL. The society "was formed as a result of a growing conviction among men, as well as women, that the delay in removal of the sex disqualification from the Parliamentary franchise was due to the determined indifference of the Government rather than to any considerable opposition in the country". The inaugural meeting of the MPU was held in the Eustace Miles Restaurant. In 1911 the society organized the legal action brought by Alfred Hawkins (*see* Alice HAWKINS) against the Bradford League of Young Liberals. By 1913 branches had been opened in Hull, Birmingham, Oxford, Norwich, Bristol, Leeds (of which, after 1912, Frank RUTTER was secretary), Newcastle, Manchester, Edinburgh, Bradford, Glasgow, Leicester, Dundee, Reading, Harrow, Holloway, West Ham and Scarborough. There was also an Oxford University branch, for which H.W. NEVINSON wrote a pamphlet, *New Tracts for the Times No II, The Claim on Oxford*; Gerald Gould and G.D.H. Cole wrote others. In August 1913 the MPU was planning to open an Eastbourne branch; by April 1914 Hackney, Kingsland and Stoke Newington branches had been founded. By July 1914, as the militant campaign became ever more dangerous, the MPU organized a Suffrage Speakers Defence Corps. The MPU appears to have remained active during the First World War; a North London branch was opened by 1915. There is a suggestion that as the EAST LONDON FEDERATION OF SUFFRAGETTES became less exclusively a woman's organization, the MPU merged with it to become the Workers' Suffrage Federation The Union's colours echoed those of the WSPU – purple, white and green.

Honorary organizing secretary (1910, 1913) Victor Duval; honorary assistant organizer (1913) Hugh FRANKLIN; honorary parliamentary secretary (1910, 1913) D. Cameron-Swan; honorary treasurer (1910, 1913) H.D. HARBEN; chairman of the committee (1913) H.W. Nevinson.

Address: (1913) 13 Buckingham Street, Strand, London (which was also the address of Duval & Co.).
Archival source: Men's Political Union for Women's Enfranchisement 1911, 1912, Fawcett Library.

MEN'S SOCIETY FOR WOMEN'S RIGHTS A militant society, founded by A.W.G. Jamrach, who was editor of the *Awakener* from 1912 until June 1914, when he resigned because his readership thought him too closely allied to the WOMEN'S SOCIAL AND POLITICAL UNION. He was editor of the *Altruist* from November 1913 until April 1915, which was described as the monthly paper of the Men's Society of Human Rights.

The society's executive committee comprised: Capt. C Gonne, W. Boulting, and Wyndham Hart; honorary secretary (1913) Lieut J.L. Cather; honorary treasurer, A.W.G. Jamrach; honorary propaganda secretary, Frank Witty. William Boulting wrote for the society a pamphlet, *An Old Doctor's View of the Women's Movement, c. 1912*.

Address: (1913, 1916) 65 Avenue Chambers, Southampton Row, London WC.

MERIONETHSHIRE (NUWSS) In 1913 the society was a member of the WEST LANCS, WEST CHESHIRE, AND NORTH WALES FEDERATION OF THE NATIONAL UNION OF WOMEN'S SUFFRAGE SOCIETIES. Secretary (1913) Mrs Francis Lewis, Balkan Hill, Aberdovey, Wales.

MERRYWEATHER, MARY (c. 1813–1880) Quaker. Around 1850, at the behest of Ellen Courtauld, she started a day nursery and a night school for women working at COURTAULD's silk factory at Halsted in Essex. A close friend of Bessie Rayner PARKES, in 1859 Mary Merryweather held a few shares in the *English Woman's Journal*. She trained at the St Thomas's Hospital Nursing School and then, in 1862, founded a Training School for Nurses in Liverpool and organized there schemes for district nursing. She signed the women's suffrage petition in 1866, was a member of the Society for Promoting the Employment of Women in 1867 and a member of the governing council of the London School of Medicine for Women.

Address: (1866) Dover Street, Liverpool.

MERTHYR AND DISTRICT (NUWSS) In 1913 the society was a member of the SOUTH WALES AND MONMOUTH FEDERATION OF THE NATIONAL UNION OF WOMEN'S SUFFRAGE SOCIETIES. Secretary (1913) Mrs M.J. Williams, 1 Lewis Terrace, Heolgerrig, Merthyr Tydfil, Wales.

METHVEN, JESSIE CUNNINGHAM (1856–1917) In the 1890s was secretary of the EDINBURGH NATIONAL WOMEN'S SUFFRAGE SOCIETY, in 1895 was a member of the CENTRAL NATIONAL SOCIETY FOR WOMEN'S SUFFRAGE, in 1896 was a member of the SPECIAL APPEAL COMMITTEE, in 1897 was one of the two representatives from the Edinburgh Society on the NATIONAL UNION OF WOMEN'S SUFFRAGE SOCIETIES Parliamentary Committee and in 1899 succeeded Eliza WIGHAM as representative from Edinburgh on the executive committee of the NUWSS. She was also a member of the Scottish Women's Liberal Association. In 1901–2 Jessie Methven gave a donation to the Special Organizing Fund of the NORTH OF ENGLAND SOCIETY FOR WOMEN'S SUFFRAGE, through which factory women petitioned for enfranchisement, and of which Priscilla Bright MCLAREN, the president of the Edinburgh National Society, was a keen supporter.

Jessie Methven signed, as an "Independent Socialist", the joint WOMEN'S SOCIAL AND POLITICAL UNION/Independent Labour Party manifesto that was issued at the January 1906 general election. On 1 May 1906 she contributed a letter, supporting militancy, to a correspondence in the *Glasgow Herald* concerning the disturbance created by the WSPU in the Ladies' Gallery of the House of Commons at the end of April. She joined the WSPU at the end of 1906, immediately after the death of Priscilla Bright McLaren, continuing to support it, and the MEN'S POLITICAL UNION, to whom she gave handsome donations in 1910 and 1911, until the outbreak of war. In 1911 she gave a hand printing press to the Edinburgh WSPU and on 24 November 1911 she was sentenced to ten days' imprisonment after breaking a window in the Home Office during the demonstrations following the "torpedoing" of the Conciliation Bill.

Address: (1917) 25 Great King Street, Edinburgh.
Bibliography: J.C. Methven, "Women's Suffrage in the Past: A Record of Betrayal", the *Suffragette*, 17 January 1913; L. Leneman, *A Guid Cause: The Women's Suffrage Movement in Scotland*, 1991.

MIDDLESBOROUGH (NUWSS) In 1913 the society was a member of the NORTH AND EAST RIDINGS FEDERATION OF THE NATIONAL UNION OF WOMEN'S SUFFRAGE SOCIETIES. Secretary (1913) Mrs Steel, 1 Southfield Villas, Middlesborough, Yorkshire.

MIDDLESBOROUGH (WFL) Secretary (1913) Miss A. Mahony, 35 Albert Terrace, Middlesborough, Yorkshire. In 1910 the North-East Yorkshire organizer, based in Middlesborough, was Alice Schofield (*see* Alice Schofield COATES), Northgate, Roman Road, Linthorpe, Middlesborough.

MIDDLESBOROUGH (WSPU) Secretary (1906) Miss D. Coates, Northgate Roman Road, Linthorpe, Middlesborough, Yorkshire.

MIDDLESBOROUGH, SOUTH BANK (WSPU) Secretary (1906) Mrs Smith, 33 Pearl Street, Middlesborough, Yorkshire.

MIDDLETON (NUWSS) By 1912 the society was a member of the MANCHESTER AND DISTRICT FEDERATION OF THE NATIONAL UNION OF WOMEN'S SUFFRAGE SOCIETIES. Secretary (1913) A.H. Valentine, Esq., Limefield, Middleton, Lancashire.

MIDLANDS FEDERATION OF THE NATIONAL UNION OF WOMEN'S SUFFRAGE SOCIETIES Formed in 1910 and by 1913 had divided into the MIDLANDS (EAST) FEDERATION OF THE NATIONAL UNION OF WOMEN'S SUFFRAGE SOCIETIES and the MIDLANDS (WEST) FEDERATION OF THE NATIONAL UNION OF WOMEN'S SUFFRAGE SOCIETIES.

MIDLANDS (EAST) FEDERATION OF THE NATIONAL UNION OF WOMEN'S SUFFRAGE SOCIETIES Secretary (1913) Miss Maud Dowson, Sulney Fields, Upper Broughton, Melton Mowbray, Leicestershire (*see* Helena DOWSON).

MIDLANDS (WEST) FEDERATION OF THE NATIONAL UNION OF WOMEN'S SUFFRAGE SOCIETIES Honorary secretary (1913) Miss Noel Herbert Wright, Sutton Lodge, Solihull; secretary (1913) Miss Harding, Southside, Warwick Road, Solihull, Warwickshire. The Federation's BANNER, made in 1912, is now held in Birmingham City Museum and Art Gallery.

MID-LONDON (WFL) Secretary (1913) Mrs Tritton, 1 Northcote Avenue, Ealing, London W.

MIDLOTHIAN (a branch of the EDINBURGH NATIONAL SOCIETY FOR WOMEN'S SUFFRAGE, NUWSS) Secretary (1909) Mrs Ross Cooper, Kingarth, Colinton, Midlothian. The society appears to have been no longer in existence by 1913.

MILL, JOHN STUART (1806–1873) Political economist and philosopher, the eldest child of Harriet and James Mill, writer and journalist. John Stuart Mill had, as he wrote in *The Subjection of Women*, 1869, "from the very earliest period" believed that the legal subordination of one sex by another is wrong. *The Subjection of Women* stemmed from the same root as Mary Wollstonecraft's *Vindication of the Rights of Woman*, the enlightened feminism of Unitarian dissenters and philosophic radicals. Mill was influenced by the Saint Simonians and early French and English socialists such as William Thompson and Robert Owen. As a boy Mill had met William Thompson, whose *Appeal of One half of the Human Race, Woman, against the Pretensions of the other half, Men, to retain them in Political and Thence in Civil and Domestic Slavery*, 1825, had been written, with Anna Wheeler, to refute the opinion of James Mill that women did not need the vote. It was sexual equality that Mill singled out as being one of the most important aspects of socialism. He revealed his commitment to women's equality as early as 1824 in his first article for the *Westminster Review*.

After Mill met Harriet TAYLOR in 1830 he was drawn into the circle of Unitarian radicals, contributing articles to Fox's *Monthly Repository* and, stimulated by the predicament in which their devoted friendship placed them, in 1832 committing to paper, for her eyes only, his thoughts on marriage. Mill was able to put theory into practice when in March 1851, a month before he and Harriet Taylor finally married, he formally renounced all the legal rights that accrued to a man on marriage. In the same month he offered to the *Westminster Review* an article written by Harriet Taylor at his suggestion, inspired by the Convention of Rights for Women in Massachusetts. This article was published as "The Enfranchisement of Women", in July 1851. The death of Harriet in 1858 left Mill bereft, comforted only by the constant companionship of her daughter, Helen TAYLOR. Mill took more than a theoretical interest in the position of women. Practically, in 1864 he subscribed to the Society for the Promotion of Employment of Women and in 1866 he was a member of the first general committee of Elizabeth Garrett's St Mary's Dispensary for Women and Children. In a letter to Helen Taylor, 21 February 1860, he wrote that in a discussion on "the woman question" with Henry FAWCETT and Thomas HARE they had agreed that:

> all employments & positions should be open to women & that then each would fall naturally into what it turned out they were fittest for individually. It appears that Fawcett presses the matter on his friends . . . Hare said if he were in Parliament he would bring it forward (the question of the suffrage for women, as I understood) . . . Various things he [Fawcett] says incline me to attach more importance than I did to what Miss Parkes & her set are doing . . . He says the E[nglish] W[oman's] J[ournal] increases in sale and has got into places where it was scouted at first.

By the end of the year Mill mentioned in a letter to Henry Fawcett that he was making good progress with the book that was eventually published, in 1869, as *The Subjection of Women*. Later editions of Mill's *Autobiography* reveal that *Subjection* was a joint work with Helen Taylor, and he further diminishes his part in it by stating that all that was most striking and profound in it resulted from conversations with his wife. Millicent Garrett FAWCETT, in her introduction to the 1912 edition of the World's Classics edition of Mill's work that included *Subjection of Women*, stresses that he always attached considerable importance to the timing of the publication of his books. Although first written in 1860–61 it had stayed as a draft, only going to press, published by Longmans, in early 1869. By this time Mill had received widespread publicity as the parliamentary champion of women's enfranchisement. In March 1865 Mill was asked to stand as one of two Liberal candidates for the Westminster constituency. He agreed to his name being put forward, although stating that his personal inclination was against going into parliament. He was firmly against the expenditure of money on political campaigning and against personal canvassing. He therefore spent from early April until the end of June in France, demonstrating himself a disinterested candidate by refusing to return, until finally persuaded by his election committee to do so. He then addressed a few meetings in person in the week before the election. Labelled an "advanced liberal", he introduced in his election address the subject of women's suffrage. Mill wrote from Avignon on 17 April to James Beal, the radical politician who had proposed him as a candidate, a letter published in *The Times* on 21 April 1865, stressing that he would be in favour of opening the suffrage to "all grown persons, both men and women, who can read, write, and perform a sum in the rule of three, and who have not, within some small number of years, received parish relief" as well as "utterly abominating all class ascendancy". Thus Mill advocated an extension of the franchise by both class and gender. Among the members of his election committee were Edward Sterling (*see* Bertha STERLING) and Frank Malleson (*see* Elizabeth MALLESON). When this committee offered to reprint any of Mill's articles he thought might be beneficial to his candidacy the only one he suggested was "the article on 'Enfranchisement of Women', but it must be as my wife's, not as mine". Although this particular gesture towards publicity came to nothing, as Mill wrote to Thomas Hare on 29 May, "this election affair is a better *propaganda* for all my political opinions than I might have obtained for many years; and it is selling my cheap editions, and indeed the dear ones too, in a most splendid manner".

Barbara BODICHON, Isa CRAIG, Emily DAVIES and Bessie Rayner PARKES were enthusiastic supporters of his campaign. At an election committee meeting in St James's Hall on 1 June addressed by, among others, Professor David MASSON, *The Times* reported Sargeant Parry as saying, "With respect to giving the suffrage to the ladies (a laugh), if any man but Mr Mill had put forward that opinion he would have been ridiculed and hooted by the press; but the press had not dared to do so with him." Mill himself was not at that meeting but was present to impress Elizabeth Wolstenholme (see Elizabeth Wolstenholme ELMY) at the meeting she attended on 5 July in the same hall. *The Times* reported that Henry Fawcett was among the speakers at this meeting as was an, alas unnamed, lady. Agnes GARRETT reported to her mother on 11 July, nomination day, that she and her sister Millicent had attended one of Mill's meetings, perhaps the one held the day before, 10 July, at St Martin's Hall in Long Acre and eloquently described by Moses Coit Tyler in *Glimpses of England*, 1898. In a letter to *The Times* on 21 May 1905, the day after the centenary celebrations for Mill's birth, Thomas Hardy described having seen him on the hustings in Covent Garden during the 1865 election, where he looked "a man out of place" and "personified earnestness". After the election result was known, *The Times* stated that

> The very circumstance that this eminent writer declared his most controverted opinions in his address, and in his subsequent speeches, makes his return the more significant. Hundreds who voted for Mr Mill probably disagreed with him philosophically, and a still greater number politically. But it is creditable to the electors, and a hopeful sign for the metropolitan boroughs, that the Westminster people will rather have a man who thinks for himself, even though his conclusions may be different from their own...

A year later, with parliament discussing the Reform Bill, Mill intimated that he would be happy to present a petition in favour of women's suffrage (*see* WOMEN'S SUFFRAGE PETITION COMMITTEE). After the organizational success of this petition, which he duly presented on 7 June, Mill was prepared to present further petitions from women householders (*see* LONDON PROVISIONAL PETITION COMMITTEE). After the emergence of a more stable group, the ENFRANCHISEMENT OF WOMEN COMMITTEE, in November 1866, differences began to emerge between the strong personalities involved. Mill took a gradualist, *realpolitik* approach; the London society's full title as printed on its notepaper, "Enfranchisement of Unmarried Women and Widows, Possessing the Due Property Qualification", reflected the group of women whom he thought it might be feasible to enfranchise. On 19 March 1867 he gave notice that he would move that in clauses 4, 5 and 6 of the Reform Bill the word "man" be omitted and the word "Person" be substituted. This statement was greeted in the House of Commons by laughter and cheers. When, on 20 May 1867, he moved his amendment, among those in the Ladies' Gallery to listen to the debate were Millicent Fawcett and Lady AMBERLEY. Mill's main line of attack was the one to which the suffrage movement was to return time and time again in the course of the next 51 years, "that taxation and representation go hand in hand". The amendment was lost by 73 votes to 196, but Mill and his supporters were gratified by the size of the minority vote and the Enfranchisement of Women Committee immediately gave an order to the publisher, Trubner, to reprint Mill's 20 May speech. *The Times* gave the flavour of the occasion when it reported the short debate as "more jocular than serious in tone". Mr Karslake, MP for Colchester, opposed the amendment on the grounds that no woman in Essex had asked him to support it and it would lead to the enfranchisement of married women, a state of affairs that he patently felt to be so ludicrous as to need no further explanation. His was the constituency selected the following month by Helen Taylor and Clementia TAYLOR to be visited by Lydia BECKER with the purpose of organizing there support for the women's suffrage cause.

Mill was active in his support for the setting up of the LONDON NATIONAL SOCIETY FOR WOMEN'S SUFFRAGE, in August 1867 writing letters to men and women, the "good" rather than the conventionally "great", in an attempt to enlist support for the society's general committee. He makes a point in these letters that the executive committee was to consist of "ladies" only, a point on which he firmly backed Helen Taylor. Of the London National Society's first public meeting, at which women had been among the speakers, he commented in a letter of 19 July 1869 that "the meeting was a far greater success than the newspaper would lead you to imagine. The uniform level of the speaking was quite unprecedently good, and I believe it has struck a really important blow." He encouraged the leading ladies of the society, particularly Millicent Fawcett and Mentia Taylor, to address public meetings. In a letter to Mentia Taylor, 7 October 1869, he wrote, "The cause has now reached a point at which it has become extremely desirable that the ladies who lead the movement should make themselves visible to the public, their very appearance being a refutation of the vulgar nonsense talked about 'women's rights women'." However, the next year it was with reluctance that he consented to speak at the meeting organized by the London National at the Hanover Square Rooms on 20 March 1870 in support of the Women's Disabilities Removal Bill introduced in parliament by Jacob BRIGHT and Sir Charles Dilke (*see* Emilia DILKE). In a letter to Mentia Taylor written on 21 February, Mill explained that:

> as the promises are as yet so few . . . I think the second meeting in some respects more critical than the first because many who have heard of the success of the first will come, and it will be mischievous if they go away disappointed. I cannot pledge myself to speak and I do not see a prospect of a successful meeting, whether I speak or not, unless Mr Maurice and Mr Cairnes consent. I do not see, without them, enough speakers of the first class . . . Still we think that few lady speakers are better than having any who are not all that could be desired . . .

In January 1871 Mill travelled to Edinburgh to address a meeting of the EDINBURGH NATIONAL SOCIETY at which he was received, according to the report in *The Times*, with "great enthusiasm, the audience rising and waving their hats and handkerchiefs". By May 1871 Mill was at the heart of what proved to be an unsuccessful move by the London National Society to stave off the setting up of the CENTRAL COMMITTEE OF THE NATIONAL SOCIETY FOR WOMEN'S SUFFRAGE. He and Helen Taylor had resigned as members of the MANCHESTER NATIONAL SOCIETY in December 1868, in protest against Lydia Becker's style and methods. Mill strongly disapproved of the involvement of the Manchester "Bright and Becker set" in the Campaign for the Repeal of the Contagious Diseases Acts. Although personally in favour of the repeal of the acts, and in 1870 subscribing in his private capacity to the campaign and testifying against the acts to the Royal Commission, he felt it was disastrous for the women's suffrage cause to be associated in the public mind in any way with woman in her less moral aspects.

Apart from his work for the London National Society, Mill in his correspondence with men from the working class stressed the importance of women's suffrage. In a letter of 28 July 1868 to William Wood, a Hanley potter, thanking him for signatures obtained for one of the women's suffrage petitions, Mill commented that, although the women's suffrage cause was prospering, it "will prosper more and more if taken up by the enlightened among the working men". Although himself in favour of extending the franchise to the working classes, Mill in a letter to Sir Charles Dilke, 28 May 1870, advised against mixing women's with universal suffrage, writing, "Women's suffrage has quite enemies enough, without adding to the number all the enemies of universal suffrage. To combine the two questions would practically suspend the fight for women's equality, since universal suffrage is sure to be discussed almost solely as a working men's question: and when at last victory, comes, there is sure to be a compromise, by which the working men would be enfranchised without the women". This was the rationale that dominated the thinking of the women's suffrage movement for the next 45 years.

Although feeling that it would cripple the cause to attempt at this stage to enfranchise married women, Mill was one of the sponsors of the Married Women's Property Bill in 1868, but was out of parliament by the time it was enacted in 1870. As part of his gradualist, pragmatic approach, the rationale was that once a married woman was able to hold property in her own right, she would then satisfy the property qualification attached to the vote and it would be more difficult to exclude her from any opening of the franchise to women.

While still in parliament, Mill played his part by continuing to present the petitions in favour of women's suffrage organized by the London National Society. However, he lost his seat in the Westminster election held on 17 November 1868. The same candidates stood as had in 1865 but Mill was beaten into third place by the Conservative, who had a majority of 300 votes. On 1 December 1868 Mill wrote from Avignon to S.A. STEINTHAL, commenting that the result of the new elections

> appears to be on the whole unfavourable to the cause of women's suffrage. The new members in favour of it are but few, and there have been losses among both its Tory and Liberal supporters. It appears therefore improbable than any efficient stand can be made on this subject in the House of Commons this session; and I have long been of opinion, and expressed myself strongly to that effect last year, that it would be injurious to the cause if a division should take place leaving us with smaller numbers than in the former division. It would be doubly injurious, first by seeming to show a reaction in public opinion against us, and secondly, by depriving us, as it very probably would, of the prestige of Mr John Bright's name, which at present we are able to boast.

John Bright had, to the general surprise, voted in favour of Mill's 20 May 1867 amendment. Commenting adversely on a circular he had received, which reading between the lines had probably emanated from Lydia Becker, Mill advised Steinthal, and presumably through him the Manchester National Society, to continue petitioning parliament and to abjure any "desire to produce *éclat* and great results with small means". Mill recommended that Steinthal should "encourage them [women] to begin that great lesson of steady, silent, persevering effort by which every class and nation has to be fitted for freedom". In 1870, after the failure of the Disabilities Removal Bill, which had been sponsored by Jacob Bright, Mill felt that it would be prejudicial to press the cause in a parliament that had judged against it and that, moreover, by so doing they might achieve an even worse result. The advice that he pressed on the members of the London National Society was that they should wait for the next parliament before recommencing the campaign. Having left parliament, Mill revised the 1860–61 draft of his work on the woman question which was published on 24 May 1869 as *The Subjection of Women*. In a letter of 9 April he explained that "it is not specially on the Suffrage question, but on all the questions relating to women's domestic subordination and social disabilities, all of which it discusses more fully than has been done hitherto. I think it will be useful, and all the more, as it is sure to be very bitterly attacked." Jessie Boucherett wrote to Helen Taylor on 14 June, "I cannot tell you how much pleasure it has given us to read 'The Subjection of Women'. I hope it will be reviewed in many periodicals, but I am afraid our enemies will think it the best policy to pass it over in silence, as the Times & Pall Mall have done to the victory on our Memorial (MWP). You have probably seen the review in the Spectator. It is the only notice I have seen yet".

Mill continued to be remembered as a champion of the women's movement. The WOMEN'S FREEDOM LEAGUE published a postcard displaying his likeness and on 21 May 1910, during the anniversary of Mill's birth and the day after the funeral of King Edward VII, the WFL, Edith CRAIG and the SUFFRAGE ATELIER organized a procession to Mill's statue in the Victoria Embankment Gardens where wreaths were laid. The accompanying speeches emphasized that the women's cause had a long and venerable tradition. At a WFL meeting in Mill's memory held that evening in Caxton Hall a letter from Elizabeth Wolstenholme Elmy, recalling the early days of the suffrage movement, was read out and, among other speakers, Walter Crane recalled that he had been present at Mill's election meeting in St James's Hall, perhaps the very one attended by the young Elizabeth Wolstenholme.

Address: (1860s) Blackheath Park, Blackheath, London SW; (1873) 10 Albert Mansions, London SW.
Portrait: Mill's portrait by G.F. Watts was commissioned by Sir Charles Dilke. Mill gave his first sitting on 17 March 1873 and the finished painting was delivered on the day of his death. A copy by Watts of the portrait is now in the National Portrait Gallery. The statue of Mill by Thomas Woolner, 1878, is in Victoria Embankment Gardens.
Archival source: Mill–Taylor Correspondence, London School of Economics.
Bibliography: M. Coit Tyler, *Glimpses of England*, 1898; H.S.R. Elliot (ed.), *The Letters of John Stuart Mill, with Notes on Mill's Private Life by Mary Taylor*, 1910; F.E. Mineka and D.N. Lindley, *The Later Letters of John Stuart Mill, 1849–1873*, 1972; G. Tulloch, *Mill and Sexual Equality*, 1989.

MILLER, FLORENCE FENWICK, MRS (1854–1935) Educated privately, in 1871 passed with distinction a portion of the preliminary examination of the

University of Edinburgh, but as the University decided against allowing women to take medical degrees, returned to London and entered the Ladies' Medical College. Beginning in 1873 she published a series of "Simple Lessons" for children on physiology and natural history. In 1877 she published, under the auspices of the Sunday Lecture Society, *The Lessons of a Life, Harriet Martineau. A Lecture*, and in 1883 a study of Harriet Martineau for the "Eminent Women" series. She married, in 1877, Frederick Arthur Ford, but retained her own name, merely adding the prefix "Mrs". The marriage was not, however, unremarked; Florence Fenwick Miller invited Helen TAYLOR to join a few friends to celebrate with her and Mr Ford on the first anniversary of their wedding. There were two daughters, Irene MILLER and Helen, who later married the publisher Leonard Parsons. Florence Fenwick Miller noted in an interview she gave to the *Women's Penny Paper*, 23 February 1889, that she had "a singularly good collection of works by women, including the now rare 'Vindication of the Rights of Woman'".

Florence Fenwick Miller first spoke at a women's suffrage meeting in 1873 and in the course of the next year did so again on at least two occasions, once at Ipswich and once at Haverfordwest. In 1876 she was elected as a Liberal to the Hackney division of the London School Board, attracting some opposition the next year when, on marrying, she did not take her husband's name and, a member of the Malthusian League, supported Annie Besant in the course of her trial for disseminating birth-control literature. She was, however, elected for a second term in 1882, considered an excellent public speaker, the acme of the new "platform women". In the 1880s she was a member of the Vigilance Association for the Defence of Personal Rights. By 1883 she was a member of the CENTRAL COMMITTEE FOR WOMEN'S SUFFRAGE, giving for them in that year, for instance, "seaside lectures" at Worthing and Littlehampton and ten lectures at Working Men's Clubs, the latter for a fee of £25. After the split in 1888 she stayed with the CENTRAL NATIONAL SOCIETY FOR WOMEN'S SUFFRAGE.

Having, at the March 1889 annual general meeting of the Central National Society, condemned its support of the Woodall couverture clause in the franchise bill, she joined the WOMEN'S FRANCHISE LEAGUE as soon as it was founded and was a member of its executive committee. She wrote and delivered at the National Liberal Club on 25 February 1890 an address "On the Programme of the Women's Franchise League". Elizabeth Wolstenholme ELMY, one of the founders of the League, resigned in May 1890, having been, she felt, bitterly insulted by Florence Fenwick Miller. The precise insult is veiled in the extant correspondence but it would appear that Mrs Miller had referred disparagingly to the fact that Elizabeth Wolstenholme Elmy held a *paid* position with the League. Mrs Elmy, in her letters to Harriet MCILQUHAM at this time, implies that Mrs Miller had hurried the publication of the February address through the press, giving herself credit for founding the League, and that she was planning to use the WFL to further her personal ambitions. In a letter to Mrs McIlquham of 27 April 1890, Mrs Elmy writes, "one must remember that the upbringing has been that of slaves and that it will take generations of freedom to eradicate the vices of slavery and in Mrs Miller's case that she had at too early in life, as a mere girl of 18 or 19, personal successes – which turned her head – and that for the rest she lives on and by rich people, mixes with them whilst poor – and is corrupted thereby. She *longs* to be rich". In a letter of 11 April, Mrs Elmy told Mrs McIlquham that one of the wealthy members of the WFL, Ursula BRIGHT, did not care for Florence Fenwick Miller and was particularly anxious that she should not speak at a drawing-room meeting she was giving for the WFL in May, ending "Mrs Miller is certain to be offended".

From 1883 until 1890 Florence Fenwick Miller wrote a weekly column, "Filomena's Letter", that appeared in a number of provincial newspapers and in 1886 she began "Ladies Notes", which ran weekly in the *Illustrated London News* for the next 33 years. From 1895 until 1899 she was editor and sole proprietor of the *Woman's Signal*, which was founded by Lady Henry Somerset, who had bought up the *Woman's Herald*, described by Mrs Miller in a letter to the editor of the *Daily Chronicle* (*c*. March 1898) as Henrietta MULLER's "little venture", "in order that there should be no rival in the field in the shape of any other journal standing for women's interests and progress in the wide world". Mrs Sibthorp, the owner and editor of *Shafts*, took exception in the April 1898 issue to this disparagement of the *Woman's Herald*. For some of the period of her ownership of the *Woman's Signal*, Florence Fenwick Miller had a contract with the Central National Society to supply it with 500 copies of each issue; she was a speaker at that society's annual general meeting in 1896. From 1902 to 1904 she was a staff writer for the *London Daily News*.

In 1893 Florence Fenwick Miller attended, with Alice Cliff SCATCHERD, Ursula Bright and Jane Cobden UNWIN, fellow members of the Women's Franchise League, and Laura Ormiston CHANT of the Central National Society, the World's Congress of Representative Women in Chicago and gave there a paper on "Wives and Mothers: their civil duties". She wrote an article, "Art in the Women's Section of the Chicago Exhibition", published in the Chicago supplement to the *Art Journal*, in which she revealed that she loathed Mary Cassatt's mural *Modern Women*, and criticized the unflattering manner in which Annie SWYNNERTON's canvas, *Florence Nightingale in the Crimea*, was hung.

In February 1902 Florence Fenwick Miller represented Britain at the founding conference, held in Washington, of what was to become the INTERNATIONAL WOMAN SUFFRAGE ALLIANCE. She had been given a grant of £5 towards the cost of her journey by the NATIONAL UNION OF WOMEN'S SUFFRAGE SOCIETIES. She became first treasurer of what was then called the International Women's Suffrage Committee and, while in Washington, delivered a speech before the Committee on the Judiciary of the House of Representatives. She resigned from the International Women's Suffrage Committee in 1904. On 29 October 1906 *The Times* published a long letter from Florence Fenwick Miller occasioned by the arrest and imprisonment of her daughter Irene during the WOMEN'S SOCIAL AND POLITICAL UNION demonstration in the Lobby of the House of Commons and on 11 December 1906 she was present at the banquet at the Savoy given by Mrs FAWCETT to celebrate the release of the prisoners. She subscribed to the WSPU in 1906–7. In 1915 she was elected president of the WOMEN WRITERS' SUFFRAGE LEAGUE, although she had made no obvious contribution to its work in the years of main suffrage activity before the First World War.

Address: (1878) 129 Thomas Road, Finsbury Park, London N; 59 Francis Terrace, Victoria Park, Hackney, London N; (1930s) 23 Brunswick Road, Hove.

Photograph: as a young woman, by Fradelle and Marshall, in the Helen Blackburn Collection, Girton College Archives.

Archival source: Mill–Taylor Papers, London School of Economics and Political Science; Elizabeth Wolstenholme Elmy Papers, British Library.

Bibliography: R.T. Van Arsdel, *Florence Fenwick Miller, Feminism and the* Woman's Signal, 1979.

MILLER, IRENE (1880–1964) Daughter of Florence Fenwick MILLER and Frederick Arthur Ford. She always used the surname Miller, although her death, for instance, is registered as Ford. In her entry in the *Suffrage Annual and Women's Who's Who* she notes that she "was born and brought up in a Suffragist home circle". She was a childhood friend of the PANKHURSTS, their mothers both being very active in the WOMEN'S FRANCHISE LEAGUE. Minnie BALDOCK, in a letter written to Dora MONTEFIORE, mentions that Irene Miller had written to her after reading newspaper reports of their heckling of Asquith at the Queen's Hall on 19 December 1905. "She belongs to no organisation, but is very strong *re* Women's Suffrage, and also very brave. She asked me to come to one of Sydney Buxton's meetings. Although very busy, I felt that I could not damp her ardour, so we went. She was to do all the shouting and would not mind so long as I was with her. We went to a crowded meeting held at the Poplar Town Hall". In early 1906 Irene Miller was a member of the first London committee of the WOMEN'S SOCIAL AND POLITICAL UNION, was arrested (later esteemed by the WOMEN'S FREEDOM LEAGUE as their first member to be arrested in London although, with Annie KENNEY and Flora DRUMMOND, she was released, at the direction of Campbell-Bannerman, without charge) after taking part in a deputation to Downing Street on 9 March, spoke at her first WSPU meeting, at the CANNING TOWN branch, on 24 April, and helped orchestrate the demonstration in the Ladies' Gallery of the House of Commons on 25 April after Keir HARDIE's Resolution was talked out.

In May and June 1906 Irene Miller was present, with Annie Kenney, Minnie Baldock and women from Canning Town at Dora Montefiore's tax-resistance siege in Hammersmith. In October 1906 she was one of the WSPU women arrested and imprisoned after taking part in a demonstration in the Lobby of the House of Commons and was, of course, present at the dinner given at the Savoy on 11 December by Mrs FAWCETT to celebrate the prisoners' release. In September 1907 Irene Miller was one of the members of the provisional committee who refused to accept Mrs Pankhurst's authority in dispensing with the WSPU constitution and thereby founded the group that became the Women's Freedom League. She spoke frequently in public in support of the suffrage cause, but was involved in no further militancy. She worked as a journalist and a black-and-white illustrator; her novel, *Sekhet*, was published in 1912.

Address: (1906) 15 Newport House, Charing Cross Road, London W; (1913) 30 Long Acre, London W.

Archival source: Minnie Baldock Papers, The Suffragette Fellowship Collection, Museum of London.

MILLOM (NUWSS) In 1913 the society was a member of the NORTH-WESTERN FEDERATION OF THE NATIONAL UNION OF WOMEN'S SUFFRAGE SOCIETIES. Secretary (1913) Miss G.A. Lawrence, Bank House, Millom, Cumberland.

MILLS, ERNESTINE, MRS (1871–1959) Born at Hastings, daughter of Major Thomas Evans Bell and Emily Ernst Bell, née Magnus. Major Evans Bell, the author of several books on India, was an active member of the Secular Society, an associate of F.W. NEWMAN and patron of George HOLYOAKE. In 1868 he was a member of the LONDON NATIONAL SOCIETY FOR WOMEN'S SUFFRAGE. Mynie (Emily) Evans Bell signed the 1866 women's suffrage petition. She had studied at the Royal Academy of Music, attempted to rescue her father's failing company, the Pimlico Slate Works, and then turned to the stage as a profession, using the name "Mrs Fairfax". In 1872 she wrote a novel, *A First Appearance*, dedicated to Mary Eliza Rogers (author of *Domestic Life of Palestine*), based on her family circumstances (a Jewish father, an Irish mother and theatrical experiences). In 1871–2 both Major and Mrs Evans Bell were members of the CENTRAL COMMITTEE OF THE NATIONAL SOCIETY FOR WOMEN'S SUFFRAGE. After the early death of her parents, Ernestine was placed in the guardianship of Professor William Ayrton and his first wife, Matilda Chaplin Ayrton (*see* Hertha AYRTON). In 1898 she married, at Kensington Register Office with Hertha and Edith Ayrton as witnesses, Dr Herbert Mills (1868–1947) of Westminster Hospital who was later, in 1909, to tend Harry, the dying son of Emmeline PANKHURST, and in 1911 to serve on the council which advised on the introduction of the National Insurance Act. It was in the Mills's back garden, during the First World War, that Hertha Ayrton conducted experiments with the gas fans she had devised for use in trench warfare. The Mills had one daughter, Hermia (1902–87), who became a doctor.

Ernestine Mills studied at the Slade School, at the Finsbury Central Technical School and South Kensington School of Art, where she was a pupil of Alexander Fisher. She was an associate of the Society of Women Artists in 1919, a member of the Society of Women Artists, 1920, and subsequently a member of council, treasurer and vice-president of the crafts section. She exhibited at the Royal Academy, for the first time, an enamel on copper, in 1900; at the Royal Miniature Society; at the Royal Scottish Academy; at the Society of Women Artists; and many times at the Walker Art Gallery. She served as an apprentice to Frederic Shields, a member of the Pre-Raphaelite Circle and a friend of her mother's, and edited *The Life and Letters of Frederic Shields*, 1912. By July 1909 Ernestine Mills was a member of the FABIAN WOMEN'S GROUP and contributed a paper on the "Origin of the Physical Disability of Women" to a series on the subject read by the Group in 1908–9. She published in the *Englishwoman* in 1915 an article, "Misapplied Industry", which advocated the necessity of eliminating shoddy, tasteless "fancy goods".

Ernestine Mills joined the WOMEN'S SOCIAL AND POLITICAL UNION in 1907. Although apparently not a member of either of the artists' suffrage societies, she published herself two suffrage propaganda POSTCARDS, one, "The Anti Suffragist", including a verse by Charlotte Perkins Gilman, and another, "The New Mrs Partington". She may have produced purple, white and green enamel badges for the WSPU (*see* JEWELLERY AND BADGES). She certainly sent enamel jewellery for sale, in aid of the Self-Denial Fund, at weekly WSPU "At Homes" at the

Portman Rooms in February 1908. In May 1909 she made a pendant in silver enamel, representing the winged figure of Hope singing outside the prison bars, which, attached to a chain with stones of purple, white and green, was presented to Louise EATES by the Chelsea WSPU on her release from prison. In May 1909 Ernestine Mills supplied enamel work to be sold on the Chelsea stall at the WSPU Prince's Rink Exhibition. In 1950 she was commissioned by the SUFFRAGETTE FELLOWSHIP to produce an enamelled plaque, costing £35, to commemorate the BRACKENBURY sisters and their mother, to be installed in their house, the erstwhile "Mouse Castle" at 2 Campden Hill Square which had been left to the "Over Thirty Association". The plaque was unveiled in 1951 by Winifred MAYO and is now on display in the Museum of London.

Address: (1898) 23 Holland Park Avenue, London W; (1934) 21 St Mary Abbotts Terrace, London W; (1950) 57 Addison Road, London W14.

MILLS, (MARY) THEODORA (c. 1870–1958) Unitarian, from 1902 secretary of CHELTENHAM WOMEN'S SUFFRAGE SOCIETY. She wrote five suffrage propaganda songs published by the WOMEN'S SOCIAL AND POLITICAL UNION in 1906–7, including "Rise Up Women! For the fight is hard and long", to be sung to the tune of "John Brown's Body" and won a competition sponsored by the INTERNATIONAL WOMAN SUFFRAGE ALLIANCE with an International Suffrage song, "Forward, Sister Women!", which was translated into several languages (*see* SONGS, MUSIC AND POETRY). In her will she left money to the Peace Pledge Union, the British Union for the Abolition of Vivisection, and money and her unpublished novels to the General Assembly of the Unitarian Church.

Address: (1913, 1958) Lowmandale, Leckhampton Road, Cheltenham, Gloucestershire.

MITCHELL, HANNAH MARIA, MRS (1871–1956) née Webster One of six children, born on a small farm in the Peak district of Derbyshire, the granddaughter of a Chartist. Her childhood was made unhappy by her own lack of access to education and by her mother's violent temper. When she was 14, after a final argument with her mother, she left home. After a short time in domestic service, she obtained work as a dressmaker's assistant. Her continuing search for knowledge and intellectual stimulus led her into the Socialist movement and marriage to Gibbon Mitchell, a young adherent. She had one son, but a difficult birth and the knowledge that a larger family would mean poverty, both physical and mental, convinced her and her husband of the imperative of birth-control and they had no more children. They did, however, later take into their houshold an orphaned niece. After moving to Ashton-under-Lyne in 1900, Hannah Mitchell became active in the local Socialist group, which was affiliated to the Independent Labour Party, eventually becoming lecture secretary of the local branch of the Labour Church. Through this activity she came into contact with many of the leading Socialists in the north of England, including Isabella FORD and Emmeline PANKHURST, and herself became a speaker. In 1904, nominated by the ILP, she was elected to the Ashton-under-Lyne Board of Guardians, filling the seat vacated by Bertha MASON. At the same time, realizing that there was a danger that the ILP might advocate manhood suffrage and ignore the woman's cause, she joined the WOMEN'S SOCIAL AND POLITICAL UNION, actively campaigning with them around Manchester in the winter 1904–5.

The following summer, with Nellie Alma MARTEL, Teresa Billington (*see* Teresa BILLINGTON-GREIG), Flora DRUMMOND and Annie KENNEY, Hannah Mitchell spoke for the WSPU in the surrounding Lancashire towns. In October she was waiting, with other WSPU supporters, at the gates of Strangeways prison in Manchester when Christabel PANKHURST was released and attended the celebratory meeting organized by the ILP held at the Free Trade Hall that evening. As the WSPU made its presence felt during the election campaign in early 1906, Hannah Mitchell became adept at heckling Cabinet ministers and as the WSPU focused more on London she was often called upon to deputize at northern meetings for the Pankhursts or Annie Kenney. She took the time out from campaigning to write to the *Labour Leader*, 16 March 1906, to complain about the introduction of a woman's page in this journal. "We don't want to read about food and clothes", she wrote, "our lives are one long round of cooking and sewing". In the summer of 1906, after she had been thrown out of a Liberal meeting, she was sentenced to three days' imprisonment on a charge of obstructing the police. However, she only spent one night in Strangeways; her husband had, against her wishes, paid her fine. In her autobiography she describes in some detail the viciousness of the attacks on WSPU speakers at this time, necessitating protection by ILP men.

In October 1906 Hannah Mitchell attended the WSPU conference in London, billeted for the occasion at the home of Louise CULLEN, with whom she remained friendly for the rest of her life. After seeing her (Liberal) MP in the Lobby of the House of Commons and, in vain, asking him to move an amendment to the Plural Voting Bill in favour of women's enfranchisement, she took part in the demonstration that resulted in the arrest of, among others, Anne Cobden SANDERSON, Dora MONTEFIORE and Mary GAWTHORPE. She then worked with Mrs Pankhurst in the Huddersfield by-election campaign. Until now Hannah Mitchell had given her services voluntarily to the WSPU but she was then asked to become a part-time ORGANIZER in Oldham, grateful for the small salary offered. She also undertook suffrage speaking tours in the north-east and in London, where again she stayed with Louise Cullen. In the summer of 1907 she spent some more time away from home campaigning first at the Jarrow and then at the Colne Valley by-elections. She eventually suffered a nervous breakdown, brought on, according to her doctor, by overwork and under-feeding. Mrs DESPARD visited her and later sent money to ensure that she suffered no further malnourishment.

After her recovery, Hannah Mitchell joined the WOMEN'S FREEDOM LEAGUE; the break with the WSPU had occurred during her illness. She particularly noted in her autobiography how hurt she was that none of the Pankhursts, for whom she had worked so devotedly, had bothered even to write to her when she was ill. By the summer of 1908 she was sufficiently recovered to go with her son for a short time to East Fife, Asquith's constituency, as a WFL organizer, helped there by Arabella and Muriel SCOTT. When she spoke in Dundee she stayed with Agnes Husband and her sisters. On her return she worked as a paid organizer for the WFL in Manchester, before coming to the conclusion that her nerves could no longer stand the strains of militancy. While maintaining her interest in the suffrage cause, and the WFL in particular, she continued with her work for the Board of Guardians and for the Manchester ILP.

During the First World War Hannah Mitchell was a pacifist, working as a volunteer for the ILP, the No-Conscription Fellowship and the Women's International League. In 1924, nominated by the ILP, she was elected a member of the Manchester city council, remaining in office until she retired in 1935, and from 1926 until 1946 she was a justice of the peace. Of the latter position she rightly wrote, "Of the many women who have received this honour, few indeed can have attained it in the face of so many handicaps as I had. Ignorance, poverty, the disabilities of women in general and married women in particular, had all been faced in the years of service and study which had preceded this result".

Photograph: in H. Mitchell, *The Hard Way Up: The Autobiography of Hannah Mitchell, Suffragette and Rebel*, 1968.
Bibliography: H. Mitchell, *The Hard Way Up: The Autobiography of Hannah Mitchell, Suffragette and Rebel*, 1968.

MITCHELL, LILIAS (1884–1940) Born in Leith, Edinburgh, where her father ran a prosperous timber business, she joined the WOMEN'S SOCIAL AND POLITICAL UNION in 1907 or early 1908, having attended, with her mother, a meeting addressed by Emmeline PANKHURST and Emmeline PETHICK-LAWRENCE. She was imprisoned for a fortnight in 1910 and was sentenced to a further four months in Holloway in March 1912, after taking part in the WSPU window-smashing campaign. She took part in the hunger strike on this occasion and, having been forcibly fed, was released before the expiry of her sentence. By December 1911 she was WSPU ORGANIZER in Aberdeen, moved to Newcastle as organizer there, and in July 1913 took over the WSPU campaign in the Midlands, based in Birmingham. Lilias Mitchell worked hard there to recruit paper sellers for the *Suffragette* and by October was selling from Birmingham 450 to 500 copies a week. Mary RICHARDSON describes how, early in 1914, she and "Lilian" (*sic*) Mitchell, deployed a bomb, made by a woman chemist, to destroy a railway station in Birmingham. Lilias Mitchell was arrested in May 1914 for causing a breach of the peace; in retaliation the Castle Bromwich racecourse was attacked, causing thousands of pounds worth of damage. She was sent to Winson Green Prison, became ill after hunger striking, was released on licence and then re-arrested in June under the "Cat and Mouse" Act. After the First World War she was secretary of the Edinburgh and South Area of the Young Women's Christian Association.

Address: (1934) Central Buildings, 116 George Street, Edinburgh.
Archival source: L. Mitchell, "Suffrage Days", memoir in private collection.
Bibliography: L. Leneman, *A Guid Cause: The Women's Suffrage Movement in Scotland*, 1991.

MONMOUTHSHIRE committee of the NATIONAL SOCIETY FOR WOMEN'S SUFFRAGE Founded in 1871 with Lady AMBERLEY, Ravenscroft, Chepstow, as the secretary and with Lord Amberley as a member of the committee. In 1872 the Monmouth society associated itself with the new CENTRAL COMMITTEE OF THE NATIONAL SOCIETY FOR WOMEN'S SUFFRAGE.

MONTEFIORE, DORA BARROW, MRS (1851–1934) née Fuller Born in Surrey, daughter of a land surveyor, educated in Brighton. She went to Australia to be housekeeper to her brother and there married, in 1879, George Barrow Montefiore. He died ten years later, leaving her with two young children. When she discovered that she had no guardianship rights over her own children, she became a campaigner for women's rights. In 1891, with a few others, she founded, in Sydney, the Womanhood Suffrage League of New South Wales. She became honorary secretary of the League but returned to Europe in 1892, living for a time in Paris, where she joined the THEOSOPHICAL SOCIETY, lapsing as a member by 1900. In 1893 she returned to England, joining the Women's Liberal Association and the executive committee of the CENTRAL COMMITTEE FOR WOMEN'S SUFFRAGE. In July 1893 she displayed her feminist credentials by contributing to *Shafts*, in which were regularly to appear examples of her poetry and in 1896 an article, "Why We Need Woman Suffrage, and why we need it now". In 1894 she joined the Pioneer Club (*see under* CLUBS).

In 1896 she was elected to the executive committee of the CENTRAL NATIONAL SOCIETY FOR WOMEN'S SUFFRAGE, like Eva McLaren belonging to both branches of the central suffrage society. In 1897, representing the Central Committee, she read a paper, for which Elizabeth Wolstenholme ELMY furnished her with material, at the Women's International Congress in Brussels. In March of the same year she suggested to the Central National Society that a demonstration might be held in Hyde Park on the Sunday preceding 23 June, which was the date on which Mr Faithfull Begg's women's suffrage bill was expected to reach its committee stage, in order that "working women might show their support for the suffrage". This suggestion, which was at the time rather startling, was deemed inadvisable, although the committee did think it not inconceivable that an indoor public meeting might be held in the East End of London. In 1900, with Lady GROVE, Dora Montefiore again attended the International Women's Congress at Brussels and gave a paper, in French, on the history of the English women's movement.

In 1898, with Louisa MARTINDALE, Dora Montefiore, as a member of the WOMEN'S LOCAL GOVERNMENT SOCIETY, campaigned in Sussex to raise awareness of the importance of the election of women as parish councillors. In 1898 she spoke at one of the first meetings held by the Horsted Keynes Women's Liberal Association, which had been founded by Louisa Martindale. Dora Montefiore was a member of the executive committee of the UNION OF PRACTICAL SUFFRAGISTS, which had been founded by 1896 to put the "test" question to Liberal candidates – i.e. if they were in favour of women's suffrage. In 1899 the Union of Practical Suffragists published Dora Montefiore's pamphlet *Women Uitlanders*, which had originally appeared in the *Ethical World*; she was still a member of its executive committee in 1900. In 1898 she began writing a column, "Women's Interests", in the *New Age*; she was still a contributor to this journal in 1905. While yet a member of the Union of Practical Suffragists, a Liberal party organization, she was, in 1898, travelling in the Clarion Van, campaigning for the Independent Labour Party. During the course of this journey Dora Montefiore appears to have formed a relationship, possibly platonic, with a fellow caravanner, George Belt, a bricklayer's labourer and a member of the ILP National Administration Committee. An indiscreet letter from Dora Montefiore, intercepted by his wife, led to his being sacked from his position as an ILP organizer in Hull. When Margaret MacDonald, wife of the ILP leader, mentioned the scandal to Lady ABERDEEN, Dora Montefiore was forced to retire from her position as recording secretary at the 1899 International Women's Congress in London and was unable to read her prepared paper. George Belt, presumably financed by Dora, brought a libel case against Margaret MacDonald. Ramsay MacDonald settled the case out of court for £120. It is likely that Dora Montefiore's relationship with George Belt continued for several years. In 1906 George Belt, having left his wife, was proposed as the ILP general election candidate for Hammersmith, at a time when Dora Montefiore was a member of the Hammersmith Trades and Labour Council. Ramsay MacDonald, unforgiving, refused to give him the backing of the Labour Representation Committee. Dora Montefiore, in spite of these personal difficulties, did attend the 1899 ILP conference. She became increasingly interested in social questions and at some point joined the Social Democratic Federation. In 1900 she was speaking on women's suffrage in Ealing with a prominent SDF member, Amie HICKS, by 1901 she was writing for *Justice* and the *Social Democrat* and from 1903 to 1905 she was a member of the executive committee of the SDF. In March 1904 she was the instigator of a women's branch of the SDF, forming what were known as Women's Socialist Circles, and became its first treasurer. Dora Montefiore resigned from the woman's branch of the SDF in 1905 when it became clear that the Women's Socialist Circles were to be more social than Socialist. It is likely that it was through this work, as well as her involvement in the Hammersmith Distress Committee, that she came into contact with the women in West Ham and Canning Town who were in March 1906 to form the first branch of the WSPU in London. With Keir HARDIE and George LANSBURY she organized, in June 1905, a march of 1000 of these women to the House of Commons during a period of government intransigence over the Unemployment Bill. Dora Montefiore had maintained her close contact with Elizabeth Wolstenholme Elmy, sending her a guinea in 1901, and when in July 1903 W.T. Stead organized an independent conference at Mowbray House to discuss plans for an autumn suffrage campaign, it was with Dora Montefiore that Mrs Elmy stayed while attending it. On the way back from the SDF annual general meeting at Burnley in 1904 Dora Montefiore spent the Easter weekend in Manchester, visiting Elizabeth Wolstenholme Elmy and the Pankhursts. Shortly afterwards she appears to have represented the WOMEN'S SOCIAL AND POLITICAL UNION at the Berlin conference of the International Council of Women.

Dora Montefiore was present with Mrs PANKHURST and other members of the WSPU at the House of Commons on 12 May 1905, only to hear Bamford Slack's women's suffrage bill talked out. In May 1906, when she was in London to take part in the deputation to Campbell-Bannerman, Elizabeth Wolstenholme Elmy again stayed with Dora Montefiore. The two women maintained a constant correspondence, unfortunately now lost, and it is clear that Dora Montefiore was for Elizabeth Wolstenholme Elmy an important source of information on the suffrage cause in London. Doubtless both information and interpretation were shared with other members of Mrs Elmy's circle of friends and correspondents, including Mrs Pankhurst. It was at an open-air meeting arranged by Dora Montefiore, held in Ravenscourt Park in west London, probably in 1904, that Sylvia Pankhurst made her first suffrage speech. In her autobiography Dora Montefiore writes that "The work of the WSPU was begun by Mrs Pankhurst in Manchester and by a group of women in London who had revolted against the inertia and conventionalism which seemed to have fastened upon the Victoria Street Union of Suffrage Societies." She then invokes the name of Elizabeth Wolstenholme Elmy as the link between these groups, that she knew of and approved of the work of both the embryonic WSPU in Manchester and in London that of "a group of women, myself included, who undertook to attend political meetings and question speakers about their intentions towards the enfranchisement of women, keeping that before the meeting as our supreme aim and if necessary, holding up proceedings until an answer was obtained". Mrs Montefiore stresses that what she calls "the London Committee of the W.S.P.U." had already "been doing good work in London long before Annie KENNEY arrived on the scene". It is clear that, with some justice, she saw herself as a leader of the beginnings of an alternative suffrage movement in London and takes Sylvia PANKHURST to task for ignoring, in both the original history of the suffrage movement that appeared weekly in *Votes for Women* and in *The Suffragette*, 1911, the part she played in this transitional period. In particular she cites the suppression of her presence on the occasion at which Annie Kenney, Minnie BALDOCK and "another woman" had heckled Asquith at the Queen's Hall on 19 December 1905. She indignantly points out that not only was she the other woman but that it was she who organized the whole stunt, obtained the tickets from the Liberal Association and was the principal questioner. Her lengthy description of the sequence of events that evening accords well with the report published in *The Times* the next day. However, the disinterested contemporary report in the *Labour Leader* makes no mention of her. Dora Montefiore also disputes Sylvia Pankhurst's statement (although it is repeated by Annie Kenney in her autobiography) that it was with Sylvia, rather than with Mrs Montefiore, that Annie Kenney first stayed when she came to London. She writes that when, years later, she tackled Sylvia Pankhurst about these "intentional mis-statements" she was told "that she [Sylvia Pankhurst] was very young at the time and entirely under the influence of her mother, who wished my name to be suppressed".

In January 1906 Dora Montefiore went to Wigan to campaign on behalf of Thorley Smith who, sponsored by the LANCASHIRE AND CHESHIRE WOMEN TEXTILE AND OTHER WORKERS' REPRESENTATION COMMITTEE, was standing as a women's suffrage candidate. On 2 March 1906 Mrs Montefiore took part in a deputation, with Annie Kenney and Frances ROWE, to Campbell-Bannerman; he was ill and could not see them. It was a precursor of others, but as it had no direct result Sylvia Pankhurst did not mention it. Mrs Montefiore not only mentions it in her autobiography, but includes a photograph of the deputation on the doorstep of No. 10. In June 1906 Dora Montefiore was arrested for distributing leaflets in Hyde Park at a meeting to protest at the arrest of Annie Kenney, Mrs KNIGHT and Mrs SBARBORO. She was released without charge, again not worthy of mention by Sylvia Pankhurst, but evidence of Mrs Montefiore's active involvement. She was also not averse to advocating direct action. *The Times* reported on 25 May that, during the course of her "siege" the day before, Mrs Montefiore had said, "If she were free she would at once go to demonstrate before Mr Asquith's house and break his windows." This declaration was sufficiently noteworthy for the Hon. Charles Lister to write in the *Labour Leader*, 1 June, "We would respectfully exhort Mrs Montefiore to remember that it is futile for a *few* enthusiasts to break these windows. A surging mob should fill Cavendish Square and clamour for its right and duties, a surging mob 20 000 strong". It is entirely likely that Dora Montefiore was always unacceptable to Mrs Pankhurst. A financially independent widow, tainted by rumours of scandal, extremely active in promulgating her politically radical views, intent on running any society she joined, was anathema. When in 1931, some years after this conversation, Sylvia Pankhurst wrote an expanded version of her history, *The Suffragette Movement*, Mrs Montefiore is accorded a grudging six entries in the index.

Dora Montefiore must have been particularly incensed by Sylvia Pankhurst's failure to include any mention in *The Suffragette* of the tactic which she saw as her main contribution to the suffrage cause in these years. During the Boer War she had refused to pay income tax because the money was used to finance a war in the making of which she had no voice. She employed the same reasoning when, in late May 1904, she refused to pay income tax because she had no vote. Elizabeth Wolstenholme Elmy wrote to Harriet MCILQUHAM on 25 May 1904 that "I am hoping that the sale of Mrs Montefiore's distrained goods next Monday may be made a WS [women's suffrage] demonstration. Many women, I hear, are preparing to follow her example." On 1 June she wrote:

> I was very glad Mrs Montefiore's sales were so well attended. The previous "resisters" have only invited a few private friends to their houses to witness the removal of their goods, and nothing more has been attempted. I hope that now we shall have the nucleus of a League of women

pledged to do likewise, though of course, only the minority of well-to-do women, even amongst widows and unmarried women, can be free to act thus. Married women are practically shut out from doing it by the joint assessment of husband and wife.

In 1905 Elizabeth Wolstenholme Elmy reveals in a letter, dated 12 July, that Dora Montefiore was prepared to go to prison rather than pay her tax and in an article in the July 1905 edition of the *Westminster Review* she urged women to support Mrs Montefiore in her tax resistance. In fact, as Mrs Montefiore makes clear in her autobiography, the sales of her distrained goods in 1904 and 1905 did not attract much publicity and it was only in 1906, with the backing of WSPU members, particularly from the East End branch, that she achieved a suitable degree of publicity when she not only refused to pay her tax but also barricaded herself into her house against the bailiff. She had been present in the deputation to Campbell-Bannerman on 19 May 1906 and offered her tax resistance as a rejoinder to Sir Henry's suggestion that women should educate parliament. The "Siege of Fort Montefiore" was well covered in the press. Annie Kenney and Teresa Billington (*see* Teresa BILLINGTON GREIG) arrived with 50 women from Canning Town, carrying red BANNERS bearing the message "We demand the vote this session" and "We demand votes for women" and sang "The Scarlet Standard". Dora Montefiore's goods were eventually sold at public auction in July and she herself bought them back at a cost of £19 11s; her tax bill had been £18. In early 1910 she attended a meeting of the newly-founded TAX RESISTANCE LEAGUE.

The only mention Sylvia Pankhurst makes of Dora Montefiore in *The Suffragette* (although her name is not indexed) is in the context of her imprisonment, with her neighbour in Upper Mall, Anne Cobden Sanderson, and others, after being arrested in the Lobby of the House of Commons on 23 October 1906. Indeed, her name is only mentioned to draw attention to her early release from prison, apparently due to "serious illness". In *The Suffragette Movement* Sylvia Pankhurst elaborates on the cause of release, now describing it as due to Mrs Montefiore's having contracted an infestation of head lice in prison. Sylvia Pankhurst is certainly not prepared to invest Dora Montefiore's imprisonment with the same glamour she accorded the other women involved, including Mrs PETHICK-LAWRENCE, who, unable to stand the strain, was released a day before Mrs Montefiore. Dora Montefiore had, however, by 31 October recovered sufficiently from her ordeal to write a short foreword to *The Woman's Calendar* that she had compiled for publication by A.C. Fifield, noting that "Women are beginning to take themselves seriously".

On the Saturday before the opening of parliament in October 1906 Elizabeth Wolstenholme Elmy and Dora Montefiore attended a meeting held to discuss the WSPU constitution. It is clear from a letter written by Elizabeth Wolstenholme Elmy to Harriet McIlquham that Dora Montefiore was by now deeply unhappy with the WSPU organization in London. An element of confusion has entered into the train of events because this letter was written at the turn of the year 1906–7, on 6 January, and was mistakenly dated by Elizabeth Wolstenholme Elmy "1906". This has meant that it has been mis-sequenced when her papers were catalogued, although it is quite clear from the contents of the letter that it could not possibly have been written in January 1906. There is little doubt that it was only after the arrival of Mrs Pankhurst and Christabel in London in June 1906 that Dora Montefiore began to feel less certain about her position at the heart of the (comparatively) militant suffrage movement in London. In the letter of 6 January (1907) Elizabeth Wolstenholme Elmy gives a very clear description of Mrs Montefiore's state of mind in October 1906, just prior to her arrest and imprisonment:

Whenever she and I – or she and I, and Frank were alone together, it was one continuous wail of discontent against everybody else. Everything other people did was wrong, everybody slighted her – nothing she did was recognized or acknowledged. . . . The Sunday [the day after the meeting to discuss the WSPU constitution] we went with her to Victoria Park she did nothing but find fault all the way with every body and everything connected with the W.S.P. &U. Movement. They undertook to do things but left all the doing to her. At last, at the second station, at which we had to change, I could bear it no longer and worn out with work and excitement – burst out crying and told her I could not go any further with her unless she desisted from all this fault-finding and blaming of the absent. For a few minutes she talked of other things; but long before we reached the Park, she was at it again. The meeting would be a failure, they promised to make all arrangements – but never did anything. The evidence was to the contrary. They sent a splendid platform to support her in the chair. Annie Kenney, Teresa Billington, Irene Fenwick MILLER, Mrs Sbarbaro, Mrs Baldock and others. Elizabeth Wolstenholme Elmy adds in this letter that:

Frank tells me he is satisfied that the *awful change* in her (for she was not thus self-absorbed, & egotistic and pathetic of old) is due to her extravagant use of *cocaine* lozenges – which she takes for a cough of which she complained – and which easily becomes quite as dangerous and demoralizing as the "morphia" habit – and he fears, that unless she will give it up it will be her destruction intellectually and morally. I tell you all this in confidence, in the hope that Mrs Rowe (who I think should know this) may be able to ascertain whether she still continues the dangerous habit if so, to warn her, to get her medically warned of the danger . . . That she was continually sucking some lozenges I know, but I *know* nothing more, except the sorrowful change in her.

Harriet McIlquham passed on the news to Frances Rowe, who replied to her in a letter dated 9 January 1907 that she knew nothing of cocaine lozenges and that it was not even "the old scandal" that had influenced the WSPU's current attitude to Dora Montefiore, but "they cannot have her on any terms. Self aggrandisement seems to be inseparable from her. While she can lead an admiring entourage all goes well."

There is no doubt, however, that after she was released from prison Dora Montefiore broke off her association with the WSPU. According to Frances Rowe this was as a result of an interview with Mrs Pankhurst at which the latter "was heated and spoke plainly – as she can!" and to all intents dismissed Mrs Montefiore from the WSPU. Dora Montefiore did not attend the banquet at the Savoy on 11 December given by Mrs FAWCETT to honour the prisoners and in a letter to Adelaide KNIGHT was scathing about it, warning her that the East End women were being falsely flattered by both "the Tory women" of "the old Suffrage Society" and the undemocratic WSPU. In her autobiography she explains that she could not countenance the WSPU's encouragement of physical resistance to the police, nor could she support a society that failed to publish its accounts, and makes it clear that she considered Mrs Pankhurst an autocrat. Her break with the WSPU preceded that of Mrs DESPARD, and although the two shared similar social commitment, Mrs Montefiore does not appear to have joined the WOMEN'S FREEDOM LEAGUE. She certainly does not mention such membership in her autobiography, although June Hannam in her biography of Isabella Ford records that Dora Montefiore was present at an INTERNATIONAL WOMAN SUFFRAGE ALLIANCE conference at the Hague in 1908 as a "socialist member of the WFL". Dora Montefiore was treasurer of the HAMMERSMITH SUFFRAGE SOCIETY, of which Frances Rowe was honorary secretary, which had been affiliated to the WSPU, and which carried on independently for some years.

In August 1906 Dora Montefiore had attended, as the WSPU's delegate, the International Woman Suffrage Alliance meeting at Copenhagen and by doing so had been reviled by the SDF journal *Justice* for her implied support for propertied women. In 1907, after leaving the WSPU, she joined the Adult Suffrage Society, which had the backing of the SDF, and from January 1909 until 1912 was its honorary secretary. She explains in her autobiography that she had "always been a staunch adult suffragist" but had felt that because the term "adult suffrage" carried such a strong connotation of "manhood suffrage" she had thought it necessary to pursue the goal of women's enfranchisement by whichever method was most likely to succeed. For a time it seemed that the WSPU provided the best means. She kept in close touch with Adelaide Knight, who had also been a member of the SDF and the WSPU, and who then became secretary of the Canning Town branch of the WSS. Dora Montefiore, always an internationalist, kept up a tireless round of travel, speaking at suffrage conferences in Europe, America (1910–11), South Africa and Australia (1911–13). She was a close friend of Clara Zetkin and of Alexandra

Kollantai. In 1913 she gave active support to the strikers in the Dublin Lock-Out. With, among others, Julia SCURR, she attempted to organize the evacuation of starving Irish children to England. This scheme invoked the wrath of the Irish Catholic church and Dora Montefiore, around whom rumours of involvement in the White Slave Trade were now swirling, was bailed out of prison by Constance Markievicz, sister of Eva GORE-BOOTH. On 10 August, with John Scurr and Sylvia Pankhurst, she was among the speakers at a rally organized by the *Daily Herald* League in Trafalgar Square to protest against the imprisonment of George Lansbury. She was in South Africa from January to May 1914 and on her return founded a new journal, the *Adult Suffrage*, but was sufficiently ecumenical to attend the Costume Dinner organized by the ACTRESSES' FRANCHISE LEAGUE and the WOMEN WRITERS' SUFFRAGE LEAGUE held at the Hotel Cecil on 29 June 1914.

Early in the First World War Dora Montefiore worked in England with Charlotte Despard and with the WFL and from 1915 to 1916 for the "Cantine des Dames Anglaises" in France. On 28 January 1918 she presided over a dinner held at the Lyceum Club (*see under* CLUBS) to celebrate women's limited enfranchisement. Among the guests were H.W. NEVINSON, Evelyn SHARP and Olive Schreiner. Mary Sheepshanks, the editor of *International Suffrage News*, read out a message of congratulations from a German suffragist, which unpatriotic behaviour led to her being excluded from the Club. Dora Montefiore put her internationalist sympathies before the convenience of a London *pied-à-terre* and resigned in sympathy.

In February 1919 Dora Montefiore stood, unsuccessfully, as Labour candidate for Hammersmith in the LCC elections. In 1920 she was the British Socialist Party delegate to the convention that founded the British Communist Party and, never one to be a mere rank and file member, was elected onto the executive committee. She was international secretary of the first International Conference of Communist Women and in 1924 attended the Moscow International Congress as delegate from the Australian Communist Party. Despite the continuous widening of her horizons Dora Montefiore liked to keep in touch with the past. In the early 1920s she organized a dinner at the Minerva Club (*see under* CLUBS) and included among the guests Charlotte Despard, Dr Elizabeth KNIGHT, Edith How MARTYN, Teresa Billington-Greig, Minnie Baldock, Sylvia Pankhurst, Nellie MARTEL, Emma SPROSON, Nina BOYLE and Octavia LEWIN. In her will, dated 1933, she asked that Florence UNDERWOOD, secretary of the WFL, "and any other friends who may be interested" should be informed of her death and that "an announcement of my death and the mode of my burial . . . be inserted in the obituary column of the *Times*".

Among Dora Montefiore's published work are: *Singings in the Dark*, 1898; *Woman Uitlanders*, 1899; *A Woman's Calendar*, 1906; *Some Words to Socialist Women*, 1908; *The Position of Women in the Socialist Movement*, 1909.

Address: (1900) 63 Philbeach Gardens, London, W; 52 Upper Mall, Hammersmith, London W; (October 1906) 8 Westminster Mansions, London SW; (1934) Melbourne, Edwin Road, Clive Vale, Hastings; Araluen, Beacon Gardens, Crowborough, Sussex; The Cot, West Coker Road, Yeovil, Somerset.
Photograph: in D.B. Montefiore, *From a Victorian to a Modern*, 1927.
Archival source: Elizabeth Wolstenholme Elmy Papers, British Library; Frances Rowe Papers, Autograph Collection, Fawcett Library; Hammersmith and Fulham Archives and Local History Centre.
Bibliography: D.B. Montefiore, *From a Victorian to a Modern*, 1927; C. Collette, "Socialism and Scandal: The Sexual Politics of the Early Labour Movement", in *History Workshop Journal*, 23, Spring 1987; C. Collette, *For Labour and For Women: The Women's Labour League, 1906–18*, 1989; J. Hannam, *Isabella Ford*, 1989; A. Oldfield, *Woman Suffrage in Australia: A Gift or a Struggle?*, 1992; K. Hunt, *Equivocal Feminists: The Social Democratic Federation and the Woman Question 1884–1911*, 1996.

MONTGOMERY BOROUGH (WFL)   Secretary (1913) Miss Clark, 11 Severn Street, Newtown, North Wales.

MONTROSE committee of the NATIONAL SOCIETY FOR WOMEN'S SUFFRAGE   Formed in 1872. In 1913 the society was a member of the SCOTTISH FEDERATION OF THE NATIONAL UNION OF WOMEN'S SUFFRAGE SOCIETIES. Secretary (1913) Miss Hossack, 89 Bridge St, Montrose, Angus.

MOORE, DECIMA (LADY GUGGISBERG) (*c.* 1871–1964)   Educated Boswell House, Brighton, actress, sister of Eva MOORE, member of the executive committee of the ACTRESSES' FRANCHISE LEAGUE. When on tour she alternated theatrical performances with suffrage meetings. She opened the third day of the WOMEN'S SOCIAL AND POLITICAL UNION Scottish Exhibition in Glasgow in April 1910. In June 1911 she appeared as a suffragette in Barker's Motion Photography FILM of Inez Bensusan's *True Womanhood*. She was particularly renowned as the reciter of *Woman This and Woman That*, the monologue written by Laurence HOUSMAN. Decima Moore was also a supporter of the TAX RESISTANCE LEAGUE, the NEW CONSTITUTIONAL SOCIETY FOR WOMEN'S SUFFRAGE, 1910 and the MEN'S POLITICAL UNION in 1911. In August 1914, with her sister and Evelina HAVERFIELD, she formed the Women's Emergency Corps to provide women as paid, not voluntary, helpers at the time of national crisis. In 1958 she was a member of the committee formed to organize a memorial for Christabel PANKHURST.

Bibliography: J. Holledge, *Innocent Flowers: Women in the Edwardian Theatre*, 1981.

MOORE, EVA (MRS HENRY ESMOND) (1868–1955)

Born in Brighton, with eight sisters and a brother, actress, sister of Decima MOORE, mother of a son and a daughter, she spoke at the inaugural meeting of the ACTRESSES' FRANCHISE LEAGUE held in the Criterion Theatre in 1908 and became one of its vice-presidents. Her husband wrote *Her Vote: a comedy in one act*, 1910, a suffrage propaganda PLAY in which she took the lead. The propaganda element in this sketch was a little too light-hearted for the AFL and Eva Moore was asked not to play it again. She refused and resigned from the AFL, although she rejoined later. Eva Moore was a supporter of the TAX RESISTANCE LEAGUE and gave a recitation at the "John Hampden" dinner held by the TRL in December 1911. In 1911 she gave a donation to the Hawkins Legal Fund organized by the MEN'S POLITICAL UNION. She became a member of the UNITED SUFFRAGISTS and in 1914, after the outbreak of war, was involved with her sister in the founding of the Women's Emergency Corps. In the 1930s she was a vice-president of the Six Point Group.

Address: (1901) 21 Whiteheads Grove, Chelsea, London SW; (1934) 5 Cresswell Place, The Boltons, London SW; Apple Porch, Maidenhead, Berkshire.

Photograph: in Fawcett Library Collection.
Bibliography: E. Moore, *Exits and Entrances*, 1923; J. Holledge, *Innocent Flowers: Women in the Edwardian Theatre*, 1981; S. Stowell, *A Stage of Their Own: Feminist Playwrights in the Suffrage Era*, 1992

MOORHEAD, ETHEL AGNES MARY (c. 1877–?)

Roman Catholic, one of six children of an Army surgeon of Irish extraction, who spent most of his life in India, Mauritius and South Africa until the family returned to Dundee at the end of the nineteenth century. Ethel Moorhead's elder sister Alice, encouraged by her father, qualified as a doctor in 1891, was in practice in Dundee, was elected a member of the parish council, married in 1908 a doctor in Leith and died a year after the marriage. One of her brothers, Rupert Moorhead (d. 1939) lived in Batheaston in Somerset and was family doctor to the BLATHWAYTS; her other brother Arthur, a brevet colonel, died at Batheaston in 1916 and left the residue of his estate in trust to her, thus providing her with an income. Ethel had been allowed to study painting in Paris, at the end of the nineteenth century, supported by her sister, but it was never considered by the family that she should become a professional artist. From around 1897 Ethel Moorhead was the daughter-at-home, her presence there assuaging the conscience of her siblings. Her mother died in 1902 and, painting for pleasure, with much encouragement from her father, whom she loved, she kept house until he died, leaving an estate worth £67, in 1912. She then went to Edinburgh.

In the period immediately before the First World War Ethel Moorhead achieved noteriety in the Scottish press and, because of this, was deemed by the public to be a leader of the suffragettes in Scotland. In fact she never held any organizational post in the WOMEN'S SOCIAL POLITICAL UNION and, like Emily Wilding DAVISON in England, acted on her own initiative to draw attention to the suffrage campaign. She had first spoken at a WSPU meeting in Dundee in 1910 and at the end of that year threw an egg at Winston Churchill when he came to speak there. Her cats were called "the Panks". In January 1911, a member of the TAX RESISTANCE LEAGUE, she refused to pay her tax and the bailiffs removed a candelabrum in lieu, which was bought back by friends, much to her father's amusement. In March

1912 she took part in London in the WSPU window-smashing campaign, choosing as one of her targets that of Thomas Cook, her brother Arthur's agent. After being held on remand in Holloway, she was released on bail of £300, guaranteed by friends of Janie ALLAN, who had taken charge of what Ethel Moorhead refers to as "the Scotch batch". Among the latter was Frances PARKER, whom she now met for the first time and with whom she was to be close for the rest of "Fan's" life. As Ethel Moorhead tellingly describes in *Incendaries*, at this time of increasing militancy, "They snatched friendship as they rushed past on mad quests". When her case came to trial the main witness against her, much to her surprise, muddled his evidence, on purpose she thought, in such a way that the judge had no option but to advise the jury that they must return a verdict of "not guilty". In August 1912, as "Edith Johnston" she was arrested for breaking the glass of the case containing William Wallace's sword at the Wallace Monument in Stirling and was sentenced to seven days' imprisonment in Perth prison. On 25 October 1912 she entered a classroom at Broughton Higher Grade School and, with a dog whip, struck Peter Ross, who had been responsible for ejecting her from a meeting being held by Sir Rufus Isaacs. The fine of £1 to which she was sentenced was paid without her consent and she was released. On the same day she broke seven panes of glass in a police cell. In late 1912 she was arrested in Aberdeen as "Mary Humphreys", with, among others, Olive WHARRY, Frances Parker and Emily Wilding Davison, after a disturbance at a meeting being held by Lloyd George and was sentenced to ten days' imprisonment. The women went on hunger strike until their fines were paid, without their consent, by sympathizers.

In January 1913 Ethel Moorhead was arrested, this time as "Margaret Morrison" (Margaret had been her mother's name), in Leven. While Asquith was addressing his constituents, she threw pepper into the eyes of a policeman and was found to have in her possession a metal hammer and pieces of lead for the commission, it was thought, of acts of mischief. She was imprisoned, awaiting trial, in Dundee prison, where she broke panes of glass and went on hunger strike. On 3 February a letter she wrote as "Margaret Morrison" from Dundee prison to Arabella SCOTT was suppressed by prison officials. In it she had asked Arabella Scott to inform "my people... and friends that there is a plot hatching – was visited today by a blurry-eyed doctor (I thought smelling of whiskey) and with an affectionate manner!" She was sentenced to 30 days' imprisonment and taken to Perth prison where there were facilities for forcible feeding. She refused to be examined by the prison doctor, who felt unable to feed her without so doing, and she was discharged on 6 February. In July 1913, again as "Margaret Morrison", she was arrested, having been caught red-handed with petrol and suffrage literature inside an empty house and, when tried in October, was sentenced to eight months' imprisonment. Dorothea Chalmers SMITH was involved in this attempt at arson. After sentence Ethel Moorhead went on hunger strike, was released under the "Cat and Mouse" Act and disappeared. She describes most graphically, in *Incendaries*, how Frances Parker protected her from the "cats", organizing sanctuaries and disguises. She was re-arrested on 17 February 1914 after having been found acting suspiciously at Traquair House. She was identified from her photograph in the *Police Gazette*. The Criminal Record Office photograph of her is less than flattering; she is described as aged 44, 5ft 6in tall, with brown eyes, "(wears pince-nez), oblong face, receding chin, slim build, stooping shoulders". It was thought that she had been responsible for at least four fires, three in Perthshire and one in Renfrewshire, which had occurred in the period between October and February when she was "on the run". From the case papers it is clear that the prison commissioners in Calton gaol in Edinburgh, to where she had been taken, were prepared to go to some lengths to ensure that Ethel Moorhead remained in prison, feeling it necessary to protect the public from her. She went on hunger, thirst, and sleep strike and from 19 February was fed by force. This was the first time that "artificial feeding", as it was termed, had been used on a suffragette in Scotland. The prison authorities were also prepared to supply comforts such as books, flowers and her own clothing. There was a suggestion that she might be certified as insane, but this was dismissed. The authorities at Calton gaol brought in the doctor from Peterhead prison, practised in dealing with Scotland's worst criminals, to administer the feeding to Ethel Moorhead. On 23 February she asked to see her solicitor in order to make her will. By this date the police had a warrant, naming her as Ethel Moorhead, for her arrest on a charge of having set fire to three houses in Comrie district on the night of 3/4 February, hoping thereby to re-arrest her if she was released from prison. She was visited each day by the Catholic prison chaplain, at the request of Frances Parker, of whom he brought news. By 25 February the prison medical report mentions that she exhibited symptoms of pneumonia, though hastening to add that this was in no way associated with forcible feeding, but the result of a chill brought on by her own behaviour. She did develop double pneumonia, caused, her doctor insisted, by food entering her lungs during the course of being fed, and was so ill that she received the general absolution from the Catholic chaplain. She was finally released that day, under the "Cat and Mouse" Act, after the intervention, at the suggestion of a sympathetic prison wardress, of Joseph Dobbie, an Edinburgh lawyer, who threatened the prison officials with prosecution if they continued to attempt to feed her. In *Incendiaries* she gives an eloquent, anguished account, couched in suitably staccato modernist prose, of the horrors of her incarceration. A few hours after her release Whitekirk in East Lothian was burned down. Janie Allan certainly believed that the destruction of the church was a direct result of the forcible feeding of Ethel Moorhead. It is clear, reading between the lines of *Incendiaries*, that the arson was committed by Frances Parker. With the help of the latter and of Janie Allan, Ethel Moorhead escaped from the home of the doctor caring for her and was not recaptured by the time war broke out in August. It is virtually certain that she was the companion, who escaped, when Frances Parker was arrested in July 1914 while attempting to set fire to Burns's cottage in Alloa.

During the First World War Ethel Moorhead worked in London with Frances Parker, as joint organizers for the Women's Freedom League's National Service Organisation, based at 144 High Holborn. In 1915 Ethel Moorhead was a member of the Emily Wilding Davison Lodge (*see under* CLUBS) which was based at the same address. In the early 1920s she lived in France, probably with Frances Parker. In 1922 she befriended Ernest Walsh, a young, ill, American poet, a protégé of Harriet Monroe and Ezra Pound. She travelled Europe and North Africa with him, as he searched for surroundings congenial to his mind and body. Ethel Moorhead and Walsh spent the winter of 1923 at Archacon near Bordeaux and it was there that Frances Parker died in January 1924. Although Ethel Moorhead does not mention this event in her memoir of Ernest Walsh, it is inconceivable that the two women could not have been there but together.

With Walsh, Ethel Moorhead founded *This Quarter*, an English-language review of art and literature, "because he believed in himself. Because I believed in him and his poems". They co-edited the first two issues and after his death in Monaco in 1926 she continued as sole editor for two more issues, until spring 1929. The first issue of *This Quarter*, published in Paris in 1925, contains reproductions of four paintings by Ethel Moorhead and a wry line and prose observation of Ezra Pound. The second issue, published from Milan, contains, alongside contributions from James Joyce and Djuna Barnes, "Incendiaries (Work in progress)" by Ethel Moorhead, a moving, autobiographical account of her early life and suffragette activities. She records in *This Quarter*, no. 3, 1927, that the journal had been founded "on the strength of a legacy left me by a friend, Frances Mary Parker". She reveals in an editorial that she was severely disappointed with the manner in which Janie Allan had exercised her function as Frances Parker's executor and includes her, along with sundry Scottish lawyers, in "*This Quarter*'s Unrecommended List".

Address: (1910) The Weisha, Ninewells, Dundee, Fife; (1913) Argyll Cottage, Liberton, Midlothian; (1929) 5 Descente de Larvotto, Monte Carlo, Monaco.
Photograph: Criminal Record Office – no. M/19433.
Archival source: Scottish Office Prison Commission files, Scottish Record Office; *Ethel Moorhead* video film written and directed by Mary Gordon, a Moorhead Production for First Reels, 1995, Fawcett Library.
Bibliography: E. Moorhead and E. Walsh (eds), *This Quarter*, nos 1 and 2, 1925; E. Moorhead (ed.), *This Quarter*, no. 3, 1927, no. 4, 1929; E. Walsh, *Poems and Sonnets: With a Memoir by Ethel Moorhead*, 1934; L. Leneman, *A Guid Cause: The Women's Suffrage Movement in Scotland*, 1991; L. Leneman, *Martyrs in Our Midst: Dundee, Perth and the Forcible Feeding of Suffragettes*, 1993.

MORDAN, CLARA EVELYN (1844–1915) Born in South Kensington, the daughter of a prosperous manufacturer of propelling pencils. In 1866 she was taken by her father to hear J.S. MILL advocating the enfranchisement of women. In July 1869, again accompanied by her father, she attended the first public meeting held in London to discuss women's suffrage. By 1878 she was a member of the MANCHESTER NATIONAL SOCIETY FOR WOMEN'S SUFFRAGE and was a frequent speaker on women's suffrage at London drawing-room meetings. In the 1880s she gave generously to the CENTRAL COMMITTEE OF THE NATIONAL SOCIETY FOR WOMEN'S SUFFRAGE, remaining with that society after the 1888 split, and was a member of its executive committee from 1889 until at least 1893. In 1889 she was honorary secretary of the "Caroline Ashurst Biggs Memorial Fund". Clara Mordan was prepared to travel outside London in support of the cause; in November 1892 she was a member of a deputation of the Central Committee to a meeting in support of women's suffrage held in the Town Hall, Luton.

Clara Mordan was a member of the executive committee of the CENTRAL SOCIETY FOR WOMEN'S SUFFRAGE after it was re-formed in 1900 and still subscribed to it in 1905. In 1894 she was a member of the SPECIAL APPEAL COMMITTEE, formed by women from all parties and societies, that organized the collection of nearly a quarter of a million signatures of women who supported women's enfranchisement. In 1898 she subscribed to the WOMEN'S EMANCIPATION UNION and in 1901–2 she supported the Special Organising Fund run by the NORTH OF ENGLAND SOCIETY to produce the petitions from textile workers.

Mrs BLATHWAYT records in her diary in 1910 that Clara Mordan, while staying at Batheaston, had told her that she was brought into the WOMEN'S SOCIAL AND POLITICAL UNION "from the beautiful and simple way in which Annie [KENNEY] laid the case before her. She had worked all along with the non-militant society and had given up the movement in despair." In *Memories of a Militant*, Annie Kenney describes how Miss Mordan attended the first WSPU meeting held in Caxton Hall in February 1906, and afterwards sent £20 towards expenses. She continues, "I went to see her afterwards, and she became one of our most loyal members and most generous subscribers." By February 1907 Clara Mordan had given at least £172 to the WSPU; in July 1907 she gave a further £10; in 1908–9 a total of £577; in April 1909 a further £100 to be towards the cost of the Prince's Rink Exhibition; £60 in October 1909, and a further £100 in December, specifically for the General Election Fund, a further £100 in March 1910, and £200 in June 1912 to support the renewal of militancy.

Clara Mordan was present at the banquet held at the Savoy by Mrs FAWCETT on 11 December 1906 to welcome the released WSPU prisoners. In 1908 she spoke at suffrage meetings in Bristol and Plymouth, doubtless at the behest of her favourite, Annie Kenney, who was by then WSPU organizer in the west country. In June 1908 Clara Mordan donated one of the commercially manufactured silk WSPU BANNERS unfurled with ceremony on 17 June, prior to their being carried in the Hyde Park Demonstration. Her banner, worked in gold on a green ground, bore the motto "Hope is Strong" and eagles bearing standards with the words "Awake", and "Arise"; unfortunately it does not appear to have survived. On 14 January 1909 Clara Mordan, at a ceremony held in the Queen's Hall, presented Emmeline PANKHURST, on her release from prison, with an amethyst, pearl and emerald necklace; it is very likely that she contributed generously towards its purchase. In January 1910 she spoke on "The Evolution of Women" at a meeting of the Crouch End WSPU in north London. On 16 November 1910 she sent a postcard to Mary CLARKE in Brighton saying that she was "no longer a 'worker' save a little with my pen. I have never been well since the Procession of July 23 [1910] when I played my part on Annie Kenney's platform". In the same week she gave £200 to the WSPU "war chest". She had developed the consumption from which she eventually died and was writing from the East Anglian Sanatorium at Nayland, near Colchester, founded and superintended by Dr Jane Walker, housed in a purpose-built Arts and Crafts building, and run by women for tubercular patients of both sexes. Millicent Garrett Fawcett had been active in its founding in 1899 and was chairman of the hospital for most of her life. Obviously a committed feminist, Clara Mordan published a letter in the 21 October 1910 edition of *Votes for Women* in which she wrote that "I have impressed upon my doctor that she really must keep me alive till I can have a reasonable prospect of feeling that my last bed will be a coffin some woman has earned her living by making."

In addition to her support for the WSPU Clara Mordan subscribed in 1910 to the NEW CONSTITUTIONAL SOCIETY FOR WOMEN'S SUFFRAGE, supported the TAX RESISTANCE LEAGUE, in 1911 was a member of the CHURCH LEAGUE FOR WOMEN'S SUFFRAGE and in 1913 supported the NATIONAL POLITICAL LEAGUE. In November 1912 she contributed towards the expenses of George LANSBURY when he stood as a suffrage candidate.

For 16 years Clara Mordan was honorary treasurer of the London branch of the Ladies' National Association for the Repeal of the Contagious Diseases Act. In 1895 she wrote a letter published in *Shafts* in the course of a correspondence on "missions to fallen women", commenting on the temerity of men referring to women as "fallen". She was a member of the executive committee of the SOCIETY FOR PROMOTING THE RETURN OF WOMEN AS POOR LAW GUARDIANS. She spoke at a meeting at the Pioneer Club in 1897 (*see under* CLUBS).

Clara Mordan was the first major benefactor of St Hugh's College, Oxford, which she first visited in 1897 after hearing Miss Rogers lecture in London on the subject of women's education. On the day after this first visit she sent the college £1000 with which to endow a scholarship, the only condition being that the scholar should not perform or witness any experiment or demonstration on a living animal. She was a co-opted member of the College Council in 1902 and a trustee in 1907. In her will, of which the principal and treasurer of St Hugh's were appointed among the executors, she left a legacy to the college which largely funded the first purpose-built collegiate building; the library in this building was named the "Mordan Library".

Address: (1895 and 1909) 28 Bedford Place, Bloomsbury, London WC; Stone House, Reigate; (1912) 131 Bedford Court Mansions, Bloomsbury, London WC; 18 Marine Mansions, Bexhill-on-Sea, Sussex.
Photograph: in E.Hill and O.F. Shaffer, *Great Suffragists – and Why*, 1909; in Fawcett Library Collection.
Bibliography: E. Hill and O.F. Shaffer, *Great Suffragists – and Why*, 1909; P. Griffin (ed.), *St Hugh's: One Hundred Years of Women's Education in Oxford*, 1986.

MORECAMBE (NUWSS) In 1913 the society was a member of the NORTH-WESTERN FEDERATION OF THE NATIONAL UNION OF WOMEN'S SUFFRAGE SOCIETIES. Secretary (1913) Miss Wolstenholme, Westbourne, Morecambe, Lancashire.

MORPETH (NUWSS) In 1913 the society was a member of the NORTH-EASTERN FEDERATION OF THE NATIONAL UNION OF WOMEN'S SUFFRAGE SOCIETIES. Secretary (1909) Miss Ayre, 1 Howard Terrace, Morpeth, Northumberland; (1913) Miss McDowell, East Collingwood, Morpeth, Northumberland.

MULLER, [FRANCES] HENRIETTA (*c.* 1851–1906) Born in Valparaiso, Chile. Her father William Muller was a German businessman and her mother was English. Henrietta Muller was the sister of Eva McLAREN, to whom in her will she left her entire estate; she also had at least two other sisters and one brother, William Burdon Muller. When she was nine years old, the family left Chile, sailing round Cape Horn to Boston and then to London, where she was privately educated for two years before the family went back to Chile. After another two years they returned, finally, to England. Henrietta Muller went to school in London and then, after some opposition from her father, read the Moral Science Tripos at Girton, 1873–6, where she was a contemporary of Hertha AYRTON and of the daughter of Louis BORCHARDT. Henrietta Muller was a good linguist, speaking French, Spanish, German, Italian and having a smattering of Latin and Greek.

The female side of the Muller family, whatever the views of the patriarch on the suitability of higher education for women, established a feminist tradition (*see* Appendix). In 1873 Mrs Muller gave 1/– subscription to the CENTRAL COMMITTEE FOR WOMEN'S SUFFRAGE, was a member of the managing committee of the Society for Promoting the Employment of Women from 1880 until at least 1902, in 1889 signed the Declaration in Favour of Women's Suffrage compiled by the Central Committee, in 1892 held a Peace Meeting at her home, in 1891 was the hostess of a conference of the Ladies' National Association for the Repeal of the Contagious Diseases Act (at which Eva McLaren took the chair), from 1889 was a member of the executive committee of the CENTRAL NATIONAL

SOCIETY FOR WOMEN'S SUFFRAGE and in 1906 was a vice-president of the CENTRAL SOCIETY. In the 1880s both Mrs Muller and Henrietta Muller were members of the Vigilance Association for the Defence of Personal Rights. While still at Girton, Henrietta Muller was involved in the founding of the Women's Printing Society (which later was the printer of and regular advertiser in the *Woman's Herald*) and was in touch with Emma PATERSON's effort to establish women's trade unions.

In July 1879 Priscilla MCLAREN wrote to Helen TAYLOR saying that she was glad that Miss Taylor was "taking up" Henrietta Muller, writing "she has great energy and that is a very important qualification – if her judgment be good and I can hear nothing to the contrary – I really have no right to interfere about candidates and do not wish to do so". In November 1879, presumably having benefited from Helen Taylor's advice, Henrietta Muller was elected, at the head of the poll, to the London School Board, on which she remained until 1885. She reckoned that her three elections cost her £12,000; luckily she had the means to finance such excursions into local government. Henrietta Muller was a member of the Central Committee of the National Society for Women's Suffrage in 1880 and spoke at the Grand Demonstration in favour of women's suffrage held at the Colston Hall, Bristol, on 4 November. On 27 February 1882, with Viscountess HARBERTON, Eliza STURGE, Miss Carbutt and Lydia BECKER, she spoke at the Sheffield Grand Demonstration. She was prepared to undertake lectures on the subject of women's enfranchisement at more intimate venues; in the course of 1884 she also spoke at local suffrage meetings in Beckenham and Halifax. She was a regular speaker for the suffrage cause at London Liberal and radical clubs; an account of one of these talks is given in the *Women's Penny Paper*, 22 November 1890. In January 1884 she was "a lady patroness" of a subscription ball in aid of funds for the Central Committee, of which society she was by now a member of the executive committee, and in the same year, as reported in an interview in the *Women's Herald*, she "resolved upon the novel and unusual resolution not to pay my taxes as a protest against being denied the right to vote". She barred her doors for a short time against the bailiffs, who eventually seized goods to cover the amount due and sold them at public auction, at which they were bought by Mr and Mrs J.P. THOMASSON. Henrietta Muller was being a little disingenuous in implying that such tax resistance in the suffrage cause was "novel and unusual"; Charlotte BABB, with whom she was acquainted, had been doing just that for the previous 13 years. However, Henrietta Muller was well satisfied with the publicity her action brought, saying in the *Woman's Herald* interview, "to my great surprise the Woman's Suffrage cause had a splendid boom in the papers". Although herself privately outspoken against marriage, she supported those protesting against Woodall's clause which would exclude married women from enfranchisement and in 1889 became a member of the executive committee of the Central National Society for Women's Suffrage. In 1892 she was a vice-president of the WOMEN'S PROGRESSIVE UNION. In 1900 she was a member of the Central Society for Women's Suffrage.

In 1888 Henrietta Muller had founded and as "Helena B. Temple" was editor of the *Women's Penny Paper*, "the only paper in the world conducted, written, printed and published by women". It began as an eight-page paper but soon increased its size. In 1889 Henrietta Muller agreed that a column of women's suffrage news should be inserted weekly by the Central National Society for Women's Suffrage, at a cost of £52 per annum. Despite Henrietta Muller's opposition to the Woodall clause, the *Women's Penny Paper* was deemed by Elizabeth Wolstenholme ELMY habitually to show hostility to the claims of married women. She thought that a report in the *WPP* about one of the meetings held by the WOMEN'S FRANCHISE LEAGUE was damaging to their cause and because of the perceived uselessness of the reporting returned a supply of copies of the *WPP* ordered by the committee of the WFL, offering to pay 10/– in consideration of any extra cost to which the proprietor had been put. Henrietta Muller replied by suing Elizabeth Wolstenholme Elmy for £2, the value of the papers supplied. Mrs Elmy eventually paid the £2 owing and wrote on 3 May 1890 to Harriet MCILQUHAM, "*Can* such women as this help forward the progress of others?" In 1891 the paper changed its name to the *Woman's Herald* and continued to be edited by

Henrietta Muller until 1891, when she went to India. It was then carried on by Eva McLaren, becoming from May 1892 until February 1893 the organ of the WOMEN'S LIBERAL FEDERATION, edited first by Mrs Frank Morrison and then by Christina Bremner. Eva McLaren's advocacy of temperance, as well as of Liberalism, had its effect on the character of the paper, which from February until December 1893 was edited by a leading temperance worker, Lady Henry Somerset. From the beginning of 1894 it was reborn as the *Woman's Signal*, eventually being owned and edited by Florence Fenwick MILLER. When the latter dismissed the original paper as Henrietta Muller's "little venture" Mrs Sibthorp leaped to the defence in *Shafts*, April 1898, writing "it was edited and superintended by a woman of unique force of character; it never aimed at anything short of the emancipation of women, socially, industrially, educationally, and politically, and therefore took no party side".

In 1882 Henrietta Muller was visited by Elizabeth Cady Stanton, who described her as "fearless, aggressive and self-centred", commenting that "she has a luxurious establishment of her own, is fully occupied in politics and reform, and though she lives by herself she entertains her friends generously, and does whatever it seems good to her to do", and remarking on her devoted friendship with Frances LORD. At a meeting held in her house, at which Elizabeth Cady Stanton was present, Henrietta Muller read a paper on the dignity and office of single women, which was probably that later published in the *Westminster Review*, January 1884, as "The Future of Single Women". On the eve of their departure for America in November 1883 Henrietta Muller gave a farewell reception, attended by all the radical feminist great and good, for Elizabeth Cady Stanton and Susan B. Anthony,

From 1885 until 1888 Henrietta Muller was a member of Karl Pearson's Men and Women's Club. Olive Schreiner described her to Pearson as "a plucky, fearless, brave, true little woman". In 1887 Henrietta Muller gave a course of four lectures, for women only, in the Westminster Town Hall. They were titled "Woman and the Bible", "The Dominion of Man", "Real Women" and "Ideal Women". She was also a member of the Moral Reform Union, the Personal Rights Association and, until resigning in 1888, a member of the executive committee and of a legal sub-committee of the National Vigilance Association. In 1885 she led employees of the Army Clothing Establishment in a demonstration in Hyde Park, demanding rigorous enforcement of the new age-of-consent legislation.

In 1891 Henrietta Muller became a member of the THEOSOPHICAL SOCIETY and left England to work in India with Annie Besant. In 1895 she adopted a young Bengali and resigned from the Theosophical Society. She later spent some time in China and America, where, in Washington, she died. She left two watercolours by John Varley to Girton.

Address: (1882) 86 Portland Place, London W; (1884) 58 Cadogan Place, London SW; (1901) Hyde Park Court, Albert Gate, London SW; Mrs Muller (1891) 86 Portland Place, London W.

Photograph: in the *Woman's Herald*, 28 November 1891; carte de visite in Josephine Butler Collection, Fawcett Library; of Mrs Muller in the *Woman's Herald*, 18 February 1893.

Archival sources: Elizabeth Wolstenholme Elmy Papers, British Library; Mill–Taylor Papers, London School of Economics and Political Science.

Bibliography: E.C. Stanton, *Eight Years or More (1815–1897): Reminiscences of Elizabeth Cady Stanton*, 1898; L. Bland, *Banishing the Beast: English Feminism and Sexual Morality 1885–1914*, 1995.

MUNRO, ANNA GILLIES MACDONALD (*c.* 1883/4–1962) (from 1913 Mrs Munro-Ashman) Born in Glasgow, the elder daughter of a schoolmaster, she worked for three years, through the non-conformist Sisterhood of the Poor Movement, among the sweated workers in the East End of London and in Edinburgh and Glasgow before she joined the WOMEN'S SOCIAL AND POLITICAL UNION in October 1906, becoming its organizer in Dunfermline. She followed Teresa BILLLINGTON-GREIG into the WOMEN'S FREEDOM LEAGUE, becoming her private secretary in late 1907. In January 1908 Anna Munro was arrested and imprisoned in Holloway for six weeks after taking part in a deputation to see Haldane. A month later she was appointed organizing secretary of the Scottish Council of the WFL. She addressed the women taking part in the Women's March organized by Florence DE FONBLANQUE in the autumn of 1912 both at the start in Edinburgh and at the finale in London, having walked the entire route. She married Sydney Ashman, a supporter of the MEN'S LEAGUE FOR WOMEN'S SUFFRAGE, in Wandsworth in April 1913. His sister was secretary of the Newbury and Thatcham WFL group and he had heard Anna Munro speak when she was travelling in the area in the WFL CARAVAN. She was a tall, elegant woman and an eloquent speaker. Anna Munro, who kept her maiden name for professional purposes so as not to jeopardize her husband's road haulage business, became the mother of a son and a daughter. Soon after her marriage she was, with Nina BOYLE, arrested and imprisoned for holding an illegal suffrage meeting in Hyde Park. In 1956 she gave a radio talk, titled "A Honeymoon in Prison", based on her experience at this time. After the First World War she became a magistrate in England and president of the Women's Freedom League, in which she remained active up until its disbanding in 1961. She remained throughout her life a Labour Party supporter, serving on local committees, and as both chairman and president of her local party.

Address: (1913) 28 Albert Palace Mansions, Lurline Gardens, Battersea, London SW; (1962) Venturefair, Padworth, near Reading, Berkshire.
Photograph: in the Suffragette Fellowship Collection, Museum of London.
Bibliography: L. Leneman, in *A Guid Cause: The Women's Suffrage Movement in Scotland*, 1991; E. King, *The Hidden History of Glasgow's Women: The Thenew Factor*, 1993.

MURDOCH, MARY CHARLOTTE (1864–1916) Born in Elgin, one of six children of a solicitor who died in 1871. She was educated in Elgin, at Manor Mount Girls' Collegiate School at Forest Hill in south London, and then at Lausanne. In 1883 she returned to Elgin, as the "daughter-at-home" but, after her mother's death, in 1888 she entered the London School of Medicine for Women. While studying in London she attended many women's suffrage meetings, as well as experiencing a range of ideas proferred by the Secular Society, the Theistic Church, by Stanton COIT at South Place, and the various branches of the Anglican Church. In 1893 she was appointed house-surgeon at the Victoria Hospital for Children in Hull and in 1895 she returned to London as assistant medical officer at the Tottenham Fever Hospital. After an illness she returned to Hull in 1896 and set up as a general practitioner, taking Louisa MARTINDALE (1872–1966) into partnership in 1900. On her return to Hull she was appointed honorary assistant physician to the Victoria Hospital for Children and in 1910 became honorary senior physician.

By 1904 she had founded and become president of the HULL WOMEN'S SUFFRAGE SOCIETY, which was affiliated to the NATIONAL UNION OF WOMEN'S SUFFRAGE SOCIETIES. She became a very active public speaker for the cause. In the autumn of 1909, when the NUWSS publicly disassociated itself from the militancy of the WOMEN'S SOCIAL AND POLITICAL UNION, Mary Murdoch resigned from the NUWSS, although retaining a close personal friendship with Millicent FAWCETT. She then joined the WSPU although she was not sympathetic towards its autocratic constitution and did not approve of the increasing militancy. In 1911, despite her change of society, she represented Mrs Fawcett at the meeting of the International Council of Women held in Stockholm and in 1913 once again stood proxy at the meeting of the standing committee of the ICW at the Hague and attended the Rome convention in 1914. Among her many other activities Mary Murdoch had founded in 1905 and become president of a Hull branch of the National Union of Women Workers, was elected a member of the executive committee of the NUWW in 1908 and became vice-president in 1910. She appointed Dr Louisa Martindale as one of her executors, bequeathing to her all her medical books and surgical equipment, and her dogcart and jewellery to her mother, Mrs Louisa Martindale.

Address: (1909) 102 Beverley Road, Hull, Yorkshire.
Bibliography: H. Malleson, *A Woman Doctor: Mary Murdoch of Hull*, 1919.

MURRAY, EUNICE GUTHRIE (1877–1960) Scottish, one of three daughters, all of whom were committed to the suffrage movement, of a Glasgow lawyer and his wife, who was herself a member of the WOMEN'S FREEDOM LEAGUE. Eunice Murray was educated at St Leonards School, St Andrews. She attended the Green, White and Gold Fayre organized by the Women's Freedom League in April 1909, became president of the Glasgow branch of the WFL, by 1913 was president of the WFL in Scotland, and was the author of suffrage pamphlets, including *The Illogical Sex, Prejudices Old and New* and *Liberal Cant*, which were published by the Scottish Council of the WFL. She attended the INTERNATIONAL WOMAN SUFFRAGE ALLIANCE conference at Budapest in 1913. After her return, on 17 November, she was arrested for obstruction after attempting to address a meeting near Downing Street. In 1917 she published a novel, *The Hidden Tragedy*, which centres on its heroine's involvement in the militant suffrage movement. In April 1918 Eunice Murray was "commemoration orator" at a ceremony organized by the GLASGOW AND WEST OF SCOTLAND ASSOCIATION FOR WOMEN'S SUFFRAGE in Kelvingrove Park, at which Louisa Lumsden planted a tree. Eunice Murray stood in the 1918 general election as an independent candidate at Glasgow (Bridgeton). She was unsuccessful but did have the distinction of being the first woman to stand in a parliamentary election in Scotland. She was the author of books on the history of costume and of *Scottish Women of Bygone Days*, 1930, and *A Gallery of Scottish Women*, 1935. In 1938 she chaired a Status of Women Conference in Glasgow, at which Helen FRASER was one of the speakers. In 1940 Eunice Murray was the executor of the will of Nina BOYLE.

Address: Moore Park, Cardross, Dumbarton.
Photograph: in E. King, *The Hidden History of Glasgow's Women: The Thenew Factor*, 1993
Bibliography: L. Leneman, *A Guid Cause: The Women's Suffrage Movement in Scotland*, 1991; E. King, *The Hidden History of Glasgow's Women: The Thenew Factor*, 1993.

MURRAY, FLORA, DR (*c.* 1870–1923) In November 1908, while assistant anaesthetist at the Chelsea Hospital for Women, she signed a letter, sponsored by the NATIONAL UNION OF WOMEN'S SUFFRAGE SOCIETIES, requesting Asquith to receive a deputation of medical women. In 1908 she joined the WOMEN'S SOCIAL AND POLITICAL UNION. In 1909 she stood surety for Marion Wallace-DUNLOP when she was released on bail after stencilling the walls of St Stephen's Hall. By 1909 she had organized a first-aid unit to treat women injured in the course of their militancy; this contingent was at work, ministering to the injured, on "Black Friday" in November 1910. Flora Murray was a member of the KENSINGTON WSPU and in January 1910, with Gertrude Eaton, held voice production and public-speaking classes for the Kensington committee of the CONSERVATIVE AND UNIONIST WOMEN'S FRANCHISE ASSOCIATION. On 23 July 1910, when she chaired one of the platforms at the Hyde Park Demonstration, Louisa Garrett ANDERSON, her devoted friend, was one of her speakers. In 1910 Flora Murray gave her support to the NEW CONSTITUTIONAL SOCIETY FOR WOMEN'S SUFFRAGE. She acted as doctor to the nursing home, where hunger-striking suffrage prisoners were treated when released on licence, which was run by Nurse PINE in Notting Hill Gate.

Flora Murray was in constant attendance on Mrs PANKHURST in the final years of suffrage militancy, visiting her, for instance, in May 1913 when she was recuperating from a hunger strike at Ethel SMYTH's house, the "Coign". In 1914 she collected evidence in an attempt to discover whether hunger-striking suffragettes, among them Grace ROE, had been drugged with bromides when in prison in order to make them more amenable to forcible feeding.

In 1912, with Louisa Garrett Anderson, Flora Murray founded a Women's Hospital for Children in the Harrow Road in Marylebone, and appointed Dr Mary MURDOCH honorary consulting physician. During the First World War, with Louisa Garrett Anderson, Flora Murray ran the Endell Street Military Hospital. She described her war work in *Women As Army Surgeons*, 1920. In 1919 she was chairman of a committee which approached former members of the WSPU with the aim of raising a monetary testimonial to Emmeline and Christabel PANKHURST. She appears to have been practising from Penn at the time of her death. By her will she left her entire estate to Louisa Garrett Anderson.

Address: (1912) 85 Campden Hill Court, London W; (1921) 60 Bedford Gardens, Campden Hill, London W; (1923) Paul End, Penn, Buckinghamshire.
Portrait: in oil by Francis Dodd, *An Operation at the Military Hospital, Endell Street*, 1920; in charcoal by Austin O. Spare, *Dr Flora Murray: Endell Street Hospital*, both in Imperial War Museum; another portrait by Francis Dodd was owned by Louisa Garrett Anderson, who left it in her will to her nephew.
Bibliography: F. Murray, *Women as Army Surgeons*, 1920.

MURRELL, CHRISTINE MARY, DR (1874–1933) Born in London, she qualified as a doctor in 1899 and in 1903 set up as a general practitioner with Dr Honor Bone. In 1906 she was a member of the South

Paddington branch of the NATIONAL UNION OF WOMEN'S SUFFRAGE SOCIETIES. By 1907 she was a member of the WOMEN'S SOCIAL AND POLITICAL UNION. In 1911 she was the marshal for the contingent of women doctors in the Coronation Procession organized by the WSPU. As militancy increased, although she took no part in it herself, she did care for released hunger strikers in her own home. During the First World War she was one of the doctors attached to Evelina HAVERFIELD's Women's Emergency Corps. After the partial enfranchisement of women in 1918 Christine Murrell joined the Women's Election Committee, working for the adoption of women parliamentary candidates. Shortly before her death she was elected as the first woman member of the General Medical Council. From 1922 she had been a close friend of Marie LAWSON and in 1929 became a director of the Sheridan Machinery Company. She had backed Marie Lawson by guaranteeing £4000 in order that she could buy the company from its previous owners. In her will she left to Marie Lawson £5000 and all the shares she owned in the Sheridan Machinery Company. She also left £2000 to the British Medical Association to start a loan fund, to be known as the Murrell Loan Fund, for men and women starting in general practice, and £1000 to the "John Rains Loan Fund" of the Medical Women's Federation, which she had initiated in memory of her grandfather who had given the money to enable her to set up in practice. The residue of her estate was left to her partner, Honor Bone.

Address: (1910) 86 Porchester Terrace, London W; (1932) 21 North Gate, Regents Park, London NW8; Four Winds, Frimley, Surrey.

Photograph: in C. St John, *Christine Murrell, M.D.: Her Life and Work*, 1935.

Bibliography: C. St John, *Christine Murrell, M.D.: Her Life and Work*, 1935.

MUSWELL HILL (branch of the LONDON SOCIETY FOR WOMEN'S SUFFRAGE, NUWSS)   Secretary (1913) Miss Agnes Wilkie, 59 Hillfield Park, Muswell Hill, London N.

MYERS, ELSA (1888–1926)   Trained as a school teacher, a member of the Industrial Women's Council, she had joined the WOMEN'S SOCIAL AND POLITICAL UNION by 1910 when she took part as a speaker in the 1910 Hyde Park Demonstration. She was also a member of the TAX RESISTANCE LEAGUE and the JEWISH LEAGUE FOR WOMEN'S SUFFRAGE and campaigned at many by-elections and took part in many political protest meetings, being present at Llanystudmdwy when other suffragettes were viciously attacked, but, being a teacher, felt unable to prejudice her chances of employment by going to prison. However, she felt her chance had come when in March 1913 her school was closed for a month. She broke a pane of glass at the War Office and was sentenced under the name of "Marjorie Manners" to one month's imprisonment. She went on hunger strike, was forcibly fed, was released on the morning that the school was reopened, and at 9 am was at school, her exploit unremarked. Her fiancé was killed during the First World War and Elsa Myers became headmistress of a London school. She qualified as a solicitor, but developed tuberculosis and died.

Address: (1913) 16 Mowbray Road, Brondesbury, London NW.

Archival source: The Suffragette Fellowship Collection, Museum of London.

Bibliography: M. Richardson, *Laugh a Defiance*, 1953.

N

NAIRN committee of the NATIONAL SOCIETY FOR WOMEN'S SUFFRAGE Was in existence in 1872 when its convenor was Provost Mackintosh. In 1913 the society was a member of the NORTH OF SCOTLAND FEDERATION OF THE NATIONAL UNION OF WOMEN'S SUFFRAGE SOCIETIES. Secretary (1909) Miss Janet Clunas, Cawdor Place, Nairn; (1913) Miss Laing, Holmwood, Nairn.

NATIONAL COUNCIL FOR ADULT SUFFRAGE Formed in September 1916 by a combination of dissidents from the NATIONAL UNION OF WOMEN'S SUFFRAGE SOCIETIES and the UNITED SUFFRAGISTS, together with Labour and Socialist leaders, to bring pressure to bear on the Speaker's conference that had been convened to discuss the suffrage question. Sylvia PANKHURST had been instrumental in its formation but left when it became apparent that its aims and methods were not likely to be as radical as she had hoped. Chairman: Henry NEVINSON; treasurer: Emmeline PETHICK-LAWRENCE; secretaries: Kathleen COURTNEY and James Middleton (of the ILP). Among the members of its executive committee were Catherine MARSHALL, George LANSBURY, Maude ROYDEN, Helena SWANWICK and Evelyn SHARP.

NATIONAL INDUSTRIAL AND PROFESSIONAL WOMEN'S SUFFRAGE SOCIETY Founded at the end of 1905 to accommodate those women who wished to resign from the NORTH OF ENGLAND SOCIETY FOR WOMEN'S SUFFRAGE along with Esther ROPER, Eva GORE-BOOTH and Christabel PANKHURST, but who did not wish to ally themselves directly with textile workers and trade unionists. Katherine THOMASSON, a radical Liberal, although reluctant to finance the LANCASHIRE AND CHESHIRE WOMEN TEXTILE AND OTHER WORKERS' REPRESENTATION COMMITTEE, immediately gave the National Industrial and Professional Women's Suffrage Society £210 and in 1913 was still a member of its executive committee. The National Industrial and Profesional Women's Suffrage Society, besides being a group in its own right, was also an umbrella society for the LCWTOWRC and the MANCHESTER AND SALFORD WOMEN'S TRADE AND LABOUR COUNCIL. It was "a society composed of women workers of all grades, and of others interested in the industrial aspect of the Suffrage question" (*Suffrage Annual and Women's Who's Who*, 1913). The society saw the franchise as the means of achieving industrial and economic rights for women and was particularly concerned with combating protective legislation which would have deprived such women as barmaids and workers at the pit brow of their livelihood. In October 1911 the society organized a public meeting in London, at the Memorial Hall, Farringdon Street (home of radical causes), to protest against the abolition of women's work at the pit brow and to demand the franchise. Walter McLaren (*see* Eva McLAREN), Sarah Dickenson, Sarah REDDISH and Esther Roper were among the speakers. The National Industrial and Professional Women's Suffrage Society was represented at the NUWSS celebrations on 13 March 1918 to mark the partial enfranchisement of women.

Secretary (1913) Esther Roper; treasurer (1913) Mrs Elizabeth Howarth, who had been a member of the executive committee of the NEWSS, but resigned with Esther Roper in 1905.

Address: (1913) 5 John Dalton Street, Manchester; 33 Fitzroy Square, London W1.
Bibliography: J. Liddington and J. Norris, *One Hand Tied Behind Us: The Rise of the Women's Suffrage Movement*, 1978.

NATIONAL POLITICAL LEAGUE For men and women, founded in 1911 by Mary Adelaide Broadhurst, who had been the WOMEN'S FREEDOM LEAGUE organizer in Liverpool. The NPL aimed to further social and political reforms on a non-party basis.

The extension of the suffrage to duly qualified women was considered the necessary precursor of any such reform. By 1913 the League intimated that it had begun collecting and classifying information on existing social and industrial conditions in order that future political activity, after enfranchisement, might be based on an asssured grasp of the subject. The League had also set up a publishing department, an intelligence bureau and a press agency. Vice-presidents of the League included Lady Aberconway (see Laura McLaren), Janie Allan, Lady Cowdray, Lady Wright and Ethel Snowden; George Lansbury, Henry Harben and John Scurr were supporters. An impassioned meeting attended by 1500 people held by the League at the Kingsway Hall on 19 March 1913 to protest against forcible feeding was reported verbatim by the police to the Home Office and received the laconic annotation, "Mr G.B. Shaw makes jokes – and Dr Mansell Moulin [sic] tells lies." The League held a meeting in the Queen's Hall on 8 July 1913 to protest against the "Cat and Mouse" Act and was of assistance to Maud Arncliffe Sennett and the Northern Men's Federation when the men from Scotland arrived in London later that month. During the First World War the NPL organized the National Land Council, setting up 11 centres at which women were trained to work on the land. By 1917, with the same London address, it was renamed the National Political Reform League.

National organization and north-western centre: founder and honorary president (1913) Miss Mary Adelaide Broadhurst; secretary (1913) Margaret Milne Farquharson; honorary treasurers (1913) Muriel, Countess de la Warr, W. Lyon Blease and Mrs F.C.B. Carpenter. North-eastern centre: chairman (1913) Mona Taylor; honorary treasurer (1913) Violet Taylor; organizer and secretary (1913) Laura Ainsworth.

Address: (1913, 1917) Lloyd's Bank Buildings, 14 St James's Street, London W; north-western centre (1913) 6 Prince's Road, Liverpool; north-eastern centre (1913) 51 Blackett Street, Newcastle, a short distance away from the WSPU shop.

Bibliography: *Suffrage Annual and Women's Who's Who*, 1913.

NATIONAL SOCIETY FOR WOMEN'S SUFFRAGE

Throughout the summer of 1867 Clementia Taylor, Helen Taylor and Lydia Becker were working their way towards establishing a partnership of the women's suffrage societies recently set up in London, Manchester, Edinburgh and Dublin, that would see them, in Mentia Taylor's words, "united yet independent" (see London National Society, Manchester National Society and Edinburgh National Society). On 6 November 1867 the societies combined, rather warily, as the National Society for Women's Suffrage. In 1868 societies at Birmingham and Bristol were founded, as branches of the National Society. In 1869 the National Society resolved to organize a petition from every borough in England, each to be presented to parliament by an MP for that borough.

The National Society published leaflets in 1868 giving instructions to women who possessed county qualifications about how they should register themselves as voters and held, in London at the Langham Hotel, a Women's Suffrage Conference, jointly organized by the committees of London, Edinburgh, Dublin, Manchester, Birmingham and Bristol, on 28 April 1871 in order to organize a memorial to Gladstone on the occasion of the Second Reading of the Electoral Disabilities Removal Bill, which was to be proposed by Jacob Bright on 3 May. The memorial was signed by 2000 women, including Florence Nightingale, Harriet Martineau, Augusta Webster and Frances Power Cobbe.

Despite these manifestations of concerted action the National Society suffered from the lack of an actual presence. It had no powers or officers and it was this lack that Jacob Bright intended to rectify by his proposal, made in November 1871, for the setting up in London of a Central Committee of the National Society for Women's Suffrage.

Bibliography: H. Blackburn, *Women's Suffrage: A Record of the Women's Suffrage Movement in the British Isles*, 1902.

NATIONAL UNION OF SOCIETIES FOR EQUAL CITIZENSHIP

The name given to the National Union of Women's Suffrage Societies after it had agreed at its annual general meeting in March 1919 to revise its constitution to allow other women's groups with similar aims to affiliate to it. Eleanor Rathbone succeeded Millicent Fawcett as president of the new body. Local suffrage societies either disbanded, a measure of enfranchisement having been achieved, or transformed themselves into local branches of NUSEC and carried on campaigning.

Although NUSEC lobbied for the franchise to be extended to all women, on the same terms as it was given to men, it also campaigned for other feminist causes, such as family allowances and the political education of women. The 1918 franchise act had given the vote to women over 30 who were qualified to vote at local elections; suitably qualified women over 21 were entitled to vote at local but not at parliamentary elections. Occupation of premises, as defined by the act, either by a woman over 30 or by her husband, was the qualification on which citizenship was based. Women qua women were in certain circumstances, even if so qualified, debarred from voting. The extension of the franchise was by no means an inevitability. NUSEC, relying on its history of close co-operation with the Labour Party, put its faith in the Labour government under Ramsay MacDonald and was bitterly disappointed when it saw repeated the obstructive strategies employed by the pre-war Liberal government. It was only in March 1927 that a prime minister (by now Stanley Baldwin) agreed to receive a deputation from NUSEC and other interested groups. A small but vociferous campaign by the Six Point Group, coupled with the more sedate lobbying of NUSEC and a recognition that the political process had not been shaken by allowing six million women to vote in the course of the previous ten years, eventually resulted in the passing of the People (Equal Franchise Bill) in March 1928. Address: (1923) 15 Dean's Yard, Westminster, London SW1; president (1923) Eleanor Rathbone; secretary (1923) Elizabeth Macadam; parliamentary secretary (1923) Eva Hubback.

Bibliography: C. Law, "The old faith living and the old power there: the movement to extend women's suffrage", in M. Joannou and J. Purvis (eds), *The Women's Suffrage Movement: New Feminist Perspectives*, 1998; C. Law, *Suffrage and Power: The Women's Movement, 1918–1928*, 1998.

NATIONAL UNION OF WOMEN'S SUFFRAGE SOCIETIES Formed as a result of a proposal at a special conference of all the suffrage societies held in Birmingham in October 1896. The idea of holding the conference had first been mooted in June; the proposal was to unite the collection of district societies which made women's suffrage their sole object on a non-party basis. The societies had worked successfully together, in the course of the previous year, on the SPECIAL APPEAL COMMITTEE and on a combined sub-committee of the societies which directly lobbied MPs to support the suffrage bill introduced by Mr Faithfull Begg. After a year in which the idea was tentatively put into practice under the title the "Combined Societies for Women's Suffrage", with the country divided between the main societies for the purpose of campaigning, the NUWSS was formally constituted on 14 October 1897. The scheme had been drawn up by Mona TAYLOR and resulted in the union of the CENTRAL NATIONAL SOCIETY, the CENTRAL COMMITTEE OF THE NATIONAL SOCIETY, the MANCHESTER NATIONAL SOCIETY, the Birmingham, Bristol, Leeds, Liverpool, Luton, Nottingham, Leicester, Mansfield, Southport, Birkenhead and Cambridge Women's Suffrage Societies, the WOMEN'S FRANCHISE LEAGUE, the PARLIAMENTARY COMMITTEE FOR WOMAN SUFFRAGE and the Edinburgh National Society, together with the Dublin and North of Ireland Women's Suffrage Societies. The Cheltenham and Halifax societies also soon joined. It was recognized that there was a need to present a common front from the centre, to concentrate the maximum pressure behind the annual presentation of the parliamentary bill. This was the policy that had been developed by Lydia BECKER when she was parliamentary agent of the Central Committee and, although it had not proved very successful, the NUWSS had no alternative strategy. Between 1897 and 1904 no women's suffrage bill was discussed in the House of Commons. The parliamentary committee comprised, from the Central and East of England Society: Lady Frances BALFOUR, Helen BLACKBURN and Millicent FAWCETT; from the Central and Western Society: Mrs Russell Cooke (*see* Maye DILKE), Eva McLAREN and Mrs Wynford Philipps; from the North of England Society: Hon. Mrs Arthur Lyttelton; Rev. S.A. STEINTHAL and Esther ROPER; from the Edinburgh National Society: Louisa STEVENSON and, at first, Elizabeth WIGHAM, and then, Jessie METHVEN; from the Bristol and West of England: Lilias Ashworth HALLETT and Agnes BEDDOE. The secretaries were Edith PALLISER, Esther Roper and Gertrude Stewart, the secretaries of the three main constituent societies. There was at this stage no president or honorary secretary representing the NUWSS *per se*.

While the executive committee concentrated, to little effect, on parliament, the local societies put their energies rather more successfully to building up local support. The "Local Associate Scheme" was begun in 1897, from an idea that was originated by its Kensington Association, by the Central and East of England Society in order to expand the suffrage association to all the parliamentary constituencies within their territory. The idea was that small societies should be seeded in each constituency, and would then liaise with the central society. "Associate members" were those who sympathized with the cause and were prepared to sign petitions and distribute tickets and handbills for meetings, but could not afford to become subscribing members. Although in October 1898 the CAMBRIDGE ASSOCIATION FOR WOMEN'S SUFFRAGE rejected the idea as "impractical at present", the scheme was sufficiently successful for the North of England and Central and Western societies to adopt it. In 1899 Sybil Dilke, daughter of the erstwhile Mrs Ashton Dilke, was the honorary secretary in the Paddington area of the Associate scheme, visiting in their own homes women who would not otherwise attend suffrage meetings. In the north Esther Roper and Eva GORE-BOOTH built up a network of local suffrage committees in the Lancashire textile towns.

On 16–17 October 1903 the National Convention for the Civic Rights of Women, held at the insistence of Elizabeth Wolstenholme ELMY, backed by W.T. Stead and sponsored by the NUWSS, took place in Holborn Town Hall. It was attended by 200 delegates, representing both the women's suffrage societies and such other women's organizations as the British Women's Temperance Association and the WOMEN'S LIBERAL FEDERATION. As a result of the convention the NUWSS was instructed to ask all Cabinet members and leaders of the opposition to receive deputations on women's suffrage, to write to all MPs on the subject and to raise a fund of £2000 a year for three years in order to undertake an active campaign. Elizabeth Wolstenholme Elmy, having consulted with Isabella FORD, was particularly keen on this method of attack, writing, "We want mass meetings in all the great towns of the U.K. – and as the local workers will seldom be rich enough personally to defray the costs, grants should be made towards the cost of these and of the many smaller meetings required to work them up." "The manifest incapacity of the NU to take charge of a great national campaign has driven us all to the conclusion that there must be, for its conduct, a special Committee, on which the NU should be represented but not predominant – with its own treasurer and secretary." Finally the NUWSS was instructed to form committees in every borough and county in order to press the question of women's suffrage, irrespective of party, upon every MP and candidate before the next general election and that local party associations should be pressured to select only candidates in favour of women's suffrage. As a result of its attempts to implement the convention's resolutions, the executive committee of the NUWSS began to be more active and less of a purely liaison committee. In the spring of 1905 the NUWSS held a meeting at the Queen's Hall in support of the bill promoted by the newly formed WOMEN'S SOCIAL AND POLITICAL UNION and due to be introduced on 12 May by Bamford Slack.

After the Liberal success in the January 1906 general election, the NUWSS organized on 19 May a deputation, comprising women from many organizations, to the new Prime Minister, Campbell-Bannerman; Emily DAVIES spoke on behalf of the NUWSS. After their dismissal, the realization that, despite a Liberal government and a supposedly sympathetic prime minister, the cause was no nearer achievement galvanized the NUWSS into greater activity. Henceforward it began to exert greater central control over policy and the activities of its member societies.

The arrest of Anne Cobden SANDERSON, an erstwhile member of the NUWSS, in October 1906 while protesting with the WSPU in the Lobby of the House of Commons, brought support from the NUWSS, who organized a banquet at the Savoy on 11 December to celebrate the release of the prisoners. Many NUWSS members gave donations to the WSPU on this occasion; the harmony between the two suffrage camps did not, however, continue as the NUWSS began to fear that increasing WSPU miltancy was positively harming the cause.

In January 1907 the NUWSS adopted a new constitution, strengthening its organizational structure. A council, meeting four times a year and comprising representatives from the local societies was formed to formulate policy; an executive committee of elected members was to be responsible to the committee for the implementation of the policy. As neither political party was prepared to sponsor a women's suffrage bill, it was thought necesssary to begin work on a private member's bill, which would have little hope of success, but would keep the issue alive. In order to demonstrate public support for women's suffrage the NUWSS organized the first large-scale demonstration. It took place, processing from Hyde Park Corner to Exeter Hall, in the Strand, on 9 February 1907 and has earned the sobriquet, "The Mud March", descriptive of the state of shoes and skirts at its end. Three thousand women, representing 40 groups, were led by Millicent Fawcett, Lady Frances Balfour and Lady Strachey (see STRACHEY FAMILY), whose daughter Philippa had been responsible for its organization. On 8 March, W.H. Dickenson, Liberal MP for St Pancras, introduced a Women's Enfranchisement Bill; it was talked out. Despairing of making progress through the conventional parliamentary channels, the NUWSS decided to concentrate on by-elections, their aim being to give support to any candidate, irrespective of party, in favour of women's suffrage. In May 1907 the NUWSS sponsored Bertrand Russell, son of Lady AMBERLEY, one of the earliest supporters of women's suffrage, as an unofficial Liberal candidate at the Wimbledon by-election. Between 1907 and 1909 the NUWSS campaigned in 31 by-elections and by 1909 employed ten ORGANIZERS. In February 1908 H.Y. Stanger, Liberal MP for North Kensington, introduced a women's suffrage bill, which passed its second reading before being blocked. This was the greatest progress that a suffrage bill had made since 1897. After Asquith replaced the dying Campbell-Bannerman in April, a deputation from the NUWSS to Winston Churchill, now president of the Board of Trade, came away believing that he was prepared to influence the cabinet in their favour. On 13 June 1908 the NUWSS organized a large procession in London and local societies held similar gatherings throughout the country. The first issue of the NUWSS's paper the *Common Cause*, edited by Helena Swanwick, appeared on 15 April 1909 and enabled the local societies to keep in touch weekly with both the activities of the executive committee and with each other. The general elections of 1910 kept the suffrage issue to the fore, the NUWSS working to secure the return of MPs in favour of women's suffrage. Voters' petitions, totalling 280 000 signatures, were collected during the January election in over 290 constituencies and presented to the House of Commons in March.

In January 1910 H.N. BRAILSFORD approached the NUWSS with the idea of forming an all-party Conciliation Committee to draft a women's suffrage bill and guide it through parliament. This committee, comprising 36 MPs, was chaired by Lord Lytton with Brailsford as secretary, and formulated a bill based on the municipal franchise. Once more optimistic, the NUWSS rallied its forces to show support for the new bill; the WSPU had suspended its hostilities. The NUWSS and the Women's Liberal Federation, represented respectively by Mrs Fawcett and Lady McLaren, were received in deputation by Asquith, the first such he had seen since he had become prime minister. His response to their representations was, as usual, guarded. On 12 July the bill passed its second reading but was sent to a committee of the Whole House, rather than to a Grand Committee, with the result that it was unlikely that the government would find time to consider it. On 23 July the NUWSS and the WSPU co-operated in staging another grand rally in London, known as the "From Prison to Citizenship" procession, to demonstrate a united front, despite continuing back-room squabbles. At the beginning of the new parliamentary session in mid-November it became clear that the government was not prepared to give time for the bill. The WSPU broke its truce on "Black Friday", 18 November, and clashed with police in Parliament Square. The NUWSS and the Conciliation Committee placed their faith in Asquith's vague promise to give facilities to a woman's suffrage bill sometime in the new parliament. In the December general election the NUWSS sponsored three women's suffrage candidates. One of these, Brailsford, withdrew before the election after the Liberal Party had withdrawn its first choice and substituted a suffragist; the other two were ignominiously defeated.

E.M. Gardner's caravan in Yorkshire with NUWSS banner. Taken from The Fawcett Library and reproduced by kind permission of the Mary Evans Picture Library.

Although the NUWSS was little nearer its goal, the publicity given to the suffrage cause had increased its membership from 13 429 in 1909 to 21 571 in 1910; the number of its societies from 130 to 207, and its income from £3385 to £5503. In addition the aggregated income of the affiliated societies had amounted to £14 000 by 1910. This growth led to a restructuring of the Union in 1910. Regions of the country were allotted to federations, each comprising the local affiliated societies. Each federation was headed by a committee consisting of one representative from each society, together with a representative from the NUWSS executive. By 1911 the NUWSS comprised 16 federations and 26 000 members. Delegates from the federations met twice a year at the provincial councils of the NUWSS, in order that the executive committee might be kept fully informed of opinion in the country. Both the NUWSS executive and the federations employed organizers.

The NUWSS continued in 1911 to campaign throughout the country, in drawing rooms, garden parties, and at public meetings, and to lobby in parliament for the Conciliation Bill, which passed its first reading in February and its second, by a large majority, in May. The NUWSS then continued lobbying the government to give time for the bill, which was refused, Lloyd George announcing that the cabinet would give a week in the next session of parliament, after another second reading. After clarification was given by Sir Edward Grey, the NUWSS was reasonably optimistic, despite past experience, that the government would hold to its word. The WSPU again suspended its hostilities and the two major suffrage groups united in staging the Coronation Procession on 17 June. Once the new parliamentary session opened, hopes for the Conciliation Bill were dashed by the government's proposal to introduce its own reform bill. The proposal was that this might, once passed, be amended to include wider categories of women, including "working men's wives", than the Conciliation Bill would enfranchise. The NUWSS, unlike the WSPU, whose renewed militancy an NUWSS manifesto denounced, was by no means unenthusiastic and prepared to map out strategy, while keeping the Conciliation Bill in reserve. However, the Conciliation Bill was defeated on its second reading on 28 March 1912, the result, it was felt by the NUWSS, of WSPU militancy, although, as usual, other factors such as the voting tactics of the Irish MPs and the absence of many Labour Party members, who were dealing with a coal miners' strike, played their part. With the defeat of the bill, the Conciliation Committee dissolved, and the NUWSS's links with the Liberal Party were severely weakened, although they continued in the course of the next year to lobby Liberal MPs in the hope of rebuilding support in the House of Commons.

However, within a month of the defeat of the Conciliation Bill the NUWSS, having remarked that at its annual party conference in January the Labour Party had passed a resolution committing itself to supporting women's suffrage, and that those Labour MPs who were present in the House on 28 March had all voted for the bill, began to look for an alliance with the Labour Party. H.N. Brailsford made the initial approach on behalf of the NUWSS and by the end of April Kathleen COURTNEY was involved in formal negotiations with the secretary of the Labour Party. The NUWSS planned to finance an Election Fighting Fund, in order to support Labour candidates at by-elections and thereby subject the Liberal Party to greater opposition than that afforded by the usual one Conservative candidate. It was hoped that between £10 000 and £20 000 could be raised for the purpose. The adoption of the EFF policy proved unacceptable to some members of the NUWSS; both Emily Davies, a Conservative, and Margery Corbett ASHBY, a Liberal, felt constrained to resign. However, many of the leaders of the local suffrage societies, such as Catherine OSLER in Birmingham, who had been life-long Liberals, resigned from their Women's Liberal Associations in protest against the government's attitude to the suffrage question and this eased to some extent the difficulty of henceforward backing Labour Party candidates. It was, however, agreed that Liberal Party candidates who had consistently supported women's enfranchisement would not be opposed. By this strategy it was also hoped that pressure would be put on the Liberal Party to deselect anti-suffragist candidates. A special council of the NUWSS ratified the EFF policy at a meeting held on 14 May 1912. The EFF Committee, which administered the Fund, was responsible to the executive committee of the NUWSS; pro-Liberal members were worried that the Labour Party might control the Fund and, hence, NUWSS policy. The first EFF Committee comprised Mrs Anstruther, Margaret ASHTON, Mrs Auerbach, Ruth Cavendish-BENTINCK, Mrs Stanton COIT, H.N. Brailsford, Kathleen Courtney, Lady DE LA WARR, Mrs Fawcett, Isabella Ford, Mrs Homan, Laurence HOUSMAN, Margory LEES, Lord Lytton, Catherine MARSHALL (who was its secretary), Lady Meyer, Edith Palliser, Julia Reckitt, Ethel SNOWDEN, Mrs Stanbury and Mr G.E.S. Streatfield. Not all were members of the NUWSS. Margaret Robertson was the EFF's national organizer and the federations increasingly employed local organizers, such as Annot ROBINSON, Ada Nield CHEW and Selina COOPER, who were Labour Party supporters. The FRIENDS OF WOMEN'S SUFFRAGE scheme was also inaugurated on 14 May.

The NUWSS employed its EFF policy, with some success, at by-elections at Holmfirth, Crewe and Midlothian, but with no success at Hanley. By July 1912 the decision was taken to establish local EFF committees within each federation and commitment made to develop local Labour Party electoral organization in the seats of Labour MPs and in those of leading Liberal anti-suffragists. There were distinct differences between the federations in level of support for the EFF policy; the North-East, for example, supported it and South Wales was against it. As by-election results proved the effectiveness of the policy, the Labour Party, both nationally and at a local level, began to work in even closer co-operation with the NUWSS. Fenner Brockway, later a Labour MP, relates in his autobiography, *Inside the Left*, 1942, how as a young man, greatly impressed by NUWSS organization of the events, he spoke with Mrs Fawcett and Margaret Robertson at meetings in the Usher Hall in Edinburgh and the Albert Hall in London. In the spring of 1912 the NUWSS, in an attempt to neutralize the Irish Nationalist vote in the House of Commons, also lobbied, with scant success, for an amendment to the Irish Home Rule Bill, by which women on the municipal register in Ireland would be enfranchised.

At the same time the NUWSS was involved in complicated lobbying in order to ensure the best possible outcome from the four proposed women's suffrage amendments to the Franchise and Registration Bill. All came to nothing in January 1913 after the Speaker ruled the women's suffrage amendments out of order, strengthening NUWSS disillusionment with the Liberal Party and consequent support for Labour. Since no further measure of women's suffrage was likely to make serious progress in parliament before the next general election, due at the latest in 1915, the NUWSS turned its attention to building up its campaign in the country. By 1913 it had over 400 societies in 19 federations; in 1914 the number of societies had grown to 600. By 1914 the NUWSS, including the EFF, was spending over £45 000. Organizers in all the federations worked steadily at collecting resolutions from local trade union branches in favour of women's suffrage. In the summer of 1913 NUWSS members, whether supporters of the EFF policy or intransigent Liberals, were able to demonstrate their support for the cause by taking part in the NUWSS PILGRIMAGE. Marchers carried placards claiming that they were "Non-Party", as well as "Constitutionalist". The government appeared to have been impressed by the event; Asquith agreed to receive a deputation of pilgrims.

Later that summer, as part of this campaign of political education the NUWSS organized Suffrage Summer Schools at Oxford and St Andrews. The Midlands Federation had run such a school (it had even made a profit) at Malvern the previous year. The Oxford school was held between 11 and 25 August at St Hugh's (board, two sessions, lodgings and lectures 35s a week). Emily MANNERS of the Mansfield Women's Suffrage Society was one of those who attended the Oxford school. The St Andrews schools, held at University Hall in both 1913 and 1914, were organized by the Scottish Federation. The Glasgow and West of Scotland Association for Women's Suffrage agreed to send their secretary to the St Andrews school in 1913. In 1914 the St Andrews Summer School ran from 11 August to 8 September. To this the Glasgow Association sent their trainee secretary/office girl, although it was minuted that her salary would not be paid while she was there. In addition, in 1913 the NUWSS ran a smaller summer school at Tal-y-Bont in the Conwy Valley to help train women in public speaking. In July 1914, Violetta Thurstan, organizer to the West of England Federation, ran a Suffrage Camp at Upwey near Weymouth. The idea was to mix working-class and middle-class suffragists, setting up reading groups to discuss social policy. Among those attending were Katherine HARLEY and Alice CLARK, with, for a short time, her mother Helen Bright CLARK and her aunt Dr Annie Clark. A photograph of the camp was reproduced as a postcard. As part of the continuing education process another suffrage summer school, organized by Dora MASON, was held at St Andrews in 1915. Among the speakers attending were Katherine Harley, Muriel MATTERS, Mary Sheepshanks and Chrystal MACMILLAN.

The NUWSS, working in conjunction with the CONSERVATIVE AND UNIONIST WOMEN'S FRANCHISE ASSOCIATION, did manage to engineer a debate, and attendant publicity, on women's enfranchisement in the House of Lords in April 1914. On the evening of 4 August, a few hours before Britain was at war, the NUWSS, apparently believing that Sir Edward Grey was endeavouring to maintain British neutrality, took part in a meeting at the Kingsway Hall with, among other bodies, the Women's Labour League and the Women's Co-operative Guild, calling on governments to work for a settlement by reason not force, and, in the event of war, encouraging the women's societies to make use of their organizations to alleviate the ensuing economic and industrial distress. After 4 August the NUWSS suspended political activity and concentrated its organizing capacity on relief work, the hospital units sent to the fighting fronts being its most ambitious achievement. The war caused a split in the executive committee of the NUWSS when all officers, except the president and treasurer and ten members of the executive committee, resigned in April 1915 over the decision not to support the Women's Peace Congress at the Hague.

The coalition government formed in 1915, which included more suffragists than had the Liberal government, appointed an Electoral Reform Conference in October 1916. A consultative committee of constitutional women's suffrage societies, representing 20 different organizations, which was at work under the chairmanship of Eleanor RATHBONE, was not allowed to give evidence to the conference. However, Asquith's removal as prime minister in December 1916 and his replacement by Lloyd George, who although by no means a reliable friend of women's suffrage at least was not entirely unsympathetic, facilitated the inclusion of women in a new Representation of the People Act. The question of women's suffrage, which had, tortuously, over 50 years come to be recognized as a serious political issue was partially resolved by the 1918 Representation of the People Act, which enfranchised women over the age of 30. On 13 March the NUWSS victory celebration, to which representatives of many other suffrage societies were invited, was held at the Queen's Hall, which was decorated for the party by the ARTISTS' SUFFRAGE LEAGUE. The musical accompaniment to the celebrations included, very suitably, Beethoven's "Fidelio" overture and stanzas from William Blake's *Prophetic Books* which had, in 1916, been set to music as *Jerusalem*, by Hubert Parry. This rousing chorus was conducted on the night by the composer, who had long been a close friend of Agnes Garrett and Millicent Fawcett. In her letter to thank him, on 15 March, Mrs Fawcett wrote, "Your 'Jerusalem' ought to be made the Women Voters' Hymn", which, of course, in a way it was, being adopted by the Women's Institute movement. The speakers in the Queen's Hall were Mrs Fawcett, the Earl of Lytton, Sir John Simon, Arthur Henderson and Maude ROYDEN. In April 1919 the NUWSS changed its name to the NATIONAL UNION OF SOCIETIES FOR EQUAL CITIZENSHIP and allowed all societies which had the equality of men and women as their objects to affiliate.

President: Millicent Garrett Fawcett. Secretary (parliamentary) (1909–10) Bertha Mason; (1911–January 1913) Edith Palliser; (1913–15) Catherine Marshall; (1916–18) Ray Strachey. Joint secretaries (1897–1906) Edith Palliser, Gertrude Stewart and Esther Roper. Joint honorary secretaries (1903–9) Frances Sterling and (?–1909) Frances Hardcastle; and (1909–11) Edith Dimock; honorary secretary (1911, 1915) Kathleen Courtney; (1916) Miss E.M. Atkinson. Honorary treasurer (1913, 1916) Mrs Auerbach.

Address: The NUWSS did not have an office in London separate from the Central/London Society until 1911. It gave equal billing to the addresses of its three regional centres, London, Manchester and Bristol. (1898, 1900) 20 Great College Street, London SW and 39 Victoria Street, London SW; (1900–1903) 28 Millbank, London SW (office of the Central Society); (1903–10) 25 Victoria Street (office of the Central Society and then of the London Society); (1910) 58 Victoria Street, London SW (office of London Society); (1911–17) Parliament Chambers, 14 Great Smith Street, London SW; (1918) 62 Oxford Street, London W.

Archival source: NUWSS annual report 1897–1918 (incomplete); NUWSS executive minutes 1897–1918 (incomplete); Election Fighting Fund Committee Minutes June–December 1912; NUWSS quarterly council reports 1907–9 (incomplete), Fawcett Library.

Bibliography: M.G. Fawcett, *The Women's Victory – and After: Personal Reminiscences, 1911–1918*, 1920; C. Rover, *Women's Suffrage and Party Politics, 1866–1914*, 1967; L.P. Hume, *The National Union of Women's Suffrage Societies, 1897–1914*, 1982; S.S. Holton, *Feminism and Democracy: Women's Suffrage and Reform Politics in Britain, 1900–1918*, 1986; J. Vellacott, *From Liberal to Labour with Women's Suffrage: The Story of Catherine Marshall*, 1993.

NAYLOR, MARIE ISABEL (c. 1866–1940)   An artist, she studied at the Royal Academy and afterwards in Paris, where in 1898 she had a one-woman exhibition at the Galerie Dosbourg, 27 rue le Peletier. She later exhibited at the Royal Academy in London. She had been a member of the NATIONAL UNION OF WOMEN'S SUFFRAGE SOCIETIES, subscribing to the CENTRAL/LONDON SOCIETY FOR WOMEN'S SUFFRAGE in 1906–7, "but longed for some fresher spirits to step out and take bolder and more effective action". At a meeting in the Suffolk Street Galleries she met the leaders of the WOMEN'S SOCIAL AND POLITICAL UNION and as recorded in a short biography in *Votes for Women*, 18 June 1908, she felt that she "could follow these women to prison or to death". She was a speaker for the WSPU by 1907 when she took part in the demonstrations surrounding the first Women's Parliament; the case against her was dismissed. She was arrested in February 1908 after taking part in the "pantechnicon raid" and sentenced to six weeks' imprisonment in Holloway. In June 1908 Marie Naylor was chairman of one of the platforms at the Hyde Park Demonstration. She undertook several speaking tours in the west country, staying with the Blathwayts at Eagle House, Batheaston, in January 1909. Mrs BLATHWAYT wrote of Marie Naylor in her diary that she was "One of their best London speakers". In November 1911 she broke a pane of glass in a Home Office window, saying at her trial that it was the only act of wilful damage that she had ever committed, and was sentenced to ten days' imprisonment. Marie Naylor was one of the pallbearers at Mrs PANKHURST's funeral. She was killed in an air raid during the Second World War.

Photograph: *Votes for Women*, 7 May 1908; in B.M. Willmott Dobbie, *A Nest of Suffragettes in Somerset*, 1979.

NEAL, MARY CLARA SOPHIA (1860–1944) CBE Educated at the Ladies' College, Birmingham. She studied economics and lectured at Labour Churches; at the Nottingham Labour Church her subject was Maeterlinck's "Treasure of the Humble". By 1890 she had left her family home in Bournemouth to become "Sister Mary", a member of the West London Sisterhood, responsible for the Mission's Working Girls' Club. Emmeline Pethick (*see* Emmeline PETHICK-LAWRENCE), who worked with her, described her as having "a strong sense of humour and a profound aversion from unreality; she had also a sharp tongue". She espoused the socialism of Keir HARDIE and Edward Carpenter and was adept at dealing with the young factory girls who attended the Club. In 1895, with Emmeline Pethick, Mary Neal left the Mission in order that they might carry on their social missionary work free from what they had come to perceive as the restrictions of its Methodist ethos and without the restrictions of institutional living. They shared a flat in a block designated for working men, "to get out of the plush sofa ideal", and opened in Wigmore Street a dress-making firm, Maison Espérance, in order to give steady, controlled employment, paying a minimum wage double that which they might otherwise command, to the girls among whom they were working. With Lily Montagu, doyenne of a Jewish working girls' club, they bought a large house in Littlehampton and, naming it "The Green Lady Hostel", opened a country holiday home in which girls could spend their annual holiday. In 1899 Mary Neal attended the London International Congress of Women. In 1901, after Emmeline Pethick's marriage, Mary Neal joined Cecil Sharp (see Evelyn SHARP) in the work of reviving English Folk Dance. The Folk Songs and Dances that he published were soon taught to the girls of the Espérance Club, who themselves then taught them to elementary schoolteachers. Morris dancing was eventually incorporated into the school curriculum. In 1910 Mary Neal published *The Espérance Morris Book*, which includes detailed description of 12 Morris dances and a selection of folk songs, and later gave a course of lectures on English folk dancing in the United States. She was a regular contributor at this time to the *Observer*, and wrote also for *The Times* and the *Pall Mall Gazette*. Between 1910 and early 1912 she carried her folk dance mission to the United States.

In February 1906 Mary Neal accompanied Emmeline Pethick-Lawrence to the meeting at Sylvia PANKHURST's lodgings in Park Walk, Chelsea, at which the London committee of the WOMEN'S SOCIAL AND POLITICAL UNION, of which she was subsequently a member, was formed. She was also a member of the national committee of the WSPU as it was reconstituted in 1907 after the WOMEN'S FREEDOM LEAGUE had broken away. This, however, meant nothing more than that she had her name on the WSPU notepaper; the committee seldom met. On 19 September 1908 Mary Neal wrote from the West London Social Guild to Minnie BALDOCK telling her that she wanted to start a WSPU branch at the Espérance Club and asking if she would come and talk to the club members. Mary Neal did some speaking for the WSPU cause (in 1908, for instance, she did so in Bristol) but never took part in any militant action. After the WSPU break with the Pethick-Lawrences she acted as a "special commissioner" for their paper *Votes for Women*. In this capacity she went to Dublin in 1913, during the Lock-Out, and brought back five children to be cared for by the Pethick-Lawrences. Mary Neal was more successful than Dora MONTEFIORE in circumventing the wrath of the Catholic church and the children spent three happy months in Surrey. Mary Neal joined the UNITED SUFFRAGISTS; *Votes for Women*, 21 May 1915, records that she made "one of her witty and racy speeches" at a meeting of that society. With the Espérance Club she raised funds for the US. She was also a member of the TAX RESISTANCE LEAGUE.

In 1934 Mary Neal was a justice of peace in West Sussex, specializing in child delinquency, and was a member of the Howard League for Penal Reform. Her will was witnessed in 1940 by May Pethick, sister to Emmeline Pethick-Lawrence.

Address: (1903) 20 Somerset Terrace, Duke's Road, London WC; (1915) 50 Cumberland Market, London NW (the address of the Espérance Club); (1934) Green Bushes, 31

St Flora's Road, Littlehampton, Sussex; (1944) The Retreat, Rad Lane, Peaslake, Surrey.
Bibliography: R. Hyde, "Mary Neal and her work", *T.P.'s Weekly*, 17 May 1912; E. Pethick-Lawrence, *My Part in a Changing World*, 1938.

NEILANS, ALISON ROBERTA NOBLE (1884–1942) Born in Camberwell, became an ORGANIZER for the WOMEN'S FREEDOM LEAGUE and by 1910 was a member of its executive committee. In 1908 she served two terms of imprisonment, sentenced on 30 January to one month and on 7 December to another. She achieved some noteriety when, at the Bermondsey by-election in 1909, she poured a liquid into the ballot boxes, for which she received a sentence of three months' imprisonment. She went on hunger strike in Holloway and was forcibly fed twice a day. In 1913 she organized the WFL summer campaign on the west coast of Scotland. In 1911 she was also a member of the CHURCH LEAGUE FOR WOMEN'S SUFFRAGE and in 1915 worked with Sylvia PANKHURST in the EAST LONDON FEDERATION OF THE SUFFRAGETTES. Alison Neilans was secretary of the Association for Moral and Social Hygiene from 1917 for many years and was editor of its journal, the successor to the *Shield*, the *British Review of Moral and Social Hygiene*. In 1934 she was a member of the executive council of the Open Door Council. From 1929 until 1935 she was a member of the board of the INTERNATIONAL WOMAN SUFFRAGE ALLIANCE. She contributed the section on "Changes in Sex Morality" to *Our Freedom and Its Results*, edited by Ray Strachey in 1936.
Portrait and photograph: both in Josephine Butler Collection, Fawcett Library.

NELIGAN, DORINDA (1833–1914) Born in Cork, educated at the Sorbonne, served with the British Red Cross during the Franco-Prussian war, headmistress of Croydon High School from 1874 to 1901, from 1893 a vice-president of the Association of Headmistresses. She was a supporter of the WOMEN'S EMANCIPATION UNION in 1894, subscribed to the CENTRAL SOCIETY FOR WOMEN'S SUFFRAGE in 1900 and to the WOMEN'S SOCIAL AND POLITICAL UNION in 1909. She was also at one time a member of the WOMEN'S FREEDOM LEAGUE and of the CHURCH LEAGUE FOR WOMEN'S SUFFRAGE and was a patroness of the ACTRESSES' FRANCHISE LEAGUE. Her sister was a member of the Committee of the Croydon branch of the NATIONAL UNION OF WOMEN'S SUFFRAGE SOCIETIES. Dorinda Neligan was arrested on 29 June 1909, having taken part in the WSPU deputation with Mrs PANKHURST and Mrs Saul SOLOMON and six other women, from Caxton Hall to present a petition to Asquith, but the case against her was dropped. On "Black Friday", 18 November 1910, she was one of the leaders, with Mrs Pankhurst and Elizabeth Garrett ANDERSON, of the deputation to the House of Commons. She also supported the TAX RESISTANCE LEAGUE and her distrained goods were sold in April 1912.
Address: (1913) Oakwood House, Croydon, Surrey.

NELSON Women's Suffrage Society Formed by Selina COOPER in 1906 and affiliated to the NATIONAL UNION OF WOMEN'S SUFFRAGE SOCIETIES. In 1909 it was renamed the CLITHEROE Society when societies were realigned on constituency lines.

NEVINSON, HENRY WOOD (1856–1941) Radical journalist, born in Leicester, educated at Christ Church, Oxford. In 1884 he married Margaret Jones (*see* Margaret Wynne NEVINSON) although he only refers to her once, tangentially, in *Fire of Life*, the distillation of his three autobiographies and even then does not claim her as his wife. In 1889 he joined the Social Democratic Federation and was persuaded by Samuel Barnett to join Toynbee Hall. From 1897 Nevinson was a prolific war correspondent and during intervals back in England was a wholehearted supporter of the militant suffrage movement, as he was of many other radical causes. He made his first women's suffrage speech on 27 February 1907 on the occasion of a breakfast to celebrate the release from prison of women arrested after taking part in a WOMEN'S SOCIAL AND POLITICAL UNION deputation to the House of Commons. His wife had taken part in this deputation, although he chose not to record that fact. Charmed and intrigued by Christabel PANKHURST, he particularly noted that she sat beside him on this occasion. Although in September 1907 his wife left to join the WOMEN'S FREEDOM LEAGUE, Nevinson continued to support the WSPU with money, spoke at its meetings (although he commented that he was too cool and restrained to be a moving speaker) and carried banners in its processions. He attended the meeting held by Lloyd George for members of the WOMEN'S LIBERAL FEDERATION in the Albert Hall on 5 December 1908 and, appalled by the treatment of WSPU hecklers, joined in the melée until evicted from the hall. As a result his editor suspended him from his position on the *Daily News*. H.N. BRAILSFORD threatened to resign in sympathy. In September 1909 they did indeed both resign from the paper over its refusal to condemn the government's decision to feed suffragette prisoners by force. On 4 October Mrs PANKHURST wrote to Nevinson to express her regret that he had been forced so to act, fully appreciating the material loss he would suffer. Indeed Nevinson recorded in his autobiography that he and Brailsford had never "obtained regular work on any daily paper since".

Nevinson was at first a member of the committee of the MEN'S LEAGUE FOR WOMEN'S SUFFRAGE but increasingly thought it insufficiently radical and left in 1910 to become a founding member of the MEN'S POLITICAL UNION FOR WOMEN'S ENFRANCHISEMENT. On 17 June 1911 he rode "on a wise and beautiful mare" in the women's suffrage Coronation Procession, standard bearer for the MPU. The next month he introduced to Christabel Pankhurst Yoshio Markino, a Japanese writer and artist, who included delineations of her, in both word and pen, in his delightful *My Idea26led John Bullesses*, 1912. Nevinson sat through the PETHICK-LAWRENCES' trial in 1912 but was in Bulgaria when he learned in October of the split between them and the Pankhursts. He thought the news "fatal" and throughout 1913 felt that the WSPU cause was weakening, that relations between headquarters and loyal supporters had become increasingly strained and eventually hostile. Hindsight tells us that his interpretation was correct and that his exclusion derived from Christabel Pankhurst's growing conviction that the militant suffrage movement should rely only on women. On 29 July 1913 he attended the costume dinner given by the WOMEN WRITERS' SUFFRAGE LEAGUE and the ACTRESSES' FRANCHISE LEAGUE in the guise of Garibaldi, the hero of so many of his fellow diners. Nevinson sympathized with Sylvia PANKHURST'S East End campaign and in July 1914 wrote for her paper, the *Women's Dreadnought*. In his autobiography he recorded that it was with reluctance that erstwhile members of the WSPU in 1914 formed the UNITED SUFFRAGISTS.

Nevinson's close companion throughout these years was Evelyn SHARP, who later became his wife and whom he lauded for her work for the United Suffragists throughout the years of the First World War. In 1916 Nevinson was appointed chairman of the NATIONAL COUNCIL FOR ADULT SUFFRAGE and in 1917 reluctantly acquiesced to the suggestion that there should be an age restriction placed on women's enfranchisement. With Evelyn Sharp, he was in the House of Commons on 6 February 1918 and at 8.45 that evening was relieved to learn that the Franchise bill had been given the Royal Assent. Nevinson's pamphlets in support of the women's suffrage cause include *Women's Vote and Men*, Woman's Press, reprinted from the *English Review*, October 1909.

Address: (1903, 1941) 4 Downside Crescent, London NW.
Portrait: by Sir William Rothenstein, 1918, reproduced in *Fire of Life*, 1935.
Archival source: H.W. Nevinson Papers, Bodleian Library, Oxford.
Bibliography: E. Sharp, *Unfinished Adventure: Selected Reminiscences from an Englishwoman's Life*, 1933; H.W. Nevinson, *Fire of Life*, 1935; A.V. John and C. Eustance (eds), *The Men's Share?: Masculinities, Male Support and Women's Suffrage in Britain, 1890–1920*, 1997.

NEVINSON, MARGARET WYNNE (1858–1932) Born in Leicester, she was the only daughter of the Rev. Timothy Jones, vicar of St Margaret's; she had five brothers. She was educated at home and then at St Anne Rewley, Oxford; in Paris; in Cologne; and then, while teaching at South Hampstead High School, worked for an LLA from St Andrews, qualifying in 1882 with classes in Latin, Education (Hons) and German (Hons). She was married in 1884 to H.W. NEVINSON, whom she had known since her childhood in Leicester, and became the mother of a son, later celebrated as the painter C.R.W. Nevinson, and of a daughter. She worked as a rent collector for charitable organizations in London's East End. She was a member of the WOMEN'S FRANCHISE DECLARATION COMMITTEE in 1906, was a member of the Hampstead branch of the NATIONAL UNION OF WOMEN'S SUFFRAGE SOCIETIES, took part in the "Mud March" in February 1907 and subscribed to the WOMEN'S SOCIAL AND

POLITICAL UNION. However, she does remark in her autobiography that when she visited Clement's Inn she "was not favourably impressed with several of the Committee". She attended the first Women's Parliament in Caxton Hall in February 1907 and then took part in the deputation to the House of Commons. However, in September, unable to accept Pankhurst autocracy, she left the WSPU, with Charlotte DESPARD and Edith How MARTYN, in order to found the WOMEN's FREEDOM LEAGUE. She was a very active member, speaking at meetings on an average of four or five times a week, contributing to the *Vote* and taking part in the picketing of the House of Commons that lasted from 5 July until 28 October 1910. At the beginning of the campaign she felt unable to speak at open-air meetings, but she soon forced herself to overcome the prejudices instilled by her upbringing and endured the gamut of rotten vegetables, eggs, cayenne pepper, rats and indecent heckling. She took part in a WLF CARAVAN tour through Kent.

Margaret Nevinson was an early member of the WOMEN WRITERS' SUFFRAGE LEAGUE and treasurer for most of the ten years of its existence. For its costume dinner at the Hotel Cecil on 29 June 1914 she went as "a mother of the Futurists", a witty allusion to her son's distinction of being, as Frank RUTTER later described, "the only English Futurist". She was also a founding member of the CHURCH LEAGUE FOR WOMEN'S SUFFRAGE, was active in the TAX RESISTANCE LEAGUE, declining to pay all taxes during her husband's long absences abroad, and subscribed to the NEW CONSTITUTIONAL SOCIETY FOR WOMEN'S SUFFRAGE in 1910. Among her writings are two pamphlets published by the WFL, *Ancient Suffragettes*, c. 1910, and *Five Years Struggle for Freedom: A History of the Suffrage Movement from 1908 to 1912*, c. 1913. She dramatized, at the request of Edith CRAIG, a sketch "Detained by Marital Authority" that she had written for the *Westminster Gazette*. The resulting play, *In the Workhouse*, was staged in 1911 by the Pioneer Players. She later published a book of the *Westminster Gazette* sketches as *Workhouse Characters*, 1918. Margaret Nevinson was a member, for the Kilburn ward, of the Hampstead Board of Guardians from 1904 until 1922 and was a School Board manager. In 1920, having been proposed by the WFL, she was appointed a JP for the County of London, becoming the first woman to adjudicate at criminal petty sessions. She was a member of the Council of Woman Journalists, 1924 and vice-president of the British-American Women's Peace Crusade, 1928.

Address: (1903) 4 Downside Crescent, London NW.
Photograph: by Lena Connell on WFL postcard, John Johnson Collection, Bodleian Library, Oxford.
Bibliography: M. Wynne Nevinson, *Life's Fitful Fever: A Volume of Memories*, 1926.

NEW, EDITH BESSIE (1877–?) Born in Swindon, was a school-teacher in Greenwich, joined the WOMEN'S SOCIAL AND POLITICAL UNION in 1906, and by 1908 was one of its ORGANIZERS. She was arrested in March 1907 following a raid on the House of Commons and sentenced to two weeks' imprisonment. In January 1908 she chained herself to the railings of 10 Downing Street and was subsequently imprisoned for three weeks. In March she was in Hastings organizing the WSPU campaign at the by-election. She wrote a letter to *The Times*, 5 March, to highlight the success of the WSPU by-election policy, noting that, when canvassing, she was told by many erstwhile Liberals that, having been enlightened by the WSPU, they were now voting Conservative. She was again in Holloway for two months in mid-1908 after, with Mary LEIGH, throwing stones at the windows of 10 Downing Street. Edith New and Mary Leigh, acting without the sanction of the WSPU leadership, were the first two suffragettes to use stone throwing as a political weapon. On their release from Holloway they were taken in a carriage pulled by six suffragettes to a celebration breakfast in Holborn. Later in 1908 Edith New was the WSPU organizer in Newcastle, moving for a short time to Leicester, and then back to Newcastle in February 1909. In September 1909 she was imprisoned in Dundee following her arrest for breach of the peace at a meeting being held by Herbert Samuel. She was one of the first suffragettes to go on hunger strike in Scotland and after five days was released on the order of the secretary for Scotland without having been forcibly fed.

Address: (1908) 68 Royal Hill, Greenwich, Surrey; (1913) 1 Diamond Terrace, Greenwich, Surrey.
Photograph: in *Votes for Women*, 7 May 1908.
Archival source: Scottish Record Office.

NEWARK committee of the National Society for Women's Suffrage   Was in existence in 1872.

NEWBURY (NUWSS)   Formed in 1913. Chairman Miss Henry, secretary Mrs Sharwood Smith.

NEWBURY (WSPU)   Secretary (1913) Miss Daulkes, Diglis, Newbury, Berkshire.

NEWBURY AND THATCHAM GROUP (WFL) Secretary (1913) Miss M. Ashman, Broad Street, Thatcham, Berkshire (sister-in-law of Anna MUNRO).

NEW CONSTITUTIONAL SOCIETY FOR WOMEN'S SUFFRAGE   Founded in January 1910 (probably in the immediate aftermath of the general election) "in order to unite all suffragists who believe in the anti-Government election policy, who desire to work by constitutional means, and to abstain from public criticism of other suffragists whose conscience leads them to adopt different methods". It was, thus, carrying out the election policy of the WOMEN'S SOCIAL AND POLITICAL UNION, but entirely eschewing the WSPU's other weapon, militancy. The NCSWS campaigned at London by-elections in 1910 and ran committee rooms in three constituencies during the December general election. Its policy was to work with all other societies whenever possible. In 1910 the NCSWS took part in both the WSPU procession on 18 June and in that organized by the NATIONAL UNION OF WOMEN'S SUFFRAGE SOCIETIES on 9 July, and stated in the *Suffrage Annual and Women's Who's Who* in 1913 that it had "taken part in almost all the joint demonstrations and processions organised by other societies in 1910, 1911 and 1912". By the end of 1910 it had issued three different badges and various posters.

In 1911 the NCSWS suspended its campaign until the fate of the Conciliation Bill was sealed by Asquith's announcement in November of the government proposal to introduce a manhood suffrage bill. It then reverted to its original policy of campaigning against all government candidates at by-elections and supported George LANSBURY at the Bromley and Bow by-election in 1912. The NCSWS affiliated to the FEDERATED COUNCIL OF SUFFRAGE SOCIETIES in 1912, by which time it had seven London branches and ten in the country, and employed several organizers. It held weekly afternoon "At Homes" at its office.

The NCSWS published *Woman Under a Liberal Government, 1906–14* by Winifred Holiday (daughter of the artist Henry Holiday), which was subtitled "an account of the manner in which Liberal Principles are applied to 'the protected Sex'". During the First World War the NCSWS devoted itself to war work and on 13 March 1918 took part in the celebrations organized to celebrate women's partial enfranchisement by the National Union of Women's Suffrage Societies at the Queen's Hall.

President: (1913) Adeline CHAPMAN; honorary treasurer (1913) Mrs Hartley (who had been adopted by Eliza Lynn Linton and had been honorary secretary of Hampstead branch of London Society for Women's Suffrage (NUWSS), but resigned to help form this new society); honorary organizer (1913) Alexandra Wright; honorary secretary (1913, 1917) Jean Forsyth; secretary (1913) Gladys Wright (*see* WRIGHT SISTERS).

Address: (1910, 1917) 8 Park Mansions Arcade, Knightsbridge, London, SW. The premises originally comprised only an office and were enlarged in 1911 to include a shop. It advertised to other societies that it had meeting rooms to let. From 1912 it shared an address with the QUI VIVE CORPS, although this arrangement was probably merely financial rather than indicating any particular shared philosophy.

Archival source: New Constitutional Society for Women's Suffrage annual reports 1–3, 1910–12, Fawcett Library.

NEW FOREST (NUWSS)   In 1913 the society was a member of the SURREY, SUSSEX, AND HANTS FEDERATION OF THE NATIONAL UNION OF WOMEN'S SUFFRAGE SOCIETIES. Secretary (1909, 1913) Miss Anna BATESON, Bashley Nursery, New Milton, Hampshire.

NEW UNION FOR MEN AND WOMEN   Was formed by July 1909, when it joined with the MEN'S LEAGUE FOR WOMEN'S SUFFRAGE and the MEN'S COMMITTEE FOR JUSTICE TO WOMEN, in appealing to the Home Secretary to treat members of the WOMEN'S FREEDOM LEAGUE, arrested while attempting to present a petition to Asquith, as political prisoners. The Union organized meetings during the January 1910 general election, at which the speakers included Emily, Ernest and Victor DUVAL. **Address:** (1910) W. Wilson Horn, 52 Maddox Street, Hanover Square, London W.

NEWCASTLE branch of the MEN'S POLITICAL UNION FOR WOMEN'S ENFRANCHISEMENT   Founded in 1910.

NEWCASTLE (WSPU)   Founded in July 1908 by Mona TAYLOR and other experienced suffrage workers. At first the WOMEN'S SOCIAL AND POLITICAL UNION members met at Fenwick's Drawing-Room Cafe on Wednesday afternoons and evenings, but later moved across the road to Crosby's Cafe, which was also the meeting place of the local branch of the Women's Liberal Association. The WSPU SHOP was opened in February 1910 at 77 Blackett Street. The WSPU ORGANIZER at that time was Annie WILLIAMS, who by November 1910 had particularly noted that "Co-operative women are very keen to know more about Votes for Women" and was speaking at many Co-operative Women's Guild meetings. Laura AINSWORTH took over as organizer in July 1911 until she resigned from the WSPU in September 1912, in protest against the Pankhurst/Pethick-Lawrence split. She was succeeded as organizer by Lilias MITCHELL.
Shop and office (1913) 77 Blackett Street, Newcastle.

NEWCASTLE WOMEN'S SUFFRAGE SOCIETY AND DISTRICT   Founded in 1900. A Newcastle committee of the CENTRAL COMMITTEE OF THE NATIONAL SOCIETY FOR WOMEN'S SUFFRAGE had been in existence in Newcastle in 1872, when its honorary secretary was Mrs Wilson, 1 Hawthorn Terrace, but had presumably lost impetus. Mrs Mona TAYLOR, one of the founders of the new society, was its representative on the NATIONAL UNION OF WOMEN'S SUFFRAGE SOCIETIES executive committee. In 1900 the executive committee of the Newcastle society comprised Mrs George Renwick, Mrs Spence WATSON (who was the society's representative on the committee of the NORTH OF ENGLAND SOCIETY), Dr Ethel BENTHAM, Mrs Edwards Lawrence (a dame of the Primrose League), Miss Moffat (the honorary secretary of the local Women's Liberal Association), Mrs Pease (a poor law guardian), Miss Storey (a member of the Primrose League) and Miss Telford (a member of the WLA). The president of the society was Dr Ethel WILLIAMS, the treasurer was Mrs Barnett and the honorary secretary was Mona Taylor. The society organized meetings in the open air and at factory gates, as well as in drawing rooms, and gathered in Fenwick's Drawing-Room Cafe on Monday nights, in order that women otherwise occupied during the day might attend. By July 1908, however, tensions in the society over whether to support Liberal or Labour candidates at by-elections led Mona Taylor and 12 other women to break away from the Newcastle NUWSS society and form a branch of the WOMEN'S SOCIAL AND POLITICAL UNION. She was succeeded as secretary by Florence Harrison BELL. In 1910 the society became a member of the NORTH-EASTERN FEDERATION OF THE NATIONAL UNION OF WOMEN'S SUFFRAGE SOCIETIES and in 1912 was a promoter of the Election Fighting Fund policy.
Secretary (1909, 1910) Mrs Harrison Bell, 6 Hotspur St, Heaton; (1913) Dr Charlotte Brown; secretary and office, Mrs Johnson, 27 Ridley Place, Newcastle-on-Tyne.

Bibliography: D. Neville, *The Women's Suffrage Movement in the North East of England, 1900–14*, M.Phil Thesis, Newcastle-upon-Tyne Polytechnic, 1991; D. Neville, *To Make Their Mark: The Women's Suffrage Movement in the North East of England, 1900–1914*, 1997.

NEWCOMBE, BERTHA (1857–1947)   Born at Priory House, Lower Clapton, the daughter of Samuel Prout Newcombe and his wife Hannah, both of whom subscribed to the WOMEN'S EMANCIPATION UNION in 1896. In 1889 a Miss Prout Newcombe attended a conference of the WOMEN'S FRANCHISE LEAGUE; this may have been Bertha. Her father conducted a school, was the author of an improving work, redolent of its time, *Fireside Facts from the Great Exhibition*, and is recorded by Huon Mallieliu in *British Watercolour Artists*, 2nd edn, 1986, as an artist. The family was without doubt related to the eminent topographical artist, Samuel Prout (1783–1852), five of whose works Bertha Newcombe left to the Southampton Art Gallery. Carrying on the family's artistic tradition, Bertha Newcombe studied at the Slade, 1876, and from 1888 was a member of the New English Art Club. She exhibited there, at the Royal Academy (*Primrose Copse*, 1905), and with the Society of Women Artists. She was a keen member of the Fabian Society and in 1893 painted George Bernard Shaw as *The Platform Spellbinder*. She was a great admirer of Shaw and, around 1895–7, may have entertained thoughts, even hopes, of marrying him. Long after, in 1909, she approached him about the possibility of acquiring the performing rights in his suffrage play *Press Cuttings*, but friendship did not prevail against the mechanics of play licensing. Bertha Newcombe was a member of the committee of the ARTISTS' SUFFRAGE LEAGUE and a friend of Christiana HERRINGHAM. In 1910, she painted *Emily Davies and Elizabeth Garrett presenting the first Women's Suffrage Petition to J.S. Mill, 1866*, now in the Fawcett Library collection. In it the two women, dressed in crinolines and bonnets, are depicted coyly displaying to Mill the petition hidden under the apple-seller's stall. As a non-militant, Bertha Newcombe was keen to emphasize the constitutional *fons et origo* of the suffrage movement, in clear contrast to the revolutionary and satirical suffrage images more commonly seen. In 1913 Bertha Newcombe was a member of the executive committee of the LONDON SOCIETY FOR WOMEN'S SUFFRAGE.

Bertha Newcombe had money invested in the Shoreditch Housing Association and in the Women's Pioneer Housing Association (*see also* Gertrude LENNOX) and in her will requested that the proceeds of the sale of her house should be given to the Shoreditch Housing Association to be devoted to the housing in flats or rooms of elderly women of limited means, and that the residue of her estate be left to the Society for the Protection of Ancient Buildings to be used for the preservation or repair of almshouses, preferably those suitable for women. She left all her books to the public reference library at Winchester, although, unfortunately, the library cannot now trace this bequest, which might have given a further interesting insight into Bertha Newcombe's life.

Address: (1905) 1 Cheyne Walk, Chelsea, London SW; (1947) Redlynch, Tilmore, Petersfield, Hampshire.

NEWHAVEN (NUWSS) In 1913 the society was a member of the SURREY, SUSSEX, AND HANTS FEDERATION OF THE NATIONAL UNION OF WOMEN'S SUFFRAGE SOCIETIES. Secretary (1913) Miss Hunt, 8 Railway Road, Newhaven, Sussex.

NEWMAN, FRANCIS WILLIAM, PROFESSOR (1805–97) Unitarian, younger brother of Cardinal Newman, leader of the Oxford Movement. From 1846 he was professor of Latin at University and was one of the founders in 1849 of Bedford College for Women, at which, until 1851 when he resigned over controversies concerned with the appointing of teaching staff, he lectured on ancient history, mathematics, philosophy and political economy. In 1851 Newman was, with P. A Taylor (*see* Clementia TAYLOR) and David MASSON, a member of the Friends of Italy. With John Stuart MILL, Newman was associated with George HOLYOAKE in founding the London Association for the Promotion of Co-operation. Newman subscribed to the ENFRANCHISEMENT OF WOMEN COMMITTEE in 1866–7 and joined the LONDON NATIONAL SOCIETY in 1867. In 1868 he became honorary secretary of the Bristol and Clifton branch of the National Society for Women's Suffrage (*see* BRISTOL AND WEST OF ENGLAND SOCIETY) and wrote a circular explaining its objects. In the same year he wrote *Old England – Women's Right of Suffrage*, which was published by the Bristol society. He was an active speaker for the society, addressing large meetings in Bath and Bristol in 1870. Newman was a member of the general committee of the CENTRAL COMMITTEE FOR WOMEN'S SUFFRAGE from 1872 until at least 1897 and subscribed to the WOMEN'S EMANCIPATION UNION in 1894 and 1896. On 1 January 1882 when sending his annual subscription to the Central Committee he added optimistically that he "heartily wish[ed] success may crown the cause this year". In addition to his suffrage activities Newman was a supporter of the Vigilance Association for the Defence of Personal Rights in 1872 and was for 20 years president of the Vegetarian Society.

Address: in Weston-super-Mare, 1882.
Photograph: carte de visite in Josephine Butler Collection, Fawcett Library.
Bibliography: I. Giberne Sieveking, *Memoir and Letters of Francis W. Newman*, 1909.

NEWNHAM COLLEGE Had a suffrage society by 1907 and in 1908 amalgamated with that of GIRTON to form the CAMBRIDGE UNIVERSITY WOMEN'S

Suffrage Society. In 1910, however, the College magazine *Thersites* noted that a meeting organized in Newnham by the society was very poorly attended. Secretary (1909) Miss H. Gardner, Newnham College, Cambridge.

NEWPORT (MONMOUTHSHIRE) (NUWSS) In 1913 the society was a member of the South Wales and Monmouth Federation of the National Union of Women's Suffrage Societies. Secretary (1913) Miss Acomb, Tr-gwyn, Clytha Park, Newport. The society's banner, designed by Mary Lowndes, is now in Newport Museum and Art Gallery.

NEWPORT (MONMOUTHSHIRE) (WSPU) Organizer (1910) Rachel Barrett, 46 Clarence Place, Newport. Secretary (1913) Mrs Humphrey Mackworth (*see* Lady Rhondda), Oaklands, Caerleon. The society's banner, probably made for the 18 June 1910 "Prison to Citizenship" procession in London, is now in Newport Museum and Art Gallery.

NEWQUAY (WSPU) Secretary (1913) Miss Clemes, Llangarth, Newquay, Cornwall.

NEWSOME, STELLA WINIFRED (1889–1969) A teacher, she was an early member of the National Federation of Women Teachers. She joined the National Union of Teachers in Leicester, but left the Union after two months when her local branch refused to discuss a motion on votes for women. She was a very active undercover worker for the Women's Social and Political Union in 1914 and was enraged when the Pankhursts arbitrarily stopped the campaign after the outbreak of war, especially detesting *Britannia*. Stella Newsome was a member of the Independent WSPU and by 1918 was a member of the United Suffragists before joining the Women's Freedom League. She assisted Emmeline Pethick-Lawrence in compiling the latter's memoirs, *My Part in a Changing World*, 1938. Stella Newsome was president of the Suffragette Fellowship in 1950 and later she worked for the Six Point Group, being honorary editor of its newsletter in the 1960s and publishing a brief history of the WFL, *The Women's Freedom League, 1907–1957*, 1960. She died after being hit by a car.

Address: (1950) Appletree Cottage, Peaslake, Surrey; (1968) 26 West End Lane, London NW6.

NEWSPAPERS AND JOURNALS In the nineteenth century journalism in support of the campaign for women's enfranchisement was in the main confined to small-circulation periodicals, such as the politically radical *Westminster Review*, the *Contemporary Review* and the *Fortnightly Review*. In the second half of the nineteenth century the number of newspapers, particularly those published outside London, increased dramatically, a result of the abolition of stamp duty in 1855 and of paper duty in 1861. Many of the new papers, seen as potential agents of social and political change, supported the Liberal Party, backed by radical pressure groups and aspiring Liberal politicians. As literacy increased, stimulated by the 1870 Education Act, so the market for newspapers developed. In the last decade of the century the economic, organizational and technological advances, the foundations of which had been laid in the 1850s and 1860s, bore fruit as the "New Journalism", which Miss March Phillips, in a talk on that subject to the Pioneer Club in 1895, applauded for its liveliness. The use of illustrations and investigative reporting appealed to the appetite of the new newspaper readers, both male and female. The great increase in the scale of production of the papers and the speed of their nationwide distribution ensured that the increasing demand could be met. However, despite the greater number of Liberal papers, despite the greater representation of Liberal newpaper proprietors, journalists and authors in parliament, despite the larger newspaper readership with its potentially more diverse opinions, the women's suffrage campaign received little attention from the popular press in the nineteenth century. Although it was recognized that the electorate enfranchised by the 1884 Reform Act might well be manipulated at elections by an increasingly powerful press, there was no will or interest on the part of any popular paper to campaign for women's enfranchisement. Indeed, amongst the established press it was only the *Manchester Guardian* that consistently supported the cause.

In the twentieth century the women's suffrage movement did become "news". *The Times Index* gave the subject a mere two entries in the course of 1905; in 1913 it was forced to devote to it 12 double-columned pages. By 1910 nearly 70 per cent of the circulation of the morning metropolitan press and 82.6 per cent of that of the evening papers were controlled by three companies, Northcliffe, Morning Leader Group and Pearson; 80.7 per cent of the circulation of the Sunday papers was divided between four companies, those owned by Dalziel, Riddell, F. Lloyd and Northcliffe. Of these only Dalziel introduced a column covering the women's suffrage campaign; the others only responded to the campaign when it presented itself as "news". Their coverage, driven by the desire to supply their readers with dramatic pictures and snappy stories, necessarily highlighted spectacle and extremes. The WOMEN'S SOCIAL AND POLITICAL UNION from its earliest days in London grasped the principle of providing the "news" that the popular press could communicate to its readers. To precede its very first meeting in London in February 1906 the WSPU organized a straggly procession from St James's Park tube station round the corner to Caxton Hall and arranged for the *Daily Mirror* photographer to be there to record it for the next day's paper. A year later the *Daily Mirror* was on hand to photograph the next suffrage procession, the NATIONAL UNION OF WOMEN'S SUFFRAGE SOCIETIES' "Mud March". The type of increasingly grand spectacle for which the Edwardian suffrage campaign is remembered was in part driven by the needs of the newspapers. Images of orderly, elegant, banner-bearing women were more likely to be included than their speeches. So powerful is the visual image that these processions and pilgrimages, besides making an impact on their contemporaries, have become woven into the history of the suffrage campaign. The "Grand Demonstrations" of the 1880s, which greatly impressed those who attended them, lack any visual legacy and, despite the descriptive power of recording journalists, have been forgotten. The WSPU's tactics brought the suffrage campaign into the popular newspapers, indeed it was in a newspaper that the sobriquet "suffragette" was coined.

Once they had embarked on their London campaign the WSPU quickly realized that there was little point in demonstrating unless the press was present to communicate the protest. On 2 March 1906 a press photographer was on hand to record a very small WSPU deputation, led by Dora MONTEFIORE, standing on the doorstep of 10 Downing Street. This occasion was quiet and orderly but within the next few months the attendant photographers were rewarded as similar deputations resulted in skirmishes and arrests, allowing them to capture and deliver to their readers the visual representations of "news". The image of Ada WRIGHT, knocked to the ground on "Black Friday", pictured on the front page of the *Daily Mirror*, 19 November 1910, was sufficiently powerful for the government to attempt to suppress copies of the paper and order negatives of the photographs to be destroyed. However, the newspapers, while having the power to bestow publicity, could also deny it. Maud Arncliffe SENNETT chose to break a window in the *Daily Mail* office in November 1911 because the paper had not reported an enthusiastic WSPU rally in the Albert Hall a few days earlier at which over £4000 had been raised. Lord Northcliffe, the proprietor of the *Daily Mail*, negated her protest by paying her fine and depriving her of the publicity of imprisonment for the cause. The lack of interest by the press in the women's suffrage campaign, unless windows were broken, was a constant complaint by suffrage workers of all opinions. Frederick PETHICK-LAWRENCE addressed the problem in an article, "Is there a press boycott of woman suffrage?" in *Votes for Women*, 25 June 1909, deploring the lack of coverage in the daily press and suggesting that the remedy lay in increasing the readership of *Votes for Women*. The suffrage societies, both militant and constitutional, were very aware of the necessity of harnessing to their interest whatever they could stimulate the national and local press to produce. Both the NUWSS and the WSPU ran efficient press departments, subscribing to cuttings agencies, liaising with press agencies and placing articles by their members in papers and journals. Mary Home, described as the WSPU "Cuttings Girl", put together a display of press photographs of the suffrage campaign that was one of the main attractions at the 1909 WSPU Prince's Skating Rink Exhibition. A surprising number of books of newspaper cuttings about the suffrage campaign have survived, testifying to the contemporary interest in the campaign as mediated by the press.

As a consequence of their lack of coverage by the general press, the nineteenth-century women's suffrage campaign supported several journals specific to its cause in which news and comment were disseminated amongst supporters. The twentieth-century campaign, with its myriad of societies, stimulated the publication of a range of associated papers. Of these the best-known, *Votes for Women*, eventually became its own *raison d'être* as the centre of a society, the Votes for Women Fellowship, the paper binding together its readers in a common purpose. All the suffrage papers suffered difficulties over distribution, relying on their readers to drum up new subscriptions from friends and acquaintances. The smaller papers suffered the drawback of insignificance and *Votes for Women* and later the *Suffragette*, from worries of stockists over handling papers that might be deemed subversive. Members of the societies themselves took to the streets to sell their papers, an act of moral bravado that signified a very real commitment to the cause.

MAIN NATIONAL AND PROVINCIAL NEWSPAPERS
Votes for Women included, in a column headed "From the Press", regular extracts from the national and local press's treatment of the suffrage campaign. When studying these or when using local or national papers as source material on the women's suffrage movement it is worthwhile establishing the general tenor of the politics and the family and friendship networks of the paper's owner and editor.

BIRMINGHAM DAILY GAZETTE   Founded in 1861, Liberal, later tending towards Conservative.

BIRMINGHAM DAILY MAIL   Founded in 1870, Liberal.

BIRMINGHAM POST   Founded in 1857, supported Joseph Chamberlain after the division in the Liberal party over Home Rule. According to Millicent FAWCETT, in *Victory and After*, it was anti-suffrage.

BOLTON DAILY CHRONICLE   Founded in 1870, Conservative.

BOLTON EVENING NEWS   Founded in 1867, Liberal.

BRISTOL TIMES AND MIRROR   Founded in 1865, Conservative.

BRADFORD DAILY TELEGRAPH   Founded in 1868, Liberal evening paper.

BRADFORD OBSERVER   Founded in 1868, Liberal.

DAILY CHRONICLE   Founded in London in 1856, became a daily in 1869, and was bought in 1876 by Edward Lloyd who built it up into a national Liberal daily. H.W. Massingham (*see* Clementina BLACK) was editor 1895–9. In 1918 the paper was bought by a syndicate led by Lloyd George.

DAILY CITIZEN   Launched in Manchester in 1912, backed by the Labour Party. It ceased publication in 1915.

DAILY EXPRESS   Popular daily, launched by C. Arthur Pearson in 1900.

DAILY GRAPHIC   First pictorial morning paper, launched in London in 1890.

DAILY HERALD   Founded in 1912 by George LANSBURY and Ben Tillett, with official Labour Party backing. It grew out of the *Worker*, the monthly organ of the Labour Representation Committee in Bow. Rowland Kenney (*see* Annie KENNEY) was the paper's first editor. Lansbury ensured that the *Daily Herald* gave prominent support to the women's suffrage cause and reportedly recruited capital for the paper from such wealthy suffrage supporters as the Countess DE LA WARR and her friend Mary Dodge. From 1913 Will Dyson was the paper's mordant cartoonist. In 1919 Lansbury became the *Daily Herald*'s editor, with Gerald Gould (*see* Barbara Ayrton GOULD) as associate editor.

DAILY MAIL   Founded in 1896 by Alfred Harmsworth (later Lord Northcliffe) and owned by him until his death in 1922, and after that by his younger brother Viscount Rothermere. The paper was extremely successful and influential. In 1906 it was Charles Hands writing in the *Daily Mail* who first used the term "suffragette". In 1917, because it was giving general support to Lloyd George, the *Daily Mail* supported the move towards women's enfranchisement. However, after the First World War the paper was distinctly opposed to universal female enfranchisement, partly as a result of a breach between Rothermere and Stanley Baldwin.

DAILY MIRROR   Launched by Alfred Harmsworth (later Lord Northcliffe) in November 1903 as a paper for women. It initially had a woman editor and was staffed mainly by women. It was not a success, circulation plummeted, and the editor,

Mary Howarth, was soon fired and replaced by Hamilton Fyfe. In early 1906 the *Daily Mirror* gave full coverage to the first WSPU rally at Caxton Hall. The paper sent along a photographer and it was one of his photographs that was then issued as the first WSPU postcard.

DAILY NEWS Founded by Charles Dickens in 1845 as a London Liberal daily and managed by Charles Dilke, grandfather of Sir Charles DILKE. It was bought in 1869 by, among others, Henry Labouchere, MP for Northampton from 1880 (and founder and editor of *Truth*, 1877). A.G. Gardiner was editor 1902–18, by which time the proprietor was George Cadbury. The paper was closely associated with nonconformism. Harold Spender (*see* Emily SPENDER), Frances Power COBBE, Florence Fenwick MILLER, H.W. NEVINSON and H.N. BRAILSFORD all worked on or contributed to the *Daily News*. The last two resigned from the paper in 1909 in protest at its refusal to condemn forcible feeding. In 1906 the *Daily News* sponsored the six-week exhibition on sweated labour at the Queen's Hall, an exhibition that stimulated many women to join the women's suffrage movement. The paper merged with the *Morning Leader* in 1912, to become the *Daily News and Leader*. In 1928 this merged with the *Westminster Gazette* and in 1930 with the *Daily Chronicle*, ending up as the *News Chronicle*.

DAILY POST Founded in Liverpool in 1855 as the *Liverpool Daily Post*. Edward Russell, a Gladstonian Liberal, was editor from 1869 for nearly 50 years.

DAILY RECORD Launched in Glasgow by the Harmsworths as a morning paper, with pictures, in 1895.

DAILY SKETCH Launched in Manchester by Edward Hulton Jnr in 1908.

DAILY TELEGRAPH Founded in 1855 and became London's first penny daily. It was taken over in 1856 by Joseph Levy and in practice edited by his son, Edward Levy (later Levy Lawson, Lord Burnham). It was in the mid-nineteenth century a Liberal paper, with which Gladstone had a close association. In the 1865 election the paper supported John Stuart MILL. It moved towards the centre of the political spectrum, not abandoning the Liberal label until 1886. By 1877 it had the largest circulation of any newspaper in the world, maintaining this as it changed its politics. By 1913 the *Daily Telegraph* ran a column, "Women in Public Life", which included coverage of the suffrage campaign.

EASTERN DAILY PRESS Founded in Norwich in 1870, Liberal.

EASTERN MORNING NEWS Founded in 1864 in Hull, by William Saunders (*see* Emily SPENDER). It was a Liberal paper, strenuously pro-Home Rule towards the end of the century.

ECHO Founded in 1868 in London by Cassell, Petter and Galpin as a Liberal $\frac{1}{2}$d evening paper. It passed through several owners and by 1895 is described as Liberal Unionist in tone. In 1901 it was bought by Frederick PETHICK-LAWRENCE, who was its editor until closing the paper, which was losing money, in 1905. H.J. Wilson, Liberal MP for Holmfirth, had been a financial supporter.

EVENING NEWS Founded in London in 1881, bought by Harmsworth brothers in 1894, Conservative.

EVENING STANDARD Relaunched in London as a Conservative evening paper in 1859. In 1904 it was owned by C. Arthur Pearson, who sold it to Davison Dalziel, who in turn sold it in 1915 to Edward Hulton Jnr.

FORWARD Socialist newspaper published in Glasgow, edited by Thomas Johnston, that gave a platform to the women's suffrage campaign. Mary PHILLIPS was one of the paper's regular columnists.

GLOBE Launched in 1803 as a Conservative London evening paper. It was absorbed by the *Pall Mall Gazette* in 1921 and incorporated in the *Evening Standard* in 1923.

LEEDS MERCURY Founded in 1861, Liberal.

LIVERPOOL DAILY COURIER Founded in 1863, Conservative.

LIVERPOOL EVENING EXPRESS Founded in 1870, Conservative.

MANCHESTER COURIER Founded in 1864, Conservative.

MANCHESTER EVENING NEWS Founded in 1868, independent.

MANCHESTER GUARDIAN Founded in 1821 as a bi-weekly and in 1855 became a daily. In the late 1860s it established a London office near the House of Commons. In 1872 a youthful C.P. Scott, cousin of the proprietor, took over as editor, remaining in this position until 1929. The paper was strongly Liberal and by 1880 was the voice of Home Rule.

Scott married Rachel Cook (*see* Harriet Cook), one of the first women to have been educated at Girton and the successor to Lydia Becker's seat on the Manchester School Board. Scott was a strong advocate of women's enfranchisement and worked on the Conciliation Committee in 1911. Under his editorship the *Manchester Guardian*, of which, from 1907 to 1913, he was sole proprietor as well as editor, firmly backed the women's cause. Scott was closely associated in Manchester with Elizabeth Wolstenholme Elmy, Susan Dacre and Helena Swanwick. H.W. Massingham and Harold Spender (*see* Emily Spender) were based in the paper's London office, which also fostered Evelyn Sharp's career.

MIDDLESBOROUGH DAILY GAZETTE Founded in 1869, Liberal.

MORNING ADVERTISER Founded in 1794, a London daily, Liberal.

MORNING LEADER Launched in London in 1892 by the Colman family of Norwich as a Liberal daily. It merged in 1912 with the *Daily News* as the *Daily News and Leader* (*see under* GAMES).

MORNING POST Founded in London in 1722. From 1876 to 1908 it was owned by Algernon Borthwick (later Lord Glenesk) and then by his daughter Lady Bathurst (1908–24). Its editors were (1905–11) Fabian Ware and (1911–37) H.A. Gwynne, who had previously been editor of the *Standard* but had left after disagreements with its new proprietor, Dalziel. The *Morning Post* was anti-suffrage and right-wing; it merged in 1937 with the *Daily Telegraph*.

NEWCASTLE DAILY CHRONICLE A Liberal paper founded in 1858.

NEWCASTLE JOURNAL Founded as a Conservative paper in 1861.

NORTHERN ECHO (Darlington) Founded in 1870 as a $\frac{1}{2}$d morning paper by a group of northern businessmen to advocate advanced liberal opinion in the north-east and north Yorkshire. W.T. Stead became its editor in 1871. In 1904 the *Echo*, still Liberal, was taken over by the Rowntree Social Service Trust, becoming part of the North of England Newspaper Co.

NOTTINGHAM DAILY EXPRESS Founded in 1860, Liberal.

NOTTINGHAM DAILY GUARDIAN Founded in 1861.

OBSERVER Founded in 1791. It was edited from 1891 until 1905 by Rachel Beer, wealthy wife of the proprietor. She also edited the *Sunday Times*, 1893–7, after it had been bought by her husband. She was a member of the Institute of Journalists and the Society of Women Journalists. The *Observer* was bought by William Waldorf Astor in 1911.

PALL MALL GAZETTE Founded in 1865 as a London evening paper, by George Smith of the publishers Smith, Elder. Originally Conservative, it was modelled on the *Anti-Jacobin*. In 1880 Smith gave the paper to his son-in-law Henry Yates Thompson, a Liberal, and it was edited from 1880 until 1883 by John Morley, with W.T. Stead as his assistant. Three years later W.T. Stead became editor, holding the position until 1889. Under his editorship the paper became the champion of all oppressed causes. Stead became closely associated with Millicent Fawcett, Elizabeth Wolstenholme Elmy, and Richard Pankhurst. In 1885 Stead published in the *Pall Mall Gazette* his now famous article, "Maiden Tribute of Modern Babylon", in which he exposed the white slave traffic in London. As a result of his methods of investigative journalism he was imprisoned in Holloway (which was not then a woman's prison) for three months. From 1882 a woman, Hulda Friedrichs, was a senior journalist on the *Pall Mall Gazette*. In 1892 J.A. Spender became assistant editor but when, around late 1892, Yates Thompson was offered £50 000 for the paper from the Conservative Lord Astor, Spender, a Liberal, resigned and joined the newly founded *Westminster Gazette*. It was in the *Pall Mall Gazette* that Keir Hardie managed to place Sylvia Pankhurst's articles on prison life in early 1907. In 1915 the *Pall Mall Gazette* was bought by Davison Dalziel, the owner of the *Evening Standard*, with which it was incorporated in 1923.

PRESS AND JOURNAL An amalgamation of two papers, the elder of which was founded in Aberdeen in 1748. In 1913 Millicent Fawcett singled the paper out as one of the few that consistently supported women's suffrage.

SCOTSMAN Launched in Edinburgh in 1817. Its editor, 1848–76, was Alexander Russel, father of Helen Archdale. Isa Craig may have had a post on the paper during the course of his editorship.

SHEFFIELD INDEPENDENT Founded in 1861, Liberal. H.J. Wilson, the radical MP for Holmfirth, put money into the paper in the early twentieth century.

SHIELDS DAILY NEWS   Founded in 1864, Liberal.

STANDARD   In the nineteenth century the *Standard* was a Conservative equivalent of the *Daily News*. It was the morning sister paper of the *Evening Standard*, both, from 1910 until 1915, in the ownership of Davison Dalziel, who then sold the *Evening Standard* to Edward Hulton Jnr and closed the *Standard*. In the *Standard*, which under its previous owner had been anti-suffrage, Dalziel, a Unionist, in 1911 introduced a column, "The Woman's Platform", which was devoted to the issue of women's suffrage, treating impartially supporters and opponents. H.A. Gwynne, the incumbent editor when Dalziel took over the *Standard*, objected to such editorial interference from the proprietor and soon left to join the *Morning Post*.

SUNDAY TIMES   Founded in London in 1821 and bought in 1887 by Alice Cornwell, who gave it to her future husband. In 1893 it was bought by the husband of Mrs Rachel Beer, who took over the editorship, while also editing her Sunday rival, the *Observer*.

THE TIMES   Founded in London in 1785, remaining in the Walter family until 1908 when it was bought by Alfred Harmsworth (later Lord Northcliffe). J.L. Garvin was editor from 1908 until 1942. *The Times* was anti-suffrage for 50 years, only becoming less so towards the end of 1913. At Christmas 1916 Northcliffe complained to Lady Betty Balfour that there was insufficient demand from women for their own enfranchisement and urged her to get up a public meeting. Lady Betty sent this letter to Millicent Fawcett who wrote that "because we break no windows, Lord Northcliffe thinks there 'is no movement for women's suffrage any-where'". In a further letter Northcliffe again suggested a large deputation, making it clear that this was in order to get the subject into the newspapers, and said that he would speak to the prime minister. Northcliffe also wrote that he had spoken to the editor of *The Times*, who was entirely favourable to supporting a new campaign. This episode can be read either as the power of a newspaper proprietor to manipulate both press and government or, perhaps rather more likely, the desire of the government to manipulate public opinion through the press. Lloyd George, close associate of Northcliffe, had become prime minister barely three weeks before Northcliffe's first letter to Lady Betty. A CD-ROM, *Women's Rights: Extracts from the Times*, issued by Linton Healey Multimedia, contains both news items and photographs from THE TIMES covering the women's suffrage campaign.

TRIBUNE   First appeared on 15 January 1906. It was a Liberal daily founded by Franklin Thomasson, who was described by one of the paper's journalists, Philip Gibbs, in *Adventures in Journalism*, 1923, as "a very tall, handsome, and melancholy young man" "who started the Tribune as a kind of sacred duty which he inherited with his money". The launching of the paper had been a condition of J.P. Thomasson's will. The paper's editor was William Hill, who previously worked on the *Westminster Gazette*. H.N. Brailsford also joined the paper's staff. In 1906 the *Tribune*'s address was that used by the Women's Franchise Declaration Committee, organized by Clementina Black. However, by the summer of 1907 Frances Rowe noted in a letter that the *Tribune* now hardly covered the issue of women's suffrage and she no longer took it. Circulation did indeed drop very quickly and by 1908, when it ceased publication, the paper had lost £300 000.

WESTERN DAILY MERCURY   Founded in Plymouth in 1860, Liberal.

WESTERN DAILY PRESS   Founded in Bristol in 1858, Liberal.

WESTERN DAILY TIMES   Founded in 1866 in Exeter, Liberal.

WESTERN MAIL Founded as a Conservative daily in Cardiff in 1869 by the Marquis of Bute. By 1903 the chairman of the company that owned the *Western Mail* and the *News of the World* was George Riddell (knighted 1909, baronetcy 1918), golfing companion of Lloyd George, for whom he was building the house at Walton Heath that was blown up by WSPU arsonists on 19 February 1913. A reporter from the *Western Mail* supplied to the Home Office the verbatim transcript of the speech that Mrs Pankhurst delivered on 20 February at the Cory Hall, Cardiff, on the basis of which the decision was taken to prosecute her.

WESTERN MORNING NEWS   Founded in Plymouth as an independent daily in 1860 by William Saunders, with his brother-in-law Edward Spender as editor (*see* Emily Spender). In 1875 Edward

Spender subscribed to the CENTRAL COMMITTEE OF THE NATIONAL SOCIETY FOR WOMEN'S SUFFRAGE.

WESTMINSTER GAZETTE Founded by George Newnes as a Liberal London evening paper in 1893 after the *Pall Mall Gazette* had reverted to conservatism. The paper's editor from 1896 to 1921 was J.A. Spender, who had been a leader writer on the *Echo*, then editor of the *Eastern Morning News*, which had been founded by his uncle. Stephen Koss describes Spender as "the doyen of political journalists". The *Westminster Gazette* was more or less the accredited organ of parliamentary Liberalism, by no means radical. In 1908 Sir W.D. Pearson (*see* Lady COWDRAY) was part of a syndicate that bought the paper from Newnes and by 1911 was virtually its sole owner, although Lord Aberconway (*see* Laura McLAREN) had an interest in the paper. By 1918 Lord Cowdray was the chief proprietor of the *Westminster Gazette*.

YORKSHIRE POST Founded as a weekly in 1754, became a daily in 1866, Conservative. According to Millicent FAWCETT, in *Victory and After*, the paper was firmly anti-suffrage.

JOURNALS

ATHENAEUM From 1869 was owned by Sir Charles DILKE (*see also* J.E. Francis *under* PRINTERS AND PUBLISHERS).

CLARION Radical weekly, founded and edited from 1891 by Robert Blatchford. The PANKHURST sisters belonged to the Clarion Cycling Club and Dora MONTEFIORE was compromised after a putative affair while proselytizing from a Clarion van.

CONTEMPORARY REVIEW Launched on 1 January 1866 by Alexander Strahan (*see under* PUBLISHERS AND PRINTERS) with Alford, Dean of Canterbury (1810–71), as editor. The latter, who remained editor until his death, was a populizer, his obituarist remarking that "Very few indeed of our dignitaries thought so much of the people, and worked so hard to teach them". The journal's prospectus promised that it "would number among its contributors those who, holding loyally to belief in the Articles of the Christian Faith, are not afraid of modern thought in its varied aspects and demands, and scorn to defend their faith by mere reticence, or by the artifices too commonly acquiesced in". According to Emily DAVIES in December 1866 Alford, who was a member of the LONDON PROVISIONAL PETITION COMMITTEE, asked her to find for publication in the *Contemporary Review* an article on women's suffrage. The result was Lydia BECKER's "Female Suffrage", which appeared in the March 1867 edition. The *Contemporary Review* also published Jessie BOUCHERETT, "Condition of Women in France", May 1867; Emily Davies, "Some Account of a Proposed New College for Women", December 1868; Lydia Becker, "On the Study of Science by Women", March 1869; Julia Wedgwood, "Female Suffrage in its Influence on Married Life", August 1872; Millicent Garrett FAWCETT, "The Women's Suffrage Question (No I)"; Leonard Courtney, "The Women's Suffrage Question (No II)"; Emily Pfeiffer, "Woman's Claim", 1881; Sarah M. Sheldon AMOS, "The Women's Suffrage Question (No III)", June 1892. Millicent Garrett Fawcett had a total of ten articles published in the *Contemporary Review*. In 1870–72 Emilie Ashurst VENTURI sent two articles of her own and five by Mazzini to the *Contemporary Review*. In 1877 Strahan sold the *Contemporary Review* to a group that continued publishing as Strahan and Co. In 1882 Percy Bunting (*see* Sarah AMOS), a Gladstonian Liberal, became editor of the journal, which henceforward was at the vanguard of social reform. In 1911 Teresa BILLINGTON-GREIG published an important article, "Feminism and Politics", in the *Contemporary Review*.

EXAMINER A radical weekly supporting the philosophy of John Stuart MILL. It had been owned by Albany Fonblanque who sold it in 1867 to William Torrens McCullagh. It then sank and was relaunched as the organ of "Radical opinion in political, social, and theological questions" in 1871 with Millicent FAWCETT, Mill, and Swinburne among its contributors. In 1871 Fox Bourne in a letter to Mill, the day before the latter's death, mentioned that he had heard that Helen TAYLOR was thinking of starting a paper and wondered if she would be interested in acquiring an interest in the *Examiner*. Mill's death, however, negated Helen Taylor's plans and she never launched a paper. In 1872 a collection of papers from the *Examiner*, edited by R.H. Lapham, was reprinted as *The Woman Question*. In late 1873 P.A. TAYLOR bought the *Examiner*, apparently thereby annoying Helen Taylor. P.A. Taylor

Bristol Central Library's
Lunchtime Lectures
September/October 2024

Handwritten annotations:
- maid Ellen Morgan → Mary Blathwayt + Aethel + Grace Tollemache
- attended WSPU Bristol 1907
- "No militancy" father "wd not like it"
- Trees + rest
- Mary resigned WSPU Sept Jun 1913

Thursday 26th September

Reading, Self-Improvement and Library Culture in Eighteenth-Century Britain

Professor Mark Towsey, University of Liverpool

Reading became increasingly popular in the 1700s to a wider range of people than ever before. To accompany our current exhibition on the Bristol Library Society of the 1770s, this talk looks at library provision in the eighteenth century and what library records can tell us about this pivotal moment in the development of the modern world.

Handwritten annotations:
- Local house burned - Tollemache
- Sisters disguised as "market women"
- Mary's diarie "suffocatingly naieve"
- The "Mr Pooter of the suffrage movement"
- Never threw stones.

Thursday 3rd October

The Bristol Sound, Multiculturalism and Anti-racism

Dr Pete Webb, UWE Bristol

Handwritten: no ref to sex with Kenney

The "Bristol Sound," pioneered by artists like Massive Attack, Portishead, and Tricky, emerged from the city's diverse musical subcultures like Punk, Reggae, and Hip-hop. Developed away from mainstream media, the music was shaped by the city's ethnic and class diversity and strong anti-racist activism. This talk explores the significance of events like the St Pauls riots, and the connection between music and political activism.

To stay up to date with upcoming events and lectures, follow us on Eventbrite:
https://www.bristollibraries.eventbrite.co.uk

Bristol Libraries
www.bristol.gov.uk/libraries

12.30-1.20pm
Every Thursday - FREE

Bristol Central Library's
Lunchtime Lectures
September 2024

[Handwritten notes across top: Tillemache "market woman disguise" Trowbridge protest / Smashed window / NWU she came out madder than she went in / Grace / Smashed Buck House / banquet. King didn't press / window dung]

Thursday 12th September

Heritage Open Days: *Electrical Networks Then and Now*

Join the Women's Engineering Society in their Electric Dreams series of talks as they celebrate the formation of the Electrical Association for Women 100 years ago. This talk is delivered by **Fiona Gleed** in partnership with the Open University and Bristol Libraries.

[Handwritten: no rg to sex with anyone]

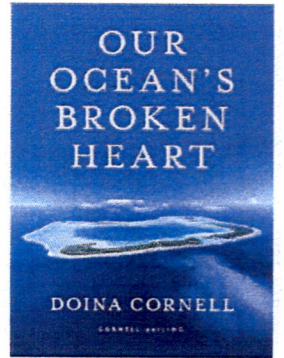

Thursday 19th September

Our Ocean's Broken Heart by **Doina Cornell** depicts one woman's journey across the ocean and into the heart of those places most threatened by climate change.

In her new book she tells the story of sailing voyages she made to the Arctic and the Pacific accompanied by her children, exploring what it means to be a sailor and our relationship with the ocean.

To stay up to date with upcoming events and lectures, follow us on Eventbrite:
https://www.bristollibraries.eventbrite.co.uk

Bristol Libraries
www.bristol.gov.uk/libraries

12.30-1.20pm
Every Thursday - FREE

did not own the *Examiner* for long and it ceased publication in 1881.

FORTNIGHTLY REVIEW Founded as a journal of secular radicalism in 1865. From 1865 until December 1866 its editor was G.H. Lewes; from 1867 until 1882, John Morley (who in 1880 also took over the editorship of the *Pall Mall Gazette*); from 1882 until 1886, T.H.S. Escott; from July 1886 until 1894 Frank Harris; from December 1894 until 1928, William Leonard Courtney. The *Fortnightly Review* published Richard PANKHURST, "The Right of Women to Vote under the Reform Act, 1867", 1868; Millicent Garrett FAWCETT, "The Electoral Disabilities of Women", 1870, and "The Women's Suffrage Bill", 1889; and in November 1891 she replied in the journal to an article the month before by Frederic Harrison. The *Fortnightly Review* published articles by Charlotte Carmichael STOPES and Teresa BILLINGTON-GREIG's "Suffragist Tactics: Past and Present", 1907, and "The Government and Women's Suffrage", 1910.

NINETEENTH CENTURY Published first by Henry S. King and then by Kegan Paul. The journal, which represented a group of people who had broken away from the *Contemporary Review*, was edited by James T. Knowles from 1877 until 1900. Articles on the subject of women's suffrage include Millicent Garrett FAWCETT on "The Future of Englishwomen: A Reply", 1878, and "Women and Representative Government", 1883. In June 1889 the journal published an appeal against female suffrage and in July "A Reply" by Millicent Garrett Fawcett and Mrs Ashton DILKE. In 1907 Eva GORE-BOOTH published in the *Nineteenth Century*, "Woman and Politics: A Reply", and another article in 1908, responding to anti-suffrage articles.

PUNCH Launched in 1841, published weekly. Originally a journal of advanced Liberal opinion, even when it became more conservative and depicted the suffragist as bespectacled and rednosed, it consistently and sympathetically covered the women question. The social and political problems of the day are reflected in its cartoons; 1913 was a bumper year. Its editor from 1906 to 1932 was Owen Seaman.

REVIEW OF REVIEWS Founded by W.T. Stead in 1890 as a monthly digest of the chief British and foreign reviews and magazines. Stead was an ardent supporter of the women's suffrage movement and the *Review of Reviews* office in Norfolk Street, off the Strand, was often visited by Elizabeth Wolstenholme ELMY when in London. In early 1906 Stead published in the *Review of Reviews* a "Character Sketch" of Annie KENNEY, by whom he had clearly been impressed. The *Review of Reviews* also published articles by the constitutional suffragists, for instance one by Millicent FAWCETT in September 1913.

WESTMINSTER REVIEW The original *Westminster Review* was founded in 1824 by James Mill with money given to him by his friend Jeremy Bentham; its writers were drawn from members of the Utilitarian Society. After several changes of proprietor, from 1836 until 1840 John Stuart MILL was the real, but unnamed editor of what was by then the *London and Westminster Review*. It was generally held by his contemporaries that Harriet TAYLOR exercised some influence on the policy of the *Review* at this time. The journal was bought by W.E. Hickson, a retired shoe manufacturer, in 1840, and again changed proprietors in 1852 when it was bought by John Chapman, who was editor from 1854 until 1894, for some of that time jointly with George Eliot. Their first issue, January 1852, contained an article by W.J. Fox on "Representative Reform". In 1852 the journal was saved by an injection of £600 from Samuel COURTAULD and in 1854 by £500 from Harriet Martineau; the print run for the *Review* at this time was only 650 copies. Further loans came from Courtauld and from Octavius Smith, uncle to Barbara BODICHON. With the latter, while she was still Barbara Leigh Smith and a near neighbour in Blandford Square, Chapman had an affair of some seriousness. It is not inconceivable that his interest in Barbara Leigh Smith was stimulated by his knowledge of her personal wealth; Chapman's finances, as those of the *Review*, were always parlous. In March 1860 Chapman sold the *Westminster Review* to George Manwaring, remaining as its publisher. However, by the end of 1861 Manwaring had sold the journal back to Chapman, who eventually sold it to Nicholas Trubner, remaining as editor, even after moving to Paris in 1874. The *Westminster Review* published articles in support of women's suffrage from 1851 until its demise in 1914. Among these were Harriet TAYLOR, "The Enfranchisement of Women", published in July 1851, while the *Review* was still in the hands of W.E. Hickson although in the process of being transferrred to Chapman;

Anon, "The Emancipation of Women", 1874; three articles on the emancipation of women and laws related to women, 1887; and Amy Bulley, "The Political Evolution of Women", 1890. Mona CAIRD was an occasional and Elizabeth Wolstenholme ELMY ("Ignota") and Harriet McILQUHAM regular contributors well into the twentieth century, when, after Chapman's death, the editorship was held by his second wife, Hannah Chapman. In 1915 Anne Cobden SANDERSON assumed some responsibility for the welfare of the now elderly and ill second Mrs Chapman.

WOMEN'S SUFFRAGE NEWSPAPERS AND JOURNALS

ABERDEEN WOMEN'S SOCIAL AND FRANCHISE LEAGUE   First (and only?) issue, March 1912.
ALEXANDRA MAGAZINE   Published 1864–65, editor Susannah Meredith.
ALTRUIST   Published 1913–15 by the MEN'S SOCIETY FOR WOMEN'S RIGHTS.
AWAKENER   Published 1912–14, issued by the MEN'S SOCIETY FOR WOMEN'S RIGHTS. The journal was particularly concerned with the suppression of the white slave trade.
BALANCE   Issued by the Society for the Study of Women's Franchise, Bedford College, London. The first (and only?) issue, November 1913.
BRITANNIA   Published 1915–18, editors Christabel PANKHURST, Emmeline PANKHURST, Flora DRUMMOND, Annie KENNEY. The official organ of, first, the WOMEN'S SOCIAL AND POLITICAL UNION and then the WOMEN'S PARTY.
CALLING ALL WOMEN   Published 1947–77, the newsletter of the SUFFRAGETTE FELLOWSHIP.
CATHOLIC CITIZEN   Published 1918–?, organ of the CATHOLIC WOMEN'S SUFFRAGE SOCIETY and then of St Joan's Social and Political Alliance.
CATHOLIC SUFFRAGIST   Published 1915–18, organ of the CATHOLIC WOMEN'S SUFFRAGE SOCIETY.
CHURCH LEAGUE FOR WOMEN'S SUFFRAGE   Published 1912–17, monthly paper of the CHURCH LEAGUE FOR WOMEN'S SUFFRAGE.
COMMON CAUSE   Published 1909–20, for most of that time as the organ of the NATIONAL UNION OF WOMEN'S SUFFRAGE SOCIETIES. In 1908 the NUWSS had withdrawn its support from the *Women's Franchise*, the proprietor of which, J.E. Francis, had refused to exclude from it reports of the activities of the WOMEN'S FREEDOM LEAGUE, of which the NUWSS was critical. The *Common Cause* was launched as "The organ of the women's movement for reform", to represent the view of the constitutionalists, in April 1909. At first it was published by an independent company, mainly financed by Margaret ASHTON, and was only formally adopted by the NUWSS in the autumn of 1909. Helena SWANWICK was the first editor, at an annual salary of £200. Initially based in Manchester, as a tyro editor she was grateful for the advice she received from C.P. Scott, editor of the *Manchester Guardian*. The paper moved to London in 1911 and later editors included Clementina BLACK and Maude ROYDEN. Appeals continually went out to members of societies of the NUWSS to help increase the paper's circulation. In 1910 the CAMBRIDGE WOMEN'S SUFFRAGE ASSOCIATION distributed specimen copies (the cost of which was borne by Margaret HEITLAND) to likely subscribers. For a time a newsboy was engaged to sell the paper in the Cambridge streets on Saturday mornings. Members of the NUWSS, unlike those of the WSPU, were less inclined to volunteer to sell copies in the street themselves. In 1914 the GLASGOW AND WEST OF SCOTLAND ASSOCIATION approached the local Labour Exchange for people to act as street vendors for the *Common Cause* and when there proved to be no suitable applicants, applied instead to the Women's Employment Bureau. Periodically new capital was raised for the paper by the issue of shares; in July 1912 the Cambridge Association, in response to an appeal from Mrs FAWCETT, agreed to take three £1 shares in the paper. In 1919 in order to raise money to keep the paper going and raise fresh capital, new shares were again issued. The NUWSS was keen to exploit the educative and propaganda aspects of the *Common Cause*. In March/April 1912 an appeal was sent to its member societies asking them to send the *Common Cause* to their MPs and to the Free Libraries in the neighbourhood. The SOUTHAMPTON branch, always feeble, was unable, due to lack of funds, to carry out the proposal. The Cambridge Association agreed "to have sent from the Common Cause office every week for 6 months free copies to local MPs". The *Common Cause* played its part in cementing the NUWSS realignment with

the Labour Party after the setting up of the Election Fighting Fund in 1912. In January 1913 the Cambridge Association agreed that the *Common Cause* should be sent regularly to the secretary of the local ILP at the expense of the Association and in February even the Southampton branch agreed to leave the *Common Cause* regularly in the local Morris (ILP) Hall. In 1920 the *Common Cause* was succeeded by the *Woman's Leader*.

CENTRAL AND EAST OF ENGLAND SOCIETY FOR WOMEN'S SUFFRAGE Published 1891–1900, an occasional paper.

COMING DAY Published 1916–20, by the FREE CHURCH LEAGUE FOR WOMEN'S SUFFRAGE, incorporating the *Free Church Suffrage Times*.

CONSERVATIVE AND UNIONIST WOMEN'S FRANCHISE REVIEW Published 1909–16.

ENGLISH WOMAN'S JOURNAL Published 1858–64, edited by Bessie Rayner PARKES and Matilda Hays. The journal was published by a limited company, of which the first three male shareholders were Samuel COURTAULD, James Vaughan (widower of Esther Bright, sister of Jacob BRIGHT and Priscilla Bright McLAREN), and William Strickland Cookson. The women shareholders were Barbara BODICHON (whose shares, in the days before the Married Women's Property Act, were held in the name of her unmarried sister), Matilda Hays, and Maria Rye. In 1860 shares were taken by, among others, P.A. TAYLOR, Laura Herford, Mary MERRYWEATHER, Emily FAITHFULL and Jane Crow. By the end of 1859 the offices of the *Journal* moved from 14a Princes Street, off Oxford Street, to 19 Langham Place.

ENGLISHWOMAN Published 1909–21. The first editor was Elisina Grant Richards (*see under* PUBLISHERS AND PRINTERS) and the editorial committee included Lady Frances BALFOUR, Lady STRACHEY, Cicely HAMILTON and Mary LOWNDES.

ENGLISHWOMAN'S REVIEW A successor in spirit to the *English Woman's Journal*, published 1866–1910, edited by Jessie BOUCHERETT (1870); Caroline Ashurst BIGGS (1871–89); Helen BLACKBURN and Antoinette M. Mackenzie (1889–1902); Antoinette M. Mackenzie (1903–10). The *Englishwoman's Review* was published, as was the *Women's Suffrage Journal*, on commission by Trubner. The publisher's accounts show that in the 1870s and 1880s many copies were sold for waste.

FREE CHURCH SUFFRAGE TIMES Organ of the FREE CHURCH LEAGUE FOR WOMEN'S SUFFRAGE, published 1913–15 and then succeeded by the *Coming Day*.

FREEWOMAN Published 1911–12, edited, at first jointly, by Dora MARSDEN and Mary GAWTHORPE, and then by Dora Marsden alone. It is interesting for its criticism of the WSPU and the reaction this produced.

FRIEND OF WOMEN'S SUFFRAGE Issued, 1913–14, by the NATIONAL UNION OF WOMEN'S SUFFRAGE SOCIETIES as an adjunct to its FRIENDS OF WOMEN'S SUFFRAGE scheme.

INDEPENDENT SUFFRAGETTE Published in 1916 and 1917, by the INDEPENDENT WOMEN'S SOCIAL AND POLITICAL UNION, a WSPU breakaway paper. Contributors included Charlotte MARSH and Dorothy E. EVANS.

JUS SUFFRAGII Published 1906–29, journal of the INTERNATIONAL WOMAN SUFFRAGE ALLIANCE. Its editors included Martina G. Kramers, Mary Sheepshanks and Margery Corbett ASHBY. When the paper was first launched the GLASGOW AND WEST OF SCOTLAND ASSOCIATION FOR WOMEN'S SUFFRAGE "agreed to subscribe for 60 copies for distribution amongst the Committee".

LIBERAL WOMEN'S REVIEW Published, probably for one issue only, in June/July 1914, by the LIBERAL WOMEN'S SUFFRAGE UNION. Edited by Mary Somerville, it represented the views of such Liberal women as Eva and Laura McLAREN.

MEN'S LEAGUE FOR WOMEN'S SUFFRAGE Published 1909–14, the paper of the MEN'S LEAGUE FOR WOMEN'S SUFFRAGE.

MONTHLY NEWS OF THE CONSERVATIVE AND UNIONIST WOMEN'S FRANCHISE ASSOCIATION Published 1914–24 as a supplement to the *Conservative and Unionist Women's Franchise Review*.

NATIONAL SOCIETY FOR WOMEN'S SUFFRAGE Published 1891–1900, described as an "occasional paper", published annually.

ONLY WAY Published 1909–10, the magazine of the EDINBURGH WOMEN'S SUFFRAGE SOCIETY.

PELICAN Subtitled "A Quarterly magazine, Advocating the Social and Educational Progress of Woman". Published by Simpkin Marshall, 1874–5 (five issues and then discontinued). Edited by Richard King Jnr.

PERSONAL RIGHTS JOURNAL Published 1881–1903, until October 1886 as the *Journal of the Vigilance Association for the Defence of Personal Rights*. Elizabeth Wolstenholme ELMY was a contributor, linking this journal and society with the WOMEN'S FRANCHISE LEAGUE and the WOMEN'S EMANCIPATION UNION.

SCOTTISH VOTES FOR WOMEN Intended to be launched on 21 May 1908, published from the headquarters of the SCOTTISH WOMEN'S SOCIAL AND POLITICAL UNION at 141 Bath Street, Glasgow. It is not clear if the paper was published; no copies appear to have survived.

SHAFTS Published 1892–1900, edited by Margaret Shurmer Sibthorpe, radical feminist paper, with coverage of the suffrage movement, particularly from Elizabeth Wolstenholme ELMY. Contributors also included Dora MONTEFIORE, Laura Morgan-Browne and Charlotte Carmichael STOPES.

SUFFRAGETTE Published, after the PANKHURSTS split with the PETHICK-LAWRENCES, 1912–15, as the organ of the WOMEN'S SOCIAL AND POLITICAL UNION. The Home Office tried to suppress the paper. On 2 May 1913 Sidney Granville Drew, manager of Victoria House Printing Co. which had printed that week's issue of the *Suffragette*, was arrested. On 8 May the Home Office thought it likely that copies of the paper might have been printed in Holland and then imported. In fact the 8 May issue was printed by the National Labour Press Ltd in Manchester. On 10 May that printer was remanded on bail on an undertaking not to assist in the meantime in publishing the *Suffragette*. According to Helen CRAWFURD the *Suffragette* was subsequently printed by the presses of the *Forward* and the *Socialist*. Jessie KENNEY's reminiscences confirm this; from May to August 1914 she travelled each week from Paris to Glasgow (where the *Forward* was based) to see the *Suffragette* through the press. The circulation of the paper was about 17 000 for its early issues, falling to about 10 000 as the police successfully intimidated stockists.

SUFFRAGETTE NEWS SHEET Produced, apparently weekly, from 1916 until 1918 by the SUFFRAGETTES OF THE WOMEN'S SOCIAL AND POLITICAL UNION.

SUFFRAGIST Published in October 1909 from the address of the SUFFRAGISTS' VIGILANCE LEAGUE. It included an article by Rose Lamartine YATES on "A Warning to Anti-suffragists and Anti-Militants" and a plethora of cartoons and comic rhymes. The paper was printed by the Athenaeum Press, which was owned by J.E. Francis, erstwhile publisher of *Women's Franchise*.

TIME AND TIDE Launched as a feminist weekly by Lady RHONDDA in 1920.

VICTORIA MAGAZINE Published 1863–80, edited by Emily FAITHFULL.

VOTE Published by the Minerva Publishing Co., 1909–33, as the organ of the WOMEN'S FREEDOM LEAGUE. Its first editor was Charlotte DESPARD.

VOTES FOR WOMEN Published 1907–18, edited by Emmeline and Frederick PETHICK-LAWRENCE, and printed by the St Clement's Press. It appeared monthly from its launch in October 1907 until the end of April 1908, apparently with weekly updating supplements, and then became a weekly. Its price was reduced from 3d to 1d from the issue of 21 May 1908. Until the split between the Pankhursts and the Pethick-Lawrences in 1912 the paper was the official organ of the WOMEN'S SOCIAL AND POLITICAL UNION. It then was continued by the Pethick-Lawrences as a paper around which they grouped their VOTES FOR WOMEN FELLOWSHIP, until handing it over to the UNITED SUFFRAGISTS in August 1914. Throughout its life a great deal of effort was expended on increasing the circulation of *Votes for Women*. Summer holiday campaigns, when supporters holidaying at the seaside were urged to recruit new subscribers, were a feature. At the beginning of October 1909, coinciding with a redesign and increased page size, the WSPU launched an aggressive advertising campaign for *Votes for Women*, permanent pitches were established in central London and the Suffragette Bus, advertising the paper, toured London streets. The paper's circulation rose from 5000 per month in April 1908 to 22 000 per week in May 1909, to over 30 000 a week in early 1910. However, after the break with the WSPU the Pethick-Lawrences had a struggle keeping the paper solvent. As a small compensation for the loss of its committed WSPU readership it was able to attract readers from non-militant societies; in October 1912 the Southampton NUWSS branch ordered a dozen copies of *Votes for Women*, rather than the *Common Cause*, to sell at a social evening. The paper's end mirrored its beginnings. After the Pethick-Lawrences gave it to the United Suffragists it was always in dire financial straits. A call for funds for the paper went out in October 1915. By 1917 its layout had reverted to a design not dissimilar to that of 1907 and it became a monthly, rather than a weekly. "A Patriot's" cartoons disappeared from the front page. As soon as the Representation of the People Act was passed in February 1918 *Votes for Women* ceased publication, its work accomplished.

WOMAN   Published in 1887, running for eight issues, by G. Hill, publisher of the *Westminster and Lambeth Gazette*.

WOMAN'S HERALD   Successor to the *Women's Penny Paper*, published 1891–3, edited by "Helena B. Temple" (Henrietta MULLER); then Mrs Frank Morrison, then Christina S. Bremner, by which time it was the "organ of the Women's Liberal Federation"; then edited by Lady Henry Somerset, "for God and every land: a weekly record of the progress of the woman's movement". In 1894 it became the *Woman's Signal*.

WOMAN'S LEADER   Published 1920–32, succeeded the *Common Cause* as the official organ of, first, the NATIONAL UNION OF SOCIETIES FOR EQUAL CITIZENSHIP and then of the National Union of Townswomen's Guilds.

WOMAN'S OPINION   Published 1874, edited by Mrs Amelia Lewis.

WOMAN'S SIGNAL   Published 1894–9, successor to the *Woman's Herald*, edited until September 1895 by Lady Henry Somerset and Annie E. Holdsworth, then by Florence Fenwick MILLER. In 1896 the *Woman's Signal* had a contract to supply 500 copies of each issue to the CENTRAL NATIONAL SOCIETY, but the society had only 209 subscribers and asked if the "surplus copies [which] were accumulating and filling up the office" could be passed on to affiliated societies. Elizabeth Wolstenholme ELMY, no friend of the editor, wrote in 1898, "The *Woman's Signal* is altogether painful in its inaccuracy. Scarcely a week passes but I find some statement or statements so outrageously wrong that I dare not trust others which I have not the means of verifying."

WOMEN'S DREADNOUGHT   Published 1914–24 (latterly as the *Workers' Dreadnought*), paper of the EAST LONDON FEDERATION OF SUFFRAGETTES, later of the Workers' Suffrage Federation, then of the Workers' Socialist Federation, and then an organ of the Communist Party of Great Britain. It was edited by Sylvia PANKHURST and was the only suffrage paper that made a distinct appeal to working people.

WOMEN'S FRANCHISE   Published 1907–11 by John E. Francis, owner of the Athenaeum Press, and a prominent member of the MEN'S LEAGUE FOR WOMEN'S SUFFRAGE. The paper represented all major tendencies within the suffrage movement (especially WSPU, WFL and the NUWSS, which had been thinking of publishing its own paper, but decided instead to support the *Women's Franchise*). Mary BLATHWAYT was a subscriber to the *Women's Franchise*, and sent it to her friends and ordered extra copies for the Bath Reference Library and the Bath and Counties Ladies' Club. As the suffrage societies each launched their own papers, demand for the *Women's Franchise*, which was a bulletin board rather than a crusading journal, fell away.

WOMEN'S FREEDOM LEAGUE BULLETIN   Published 1934–61, the successor to the *Vote*.

WOMEN'S FREEDOM LEAGUE TEMPORARY NEWS SHEET   Published in 1909, printed by J.E. Francis, immediately prior to the publication of the *Vote*.

WOMEN'S GAZETTE   Published 1888–91, from 1 September 1889 as the official organ of the WOMEN'S LIBERAL FEDERATION, from 2 Tokenhouse Buildings, London EC. It was then edited and managed by Eliza ORME and contained a column of "News and Notes on the Suffrage Question". At this time many local Women's Liberal Associations held shares in the company as did such individuals as the Countess of ABERDEEN, Mrs Anna BATESON, Dr Sophie Bryant, Isabella FORD, Henry Holiday, Margaret Illingworth, Mrs Isabella Mills, Walter and Eva McLAREN, Arabella SHORE, Ursula BRIGHT, Emilia DILKE, George HOLYOAKE, Bertha MASON and Hannah Withall Smith (*see* STRACHEY FAMILY). From September 1891 Eliza Orme became publisher as well as editor and manager of the *Gazette*; the company was finally wound up in 1894.

WOMEN'S INTERNATIONAL LEAGUE   Published 1916–52, the paper of the Women's International League for Peace and Freedom.

WOMEN'S PENNY PAPER   Published 1888–90, edited by "Helena B. Temple" (Henrietta MULLER) as "the only paper in the world conducted, written (printed and published) by women".

WOMEN'S SUFFRAGE JOURNAL Published on commission, 1870–90, by Trubner (*see under* PUBLISHERS AND PRINTERS), edited by Lydia BECKER. In 1875 the print order was for 400 copies. After the rupture in the National Society in 1888, the *Women's Suffrage Journal* became the paper of the CENTRAL COMMITTEE OF THE NATIONAL SOCIETY, the interests of the CENTRAL NATIONAL SOCIETY being represented by the *Women's Penny Paper*. The journal's accounts may be traced through Trubner's commission ledgers.

WOMEN'S SUFFRAGE NEWS Published in 1894, edited by A.B. Louis, distributed by the CENTRAL COMMITTEE OF THE NATIONAL SOCIETY FOR WOMEN'S SUFFRAGE.

WOMEN'S SUFFRAGE RECORD Published 1903–6, edited by Edith PALLISER for the NATIONAL UNION OF WOMEN'S SUFFRAGE SOCIETIES. Elizabeth Wolstenholme ELMY wrote to Harriet McILQUHAM on 17 September 1904, "I only learned the other day that the WS Record is a *private* effort of Miss Palliser's own – the National Union contributing not one penny." The CAMBRIDGE ASSOCIATION FOR WOMEN'S SUFFRAGE for a time, before May 1905, supplied the paper free to members.

WOMEN'S TRIBUNE First issue 18 May 1906, the paper of the WOMEN'S DECLARATION COMMITTEE, continued from November 1906 until June 1907 as *Women and Progress*. When the paper was founded in April 1906 its only director and sole managing director was Christiana HERRINGHAM and the Women's Tribune Co. Ltd was wound up in October 1906, shortly before she departed for India. Among the company's shareholders was Nora Vynne. In December 1906 the paper carried as its back page a copy of the petition organized by the WOMEN'S FRANCHISE DECLARATION COMMITTEE. The paper is particularly useful as a source of information on the WSPU's early days in London.

Archival source: The archives of Kegan Paul, Trench, Trubner and Henry S. King, 1858–1912, on microfilm, British Library; Papers of the Women's Gazette Publishing Co. Ltd, Public Record Office; Papers of the Women's Tribune Co. Ltd, Public Record Office.

Bibliography: *Deacon's Newspaper Handbook*; *May's Press Guide* (late nineteenth century editions); J.L. Hammond, *C.P. Scott of the Manchester Guardian*, 1934; F.W. Pethick-Lawrence, *Fate Has Been Kind*, no date (1942); W. Harris, *J.A. Spender*, 1946; *The Wellesley Index to Victorian Periodicals, 1966–89*; C. Rover, *Punch Book of Women's Rights*, 1967; G.S. Haight, *George Eliot and John Chapman*, 2nd edn, 1969; P. Ferris, *The House of Northcliffe: The Harmsworths of Fleet Street*, 1971; A.L. Lee, *The Origins of the Popular Press 1855–1914*, 1976; S. Koss, *The Rise and Fall of the Political Press in Britain*, vol. 2, *Twentieth Century*, 1984; B. Harrison, "Press and Pressure Group in Modern Britain", in J. Shattock and M. Wolff, *The Victorian Periodical Press: Samplings and Soundings*, 1982; L. Brown, *Victorian News and Newspapers*, 1985; D. Doughan and D. Sanchez, *Feminist Periodicals 1855–1984: An Annotated Critical Bibliography of British, Irish, Commonwealth and International Titles*, 1987; J. Rendall, "'A Moral Engine'? Feminism, Liberalism and the *English Woman's Journal*", in J. Rendall (ed.), *Equal or Different: Women's Politics 1800–1914*, 1987; B. Melman, *Women and the Popular Imagination in the 1920s: Flappers and Nymphs*, 1988; D. Griffiths (ed.), *The Encyclopaedia of the British Press, 1422–1992*, 1992; A. Jones, *Powers of the Press: Newspapers, Power and the Public in Nineteenth-century England*, 1996; S. Taylor, *The Great Outsiders: Northcliffe, Rothermere and the* Daily Mail, 1996.

NEWTON ABBOT (NUWSS) In 1913 the society was a member of the SOUTH-WESTERN FEDERATION OF THE NATIONAL UNION OF WOMEN'S SUFFRAGE SOCIETIES. Secretary (1913) Miss A. Davies, Wrington House, Chudleigh, S. Devon.

NEWTON STEWART branch of the WOMEN'S EMANCIPATION UNION President (1895) Mrs Watson; honorary secretary Mrs John Stroyan.

NEWTON-LE-WILLOWS (NUWSS) In 1913 the society was a member of the WEST LANCS, WEST CHESHIRE, AND NORTH WALES FEDERATION OF THE NATIONAL UNION OF WOMEN'S SUFFRAGE SOCIETIES. Secretary (1913) Miss Watkins, Kirkby, Newton-le-Willows, Lancashire.

NICHOL, ELIZABETH PEASE, MRS (1807–97) Quaker, daughter of Elizabeth and Joseph Pease, a Darlington manufacturer. She was a cousin of the mother of Isabella and Emily FORD, and a friend of Harriet Martineau. Elizabeth Pease worked as her father's secretary in the campaigns for Catholic Emancipation, abolition of the Test Acts and abolition of the slave trade. Around 1836 she founded in Darlington a Women's Abolition Society, of which she was co-secretary. By 1837 she was conducting a transatlantic correspondence with the Grimké sisters and on 6 June 1840, during the London

Anti-Slavery Convention, she called on Lucretia Mott at the latter's lodgings in Cheapside. Lucretia Mott described her on this occasion as "a fine, noble-looking girl". She also met Elizabeth Cady Stanton and was incensed at the exclusion of women from the Convention. By 1847, presumably through their mutual interest in the anti-slavery campaign, she knew Eliza WIGHAM. In that year at the Ben Rhydding hydropathic centre, a venue much favoured by the radical Liberals, Elizabeth Pease met Priscilla Bright McLAREN, the STANSFELDS and the ASHWORTH sisters. It was here on a later occasion that she met for the first time John Pringle Nichol, professor of astronomy at Glasgow University, whom she married in 1853, by so doing being compelled to leave the Society of Friends. Until his death in 1859 the Nichols lived in Glasgow, where they were friendly with Rev. H.W. CROSSKEY. George HOLYOAKE visited Nichol when in Glasgow in 1851 and, after their marriage, both Nichols were friendly with Mazzini.

In 1842 Elizabeth Pease described herself as a Chartist, writing "I believe the Chartists generally hold the doctrine of the equality of women's rights – but, I am not sure whether they do not consider that when she marries, she merges her political rights with those of her husband". In 1866 she signed the women's suffrage petition and by 1870 was treasurer of the EDINBURGH NATIONAL SOCIETY FOR WOMEN'S SUFFRAGE. In September of that year Elizabeth Nichols attended the Social Science Congress in Newcastle, along with Mrs PENNINGTON, Elizabeth Wolstenholme (*see* Elizabeth Wolstenholme ELMY), Rev. S.A. STEINTHAL, Priscilla Bright McLAREN, Anna Maria PRIESTMAN and Mary ESTLIN. In February 1880 she was present at the Grand Demonstration of Women at the Free Trade Hall in Manchester and, as reported in the *Women's Suffrage Journal*, was singled out by Priscilla Bright McLaren as by her presence still testifying "for that political freedom which has, years ago, been granted to the negro whom she helped make free". In May 1884 she signed the Letter from Ladies to Members of Parliament, asking for the inclusion of women heads of householders in the government Franchise Bill. Elizabeth Pease Nichol was also a member of the executive committee of the Ladies' National Association for the Repeal of the Contagious Diseases Act, in 1871 was a member of the Committee for Securing Complete Medical Education to Women in Edinburgh and in 1877 was a member of the governing council of the London School of Medicine for Women. She was a shareholder in St Leonard's School at St Andrews, holding at the time of her death £100 worth of shares in the "St Andrews School Company Ltd for Girls". After the abolition of slavery she gave her files of the *Liberator*, from its earliest issues, to the British Museum. At the suggestion of R.D. Webb she gave her anti-slavery library of 350 books and pamphlets to Cornell University. She later gave to the Library of the Veterinary College in Edinburgh a number of books and pamphlets on animals and their treatment, which she had collected during her involvement with anti-vivisectionism. Her biographer does not, however, allude to any corresponding collection made by Elizabeth Pease Nichol of material pertaining to her involvement in the women's suffrage campaign.

Address: (from 1861) Huntly Lodge, Merchiston, Edinburgh.

Photograph: carte de visite in Josephine Butler Collection in Fawcett Library; photograph in A.M. Stoddart, *Elizabeth Pease Nichol*, 1899.

Bibliography: A.M. Stoddart, *Elizabeth Pease Nichol*, 1899; F.B. Tolles (ed.), *Slavery and "The Woman Question": Lucretia Mott's Diary, 1840*, 1952; C. Midgley, *Women Against Slavery: The British Campaigns 1780–1870*, 1992.

NINE ELMS (WSPU) Secretary (1906) Miss Mansel, 2 Currie St, Nine Elms Lane, London SW (address of Charlotte DESPARD).

NORMANTON (NUWSS) Founded in 1904 and by 1913 was a member of the WEST RIDING FEDERATION OF THE NATIONAL UNION OF WOMEN'S SUFFRAGE SOCIETIES. Secretary (1913) Miss Marguerite Pearson, Yorke Villa, Normanton, Yorkshire.

NORTH AND EAST RIDINGS FEDERATION OF THE NATIONAL UNION OF WOMEN'S SUFFRAGE SOCIETIES Honorary secretary (1912) Miss E. Bateson, Robin Hoods Bay, Yorkshire.

NORTH HERTS WOMEN'S SUFFRAGE ASSOCIATION (NUWSS) Founded in 1909, with Lord Lytton as president. His sisters, Lady Betty Balfour and Lady Constance LYTTON were associated with the society. Lady Constance attended the inaugural meeting, but does not appear to have attended any subsequent ones. Bernard Shaw was a vice-president of the Association. In 1911 the society had grown so large that it decided to split into two societies: HITCHIN AND DISTRICT and LETCHWORTH AND DISTRICT, with each society affiliating separately to the NATIONAL UNION OF WOMEN'S SUFFRAGE SOCIETIES. The Association played its part in entertaining members of the PILGRIMAGE, giving them, on 21 July 1913, luncheon and a midday meeting at Hitchin, followed by tea at Stevenage, and the next day repeating the hospitality at Welwyn. The Association had its own BANNER. The North Herts Association continued its existence to 1918, when it turned itself into a Women's Citizens Association under the auspices of the NUWSS.

Archival source: Minutes of the North Herts Women's Suffrage Association, Fawcett Library.

NORTH LONDON branch of the NATIONAL SOCIETY FOR WOMEN'S SUFFRAGE Founded in 1871. Its secretary was Mrs H. Browne, 40 Camden Square, London N, who had signed the 1866 women's suffrage petition.

NORTH OF ENGLAND SOCIETY FOR WOMEN'S SUFFRAGE The name given in 1897 to the erstwhile MANCHESTER NATIONAL SOCIETY FOR WOMEN'S SUFFRAGE when a more rational geographical structure was given to the main suffrage societies in order that they might work for the cause in a more concentrated manner. Until then it has been affiliated to the CENTRAL COMMITTEE OF THE NATIONAL SOCIETY, and then, briefly, until early 1898, to the CENTRAL AND EAST OF ENGLAND SOCIETY, but it then dropped this by now purely historical association and affiliated to the new NATIONAL UNION OF WOMEN'S SUFFRAGE SOCIETIES. In 1897 Elizabeth Wolstenholme ELMY reported that the North of England Society was so poor that it had to dismiss one member of its staff, and that it had received many letters from former members who thought it was no use subscribing to or working for women's suffrage any longer, since a bill never got further than its second reading. Esther ROPER and Eva GORE-BOOTH set about building up support for the society from working women and were particularly successful in attracting those employed in the cotton trade. In 1901 and 1902 the NESWS presented petitions signed by 66 835 women factory workers in Yorkshire, Cheshire and Lancashire. In 1903 the radical suffragist element in the NESWS, while still individually remaining members of the NESWS, formed the LANCASHIRE AND CHESHIRE WOMEN TEXTILE AND OTHER WORKERS' REPRESENTATION COMMITTEE in order to sponsor a women's suffrage candidate at the next general election.

During the years of her secretaryship Esther Roper broadened the social and economic mix of the NESWS's executive committee. In 1899 it comprised, in the main, middle-class liberals: Miss Atkinson, The Countess of Bective, Mrs Allen Bright (Liverpool), Miss A.M. Cooke, Miss Cox, Miss Eva Gore-Booth, Miss Hatton, Mrs Hayes, Mrs Gray Heald (Leeds), Miss Higginson, BA, Miss B. McGowan, MA, Miss Bertha MASON, Mrs Morrell, Miss Eleanor RATHBONE (Liverpool), Rev. S. STEINTHAL, Mrs Mona TAYLOR (Northumberland), Mrs Thew, Miss Wakefield, Miss J.H. Willmer (Birkenhead) and Mrs Wilkinson (Leeds). In 1901 Sarah REDDISH, Mrs THOMASSON and Mrs Spence WATSON joined the executive committee. By 1903 Sarah Dickenson and Christabel PANKHURST had also joined. After the annual general meeting of the NESWS held at the end of 1905, Eva Roper, Sarah Dickenson, Eva Gore-Booth, Mrs Haworth (who in 1902 had taken part in the graduates' suffrage deputation to parliament and was a member of the Accrington Suffrage Society), Miss Nellie Keenan (secretary of the Salford Power-Loom Weavers' Association), Christabel Pankhurst, Sarah Reddish, Mrs Thomasson and Rev. S.A. Steinthal resigned from the society, all refusing to condemn Christabel Pankhurst's performance in interrupting Sir Edward Grey's meeting at the Free Trade Hall in Manchester in October. The members remaining (what Elizabeth Wolstenholme Elmy termed the "Liberal gang") on the executive committee were Mrs Bauer, Mrs Brigden, Countess of Bective, Miss Cox, Mrs d'Auquier, Miss Fox, Miss Foxley, Miss Hatton, Mrs Gray Heald, Mrs Herford, Mrs Nixon, Miss Bertha Mason, Miss Eleanor Rathbone, Mrs Redford, Mrs Hans Renold, Miss Rowton, Mrs Sale, Mrs Thew, Miss Wakefield, Miss Wyse and Mrs Muter Wilson. The membership of the committee remained more or less constant between then and 1908. In the latter year C.P. Scott, editor and proprietor of the *Manchester Guardian*, was co-opted onto the committee. In 1908 a BANNER had been commissioned by the North of England Society in honour of his wife, which was carried in a procession on 24 October. In 1911 the North of England Society for Women's Suffrage changed its name back to the MANCHESTER SOCIETY FOR WOMEN'S SUFFRAGE; so many new societies had been formed in the north that it was no longer pre-eminent. A banner devised in 1908 for the society by Mary LOWNDES is now held in the Manchester Central Library Archive. Chairman: (1899–1903) Bertha Mason; (1903–6) Mrs Redford; (1906–11) Margaret ASHTON.

Honorary secretaries: (1899–1900) Miss Atkinson and Miss Higginson, BA; (1904–6) Miss Hatton, Grove House, Gorton; (1907–11) Helena SWANWICK. Secretary (1897–1905) Esther Roper; (1906–7) Mrs Darlington; (1908–11) Miss Kathleen COURTNEY. Honorary treasurer: (1899–1905) Rev. S. Steinthal; (1906) James T. Travis-Clegg, Whalley Abbey, Whalley, Lancs; (1907–8) F.A. Bruton, MA. Petition workers/organizers: (1901, 1903) Sarah Reddish and Miss Rowton.

Address: (1897–1908) Queen's Chambers, 5 John Dalton Street, Manchester; (1908–11) 85 Deansgate Arcade, Manchester.

Archival source: Annual reports of the North of England Society for Women's Suffrage, 1899–1911, Manchester Central Library.

Bibliography: J. Liddington and J. Norris, *One Hand Tied Behind Us: The Rise of the Women's Suffrage Movement*, 1978.

NORTH OF SCOTLAND FEDERATION OF THE NATIONAL UNION OF WOMEN'S SUFFRAGE SOCIETIES Honorary secretary (1912) Miss A. Black, 9 Victoria Terrace, Inverness, Invernesshire.

NORTHALLERTON (NUWSS) In 1913 the society was a member of the NORTH AND EAST RIDINGS FEDERATION OF THE NATIONAL UNION OF WOMEN'S SUFFRAGE SOCIETIES. Secretary (1913) Mrs Thornton, Moor House, Thornton-le-Moor, Northallerton, Yorkshire.

NORTHAMPTON (NUWSS) In 1913 the society was a member of the MIDLANDS (EAST) FEDERATION OF THE NATIONAL UNION OF WOMEN'S SUFFRAGE SOCIETIES. Secretary (1913) Miss K.M. Harvie, 67 Colwyn Road, Northampton, Northamptonshire.

NORTHAMPTON (WSPU) Organizer (1913) Miss Miller, 30 Bridlesmith Gate, Nottingham, Nottinghamshire.

NORTH-EASTERN FEDERATION OF THE NATIONAL UNION OF WOMEN'S SUFFRAGE SOCIETIES Formed in 1910, comprising all the societies in Northumberland and Durham. This Federation was a driving force behind the adoption of the NUWSS Election Fighting Fund policy in 1912. Honorary secretary (1912) Miss Hardcastle, 3 Osborne Terrace, Newcastle-upon-Tyne; organizing secretary (1912) Clementina Gordon. Chairman (1915) Dr Ethel WILLIAMS.

Archival source: 5th annual report of the North-Eastern Federation, 1915, Fawcett Library.

NORTHERN HEIGHTS (WFL) Secretary (1913) Miss Ada Mitchell, Merok, Great North Road, Highgate, London N.

NORTHERN HEIGHTS (WSPU) Secretary (1906) Miss L. Thompson, 43 Rosebery Gardens, London N.

NORTHERN MEN'S FEDERATION FOR WOMEN'S SUFFRAGE Founded by Maud Arncliffe SENNETT, inspired by the funeral of Emily Wilding DAVISON in June 1913. The original idea was to form a deputation to Asquith of Scotsmen, leading members of Edinburgh and Glasgow Town Councils, clergymen, church elders, solicitors and other professional men. Maud Arncliffe Sennett asked Christabel PANKHURST to help finance this first deputation, but this request was refused; the WOMEN'S SOCIAL AND POLITICAL UNION had no cash to spare. The first deputation took place in July 1913, timed to coincide with the NATIONAL UNION OF WOMEN'S SUFFRAGE SOCIETIES' PILGRIMAGE. Although Asquith refused to see the deputation the resultant publicity given to the Scotsmen's speeches and publications led to the founding of the Northern Men's Federation, which was then very active in the months leading up to the First World War.

The Federation had no politicial affiliation, although most of its supporters were Liberals. Its policy was to oppose, by non-militant methods, any government whose leader declined to make suffrage a government measure. Among the NMF's supporters were the NATIONAL POLITICAL LEAGUE, Lady DE LA WARR and Lady COWDRAY and, on account of Maud Arncliffe Sennett's past association, it was strongly backed by the ACTRESSES' FRANCHISE LEAGUE. The NEW CONSTITUTIONAL SOCIETY gave the NMF initial support, which it then seems to have retracted. In December 1913 the GLASGOW AND WEST OF SCOTLAND ASSOCIATION FOR WOMEN'S SUFFRAGE received a letter from Janie ALLAN, who was at least for a short time the secretary of the Glasgow branch of the NMF, asking the executive committee to support an appeal to the Glasgow Presbyteries in support of the NMF. Branches besides those in Edinburgh and Glasgow were formed in Newcastle, Manchester and Lancashire, although in her autobiography Maud Arncliffe Sennett remarks, typically, that "the three lady organizers for Manchester, Dundee and Liverpool vanished into thin air when the work and sacrifice needed was fully appreciated". Henceforward the NMF focused on Edinburgh, Glasgow and Berwick-on-Tweed. Maud Arncliffe Sennett did not want the Federation to have committees; "a great deal of unnecessary time is wasted in Committee work, and individual ideas and enthusiasms get tied up in Red Tape, and the Missionary Spirit" she wrote in the Federation's manifesto. The Glasgow branch sent a "Protest Against Forcible Feeding" to the Secretary for Scotland. There was a second deputation, which included the lord provost and the senior magistrate of Glasgow, to Downing Street in February 1914. Asquith again refused to receive them.

The NMF continued its suffrage campaign during the First World War, holding a large demonstration in Edinburgh in 1915 to publicize women's contribution to the war and from 1916 campaigned vigorously against the Contagious Diseases Acts contained in 40D DORA. The NMF was not asked to take part in the Speaker's conference that considered the bill that eventually led to women's partial enfranchisement and did not participate in the NUWSS victory celebrations on 13 March 1918. Maud Arncliffe Sennett was reluctant to disband the NMF, widening its scope to include land reform and changing its name to the Northern Men's Federation for Women's Suffrage and Land Reform. However, by September 1919 the NMF was defunct and its remaining funds were handed over to the WOMEN'S FREEDOM LEAGUE. Maud Arncliffe Sennett commissioned two BANNERS for the NMF from the SUFFRAGE ATELIER. That for the Edinburgh branch of the NMF in 1914 is now in the collection of the National Museum of Antiquities in Edinburgh and that for Berwick-on-Tweed is now in Museum of London. A banner for the Glasgow branch is now held by the People's Palace, Glasgow.

Founder and organizer (1913, 1919) Maud Arncliffe Sennett, 6 Wellington Road, St John's Wood, London N.W.

Archival source: Maud Arncliffe Sennett Collection, British Library.

Bibliography: *"Scotchmen at Downing Street": Speeches of the Delegates 18 July 1913*; M. Arncliffe Sennett, *The Child*, no date (1938); L. Leneman, *A Guid Cause: The Women's Suffrage Movement in Scotland*, 1991; L. Leneman, "Northern Men and Votes for Women", in *History Today*, December 1991; C. Eustance, "Citizens, Scotsmen, 'bairns': manly politics and women's suffrage in the Northern Men's Federation, 1913–20", in A.V. John and C. Eustance (eds), *The Men's Share?: Masculinities, Male Support and Women's Suffrage in Britain, 1890–1920*, 1997.

NORTH-WEST LONDON branch of the WSPU Honorary secretary (1910) Eleanor Penn GASKELL. Office: 310 High Street, Kilburn, London NW.

NORTH-WEST LONDON branch of the UNITED SUFFRAGISTS Formed in June 1915. Honorary secretary (1915) Eleanor Penn GASKELL. Office: 310 High Street, Kilburn, London NW.

NORTH-WESTERN FEDERATION OF THE NATIONAL UNION OF WOMEN'S SUFFRAGE SOCIETIES Honorary secretary (1911–September 1912) Miss Catherine MARSHALL, Hawse End, Keswick, Cumberland.

NORTHWICH (NUWSS) Formed in 1911 and joined the MANCHESTER AND DISTRICT FEDERATION OF THE NATIONAL UNION OF WOMEN'S SUFFRAGE SOCIETIES. Secretary (1913) Miss E. Brock, Mossfield, Winnington, Northwich, Cheshire.

NORTHWOOD (branch of the LONDON SOCIETY FOR WOMEN'S SUFFRAGE, NUWSS) Secretary (1913) Miss K. Phillips, Middlegate, Northwood, Middlesex.

NORWICH (NUWSS) In 1913 the society was a member of the EASTERN COUNTIES FEDERATION OF THE NATIONAL UNION OF WOMEN'S SUFFRAGE SOCIETIES. Secretary (1910) Miss E.L. Willis, Southwell Lodge, Ipswich Road, Norwich, Norfolk.

NORWOOD (NUWSS) Secretary (1913) Miss L.G. Archer, 3 Westbourne Road, Sydenham, London SE. Office, 42 Anerley Road, Upper Norwood, London SE.

NOTTINGHAM (WSPU) Honorary secretary (1910) Miss C.M. Burgis, 21 Chaucer Street, Nottingham; Miss Nellie CROCKER and Miss Roberts, 6 Carlton Street, Nottingham. Organizer (1913) Charlotte MARSH, 30 Bridlesmith Gate, Nottingham; 31 Derby Road, Nottingham.

NOTTINGHAM WOMEN'S SUFFRAGE SOCIETY (NUWSS) A Nottingham committee of the LONDON NATIONAL SOCIETY FOR WOMEN'S SUFFRAGE was founded in 1871, when its president was Richard A. Armstrong and its honorary secretary was Elizabeth Sunter, 40 Bilbie St., Nottingham, who had signed the 1866 women's suffrage petition. In 1872 Nottingham associated itself with the new CENTRAL COMMITTEE OF THE NATIONAL SOCIETY FOR WOMEN'S SUFFRAGE, in 1890 with the CENTRAL NATIONAL SOCIETY and in 1898 joined the NATIONAL UNION OF WOMEN'S SUFFRAGE SOCIETIES.

Anderson Brownsword chaired the first women's suffrage meeting in Nottingham and Alice Dowson, by 1894 the society's honorary secretary, had been one of the speakers at the Grand Demonstration of Women held at Nottingham in November 1881. Helena DOWSON, the daughter of Anderson Brownsword, married Alice Dowson's son W.E. Dowson and from 1895 was the secretary of the Nottingham society. She later became president of the society and was succeeded as secretary by her sister-in-law Hilda Dowson. In 1913 the society was a member of the MIDLANDS (EAST) FEDERATION OF THE NATIONAL UNION OF WOMEN'S SUFFRAGE SOCIETIES and affiliated to the National Union of Societies for Equal Citizenship in 1923.

Secretary (1891, 1913) Mrs Helena Brownsword Dowson, Felixstowe, The Park, Nottingham. Office (1912/13) Regent Chambers, 54 Long Row, Market Place, Nottingham.

Archival source: Minute Books of the Nottingham Women's Suffrage Society, 1909–24, Nottinghamshire Archives.
Bibliography: C. Weir, *Women's History in the Nottinghamshire Archives Office, 1550–1950*, 1989; Dame A. Meynell, *What Grandmother Said: The Life of Alice Dowson*, 1998.

NOVELS This list of novels that contain suffrage scenes, characters, or allusions does not claim to be exhaustive, but does give an indication of the extent to which the women's suffrage movement penetrated the popular novel. Apart from those novels dedicated to the cause, others used support for, or antipathy to, the suffrage as a shorthand by which to delineate characters, or to put plot machinery into gear by such devices as the introduction of a by-election (a much more frequent occurrence before the First World War when politicians taking up a cabinet appointment had to apply for reselection at a by-election), by which interesting outsiders were brought into a small community and political issues of the day were aired, or to add excitement by positioning characters in the melée of a suffrage rally. Many novels deal primarily with other feminist issues, such as prostitution, venereal disease, divorce, children, or poverty and women's enfranchisement is discussed as a necessary precursor to the rectification of these evils.

A DAME OF THE PRIMROSE LEAGUE [Mrs Meredith], *A Woman's Crusade*, Kegan Paul, 1893 (400 copies printed, 200 sold; one was presented to the Princess of Wales, 6 to Clubs, the remaining 200 were sold as waste paper. One of the novel's readers, in 1896, was Elizabeth Wolstenholme ELMY.)
ABBOTT, Nina, *Shadow Drama*, Duckworth, 1940 (arranged and edited by her daughter, Naomi Jacob).
AINSLIE, Kathleen, *Votes for Catharine Susan and Me*, Castell Brothers, no date (c. 1910). Delightful children's picture book, containing all the stereotypical images of the militant suffragette campaign.
ALLEN, Grant, *The Woman Who Did*, John Lane, 1895.
AMBER, Miles (Ellen Melicent Cobden SICKERT), *Sylvia Saxton; Episodes in a Life*, T. Fisher Unwin, 1914. The novel is dedicated to the artist Emily Mary Osborn (*see* Barbara BODICHON *and* Jane Cobden UNWIN) and her companion, Mary Elizabeth Dunn.

ANDREW, Stephen, *Doctor Grey*, Greening & Co., 1911. Reviewed in *Votes for Women*, 20 January 1911.
ANON, *Daughters of the City*, Harcourt, Simpkin, Marshall, 1899. Advertised in *Votes for Women*, May 1909, as "The story of a woman's battle for what she believed to be her rights and duties".
ANON, *For a God Dishonoured*, John Long, 1899.
ANON, *A Suffragette's Love Letters*, Chatto & Windus, 1907.
ANON (Millicent Heathcote), *Eve-Spinster*, Mills & Boon, 1912.
ANSTRUTHER, E.H., *The Husband*, John Lane, 1919.
ARMOUR, Margaret, *Agnes of Edinburgh*, A. Melrose, 1911. Margaret Armour was Mrs W.B. Macdougall, whose grandmother, also Margaret Armour, was a close friend of Priscilla Bright McLaren.
ATHERTON, Gertrude, *Julia France and Her Times: A Novel*, John Murray, 1912.
BAILLIE REYNOLDS, Mrs, *The Cost of a Promise; a Novel in Three Parts*, Hodder & Stoughton, 1914.
BALLYN, Deane, *The Price of Freedom: A Tale of To-day*. Creating an Entirely New Literary Form, and an introduction thereto, Walter Scott Publishing, 1910.
BENNETT, Arnold, *The Regent*, Methuen, 1913.
BENNETT, Arnold, *The Lion's Share*, Cassell, 1916.
BENSON, E.F., *Mrs Ames*, Hodder and Stoughton, 1912.
BENSON, Stella, *I Pose*, Macmillan, 1915.
BIGGS, Caroline Ashurst (ed.), *Suffrage Stories*, published by the National Society for Women's Suffrage, 1882. A series of pamphlet stories: *Jane Crump's Politics* by A Quiet Woman; *Mrs Mabury's Petition*, by the author of *Rachel's Secret*; *A Sylvan Queen*; *A Woman's Duty* by the author of *The Master of Winbourne* (Caroline Biggs); *Annie's Baby* by Carey Search; *Mrs Truffles on the Woman Question* by the author of *St Olave's* (Eliza Tabor); *What the Widow Thinks* (a long poem) by Laura Ormiston CHANT; *Where the Shoe Pinches* by A Barrister; *Mother and Child* by A Lawyer.
BRITTAIN, Vera, *Honourable Estate*, Gollancz, 1936.
BROUGHTON, Rhoda, *Dear Faustina*, Richard Bentley, 1897.
BURTON, Betty, *Goodbye Piccadilly*, Grafton, 1991.
BURTON BALDRY, William, *From Hampstead to Holloway: The Journey of a Suffragette*, John Ouseley, 1909.
CAINE, William, *The Victim and the Votery* (A Guignolerie), Greening & Co., 1908.

CARTLAND, Barbara, *Vote for Love*, Bantam Books, 1977.
CLEEVE, Lucas (Adeline Georgina Isabella Kingscote), *A Woman's Aye & Nay*, John Long, 1908.
COLE, Sophie, *A Plain Woman's Portrait*, Mills & Boon, 1912.
COLEBROOKE, Helen, *Winged Dreams*, Blackwood, 1908.
COLMORE, Gertrude, *The Crimson Gate*, Stanley Paul, 1910.
COLMORE, Gertrude, *Suffragette Sally*, Stanley Paul, 1911 (republished, Pandora, 1984, as *Suffragettes: A Story of Three Women*). In a letter of 8 October 1911 to Minnie BALDOCK, Julie East, a WSPU member living in Gunnersbury, mentioned that her husband "was on the sofa reading 'Suffragette Sally' and every now and then I hear a little gurgle of amusement. Have you read it? It is very good." (See Gertrude Baillie-WEAVER).
COLMORE, Gertrude, *Mr Jones and the Governess and other stories*, published by the Women's Freedom League, 1913. (See Gertrude Baillie-WEAVER).
COURTNEY, W.L., *The Soul of a Suffragette*, Chapman and Hall, 1913.
CROSS, Victoria (pseudonym of Vivian Cory), *Martha Brown, M.P. A girl of to-morrow*, T. Werner Laurie, 1935.
DANBY, Frank (pseudonym of Julia Frankau), *Joseph in Jeopardy*, Methuen, 1912.
DE PRATZ, Claire, *Elizabeth Davenay*, Mills & Boon, 1909.
DE SELINCOURT, Hugh, *Women and Children*, Leonard Parsons, 1921. The book was dedicated "with permission" to Emmeline PETHICK-LAWRENCE.
DESPARD, Charlotte and COLLINS, Mabel, *Outlawed: A Novel on the Woman Suffrage Question*, H.J. Drane, 1908. (Like Charlotte DESPARD, Mabel Collins was a theosophist.)
DIVER, Maud, *Unconquered: A Romance*, G.P. Putnam's, 1917.
EDGINTON, May, *The Sin of Eve*, Hodder & Stoughton, 1913.
FAIRBAIRNS, Zoe, *Stand We at Last*, Virago, 1983.
FAIRFAX, G.V., *The Working-Day World; or The Stronger Portion of Humanity*, Digby, 1893.
FORD, Ford Madox, *Some Do Not*, Duckworth, 1924.
FRASER, George, *The Humby Election: a sketch*, published on commission by Trubner, 1873. (George

Fraser was a partner in a firm of solicitors, James Fraser & Sons, 31 Copthall Ave, London EC and secretary of the the Women's Gazette Printing and Publishing Company Ltd (*see under* NEWSPAPERS AND JOURNALS).

FURSDON, F.R.M., *The Story of Amanda*, Simpkin & Marshall, 1914.

GEORGE, W.L., *A Bed of Roses*, Frank Palmer, 1913.

GIBBS, Philip, *Intellectual Mansions*, Chapman and Hall, 1910. The first edition was bought up by the WSPU and bound in a cover of purple, white and green; according to Gibbs this killed it stone dead. The novel was reviewed in *Votes for Women*, 27 May 1910.

GODDARD, Robert, *Past Caring*, Robert Hale, 1986.

GOLDIE, V., *The Declension of Henry D'Albiac*, Heinemann, 1912.

GORING-THOMAS, A.R., *The Strong Heart*. Being the Story of a Lady, John Lane, Bodley Head, 1914.

GRAHAM, Winifred, *The Enemy of Woman*, Mills & Boon, 1910.

GRAND, Sarah, *The Beth Book*, Heinemann, 1898.

GRAY, Maxwell (Mary Gleed Tuttiett), *Sweethearts and Friends, A Novel*, Marshall, Russell, 1897.

GREEN, Evelyn Everett, *Ursula Tempest*, RTS, 1910.

HAMILTON, Cicely, *William – an Englishman*, Skeffington, 1919.

HARGROVE, Ethel C., *The Garden of Desire: A Story of the Isle of Wight*, Grafton, 1916.

HARKER, L. Allen, *The Ffolliots of Red Marley*, John Murray, 1913.

HARRADEN, Beatrice, *Interplay*, F.A. Stokes, Methuen, 1908.

HAWKE, Napier, *The Premier and the Suffrage*, Henry J. Drane, 1909.

HINE, Muriel, *The Hidden Valley*, John Lane, 1919; *The Man with the Double Heart*, John Lane, 1914.

HOBSON, Mrs Coralie, *The Revolt of Youth*, T. Werner Laurie, 1919.

HOUSMAN, Laurence, *Trimblerigg*, Jonathan Cape, 1924.

HOWELL, Constance, *Chester Chase*. Digby Long, 1914.

HUTCHINSON, A.S.M., *If Winter Comes*, 1921.

JAGGER, Mrs, *"Is Love a Crime?": A Novel*, Swan Sonnenschein, Lowrey & Co., 1886. Swan Sonnenschein wrote to Mrs Jagger on 15 June, "We think your book decidedly interesting – it is certainly above the average merit of the novels issued every week".

JAMES, Norah, *Sleeveless Errand*, Babou & Kahane (Paris), 1929.

JAMESON, Storm, *The Pot Boils; A Novel*, Constable, 1919.

JOHNSTON, Sir Harry, *Mrs Warren's Daughter: A Story of the Woman's Movement*, Chatto & Windus, 1920.

JONES, F.L. Wilson, *A Would-Be Suffragette*, Digby, Long and Co., 1911.

KEENE, Leslie, *The Suffrage and Lord Laxton*, Digby, Long, 1914.

KENEALY, Annesley, *The Poodle-Woman. A Story of "Restitution of Conjugal Rights"*, Stanley Paul, 1913. (The author was a sister of Dr Arabella Kenealy and was herself a nurse who had nursed during a cholera epidemic in Hamburg *c.* 1892). This title was advertised as the first in "The Votes for Women Series"; no others appear to have been published.

LATIMER, S.F., *A Life Laid Bare or the Battle of the Suffrage*, The Standard & Current Library (Newton Abbott), 1907.

LEFROY, Ella Napier ("E.N. Leigh Fry"), *The Man's Cause*, John Lane, 1899.

LEGGE, Margaret, *A Semi-detached Marriage*, Alston Rivers, 1912.

LESLIE, Henrietta (pseud. Gladys SCHÜTZE), *A Mouse with Wings*, Collins, 1920.

LINTON, E. Lynn, *In Haste and At Leisure*, Heinemann, 1895.

LUCAS, E.V., *Mr Ingleside*, Methuen, 1910. Reviewed by Emmeline PETHICK-LAWRENCE in *Votes for Women*, 28 October 1910.

LYALL, David (pseudonym of either Annie S. Swan or Helen Mathers), *The One Who Came After; a Study of a Modern Woman*, Hodder & Stoughton, 1910.

MACKERLIE, H.G., *The Radical's Wife*, J. Macqueen, 1896.

MACNAUGHTON, S., *Some Elderly People and their Young Friends*, Smith, Elder, 1915.

MAGUIRE M.P., *John Francis, The Next Generation*, Hurst & Blackett, 1871.

MARRIOTT, Charles, *Now*, Hurst and Blackett, 1910. Reviewed in *Votes for Women*, 24 June 1910. Marriott's wife, Bessie Wigan, was a member of the committee of the ARTISTS' SUFFRAGE LEAGUE.

MASEFIELD, John, *The Street of Today*, J.M. Dent, 1911.

MASSIE, Chris, *Esther Vanner*, Sampson Low, 1937.
MAUD, Constance, *No Surrender*, Duckworth, 1911. Reviewed in *Votes for Women*, 24 November 1911. Constance Maud became a member of the WSPU in 1908.
MCLEOD, Irene Rutherford, *Graduation: A Novel*, Chatto & Windus, 1918. (*See also* DRUMMERS' UNION; YOUNG PURPLE, WHITE AND GREEN CLUB.)
MINNETT, Cora, *The Day After Tomorrow*, F.V. White, 1911.
MOLLWO, Adrienne, *A Fair Suffragette*, Henry J. Drane, 1909.
MUIR, Kate, *Suffragette City*, Macmillan, 1999.
MURRAY, Eunice, *The Hidden Tragedy*, C.W. Daniel, 1917. Dedicated to "My Colleagues, Friends and Fellow Workers in the Women's Freedom League". (*See* Eunice MURRAY).
NETHERSOLE, S.C. [Susie Colyer], *The Game of the Tangled Web*, Mills & Boon, 1916.
NORTH, Laurence (pseudonym of James David Symon), *Impatient Griselda*, Martin Secker, 1910/11.
OLDMEADOW, Annie Cecilia, *A Box of Chocolates*, Grant Richards, 1913. Dedicated "To the Militant Suffragists".
PAGE, Gertrude, *Winding Paths*, Hurst & Blackett, 1911.
PECK, Winifred, *The Skirts of Time*, Faber, 1935.
PENNELL, Elizabeth Robins, *Our House and the People in It*, T. Fisher Unwin, 1910.
RAMSAY, Miss, *Mildred's Career: A Tale of the Women's Suffrage Movement*, C. Skeet, 1874. The novel contains the printed dedication to Lady Anna GORE LANGTON "to whose generous efforts the women's suffrage movement owes so much". The novel was reviewed in the *Women's Suffrage Journal*, 1 July 1874. The author is doubtless the Miss Ramsay of 40 Royal York Crescent, Clifton, who was secretary of the Clifton section of the BRISTOL AND WEST OF ENGLAND branch of the National Society for Women's Suffrage in the 1870s, at a time when Lady Anna Gore Langton was president. A copy of the novel is held in the Blackburn Collection, Girton College; it is not in the British Library.
RAWSON, Maud Stepney, *Splendid Zipporah*, Methuen, 1911.
RE-BARTLETT, Lucy, *Transition*, Longmans Green, 1913.

ROBERTS, Mrs Katherine (probably a pseudonym), *Pages from the Diary of a Militant Suffragette*, Garden City Press, Letchworth, 1910. "Dedicated to the brave women who to-day are fighting for freedom". Reviewed in *Votes for Women*, 11 November 1910.
ROBINS, Elizabeth, *The Convert*, Macmillan, 1907.
ROBINS, Elizabeth, *Under His Roof*, 1912, Women Writers' Suffrage League pamphlet, 1912. A short story.
RYLEY, M. Beresford (pseudonym), *"Ma'am"*, Hutchinson, 1917. "The author of this novel having died while it was still in manuscript, it has been revised for the press by her friend Mr E.V. Lucas."
SAGE, E.P. Ramsay, *A Fair Field and No Favour*, H.J. Drane, 1912. Subtitled "To the women of England, this volume is offered by one of themselves".
ST JOHN, Christopher, *Hungerheart: The Story of a Soul*, Methuen, 1915. "When I went to suffragette meetings in the character of a sympathetic onlooker, I found that the 'suffragettes' were not a race apart, but a collection of ordinary wives, mothers, sisters and daughters, with all the virtues and faults of ordinary women . . .". (*See* Christopher ST JOHN).
SHARP, Evelyn, *The Making of a Prig*, John Lane, 1897. (*See* Evelyn SHARP.)
SHARP, Evelyn, *Rebel Women*, A.C. Fifield, 1910. (*See* Evelyn SHARP.)
SKELTON, Margaret, *The Book of Youth*, Collins, 1920.
SIDGWICK, Ethel, *Jamesie*, Sidgwick & Jackson, 1918.
SIEVEKING, Lance, *The Woman She Was*, Cassell, 1934.
SIMMONDS, Nita, *The House of the Suffragette*, Doherty & Co., 1911.
SINCLAIR, May, *The Tree of Heaven*, Cassell, 1917. (*See* May SINCLAIR.)
SKETCHLEY, Arthur (pseudonym of George Rose), *Mrs Brown on Woman's Rights*, Routledge, 1872.
SMEDLEY, Constance (Mrs Maxwell Armfield), *The Daughter: A Love Story*, Constable, 1908.
SMEDLEY, Constance (Mrs Maxwell Armfield), *Commoners' Rights*, Chatto & Windus, 1912.
SMEDLEY, Constance (Mrs Maxwell Armfield), *On the Fighting Line*, G.P. Putnam's Sons, 1915.
SMITH, Isabel, *Nevertheless*, Alston Rivers, 1913.

SPENDER, Emily, *Son and Heir*, Restored, Hurst & Blackett, 1871 (*see* EMILY SPENDER).

SPRING, R. Howard, *Fame is the Spur*, Collins, 1940.

STAINTON, J.S., *The Home-Breakers* (An Anti-Militant Suffragist Novel), Hurst & Blackett, 1913.

STEWART, Edith Anne, *Love and the People*, Lynwood, 1911.

SWAN, Annie S., *Margaret Holroyd; or, the Pioneers*, Hodder & Stoughton, 1910.

SYRETT, Netta, *Troublers of the Peace*, Chatto & Windus, 1917.

SYMONS, Geraldine, *Miss Rivers and Miss Bridges*, Macmillan, 1971.

MRS TIBBITS (Annie O. Tibbits), *At What Sacrifice*, Digby, Long & Co., 1912.

TOMLINSON, H.M., *The Day Before*, Heinemann, 1940.

TRAVERS, John (pseudonym of Eva Mary Bell), *In the World of Bewilderment: A Novel*, Duckworth, 1912.

TROUBRIDGE, Laura, *Body and Soul*, Mills & Boon, 1911.

TRUSCOTT, Parry, *Hilary's Career*, T. Werner Laurie, 1913.

TWEEDALE, Violet, *The Veiled Woman*, Herbert Jenkins, 1918.

U AND I, *Divers Dialogues*, R.W. Hunter (Edinburgh), 1893.

VYNNE, Nora, *The Pieces of Silver*, Andrew Melrose, 1911. One of the dedicatees is Franklin THOMASSON. (*See also* NEWSPAPERS AND JOURNALS (*Women's Tribune*); Helen BLACKBURN.)

WARD, Mrs Humphry, *Delia Blanchflower*, Ward, Lock & Co., 1914.

WELLS, H.G., *Ann Veronica*, T. Fisher Unwin, 1909. Although immensely popular with young "new women", this novel received an unsympathetic review in the *Vote*, 23 December 1909, and, for quite contradictory reasons, was accorded the distinction of being put on the "restricted list" of the Circulating Libraries Association.

WELLS, H.G., "*The New Machiavelli*", John Lane, 1911. Reviewed in *Votes for Women*, 10 February 1911. It contains a chapter devoted to the WFL 1909 picket of the House of Commons.

WELLS, H.G., *The Wife of Sir Isaac Harman*, Macmillan, 1914.

WEST, REBECCA, *The Judge*, Hutchinson, 1922.

WHITE, Percy, *To-day*, Constable, 1912.

WILSON, Jesse, *When the Women Reign. 1930*, Arthur Stockwell, 1909.

WINTER, John Strange (pseudonym of Henrietta Eliza Vaughan Stannard), *I Married a Wife; A Novel*, F.V. White, 1895.

WOOLF, Virginia, *The Voyage Out*, Duckworth, 1915; *Night and Day*, Duckworth, 1919; *The Years*, Hogarth Press, 1937.

WYLLARDE, Dolf, *The Holiday Husband*, Hurst & Blackett, 1919.

ZANGWILL, Edith, *The Call*, Allen & Unwin, 1924.

See also PRINTERS AND PUBLISHERS.

Bibliography: J. Grimes and D. Daims, *Novels in English by Women, 1891–1920: A Preliminary Checklist*, 1981; D. Daims and J. Grimes, with editorial assistance of Doris Robinson, *Towards a Feminist Tradition: An Annotated Bibliography of Novels in English by Women 1891–1920*, 1982; D. Robinson, *Women Novelists 1891–1920: An Index of Biographical and Autobiographical sources*, 1984; K. Flint, *The Woman Reader 1837–1914*, 1993; A. Ingram and D. Patai (eds), *Rediscovering Forgotten Radicals: British Women Writers, 1889–1939*; 1993; J.E. Miller, *Rebel Women*, 1994; Glenda Norquay, *Voices and Votes: A Literary Anthology of the Women's Suffrage Campaign*, 1995; M. Joannou, "Suffragette fiction and the fictions of suffrage", in M. Joannou and J. Purvis (eds), *The Women's Suffragette Movement: New Feminist Perspectives*, 1998.

NUNEATON (NUWSS) In 1913 the society was a member of the MIDLAND (WEST) FEDERATION OF THE NATIONAL UNION OF WOMEN'S SUFFRAGE SOCIETIES. Secretary (1913) Miss Agnes Dilger, 194 Coton Road, Nuneaton, Warwickshire.

O

OBAN committee of the EDINBURGH SOCIETY FOR WOMEN'S SUFFRAGE Formed in 1871 as a result of lecture tour there by Jane TAYLOUR and Agnes MCLAREN. The Oban society associated itself with the new CENTRAL COMMITTEE OF THE NATIONAL SOCIETY FOR WOMEN'S SUFFRAGE in 1872. By 1913 the society had been revived by an organizer working for the GLASGOW AND WEST OF SCOTLAND ASSOCIATION FOR WOMEN'S SUFFRAGE and was a member of the SCOTTISH FEDERATION OF THE NATIONAL UNION OF WOMEN'S SUFFRAGE SOCIETIES. Secretary (1913) Miss Busby, at Dungallan House, Oban, Argyll.

OGSTON, HELEN CHARLOTTE ELIZABETH DOUGLAS (1883–?) (later Mrs Townroe and then Mrs Bullimore) and **CONSTANCE AMELIA** (1884–?) Both born in Aberdeen. They were the daughters of Francis Ogston, professor of forensic medicine at Aberdeen University; in the 1870s he abstained from voting on a proposal that Aberdeen University should admit women as students. Helen Ogston graduated with a science degree from Aberdeen University and then came to London where she qualified as a sanitary inspector. The Ogston sisters joined the WOMEN'S SOCIAL AND POLITICAL UNION in 1908 and in June Helen Ogston was a speaker, on the same platform as Marie BRACKENBURY and F.E.M. MACAULAY, at the Hyde Park Demonstration. In October she was speaking for the WSPU in Battersea Park. Constance may have remained in Aberdeen; she was certainly supporting the WSPU there in early 1909. On 5 December 1908 Helen Ogston achieved a measure of notoriety by wielding a dog-whip in the Albert Hall. She volunteered to attend, as a WSPU heckler, a meeting held by the WOMEN'S LIBERAL FEDERATION, chaired by Lady MCLAREN and with Lloyd George as its principal speaker, at the Albert Hall. However, before the meeting she told Sylvia PANKHURST, who was expecting the women to be attacked by Liberal stewards and had organized in advance a press conference at which their injuries were to be displayed, that she intended to take a dog-whip to defend herself from "indecent assault". Sylvia Pankhurst attempted to dissuade her, thinking that a whip would be too deliberate and indiscriminate a weapon and suggesting that instead she arm herself with an umbrella. In spite of this advice Helen Ogston took the whip and used it, she said, when a man put the lighted end of a cigar on her wrist and another struck her on the chest. Although Frederick PETHICK-LAWRENCE deplored both Helen Ogston's action and the fact that she had acted on her own initiative, Sylvia Pankhurst thought that, on balance, the incident attracted sympathy to the WSPU, highlighting the violence of the treatment to which its members were subjected. Before the WLF meeting the WSPU had been in correspondence with Lloyd George, intimating that unless he pledged government action on women's suffrage, or at least himself resigned from the cabinet on the issue, he would be subjected to WSPU heckling. It is now clear that Lloyd George considered that the WSPU could only do its cause harm by disrupting a meeting held to discuss the suffrage issue, and that in the event Helen Ogston's action, on which the press concentrated, may, from the government point of view, have distracted attention from the fact that he had nothing new to offer. One side-effect of the turmoil at the Albert Hall was that Lloyd George in future barred women from all his meetings and the government introduced the Public Meetings Bill.

In 1909 Helen Ogston was based in Brighton, certainly speaking in the town in January and June and conducting a campaign through southern England in November. In 1910 she presumably left the WSPU when she was appointed as an organizer for the newly founded NEW CONSTITUTIONAL SOCIETY FOR WOMEN'S SUFFRAGE. Helen Ogston married,

first in 1912 and for the second time in 1929; Constance married in 1920.
Portrait: representation of Helen Ogston with dog-whip in Albert Hall, in *Illustrated London News*, 12 December 1908.
Bibliography: *Votes for Women*, 10 December 1908; A. Rosen, *Rise Up Women!; The Militant Campaign of the Women's Social and Political Union 1903–14*, 1974; L. Moore, *Bajanellas and Semilinas: Aberdeen University and the Education of Women, 1860–1920*, 1991.

OLDHAM (WSPU)   Secretary (1906) Miss Ogden, 275 Waterloo Street, Oldham, Lancashire.

OLDHAM WOMEN'S SUFFRAGE SOCIETY (NUWSS)   Formed in 1910, with Margory LEES as president. Mrs FAWCETT spoke at a meeting in the town on 8 November 1910 to discuss the formation of a suffrage society. The society joined the MANCHESTER AND DISTRICT FEDERATION OF THE NATIONAL UNION OF WOMEN'S SUFFRAGE SOCIETIES. Membership grew rapidly from 130 members in 1911 to 857 members in 1913. Twenty-three members of the Oldham society took part in the Suffrage Coronation Procession in June 1911, carrying the society's banner. By November 1911 the Oldham society had opened a suffrage shop. Margory Lees and other members of the Oldham society took an enthusiastic part in the PILGRIMAGE in July 1913. The Oldham society fully supported the FRIENDS OF WOMEN'S SUFFRAGE scheme, by which membership was opened up to the poorer members of the working classes. After 1919 the Oldham Women's Suffrage Society was reformed into a Women Citizens' Association and subsequently amalgamated with the National Council of Women in 1921.
Secretary (1913) Mrs Bridge, 82 Greengate St, Oldham.
Photograph: of Oldham NUWSS shop, taken in November 1911, Fawcett Library.
Archival source: Lees Papers, Oldham Local Studies Library.

OLTON (NUWSS)   In 1913 the society was a member of the MIDLAND (WEST) FEDERATION OF THE NATIONAL UNION OF WOMEN'S SUFFRAGE SOCIETIES. Secretary (1909) Mrs H. Small, Orielton, Olton, Birmingham; (1913) Miss Bennett, Trimpley, Kineton Road, Olton, Birmingham.

O'MALLEY, IDA BEATRICE (1874–1939)   Born at Waltham Abbey, Essex, daughter of a major in the Royal Artillery whose family came from Co. Mayo. After spending her childhood years in Halifax, Nova Scotia and Gibraltar, she was educated from the age of 15 at St Leonards School, St Andrews, and at Lady Margaret Hall, Oxford, from where she graduated in Modern History in 1896. While continuing to live with her family in Oxford she was a close friend of Maude ROYDEN and Kathleen COURTNEY and was a member of the executive committee of the OXFORD SOCIETY FOR WOMEN'S SUFFRAGE. After moving to London after the death of her father in 1909 she was a vice-president of the Oxford Old Students' Women's Suffrage Society, a member of the executive committee of the LONDON SOCIETY FOR WOMEN'S SUFFRAGE, a member of the executive committee of the NATIONAL UNION OF WOMEN'S SUFFRAGE SOCIETIES, by 1911 honorary secretary of its literature sub-committee and, after 1912, of the FRIENDS OF WOMEN'S SUFFRAGE sub-committee. Her work for the NUWSS was unpaid; she presumably had private means. Ida O'Malley was a close friend of Maude Royden and Catherine MARSHALL, subscribed to the NUWSS Election Fighting Fund in 1912, and was a member of the committee of the Whitechapel and St George in the East branch of the LSWS in 1913. In addition to her involvement with the NUWSS Ida O'Malley was in 1910 a supporter of the TAX RESISTANCE LEAGUE and a member of the executive committee of the CHURCH LEAGUE FOR WOMEN'S SUFFRAGE. Converted from agnosticism to Christianity, she became devoutly high church. Her niece thought that she was much influenced by the novels of Charlotte M. Yonge. From 1917 until 1920 Ida O'Malley was editor of the *Common Cause* and *Woman's Leader*. From around 1920 she informally adopted her two nieces, daughters of her younger brother, devoting herself to their upbringing, relinquishing her suffrage involvement, and contributing anonymously "The Diary of The Woman in the Home" to the *Woman's Leader*. She later was the author of a biography of Florence Nightingale, 1931, and of *Women in Subjection*, 1933.

Address: (1892) Belview, Exeter; (1913) 51 Paulton's Square, Chelsea, London SW; (1913–1930s) 6 Steeles Road, London NW3.

Archival source: B. Harrison, taped interview with Mrs Mary Dunlop, adopted daughter (and niece) of Ida O'Malley, 1977.

ORCADIAN WOMEN'S SUFFRAGE SOCIETY (NUWSS) Although Orkney had been visited in the autumn of 1871 by Agnes MCLAREN and Jane TAYLOUR who addressed public meetings on the question of women's suffrage, it was only on 25 September 1909 that a formal society was founded on the island. The OWSS held seven public meetings in its first year, by the end of which it had 55 members. In June 1910 Miss Lamond (*see* Elizabeth ABBOTT), the organizer for the SCOTTISH FEDERATION OF WOMEN'S SUFFRAGE SOCIETIES, of which the society was a member, visited Orkney to address a meeting of the society. In 1911 a branch of the WOMEN'S SOCIAL AND POLITICAL UNION that had been formed at Stromness converted itself into a branch of the OWSS. In 1911 the Orcadian society's BANNER, designed by Stanley Cursitor and Christina JAMIESON, was taken to London to be carried in the suffrage Coronation Procession on 17 June. In April 1912 Dr Elsie INGLIS visited Orkney to address a meeting of the society and later that year the OWSS was the only Scottish NUWSS society to contribute towards the cost of Mrs DE FONBLANQUE's "Woman's March" from Edinburgh to London. Secretary (1913) Mrs Bina Cursitor, Daisybank, Kirkwall, Orkney. In 1916, by which time membership of the society had risen to almost 100, Mrs Cursitor moved to Edinburgh and, on her departure, was presented with a gold watch in appreciation of her service to the OWSS.

Archival source: The *Orkney Herald*, 1909–17, references supplied by The Orkney Library, Kirkwall, Orkney.

ORGANIZER The term used to denote a paid peripatetic employee of the women's suffrage campaign. Throughout the 58 years of campaigning for women's enfranchisement prior to the First World War the majority of the women involved in the movement gave their services voluntarily. There was a clear social distinction between these women and those whom they employed. During the nineteenth century the paid secretaries of societies, many of whom are now known only as names, occupied an anomalous position between that of honorary secretary and organizer. They were ladies, but the necessity of earning their own living deprived them of moral authority. Helen BLACKBURN, secretary at various times to the societies in Bristol and London, by contributing a history of the movement and leaving behind an extensive archive, has a stronger corporeal presence than many of the other women in similar positions, but was considered by her contemporaries to be a "character" rather than a champion. Lydia BECKER, who built up for herself the reputation of a "champion", was always at pains to stress that she gave her services voluntarily to the MANCHESTER NATIONAL SOCIETY, although she did accept the payment of expenses when offered. Elizabeth Wolstenholme ELMY maintained that it was because she accepted a salary as secretary of the WOMEN'S FRANCHISE LEAGUE that her position had been so weakened as to allow others to force her to resign. Although in dire financial straits, she never made what she saw as the mistake of accepting a salary again, although prepared to receive donations from the "Grateful Fund" organized by her supporters. By the turn of the century, as the numbers of middle-class working women increased, the stigma attached to the position of paid secretary appears to have evaporated and the new generation of women, such as Esther ROPER in Manchester and Edith PALLISER in London, carried with them real authority.

Interestingly, it is Lydia Becker who could claim the title of the first "organizer" for the women's suffrage movement. In June 1867 she was asked by Helen TAYLOR and Mentia TAYLOR to travel to Colchester to organize there a petition to present to the local MP, Mr Karslake, and to set up a committee of ladies in favour of women's suffrage. Lydia Becker had already intimated that she was willing to go anywhere to undertake such work, provided her travelling expenses were paid. A letter from Helen Taylor delicately asked whether Lydia Becker would mind staying in a hotel in Colchester, because, although the London committee was able to provide her with introductions to some local ladies, these were not personal friends and she could not therefore expect to stay with them. This social minefield was successfully negotiated; Lydia Becker's social status and respectability were preserved, and she received out-of-pocket expenses while she was organizing the Colchester petition.

The correspondence surrounding this episode does reveal a tension. Lydia Becker was, at this very early stage of the campaign, willing to be helpful and particularly grateful to be in contact with a man as eminent as John Stuart MILL, but once she established her position as honorary secretary of the Manchester National Society, she did not wish to risk losing authority by accepting payment for work undertaken in the campaign. When in 1881 she was persuaded to act as secretary to the CENTRAL COMMITTEE OF THE NATIONAL SOCIETY FOR WOMEN'S SUFFRAGE considerable pains were taken to preserve her *amour propre* by stressing that the payment she received was only to assist her with her travelling expenses between London and Manchester.

Very soon after her return from Colchester in 1867 Lydia Becker employed, on behalf of the Manchester National Society, a Miss Knott to canvass in Bolton and Liverpool for names for the women's suffrage petitions. Lydia Becker described Miss Knott in a letter to Helen Taylor as "an intelligent superior person of her class, and [with] a very pleasing manner, simple and unobtrusive so that there is nothing about her which could possibly repel or produce an unfavourable impression on the people she visits". This short description, besides telling us about Miss Knott, also reveals the expectations and fears of both Lydia Becker and Helen Taylor. Miss Knott was paid £2 a week. At the same time Clementia TAYLOR, on behalf of the London National Society, employed Mary Grant, the eminently respectable wife of her husband's secretary and the mother of a future Liberal MP, to act as a canvasser in Southwark, collecting names for the LONDON NATIONAL SOCIETY's petition. The London society did not, however, continue with this method of canvassing, preferring to approach likely signatories by means of a letter from its principals rather than by a paid intermediary. This method of working was stigmatized by Lydia Becker as unnecessarily expensive. The Manchester society continued to be the most organizationally innovative of the national suffrage societies, by 1877 employing a full-time agent, Mrs McCormick, who travelled all over the north of England, arranging and attending the public meetings organized by the society. In that year she also accompanied Alice SCATCHERD to Grimsby and north Northamptonshire during the parliamentary elections, attended deputations to the candidates, and devoted 156 days to office and other work in Manchester. She was probably employed by the Manchester society until 1885 after which time the society apparently no longer wished, or perhaps could not afford, to retain an organizer. In 1886 Alice Scatcherd tried to arrange an annuity for Mrs McCormick, with whom she remained personally friendly well into the 1890s. In 1890 Mrs McCormick became organizer to the WOMEN'S FRANCHISE LEAGUE, as successor to Agnes SUNLEY. The latter had remained loyal to Elizabeth Wolstenholme Elmy, joining her in the WOMEN'S EMANCIPATION UNION, thereby sacrificing her much-needed salary. The WEU could not afford such a luxury as an organizer.

In 1877 Mrs McCormick besides her work for the Manchester National Society had also assisted the Central Committee of the National Society for Women's Suffrage. By 1883 the Central Committee employed its own organizing agent, Miss Moore. After the division in the Central Committee, the CENTRAL NATIONAL SOCIETY by 1890 employed Caroline Fothergill as a special organizing agent and in 1896 a Miss Cameron. In order to put into effect the campaign amongst the women texile workers in their area, in 1899 and 1900 the NORTH OF ENGLAND SOCIETY (the renamed Manchester society) launched a "Special Organising Agents' Fund". Katherine Rowton, Mrs Hodgson Bayfield, Mrs Ramsbottom, Mrs Green and Sarah REDDISH were the organizers paid for by this fund, to which Agnes POCHIN and Priscilla Bright McLAREN, two of the stalwarts of the suffrage campaign, contributed. Sarah Reddish was by this time a professional, having been employed in 1893 as the first organizer (at a salary of £1 a week plus expenses) for the Women's Co-operative Guild. Between them these women collected 29 359 signatures for the petition from Lancashire women cotton factory operatives.

Agnes Sunley and Sarah Reddish certainly, and Mrs McCormick probably, were working-class women. Jessie CRAIGEN and Jane TAYLOUR, two other peripatetic workers connected to the nineteenth-century women's suffrage movement, occupied a rather more anomalous position. They were freelance workers rather than being directly employed by a suffrage society and their idiosyncracies and devotion to the cause appear to have overridden class distinction. Although not organizers, Helena DOWNING and Mme Jane RONNIGER were middle-class women who lectured, presumably for payment, on behalf of the suffrage cause. The fact that the former was Irish and the latter, although leaving no clues as to her origin, would appear to have been married to, or the widow of, a Frenchman doubtless vitiated the restrictions that might have conventionally been imposed on them. In the last quarter of the nineteenth century, when it was generally still considered socially reprehensible for middle-class women to work for money outside the home, the peripatetic nature of the organizer's work, travelling alone around the country and staying in a series of lodgings, would have additionally limited its appeal to all but the most dedicated to the cause. As a corollary those who did undertake the work might well have been seen at best as eccentric.

In terms of census categories the work of a female organizer most closely resembled that of a female clerk, the numbers of which increased in England and Wales from 279 in 1861, to 18 947 in 1891 and to 124 843 in 1911. In the same way as it became economically possible and socially acceptable for middle-class women to work as clerks, so it became possible for them to work as employees of the suffrage societies. The growth in the work of the suffrage movement in the early years of the twentieth century was a factor of the growth in the numbers of educated women able and willing to exchange their homes for "digs". When in 1903 the NATIONAL UNION OF WOMEN'S SUFFRAGE SOCIETIES began to find a new cohesive identity, Isabella FORD suggested to its executive committee that an organizer should be sent round once a year to offer help to the different societies in the Union, and that an organizer should be employed at election times. During the course of 1904 the NUWSS appointed two national organizers at a salary of £70 to £80 per annum. The experiment presumably was initially not deemed a success because by 1905 it was decided that the local societies should instead employ their own organizers and that the Union would give grants towards this expense rather than employing an organizer directly. However, by 1907 the NUWSS was again employing two organizers, one of whom, Mrs Bertram, was paid £120 per annum and still held her position in 1913. As the suffrage campaign gained momentum, by 1908 the NUWSS employed six organizers and in 1909, ten. One of them, Margaret Robertson, gave a good description of her hectic peripatetic life at this time in an article, "An Organiser's Work", in the *Common Cause*, 29 April 1909. The NUWSS sent out its organizers to give added support to local societies. In February 1912 Miss Fielden was sent to help the BEDFORD WOMEN'S SUFFRAGE SOCIETY for two weeks. In that time she arranged three drawing-room meetings and herself addressed meetings of the ILP, the Women's Adult School, the Women's Liberal Association, the Women's Temperance Association and an open meeting at the Co-operative Hall, as well as organizing a very successful social evening. Over 50 new members were enrolled during that fortnight. Miss Fielden also arranged a deputation to Mr Kellaway, the MP for Bedford, at which both she and Edith Palliser spoke.

After the NUWSS regrouped its branches into federations in 1910, organizers were employed at federation level. In the summer of 1911 the Surrey and Hants organizer, Mrs Dempster, spent four days working in Southampton. For the occasion she stayed with one of the Southampton committee members, who received a vote of thanks but apparently no payment for her board and lodging. In November 1912 Mrs Dempster returned to Southampton for another five days' work. The Southampton committee was adamant that it could not afford to pay for her stay; hospitality had to be supplied by individual members. However, when another organizer was sent to Southampton a couple of months later in order to arrange a postal campaign, the committee was able to pay for her board and lodging although, rather grudgingly, the minutes record that they thought it rather expensive. On such minutiae are great campaigns built.

The larger NUWSS societies had their own full-time organizer. From July 1910 the NEWCASTLE SOCIETY had employed in this capacity, Clementina Gordon, a middle-class socialist whose sister Lisa was in 1913 secretary of the Edinburgh society. In January 1914 the OXFORD NUWSS society employed Helga Gill as organizer at a salary of £120 per annum, plus travelling expenses and half-board and lodging expenses. Her lodgings in Oxford were, however, to be approved by the executive committee of the Oxford society. She was allowed eight weeks' holiday in the year (including bank holidays) and was required to make a weekly report to the society's secretary.

In Scotland it is not clear if the Edinburgh society employed an organizer before 1904 when it appointed Miss Andrew at a salary of £2 2s a week plus travelling expenses. In the 1870s Agnes McLaren and Jane Taylour had undertaken extensive missionary work around the country, but presumably this was on a voluntary basis. As the NUWSS suffrage campaign became increasingly professional Wilhelmina Lamond (see Elizabeth Abbott) was employed in 1909 as an organizer by the Edinburgh society and the NUWSS. In 1911–12 the minutes of the Glasgow and West of Scotland Association contain extensive discussion of the desirability of "joining with the Scottish Federation in engaging an Organizer for 6 months at a salary of £2 per week and out of pocket expenses amounting in all to a total of £90 payable equally £45". The search for a suitable organizer turned into a saga that occupied the Association until the outbreak of war in August 1914. In May 1912, after various unsuccessful attempts, the GWSAWS eventually hired a Miss Watson, who was also a NUWSS organizer. She spent five weeks of the summer resuscitating societies at Oban and Gourock and starting new ones at Largs and Blairmore, injecting some vitality into the somewhat torpid GWSAWS. However, a suggestion that Miss Watson should be co-opted as a member of the executive committee was rejected in favour of offering her an invitation to attend the committee meetings only when her presence was required. The GWSAWS was not yet ready for a level of democracy that would include employees in its discussions. Miss Watson may have left when her contract came to an end because in December 1912 her successor, Miss Marion Kerr, was appointed as an organizer to GWSAWS on an initial contract of six months at a salary of £100 per annum, with five weeks' holiday a year (one month to be taken in the summer and one week either at Easter or at Christmas, besides the public holidays and the Fair weekend). Miss Kerr was the first organizer that the Association supported in attending the NUWSS annual meeting "as it was most important that she should get into touch with all the work and with other organizers" (Minutes 19 February 1913). Miss Kerr, however, took her holiday from 24 to 31 March 1913 and then handed in her notice on 14 April as "she found the work too heavy". She offered to work half of each day, as did a Miss Kirby; they were presumably offering a job share. However, Miss Kerr's resignation was accepted and she was asked to carry on working half-time until another organizer could be appointed. Miss Kirby's offer was not accepted. Miss Kerr then asked for ten days' holiday before starting half-time work. None of the applicants for her job proved suitable so Miss Watson was asked to come back from September until the end of April. It was agreed that she should be paid the salary she suggested, £175 per annum, travelling and other expenses, three weeks' holiday at Christmas, a fortnight at Easter, and Saturday afternoons and the usual public holidays off. However, after this was acceded to, Miss Watson then let it be known that she could not accept a short-term contract and the GWSAWS agreed, in desperation, to accept her on her own terms, that is, as a permanent appointment with one month's notice each side. They did, however, ask that she take only a fortnight's holiday at both Christmas and Easter. However the GWSAWS, despite all this negotiation, then decided that it would look for someone less expensive. By 1 September 1913 it had employed Miss Shakespeare, who had been recommended by the NUWSS, at a salary of £120 per annum, all travelling expenses in town and personal expenses out of town when hospitality was not given. She was to have one month's holiday in the summer, a week at Christmas, a week at Easter, all public holidays, the whole of every second Saturday and the afternoon of the other. By November Miss Shakespeare had been accorded the honour of being invited to attend executive committee meetings. By May 1914, for whatever reason, the GWSAWS minutes record that "Miss Shakespeare was not suited to Glasgow and Glasgow was not suited to her." The tricky matter of a replacement was solved by the outbreak of war and the resolve of the GWSAWS executive committee to do without an organizer.

The WOMEN'S SOCIAL AND POLITICAL UNION, being a creature of the twentieth century, does not appear to have suffered from the social tensions between its paid and voluntary workers that beset the early days of the NUWSS. By 1906, when the campaigns of both the NUWSS and the WSPU began in earnest, the work of an organizer was acceptable to women from a wide variety of backgrounds. Although there was nothing particular in the work of hiring speakers, halls and sandwich men, dealing with printers, the police and newspaper offices that made the work of an organizer "middle class", women who competently negotiated these hurdles gained confidence and authority. For Annie KENNEY, who could claim to be the WSPU's first organizer, the acceptance of this position, allied to her own natural charm, meant that she was able to move with ease between the factory and the drawing room. Minnie BALDOCK, Selina COOPER, Emma SPROSON and Ada CHEW were all working-class women who clearly possessed excellent speaking and organizational skills, which, allied with a natural dignity, made them respected employees of the mainly middle-class suffrage societies. Most WSPU organizers, if not born into the middle class, had acquired an education, always a key to social mobility. Teresa Billington (see Teresa BILLINGTON-GREIG), having been first a teacher and then the ILP's first woman organizer, transferred her undoubted ability to the WSPU at Easter 1906. She and Mary GAWTHORPE, who also had teaching qualifications and became an organizer in 1906, were paid £2 a week. This was the rate of pay that in 1909 Mary BLATHWAYT, herself a voluntary worker, recorded that organizers were then paid, and which Olive BARTELS received in 1913. An organizer's remuneration, the average for a woman clerk in a good-class business house, thus stayed constant throughout the militant campaign. Grace ROE initially received £2 a week, but as her responsibility increased so her salary rose to £2 10s by June 1914. Mary PHILLIPS, who had been a WSPU organizer since 1907, was earning £2 15s a week in 1912.

After the WSPU established a presence in London the campaign developed rapidly and by 6 September 1906 Elizabeth Wolstenholme Elmy was able to record in a letter to Harriet MCILQUHAM that besides Christabel PANKHURST, Teresa Billington and Annie Kenney, "there are now 5 women organizers actively at work". By February 1909 the WSPU employed 30 organizers throughout the country, which was then divided into eight districts. A year later it increased its districts to 23, each in the charge of a paid organizer, as well as employing peripatetic organizers. Unlike the NUWSS, whose constituent societies were run by local women, WSPU branches were managed by organizers appointed by Clement's Inn. The organizers were moved around from district to district quite frequently. This was in part dictated by the exigencies of the campaign and in part to dissuade any building up of personal support. Clement's Inn controlled its organizers by keeping a tight rein over the expenses they incurred and even at one stage in the campaign required them to send in a weekly diary of the work they had undertaken. A sample diary was provided by Clement's Inn in order to indicate how the days should be spent. At all stages of the militant campaign WSPU headquarters had difficulty in restraining organizers from volunteering for deputations or demonstrations that might attract imprisonment. In the last phase of the militant campaign very clear instructions were issued requiring organizers to stay at their posts and allow activists, who were considered more expendable, to commit acts of terrorism. The role of the organizer was not universally applauded. Rebecca West reiterated her concern in the *Daily Herald,* 5 and 11 September 1912 and in the *Clarion,* 24 January 1913, in which she wrote that the WSPU had "wasted a wonderful opportunity when it encouraged its working-class women with a genius for revolt to leave their mills and go to south-coast watering-places to convert retired Anglo-Indian colonels". She thought that it would have been preferable for the mill girls to stay in their mills, the teachers in their schools, and shop assistants in their shops and to conduct a revolution from within their workplace rather than travelling over the country and living in commercial hotels.

Britain's extensive train network did indeed allow organizers to reach every corner of the country. Sometimes hospitality was provided by sympathizers. For instance Miss I. Carrie, a teacher from Arbroath, agreed to allow WSPU speakers to stay in her house in Dundee, although reluctant to let this be generally known. When interviewed, she described how she "got the bedroom ready, leaving a gas on, food ready if needed, and all the lights on that were necessary and left the door unlocked and they just stepped in. I did not stay up to meet them as they were usually late and I left breakfast for them in the kitchen and they prepared their own breakfast and I was usually away before they got up." At the height of the militant campaign such was the trust felt by sympathizers for activists that Eileen CASEY's parents were prepared to leave a door unlocked at night in order that two women, whom they must have suspected were guilty of some form of criminal damage and who were previously unknown to them (it was the latter fact that caused consternation at the trial), could slip into the house. It was, however, more usual for organizers to stay in commercial lodgings. In response to a query from Ada FLATMAN, Decima MOORE, an actress and therefore a seasoned peripatetic, gave details of digs in Cheltenham, writing, "they are theatrical women and used to serving meals at all hours". Thus Ada Flatman, while supervising an election campaign was able to make use of this advice, renting three rooms, with a bath, for 20s a week. *The Women's Suffrage Cookery Book*, compiled by Mrs Aubrey Dowson (a member of the Birmingham NUWSS society and related by marriage to the Dowsons of Nottingham), a fund-raising venture that solicited recipes from NUWSS activists, included "Menus for Meals for Suffrage Workers". "It is essential that the meals should be sustaining and yet they must be simple and such as can be eaten quickly, and also made up of dishes which will keep hot without spoiling and can be eaten with impunity at any hour." "Gravy Soup, Galatine of Turkey and Tongue, and Summer Pudding" was one of the menus that a fortunate organizer might expect at the end of an exacting day. In some towns there was a "suffrage" lodging in which organizers always stayed. Minnie TURNER's boarding house was Brighton's such centre. In Folkestone a boarding house, "Treverra", 30 Bouverie Road West, was used both as a base by WSPU organizers and as a hiding place for escaped "mice". However, not all organizers were prepared to endure a nomadic existence. Annie Kenney, who remained in Bristol working as WSPU organizer for a longer period than was usual, moved through a series of digs before adopting a radical alternative and renting a flat. When she moved back to London she continued this independent way of life in a rented flat in Mecklenburgh Square.

Women such as Ada Flatman, Lillian LENTON, Kitty MARION and Selina Cooper attempted to prolong their careers as organizers after the ending of the campaign for the vote. The world had, however, moved on and political campaigning had become less women-orientated. After 1918 the political parties did employ a certain number of women as constituency organizers and assistant election agents and women might also hold similar posts in pressure groups, but there was no longer the necessity to organize the country. Doubtless the women who had worked for the suffrage societies and who, after taking advantage of whatever the First World War had to offer them, were still of an age to develop a career, derived considerable benefit from their experience as organizers. Older unqualified women for whom their time as organizers had come as a welcome solution to the problem of employment discovered that the post-war world little valued their experience.

Archival sources: Lydia Becker Papers, Manchester Central Library; Mill–Taylor Papers, London School of Economics and Political Science; Elizabeth Wolstenholme Elmy Papers, British Library; Minutes of the Glasgow and West of Scotland Association for Women's Suffrage, Department of Rare Books and Manuscripts, Mitchell Library, Glasgow; Documents relating to the Bedford Society for Women's Suffrage, Bedfordshire Record Office; interview with Miss I Carrie, December 1976, by Dr Sheila Hamilton, Dundee Archives.

Bibliography: L. Holcombe, *Victorian Ladies at Work: Middle-class Working Women in England and Wales 1850–1914*, 1973; J. Marcus (ed.), *The Young Rebecca: Writings of Rebecca West 1911–1917*, 1982.

ORME FAMILY Mrs Eliza Orme (always known as Mrs Charles Orme) (1816–92) was born in Romford, Essex, eldest daughter of Rev. Edward Andrews, a nonconformist minister who in 1829 started teaching Latin and Greek to the young John Ruskin. One of her sisters, Emily, in 1847 married the poet Coventry Patmore and in 1854 was immortalized as *The Angel in the House*. Another sister, Georgiana, in 1854 married Coventry Patmore's brother George. Eliza Andrews in 1832, a year after the death of her mother, married Charles Orme, the son of a wealthy brewer. She and her husband cultivated a large literary and artistic circle, including Pre-Raphaelites, Carlyle, Ruskin and Tennyson. Emily Patmore died in 1863 and Eliza Orme, to whom she had been very close, was subsequently considered by Coventry Patmore to take insufficient interest in himself and his four children. He formally broke off relations with the Ormes. Perhaps Eliza Orme was out of sympathy with his attitude to women; certainly in 1866 she signed the women's suffrage petition, subscribed to the ENFRANCHISEMENT OF WOMEN COMMITTEE in 1866–7 and joined the LONDON NATIONAL SOCIETY FOR WOMEN'S SUFFRAGE in 1867. One of her daughters, [Emily] Rosaline, married David Masson (see MASSON FAMILY), and another, Eliza (1849–1937), was in 1872 joint secretary of the London National Society and a member of the EDINBURGH NATIONAL SOCIETY. Eliza Orme the younger was also a member of the managing committee of the Society for Promoting the Employment of Women from 1873 until 1877. In that year she was also a member of the governing council of the London School of Medicine for Women. In 1872 she wrote to Helen TAYLOR to tell her that she had just resigned her post as secretary of the LNS in order to undertake some practical work and that she was interested in entering the legal profession. In 1873–4 Helen Taylor paid £75 for Eliza Orme to work as a pupil to Mr Vaizey in Old Square, Lincoln's Inn; the introduction was arranged through Alice WESTLAKE's husband John. It is interesting to speculate as to why Helen Taylor paid this fee; it would seem unlikely that neither Eliza Orme nor her family could have afforded to have paid it. It is possible that there was family disapproval, although Helen Taylor was keen for women to test entry to the legal profession and may have insisted on paying. In 1881 Eliza Orme was still living at home and gives herself no occupation in her census return. However, by 1882 she is described as a legal conveyancer and in 1888 was working in partnership with a Miss Richardson. In 1875 it was Eliza Orme who alerted Helen Taylor to a girl, Phoebe Sarah Marks (see Hertha AYRTON), to whom she had taught mathematics, who wanted to study at Girton. Coincidentally it was Eliza Orme who wrote the obituary in the *Englishwoman's Review*, 15 August 1883, of Matilda Chaplin Ayrton, Professor Ayrton's first wife. In the 1880s she was a member of the Personal Liberty Club, delivering to it an address on "The Evils of Compulsory Education" on 19 October 1880.

In 1875 Eliza Orme (the younger) was, although no longer secretary, an active member of the London National Society for Women's Suffrage, speaking that year at a suffrage meeting in St Pancras. In 1882 she was a member of the general committee of the Beckenham branch of the CENTRAL COMMITTEE FOR WOMEN'S SUFFRAGE and spoke at a women's suffrage meeting there. In 1885 she signed a petition to the House of Lords in support of the Woman's Suffrage Bill. She was a member of the Royal Commission of Labour: The Employment of Women, 1893, one of four women assistant commissioners. She was editor and manager of the *Women's Gazette*, the organ of the Women's Liberal Federation (see NEWSPAPERS AND JOURNALS), and secretary of the Home Rule Union. In 1899 she was a member of the executive committee of the Women's National Liberal Association.

Address: Eliza (Mrs Charles) Orme (1866) 81 Avenue Road, Regent's Park, London; Eliza Orme, the younger (1882) The Orchard, Bedford Park, Chiswick, London W and 27 Southampton Buildings, London WC; (1908) 118 Upper Tulse Hill, London SW; (1937) Dunstanton, Christchurch Road, Streatham, Surrey.
Portrait: Eliza (Mrs Charles) Orme in I. Anstruther, *Coventry Patmore's Angel*, 1992.
Archival source: Mill–Taylor Papers, London School of Economics and Political Science.
Bibliography: F. Masson, *Victorians All*, 1931; E. Sharp, *Hertha Ayrton*, 1926; I. Anstruther, *Coventry Patmore's Angel: A Study of Coventry Patmore, His Wife Emily and The Angel in the House*, 1992.

O'SHEA, NORAH (1865–1953) Born in South Stoneham. Despite her name and red hair she was not, as Lancelot Surry (see PILGRIMAGE) thought, Irish-born. Her sister Margaret was a member of the CENTRAL SOCIETY FOR WOMEN'S SUFFRAGE in 1905. In 1907 Norah O'Shea gave a drawing-room meeting for the LONDON SOCIETY FOR WOMEN'S SUFFRAGE and in the ensuing years was the very efficient secretary of the Portsmouth branch of the NATIONAL UNION OF WOMEN'S SUFFRAGE SOCIETIES and had, it would appear, responsibility for some of the time for the Southampton branch. In 1912 she offered a collection of books to the Southampton branch to be sold in aid of the society; the offer was rejected. She put together a selection of books of feminist interest which acted as the Portsmouth branch's lending LIBRARY; a few of the books survive in the Portsmouth Record Office. Besides speaking at suffrage meetings in the area, Norah O'Shea in 1910 opened her garden for a party organized by the Portsmouth branch of the NUWSS. In 1913 she was the parliamentary secretary to the SURREY, SUSSEX AND HAMPSHIRE FEDERATION of the NUWSS. In May 1913 she was presented with a beautiful album, decorated in red, white and green, by the Portsmouth branch of the NUWSS and its Gosport and Cosham branches "in recognition of her devoted services as honorary Secretary and her long and self-sacrificing work in the cause of Women's Suffrage". The album contains 133 signatures, including that of Harriet Blessley (see PILGRIMAGE), but it is not clear what occasioned the testimonial at this time. Two months later Norah O'Shea organized the Portsmouth contingent of the NUWSS Pilgrimage, paying for the pilgrims' first lunch, taken at a pub, speaking at meetings along the way and chairing the platform of the Surrey, Sussex and Hampshire Federation at the final rally in Hyde Park on 26 July. Her sister Margaret described as "dark, quiet and stately" (*Portsmouth Evening News*, 7 May 1963), wrote a suffrage song, "Forward, brave and dauntless/ Daughters of the earth,/ Let your dormant talents/ Spring to glorious birth". Both Norah O'Shea and her sister were vegetarians, were involved in campaigns for animal welfare and were interested in herbal remedies. Norah O'Shea had a letter published in the *Freewoman*, 25 July 1912, from which it would appear that she was a regular reader of that emancipated journal. During the First World War Norah O'Shea, an anti-militarist member of the NUWSS, was a leader of the Women's Union of Peace. The sisters may have had socialist leanings; they lent a copy of M.P. Price, *The Diplomatic History of the War*, 1914, to the Cosham Labour Party's library. In 1917 Norah O'Shea became honorary secretary of the newly formed PORTSMOUTH branch of the UNITED SUFFRAGISTS. The first meeting of the society was jointly arranged with the Portsmouth Trades and Labour Council. Although there is no indication that either Margaret or Norah worked for their living, they were certainly by no means wealthy. In her will Norah O'Shea, the surviving sister, left the remainder of her estate, after four bequests of family pictures and papers, to her solicitor "in recognition of many acts of unfailing kindness, consideration and help given during many years of financial strain and trouble to myself, my sister Margaret O'Shea".

Address: (1907) The Cottage, Cosham, Portsmouth; (1923) may be same address – 53 Havant Road, Cosham, Portsmouth; (1950) 21 Weston Avenue, Milton, Southsea, Hampshire.
Archival sources: Portsmouth Record Office; Southampton Archives Service.
Bibliography: S. Peacock, *Votes for Women: The Women's Fight in Portsmouth*, 1983.

OSLER, CATHERINE COURTAULD, MRS (1854–1924) Unitarian, born at Bridgwater, Somerset, daughter of William and Caroline TAYLOR, niece of P.A. and Clementia TAYLOR (see Appendix). Her parents were founding members of the BIRMINGHAM WOMEN'S SUFFRAGE SOCIETY and, as Miss C.C. Taylor, she subscribed 1/– to the BWSS in 1868–9. In 1873 she married Alfred Clarkson Osler, a wealthy glass manufacturer, who was for many years president of the Birmingham Liberal Association, started the Birmingham Public Picture Fund and was involved in the free libraries movement and the movement for opening museums and art galleries on Sundays. In 1880 Catherine Osler gave "a clear and incisive speech" at the third Demonstration of Women, held in Bristol. In 1881 she moved the second resolution, which was to appoint a deputation to the prime minister, at the fifth Demonstration of Women, held in Birmingham. The resolution was supported by Florence Fenwick MILLER, Caroline Ashurst BIGGS, Jessie CRAIGEN and Helena DOWNING. From 1885 Catherine Osler was secretary of the BWSS and her sister Edith (b. 1860) was treasurer; her father was still at that time a member of the executive committee. From around 1884 she was president of the Birmingham Women's Liberal Association, in 1888 presiding over a conference of the WOMEN'S LIBERAL FEDERATION held at Birmingham. In 1891 she brought a women's suffrage resolution, which was well received, before a general meeting of the Birmingham Liberal Association. In a letter to Harriet McILQUHAM on 5 September 1892 Elizabeth

Wolstenholme ELMY described Catherine Osler as "more than willing to help with our Conference meeting so I hope we may have a real good time there". It is doubtful that Catherine Osler was actually a member of the WOMEN'S EMANCIPATION UNION but, as Elizabeth Wolstenholme Elmy had hoped, she took the chair at an afternoon session of the Inaugural Meeting organized by the WEU at Birmingham in October 1892.

In 1881 Catherine Osler founded the Birmingham Ladies' Debating Society and from the 1890s was a member of the Birmingham branch of the National Union of Women's Workers, the meetings of which over the next few years progressed from being that of a genteel debating society (in 1896 Mrs Osler spoke for the motion "That a sense of humour is more to be desired than many virtues") to one at which, in 1908, at the end of a debate discussing the motion "That the time has now come for granting the franchise to women on the same terms as it is or may be granted to men", she delivered a speech fully in favour of the enfranchisement of women.

By 1901 Catherine Osler had become president of the BWSS and had supervised the opening of new branches in 1903–4 at Coventry, Warwick, Leamington and Redditch. In 1909 Catherine Osler and the BWSS were criticized by Ethel SNOWDEN for sitting on the same platform as Asquith at a Liberal meeting. Later that year Catherine Osler resigned as president of the Birmingham Women's Liberal Association as a protest against the government's policy of forcibly feeding hunger-striking suffragette prisoners. She did not, however, condone militancy. An article she had written, "Why Women Need the Vote", was at this time reprinted from the *Common Cause* and published as a pamphlet. Oslers regularly advertised in the *Common Cause* its glass and chinaware shop at 100 Oxford Street, London (which was the responsibility of her son John, whose wife in 1909 was secretary of the Hampstead NUWSS branch). In 1911 Catherine Osler presided over a meeting of the BWSS at which Anne Cobden SANDERSON talked on tax resistance. From 1911 Catherine Osler was a member of the executive committee of the NATIONAL UNION OF WOMEN'S SUFFRAGE SOCIETIES. In 1912 she subscribed to the NUWSS Election Fighting Fund.

During the First World War Catherine Osler was a member of the executive of the Citizens' Committee, which acted as a control committee for distributing grants to alleviate distress caused by the war. In March 1917 she presided at a suffrage demonstration held at the Midland Institute in favour of the inclusion of women in the proposed Electoral Bill. She was in the chair when the amalgamation between the BWSS and the NUWW was discussed and was keen that the lack of representatives of women's labour organizations on the new body should be rectified, suggesting that the Women's Co-operative Guild should be offered three representatives. She finally resigned as president in 1920.

In 1908 Catherine Osler was a leading member of the executive committee of the newly founded Birmingham Society for Promoting the Election of Women on Local Government Bodies, which was jointly instituted by the Birmingham branch of the NUWSS and the Birmingham Society for the Promotion of the Election of Women Guardians. Her daughter-in-law, Mrs Julian Osler, was honorary treasurer of the new society, which by 1913 had become the Birmingham Women's Local Government Association. In 1918 the secretary of the BWSS, Mrs Ring, became the paid secretary of the BWLGA until 1921 when the society dissolved, its aims having been achieved. Catherine Osler was present at its final meeting. She is doubtless the "C.C.O." commemorated, among the initials of other pioneers, by Millicent FAWCETT in her dedicatory preface to *The Women's Victory – and After*, 1920.

Catherine Osler had three sons and two daughters. One son, Philip, died in 1897, aged 21, after a fall during the construction of the New General Hospital in Birmingham. Her son Julian was a member of the MEN'S LEAGUE FOR WOMEN'S SUFFRAGE by 1909 and his wife was a member of the executive committee of the Birmingham NUWW in 1915 and, after the amalgamation, of the Birmingham National Union of Societies for Equal Citizenship. Catherine Osler's daughters Nellie and Dorothy were members of the BWSS by 1906 and in 1909 Dorothy was listed as one of the stewardesses for NUWSS meetings. The latter was also a member of the Birmingham NUWW, taking part in a reading of Ibsen's *Enemy of the People* at a NUWW meeting in 1910.

Catherine Osler in 1888 wrote an article for the *Women's Penny Paper*, newly founded by Henrietta MULLER, and in 1911 published *A Book of the Home*, an extremely interesting and sensible study of family life. In it she shows a considerable breadth of reading and is emphatic that there are no "natural spheres" for men and women. Catherine Osler was made an Honorary MA of Birmingham University in 1919. Around 1920 a portrait of her, painted by Edward Harper, was presented to the City Council to be hung in the Art Gallery. The surplus from the money raised to pay for this, together with an additional donation from her family, funded a Birmingham University scholarship in order to allow women BA students to read for a postgraduate degree in the Faculty of Arts. This scholarship is still (1999) awarded from time to time. In her will the only bequest made outside her family, except to her maids, was to "my friend Florence Carol Ring", who had been for many years the very efficient secretary of the BWSS.

Address: Fallowfield, Norfolk Road, Edgbaston, Birmingham.
Portrait: by Edward Harper, *c.* 1920, presented to Birmingham City Council, now on loan to Highbury, Joseph Chamberlain's former home in Birmingham.
Photograph: by Lallie Charles, in *Why Women need the Vote*, *c.* 1909.
Archival source: Birmingham Archives and Local History Library; Elizabeth Wolstenholme Elmy Papers, British Library.

OSWESTRY (NUWSS) In 1913 the society was a member of the MIDLAND (WEST) FEDERATION OF THE NATIONAL UNION OF WOMEN'S SUFFRAGE SOCIETIES. Secretary (1913) Mrs M.C. Cartwright, Brook Street House, Oswestry, Shropshire.

OTTERY ST MARY (NUWSS) In 1913 the society was a member of the SOUTH-WESTERN FEDERATION OF THE NATIONAL UNION OF WOMEN'S SUFFRAGE SOCIETIES. Secretary (1913) Miss Moore, Coleby House, Ottery St Mary, Devonshire.

OUNDLE AND DISTRICT (NUWSS) In 1913 the society was a member of the MIDLAND (EAST) FEDERATION OF THE NATIONAL UNION OF WOMEN'S SUFFRAGE SOCIETIES. Secretary (1913) Miss Helen Smith, The Rectory, Oundle, Northamptonshire.

OXFORD (NUWSS) Founded in 1904 and in 1913 was a member of the OXON, BERKS, BUCKS, AND BEDS FEDERATION OF THE NATIONAL UNION OF WOMEN'S SUFFRAGE SOCIETIES. Secretary (1909) Miss Rhys, Jesus College, Oxford; (1913) Mrs Haverfield, Winshields, Headington Hill, Oxford; (1917) Mrs W.M. Geldart, 10 Chadlington Road, and Miss Eden Lewis, 13 Rawlinson Road. An office was opened at 35 Holywell, Oxford, in October 1911. Leading members of the society were, in April 1913, opposed to the proposed Election Fighting Fund policy. Mrs Haverfield accepted the policy for a while before, in April 1914, resigning, with Eleanor RATHBONE and Margery Corbett ASHBY, from the NUWSS executive.

OXFORD branch of the WOMEN'S EMANCIPATION UNION Honorary secretary (1895) Mrs J.G. Grenfell.

OXFORD (WSPU) Honorary secretary (1910) Mrs E.F. Richards, 209 Woodstock Road, Oxford; shop 15 High St., Oxford; secretary (1913) Miss Graham, 27 Norham Road, Oxford. The first WSPU meeting in Oxford was held in February 1908. In the summer of 1909 the society ran a summer campaign to coincide with University Extension lectures.

OXFORD MEN'S POLITICAL UNION FOR WOMEN'S ENFRANCHISEMENT Founded in 1910.

OXFORD WOMEN STUDENTS' SOCIETY (NUWSS) Comprised the suffrage societies of Lady Margaret Hall, Somerville, St Hugh's, St Hilda's and the Oxford Home Students (later St Anne's). Secretary (1913) Miss R. Giles, 178 Sinclair House, Thanet Street, London WC. A BANNER for the society was designed by Edmund New; it does not appear to have survived, but the design was published as a postcard – and in the 1990s was "republished" on a mug by the Bodleian Library, Oxford.

OXON, BERKS, BUCKS, AND BEDS FEDERATION OF THE NATIONAL UNION OF WOMEN'S SUFFRAGE SOCIETIES Formed in 1910 and comprised the societies in the counties of Oxfordshire, Berkshire, Buckinghamshire, the Watford division of Hertfordshire and, by 1913, Bedfordshire. The Federation organizers worked hard among the trade unions in Aylesbury, Bletchley, Luton, Oxford, Reading, Watford, Windsor, Wokingham and High Wycombe, sending speakers to meetings and asking for a resolution in favour of women's suffrage to be passed; 54 were passed in the year 1913–14. The Federation's BANNER, probably designed by Mary LOWNDES and executed by the ARTISTS' SUFFRAGE LEAGUE, and still being paid for in 1914, is held in the Fawcett Collection.

President (1912–14) Mrs F.J.K. Cross, Aston Tirrold Manor, Wallingford; honorary secretary Miss Dunnell, Chesterton, Banbury, (1913–14) Miss C.C. Lyon, Ashcroft, Prestwood, Great Missenden; honorary treasurer Mrs Berney, Ulverscroft, High Wycombe.

Archival source: Annual report, 1913–14, Fawcett Library.

OXTED AND LIMPSFIELD (NUWSS) In 1913 the society was a member of the SURREY, SUSSEX, AND HANTS FEDERATION OF THE NATIONAL UNION OF WOMEN'S SUFFRAGE SOCIETIES. Secretary (1909) Miss A. Jacomb Hood, Hillandale, Oxted, Surrey; (1913) Mrs Seyd, Spinney Mead, Rockfield Road, Limpsfield, Surrey.

P

PADDINGTON (NORTH) (branch of the LONDON SOCIETY FOR WOMEN'S SUFFRAGE, NUWSS) Secretary (1909) Mrs Bertram, 38 Palace Mansions, Addison Bridge, London W.

PADDINGTON (SOUTH) (branch of the LONDON SOCIETY FOR WOMEN'S SUFFRAGE, NUWSS) Secretary (1909) Mrs Bertram, 38 Palace Mansions, Addison Bridge, London W; (1913) Miss Boyd, 5 Onslow Place, London SW.

PADDINGTON AND MARYLEBONE (WSPU) Secretary (1906) Miss Hooper, 34 St Ervan's Road, Paddington, (1913) Mrs Cooke, 52 Praed Street, Paddington, London W.

PAISLEY committee of the NATIONAL SOCIETY FOR WOMEN'S SUFFRAGE Formed in 1872. Treasurer Mrs S. Robertson, Castlehead, Paisley. In 1913, refounded, the society was a member of the SCOTTISH FEDERATION OF THE NATIONAL UNION OF WOMEN'S SUFFRAGE SOCIETIES. Secretary (1913) Miss Risk, 36 Whitehaugh Drive, Paisley, Renfrewshire.

PAISLEY (WFL) Secretary (1913) Miss Dracup, 10 Townhead Terrace, Paisley.

PALLISER, EDITH (1859– alive 1925) Born in Comragh, Co. Waterford, she became secretary of the CENTRAL COMMITTEE OF THE NATIONAL SOCIETY FOR WOMEN'S SUFFRAGE in 1895, succeeding Helen BLACKBURN. She also at this time became, with Esther ROPER, joint secretary of a group drawn from the different suffrage societies to promote joint parliamentary action. Between 1903 and 1906 she funded and edited the *Women's Suffrage Record* for the NATIONAL UNION OF WOMEN'S SUFFRAGE SOCIETIES. Elizabeth Wolstenholme ELMY wote to Harriet McILQUHAM on 17 September 1904, "I only learned the other day that the WS Record is a *private* effort of Miss Palliser's own – the National Union contributing not one penny." After 1907, when the society renamed itself the LONDON SOCIETY FOR WOMEN'S SUFFRAGE, Edith Palliser became chairman of the committee and Philippa STRACHEY succeeded her as secretary. From 1897 Edith Palliser was also co-secretary of the NATIONAL UNION OF WOMEN'S SUFFRAGE SOCIETIES, of which, with Frances STERLING, she was one of the architects, taking over in 1911 as parliamentary secretary from Bertha MASON. Having suffered from periods of ill health, she resigned from this position in January 1913, being succeeded in it by Catherine MARSHALL. In 1903 Edith Palliser was secretary of the English National Subcommittee of the International Woman Suffrage Committee which advised on the formation of the INTERNATIONAL WOMAN SUFFRAGE ALLIANCE, in 1904 attended the Alliance's first meeting in Berlin and in 1908 that in Amsterdam. In 1907 she contributed an essay, "The International Movement for Women's Suffrage", to Brougham Villiers (ed.), *The Case for Women's Suffrage*. In 1900 Edith Palliser wrote a leaflet, *Some Reasons Why Working Women Want the Vote*, and in 1906 she attended, in her individual capacity, the annual conference of the LANCASHIRE AND CHESHIRE WOMEN TEXTILE AND OTHER WORKERS' REPRESENTATION COMMITTEE. Also in that year, as she had in 1902, she attended the annual conference of the National Union of Women Workers. In 1915 she became chairman of the newly formed London Committee for the Scottish Women's Hospitals and remained in this position for the duration of the war. She subscribed to the London Society until 1926. There is no trace, in Britain, of her death; she may have returned to Ireland. Esther Palliser, who may have been her sister, wrote songs for a matinee given by the ACTRESSES' FRANCHISE LEAGUE at the Scala Theatre in November 1909.

Address: (1913) 26 Pembroke Square, London W.
Photograph: in Fawcett Library Collection.

PANGBOURNE (NUWSS) In 1913 the society was a member of the OXON, BERKS, BUCKS, AND BEDS FEDERATION OF THE NATIONAL UNION OF WOMEN'S SUFFRAGE SOCIETIES. Secretary (1913) Miss L. Jones, Jesmond Hill, Pangbourne, Berkshire.

PANKHURST, ADELA CONSTANTIA MARY (1885–1961) (later Mrs Walsh) Youngest daughter of Emmeline and Richard PANKHURST. She was involved with the WOMEN'S SOCIAL AND POLITICAL UNION from its earliest days and by 1906, having undergone some training as a pupil-teacher, was working as an elementary school teacher in Manchester. In that summer she was, with Hannah MITCHELL, imprisoned there for a week after taking part in a WSPU demonstration. After her release she worked in Yorkshire, raising WSPU support for a textile-workers' strike at Hebden Bridge. Articles she wrote about this campaign appeared in the *Labour Record*. Like Sylvia PANKHURST, she retained her association with the Independent Labour Party after her mother and Christabel had broken away. In October, with Anne Cobden SANDERSON, Dora MONTEFIORE and others, Adela Pankhurst was arrested at the House of Commons and sentenced to two months' imprisonment. In early 1907, despite arriving with pneumonia, she worked with Helen FRASER, organizing the campaign at the Aberdeen South by-election, and from there moved on to Cardiff. In the summer of 1908 Adela Pankhurst was working in Bristol with Annie KENNEY and in August paid a visit to the BLATHWAYTS at Batheaston. Emily Blathwayt at this time described her as "a dear little thing of 23 and except when she speaks looks a timid little child".

In the autumn of 1908 Adela Pankhurst succeeded Helen ARCHDALE as WSPU organizer in Yorkshire and in February 1909 worked at four by-election campaigns in Scotland. She was arrested in Edinburgh in July 1909 and in Glasgow in August, although on neither occasion were charges pressed. In September 1909, after the release of Edith NEW, Lucy BURNS and Alice PAUL, who had been the first suffragette prisoners to hunger strike in a Scottish prison, Adela Pankhurst addressed a large meeting in Dundee. While they were in prison Adela Pankhurst wrote in their support to the governor. In October 1909 she was imprisoned there herself, having been arrested with Helen Archdale, Maud JOACHIM and Catherine Corbett on a charge of breach of the peace, and, with the others, she went on hunger strike. The prison doctor described her on this occasion as "a slender undersized girl five feet in height and (in health) 7 stones in weight" and commented that "Dr Sturrock, the Superintendant of the Perth Criminal Lunatic Department, was impressed by her extraordinary appearance and bearing and did not hesitate to say that she was of a 'degenerate type'". She was deemed unfit for forcible feeding and released. Although Emily Blathwayt had just resigned from the WSPU she and Colonel Blathwayt invited Adela Pankhurst to Eagle House, Batheaston, to recuperate.

In October 1909 Adela was back in Edinburgh, speaking at meetings with Emmeline and Christabel Pankhurst and Emmeline PETHICK-LAWRENCE. In January 1910 she organized the WSPU general election campaign in Scarborough and remained there, working in Scarborough and Sheffield, until the end of February 1911. In Sheffield and later in 1911 in London she lived with Helen Archdale, caring for the latter's children when she was in prison at the end of the year. By 1912 a combination of a dislike of militant tactics and ill-health forced Adela, who had never been strong, to give up her work with the WSPU. According to Sylvia Pankhurst Adela's final campaign was the North-West Manchester by-election in August 1912. Her mother had given her £200 to pay for a course at Studley Agricultural College in Worcestershire, where she was in residence by June 1912. Having received her diploma, Adela, according to the Blathwayt diaries, was in April 1913 employed as head gardener at Road Manor near Bath, the home of Mrs Batten Pooll. The latter was a WSPU supporter; a Miss Batten Pooll went with Annie KENNEY to the USA during the First World War. However, Adela Pankhurst is quoted by David Mitchell in *Queen Christabel* as saying that no-one in the suffrage movement would employ her. She later accompanied friends as a companion-governess, travelling with them in Europe.

On 2 February 1914 Adela Pankhurst emigrated to Australia, travelling on the *Geelong*. She had been offered by Vida GOLDSTEIN a post as organizer with the Women's Political Association in Melbourne and during the First World War continued working with

Goldstein and Jennie BAINES after the WPA became the Women's Peace Army, campaigning against the war and against conscription. Her pacifist pamphlet *Put Up the Sword!* was published in 1915 by Melbourne's Peace Army. In 1917 she resigned from the Women's Peace Army and joined, as Jennie Baines had already done, the Victorian Socialist party. In 1917 she wrote a five-act anti-conscription play, *Betrayed*. In September 1917 Adela Pankhurst married Tom Walsh, an active Socialist, a widower with three children, and shortly afterwards was sentenced, with Jennie Baines, to nine months' imprisonment after leading processions of the Socialist Women's League. She was released in January 1918 and in 1921 joined the executive committee of the newly formed Australian Communist Party. She maintained contact with Sylvia Pankhurst, writing an article on "Communism and Social Purity" that appeared in the *Dreadnought* in February 1921. The Walshs were sceptical adherents of communism and by 1923 Adela had rejoined the VSP as honorary organizer. Dora Montefiore visited Adela Walsh at this time and describes her life, the mingling of babies with politics. Besides caring for her three step-children Adela Walsh had five children of her own (Richard, Sylvia, Christian, Ursula and Hope, the latter dying shortly after birth). In 1929 Adela Walsh was one of the founders of the Australian Women's Guild of Empire, which campaigned against communism and for industrial peace, the family, Christian ideals and the development of Australia as part of the British Empire. She was editor of the Guild's *Empire Gazette*. Lady RHONDDA was an overseas patron of the Australian Women's Guild of Empire. Elsie BOWERMAN was at pains to point out that the Australian organization was quite independent of the Guild of Empire for which she and Flora DRUMMOND worked in Britain. In 1939 after the Walshes espoused support for Japan, the Guild of Empire was closed down, to be reopened as the People's Guild by Adela Walsh in 1940. In 1942, still supporting Japan, she was interned. After the war, her husband having died, she worked as a nurse at a home for children with learning disabilities. She was received into the Roman Catholic Church a few months before she died.

Address: (1912) 45 Albert Bridge Road, Battersea, London SW.

Photograph: in D. Mitchell, *The Fighting Pankhursts*, 1967.
Archival source: Mitchell Papers, Museum of London; Scottish Office Prison Commission files, Scottish Record Office.
Bibliography: D. Montefiore, *From a Victorian to a Modern*, 1927; D. Mitchell, *The Fighting Pankhursts*, 1967; D. Mitchell, *Queen Christabel*, 1977; V. Coleman, *Adela Pankhurst*, 1996.

PANKHURST, CHRISTABEL HARRIETTE (1880–1958)
Born in Manchester, the eldest child of Richard and Emmeline PANKHURST. It appears to have been accepted in the family that she was her mother's favourite and the natural leader among her brothers and sisters. She was educated, doubtlessly inadequately, at home, by a series of governesses and then, after the family's return to the north from London in 1893, first at Southport High School for Girls and, a little later, at Manchester High School for Girls. Christabel was an accomplished dancer, a talent put to good use at Independent Labour Party and Clarion Club functions. In 1897, having left school, she attended classes in Manchester in French, logic and dressmaking and in the summer of 1898 she had just begun a stay in Geneva to perfect her French when news arrived of her father's death. She stayed there until the autumn but then travelled back to Manchester to take up work at her mother's shop, Emerson's, an employment she did not find congenial.

On 11 October 1900 Christabel Pankhurst attended a meeting of the Owen's College Women's Debating Society at which the principal of the college, Sir Alfred Hopkinson, gave a talk on "The Politics of the Poets". Christabel, who by then lived just around the corner in Nelson Street, attended the meeting as a "friend'; she was not yet a member of the college although she was attending its classes in logic. Her involvement in the discussion at the end of the talk attracted the attention of the chairman of the society, Esther ROPER. Christabel took part in six further debates held by the college society between then and February 1902 and developed her friendship with Esther Roper and Eva GORE-BOOTH. In 1902–3 she joined the executive committee of the NORTH OF ENGLAND SOCIETY FOR WOMEN'S SUFFRAGE, of which Esther Roper was secretary and which still included members who had been contemporaries of Richard Pankhurst. In her autobiography Christabel Pankhurst noted that she quickly determined that, as a member of "the third generation of women to claim the vote,... the vote must now be obtained". She launched her career as a suffrage campaigner among the working women of Lancashire, Cheshire and Yorkshire. In 1902 a Miss Palliser of the North of England Society wrote to the GLASGOW AND WEST OF SCOTLAND ASSOCIATION FOR WOMEN'S SUFFRAGE, asking them to meet Miss Pankhurst, "a member of the North of England Society for the purpose of hearing from her about the Petition work amongst the textile workers which had been organized by her Society". The Glasgow Association, always somewhat ponderous, replied that they did not have time to arrange such a meeting. In April 1902 Elizabeth Wolstenholme ELMY, the pioneer Manchester suffragist, wrote to tell Harriet McILQUHAM of one of Christabel's earliest publications: "I was particularly delighted to see 'Christabel's letter'. She is, I think, the *youngest* daughter... and was, when I last saw her, a *bright little thing* of 7 or 8 – so that she cannot be now much more than 20! So that letter gives a promise of a future useful worker." From May 1902 Esther Roper was chairman of Owen's College Women's Union, with a strong interest in encouraging women to enroll for degree courses. In the autumn term of 1903 Christabel Pankhurst began reading for a law degree, while maintaining her involvement in the suffrage movement.

In October 1903 Emmeline Pankhurst founded the WOMEN'S SOCIAL AND POLITICAL UNION. Christabel was not, apparently, at its first meeting; although obviously interested, she continued her association with the North of England Society. On 2 December 1903 Mrs Elmy noted, "Today Christabel Pankhurst has a capital little letter in the Manchester Guardian – on the 'Liberal leaders and Women's Franchise'." In February 1904 Christabel took what she later described as her first militant step when, at a meeting addressed by Winston Churchill in the Free Trade Hall in Manchester, she asked to be allowed to move a woman's suffrage amendment to a resolution on free trade. She wrote in *Unshackled*, "To move from my place on the platform to the speaker's table in the teeth of the astonishment and opposition of will of that immense throng, those civic and county leaders and those Members of Parliament, was the most difficult thing I have ever done." She quickly regretted that she had not pressed her point on this occasion and resolved to make her mark when the next opportunity presented itself.

In March 1904 Mrs Elmy went to Manchester for a day of women's suffrage meetings and passed on to Harriet McIlquham this vignette of the early days of the WSPU:

Soon after 5 Christabel Pankhurst came for me and I dined with herself, her mother & 2 sisters, and Mrs Scott, the President of the Women's Political and Social Union, and had a most loving and hearty welcome. Christabel and Mrs Scott travelled with me as far as Stockport as they were going to speak on WS at a great Labour meeting at Heaton Moor. Mrs Pankhurst is immensely improved though she has nothing like the brain of her husband and oldest daughter. The other 2 girls are clever and sweet, but have not Christabel's force & originality. The boy, the baby I knew, is at school near London, so I did not see him.

Christabel Pankhurst published, c. 1904, a 16-page pamphlet, printed by Abel Heywood, Manchester, titled, *Parliamentary Vote for Women*. The pamphlet carries the Pankhurst address, 62 Nelson Street, but makes no mention of the WSPU. In the pamphlet Christabel wrote, "working men show little desire to give to women the rights which they possess... It is only when all men and all women stand on an equal footing that their interests become the same ... how important it is to break down the oldest and strongest of tyrannies – the tyranny of sex." Interestingly, this pamphlet was never advertised as being stocked by the Woman's Press, the WSPU's literature department, and its existence has been overlooked.

In "The Woman's Letter" column of the *Clarion*, 6 May 1904, Julia Dawson quoted a letter from Christabel Pankhurst in which she wrote:

As for suffrage the ILP has always given preference to other questions. Bruce Glasier, for one, has said on platforms that "we have votes enough. What we must do is learn to use them". That is all very well for men who have two-thirds of a loaf, while we have not a crumb... lately Keir HARDIE has introduced what he calls a Franchise Bill, which has as much chance of passing, as one Bill, as the whole Socialist programme. It is most unpractical. The conference instructed the NAC to introduce a Disabilities Removal Bill, so the rank and file are with us. If the leaders loyally carry out their instructions it will be a great help. It is clear that, very soon after the formation of the WSPU, a month after her mother joined the National Administrative Council of the ILP, and two years before the WSPU moved its main activity to London, which is the point at which its break with Labour is usually identified, Christabel did not intend to place any faith in the ILP.

On 25 July 1904 Christabel Pankhurst published a long article in the *Daily Dispatch*, "Woman's Rights: an American reformer in Manchester"; Susan Anthony was visiting Manchester that day. It is likely that Elizabeth Wolstenholme Elmy, a friend and admirer of both Susan Anthony and Christabel had suggested the commission. In November 1904 Christabel was a delegate from the North of England Society to the NATIONAL UNION OF WOMEN'S SUFFRAGE SOCIETIES convention in London, staying with her sister Sylvia, and prepared to make a speech. In April 1905 Mrs Elmy told Harriet McIlquham that "Christabel has been using her Easter holidays to plentiful effect – speaking every day for the Bill and roaming everywhere. It is delightful to feel how true . . . and earnest these young workers are who will carry on the work . . . when we are gone." Mrs Elmy makes clear that most of the "roaming" was done by rail. In August she was able to report that "Christabel speaks twice today in Albert Square, Manchester last Sunday from 7000 to 8000 persons attended the meetings. They are *primarily* on the unemployment question, but she always works in W.S." Still studying in Manchester, Christabel was unable to accompany her mother on her expeditions to London to lobby at the House of Commons and doubtless felt frustrated by the lack of progress made by these conventional means of campaigning. Mrs Elmy sang her praises to Harriet McIlquham, writing on 5 July 1905, "how grandly dear Christabel and her mother are working for WS. It is holiday time just now, and she is speaking 3 or 4 times each week, and twice or thrice each Sunday for WS and Mrs Pankhurst almost as often. The best work for WS is being done by the splendid workers outside the NU which seems quite incapable of rising to the greatness of the question". In a further letter, dated 12 July, again extolling the work being done by Christabel and Emmeline Pankhurst, Mrs Elmy made the point that "in nine cases out of ten they have to pay their own expenses, which is a very heavy pull on a small income".

On 13 October 1905, with Annie KENNEY, Christabel Pankhurst rose to the occasion by putting into practice a plan she had made to interrupt another Liberal meeting in the Free Trade Hall. Male hecklers had been dealt with humorously by the speakers earlier in the evening, but when Annie Kenney put to Sir Edward Grey the question, recorded by Christabel in her autobiography as "Will the Liberal government give votes to women?" and unfurled their banner, the meeting was, Christabel related, "aflame with excitement". At the request of the chief constable of Manchester, the question was sent up in writing to the platform to be answered at the end of the meeting. When it was not, they felt free to renew their questioning and were then dragged from their seats. Christabel Pankhurst later made clear that she intended to provoke arrest and did so by committing a technical assault on a policeman, by spitting. In *Unshackled* she wrote, "It was not a real spit but only, shall we call it, a 'pout', a perfectly dry purse of the mouth. I could not *really* have done it, even to get the vote, I think." This coyness, whether it represented her attitude in 1905 or in the 1930s when *Unshackled* is thought to have been written, is rather astonishing from one who was very soon prepared to allow women to starve themselves "to get the vote". Although the two women refused to be bailed, they were sent home without bail having been set and appeared in the police court the next morning, Saturday, for sentencing. Having refused to pay a fine, Christabel Pankhurst was sentenced to seven days' imprisonment. Such was the publicity engendered by the case that even *The Times* gave it coverage on Monday, 16 October.

A week after their defiance of Liberal ministers, the released prisoners returned to the Free Trade Hall, to be welcomed by an enthusiastic meeting organized by the Manchester Central Branch of the ILP. Elizabeth Wolstenholme Elmy has left a vigorous account of the occasion. Christabel Pankhurst was threatened with expulsion from Owen's College and as a condition of being allowed to complete her degree gave an undertaking that she would not be involved in any other disturbance. She was, however, able to combine her studies with speaking at meetings as before and to organize the WSPU's campaign during the January 1906 general election, allowing other members to undertake the heckling of cabinet ministers. She led a deputation of WSPU members to see A.J. Balfour, who represented a Manchester constituency, and recorded him as replying, when asked why the Conservative party had not done anything to promote women's enfranchisement when they were in power, "Well, to tell you the truth, your cause is not in the swim." This dismissal clearly strengthened Christabel's resolve.

For the first six months of 1906 Christabel Pankhurst remained in Manchester, studying, addressing meetings and deputizing as registrar when her mother was working for the WSPU in London. In July 1910 Elizabeth Wolstenholme Elmy sent to Sylvia Pankhurst "the list of the 50 or more W.S. lectures and addresses that dear Christabel gave *during her final* session at Owen's College, preparing for her finals exam". In March Christabel became vice-chairman of a newly founded Socialist Society at Owen's College; Victor Grayson, the future Labour MP, was its chairman. It was obviously difficult to control developments in London at a distance; it is not clear if Christabel even attended the first London WSPU rally in Caxton Hall on 19 February. In *Unshackled*, her description of the meeting does not seem to be a first-hand account. On 30 June Christabel Pankhurst, who had been the only woman law student at Owen's College, graduated with a first-class degree, bracketed with one other at the top of the examination list. She also won a prize in international law. Besides the Pankhurst family, both Esther Roper and Elizabeth Wolstenholme Elmy attended the ceremony.

Christabel Pankhurst immediately left Manchester for London, where she lived with the PETHICK-LAWRENCES in rooms in Clement's Inn and was employed, from 4 July, as the WSPU's chief ORGANIZER, at a salary of £2 10s a week. She arrived in time to witness the trial of Annie Kenney, Adelaide KNIGHT and Jane SBARBORO. She was delighted now to be at the centre of the campaign, able personally to control the publicity generated by the trial and to alter the WSPU's course from reliance on poor women from the East End of London to one of attracting members from what she termed "the feminine bourgeoisie". She herself spoke weekly near the Reformer's Tree in Hyde Park and many new adherents to the cause were first attracted by hearing her there. In August she went alone to Cockermouth to implement the WSPU's new election policy, of which she was the architect, of attacking the government candidate. She related in *Unshackled* how she conducted the campaign single-handedly for its first few days. In September she defended to the Manchester Central branch of the ILP her action, while accepting hospitality and help from the local ILP branch, in giving no support to the ILP candidate at Cockermouth. She was not, in the event, required to resign, although she did so of her own accord within nine months.

The arrest of Anne Cobden SANDERSON, together with, among others, Emmeline Pethick-Lawrence and Minnie BALDOCK, in the Lobby of the House of Commons in October marked an end and a beginning in Christabel Pankhurst's strategy. By influencing women of substance such as Mrs Cobden Sanderson to go to prison for their cause, the WSPU was able to attract very many more middle-class women, those with both a social conscience and money, to their standard. The banquet organized by Mrs FAWCETT for the WSPU prisoners at the Savoy on 11 December 1906 marks the cusp of the change. The WSPU was able that evening to legitimize its militancy, clothing its perpetrators in evening dress and drawing plaudits and subscriptions from middle-class suffragists. It was then able to dispense with the women from Canning Town and West Ham who, although raising the body count, could not contribute what Christabel deemed necessary to influence the government. Ironically, Anne Cobden Sanderson was herself too committed a socialist to countenance this change of tack. An indication of the direction that Christabel's thinking was taking can be gleaned from a letter Mrs Elmy wrote to Harriet McIlquham on 5 February 1907, in which she asked if she would ask Anna Maria PRIESTMAN in Bristol if Christabel could address her "set of Liberal women – she is anxious to . . . move into touch with Liberal women – especially to address

Women's Liberal Associations". Christabel Pankhurst saw these women as the WSPU's natural membership, politically and socially aware, financially comfortable and likely to become disillusioned with the Liberal Party which, though in power partly through their efforts, did nothing to enfranchise women.

On 13 February 1907 Christabel Pankhurst was arrested, leading a deputation from the Women's Parliament in Caxton Hall to the House of Commons. In *The Suffragette Movement*, 1931, Sylvia Pankhurst stated that Christabel had judged it necessary to maintain credibility by going to prison once in London and had judged it best to do so at this stage of the campaign, while sentences were still short, in order not to lose control by a prolonged absence. This gloss on Christabel's action, deemed heroic at the time, did not, of course, appear in Sylvia's earlier history, *The Suffragette*, 1911. Christabel, at Westminster Police Court, asked, as organizer of the WSPU's demonstration, to be tried first and the dock provided a splendid public platform from which to attack the government. She was sentenced to 14 days' imprisonment, gaining kudos and keeping control of the movement. She demonstrates in *Unshackled* how necessary she felt it was to be alert to what were perceived as attempts to subvert the Union. She dismisses as schismatics those who left to set up the WOMEN'S FREEDOM LEAGUE in the autumn of 1907 and characterizes their bid to democratize the WSPU "as though in the midst of a battle the Army had begun to vote upon who should command it, and what the strategy should be".

In early issues of *Votes for Women*, which commenced publication in November 1907, Christabel set out each month "The National Campaign", describing meetings to be attended and tactics to be pursued throughout the country. She was also masterminding the campaign behind the scenes. By October 1907 she was in correspondence with Balfour, attempting to get him to commit the Conservative party to support women's suffrage if reelected. From the correspondence it does not appear that Balfour took her too seriously as a politician; he, like Asquith, merely asked for more proof that women were in favour of their own enfranchisement. These requests were addressed by vigorous

Christabel Pankhurst (1880–1958), photographed *c*. 1908. The circular brooch she is wearing was probably designed by C.R. Ashbee. (Author's collection)

WSPU campaigning, organized by Christabel, at the many by-elections in the first few months of 1908, nine of them occasioned by the cabinet reshuffle following Campbell-Bannerman's resignation, and at the Women's Sunday WSPU rally in Hyde Park on 21 June 1908. When the resolution carried by the hundreds of thousands present that day, "that this meeting calls upon the Government to grant votes to women without delay", was dismissed by Asquith, who did not even trouble to consult his cabinet, Christabel resolved to put into effect the threat in the press statement that had been issued by the WSPU. Its last sentence read, "It is thus quite evident that agitation by way of public meetings will have no effect in inducing the Government to grant votes to women, and that in order to secure this reform militant methods must once more be resorted to." A report in *Votes for Women*, 25 June, of the WSPU reception held in the Queen's Hall on Monday 22 June, in the aftermath of the tremendous success in Hyde Park the day before, gives a vivid picture of Christabel's decisiveness and assurance, qualities that appear to have been her main attraction: "It will not do", she declared, "We want the government to take direct responsibility. Let the politicians be under no mistake or delusion as to this. They will not stem our agitation.... If Mr Asquith's reply is unfavourable, well – what next? You have got to do something – surely you can all see that. We must take the militant action we have adopted before now, and we call upon you women to be ready for it."

Christabel Pankhurst did not join the deputation to Asquith from the Women's Parliament held in Caxton Hall on 30 June. She remained in the hall, addressing the members of the convention with, according to the report in *Votes for Women*, 2 July, such pithy statements as "one had sometimes to be a law-breaker before one could be a law-maker" and legitimizing their protest by quoting John Bright. She had taken his advice, given in respect of the agitation for the 1867 Reform Bill, "to fill the streets with people from Westminster Bridge to Charing Cross", by issuing an invitation to men and women to assemble that evening outside the House of Commons to offer support to the WSPU deputation. Asquith, of course, refused to be interviewed, but thousands filled Parliament Square, some arrests were made, including the "women of distinction and influence" whom Christabel had, candidly, particularly requested to do their duty, and the WSPU's initiative was maintained. As a precursor to future developments, two WSPU members, Mary LEIGH and Edith NEW, by breaking the windows of 10 Downing Street, took Christabel's call to militancy further than she had explicitly requested. However, neither had she requested women to refrain from violence; "militancy" was undefined. Christabel's justification was that it was the government, by its intransigence, that forced the WSPU to act. This certainly was the justification given by Edith New when at Bow Street Police Court she stated, "I wish to say we have no other course to pursue. We have tried every other means to attain our end, and, having failed, we have had to take more militant measures. The responsibility for everything that has been done rests on those who make us outlaws by the law of the land". In her "Political Notes" in *Votes for Women*, 9 July, Christabel Pankhurst condoned this escalation of militancy and in an article in the next issue put the responsibility squarely back on the government that, by withholding their political rights and provoking women to violence, had "already incurred unforgettable disgrace".

Christabel Pankhurst spent some time during the summer of 1908, probably in August, on holiday at a German spa, but her articles, even during her absence, continued to appear weekly in *Votes for Women*. The autumn campaign was planned around, first, a rally in the Albert Hall on 29 October. To this was added, by 10 September, another Caxton Hall convention, to be held on the evening of 13 October, and from which another deputation would set forth in an attempt to see Asquith. The date, the day after the opening of parliament and the third anniversary of the Free Trade Hall incident, was chosen deliberately. A handbill advertising the deputation was distributed at a meeting held in Trafalgar Square a few days earlier and read, "Men and Women – Help the Suffragettes to Rush the House of Commons". In *Unshackled* Christabel Pankhurst explained that "Rush" had been suggested by Mabel TUKE; she does not claim that the wording was deliberately selected in order to provoke action by the Home Office. Sylvia Pankhurst in *The Suffragette Movement* does, however, clearly suggest that the wording was provocative. The fact that the WSPU chose to insert in *The Times* on 9 October a notice drawing attention to the fact that they were publishing a handbill, for which they gave the full wording, lends credence to this interpretation. Indeed, on 10 October there was a statement in *The Times* to the effect that "The officers of the Union ... assert that the word 'rush' in this appeal is used deliberately". Christabel, her mother, and Flora DRUMMOND, all of whom had addressed the Trafalgar Square meeting, were served with a summons on a charge of conduct likely to provoke a breach of the peace. After eluding the police for a day, in order symbolically to prove they were in control of the situation, the three women eventually summoned the police to arrest them at Clement's Inn; they were in police detention when the convention was held in Caxton Hall.

At her trial at Bow Street on 14 October Christabel Pankhurst defended herself, having elected in vain for trial by jury. She assured maximum publicity by serving subpoenas on two cabinet ministers, Lloyd George and Herbert Gladstone; the former had been present at the advertising meeting in Trafalgar Square and the latter had witnessed the scenes in Parliament Square on 13 October. Christabel Pankhurst was labelled by the press "The Suffragette Portia" as a consequence of her cross-examination of the two men. The result was, however, a guilty verdict and a sentence of 10 weeks' imprisonment. It is difficult to imagine that, whatever the publicity gained, Christabel Pankhurst had intended to put herself in this position, removed from day-to-day control of the WSPU. She appeared to have underestimated the government's determination to extinguish the militant movement, although in her nimble mind even this misjudgement was put to good use as evidence that the power of the WSPU leaders was such that the government was compelled to imprison them.

Christabel Pankhurst hoped to spend her time in Holloway writing a popular book on the suffrage movement and apparently secured the offer of an advance from a literary agent; the Home Office, not unsurprisingly, refused permission. She, with her mother, was released from Holloway on 19 December and a rapturous reception was held for them at the Inns of Court Hotel on 22 December. In the evening, at a rally at the Queen's Hall, Christabel Pankhurst made a long speech that was reprinted verbatim in *Votes for Women*, 31 December. In it she mentions that during the two months of her imprisonment "airships came out of the region of theoretical and problematical things into being something quite practical – they are to be as useful to us as motor-cars" and drew from this the moral that conditions of life were changing all the time and that if "we are to hold our own in the world in the future, we men and women of Great Britain, we have got to be well equipped". She ended by saying that she did not think that "the physical condition, or the mental or spiritual condition of the mass of our people is what it ought to be; and therefore it is as patriots that we are here tonight; we want to take our share in saving the country." It was a line of thought that was to be taken to an extreme after August 1914.

During the first half of 1909 Christabel Pankhurst maintained the established course, pursuing an anti-government policy at by-elections, sending deputations of women publicly to battle with the police and letting the rank-and-file set the meaning of "militancy". When Marion Wallace-DUNLOP adopted the hunger strike in June 1909 in protest against the refusal to treat her as a political prisoner it was gratefully accepted by Christabel as another means of circumventing government control. Still in desultory correspondence with Balfour, she wrote to him on 22 July, "They will never in future be able to keep us in prison more than a few days, for we have now learned our power to starve ourselves out of prison, and this power we shall use – unless of course the Government prefer to let us die. I hardly think, however, that even they will adopt so extreme a course, if only for the reason that it would not pay them politically to do so." In *Unshackled* Christabel revealed that she was including herself among the potential hunger strikers; she was well aware that the government would find it convenient and, eventually, necessary to imprison the WSPU leaders for considerable lengths of time and she felt that the hunger strike was a weapon of retaliation to keep in reserve. The government, of course, soon introduced methods of reducing women's freedom to starve themselves. Christabel capitalized on the introduction of forcible feeding by organizing a petition from medical practitioners protesting against the torturing of women. She herself spent some of the summer taking "the cure" at the German spa she had attended the previous year. She published no signed articles in *Votes for Women* between 30 July and 17 September and, unlike Emmeline Pankhurst, is not listed as attending any of the summer campaign meetings; this was at a time when the pages of the paper were full of tales told by the hunger strikers. If she did feel able to be out of the country for most of this period and to relax her weekly public identification in *Votes for Women* with developments in the campaign, one might deduce that Christabel Pankhurst felt very confident about her position within the WSPU. She had been sent to the spa by the Pethick-Lawrences and presumably trusted them not to effect a palace revolution.

On her return to work Christabel Pankhurst travelled to Birmingham with her mother in an attempt to institute legal proceedings on behalf of the hunger strikers in Winson Green prison. This came to nothing, but she did address a meeting in Birmingham on 28 September. From 1 October the redesigned, larger, *Votes for Women* usually carried a weekly leading article signed by Christabel Pankhurst. She was able to use this platform to hammer home WSPU policy and its justifications and to turn to the WSPU's advantage all political developments. On 12 November her leader was devoted to highlighting the inconstancy and hypocrisy of Asquith in taking up battle as the defender of freedom against the power of the House of Lords to exercise control over the budget when "he himself has no right to tax the women of the country, whom he and his followers in the House of Commons in no way represent".

For the general election in January 1910 Christabel Pankhurst produced a leaflet, *Militant Methods,* a defence of the policies adopted by the WSPU, interspersed with the sayings of Liberal statesmen, highlighting the dichotomy between words and deeds, at least as far as they affected women's enfranchisement. The result of the election, which left the Liberals dependent on the support of the Labour Party and Irish Nationalists, was, of course, claimed by Christabel in her leader in *Votes for Women*, 4 February 1910, as attributable to the campaigning efforts of the WSPU whom, she revealed, had little suspected quite how damaging their attack on the Liberal government would be at a general election. The WSPU announced its truce on 31 January and in her leaders of 4 February and 11 March Christabel made clear that, "if the Government refuse to take this opportunity of settling the question on terms honourable to themselves, to women, and to the nation as a whole, then the women of the country must... win their enfranchisement... by methods of protest and of revolution". The truce was a shrewd tactic, although it is doubtful if Christabel in truth expected much of Asquith's government. It did give her time to take stock; militancy as practised had not won instant enfranchisement, the government was protecting itself from all the tried ruses to engage them and the law of diminishing returns was setting in as MPs and newspaper readers became inured to stories of prison hardship and martyrdom lost its potency. The death of her brother Harry, although it was to Sylvia rather than to Christabel to whom he turned in life, doubtless contributed towards a desire for a moratorium. At the end of March she went with Annie Kenney for a holiday on Sark.

The summer was spent in politicking and pageantry, but Christabel could do little to affect the working of the Conciliation Committee and doubtless felt frustrated by the lack of progress. Her editorials, which did not endear her to H.N. BRAILSFORD, the instigator of the conciliation strategy, repeatedly stressed that militancy would be renewed if she felt it necessary. By early August she was laying plans to send a large deputation of women to the House of Commons if the Conciliation Bill failed. The moment came when, on 18 November, Asquith announced the dissolution of parliament without any mention having been made of a bill for women's enfranchisement. Christabel Pankhurst was not one of the 300 women who took part in the deputation from Caxton Hall to the House of Commons; doubtless discretion demanded that she stayed out of the fray both then and on the following Tuesday when Mrs Pankhurst led another battling deputation to Downing Street. As Christabel wrote in her leader in *Votes for Women* on 25 November, "Negotiations are over. War is declared."

The truce was, however, temporarily renewed during the ensuing general election, maintained as a second Conciliation Bill was prepared, and lasted throughout the summer, allowing the WSPU to be relieved of any necessity of disrupting Coronation celebrations. At the same time Christabel Pankhurst reiterated throughout the period the call for volunteers to be ready and waiting to take part in the next deputation, which she promised would be very large, should the political process fail. In the early part of the year she left Clement's Inn, where she had been living with the Pethick-Lawrences since July 1906, and moved into a nearby flat, probably that rented by Jessie STEPHENSON in Staple Inn. Very little is known of her day-to-day existence: Did she have a housekeeper? Where did she eat? Who did her washing? There was, presumably, no life other than the WSPU.

On 17 November, with Emmeline Pethick-Lawrence, Christabel Pankhurst led the WSPU delegation in the deputation of all women's suffrage societies that Asquith and Lloyd George, following the announcement of the proposed Manhood Suffrage bill, had agreed to receive. She dressed for the occasion in a coat, which with its wide striped, satin lapels advertised the colours of the WSPU. Henry NEVINSON commented to his diary that it was "fine – but a little overdone for the morning". Asquith and Lloyd George were, however, moved by neither costume nor oratory. Helena SWANWICK, also present representing the NUWSS, in a letter written that evening to her husband, described Christabel Pankhurst's performance as ineffective, relating that she "read most of her very halting speech and defiance does not read well". The Conciliation Bill having been "torpedoed", Christabel Pankhurst presided over the women's convention held in Caxton Hall on 21 November. As Henry Nevinson reported in *Votes for Women*, 24 November, "in that stirring voice of hers, an excellent thing in warfare, she read the resolution that was to be taken to the House". During the course of the delivery of that resolution, 220 women and three men were arrested, and militancy, in the form of window breaking, was renewed. Christabel Pankhurst said nothing beforehand in her speeches to encourage this attack, but the militants were supplied with their tools by Clement's Inn. She, as usual, remained in Caxton Hall while Mrs Pethick-Lawrence led the deputation into the hands of the police and to Holloway. Coincidental with the ending of the Conciliation truce came the first open attack by a former member of the WSPU on Christabel's leadership. In the first issue of the *Freewoman*, 23 November, Dora MARSDEN accused Christabel of political ineptitude.

The organized militancy and window smashing in the West End of London that took place on 1 March was followed by a warrant issued on 5 March for the arrest of the Pethick-Lawrences and Christabel Pankhurst on a charge of conspiring to commit damage. The Pethick-Lawrences were discovered in Clement's Inn and taken into custody by the police. Christabel was living out of the Inn, perhaps still in Jessie Stephenson's flat or perhaps in another, as she intimated in *Unshackled* that she had only very recently moved. It does not reflect too well on Scotland Yard, who had had Clement's Inn under observation for some time, that they did not know where Christabel might be found. Although in *Unshackled* she does not suggest that she had, at this stage, gone to any trouble to conceal her whereabouts, it is unlikely, tactician that she was, that she was unaware of the danger of arrest. She had shown in the past that she did not feel that imprisonment was the best way that she could serve the WSPU. In *Unshackled*, Christabel revealed that she had, when incarcerated in Holloway in late 1908, come to the conclusion that "to avoid imprisonment, one could escape to a foreign country and as a political offender be able to stay there". She may not have known when exactly this plan was to be activated, but it is inconceivable that in the intervening three years she had not elaborated on it. In January 1911 Emmeline Pankhurst and Emmeline Pethick-Lawrence had spent a week in Paris, adulated by both French and American women of influence. In the event, on 5 March 1912, Frederick Pethick-Lawrence sent Evelyn SHARP to warn Christabel of the warrant for her arrest and to ask her to countersign the cheque which diverted most of the WSPU's funds into Hertha AYRTON's bank account. Christabel then slipped out of the building when another WSPU member called with a message, and eventually made her way to Nurse PINE's nursing home in Notting Hill. In *Unshackled*, when describing this adventure she mentioned a discussion that had taken place some time previously in which the suggestion had been made that she might need somewhere to hide. She received funds, apparently 100 gold sovereigns, from a supporter and escaped in disguise to Paris.

She quickly settled in the centre of the city, in the 8th *arrondissement*. She lived first at 9 rue Roy, then, as now, a hotel in a side road off Boulevard Haussmann at Place St Augustine, from where she continued to control the WSPU. She appointed Annie Kenney her deputy in London and a constant flow of messengers across the Channel kept her in contact with Clement's Inn. Immediately after her departure she was able to quash a suggestion that the WSPU, in the absence of its leaders, should be run by a small committee. There was never afterwards any direct threat to her leadership. She continued contributing leading articles to *Votes for Women*, although, until 13 September, by which time she was assured that she could not be extradited, they were unsigned. Despite Evelyn Sharp having been given by Frederick Pethick-Lawrence the editorship of *Votes for Women* during his imprisonment, Christabel insisted that Annie Kenney should have overall control of the paper's content, a move that clearly caused resentment from those who regarded themselves as professional journalists. Christabel's life henceforward took on a more leisurely pace; she no longer had to devote much time to public speaking, although she did occasionally address a drawing-room meeting, and the only travelling necessary was spent in trips to Boulogne, Deauville or St Malo where she would on occasion meet her lieutenants from England. Life was no longer solely concentrated on political activity; Ethel SMYTH had given her an entrée to Parisian society through Winnaretta Singer, Princess de Polignac, whose house she was already visiting a mere four or five days after her arrival in Paris. Annie Kenney was directed to find her there when she arrived in Paris to receive her first instructions. In *Unshackled* Christabel gave no real details of her Parisian life. Annie Kenney described Christabel during this time as "fresh, virile, energetic", a contrast no doubt to the hunger strikers as they emerged from Holloway. When Emmeline Pankhurst, Annie Kenney, Mabel Tuke, or Grace ROE visited her they had a merry time going to the theatre, concerts and shopping. Christabel also commented in *Unshackled*, rather disingenuously, that, although never being "off duty", she could "at the same time, maintain behind the line a haven of rest for those who came from London". On Christmas Day 1912 she dined in the company of WSPU members, including Hilda and Irene Dallas, at the Restaurant Mollard. The evening ended with the singing of the "March of the Women".

Christabel Pankhurst moved to Boulogne for the summer of 1912, meeting there with her mother and the Pethick-Lawrences in order to discuss her plan for a more destructive militancy than had hitherto been employed. It was to involve attacks on public and private property. In July she had specifically requested Sylvia Pankhurst to set fire to Nottingham Castle. The Pethick-Lawrences were entirely taken aback by what they perceived as a politically ill-judged policy. They suggested, rather, that Christabel should return to England and court arrest in order to capitalize on the public support that the Pethick-Lawrences felt had been engendered by their trial. In *Unshackled* Christabel referred to calls that were made for her return and did feel it necessary, even 40 years later, to explain why she did not go back. Her reasons were that she was the only one who could be counted on to stay out of the fray and not be "disabled for command", and, moreover, the only one who had "the capacity to read the mind of particular Cabinet ministers and of the Government in general". Emmeline Pethick-Lawrence explains in her autobiography that, although in the past Christabel had preferred to advance "militancy by slow degrees in order to give the average person time to understand", since moving to Paris she had adopted what Mrs Pethick-Lawrence characterized as Emmeline Pankhurst's extreme, dramatic, militancy. In September Christabel Pankhurst returned to London, in disguise, in order to inform the Pethick-Lawrences in person that she wished them to leave the WSPU and that she intended in future to have sole control of the Union. Her plans were well laid and the *Suffragette*, of which she was editor, appeared as the new official paper of the WSPU on 17 October, the day of the meeting at the Albert Hall at which the parting with the Pethick-Lawrences was announced.

In November George LANSBURY, who had resigned his parliamentary seat at Bow, met Emmeline and Christabel Pankhurst at Boulogne and it was decided that he would stand for re-election, backed by the WSPU, as an independent Labour candidate on a "Votes for Women" platform. Christabel, through Grace Roe, directed the WSPU's ill-judged campaign at the by-election; Lansbury was defeated. As the months passed it was felt, even by those who had hitherto been fervent admirers, that Christabel Pankhurst was losing touch with the realities of the WSPU campaign as they experienced it. After the police raid on Lincoln's Inn House at the end of April 1913 it became increasingly difficult for the WSPU to give support to women who were on the run as "mice". Mary Leigh, with two other militants, travelled to Paris in order to present Christabel with the facts. In an interview in 1965 Mary Leigh revealed, "She treated me like some crazy stranger. I didn't stay long and I didn't get anywhere". Perhaps in order to give added cohesion to the WSPU, startling members into a tighter loyalty as the shock of militant tactics dulled with repetition, in April Christabel Pankhurst launched in the *Suffragette* a series of articles on prostitution, venereal disease and the white slave trade. They were later published as *The Great Scourge, and How to End It*. Although the gist of the articles was by no means original (*Under the Surface*, Dr Louisa Martindale's book dealing with the same subject, had been published in 1909), she applied startling statistics to a mixture of fact and urban myth and was able to make such appeals as, "Let all women who want to see humanity no longer degraded by impure thought and physical disease come into the ranks of the Women's Social and Political Union, and help to win the Vote!" Her message was, "The real cure is a two-fold one – Votes for Women, which give women greater self-reliance and a stronger economic position, and Chastity for Men". The circulation of the *Suffragette* increased; W.T. Stead had run a similar campaign 30 years before with the same result. *The Great Scourge* entered the most unlikely homes; Mary BLATHWAYT gave copies to at least two friends and read it aloud to her maiden aunt. While the articles were appearing, Christabel Pankhurst was staying with her mother and Annie Kenney at Les Abeilles, Deauville, the home of Mrs Belmont, a wealthy American suffragist who in January 1911 had spent some time in London conferring with Mrs Pankhurst. It was from here on 1 August that Christabel wrote an extraordinarily vitriolic letter to Mary PHILLIPS, who, after six years of involvement with the WSPU, had been dismissed as an organizer. In 1913, over a period of four months, Christabel was paid by the WSPU £175, which covered rent and stationery for a Paris office, although it is not clear if this was separate from her own apartment, now at 8 Avenue de la Grande Armée. The average wage at this time to WSPU staff was £2 a week. In November 1913 she wrote to Mrs Badley, wife of the founder of Bedales, asking directly for money. In early 1914 Jessie KENNEY joined her in Paris to act as her secretary.

Christabel Pankhurst maintained her concern to protect the WSPU from deviationists. In early 1914 she summoned Sylvia Pankhurst to Paris and, in their mother's presence, asked her to take her EAST LONDON FEDERATION OF SUFFRAGETTES out of the WSPU. Christabel was not interested in developing a movement of working women, nor with working in association with the men of the *Daily Herald* League, and suspected that funds were being diverted to the East End that might be used by Lincoln's Inn House. At around the same time Christabel received at least two letters, one from Henry HARBEN and one from Beatrice HARRADEN, both quite separately and severely criticizing her handling of the WSPU's affairs. Elizabeth Robins had written 16 pages in a similar vein in November 1912; there doubtless were others. Harben and other supporters then broke away to found the UNITED SUFFRAGISTS. Christabel continued to place her faith in ardent militancy, given added conviction by the success of the Irish Unionists in defeating a Home Rule bill by threatening to use force. She was, however, sufficiently worried by the police raid on Lincoln's Inn House at the end of May not to leave her Parisian apartment from then until the end of July, when, with war threatening, she travelled to Britanny to meet Emmeline Pankhurst and Ethel Smyth. With the WSPU's organization under constant harassment from the police, its funds depleted, and her mother suffering from her repeated hunger strikes, Christabel Pankhurst's luck held; war was declared, the government gave WSPU prisoners an amnesty, and a final cessation of WSPU militancy was declared on 10 August 1914.

On 5 September Christabel Pankhurst returned to London, on 8 September was fêted at a WSPU meeting at the London Opera House, very close to Lincoln's Inn House in Kingsway, and there revealed that WSPU policy was to abandon "Votes for Women" and to support the government in its execution of the war. The Social Evil was replaced by the German Peril and in October Christabel set off on her first trip to the USA. Backed by Mrs Belmont and with the approval of the British government, her role was to urge America to support the Allies by entering the war. In 1915 the WSPU published as a pamphlet titled *International Militancy*, a speech given by Christabel Pankhurst in the

Carnegie Hall, New York on 13 January 1915. In the course of it she had said, "You would not have thought much of our intelligence, our patriotism, our love of freedom, if we had let (German) militarism ... use us suffragettes ... to destroy the mother of Parliament ... We shall have plenty of time when this war is over to fight our Civil War for votes for women." Olive BARTELS accompanied her on this trip and mentioned, when interviewed in the 1970s, that when she and Christabel returned to Paris at the end of this trip, she was surprised to discover in Christabel's room a heavily annotated copy of the New Testament. Olive Bartels specifically remarked that this predated Christabel's known attachment to Second Adventism. She commented that she thought Christabel's "mind was affected in some way". Christabel Pankhurst continued living in Paris until 1917, describing in *Unshackled* that it "was useful ... as a point of information and observation". She conducted the WSPU's campaign through *Britannia*, the successor to the *Suffragette*, attacking Asquith as pro-German. This policy brought retribution in the form of raids on the WSPU's new premises in Great Portland Street and on its printer. When Lloyd George and the National Government succeeded Asquith, Christabel Pankhurst was prepared to take the credit. In 1917, the funds of the WSPU having been diverted into the purchase of Tower Cressy and the establishment of Mrs Pankhurst's nursery for "war babies", Christabel relaunched the WSPU as the Women's Party. The programme of the new party was based on "equality of rights and responsibilities in the social and political life of the nation" and presupposed that women would be voters at the next general election. From late 1917 Christabel, with the other leading members of the Women's Party, campaigned in the industrial heartlands, advocating industrial peace and warning against the dangers of Bolshevism.

Christabel Pankhurst stood at Smethwick in the December 1918 general election, as the Women's Party candidate, with the backing of the Coalition government, the only woman candidate to be so endorsed. Her platform was: to secure a lasting peace based on obtaining material guarantees against future German aggression; to improve the social conditions of the working classes by a levelling up in society, by industrial salvation and wealth production; and to crusade against Bolshevism and "shirkers". She was also in favour of co-operative housekeeping and the provision in public houses of music and refreshment in order to make them sufficiently pleasant for women to enter. She lost to the Labour candidate by only 775 votes, but never repeated the experience.

This marked the end of Christabel Pankhurst's involvement in politics. She spent most of the rest of her life in the USA, becoming a travelling evangelist for Second Adventism, having as Grace Roe remarked when interviewed in the 1970s, a tiny income but a lot of friends. Grace Roe also remarked that, unlike herself, Christabel Pankhurst had not been influenced by theosophy. Christabel adopted one of Mrs Pankhurst's "war babies", Aurea Elizabeth Pankhurst, who, in her frequent absences, spent lengths of time boarded with an Adventist couple in Bournemouth and then at boarding school in Oxfordshire. In 1928 Christabel accepted an invitation from Edith How MARTYN to attend a suffragette reunion and in 1936 was made a Dame Commander of the British Empire (DBE) in recognition of her work for women's enfranchisement. She spent her later years in Santa Monica, California, overlooking the Pacific, and was buried at Woodlawn Cemetery. Her executrixes and beneficiaries were Grace Roe and a Mrs Grace Harris. In her will Christabel Pankhurst recorded, "I leave my eyes to the Eye Bank ... so that having served me perfectly during my whole lifetime, they may serve to restore sight to others". A memorial service was held for her in London, attended by many members of the SUFFRAGETTE FELLOWSHIP and, as a permanent commemoration, a stone semi-circle – with, at one end, a bronze relief of Christabel's profile and, at the other end, a representation of the "Holloway" badge – was added at the base of her mother's statue next to the House of Commons. After her death the manuscript of what Frederick Pethick-Lawrence described in his preface as "the personal narrative of the epic struggle" was discovered. This had apparently been written in the 1930s and was published in 1959 as *Unshackled: The Story of How We Won the Vote*. It is no rival to Sylvia Pankhurst's *The Suffragette Movement*, which was written about the same time and is interesting as much for what it omits as for what it reveals.

Besides the works mentioned, Christabel Pankhurst's pamphlets include *The Commons Debate on Woman Suffrage with a Reply by Christabel Pankhurst*, Woman's Press, 1908, and *Industrial Salvation*, The Woman's Party, 1918.

Address: (1900) 62 Nelson Street, Manchester; (1906) Clement's Inn, London WC; (1912) 9 rue Roy, Paris; (1913) 11 Avenue de la Grande Armée, Paris; (1917) 4 William Street, Knightsbridge, London SW; (1935) 5 Vincent Square, London SW1; (1942) 2172 Vista del Mar Ave, Los Angeles; (1956) 943 Ocean Ave, Santa Monica, California.

Portrait: caricature by Max Beerbohm exhibited at New English Art Club, 1909; Leicester Galleries, 1911; Piccadilly Gallery, 1996. Original pencil sketch for this caricature is in the University of Texas. Spy cartoon published in *Vanity Fair*, 15 June 1910. Drawing by Jessie Holliday (who had been admitted to the Royal Academy school in 1903, aged 19) given to National Portrait Gallery by wish of Iola A. Williams, 1961. Portrait by Ethel Wright, 1909 (offered then for sale at 100 guineas, to be donated to WSPU funds), bought by Una DUGDALE (for a discussion of this portrait see "England's Suffragette Martyr" in *Harper's Weekly*, 1909). Statuette by Sir Charles Wheeler, exhibited at Summer Exhibition, Royal Academy, 1962, was owned by the family of the second Lady Pethick-Lawrence.

Archival sources: Elizabeth Wolstenholme Elmy Papers, British Library; Harben Papers, British Library; Balfour Papers, British Library; Suffragette Fellowship Collection, Museum of London; Mitchell Papers, Museum of London.

Bibliography: S. Pankhurst, *The Suffragette Movement*, 1931; C. Pankhurst, *Unshackled*, 1959; D. Mitchell, *Queen Christabel*, 1977; A. Rosen, *Rise Up Women!*, 1974; E. Sarah, "Christabel Pankhurst: reclaiming her power", in D. Spender (ed.), *Feminist Theorists*, 1983; J. Purvis, "Christabel Pankhurst and the Women's Social and Political Union", in M. Joannou and J. Purvis (eds), *The Women's Suffrage Movement: New Feminist Perspectives*, 1998.

PANKHURST, EMMELINE, MRS (1858–1928) Born on Bastille Day in Manchester, daughter of Robert Goulden, who by the time of her birth was a cotton printer. Her mother Jane Quine came from the Isle of Man. Emmeline Goulden was the eldest daughter of ten children, of whom her sisters Ada (later Mrs Goulden Bach) and Mary (*see* Mary CLARKE), and her brothers Herbert and Walter, were concerned and willing supporters of her later career. The Goulden family had a history of involvement in radical causes; her grandfather had been present at Peterloo in 1819 and her grandmother had been a member of the Anti-Corn Law League. As a child Emmeline Goulden was encouraged to contribute thought and effort towards the emancipation of slaves. She first attended a suffrage meeting, at which Lydia BECKER was a speaker, when she was about 14; her mother was a subscriber to the *Women's Suffrage Journal*. Shortly afterwards Emmeline Goulden left Manchester to attend school in Paris, becoming precociously acquainted with the city. The tedium of life at home in Manchester, once schooling had ended, was relieved by her marriage in 1879 to Richard PANKHURST. In the next five years she had four children, Christabel (1880) (*see* Christabel PANKHURST), Sylvia (1882) (*see* Sylvia PANKHURST), Henry Francis (Frank) (1884) and Adela (1885) (*see* Adela PANKHURST). In 1880 Emmeline Pankhurst joined the executive committee of the MANCHESTER NATIONAL SOCIETY FOR WOMEN'S SUFFRAGE and in 1881 was co-opted on to the executive committee of the Married Women's Property Committee for the last year of its life. She supported her husband in the radical ideas he espoused as an independent candidate in 1883 at a Manchester by-election and was shocked by the measure of his defeat. In the 1885 general election Dr Pankhurst stood at Rotherhithe as a candidate for the Liberal and Radical Association. In August before the election, Emmeline Pankhurst had written from Manchester to Caroline Ashurst BIGGS, whose name she had been given as one of the "ladies in London who interested themselves in electoral work", asking "if anything would be done by our suffrage friends" to assist Dr Pankhurst in his candidature. She was delighted to hear, in a letter from Florence BALGARNIE, that Helen TAYLOR would lend her support. Despite this, Richard Pankhurst was again defeated. The family's income was depleted as a result of a subsequent case for libel brought by Richard Pankhurst to defend himself against imputations of atheism spread by his electoral opponent. After the election the Pankhurst family, accompanied by Mary Goulden, moved to London, where Mrs Pankhurst, hoping to revive the family finances, rented a house and shop at 165 Hampstead Road, some way north of Tottenham Court Road. The shop they opened was styled "Emerson and Company", doubtless a nod towards the influence of Ralph Waldo Emerson, who affirmed beauty, dignity and the infinite importance of the human soul. He also is reported to have commented at the beginning of the American Civil War that "sometimes gunpowder smells good"; it was altogether a prescient choice of name. The shop, described as a "fancy stationers" in the Post Office directory, was a business failure and after the death of four-year-old Frank in 1888 Emmeline Pankhurst closed the shop and moved her family, including her sister Mary, from insalubrious Hampstead Road to a large house in Russell Square. In the 1891 census Emmeline Pankhurst is described as an "art furnisher". By 1890 "Emerson's", with a stock of "inexpensive art furniture", had been reopened first in Berners Street, off Oxford Street, and then at 223 Regent Street, an ineffectual rival to Liberty's, which lay immediately across the road. The shop advertised regularly in the *Women's Penny Paper* and in return received editorial coverage for its seasonal shows (issue of 15 November 1890). Emerson's also acted as an estate agency. In 1888 Emmeline and Richard Pankhurst had been included among the "Guarantors" listed for the first exhibition of the Arts and Crafts Exhibition Society which was held at the New Gallery in Regent Street, for which T.G. Cobden Sanderson (*see* Anne Cobden SANDERSON) was the exhibition secretary and Walter Crane was the president. The Pankhursts mixed with artistic and political bohemia; William Morris, Stepniak, Grant Allen, Louise Michel and Annie Besant were all received at Russell Square. Although, for Emerson's, she took from the Aesthetic and Arts and Crafts movements what was pretty and appealing, Emmeline Pankhurst herself remained more a figure rendered by Tissot than by Burne-Jones. She preferred Parisian modes to Pre-Raphaelite drapery and, at this time, never went outdoors unveiled. Of her mother's taste and style Sylvia Pankhurst commented, "She was a woman of her class and period, in this, as in much else."

In early 1889 Emmeline Pankhurst and her husband were associated with Elizabeth Wolstenholme ELMY, Harriet MCILQUHAM and Alice Cliff SCATCHERD in the formation of the WOMEN'S FRANCHISE LEAGUE. Mrs Pankhurst was not present on 25 July at the inaugural meeting of the League; she had given birth on 7 July to her fifth child, Harry. She was, however, probably present at a committee meeting of the League which was was held on 23 July 1889 at the Pankhursts' house and she was included as a member of the first provisional council of the League. A second round of Women's Franchise League meetings was hosted in November by the Pankhursts. The central position of Russell Square and the layout of the Pankhursts' house, in which the two first-floor rooms opened into one big enough to accommodate a conference, gave Emmeline Pankhurst an eminence in the Women's Franchise League that she might not otherwise have held. Out-of-town members were at a psychological disadvantage in having to travel to London, stay in lodgings for the occasion, and then arrive at Russell Square to receive Pankhurst hospitality. After the resignation of Elizabeth Wolstenholme Elmy as secretary of the League in May 1890, Emmeline Pankhurst became for a time, with Countess Schack, joint secretary.

In parallel with her position with the WFL, from 1889 to 1893 Emmeline Pankhurst maintained a subscription to the CENTRAL NATIONAL SOCIETY FOR WOMEN'S SUFFRAGE. On 12 December 1888 she had joined the Central Committee for Women's Suffrage, hoping thereby to be entitled to attend the special meeting that had been organized for later that day at which proposed new rules for the society were to be discussed. Although agreeing that she was technically qualified to attend the meeting, Florence Balgarnie pointed out to her in a note that it was hoped that ladies who had only recently joined the society would not press this entitlement. Emmeline Pankhurst appears to have insisted, successfully, on her right to attend and, presumably, voted for the change in the rules that led to the formation of the Central National Society for Women's Suffrage. She was interviewed for the 7 February 1891 issue of the *Woman's Herald*, a paper which supported the Central National, and is recorded as saying, "I am a radical, devoted to the politics of the people, and to progress, especially where the education, emancipation, and industrial interests of women are concerned". She and Richard Pankhurst had joined the Fabian Society in September 1890. She remained a member until 1900 when she resigned in protest against the society's refusal to oppose the Boer War. In December 1891 the Women's Franchise League held a conference, over a period of three evenings, at the Pankhursts' house in Russell Square.

In April 1892 Emmeline Pankhurst, with her husband, was involved tacitly, if not in person, in a precursor to militancy. A joint meeting held at St James's Hall by the WOMEN'S SUFFRAGE DEMONSTRATION COMMITTEE in support of Sir Albert Rollit's Parliamentary Franchise (Extension to Women) Bill was disturbed by members of the Women's Franchise League, who opposed the bill on the grounds that it did not expressly include married women in its terms of reference. The meeting was chaired by J.H. Levy of the Personal Rights Association who, although willing to accept as sincere Alice Scatcherd's subsequent apology for the disturbance, had doubts about that of the Pankhursts, who it was rumoured had intended that the meeting should be broken up. Dr Pankhurst, in the columns of the *Personal Rights Journal*, denied that this was so. By the beginning of 1893, the lease of the Russell Square house having come to an end, an unexpected and heavy bill for dilapidations having been incurred, and "Emerson's" having been less successful than hoped, the Pankhursts returned north, eventually returning to a residential part of Manchester.

From 1893 Emmeline Pankhurst was a member of the executive committee of the Manchester National Society, now freed by Lydia Becker's death from opposition to the inclusion of married women in any proposed suffrage bill, and given new life with the appointment of Esther ROPER as secretary. In June 1894, as a leading member of both the Franchise League and the Manchester National Society, Emmeline Pankhurst helped to organize a "Great Demonstration" in the Free Trade Hall to support the campaign for the Special Appeal (*see* SPECIAL APPEAL COMMITTEE) among the women textile workers of Lancashire and Cheshire. Dr Pankhurst was one of the speakers on that occasion. On 17 December 1894, taking advantage of the clauses of the newly passed Local Government Act by which married women won the right to all local franchises, she was elected to the Chorlton Board of Guardians. In July 1894 Mrs Pankhurst was adopted as the ILP candidate for the Manchester School Board, although she was not successful in the ensuing election. It was not until September that she left the Lancashire and Cheshire Union of the Women's Liberal Association, of which she had been an executive member, in order to join the Independent Labour Party. As president of the Lancashire and Cheshire Union, Ursula BRIGHT wrote to her "Must you leave the L&C.U. These continual splits among women weaken us". Mrs Pankhurst was an energetic and successful poor law guardian at a time of economic distress. In July 1895 she canvassed for Richard Pankhurst when he stood in the general election as an ILP candidate at Gorton, on one occasion undergoing a stoning. In 1896 she had her first brush with the law when she supported the stand taken by Leonard Hall (*see* Nellie HALL) at Boggart Hole Clough and, having been summonsed, conducted her own defence from the dock. The case against her was dismissed and she continued weekly to address crowds at Boggart Hole Clough. After Dr Pankhurst's sudden death in 1898 and the associated cessation of the family income, Emmeline Pankhurst was appointed to the paid position of registrar of births and deaths and on 30 August resigned from her voluntary position on the Board of Guardians. She also revived the idea of "Emerson's", opening a shop at 30 King Street, hoping that it would be more successful in Manchester than it had been in London. The family moved from leafy Victoria Park to a smaller house at 62 Nelson Street, off Oxford Road. A Testimonial Fund in memory of Dr Pankhurst raised over £1000, in order to help support his widow and children. By the end of 1902 letters between Mrs Pankhurst and Mr Nodal, one of the administrators of the fund, reveal how bitterly she resented being treated as an object of charity.

Emmeline Pankhurst actively campaigned against the Boer War and, revived by the success of Keir HARDIE at Merthyr Tydfil, she became one of the Manchester ILP delegates to the local Labour Representation Committee and stood again as an ILP candidate for the Manchester School Board; this time she was successful. She retained this position until women's eligibility was removed by the 1902 Education Act. She was, however, co-opted to the Board, remaining as a member until October 1904. The barring of women from an area of local government to which they had battled for entry 20 years before could only have made more self-evident the need for women's parliamentary enfranchisement.

In 1901 Mrs Pankhurst, accompanied by Christabel and Sylvia, attended, as a delegate, the ILP annual conference at Leicester. In 1902 she and Christabel were involved with the NORTH OF ENGLAND SUFFRAGE SOCIETY in the campaign sponsored by the Labour Representation Committee to elect David Shackleton as the MP for Clitheroe. It was hoped that Shackleton would take the fight for women's suffrage into the House of Commons, a hope that was not realized. In August 1902 she was also a founder member of the Manchester Central branch of the ILP. Jill Liddington and Jill Norris, in *One Hand Tied Behind Us*, stated that their research in Manchester revealed no strong attachment by Mrs Pankhurst at this time to women's suffrage, but rather that she was intent on furthering the cause of Labour. During these years she was, however, gaining first-hand experience, through her work as registrar and on the School Board to add to that she had already derived from her time as poor law guardian, of the ill-usage of women as members of a society whose laws were made and monitored by men. The need for social reform always informed her demand for votes for women. As so much faith had been placed in the advent of a party devoted to socialism, it was natural that she should work for the advancement of the ILP. In 1903 the Labour Representation Committee changed its policy to allow for "Labour" candidates, that is ones pledged not to promote the interests of the Conservative or Liberal parties; Will Crooks and Arthur Henderson had joined Keir Hardie in the House of Commons. Mrs Pankhurst had seen over many years that a women's franchise bill, however phrased, if introduced by a private member would, notwithstanding the number of members who had pledged their support, never succeed. In spite of an annual ceremonial lobbying by the NATIONAL UNION OF WOMEN'S SUFFRAGE SOCIETIES, no Conservative or Liberal member had introduced such a bill, however hopeless, since 1897. However much energy was expended in educating the workers, men and women, as to the desirability of women's enfranchisement, it was only in the House of Commons that the decision would be taken. The question of women's suffrage was a constant subject in the Pankhurst household; Christabel was very much involved at this time with Eva GORE-BOOTH, Esther Roper and the campaign among the women textile workers.

The timing of the formation of the WOMEN'S SOCIAL AND POLITICAL UNION was doubtless a fortuitous mix of the personal and the political. With a "real" Labour Party in the House of Commons, Mrs Pankhurst felt that now was the time for the subject of women's enfranchisement once again to be brought before the public. In October 1903 Christabel embarked on her university degree course, which had the potential to take her even further from her mother's sphere than had her friendship with Eva Gore-Booth and Esther Roper, of which, as Sylvia Pankhurst reveals in *The Suffragette Movement*, her mother was jealous. It is not known whether Emmeline Pankhurst was invited to the National Convention for the Civic Rights of Women, which was intended to promote a fresh burst of activity in the suffrage cause, held on 16–17 October 1903 in Holborn Town Hall. Esther Roper and Elizabeth Wolstenholme Elmy, with both of whom she was in close contact, attended. Emmeline Pankhurst, however, was sceptical of the ability of the NUWSS ever to campaign effectively. In addition, all the Pankhursts had been provoked to discover that a new ILP hall in Salford, named for Dr Pankhurst, and opened on 3 October by Walter Crane, was closed to women, a fact that did not bode well for future ILP support for women's issues. It may just have been a coincidence that it was on 10 October 1903, a week after the opening of the Pankhurst Hall, a week before the Convention, and the day after the prorogation of the current parliament with a new session in prospect, that Emmeline Pankhurst held a small meeting of ILP women at her home and formed then a new organization, soon named the Women's Social and Political Union, by which to accomplish women's enfranchisement.

On 3 February 1904, the day after the opening of the new parliament, Emmeline Pankhurst was present, alongside members of the NUWSS, in a committee room of the House of Commons to lobby for the inclusion of a women's suffrage measure in the coming session. *The Times* reported that the meeting, chaired by Sir Charles McLaren and attended by Keir Hardie and Lady MCLAREN, resolved to "endeavour to secure a place in the ballot for either a Bill or a motion on the subject". Emmeline Pankhurst in her autobiography is dismissive of such empty words; no women's suffrage bill had been introduced since 1897. She recollected that she asked Sir Charles "to tell us what he and the other members will pledge themselves to *do* for the reform they so warmly endorse". Her motto, which became the leitmotif of the WSPU, was "Deeds Not Words". The launching of the new society did not take Emmeline Pankhurst into unfamiliar territory. In the 14 years since her days as a member of the Women's Franchise League, she had become an experienced speaker, addressing audiences in drawing rooms, in public halls and in the open air; she had first-hand experience of work within a political party; and she was involved in local government. The immediate target of the WSPU's campaign was the ILP, to persuade the National Administrative Council to adopt a policy of votes for women on the same terms as for men. At its April 1904 conference the ILP elected Mrs Pankhurst to its executive, which body was also instructed to arrange for the introduction into parliament of a women's suffrage bill. A year later at the 1905 conference, held in late January in the Sun Hall, Liverpool, the Labour Representation Committee rejected women's suffrage in favour of a policy of adult suffrage. Mrs Pankhurst wrote to commiserate with Selina COOPER in this setback and encouraged her to work to get women sent as delegates to the next year's conference. In mid-February 1905 Emmeline Pankhurst went to London to lobby MPs who had been successful in the ballot for private members' bills, in an attempt to persuade one to use his place to introduce the Votes for Women bill. In *The Suffragette Movement*, Sylvia Pankhurst gives the impression that she and her mother worked alone in this endeavour. In fact, Harriet McIlquham, with whom Emmeline Pankhurst had been associated in the early days of the Women's Franchise League, Mrs J.G. Grenfell, who had been a member of the WOMEN'S EMANCIPATION UNION, and Isabella FORD, were also there at the House, interviewing MPs on behalf of the WSPU. Elizabeth Wolstenholme Elmy, back home at Congleton, was using her experience garnered over 30 years of political involvement, in writing to MPs she knew, asking them to use their influence. They were eventually successful in persuading Bamford Slack, a Liberal, to sponsor the bill and in April persuaded the ILP at its annual conference to pass a resolution in favour of the bill. Emmeline Pankhurst returned to Westminster on 12 May, the day on which Bamford Slack's bill was due to be debated, and was accompanied in the Lobby of the House of Commons by Elizabeth Wolstenholme Elmy, Isabella Ford, Dora MONTEFIORE, Nellie Alma MARTEL, many constitutional suffragists and a platoon from the Co-operative Women's Guild. The bill was talked out. The women demonstrated in Broad Sanctuary, under the benign eye of the police, and passed a resolution, drafted by Mrs Wolstenholme Elmy, protesting against the procedures of the House of Commons. Emmeline Pankhurst dated the beginning of the militant campaign to this demonstration.

Back in Manchester the Pankhurst household was described by Teresa Billington (*see* Teresa BILLINGTON-GREIG), one of the WSPU's earliest recruits, as being at this time "a home of love, unity, and confusion". She stresses the missionary fervour, which she characterized as "reformist, rebellious, revolutionary", that had gripped the household and which united mother and daughters, drawing Christabel back into her mother's sphere. The Pankhursts and Teresa Billington launched a speaking campaign, working throughout the summer in tandem with the local ILP. Teresa Billington has described the wide range of societies and groups they addressed: "Trade Unions, Labour churches, ILP and SDF branches, Ethical Societies, Cooperative groups, Nonconformist chapels and churches, and Clarion Scouts". The ranks of speakers were soon swelled by the addition of Annie KENNEY and Hannah MITCHELL. Although traditional, this style of campaign was likely to be excruciatingly slow in making any impact on national politics. With a general election expected, WSPU policy was redirected from pressure on the ILP to pressure on the likely new government. As the Liberals were expected to win the election, it was from potential members of a Liberal cabinet that attempts were made to elicit assurances of support for a government measure for women's enfranchisement. Although she had been involved in the planning for the evening, Emmeline Pankhurst was not present in the Free Trade Hall on 13 October when Annie Kenney and Christabel put to Sir Edward Grey the question, "Will the Liberal Government give women the vote?" She was, however, in the court room the next morning when they were sentenced to a fine, or imprisonment, on a charge of obstruction and, in Christabel's case, of assaulting a policeman. Emmeline Pankhurst relates in her autobiography that she offered then to pay the fines in order that the two young women could return home, but that she was overruled by Christabel. She appeared at the indignation meetings in Manchester during the course of the next few days and at the triumphant reception for the released prisoners at the Free Trade Hall on 20 October. During the January 1906 general election she campaigned in Merthyr Tydfil for Keir Hardie.

Emmeline Pankhurst remained in Manchester, still employed as registrar, carrying on the WSPU campaign there as the new London-based group grabbed the headlines. She was chairman of the first WSPU London meeting in Caxton Hall on 19 February 1906 and was noted by the *Daily Mirror* as concluding that as there was no mention in the King's Speech of any special legislation for women "we must take a more militant attitude. The vote is our only weapon to bring about the social legislation we want". She was present in one of the dining rooms of the House of Commons on 4 April, at a dinner given by the new Labour Party, of which Keir Hardie was chairman, to celebrate its formation. To her great dismay the Labour Party, however, would not promote a Woman Suffrage bill. She was present in the Ladies' Gallery on 25 April when some of the impetuous new recruits to the WSPU caused a disturbance towards the end of the debate on Hardie's resolution in favour of women's suffrage. Keir Hardie appeared surprised that Mrs Pankhurst was not aware of the procedures of the House; although the 11 o'clock close had only come into operation the previous day. It is rather more surprising that Mrs Pankhurst was unable to control her associates; one might deduce that she had not been so minded. On 19 May Mrs Pankhurst spoke as a member of the deputation of all suffrage workers to Campbell-Bannerman, asserting that members of her WSPU were prepared to sacrfice for the vote "Life itself, or what is perhaps even harder, the means by which we live". She was here talking from experience; Emerson's was again closed and the fees from her registrarship barely met the liabilities she had incurred and the cost of keeping her family. At the same time as Christabel graduated in Manchester, her son Harry had been removed from the school he attended in Hampstead. Adela was now an elementary schoolteacher in Manchester and presumably contributed to the family expenses. Mary Clarke kept house and acted as deputy registrar to allow Emmeline time to campaign. Writing to Sylvia Pankhurst in December 1929, Emmeline PETHICK-LAWRENCE, whom Keir Hardie had introduced to Emmeline Pankhurst early in 1906 and who became treasurer of the fledgling WSPU, remarked "I think your mother's financial affairs would not be easy to explain." This judgement was true both before and after Mrs Pankhurst, a female Micawber, launched the WSPU.

In August Emmeline Pankhurst joined in the WSPU campaign at Cockermouth, the first by-election at which the WSPU policy of attacking the government candidate was put into effect. She was present at subsequent by-elections throughout the country during the remainder of the year. On 23 October she led a deputation from the Women's Parliament in Caxton Hall to the House of Commons, but was not one of those arrested. She was still a member of the ILP, speaking in November 1906 at a demonstration in the Horticultural Hall, Westminster, organized by the Metropolitan District Council Labour Party and in early April 1907 at the ILP annual conference at Derby to explain the WSPU election policy, by which Labour Party candidates were specifically not to be supported. On 19 April 1907 she wrote from Manchester to Caroline PHILLIPS in Aberdeen that she was giving up homekeeping and was in the midst of packing and dispersing books and papers, the accumulation of many years. On 8 March the talking-out of H.W. Dickenson's Women's Enfranchisement bill had determined Emmeline Pankhurst to resign her registrarship. A few days before then she had been warned by the Registrar General that her position with the WSPU was not compatible with her official post. It was a considerable decision to give up pensionable employment for the vagaries of a political campaign. Henceforward, although she was ostensibly based in London, Emmeline Pankhurst never had a settled home, but lived an itinerant life, travelling around the country, staying in hotels and with supporters, who were only too delighted to bask in her reflected glory. Even when in London she lived in the Inns of Court Hotel (not, as Ethel Smyth described it, the "Lincoln's Inn Hotel"), on the corner of High Holborn and Lincoln's Inn Fields, rather than as one might have expected, in a room in Clement's Inn.

While Christabel Pankhurst remained in London, exercising political control from Clement's Inn, her mother was the WSPU's inspired ambassador. Kitty MARSHALL in her unpublished memoir remarks on Emmeline Pankhurst's lovely voice, which was so clear that even in the Albert Hall she never used a microphone. Even a young boy, Lancelot Surry, who had no inherent bias towards women's suffrage, who indeed might have resented being taken along to such meetings as the one he remembered, held at the town hall in Portsmouth and addressed by Mrs Pankhurst, recorded in later life, "Her personality made an indelible impression on me. I never heard a political speaker (with the possible exception of Lord Birkenhead) who was more completely master of his subject, or who seemed to welcome noisy interruptions with such zest. Before half an hour had gone by Mrs Pankhurst had them all eating out of her hand!" Such testimonials are reiterated, by friend and foe, throughout the suffrage campaign. Teresa Billington-Greig wrote of Emmeline Pankhurst's "assumption of success" as being central to her power and control; that, once her opinion had been given on any matter, she assumed that success would be ensured. She did not brook dissent. Teressa Billington-Greig described Emmeline Pankhurst in the early years of the WSPU as "a very wonderful woman, very beautiful, very gracious, very persuasive ... She was ruthless in using the followers who gathered around her as she was ruthless with herself ... a dictator without mercy." In September 1907, when discussing in a letter the split within the WSPU between the Pankhursts and the group that became the WOMEN'S FREEDOM LEAGUE, Elizabeth Wolstenholme Elmy wrote, "I have often seen and heard Mrs Pankhurst cleverly and pleasantly tide over difficult situations, keeping her own temper and soothing other people's ruffled tempers, that I cannot possibly accept the representations of her conduct and Christabel's given by Mrs Rowe." Mrs Elmy, suspicious as she had been in the past as to Mrs Pankhurst's ability to effect political change, had been quite won over by her personality and political astuteness. In the summer of 1907 Emmeline Pankhurst resigned from the Labour Party, as she had left the Liberal Party in 1894, prepared to put the cause of women's suffrage before that of a party interest, and thereby proving herself, in Mrs Elmy's terminology an "earnest worker".

Work began in earnest when, on 14 February 1908 Emmeline Pankhurst was sentenced to six weeks' imprisonment in the second division. Lame from the mobbing she had recently received at the Mid-Devon by-election, she had headed the deputation from Caxton Hall to the House of Commons and had been arrested on a charge of obstructing a policeman. On this occasion she served her entire sentence in Holloway. In October she was sentenced to a further three months' imprisonment for inciting riot as a result of the plea to "rush" the House of Commons. From the dock at Bow Street magistrates' court Mrs Pankhurst had stated that "I am here to take upon myself now, Sir, as I wish the Prosecution had put upon me, the full responsibility for this agitation." It was a responsibility that she was to claim throughout the WSPU's active years. In Holloway, with Christabel, she demanded for the suffragettes the status of political prisoners. For defiance of prison rules she was placed in solitary confinement. She was, however, released a few weeks before the due date for the expiry of her sentence. Between these two terms of imprisonment she had been at the centre of the splendid WSPU demonstration in Hyde Park on 21 June. She had shared her platform with, among others, Charlotte Carmichael STOPES and Elizabeth Wolstenholme Elmy, who, describing the occasion to Harriet McIlquham, wrote:

> We could see pretty fairly all that went on there, not distinguishing persons of course, except Christabel herself, in her simple white, but no other platform was near enough to see individuals. Four rows of spectators faced that side of the platform, and then a row of Liberal youths (showed themselves such by their occasional cries of "Torygold") and next behind a row of men whom I suppose to have been ... prize fighters. The type was unmistakeable, and these obeyed the orders of the young Liberal gang.... The three storm centres were Mrs Martel's platform,

Mrs Emmeline Pankhurst (1858–1928) photographed c. 1909, wearing a "Boadicea" brooch. (Author's collection)

Christabel's and Mrs Pankhurst's – and ours was naturally the most violent . . .

During 1909 the set pattern continued; Emmeline Pankhurst toured throughout the country, campaigning at by-elections and inspiring women to join the WSPU. The contrasting aspects of the WSPU and of her involvement in it are exemplified by events in two consecutive months. In May Mrs Pankhurst's stall at the Prince's Skating Rink Exhibition was devoted to millinery, the epitome of womanliness. On 29 June she embodied its antithesis by striking Inspector Jarvis twice on the face, while leading a deputation to Asquith, and was again arrested. The case went to appeal, due to be heard in December. In the meantime, despite knowing that her remaining son, Harry, had contracted poliomyelitis, she set sail for America, to undertake a lecture tour.

On her return, although the appeal had gone against her and her co-defendant, Evelina HAVERFIELD, the fine was deemed paid. The government had no wish to draw more attention than necessary to the WSPU. In America her tour was organized by Harriot Stanton BLATCH. The first rally, at which she was welcomed to New York by Margaret Dreier Robins, sister-in-law of Elizabeth ROBINS, filled the Carnegie Hall.

Harry Pankhurst died in January 1910, in the middle of the general election campaign. On 9 January Mrs Pankhurst wrote to Mary PHILLIPS, the WSPU organizer in Bradford, "If you can arrange it I would be grateful if Bradford friends would just behave to me as if no great sorrow had come just now. It breaks me down to talk about it although I am very grateful for sympathy. I want to get through my work and know that you will help me to do it". In September 1910 she went on a speaking tour of the Highlands, accompanied by Una DUGDALE, and then to Ireland. On 22 November, four days after "Black Friday", Emmeline Pankhurst was arrested in Downing Street while leading a deputation to the prime minister, who was determined not to see them. She was released without charge, as were all the others arrested on those two days, if they had not taken part in window smashing. Emmeline Pankhurst did not test the government's nerve further at this time. Her sister Mary was imprisoned and died suddenly, on Christmas day, while they were both visiting their brother Herbert at Winchmore Hill. On the night of the census in April 1911 Emmeline Pankhurst, according to her authobiography, attended a concert organized by the WSPU at the Queen's Hall, walked around Trafalgar Square until midnight and then joined other suffrage census resisters for the night at Aldwych skating rink, having endorsed her census form, "No vote no census". According to Ethel Smyth, in *Female Pipings in Eden*, it was on "Census night" with Emmeline Pankhurst that she watched the dawn rise over the river from the latter's room in the "Lincoln's Inn Hotel". As Ethel Smyth remarked, "Neither of us ever forgot that dawn." She has left one of the most vibrant descriptions of Mrs Pankhurst at this time: "A graceful woman, rather under middle height; one would have said a delicate-looking woman, but the well-knit figure, the quick deft movements, the clear complexion, the soft bright eyes that on occasion could emit lambent flame, betokened excellent health." Ethel Smyth comments particularly on Mrs Pankhurst's air of authority and her genius as an orator.

In October 1911 Emmeline Pankhurst made a second lecture tour of the USA, raising funds for the WSPU, and renewing contact with Harriot Stanton Blatch and with Alice PAUL. While there, she learnt that Asquith proposed to introduce a government measure of manhood suffrage, to which an amendment to include women might be inserted; she cabled "Protest imperative!". The protest led to 220 women being imprisoned. On her return Mrs Pankhurst was only too willing to enter the fray. On 1 March 1912 she took a taxi to Downing Street and threw a stone at a window of No. 10. She was sentenced to two months' imprisonment. On 3 March the governor of Holloway reported, "They [Mrs Pankhurst and two of the other WSPU leaders] informed me that they expected greater privileges this time than they have had before, and hinted that as they would be coming in large numbers, it would be necessary to let them have their way. Mrs Pankhurst refused to give up her watch and her writing-case . . . I thought it better not to use force, but to leave the matter for the Magistrates to deal with." While in Holloway she was charged with "conspiring to incite certain persons to commit malicious damage to property". In order to prepare for her defence she was allowed, while in Holloway, access to file copies of *Votes for Women*, press cuttings, books of political speeches and her secretary. She was allowed her own food, which included a daily half pint of Chateau Lafite. She was released on bail on 4 April, the Home Secretary having terminated her sentence for window breaking while she awaited trial on the conspiracy charge. In May she was sentenced with Mr and Mrs Pethick-Lawrence to nine months' imprisonment in the second division and, with them, was ordered to pay the costs of the prosecution.

The WSPU leaders were held under rule 243A and protested bitterly at not being given first division, or political, status. When Adela Pankhurst travelled to London to see her, to discuss the fees for the agricultural college course she was about to start, the authorities refused to allow the visit. On 11 June Mrs Pankhurst and the Pethick-Lawrences were moved into the first division. By this time the Home Office had been deluged by requests for visits from the good and the great – among them Lady Sybil Smith, Countess DE LA WARR, Ethel Smyth, the Ranee of Sarawak (who was sent a copy of the First Division Rules; Adela Pankhurst had been told to buy a copy from the Stationery Office) and Mrs Pankhurst's doctor. By 21 June Emmeline Pankhurst was refusing food; visits were suspended (Adela, who had come from Warwickshire, Christabel, and Herbert Goulden were all turned away). She would not allow a medical examination and Home Office officials were doubtful about how to treat her. They did not forcibly feed her, as they did the other prisoners, including the Pethick-Lawrences, all of whom had by then adopted the hunger strike. The Home Secretary finally made the order to discharge Emmeline Pankhurst on 24 June. She went immediately to visit Christabel, who was now living in Paris. The two Pankhursts then summoned the Pethick-Lawrences to meet them at Boulogne to discuss their plan for a more ardent form of militancy.

During the course of the summer, when the Pethick-Lawrences were in Canada, Mrs Pankhurst had complete control of the London headquarters for the first time. She was instrumental in finding new headquarters for the WSPU in Lincoln's Inn House in Kingsway after the the rooms in Clement's Inn had been reclaimed by the landlord. Differences in attitude towards militancy that had arisen with the Pethick-Lawrences at the Boulogne meeting hardened into a desire that they should be asked to leave the WSPU. Mrs Pankhurst, who took over from Emmeline Pethick-Lawrence the role of treasurer, appears to have had little compunction in delivering this blow. Her speech at the Albert Hall on 17 October, in which she stressed that "we [are] fighting in an army, and that unity of purpose and unity of policy are absolutely necessary", called for "a new and stronger policy of aggression". Questions about this speech were soon asked in the House of Commons; Sir Rufus Isaacs replied that "It is not proposed to take any proceedings". However, by the end of 1912 police were attending all London WSPU meetings and forwarding verbatim reports to the Home Office, who noted all the incitements to break the law. From Home Office papers it is clear that the government was biding its time, sure that Mrs Pankhurst would soon give them clear cause to prosecute. The opportunity presented itself when, on 20 February, the day after Lloyd George's house, which Sir George Riddell, the proprietor of the *News of the World*, was building for him at Walton Heath, had been destroyed, Mrs Pankhurst claimed in the course of a speech given at the Cory Hall, Cardiff, that she accepted full responsibility for this arson attack and that "I have advised, I have incited, I have conspired." Her speech was taken down verbatim by a reporter from the *Western Mail*, which was also owned by Riddell, and, this section underlined, sent to the Home Office. The decision to prosecute Mrs Pankhurst was taken at a meeting in the Home Secretary's room on 21 February. She was taken to be charged at Epsom Police court on 25 February. James Murray, formerly an Aberdeen Liberal MP, and Mrs Rosina Mary Pott of 11 Scarside Villas, Kensington, stood sureties for her. However, although bail was available, Mrs Pankhurst would not give an undertaking not to take part in agitation until the next assizes in June. She was taken back to Holloway, went on hunger strike and, eventually, having accepted bail conditions and the promise that her trial would be moved to the Central Criminal Court, where it would be heard in April, was released on 27 February. The medical officer in Holloway reported that he did not think her fit for forcible feeding ("not inconsiderable risk in performing the operation owing to condition of heart").

At her trial Mrs Pankhurst conducted her own defence to the charge of inciting certain persons unknown to place an explosive on 19 February in a building at Walton, Surrey, with intent to destroy or damage it. She was found guilty, with a strong plea for mercy from the jury, and sentenced on 3 April to three years' penal servitude. In prison she went on hunger strike and was not forcibly fed. By 9 April she was described in the prison report as emotional and depressed. She threatened to take off her clothes, or walk about all night in order to ensure her release; she was desperate to appear at an Albert Hall meeting on 10 April. The Home Office noted that she "appears to be very nervous about herself", and delayed her release until 12 April, when she was let out for 15 days on a Special Order licence. The "Cat and Mouse" Act, which had been hastily drafted to deal with this situation, did not receive the Royal Assent until 25 April. While she was in prison Keir Hardie and other sympathetic MPs had kept the question of Mrs Pankhurst's health in front of the House of Commons.

The Home Office instructed the governor of Holloway to telephone the Special Branch at New Scotland Yard as soon as Emmeline Pankhurst had left and to give them the address of her destination. She was released to Nurse PINE at 9 Pembridge Gardens, but by 22 April Dr Flora MURRAY intimated that, because the large crowd gathered outside had interfered with the running of the nursing home, Mrs Pankhurst should be moved to Hertha AYRTON's house at 41 Norfolk Square. She was still there on 28 April, demonstrating no intention of returning to Holloway. Her licence was, therefore, revoked and a warrant was issued for her arrest. She was visited by the medical inspector of prisons, Dr Smalley, who reported that her health was such as to render her removal to prison inadvisable for the present; the execution of the warrant was deferred. Dr Smalley had been roundly abused by a "very unruly crowd of women round the door" of Hertha Ayrton's house. During his visit both Hertha Ayrton and Herbert Goulden were also present. Dr Smalley reported that Mrs Pankhurst "seemed about to burst into tears"; Hertha Ayrton told him that it was Dr Murray's opinion that it would be three months before Mrs Pankhurst was convalescent. At the beginning of May she was allowed to move with Nurse Pine to "Coign", Ethel Smyth's house in Surrey, in order to recuperate. "Coign" was kept under constant surveillance; in addition to the local Surrey constabulary a Metropolitan Police officer, "who has a good knowledge of the leading members of the Women's Social and Political Union", was drafted in. The Home Office report details that "If she should attempt to escape, she will have to be arrested at once and brought before the magistrate who issued the warrant . . . If she goes back to Holloway, I think she should be kept there as long as possible and then released under the Prisoners' Temporary Discharge Act. If that is done, we cannot prevent her going abroad, but her sentence will hang over her for the rest of her life." It was therefore half-expected that she might follow Christabel's example. Dr Murray had given an assurance that for a week from the date of her departure from Norfolk Square on 3 May Emmeline Pankhurst would not escape. After the end of that week Dr Murray was not able to renew her assurance. On 26 May Mrs Pankhurst was re-arrested at "Coign" as, accompanied by Ethel Smyth, Nurse Pine and Dr Murray, she attempted to enter a motor car. This was no surreptitious attempt at flight; a photograph of an elegant Mrs Pankhurst falling, fainting, onto Ethel Smyth's stalwart knee appeared in the *Daily Sketch* on 27 May.

Emmeline Pankhurst was returned to Holloway, renewed her hunger strike and was released under the "Cat and Mouse" Act on 30 May. She was taken on this occasion to Ada WRIGHT's flat at 51 Westminster Mansions, Little Smith Street, and was due to return to Holloway on 7 June. She did not do so. Among the Home Office papers is a memo revealing that the commissioner of police did not intend to re-arrest her, and would allow her to remain at home as long as she abstained from attending WSPU meetings. However, she was re-arrested outside Ada Wright's flat on 14 June as she stepped, with Sylvia Pankhurst, into a horse brougham. She was on her way to Emily Wilding DAVISON's funeral. A Home Office official noted that "If her re-arrest is criticized it would be well to point out that she has been convicted of a serious crime and sentenced to a term of penal servitude. If she is well enough to take part in a demonstration of sympathy with an act of criminal folly which might have endangered several lives she ought not to be allowed to remain at large". On being returned to Holloway Emmeline Pankhurst immediately went on hunger strike and was released on 16 June, under the "Cat and Mouse" Act, again to Ada Wright's flat. She did not return to Holloway on 23 June as instructed.

Emmeline Pankhurst was re-arrested on 21 July and sent back to Holloway. This time she went on a hunger-and-thirst strike and refused to undress and, lying on her bed covered with blankets, refused all examinations. She smashed up all her cell utensils. The Prison Commissioners medical officer reported on 23 July, "She was evidently in an emotional state and seemed distressed at her own position and also because she thought her daughter [Sylvia] might be in the same plight as herself." She was released once more on 24 July to 51 Westminster Mansions. The Home Office received letters petitioning for less harsh treatment for Mrs Pankhurst, contrasting her case with that of a man who had been sentenced for assaults on young girls, but who was then released on grounds of ill health without finishing his sentence. Among the signatories were the Bishop of Lincoln, the Bishop of Kensington, William de Morgan, Charles Mansell-Moullin (*see* Edith MANSELL-MOULLIN), H.W. Massingham and Albert Dawson, the editor of the *Christian Commonwealth*. The London Graduates' Union (which included Karl Pearson, Sidney Webb and Sir Edward Busk) petitioned the King, asking for a free pardon for Mrs Pankhurst. A Home Office note reveals that, of course, the reply ("the S[ecretary] of S[tate] regrets he was unable to advise HM to comply with the prayer of the petitioner") had been couched before being presented to the King, who approved the proposed reply on 5 July.

A photograph of Emmeline Pankhurst's licence for release under the "Cat and Mouse" Act, dated 24 July 1913, was issued by the WSPU as a postcard, with a caption to the effect that the original had been sold for £100. It had been auctioned to an American at a WSPU rally at the London Pavilion, to which Mrs Pankhurst had been taken in an invalid chair a few days after her release, too ill to talk, but perhaps an even more potent symbol in her silence. She failed to return to Holloway on 31 July, as required, remaining at Ada Wright's flat while her hostess was visiting the United States. The police made no attempt to re-arrest her; she explained this in her autobiography by commenting on the International Medical Congress that was held in London in August and suggesting that it was the presence of so many eminent doctors in the capital that deterred the Home Office from drawing attention to their treatment of suffragette prisoners. Mrs Pankhurst herself addressed a meeting of the Congress.

Mrs Pankhurst then spent two months in Paris with Christabel and in October sailed from France for New York. It is clear from the Home Office papers that, if the British government had not wanted her to collect funds for a new campaign, the British Embassy in Washington was prepared to advise American immigration to refuse her permission to land. The government did not, however, think it wise to interfere and left it to the decision of the US immigration authorities. She was, in fact, detained on Ellis Island and appeared before a Board of Special Inquiry, before being allowed, by direct authority of the President, to continue with her visit. She records that this detention ensured her publicity and, its welcome accompaniment, enhanced donations for the WSPU "war chest". She was able to bring back over £4000. She was accompanied both on her journey to the US and on the return by Rheta Child Dorr, who used the time at sea to take down Mrs Pankhurst's dictated account of her life, later published as *My Own Story*. While in New York in October 1913, Emmeline Pankhurst played herself, as did Harriot Stanton Blatch, in a feature FILM, *What Eighty Million Women Want*, a tale of political corruption, which took its title, though not its content, from a book of the same name by Rheta Child Dorr. The film was produced by the Uneek Film Company and received its first screening, introduced by Harriot Stanton Blatch, at the Bryant Theatre, New York, on 29 November 1913.

On 4 December 1913 the *Majestic*, carrying Mrs Pankhurst and Rheta Child Dorr, steamed into Plymouth harbour to be met by an arresting force. Scotland Yard had sent from the Special Branch one first-class inspector, one second-class inspector, one second-class sergeant, and two constables for the purpose of assisting the chief constable of Plymouth to arrest Mrs Pankhurst. The police report makes clear that the arrest was planned well in advance with the White Star Line Company. Emmeline Pankhurst, refusing to co-operate, was carried off the ship and taken to Exeter jail, where she immediately went on hunger-and-thirst strike, and was released late on 8 December. The Home Office had determined even before her arrest that they must keep her in prison until at least 6 pm on 7 December. She was supposed to return to prison on 13 December. On that date she was re-arrested at Dover; she had been with Dr Frances Ede and Nurse Pine to visit Christabel in Paris. She was returned to Holloway, from where she was again released, to Lincoln's Inn House, on 17 December, after hunger striking. She was due to return on 23 December, but instead escaped again to Paris, staying there until the end of January.

The police were not unaware of Emmeline Pankhurst's haunts in London. On 10 February 1914 police were present while she addressed a meeting of, they estimated, 1200 people, from the balcony of the BRACKENBURYS' house, 2 Campden Hill Square. She defied the police to arrest her both then and on a similar occasion on 21 February when she spoke to a crowd from the balcony of Gladys SCHÜTZE's house in Chelsea. The latter event was advertised on the day in *The Times*.

On 9 March 1914 Emmeline Pankhurst was arrested, among scenes of pandemonium, at a meeting in St Andrew's Hall, Glasgow. The hall, which held 455 people, was full, with yet more people standing. The police force sent to effect her arrest consisted of 161 men, of whom 109 were in uniform and 52 in plain clothes, of whom two were officers sent from the Metropolitan Police in London to assist in her identification. She managed to pass onto the platform, unobserved even by these trained eyes. Despite orders to the contrary, the superintendent of police ordered his men to arrest her while she was on the platform. She was surrounded by her bodyguard, who wielded police batons, indian clubs, life preservers and hammers. They also threw flower pots, water bottles, glasses, chairs and buckets of water, which they had concealed for this purpose. During the commotion a revolver, which evidently contained blank cartridges, was fired by Janie ALLAN. The bodyguard consisted of I.A.R. Wylie, Flora DRUMMOND, Miss Joansen, Miss Neave, Miss Cooper, Miss Palmer, Olive BARTELS, Miss Harding, Mrs Williams and Lillian Dove-WILLCOX, all of whom were identified by the police. Mrs Pankhurst was taken back to London on a train accompanied by four detective officers and a matron, together with the two other Metropolitan Officers. Considerable care had been taken to effect the retreat from Glasgow. The police party joined the London train at Coatbridge, the exit out of Glasgow having been blocked by lorries to prevent suffragettes from following. Despite this, Mrs Dove-Willcox and Mrs Williams were on the station platform at Carlisle to call out "Are you there Mrs Pankhurst" as the carriage, with drawn blinds, went past. They then boarded the train. The driver was instructed to stop at Loudon Road Station, just north of Euston, with the front portion, which contained Lillian Dove-Willcox and other suffragettes, in a tunnel, and the rear portion, with Mrs Pankhurst, near to the station exit. Mrs Pankhurst, who refused to co-operate in any way during the journey and who had to be carried from the train, is noted by the Home Office as having said to Inspector Parker, the accompanying detective, "I wish to inform Mr McKenna that when he attempts to arrest me again he will require a regiment of soldiers; I am a prisoner of war". The next day Mary RICHARDSON slashed the *Rokeby Venus* in the National Gallery and among the other acts of damage committed in the next few days, the windows of McKenna's house were smashed. After hunger striking, Emmeline Pankhurst was again released from Holloway on 14 March, due to return on 21 March. Having failed to return, she was arrested again on 21 May in the course of attempting to petition the King at Buckingham Palace. In the last few months before the war Mrs Pankhurst had determined to bypass government ministers and deal directly with "the Throne", as she termed it. She had seen that such an appeal by Irishmen, together with a call to arms, had resulted in the convening by the King of an Irish Conference. However, suffragette outrages did not have the same impact as the threat of the Currah "mutiny'; women were unlikely ever to win the physical force argument. In the course of the 21 May deputation the police report records that Chief Inspector Rolfe of A Division, "took her up in his arms and brought her within the Police line, to the open space in front of Buckingham Palace". The photograph of Emmeline Pankhurst, tiny feet (size $3\frac{1}{2}$) off the ground, head, topped by its neat little feathered hat, thrown back, eyes closed, clasped around the waist by the inspector, has become one of the iconographic images of the suffragette movement. The next day *Primavera* was slashed in the Royal Academy, as were five pictures in the National Gallery. Mrs Pankhurst was released again on 27 May to 34 Grosvenor Place, London SW, due to return to prison on 3 June. On 9 June she wrote to Mrs Badley, who was half-sister to Rhoda GARRETT, cousin of Millicent Fawcett, the wife of the founder of Bedales, and a long-standing supporter of the WSPU, asking for money to be sent to her, as "Miss Howard", at 6 Blenheim Road, London NW, which was then possibly the address of I.A.R. Wylie. The police had control of Lincoln's Inn House and, as the WSPU's treasurer, she may well have had to write other such letters at this time in an attempt to keep the campaign active. By 23 June, according to government figures, she had served only 16 days of her three-year sentence.

On 8 July Mrs Pankhurst was back in Holloway, having been arrested in a tussle outside Lincoln's Inn House. That night Ethel MOORHEAD and Frances PARKER planted a bomb at Robert Burns's cottage in Alloway. When she reached Holloway, because Grace ROE had been caught attempting to smuggle an emetic into prison, the police insisted that Mrs Pankhurst should be thoroughly searched, although nothing except indigestion tablets was found. On 10 July she was tried before the Visiting Committee in Holloway on a charge of using unseemly language and violence. This related to her behaviour during the course of the "forcible" (i.e. "strip") search in the Reception Wing of Holloway on 8 July. After being stripped and searched she had remained lying on the floor, refusing to be helped on with her clothes. She had lambasted the matron and wardresses for their conduct towards her. The image of Mrs Pankhurst, usually so fastidious and personally reticent, lying naked, stripped, under the gaze of prison officials, is not one conjured up in detail by suffrage histories. This private view was, however, produced for public consumption, that of the Home Office. This humiliation more than her commanding oratory and platform presence represents Emmeline Pankhurst's apotheosis and perfectly demonstrates what Teresa Billington-Greig identified as her willingness to be ruthless with herself.

Having been found guilty of unseemly language and conduct Emmeline Pankhurst was sentenced to seven days' close confinement. Her conduct in general was described as "Bad – is sullen and abusive". A continuation of her hunger strike led to release from Holloway on 11 July. She was due to return on 15 July, but on 16 July she was still a patient at Nurse Pine's nursing home. She was arrested that evening as she was leaving, on a stretcher, to attend a WSPU fund-raising rally at

Holland Park Hall. Officials at the Home Office had marked in red a passage in the 10 July issue of the *Suffragette* that stated, "It is Mrs Pankhurst's intention to be present and to speak at the meeting". The Archbishop of Canterbury wrote to the Home Secretary to inform him that he had received a deputation of WSPU members, "who in the most quiet, reasonable, and orderly manner desired to lay before me their grave apprehensions as regards what may happen tomorrow if Mrs Pankhurst is arrested on her way to the Albert Hall meeting [the meeting was, in fact, held in Holland Park Hall] or is prevented from taking part in the meeting". He wrote to McKenna to inform him that these reasonable ladies had told him that in future Mrs Pankhurst would be accompanied by an armed bodyguard and that they were apprehensive of bloodshed. On 17 July, the day after Mrs Pankhurst's arrest, another picture, this time a portrait of Thomas Carlyle in the National Portrait Gallery, was attacked. Carlyle, whose *French Revolution* had inspired her, was in fact one of Mrs Pankhurst's heroes; his assailant presumably only saw that he was a man. Emmeline Pankhurst was again released from Holloway on 18 July to Nurse Pine's care. She had completed her tenth hunger strike. The Home Secretary received a letter of protest from the Bishop of Lincoln as well as letters from women containing threats, albeit couched in genteel tones, to McKenna himself. On 20 July women were arrested at the gates of Buckingham Palace waiting to deliver another letter from Mrs Pankhurst to the King as the Irish delegates arrived for their conference. Emmeline Pankhurst was due to return to prison on 22 July, but managed to slip out of the country. She was with Ethel Smyth in St Malo when war was declared. On 13 August a letter went out from the WSPU, under her name, to inform supporters that the militant campaign had ended.

Emmeline Pankhurst returned to the public platform in September 1914 to support the Allies' war policy. In 1915 the WSPU was reactivated in order to oppose the convening of the International Congress of Women at the Hague; Emmeline Pankhurst rejected any suggestion of pacifism. Her main, and most characteristic, contribution to the war effort was first mooted in the 7 May 1915 issue of the relaunched *Suffragette*. Her intention was to found a home for "War Babies", a euphemism for the illegitimate by-products of a society in turmoil. "Ex-prisoners and Active members of WSPU" issued a pamphlet protesting against Mrs Pankhurst's policy of neglecting "the Cause of Votes for Women, in order to take upon herself, in the name of the Union, without consulting its Members, responsibilities which belong to the State. Will Voteless women think twice before contributing to the scheme for 'War babies' and call upon Mrs Pankhurst to refound the WSPU on a new and democratic basis?" Despite this opposition, she acquired four babies and, funded by money she raised in early 1916 on another American lecture tour, in the autumn established a home for them at 50 Clarendon Road, Kensington. Nurse Pine was installed to care for the babies. In 1917 the remaining WSPU funds were used to purchase and furnish as a home for female orphans a house, Tower Cressy, in Aubrey Road, Kensington. The four-floor house had been built in 1854 by the architect of Westminster Bridge and was surmounted by a large turret with bulbous pinnacles. Described as vulgarily Italianate, it had once been home to the designer Christopher Dresser and his 13 children. Two of Annie Kenney's sisters, Jenny and Kitty, who had trained under Maria Montessori, worked with Mrs Pankhurst and Nurse Pine at Tower Cressy. The venture could not, however, be sustained and in 1919 was transferred to trustees and became the War Memorial Adoption Home, the original hostel of the National Adoption Association.

In 1916 Emmeline Pankhurst returned to America, this time to undertake a lecture tour in order to raise funds to provide aid for Serbia as well as for the "war babies". The next year she went to Russia, urged on by Lloyd George, to encourage Russian women to support the war. She was there during the October Revolution. In Petrograd she took the salute at a march-past of the Women's Battalions of Death, the answer to "the physical force" argument that had been used for so long to undermine women's qualification for citizenship. In 1918 she returned to America, again at the government's behest, to lecture on the evils of Bolshevism. While in Britain, Mrs Pankhurst campaigned for "industrial peace", that is, against socialism, and, with Christabel, renamed the WSPU the WOMEN'S PARTY.

Emmeline Pankhurst suffered what Ethel Smyth with typical extravagance described as "the bitterest disappointment of her life" when in 1918 Christabel failed to be elected as the Women's Party member for Smethwick. In September 1919 Mrs Pankhurst set sail for North America and was appointed a lecturer by the National Council for Combating Venereal Diseases. In 1919–20 a testimonial fund organized on her behalf in Britain by Kitty Marshall and other WSPU members raised less than £3000. Half the amount was spent on a cottage, "Westward-Ho", in Devon, which she scarcely visited and which was eventually sold at a loss. In the summer of 1920 she was joined by three of the "war babies" (Kathleen King, Joan Pembridge and Mary Gordon), Nurse Pine and a French governess, living first in Victoria and then in Toronto. In 1922 Christabel and the fourth girl, Elizabeth Tudor (later renamed Aurea Elizabeth Pankhurst), whom she had adopted, joined the household. By 1924, having worked continuously to support her household, Mrs Pankhurst became ill and went to recuperate in Bermuda with the young girls. She eventually returned two of them to England; Kathleen was adopted by John Coleridge Taylor, an *Evening Standard* journalist, and Joan was adopted by a wealthy couple in Scotland. Nurse Pine, who was not happy after Christabel's arrival, had returned to England in 1923 and the sole care of three young children was doubtless too much for Mrs Pankhurst, now 66 years old. In 1925 Emmeline and Christabel, together with Elizabeth (Betty) and Mary, left Canada for France, joining Mabel TUKE in running The English Teashop of Good Hope at Juan-les-Pins. Like Emerson's before it, this venture failed. Emmeline Pankhurst returned to London, where she lived with her sister, Ada Goulden Bach. She turned down an invitation to organize the Equal Political Rights Campaign, which had been founded by Lady RHONDDA to campaign for the extension of the franchise to women under 30. Mrs Pankhurst apparently stated that it was up to young women to win their own enfranchisement; her generation had broken the sex barrier. She did, however, take part in the demonstration organized by the Equal Political Rights Demonstration Committee in 1926 and was, in 1927, persuaded to stand as a Conservative candidate in the constituency of Whitechapel and St George's, Stepney, likely to be a hopeless cause. Her campaigning themes were national solidarity, moral rearmament and an end to class war. In early 1928 she moved into a rented room in Wapping, found for her by Kitty Marshall. She was forced to part with Mary Gordon, who was at first cared for by the Coleridge Taylors, then by Marion Wallace-DUNLOP, and was eventually adopted by a Miss Bevis.

After a short illness, Emmeline Pankhurst died at a nursing home at 43 Wimpole Street, London W, on 14 June 1928. She was buried on 18 June in Brompton Cemetery after a vigil had been kept around her coffin the previous night in St John's, Smith Square. Her pallbearers were Barbara Wylie, Marion Wallace-Dunlop, Harriet KERR, Ada Wright, Maria and Georgina Brackenbury, Rosamund MASSY, Kitty Marshall, Marie NAYLOR and Mildred MANSEL. Probate on her estate, which amounted to £86 5s 6d, was granted to Christabel Pankhurst. Katherine Marshall opened a fund for a Mrs Pankhurst Memorial, of which, with Rosamund Massy, she was joint honorary secretary and Lady Rhondda was honorary treasurer. The headstone for Mrs Pankhurst's grave was designed by Julian P. Allan, whom Kitty Marshall described as "a clever girl". The portrait of Mrs Pankhurst painted by Georgina Brackenbury was purchased and given to the National Portrait Gallery. Kitty Marshall was quite determined that Mrs Pankhurst should be commemorated by a statue in Westminster and went to considerable lengths to procure a suitable position for it in Victoria Tower Gardens, adjacent to the House of Commons. The statue was commissioned from A.G. Walker ARA, Sir Herbert Baker made the plinth, and it was unveiled (from under a purple, white and green flag) by Prime Minister Stanley Baldwin on 6 March 1930. Ethel Smyth conducted the "March of the Women" and the speakers, besides Baldwin, included Flora Drummond, Lady Rhondda and Mr Pethick-Lawrence. The SUFFRAGETTE FELLOWSHIP made sure that, when necessary works entailed the shifting of the statue in 1955, it was moved into an even more prominent position, close to the entrance to the House of Lords. With £200 left over new choir stalls, with "EP" carved on the seats, were given to Ongar Church, near to the Marshalls' home; a surprising choice of memorial to one who was not overtly concerned with church attendance. Over the following years the next generation of the Pankhurst family was represented in the Suffragette Fellowship by Emmeline Pankhurst's nieces, Enid and Sybil Goulden Bach.

When approached by Sylvia Pankhurst in December 1929 about her plan to write a biography of her mother, Emmeline Pethick-Lawrence wrote, "I believe she conceived her objective in the spirit of generous enthusiasm. In the end it obsessed her like a passion and she completely identified her own career with it in order to obtain it. She threw scruple, affection, honour, legality and her own principles to the winds." Emmeline Pankhurst's pamphlets include *The Importance of the Vote*, Woman's Press, 1908.

Address: (1886) 165 Hampstead Road, London NW; (1889) 8 Russell Square, London WC; (1894) 4 Buckingham Crescent, Daisy Bank Road, Victoria Park, Manchester; (1899) 62 Nelson Street, Manchester; (June 1913) 51 Westminster Mansions, Little Smith St., SW (Ada Wright's flat); (June 1914) 6 Blenheim Road, London NW (May have been Barbara Wylie's address); (March 1917) 50 Clarendon Road, Holland Park Avenue, London W11; (1917–18) Tower Cressy, Aubrey Road, Kensington, London W; (1921) Beach Drive, Oak Bay, Victoria, British Columbia, Canada; (1925) 2 Elsham Road, Kensington, London W (address of her sister, Mrs Ada Goulden Bach); (1928) 9 High Street, Wapping, London E.

Portrait: portrait by W.R. Sickert, owned by Dr A.W. Laing in 1960 (see *Art in Private Collections in Manchester*, 1960). By Georgina Brackenbury, painted from life c. 1927, National Portrait Gallery; a slightly smaller version of this portrait, also by Georgina Brackenbury, painted c. 1927 was given to the Museum of London by the Suffragette Fellowship in 1950. Ivory bust by A.G. Walker (who in his turn was painted by George Coates – see Dora Meeson COATES) (photograph in National Portrait Gallery Archive); bronze on marble base by Walker, probably model for next item (photograph in National Portrait Gallery Archive); statue by Walker in Victoria Tower Gardens. Photograph by Constance Marsden, reproduced in *Amateur Photographer*, 29 September 1913 (National Portrait Gallery Archive); two photographs by Olive Edis, late 1920s, National Portrait Gallery.

Archival source: Home Office Papers, Public Record Office; Papers of Sylvia Pankhurst, Internationaal Instituut voor Sociale Geschiedenis, Amsterdam; Mitchell Collection, Museum of London.

Bibliography: E. Pankhurst, *My Own Story*, 1914; E. Smyth, *Female Pipings in Eden*, 1933; S. Pankhurst, *The Life of Emmeline Pankhurst*, 1935; C. Pankhurst, *Unshackled*, 1959; B. Harrison, *Prudent Revolutionaries: British Feminists between the Wars*, 1987; S. Holton, "In sorrowful wrath: suffrage militancy and the romantic feminism of Emmeline Pankhurst", in H.L. Smith (ed.), *British Feminism*, 1990.

PANKHURST, RICHARD MARSDEN (1835–98) Son of an auctioneer, a Liberal dissenter, he was educated at Manchester Grammar School and Owen's College, Manchester, from where he finally graduated with an LLD from the University of London in 1863. After initially practising as a solicitor he was called to the Bar by Lincoln's Inn in 1867 and joined the Northern Circuit, based in Manchester. Influenced by the thinking of Ernest Jones, the Chartist, and of John Stuart MILL, he was an early member of the National Association for the Promotion of Social Science and his legal advice was sought by those interested in causes of popular reform. In 1858, following the pattern set in London by the founding of the Working Men's College, Pankhurst with others instituted evening classes at Owen's College. In 1863 he became honorary secretary of the Lancashire and Cheshire Union of Institutes, which through Mechanics' Institutes offered scientific training to workers. Rev. S.A. STEINTHAL worked with him in this endeavour. Sylvia PANKHURST writes that Richard Pankhurst was a member of the first committee formed in Manchester to support women's suffrage, although Elizabeth Wolstenholme ELMY does not note his presence when reminiscing to Harriet McILQUHAM in later years and his name does not appear on the headed notepaper of the Manchester Committee for the Enfranchisement of Women when it was founded in January 1867. He, however, quickly did become a member of the executive committee of the society and was certainly one of the speakers, with Agnes POCHIN and Jacob BRIGHT, on 14 April 1868 at the first public meeting to be held in Manchester in support of women's suffrage. His article "The Right of Women to the vote under the Reform Act of 1867" was published in the *Fortnightly Review* in 1868. Dr Pankhurst worked in close association with Lydia BECKER, who in a letter of 7 June 1868 described him as "a very clever little man – with some extraordinary sentiments about life in general and women in particular". In November 1868 Dr Pankhurst argued, unsuccessfully, before the Court of Common Pleas the case (known as *Chorlton* v. *Lings*) of 5000 Manchester women householders to be included in the voters' register, and that brought by Philippine KYLLMANN. He then drafted the Women's Disabilities Removal Bill, sponsored in parliament by Jacob Bright, that initiated 50 years of parliamentary campaigning. Dr Pankhurst was a leading member of the Married Women's Property Committee for its entire life, 1868–82, drafting the Married Women's Property Bill which was introduced in parliament in 1868. In 1869 he drafted an amendment to the Municipal Corporations Bill, restoring to women the right to vote in municipal elections, which was successfully moved in parliament by Jacob Bright. Dr Pankhurst was elected to the executive committee of the NATIONAL SOCIETY FOR WOMEN'S SUFFRAGE in 1873. In 1874 he opposed Lydia Becker in her intention of amending the women's suffrage bill to exclude married women, and in 1875 resigned from the executive committee of the MANCHESTER NATIONAL SOCIETY. In 1879 he married Emmeline Goulden (see Emmeline PANKHURST) and in the course of the following years became the father of five children, among them Christabel, Sylvia, and Adela.

In 1883 Dr Pankhurst resigned his membership of the Manchester Liberal Association and stood as an independent, supporting adult suffrage for both sexes, amongst other radical causes, at a Manchester by-election. Hugh Mason, father of Bertha MASON, although a Liberal MP, gave £100 towards his election expenses. In 1885 the Pankhursts moved to London and he fought, again unsuccessfully, a fraught campaign as a candidate sponsored by the Rotherhithe Liberal and Radical Association (which had no connection with the Liberal Party). Helen TAYLOR's candidature in the same election was backed by the Camberwell Radical Association and Dr Pankhurst went to speak in her support. In 1889 he was present at the annual general meeting of the CENTRAL NATIONAL SOCIETY FOR WOMEN'S SUFFRAGE and protested against the addition of the clause excluding married women to Woodall's Bill. On 25 July 1889 he spoke at length against the principle of couverture at the inaugural meeting of the WOMEN'S FRANCHISE LEAGUE and, with his wife, was a member of the WFL's Council. In 1890 Dr Pankhurst joined the Fabian Society, becoming president of the Manchester and District branch. In 1893 the Pankhursts returned north, living at first in Southport, then at Disley in Cheshire, finally moving back into Manchester. In 1894 he joined the Independent Labour Party and at the general election in July 1895 stood, yet again unsuccessfully, as the ILP's candidate at Gorton. In 1895 he was elected to the national executive of the ILP. His sudden death made a deep impression on Sylvia Pankhurst, who was alone with him when he was taken ill.

Address: 165 Hampstead Road, London NW; (1889) 8 Russell Square, London WC; (1894) 4 Buckingham Crescent, Daisy Bank Road, Victoria Park, Manchester.

Bibliography: S. Pankhurst, *The Suffragette Movement*, 1931; A. Rosen, *Rise Up Women!: The Militant Campaigns of the Women's Social and Political Union 1903–1914*, 1974; L. Holcombe, *Wives and Property*, 1983.

PANKHURST, [ESTELLE] SYLVIA (1882–1960) Born at 1 Drayton Terrace, Old Trafford, Stretford, Manchester, second daughter of Richard and Emmeline PANKHURST. After the family returned to the north from London, she was educated at Southport High School for Girls, 1893, and then at Manchester High School for Girls. From 1900 to 1902 she studied, on a free studentship, at Manchester Municipal School of Art. She won several prizes, including the Proctor Memorial Travelling Scholarship which, in the summer of 1902, enabled her to journey to study mosaics in Venice and Florence. She returned to Manchester in spring 1903 because her mother had organized for her a commission to devise and execute mural designs for the Pankhurst Hall, which had been built by the Independent Labour Party in Salford in honour of her father. The hall was opened in early October by Walter Crane, who had been part-time director of Design at the School of Art in Manchester, 1893–6, and who was himself accustomed to such commissions, having, with Henry Holiday, in April 1890 decorated St James's Hall, London, for a Home Rule reception in honour of Parnell. The skill of the decorator made no difference to the ILP; women were not admitted to the hall. In November 1903 Sylvia Pankhurst became one of the first Associates of the Manchester Municipal School of Art and prepared to sit the scholarship examination for the Royal College of Art in London. It was at this time that the work of the WOMEN'S SOCIAL AND POLITICAL UNION, founded by her mother in October at a meeting at which

Sylvia may have been present, was developing, still contained within the walls of the family home at 62 Nelson Street. In national competition Sylvia, coming top of the list, won one of six scholarships (worth £50 a year) to the Royal College of Art. She moved to London, living in lodgings off the Fulham Road, and joined the local branch of the ILP. She renewed her friendship with Keir HARDIE, a friend of her parents; that it was a loving relationship is clear from surviving letters. On her behalf Hardie asked a question in the House of Commons about the proportion of internal RCA scholarships given to women, against whom Sylvia thought the college discriminated. In 1904 Sylvia made her maiden speech in support of women's suffrage, at Ravenscourt Park, at the invitation of Dora MONTEFIORE. In 1904 she moved into two rooms in the house of Thomas Roe, a tailor, and his wife, Florence, in Park Walk, Chelsea, and it was here that her mother stayed in February when she came to London to lobby at the House of Commons in order to persuade an MP to adopt a women's franchise bill. Sylvia accompanied her to Westminster and in the following weeks travelled around London to garner signatures for a petition that was to accompany the bill. On 12 May she was present at the House of Commons as the bill was talked out and took part in the demonstration, with her mother and Elizabeth Wolstenholme ELMY, to protest against the arcane procedures that allowed this to happen.

It was only when she returned to Manchester for the summer that Sylvia Pankhurst met the WSPU's new recruits, Annie KENNEY and Teresa Billington (see BILLINGTON-GREIG), with whom she then spent her holiday campaigning around the towns of Lancashire. Sylvia was probably back in London for the new academic term when Christabel and Annie Kenney made their demonstration at the Free Trade Hall in Manchester on 13 October. She gives in both *The Suffragette* and *The Suffragette Movement* what appears to be an eyewitness account, but does not place herself in the scene as she would surely have done if she had been there. Elizabeth Wolstenholme Elmy, in her very full account of the events of 13 October, and of the triumphal return to the Free Trade Hall on 20 October, does not mention Sylvia. The latter was, however, soon to take her share in early WSPU militancy. When Annie Kenney came to London in December she stayed with Sylvia in Chelsea and together, with Dora Montefiore, Minnie BALDOCK and Teresa Billington (who had also come to London although Sylvia does not mention her presence in Park Walk) they arranged to interrupt Liberal meetings held in the Queen's Hall and the Albert Hall by Campbell-Bannerman and Asquith. Sylvia was present on the occasion of the demonstration in the Albert Hall on 21 December.

Sylvia Pankhurst spent her Christmas vacation in Manchester. In readiness for the general election campaign she painted "Votes for Women" on hundreds of pieces of white calico; the BANNER was merely the message at this stage of the campaign. She heckled Winston Churchill in Manchester and when she accompanied Annie Kenney to Sheffield to repeat the performance for Asquith, they were both flung out into the street. She was back in London when the election results were announced and was delighted by the success of the 29 Labour MPs. She still put her faith in socialism but in *The Suffragette Movement,* written, of course, with hindsight, she noted that at this time Christabel, in Manchester, was already moving in the opposite direction, taking a WSPU deputation to interview the defeated Conservative leader, Balfour, who had professed himself sympathetic to their cause. Sylvia was to be torn between her sympathy with Keir Hardie and socialism and the WSPU's developing policy of eschewing support from any party. A few days after the end of the election Annie Kenney arrived in London and, with considerable assistance from seasoned campaigners such as Dora Montefiore, Keir Hardie and W.T. Stead, she and Sylvia arranged for the WSPU to open its assault on London with a meeting in the Caxton Hall in Westminster on the day of the opening of parliament.

By the end of February 1906 Sylvia Pankhurst was appointed honorary secretary of the London committee of the WSPU and in this capacity backed the policy of doorstepping Campbell-Bannerman. She was in her final two terms of her RCA course, working for the WSPU in every spare moment, with no possibility of pursuing further studies, even if granted another studentship. She had previously been able to sell textile designs to a few firms, but with her mother's shop, Emerson's, of which these same firms were creditors, in terminal decline, she did not feel able to pursue that source of small additional income. In an attempt to gain some time to build up a portfolio with which to launch herself into work at the end of her college course, she suggested to her mother that she should be relieved of her secretaryship of the London branch of the WSPU. Her mother insisted that she should retain it until Christabel graduated in the summer and arrived in London to take over control. As the end of her college year approached Sylvia was bitterly hurt that her mother did not write to encourage her. Twenty-five years later she recalled this hurt, writing in *The Suffragette Movement*, "We were no longer a family; the movement was overshadowing all personal affections." Sylvia had no desire to become a paid organizer for the WSPU. In spite of her mother's wish, before Christabel's arrival, Sylvia resigned her honorary secretaryship, the responsibility for which was then shared by Edith How MARTYN and Charlotte DESPARD.

Sylvia Pankhurst moved from Park Walk to two rooms in Cheyne Walk on the Embankment, attempting, with considerable difficulty, to earn a living as an artist. Whatever other journalism she also managed to procure she was not, as Richard Pankhurst stated in *Sylvia Pankhurst: Artist and Crusader*, the "Ignota" who contributed articles to the *Westminster Review*. The author of these was Elizabeth Wolstenholme Elmy; it was doubtless a mention of the articles among Sylvia Pankhurst's papers that led to this misapprehension, which unfortunately has been repeated elsewhere. In her essay in *Myself When Young* Sylvia Pankhurst recounted the struggle she felt between her desire to put her art at the service of "the People and the Poor" and her knowledge that the only way of surviving as an artist was through the patronage of the rich. It was perhaps around this time that she designed the Member's Card for the WSPU, which portrays, in clear, bright colours, the working women, in aprons, clogs and shawls, whose lives she hoped the campaign would improve.

In October 1906 Sylvia Pankhurst went to prison for the first time, arrested on a charge of obstruction, having protested at the police court on the sentencing of the WSPU women arrested outside parliament on 23 October. Unsurprisingly the experience had a profound effect; in both *The Suffragette* and *The Suffragette Movement* she gives a detailed and evocative account of prison life. Sylvia Pankhurst was adamant that this opportunity to expose the conditions under which all convicted women, not just suffragettes, were held in prison should be grasped, despite Christabel's fear that such a campaign would divert attention from the WSPU's *raison d'être*. After her release Sylvia gave to the press interviews and sketches she had made in prison after being moved into the first division, which change in status allowed her to follow her profession. Some of these and an article she had written were published, through the influence of Keir Hardie, in the *Pall Mall Gazette,* January–June 1907. In *The Suffragette Movement* Sylvia Pankhurst remarked that there was comment about the fact that she was not invited to the banquet given by Mrs Fawcett for the released prisoners at the Savoy on 11 December. As she gives no description of this interesting occasion, she doubtless was not there. The printed seating plan and list of those invited does, however, show a place both for her and her guest. It seems likely that it was around the time of the banquet that she was in Venice, at the invitation of Emmeline PETHICK-LAWRENCE, who had managed to endure only a few days in prison after being arrested in October before suffering a nervous breakdown, and who had gone to Italy to recuperate.

On 13 February 1907 Sylvia Pankhurst was arrested again, with Christabel and over 50 others, after taking part in a deputation from the Women's Parliament in Caxton Hall to the Houses of Parliament. She had painted a banner to decorate the hall for the meeting. Still in the tradition of her design for the early WSPU membership card it depicted working women – one carrying a child and the other a sheaf of corn. The evening before, at Limehouse Town Hall, Emmeline Pethick-Lawrence presented to the new Limehouse branch of the WSPU a banner executed by Sylvia Pankhurst; it is not clear if this was different from that displayed in Caxton Hall. As a ringleader of the deputation and a previous offender Sylvia was sentenced to three weeks' imprisonment, which was spent in the first division and which she devoted to a study of prison conditions. While she was in Holloway Keir Hardie sent her a copy of *Noctes Ambrosianae* which, he explained "had a great vogue in Scotland 50 years ago". On her release, at the breakfast of welcome held at the Eustace Miles Restaurant, the Penal Reform Union was formed by Capt. Arthur St John, a useful by-product of her incarceration.

Keir Hardie was ill in the early summer and in July set off on a world tour that lasted until April 1908. Perhaps it was his absence from London that prompted Sylvia to set off for the north to study, as an artist, the lives of working women. She lived for a time at Cradley Heath with the women chainmakers, before moving to Leicester, where she lived with Alice HAWKINS and painted women shoemakers. She then travelled to Wigan to study women "pit brow" workers and, from there, back down to Staffordshire to the potteries and then onto Scarborough, on the east coast, to paint the Scottish fishwives who followed the herring fleet. North in Berwickshire she studied women agriculture workers before travelling in the winter to Glasgow, painting women cotton workers and visiting her brother Harry, who was working with a builder in the city. She published, as "Woman Workers of England" in the *London Magazine* in November 1908, an article based on her observations. It reproduced in colour her painting *The Chainmaker* and two black and white scenes, *Pit-Brow Lasses* and *Inside a Cotton-spinning Mill*. In the course of these travels she also went at her mother's request to help the WSPU campaign at the Rutland and Bury St Edmunds by-elections. In addition she embarked on a series of articles, "The History of the Suffrage Movement", which commenced in the first issue of *Votes for Women*, October 1907 and concluded in the issue of 24 September 1909. Sylvia preserved a series of letters that she received at this time from Elizabeth Wolstenholme Elmy who, to help her write the articles, gave invaluable information from her personal experience of the beginnings of the women's suffrage movement. The letters do not give any clues to Sylvia's whereabouts when she received them, although the first is dated 1 October 1907, when she was well set on her travels. Living in lodgings, she was unlikely to have had access to printed sources other than those in her possession. Teresa Billington-Greig reported that she had five or six cases of her parents' papers at her disposal,

but it is unlikely that these accompanied her around the country. Although at this stage *Votes for Women* only appeared monthly, it was a not inconsiderable feat to embark on the history under these circumstances. Mrs Elmy also took the trouble to send Sylvia, both then and after her return to London, many bound volumes of the reports of the various societies with which she had been associated and, a year later, a run of the *Englishwoman's Review*, to aid in her writing. Sylvia Pankhurst returned south by mid-December 1907, spending Christmas with her mother, Christabel and Mary GAWTHORPE at Teignmouth where they were campaigning at the Mid-Devon by-election. Sylvia managed to avoid, by her absence, personal involvement in the autumn ructions in the WSPU that led to the formation of the WOMEN'S FREEDOM LEAGUE. Unlike her mother and Christabel she did not repudiate her membership of the ILP.

During the first half of 1908, although in her two histories of the movement she gives energetic accounts of the WSPU's activities, Sylvia Pankhurst herself is noticeably absent from events. She continued contributing her instalments of suffrage history each month in *Votes for Women*, but does not appear to have taken part in the deputation from the Women's Parliament from Caxton Hall on 11 February; she certainly was not among those arrested. Neither does she appear listed as a speaker at meetings either in London or around the country and only reappears in the picture in June when she was a speaker on Platform 17 at the 21 June Hyde Park demonstration. She had, however, been busy for a considerable time before then as a voluntary organizer in Chelsea, Fulham and Wandsworth for the demonstration, training speakers for the occasion. She was also the designer of many of the special banners that were unfurled to considerable acclaim in the Queen's Hall on 17 June. The designs had been made up by a commercial firm, probably Tutills. Among these were ones for the Bradford WSPU ("Grant to womanhood the justice England should be proud to give"), another bearing the words "Human Emancipation must precede Social Regeneration", another, given by Elsie BOWERMAN's mother, bore the resounding motto, "Rebellion to tyrants is obedience to God", and another, depicting a pelican feeding its young from its breast and the words "Great souls live, like fire-heated suns, to spend their strength". This last motif was one among those used by Sylvia the next spring when designing the murals for the WSPU exhibition held in Prince's Skating Rink. She rented space in Avenue Studios, Fulham Road (also the work place of Annie SWYNNERTON), and with assistance from three young women and four men who had been students with her at the RCA, she prepared the decorations, which were to cover a hall measuring 250 feet by 150 feet and were 20 feet high. She was paid 30s a week for her work. For this commission, which was in essence to set the scene for a bazaar, an eminently middle-class endeavour, she abandoned socialist realism for Pre-Raphaelite angels and imagery. Walter Crane, mentor of radical activists, had deployed for over 20 years both styles – supplying sturdy wenches with swirling snowy aprons for the front covers of the *Labour Leader* and the *Women Worker* (both of which designs were also utilized in banners) and Mayday maidens, barefoot in flower-filled meadows, for more poetic applications of the socialist message. Sylvia took a text from the Psalms and, in the WSPU colours, delivered an accomplished and suitably uplifting mural. It is delightful to read that Sylvia Pankhurst "was thrilled by the sight of the work we had executed under such cramped conditions".

By the time that the sale of the first bound volume of *Votes for Women* was announced, on 29 October 1908, Sylvia Pankhurst had designed for its cover the angel of freedom device that was to be used on a variety of WSPU ephemera. It doubtless drew its inspiration from Walter Crane's *Angel of Freedom*, which had been exhibited at the Grosvenor Gallery in 1885, and was made the WSPU's own with the introduction of prison bars and broken prison chains. For the 1909 Prince's Skating Rink event the refreshment room was supplied with decidedly stylish plain china decorated with the angel device in a cartouche. Three angels, two with trumpets and one with a "freedom" banner, feature on the illuminated address that Sylvia designed to be given to WSPU prisoners on their release; the first were presented in September 1908. At around the same time Sylvia designed two other icons for the WSPU. One depicts a young woman emerging from the prison gate, stepping over her broken chains and accompanied by a flock of doves. This device was used on the 1908 WSPU Christmas card. The other icon is of the woman sower, which was featured, as well as angels, in the May 1909 WSPU Exhibition mural. It was also used to advertise the Albert Hall meeting held a few weeks earlier, on 29 April. At this time she also designed the "Holloway" brooch (*see* JEWELLERY AND BADGES).

Between these bursts of artistic activity for the WSPU Sylvia Pankhurst had been instructed by Emmeline Pethick-Lawrence to take control of the office in Clement's Inn when Emmeline and Christabel Pankhurst were imprisoned in October 1908 for inciting crowds to "Rush the House of Commons". It was during her period of responsibility that, on 5 December, Lloyd George was heckled at a meeting of the Women's Liberal Federation in the Albert Hall by WSPU members who filled the front seats and in the course of the evening revealed themselves to be wearing imitation prison clothes under their coats. Envisaging the damage that would be wrought on them by the meeting's stewards, Sylvia had the press ready to photograph the women as they returned battered to Clement's Inn. The meeting became notorious as the occasion on which Helen OGSTON, against Sylvia's advice, wielded a dog-whip. On her release Christabel was not pleased with the emphasis that had been placed in the press on the violence shown against the women. In *The Suffragette Movement* Sylvia Pankhurst glosses the rebuke with the explanation that Christabel "was ever a stoic in such matters", but it is difficult to escape the thought that Christabel might have been quite happy with the publicity if it had been of her making. Christabel was released from prison on 19 December; in the first week of January 1909 Sylvia Pankhurst was on her way to the far north, to Aberdeen, with instruction to bring the recalcitrant local union to heel. She remained there for the rest of the month, preparing the ground for the arrival of Ada FLATMAN.

After the end of the Prince's Skating Rink Exhibition Sylvia Pankhurst went to Kent to paint, deeply troubled by the hunger striking that resulted from escalating militancy. In *The Suffragette Movement* she states that she had not at that time thought that this policy was the best one to follow; she already thought that it was by appealing to the masses that the vote would be won. However, for the rest of 1909 her thought and time were devoted to the care of her brother Harry, who in the autumn developed poliomyelitis. Sylvia comments on Mrs Pankhurst's "ruthless inner call to action" that allowed her, when her son was so ill, to set sail for America in order to undertake a lecture tour at the end of October.

After Harry's death in January 1910 and the WSPU's truce from militancy after the general election, Sylvia Pankhurst and Annie Kenney were taken on holiday to Innsbruck and Oberammergau by Emmeline Pethick-Lawrence. Sylvia moved in the early part of the year to Cambridge Lodge Studios, 42 Linden Gardens, Kensington, working on studies, including that in charcoal now in the National Portrait Gallery, for a projected portrait in oils of Keir Hardie. She was also working on *The Suffragette: The History of the Women's Militant Suffrage Movement 1905–10*, reshaping her *Votes for Women* articles into a book. She was in correspondence in June and July 1910 with Elizabeth Wolstenholme Elmy, who supplied her with yet more background material for her history, writing, for instance on 13 July, obviously in reply to an inquiry from Sylvia, "You are quite free to make whatever you please of anything I have sent or may send you, unless I mark them 'private' and ask to have them returned. Miss Becker's letter you may of course publish". *The Suffragette* does not contain much detail of the suffrage movement prior to the founding of the WSPU, but Sylvia Pankhurst presumably kept Mrs Elmy's information and was able to use it to good effect in *The Suffragette Movement*. Rather surprisingly *The Suffragette* was first published in America by an American publisher, Sturgis and Walton Company, and printed sheets were imported to Britain where it was published by Gay and Hancock. It is very likely that this route of publication emanated from information given by Mrs Elmy, who in March 1905 had recommended Gay and Hancock to Harriet McILQUHAM, when she was looking for a publisher, as the agents in England for Charlotte Perkins Gilman, who thought well of them. If Sylvia on Mrs Elmy's advice got in touch with Gay and Hancock they might well have recommended to her an American publisher. Alternatively it is just possible, but rather unlikely, that the deal might have been concluded merely by chance during Sylvia's trip to the USA in January 1911; she was working on the book during the voyage. She had spent Christmas on her own in Linden Gardens, not joining her mother and aunt, Mary CLARKE, at her uncle Herbert Goulden's house for Christmas lunch. However, Mary Clarke's sudden death united mother and daughter and Emmeline Pankhurst accompanied Sylvia to Southampton to see her safely embarked. Sylvia was met off the boat in New York by Harriot Stanton BLATCH and other members of the Women's Political Union. The ensuing publicity accorded to the arrival of one of the leading English suffragettes ensured Sylvia a wealth of speaking dates. She then travelled the length and breadth of the USA, venturing north into Canada, and addressing on average two meetings a day. In March in Boston she addressed the Judiciary Committee of the Legislature. The tour, which was covered in the pages of *Votes for Women*, ended on 12 April. On her return, in May, she took part in a deputation of past students of the Royal College of Art to the Board of Education enquiry into the RCA. She was not involved in the preparations for the 17 June suffrage Coronation Procession, the plans for which had presumably been laid while she was abroad, but in the autumn Emmeline Pethick-Lawrence asked her to arrange the Christmas WSPU bazaar in the Portman Rooms. For this Sylvia was able to reuse the Prince's Skating Rink mural, adapted and embellished to fit the new site. She also devised for the stallholders costumes based on eighteenth-century designs taken from W.H. Pyne, *The Costume of Great Britain*, 1808, a book of some value which had been given to her by Keir Hardie. The costumes were paid for by the wearers and made up in the studio of Georgina and Maria BRACKENBURY. Writing to Minnie Baldock on 19 October, shortly after the plans for the bazaar had been published, Isabel SEYMOUR remarked, "I do wish they were not going to be in costume. I *shall* look an old guy!"

Sylvia Pankhurst was in America, on another lecture tour, when the window-smashing campaign was activated by the WSPU in London in March 1912. She commented on the distaste with which this policy was viewed by erstwhile American sympathizers and stated in *The Suffragette Movement* that this was the moment that proved decisively to her that she would have to devote all her attention to winning the vote because, while the struggle continued, all other enterprises were overshadowed by the repercussions of the campaign. She specifically stated that "I neither could nor would now withdraw to another country", a dart obviously aimed at Christabel's decision to remove herself to Paris. Sylvia, however, was not the one threatened with a charge of conspiracy. She apparently returned to England in early April and immediately, on 13 April, published a letter in the press questioning the treatment of suffragist prisoners and amplified this in a long letter, dated 23 April, published in *Votes for Women*, 26 April 1912. She then travelled to Paris to see Christabel. Sylvia related in *The Suffragette Movement* that she realized in the course of this meeting that Christabel was intent on keeping her on the sidelines, ostensibly as a reserve, but rather, Sylvia thought, because she was jealous to conserve her own power and policies. Sylvia records that, although she was willing to uphold Christabel's policy in theory, if, in practice, nothing was required of her, her own conscience would impel her to follow her own course. On 27 April she is billed as appearing at a meeting in Palmer's Green, the first, apparently, since her return from the USA. On 7 June she announced in *Votes for Women* "A Great Popular Campaign of Demonstrations", in which the ILP as well as other suffrage societies such as the NEW CONSTITUTIONAL SOCIETY FOR WOMEN'S SUFFRAGE, the TAX RESISTANCE LEAGUE and the MEN'S POLITICAL UNION had agreed to co-operate with the WSPU's London local unions. Christabel Pankhurst, as chief political organizer, had been responsible for the local unions; after her departure their care had devolved on Flora DRUMMOND. Sylvia Pankhurst was careful to defer to General Drummond, while persuading her to galvanize the London unions into holding large popular demonstrations on common land, such as Ealing, Streatham and Wimbledon commons, Regent's Park, Blackheath, Finsbury Park and Peckham Rye. All these took place throughout the summer against the background of the forcible feeding of WSPU prisoners, whom Sylvia saw as the misguided tools of Christabel's policy, and culminated in a Hyde Park demonstration on Bastille Day, Mrs Pankhurst's birthday. To finance the demonstration campaign, although she stressed that it was cheaply staged by volunteers, an appeal, of which Lady Sybil Smith was treasurer, was launched by Sylvia Pankhurst. This was the first time since 1906 that Sylvia had taken an executive role in the WSPU. The Bastille Day demonstration was held three days before the introduction of the government's despised Franchise and Registration Bill (Manhood Suffrage Bill); Sylvia Pankhurst called not for manhood suffrage alone, but also for womanhood suffrage. Besides being the organizer of the demonstration, she was also its decorator. The colours of each organization, although flown separately as banners, were united by being topped by the "scarlet caps of liberty", a reference both to the French Revolution and to the franchise demonstrations of the 1860s, which Sylvia adopted as a symbol of popular revolt.

In August 1912 Sylvia Pankhurst worked with gusto at the Crewe and North-West Manchester by-elections, writing up the campaign for *Votes for Women*. Keir Hardie was present as a Labour Party speaker during the Manchester campaign. Ironically, by now the NUWSS was supporting the Labour Party, and Sylvia, as the WSPU organizer, was working against the Liberal candidate but not directly for that of the Labour Party. In July Christabel Pankhurst had initiated the "secret arson campaign" and it was a belief that this policy was not only distasteful but mistaken that, together with the success of the popular demonstrations held in large provincial towns as well as in London, inspired Sylvia in October to launch a mass campaign in the East End of London. The ousting of the Pethick-Lawrences from the WSPU in October, a move she deplored, drew from Sylvia Pankhurst the comment in *The Suffragette Movement* that the four protagonists "differed less with each other . . . than I had often differed in view from them".

Sylvia Pankhurst's companion in the East End enterprise was Zelie Emerson, a young American woman whom she met in Chicago and who returned with her to Britain to help the cause. They opened a headquarters in the Bow Road and, with volunteers drawn mainly from the Kensington, Chelsea and Paddington unions, opened local branches in Bethnal Green, Limehouse and Poplar. Sylvia Pankhurst makes it quite clear that her intention was to instigate a mass movement that would inspire similar ventures throughout the country, the totality of which the government could not fail to notice. Coincidentally Bow and Bromley became the centre of attention when, in November, George LANSBURY resigned his seat in order, at the instigation of Christabel and Emmeline Pankhurst, to fight for re-election on a "Votes for Women" platform. Sylvia Pankhurst was not in charge of this campaign, which was conducted by Grace ROE, with whom she had previously crossed swords in Dublin during the campaign to secure the release of Mary LEIGH. After Lansbury lost his seat WSPU headquarters wanted to close down the East End operation but Sylvia managed to convince her mother that to do so would look like retreat and, in addition, suggested that a deputation of working women should seek an audience with Lloyd George. This was in the event headed by Flora Drummond. Maddened by the machinations of both the government, which had subverted the Franchise Reform Bill with the Speaker's ruling that the introduction of a woman's suffrage amendment would invalidate it, and by the WSPU's reaction of arson, Sylvia felt compelled to commit a "defiant deed". This, in the event, was the throwing of a stone at a painting in St Stephen's Hall in the House of Commons. It was, ironically, a recent depiction of a seventeenth-century Speaker, who had been forced by members of parliament to defy the King. Although she may have wished to have been charged, thanks to Keir Hardie's intervention she was not. She then took part in a militant WSPU march from a meeting in the Horticultural Hall to the House of Commons, was arrested and sentenced to 14 days' imprisonment in lieu of a fine. However, as the *Suffragette* reported on 7 February, her fine was paid later that day by "an unknown person". In *The Suffragette Movement* Sylvia Pankhurst revealed that it was in fact the WSPU that had paid the fine. This apparently was policy; the previous week Mrs Drummond and others who had been arrested at the same demonstration were similarly released. Presumably the WSPU wanted, if possible, to keep its personnel out of prison, relying on the arson campaign and the hunger striking of those who had received terms of imprisonment not redeemable by the paying of a fine, to keep the campaign in front of the public and parliament.

On 14 February Sylvia Pankhurst, after a meeting held in a hall in Bow Road, led a procession around the district and, again courting imprisonment, threw a stone at the window of the local police station. She was immediately sentenced, with Zelie Emerson, to six weeks' imprisonment, began a hunger-and-thirst strike, but again had the fine paid the next day, anonymously, by Mrs Pankhurst. However, Sylvia was not to be deterred. On 17 February she led a crowd in the Bow Road and set an example, by throwing a stone through an undertaker's window, that was quickly emulated by others. This time there was no option of a fine; the sentence was two months' hard labour. The authorities realizing that she would immediately embark on a hunger strike, she was placed in the hospital wing. At this stage Rule 243A was still in force although because of the hunger strike she lost all associated privileges, except that she was allowed to wear her own clothes while being forcibly fed. She and Zelie Emerson, who had been sentenced with her, added a refusal to drink to that of eating. A letter Sylvia Pankhurst smuggled out to her mother, describing her plight, was published in the *Daily Mail*. Although publicity was ensured, release was no nearer. In despair Sylvia resolved to attempt to hasten her departure from prison by walking night and day across her cell. She was finally released on 21 March. The *Suffragette*, 29 March, contains a long article, "They Tortured Me", in which she gives vivid details of her imprisonment. As soon as she recovered sufficiently she was instrumental in setting up a committee to lobby for the repeal of the "Cat and Mouse" Act, which received the Royal Assent on 25 April. Charles Mansell-Moullin was a leading member of the committee and his wife Edith MANSELL-MOULLIN was its honorary secretary. At the same time Sylvia Pankhurst continued building up support in the East End. On 25 May she organized a "Woman's May Day" demonstration in Victoria Park. On 27 May the East End local branches formally united as the East London Federation of the WSPU, democratically constituted but, nevertheless, Sylvia Pankhurst's power base.

On 29 June Sylvia Pankhurst brought her East End masses nearer to Westminster. A demonstration was organized in Trafalgar Square by the East London Federation, with support from the MEN'S FEDERATION FOR WOMEN'S SUFFRAGE and the Free Speech Defence League. Sylvia led a crowd from the East End and urged them to march on Downing Street. On 3 July she was served with a summons under the Statute of Edward III that was also used in an attempt to silence George Lansbury and Flora Drummond. Ignoring this, she spoke at a public meeting on 7 July and was eventually arrested after near riot. She was sentenced to three months' imprisonment, hoping that the publicity that would follow the action and reaction engendered by the application of the "Cat and Mouse" Act would, in her case, cause a mass action in the East End for its repeal. She immediately adopted the hunger-and-thirst strike to which after a few days she added constant walking. She was released on 13 July and was taken to the home of Mr and Mrs Payne at Ford Road, Bow, where she was assured of care and safety. Dr Flora MURRAY came down to Bow to attend her recuperation. Sylvia Pankhurst at this time was writing unpaid weekly articles for the *Clarion*, the *Merthyr Pioneer* and *Forward*, all socialist journals, as well as undertaking paid journalism for American publications. On 18 July she evaded detectives to address a meeting at Poplar Town Hall and on 21 July repeated the performance at Bromley Town Hall and managed to escape by a hair's breadth, rescued eventually by Willie Lansbury, George's son. She spoke a few days later at Canning Town Hall before escaping to the country for a few days in order to recover her strength.

Still a "mouse", Sylvia Pankhurst addressed a crowd in Trafalgar Square on Sunday 27 July – encouraging the people to go with her to Downing Street to present a "Women's Declaration of Independence" (an imitation of one launched by Unionist Ulster). She was arrested during the course of the day and returned to Holloway, went on hunger-and-thirst strike and was released again on 1 August. These escapades were repeated until in the middle of August she escaped to Finland, with Norah Smyth, for a respite, returning to the East End in October. She was immediately back in the fray, addressing a meeting at Bow Baths and causing another riot; Mary Leigh was knocked unconscious, Sister Townend injured her knee, Miss Forbes Robertson suffered a broken arm and the Hackney WSPU secretary a broken collar-bone. The next day, 14 October, Sylvia Pankhurst was recaptured after speaking at Poplar Town Hall. Back in Holloway she endured the hunger-and-thirst strike for another nine days before being released under the "Cat and Mouse" Act. She managed to evade the police, although still addressing public meetings protected by her followers, until re-arrested in early December at Shoreditch Town Hall. She gained her release after another six-day hunger strike.

At the end of December, on Sylvia's initiative, the East London Federation organized a two-week Suffrage School, one week being spent in Bow and the other in Kensington. The topics discussed were ones to which suffrage speakers constantly referred, such as the industrial position of women, the history of the women's movement and the legal disabilities of women. Although the NUWSS ran similar "schools", the East London Federation was the only branch of the WSPU to attempt an education programme. After another arrest in early January and another hunger-striking sojourn in Holloway, Sylvia Pankhurst was summoned by Christabel to Paris. After enduring a hazardous journey, in constant fear of arrest, she was told by Christabel, in the presence of their mother, that the East London Federation's structure and membership did not accord with her vision of the WSPU and that a clean break must be made between the two organizations. Henceforward Sylvia Pankhurst was free to develop the renamed EAST LONDON FEDERATION OF THE SUFFRAGETTES as she wished.

A new paper, the *Women's Dreadnought,* was the first evidence of Sylvia Pankhurst's autonomy. She was its editor and intended it to be a medium in which working-class women could reflect their own views and experiences. She also instigated the drilling of a "People's Army", to include women as well as men, intending that it should be used to intimidate the police. In *The Suffragette Movement* she glosses the word "Army" as being in this case a "rhetorical" usage; it doubtless was not interpreted as such at the time by the Home Office. However, in the event, the Army fell prey to a lack of commitment from outsiders; the army officers who had promised to drill the masses did not appear. Another new tactic, a "No Vote No Rent" strike, although actively promoted by Sylvia Pankhurst, also proved a non-starter; women were too frightened at the thought of eviction to put the idea into practice. She realized that the time was not yet ripe for such drastic action.

Sylvia Pankhurst's life took on even more hectic oscillations as she moved between Holloway, Bow, Westminster Abbey (carried there shoulder-high in a procession to intercede for the vote on Mothering Sunday), and Budapest, Vienna, Dresden and Paris, in which cities, having escaped from England in disguise, she gave in April and May a series of lectures. During this time she was fêted as a socialist revolutionary and, thus buoyed up, returned to Bow to open the new ELFS headquarters at 400 Old Ford Road. She was arrested again on Sunday 24 May, attempting to speak at the ELFS "Women's May Day" rally in Victoria Park. The police seized her as she was walking into the park in the centre of a group of 20 women, each of whom was chained to her. The police smashed the padlocks with their truncheons. After hunger-striking her way out of Holloway on 30 May, Sylvia Pankhurst decided that new pressure must be put on the cabinet. She organized mass rallies at which East Enders voted to support a resolution that all women over the age of 21 should be enfranchised and were intent on marching on Downing Street to present their case on 10 June to Asquith, who, of course, intimated that he would refuse to receive them. Sylvia Pankhurst then wrote telling him that if he did not receive the deputation she would hunger strike not only in prison but even after her release. Evelyn SHARP and Henry NEVINSON were accompanying the march of the people from Bow to Westminster when Sylvia Pankhurst was snatched back by the police. Asquith did not receive the deputation; the Liberal chief whip did, however, venture out of the House of Commons to see its members. When, after another hunger-and-thirst strike, Sylvia Pankhurst was released from prison on 18 June she was taken to Westminster where, in her extreme weakness, she lay down outside the House of Commons. Her plan was to lie there until Asquith promised to receive the deputation of East End women. She did not have long to wait; Keir Hardie passed on to her a message that Asquith was prepared to see the women on 20 June.

Sylvia Pankhurst did not accompany the deputation, which was led by Julia SCURR. She believed that Asquith had capitulated in receiving the deputation and that his reply to the East End women indicated that the way had been paved for a change of attitude by the government to women's enfranchisement. As she had gone to such lengths to secure this answer it is understandable, if still somewhat surprising, that she should have been so convinced. Other suffragists did not place much faith in Asquith's apparent volte-face; the NUWSS had received similar reassurance when they had met him on 8 August 1913, shortly after the end of the Pilgrimage. However, Sylvia Pankhurst felt she had done her best and now turned her attention to the plight of the hunger strikers who were being held, enduring forcible feeding, for longer periods than they had been previously. If they were released under the "Cat and Mouse" Act it was only for a short time and the police were now actively enforcing their return to prison. Sylvia had an interview with Lloyd George, who told her that he would refuse to serve in the next Liberal cabinet unless a Reform Bill was introduced and the inclusion of votes for women left to a free vote of the House. However, neither Lloyd George nor Asquith was put to the test, nor was Sylvia Pankhurst ever to be certain that the pressure she and the ELFS thought they were putting on the cabinet would have achieved the desired end. She was in Dublin, investigating the firing of soldiers on a crowd, when war was declared.

Sylvia Pankhurst devoted herself and the ELFS (from January 1916 renamed the Workers' Suffrage Federation) to social welfare work in the East End of London during the First World War. A pacifist, she was shocked by the extremist pro-war stand taken by her mother and sister. Unlike them she continued campaigning for womanhood suffrage. She became a member of the executive committee of the Women's International League for Peace and Freedom and in August 1916 took the initiative in suggesting to that organization that it should hold a conference, pulling together the suffrage societies and industrial and co-operative organizations, to discuss putting further pressure on the government to introduce "human suffrage". Although, as a result, the National Council for Adult Suffrage was formed, it proved ineffectual. Sylvia Pankhurst was then instrumental in forging an alliance between the WSF and Labour leaders, such as George Lansbury, which resulted in the formation of the Adult Suffrage Joint Committee. With deputations of women from the East End Sylvia Pankhurst continued lobbying at the House of Commons against the age limit (30 or 35) that it was proposed to impose on women. When the National Council for Adult Suffrage appeared amenable to some such restriction, Sylvia Pankhurst instigated the formation of yet another group, the Labour Council for Adult Suffrage. But, as she related in *The Suffragette Movement*, she knew that this group would have little success and that the true adult suffragists had been "out-generalled" by the National Council, whose officials were drawn from the NUWSS. When the Labour Party backed the Speaker's Conference Report, Sylvia Pankhurst knew that the adult suffrage cause was, for the moment, lost. She remarks on the irony that, in the years before the war, adult suffragist members of the Labour Party had prevented the adoption of a limited measure of enfranchisement for women; it was these same members who now were prepared to accept the imposition of an age limit on women's enfranchisement.

In 1922 Sylvia Pankhurst published a collection of poems, *Writ on a Cold Slate*, that derived from her experience of imprisonment, both as a suffrage campaigner and as a result of a five months' sentence for sedition in 1921. She joined, but soon left, the British Communist Party. In 1931 she published *The Suffragette Movement: An Intimate Account of Persons and Ideals*, part history and part autobiography, which has stood for many years as the main source of information on the militant suffrage movement. In 1936 she published *The Life of Emmeline Pankhurst: The Suffragette Struggle for Women's Citizenship*, urged to do so by Emmeline Pethick-Lawrence, to whom she remained close. When Sylvia Pankhurst's son was born in 1927 she gave him the names Richard Keir Pethick after her father, Keir Hardie, and Emmeline Pethick, to whom she also dedicated, in 1932, *The Home Front*, her description of her work during the First World War.

Address: (1904) 45 Park Walk, Chelsea, London SW; (1910) 3 Cambridge Lodge Studios, 42 Linden Gardens, Kensington, London SW; (1915,1919) 400 Old Ford Road, Bow, London E; (1920s–1950s) West Dene, 3 Charteris Road, Woodford Green, Essex.
Portrait: by H. Cole, National Portrait Gallery; self-portrait, National Portrait Gallery; Bassano photograph, 1927, National Portrait Gallery; photographs by Howard Coster, 1938, National Portrait Gallery.
Archival source: Papers of Sylvia Pankhurst, Internationaal Instituut voor Sociale Geschiedenis, Amsterdam.
Bibliography: E.S. Pankhurst, *The Suffragette*, 1911; E. S. Pankhurst, *The Suffragette Movement: An Intimate Account of Persons and Ideals*, 1931; E.S. Pankhurst, *The Home Front*, 1932; The Countess of Oxford and Asquith (ed.), *Myself When Young*, 1938; D. Mitchell, *The Fighting Pankhursts*, 1967; R. Pankhurst, *Sylvia Pankhurst: Artist and Crusader*, 1979; B. Harrison, *Prudent Revolutionaries: British Feminists between the Wars*, 1987; S. Romero, E. *Sylvia Pankhurst: Portrait of a Radical*, 1987; R. Pankhurst, "Sylvia Pankhurst in perspective: some comments on Patricia Romero's biography", in *Women's Studies International Forum*, 11, 3, 1988; I. Bullock and R. Pankhurst (eds), Sylvia Pankhurst: from artist to anti-fascist, 1992; K. Dodd (ed.), *A Sylvia Pankhurst Reader*, 1993; J. Dunham, *Amy K. Browning*, 1995; B. Winslow, *Sylvia Pankhurst: Sexual Politics and Political Activism*, 1996.

PARKER, FRANCES MARY (1875–1924) Born in Waimate, New Zealand, daughter of Frances Emily Jane Kitchener, who married H.R. Parker in 1869. Her mother's brother, the future Lord Kitchener, paid for Frances Parker's education at Newnham College, Cambridge, 1896–9. She then taught for a year at a French Ecole Normale, and in Auckland. After returning to England, she joined the WOMEN'S SOCIAL AND POLITICAL UNION in 1908, and in February was sentenced to six weeks' imprisonment after taking part in the deputation from the Women's Parliament in Caxton Hall to the House of Commons. In June 1908 she was one of the speakers on Adela PANKHURST's platform at the WSPU demonstration in Hyde Park on "Woman's Sunday". She gave £60 to the WSPU in April 1909 and was by then running what has been described as a "suffragette dairy and farming school" with [Edith] Kate le Lacheur, with whom she had been a contemporary at Newnham, in order to raise money for the WSPU and to train women to be economically self-sufficient. In September 1909 Frances Parker undertook a speaking tour in south-west Scotland with the SCOTTISH UNIVERSITY WOMEN'S SUFFRAGE UNION, in 1910 organized its CARAVAN tour and in 1911 was the SUWS delegate to the INTERNATIONAL

Woman Suffrage Alliance congress in Stockholm. In March 1912 she was imprisoned for four months in Holloway after taking part in the WSPU window-smashing campaign. Mary THOMPSON, a fellow prisoner, described her at this time as "A very determined personage and amusing too". Ethel MOORHEAD who met her at this time described her as "small and looked innocent and disarming with her charming looks, brown eyes, and silky hair. But she had an exquisite *madness* – daring, joyous, vivid, strategic".

In December 1912 with, among others, Olive WHARRY, Ethel Moorhead and Emily Wilding DAVISON, Frances Parker was sentenced to five days' imprisonment for causing a breach of the peace following a disturbance at a meeting held by Lloyd George in the Aberdeen Music Hall. She went on hunger strike but was not forcibly fed. By 1913 she was based in Dundee as WSPU ORGANIZER. In April 1913 she went to Perth to hold a meeting there, even though suffragettes were suspected as being the cause of the recent destruction by fire of the Perth County Cricket Club. Her meeting had a very hostile reception, described in contemporary reports as a riot, and she was forced to retreat, but returned the next month to face a rather more sympathetic audience. She became WSPU organizer in Edinburgh in August 1913. At the end of 1913 she spent some time sheltering Ethel Moorhead, who was on the run as a "mouse". It is more than likely that in February 1914 Frances Parker was responsible for burning down Whitekirk in retaliation for the forcible feeding of Ethel Moorhead. In July 1914 she was arrested, as "Janet Arthur", while attempting, with Ethel Moorhead, to blow up Robert Burns's cottage in Alloway. A short biographical entry in *This Quarter*, vol. 1, no. 1, states that "she allowed herself to be taken that her comrade might escape". While held on remand in Perth prison, Frances Parker went on hunger strike and was forcibly fed by tube supplemented by rectal feeding and subjected to what she described as "a grosser and more indecent outrage, which could have been done for no other purpose than to torture". The medical report by Dr Lindsay of Perth prison indicates injuries consistent with an instrument having been introduced into the vagina and that abrasions had been caused in the genital area. After the intervention of her brother she was released into a nursing home, from which after two weeks she escaped. After the outbreak of war, her solicitor, who was also acting for Ethel Moorhead, wrote to the Secretary of State for Scotland to ask if the amnesty being granted to suffrage "mice" would also apply to Frances Parker. The point was made that as a niece of Kitchener she was proposing to devote her energies to help the country's war effort. On 14 August the Lord Advocate issued an instruction to the effect that, although she was still at large, the trial for attempted arson would not go ahead and that Frances Parker was not liable to re-arrest.

During the First World War Frances Parker became honorary organizer of the Women's Freedom League National Service Organization, working in London with Ethel Moorhead "to bring women workers in touch with employers and find the right work for the right women". She became deputy controller of the WAAC at Boulogne. Her mother was chairman of the Women's Imperial Defence League, campaigned against the employment of anyone with a German-sounding name in a position of any importance and became commandant-in-chief of the Women Signallers Corps.

When Frances Parker died in early 1924, at Archacon near Bordeaux, it is virtually certain that she was living there with Ethel Moorhead and the latter's protégé, Ernest Walsh. By her will, of which Janie ALLAN was executor, apart from a small bequest to her sister, Frances Parker left all her property to Ethel Moorhead "in grateful remembrance for her care and love". The first issue of *This Quarter*, a literary magazine edited by Moorhead and Walsh, funded by this bequest, contains a poem and the reproduction of two paintings by Frances Parker, alongside contributions from Gertrude Stein, Bryher, H.D., and Ernest Hemingway.

Address: (1914) 33 Cambridge Mansions, Battersea Park, London SW; (1924) 36 George Street, Edinburgh.
Photograph: in L. Leneman, *A Guid Cause: The Women's Suffrage Movement in Scotland*, 1991.
Archival source: Scottish Office Prison Commission files, Scottish Record Office.
Bibliography: *This Quarter*, 1, 1, 1925; E. Moorhead, "Incendiaries (work in progress)", *This Quarter*, 1, 2, 1925; L. Leneman, *A Guid Cause: The Women's Suffrage Movement in Scotland*, 1991; L. Leneman, *Martyrs in Our Midst: Dundee, Perth and the Forcible Feeding of Suffragettes*, 1993.

PARKES, [ELIZABETH] BESSIE RAYNER (1829–1925) (later Madame Belloc)   Born a Unitarian, converted to Roman Catholicism under the influence of her close friend, Adelaide Procter. Her father, Joseph Parkes, in 1832 was involved with the Birmingham Political Union in pressing for the passing of the Reform Bill, and was secretary to the parliamentary commission on municipal reform which recommended the restructuring of local government in 1833 and was chief organizer of elections for the Liberal party in 1832–40. Joseph Parkes was a close friend of George and Harriet GROTE and of John Stuart MILL. Bessie Parkes's maternal grandfather was Joseph Priestley, friend of Mary Wollstonecraft and one of the most prominent dissenting radicals of his generation. Bessie Parkes was a delicate child; her family wintered abroad to protect her health and lived for much of the time in Hastings to enjoy the clement southern clime. Her brother died there, aged 25, of tuberculosis in 1850. Bessie Parkes was, by 1846, a neighbour in Hastings and close friend of Barbara Leigh Smith (*see* Barbara BODICHON) and in their correpondence the two shared thoughts on woman's lot. In a letter of 1848 Bessie Parkes wrote, "Dont you wish you were a Man! Sometimes I do, sometimes I am glad I am a woman that I may help to push on my own sex." In 1848 Bessie Parkes mused that if she had to earn her own living, "I never *would* be a governess and give up my independence but I would if cast on my own exertions set hard to learn the higher branches of bookkeeping if one may so term it and see if like so many French women, I could not get some employment in managing a warehouse or some such thing. Such people have much better payment I think than a governess . . . and all the unemployed hours to themselves. . . . What a pity English women do not do anything but be governesses and milliners". The two girls were at this time already successful in publishing articles in the *Hastings and St Leonards Gazette* and the *Birmingham Journal*. In 1849 Bessie Parkes subscribed to *Eliza Cook's Journal* and in 1852 was reading the works of John Stuart Mill. In 1855 she wrote to Barbara, "Dont you see how marvellous[ly] all manner of women are rising up". She described herself and Barbara as being "daft upon missions" and the mission at the end of that year was to organize a petition to parliament on the laws of property as they affected married women. Bessie Parkes took some part in drafting the petition and was a member of the all-women committee that organized the collection of signatures to the 70 copies of the petition that circulated throughout the country. Bessie Parkes wrote to Barbara Leigh Smith on 24 January 1856, "I am delighted at the names for the petition . . . we have now got *10 good* names, and if you will wait a bit, we shall get plenty more. It is all these things which stir the question, more than the actual presentation." This first experience of political organization by women laid the foundation for all subsequent such activity and the circulation of the petition established a feminist communication network that was reactivated in future feminist campaigns.

By May 1857 Bessie Parkes had taken over the editorship of a journal, the *Waverley*, which was then published in Edinburgh. She asked Barbara Leigh Smith to consider investing £200 in it and thought that Anna Jameson and the Brownings might also help. Her intention was to commission for the journal a series of articles on female factory life from Mary MERRYWEATHER and on reformatories from the Davenport HILLS. Bessie Parkes's aim was that the publication of the *Waverley* should be moved to London and that there "we can have our own book shop, or the beginning of a club room for exhibiting pictures etc etc. . . . I shall try to have the shop in Oxford St and Isa Craig could be put into it as Locum General. My idea is to make the whole thing *respectable and practical*". It did not, however, prove financially sensible to continue with the plan to buy the *Waverley* and, instead, by March 1858 Bessie Parkes, with Matilda Hays, was editor of the newly launched *English Woman's Journal*. By January 1859 Bessie Parkes was able to write to Barbara Bodichon that:

> Subscriptions come in steadily, we have now close upon 400, and our sales are about 250 a month. This is current; the back numbers keep constantly selling too. To build up the circulation of a new periodical is a very difficult task, but I think G[od] W[illing] that I feel amply satisfied at . . . our first year's work; . . . when I think of the number of people of all sorts who have been brought into contact . . . I have just picked up a most hearty young worker, a clergyman's daughter, by name

Miss Faithfull, who has brought me a host of subscriptions . . . On all sides we have letters and testimonials of our success, new subscribers thick as blackberries, and every reason to think that the judicious path has been chosen.

She wrote a little later in the year that "Miss Emily Faithfull is the nearest approach to my ideal of a canvasser I have yet got hold of. A clergyman's daughter, aged 23, & rather strong-minded, carried her own huge carpet bag etc." By 1859 Bessie Parkes was able to report, after a visit to Norwich to see Mr Jarrold, the printer, with a view to his republishing Mary Merryweather's articles as a book, that he had told her that "the Journal is well thought of by the trade". In late 1859 an exhibition of Barbara Bodichon's pictures was hung in the reading room at Langham Place and Bessie Parkes bought, for permanent display there, "that one of your pictures which I knew all our 70 subscribers would understand". By November 1859 circulation had risen to 700; the *English Woman's Journal* continued publication until 1864.

The work of the Langham Place group was given added publicity by the success of two papers given at the conference of the Social Science Association, held that October in Bradford. Bessie Parkes read a paper, to which Barbara Bodichon contributed, on "The Market for Educated Female Labour" and Jessie BOUCHERETT delivered "The Industrial Employments of Women". She wrote to Barbara Bodichon on 17 November 1859, "The whole kingdom is ringing with our Bradford Paper, and subscriptions pouring in at the EWJ office. . . . What a crown to our long struggle begun 10 years ago: 12 years. . . . It is the long struggle which is beginning to tell; and the having an organisation in which to receive the PUBLIC Interest." The result of this interest was the founding of the Society for Promoting the Employment of Women.

On 7 March 1860 Bessie Parkes wrote of the launching of Emily Faithfull's Victoria Press, "They will employ at least 6 girls; so here are women in the trade at last! One dream of my life!" Another of her dreams, the "club room" of which she had written in 1857, was made real in 1860 when, with Barbara Bodichon, she opened the Ladies' Institute at 19 Langham Place, just north of Oxford Street (*see under* CLUBS).

In May 1866 Bessie Parkes was, with Barbara Bodichon, Elizabeth Garrett (*see* Elizabeth Garrett ANDERSON) and Emily Davies, one of the small group of women who undertook the drafting and circulation of the petition in favour of women's suffrage that John Stuart Mill subsequently presented to parliament (*see* WOMEN'S SUFFRAGE PETITION COMMITTEE). She did not, however, subscribe to any of the societies that sprang from it. In 1867 she married a Frenchman, Louis Belloc, and until his death five years later, lived in France. Even after her return to England she took no further part in any aspect of the women's movement. Her son, Hilaire Belloc, was a determinedly anti-suffragist MP. However, among Bessie Parkes's papers in Girton College archive is her cuttings book, which she titled "On Women's Rights", a testament to her role as midwife to the infant feminist movement in the mid-nineteenth century. Bessie Parkes's books include *Remarks on the Education of Girls*, published by John Chapman in 1856, and *Essays on Women's Work*, published by Alexander Strahan in 1857 as well as later collections of poetry.

Address: (1852) 2 Savile Row, London W; (1859) 17 Wimpole Street, London W; (1882) Slindon Cottage, Slindon, Sussex; (1916) Glaston Cottage, Slindon, Sussex.
Archival source: Parkes Papers, Girton College, Cambridge.
Bibliography: J. Buckley, *Joseph Parkes of Birmingham*, 1926; J. Rendall, "Friendship and Politics: Barbara Leigh Smith Bodichon and Bessie Rayner Parkes" in S. Mendus and J. Rendall (eds), *Sexuality and Subordination*, 1989.

PARKES, MARGARET ANNE, MRS (c. 1865–1920) (Mrs Kineton Parkes)   Born in London, married in 1889 the novelist Kineton Parkes and became the mother of two sons. From 1901 to 1909 she was a member of the committee of the Women's Liberal Association for Leek, Staffordshire, where her husband was principal of the Nicholson Institute, 1892–1911. By 1909 she was living in London; her husband remained in Leek. She was a member of the WOMEN'S FREEDOM LEAGUE before becoming secretary of the TAX RESISTANCE LEAGUE. She was present at the TRL's first meeting in 1909 and presumably had a paid position in the WFL because that society initially agreed to spare her for at least three months in order that she might set up the new organization. She remained with the TRL for its entire lifetime, giving lectures to suffrage societies, both militant and constitutional, around the country. In 1911 she published the pamphlet *Why We Resist Our Taxes* and, in 1919, a pamphlet giving a history of the TRL. In 1910 she subscribed to the NEW CONSTITUTIONAL SOCIETY FOR WOMEN'S SUFFRAGE and on 29 June 1914 she was present at the Costume Dinner organized by the ACTRESSES' FRANCHISE LEAGUE and the WOMEN WRITERS' SUFFRAGE LEAGUE held at the Hotel Cecil. In August 1914 Mrs Kineton Parkes became financial secretary of the newly founded Women's Emergency Corps and in 1915 was given a cheque as a testimonial by the TRL. She died at the Mental Hospital, Seacliffe.

Address: (1909) 62 Rosslyn Hill, Hampstead, London NW; (1911) 10 Talbot House, 98 St Martin's Lane, London WC; (1915) The Acorn, Rotherfield, Sussex.

PARLIAMENTARY COMMITTEE FOR WOMAN SUFFRAGE Formed by Mary COZENS on 18 December 1893 to secure the parliamentary franchise for women. It had no association with the existing suffrage societies nor with any political party. Helen BLACKBURN, never dignifying it with a title, describes its backers as "misguided friends of the suffrage cause". The committee brought in its own bills; the first, proposed by Mr Macdona on 1 May 1895, failed, blocking the way for a motion due to be proposed by Charles McLaren (*see* Laura McLAREN) and incurring the wrath of the leaders of both the CENTRAL COMMITTEE OF THE NATIONAL SOCIETY FOR WOMEN'S SUFFRAGE and the CENTRAL NATIONAL SOCIETY. In 1896-7 Mary Cozens again lobbied leading politicians and put forward her own bill, which was introduced into the House of Lords on 8 March by Lord Templetown "to the surprise of all the leaders of the work in the House and out of it", as Helen Blackburn put it. In the May 1896 issue of *Shafts* Mary Cozens called "upon all women who have at heart the obtaining of Political Freedom, which must be the first step in the elevation of womanhood to its true place, morally, industrially, and economically, to leave no effort untried to assemble in numbers on May 20th, at 2.30p.m., in the Central Hall of the House of Commons to vindicate our demand for the extension of the Franchise". That afternoon the Parliamentary Franchise (Extension to Women) Bill was the first order of the day; the novel tactic of a mass gathering that the Committee was advocating is an interesting precursor of the tactics adopted ten years later by the WSPU. The mainstream suffrage societies did not press their members to attend Westminster that day. The Committee remained in existence until 1901, becoming a constituent member of the NATIONAL UNION OF WOMEN'S SUFFRAGE SOCIETIES in 1897, but does not appear to have sponsored any further bills or caused any further trouble to the more conventional societies. President, Sir Richard Temple (a former Anglo-Indian administrator, Conservative MP for Kingston-on-Thames, 1892-5, who had been president of the Social Science Congress, 1883); Chairman of the Executive, Miss Helen New (who was a regular correspondent to *Shafts*); Secretary, Miss Mary Cozens.

Address: (1897) 9 Victoria St., London SW.
Bibliography: H. Blackburn, *Women's Suffrage: A Record of the Women's Suffrage Movement in the British Isles*, 1902.

PARSONS, MARGUERITE [DAISY] LENA, MRS (?1890-1957) Left school at the age of 12, worked first in service and then in a cigarette factory, and in 1912, having been influenced by the work of Minnie BALDOCK, began working with Sylvia PANKHURST in the EAST LONDON FEDERATION OF SUFFRAGETTES. In 1913 she chaired the first meeting held by Mary PHILLIPS after the latter had been deputed by Sylvia Pankhurst to work for the ELFS in West Ham. By early 1914 Sylvia Pankhurst was able to write to Mary Phillips that "Mrs Parsons is getting quite responsible and can be called the Canning Town Honorary Secretary". In 1914 Mrs Parsons was one of the deputation of working women, led by Julia SCURR, to Asquith – the only such deputation he ever received. She was described on this occasion by Sylvia Pankhurst as "a frail little woman, who, having a delicate father, had worked to help her mother to support her little brothers since she was twelve years of age; and now with a husband earning a small wage, was caring for her two little girls and an orphaned niece". During the First World War she continued working with Sylvia Pankhurst, was elected to the borough council in 1922, became an alderman in 1935 and was the first woman mayor of West Ham, 1936-7.

Photograph: in R. Taylor, *In Letters of Gold: The Story of Sylvia Pankhurst and the East London Federation of Suffragettes in Bow*, 1993.

Archival source: Stratford Local Studies Library.
Bibliography: S. Pankhurst, *The Suffragette Movement*, 1931; R. Taylor, *In Letters of Gold: The Story of Sylvia Pankhurst and the East London Federation of the Suffragettes in Bow*, 1993.

PATERSON, EMMA ANN, MRS (1848–86) Daughter of Henry Smith, the headmaster of a school in Hanover Square, London, and his wife Emma Dockerill. Emma Smith was educated at home and was then apprenticed to a bookbinder, but was forced to abandon this scheme when she was 16, after her father's death. In 1866 she began work as assistant to the secretary of the Working Men's Club and Institute Union, which had been founded in 1861 by the Rev. Henry Solly (whose sister Lavinia in 1866 signed the women's suffrage petition) and Thomas Paterson, a cabinet maker. The secretary, to whom she was assistant, may have been Jane W.M. Horsburgh, who signed the 1866 suffrage petition from the address of the Working Men's Club in the Strand; whoever did hold this position was in 1867 succeeded to it by Emma Smith. In 1873 she was appointed, presumably through the connections she had made in her five years with the Working Men's Club, as secretary of the newly formed CENTRAL COMMITTEE OF THE NATIONAL SOCIETY FOR WOMEN'S SUFFRAGE. The Central Committee, although it had had some difficulty in finding a successor to Caroline Ashurst BIGGS and Agnes GARRETT, who had been acting as joint secretaries, soon dismissed Emma Smith, on the grounds of her lack of stamina and her inability to speak well in public. She was succeeded by Mary Dowling and then, after the latter's sudden death, by Helen BLACKBURN. Emma Paterson (she had married Thomas Paterson in 1873) did, however, retain some connection with the suffrage movement, being one of the speakers, whatever her aptitude, at the National Demonstration of Women held at St James's Hall in London in May 1880.

In 1874 Emma Paterson wrote an article published in the *Labour News* advocating the setting up of trade unions for women workers. She was afterwards honorary secretary of the Women's Protective and Provident League, which with Lady DILKE she had founded. She participated in the founding of the National Union of Women Workers, which resulted from a paper delivered by Anna Maria PRIESTMAN to the Economic Section of the British Association in Bristol in 1874, and in 1876, with Emily FAITHFULL, was the founder of the Women's Printing Society. Despite having Elizabeth Garrett ANDERSON as her doctor, Emma Paterson died young, of diabetes.
Photograph: on dustwrapper of H. Goldman, *Emma Paterson*, 1974.
Bibliography: H. Goldman, *Emma Paterson: She led women into a man's world*, 1974.

PAUL, ALICE (1885–1977) Quaker, American, born in New Jersey, educated in the USA, at Swarthmore College, at the New York School of Philanthropy and at the University of Pennsylvania (1906–7), where she wrote her thesis on equality for women in Pennsylvania. She was then given a fellowship to go to England to attend for a year courses at the Woodbrooke Settlement for Religious and Social Studies, Birmingham, at the same time studying economics at Birmingham University. While there she heard Christabel PANKHURST address, and be shouted down by, students at the university. At the insistence of the vice-chancellor, Sir Oliver Lodge, Christabel Pankhurst and two other speakers for the WOMEN'S SOCIAL AND POLITICAL UNION were invited back and given a chance to put their case without interruption; Alice Paul became, as she put it, "a heart and soul convert" and in 1908 joined the WSPU. She went to London, working first at settlements in Clerkenwell and Dalston and then taking a two-year course at the London School of Economics, where she met Rachel BARRETT and was introduced to such WSPU activities as selling *Votes for Women* and speaking at outdoor meetings. On 29 June 1909 she took part in the WSPU deputation to the House of Commons and was arrested. It was on this occasion, while being held in Cannon Row police station, that she first met Lucy BURNS. Alice Paul had, in fact, booked her passage home to the USA but was forced to cancel it in order to stay in England for trial. The case was finally dropped. She was soon rearrested, having held a suffrage meeting in Norwich outside a meeting addressed by Winston Churchill, but was not charged. In July she and Lucy Burns, with others, were arrested in Limehouse in the East End of London, after interrupting a meeting being held by Lloyd George. They were both sentenced to two weeks' imprisonment in Holloway, went on hunger strike and were released after five and a half days. After recovering, with Lucy Burns and Mrs PANKHURST she was driven up to Scotland in the WSPU car, with Vera HOLME at the wheel, to campaign there. In August in Glasgow Alice Paul spent a night on the roof of St Andrew's Hall, hoping thereby to gain entry to a meeting to be held by a cabinet minister. Alice Paul, with Lucy Burns and Edith NEW, were arrested in September in Dundee, having tried to force entry to another meeting, and after being sentenced to ten days' imprisonment went on hunger strike. Along with the other two, Alice Paul was released, without having been forcibly fed, after three days. She then went on to help organize the Edinburgh suffrage pageant in October. Back in London she was again arrested, after interrupting the Lord Mayor's Banquet at the Guildhall, and sentenced to 30 days' imprisonment in Holloway. She went on hunger strike and this time, being in England, she was forcibly fed. In January 1910, after her release and having recovered from her ordeal, she sailed for America. There, after Lucy Burns had returned in 1912, she and Alice Paul launched a federal campaign for women's enfranchisement. The publicity tactics used by the Woman's Party, as the Congressional Committee of the National American Woman Suffrage Association became, closely mirrored those of the WSPU. Alice Paul was imprisoned three times for picketing the White House. From 1936 she was a member from the USA on the Laws Committee of the International Council of Women.

Photograph: I.H. Irwin, *The Story of Alice Paul and the National Woman's Party*, 1977.
Bibliography: A.R. Fry, *Conversations with Alice Paul: Woman Suffrage and the Equal Rights Amendment*, 1976; I.H. Irwin, *The Story of Alice Paul and the National Woman's Party*, 1977; L. Leneman, *A Guid Cause: The Woman's Suffrage Movement in Scotland*, 1991.

PECKHAM (WFL)   Secretary (1913) Mrs Pickering, 23 Albert Road, Peckham, London SE.

PEEBLES (NUWSS)   In 1913 the society was a member of the SCOTTISH FEDERATION OF THE NATIONAL UNION OF WOMEN'S SUFFRAGE SOCIETIES. Secretary (1913) Mrs W.E. Thorburn, Hay Lodge, Peebles, Peeblesshire.

PEMBURY, MATFIELD, AND BRENCHLEY (NUWSS)   In 1913 the society was a member of the KENTISH FEDERATION OF THE NATIONAL UNION OF WOMEN'S SUFFRAGE SOCIETIES. Secretary (1913) Miss Mabel Symons, The Grange, Matfield, Kent.

PENARTH WOMEN'S SUFFRAGE SOCIETY (NUWSS)   Established in October 1910, having broken away from the CARDIFF WOMEN'S SUFFRAGE SOCIETY, of which it had been a branch. Another general election was imminent and the society was very active, immediately making plans to hold a public meeting on 14 November, at which Chrystal MACMILLAN was invited to speak and for which the Cardiff society was requested to lend red, white and green draperies with which to decorate the room. On 18 November Miss Thompson offered to present a copy of Mr Brailsford's pamphlet on the Conciliation Bill to every member of the Penarth Urban District Council. On 24 November the society decided to send a CHURCH LEAGUE FOR WOMEN'S SUFFRAGE pamphlet to every clergyman in Penarth. The literature secretary was requested to purchase 500 copies of Conservative (pro-suffrage) leaflets to be distributed at the Primrose League meeting on 30 November and to order two dozen copies of the *Common Cause* to be sold at the door. They proposed to question election candidates on their policy towards women's suffrage. It was decided that the deputation to Mr Lewis Morgan (Unionist candidate for South Glamorgan) should include only members of the Penarth society who also belonged to the Primrose League. On 2 December the deputation reported that Mr Morgan was in favour of women's suffrage. For the duration of the election campaign a suffrage shop was opened for two weeks at 107 Glebe Street, the same premises as had been used during the previous election. The Penarth society, with only one dissension, decided to send a letter to the executive committee of the National Union, protesting against the adoption of tax resistance as a strategy, and were gratified to receive a reply on 13 January 1911 that the NUWSS was determined that it should not be encouraged. Helena SWANWICK and Helen FRASER were among the speakers who addressed the society in the course of the year. Despite increasing their membership, by November 1911 funds were so low that it was necessary to organize a "Cake and Apron sale", which made just over £10. As in all societies much effort and planning was spent on activities that never materialized. A money-raising whist drive had to be substituted for the Fancy Dress Dance planned for 24 January 1912, insufficient tickets having been sold for the latter. The society resolved to apply for a box in the Grand Tier at the NUWSS demonstration at the Albert Hall on 23 February and to run an excursion train from Cardiff for the occasion. In the event they could not book the box they wanted and it was not possible to arrange for an excursion train.

At the society's annual general meeting held on 24 July a resolution was passed that the Penarth Women's Suffrage Society rejoin the Cardiff and District Women's Suffrage Society. They were then, once again, to be a local committee, subordinate to the committee of the Cardiff WSS. At this AGM Miss Janet Price gave an address on the work of the South Wales Federation and the recent development of the Election Fighting Fund policy of the NUWSS. Minutes of the Penarth society then become infrequent; the final entry is for 27 October 1913. There are no references to the NUWSS PILGRIMAGE in July 1913. The book is then reused, in 1938, to carry minutes of the Cardiff branch of the National Women Citizens' Association, although there is no obvious continuation of personnel.
Honorary secretary (1910 to end of 1911) Mrs Maillard (she was a member of the Primrose League and resigned as secretary of the Penarth WSS because she could not devote sufficient time to it. She was still working for Cardiff and District Women's Suffrage Society in 1919 and in 1920 was returned without contest as an urban district councillor for the South Ward in Penarth); honorary treasurer (1910) Mrs Hammond Robinson; literature secretary (1910) Miss Ursula Thompson; (May 1911) Miss Edith Evans Jones.

Archival source: Minutes of the Penarth Women's Suffrage Society, Glamorgan Record Office.

PENNINGTON FAMILY Frederick Pennington (1819–1914) was born at Hindley, Lancashire, where his father was a cotton spinner and merchant. He was educated at Dr Formby's School, Southport and from 1830 to 1832 in Paris. He spent his working life as an East India merchant, retiring in 1865. Frederick Pennington was a member of the council of the Anti-Corn Law League and a generous benefactor to that cause. From 1874 until 1885, an "advanced Liberal", he was MP for Stockport. Pennington was part of the radical Liberal coterie (see Appendix); one of his sisters married Joseph Mellor and was the mother of Ursula BRIGHT and another was married to Thomas THOMASSON. In 1854 Frederick Pennington married Margaret Landell Sharpe (1828–1929) daughter of Dr John Sharpe. Her brother Thomas Sharpe was principal of Queen's College, London. The Penningtons had one son and three daughters. Priscilla Bright MCLAREN often stayed with the Penningtons "in their beautiful home amid the Surrey hills". "The Saturday to Monday parties at Broome Hill included many guests of eminence in politics, art, or letters and longer visits during Parliamentary recesses afforded opportunities of ripening House of Commons acquaintances into personal friendships." During the parliamentary session the McLarens often stayed with the Penningtons in their London house. Margaret Pennington subscribed generously to the ENFRANCHISEMENT OF WOMEN COMMITTEE in 1866–7, to the MANCHESTER NATIONAL SOCIETY FOR WOMEN'S SUFFRAGE in 1868 and was also a member of the LONDON NATIONAL SOCIETY FOR WOMEN'S SUFFRAGE and, in 1873, the BIRMINGHAM NATIONAL SOCIETY FOR WOMEN'S SUFFRAGE.

Mrs Pennington also subscribed to the Society for the Promotion of Employment of Women, was from 1869 to 1872 a member of the executive committee of the Married Women's Property Committee and, a supporter of the repeal of the Contagious Diseases Act, was a very assiduous member of the committee of the Ladies' National Association after its formation in 1870. Frederick Pennington became chairman of the finance committee of the LNA. In 1872, partly as a result of her involvement with the LNA, Mrs Pennington was a founding member and honorary secretary of the CENTRAL COMMITTEE OF THE NATIONAL SOCIETY FOR WOMEN'S SUFFRAGE. The first address of the Central Committee was that of the Penningtons' London home. A letter from Mrs Pennington to Elizabeth MALLESON in 1905 highlights the nature of the relations between the London National Society and those who wished to campaign for women's causes other than suffrage. She remembered "How we poor pioneers were reviled and ridiculed. Our successors don't know at what a cost to some of us their comparative emancipation has been attained. But the bicycle has been a greater emancipation than anything. One thing I shall never forget. The W.S. [women's suffrage] funds (London Society) were very low so I gave them £50 and almost the first use the committee made of it was in printing a circular denouncing me and others for our part in the CD agitation." After the split in the Central Committee in 1888 Mrs Pennington supported the CENTRAL NATIONAL SOCIETY, giving that society £50 in 1889 and becoming a member of its executive committee. She was also interested in furthering the cause of higher education for women, giving £100 to Sophia Jex-Blake's scheme for University Endowment for Women and, in 1891, sizeable donations in 1891 to the Maria Grey Training College.

Address: (1870 and 1914) 17 Hyde Park Terrace, London W; Broom Hall, Holmwood, Dorking, Surrey.

Bibliography: J.B. MacKie, *The Life and Work of Duncan McLaren*, 1888; H. Malleson (ed.), *Elizabeth Malleson 1828–1916: Autobiographical Notes and Letters*, with a Memoir by Hope Malleson, 1926.

PENRITH (NUWSS) In 1913 the society was a member of the NORTH-WESTERN FEDERATION OF THE NATIONAL UNION OF WOMEN'S SUFFRAGE SOCIETIES. Secretary (1913) Miss May Lawrence, Newton Rigg, Penrith, Cumberland.

PENZANCE (NUWSS) In 1913 the society was a member of the SOUTH-WESTERN FEDERATION OF THE NATIONAL UNION OF WOMEN'S SUFFRAGE SOCIETIES. Secretary (1913) Mrs Glave Saunders, 1 Pendarves Road, Penzance, Cornwall.

PEOPLE'S SUFFRAGE FEDERATION Founded in 1909 by a group of women and men, drawn from both Liberal and Labour supporters. "It was the outcome of a strong belief on the part of the promoters that the enfranchisement of women ... could best be carried through in alliance with the progressive forces in politics, and could only be realised in a really effective manner by the reform of the franchise in the sense of adult suffrage" (*Suffrage Annual and Women's Who's Who*, 1913). Its formation marked a stage in the campaign for women's enfranchisement at which it had become clear to progressive thinkers that enfranchisement was necessary for all women in order that they might better their social and economic position. The existing franchise, even if it were to be granted to women on the same terms as men, would still be out of the reach of most unmarried working women and, indeed, of most married women. The executive committee of the PSF included Florence BALGARNIE, Margaret Llewelyn Davies, who brought to it the support of the Women's Co-operative Guilds, Marion Phillips and Mr and Mrs George Trevelyan. The PSF drew support from trades councils, trade unions, working women's societies and branches of the Independent Labour Party. Margaret Bondfield attempted to persuade the Women's Labour League to affiliate with the PSF. Charles McLaren (*see* Laura MCLAREN), Jane Harrison, Emily Hobhouse, Margaret McMillan, Lady Mary Murray, Canon and Mrs Barnett, George LANSBURY and Bertrand Russell were all supporters of the PSF. By 1911 a parliamentary council comprising 110 MPs had been formed, which presented a memorial to the prime minister on 7 November 1911 requesting the introduction of an adult suffrage bill. Asquith in his reply intimated that a women's enfranchisement amendment might be made to the Franchise and Registration Bill. The PSF campaigned for this amendment. Pamphlets published by the PSF included *Adult Suffrage: An Address to Democrats*, by F.D. Acland, MP, and *Anti-Suffragist Anxieties* by Bertrand Russell.

Joint honorary secretaries (1909) Mary Macarthur and Margaret Llewelyn Davies; chairman (1909) Margaret Bondfield; honorary treasurers (1913) Mrs Walter Rea and Arthur Henderson, MP; secretary (1913) Edward McGegan.

Address: Queen Anne's Chambers, Tothill Street, Westminster, London SW.

Archival source: People's Suffrage Federation 1st Report, 1909–10, Fawcett Library.

PERTH committee of the NATIONAL SOCIETY FOR WOMEN'S SUFFRAGE Formed in 1872 and in 1913 the society was a member of the SCOTTISH FEDERATION OF THE NATIONAL UNION OF WOMEN'S SUFFRAGE SOCIETIES. Secretary (1913) Mrs Slater, West Manse, Scone, Perthshire.

PERTH (WFL) Secretary (1913) Mrs Macpherson, 3 Charlotte Street, Perth, Perthshire.

PETERBOROUGH (NUWSS) In 1913 the society was a member of the MIDLANDS (EAST) FEDERATION

OF THE NATIONAL UNION OF WOMEN'S SUFFRAGE SOCIETIES. Secretary (1913) Miss P. English, Orton Longueville, Peterborough, Huntingdonshire.

PETERSFIELD WOMEN'S SUFFRAGE SOCIETY Was in existence, independent of all the main suffrage societies, by June 1911, when it sent a contingent of 24 members, with a banner, to join the suffrage Coronation procession in London. Its president was the Countess of Selborne. In August 1911 it held a fête at Bedales School, at which speeches were given by Evelyn SHARP and H.W. NEVINSON. In the course of the year the Petersfield WSS distributed over 3000 free copies of suffrage newspapers, paid for mainly by Lady Selborne. The society found that the *Hants and Sussex News* was prepared to give good coverage to its activities. Col Hanna, the chairman of the local Liberal Association, resigned his position in 1911 when a Liberal candidate opposed to women's suffrage was adopted. In 1912 the Petersfield WSS affiliated to the FEDERATED COUNCIL OF WOMEN'S SUFFRAGE.
Archival source: Annual Reports of the Petersfield Women's Suffrage Society, Fawcett Library.

PETHICK, DOROTHY (1881–1970) Born in Somerset, younger sister of Emmeline PETHICK-LAWRENCE. She was educated at Cheltenham Ladies' College and in 1906 spent a year training in social work at the Women's University Settlement in the Blackfriars Road in London, becoming in 1908 superintendent of girls' club work in Nottinghamshire. When in London in 1906 she had attended the early WOMEN'S SOCIAL AND POLITICAL UNION meetings and on 29 June 1909 was arrested after taking part in the WSPU deputation to the House of Commons. On 9 October 1909 she was arrested, with Kitty MARION, in Newcastle, having thrown a stone at a window of the General Post Office. She was sentenced to 14 days' hard labour, even though the window had not, in fact, been broken. She went on hunger strike and gave a very well observed account in *Votes for Women* of the lack of hygiene involved in the process as carried out by the prison authorities. She also commented that "I always had a very strong feeling of people like Garibaldi, Mazzini and Joan of Arc with me". After her release she went to Bristol to take part in a demonstration at which Churchill was to speak. In January 1910 she was WSPU organizer for the general election campaign in the Leicester (Loughborough) division. In November 1910 she was sentenced to 14 days' imprisonment after taking part in the demonstrations to protest against the "Black Friday" debacle; her fine was, however, paid without her consent. Shortly afterwards she was again imprisoned for demonstrating in Leicester, but because of the forthcoming general election, her fine was paid and she was released. In April 1911 she organized a census night protest for Leicester WSPU. She remained as organizer in Leicester until 1912, presumably leaving when her sister was ousted from the WSPU.

During the First World War Dorothy Pethick joined the women's police force and in 1917 was based at Gretna. In 1916 she was a member of the UNITED SUFFRAGISTS and honorary treasurer of the BRITISH DOMINIONS WOMAN SUFFRAGE UNION (and still held the position in 1918 when the society changed its name to the British Dominions Women Citizens' Union), and afterwards was for many years secretary of the Rudolf Steiner school (Waldorf School) in Hampstead. She left her collection of anthroposophical books to the Rudolph Steiner Library and the bulk of her estate to the Anthroposophical Society and the Rudolph Steiner schools, and £100 to the International Alliance of Women.
Address: (1918) 39 Meadway Court, London NW4; (1970) Cheveralls Old People's Home, Markyate, Bedfordshire.
Bibliography: E. Pethick-Lawrence, *My Part in the Changing World*, 1938.

PETHICK-LAWRENCE, EMMELINE, MRS (1867–1954) (later Lady Pethick-Lawrence) The eldest surviving child of the 13 born to her parents, brought up first in Bristol and then at Weston-super-Mare. Although her younger sisters, Marie and Dorothy PETHICK, were sent to Cheltenham Ladies' College, Emmeline received a conventional education, boarding school from the age of eight, followed by a period at a local day school, and then attending a small local boarding school to be "finished". French and German were acquired during periods spent living with families in Nancy and Weisbaden. She was brought up as a Nonconformist, first as a Methodist and then as a Congregationalist, before her father joined an evangelical Church of England congregation. Emmeline greatly admired her father, Henry Pethick, remarking in her autobiography that "the closest bond between my father and me was his passionate love of justice, which I inherited from him". She also noted his "deep strain of religious mysticism", a characteristic she also shared. In 1907, shortly before his death, he was to give £100 to the WOMEN'S SOCIAL AND POLITICAL UNION. Conscious of being the eldest daughter of several at home in Weston, where there were many such families, with no future defined except marriage, Emmeline Pethick in 1890 decided that action was required and wrote applying to become a volunteer with the Sisterhood of the West London Mission. One of the founders of this organization, Mark Guy Pearse, a Methodist preacher, had inspired her since her childhood. She was appointed as sister in charge of the Working Girls' Club to succeed Mary NEAL, who, threatened by consumption, had to leave London temporarily. After "Sister Mary's" return to London the two women became firm friends, sharing an adherence to socialism as preached by Keir HARDIE and Edward Carpenter.

After a few years working together at the Mission, in 1895 Emmeline Pethick and Mary Neal resolved to break away from institutional living and the Methodist ethos in order to live amongst the people they were intent on helping. By the turn of the century they were living in a workman's flat in Somerset Terrace, overlooking Euston Road (rent 14/6 a week). They founded the Espérance Working Girls' Club in Cumberland Market, just north of the Euston Road, and Emmeline Pethick became its musical director. They also opened in 1897 a dressmaking business, Maison Espérance at 155 Great Portland Street, paying their employees double the money they were used to receiving, restricting the working day to eight hours and spreading the work evenly throughout the year. Together with Lily Montagu, who ran a club for Jewish girls, they opened a holiday hostel in Littlehampton. This, "The Green Lady Hostel", allowed working girls to enjoy a brief holiday by the sea. In 1898 Emmeline Pethick contributed an essay on "Working Girls' Clubs" to *University and Social Settlements*, edited by Will Reason, the former secretary of Mansfield House, the settlement in Canning Town with which Frederick Lawrence was soon to be involved. In October 1901, at the Town Hall at Canning Town, with Lloyd George among the wedding guests, Emmeline Pethick married Frederick Lawrence, whom she had met when her Espérance Club dramatic group staged a performance at West Ham.

In London the Pethick-Lawrences (for they had so combined their names) lived in Clement's Inn, just off Fleet Street, close to the office of the *Echo*, of which Frederick Pethick-Lawrence was owner, manager and editor (*see* NEWSPAPERS AND JOURNALS). Here the apartments were serviced, the tenants supplied with meals by the management. In addition the Pethick-Lawrences owned a Lutyens-designed house, "The Mascot", at Holmwood, outside Dorking, to which they added a holiday home for poor London children. In 1905 the *Echo* ceased publication; Frederick Pethick-Lawrence had been running it at a loss for several years. In the spring of 1905 he launched a new monthly publication, the *Labour Record and Review*. This contained "A Page About Women" written by "Justitia". The style is very reminiscent of that of Emmeline Pethick-Lawrence. Eventually her name did appear as author; the first article to be so credited was titled "The Story of Mazzini's Life".

While the Pethick-Lawrences were enjoying an extended holiday in South Africa in the autumn of 1905, during the course of which they spent some time in the company of Olive Schreiner, they heard of the disturbances being caused by militant women suffragists in Manchester. They were back in London in January 1906 and Emmeline Pethick-Lawrence records in her autobiography that it was from her roof garden in Clement's Inn that she saw the election results "as they were thrown by a lantern-slide on the elevated-whitened board in the Strand". Sylvia PANKHURST, too, chose to remember in *The Suffragette Movement* that she watched the Labour Party successes flashed up in this manner. They both, independently, shared the same exhilaration that Keir Hardie and the Labour Party had met with such success. A month later Keir Hardie introduced Emmeline Pethick-Lawrence to Emmeline PANKHURST as "a practical and useful colleague who could develop in London the new society she had founded in Manchester – the Women's Social and Political Union". Initially Emmeline Pethick-Lawrence demurred, feeling that she was already involved in too many projects. However, once she met Annie KENNEY, who was also sent by Keir Hardie, she was captivated and agreed to become the WSPU's treasurer. In the 1950s Teresa BILLINGTON-GREIG commented on the strong emotional attraction that immediately developed between Emmeline Pethick-Lawrence and Annie Kenney, describing it as "so emotional and so openly paraded that it frightened me as I saw it as something unbalanced and primitive and possibly dangerous to the movement". Despite Emmeline Pethick-Lawrence's emotional and mystical approach to the woman's cause, Teresa Billington-Greig's fears were groundless. Emmeline Pethick-Lawrence was an astute businesswoman and a good organizer. As she wrote of the Pankhursts and their guerrilla method of political warfare, "It became my business to give their genius a solid foundation."

At this stage Emmeline Pethick-Lawrence still saw the WSPU as part of the Labour movement and was prepared for it to be associated with concerns other than women's enfranchisement. In May 1906, at her instigation, the London Committee of the WSPU sent to the government a resolution calling for a commission of inquiry into the unrest in Natal, from where she had so recently returned. After Christabel PANKHURST's arrival in London in July there was to be no more such deviation. Christabel lived with the Pethick-Lawrences in Clement's Inn for the next five years. Emmeline Pethick-Lawrence apparently had no compunction in leaving the Labour Party after Christabel formulated the WSPU by-election policy of campaigning against the government candidate, rather than for that of the Labour Party.

On 23 October 1906 Emmeline Pethick-Lawrence was arrested on a charge of disorderly conduct while taking part in the WSPU protest at the opening of parliament. She was sentenced to two months in the second division. She immediately collapsed with a nervous breakdown and two days later was released from Holloway, having given an undertaking not to take part in any further militant action for six months. She notes in her autobiography that Mrs Pankhurst gave her permission to make such a promise. She was taken to recuperate in Italy, where Sylvia Pankhurst joined her after serving her prison sentence.

In her autobiography Emmeline Pethick-Lawrence makes clear that, while agreeing with the idea of the WSPU as conceived by Emmeline and Christabel Pankhurst, she understood how difficult it was to explain its necessary lack of democracy to those such as Charlotte DESPARD and Teresa Billington-Greig who were pressing for it to be based on a working constitution. Emmeline Pethick-Lawrence remained firmly with the WSPU when these others broke away and founded the WOMEN'S FREEDOM LEAGUE in September 1907. She was a member of the titular National Committee of the WSPU, which seldom met during her membership of the WSPU. She was, however, a strong influence, with her husband, on Christabel Pankhurst, who spent most of her time in their company either at Clement's Inn or Holmwood. Together they formulated policy. In October 1907 the Pethick-Lawrences founded, and were co-editors of, *Votes for Women*, which in its layout, typeface and its eventual use of a political cartoon on the front cover, bore a strong physical resemblance to the *Labour Record and Review*. The first issue of *Votes for Women* contained a report by Emmeline Pethick-Lawrence of the meeting of the German Union for Women's Suffrage that she and Annie Kenney had lately attended in Frankfurt. Her youthful sojourn in Weisbaden reaped its just reward; she gave her speech to the conference in German. Emmeline Pethick-Lawrence contributed a signed article to most issues of *Votes for Women*. These tend towards the exhoratory, apostrophizing woman and her soul, and urging "women of every class and creed, Come and help us. Enter into our fellowship. You shall have conflict, worldly loss, suffering, but you shall have fulness of life in return, and the light which is more than sun, moon, and stars" (*Votes for Women*, January 1908). By all accounts her oratory followed the lines of her written style, uplifting, theatrical and, to some, embarrassing. There is no doubt, however, but that she was completely sincere, intent on motivating women to find fulfilment in the cause. As she wrote to Mary PHILLIPS on 22 September 1908, "I do love to have happy people in this Movement. I think they carry special power with them." She was one of the WSPU's star speakers, travelling all round the country when occasion demanded it to deliver her brand of moral uplift.

Emmeline Pethick-Lawrence kept a tight control of the WSPU's finances, at one end exhorting and wheedling donations from sympathizers and, at the other, expecting provincial organizers to be accountable for every penny they spent, constantly urging them to economize on their board and lodging. She was quite prepared to veto schemes proposed by these organizers if she did not think them financially viable. Both Ada FLATMAN and Dora MARSDEN were recipients of chastening letters from Emmeline Pethick-Lawrence. As treasurer to the WSPU she was also responsible for devising means of parting sympathizers from their money, a role in which all commentators agreed she was extremely adept. In *The Suffragette Movement* Sylvia Pankhurst remarked that none rivalled Emmeline Pethick-Lawrence in her ability to appeal to the conscience of wealthy and leisured women, urging them that if they were unable to give their time and energy to the cause, they could at least give their money. One of the first schemes she introduced, in February 1908, was "Self-Denial Week". She probably stole the idea from the Salvation Army which ran similar projects; the use of employing "self-denial", with its overtones of submissive womanhood, as a means of raising funds to promote "militancy" has a certain piquancy. In 1908 "Self-Denial Week" raised £8000. Emmeline Pethick-Lawrence had a flair for publicity and in May 1908 it was she who chose "purple, white and green" as the COLOURS by which the members of the WSPU should be unified and recognized while taking part in the procession through London to the rally in Hyde Park on 21 June. She was, as Sylvia Pankhurst put it, "fertile in picturesque ideas" and was responsible for the display of tartaned and kilted "lassies" who were waiting to escort Mary Phillips and the other Scottish prisoners released from Holloway in September 1908. In her autobiography Emmeline Pethick-Lawrence describes in detail how she manipulated one of the appeals for money that raised such impressive totals. On 29 October 1908, after the trial and imprisonment of Emmeline and Christabel Pankhurst, Emmeline Pethick-Lawrence was the only one of the advertised speakers able to appear at a WSPU rally at the Albert Hall. She had beforehand written to the WSPU's principal subscribers, asking them to promise donations that would make an impressive start to a fund-raising meeting that was intended to prove to the government that whatever legal steps were taken to suppress it, the WSPU had access to substantial sums of money. Emmeline Pethick-Lawrence describes how "promise cards like dance programmes had been placed, with a pencil attached, on every seat" in the Albert Hall and "a veritable army of white-robed young stewards, wearing wide belts of purple, white, and green to mark their office, were stationed at every row to receive the promises and bring them to the platform". Excitement mounted as, spurred on by the large sums already promised, the audience donated promises of money, as well as stripping themselves of jewellery and other valuables to offer to the treasurer. The total was displayed on a board, constantly updated by Frederick Pethick-Lawrence, and eventually reached £3000.

On 24 February 1909 Emmeline Pethick-Lawrence led a WSPU deputation from Caxton Hall to the House of Commons. She was arrested with Lady Constance LYTTON, by now a close friend, and sentenced, on a charge of obstructing the police, to two months in the second division. She spent the first month of her sentence with Constance Lytton in the hospital wing of Holloway, but for the second month was removed to the new section of the prison, relieved to find that conditions there were much better than those that had driven her to breakdown in 1906. It had taken considerable courage to place herself again in the position which had resulted previously in a deeply felt humiliation. On her release on 16 April from Holloway she was given a rapturous reception by the WSPU, a public breakfast for 600 at the Wharncliffe Rooms, and a motor car, rendered in purple, with white and green lines, which she immediately dedicated to the general use of the Union (*see* CARAVANS AND CARS).

On 17 November, while Emmeline Pankhurst was on a lecture tour of America, it was with Christabel Pankhurst that Emmeline Pethick-Lawrence represented the WSPU in a deputation of the suffrage societies to Asquith to protest against the "torpedoing" of the Conciliation bill. Asquith's response having been deemed inadequate, on 21 November Emmeline Pethick-Lawrence led a WSPU deputation from Caxton Hall to the House of Commons. In the course of the usual altercation with the police she was arrested and received a month's imprisonment for assault. Once back in Clement's Inn she did not take a stand against the WSPU's window-smashing campaign that began on 1 March 1912, although from the events that occurred later in the year it is possible that she had considerable reservations about the merits of a policy that resulted in the destruction of private property. She apparently did not actually take part in the raid herself, but on 5 March she and her husband were arrested with conspiring with Emmeline Pankhurst and Mabel TUKE to cause damage. She was held on remand in prison until committed for trial at the end of March. The result of the trial, at which she was defended by Tim Healy, the Irish politician and lawyer, which engendered considerable publicity, was a sentence of nine months' imprisonment in the second division, and an order that the three defendants should pay the whole cost of the prosecution, an unprecedented penalty. Although, after protests, the Pethick-Lawrences and Mrs Pankhurst were accorded first-division status, they could not accept it while other suffragette prisoners remained in the second division. In late June they carried out their threat to hunger strike and Emmeline Pethick-Lawrence was forced to endure one forcible feeding operation before being released two days later.

After recuperating in the country for a few weeks the Pethick-Lawrences travelled to Switzerland, stopping on the way to meet Emmeline and Christabel Pankhurst at Boulogne. In the course of this meeting it became clear that a deep division as to future policy had arisen between the Pankhursts and the Pethick-Lawrences. Emmeline Pethick-Lawrence made clear to the Pankhursts that she thought that the WSPU should capitalize on the sympathetic publicity that had accrued to the WSPU as a result of the trial, and not alienate the public by committing further damage to property. Rather than the campaign of secret terror envisaged by the Pankhursts, Emmeline Pethick-Lawrence had intended that the WSPU should embark on a series of large popular demonstrations, a development of policy favoured, independently, by Sylvia Pankhurst. Emmeline Pethick-Lawrence described the events that followed in a letter to Evelyn SHARP, written in July 1930:

Fred and I went to America after our release from prison at the suggestion of Mrs Pankhurst who wrote to us to say that she was too ill to receive a public welcome, and she thought it would be far better if we all waited to have our welcome together at the Albert Hall meeting. It would make it far easier to carry out, she wrote, if we went to visit our brother in Canada during the months of August and September, we should then come back thoroughly strong and reconstituted in health and should then have a meeting in the Albert Hall when we three, who had gone through the trial together should reap together the enthusiasm entailed by the subsequent events of that trial. We went and we returned in response to this idea, and had no conception of the movement that had been carried out during our absence until out little friend and domestic helper, May Start, met us at the boat in order to break to us the news of the intrigue that had been hatched during our absence.

In their absence Mrs Pankhurst had moved the WSPU from Clement's Inn to Lincoln's Inn House in Kingsway and when the Pethick-Lawrences called there they, who had previously been the linchpins of the business organization, found that no offices had been allotted to them. Mrs Pankhurst told the Pethick-Lawrences that she had severed her connection with them. When Emmeline Pethick-Lawrence appealed to Mabel Tuke and Annie Kenney they both refused to speak to her. Such was the Pethick-Lawrences' disbelief that they were to be removed from the organization to which they had devoted so much time, money and love, that it was only when Christabel was summoned from Paris to tell them that she had, as Emmeline Pethick-Lawrence put it, "no further use for them" that the Pethick-Lawrences accepted their ousting. Emmeline Pethick-Lawrence records that henceforward she never again saw or heard from Emmeline Pankhurst and, although there is a suggestion that she did in the future meet Christabel, it was as strangers.

The Pethick-Lawrences retained control of *Votes for Women*, which they had previously given to the WSPU. It continued publication much the same as previously and around it grew another group, the VOTES FOR WOMEN FELLOWSHIP, which aimed to promote the paper and its policies rather than stand as a new militant organization. Despite this continuity, Emmeline Pethick-Lawrence notes in her autobiography how much she missed her erstwhile colleagues and the WSPU, which "Fred and I loved as though it were our child". In addition the Pethick-Lawrences' house at Holmwood was at this time occupied by bailiffs, with the intention that its contents should be sequestered, auctioned on 31 October, and the resulting sum set against the prosecution costs for the conspiracy trial. Most of the furniture was bought back by Emmeline Pethick-Lawrence's family and friends and returned to her.

In July 1913 Emmeline Pethick-Lawrence was back in Holloway, having been arrested with Evelyn Sharp and Lady Sybil Smith, while taking part in a deputation carrying a memorial from the committee convened to protest against the "Cat and Mouse" Act to the House of Commons. Although the sentence was set for 14 days, Emmeline Pethick-Lawrence reported in her autobiography that it was the threat by Lady Sybil, who was related to members of the House of Lords, to hunger strike that inspired the Home Office to cut the sentences for all the women to four days. Soon after this episode she, like so many other suffrage campaigners, was moved to help the children suffering from their fathers' involvement in the Dublin lock-out. Emmeline Pethick-Lawrence, through her emissary Mary Neal, was rather more tactful, and as a result more successful, than Dora MONTEFIORE in securing the temporary adoption of half-a-dozen children. In July 1914 Emmeline Pethick-Lawrence, with her husband, joined the UNITED SUFFRAGISTS and together they gave *Votes for Women* to the new society.

Soon after the outbreak of war Emmeline Pethick-Lawrence was invited to speak at a meeting at Carnegie Hall to inaugurate a new suffrage campaign in the United States. She was determined to use this opportunity to promote to American women the idea of a negotiated peace, which she had already become convinced was the only just solution to the war. In February 1915 she set sail for the Hague with Jane Addams and other representatives of the National Women's Peace Party of America, in order to attend the Women's Peace Congress. Having arrived by this indirect route, she was one of only three British women able to attend the conference. In the autumn of 1915 Emmeline Pethick-Lawrence became the honorary treasurer of the newly founded Women's International League of Great Britain and as she wrote, "From this time forward the main purpose of my life was to spread as far as possible, the conviction that peace and negotiation alone could promote a stable condition in Europe".

In August–September 1915 she published "The Woman's Crusade for Peace" in the *Socialist Review*. In addition to its work for peace, the WIL supported a policy of adult suffrage, as, presumably, by then did Emmeline Pethick-Lawrence. In December 1918 she stood in the general election as the Labour candidate at Rusholme division of Manchester. Her platform was devoted to the idea that the only chance for permanent peace in Europe was a just settlement with Germany. She was defeated, although the votes of returning combatants saved her deposit, and she had the satisfaction of being placed above the Liberal candidate. She devoted the rest of her political life to campaigning for peace. In addition, from 1926 she was for nine years president of the Women's Freedom League, was for many years a member of the executive committee of the Open Door Council and was a vice-president of the Six Point Group. In 1946 Emmeline Pethick-Lawrence was technical adviser for the scenes relating to the suffrage movement in a film of Howard Spring's novel, *Fame is the Spur* (*see* FILMS). For this film, material was loaned by the Suffragette Record Room, of which she was a patron, as she was of the SUFFRAGETTE FELLOWSHIP. Besides the hundreds of articles she contributed to *Votes for Women*, Emmeline Pethick-Lawrence wrote for the WSPU 11 pamphlets, among them *The Faith That is in Us*, *The New Crusade*, the text of a speech she gave at the Exeter Hall on 30 May 1907, *The Call to Women* and *Why I Went to Prison*, 1909. Among the many bequests in her will she left £50 to the Women's Freedom League, £100 to Isabel SEYMOUR, £100 to Charlotte MARSH, £100 to Stella NEWSOME, £50 to Marion Reeves who ran the Minerva Club (*see under* CLUBS), £25 to Harriot Rozier, who had been a member of the WSPU, and an annuity of £50 to Sylvia Pankhurst.

Address: (1901) Clement's Inn, Lincoln's Inn Fields, London WC; "The Mascot", Holmwood, Surrey; (1917) 11 and 12 Old Square, Lincoln's Inn, London WC; (1920) "Fourways", Peaslake, Surrey.

Portrait: Joint portrait of Frederick and Emmeline Pethick-Lawrence by Dame Laura Knight, 1936, commissioned by a committee of their friends, which included Lady Balfour of Burleigh, "Henrietta Leslie" (*see* Gladys Schütze), and Stella Newsome. Joint portrait of Lord and Lady Pethick-Lawrence by John Baker, at Peaslake Village Hall, Surrey, unveiled by Baroness Summerskill in 1962, print of it given to National Portrait Gallery Archive by Esther Knowles in 1962. Photograph of Emmeline Pethick-Lawrence, wearing her "Holloway" badge, by Bassano, taken on 28 September 1910, National Portrait Gallery.

Archival sources: Evelyn Sharp Papers, Bodleian Library, Oxford; Teresa Billington-Greig Papers, Fawcett Library; Mary Phillips Papers, Camellia plc.

Bibliography: E. Pethick-Lawrence, *My Part in a Changing World*, 1938; F. Pethick-Lawrence, *Fate Has Been Kind*, 1942; V. Brittain, *Pethick-Lawrence: A Portrait*, 1963; B. Harrison, *Prudent Revolutionaries: Portraits of British Feminists between the Wars*, 1987; J. Balshaw, "Sharing the burden: the Pethick Lawrences and women's suffrage", in A.V. John and C. Eustance (eds), *The Men's Share*, 1997.

PETHICK-LAWRENCE, FREDERICK WILLIAM (1871–1961) (later Lord Pethick-Lawrence) Born Frederick William Lawrence into a prosperous Unitarian family, he was educated at Eton and Trinity College, Cambridge, where he read mathematics, natural science and economics, and was president of the Union. After leaving Cambridge he travelled round the world and on his return to England in 1899 worked at Mansfield House, a university settlement in Canning Town, was called to the Bar, and was selected as the Liberal-Unionist candidate for North Lambeth. At this time he met and proposed marriage to Emmeline Pethick (*see* PETHICK-LAWRENCE), who initially refused him on the grounds that she did not feel able to be the wife of an MP belonging to a traditional political party. Frederick Lawrence then set out for South Africa to investigate, as it raged around him, the merits of the Boer War and returned to renounce his allegiance to the Unionists. In his autobiography he stressed the influence of Mazzini on his outlook.

In 1901 Frederick Lawrence took a controlling interest, and became editor of the *Echo*, a London evening newspaper, married Emmeline Pethick, and identified himself very closely with all her social interests. He built as a gift to her "The Sundial", a holiday cottage for children close to their country house. In 1905 he was forced to close the *Echo*, which was still losing money, and, instead, launched the *Labour Record and Review*; he had become a close friend of Keir HARDIE. In late 1905 Pethick-Lawrence was on holiday in South Africa with his wife when they heard of the imprisonment in Manchester of Christabel PANKHURST and Annie KENNEY. On their return Emmeline Pethick-Lawrence was introduced to Mrs Pankhurst and Annie Kenney by Keir Hardie. Frederick Pethick-Lawrence soon became acquainted with the personalities of the WOMEN'S SOCIAL AND POLITICAL UNION, writing a character sketch of Annie Kenney for the April issue of the *Labour Record and Review* and one of Teresa Billington (*see* BILLINGTON-GREIG) for the July issue. The March issue contained an article by William Sanders, whose wife Beatrice (*see* Beatrice SANDERS) was recruited by Pethick-Lawrence to become the WSPU's financial secretary. Frederick Pethick-Lawrence records in his autobiography that it was in July 1906 that he first became directly involved in the WSPU cause; his wife summoned him to help secure the defence of Annie Kenney, Adelaide KNIGHT and Mrs SBARBORO, who had been arrested outside Asquith's house in Cavendish Square. Nevertheless he did not at first intend to take any active part, remarking that "the day had gone by when 'ladies' expected 'gentlemen' to be kind enough to tell them how to get the vote". However, he did feel that the WSPU could benefit from his experience of business planning and organized the acquisition of an office for them in Clement's Inn. After Emmeline Pethick-Lawrence's arrest, imprisonment and subsequent breakdown in October 1906 her husband took over in her absence the activities of treasurer of the WSPU. During this period he instituted the Literature Department, later renamed The Woman's Press, as the trading arm of the WSPU. After Emmeline Pethick-Lawrence was able to retrieve the reins of treasurer, Frederick remained as business adviser and, as militancy increased, put up bail and was the legal adviser to the ever-increasing number of arrested suffragettes. In his autobiography he relates that, after the split with those who went on to found the WOMEN'S FREEDOM LEAGUE, although Mrs Pankhurst was in theory the autocratic leader of the WSPU, in reality power was concentrated in the hands of Christabel Pankhurst, his wife and himself.

In November 1907 Frederick Pethick-Lawrence, with his wife as co-editor, put his experience and capital at the service of the WSPU and commenced publication of *Votes for Women*. He thereby gave the WSPU the medium that consolidated the Union's identity and broadcast its message so effectively for the next five years. He contributed many unsigned notes and articles to the paper, made sure that it always contained the most up-to-date news, and states that from April 1908 until his arrest in March 1912 it was only on the rarest of occasions that he was not the one who saw the paper through the press. As well as giving his time, Frederick Pethick-Lawrence was happy to put his inherited money at the service of the WSPU. In 1908–9 he and his wife are recorded in the accounts as giving £1687 to the WSPU, followed the next year by a further £1300.

In June 1908 Frederick Pethick-Lawrence was closely involved in the organization of the WSPU Hyde Park rally, indeed, in *The Suffragette Movement* Sylvia Pankhurst heralds him as "the main architect of the scheme". In November 1908, at Christabel Pankhurst's direct request, he acted as counsel for Jennie BAINES when she stood trial in Leeds on a charge of "unlawful assembly". This was the first case Pethick-Lawrence had conducted in court, but it was doubtless despite his strenuous efforts that Jennie Baines was found guilty. He became very familiar with police courts in the following years. He records that he himself never witnessed any of the WSPU "raids" on Parliament, always remaining in Clement's Inn, by the telephone, awaiting the summons to go to police stations to stand bail for those arrested. He advised the women on how they should conduct their defence. It was after bailing out the women who had been arrested on 1 March 1912 after taking part in the window-smashing raids in the West End of London and while he was writing up their exploits for the pages of *Votes for Women*, that on 5 March Pethick-Lawrence was, with his wife, arrested on a charge of conspiracy. Always the businessman, he had ready a cheque, dated 1 March, that would transfer most of the WSPU's assets from the Union's bank account into that of Hertha AYRTON. Evelyn SHARP, who fortuitously arrived soon after the police, was given the editorship of *Votes for Women* and the cheque, which required countersigning, to take to Christabel Pankhurst, who was thus warned of her danger. Pethick-Lawrence was held on remand in Brixton prison until the end of March when he was committed for trial and released on bail. With his wife he travelled, by a devious route, to Paris to consult with Christabel, with whom relations appear still to have been perfectly amicable. He conducted his own defence, intent, although certain to be found guilty, on proselytizing the cause. His speech from the dock was published as *The Man's Share* by the WSPU. Having been sentenced to nine months' imprisonment and ordered to pay the costs of the prosecution, he began his sentence in Wormwood Scrubs before being transferred to Brixton, where he was to be held under rule 243A. He was visited regularly by the Unitarian chaplain, Frederick HANKINSON, who gave him news from Holloway of Emmeline Pethick-Lawrence. After outside agitation he, with his wife and Emmeline Pankhurst, was accorded first-division status, for which he soon substituted a hunger strike when it became clear that other suffrage prisoners were not to be so elevated. He was forcibly fed twice a day until released on 27 June.

Soon after his release Frederick Pethick-Lawrence travelled with his wife to Boulogne where he had a heated discussion with Christabel Pankhurst, disagreeing with her intention of concentrating on attacks on private property and being astounded to learn that she did not intend to return to England. He was, as he termed it, "shattered" to discover in October, after a lengthy visit to Canada and the USA, that the Pankhursts had ousted himself and his wife from the WSPU. It is likely that, apart from differences over policy, Christabel was suspicious that in her absence the Pethick-Lawrences would be in a position, whether or not they used it, to exercise even more control over the WSPU than they had done in the past. It is now clear that she was becoming increasingly convinced that the WSPU should be a women-only movement and that Pethick-Lawrence's wealth was seen as an Achilles' heel through which the government could attack the WSPU. Bailiffs had already entered his country house, "The Mascot", and furniture was auctioned to raise money to pay the order for costs that was outstanding against him. Emmeline Pethick-Lawrence gave her husband the credit for deciding that no public remonstrance should be made against the Pankhursts. In his autobiography he wryly pointed out that as they had supported Mrs Pankhurst in her bid for autocracy in 1907, they could hardly dispute it now. He characterized the Pankhursts as the agents of destiny and remarked that "They cannot be judged by ordinary standards of conduct; and those who run up against them must not complain of the treatment they receive."

As co-editor of *Votes for Women*, which had now reverted to his ownership, Pethick-Lawrence continued campaigning for the suffrage cause, first as a co-founder of the VOTES FOR WOMEN FELLOWSHIP and then, in 1914, as a member of the UNITED SUFFRAGISTS. It was Frederick Pethick-Lawrence who, in the pages of *Votes for Women*, invented the sobriquet "Cat and Mouse" Act to describe the Prisoners (Temporary Discharge for Ill-Health) Act, a usage which was even adopted by the Home Office itself. The sum of money derived from the auction of the Pethick-Lawrences' furniture did not meet the costs outstanding against them and Frederick Pethick-Lawrence was declared bankrupt in order that the government could recover the required sum. As a consequence he was expelled from the Reform Club, an incident he felt worthwhile recording. The Pankhursts had been correct in assuming that Pethick-Lawrence's wealth made him vulnerable. In 1913 the firms whose windows had been attacked brought proceedings against him and his wife in an action to recover damages. In the event judgement was entered against them; Pethick-Lawrence forfeited £5000. After this call on his assets, his bankruptcy was discharged. However, if he had remained a leading member of the WSPU there would doubtless have been further attempts to embroil him in legal action. The Pankhursts, having no assets, were obviously immune from such proceedings.

In mid-1914 the Pethick-Lawrences handed over *Votes for Women* to the United Suffragists, intending to undertake a world tour; the outbreak of war, which surprised Frederick Pethick-Lawrence as much as anyone, prevented them putting this plan into operation. In 1915 he sailed for America to join Emmeline Pethick-Lawrence, who had become involved in the campaign to lobby for a negotiated peace. He returned with her, Jane Addams and other American sympathizers, travelling to the Hague to witness the Women's Peace Congress. Pethick-Lawrence was not directly involved in the negotiations that resulted in women's partial enfranchisement in 1918 but, in 1928, it was in reply to a question from him, now a Labour MP, that Prime Minister Stanley Baldwin made his announcement that his government intended to introduce and carry through a bill to enfranchise all women.

After Emmeline Pethick-Lawrence's death, Frederick Pethick-Lawrence married a former WSPU member, Helen CRAGGS. Despite the events of 1912, he remained loyal to Christabel Pankhurst's memory, organizing the addition of her name to the statue commemorating her mother, and arranging the publication of her history of the militant suffrage movement, to which he gave the title *Unshackled*. In this, rather touchingly, he included as a frontispiece a portrait of her wearing a hat he had given her. After his death, a Pethick-Lawrence Memorial Committee organized commemoration ceremonies at one of which Mary LEIGH paraded the WSPU flag that Emily Wilding DAVISON was wearing when she fell under Anmer's hooves in June 1913. The contributors to the Memorial Appeal Fund include many ex-members of the WSPU and WFL.

Among the works Frederick Pethick-Lawrence published while involved in the WSPU campaign are *Is the English Law Unjust to Women?*, *The Bye-election Policy of the WSPU*, *Women's Work and Wages*, *Treatment of the Suffragettes in Prison* and *Women's Fight for the Vote*, the latter a book based on articles he first published in *Votes for Women*.

Address: (1901) Clement's Inn, London WC; "The Mascot", Holmwood, Surrey; (1917) 11 and 12 Old Square, Lincoln's Inn, London WC; (1920) "Fourways", Peaslake, Surrey.
Portrait: Joint portrait of Frederick and Emmeline Pethick-Lawrence by Dame Laura Knight, 1936. Joint portrait of Frederick and Emmeline Pethick-Lawrence by John Baker, at the Village Hall, Peaslake, Surrey, unveiled by Baronness Summerskill in July 1962. A print of the portrait was given to the National Portrait Gallery Archive in 1962 by Esther Knowles, the WSPU's youngest office girl and, for most of his life, Pethick-Lawrence's secretary. Another portrait by John Baker, of Pethick-Lawrence alone, was unveiled by Lord Longford at Pethick-Lawrence House, Dorking, July 1962. Portrait, by Henry Coller, 1933, given to National Portrait Gallery in 1962 by Esther

Knowles. Wooden head by Albert Moroder, 1949, given to National Portrait Gallery by Theresa GARNETT in 1962.
Bibliography: E. Pethick-Lawrence, *My Part in a Changing World*, 1938; F. Pethick-Lawrence, *Fate Has Been Kind*, 1942; V. Brittain, *Pethick-Lawrence: A Portrait*, 1963; B. Harrison, *Prudent Revolutionaries: Portraits of British Feminists between the Wars*, 1987; J. Balshaw, "Sharing the burden: the Pethick Lawrences and women's suffrage", in A.V. John and C. Eustance, *The Men's Share?: Masculinities, Male Support and Women's Suffrage in Britain, 1890–1920*, 1997.

PHILLIPS, CAROLINE AGNES ISABELLA (1870–1954) Scottish, daughter of a schoolmaster, by 1907 she was a journalist with the *Aberdeen Daily Journal* and honorary secretary of the Aberdeen branch of the WOMEN'S SOCIAL AND POLITICAL UNION, which had been established early in the year to take the suffrage campaign into Scotland's Liberal heartland at the South Aberdeen by-election. The editor of the *Journal* did not approve of her suffrage activity but appears to have let her work from its premises. In January 1908 he wrote to her (and she preserved the letter) "You are identifying yourself far too closely with W.S. [women's suffrage] Movement, considering the position you hold here. I hear lots of protests, both inside and outside the office. I trust you will give me the assurance before Friday that henceforth you will mind your own affairs otherwise I will have to refer the matter to the board." In April 1907 Mrs PANKHURST, who had already visited Aberdeen in early February, wrote to Caroline Phillips to say that she was spending a few days in Scotland in early May and would be glad to visit the Aberdeen branch if a meeting could be arranged. She wrote, "We of the National Committee are very anxious to keep in touch with provincial Branches and so we arrange that from time to time visits of the kind I am now undertaking shall be made." She was subsequently booked into Aberdeen for the second week of May. Caroline Phillips organized a special train from Aberdeen to Edinburgh on 5 October 1907 in order that Aberdonians could take part in the Women's Suffrage Demonstration, which was to include representatives of all suffrage societies, and over which S.E.S. MAIR presided. She received an invitation to the celebration a week later held in the Portman Rooms in London to celebrate the second anniversary of the imprisonment of Christabel PANKHURST and Annie KENNEY. Caroline Phillips did not always approve of tactics dictated from London. In November 1907 Asquith was a candidate at the election for rector of Aberdeen University. Women, members of the WSPU, the NATIONAL UNION OF WOMEN'S SUFFRAGE SOCIETIES and the Women's Liberal Association all electioneered to keep him out in order to show disapproval of his stand on suffrage. However, as Asquith was in Aberdeen as a guest of James Murray, the Liberal MP who was very supportive of women's suffrage, Caroline Phillips thought that, whatever were London tactics regarding Asquith, it was not politic to antagonize his host. Matters appear to have been resolved amicably with London and on 18 November Christabel Pankhurst wrote to Caroline Phillips hoping that she would retain the secretaryship and adding, "I think you will get on all right in a very short while." It is possible that Caroline had threatened to resign.

During 1908 Caroline Phillips worked hard to organize the WSPU campaign in Aberdeen, despite women of the Liberal Association, on whose support they counted, having been irritated by a speech given by Christabel Pankhurst in a meeting at the end of January. Mrs Pankhurst returned to Aberdeen on 1 April and in the draft of a letter to James Murray before this occasion Caroline Phillips wrote of a recent drawing-room meeting that:

[the] remarkable feature of the meeting was that the question of women's suffrage was never lost sight of in the social gathering – votes and policies are lively interesting subjects – not the dry dreary affairs that some of the older women political organisations make them. Plans are afoot for Mrs Pankhurst's visit on 1 April – will have an Afternoon Public meeting and a semi-social gathering for the evening of the same day with invitations on a large scale. We would like to make the last-named a brilliant, dressy, affair, what Lady Ramsay calls a "real shine". I have promise already of the very best musical talent the town affords. Are we too ambitious in aspiring to hold this gathering in the Art Gallery?

This rather artless approach to the suffrage campaign and the close association with the local Liberal MP was not in tune with the developing militant attitudes of Clement's Inn, which in the course of the year dealt Caroline Phillips several rebuffs; speakers were not available, it was too late in the season for a caravan tour, but it was hoped that "active demonstrators" would travel from Aberdeen to London to take part in the Women's Parliament in Caxton Hall. The final straw came in a peremptory telegram from Christabel Pankhurst to Caroline Phillips on 5 January 1909 announcing "Sylvia Pankhurst arrives Thursday morning to take charge local work. Thursdays meeting had better be abandoned. Writing." On 11 January Caroline Phillips received a cyclostyled letter from Sylvia PANKHURST, writing from an Aberdeen address, to announce that the committee of the NWSPU was now able to send a permanent representative to Aberdeen to organize an active Votes for Women movement there in close co-operation with Clement's Inn and in conjunction with the local WSPU. The letter makes clear that:

> a large experience all over the country has shown the Committee that the movement makes very much greater headway under this system than when the provincial work is left to a number of separate and isolated local Unions, and as I am here representing the National Committee and making the preliminary arrangements on their behalf, I therefore recommend that the local Aberdeen WSPU be dissolved as under the new scheme it can no longer be recognised and I wish also most cordially to invite you to become a Member of the NWSPU.

Ada FLATMAN arrived to help Sylvia wield the new broom, writing on 10 February to Caroline Phillips, who had said that she could take no prominent part in stewarding a meeting to be held by Sylvia Pankhurst, that "you will I am sure know we shall always be grateful for any help you can give us". This must have been rather a blow for the woman who had devoted two years to nursing the Aberdeen WSPU. From a letter drafted by Caroline Phillips to Sylvia Pankhurst, who had by then returned to London, she made it clear that there was "a unanimous verdict . . . that the National have treated the local Union abominably" although she appeared to absolve Sylvia of blame. Caroline Phillips, alienated from the WSPU, does not appear to have taken any further part in the suffrage movement.

Address: (1907) 61 Albury Road, Aberdeen.
Archival source: Watt Collection, Aberdeen Art Gallery and Museum.

PHILLIPS, MARY ELIZABETH (1880–1969) Daughter of a doctor, W. Fleming Phillips, who worked in Glasgow and who encouraged her to join the suffrage campaign. She was engaged by the GLASGOW AND WEST OF SCOTLAND ASSOCIATION FOR WOMEN'S SUFFRAGE for seven weeks as a paid ORGANIZER in late 1904 and early 1905 and was still attending the society's committee meetings in 1906. In March 1907 she resigned her position as organizing secretary for the GWSAWS and as local secretary for the Largs Committee in order to join the WOMEN'S SOCIAL AND POLITICAL UNION. She later said that she had come to recognize the failure of "constitutional" agitation. A Socialist, she wrote a regular column in *Forward*, a Glasgow-based "Scots Weekly journal of socialism, trade unionism, and democratic thought", in which she dealt at length with the suffrage campaign. Mary Phillips was actively working for the Glasgow branch of the WSPU in June 1907 and in September was based at Fairlie, Ayrshire, where she worked for the WSPU on an "out-of-pocket-expenses" basis. On 12 November 1907 Christabel PANKHURST wrote to ask Mary Phillips if she would organize two campaigns in Scotland, one in East Fife and one "in Mr Morley's constituency", in order to relieve Helen FRASER of some of her workload. Mary Phillips, who seems then to have been working at the Scottish Council for Women's Trades, replied that she would be able to help the WSPU for the next month.

In March 1908 Mary Phillips was one of those who took part in the "pantechnicon raid" on parliament, relating details of the adventure in her *Forward* column after her release from a six-week prison sentence. She was arrested again after taking part in the 30 June deputation from Caxton Hall and was sentenced to three months' imprisonment. On her release on 18 September she was greeted by a bevy of WSPU members, led by Flora DRUMMOND, all of whom were attired in full Scottish regalia and accompanied by pipers. Mary Phillips and her parents were transported in a carriage pulled by the women from Holloway to the Queen's Hall.

From June 1908 until 1913 Mary Phillips was a paid organizer for the WSPU, travelling around the country as directed. After her release from her second term of imprisonment she was based in

Reading in October 1908; was in Plymouth, with Annie KENNEY and Mary BLATHWAYT, in November 1908; in Newcastle in January 1909, where she took over as organizer from Edith NEW; in Forfar, staying with Flora Drummond in a temperance hotel, in February 1909; and in Liverpool (36 Oxford Road, Liverpool) in May 1909. In June 1909 she stayed at Violet BLAND's house at Bristol (Henley Grove, Henleaze), and was in Cornwall in July, first in Truro (78 Lemon Street), and then at Tregenna House, Penzance, working in Ilfracombe and Swansea. At the end of July she was arrested, with Vera WENTWORTH and Elsie HOWEY, after interrupting a meeting being held by Lord Carrington in Exeter. She was sentenced to seven days' imprisonment, went on hunger strike for recognition as a political prisoner, and was released after three days. She had been sentenced to the third division; the magistrate had to be reminded by the Home Office that suffragist prisoners should be placed in the second division. On her release Mary Phillips stayed at the Osborne Hotel, Exeter, where Emmeline PANKHURST wrote to her on 4 August, "As for you my dear girl take great care of yourself and do everything in your power to recover your health and strength". In September Mary Phillips was sent by Mrs TUKE the hunger strike medal she had earned. In September 1909 Mary Phillips was in Bradford (9 The Parade), making a brief visit to Batheaston, where Col BLATHWAYT took her photograph on 3 October. In November 1909 she wrote to Christabel Pankhurst that she would like to take part in further militant activity and court prison for the cause. Christabel Pankhurst wrote back, "Nothing would be more mistaken at the present time. On no account run the risk of it, as the work you have been doing recently would all go to pieces. It will be necessary to get your voluntary workers to make the protest, which of course you will organize." In December 1909 Mary Phillips was taken to task by Emmeline PETHICK-LAWRENCE for a deficit of £66 in the Bradford WSPU accounts.

Mary Phillips remained in the north for the next three years, organizing WSPU campaigns throughout Yorkshire. She did, of course, go to London to take part in all the WSPU processions during the period of truce in 1910 and 1911. In November 1912, while she was campaigning at the Bolton by-election with Jennie BAINES, she received letters from Christabel Pankhurst exhorting her to think of ways of increasing sales of the *Suffragette* in her area and suggesting that "Mrs Baines may remember some of the schemes adopted by the 'Clarion' People in the old days. Why should we not try them?" In July 1912 Mary Phillips was arrested in Chester, but her fine was paid, without her consent, by a local Liberal. In December 1912 her mother died and she returned to Falmouth for a time to comfort her father, who had moved to Cornwall a few years previously. While there, she received a letter of sympathy from Christabel Pankhurst, from whom she had had over the years numerous letters of praise and affection. The contrast between this and a letter she received from Christabel on 1 August 1913 is startling. In the latter Christabel Pankhurst wrote:

> I have had a letter about you from a member in London. She encloses a letter from you in which you say that the district you were working in was not considered worth working any longer and that that is the reason why you are no longer an organiser. I want to say that if we had thought you would have made a success of another district we should have asked you to take one. I did not wish to hurt you needlessly by saying what always has been felt at headquarters that you are not effective as a district organiser. . . . As a shop secretary where you would not have so much responsibility for making things go, you would I think probably be successful. That I shall say if my opinion is asked. But I cannot say that you would make a successful head of a district campaign because I do not think it. It is not possible that members shall have the impression that you have been unjustly dealt with in spite of your having been a fully competent organiser.

This letter, sent to one who had worked tirelessly for the WSPU for six years and who had undergone several prison sentences for the cause, may be indicative of the increasing strain that the WSPU, harried by the police, was under. Mary Phillips had been dismissed from her position as organizer in Plymouth with four weeks' salary in lieu of notice on 9 July 1913. A year earlier, on 18 April 1912, she had been congratulated on her success and her salary had been increased from £2 10s to £2 15s a week.

Her papers reveal no reason for "headquarters'" belated dissatisfaction.

Mary Phillips immediately joined the EAST LONDON FEDERATION OF THE SUFFRAGETTES, working, as "Mary Paterson", for Sylvia Pankhurst from 1913 until 1915. She had obviously taken a salary cut, because on 1 January 1914 Sylvia Pankhurst *increased* her salary to £2 a week. She was credited by Sylvia Pankhurst as giving the title, "The Workers' Dreadnought", to the ELFS paper in early 1914. Mary Phillips lived above the ELFS Poplar shop, working there and in Canning Town and Poplar with, among others, Norah Smyth and May BILLINGHURST. In 1915 she joined the UNITED SUFFRAGISTS, working until February 1916 as its organizer in south London, based at the US club at 92 Borough Road, Southwark. She then worked for, in succession, the NEW CONSTITUTIONAL SOCIETY FOR WOMEN'S SUFFRAGE, the Women's International League and the Save the Children Fund. From 1928 until 1955 she was editor of a Daily News Service for the brewing trade and after her retirement worked on a semi-voluntary basis with the Publications Department of the National Council of Social Service. She was a life-long member of the Six Point Group. In July 1910 she had attended, as a visitor, a Fabian Women's Group Conference and her politics always remained what she herself described, in an autobiographical profile in *Calling All Women*, as "extreme Left".

Mary Phillips later (*c*. 1960) wrote a pamphlet, *The Militant Suffrage Campaign in Perspective*, which was published by the SUFFRAGETTE FELLOWSHIP. She had been custodian of the Suffragette Fellowship artefacts around 1934.

Address: (September 1907) 6 Allanton Park Terrace, Fairlie, Ayrshire; (1909) 37 Queen's Road, Bristol; (January 1910) 500 Leeds Road, Bradford; (March 1910) 68 Manningham Lane, Bradford; (July 1913) 4 Carlisle Terrace, The Hoe, Plymouth; (October 1913) Fairholme, Worple Road, Wimbledon, SW; (1934) 82 Church Street, Kensington, London W; (1967) Hovedene Hotel, 15/17 The Drive, Hove, Sussex.
Photograph: wearing her Holloway brooch at "Suffragettes" dinner at the Belgravia Hotel, 13 October 1933, in National Portrait Gallery Archive.
Archival source: Mary Phillips Papers, Camellia plc.
Bibliography: *The Listener*, 8 February 1968.

PHIPPS, EMILY (1865–1943) Born in Devonport, was a pupil-teacher, went to training college, and then took an external University of London degree. She became headmistress of the Swansea Municipal Secondary Girls' School. In 1903–4 she joined the Equal Pay League, a feminist pressure group within the National Union of Teachers of which Teresa Billington (*see* Teresa BILLINGTON-GREIG) was honorary secretary of the Manchester branch. In 1908 she joined the WOMEN'S FREEDOM LEAGUE in Swansea after witnessing the treatment accorded to suffragette hecklers at a Liberal meeting and became a very active member. She went to some lengths to evade the census in 1911, spending the night in question in a cave on the Gower coast. Emily Phipps became president of the National Union of Women Teachers and in 1918 stood for parliament as an independent in Chelsea, sponsored by the National Federation of Women Teachers, but failed to be elected. In 1919 she was a founder and editor of the *Woman Teacher*, a feminist weekly paper. She resigned from teaching in 1925 and in 1928 was called to the Bar. In 1928 she published *History of the National Union of Women Teachers* and in her will she left a financial legacy to the NUWT.
Address: (1943) Cremyll Cottage, Hermitage, Nr Newbury, Berkshire.
Bibliography: H. Kean, *Deeds Not Words: The Lives of Suffragette Teachers*, 1990; A. Oram, *Women Teachers and Feminist Politics 1900–39*, 1996.

PHOTOGRAPHS AND PHOTOGRAPHERS The importance of keeping a photographic representation of the women involved in the suffrage campaign was recognized in the nineteenth century by both Helen BLACKBURN and Lilias Ashworth HALLETT. We are left, however, with only a shadow of the rich collections built up by these two women. The Helen Blackburn collection at Girton does contain some very interesting photographs, many of which were used as illustrations in her *Record of Women's Suffrage*, 1902. However, these are but a fraction of the collection of prints and photographs that are detailed in the catalogue of her *Collection of Portraits of Eminent British Women*. Items from this collection, which had by then been entrusted to Bristol University, were reproduced in *The Story of the Women's Suffrage Movement*, 1912, by Bertha MASON, who, in her introduction, also gave thanks to Lilias Ashworth Hallett for the use of items from her photograph collection. For at least two years before the book's publication Bertha Mason had been using lantern slides made from these photographs to give a "limelight lecture" to NUWSS societies around the country on the history of the women's suffrage movement, applauding the pioneers. Similarly, Rose Lamartine YATES, a leading member of the Wimbledon WSPU, gave a lecture, "A true story of the militant campaign", "illustrated by actual photographs of events", to WSPU branches, and Florence HAIG has left notes of the lecture that accompanied her lantern slides, now lost, that explained the WSPU's campaign. Col BLATHWAYT of Eagle House, Batheaston, had combined his interest in the suffrage cause with his skill as a dedicated amateur gardener and photographer to produce an extremely interesting collection of photographs of visiting suffragettes and suffragists. These photographs, many of which are reproduced in Willmott Dobbie, *A Nest of Suffragettes in Somerset*, 1979, clearly capture the individuality of the women, giving life to their eyes.

An exhibition of press photographs depicting the history of the WSPU was organized by the YOUNG HOT BLOODS and shown at the WSPU Prince's Skating Rink exhibition in May 1909. However, by 1912, the WSPU's image as shown through the lens of press photographers was no longer deemed compatible with the nobility of their cause. An advertisement for a Practical Correspondence Course in Photography in *Votes for Women*, 31 May 1912, noted that "The professional press photographer, who seeks to belittle the cause of the noble women who are fighting for freedom, has done his best to picture us when we are being assaulted by roughs or hustled by the police" and suggested that women should become press photographers. "The dignity of the cause has in some rare cases suffered because pictures of prominent Suffragists have appeared in the newspapers showing these intellectual women with their hats awry and their hair straggling in unkempt coils. . . . It is the dignity of the Suffragist movement that we want to see pictured." The following photographers, mainly professional, did their part to ensure that those prominently involved in the suffrage movement, both militants and constitutionalists, were accorded their due both of dignity and womanliness. By contrast, the photographs of women who had been arrested for causing damage to works of art, issued on sheets by the Metropolitan police to art galleries and museums in 1914, show an alternative image of the reality of a life lived for the cause. Here the women are caught unawares, hair dishevelled, faces on occasion contorted in pain, pinioned by police. Deprived of the shelter of "dignity", they are real flesh and blood. Ironically it would probably have been more difficult for the inspecting warders at the art galleries to identify the wanted women from these photographs than from ones posed in the calmness of the studio with hair and dress clean and tidy.

MISS ALICE BARKER, 21 Kentish Town Road, London NW, photographed Mrs DESPARD.
BASSANO, 25 Old Bond Street, London W, photographed Emmeline PETHICK-LAWRENCE, wearing her "Holloway" badge in September 1910.
ANNIE BELL, Art Photographer, 92 Victoria Street, London SW. Her photographs of WSPU leaders sold well at the Prince's Skating Rink WSPU Exhibition in 1909. She advertised regularly in *Votes for Women* and is not to be confused with another Annie Bell, a very militant member of the WSPU who was arrested on 29 June 1909.
FLORENCE BAXTER, South Croydon, photographed Vera WENTWORTH.
BENNETT-CLARK, Wolverhampton, photographed Emma SPROSON.
ALICE BOUGHTON photographed Beatrice HARRADEN.
E.W. BRADDEN, North Street, Guildford, Surrey, photographed Muriel MATTERS in the Women's Freedom League caravan.
BRINKLEY & SON (GLASGOW) photographed Teresa BILLINGTON-GREIG.
MRS ALBERT BROOM (1863–1939) photographed the WSPU Hyde Park Demonstration, 21 June 1908; NUWSS Pageant of Trades and Professions, April 1909; the WSPU Prince's Skating Rink Exhibition, May 1909; the WSPU "From Prison to Citizenship" Procession, 23 July 1910; the Women's Coronation Procession, June 1911; NUWSS PILGRIMAGE, July 1913. In the late 1920s she photographed Mrs PANKHURST as she neared the end of her life.
Bibliography: D. Atkinson, *Mrs Broom's Suffragette Photographs: Photographs by Christina Broom 1908 to 1913*, no date (1980s).

BYLES ENGRAVERS photographed Lady Constance LYTTON.

LENA CONNELL, started as a photographer c. 1895, while in her teens, and was a winner of the gold medal of the Professional Photographers' Association. She was the first woman photographer who did not restrict herself to photographing women; Fritz Kreisler and Keir HARDIE were among her sitters. She walked in the 21 June 1908 WSPU procession, in the Pageant of Women's Trades and Professions, organized by the LONDON SOCIETY FOR WOMEN'S SUFFRAGE and the ARTISTS' SUFFRAGE LEAGUE on 27 April 1909, attended, as a visitor, a meeting of the FABIAN WOMEN'S GROUP in March 1911 and c. 1913 was a member of the Hampstead branch of the WOMEN'S SOCIAL AND POLITICAL UNION, giving for it a drawing-room meeting. Among the members of the suffrage movement photographed by her were: Mrs PANKHURST, Maud Arncliffe SENNETT, Sarah BENETT, Edith CRAIG, Charlotte DESPARD, Mrs DRUMMOND, Mrs Dacre Fox, Cicely HAMILTON, Beatrice HARRADEN, Evelina HAVERFIELD, twice, Lilian HICKS, Gladice KEEVIL, Lady Constance LYTTON, Muriel MATTERS, Margaret NEVINSON, Evelyn SHARP.

Address: 50 Grove End Road, London NW.
Photograph: The *Vote*, 7 May 1910.
Bibliography: The *Vote*, 7 May 1910; Yevonde, *In Camera*, 1940; V. Williamson, *Women Photographers*, 1986.

MURIEL DARTON, 8 Ribblesdale Road, Hornsey, London N. She advertised in *Votes for Women*, 24 December 1909, noting that she would "be very glad to undertake photographic work of any kind on terms which merely cover the actual cost of materials in all cases where it may be of service in advancing the propaganda work of the WSPU". Her photographs of Theresa GARNETT and Lillian Dove-WILLCOX appeared in *Votes for Women*, 6 August 1909.

DURRANT, Torquay, photographed Elsie HOWEY.

ELLIOT & FRY, 55 & 56 Baker Street, London W, photographed Mrs DESPARD, Mrs PANKHURST, Lady Frances BALFOUR, Georgina BRACKENBURY and Cicely HAMILTON.

FOULSHAM & BAMFIELD, 49 Old Bond Street, London W, photographed Marion HOLMES and Marguerite SIDLEY, both Women's Freedom League organizers.

R.H. FROST, 9 Hartfield Rd, Wimbledon, London SW, photographed Rose Lamartine YATES.

WERNER GOTHARD, Leeds, photographed Mary GAWTHORPE.

A.E. GRAHAM, Redcar, photographed a suffragette meeting at Redcar, 1909.

C. HERMAN, 72 Church Street, Camberwell Green, London SE, photographed Mrs MARTEL.

MARTIN JACOLETTE, 38, 40, 42 Harrington Road, South Kensington, London SW photographed Mrs PANKHURST, wearing her "Holloway" brooch.

KAY, Manchester, photographed Christabel PANKHURST, after October 1907.

F. KEHRHAHN & CO., Bexleyheath, photographed Emmeline PETHICK-LAWRENCE; Vera HOLME (in the costume designed by Sylvia Pankhurst for the WSPU Christmas bazaar, 1911); Mrs PANKHURST; The Trinity (Mr and Mrs Pethick-Lawrence, and Emmeline Pankhurst), and Emily Wilding DAVISON. The firm produced postcards of the WSPU "Prison to Citizenship" procession, 23 July 1910; the WSPU Christmas Bazaar, 1911; and the WSPU summer exhibition, 1913.

VERLAG: F. KREUZER (Munich) photographed Georgina BRACKENBURY.

LAFAYETTE photographed Lady Constance LYTTON, Margaret ASHTON and Helena SWANWICK.

MISS MARIE LEON, 30 Regent Street, SW, photographed Cicely HAMILTON and the portraits for the published edition of her *Pageant of Great Women*.

CONSTANCE MARSDEN photographed Mrs PANKHURST. In August/September 1913 a photograph of Mrs Pankhurst by Constance Marsden, "Portrait of Mrs Emmeline Pankhurst", was accepted by the Royal Photographic Society of Great Britain for an exhibition at the Royal Society of British Artists, Suffolk Street, London W. Constance Marsden was a member of the WSPU; her autograph album containing the signatures of, among others, Emmeline and Christabel PANKHURST and Emily Wilding DAVISON is held in a private collection.

RITA MARTIN photographed Mrs MASSY.

EDITH MATHEW, The County Studio, Towyn, N. Wales, photographed the NUWSS caravan.

MERCHANT PORTRAIT CO., 10 Kentish Town Road, London NW, photographed Alison NEILANS (WFL), Mrs PANKHURST, Lady Constance LYTTON, and the

WSPU band. They also were makers of celluloid badges in the colours, including the artistic green, white and gold of the WFL.

YEVONDE MIDDLETON, who was trained by Lena Connell, photographed Sylvia PANKHURST's grave in Addis Ababa (Mitchell Collection, Museum of London).

Bibliography: Yevonde, *In Camera*, 1940.

W. DENNIS MOSS, Cirencester, photographed Mrs PANKHURST with her car.

MAX PARKES photographed Anne Cobden SANDERSON.

RIBSDALE CLEARE, Lower Clapton Road, London E, photographed Edith How MARTYN.

SCHMIDT, Manchester, photographed Mary GAWTHORPE and Mrs PANKHURST.

ADA SCHOFIELD, 16 Dyke Road, Brighton, Sussex, photographed Helen OGSTON, Mary CLARKE, Isabella McKEOWN and Flora DRUMMOND.

H. SERGEANT, 159 Ladbroke Grove, London W, was a printer and stationer and probably also took the photographs published on postcards of the WSPU's 23 July 1910 "West" procession and a procession to Westminster Abbey, displaying the banners of the church suffrage societies, on 10 November 1910.

IAN SMITH, Edinburgh, photographed Evelina HAVERFIELD as the standard bearer at the suffrage demonstration in Edinburgh 9 October 1909, and other views of the procession.

LIZZIE CASWELL SMITH, 309 Oxford Street, London W. Her father, J. Caswell Smith, was also a photographer. Photographs by Lizzie Caswell Smith of Flora DRUMMOND, Mrs FAWCETT and Christabel PANKHURST appeared on postcards and she regularly advertised in *Votes for Women*.

A & G. TAYLOR, Glasgow, photographed Elizabeth Wolstenholme ELMY, 1907.

TERRY & FRYER, Worcester, photographed Gladice KEEVIL.

WINIFRED TURNER, photograph of WFL caravan on a postcard published by the WFL.

UNDERWOOD & UNDERWOOD STUDIOS, New York, photographed Christabel PANKHURST (in academic robes) and Mrs Emmeline PANKHURST.

G. WEST & SON, Portsmouth, photograph in which the NUWSS banner proclaiming "4103 men of Portsmouth petition for suffrage" is prominently displayed.

LAMBERT WESTON & SON, 29 Brompton Square, and at Dover, and Folkestone, photographed Helen CRAGGS, Annie KENNEY, Christabel PANKHURST (twice) and Mrs PANKHURST.

PILGRIMAGE The idea of holding a "Woman's Suffrage Pilgrimage" was suggested by Katherine HARLEY at a NATIONAL UNION OF WOMEN'S SUFFRAGE SOCIETY sub-committee meeting on 18 April 1913. Although the NUWSS does not appear to have acknowledged a model, it could not have failed to notice the Women's March organized by Florence DE FONBLANQUE that had arrived in London from Edinburgh just five months previously. This, although involving only a few participants (the NUWSS having declined to support it), had resonated with spirituality. In the summer of 1913 this was the quality that the NUWSS recognized it could use to gain public approval and by which it could differentiate itself from the damaging, in all senses, WOMEN'S SOCIAL AND POLITICAL UNION campaign.

The Pilgrimage began on 18 June, having been organized with exemplary speed made possible by the smooth-running system of federations that was by now firmly in place. The NORTH-EASTERN FEDERATION, the NORTH AND EAST RIDINGS FEDERATION, the WEST RIDING FEDERATION, the EAST MIDLAND FEDERATION and the EASTERN COUNTIES FEDERATION travelled the Newcastle to London route. The NORTH-WESTERN FEDERATION, the MANCHESTER AND DISTRICT, the WEST LANCS, WEST CHESHIRE AND NORTH WALES FEDERATION, the WEST MIDLANDS FEDERATION and the OXON, BERKS, BUCKS, AND BEDS FEDERATION travelled on the Carlisle to London route. The SOUTH-WESTERN FEDERATION, the WEST OF ENGLAND FEDERATION, the SURREY, SUSSEX, AND HANTS FEDERATION, and the SOUTH WALES FEDERATION walked the Lands End to London route. The KENTISH FEDERATION made its way through the County of Kent. London was approached by six main routes: from the northwest, by Watling Street, entering London on the two main northern roads, through Highgate and Tottenham; the East Coast Road entering through east London; the Kentish Pilgrim's Way entering London through Blackheath and the south-east; the Brighton Road entering London by Streatham and Brixton; the two west-country roads through

The west-country contingent of the NUWSS Pilgrimage, July 1913. The pilgrims wear the recommended raffia cockades, the red, white and green shoulder sash, and matching haversacks. These, although obviously official, do not correspond to the description that was issued by headquarters. By 1913 dress had become less fitted and hats simpler. The older woman in the foreground, although less up-to-date in her dress sense, sports a "Lands End" arm band. (Author's collection)

Richmond and Hammersmith. The Pilgrimage was confined to England. There had been an intention to hold a Scottish Pilgrimage centring on Edinburgh, but the SCOTTISH FEDERATION decided not to undertake it, "owing to lack of funds and because they did not think it would prove effective in Scotland" (Minutes of the GLASGOW AND WEST OF SCOTLAND ASSOCIATION FOR WOMEN'S SUFFRAGE, 26 May 1913).

Pilgrims were urged to wear a uniform, a concept always close to Katherine Harley's heart. It was suggested that pilgrims should wear white, grey, black, or navy blue coats and skirts or dresses. Blouses were either to match the skirt or to be white. Hats were to be simple, and only black, white, grey, or navy blue. For 3d, headquarters supplied a compulsory raffia badge, a "cockle shell", the traditional symbol of pilgrimage, to be worn pinned to the hat. Also available were a red, white and green shoulder sash, a haversack, made of bright red waterproof cloth edged with green with white lettering spelling out the route travelled, and umbrellas in green or white, or red cotton covers to co-ordinate "civilian" umbrellas. Harriet Blessley recorded that she "Felt very conspicuous in sash and cockade". The Pilgrimage culminated at 5 pm on 26 July at a meeting in Hyde Park, where speakers addressed the throng from 19 platforms representing the 19 federations. The Pilgrimage raised consciousness of the constitutional suffrage movement and £8777. Involvement in the Pilgrimage represented to some members of the constitutional society an experience as unusual and memorable as imprisonment was to members of the WSPU. The result is that accounts of participation in the Pilgrimage have been preserved.

Margory LEES left a very full chronicle of her Pilgrimage from Oldham to London, in which she stressed that participation renewed dedication to the cause, showed the strength of the non-militant suffragists, and succeeded in "visiting the people of this country in their own homes and villages, to explain to them the real meaning of the movement". Her papers include cyclostyled itineraries, revealing how detailed was the organization for each day's travel. Miss Norma Smith was organizer of the Great North Road route travelled by Margory Lees and which Mrs FAWCETT and Frances STERLING joined as star guests. Margaret ASHTON brought her car and picked up stragglers. The Pilgrims were accompanied by a lorry, containing their baggage as well as the "Non-Militant" banners that were so necessary at this time to distinguish them from the WSPU. Thought was given to spectacle and practicality; for the march from Manchester to Stockport all university students and graduates were requested to wear their caps and gowns (but to bring just one suitcase!). Margory Lees and other members of the OLDHAM WOMEN'S SUFFRAGE SOCIETY, travelling with a caravan, set off on 7 July. On 11 July Margory Lees broke her journey, catching a train back to Oldham from Wolverhampton, returning to rejoin the Pilgrimage at Birmingham on 13 July. Both open-air and indoor meetings were arranged *en route* at lunchtime and in the evening. The Pilgrims attended a large indoor meeting in Oxford on 19 July. Mrs Chapman Catt was expected as a speaker, but she failed to turn up; Margaret Ashton spoke in her place and was, according to Margory Lees, very popular. Teas, so necessary for morale, were provided by local individual sympathizers or, as in Stockport, by the Women's Co-operative Guild.

Margory Lees was not very complimentary about the Oxford society's hospitality arrangements, complaints echoed, quite independently, by two other Pilgrims. Mrs Tiffin and E. Murgatroyd wrote to Selina COOPER from Kelsale, Priory Road, High Wycombe, "You were right about the organization of this pilgrimage. We find the Liverpool Pilgrims and Warrington, have had to arrange their own meetings, find places to stay at, on several occasions. One lady from Warrington told us today, that it had cost her six pounds up to now." Selina Cooper's correspondents were taken round some of the colleges by their Oxford hostesses, but then met up with a local friend, a Mr Trotter who told them "that the Labour Party hadnt paid him anything for months they were the biggest lot of snobs in creation, if you'll come back here for a few days I'll show you the other side of Oxford. He said many times it was medicine to see and hear us in the midst of that place of make believe."

The Oldham contingent, with its accompanying caravan, was presumably relieved of the necessity of relying on local hospitality at night. However, the letters of Margaret Greg, who was travelling the same route, to her sister Hilda DOWSON, give another view of the Oldham contingent and their caravans, about which Miss Ashton was less than pleased. Margaret Greg reported that "Miss Darlington says [it] will be a nuisance all the way as you *can't* find caravan pitches in towns". When the caravans could not get down the lane to Buglawton to honour Elizabeth Wolstenholme ELMY, Margaret Greg commented, "As they were going the whole way, the Oldhamers cannot be bullied, but Miss Ashton was very cross." Another pioneer was honoured when, on the way out of Oxford, the pilgrims stopped at Florence Davenport HILL's house at Headington to have their photographs taken. At Thame in the evening their caravans and tents were surrounded by a mob. Margory's mother, Sarah LEES, motored down from Oldham, joined the pilgrims at Beaconsfield and then addressed meetings on the route into London. Once they arrived, the horses were put on a train at St Pancras to travel back to Oldham (it is not clear whether or not the caravans were also thus transported) and the Oldham pilgrims settled into the comforts of the Waverley Hotel in Bloomsbury, next door to the church in which Emily Davison's funeral had so recently taken place.

On 26 July the Watling Street pilgrims assembled at Elgin Avenue, Maida Vale, and the Oldham Suffrage Society banner was carried into Hyde Park, Mrs Lees following in her car. After the meeting Margory Lees and her companions went to Alan's Tea Rooms (*see* HALLS AND RESTAURANTS) for dinner. On the next day, Sunday, she went to a "dull service" at St Pauls, many of the prayers being inaudible. Afterwards, with others, she had tea with Dr Olive Claydon (who in 1911 had given a talk to the Oldham Women's Suffrage Society on "The New Woman") at the Lyceum Club (*see* CLUBS), and then went to the Ethical Church, Queen's Road, where Maude ROYDEN "spoke beautifully on the spirit of the Pilgrimage". The pilgrims returned to Oldham by train the next day. Margory Lees was sufficiently impressed by the experience to preserve all the associated documents and her Pilgrimage diary, in which she gives a list of all the pitches from Congleton to Uxbridge, the parts of the journey that she walked and the parts that she travelled by motor or caravan. She also kept an autograph list of people whom she met on Pilgrimage, including Katherine Harley, and recorded choice remarks about those she encountered on the way.

On 8 July Margaret Greg wrote to her sister that "My verdict on the Pilgrimage is that it is going to do a very great deal of work – the sort of work that has hitherto only been done by towns or at election times is being spread all through the country. Certainly, hereabouts, it is an astonishing advertisement – considering how small it is in actual numbers – and has created a great sensation, though not always in a favourable manner." She noted that the *Manchester Guardian* reports did not reveal how rough some of the meetings were. She described how they had to fight their way into a meeting in Macclesfield through a very hostile crowd and continued, "Mother made a very good but very short Chairman's speech", Miss Ashton surpassed herself and Fenner Brockway's speech reduced her to tears. "Friends of Women's Suffrage cards" were handed out to crowds of mill workers, which were then to be followed up by officers of the local NUWSS society.

Eliza Vaughan of Turners Rayne, Braintree, Essex set out with the East Coast contingent on 19 July, meeting her companions on St John's Green in Colchester. They were escorted on their way, accompanied by a band and by the local police, who were very helpful. The pilgrims distributed pamphlets on their way and held an open-air meeting that evening. Eliza Vaughan commented on the support the pilgrims received from Anglican vicars and Nonconformist ministers along the way, who drew attention to the spiritual side of the women's movement from their pulpits on that Sunday. On Monday the pilgrims walked as far as Mark's Tey, and then divided into two parties, one going straight by the Roman road to Kelvedon, and the other turning aside to attend meetings in Coggeshall and Braintree, from where they marched the next day to rejoin the others at Witham. They met with "antis", who assumed they were militant, in spite of the banner they carried announcing them as "Law-abiding Suffragists". After Witham, they walked to Chelmsford, where they held a "fine" meeting. Afterwards they were attacked by boys, who threw green apples at their horse and wagonette and followed them to their lodgings where, when they stopped, they destroyed the banners they were carrying. There were police in the vicinity but they did not manage to prevent this attack. The next day the pilgrims continued on their way through Ingatestone to Brentwood, where, in the evening, they gave an address from two platforms to large crowds. On Thursday they arrived in Romford, where they were welcomed by a flourishing branch of the CHURCH LEAGUE FOR WOMEN'S SUFFRAGE and invited to a special service at one of the local churches, and afterwards were escorted, with a band, through the streets – "it seemed as if everyone in the town must have seen our banners, and heard our music". The Corn Exchange was so full for their meeting that an overflow meeting was held in the market place. From Romford they travelled by train to Manor Park, where they were met by police, who were to accompany them into London. The daughter of one of the policemen was a member of the NUWSS. The pilgrims addressed a small crowd at Stratford Broadway and then continued to Bow Bridge, where a band was waiting by the side of the old church, "to cheer our way through the dreary stretches of Mile End Road and Whitechapel. Crowds soon collected on either side, all decently-behaved, and apparently interested, but it made one realise more keenly the injustice of woman's position to look upon those degraded, drink-soaked specimens of male humanity, and to think that they possessed a right denied to the ablest and noblest of our sex". She commented of the Hyde Park demonstration that it was a "triumph of organisation". She remained in town and the next day "united with Mrs Fawcett in attending service at St Paul's in the afternoon"; she did not mention if she thought the service inaudible.

The Southampton branch of the NUWSS, usually rather indecisive and ineffectual, appears to have been positively galvanized into action by the thought of the Pilgrimage. A week before it was due to start they held a garden meeting to give it publicity. It was decided not to put up the NUWSS posters as they were considered too small and expensive to be effective in a big town. They did, however, budget £4 for newspaper advertisements "in large type" and for a few advertising bills in town. They offered hospitality to the Bournemouth and New Forest Pilgrims on 18 and 19 July and organized a public meeting on the Common. For this occasion a band was hired (at the cost of £5), "literature" and copies of the *Common Cause* were sold, and members were signed up to the FRIENDS OF WOMEN'S SUFFRAGE scheme. All this was done with rather more gusto than Southampton had been wont to display.

The start of the Pilgrimage from Portsmouth was witnessed by the Portsmouth Unitarian minister and by a young boy, Lancelot Surry, whose mother was a suffrage supporter. He remembered that the attending crowd, "mostly idlers, ne'er-do-wells and urchins, with a sprinkling of respectable working men and women – were in their most repulsive mood and the expressions and oaths hurled at the little band of speakers was, indeed, revolting. There were coarse jokes about trousers, washing and immorality." One of those thus serenaded was Harriet Blessley, who has left a full description of her Pilgrimage. There were nine pilgrims, including Norah O'SHEA, nearly all of them vegetarians, on this first stage of the journey. The Portsmouth pilgrims experienced a considerable amount of hostility and aggravation and Harriet Blessley commented on how helpful the police were, writing, "It is difficult to feel a holy pilgrim when one is called a brazen hussy." She came to the conclusion that she was glad that she was non-militant when she saw the fierce animosity caused by the militants. She was in charge of handing out "literature" and selling the *Common Cause*. She noted that many working women signed "Friends of Suffrage" cards. On their arrival in London the contingent attended a welcoming meeting at Kensington Hall, addressed by Mrs Fawcett, whom Harriet described as "looking like a superior charwoman". Harriet Blessley was very impressed, and relieved, by the size of the crowd that gathered the next day in Hyde Park. Besides the St Paul's and Ethical Church services, suffragist ministers throughout the country took notice of the non-militant suffrage movement in that day's sermon. The sermon preached by the Rev. H.E.B. Speight at Essex Church, The Mall, Notting Hill Gate was reprinted in the *Inquirer* as "The Women's Pilgrimage and its Moral Significance". The Pilgrimage made its moral impact, which was then used by the NUWSS leaders as a reason for asking Asquith to receive a deputation. This, which was received at 10 Downing Street on 8 August, was the first suffrage deputation that the Prime Minister had agreed to see since November 1911. It brought no dramatic change of government policy, but was another stroke in the slow war of attrition waged by the NUWSS. As the organizers of the Women's March had followed up their initiative by founding the QUI VIVE CORPS, so the NUWSS capitalized on the success of the Pilgrimage by founding the ACTIVE SERVICE LEAGUE.

Archival sources: Lees Papers, Oldham Local Studies Library; Margory Lees's Pilgrimage diary, Fawcett Library; Dowson Papers, Nottinghamshire Archives; Papers of Selina Jane Cooper, JP, Lancashire Record Office; Papers of Eliza Vaughan, Essex Record Office; Papers of Harriet Blessley and Papers of Lancelot Surry, Portsmouth Record Office; National Union of Women's Suffrage Societies, Southampton branch Minute Book, 1911–14, Southampton Archives Service.

Bibliography: K.M. Harley, "The Pilgrimage", *Englishwoman*, September 1913; J. Vellacott, *From Liberal to Labour with Women's Suffrage: The Story of Catherine Marshall*, 1993.

PINE, CATHERINE EMILY (1864–1941) Born in Maidstone, she trained as a nurse at St Bartholomew's Hospital from 1895 until 1897. She was described during her training as being "punctual, very kind and attentive, very patient and even tempered, obedient, accurate, and clean and neat in person and work". Ward sisters recorded that "she will make a very good nurse" and that she was "a nice sensible woman". After qualifying she remained at St Bartholomew's, working as a hospital sister from 1900 until June 1907. By 1908, with Nurse Gertrude Townend, who had qualified at St Bartholomew's in 1901 and had subsequently been a Sister at (Great) Ormond Street Hospital, she was running a nursing home in Notting Hill. Nurse Townend was also a WOMEN'S SOCIAL AND POLITICAL UNION activist; on 13 October 1913 she was injured in a tussle with the police at a meeting at Bow Baths Hall at which Sylvia PANKHURST was the speaker. Nurse Pine, as she was always called, was presumably by 1908 a member of the WSPU and it was to her nursing home, then at 3 Pembridge Gardens, in April of that year that Harry, son of Emmeline PANKHURST, was taken when he first fell seriously ill. Herbert Mills, husband of Ernestine MILLS, was the doctor in attendance then and in October when Harry, having contracted poliomyelitis, was returned to the nursing home. He died in Nurse Pine's new premises at no. 9 in January 1910. The nursing home was by this time being used by suffragettes recovering from imprisonment and after the passing of the "Cat and Mouse" Act in 1913 it was to there that "mice" went to be nursed. The nursing home was, however, unable to compromise its acceptability to the authorities by allowing "mice" to escape from its premises.

In 1913 on the occasions on which Mrs Pankhurst was released from prison as the result of a hunger strike, Nurse Pine was her devoted attendant. Her own nursing home was so besieged by detectives and onlookers that, in order to maintain the calm necessary to the recovery of her patients and in order that she should not lose clients and thereby jeopardize her business, Nurse Pine looked after Mrs Pankhurst, in London, at Hertha AYRTON's house and the BRACKENBURYS' house, "Mouse Castle", and, in the country, watched by detectives, at Ethel SMYTH's house, the "Coign", in Surrey. Dr Flora MURRAY was the doctor entrusted with the care of Mrs Pankhurst at this time and was in attendance also at Nurse Pine's nursing home.

In 1915 Mrs Pankhurst resolved to set up a hostel in which to care for (illegitimate) "war babies". It was housed first in Mecklenburgh Square and then, in 1916, at 50 Clarendon Road, London W. In 1917 when it moved to Tower Cressy (a house originally designed as his family home by Christopher Dresser, and described by Annie KENNEY's husband as a "wonderful, wonderful house", "almost a dream castle") it was Nurse Pine who, with two of Annie Kenney's sisters, was in charge. In 1920 she joined Mrs Pankhurst in America; Kitty MARION claimed that the two of them "cut" her when they met by chance on a New York street. In 1921 Nurse Pine went to Canada with Mrs Pankhurst and three of the adopted "war babies" to live first in Victoria and then in Toronto. After Christabel PANKHURST and her adopted daughter joined them in the summer of 1922 the atmosphere changed and Nurse Pine returned to England in 1923. She apparently never saw Mrs Pankhurst again, although the two maintained a correspondence. Nurse Pine was present at Emmeline Pankhurst's funeral. In her will Nurse Pine left a financial bequest, and her gramophone, to Gertrude Townend, her suffragette medal to "the History Section of the British College of Nursing", and her "suffrage books and photographs pertaining to the 'Votes for Women' campaign to the Women's Social and Political Club". The latter now form part of the SUFFRAGETTE FELLOWSHIP Collection held by the Museum of London.

Address: (1894) c/o Rev. F.J. Hammond, St Cyprian's Parsonage, Brockley, London SE; (1908) 3 Pembridge Gardens, London W; (1909) 9 Pembridge Gardens, London W (which, incidentally had been in the 1880s the home of Netta Franklin, aunt of Hugh, and in 1916–17 president of the NUWSS); (1939) The Firs Bungalow, Temple Ewell, Dover; (1941) St Neots, Home St., Frindsburg, Rochester, Kent.
Photograph: in Suffragette Fellowship Collection, Museum of London, which also contains an interesting photograph of the room in Pembridge Gardens in which Mrs Pankhurst was nursed. The walls of the room can be "read" for the prints and photographs with which they are decorated.
Archival source: Nurse Pine Collection, Museum of London; Archives, The Royal Hospitals NHS Trust.
Bibliography: E. Smyth, *Female Pipings in Eden*, 1933.

PINNER (WSPU) Secretary (1913) Mrs Janie TERRERO, Rockstone House, Pinner, Middlesex.

PLAYS The potential of drama for propaganda purposes had been recognized early in the women's suffrage campaign. In a letter to the *Women's Suffrage Journal*, 1 September 1873, "E.M.L." wrote, "Is there no playwright among the friends of women's suffrage? The stage ought to be the most powerful of secular educators. The woman question is capable of a thoroughly dramatic treatment". On 2 February 1889 a joint letter from Alice Cliff SCATCHERD and Agnes SUNLEY appeared in the *Women's Penny Paper* explaining that they were often called upon to give recitations and "would be grateful if your readers can recommend to us, narratives in prose or verse, specially the latter, telling of the devotion of women to some public cause, of loyalty to other women, to their country, to some truth which wants vindicating; rather than of devotion to individuals or church. . . . Public recitation is a valuable means of education on the women's question which should be diligently used". Laurence HOUSMAN (*see under* SONGS, MUSIC AND POETRY) provided the suffrage campaign with its most popular monologue and a plethora of playwrights rallied, belatedly, to the call, producing a prodigious number of plays. The ACTRESSES' FRANCHISE LEAGUE, through its Play Department, ran a publishing programme, concentrating on one-act plays with a small cast list, suitable for slotting in as propaganda in an evening's amateur entertainment. In *Victory – and After*, 1920, Millicent FAWCETT noted that while some plays, for example *How the Vote Was Won*, *Votes for Women* and *Press Cuttings*, were "propaganda plays pure and simple, and very good propaganda, too, extremely witty and amusing", there were others by Sir James Barrie, Arnold Bennett, and many by Bernard Shaw, that were "even more telling because a good deal more subtle in method". The following list includes only those that are directly related to the women's suffrage campaign. There are, in addition, a number of other plays, the names of which are known, but which it has proved impossible to locate or to check their content.

ALLEN, Inglis, *The Suffragette's Redemption*, French's Acting Edition, 1913.
ANCKETILL, Henry, *The Case in a Nutshell: a dramatic dialogue on woman's franchise* (for three characters), P. Davis & Sons, printers, Durham, *c.* 1890.
ANON, *Helping the Cause*, 1912. Lillie Langtry appeared in this sketch at the Coliseum in February 1912.
ARNCLIFFE SENNETT, H., *An Englishwoman's Home*, Actresses' Franchise League, 1911.
BALLYNN, Deane, *The Price of Freedom: a Tale of Today, creating an entirely new literary form and an introduction thereto*, W. Scott, 1910.
BENNETT, P.R., *Mary Edwards – an anachronism in one act*, published by the Actresses' Franchise League, 1911. Produced by Miss Horniman's company at the Gaiety Theatre, Manchester on 8 May 1911.
BENSUSAN, Inez, *The Apple: an episode of today in one act*, published by Actresses' Franchise League, 1911.
CHAPIN, Alice, *At the Gates*, 1910 (she was a member of the AFL and of the Women's Freedom League, was sentenced to four months' imprisonment in November 1909, for having, with Alison Neilans, poured fluid into a ballot box at the Bermondsey by-election.)
CHAPIN, Alice and COLLINS, Mabel, *Outlawed: a drama in three Acts*, performed at the Royal Court in November 1911. The play is based on the novel by Charlotte Despard and Mabel Collins, *Outlawed: A Novel on the Woman Suffrage Question*, H.J. Drane, 1908.
CHOLMONDELEY, Mary, *Votes for Men a Dialogue*, 1909 – appeared in *Cornhill Magazine*, December 1909.
COWEN, Louis, *Unexpected Circumstances*, performed by the AFL, 1910.
CRAWLEY, E.A., *The Suffragette*. Performed in Birmingham on 18 April 1908.
CRAWLEY, Muriel, *The Cause and Lady Peggy*, 1909.
CUDMORE, Angela and DAVEY, Peter, *We Dine at Seven; sketch for two ladies*, Samuel French, 1909.
DALTON, John Philip, *The Suffragette*, 1909. He was vicar of St Paul's, Forest Hill, London SE. The play was first produced in his church hall on 19 November, 1908.
DANCE, George, *The Suffragette*, 1907. A musical.
DIX, Frank, *Signposts*, 1912.
DORYYNNE, Jess, *Surprise of His Life*, 1912. She was a member of the AFL and had been abandoned by Edy CRAIG's brother, Gordon, when pregnant with his child.
DOUGLAS, G.A.H., *Rab Hewison defeats the Suffragettes, and other readings*, no date. A recitation.
DUGDALE, Joan, *Clowning Street*, 1913. She was organizing secretary of the Actresses' Franchise League (*see* Una DUGDALE).
ESMOND, Henry Vernon, *Her Vote: a comedy in one act*, 1910. The author was the husband of Eva MOORE.
GARLAND, Alison, *The Better Half*, 1913, published by *Daily Post*, Liverpool, 1913. Copies of the play could be obtained from her sister, Miss E.A. Garland, Pengwerne Terrace, New Brighton (*see* Alison GARLAND).
GLOVER, Evelyn, *A Chat with Mrs Chicky: a duologue*, published by AFL, 1912; *Mrs Appleyard's Awakening: a play in one act*, published by AFL, 1911; *Showin' Samyel*, a suffrage recitation, 1914.
GROSSMITH, George, *The Suffrage Girl*. *Votes for Women*, 10 March 1910, mentions this "dainty musical comedy" at the Court Theatre and comments, "All

allusions to the Suffrage are quite sympathetic, and mark the great change that has come over the playgoing public". It was a sketch in the *Coronation Revue*, "By George". George Grossmith's wife had subscribed to the CENTRAL AND EAST OF ENGLAND SOCIETY FOR WOMEN'S SUFFRAGE in 1897.

HAMILTON, Cicely, *Anti-Suffrage Waxworks*, first performed at a Women's Freedom League bazaar in March/April 1908 (*see* Cicely HAMILTON). It included *The Ideal Woman, The Early Victorian Maiden, Queen Elizabeth, The Objector, The Policeman* and *The Suffragette*. It was shown at the WFL Pageant in Swansea in 1910 when the "Showman" was played by Cicely Hamilton and "Alexander" was played by Erick Cleeves (*see* Mary CLEEVES).

HAMILTON, Cicely, *A Pageant of Great Women*, published by the Suffrage Shop, 1910. First performed at the Scala Theatre on 10 November 1909 (*see* Cicely HAMILTON).

HAMILTON, Cicely, *The Home Coming*, 1910.

HAMILTON, Cicely and ST JOHN, Christopher, *How the Vote was Won*, published by the Woman's Press, 1909. It was produced for the first time at the Royalty Theatre, 13 April 1909, when the cast included Nigel Playfair, Athene Seyler, Winifred MAYO and Beatrice Forbes Robertson. It was very popular with local suffrage societies, performed, for instance, at a meeting of the Bedford Women's Suffrage Society in December 1912. In March 1914 it was staged at the Kunstlerhaus Theatre in Berlin, by German suffragists.

HAMILTON, Cicely and ST JOHN, C., *Pot and Kettle*, 1909.

HARKNESS, Mrs A. Lawson, *Votes for Women. A Suffragette Comedy in One Act*, Abel Heywood & Son, Manchester, c. 1909.

HARRADEN, Beatrice, *Lady Geraldine's Speech*, 1909. It was originally written for the NUWSS, but was not performed because the characters in the play were supporters of WSPU. It was published in *Votes for Women*, 2 April 1909 (*see* Beatrice HARRADEN) and then by the Woman's Press.

HARRADEN, Beatrice and HATTON, Bessie, *The Outcast*, 1909 (*see* Bessie HATTON).

HARVEY, Josephine, see L. Morton, below.

HATTON, Bessie, *Before Sunrise*. Its private printing was organized by Edith Craig. It was first produced on 11 December 1909 at the Albert Hall Theatre and was then performed at the WSPU Christmas bazaar.

HEATHCOTE, Arthur M., *A Junction*, published by AFL, 1913.

HERRINGHAM, Mrs and HODGSON, Miss, *Granny's Decision: a Duologue*, performed at WFL bazaar in March/April 1908. Caroline Hodgson was one of the founding members of the WFL in 1907, having resigned from the WSPU. (*See* Christiana HERRINGHAM.)

HOLMES, Marion, *Brass and Clay*. (*See* Marion HOLMES.)

HOUSMAN, L., *Lysistrata*, published by the Woman's Press, 1911. *Votes for Women*, 17 March 1911, included an advertisement for this "clever and up-to-date paraphrase of Aristophanes".

HOUSMAN, Laurence, *Alice in Ganderland*, published by the Woman's Press, 1911. The AFL put on a performance at the Lyceum in October 1911; on the same bill were scenes from Ibsen's *The Doll's House* and a *Pageant of the Leagues*, which included individuals or groups symbolizing all the suffrage societies.

HUTCHINSON, M.F., *When Woman Rules: a merry comedy for girls, in two acts*, Joseph Williams, 1908.

JENNINGS, Gertrude, *A Woman's Influence*, published by AFL, 1913.

JEROME, Jerome K., *The Master of Mrs Chilvers: an improbable comedy*, published in Plays of To-day and Tomorrow series, 1911. Lena ASHWELL played the lead in its first production at the Royalty Theatre in April 1911.

JONES, Henry Arthur, *The Case of Rebellious Susan: a comedy in three acts*, Chiswick Press, 1894. Reprinted by Macmillan, 1897, 1901, Samuel French, 1909.

MARGETSON, W.H., *A Suffrage Tableau*, a joint production of AFL and Women Writers' Suffrage League on 12 November 1909. The tableau was based on the painting by Margetson that he produced for the WWSL.

MCLEOD, Irene Rutherford, *Reforming of Augustus*, 1910. (*See* DRUMMERS' UNION *and* YOUNG PURPLE, WHITE, AND GREEN CLUB.)

MILMAN, Rita, *A Suffrage Episode*, a sketch written for performance at the Prince's Rink May 1909 exhibition.

MOFFAT, Graham, *The Maid and the Magistrate. A duologue in one act*, AFL, 1913. Performed at GLASGOW

MEN'S LEAGUE FOR WOMEN'S SUFFRAGE At Home in November 1909 and at WSPU Christmas bazaar 1911.

MORTON, L. (pseudonym of Josephine Harvey), *Deeds Not Words*, performed at the April 1910 Glasgow WSPU Exhibition. According to Edith Craig, Josephine Harvey was a young writer from Bournemouth.

MOUILLOT, Gertrude, *The Master*, 1909. The author was a member of the AFL.

NEVINSON, Margaret, *In the Workhouse*, published by the International Suffrage Shop, 1911. (*See* Margaret NEVINSON.)

NEWMARCH, E., *Cynthia; a suffragette, comedietta in one act*, Drane's, c. 1910.

NIGHTINGALE, Miss H.M., *A Change of Tenant*, c. 1909. Helen Margaret Nightingale was a member of the AFL. Isabella FORD took part in a production of the play staged by the LEEDS WOMEN'S SUFFRAGE SOCIETY.

PADDEY, W.G., *The Suffragette*, C. Arthur Pearson, c. 1910. A play for one male, three females.

PALMER, T.A., *Women's Rights: a comedietta (in one act and in prose)*, Lacy's Acting Edition, 1884.

PAULL, H.M., *An Anti-suffragist, or The Other Side: a monologue in one act*, published by AFL, 1913.

PHIBBS., Mrs Harlow, *The Rack*, 1912; *The Mother's Meeting: a monologue*, published by AFL, 1913.

PHIBBS, L.S., *Jim's Leg: a monologue*, 1911.

ROBINS, Elizabeth, *Votes for Women!: a play in three acts*. The play was in production at the Court Theatre on 9 April 1907. It was published by Mills & Boon, 1909.

"S", *Lady Butterby and Mrs MacBean*, c. 1912.

ST CLAIR, Oswald, *Ladies' Logic: a dialogue between a suffragette and a mere man*, Digby Long, 1907.

SEXTON, James, *The Riot Act*, Constable, 1914.

SHAW, Bernard, *Press Cuttings: a topical sketch compiled from the editorial and correspondence columns of the daily papers*, Constable, 1909. The play was first performed "privately" in London in July 1909, and given a public performance at Miss Horniman's theatre in Manchester in September. The rights for London performances were vested in the LONDON SOCIETY FOR WOMEN'S SUFFRAGE, for whom it had been written, and provincial performances in the AFL. It was for a time banned by the Censor.

SHAW, Bernard, *Fanny's First Play*, 1911. Performed for the first time at the Little Theatre in the Adelphi, 19 April 1911.

SHEEY SKEFFINGTON, Frank, *The Prodigal Daughter*, 1915.

SMILEY, G.R., *Petticoat-Utopia or When the Women Rule*, H.E. Morgan, 1910. "A topical comedy (partly musical)".

SUTRO, Alfred, *The Perplexed Husband: a comedy in four acts*, Samuel French, 1913. First performed on 12 September 1911 at Wyndham's Theatre, when the cast included Gerald du Maurier and Athene Seyler. Reviewed in *Votes for Women*, 22 September 1911.

THORNE, George, *The Suffragettes*, 1909. Staged at the Middlesex Music Hall, Drury Lane, in February 1909 by Miss Ada Francis and Company.

TONSLEY, C.J., *Sir Robin Hall; or, the Fairy Suffragettes, Opera fantastic in 4 acts*, libretto by C.J. Tonsley, music by C.E. Cowlrick, Boosey & Co., 1912.

VAUGHAN, Gertrude, *The Woman with the Pack*, published by W.J. Hams-Smith, 1912. It was performed at the WSPU Christmas bazaar, 1911.

WADHAM, Millicent, *Ideal Woman*, 1912. It was probably published by the London Society for Women's Suffrage.

WARD, Mrs J., *Man and Woman*, published by the author, c. 1908. The play was performed, for the first time in London, under the auspices of the HAMMERSMITH WSPU, on 23 April 1908. An advertisement in *Votes for Women*, 19 January 1912, described the play as dealing "with all the main arguments for Votes for Women, in all classes and conditions". (*See* Mary WARD.)

WENTWORTH, Vera, *An Allegory*, published by AFL, 1913. It may be synonymous with Vera Wentworth's *The Awakening* (performed at the WSPU Christmas bazaar, 1911). *An Allegory* was certainly staged by suffragette prisoners in Holloway in March 1912. (*See* Vera WENTWORTH.)

Bibliography: J. Holledge, *Innocent Flowers: Women in the Edwardian Theatre*, 1981; D. Spender and C. Hayman, *How the Vote Was Won and Other Suffragette Plays*, 1985; S. Stowell, *A Stage of Their Own: Feminist Playwrights of the Suffrage Era*, 1992; K. Cockin, "Women's Suffrage Drama", in M. Joannou and J. Purvis, *The Women's Suffrage Movement: New Feminist Perspectives*, 1998.

POCHIN, AGNES, MRS (1825–1908) Youngest daughter of George and Hannah Heap of Timperley,

Cheshire. In 1852 she married, at the Unitarian Cross Street Chapel in Manchester, Henry Davis Pochin, an industrial chemist who was later to become Liberal MP for Stafford, a seat later held by his son-in-law Charles McLaren. Agnes Pochin's sister was the widow of Pochin's erstwhile business partner. H.D. Pochin was a radical Liberal, part of the coterie (*see* Appendix) surrounding Garibaldi, for whom he at one time organized a financial loan. In 1855, as "Justitia", Agnes Pochin wrote *The Right of Women to Exercise the Elective Franchise*, which was published by John Chapman. In later years Elizabeth Wolstenholme ELMY, who was still in correspondence with Agnes Pochin in 1906, noted that this pamphlet was the next work on women's suffrage, in order of appearance, after Harriet TAYLOR's essay *The Enfranchisement of Women*, which had been published in the *Westminster Review* in July 1851. Although both Elizabeth Wolstenholme Elmy and Helen BLACKBURN held the tract in high regard and although it was reprinted, under Mrs Pochin's own name, in 1873 for the NATIONAL SOCIETY FOR WOMEN'S SUFFRAGE, it has been overlooked by most twentieth-century commentators. In it Agnes Pochin wrote, "If laws are made, affecting our persons, property, and children; if taxes are imposed, which we have to pay; if other classes enjoy certain privileges which we do not; it *is* very natural to take some interest in such matters, and ask the reason why". She argues cogently, with verve and wit, that women should have the right to the parliamentary franchise on the same conditions as men; that women should be given the municipal franchise; that mere sex should be considered no barrier in the recognition of talent, or its advancement in the social scale. She also considered that women should have the right to the same terms as men in divorce; that marriage should not necessarily put a stop to a career previously marked out for a woman; and that the education of women should train them for a career.

> Woman's life in the middle classes is, and has been rendered essentially a dull one. The necessity she is thought to be under of confining herself almost exclusively to one spot; the little variety she sees, whether of scene or character; the small number of her Creator's works upon which she is permitted to render her perceptive faculties; her entire withdrawal from the investigation of her Creator's laws; the necessity she is under of conforming to a stereotyped conventional standard of character; and the dedication of so considerable a portion of her time to a mere series of mechanical details of the humblest class (I call them humble and mechanical, because they merely take time, and leave the faculties unexercised); all combine to produce what may be emphatically designated a dull life.

In 1858 when John Bright introduced his Reform Bill Agnes Pochin tried to persuade him to include a clause on women's suffrage, but he declined, saying that, although he knew no argument against women's suffrage, he thought the existing state of public opinion would mitigate against the success of such a notion and would harm the cause of reform. Rather surprisingly, Agnes Pochin did not sign the 1866 women's suffrage petition. It is extremely unlikely that this omission was due to anything other than mischance; perhaps she was away from home when signatures were gathered. She would have by then been known to Jacob and Ursula BRIGHT and more than likely known by Elizabeth Wolstenholme Elmy, who was responsible for gathering many of the Manchester signatures. In any case, by 14 April 1868 Agnes Pochin was a leading protagonist in the Manchester suffrage campaign, sitting on the platform of the Free Trade Hall in Manchester at the first public meeting held to discuss women's suffrage. She spoke publicly, introducing the second resolution of the evening: "That this meeting expresses its cordial approval of the objects of the National Society for Women's Suffrage, and of the course it has hitherto pursued, and pledges itself to support the future efforts by all practical and constitutional methods, especially by urging women possessing legal qualifications to claim to be put on the Parliamentary register". Her husband, now mayor of Salford, chaired the meeting. Her presence on the platform did not pass uncriticized. On 17 April Lydia BECKER replied to a correspondent, Sarah Jackson, who had accused Mrs Pochin of disobeying the Scriptures by neglecting her family to attend the suffrage meeting. Lydia Becker defended Agnes Pochin, writing, "Mrs Pochin is a most devoted wife and mother. They are a model couple as regards happiness ... [she] isn't leaving her children to cry out in their cots, if they were that way disposed". In fact it appears that the Pochins' young daughter Laura (*see* Laura McLaren) probably attended the meeting.

In 1869, putting the resolution she had proposed into practice, Agnes Pochin paid for the organization of a petition of 870 Salford women and, in consequence of the arguments she and her husband put forward, 1248 women were added to the borough parliamentary register. When two major appeals on the point were heard, the Pochins bore the costs. In 1870 and 1871 Agnes Pochin subscribed to the Manchester National Society for Women's Suffrage and in 1872 was a member of the newly formed executive committee of the Central Committee for Women's Suffrage. Speaking on 15 January 1872 at the first general meeting of the Central Committee, H.D. Pochin declared "This question has as good a foundation as the temperance question or as the free trade question; no one who has thought about it can doubt of its ultimate success, and I for my part am convinced that this meeting will be looked back to as marking a great epoch in the history of the Constitution of the British Empire." At a public meeting held by the Committee in July 1872 Agnes Pochin, who was no less radical than her husband, remarked that she thought "it would be well on some future occasion to make some appeal to [the working classes], and elect some working men on the Committee". In 1873 the Pochins gave £50 each to the Manchester Society and the Central Committee. In 1875 Mr Pochin gave £25 to the Manchester Society.

In 1892 Agnes Pochin joined the council of the newly formed Women's Emancipation Union, donated £10 to the WEU and £5 towards the cost of the circulation of Harriet McIlquham's pamphlet *The Enfranchisement of Women: An Ancient Right, A Modern Need*. From internal evidence it would seem that she gave money to the WEU in September 1897; Elizabeth Wolstenholme Elmy writes that "she had done splendid work". Agnes Pochin maintained her links with the mainstream suffrage societies, donating, in 1900–1901, £10 to the Central and East of England Society, £10 to the Central and Western Society and then £20 to the amalgamated Central Society.

Agnes Pochin was concerned with all aspects of the women's movement. In the early 1850s her husband founded the Salford Working Men's College and by 1860 Agnes Pochin was teaching classes of girls there. The College later ran a school for girls. When in 1892 Agnes Pochin launched HM Warship *Revenge* at Jarrow the *Woman's Herald* (3 December) reported that she took the opportunity to allude to "the silence the Church had imposed on women, and then proceeded to show the part women had played in maritime enterprise". In 1870 the Pochins left Salford and moved, to be nearer the House of Commons, to Barn Elms in south-west London. In 1874 they bought the Bodnant estate in the Conwy valley, which was eventually inherited by their daughter, Laura McLaren, their surviving son, the male heir, proving unsatisfactory.

Address: (1852) Bank Place, Salford; (1868) Broughton Old Hall, Salford; (1870) Barn Elms, Barnes, London SW; (1874) Bodnant Hall, Denbighshire.

Portrait: by Isabel Dacre in Bodnant Hall collection; by Duval (of Manchester) – mention is made of this portrait in Priscilla Bright McLaren's will (for whom Laura McLaren had made a copy, which she left to Esther Bright Clothier).

Photograph: (with H.D. Pochin) in H.T. Milliken, *The Road to Bodnant*, 1975.

Archival source: Women's Suffrage Collection, Manchester Central Library; Elizabeth Wolstenholme Elmy Papers, British Library.

Bibliography: H.T. Milliken, *The Road to Bodnant*, 1975.

POLICE The militant women's suffrage campaign, whatever else its effect, did for eight years, 1906–14, occupy a great deal of police time. The earliest police report in the Home Office files is of the disturbance in Downing Street on 9 March 1906. Despite the police having taken details of all the women involved, the Prime Minister, Campbell-Bannerman, refused to press charges. By 23 October the police in Plaistow were sufficiently aware of the Women's Social and Political Union's propensity for disruption, to keep observation at the local underground station and send to the Metropolitan Police a telegram notice of the movements of "about 30 women suffragettes". Thus alerted, plain-clothes policemen from Cannon Row were at the House of Commons, already able to recognize such ring leaders as Mrs Pankhurst, Mrs Pethick-Lawrence, Mrs Montefiore, Mrs Despard and

Mrs Cobden SANDERSON. The police were again in readiness in Westminster to meet the 300–400 women who gathered on 13 February 1907, on the occasion of the first Women's Parliament. The arrests took place about 9 pm; the police rejected allegations of brutality. The conjuction of policemen and suffragettes had by now entered the comic repertoire. Maud Arncliffe SENNETT in her suffrage scrapbook annotated a 1907 *Punch* cartoon, which showed policemen holding battered women in the air, with "This is the sort of 'humour' women are expected to appreciate."

By April 1907 plain-clothes policemen from Rochester Row police station were keeping a watch on Clement's Inn, attending WSPU meetings and reporting back. By 1909 the Home Office was forced to give serious consideration to the protection of ministers. The Special Branch of the Criminal Investigation Department was given the task, and there was discussion within the Home Office as to what department should pay for this extra policing. On 9 September 1909, a few days after Asquith had been accosted by Elsie HOWEY, Jessie KENNEY and Vera WENTWORTH at Lympne in Kent, the Home Secretary addressed a memorandum to Sir Edward Troup, the chief of police:

> I think it should be considered whether the time has not come for special police organization for countering suffragette violence... There are some specially active centres which supply or supplement disorderly women in localities lacking the article. There are some women who from nervous excitability or otherwise are specially dangerous. Where did the Lympne gang come from? Who housed and cooperated with them at Hythe? It is not enough to deal with these people if and when they come. We ought to know what they are up to locally and all the more dangerous should be known...

By July 1910 arrangements had been made for any person standing outside a minister's house or near to him in the street, whether or not they were causing a nuisance, to be cautioned and if they did not leave, to be liable to arrest. The police were instructed to act with firmness as well as tact.

Police action on "Black Friday", 18 November 1910, marked a watershed in the relationship between the militant suffrage movement and the police. H.N. BRAILSFORD's memorandum "The Treatment of Women's Deputations by the Police" included a considerable weight of evidence to support the allegations of unnecessary violence and indecency, both of usage and language, towards the women who gathered that evening in Parliament Square. The window-smashing tactic was adopted to hasten, by giving clear cause, the actual moment of arrest, otherwise the women were pushed and battered before it was judged that they had committed sufficient "obstruction". The report from the police commissioner revealed that that evening 22 arrests were made in the first hour, 30 during the second, 31 during the third, 6 during the fourth and 27 during the fifth, each arrest involving two police constables, who then had to stay at the police station until all the formalities had been completed.

By January 1912 the police had instructions to arrest all persons taking part in these organized disorders as soon as lawful occasion was thought to exist. "Any act of obstruction, assaulting or pushing the police in an endeavour to force the cordon constitutes a lawful occasion, especially when the deliberate purpose of the offenders is notorious. The Police are not to allow the women to exhaust themselves in repeated rushes at the entrance to Palace Yard or elsewhere. One rush, one arrest is to be the rule." Such was the disruption caused by the 4 March 1912 window-smashing campaign and the crowds that gathered that evening in Parliament Square that the police had to work late into the night; the lift attendant at New Scotland Yard was paid five hours' overtime.

As well as providing the thick blue line, protecting parliament and ministers, the police were also very necessary to protect both militant and constitutional suffrage speakers from the ravages of mocking crowds. Anecdotes of CARAVAN tours and the National Union of Women's Suffrage Societies' PILGRIMAGE reveal how grateful women were for a police presence. It is clear that payment to the police was an item that had to be considered when striking accounts for a meeting; Mary Ann RAWLE costed in the police presence at 6s 5d for one meeting. As militancy increased, the CID intensified its attendance at WSPU meetings, took down verbatim reports of speeches and forwarded them to the

Home Office. In May 1913 a pantechnicon was used by the police when they raided Lincoln's Inn House to load up and carry away WSPU paper work, none of which was, apparently, returned. Presumably a considerable amount of police time was expended on reading through this mixture of correspondence and accounts. Police inspectors acquainted with the appearance of "mice" were sent around the country, posted at WSPU meetings, in order to aid the local police with identification. Photographs of "wanted" suffragettes were also exchanged; Frances PARKER's photograph was sent to New Scotland Yard by the Edinburgh police and New Scotland Yard thanked the Scottish Prison Commissioners for a photograph of Helen CRAWFURD. Sheets of photographs of suffragettes deemed most dangerous to works of art were sent to museums and art galleries. Except in cases where the culprits were caught red-handed slashing pictures or firing buildings, it is clear from the detailed table compiled by A.E. Metcalfe in *Woman's Effort*, 1917, that the police did not have much success in detecting the perpetrators. Not all police work was undercover. A Home Office file contains a copy of the WSPU Seventh Annual report (1913), which is annotated by the policeman on the beat to the effect that he had entered Lincoln's Inn House in order to buy it. The printed lists of subscribers was doubtless then studied in order to identify sympathizers. Inspectors Jarvis and Riley, and Superintendent P. Quinn were the policemen who, in London, took primary responsibility for dealing with the effects of the militant campaign. Inspector Jarvis attended a SUFFRAGETTE FELLOWSHIP reunion dinner in 1936.

Archival source: Home Office Papers, Public Record Office.

Bibliography: *Treatment of Women's Deputations by the Police*, evidence collected by Dr Jessie Murray and Mr Brailsford (Woman's Press pamphlet), no date (1912); C. Morrell, *"Black Friday": Violence against Women in the Suffragette Movement*, 1981.

POLLOKSHIELDS (WFL) Was in existence in 1910. Honorary secretary, Lavinia Stewart, 4 Hampden Terrace, Pollokshields.

PONTYPOOL AND GRIFFITHSTOWN (WSPU) Secretary (1913) Miss Wilton, Trefloyd, Pontypool, Gwent.

PONTYPRIDD (NUWSS) In 1913 the society was a member of the SOUTH WALES AND MONMOUTH FEDERATION OF THE NATIONAL UNION OF WOMEN'S SUFFRAGE SOCIETIES. Secretary (1909, 1913) Mrs Parry, Eirlanfa, Pontypridd, Mid Glamorgan.

POPLAR (WSPU) This was the second branch of the WSPU to be formed in London, *c*. March 1906. Secretary (1906) Mrs Ensor, 49 Ontario Buildings, Preston's Road, Poplar, London E.

PORTISHEAD WOMEN'S SUFFRAGE SOCIETY (NUWSS) Formed in December 1913 and joined the WEST OF ENGLAND FEDERATION OF THE NATIONAL UNION OF WOMEN'S SUFFRAGE SOCIETIES. Miss Tanner, from the BRISTOL AND WEST OF ENGLAND SOCIETY FOR WOMEN'S SUFFRAGE, came to a meeting of the Portishead society, to give advice about stationery, to advise all members to take the *Common Cause* and to try to enlist people as FRIENDS OF WOMEN'S SUFFRAGE. In May 1914 members of the Portishead society were strongly resistant to the proposed ACTIVE SERVICE LEAGUE. After the outbreak of war the society involved itself in opening a "School for Mothers". In June 1915 the society passed a resolution "that the Propaganda of the National Union should be directed to Women's Suffrage only and approves the action of the executive committee at headquarters, in declining to sanction the official representations of the National Union at the Conference recently held at The Hague". The Society supported the "Millicent Fawcett Hospital" in Russia during the war, and carried on meeting and supporting pressure for the inclusion of women in electoral reform at the end of the war. In May 1918 it turned itself into the Portishead Women's Citizenship Association.

Secretary (1913) Miss Butterworth.

Archival source: Minute Book of the Portishead Society for Women's Suffrage, in a private collection.

PORTSMOUTH (NUWSS) In 1913 the society was a member of the SURREY, SUSSEX, AND HANTS FEDERATION OF THE NATIONAL UNION OF WOMEN'S SUFFRAGE SOCIETIES and had branches at Cosham and Gosport. Secretary (1909, 1913) Miss Norah O'SHEA, The Cottage, Cosham, Hampshire. An office was opened in 1913 at 2 Kent Road, Southsea, Portsmouth, Hampshire.

Bibliography: S. Peacock, *Votes for Women: The Women's Fight in Portsmouth*, 1983.

PORTSMOUTH branch of the UNITED SUFFRAGISTS Formed in 1917. Honorary secretary: Norah O'SHEA, The Cottage, Cosham, Portsmouth, Hampshire.

PORTSMOUTH (WFL) Secretary (1913) Mrs Whetton, 64 Devonshire Avenue, Southsea, Portsmouth, Hampshire.
Bibliography: S. Peacock, *Votes for Women: The Women's Fight in Portsmouth*, 1983.

PORTSMOUTH (WSPU) Secretary Miss Peacock (1910) 7 Craneswater Ave, Southsea; (1913) 4 Pelham Road, Portsmouth. A description of WSPU activities around Portsmouth is given in Lancelot Surry's typescript autobiography in Portsmouth Record Office.
Bibliography: S. Peacock, *Votes for Women: The Women's Fight in Portsmouth*, 1983.

POSTCARDS The increased activity of the women's suffrage campaign in the early years of the twentieth century coincided with the golden age of the postcard. At a pragmatic level, frequent posts (and the paucity of telephones) meant that a short message on a postcard, for which the stamp cost only a halfpenny, was a favoured means of communication. In addition, by 1905 a craze for postcard collecting was in full swing, fuelling an explosion in the number of postcard publishers, who used their ingenuity to devise material that would appeal to all sectors of the public. In the first years of the century mainstream politics had been represented on postcards in a quiet way by photographs and cartoons of men such as Chamberlain and Salisbury, and the emerging socialist movement by such series as that produced of their heroes and heroines by the Newcastle Socialist Society. In the years between 1906 and 1914 hundreds of images derived from the women's suffrage campaign were published on postcards, outnumbering those relating to other contemporary campaigns, such as tariff reform and home rule. The images may be roughly divided into two types, real photographs and line drawings. As a rough rule the former tend to be portraits of suffrage personalities and scenes of suffrage activity and are sympathetic to the cause; the latter, comic and, except for those issued by the suffrage societies, representing the received opinions and mores of the day, might be construed as "anti". The spirit of the Edwardian age is distilled in all these cards.

The WOMEN'S SOCIAL AND POLITICAL UNION, the fresh breeze sweeping through the suffrage campaign, was responsible for the first "suffrage" postcard – a *Daily Mirror* photograph of the procession of mainly East End women, carrying their home-made banners, on the way to the first public WSPU London meeting in the Caxton Hall on 19 February 1906. This card does not carry the name of any publisher; it may have been issued by the Independent Labour Party, from whose office it was certainly available. The first postcard that can be directly attributed to the WSPU (it bears the caption "Votes for Women! The Price We Pay For Demanding Our Rights. Issued by the Women's Social and Political Union") is a photograph of a woman (possibly Irene MILLER) being marched down the street between two policemen. The photograph is, again, credited to the *Daily Mirror*. By April 1906 the *Labour Record and Review* advertised that WSPU postcards could be obtained from 45 Park Walk, Chelsea, the address of Sylvia PANKHURST.

Once the WSPU settled into Clement's Inn and appointed its ORGANIZERS, these were in turn the subject of photographic postcards, with their name and society prominently displayed. The WOMEN'S FREEDOM LEAGUE continued the policy of publicizing its organizers, the WSPU tending increasingly to concentrate on portraits of Emmeline and Christabel PANKHURST and Emmeline PETHICK-LAWRENCE; in such a manner is the cult of leadership effected. By July 1909 the only women other than the leaders who featured on WSPU postcards, as advertised in *Votes for Women*, were Jennie BAINES, Flora DRUMMOND, Mary GAWTHORPE, Gladice KEEVIL and Rosamund MASSY. Several images of, for instance, Annie KENNEY and Lady Constance LYTTON, had earlier been available, but apparently were no longer so. One of the items sold by the WSPU in its shops was a postcard album in "the colours". The Women's Freedom League issued a series of cards in which its activists, presumably to rebut taunts of unwomanliness, were photographed engaged in household chores. Mrs DESPARD is knitting and Mrs

How Martyn is making jam; the WFL was not seeking for them combatative glory. The NUWSS did not pander to the cult of personality. Two different photographs, by Lizzie Caswell Smith, of Mrs Fawcett appear on postcards with the caption "President of the National Union of Women's Suffrage Societies" and there does exist a photographic postcard each of Lady Frances Balfour and Margaret Ashton, on which their names appear in the same typeface and which have identical backs. Neither of these cards identify the sitters as presidents respectively of the London and Manchester suffrage societies, but the coincidence of their similarity would suggest that they were produced on account of their suffrage connection. Other suffrage societies, such as the Women Writers' Suffrage League and the Tax Resistance League, issued at least one postcard each. Local NUWSS branches such as the Street Women's Suffrage Society and the Oxford Women's Students' Society published their own cards. The former is a group photograph, the latter, in colour, is of the banner designed for the society by Edmund Hort New.

The militant campaign, with its drama and spectacle, was attractive to the camera (see also film). Large London demonstrations and processions, local marches, outdoor meetings in market squares and on seaside promenades were all captured in photographs that were then produced as postcards. Real photographic cards could be processed very quickly and were often on sale the same day as the event photographed. Although the WSPU issued a few postcards of, for instance, the June 1908 Hyde Park demonstration, the great majority of the photographs of events were issued on postcards by independent publishers. Mrs Albert Broom photographed and published postcards of the May 1909 WSPU exhibition at the Prince's Skating Rink, H. Serjeant the 23 July 1910 "Prison to Citizenship" procession, and F. Kehrhahn the WSPU Christmas Bazaar, December 1911. These cards were on sale at events organized by the WSPU; a Mrs Broom postcard of the WSPU band carries a handwritten message to the effect that the sender bought it at a Queen's Hall meeting on 7 June 1908, "The stewards pestered us per usual to buy things, but these pcs took fancy [sic] and were about my price...". The publisher of the "London Life" series, the Rotary Photo Co., included at least three suffrage images in its series; two are sellers of the *Suffragette*, one doing so from a little horse-drawn cart, and the third shows the arrest of a "Militant Suffragette", now identified as Mary Phillips. Postcards were issued by local photographers such as Emeny of Felixstowe, Phillips and Lees, Ilfracombe, Allworth Bros, Tonbridge, and Graham of Morpeth to record local milestones in the suffrage campaign. Interest in the English suffragettes was also shown by at least one firm of German publishers; a photographic postcard of a WSPU demonstration in Trafalgar Square was published in Germany in November 1906. As militancy moved on from organized spectacle to acts of damage and arson, so it continued to provide the dramatic images attractive to postcard publishers. The scene outside St Catherine's Church, Hatcham, on the morning of 7 May 1913 was awash with photographers. One postcard photograph of the gaunt ruins includes the figure of a photographer with his tripod. The product of that man's work also appeared as a postcard, with the church, of course, in greater close-up. The Pathé film camera also recorded the scene. Two Derby firms of photographer publishers, Hurst and Wallis and F.W. Scarrett issued postcards of the burnt-out remains of Breadsall church and several views exist on postcard of the remains of Levetleigh at St Leonards and the Grand Stand at Hurst Park, both, coincidentally, destroyed by Kitty Marion. Retribution was also recorded; there are six different photographs, issued as postcards, captioned "Students' Revenge on Suffragettes' Headquarters, Bristol", depicting the trashed WSPU shop at 37 Queens Road. There are very few extant photographic postcards of Welsh or Scottish suffrage demonstrations or events, although an Aberdeen firm, Holmes, did record Lady Cowdray's reception for Mrs Pankhurst at Dunecht House in September 1911. There appear to be no postcards of the NUWSS London processions and it was only with the Pilgrimage in the summer of 1913 that NUWSS members featured on postcard propaganda. The event made sufficient impression for local photographers to record the women on the various routes accompanied by their banners, with "Non-Militant" prominently displayed. Helen Fraser is named on one postcard of the contingent setting out from Land's

End. Both the ARTISTS' SUFFRAGE LEAGUE and the SUFFRAGE ATELIER cartooned for the cause, asserting a positive image of women's role and lampooning politicians. Many of their designs were used on both posters and postcards; the cards were printed in black and white, the posters were often hand-coloured. These cards, together with cartoons by "A Patriot" (Alfred Pearse) issued by the WSPU, were probably produced in relatively few numbers; they are scarce today. In their time they were swamped by the comic postcards that emanated from the commercial publishers and which drew on society's uneasiness, indeed fear, of what was construed as unwomanly behaviour. The still-perceived incongruity of women banding together, of women addressing meetings, of the chaos that reigns at home when the wife and mother leaves to attend such a meeting, the hilarity at the thought of women in parliament, the utter impossibility of a woman in the Speaker's chair, all opinions to be found in contemporary news and parliamentary reports, were all turned by comic artists into images with which they were certain to find commercial success. The militant suffrage campaign as it developed gave the artists a golden opportunity to develop themes that featured harridans with big feet, buck teeth, long noses, hatpins, waving umbrellas or hammers, rushing the House of Commons, leaping on chairs as mice run through their meeting, being manhandled by policemen (bottoms to the fore), breaking windows, attacking pillar boxes, carrying bombs, arraigned in the dock, thrown into prison, and forcibly fed with giant syringes. There is an interesting anthropomorphic sub-section in the range of comic cards. A considerable number of the designs feature cats, some cosy, some, such as Misch & Co.'s "The Vote" series, extraordinarily vicious. All the popular postcard artists, such as Arthur Moreland, John Hassall, Donald McGill, "Cynicus" (Martin Anderson), Reg Carter and Lawson Wood produced "comic" suffrage postcards and they were published by firms great and small, including Bamforth, Valentine and Raphael Tuck. At least one German card depicts the "Sufragetten mobililiert" armed with whip, bomb, revolver, sword and spectacles. The messages these postcards bore were often irrelevant ("Come to tea") but are sometimes found to reflect the view on the suffrage campaign held by the sender. For instance, on the reverse of a card showing a "comic" forcible feeding the message from "Joan" reads "This is the way to feed these *beastly* suffragettes with *sour milk* what are they *coming to I say hang them . . .*'.

A measure of the absorption of the women's suffrage campaign into the nation's consciousness is evidenced by the number of real photographic postcards of carnivals or fancy dress parades featuring "suffragette" characters. Some include only one figure bearing, say, a placard, "Votes for Women", among others on a float. Others show groups, each individual dressed as a character in the campaign, suffragette or policeman, lined up for the photographer. Very often all the "suffragettes", brandishing their umbrellas, hammers and bombs, are men. The messages on this type of card reveal how droll contemporaries found the impersonation.

Once the vote had been partially won in 1918 the suffrage campaign, whether reality photographed or stereotypical images filtered through the sensibilities of comic artists, was no longer of much interest to the general public or, as a corollary, to postcard publishers. A flurry of interest at the time of the "Flapper" election in 1929, drawing the last drop of comedy out of the contrast between young short-skirted, shingled-haired women and the solemnity of the polling booth, marked the end of the entertaining and illuminating phenomenon of the "suffragette postcard". (*See also* PHOTOGRAPHERS.)

Bibliography: F. Staff, *The Picture Postcard and its Origins*, 2nd edn, 1979; L. Tickner, *The Spectacle of Women: Imagery of the Suffrage Campaign 1907–14*; I. McDonald, *Vindication!: A Postcard History of the Women's Movement*, 1989.

POTTERIES (WFL)   Secretary (1913) Mrs Pedley, 18 Bower Street, Hanley, Staffordshire.

PRESTON branch of the MANCHESTER NATIONAL SOCIETY FOR WOMEN'S SUFFRAGE   Founded in the 1870s. In 1913 the society was a member of the WEST LANCS, WEST CHESHIRE, AND NORTH WALES FEDERATION OF THE NATIONAL UNION OF WOMEN'S SUFFRAGE SOCIETIES. Secretary (1913) Mrs Todd, Penwortham House, nr Preston, Lancashire.

PRESTON, ST ANNE'S AND DISTRICT (WSPU) Secretaries (1906 and 1913) Mrs RIGBY, 24 Winckley Square, Preston, with (1906) Miss Alderman, 34

Broadgate, Preston and (1913) Miss Johnson, The Hydro, Lytham, Lancashire. In 1908 the Preston WSPU had a BANNER, painted in oil by Pattie Meyer, depicting "a Lancashire lassie" and the legend "Preston lassies mun hae th' voat".

PRIESTMAN SISTERS: Anna Maria Priestman (1828–1914) and Mary Priestman (1830–1914) Quakers, born in Newcastle, younger sisters of Margaret TANNER, sisters-in-law to John Bright (their sister Elizabeth was his first wife), and aunts of Helen Bright CLARK. They were therefore related by marriage, as they were by inclination, to the Bright/McLaren/Ashworth radical Liberal kinship and friendship network (see Appendix). In 1869 Mary Priestman wrote to Helen McLaren, the daughter of Priscilla Bright McLAREN, "I hope you will believe that your Mother's children feel like near and dear relations to us though they are not really so". They were also close friends of Sophia COURTAULD, aunt of P.A. Taylor (see Clementia TAYLOR) and of Mary ESTLIN. Their mother, born Rachel Bragg, was active in the anti-slavery agitation, and avoided as far as possible the use of articles produced by West Indian slave labour, or American cotton or other "slave" products. Rachel Priestman was an active religious worker, preaching in towns around Britain and even left her young children in order to undertake a preaching tour of Pennsylvania, New England and Maryland. In 1896 Anna Maria Priestman is quoted as saying, "Our father [Jonathan Priestman] was a very just man, and I always heard him speak of the perfect equality of men and women, and he liked women to take an interest in political questions". She herself did her womanly part, sewing for the Anti-Corn Law League and anti-slavery bazaars in the 1840s. By 1870, after the death of their father, both sisters moved to Bristol, perhaps to be near their newly widowed sister, Margaret Tanner.

Anna Maria and Mary Priestman had radical friends outside their family network; both were very fond of Elizabeth Wolstenholme ELMY, whom they certainly knew by 1872. In 1874, privy to the nature of Elizabeth Wolstenholme's relationship with Ben Elmy, which at that stage was unblessed by the state, Mary Priestman took care of her. Anna Maria Priestman in later years was prepared to give money to ensure Elizabeth Wolstenholme Elmy's well-being, although this was always done discreetly, through Harriet McILQUHAM. She was also one of the organizers of the "Grateful Fund" which, from 1895, aimed to give Elizabeth Wolstenholme Elmy a regular small income and in 1894 she subscribed 10/– to the WOMEN'S EMANCIPATION UNION. The Priestman sisters were also supporters of Jessie CRAIGEN, another of the more outrageous workers for the suffrage cause; they were very impressed by a speech she gave at the Grand Demonstration held at the Colston Hall in 1880 and remained her steadfast friends when others deserted her; in 1886 they raised money to provide a "Jessie Craigen Lecture Fund".

In 1874 Anna Maria Priestman read a paper on "The Industrial Position of Women as affected by their exclusion from the Suffrage" to the British Association meeting, held that year in Bristol. She was concerned that protective legislation was imposed on women workers and that this was likely to lead to their exclusion from more skilled work. This paper is interesting both because it demonstrates that the pioneers of the suffrage movement were well aware that there was more than abstract principle involved in being voteless and because it resulted, after discussions with Emma PATERSON, in the Priestman sisters, with Mary Estlin, forming in Bristol the first branch of the National Union of Women Workers. Their nieces, Lilias (see Lilias Ashworth HALLETT) and Anne ASHWORTH, were members of its committee and Clementia TAYLOR and Margaret Bright LUCAS were among its subscribers. Alice SCATCHERD soon founded a branch of the NUWW in Yorkshire. In 1889 both Priestman sisters put principle into practice and set up a soup kitchen for striking Bristol cotton workers. Their support of the women's movement embraced all radical causes. Mary Priestman in particular, with Margaret Tanner and Mary Estlin, was closely associated with Josephine Butler's campaign to repeal the Contagious Diseases Acts. She was also president of the Bristol branch of the British Women's Temperance Association.

While still living in the family home in Newcastle, both Anna Maria and Mary Priestman signed the 1866 women's suffrage petition. In April 1866 Mary Priestman was taken by Duncan McLaren to the House of Commons to hear John Stuart MILL's speech in favour of women's suffrage. Anna Maria subscribed to the ENFRANCHISEMENT OF WOMEN COMMITTEE in 1866–7 and, while still in Newcastle, in 1867 she joined the LONDON NATIONAL SOCIETY FOR WOMEN'S SUFFRAGE. In 1870 Anna Maria Priestman joined the committee of the WEST OF ENGLAND BRANCH OF THE NATIONAL SOCIETY FOR WOMEN'S SUFFRAGE and was in 1908 still a member of the executive committee of the BRISTOL AND WEST OF ENGLAND SOCIETY FOR WOMEN'S SUFFRAGE. In 1870 she and Mary Priestman employed the Quaker weapon of passive resistance by refusing to pay their taxes as a protest against the exclusion of women from the franchise. Their dining chairs were distrained in lieu of the tax; the fine was, however, paid anonymously and the chairs returned. They continued the protest the next year. In 1881 Anna Maria Priestman, with Emily STURGE, founded in Bristol the first Women's Liberal Association, which was prepared to put the "test question" (i.e. would they support women's enfranchisement?) to candidates in parliamentary and local government elections. As she remarked in an interview with Sarah Tooley published in the *Woman at Home* in 1895, "[we] determined that we would not work for any Parliamentary candidate who was not in favour of equal laws for men and women". A supporter to whom she mentioned this rule agreed that for women to work to elect men who were opposed to their enfranchisement "is like speaking through a telephone with no one at the other end".

In the years before the 1884 Reform Bill Anna Maria Priestman, like other radical suffragists, became increasingly out of sympathy with the London-based parliamentary tactics to achieve reform employed by Lydia BECKER. Favouring a mobilization of public opinion, from both the middle and the working classes, Anna Maria Priestman was chiefly responsible for raising £1000 in order that "organizing work" could be carried out in the area covered by the West of England Branch of the National Suffrage Society. After the defeat of the women's suffrage amendment in 1884 Anna Maria Priestman concentrated on trying to ensure that Women's Liberal Associations and, after its formation in 1886, the WOMEN'S LIBERAL FEDERATION, gave support to the cause of women's enfranchisement. Mary Priestman was certainly a member of the executive committee of the WLF in 1898. After the split in the CENTRAL COMMITTEE FOR WOMEN'S SUFFRAGE in 1888 Anna Maria Priestman remained with the CENTRAL NATIONAL SOCIETY, becoming a member of its executive committee. On 22 December 1888 the *Women's Penny Paper* recorded that "Miss Priestman proposed to carry on a Suffrage campaign amongst the Liberal Associations of the country." In 1896, after an attempt to commit the WLF to work only for candidates who supported women's enfranchisement was defeated, she formed, and became president of, the UNION OF PRACTICAL SUFFRAGISTS. Mary Priestman was a member of the Union's executive committee. Anna Maria Priestman wrote a pamphlet, *Women and Votes*, which was published *c.* 1896 by the Union of Practical Suffragists. In 1903 she brought this campaign to what appeared to be a successful conclusion when the WLF agreed to give its support only to candidates who were in sympathy with women's enfranchisement. However, her success was short-lived and by 1905 Anna Maria Priestman was removed as president of the West Bristol Women's Liberal Association, which she had formed 24 years earlier, and the debate over the test question was re-opened. Perhaps unsurprisingly, in view of this lack of progress, the Priestman sisters subscribed to the WOMEN'S SOCIAL AND POLITICAL UNION in 1907 and gave active support, when she arrived in Bristol as WSPU organizer in the west of England, to Annie KENNEY, about whom they must already have heard glowing reports from Elizabeth Wolstenholme Elmy. They gave £25 to the WSPU in September 1908, £10 in both September and October 1909 and £5 in October 1910. As militancy increased it is likely that the Priestman sisters became disenchanted with the WSPU. Stressing their support for the constitutional society, in 1910 Anna Maria Priestman was the author of an appeal from women members of the Society of Friends for the matter of women's suffrage to be considered at the Society's yearly meeting. She wrote, "We belong to a body that has always recognised the strength and uplifting influence of women in both public and private life; and we should like to show in some united way our sympathy and interest in this movement, thus adding our testimony to those who are working in a constitutional way, for the Cause we have so much at heart." Among the signatories are Mary Priestman, Sarah Bancroft Clark, Lucy Bancroft Gillett, Sophia S. Clark, Emily MANNERS, Eva McLAREN, Helen Bright Clark, Esther Bright CLOTHIER, Alice CLARK and Margaret Gillett. However, in 1912 the Priestman sisters contributed to the election expenses of George LANSBURY, who stood as a suffrage candidate at the instigation of Christabel PANKHURST. Their espousal of pacifism was deeply felt. Anna Maria Priestman had attended the Peace Congress at Berne in 1892, both sisters had been deeply distressed by the Boer War, and they died, within five days of each other, in October 1914, the inference being that they were heart-broken by the thought of world conflict.

Address: (from 1870) The Nook, 37 Durdham Down, Redland, Bristol.
Photograph: in S.J. Tanner, *How the Women's Suffrage Movement began in Bristol Fifty Years Ago*, 1918.
Archival source: Friends' Library, London; Priscilla Bright McLaren Papers, National Library of Scotland.
Bibliography: S.J. Tanner, *How the Women's Suffrage Movement began in Bristol Fifty Years Ago*, 1918; E. Malos, *Bristol's Other History*, 1983; S.S. Holton, *Suffrage Days*, 1996.

PRIMROSE LEAGUE The Conservative party's support group, with concerns more social than political, admitted women soon after its formation in 1883. In 1885 Lydia BECKER welcomed the formation of the Primrose League's Ladies' Grand Council, writing in the *Women's Suffrage Journal*, 1 July, "It is, I believe, a unique and unparalleled circumstance that a meeting of ladies only should be convened for such an object, and addressed by so many statesmen in the first rank of politics, and the fact is, no doubt, to be regarded as a significant sign of the advance of public opinion as to the political influence and duties of woman". Indeed any organization that drew women together for a common purpose was to be welcomed, even though, as with the Primrose League, involvement in the suffrage movement was outside its remit, in fact was banned. The Primrose League did have a considerable indirect impact on the women's suffrage movement. Because Primrose League branches ("habitations"), unlike Women's Liberal Associations, were constitutionally debarred from affiliating with other organizations, such as the CENTRAL COMMITTEE FOR WOMEN'S SUFFRAGE, non-Liberal (Conservative and Liberal Unionist) members of the Central Committee were in 1888 opposed to the introduction of new rules that would allow such affiliation, fearing that the political balance in the society would be upset. This led to a damaging split in the main women's suffrage society; Millicent FAWCETT retained the redoubt of the Central Committee, while Liberals formed the CENTRAL NATIONAL SOCIETY FOR WOMEN'S SUFFRAGE, which allowed affiliation from other organizations.

Bibliography: D. Rubinstein, *Before the Suffragettes: Women's Emancipation in the 1890s*, 1986; L. Walker, "Party political women: a comparative study of Liberal women and the Primrose League, 1890–1914", in J. Rendall (ed.), *Equal or Different: Women's Politics 1800–1914*, 1987.

PRISON Andrew Rosen has calculated that during the course of the women's militant suffrage campaign 1085 women served prison sentences for the cause. The entry of these women into the prison system had two repercussions. The more highly publicized was the initiation of a policy of hunger striking in order to force the government to accord suffrage prisoners the status of political offenders. The other, perhaps more long-lasting, was that, by suffering imprisonment, women not only acquired an experience that was to be a measure of their commitment to the cause and, indeed, a test of their own inner resources, but gave them the evidence with which to launch a campaign against the conditions in which "normal" prisoners were held. Indeed what was perceived as the callous treatment of women prisoners, of whom, it was calculated in 1910–11, 85 to 90 per cent were convicted for offences relating to prostitution, was taken by the suffrage societies as yet one more example of the economic and social ills that would be rectified if women had a share in government. The Prisons Act of 1877 had transferred the control of local prisons to the Home Office. Because the majority of the most highly publicized acts that led to arrest were perpetrated by suffragettes in London, it is with details of treatment in Holloway Prison – which since 1902 had been a prison for women only and in which they served their sentences, rather than taking the proffered alternative of a fine – that most contemporary comment and later reminiscences were concerned. Women suffrage prisoners were also held in prison in Manchester (Strangeways),

Liverpool (Walton), Aylesbury, Stafford, Maidstone, Ipswich, Stafford, Lewes, Exeter, Bristol (Horfield), Edinburgh (Calton Jail), Perth and Dundee; men were held in Wormwood Scrubs, Brixton and Pentonville. The Penal Reform Union was formed by Capt. Arthur St John in February 1907 at the breakfast held to welcome Sylvia PANKHURST on her release from prison. It is not clear what work this body actually accomplished, but its formation was a testimony to the recognition that, having seen conditions at first hand, reform was necessary. Sylvia Pankhurst published an article and sketches based on her prison experience in the *Pall Mall Gazette,* January–June 1907. Miss G.M. Alderman described, in an undramatized fashion, her imprisonment in Holloway in February 1908:

> I could see a spire of a church and most days pigeons flying and sometimes in the grounds a white persian cat. We wore a uniform – a green dress, thick serge, a little white cap on one's head, an apron of blue and white check cotton and a round disc the colour of wash leather which had a number. From the time I arrived until I left I never saw a fire or a clock – the rooms were heated by pipes – which were barely lukewarm. The floor was concrete and so were the walls. No wonder it was cold. Furniture was scarce – only a stool to sit on, a fixed shelf in one corner for a table just about big enough to hold a dinner plate. There was a mug to drink from – a little round wooden box with salt in – a comb and brush. No handle it was a man's brush. There is a knack in using this kind, it flings itself out of your hand at first and a lot of time is spent in retrieving it. The room was small – four paces across – but you could make it five by going across from corner to corner if one became restless and desired a little exercise.

The sight of the London pigeons was important to the WSPU prisoners, recurring as an image in their prison poetry. For publication in *Votes for Women,* 1 October 1908, Maud JOACHIM, having just completed a three-month sentence, the longest then served, gave a description of life in Holloway. She reported that she was allowed a bath once a week, that the cell, in the new wing, was clean and well lit by electric light, which was turned out soon after 8 pm, that the bedstead consisted of three planks, fastened to cross-pieces so as to stand about 4 inches from the ground, about 27 inches wide, and that the mattress was hard, and full of lumps. The cell furniture consisted of a little hard stool, and a table fixed into the angle of the wall near the door. In the door there was a spy hole, through which the wardresses looked in. The window was so high up that one could see out of it only by standing on the stool. About 5.30 am a bell was rung to warn that it was time to rise, breakfast arrived at 7.15 and then prisoners were required to scrub their cell floor and boards, fold up bedclothes into a roll, stow them away, and then polish the tin cell utensils with soap and bath-brick. They then, in silence, went down to chapel. She remarks that the suffragettes were separated from ordinary prisoners during exercise and chapel, not, she thinks, for their own good, but because they were vocal in their exposure of abuses. She noted that prisoners were allowed two books a week from the prison library (*see* LIBRARIES). After the initial four weeks of solitary confinement prisoners were allowed "associated labour", that is working, usually at sewing, with others in a downstairs hall, although no talking was allowed. As a special favour suffrage prisoners were allowed "association" and a second hour of exercise. But this was in a gravelled yard in the hottest part of the day (from July to September) without any head covering until they did eventually obtain sun bonnets. A vegetarian, she was allowed a special vegetarian diet, which she reported was of good quality, although monotonous. She mentioned that since suffragettes first served sentences in Holloway in 1906 a woman medical inspector of prisons had been appointed. This was Dr Mary Gordon, who gave a £5 donation to the WSPU in October 1908 and £20 in January 1909. Such detailed publicity of conditions coupled with pressure from the suffrage societies and their supporters led to an amelioration in conditions for all second-division prisoners. They were allowed better washing facilities, were not strip searched, were allowed to meet their visitors in a special room, were allowed to work "in association", and were allowed more books.

In *Votes for Women,* 30 April 1909, Emmeline PETHICK-LAWRENCE wrote that there had definitely been "hygienic ameliorations" in conditions since her first imprisonment in 1906, the horrors of which had quickly caused her to break down, and was assured that these were also enjoyed by conventional prisoners, although noting that "the utmost precautions are taken to cut us off from sight and knowledge of the condition of our fellow-inmates". She remarks that in the new wing, where suffragettes are always put (although, presumably, "ordinary" prisoners were still held in the old wing), the cells were clean, with "more than a mere superficial cleanliness", well lit, and the ventilation an improvement on the old cells where moisture from breath condensed on walls. She reported that the underclothing, although patched and often stained, was no longer foul or evil-smelling, that they were now given a nightdress, and a new brush and comb, or at least a thoroughly cleaned one (the fear and the reality of head lice was a particular cross to be borne by the middle-class prisoner) and that each woman was given a new toothbrush. Cells now had a chair instead of a stool and each cell was now allocated its own earthenware mug and plate. Prisoners were allowed to spend three hours a day in associated labour, although still in silence. She was certain that it was the publicity surrounding the imprisonment of suffragettes that had improved the prison system. The WOMEN'S FREEDOM LEAGUE as well as the WSPU was concerned in lobbying for prison reforms. From 1913 Nina BOYLE campaigned to improve the conditions in which women were taken to Holloway in "Black Marias", involving the Home Office in a considerable amount of correspondence and even forcing it to commission plans for new motorized vans.

By the Prison Act of 1898, when sentenced, prisoners could be allocated, at the magistrate's discretion, to one of three divisions; when this was not specified it was left to the decision of the Home Secretary. The first division was available for those who had committed contempt of court or sedition; prisoners were not required to work, were allowed books and newspapers, visits from three friends once a fortnight, a letter in and out once a fortnight, were allowed to follow their trade or profession, and receive payment for it, to wear their own clothes, to rent a furnished cell and to buy in food and wine. Between the other two divisions there was not much difference in substance; those offenders whose character and antecedents were "respectable" and whom it was desired to keep entirely apart from ordinary prisoners of undesirable character were allocated to the second division. They were, however, required to wear prison dress, eat prison food, in the first four weeks of their sentence were kept in cells in solitary confinement for 23 out of 24 hours, had no access to one another, and were not allowed papers or letters or visits from friends. The hour out of the cell was accounted for by 30 minutes a day for exercise and 30 minutes in chapel. During the day they were required to make mail bags or darn. After 5 pm they could, if they liked, read one of the books from the prison library. After they completed four weeks of their sentence they could write and receive one letter and were entitled to one visit by no more than three people, who were required to talk to the prisoner through bars and in the presence of a wardress. Such visits were subject to the approval of the prison governor. The Home Office could grant special permits for visits on other occasions and could allow visits to be conducted in a separate room. MPs were able to obtain these special privileges and were the recipients of many such requests from the families of suffrage prisoners. Second-division prisoners might also be sentenced to "hard labour". Dr Mary Gordon commented that when she arrived at Holloway she was "surprised to find that hard labour meant an exceedingly moderate day's work in scrubbing, or at the wash tub".

Of the first four members of the WSPU sentenced in London, on 19 June 1906, to terms of imprisonment, in the second division three (Annie KENNEY, Mrs SBARBORO and Adelaide KNIGHT) would have been thought of by their contemporaries as "working-class". Mrs Sbarboro and Adelaide Knight, both poor, though vociferous, women from the East End, and Annie Kenney served a month of their sentence, which the Home Secretary had reduced from six weeks. Dora MONTEFIORE in her memoir made the specific point that it was in every way worse for working-class women to suffer imprisonment for the cause; not only did they lose their income, but they suffered the stigma of jail at a time when the concept of suffrage martyrdom was not yet understood, least of all by their peers. The fourth to be arrested, the more newsworthy, more middle-class Teresa Billington (*see* Teresa

BILLINGTON-GREIG), had her fine paid, presumably without her consent, by an anonymous reader of the *Daily Mirror* (or by the paper itself) and was quickly released. It was only with the arrests in October 1906 of the first middle-class members of the WSPU (it is Anne Cobden-SANDERSON's name with which the Home Office chose to label its file on the episode) that the question of the status of suffrage prisoners was seriously raised. Having been sentenced to the second division, the prisoners were all elevated to the first and released before the end of their term. In February 1907 some of the women arrested after taking part in the deputation from Caxton Hall to the House of Commons were allocated to the first division and some to the second; the magistrate did not reveal his reasoning behind the discrimination. A fortnight later all 67 arrested during the course of the next deputation were sent to the first division. Neither sentencing of suffrage prisoners nor their treatment once in prison was ever consistent, the Home Office reacting in whatever way was expedient. Prisoners with connections to the political or social establishment, even if not accorded first-division status, were likely to spend much of their sentence in the relatively better conditions of the prison wing.

In the early years of the WSPU campaign, when militant actions might have seemed an aberration and likely to be a transient phenomenon, the government was not unwilling to allow suffrage prisoners to be held in the first division. As the numbers of suffrage prisoners passing through the prison system increased, this tolerance was forfeited. In October 1908 when Emmeline and Christabel PANKHURST were sentenced to three months' imprisonment in the second division in Holloway Mrs Pankhurst petitioned that they should be treated as political offenders and placed in the first division. The government's denial of the petition led to such protests as the rally organized by the WSPU on 5 November at the Free Trade Hall, Manchester. Mrs Pankhurst broke the prison rule of silence in order to be able to talk to Christabel while they were in the excercise yard, initiating a campaign of disobedience that was continued when, in February, Emmeline Pethick-Lawrence, after she had been arrested with other suffragettes, informed the governor of Holloway that the women would cause no trouble so long as there was no strip search, and they were allowed to exercise in pairs and were allowed to talk while exercising. As the militant campaign showed no sign of abating magistrates became more resolute; suffrage prisoners were sentenced to serve hard labour in the third division for obstructing the police. Indeed by May 1911 an act of civil disobedience, of failing to pay for a dog licence, put Emma SPROSON, a working-class woman, into the third division of Stafford Jail. She went on hunger strike and was moved by the governor, on his personal responsibility, into the first division. Four months later, in London, Clemence HOUSMAN, undoubtedly middle-class and backed by a strong publicity campaign, was allocated to the first division and indeed served only a week of her sentence for non-payment of tax. *Votes for Women*, 2 April 1909, noted that the Home Secretary's treatment of suffragette prisoners had been criticized in the House of Commons. Mr Swift MacNeil had stated that the offence was clearly a political one and should be treated as such. John Dillon backed him up and pointed out that the prison was no disgrace for the suffragettes, that nothing was more calculated to strengthen the movement, that they were honoured by their friends on their release and by the public and that many people thought their treatment vindictive. At the WSPU exhibition at the Prince's Rink Exhibition in May 1909 prison cells were erected, one recreating the type of second-division cell in which, by then, nearly 400 suffragette prisoners had been held, and another the first-division cell available for the "ordinary male political prisoner" (*Votes for Women*, 28 May 1909).

Marion Wallace-DUNLOP was sent to prison on 2 July, allocated to the second division. She warned the governor that unless she were placed in the first division and treated as a political prisoner she intended to hunger strike. It seems clear that this was a decision she made without consulting the WSPU leadership. In the event her hunger strike began on Monday 5 July, carried on for 91 hours, and she was set free on 9 July, without having been forcibly fed. She reportedly said, "You may feed me through the nostrils or the month, but suppose you got 108 women in here on Friday all requiring to be fed through the nostrils. At this the doctor's face was a delightful study" (*Votes for Women*,

16 July 1909). Having noted that Marion Wallace-Dunlop had successfully made her protest and shortened her prison sentence, her example was emulated by the WSPU members arrested after taking place in the deputation to the House of Commons on 29 June. When they were taken from court on 12 July they informed the officers of the WSPU that it was their intention, if denied the rights of political prisoners, to carry out "effective protest" in prison. When ordered to take off their own clothes and put on prison clothes they would refuse to do so, and would refuse to be put in second-division cells. If put in cells by force and undressed they would refuse in the morning to get up and dress except in their own clothes. They would refuse to obey the rule of silence, but would talk to each other whenever they wanted, and sing aloud during detention. Twelve of the prisoners went on hunger strike and were released after six days, without having been forcibly fed; Florence Cooke gave a very graphic account of the ordeal in *Votes for Women,* 23 July 1909. There was another hunger strike in Holloway in July, carried out by Mary LEIGH, Alice PAUL and others; they were released after having served only five-and-a-half days of their sentence. At the end of August the Home Office expressly decided not to forcibly feed hunger-striking prisoners, who again included Mary Leigh, in Liverpool's Walton Gaol. The medical officer there was quite prepared to undertake the operation, indeed he asked if he should. After the arrest of Dora MARSDEN, Emily Wilding DAVISON and others in Manchester, the Home Office minuted on 8 September that, "It is clear that if they go much further in the use of violence, the suffragettes will have to be held to serve their sentences even if it means artificial feeding. The only question is whether this is the right case to begin." It was decided not to use forcible feeding because the offence for which the women were convicted was only damage to glass and their unpaid fine only £5. On 9 September an assistant secretary in the Home Office wrote to the governor of Strangeways prison in Manchester to say that forcible feeding of suffragette prisoners there was not authorized; if the women's condition became, according to the prison medical officer's opinion, critical and there was not time to report back, the governor could release them. The governor was asked to give the Home Office a daily report on the suffragette prisoners. He was specifically asked if they were searched on arrival and if they were made to change into prison clothes. However, the Home Office was then annoyed when the Manchester prisoners, who included Dora Marsden and Emily Wilding Davison, were released after only 60 hours' detention. The Home Office official thought that the Manchester medical officer had been too lenient, writing, "Other medical officers who had better judgment or more courage, would in similar circumstances not have given the same certificates for two days more. It is particularly unfortunate that this happened in the case of the Manchester women whose offence was far more serious than any of the others." The local press was clearly amazed at the speed with which the women were released. During the short time she spent in Strangeways Dora Marsden petitioned for political status. After this experience the Home Office clearly decided that the time had come to introduce forcible feeding and it was used, for the first time, at Winson Green Prison, Birmingham, in late September 1909 on Mary Leigh, Charlotte MARSH, Laura AINSWORTH, Evelyn BURKITT and Mabel CAPPER.

The 1 and 8 October 1909 issues of *Votes for Women* carried articles on forcible feeding and warnings from doctors of its dangers. The Scottish Office did not follow the example set by England in the treatment of hunger-striking prisoners. Lucy BURNS, Alice Paul and Edith NEW, held in September on hunger strike in Dundee prison were not forcibly fed; Lucy Burns even wrote to the prison governor after her release to distance herself from the press reports that maintained that she had complained about foul air in the prison. Adela PANKHURST sent the governor a card thanking him and his staff on behalf of the released prisoners for their kindness and inviting them to a WSPU meeting. By way of contrast an unsigned card, dated 14 September 1909, from a member of the public was sent to the governor, who forwarded it to the prison medical officer. The message suggested that "there is reason to believe that the starvation dodge would cease if, instead of liberating them, they were put in the infirmary ward, and the food injected as is done in the case of lunacy patients". On 21 October permission was given from the Under-Secretary for Scotland to use forcible feeding if necessary on five new suffragette prisoners in Dundee Jail (Adela Pankhurst, Laura Evans, Helen ARCHDALE, Catherine CORBETT, Maud JOACHIM), with the suggestion that perhaps an officer should be sent to Newcastle to consult with the governor there who had recent experience of the operation. The file on these Dundee prisoners includes a copy of Mary Leigh's statement about forcible feeding, published by the WSPU, and H.N. BRAILSFORD's article on "Militant Suffragists in Newcastle" reprinted from the *Newcastle Daily Chronicle,* 11 October 1909; the governor was obviously keen to keep abreast with developments in the forcible feeding debate. Questions were asked by Philip Snowden and Keir Hardie in the House of Commons about the treatment of forcibly fed prisoners; the government preferred use of the term "artificial" to "forcible" feeding. That Home Office policy over "artificial" feeding was no more consistent than any other facet of its handling of suffragette prisoners, was demonstrated in October by the release of Lady Constance LYTTON and Jane BRAILSFORD from prison in Newcastle, after hunger striking for two days, without having been forcibly fed. It was generally accepted that it was the relationship of the two women to the social, political, and press establishment that secured their release. Indeed there had even been inconsistencies over the sentencing at Newcastle; Lady Constance was serving one month in the second division in lieu of a refusal to be bound over; the women arrested with her were sentenced to hard labour in the third division. However, in January 1910, it was to 14 days' imprisonment in this division in Walton Gaol, Liverpool, that she was sentenced, when disguised as the working-class "Jane Warton". Her hunger strike was terminated by forcible feeding; "Jane Warton" did not merit a medical examination. The ensuing controversy ensured that henceforward all prisoners were examined before being forcibly fed. For the January 1910 election campaign a WSPU supporter in Liverpool designed a poster headed "Walton Liverpool" showing a woman lying in a prison cell, hands handcuffed behind her back, with the caption "This is the way political prisoners are treated by a Liberal government." The case of Selina Martin, whose treatment in Walton had aroused much public controversy and inspired Lady Constance to become "Jane Warton", forced the Home Office to instigate an inquiry at the gaol, taking statements from all the warders. WSPU election campaigning maintained the pressure; by early February they had for sale a poster by "A Patriot" (Alfred Pearse) in four colours, showing with dramatic force a woman being fed by a nasal tube. A system of daily reports on forcibly fed prisoners was instigated, initially handwritten, but by 1912 the Home Office had devised a printed form. By April 1912 it also had printed a standard letter to send in reply to enquiries, of which there were so many, about suffragette prisoners.

In March 1910 the new Home Secretary, Winston Churchill, had taken a pragmatic view of the situation as he found it and introduced Rule 243A (*Votes for Women,* 18 March 1910) to deal with suffrage prisoners (and passive resisters). His aim was "to restrain the liberty of the prisoner, and by restraining his [sic] liberty to punish him, without the enforcement of conditions calculated to degrade or humiliate his dignity and self-respect". Rule 243A was a compromise; while bestowing privileges such as fortnightly visits and letters, the wearing of the prisoner's own clothes, exercise twice a day "in association", first-division food, a supply of books and permission to do her own work, it did not give first-division status. As a result of the WSPU window-smashing campaign in London in March 1912, of 42 women sentenced to terms of imprisonment in the second and third divisions, 33 were treated under Rule 243A. In six cases the privileges of 243A were forfeited for "gross misconduct" such as damage to prison property; the other three women were held in the prison hospital. In addition, 76 women were sentenced to hard labour and to these Rule 243A did not apply. However, this decision was reversed by Reginald McKenna, who was now Home Secretary, and the privilege of Rule 243A was extended to all suffrage prisoners. In May 1912 its terms were slightly altered so that prisoners were to be employed only on lighter forms of prison work, were restricted to one food parcel up to 11lb in weight, and visits were limited to 15 minutes once a month. In March 1912 the influx of suffragette prisoners into Holloway had caused difficulties for the authorities. Some prisoners were moved to

Aylesbury and Maidstone and in Birmingham 20 "ordinary" women prisoners were moved from Winson Green in order to make way for 25 suffragettes. The Prison Visiting Committee reported that "Notwithstanding the concessions granted to these women and their entire disregard of all discipline, . . . the ordinary prisoners behaved in an exemplary manner, although the actions of the suffragettes tended to excite them to troublesome conduct."

In May 1912 the Pethick-Lawrences and Mrs Pankhurst were sentenced to nine months' imprisonment in the second division on a charge of conspiracy. They were initially held under Rule 243A until a judge, as a result of their protests, agreed on 11 June to their transfer to the first division. However, there was then an outcry when all the other suffrage prisoners, still held as a result of the March window-smashing campaign, were not also given first-division status. The result was a mass hunger strike at Holloway, Winson Green, Maidstone and at Aylesbury, resulting in the forcible feeding of some prisoners, and the release of many before the end of their sentence. In mid-1912 the WSPU issued as a pamphlet, by George Sigerson, with an introduction by Henry NEVINSON, *"Custodia Honesta": Treatment of Political Prisoners in Great Britain*, which sought to place the struggle of suffrage prisoners for recognition as political offenders in a wider historical context.

The government, having appreciated how difficult it was to deal with hunger-striking prisoners and McKenna having made it clear that he would not allow them to die in custody, devised the Prisoner's (Temporary Discharge for Ill-Health) Bill, details of which were discussed by the cabinet as early as February 1913. What became popularly known as the "Cat and Mouse" Act received the Royal Assent on 25 April 1913. By this Act the Home Secretary was given the power to set a hunger-striking suffrage prisoner free temporarily, without remission of her sentence, thereby avoiding the need for forcible feeding. The prisoner was required to sign a form which gave the date required for her return to prison. A medical examination had to be undergone in order for this date to be extended. The prisoner was required to give an address and to agree to stay there, unless she gave one day's notice of a change, and was not to be absent from that address for more than 12 hours. In a letter written that month to Hugh FRANKLIN, Keir HARDIE commented, "Before the bill was passed McK told me in conversation that in practice the 'Licence' would run on indefinitely so long as its holders refrained from advocating or practising acts of violence. I dont suppose he could make that statement in public". This information, on the whole, proved to be correct. The police made no serious attempts to recapture many of the "mice", as long as they were not known to be involved in further militant actions. Even the most notorious were not necessarily pursued; for instance Mrs Pankhurst, while still a "mouse", was allowed to sail to America to raise funds for the WSPU with the full knowledge of the Home Office.

However, by the time Mrs Pankhurst was due to return to England, in December 1913, the government's attitude had changed and she was arrested on her arrival. By early summer 1914, as the acts of arson and criminal damage perpetrated by suffragettes increased in number and daring, the Home Office was no longer prepared to release known repeat offenders under the "Cat and Mouse" Act. Sylvia and Emmeline Pankhurst who could attract publicity by their hunger-and-thirst strikes were repeatedly released, recaptured and returned to Holloway. The Home Office never dared forcibly to feed Mrs Pankhurst, although it is doubtful if her medical history, if it had not been hers, would have precluded it. However, it is often forgotten that women whom the Home Office deemed dangerous, such as Grace ROE, Gertrude ANSELL and Olive WHARRY, were kept in prison, forcibly fed for several months and only released under the amnesty on the outbreak of war in August 1914. The prison medical officers appear to have perfected a regime of forcible feeding that did not damage the health of the prisoners to such a degree that it was necessary to release them. A much-publicized exception was the gross mishandling of Frances PARKER in Perth prison in July 1914. The Scottish Office had stressed that "this form [rectal] of feeding should not be resorted to except in a case where medical reasons, independent of the desirability of keeping the prisoner in prison, render it absolutely necessary". However, it was the suggestion, with medical verification, that an attempt had been made to "feed" her through the vagina that led to her hasty release. Suffrage prisoners, although gaining over the eight years of the militant campaign amelioration of prison conditions both for themselves and for the ordinary prisoners, were never successful in claiming that, because politically motivated, they were exempt from the criminal law.

Representing an episode so remarkable in otherwise humdrum lives, it is no surprise to realize that there is a wealth of first-hand accounts, both published and unpublished, relating to suffrage imprisonment. Until these women recounted their stories in the first decade of the twentieth century there were few published experiences of prison life, Oscar Wilde, W.T. Stead and Michael Davitt, none of them typical prisoners, being among the few exceptions. Few had previously recorded details of life in Holloway. Some of the suffragette experiences are contained in articles and letters written at the time, but many represent the result of a request from the fledgling SUFFRAGETTE FELLOWSHIP for reminiscences, particularly mentioning this one aspect of involvement in the suffrage campaign. Because these have been held as a coherent collection, relatively accessible to researchers, academic or otherwise, imprisonment has become a dominant trope of the suffrage campaign. In later years, when interviewed or writing their memoirs, ex-suffragettes assumed that it was in their prison experiences, particularly the horrors of forcible feeding, that historians and readers would be interested. Those who had endured it tended to bring the experience to the fore, those who had not felt forced to explain and apologize. A small collection of poems, *Holloway Jingles*, published by the Glasgow branch of the WSPU, possibly in 1913, to commemorate the experience of imprisonment in March and April 1912, radiates the atmosphere of comradeship that developed among those sharing a common ordeal. There is no doubt that for some suffragettes prison was a forcing ground for the deep friendships to which wills and bequests enacted 30 or 40 years later bear witness. The "new" wing of Holloway in which suffragette prisoners were held was demolished in 1977, with Enid Goulden Bach, representing the Suffragette Fellowship, at the controls of the demolition vehicle.

Archival source: Suffragette Fellowship Collection; Helen Watt Papers, Nottingham Archive; Mary Anne Rawle Papers; May Billinghurst Papers, Fawcett Library; Winson Green Visiting Committee, Birmingham Archives; G. Alderman Papers, Essex Record Office; Home Office Papers, Public Record Office.

Bibliography: D. Montefiore, *Prison Reform: From a Social-democratic Point of View*, 1909; W. Lyon Blease, *Concerning the Status of Political Prisoners*, no date (1910?); H. Blagg and C. Wilson, *Women and Prisons*, Fabian Women's Group Series No. 3, 1912; G. Sigerson, *"Custodia Honesta": Treatment of Political Prisoners in Great Britain*, with an introduction by Henry W. Nevinson, 1912; Lady C. Lytton, *Prisons and Prisoners*, 1914; A.E. Metcalf, *Woman's Effort: A Chronicle of British Women's Fifty Years' Struggle for Citizenship (1865–1914)*, 1917; M. Gordon, *Penal Discipline*, 1922; M.E. and M.D. Thompson, *They Couldn't Stop us! Experiences of Two (usually Law-abiding) Women in the Years 1909–1913*, 1957; Z. Procter, *Life and Yesterday*, 1960; A. Rosen, *Rise Up Women!: The Militant Campaign of the Women's Social and Political Union, 1903–1914*, 1974; J. Camp, *Holloway Prison: The Place and the People*, 1974; P. Priestley, *Victorian Prison Lives: English Prison Biography, 1830–1914*, 1985; L. Radzinowicz and R. Hood, *A History of English Criminal Law*, Vol. 5, *The Emergence of Penal Policy*, 1986; L. Leneman, *Martyrs in Our Midst: Dundee, Perth and the Forcible Feeding of Suffragettes*, 1993; J. Purvis, "The prison experiences of the suffragettes in Edwardian Britain", *Women's History Review*, 1, 1995.

PROCTER, ZOE (1867–1962) Born in India, the niece of Adelaide Procter, who was a member in the 1850s of the Langham Place Group, a close friend of Barbara Leigh Smith BODICHON and Bessie Rayner PARKES. Zoe Procter was educated at Clapham High School and eventually found work as a private secretary, from 1895 working as such for both Pearl Craigie ("John Oliver Hobbes") and Marie Belloc Lowndes, daughter of Bessie Rayner Parkes. In 1911, after returning from a winter in Italy, she was taken by her sister to a meeting of the WOMEN'S SOCIAL AND POLITICAL UNION and, as she records "From that moment I devoted myself to the Cause". Through a meeting with Maud JOACHIM she became involved with the work based in the SHOP run by the CHELSEA branch of the WSPU, running its lending LIBRARY. In her autobiography she describes the work undertaken in the shop to produce BANNERS for the 1911 Coronation Procession. In early 1912 Zoe Procter was inspired by hearing Christabel PANKHURST make an impassioned appeal, to volunteer to take part in the 1 March window-smashing campaign. Nina BOYLE lent her a large muff in which she concealed a hammer; she broke her window, was remanded in Holloway and eventually sentenced to six weeks' imprisonment. In her autobiography she gives a full description of this experience and of some of her fellow prisoners. It was there, in those dramatic surroundings, that she met Dorothea ROCK, with whom she lived for the rest of her life. After the beginning of the First World War Zoe Procter continued working in the Chelsea shop, gaining permission from Florence HAIG to sell toys made by Sylvia PANKHURST's East End factory. She became a member of the INDEPENDENT WSPU and was especially interested in the campaign to repeal Clause "40D" by which it was proposed to legalize brothels for the army. She was also a member of the CHURCH LEAGUE FOR WOMEN'S SUFFRAGE. By this time she was working as secretary to Gladys SCHÜTZE, who wrote as "Henrietta Leslie" and had actively supported the WSPU, and in later years she was involved with Maude ROYDEN and the Guildhouse Players.

Address: (1910) 36 Chester Terrace, London SW; (1920) 81 Beaufort Mansions, Chelsea, London SW; (1962) Shepherd's Corner, Gregories Farm Lane, Beaconsfield, Buckinghamshire.

Bibliography: Z. Procter, *Life and Yesterday*, 1960.

PUBLISHERS AND PRINTERS Works written in support of women's enfranchisement throughout the campaign had little difficulty in achieving publication. Emanating from the articulate radical middle-classes, the campaign had close contacts with communicators. Amongst the women signing the 1866 women's suffrage petition were those who had close family associations with publishers and printers particularly interested in promoting socially and politically radical works. It must also be borne in mind that in the nineteenth century the justification for a book's existence was not measured in the same commercial terms as those employed in the second half of the twentieth century. Throughout the nineteenth century it was very common for books to be published on commission for an author or society. This meant that the author undertook all the risk of publication, while the publishers merely provided the service of organizing printing, binding and distribution, for which they gave the book their imprint, charged a fee, and took a percentage of all sales. Thus, because a book or pamphlet was published, it did not necessarily mean that it was expected to achieve a widespread sale. Many works in support of women's emancipation appeared under the imprint of publishers such as Trubner or Swan Sonnenschein because the proprietor was known to be in general sympathy with the cause. However, although sympathetic, Nicholas Trubner and Willian Swan Sonnenschein were businessmen, knew that there was little possibility of commercial success for such works and only agreed to their publication on commission. Matters changed in the first decade of the twentieth century when the upsurge of interest in the suffrage campaign created a market for information that publishers fed both from their backlists, by publishing new editions of existing works, and by the publication of new works on all facets of the woman question.

Among those who signed the 1866 women's suffrage petition was Elspet Strahan whose brother Alexander, proprietor of the eponymous publishing house, had in 1857 published Bessie Rayner PARKES, *Essays on Women's Work*. When he launched a monthly literary magazine, the *Argosy*, in December 1865, Isa CRAIG was its first editor. Strahan's biographer described him as a Gladstonian Liberal with a zeal for social reform; he was one of a group, which included Douglas Jerrold and the Howitts, that pioneered the publishing of "improving literature for the working classes". On 1 January 1866 Strahan launched the *Contemporary Review*, a journal to promulgate ideas of social and political reform, the March 1867 number of which included an article by Lydia BECKER on "Female Suffrage" (*see under* NEWSPAPERS AND JOURNALS). In 1868 Strahan published Jessie BOUCHERETT, *The Condition of Women in France*, reprinted from the *Contemporary Review*. He was also the publisher of Henry Alford, a leading member of the LONDON NATIONAL SOCIETY FOR WOMEN'S SUFFRAGE, and of George MacDonald, whose wife Louisa signed the 1866 petition, and, in the late 1860s, of F.W. NEWMAN and the 8th Duke of Argyll, father of Lady Frances BALFOUR. In 1871 Alexander Strahan was a member of the executive committee of the CENTRAL COMMITTEE OF THE NATIONAL SOCIETY. In 1872 commercial pressures led to his resignation from his firm; he was given help at this critical time by a like-minded publisher, H.S. King.

John Chapman in 1855 put his imprint to *The Right of Women to Exercise the Elective Franchise*, written by "Justitia" (Agnes POCHIN), the first tract on the subject since Harriet TAYLOR's essay, which had been published in 1851 in the *Westminster Review*, a few months before that journal was bought by Chapman. Carlyle described Chapman to Robert Browning as a "Publisher of Liberalisms", an area of commerce that was, and is, notoriously unrewarding; in 1855 Chapman's business was declared insolvent. It is therefore most probable that the Pochins paid for the publication of the pamphlet. Lack of archival evidence makes it impossible to trace a direct link between the Pochins and Chapman but, advanced liberals all, they moved in the same circles, presumably read the *Westminster Review*, and selected Chapman, with his central London bookshop, rather than one of the local Manchester firms of radical printer/publishers, to disseminate the pamphlet. Among Chapman's other authors were George Eliot, Harriet Martineau, Thomas Evans Bell (*see* Ernestine MILLS), Bessie Rayner Parkes and the Unitarians Rev. H.W. CROSSKEY and Lant Carpenter. Chapman's own medical treatises, including *Functional Diseases of Women*, 1863, a subject on which he was prone to give advice to his *inamoratae*, were published by Nicholas Trubner, who started his publishing business in 1851 and was in his day noted mainly as a promoter of works about the Orient. However, Trubner was also the publisher for George HOLYOAKE's radical journal *The Reasoner* and, from 1862 until 1889, of the *Westminster Review*. Trubner published the works of Jeremy Bentham; Sophia Dobson Collett's critique of Holyoake and atheism, 1855; and, in the 1860s, Thomas Evans Bell's works on India. Trubner published, on commission, the *Englishwoman's Review*. In June 1867 it was to Trubner that the ENFRANCHISEMENT OF WOMEN COMMITTEE gave an order to reprint the speech made by J.S. MILL on 20 May in the House of Commons in support of the women's suffrage amendment to the Reform Bill. The Committee and its successor, the London National Society, managed to use (if not sell) 4500 copies of this pamphlet in less than a year. Trubner subsequently published both for the London National Society for Women's Suffrage (for instance Helen TAYLOR's *The Claim of Englishwomen to the Suffrage Constitutionally Considered*, 1867, which was reprinted from the *Westminster Review*, and Frances Power COBBE's *Why Women Desire the Franchise*, 1869) and for Lydia BECKER and the MANCHESTER NATIONAL SOCIETY, from 1870 publishing on commission the *Women's Suffrage Journal*. The firm also published for the London National a pamphlet giving details of *The Debate in the House of Commons on the Women's Disabilities Bill, 3 May 1871*. In 1879 Trubner co-published, with Alexander Ireland in Manchester, a pamphlet by Sidney Smith, *The Enfranchisement of Women and the Law of the Land*, and in 1888 was the publisher of Emily Pfeiffer, *Women and Work*, in 1889 of Mona CAIRD's novel *The Wings of Azrael*, and in 1893 of Mrs Meredith's *A Woman's Crusade* (*see under* NOVELS). In addition, for the last quarter of the nineteenth century Trubner regularly published the work of Sheldon AMOS, Frances Power Cobbe, George Holyoake and Moncure Conway. In 1892 Nicholas Trubner was joined in his business by Alfred Trench and Charles Kegan Paul, who had taken over the business of Henry S. King.

Henry King had been a partner in Smith, Elder, publisher of the Brontes. His first wife had been the sister of George Smith's wife and, sometime after her death and his remarriage, King left Smith, Elder and in 1871 set up a publishing firm of his own. King's second wife, whom he had married in 1863, was a devotee of Mazzini and a friend of Emilie Ashurst VENTURI. While King was still with the firm, Smith, Elder published six volumes of Mazzini's works, 1864–7, for which George Meredith acted as publisher's reader. Interestingly the ledgers of H.S. King reveal that the firm published on commission in 1875 *The Rights of Women*, for a Mme A.M. Venturi, of 30 Ennismore Gardens, Princes Gate, London SW. In March 1875 one copy was sent to the *Englishwoman's Review*, one to the *Westminster Review* and one to Helen Blackburn. There is no copy of the book in the British Library, nor in Helen Blackburn's Library at Girton; the Fawcett Library copy, which bears the Trubner imprint rather than that of H.S. King, carries the ownership inscription of Caroline Ashurst BIGGS, niece of Emilie Venturi. Neither the book itself nor the favourable review in the *Englishwoman's Review*, March 1875, reveal the name of the author. The book is based on an evident acquaintance with the technicalities of law and a reading reveals that the writer was an English woman. Although unable firmly to place Emilie Venturi at 30 Ennismore Gardens in 1875, it would seem unlikely that any other author with that surname would have been writing such a book at this date. In 1877 King sold his firm to Charles Kegan Paul, who in 1881 was joined by Alfred Chenevix Trench. In that year Charles Kegan Paul published 500 copies of a short work, *Women's Rights as Preached by Women*, written by the tantalizingly anonymous "A Looker On". The work is dedicated to Col Thomas Wentworth Higginson, an American who had then been writing in support of women's rights for 30 years, and is a plea for universal suffrage, using the work of Mary Wollstonecraft and "Sophia" to protest against the work of contemporary suffragists who would limit their efforts for women's suffrage to unmarried property owners. Study of the sales ledger of Kegan Paul, Trench, Trubner reveals that the book is credited to "Madame Venturi" and in 1886 the firm was still paying to her a small amount on account of its sale. Elizabeth Wolstenholme ELMY made a reference, in a letter to Harriet McIlquham, to Mme Venturi's "Sophia pamphlet". It is likely, therefore, that Emilie Venturi was "A Looker On" and the author of this tract which can, with profit, be read in the British Library. In 1889 the firm of Kegan Paul, Trench, and King was merged, by Horatio Bottomley, with that of Nicholas Trubner as the ill-fated Hansard Publishing Union. It was under this imprint that Harriet MCILQUHAM's pamphlet *The Enfranchisement of Women: An Ancient Right, A Modern Need* was published in 1892. At this time the manager of the firm was George Redway who in 1895 left to set up his own small firm, which in its short life had a reputation for publishing esoteric works. Among these were Mona Caird's *Morality of Marriage*, 1897 and books by Mabel Collins, a theosophist who later co-authored Charlotte DESPARD's suffrage novel, *Outlawed*. In 1911 Kegan Paul, Trench, Trubner was taken over by the firm of George Routledge, which had been reconstructed in 1902 under William Swan Sonnenschein and A.E. Franklin, whose wife was by 1906 a member of the London Society for Women's Suffrage. Franklin's son Cecil joined the firm in 1906 and in 1912 became a director of the amalgamated firm of Routledge, Kegan Paul, Trench, Trubner. Cecil was the older brother of Hugh FRANKLIN.

William Swan Sonnenschein, as well as being the publisher of Shaw's *Unsocial Socialist*, of George Moore, of Edward Carpenter, of Frances Power Cobbe, and of the first English edition of *Das Capital*, had published *Woman Suffrage* by Mrs Ashton DILKE in 1885, in The Imperial Parliament series, which aimed "to place within reach of the general public, at a very cheap rate short volumes dealing with those topics of the day that lie within the range of practical politics". In 1886 the firm published a novel by Mrs Jagger, *"Is Love a Crime?"*, which included references to the suffrage campaign. In 1888 Swan Sonnenschein published Jane Hume CLAPPERTON's novel of co-operative living, *Margaret Dunmore*. A mere two years later the book's earnings were pitifully small and the author eventually acquired the remaining stock. Swan Sonnenschein published several novels by Mrs J.K. Spender, sister-in-law of Emily SPENDER; her proofs were on occasion read for her by her brother-in-law, the journalist Harold Spender. Among the other novels published by the firm in 1888 was one, *By the Tide*, by Alison GARLAND. By the 1890s the firm had acquired a reputation for publishing work sympathetic to the women's cause. Among the unsolicited manuscripts it received in 1892 was that for *Woman Free* which, on 4 April, elicited the following letter from William Swan Sonnenschein to Elizabeth Wolstenholme Elmy: "We have read your ms. entitled 'Woman Free' but do not think it is likely to have a remunerative sale. We are not therefore prepared to make you any proposal for publication, and return the m.s. with thanks". It is worth noting that he did not, as he often did, propose that the firm should publish the work on commission. The following year the firm published M. Ostrogorski, *The Rights Of Women: A Comparative Study in History and Legislation*, in 1894 Charlotte Carmichael STOPES's *British Freewomen*, and in 1897 *Education of Girls and Women in Great Britain* by Christina S. Bremner, who had been an editor of the *Woman's Herald*. William Swan Sonnenschein was a member of the Ethical Society and published its literature. Stanton COIT was one of the firm's most prolific authors and was invited to select books from the firm's list for donation to the library of his Working Men's Club.

William Swan Sonnenschein was forced into retirement at the turn of the century, sold most of his copyrights to George Allen and was then in 1902 invited to join the board of the revitalized firm of Routledge. He made a total break with his erstwhile firm in 1906. The firm of Swan Sonnenschein, however, maintained its interest in the women's cause, an interest fostered by the prospect of increased sales as militancy focused attention on the suffrage campaign. The firm reissued, as a posthumous edition, Frances Power Cobbe's *Duties of Women* in 1905 and reprinted Ostrogorski's book in 1908. Unfortunately they had lost touch with the author, had not heard from him for 12 years and had failed to inform him of their intention. They had taken advice from Charlotte Carmichael Stopes in May 1908 about the advisability of reprinting the book, noting that "The sales have been very slow but lately a small demand [emanating from?] the Women's Social and Political Union has sprung up". Having been apprised of the new printing, Ostrogorski was irate at having lost the opportunity of updating the work. As the firm explained to him in a letter of 15 November 1908, "Lately there has been an increased demand for books on Women's Rights and this, we think, is likely to continue". After prompting from Mrs Stopes, Swan Sonnenschein proposed a fourth edition of her own book, *British Freewomen*, which, incorporating some updating, was published in August 1909. As the firm wrote to her, "The book seems to be selling so well, that we should propose this time to do 1000 instead of 500". The firm had taken out a half-page advertisement in the third issue of *Votes for Women*, December 1907, grouping together eight books from its list for promotion. The firm was, in fact, the first advertiser to show such confidence in the new paper. In 1911 Swan Sonnenschein amalgamated with George Allen & Sons, publisher of Ruskin, and from 1913 its affairs were directed by Stanley Unwin, nephew of T. Fisher Unwin. The firm of George Allen, which was in financial difficulties, had moved from its office at 156 Charing Cross Road in 1909, the rent of which was considered too costly, and the remainder of its lease was taken over by Frederick PETHICK-LAWRENCE, who opened there the Woman's Press, the office and shop of the WOMEN'S SOCIAL AND POLITICAL UNION.

Thomas Fisher Unwin subscribed to the Central Society for Women's Suffrage in 1890. In 1892 he married Jane Cobden (*see* Jane Cobden UNWIN); two of his brothers had married sisters of Louisa MARTINDALE. His publishing house, T. Fisher Unwin, was a promoter of works by women. In 1891 he published a new edition of Mary Wollstonecraft's *Vindication of the Rights of Woman*, the first for 50 years, to which Millicent Garrett FAWCETT contributed an interesting foreword. Fisher Unwin sold copies of the book to members of the Central National Society at half the published price, and six copies were ordered for the Society's library. That year Elizabeth Wolstenholme Elmy wrote to Harriet McIlquham that "different people have independently recommended Fisher Unwin as a fair dealer and a friend of women, and we are going to try him". This was for *Woman Free*, which she described as Mr Elmy's latest work. The Elmys were in the event as disappointed by Fisher Unwin as they were by Swan Sonnenschein, and *Woman Free* was eventually self-published by the WOMEN'S EMANCIPATION UNION. Fourteen years later, on 13 March 1905, Mrs Elmy, disillusioned, wrote to Mrs McIlquham that "There is only one word for F.U. – Shark. The old class of publishers, who were the friends and helpers of authors (Blackwoods, the older Macmillan) is dead – and the present class is grasping . . . He has done *nothing* absolutely nothing to promote the sale of the American History of Woman Suffrage or of Susan Anthony's life". Fisher Unwin had published the English editions of *The Life and Times of Susan B. Anthony*, c. 1894, and Elizabeth Cady Stanton's *Eighty Years and More (1815–1897): Reminiscences*, 1898. Anne Cobden SANDERSON, Fisher Unwin's sister-in-law, gave Mrs Elmy a gift of the Susan B. Anthony autobiography. In 1900 Fisher Unwin published the seven volumes of the *Transactions of the International Council of Women* and in 1906 George Holyoake's autobiography, *60 years of An Agitator's Life*. In 1907, as the suffrage campaign gathered momentum, the firm published a 16-page pamphlet by Robert Cholmeley, *Women's Suffrage: The Demand and its Meaning*, and a short work by Charlotte Carmichael Stopes, *The Sphere of "Man" in relation to that of "Woman"*, in which she employed an argument similar to that used in *British Freewomen*. In 1908 Unwin published an interesting collection of essays edited by Brougham Villiers (the pseudonym, linking the names of two reformers, of F. Shaw), *The Case for Women's Suffrage* (which included contributions from, among others, Emmeline PANKHURST, Keir HARDIE, Eva GORE-BOOTH and Edith PALLISER); Joseph King, *Electoral Reform: An Inquiry into Our System of Parliamentary Representation*, which despite having a foreword by Lewis Harcourt, the notoriously anti-suffragist cabinet minister, was a work sympathetic to the women's cause and offered advice as to how their goal might be attained; and Laura McLAREN, *"Better and happier": an answer from the Ladies' gallery to the speeches in opposition to the women's suffrage bill, February 28th, 1908*. In 1909 Unwin published H.G. Wells's novel of emancipated womanhood, *Ann Veronica*, and in 1911 another book by Brougham Villiers, *Modern Democracy*, in which, in the chapter "Women and Democracy" he predicates the existence of democracy on the emancipation of women. In the same year the firm also published Olive Schreiner, *Woman and Labour*, which was dedicated to Lady Constance Lytton. In February 1912 Fisher Unwin was allowed to visit Emily Wilding DAVISON while she was imprisoned in Holloway, a rather unusual occurrence as she was only allowed visits from family or close friends. It is not clear why he was required, but around this time the *Standard* published a letter purportedly from Emily Wilding Davison to Sylvia PANKHURST, in which she mentions that she had appealed for writing facilities "both because I am a journalist and because I have written a book which at the time had every chance of being published". Perhaps Unwin had visited her in his capacity as publisher.

Two works central to an understanding of the woman's cause were published by firms that had little else similar in their lists and which made no effort to attract books on related themes. In 1902 Helen Blackburn, *Women's Suffrage: A Record of the Women's Suffrage Movement in the British Isles*, was published by Williams and Norgate. This firm was a rather surprising choice, its only previous venture into this field being the publication in 1882 of the first edition of Frances Power Cobbe, *Duties of Women*, although, as Herbert Spencer's publisher, the imprint clearly gave a suitably philosophical cast to the book. Longmans, as publisher of Mill's work, did not attempt to attract any titles to complement *The Subjection of Women*. In 1904 the NUWSS backed Stanton Coit in trying to arrange for a new 6d edition of the book. Longmans organized the publication in 1906 of a new cheap, paper-covered edition, to sell to the many newly converted to the cause at public meetings and bazaars. Stanton Coit was commissioned to write a new introduction, part of it using information provided by Elizabeth Wolstenholme Elmy. It was hoped that the NUWSS would take 10 000 copies.

The firm of David Nutt, which had in a minor way shown an interest in the nineteenth century in the women's cause, publishing in 1869 the *Reports of the Schools' Inquiry Commission* as edited by Dorothea Beale, built up an interesting "women's" list in the early twentieth century. The son of the founder, Alfred Trubner Nutt (his father had been in partnership with Nicholas Trubner in the 1850s) carried on the business after 1878 and after his death in 1910 the firm was run by his widow. She, Marie Nutt, had subscribed to the London Society for Women's Suffrage in 1906, taken part in the "Mud March" and by 1910 was a vice-president of the NATIONAL POLITICAL LEAGUE. It was doubtless this connection that resulted in the firm of David Nutt being the publisher in 1913 of the second edition of *Emancipation of English Women* by Lyon Blease, honorary treasurer of the National Political League and at that time lecturer in law at Liverpool University. The book had first been published in 1910 by Constable. In 1911, very soon after coming into Marie Nutt's control, the firm of David Nutt published Jane Brownlow, *Women's Work in Local Government in England and Wales*; Cecil Chapman, *Marriage and Divorce. Some Needed Reforms in Church and State*; and the Women's Co-operative Guild, *Working Women and Divorce. An Account of Evidence Given on Behalf of the Women's Co-operative Guild before the Royal Commission on Divorce*. In 1913 the firm published *The Englishwoman's Legal Guide: A Popular Handbook of the Law as it Affects Women and Their Property* and Marie Nutt's own novel, *A Woman of Today*.

Grant Richards, nephew of Grant Allen, author of *The Woman Who Did*, founded his publishing firm in 1897, aged 25, having left school at the age of 15 and, as he put in his *Who's Who* entry, having gained an education working for seven years in the office of W.T. Stead's *Review of Reviews*. Besides publishing books by Stead, Richards was clearly influenced by his mentor's social conscience, publishing Emma Brooke, *Tabulation of Factory Law: Special Legislation for Women and Children*, 1898; Beatrice Potter, *Case for Factory Acts*, 1901; Maude Stanley, *Clubs for Working Girls*, revised edition, 1904; Laura McLaren, *Women's Charter*, 1909; in 1913 *A Box of Chocolates* by Annie Cecilia Oldmeadow, a quaint story dedicated "To the Militant Suffragists"; and, in 1913, Belfort Bax, *Fraud of Feminism*. Rebecca West reviewing the latter in the *Clarion*, described it "as a fever against feminism", "which Mr Grant Richards is offering to England for half-a-crown"; Richards was able to redeem this idiosyncrasy by publishing in 1916 Wilma Meikle's *Towards a Sane Feminism*, which Rebecca West hailed as "a little river of wit leaping from rock to rock of solid argument. This is one of the few feminist books that have a style". Grant Richards' first wife, Elisina, was the first editor of the *Englishwoman*, which his firm published from 1909 until 1921 (*see under* NEWSPAPERS AND JOURNALS).

Among the small radical publishers who fostered the literature of the women's movement was A.C. Fifield, well-known as an "anarchist" publisher. In 1906, perhaps for the Christmas market, the firm published Dora MONTEFIORE's *The Woman's Calendar*, which comprised telling quotes apposite to the women's cause. In the same year the firm published a rather more philosophical work on the woman question, H.T. Buckle, *The Influence of Women on the Progress of Knowledge*, 1906. In 1909 the firm published Lady Constance Lytton's pamphlet, *No Votes for Women*, 1909. The conjunction between Lady Constance and anarchist publishing is perhaps explained by the fact that in the same year Fifield published her brother's tract on a comprehensive temperance policy. In 1910 Fifield was the publisher of Evelyn Sharp's *Rebel Women*, Laurence Housman's *Articles of Faith in the Freedom of Women* (in their Heretical Booklets series), and in 1912 Caroline Eccles's *Of the Emancipation of Women*.

Another small publisher, Frank Palmer, in 1910 printed a pamphlet by Margaret Clayton, *Mary Wollstonecraft and the Women's Movement Today*, which was an article reprinted, with additions, from the *Humane Review*. At that time Palmer had no similar books from his list to include amongst those advertised on the final three pages. However, in 1911 the firm published Teresa BILLINGTON-GREIG's critique *The Militant Suffrage Movement: Emancipation in a Hurry*, and in 1912 a work that it may have inspired. This, titled *Women's Suffrage and Militancy*, edited by Huntly Carter, is a collection of responses to a questionnaire sent out to around 60 men and women (mainly men), most of whom might be described as "suffragists", asking their opinion on the arguments for and against women's suffrage, whether they thought that women were likely to be enfranchised in the current parliament, and whether they thought militant methods had failed or succeeded. The result is an interesting snapshot of opinion in, it may be deduced, early 1912. In 1913 Frank Palmer published a novel by W.L. George, *A Bed of Roses*, which contains allusions to the suffrage campaign. H.J. Drane was a small general publishing firm which in 1908 published Charlotte Despard's novel *Outlawed*, in 1909 *Great Suffragists – and Why*, an interesting collection, edited by E. Hill and O.F. Shafer, of short biographies of suffragists, and two suffrage novels (Napier Hawke, *The Premier and the Suffrage*, and Adrienne Mollwo, *A Fair Suffragette*). In 1912 the firm published a further suffrage novel, E.P. Ramsay Sage's *A Fair Field and No Favour*. A Miss F. Drane was a member of the London Society for Women's Suffrage in 1906–7, but it is not clear if she had any connection with the firm.

Only two publishers appear to have had the idea of publishing a series of books to capitalize on the manifest interest in the woman question. One, a nonfiction series titled "The Women's Rights Library", republished *Women's Political Rights* by the Marquis of Condorcet and, in 1912, another edition of *Woman's Influence on the Progress of Knowledge* by H.T. Buckle. Stanley Paul, a general publisher who already had in his list Gertrude Colmore's *Suffragette Sally*, its pro-WSPU content balanced by Harold Owen's *Woman Adrift: The Menace of Suffragism*, which the firm published in 1912, launched with a fanfare in January 1913 the "Votes for Women Series". Its first, and as it transpired, only book was *The Poodle-Woman* by Annesley Kenealy, a novel that did not receive an over-effusive welcome from the reviewer in *Votes for Women*, 21 February 1913. After dismissing its contents as insufficiently stimulating she wrote, "Time was when publishers turned a cold eye on fiction in which this question played a prominent or even a serious part; time was when commercial success was incompatible with Suffrage propaganda." Stanley Paul did not presumably find the venture sufficiently rewarding to invest further in the concept of the "Votes for Women Series". However, later that year the firm published the useful and informative *Suffrage Annual and Women's Who's Who*, containing details of contemporary suffrage societies and activists. It was edited by the resolutely anonymous "A.J.R." who in all probability canvassed for candidates for inclusion. The *Suffrage Annual* leans decidedly towards the constitutional wing of the movement.

All the foregoing publishing firms included books on the women's cause amongst a range of other works. At least four firms were formed specifically to publish books and pamphlets directly related to the suffrage campaign. The Woman's Press was founded in 1906 as the publishing arm of the WSPU; among its earliest publications was Annie Kenney's *Character Sketch and Prison Faces*. Its output was concentrated on penny pamphlets and leaflets, reprinting speeches and lectures, as well as publishing original tracts, both fact and fiction. For example it published both *The Trial of the Suffragette Leaders*, a transcription of the October 1908 trial and, in 1911, Laurence Housman's light-hearted one-act play *Alice in Ganderland*. As the campaign developed, the WSPU, through the Woman's Press, published material to explain tactics and political developments to its sympathizers and to convert unbelievers to the cause. For its first four years the Woman's Press was based within the WSPU headquarters in Clement's Inn. Its printers included both the St Clement's Inn Press, handily located round the corner in Portugal Street, and the Garden City Press in Letchworth, printer to many radical causes. When, in May 1910, under Frederick Pethick-Lawrence's direction, the WSPU opened its Woman's Press shop and offices at 156 Charing Cross Road, it was fitting that the first title published with that address included in the imprint was his own *Women's Fight for the Vote*. In October 1912, after the split between the Pethick-Lawrences and the Pankhursts, the Woman's Press left Charing Cross Road and moved into the new WSPU headquarters in Lincoln's Inn House. The Woman's Press published Christabel Pankhurst's *The Great Scourge and How to End It* at the end of 1913, but thereafter the publishing programme faltered to a standstill as the police raid on the WSPU headquarters drove the staff to a succession of temporary quarters.

The WOMEN'S FREEDOM LEAGUE and the Suffrage Shop (*see under* SHOPS) both had their own publishing departments. Among the productions of the former were W.G. Earengey, *Woman under the Law* (*see* Florence EARENGEY); *Towards Woman's Liberty* by Teresa Billington-Greig; *One and One are Two* by Israel ZANGWILL; and *Five Years' Struggle for Freedom: A History of the Suffrage Movement from 1908 to 1912* by Margaret Wynne NEVINSON. The WFL set up the Minerva Publishing Company to publish its paper, the *Vote*, but did not use that imprint on its campaign literature. The Suffrage Shop in 1910 published Cicely HAMILTON's *Pageant of Great Women* and Charlotte Despard's *Woman in the New Era, with an Appreciation by Christopher St John*.

Many of the other suffrage societies issued proselytizing material under their own imprints, but John E. Francis, publisher of the suffrage journal *Women's Franchise* (*see under* NEWSPAPERS AND JOURNALS) and manager of the Athenaeum Press, appears to have been the only individual to found an independent publishing company, the Woman Citizen Publishing Co., to issue works solely related to the women's campaign. He was the son of John Collins Francis (1837–1916), the publisher of the *Athenaeum*, who in 1911 became its proprietor after the death of Sir Charles Dilke (*see* Lady DILKE). John Collins Francis's father, John Francis (1811–82), had been, with George Holyoake, a leading opponent of "taxes on knowledge" and was junior clerk in the office of the *Athenaeum*, which had been launched by James Silk Buckingham in 1831, eventually becoming its publisher and manager of the associated publishing firm. John Sterling, friend of John Stuart Mill, bought the *Athenaeum* from Buckingham in 1829 and it was then acquired by the Dilke family in 1830. Sir Charles Dilke inherited it on the death of his father in 1869 and the firm was eventually inherited in 1916 by J.E. Francis on the death of his father. The Woman Citizen Co. in 1908 published the *Scottish Women Graduates' Appeal in the House of Lords*, and in 1909 Alice Zimmern, *Women's Suffrage in Many Lands*, and Ralph Thicknesse, *The Rights and Wrongs of Women*. The firm also published material for the TAX RESISTANCE LEAGUE and in 1919 printed Margaret Kineton PARKES's history, *The Tax Resistance Movement in Great Britain*. John E. Francis was a member of the MEN'S LEAGUE FOR WOMEN'S SUFFRAGE and was the printer of the League's 1910 annual report. His wife was active in the CHURCH LEAGUE FOR WOMEN'S SUFFRAGE in 1913. From 13 May until 6 June 1913 Francis took over the printing of the *Suffragette*, at a time when the paper was being harried by the police and Home Office, only agreeing to do so as long as it contained no incitement to commit damage and removing anything that he thought might jeopardize his position. In the 1920s Francis was associated with Dick Sheppard in the relief work operating from St Martin's-in-the-Fields; "down and outs" were given work at the Athenaeum Press.

The post-First-World-War younger generation of publishers with personal connections to the suffrage campaign included Victor Gollancz, who edited and contributed an essay to *The Making of Women: Oxford Essays in Feminism*, which was published by Allen and Unwin in 1917. He later married Ruth LOWY and it was to his firm that in the late 1940s Rachel BARRETT thought of submitting Kitty MARSHALL's memoir of her suffragette days. Leonard Parsons, who was married to Helen, the younger daughter of Florence Fenwick MILLER, published in 1921 a novel by Hugh de Selincourt, *Women and Children*, which was dedicated "with permission" to Emmeline Pethick-Lawrence, and *Land Nationalisation* by Emil Davies and Dorothy EVANS. In 1922 the firm published a novel by Rachel Ferguson (erstwhile member of the YOUNG PURPLE, WHITE, AND GREEN CLUB) and in 1923 *Theodore Savage* by Cicely Hamilton. In 1925 Parsons published a collection of the speeches and writings of Lord Courtney of Penwith, who had for so long been a supporter in the House of Commons of the women's campaign.

Printers, too, played their part in disseminating material in favour of the women's suffrage campaign. One of the signatories of the 1866 petition, a friend of Frances Power Cobbe, was Augusta Spottiswoode who became a member of the London National Society for Women's Suffrage. She was doubtless related to the printing firm Spottiswoode, which had a historic link to the precursor of Alexander Strahan's publishing firm. Spottiswoode was given the order in August 1867 for printing the note paper for the London National Society and in 1868 printed for the society as a leaflet a reprint of a speech W.J. Fox had given on "Woman Suffrage" at Oldham on 4 February 1853. Spottiswoode also printed for the London National the report of the society's first public meeting, on 17 July 1869, and the report of its next meeting, at the Hanover Square rooms on 26 March 1870. Another of the signatories to the 1866 petition was Florence Waterlow, wife of Alfred Waterlow, senior partner in Waterlows, the very successful firm of printers, which, after internal rearrangements, as Waterlow Bros and Layton published J.S. Rubinstein, *Married Women's Property Act*, 1882. In 1891 her niece Mrs Ruth Homan, daughter of Sir Sydney Waterlow (printer and philanthropist, a trustee for South Place Chapel, a friend of John Stuart Mill and in 1872 lord mayor of London), headed the local election poll in Tower Hamlets as a Progressive.

The report of the Manchester National Society's first meeting in 1868 was printed by John Heywood, of 141 and 143 Deansgate, an established Manchester firm of printers, but work for the society was soon transferred to the firm of Alexander Ireland, who also printed material for the Married Women's Property Committee. The link between the printer and the two societies was Lydia Becker, whose pamphlet *The Political Disabilities of Women* it had reprinted from the *Westminster Review*. Alexander Ireland subscribed to the Manchester National Society in 1867–8; his wife was a close friend of Geraldine Jewsbury and in 1892 edited *Selection from Letters of G.E. Jewsbury to Jane Welsh Carlyle*. In 1898 Ireland's collection of books by Ralph Waldo Emerson, in many of which the author had written to him personal inscriptions, was given to the Manchester Free Reference Library, to be housed in its King Street premises very close to Mrs Pankhurst's newly refounded venture, "Emerson's". In 1873

Alexander Ireland reprinted for the Manchester National Society Agnes Pochin's treatise *The Right of Women to Exercise the Elective Franchise* and, in 1874, Lydia Becker's *Liberty, Equality and Fraternity*, reprinted from the *Women's Suffrage Journal*. The association through the Manchester National Society led to the anomaly of Alexander Ireland, in Manchester, being the printer for the Central Committee of the National Society after it was set up in London in 1872. In 1880 Alexander Ireland printed Elizabeth Wolstenholme Elmy's *The Criminal Code in its Relation to Women: A Paper read before the Dialectical Society on 3 March 1880* and also printed lectures by Francis Newman. Mrs Abel Heywood, the wife of another Manchester printer/publisher, also subscribed to the Manchester Society in 1868; she was probably the Hannah Heywood who had signed the 1866 women's suffrage petition. The firm of Abel Heywood had been established in 1832 and was at the forefront of the battle to force the repeal of stamp duty on newspapers, its proprietor being imprisoned for four months as a result. The firm was, around 1904, the printer of Christabel Pankhurst's first, and now extremely scarce, pamphlet, *Parliamentary Vote for Women*.

In London the Women's Printing Society had printed reports for the Central Committee of the National Society until at least 1893 and for the Central National Society for most of the years between 1889 and 1900. The Women's Printing Society was a natural, but by no means inevitable choice of printer for works connected with the women's movement. It printed in 1883 *What is women's suffrage and why do women want it* by "Veritas"; Elizabeth Wolstenholme Elmy's *A Woman's Plea to Women* (reprinted from the *Macclesfield Courier*), 1886; Millicent Garrett Fawcett, *Home and Politics. An Address*, 1894; Frances Hoggan, *Swimming and its relation to the Health of Women*, 1879, and *Education for Girls in Wales*, 1882. It was clearly also the choice of those of discriminating taste, who wished to see their literary efforts enhanced by good quality typography and paper. It was doubtless Christiana HERRINGHAM who suggested to her two siblings that the Women's Printing Society would be a suitable printer for a memoir of their father, *Thomas Wilde Powell*, 1903; she herself used the Women's Printing Society in 1907 for the printing of the *Papers of the Society of Painters in Tempera*. In 1909 the Women's Printing Society printed and published *Woman Suffrage and the Anti-militants* by Ennis Richmond, offering special terms for supplying it to suffage societies. The Garden City Press in Letchworth was another firm that acted as publisher as well as printer. It is possible that it was acting on commission when it published Constance Smedley's *Woman: A Few Shrieks* and Katherine Roberts' *Pages from the Diary of a Militant Suffragette*.

Amongst firms that were sympathetic to the cause it was not only printers that served to produce the necessary propaganda. Carl Hentschel (1869–1920) was the owner of the largest firm of process engravers in London. His wife was an active member of the London Society for Women's Suffrage in 1906 and in January 1910 was one of the founders of the new CONSTITUTIONAL SOCIETY FOR WOMEN'S SUFFRAGE. Carl Hentschel printed for the ARTISTS' SUFFRAGE LEAGUE a New Year card and calendar for 1912 and a card for 1913.

Archival source: Archives of Kegan Paul, Trench, Trubner and Henry S. King, 1858–1912; Archives of Swan Sonnenschein & Co., 1878–1911.

Bibliography: J.C. Francis, *John Francis, Publisher of the Athenaeum: A Literary Chronicle of Half a Century*, 1888; *Catalogue of the Alexander Ireland Collection*, 1898; A. Heywood, *Abel Heywood & Son, 1832–1899*, 1899; J. Boon, *Under Six Reigns: The House of Waterlow*, 1925; G. Richards, *Author Hunting*, 1934; F.A. Mumby, *The House of Routledge, 1834–1934*, 1934; J.E. Francis, *Dick and JEF*, 1939; F.A. Mumby and F.H.S. Stallybrass, *From Swan Sonnenschein to George Allen & Unwin Ltd*, 1955; P.T. Srebrnik, *Alexander Strahan, Victorian Publisher*, 1986; L. Howsam, "Forgotten Victorians: Contracts with Authors in the Publication Books of Henry S. King and Kegan Paul, Trench, 1871–89", *Publishing History*, 34, 1993.

PURLEY (Conservative and Unionist Franchise Suffrage Association)   Secretary (1913) Mrs Edith Moore, Glan Aber, Purley, Surrey.

PURLEY (NUWSS)   In 1913 the society was a member of the SURREY, SUSSEX, AND HANTS FEDERATION OF THE NATIONAL UNION OF WOMEN'S SUFFRAGE SOCIETIES. Secretary (1913) Miss Wallis, Birkdale, Foxley Lane, Purley and Miss Brailsford, Highwood, Peaks Hill, Purley, Surrey.

PUTNEY AND FULHAM (WSPU) Secretary (1913) Miss Cutten, 905 Fulham Road, London S.W.

PWLLHELI (NUWSS) In 1913 the society was a member of the West Lancs, West Cheshire, and North Wales Federation of the National Union of Women's Suffrage Societies. Secretary (1913) *pro tem* Mrs D.H. Williams, Arden, Cardiff Road, Pwllheli, Wales.

Q

QUI VIVE CORPS At first called, rather clumsily, the "Marchers' Qui Vive Corps", founded in 1912 by Florence DE FONBLANQUE as the result of the enjoyment derived from involvement in the Women's March and the sense that the country was, whatever the political parties might think, supportive of women's enfranchisement. Its aim was to bind members from all suffrage societies in a body that could be "mobilized", offering its services to different societies impartially and whenever extra workers were required for any definite purpose. One of its objects was, "To show that the women of England are as capable of organisation, comradeship and discipline, as the men." The members were pledged to abstain from militant action while actually wearing the "Q.V." uniform of brown with green cockade and badge.

The Corps, although not militant, was distinctly militaristic. Its orders for the day, issued in Sussex in 1913, mentioned rallying at the "Depot" on Saturday afternoons and making a "March" on an outlying district to hold a meeting there. Members were prepared periodically to make longer marches to Brighton, Shoreham, Worthing, Hastings, Eastbourne and the west of England. Although intended as a national movement, it does not appear to have spread beyond Sussex, the centre of influence of its founder. In 1913 Lady COWDRAY entertained the Qui Vive Corps at Cowdray Park. Just as the NATIONAL UNION OF WOMEN'S SUFFRAGE SOCIETIES adopted the idea of the Women's March as the basis for its 1913 PILGRIMAGE, so in 1914 it produced its own version of the Qui Vive Corps, the ACTIVE SERVICE LEAGUE. The Qui Vive Corps participated in the NUWSS victory celebrations on 13 March 1918. Leader and honorary organizer (1912) Florence de Fonblanque; honorary treasurer, Miss M.E. Byham; honorary secretary Miss A.N. Roff, Easebourne, Midhurst, Sussex; secretary *pro tem* Ruth Cavendish-BENTINCK.

Address: (1913) 8 Park Mansions Arcade, Knightsbridge, London SW; (1914 and 1917) Duncton, Petworth, Sussex. In 1913 a Qui Vive Corps shop was opened at 60 West Street, Horsham, Sussex.

Archival source: Papers of Margaret Byham, Fawcett Library.

R

RADCLIFFE (NUWSS) In 1910 the society joined the MANCHESTER AND DISTRICT FEDERATION OF THE NATIONAL UNION OF WOMEN'S SUFFRAGE SOCIETIES. Secretary (1909) Miss Allen, Holly Bank, Whitefield; (1913) Miss K. Schofield, Stanley House, Besses o' th' Barn, Lancashire.

RADIO, TELEVISION, RECORDINGS AND RECORDS
It is ironic that it is the contemporary spoken force of the women's suffrage campaign that is today least well represented in archives. The reality of the campaign has been captured on film, but there is apparently no surviving recording of the voices of Mrs PANKHURST, Mrs FAWCETT, or Mrs DESPARD. Thomas Edison had invented the phonograph in 1877 but it was only at the end of the century that the "phonograph" or "gramophone" industry began to develop. In its early days there was no preconceived notion that the gramophone should be used to transmit only music. *The Electric World* suggested in 1890 that interviews with statesmen such as Gladstone and Bismarck could be reproduced via the phonograph. In 1911 HMV had in its catalogue "Political Records" by (speaking on the budget) Asquith, Lloyd George and Churchill, others speaking about the navy and, to do something to rectify the political balance of the list, a message recorded by Bonar Law. In the early twentieth century the women's suffrage societies were aware of the possibilities of this new medium. Pathéphone speeches had been recorded at some point before April 1908, when they were mentioned during the course of a WFL bazaar at Caxton Hall, by Mrs Despard, Lady GROVE, Edith How MARTYN and Teresa BILLINGTON-GREIG. The latter had recorded c. 1907 a "Votes for Women" speech for use in the campaign, perhaps the one mentioned in 1908. In April 1914 gramophone speeches were heard from Chrystal MACMILLAN and Dr Drysdale at a meeting of the NATIONAL UNION OF WOMEN'S SUFFRAGE SOCIETIES. There is one extant recording of a speech given by Christabel PANKHURST. This is now available as a track on a Pavilion Records CD, *Blaze of the Day*. The accompanying notes give the date of its recording as 18 December 1908. However, this cannot be correct, as on that day Christabel Pankhurst was still serving a prison sentence in Holloway and was not released until the evening of 19 December 1908. Another source refers to "Christabel Pankhurst's 'Suffrage for Women' Speech", presumably the same one, which was issued by the Gramophone Company in 1909. Whatever its date, it is likely to be the speech mentioned in the *Woman's Leader*, 28 August 1925, as having been recently re-released. It is rather surprising that the marketing strategists at the WOMEN'S SOCIAL AND POLITICAL UNION did not do more to capitalize on the oratorical power of their leaders. There is no mention in any WSPU literature of records for sale of speeches by Emmeline and Christabel Pankhurst, which assuredly would have been very popular. The SUFFRAGETTE FELLOWSHIP in 1947 commissioned a record from GB Ltd, a gramophone company. On one side it carries a speech by Frederick PETHICK-LAWRENCE and on the other one by Emmeline PETHICK-LAWRENCE.

The BBC did not begin broadcasting until 1922 and the earliest recording in the BBC archive of a suffrage activist is of Ethel SMYTH and dates from 1937. The BBC had broadcast the unveiling of Mrs Pankhurst's statue on 6 March 1930, but no recording survives. The BBC played its part in making the women's suffrage campaign synonymous in the mind of the general public with that of the WSPU. It is clear that from the late 1940s members of the Suffragette Fellowship had a degree of access to the BBC. No recordings, if they were made, survive of any interviews made between the end of the Second World War and 1980 with any constitutional suffragist; even the 1980 interviews with Margery

Corbett ASHBY and Hazel Hunkins Hallinan were inspired by the centenary of the birth of Christabel Pankhurst. On 13 March 1951 the BBC broadcast a play by Jill Craigie, *The Women's Rebellion* subtitled "A dramatised impression of the Suffragette Movement". The characters around whom the play was based are shown in the cast list as Emmeline Pankhurst, Christabel Pankhurst, Annie KENNEY, Emmeline Pethick-Lawrence, Irene MILLER, Charlotte MARSH, Mary LEIGH, Lloyd George, Herbert Gladstone, Sir Edward Grey, a prison governor and, rather intriguingly, Emily DAVIES. One cannot help but wonder if, in this company, the last named (played by Violet Carson) has not been confused with Emily Wilding DAVISON. Charlotte Marsh was an adviser to the production. No recording of the play survives, although the text is presumably still in the possession of the author. From the cast list one can deduce something of the play's scope. Jill Craigie wrote an article "Honourable Gaol-birds", published in the *Radio Times*, 9 March 1951, revealing that "Today I have what I think must be the largest suffragette library outside the suffragette museum [then the Suffragette Fellowship Record Room], not to mention the many hundreds of photographs, letters and mementoes that suffragettes so kindly sent me." This material and, presumably, conversations with its donors had led her to conclude that "it was the fear of a renewal of militant activities that enabled the first Bill granting the vote to women over the age of thirty to be passed without a hitch."

Radio and television treatment of such historical episodes necessarily relies for dramatic effect on the clear thinking and decisive action of a few colourful characters. The talks recorded for the BBC by Mary RICHARDSON and Ada FLATMAN also conjure up such effective scenes. Mary Richardson's talks in particular make very good radio. The incidents she describes are, as one would expect, closely modelled on the scenes set out in her autobiography, vignettes of action with herself at the centre. It seems presumptuous for the present-day listener, even if not persuaded by the same words on the printed page, to doubt the truthfulness of the spoken words of a participant in a historical episode. However, whatever listeners thought at the time, it is difficult now to give credence to Mary Richardson's avowal that Emily Wilding Davison discussed with Emmeline Pankhurst, on the evening before the 1913 Derby, her plan to halt the King's horse. Whatever other claims she made, Mary Richardson did not include herself in this particular conversation, although she was able to record that Mrs Pankhurst was worried that the jockey might be hurt but was assured by Emily Davison who was convinced that she would be the only one injured. Mrs Pankhurst was at that time, under the "Cat and Mouse" Act, living in a flat in Westminster. She never gave any indication that Emily Davison's plan had been divulged to her in advance; she surely would have made much of the responsibility if this had been so. It is necessary to be wary of taking at face value the historical veracity of such sources, the original purpose of which was primarily to entertain. The close involvement with the BBC of a small group drawn from a particular section of the Suffragette Fellowship had, in the post-Second-World-War years, the effect of obliterating from public awareness anything of the movement for women's suffrage other than colourful highlights of the militant campaign. The subtleties of NUWSS parliamentary tactics could not hope to compete with uninhibited tales spoken with conviction by strong-minded, articulate women. Even Sylvia Pankhurst, every thought and fact ringing true, was only recorded talking about her mother. She did it memorably well but was, presumably, not required (or even was required not) to mention any dissension within the WSPU. BBC radio produced other programmes, of which there do not appear to be recordings now available. Among these are *Edwardian Patchwork*, 3 March 1958, compiled from existing BBC recordings including reminiscences of Ada Flatman, Lady Keeble (Lillah MCCARTHY), Lady Violet Bonham-Carter and Una DUVAL (Home Service); Anna MUNRO, *A Honeymoon in Prison*, 1956; Christopher ST JOHN on Ethel SMYTH's suffragette days, 1958; Profile of Victoria Lidiard on Radio Four, *c.* 1988; Mrs Louise CULLEN on Australian Broadcasting about her memories of the militant campaign (no date).

BBC Television, while still based at Alexandra Palace, broadcast a play by Norman Swallow called *The Suffragette*, for which Charlotte Marsh and Jessie KENNEY acted as technical advisers, with Warwick Kenney Taylor as adviser for the character of his mother, Annie Kenney. BBC Television on 14 May 1957 presented a telvision documentary, *Fighting for the Vote*, which included interviews with, among others, Christabel Pankhurst, described in the *Radio Times* as "a leading member of the Suffragette Fellow-ship", Lady Astor, Lady Violet Bonham-Carter and Lord Pethick-Lawrence. Other participants included Winifred MAYO, Jessie Kenney, Charlotte Marsh and Mary Stocks. The accompanying note in the *Radio Times* writes of "Stories of courage and ingenuity which have almost the character of an underground resistance movement – from code telegrams and clandestine newspaper publication to disguised escapes, capture, and imprisonment". There is no extant recording of the programme; but, again, it would seem to have drawn mainly on the militant experience. Only Mary Stocks could have spoken for the constitutional movement; neither Lady Astor nor Lady Violet Bonham-Carter (Asquith's daughter) could be considered its representatives. A typescript of the interview with Christabel Pankhurst, filmed in California, is now held as part of the Mitchell Collection in the Museum of London. On 1 February 1968 BBC Television broadcast a 50-minute documentary, *Votes for Women: The Story of the Suffragettes*, which included "eye-witness accounts" from Charlotte DRAKE, Lilian LENTON, Mary PHILLIPS and Grace ROE, together with "authentic film illustrating the masculine world of British politics at the beginning of the century". *The Listener*, 8 February 1968, carried excerpts from the interviews and a flavour of the programme, accompanied by a wicked Mark Boxer cartoon.

The BBC involvement with the women's militant suffrage campaign reached its apogee with the production *Shoulder to Shoulder*, first shown in April 1974. A lavish, well researched television drama series, it is more historically accurate than some of the broadcast personal reminiscences. *Shoulder to Shoulder* was accompanied by an interesting *Radio Times Special* and in the *Radio Times*, 30 March 1974, Grace Roe in an interview with Margaret Drabble stressed that she did not want the achievements of the WSPU to be obscured by personalities. More recent BBC Television programmes, *Voices from the Doll's House* and *Skirts Through History*, 1994, have also included coverage of the women's suffrage campaign; recordings of neither are available commercially.

The following items are listed in the BBC Sound Archive catalogue; some, where indicated, are also included in the National Sound Archive.

Philip Snowden, *I Knew a Man – Keir Hardie*, 13 December 1935.

Scrapbook of 1912, Dame Ethel Smyth on Suffragettes and Vera Brittain on forcible feeding, 9 March 1937.

Ethel Smyth *Talk on the Suffragettes*, 1937, preceded by a recording of "The March of the Women" (and in the National Sound Archive).

Speeches by Eleanor Rathbone, Maude Royden, and Edith Sumerskill on "Votes for Women" at luncheon on 21st anniversary of first women's suffrage act, 17 March 1939.

Scrapbook for 1909. Mrs Muriel MATTERS Porter on leaflet exploit from airship, no date.

Talk by Lady Astor in *As I See It*, no date.

Twenty-fifth anniversary programme *Women and the Vote*, discussion, 2 April 1943.

Scrapbook for 1906, Lady Keeble (Lillah McCarthy) on memories of suffragettes, 17 and 27 October 1946.

Ada Flatman, *Reminiscences of a Suffragette*, 30 December 1946 (and in the National Sound Archive.

Lillah McCarthy, *Memories of the Suffragettes*, 17 October 1947.

Sylvia Pankhurst, *Memories of Mrs Pankhurst* (30 June 1953; and in National Sound Archive).

Scrapbook for 1903, reference to Mrs Pankhurst and suffragette movement, 18 November 1953.

Scrapbook for 1914, reference to Votes for Women, 22 December 1954.

Mary Richardson, in *Forty Years On*, 12 September 1957 (and in the National Sound Archive).

Mary Richardson and Charlotte Marsh took part in *Was it all worth while?*, 14 July 1958.

The Suffragette Movement: Memories of Emmeline Pankhurst by Winifred Mayo, Sylvia Pankhurst, Enid Goulden Bach, Lord Pethick-Lawrence, Mary Richardson and others, broadcast on *Woman's Hour* on 13 July 1958 to mark the centenary of her birth (and held in the National Sound Archive).

Mary Richardson, 21 December 1960 (and in the National Sound Archive).

Lilian Lenton remembers the "Cat and Mouse" Act, 1960.

Dora Herbert Jones makes reference to Christabel Pankhurst when interviewed on 29 March 1961.

Reminiscences of *Sir Almroth Wright, the provocative doctor*, 30 March 1961.

A.E. Blackwell on the extra work caused by suffragettes in a talk, *A London Bobby, 1910*, 14 June 1961.

St John Irvine describes how he saw Emily Davison throw herself under the King's horse, 1913 Derby, 16 June 1961.

L. Sieveking recalls helping his mother at women's suffrage campaign meetings in a talk, 18 January 1962 (*see under* NOVELS).

A. Graham-Jones, *Driving Mrs Pankhurst*, her experience as a chauffeur in 1911, 28 September 1962.

Fenner Brockway refers to his support of the women's suffrage movement in an interview in *Frankly Speaking*, 20 December 1962.

Adeline BOURNE on her work as a suffragette, 27 February 1964.

Edith Lester Jones on part she played in the suffragette movement, 31 March 1965.

Grace Roe interviewed on her experience, 18 January 1968.

Jane Wyatt, aged 88, interviewed on her activities as a suffragette, 31 January 1968.

Former suffragette, Mrs Harrison Broadley, interviewed on the suffragette movement, 6 February 1968.

Interviews with two ex-suffragettes (unnamed) on *Woman's Hour*, 6 February 1968.

Leonora COHEN interviewed 3 April 1973, and again on her 100th birthday, 14 June 1973.

Edith Pepper, former suffragette, interviewed in series *Prisoners of Conscience*, 1 October 1973.

Gladys Griffith interviewed about white slave traffic in London, with account of a case which resulted in the mother of a kidnapped girl becoming a suffragette, 9 September 1977.

Margery Corbett Ashby and Hazel Hunkins Hallinan interviewed on the centenary of the birth of Christabel Pankhurst, 18 September 1980.

Archival source: BBC Sound Recordings Catalogue British Library; National Sound Archive Catalogue, British Library.

In the 1970s the developing discipline of oral history captured on tape the recollections of the survivors of some of those involved in the women's suffrage campaign. The tapes recorded by Dr Brian Harrison are a superb resource. The following, a selection of those most obviously pertinent to the women's suffrage campaign, are illuminating, entertaining, evocative and a mine of information.

Margery Corbett ASHBY, 7 and 28 May 1974, 8 April 1975, 21 September 1976, 23 November 1976.

Fiona Billington-Greig (daughter of Teresa Billington-Greig), 24 August 1974, 19 September 1974.

Mrs Blackman (niece of Teresa Billington-Greig), 19 September 1974.

Grace Roe, 23 September 1974.

James Taylor (husband of Annie Kenney), 23 October 1974.

Mrs Leonora Cohen, 26, 27 October 1974.

Cicely HALE, 6 November 1974.

Marie LAWSON, 14, 20 November 1974.

Mrs Annie Barnes, 27 November, 18 December 1974.

Hazel Hunkins Hallinan, 8 February 1975.

Lyndal Evans (daughter of Dorothy EVANS), 22 March 1975.

Mrs Naomi Lutyens (daughter of H.D. HARBEN), 28 March, 10 April 1975.

Doris Chew (daughter of Ada Nield CHEW), 31 March 1975.

Sybil Morrison, 3 April 1975.

Reginald Price (husband of Millicent Brown), 5 April 1975.

Mrs Marion Johnson (daughter of Alice Schofield COATES), 12 April 1975.

Alice Schofield Coates, 12 April 1975.

Vera Douie, 18 April 1975.

Edith Pepper, 27 April 1975.

Elisabeth Lutyens (niece of Lady Constance LYTTON), 3 June 1975.

Dr Donald Munro-Ashman (son of Anna Munro), 30 July 1975.

Helen Moyes (formerly Helen FRASER), 19 August 1975.
Mary Tabor (niece of Mrs C.D. Rackham), 25 November 1975.
Dame Sybil Thorndike, 2 December 1975.
Dr Barclay Barrowman (brother of Janet Barrowman), 2 March 1976.
Hazel Inglis, 21 February, 16 March 1976.
Olive BARTELS, 27 March 1976.
Mrs Victoria Lidiard, 28 March 1976.
Louisa Beeston and E.M. Jackson, 30 March 1976.
Roger Fulford, 13 April 1976.
Mrs Connie Lewcock, 15 April 1976.
Mrs Nita Needham (cousin of Esther Knowles), 31 May 1976.
Mrs Vere Hinton, 1 June 1976.
Elsie Lagsding, 15 June 1976.
Mrs Eileen Sturges, 15 June 1976.
Mrs Gladys Groom-Smith, 9 June, 11 August 1976.
Mrs Peggy Goodman, 2 September 1976.
Mrs Konter and Mrs Hunter, 7 October 1976.
Mrs Margaret Dunnett (niece of Olive WALTON), 2 November 1976.
Vera Douie, 12 December 1976.
Mrs Barbara Halpern (daughter of Ray STRACHEY) 5 January, 22 January 1977, 18 August 1979.
Mrs Mary Dunlop (niece of Ida O'MALLEY), 22 January 1977.
Dr Letitia Fairfield, 21 December 1976, 17 February 1977.
Irene Hilton, 24 February 1977.
Mr and Mrs Cyril Wentzel, 1 March 1977.
Mrs Myra Stedman (daughter of Myra Sadd BROWN), 2 March 1977.
Miss E. Furlong (cousin once removed of Kathleen COURTNEY), 10 March 1977.
Mrs Alice Richards (daughter of Alice Schofield-Coates), 29 March 1977.
Mrs Groves, 30 March 1977.
Norah Balls, 16 April 1977.
Colin Franklin (nephew of Hugh FRANKLIN), 20 June 1977.
Jessie STEPHEN, 1 July 1977.
Mrs Margaret Ridgeway (daughter of Anna Munro), 16 July 1977.
Norman Franklin (nephew of Hugh Franklin), 18 September 1979.
Lord Brockway, 29 April 1980.
Mrs Helen Wilson (daughter of Annot ROBINSON), 5 September 1981.
Mrs Sue Hogan (grand-daughter of Adela PANKHURST), 3 December 1981.
Mrs Rita Pankhurst (daughter-in-law of Sylvia Pankhurst), 2 February 1982.
Dr Michael Ashby (son of Dame Margery Corbett Ashby), 15 October 1982.

Archival source: Brian Harrison tapes, Fawcett Library.

The North-West Sound Archive holds a selection of relevant recordings, some radio recordings and some the product of individually taped interviews:

Mrs Ethel Derbyshire from Blackburn, suffragette sympathizer/supporter talks about the movement, 13 February 1974.
A Voice in the Crowd, 30 March 1974, a suffragette discusses the movement and her interest in politics.
Phoebe Hesketh talks about her aunt, Edith RIGBY, 27 November 1977.
Woman b. 1904 recalls her childhood in Bolton – including memories of the suffragette movement, 24 September 1981.
Woman b. 1903 recalls memories of suffragettes, 18 December 1981.
Woman b. 1902 recalls memories of suffragettes, Bolton, 21 October 1981.
Man b. 1900 remembers his mother's suffragette activities, Bolton, 30 November 1981.
Dr Richard Pankhurst's memories of his mother, Sylvia Pankhurst, 1983.

Archival source: North-West Sound Archive, Clitheroe Castle, Lancashire (copies kept at Greater Manchester County Record Office).
Bibliography: A. Ross, *British Documentary Sound*, 1976; *Oral History: The Journal of the Oral History Society: Women's History Issue*, 5, 2; J. Liddington, *Working Class Women in the North West*, 1977.

See also FILMS; SONGS, MUSIC AND POETRY.

RADLETT (WSPU) Secretary (1913) Mrs White, Gravels, Radlett, Hertfordshire.

RAMSGATE (NUWSS) In 1913 the society was a member of the KENTISH FEDERATION OF THE

NATIONAL UNION OF WOMEN'S SUFFRAGE SOCIETIES. Secretary (1909, 1913) Miss Margaret E. Sale, 8 Royal Crescent, Ramsgate, Kent.

RATHBONE, ELEANOR FLORENCE (1872–1946) Born in London, daughter of William S. Rathbone, a Liberal MP and philanthropist. The Rathbone heritage, founded on merchant shipping, embraced Unitarianism and anti-slavery. Jane S. Rathbone of Greenbank, Liverpool (the family home) was one of the signatories to the 1866 women's suffrage petition. William Rathbone in the 1880s attended meetings in support of women's suffrage. Eleanor Rathbone was educated at Somerville College, Oxford (1893–6), a contemporary there of Maude Royden, on graduating worked for the Liverpool Central Relief Centre, and in 1898 became secretary of the LIVERPOOL SOCIETY FOR WOMEN'S SUFFRAGE, which position she still held in 1913. She was chairman of the WEST LANCASHIRE, WEST CHESHIRE, AND NORTH WALES FEDERATION, was a member of the executive committee of the NATIONAL UNION OF WOMEN'S SUFFRAGE SOCIETIES from 1900 until 1919, and from then until 1929 was president of its successor, the National Union of Societies for Equal Citizenship. From 1909 until 1935 Eleanor Rathbone was a member of Liverpool City Council, the first woman so elected. In 1913 she opposed the establishment of the NUWSS Election Fighting Fund, by which NUWSS support would be withdrawn from Liberal candidates. She saw this policy as tantamount to constitutional coercion rather than the erstwhile policy of constitutional persuasion. However, once the strategy was adopted she did in 1913 contribute towards the salary of an extra organizer to implement the policy in her federation. In early 1914, however, her opposition to the EFF hardened and she resigned from the NUWSS executive.

Eleanor Rathbone was opposed to all force in the cause of enfranchisement and signed the letter of protest against WOMEN'S SOCIAL AND POLITICAL UNION militancy that appeared in *Votes for Women* on 26 July 1912. In 1912 the Liverpool Society for Women's Suffrage published her pamphlet *What Anti-Suffragist Men really think about Women: Sir Almroth Wright and his Critics*. During the First World War Eleanor Rathbone supported Millicent Garret FAWCETT's pro-war section of the NUWSS. After the war she became president of the National Union of Societies for Equal Citizenship, of which her companion, Elizabeth Macadam, was honorary secretary. In 1922 Eleanor Rathbone stood unsuccessfully as an independent parliamentary candidate in Liverpool, but in 1929 was successful as the Independent candidate for the Combined English Universities seat, remaining in parliament until 1946. As an MP she campaigned strenuously to improve the condition of Indian women and for the introduction of family allowances, putting into practice the hopes for enfranchisement that suffragists had nursed since the nineteenth century.

Address: (1913) Greenbank, Greenbank Lane, Toxteth, Liverpool.

Bibliography: M. Stocks, *Eleanor Rathbone*, 1949; S.S. Holton, *Feminism and Democracy: Women's Suffrage and Reform Politics in Britain, 1900–1918*, 1986; M. Van Helmond, *Votes for Women: The Events on Merseyside 1870–1928*, 1992; J. Alberti, *Eleanor Rathbone*, 1996.

RAWLE, MARY ANNE, MRS (1878–?) Born in Lancashire, from the age of 10 she worked half-time and from 13 full-time in a cotton mill. In 1900 she married Francis Rawle, an iron turner. She was one of the 400 women who travelled to London to represent the textile workers in the deputation to the prime minister on 19 May 1906. She remembered that "One banner was the most striking; it was a big red one with 'Votes for Women SPU'." She mentions that Miss Billington (*see* Teresa BILLINGTON-GREIG) and Miss KENNEY organized the women into their places and that they walked, headed by Christabel PANKHURST, Irene MILLER and Annie Kenney, along Westminster Bridge and Whitehall to Downing Street. As a delegate from the WSPU Mrs Rawle was allowed into the Foreign Office with Annie Kenney, Mary NEAL, Emmeline PETHICK-LAWRENCE, Nellie Alma MARTEL, Mrs Harker and Edith How MARTYN, with Mrs Pankhurst as their speaker. She mentions that Sir Charles McLaren introduced the speakers to Campbell-Bannerman, and also mentions the presence there of Emily DAVIES, Margaret ASHTON and Eva GORE-BOOTH. In the autumn of 1906 Mrs Rawle helped Hannah MITCHELL, already a friend, when the latter was appointed part-time WSPU ORGANIZER in Oldham. Mrs Rawle went again to London, dressed in clogs and shawl, in March 1907 in order to take part in the second Women's Parliament. She was sentenced to two weeks' imprisonment in Holloway and mentions that on her reception there, she had to hand over pawn tickets as well as her money. After her release she received a letter of support, composed at its annual conference in Derby in early April, from fellow members of the Independent Labour Party and a touching letter from the secretary of her Socialist Sunday school on behalf of its children. She attended the release breakfast, held at the Eustace Miles restaurant, and received a badge and illuminated address. She was given a welcome by the Ashton-under-Lyne ILP on her release.

In 1907 Mary Anne Rawle joined the newly formed WOMEN'S FREEDOM LEAGUE, becoming its branch secretary in Ashton-under-Lyne. In 1910 Mrs Rawle moved to Grantham, Lincolnshire, and in December 1912 sent a photographic postcard of "The woman's march through Grantham", a photograph of one moment in the Women's March from Edinburgh to London organized by Florence DE FONBLANQUE, to "Mrs [Lilian?] HICKS", commenting that "if there is no other good thing that the Womens movement has done in this is as [sic] done much in bringing Rich and poor together in one great cause". In 1913 Mrs Rawle presided at a meeting of the Grantham branch of the NATIONAL UNION OF WOMEN'S SUFFRAGE SOCIETIES. It is not clear why she transferred her allegiance from the WFL, but it is likely that, her sympathies lying firmly with the ILP, she supported the NUWSS policy of backing Labour Party candidates. She herself stood as a Labour candidate in the Grantham Municipal Election. She was chairman of her local branch of the Women's Co-operative Guild for 17 years and chairman of the Grantham branch of the Old Age Pensions Association in 1945.

Address: 6 Springfield Street, Hooley Hill, Manchester.
Archival source: M.A. Rawle Papers, Fawcett Library.

RAWTENSTALL (NUWSS) By 1912 the society was a member of the MANCHESTER AND DISTRICT FEDERATION OF THE NATIONAL UNION OF WOMEN'S SUFFRAGE SOCIETIES. Secretary (1913) Mrs Robert Kay, 1 Waingate, Springside, Rawtenstall, nr Manchester, Lancashire.

RAYLEIGH (WSPU) Secretary (1910 and 1913) Mrs Warren, The White Cottage, Rayleigh, Essex.

READING branch of the MEN'S POLITICAL UNION FOR WOMEN'S ENFRANCHISEMENT Founded in 1910.

READING (NUWSS) In 1913 the society was a member of the OXON, BERKS, BUCKS, AND BEDS FEDERATION OF THE NATIONAL UNION OF WOMEN'S SUFFRAGE SOCIETIES. Secretary (1909) Miss Dale, Earlham, Kendrick Road, Reading, Berkshire; (1913) c/o 7 Town Hall Chambers, Blagrave Street, Reading, Berkshire.

READING AND NEWBURY (WSPU) Organizer (1910) Miss Catherine Margesson (*see* Lady Isabel MARGESSON); shop 39 West Street; secretary (1913) Miss Cobb, 49 Market Place, Reading, Berkshire.

REBELS' SOCIAL AND POLITICAL UNION A men's association founded *c.* 1913 in the East End of London to give support to the EAST LONDON FEDERATION OF SUFFRAGETTES. George LANSBURY's son Willie was a leading member.

REDCAR (NUWSS) In 1913 the society was a member of the NORTH-EASTERN FEDERATION OF THE NATIONAL UNION OF WOMEN'S SUFFRAGE SOCIETIES. Secretary (1913) Mrs Fothergill, 9 Nelson Terrace, Redcar, Yorkshire.

REDDISH, SARAH (1850–1928) Born in Bolton, where her father was an active member of the Co-operative society education committee, she left school at the age of 11 and began work at home, winding silk on a frame and preparing it for weaving. She later entered a cotton mill as a winder and reeler and afterwards was a forewoman in a hosiery mill. In 1879 she joined the local branch of the Co-operative Society and from 1886 until 1906 she was president of the Bolton Women's Co-operative Guild, in 1889–91 and 1895–8 was a member of the Guild's central committee and in 1897 was its president. From 1893 for two years she was the Guild's organizer, its first, in the north of England. Catherine Webb, writing the Guild's history, *The Woman with the Basket*, refers specifically to Sarah Reddish's "clear, logical, and convincing speech [which] came as a revelation of women's power". Travelling extensively through her region, in 1894–5 she attended over 100 Guild meetings. For instance, in the company of Alice SCATCHERD, Sarah Reddish was present in June 1894 at the inaugural meeting of the Morley Co-operative Guild. Her loyalties did not, however, lie solely with the Women's Co-operative Guild; in 1896 Sarah Reddish was both a supporter of the WOMEN'S EMANCIPATION UNION and took part in a propaganda tour in the Clarion van. In 1897 she stood, unsuccessfully, for election to the Bolton School Board. When in 1899 a vacancy occurred on the Board it was expected that she would be co-opted to fill it, as it was usual to select the defeated candidate who had attracted the most votes. However, because she was a woman, the Board chose to depart from this custom. She was, nevertheless, returned at an election a few months later. In 1899 she was appointed a part-time organizer for the Women's Trade Union League and in 1900 was also employed as a "petition worker" or organizer by the NORTH OF ENGLAND SOCIETY FOR WOMEN'S SUFFRAGE, of which she was also a member of the executive committee. In March 1901, as a consequence, she was, with Selina COOPER who had also gathered signatures, a member of the deputation that took the petition, which contained 29 359 names, to the House of Commons. Sarah Reddish was the first speaker when the petition was presented to Lancashire MPs.

In 1902 Sarah Reddish was actively involved, as a representative of both the WTUL and the NESWS, in the campaign to elect David Shackleton as a Labour Representation Committee member at the Clitheroe by-election and, once he was elected, his salary largely composed of levies from voteless women members of the weaving trade unions, campaigned to put pressure on the local male trade union branches to make the issue of women's suffrage a policy to be debated at Congress. In 1903 she collected signatures for a suffrage petition from women textile workers in eastern Scotland and in March 1904 she and Esther ROPER took a deputation of women trade unionists engaged in chain-making at Cradley Heath and of hosiery workers from Leicestershire factories to present a large petition to Sir Charles McLaren, the Leicestershire MP, whose mother, Priscilla Bright McLAREN, took a very keen interest in the work of the radical suffragists. In 1903, with Selina Cooper, Sarah Dickenson, Esther Roper and Eva GORE-BOOTH, she formed a new group, the LANCASHIRE AND CHESHIRE WOMEN TEXTILE AND OTHER WORKERS' REPRESENTATION COMMITTEE (LCWTOWRC) with the aim of themselves sponsoring an MP. Many of LCWTOWRC's early members were drawn from the Women's Co-operative Guild. Sarah Reddish became treasurer of LCWTOWRC, still holding the position in 1913.

In 1905, with the other radical suffragists, Sarah Reddish broke away from the NESWS, unable to support that society's condemnation of the action taken by Christabel PANKHURST and Annie KENNEY at the Free Trade Hall in Manchester in October 1905 and, yet, unable to join the fledgling WOMEN'S SOCIAL AND POLITICAL UNION. After it was formed in 1908 she worked with the BOLTON SUFFRAGE SOCIETY, being in that year a member of a sub-committee formed to arrange public meetings. The Bolton Suffrage Society worked in conjunction with LCWTOWRC in organizing the gathering of signatures for yet more petitions. Mary HASLAM, founder and president of the Bolton Suffrage Society, left a bequest in her will to Sarah Reddish.

A strong supporter of women's involvement in local government, in 1903 Sarah Reddish wrote *Women and County and Borough Councils: A Claim for Eligibility*, and from 1905 until 1921 she was, along with Mary Haslam, a poor law guardian in Bolton. However, in 1907 she was defeated when she stood in Bolton in the first city council elections for which women were eligible. In that year she was also one of a group of Co-operative Guildswomen who went to Ghent and Brussels to study the initiatives in child care taken there. As a result, on her return, she founded a "School for Mothers" in Bolton. In 1911, intent on passing on her years of public-speaking experience, she established classes for women speakers for the Women's Co-operative Guild. Sarah Reddish was also a member of the local Distress Committee, the Insurance Act Local Committee, and was a governor of Bolton Girls' High School. In 1915 she was a member of the organizing committee of the National Conference of Women held to discuss the basis of a permanent peace settlement. In her will she left, among other

bequests, £300 to the Bolton Infirmary and Dispensary and £200 to the Bolton School for Mothers.
Address: (1913, 1928) 9 Bertrand Road, Bolton, Lancashire.
Photograph: in M. Llewellyn Davies, *The Women's Co-operative Guild, 1883–1904*, 1904 and in C. Webb, *The Woman With the Basket: The Story of the Women's Co-operative Guild, 1883–1927*, 1927.
Archival source: Bolton Women's Suffrage Association Papers, Bolton Archives.
Bibliography: M. Llewelyn Davies, *The Women's Co-operative Guild, 1883–1904*, 1904; C. Webb, *The Woman with the Basket: The Story of the Women's Co-operative Guild, 1883–1927*, 1927; J. Liddington and J. Norris, *One Hand Tied Behind Us: The Rise of the Women's Suffrage Movement*, 1978; J. Gaffin and D. Thomas, *Caring and Sharing: The Centenary History of the Co-operative Women's Guild*, 1983; J. Liddington, *The Life and Times of a Respectable Rebel: Selina Cooper 1864–1946*, 1984.

REDDITCH (NUWSS) In 1913 the society was a member of the WEST RIDING OF YORKSHIRE FEDERATION OF THE NATIONAL UNION OF WOMEN'S SUFFRAGE SOCIETIES. Secretary (1913) Frederick J. Barker, Esq., 10 Unicorn Hill, Redditch, Worcestershire.

REDHILL (WSPU) Secretary (1910) Mrs Richmond, Fengates House, Redhill, Surrey.

REID, MARION, MRS (1817–1902) Born in Scotland, daughter of Marion Rennie and William Kirkland, a Glasgow merchant, she married Hugo Reid on 7 January 1839 and their daughter, Janet (Jessie) Finlay Arnot Reid, was born in Edinburgh on 24 November 1839. Despite the claims of motherhood, Marion Reid attended the World's Anti-Slavery Convention in London in 1840 and met Lucretia Mott socially on several occasions during this period. In 1843 Marion Reid wrote *A Plea for Woman*, which was published in Edinburgh by William Tait and had a considerable influence on the thinking of women on both sides of the Atlantic. It went through several editions before 1852. Anne KNIGHT's annotated copy is preserved in the Friends' Library in London. Although Caroline Ashurst BIGGS mentions the book in her chapter in *History of Women's Suffrage*, vol. 3, edited by Elizabeth Cady Stanton and Susan B. Anthony, there is no evidence that Marion Reid took any active part in the women's suffrage campaign in the second half of the nineteenth-century. Her husband, who was known to George HOLYOAKE, died in London in 1872. By 1891, described in the census as living on her own means, she lived in west London with her daughter, who was a teacher of music.
Address: (1891–1902) 3 Godolphin Road, Shepherds Bush, London W.
Bibliography: M. Reid, *A Plea for Woman*, with an introduction by Suzanne Ferguson, 1988.

REIGATE AND REDHILL (NUWSS) In 1913 the society was a member of the SURREY, SUSSEX, AND HANTS FEDERATION OF THE NATIONAL UNION OF WOMEN'S SUFFRAGE SOCIETIES. Secretary (1909) Miss R.I. Pym, Firle, The Way, Reigate; (1913) Miss Crosfield, Undercroft, Reigate, and Miss Woodhouse, Twyford, Lynwood Road, Redhill, Surrey.

REMOND, SARAH PARKER (1824–94) Black American, one of the daughters of Nancy and John Remond of Salem, who were both free born, she grew up in the anti-slavery movement. Her father was a life-member of the Massachusetts Anti-Slavery Society, her brother was the Society's first black lecturer and her mother and sisters were members of the Salem Anti-Slavery Society and were hosts to such visiting lecturers as Lloyd Garrison and Wendell Phillips. Sarah Remond toured Britain between 1859 and 1861 under sponsorship of the Ladies' and Young Men's Anti-Slavery Society and was the first woman to address mass mixed audiences with lectures that covered both anti-slavery and women's rights. "I have been received here as a sister of the white women", she wrote. She studied at Bedford College and was a member of both the London Emancipation Society and the Freedmen's Aid Association. When in London she lived with Clementia TAYLOR, writing, "I am residing with a dear friend, Mrs P.A. Taylor, the honorary secretary of the Ladies' London Emancipation Society. Mrs Taylor is the wife of P.A. Taylor, Esq M.P. whose voice in and out of Parliament, has been heard on behalf of the American slave, and whose testimony is recorded against a Southern Confederacy based upon chattel slavery." Frances Power COBBE, in her autobiography, mentions taking part in a conversation with "Miss Remond, a Negress, Mrs Taylor's companion". In 1866, while training to be a nurse at London University Hospital,

Sarah Remond signed the women's suffrage petition, possibly the only black woman to do so. Shortly afterwards she entered medical school in Florence and married an Italian.

Bibliography: "A colored lady lecturer", *English Woman's Journal*, June 1861; F.P. Cobbe, *Life of Frances Power Cobbe*, 1894.

RENDEL, [FRANCES] ELINOR (1885–1942) Granddaughter of Lady [Jane] Strachey (*see* STRACHEY FAMILY), niece of Marjorie, Pernel and Philippa Strachey, educated at Kensington High School, Newnham 1904–8, Bryn Mawr 1908–9. Her mother held a drawing-room meeting for the LONDON SOCIETY FOR WOMEN'S SUFFRAGE in 1907 and Elinor, after an apprenticeship as secretary to the CAMBRIDGE UNIVERSITY WOMEN'S SUFFRAGE SOCIETY, worked for the NATIONAL UNION OF WOMEN'S SUFFRAGE SOCIETIES between 1909 and 1912. She was a close friend of Ray Strachey, with whom she had been at school and university, and who became, such is Bloomsbury generational confusion, her aunt by marriage. In 1912 Elinor Rendel began a medical training and in 1916 went out to Serbia with the Scottish Women's Hospitals Unit. After the war she worked at Great Ormond Street Hospital and ran a successful private practice, being doctor to, among other members of the Bloomsbury Group, Virginia Woolf.

Address: (1900) Melbury Road, Kensington.
Bibliography: M. Stocks, *My Commonplace Book*, 1970.

RHONDDA, VISCOUNTESS (1883–1958) (known during the suffrage years as Mrs Humphrey Mackworth) née Margaret Haig Thomas Daughter of D.A. Thomas, who from 1888 was Liberal MP for Merthyr. She was educated at Notting Hill High School and St Leonards School, St Andrews, and spent a short time at Somerville, Oxford, leaving without completing her course, after which she lived as a "daughter at home" until her marriage in 1908. Shortly before that her cousin Florence HAIG, who had come to Llanwern to recuperate after being imprisoned for her part in the "pantechnicon raid" of February 1908, inspired Margaret Thomas to take part, less than three weeks before her wedding, in the WOMEN'S SOCIAL AND POLITICAL UNION Demonstration in Hyde Park on 21 June. She then joined the WSPU, began educating herself in the arguments for women's suffrage and in feminism in general and, as honorary secretary of the Newport branch of the WSPU, organized a campaign in South Wales. She became a prolific contributor to local papers and to *Votes for Women*, writing articles supporting militancy and reviewing suffrage books, laying the foundations of her later successful career in journalism. During one of the 1910 general elections she campaigned with her cousin Cecilia HAIG in St Andrews, it being impolitic to do so in Monmouthshire, where her father was a Liberal candidate. In July 1913 Margaret Mackworth was sentenced to a month's imprisonment in Usk gaol after being found guilty of setting fire to a pillar box, went on hunger-and-thirst strike and was released under the "Cat and Mouse" Act after five days; her fine was paid before she was re-arrested.

Lady Rhondda's mother, Mrs D.A. Thomas, was in 1892 a member of the executive committee of the WOMEN'S LIBERAL FEDERATION, by 1895 was a member of the executive committee of the CENTRAL NATIONAL SOCIETY FOR WOMEN'S SUFFRAGE and in 1906 was a vice-president of the CENTRAL SOCIETY. Although her daughter, in her autobiography, says that her mother was never a member of the WSPU, feeling unable to condone acts of violence, she did in fact give a donation to it in 1907 and by 1913 was giving quite substantial sums to the WSPU Prisoners' Fund. In 1909 Mrs Thomas was hostess of a reception given by the WOMEN'S FREEDOM LEAGUE at the Royal Hotel, Cardiff and in July provided hospitality for Annie KENNEY. In September 1911 she hosted a reception at her own home for Mary ALLEN and Lillian Dove-WILLCOX. Feeling herself unable to commit an act of violence, as a compromise she engineered her own arrest, and a technical one day's imprisonment, by taking part in a suffrage meeting held immediately outside the House of Commons, where such meetings were by then prohibited. In 1910 she subscribed to the NEW CONSTITUTIONAL SOCIETY FOR WOMEN'S SUFFRAGE and in November 1912 she contributed towards the expenses of George LANSBURY when he stood at Bow, at the instigation of Christabel PANKHURST, as a suffrage candidate. From 1911 Mrs Thomas was president of the CYMRIC SUFFRAGE UNION but could not condone Edith MANSELL-MOULLIN's call for militancy in 1912, which led to a split in the society and the formation of the FORWARD CYMRIC SUFFRAGE UNION. In 1913 she was both a vice-president of the LONDON SOCIETY FOR WOMEN'S SUFFRAGE, and ran the Antiques Stall at the WSPU's Summer Fair. In 1914 she joined the UNITED SUFFRAGISTS, and in that year was also the temporary treasurer of the EAST LONDON FEDERATION OF THE SUFFRAGETTES. In February 1914, shortly before the formation of the United Suffragists she took part with Henry NEVINSON, Laurence HOUSMAN, Henry HARBEN and Francis Meynell in a demonstration in Parliament Square against the "Cat and Mouse" Act. In 1913 D.A. Thomas, no longer an MP, was a vice-president of the MEN'S LEAGUE FOR WOMEN'S SUFFRAGE. On 4 August 1914 Mrs Thomas was involved in discussions with McKenna, the Home Secretary and Lord Riddell, the press baron, to discuss the terms under which suffragette prisoners would be given amnesty.

After the death of her father in 1918 Margaret Mackworth succeeded to his title, as Viscountess Rhonda. In 1921 she launched a long legal campaign to gain for women admission to the House of Lords and in 1923 she and her husband were divorced. In that year she founded the Six Point Group and was later a founding member of the Open Door Council. In November 1918 she had founded the Women's Industrial League, which campaigned for equal pay. In 1926 she was chairman of the EQUAL POLITICAL RIGHTS CAMPAIGN COMMITTEE, which organized an intensive campaign to equalize the franchise. In 1920 she launched *Time and Tide* as a feminist journal, with such fellow suffrage workers as Elizabeth ROBINS and Cicely HAMILTON as prominent contributors. In the 1920s Lady Rhondda shared a working relationship, a London flat and a country home with Helen ARCHDALE. In her will, besides providing means to ensure that *Time and Tide* could continue publication, Lady Rhondda left money to provide for "young women graduates of any University in the United Kingdom" who might wish to gain further experience or qualifications to become journalists. In 1923 she was president and chairman of the National Women Citizens' Association.

Address: (1913) Oaklands, Caerleon, Monmouthshire; (1920s) Stonepitts, Kent; (1958) 70 Arlington House, St James, London SW1; Churt Halewell, Shere, Surrey.

Photograph: in Viscountess Rhondda, *This Was My World*, 1933.
Bibliography: Viscountess Rhondda, *This Was My World*, 1933; S.M. Eoff, *Viscountess Rhondda: Equalitarian Feminist*, 1991.

RHONDDA FACH (NUWSS) In 1913 the society was a member of the SOUTH WALES AND MONMOUTH FEDERATION OF THE NATIONAL UNION OF WOMEN'S SUFFRAGE SOCIETIES. Secretary (1913) Miss Sarah A. Griffiths, 1 Elm Street, Ferndale, Glamorgan, Glamorganshire.

RHYL AND DISTRICT (NUWSS) In 1913 the society was a member of the WEST LANCS, WEST CHESHIRE AND NORTH WALES FEDERATION OF THE NATIONAL UNION OF WOMEN'S SUFFRAGE SOCIETIES. Secretary (1909, 1910) Miss M. Williams, 75 West Parade, Rhyl; (1913) Mrs Williams, The Studio, High Street, Rhyl; Wales.

RICHARDSON, MARY (c. 1883–1961) Born in Canada, she came to Europe with friends when she was 16 and, after a period in Paris, remained in London. She joined the WOMEN'S SOCIAL AND POLITICAL UNION, c. 1909, and was sent to work in Kilburn with Eleanor Penn GASKELL. After six months she went to work, with Helen CRAGGS, in the WSPU shop in Charing Cross Road. In her autobiography she writes that she was present but did not take part in the affray on "Black Friday" in November 1910 and that during the next autumn, that is, of 1911, she took part, as her first act of militancy, in the window-smashing campaign, breaking three windows in the Home Office. A careful perusal of the reports of arrests, which are given in detail in *Votes for Women*, does not reveal any imprisonment of Mary Richardson in either the autumn of 1911 or the spring of 1912. She records that she received a sentence of six months' imprisonment; only Charlotte MARSH, a persistent offender, received a sentence of this length. In Mary Richardson's account, which is strong on atmosphere, events have certainly been elided and massaged to fit a simple narrative. It may be that she was using a pseudonym when sentenced, but police reports record her first prosecution as having taken place on 11 March 1913, when she received a sentence of one month's imprisonment, in lieu of a fine, for wilful damage. She had broken windows in the Home Office in protest at the arrest earlier in the day of WSPU members, among them Lillian Dove-WILLCOX, who had attempted to petition the King at the opening of parliament. By the summer of 1913 Mary Richardson, however, could certainly be regarded as a persistent offender, arrested on several occasions, hunger striking, and released under the "Cat and Mouse" Act, only to be re-arrested after committing another offence. She claims to have been present, in one brief period out of Holloway, at Epsom on Derby Day, in June 1913, and to have witnessed, at close hand, Emily Wilding DAVISON rush onto the track. No other account mentions Mary Richardson's presence there that day. However, her description of spending time recuperating from one of her hunger strikes at a cottage belonging to Lillian Dove-Willcox above Tintern Abbey has the very ring of truth. One of the poems included in her collection *Symbol Songs*, published by Erskine MacDonald, 1916, is "The Translation of the Love I Bear Lilian Dove" ("My heart longs to love thee/ Lilian Dove,/ My heart's arms incline/ To thine own in pure love,/ But the finger of silence/ Parts us between/ So my love is made breath-like/ Turned into a dream..."). In August 1913 a report in the *Suffragette* described how the prison authorities hinted that if Mary Richardson persisted in committing militant acts on her release, her next term of imprisonment would result in her being sent to a lunatic asylum. In October 1913, while attempting to evade recapture as a "mouse", she was caught close to a burning house, "The Elms", owned by the Countess of CARLISLE, at Hampton-on-Thames. She was charged with arson and, while she was still on remand, forcible feeding was reintroduced to deal with her ensuing hunger strike, her fourth that summer. The authorities came to the conclusion that such a dedicated militant was a danger if released under the "Cat and Mouse" Act. The Home Office papers make clear that she violently resisted forcible feeding. On 19 October Ellen N. La Motte, who had been superintendent of the Tuberculosis Division of the Health Department of Baltimore, wrote from 166 Boulevard du Montparnasse in Paris to Christabel PANKHURST, who was also in Paris, to report on Mary Richardson's condition. Mary Richardson had gone to Paris, while evading re-arrest, at the beginning of October to stay with Miss La Motte, who thought she might have TB. The Home Office was already aware that Mary Richardson had been treated "for lung trouble" about five years previously. She was released from Holloway under the "Cat and Mouse" Act on 25 October after consultants called in by the Holloway medical officer confirmed symptoms of appendicitis.

In March 1914, the day after Mrs Pankhurst was arrested in St Andrew's Hall in Glasgow, Mary Richardson committed her most notorious militant act for the cause, slashing Velázquez's *Rokeby Venus* in the National Gallery in London. Mary Richardson wished to draw attention to "the public's indifference to Mrs Pankhurst's slow destruction" and thought to draw a parallel between this and "the destruction of some financially valuable object". She apparently had no knowledge of the part that another supporter of the militant suffrage campaign, Christiana HERRINGHAM, had played in the acquisition of this object for the nation. In an interview recorded by the BBC on 31 December 1960 and broadcast on 23 April 1961, Mary Richardson revealed that she had chosen the *Rokeby Venus* because she hated women being used as nudes, she had seen the picture gloated over by men, and she "thought it sensuous". Mary Richardson was sentenced to six months' imprisonment, went on hunger strike and was forcibly fed. She was released in April, again showing symptoms of appendicitis, to the care of Dr Flora MURRAY and Nurse PINE. Dr Murray came to the conclusion that, while imprisoned, Mary Richardson had been given bromide by the prison authorities to reduce her resistance to forcible feeding. Perhaps it was coincidence that the Prison Department denied that any bromide or like drug had been administered to any prisoners, in response to a medical statement sent to them by Dr Murray on 8 June, and reported on 9 June that they had discovered Mary Richardson, once more in Holloway, in possession of tablets which, after analysis by the Home Office, proved to be Emetine Hydrochloride, which when taken would induce the vomiting from which she had suffered. The Home Office, despite extensive inquiries, was unable to discover the supplier of the tablets, which could only be procured by doctors or pharmacists.

It is not entirely clear from the Home Office report how she was thought to have had access to the tablets which she had apparently brought into prison with her, but which were, with the other contents of her bag, held in the reception area. All Home Office files on Mary Richardson relevant to the period between her release from Holloway in October 1913 and 17 April 1914, when the question of the use of bromides was raised, have been destroyed. Mary Richardson certainly did develop appendicitis, for which she was operated on at the end of July 1914. Dr Murray noted at this time that Mary Richardson's mouth was scarred and painful from the nails of prison officials. She returned to London from a lengthy convalescence in Madeira in January 1915.

Mary Richardson stressed in her autobiography that it was her rootlessness that gave her the ability to devote herself so totally to the militant cause. During the First World War she worked for a time with Sylvia PANKHURST in the East End of London; in 1915 joined the UNITED SUFFRAGISTS, published a feminist novel, *Matilda and Marcus*, 1915, and several volumes of poetry (one dedicated to Edith Picton-Turbervill), and edited the *YWCA Magazine*, 1914–18. After the war she stood for parliament three times as a Labour candidate, without success, then became a leading member of the British Union of Fascists; thought of entering a religious sisterhood; adopted a son; and suggested, at one time, to Sylvia Pankhurst that they establish a Communist nunnery of social and religious service.

Address: (1920) The Red House, Haslingfield, Cambridge; (1923) 6 North Street, Westminster, London SW.
Photograph: in Suffragette Fellowship Collection, Museum of London.
Archival source: Home Office Papers, Public Record Office.
Bibliography: M. Richardson, *Laugh a Defiance*, 1953.

RICHMOND (branch of the LONDON SOCIETY FOR WOMEN'S SUFFRAGE, NUWSS) Was in existence in 1906. President (1906) Lady Frances BALFOUR; honorary secretary (1906) Mrs Tempany, Fernleigh, King's Road, Richmond, Surrey; (1913) Mrs Bailey, 16 Marlborough Road, Richmond, Surrey, and Olive Garnett.

RICHMOND (WFL) Secretary (1913) Mrs Shelton, 30 Graemsdyke Avenue, East Sheen, Richmond, Surrey.

RICHMOND AND KEW (WSPU) Secretary (1913) Mrs Clayton (*see* Edwy CLAYTON), Glengariff, Kew Road, Richmond, Surrey.

RIDDING, LAURA, LADY (1849–1939) Daughter of the 1st Earl of Selborne. Her sister-in-law, the Countess of Selborne, was president of the CONSERVATIVE AND UNIONIST WOMEN'S FRANCHISE ASSOCIATION. A long-standing supporter of women's suffrage, Lady Laura Ridding was president of the Winchester branch of the NATIONAL UNION OF WOMEN'S SUFFRAGE SOCIETIES. In reply to a speech given by Lord Curzon at the Hotel Cecil on 18 May 1909, in which he cited "15 sound, valid, and incontrovertible arguments against the grant of female suffrage", Lady Laura Ridding drafted a spirited and amusing reply which began,

> Fifteen valid arguments, all as yellow mustard keen!
> A Mother's Clinic doctored one: and then there were fourteen!
> Fourteen valid arguments on domestic sorrow lean.
> The happy homes of Wyoming drew one and left thirteen!

Lady Laura Ridding was active in local government, both as a poor law guardian and as a member, from 1902 until 1905, of the Nottinghamshire County Education Committee, and the author of a pamphlet, *Women on Education Authorities* (undated). She was one of the founders, in 1895, of the National Union of Women Workers and was its president from 1909 until 1911.

Address: (1913) The Old House, Wonston, Micheldever, Hampshire.
Archival source: The manuscript diaries, 1884–1939, of Lady Laura Ridding, Hampshire Record Office.
Bibliography: Angeli Vaid, "Fifteen Valid Arguments", in Hampshire Archives Trust *Newsletter*, Spring 1993.

RIGBY, EDITH, MRS (1872–1949) Born in Preston, the daughter of a doctor, educated at Penrhos College in North Wales. In 1893 she married Charles Rigby, a doctor; they had no children of their own and, after 12 years, adopted a son. Shortly after her marriage Edith Rigby set up a night-school for mill girls in Preston. Her concern for the position of poor and oppressed women led her to take an active part in the movement for women's suffrage.

She was for a time a member of the Liverpool branch of the NATIONAL UNION OF WOMEN'S SUFFRAGE SOCIETIES, but joined the WOMEN'S SOCIAL AND POLITICAL UNION in 1904, when meetings were held in the Pankhursts' house in Manchester. She took part in the NUWSS "Mud March" in February 1906 and by 1907 was secretary of its Preston branch. She joined the Independent Labour Party in December 1905, organized the local branch of the Women's Labour League and became a member of its national executive council, resigning in February 1907. In that month, a few days after taking part in the NUWSS "Mud March", she attended the first WSPU Women's Parliament in Caxton Hall and took part in the deputation to the House of Commons. She was arrested and sentenced to two weeks' imprisonment, which she relished. In October she volunteered for another deputation and again received a two-week sentence of imprisonment. In February 1908 Edith Rigby took part in the "pantechnicon raid" on the House of Commons and this time was sentenced to a month's imprisonment in the third division. On her release she arranged for the Labour MP for Preston to take her and two other local WSPU ex-prisoners to tea in the House of Commons. In December 1908 Edith Rigby was arrested in Preston while holding meetings outside the hall in which Churchill was speaking, and from which women were barred. Her father insisted on paying her fine; it was too embarrassing, he thought, for her to be imprisoned where lately she had been a prison visitor. In retaliation Edith Rigby went, three days later, to Liverpool, where Churchill was due to speak and there broke a window at the police station. She was sentenced to 14 days' imprisonment in Walton Gaol, went on hunger strike and was forcibly fed. She took part in the window-smashing campaign of November 1911, breaking a window in the Local Government Board Office in Whitehall, and receiving a three-week sentence. While in Holloway she discussed church and religion with Margaret THOMPSON. By 1913 Edith Rigby was prepared to undertake even more militant acts, defacing a statue of Lord Derby in Miller Park, Preston, and two months later burning down a bungalow belonging to Sir William Lever (later Lord Leverhulme). She then gave herself up to the police and was sentenced to nine months' hard labour. In December, having been released under the "Cat and Mouse" Act, she was re-arrested while attempting to place a bomb in the Liverpool Cotton Exchange. She was again imprisoned in Walton Gaol, went on hunger strike and was released under the "Cat and Mouse" Act. She escaped to the west of Ireland where she remained in hiding for several weeks. She was re-arrested in Preston after appearing, in disguise, as a speaker at a meeting alongside John SCURR MP.

After the outbreak of war, Edith Rigby, disagreeing with the Pankhursts' decision to abandon the suffrage fight, joined the INDEPENDENT WSPU, forming a branch in Preston. In November 1914 she was a member of the FABIAN WOMEN'S GROUP. She joined the Women's Land Army and ran a smallholding. She was by this time a committed vegetarian and became an anthroposophist, a follower of Rudolf Steiner.

Address: (1913) 28 Winckley Square, Preston.
Photograph: in P. Hesketh, *My Aunt Edith*, 1966.
Archival source: North-West Sound Archive: recording of a talk by Phoebe Hesketh about Edith Rigby, 27 November 1977.
Bibliography: P. Hesketh, *My Aunt Edith*, 1966.

RINGWOOD (NUWSS) In 1913 the society was a member of the SURREY, SUSSEX, AND HANTS FEDERATION OF THE NATIONAL UNION OF WOMEN'S SUFFRAGE SOCIETIES. Secretary (1913) Mrs Pennington, Moortown House, Ringwood, Hampshire.

RIPON (NUWSS) In 1913 the society was a member of the NORTH AND EAST RIDINGS FEDERATION OF THE NATIONAL UNION OF WOMEN'S SUFFRAGE SOCIETIES. Secretary (1913) Miss Tyler, Training College, Ripon, Yorkshire.

ROBINS, ELIZABETH (1862–1952) American actress and writer, born in Kentucky, married in 1885 to a fellow actor, George Parks, who four years later committed suicide. After a brief visit to Norway, Elizabeth Robins arrived in London and, seeking employment as an actress, was introduced to Herbert Beerbohm Tree by Oscar Wilde. In 1891 she played Hedda Gabler in an acclaimed production of Ibsen's play, on the translation of which she had collaborated with William Archer, for whom she came to care deeply; she became the Ibsen actress *par excellence*. At this time she met and cemented a friendship with Henry James. As "C.E. Raimond", encouraged by W.T. Stead, she published in the 1890s novels of a decidedly feminist slant, including the wry and ironic *George Mandeville's Husband*. In 1902 she undertook her final professional acting role in a play based on Mrs Humphry Ward's *Eleanor*, intending henceforward to devote herself to writing. In mid-1905 Elizabeth Robins travelled to America to attend the wedding of her brother, Raymond, to Margaret Dreier, who by 1907 was president of the American Women's Trade Union League and who was later to provide Mrs PANKHURST with useful introductions when she lectured in America.

Although she was a close friend of Sir Edward Grey, the Liberal politician attacked by Christabel PANKHURST and Annie KENNEY a month earlier, by November 1905 Elizabeth Robins had, after due reflection, decided that she was in principle a supporter of women's suffrage and in 1906 began focusing on the woman's cause as a subject for drama. She did not immediately concentrate on the contemporary, but as the WOMEN'S SOCIAL AND POLITICAL UNION's London campaign gathered followers and publicity during the early part of 1906, she drew on its interesting personalities and inherent drama as a source of inspiration. In the interlude between the arrival in London of Annie Kenney in late January and that of Christabel Pankhurst in July, Elizabeth Robins became a member of the Central London committee of the WSPU. Observation and ideas crystallized into her play *Votes for Women*, written during the autumn of 1906. She had attended eight large suffrage meetings between July and October and then went to Huddersfield to sample the atmosphere of the WSPU's by-election campaign. Hannah MITCHELL later described how she had related to Elizabeth Robins several of the incidents that appeared in *The Convert*, the novel based on *Votes for Women*. Of the leading characters, "Vida Levering" is modelled on Christabel Pankhurst and "Ernestine Blunt" on Teresa BILLINGTON-GREIG. "Vida" had originally been "Christian" but, after an exchange of letters with Mrs Pankhurst, Elizabeth Robins changed the name in order that Vida's interesting past might not be confused with Christabel's unblemished character.

Elizabeth Robins was present at the opening of parliament on 23 October 1906 and witnessed the arrest of Anne Cobden SANDERSON and other members of the WSPU. She was shocked by the biased press accounts of the demonstration, writing to *The Times* on 6 November to remonstrate both against this and against a letter from Sir Philip Burne-Jones, who had accepted the press interpretation of events. Letters from Walter Crane and Lady Frances Balfour, making similar points, also appeared on the same page. When she attended the annual conference of the National Union of Women Workers at Tunbridge Wells she discovered that those attending had also accepted the press interpretation of events; she intervened to protest. She was then asked by Mrs FAWCETT, a vice-president of the NUWW, to convey to the WSPU prisoners the sympathy of the NATIONAL UNION OF WOMEN'S SUFFRAGE SOCIETIES. Elizabeth Robins visited both Sylvia PANKHURST and Minnie BALDOCK in Holloway. On 11 December she proposed a toast, "Success to the Cause of Women's Suffrage", at the banquet organized at the Savoy to celebrate the release of the prisoners. This speech is included in *Way Stations*, a collection of her writing on the women's movement. Initially a supporter of both wings of the suffrage movement, in 1907 she gave £20 6s 6d to NUWSS as part proceeds of *Votes for Women*. Another share went to the WSPU. The Pankhursts had been, with W.T. Stead, J.M. Barrie and Arthur Pinero, among the first-night audience for the play. The realities of early WSPU meetings, when both speakers and audience were fresh to the cause, still leap off the pages of *The Convert*, which was published in October 1907. Mrs Pankhurst read an advance copy and congratulated Elizabeth Robins on making the political part interesting.

Elizabeth Robins remained with the WSPU after Teresa Billington-Greig and others broke away in September 1907 to found the WOMEN'S FREEDOM LEAGUE. She was a member of the titular committee of the WSPU, with her name on the notepaper, although, as with most of the other members, not required to exercise any direct control on the running of the Union. It is clear from entries in her diaries that the committee did in fact meet, but that only the PETHICK-LAWRENCES and Pankhursts, based in Clement's Inn, could be counted on as regular attenders. Elizabeth Robins was a reluctant, although much-admired, speaker for the WSPU, undertaking speaking tours around the country. Evelyn SHARP later recorded that she was inspired to join the WSPU after being moved by Elizabeth Robins's intervention at the NUWW conference in Tunbridge Wells. Several of Elizabeth Robins's lectures are reprinted in *Way Stations*. She continued to be concerned by the press's biased reporting of the suffrage campaign. In September 1908 her report on the Newcastle by-election for *Votes for Women* stressed that the daily newpaper coverage invariably depicted such campaigns as meeting with violence and ill-will from the populace; she eloquently assured her readers that this was not the case. Elizabeth Robins contributed articles on aspects of the suffrage movement to a variety of journals in Britain and in America. *The Feministe Movement in England*, published in *Collier's Weekly*, New York, 29 June 1907, alerted US readers to the lengths to which WSPU members were prepared to go in their fight for enfranchisement.

As well as contributing her active presence in public halls, Elizabeth Robins was asked in October 1908 by Emmeline Pethick-Lawrence to use her influence behind the scenes by asking Sir Edward Grey to mitigate the prison treatment of Emmeline and Christabel Pankhurst, and she was frequently asked by the latter to give names of people of influence who might prove useful. At the same time as campaigning for the cause, Elizabeth Robins managed to maintain her acceptability to society friends who were not sympathizers, even, for instance, being a guest at a private dinner given by Asquith. In 1908 she became one of the first members and president of the WOMEN WRITERS' SUFFRAGE LEAGUE. In that year she also attended the inaugural meeting of the ACTRESSES' FRANCHISE LEAGUE. On 21 June 1908, wearing a scarf in the WSPU colours and a hat trimmed in purple, white and green, she took part in the WSPU rally in Hyde Park, writing up a description of the event for the *Daily Mail*. She also took part in the 23 July 1910 "Prison to Citizenship" and the 17 June 1911 Coronation processions. To publicize the latter she wrote an article, "Come and See", which was published in the *Westminster Gazette* on 16 June 1911. On 18 November 1910 she was present in Parliament Square to bear appalled witness to scenes of violence against women, although she herself kept out of the fray. A year later, on 18 November, Elizabeth Robins was one of the members of the small deputation from the WSPU that Asquith agreed to meet after announcing that the government proposed to introduce a Manhood Suffrage Bill. She had apparently been in a quandary as to whether or not she should attend, wishing to reserve her independence, presumably doubtful about the ethics of full-scale militancy as proposed by Christabel Pankhurst. In *Way Stations* Elizabeth Robins described Asquith as incompetent and blundering, rather than mendacious and vindictive in his handling of the women's suffrage question both on this occasion and on "Black Friday" the previous November. At this time she was in close touch with Grey; presumably her insights derived from their conversations.

On 7 March 1912 Elizabeth Robins wrote a letter to *The Times* in which she dismissed the government's ability to harm the WSPU by making its subscribers financially liable for damage caused by its campaign. She likened the women's suffrage cause to a religion and stressed that it was its adherents' faith and self-denial that gave it strength. She had witnessed on 4 March some of the arrests of window smashers. Elizabeth Robins contributed an article, "The Perfidy of Sympathisers", to one of the first issues of *Votes for Women* edited by her close friend Evelyn Sharp, who had taken over responsibility for the paper after the raid on Clement's Inn and the arrest of the Pethick-Lawrences. On 28 March Elizabeth Robins addressed a packed meeting in the Albert Hall, particularly lauding the contribution made by Frederick Pethick-Lawrence to the WSPU and denying the notion that there was any "sex-antagonism" among its members. While openly supporting militancy, she was herself careful not to put her signature to any office instructions in Clement's Inn, lest she too might attract a conspiracy charge; she had no wish to go to prison or, as an American citizen, to risk deportation. She felt that she could contribute most to the cause by publicizing and explaining through her writing the defiant deeds of others. In her article "Sermons in Stones", published in the *Contemporary Review* in April 1912, she justified stone throwing and window smashing, and in "Woman's War", published in March 1913 in *McClure's Magazine*, she highlighted the violence done to women at Llandystymdwy. Besides published articles she also contributed letters to *The Times*. In December 1912 Christabel Pankhurst wrote to her from Paris, congratulating her on her work in explaining militancy to the general public. It had, of course, been her perception that the conventional press was not prepared to report the suffrage campaign fairly that had drawn Elizabeth Robins into the WSPU in 1906. In 1913, by which time Elizabeth Robins's mail was being intercepted by the police, she published *Way Stations*, giving continuity and context to the collection of speeches and articles with a series of linking "Time Tables".

On 27 July 1912 Elizabeth Robins wrote to *The Times* a riposte to a letter published on 23 July from 26 eminent supporters of women's suffrage, among them Millicent Garrett Fawcett, Elizabeth Garrett ANDERSON, Sir Edward Grey and Lord Haldane, who warned that the escalating militant campaign would do serious harm to the suffrage cause. In it she attacks the two government ministers for doing so little in the House of Commons for a cause they professed to support. Although she had conceded to the WSPU's request to write such a letter, it appears that Elizabeth Robins had been shaken both by the published opinions of those whom she respected and by her own dislike of violence, whether perpetrated against or by women. The ousting of the Pethick-Lawrences from the WSPU in October concentrated her mind and, although still prepared publicly to give a voice to the WSPU, Elizabeth Robins resigned from its committee. She remained friendly with the Pethick-Lawrences for the rest of her life. Christabel Pankhurst received from her at the end of November a 16-page critique of her handling of the WSPU, which attracted a similarly lengthy defence. In October 1912 Elizabeth Robins also resigned her membership of the WWSL, although she rejoined during the First World War and was a party to its final dissolution in 1919. In 1913 she was a supporter of the NATIONAL POLITICAL LEAGUE and of the VOTES FOR WOMEN FELLOWSHIP. She contributed a preface to a second edition of Evelyn Sharp's *Rebel Women* that was published by the UNITED SUFFRAGISTS in 1915. On 13 March 1918 she was present at the NUWSS victory celebration in the Queen's Hall.

Although no longer so actively involved in the militant suffrage movement after October 1912, Elizabeth Robins maintained her concern for topical feminist issues. Her novel *Where Are You Going To . . . ?*, published in Britain in January 1913, had prostitution as its theme; as was her wont, Elizabeth Robins had researched the question thoroughly. Christabel Pankhurst quoted from the novel when writing "The Government and White Slavery" for the *Suffragette*, April 1913. For a time in 1915 Elizabeth Robins worked with Beatrice HARRADEN as librarian for the Endell Street Hospital run by Louisa Garrett ANDERSON and Flora MURRAY before leaving to visit her family in America. In March 1915 she had been thinking of attending the congress of the Women's Peace Congress at the Hague but, like all the other hopefuls, was prevented from doing so. She remained a member of the Women's International League until 1925. In 1922 she was a vice-president of the South London Hospital for Women and a vice-president and a member of the board of management of the New Sussex Hospital for Women and Children at Brighton. In 1920 Elizabeth Robins became one of the first seven directors of Lady RHONDDA's journal *Time and Tide*, which had been launched as a means of rectifying the unfair treatment of women by the press, a leitmotif that ran through her career. The first issue of *Time and Tide* contained an appreciation of Elizabeth Robins by her old friend and co-author, Lady Florence Bell. In 1921 she was named as one of the vice-presidents of the newly formed Six Point Group. In 1924 she published, anonymously, *Ancilla's Share: An Indictment of Sex-antagonism*, a wide-ranging denunciation of sexism and a plea for pacifism. In 1927, at the suggestion of Dr Octavia Wilberforce, a younger woman with whom she had lived, Elizabeth Robins turned Backset Town, her Sussex home, into a convalescent home for overworked professional women.

Address: (1890) Manchester Square Gardens; (1907) 24 Iverna Gardens, Abingdon Villas, Kensington, London; (1909–54) Backset Town Farm, Henfield, Sussex; (1927) 36 Albion Street, London W2.

Photograph: in A.V. John, *Elizabeth Robins: Staging a Life, 1862–1952*, 1995.

Bibliography: E. Robins, *Way Stations*, 1913; E. Robins, *Both Sides of the Curtain: Memoirs*, 1940; E. Robins, *The Convert*, reissued 1980, with introduction by J. Marcus; J. Holledge, *Innocent flowers: Women in the Edwardian Theatre*, 1981; P. Jalland (ed.), *Octavia Wilberforce: The Autobiography of a Pioneer Woman Doctor*, 1989; S. Stowell, *A Stage of Their Own: Feminist Playwrights of the Suffrage Era*, 1992; A.V. John, *Elizabeth Robins: Staging a Life, 1862–1952*, 1995.

ROBINSON, (ANNIE) ANNOT ERSKINE, MRS (1874–1925) née Wilkie Born on the east coast of Scotland, the daughter of an impoverished draper, she attended Montrose Academy and worked as a pupil-teacher until she was 16. She then attended teacher-training college and in 1900 and 1901 she took, externally, courses at St Andrews in English, French, Astronomy, Comparative Religion and History, graduating with an LLA degree. She taught in Dundee and there was influenced by Agnes Husband, a member of the Dundee Labour Party. Annot Wilkie joined the WOMEN'S SOCIAL AND POLITICAL UNION in 1906, becoming the first secretary of the Dundee branch. She left Scotland for Manchester in 1907, joined the Central branch of the Manchester ILP in June and was appointed a WSPU ORGANIZER. Early in 1908 she married Sam Robinson, secretary of the influential Manchester branch of the Independent Labour Party; it was he who had helped to arrange the meeting held at the Free Trade Hall on 20 October 1905 to greet Christabel PANKHURST and Annie KENNEY after their release from prison. The Robinsons were to have two children; the marriage was unhappy, and ended by 1918. In February 1908, after her marriage, Annot Robinson took part in the "pantechnicon raid" on the House of Commons and, as a result, spent six weeks in Holloway. In June she was one of the speakers at "Woman's Sunday" in Hyde Park. Her sympathies with the WSPU must have diminished as it put distance between itself and the Labour Party. In early 1910 she was appointed a part-time organizer for the Women's Labour League and later that year attended the Labour Party conference, putting forward a resolution condemning the party's leadership for supporting neither women's enfranchisement nor the WLL. In 1911 she attended the annual conference of the WLL and moved an amendment to an adult suffragist resolution put forward by Florence Harrison BELL, by which she advocated supporting the policy followed by the main suffrage groups, the enfranchisement of women on the same basis as it was accorded to men. This amendment was defeated and later that year Annot Robinson became a paid organizer for the NATIONAL UNION OF WOMEN'S SUFFRAGE SOCIETIES. In October 1911 she was approached by the Suffrage Section of the FABIAN WOMEN'S GROUP with the suggestion that she might work for them as an organizer. After 1912 she travelled around the country speaking at NUWSS meetings in support of the Election Fighting Fund; it was the work of women such as her that had brought the NUWSS and Labour Party together. By 1914 she was organizer in Blackburn, with Ellen Wilkinson as her assistant. A pacifist, in December 1914 Annot Robinson signed the "Open Christmas Letter" to the women of Germany and Austria. In 1915 she acted as chairman for the Voluntary Workers' Committee for the Ancoats Settlement in Manchester and kept in touch with the local Labour Party. In 1917 she addressed a garden party for munition and other workers organized by the BOLTON SUFFRAGE SOCIETY and took part in the Women's Peace Crusade campaign. In 1918 she became a full-time organizer for the Women's International League for Peace and Freedom and in 1920 took part in the investigation of atrocities alleged to have been committed by the British army. After her sudden death the WILPF organized an Annot Robinson Memorial Fund on behalf of her daughters.

Address: (1901) 222 High Street, Montrose; (1906) 101 Rosebery Street, Lochee, Dundee, Fife; (1912) 73 Caroline Street, Ancoats, Manchester.
Archival source: Annot Robinson Papers, Manchester Central Library.
Bibliography: C. Collette, *For Labour and For Women: The Women's Labour League, 1906–18*, 1989.

ROCHDALE (NUWSS) In 1913 the society was a member of the MANCHESTER AND DISTRICT FEDERATION OF THE NATIONAL UNION OF WOMEN'S SUFFRAGE SOCIETIES. Secretary (1909) Mrs Toyne, 144 Tweedale Street, Rochdale, Lancashire; (1911, 1913) Miss G. Starkie, 12 Roach Place, Rochdale, Lancashire.

ROCHDALE (WSPU)   Secretary (1906) Mrs Atkinson, 15 Percival Street, Rochdale; (1913) Mrs V. Walker, 1 Aubrey Street, Rochdale, Lancashire.

ROCHESTER (NUWSS)   In 1913 the society was a member of the KENTISH FEDERATION OF THE NATIONAL UNION OF WOMEN'S SUFFRAGE SOCIETIES. Secretary (1913) Miss V. Conway GORDON, Longley House, Rochester, Kent.

ROCHESTER (WSPU)   In existence in 1910, when the honorary secretary was Mrs Gundry, 32 Stuart Road, Gillingham, Kent.

ROCK, [MADELEINE] CARON (1884–1954)   Sister of Dorothea ROCK, joined the WOMEN'S SOCIAL AND POLITICAL UNION in 1908 and was sentenced to seven days' imprisonment for window breaking in December 1911. She was also sentenced to two months' hard labour in Holloway in March 1912 after more window smashing. On 22 July 1914 she was charged with assaulting police officers while attempting to prevent Mrs PANKHURST's re-arrest at the London Pavilion. The outbreak of war saved her from further imprisonment. One of her poems, published under her initials, M.C.R., was included in *Holloway Jingles*, 1912/13. She was subsequently the author of two collections of poems, *Or in the Grass*, 1914 and *On the Tree Top*, 1927. In her will she left Marjorie Potbury, her cousin and fellow suffragette prisoner, a half share in the residue of her estate.
Address: (1912) The Red House, Ingatestone, Essex; (1954) 270 Russell Court, Woburn Place, London WC1.

ROCK, [EDITH] DOROTHEA MERIET (1881–1964)   Sister of Caron ROCK, joined the WOMEN'S SOCIAL AND POLITICAL UNION in 1908 and was sentenced to seven days' imprisonment after breaking windows in the Board of Trade Office in November 1911. In March 1912 she was sentenced to two months' hard labour after taking part in the second window-smashing campaign. While in Holloway she was the subject of a poem, "To D.R.", which was subsequently published in *Holloway Jingles*. The author "Laura Grey" was in fact Joan Baillie Guthrie, another suffragette, who soon after, as Sylvia PANKHURST records in *The Suffragette Movement*, took to drugs after being deserted by a man and then committed suicide. In Holloway Dorothea Rock met Zoe PROCTER, gave her a bunch of primroses and violets, "leading", wrote the latter, "to a friendship which was to last a life-time". Dorothea Rock was also a member of the CHURCH LEAGUE FOR WOMEN'S SUFFRAGE, a vegetarian and a member of the International Women's Franchise Club (*see under* CLUBS). During the First World War Dorothea Rock and Zoe Procter were members of the INDEPENDENT WSPU and of "The Little Company of Christ", a group led by Maude ROYDEN which met for spiritual study. Dorothea Rock eventually inherited a substantial estate from Zoe Procter and among the bequests in her own will was one to Grace Chappelow, with whom she had been arrested when window breaking in 1911, and one to her cousin, Marjorie Potbury, who had joined her in Holloway on both occasions.
Address: (1912) The Red House, Ingatestone, Essex; (1920–60) 81 Beaufort Mansions, Chelsea, London SW; (1963) Shepherd's Corner, Gregories Farm Lane, Beaconsfield, Buckinghamshire.
Bibliography: Z. Procter, *Life and Yesterday*, 1960.

ROE, [ELEANOR] GRACE WATNEY (1885–1979) Born in south London, brought up in a large Victorian household in which the emphasis was placed on etiquette and household skills, although her parents were interested in socialism and women's suffrage. Her mother died when Grace was 12 years old and she was then sent to one of the first co-educational boarding schools, becoming at this time a vegetarian. The school may have been Bedales; Mrs Badley, the wife of the founder, became a loyal supporter of the WOMEN'S SOCIAL AND POLITICAL UNION. Grace Roe became an art student and, while walking one day down Kensington High Street was given, by Florence HAIG, a handbill advertising the 21 June 1908 Hyde Park demonstration. She was interested in the women's suffrage movement, but was afraid, having read press reports, that Mrs PANKHURST and Christabel PANKHURST might be "unwomanly women". She went to Hyde Park with her aunt and brother and reported that "It was a bright, sunny day. There was Mrs Pankhurst, this magnificent figure, like a Queen." Christabel "had taken off her bonnet and cloak, and was wearing a green tussore silk dress. She was very graceful, had lovely hands and a wonderful way of using them." Grace joined the WSPU in October 1908, finally convinced after hearing Emmeline PETHICK-LAWRENCE speak at a Queen's Hall meeting. She had an independent income sufficient to allow her to act as she chose, without the necessity of earning a living. In June 1909 she was asked to organize the West London area, advertising there the deputation to the House of Commons to take place at the end of the month. Flora DRUMMOND's only instruction to her was "to hold six meetings every day and make things go". She was arrested in the fracas surrounding the deputation on 29 June.

During the January 1910 general election Grace Roe was WSPU organizer in Brixton. Later that year she became ORGANIZER in East Anglia, with headquarters in Ipswich. There was, apparently, only one member of the WSPU in Ipswich when she arrived. Within six weeks many drawing-room meetings had been held, with such speakers as Marie BRACKENBURY and Mildred MANSEL travelling from London to help. Christabel Pankhurst held a meeting at the Corn Exchange. Olive BARTELS worked as Grace Roe's deputy in the area for much of this period. Holiday campaigns were arranged along the East Anglian coast at which Emmeline PANKHURST, Emmeline Pethick-Lawrence, Lady Constance LYTTON and Lady Isabel MARGESSON spoke. At the general election in December 1911 Grace Roe was organizer for Mrs Pankhurst, who, speaking at least five times daily, concentrated her efforts on the Wisbech division. She was also the WSPU organizer at the Bromley and Bow by-election in 1912 in which George LANSBURY stood, unsuccessfully, as a woman's suffrage candidate. Sylvia PANKHURST in *The Suffragette Movement*, although she does not name her, is scathing about Grace Roe's handling of this important campaign. At this time Grace Roe also made several visits to Dublin to conduct the campaign for the release of Mary LEIGH, Gladys Evans and Jennie BAINES.

At Christmas 1912 Grace Roe was urged by Christabel Pankhurst to go to Switzerland for a rest. She went with her father and returned by way of Paris in order to meet Christabel. She was then told that she was to be understudy for Annie KENNEY. Grace Roe's moment arrived when, in April 1913, Annie Kenney was arrested a few days before the WSPU headquarters at Lincoln's Inn House were raided and the heads of its departments were removed. The printers of the *Suffragette* were also raided and Grace Roe found a new printer and drove with him to Maud JOACHIM's flat near Victoria where a makeshift Information Department under Cicely HALE had set to work. The printer told her that there was sufficient material for an eight-page paper, the famous "Raided" issue. Later that evening, disguised in Kitty MARSHALL's clothes, Grace Roe went across the Channel to meet Christabel. On her return Arthur Marshall, the WSPU's solicitor, told her that there was a warrant for her arrest and, henceforward, she spent her time in various disguises, with help from members of the ACTRESSES' FRANCHISE LEAGUE. She made constant visits to Paris and records that "The telephone was in much use and we were in touch with Christabel also by letters and messengers. I spent my late evenings at 'Mouse Castle' [the Brackenburys' house in Campden Hill]."

In May 1914 when Lincoln's Inn House was again raided Grace Roe, who was by then living in a room on the third floor, was arrested and charged with conspiracy. She was held in prison from 23 May, on hunger strike and forcibly fed, both before and after sentencing. She attempted to shorten her sentence by arranging for one of Arthur Marshall's solicitors' clerks to smuggle into her an emetic which would cause her to vomit when forcibly fed. The drug was discovered by the prison authorities and led to the forcible searching of suffragette prisoners on their reception into prison. Grace Roe was finally released from Holloway on 10 August, under the government's amnesty.

Throughout the First World War Grace Roe worked with Christabel and Emmeline Pankhurst, organizing the campaign against the Contagious Diseases Acts in 1914 and, in Newcastle, speaking out against labour unrest. She worked closely with Lloyd George, was chief organizer of the Women's War Work procession in July 1915 and organizer of the Victory Fund for the Campaign against Compromise Peace in 1916. She was friendly with Frances Stevenson, who was Lloyd George's secretary and later his wife. After the war Grace Roe spent a winter living at St Leonards, studying theosophy there with Annie Kenney. When interviewed in 1974 she remarked on the part played by theosophists behind the scenes of the militant suffrage movement.

She made the point that theosophy not only gave a spiritual dimension to their lives but, cutting across class, put people in touch with each other who would have been unlikely otherwise to meet. She was present at Annie Kenney's wedding at Lytham in 1920, found for her a publisher willing to give an advance for *Memoirs of a Militant* and lived with the married couple until Warwick Kenney Taylor was born. In 1921 Christabel Pankhurst, who had been unable to find employment in Britain, asked Grace Roe to travel with her first to Canada and then to the USA. They eventually both settled in California, first in Santa Barbara and then in Hollywood. Grace Roe acted as Christabel Pankhurst's aide during the latter's involvement in Second Adventism. Grace Roe lived in the USA for the next 40 years, involved in social work in Los Angeles and, from the mid-1930s, working as an assistant to a Mrs Roland Gray. After the Second World War she lived outside Santa Barbara, running a bookshop and metaphysical library. She was with Christabel Pankhurst when she died, was appointed Christabel's literary executor and was responsible for tracking down the manuscript of *Unshackled* and showing it to Lord Pethick-Lawrence. In 1961 she was vice-president of the SUFFRAGETTE FELLOWSHIP. In an interview given in 1974 before the television showing of *Shoulder to Shoulder*, Grace Roe, unsurprisingly, remarked that she thought that *Unshackled* gave the truest account of the suffrage movement. Significantly, and to her great credit, she stressed that the political motives of the movement should be emphasized and that the history should not be obscured by mythology. In another 1974 interview she commented, "Christabel was the apple of *my* eye."

Address: (1950s) Ojia, near Santa Barbara, California; (1968) 12 The Chase, Bishop's Stortford, Hertfordshire; (1974) Green Cottage, Hastings Road, Pembury, Tunbridge Wells, Kent.
Photograph: in the Suffragette Fellowship Collection, Museum of London.
Archival source: B. Harrison, taped interview with Grace Roe, 1974, Fawcett Library.
Bibliography: Grace Roe, *A Suffragette's Story*, reprinted as a pamphlet from *Calling All Women*, no date (*c.* 1960).

ROEHAMPTON (branch of the LONDON SOCIETY FOR WOMEN'S SUFFRAGE, NUWSS)   Secretary (1913) Mrs Walker, Willerby, Roehampton, London SW.

ROMFORD (WSPU)   Was in existence in September 1908. Secretary (1908) Mrs A.H. Ames, Wing-Eyte, Partstone Avenue, Hornchurch, Essex.

ROMILEY (NUWSS)   In 1910 the society joined the MANCHESTER AND DISTRICT FEDERATION OF THE NATIONAL UNION OF WOMEN'S SUFFRAGE SOCIETIES. Secretary (1909, 1913) Mrs F.B. Wild, 23 Warwick Road, Romiley, Lancashire.

RONNIGER, M. JANE, MADAME (?–still alive 1892)   A member of the KENSINGTON SOCIETY in 1865, she signed the women's suffrage petition in 1866, and in 1868–9 joined the LONDON NATIONAL SOCIETY FOR WOMEN'S SUFFRAGE and in 1872 the MANCHESTER NATIONAL SOCIETY. From 1871 to 1874 she travelled the country, lecturing on women's suffrage on behalf of the London National Society. For instance, on 12 January 1872 she addressed a meeting at the Mechanics' Hall, Rotherham, on "The desirability and importance of conferring the Parliamentary Franchise upon women". This may have been the lecture referred to by Prof. George Croom Robertson in a letter to J.S. MILL, 28 October 1872, when he wrote, "Mrs Ronniger brings nothing to the advocacy of the cause but a pretty face. She has only one lecture, which is a very poor one, and she has no power of fence when troublesome people get up at the end and cross-question her." Croom Robertson does not, however, appear to have been successful in his plan to replace her with another lady lecturer; Mill replied "You seem to underrate the value of 'a pretty face' in a lecturer on women's rights."

Mme Ronniger was, by profession, a teacher of voice and recitation, giving lectures and readings at provincial literary institutes, for instance in Aberdeen in February 1876 and in London to the Women's Protective and Provident League in 1877. She also wrote songs and painted portraits; she exhibited at the Female Art Institute in 1879. From 1876 until 1880 she was the editor of the *Aesthetic Review and Art Observer*, a journal which described itself as "Devoted to Literature, Art, and General Intelligence", and was at first published by Farmer and Sons, 1 Edwardes Terrace, Kensington, and, from April 1879, by the Women's Printing Society. The journal was orientated towards the interests of radical women. Among its articles were reviews of Frances LORD's *How to Influence Little Children*, of a book by E.A. Manning (another erstwhile member of the Kensington Society) on the kindergarten system, of George Fraser's *The Humby Election* (1873), which contains support for women's suffrage (*see under* NOVELS), and an article on vegetarian diet. For a time the journal contained advertisements for the *Women's Suffrage Journal* and in 1876 it covered a report of a drawing-room meeting held by the Chelsea branch of the London National Society for Women's Suffrage. In 1889 Madame Ronniger signed the petition to commemorate the 23rd anniversary of the first women's suffrage petition and in 1892 donated 1/- to the WOMEN's EMANCIPATION UNION.

Address: (1865) 47 Bedford Gardens, Campden Hill, London W; (1876) 1 Abingdon Villas, Kensington, London W.

ROPER, ESTHER (1868–1938) Born in Cheshire, the daughter of a clergyman who, from a working-class background, had become, first, a missionary in Africa with the Church Missionary Society and had then been ordained in the Church of England. From the age of four, Esther Roper, while her parents were in Africa and then after her father's death in 1877, was educated at the Church Missionary Children's Home in Highbury in north London. In 1886 she became one of the first women to attend Victoria University, Manchester, finally taking her degree in History in 1891. In 1893 she was appointed secretary of the MANCHESTER NATIONAL SOCIETY FOR WOMEN'S SUFFRAGE, in 1895, with Edith PALLISER, became joint secretary of a group drawn from the different suffrage societies to promote joint parliamentary action, in 1896 joined the executive committee of the CENTRAL NATIONAL SOCIETY FOR WOMEN'S SUFFRAGE and in 1897 became the representative of the Manchester Society on the executive committee of the NATIONAL UNION OF WOMEN'S SUFFRAGE SOCIETIES. She was a leading member of the Victoria University women's debating society, and in the late 1890s took part in many debates centring on women's suffrage. In 1895 she became a member of the newly formed university settlement, which aimed to bring entertainment and education to the slum area of Ancoats. In 1896, exhausted through overwork, she went to Italy, with a letter of introduction to the mystical novelist George McDonald, and at his house at Bordighera met Eva GORE-BOOTH. After their return from Italy Eva Gore-Booth moved from Ireland to Manchester to live with Esther Roper and they were together until Eva's death in 1926.

In 1899 Esther Roper was a member of the executive committee of the NATIONAL UNION OF WOMEN'S SUFFRAGE SOCIETIES. After her appointment in 1893 as secretary to the Manchester National Society (from 1897 known as the NORTH OF ENGLAND SOCIETY FOR WOMEN'S SUFFRAGE), Esther Roper was responsible for putting into practice the "Special Appeal", a petition to be signed by women from all classes which was intended, by showing the strength of feeling for women's suffrage, to give an impetus to the suffrage campaign (*see* SPECIAL APPEAL COMMITTEE). Esther Roper concentrated on bringing the Special Appeal to the mill-working women of Lancashire and Cheshire and in 1901 produced, with the aid of such organizers as Sarah REDDISH and Selina COOPER, another petition signed by 29 359 mill women. Priscilla Bright McLAREN gave Esther Roper warm support in this attempt, by demonstrating the interest in the cause felt by working women, to sway parliament. She also took a great interest in the petition presented in 1903 by women graduates, who included Esther Roper. Elizabeth Wolstenholme ELMY was another of the "old guard" who gave enthusiastic support to the campaign among women workers; she often stayed with Esther Roper and Eva Gore-Booth when she visited Manchester. The household was vegetarian. From 1900 until 1904 Esther Roper with Eva Gore-Booth edited *Women's Labour News*, a journal of which no copies can now be located. In 1902 Esther Roper helped organize the campaign in support of David Shackleton, the Labour Party candidate, at the Clitheroe by-election. It was hoped that Shackleton would further women's interests in parliament, but when these hopes proved futile, Esther Roper, with Eva Gore-Booth, Sarah Reddish and Sarah Dickenson, in 1903 formed the LANCASHIRE AND CHESHIRE WOMEN TEXTILE AND OTHER WORKERS' REPRESENTATION COMMITTEE to back a more reliable suffrage candidate. Esther Roper and Eva Gore-Booth had met the young Christabel PANKHURST in 1900 and it was Esther who suggested that Christabel should study for a law degree at the university in Manchester. Until late 1905 the three worked, and holidayed, together but the friendship broke after Christabel's disruption of Sir Edward Grey's meeting in the Free Trade Hall in Manchester. Although Esther Roper did not condone violence it was apparently Christabel Pankhurst's varying explanation of events rather than the act of disruption that caused the breach. However, notwithstanding the ending of a personal friendship, Esther Roper, with other radical suffragists, resigned from the North of England Society for Women's Suffrage at the end of the year, refusing to condemn Christabel's tactics. After this she devoted her energies to her work as secretary of the NATIONAL INDUSTRIAL AND PROFESSIONAL WOMEN'S SUFFRAGE SOCIETY, an organization which embodied her ideal of cross-class co-operation between women, and to campaigns against protective legislation which was seen as a threat to the ability of, for instance, pit-brow women and barmaids to earn a living. Among the pamphlets she published are *The Industrial Position of Women and Women's Suffrage* and *The Cotton Trade Unions and the Enfranchisement of Women*. She was also a contributor to the *Common Cause*.

An "extreme pacifist", in December 1914 Esther Roper was one of the signatories to the Open Christmas Letter to the Women of Austria and Germany, joined the Women's Peace Crusade and, from 1916, became an active member of the No-Conscription Fellowship. She was involved, with Eva Gore-Booth, in supporting the latter's sister, Constance Markievicz, when she was imprisoned for her part in the Irish Rebellion. After Eva Gore-Booth's death Esther Roper edited her *Complete Poems*, 1929, writing an introductory memoir for it, and edited the *Prison Letters of Countess Markievicz*, 1934. At the time of her death she was a member of the executive committee of the Open Door Council.

Address: (1905) Cringlebrook, Victoria Road, Manchester; (1914) 14 Frognal Gardens, London NW3.
Photograph: in G. Lewis, *Eva Gore-Booth and Esther Roper*, 1988.
Archival source: Elizabeth Wolstenholme Elmy Papers, British Library.
Bibliography: E. Roper (ed.), *Collected Poems of Eva Gore-Booth*, 1929; G. Lewis, *Eva Gore-Booth and Esther Roper*, 1988.

ROSS (NUWSS) In 1913 the society was a member of the MIDLAND (WEST) FEDERATION OF THE NATIONAL UNION OF WOMEN'S SUFFRAGE SOCIETIES. Secretary (1913) Mrs Thorpe, Wyton, Ross, Herefordshire.

ROTHERFIELD AND MARK CROSS (NUWSS) In 1913 the society was a member of the SURREY, SUSSEX, AND HANTS FEDERATION OF THE NATIONAL UNION OF WOMEN'S SUFFRAGE SOCIETIES. Secretary (1913) Miss White, Longcroft, Rotherfield.

ROTHERHAM (NUWSS) In 1913 the society was a member of the WEST RIDING FEDERATION OF THE NATIONAL UNION OF WOMEN'S SUFFRAGE SOCIETIES. Secretary (1913) Mrs Oldham, 21 Boston Castle Grove, Rotherham, Yorkshire.

ROTHERHAM (WSPU) Secretary (1913) Mrs Slack, 3 Highfields, Doncaster Road, Rotherham, Yorkshire.

ROTHES (NUWSS) In 1913 the society was a member of the NORTH OF SCOTLAND FEDERATION OF THE NATIONAL UNION OF WOMEN'S SUFFRAGE SOCIETIES. Secretary (1913) Miss Annie Robb, 31 Green Street, Rothes, Morayshire.

ROTHESAY (WFL) Secretary (1913) Miss Brown, Hillfoot, 27 Argyll Road, Rothesay, Bute.

ROWE, FRANCES ELIZABETH, MRS (1855–c. 1940s) Born in Manchester, daughter of Isaac Hoyle, who was a strong supporter of the higher education of women and at one time an MP. She was educated at Elizabeth Wolstenholme ELMY's school at Congleton and then as a boarder in London at Miss Pipe's school, Laleham Lodge, at Clapham Park. Miss Pipe, who originally came from Manchester, was one of the signatories of the 1866 women's suffrage petition. Frances Hoyle attended Newnham College, Cambridge, graduating with second-class honours in the Moral Sciences Tripos in 1880 and married Louis Thompson Rowe, a solicitor, in 1883. They do not appear to have had any children. Frances Rowe remained in close touch with Elizabeth Wolstenholme Elmy and was part of the latter's circle of correspondence, but does not appear to have been a member of the WOMEN'S EMANCIPATION UNION. She was, however, in the late 1890s a member of the Legitimation League. In 1901 Harriet

McIlquham wrote to Frances Rowe, "I think you are the lady whom Mrs Elmy has written once or twice to me about with affection". In 1900 Frances Rowe subscribed to the CENTRAL SOCIETY FOR WOMEN'S SUFFRAGE and in 1902 was associated with Dora MONTEFIORE and Harriet McIlquham in lobbying MPs at the House of Commons. In 1903 Elizabeth Wolstenholme Elmy remarked in a letter that Frances Rowe lived near to Dora Montefiore "and they are great friends". In May 1905 Frances Rowe had a letter published in the *Daily News* that Elizabeth Wolstenholme Elmy described as "admirable, short, temperate, dignified and most pertinent". Frances Rowe was at this time the honorary secretary of the HAMMERSMITH NATIONAL UNION OF WOMEN'S SUFFRAGE SOCIETIES branch. She took part in the abortive deputation on 2 March to Campbell-Bannerman at 10 Downing Street that was led by Annie KENNEY and Dora Montefiore. He was ill and could not see them. On 4 March Annie Kenney wrote to Frances Rowe asking her to bring as many women as she could to join another deputation to Campbell-Bannerman on 9 March and to tell Mrs Montefiore to do likewise. Frances Rowe was by now a strong advocate for the WOMEN'S SOCIAL AND POLITICAL UNION in London. She wrote a letter that appeared in the *Labour Leader*, 23 March 1906, urging women to think carefully before joining the Woman's Labour League that had just been proposed by the ILP as a counter to the WSPU. She declared, "There is already a women's organization in the Labour field, the Women's Social and Political Union. This, originating in Manchester, is taking root and growing rapidly wherever our woman organizers are at work". In October 1906 Frances Rowe was present at the meeting held in London by the WSPU to discuss its constitution. In January 1907 she attempted to subvert her NUWSS society, to turn it towards the WSPU, and when this attempt failed she broke away to found a local branch of the WSPU. Despite this change of allegiance, she took part the next month in the NUWSS "Mud March" from Hyde Park Corner to Exeter Hall. A few days later she was arrested after taking part in the deputation organized by the WSPU to the House of Commons from the first "Women's Parliament". She was fined 20/- or 14 days' imprisonment, and chose the latter, but her fine was paid anonymously on the second day of her prison term. Her father, sisters and brother "most strongly resented", as she put it, her arrest. She was worried in case her father, from whom she received an allowance, might in his will add restrictions to the money he left her, preventing her from spending it on the women's movement. Frances Rowe was in close touch with Minnie BALDOCK, who spoke at a meeting of the Hammersmith WSPU in December 1907. Mrs Rowe herself addressed meetings; for instance, in February 1908 speaking at a WSPU meeting at Wood Green and later that year, wearing one of the WSPU's new pieces of merchandise, a silk motor scarf in purple, white and green, at a meeting of the Hammersmith Ethical Society. In 1908 she published an article, *Healthy and Artistic Dress* in *Dress Review*. In November 1911 Frances Rowe was arrested, having dropped a bag containing stones, after smashing the National Bank's windows near the Strand. She is recorded in *Votes for Women*, 15 December 1911, as saying at her trial, "I have not fallen into the ranks of the criminal class. We are out to destroy other things than windows. We are out against worn-out ideas. Men regard us partly as stupid angels and partly as silly children. They never take us seriously. We want your attention, and not only your attention but the attention of the Government." She was sentenced to two months' imprisonment. When in Holloway, she signed Olive WHARRY's prison album. At the dinner held in February 1912 to welcome released prisoners Frances Rowe remarked that:

> Years ago she had begun to see that it was just in that part of life which is called the best and the most beautiful that much that was worst occurred – in the relationship of men and women. It was because so much was wrong there that so much was wrong elsewhere. She saw that the aim of the Suffrage workers was to bring woman out of the depth where she was, so she joined a Suffrage Society and worked with them. When the militant movement began, Mrs Wolstenholme Elmy, who had been her teacher since she was 14 years old, had told her that in her opinion the great hope for women lay with what she called the insurgents. As soon as she heard of the movement it had her allegiance, and as soon as she saw the orginators it had her heart.

Frances Rowe was in March 1909 a member of the FABIAN WOMEN'S GROUP, was a supporter of the TAX RESISTANCE LEAGUE and herself had goods distrained. She still subscribed to the WSPU in 1913.

Address: (1891, 1903) 11 Hammersmith Terrace, London W; (1907) 15 Hammersmith Terrace, London W; (1910) she also had a country house at Holford, near Bridgwater, Somerset (her husband came from Bridgwater) from where, through a classified advertisement in *Votes for Women*, she offered daffodil bulbs for sale.

Archival source: Elizabeth Wolstenholme Elmy Papers, British Library; Harriet McIlquham Papers, Autograph Collection, Fawcett Library.

ROWE, LOUISA JOPLING, MRS (1843–1933) Artist, in May 1884 signed the "Letter from Ladies to Members of Parliament" asking for heads of households to be included in the government franchise bill and in 1889 the Declaration in Favour of Women's Suffrage organized by the CENTRAL COMMITTEE OF THE NATIONAL SOCIETY FOR WOMEN'S SUFFRAGE. In 1890 she held a drawing-room meeting for the WOMEN'S FRANCHISE LEAGUE. In 1898 she was a vice-president of the CENTRAL AND WESTERN SOCIETY FOR WOMEN'S SUFFRAGE. Louise Jopling Rowe subscribed to the WOMEN'S SOCIAL AND POLITICAL UNION in 1907, but may have left to join the WOMEN'S FREEDOM LEAGUE. The latter society certainly held a drawing-room meeting, at which Emma SPROSON was a speaker, at Louise Jopling Rowe's house in 1909. She was a member of the NEW CONSTITUTIONAL SOCIETY FOR WOMEN'S SUFFRAGE in 1910 and, living round the corner from Laurence and Clemence HOUSMAN, a supporter of the SUFFRAGE ATELIER. In 1914 Louise Jopling Rowe joined the UNITED SUFFRAGISTS.

Address: (1880) 28 Beaufort Street, Chelsea, London SW; (1890) 8 Cranley Place, Onslow Gardens, London SW; (1908) 7 Pembroke Gardens, Kensington, London W; (1933) Manor Farm, Chesham Bois, Buckinghamshire.

Portrait: by Millais, 1879, exhibited at the Grosvenor Gallery in 1880 (photograph in National Portrait Gallery Archive); self-portrait in Oldham Art Gallery.

ROXBURGHSHIRE (a branch of the EDINBURGH NATIONAL SOCIETY FOR WOMEN'S SUFFRAGE) Secretary (1909) Mrs Mein, Croft House, Kelso, Roxburghshire.

ROYAL HOLLOWAY COLLEGE (OLD STUDENTS) (NUWSS) Secretary (1909) Miss Marjorie Richmond, Royal Holloway College, Englefield Green, Surrey; (1913) Miss M.C. Anderson, 120 Burnt Ash Hill, Lee, London SE.

ROYDEN, [AGNES] MAUDE (1876–1956) Daughter of Sir Thomas Royden, a Liverpool shipowner, educated at Cheltenham Ladies' College and Lady Margaret Hall, Oxford, where she was particularly friendly with Kathleen COURTNEY and Ida O'MALLEY. A Christian, after graduating she undertook settlement work in Liverpool and then parish work, with Hudson Shaw, in South Luffenham. From 1905 she lived again in Oxford, lecturing for the Oxford University Extension scheme, and from this time became involved in the constitutional women's suffrage movement. After its launch in 1909, she was a regular contributor to the *Common Cause*, becoming its editor in April 1913. Her lecturing experience stood her in good stead and she became recognized as one of the NATIONAL UNION OF WOMEN'S SUFFRAGE SOCIETIES's most polished speakers. She gave classes to tyro speakers; her rate of pay, according to the minutes of the GLASGOW AND WEST OF SCOTLAND ASSOCIATION FOR WOMEN'S SUFFRAGE, was 2/– for one class, 3/– for two. From 1909 she lived in Cheshire with Hudson Shaw and his wife. He had been appointed rector of Old Alderley and Maude Royden regularly held suffrage meetings in the surrounding area. In 1910 she was a supporter of the TAX RESISTANCE LEAGUE and first chairman of the CHURCH LEAGUE FOR WOMEN'S SUFFRAGE. In 1911 Maude Royden was elected to the executive committee of the NUWSS and in October of that year she undertook a speaking tour of the USA, her itinerary including talks on literary subjects and suffrage meetings. After her return she devoted herself to the suffrage cause, speaking in 1912 at 267 meetings all over the country. She was now based in London, Hudson Shaw having been appointed rector of St Botolph's, Bishopsgate. By 1913 she was, as well as being a member of the NUWSS executive committee, president of the CHESTER WOMEN'S SUFFRAGE SOCIETY, vice-president of the OXFORD WOMEN STUDENTS' SUFFRAGE SOCIETY and a member of the executive committee of the LONDON WOMEN'S SUFFRAGE SOCIETY. In that year she attended the meeting of the INTERNATIONAL WOMAN SUFFRAGE ALLIANCE in

Budapest. She supported the NUWSS's rapprochement with the Labour Party and in February 1914 was one of the speakers at a joint demonstration between the two movements held in the Albert Hall.

After the outbreak of war, Maude Royden signed the Open Christmas Letter to the Women of Austria and Germany at the end of 1914 and became secretary of the Fellowship of Reconciliation, formed by a group of fellow Christian pacifists. On 18 February 1915 she resigned her editorship of the *Common Cause* and her place on the national executive of the NUWSS, followed quickly by other radicals, such as Kathleen Courtney and Catherine MARSHALL, all differing with the leadership over the direction the society should take in wartime. Maude Royden attempted to attend the congress of women held at the Hague in 1915, at which was founded the Women's International League for Peace and Freedom, but, with 180 other women, was prevented from so doing by the closure of the North Sea to passenger shipping. Instead she took the message of Christian pacifism to the country, joining a caravan crusade organized by the Fellowship of Reconciliation. This ended in disaster at Hinckley in Leicestershire after the pacifists were attacked by a mob and the caravan burnt. At the end of the year Maude Royden was appointed a vice-president of the Women's International League for Peace and Freedom. In 1916 she was a member of the national executive of the newly formed NATIONAL COUNCIL FOR ADULT SUFFRAGE. In 1918 she was one of the speakers at the meeting held in the Queen's Hall, presided over by Mrs Fawcett, to celebrate the granting of the limited franchise to women. She then devoted herself to the campaign for the ordination of women, founding the Fellowship Guild, with its home at the Guildhouse in Eccleston Square, and becoming herself a renowned preacher. She was also an active supporter of the campaigns for birth-control and for family allowances.

Maude Royden's suffrage pamphlets include *How Women Use the Vote*, NUWSS, 1912; *Votes and Wages: How Women's Suffrage Will Improve the Economic Position of Women*, NUWSS, 1911, 4th edn, 1914; *Physical Force and Democracy*, NUWSS, 1912; *The True End of Government; Chance – The Predominance of Men in Anti-Suffrage Finance and Organisation*, 1913. She contributed two essays, "Modern Love" and "The Future of the Women's Movement" to *The Making of Women*, edited by Victor Gollancz, 1917.
Address: (1913) Frankly Hall, Birkenhead, Cheshire.
Photograph: in S. Fletcher, *Maude Royden: A Life*, 1989.
Bibliography: M. Royden, *A Three-Fold Cord*, 1947; S. Fletcher, *Maude Royden: A Life*, 1989.

RUGBY (NUWSS) In 1913 the society was a member of the MIDLAND (WEST) FEDERATION OF THE NATIONAL UNION OF WOMEN'S SUFFRAGE SOCIETIES. Secretary (1913) Mrs Parnell; office, 27 Regent St., Rugby, Warwickshire.

RUTHERGLEN, Lanarkshire, committee of the NATIONAL SOCIETY FOR WOMEN'S SUFFRAGE Formed in 1873.

RUTTER, FRANK [FRANCIS VANE PHIPSON] (1876–1937) Born in London, the son of the solicitor who acted for Ruskin when he was sued by Whistler. Frank Rutter was educated at Merchant Taylors' School and Queens' College, Cambridge, where he studied oriental languages. In 1906 he set up the French Impressionist Fund to buy pictures for the National Gallery, in 1908 he was the art critic for the *Sunday Times* and he became secretary of the Allied Artists' Association (AAA), which, in an attempt to break the power of the Royal Academy, he founded in 1908 in order to enable artists and craft workers to submit their work freely and without restriction to the judgement of the public. His *Revolution in Art: An Introduction to the Study of Cézanne, Gauguin, Van Gogh, and Other Modern Painters*, 1910, is dedicated "To the rebels of either sex all the world over who in any way are fighting for freedom of any kind", a commendation noted by *Votes for Women* when it drew attention to the Post-Impressionist Exhibition at the Grafton Gallery, 20 January 1911. In 1910 he advertised the AAA in the WOMEN'S FREEDOM LEAGUE's Suffrage Fair catalogue and in July 1913 the 6th London Salon of the AAA, held at the Albert Hall, included two pictures of suffrage interest. One, by Mary Robinson, was titled *The Most Sensational Derby on Record. Suffragette and the King's Horse, Anmer* and the other, by Mrs Lily Delissa Joseph (who at the end of the nineteenth century had been art critic of the

Women's Gazette, the organ of the Women's Liberal Federation, and who in 1931 painted the portrait of her sister Henrietta Lowy), titled *The Woman's March*, presumably depicted the 1912 March organized by Florence DE FONBLANQUE rather than the NUWSS PILGRIMAGE, which was taking place while the exhibition was being held. On 12 January 1910 Frank Rutter took the chair at the first meeting, held at the Eustace Miles Restaurant, of what was to become the MEN'S POLITICAL UNION FOR WOMEN'S ENFRANCHISEMENT and in May, representing the Press, was a speaker at the John Stuart MILL Celebrations organized by the WOMEN'S FREEDOM LEAGUE. He was a friend of long-standing of the Duval family; it was at his wedding in 1909 that Una DUGDALE and Victor DUVAL had met and in 1913 he gave Elsie DUVAL a character reference to enable her to find work in Europe after her escape as a "mouse". In 1912 Rutter moved to Leeds where he became director of the City Art Gallery. His house there was used by suffragettes recovering from hunger strike. From there, in mid-1913, Lilian LENTON, on release under the "Cat and Mouse" Act, escaped to France. There were doubtless other such incidents which, by their very nature, were kept secret at the time and which, on account of Rutter's reticence, have not been mentioned in suffragette memoirs. In his autobiography Frank Rutter, in an epilogue, particularly mentions that "the only furiously active part of my life was the few years during which I was connected with the militant suffrage movement, and of this I have said nothing, because if I once began I should want to fill a volume with my experiences during this exciting time. It is all over now, the battle has been won, and this is not the place in which to recount the skirmishes in which I had the honour to take part." He mentions that, although he did not see eye to eye with the leaders of the WSPU during some of the later phases of the campaign, he had for them the deepest respect and most profound admiration.

Address: (1913) 7 Westfield Terrace, Chapel Allerton, Leeds.

Portrait: given to Mr and Mrs Duval, now in a private collection.

Bibliography: F. Rutter, *Since I Was Twenty-Five*, 1927; T. Steele, *Alfred Orage and the Leeds Art Club, 1893–1923*, 1990.

RYDE (ISLE OF WIGHT) (NUWSS) In 1913 the society was a member of the SURREY, SUSSEX, AND HANTS FEDERATION OF THE NATIONAL UNION OF WOMEN'S SUFFRAGE SOCIETIES. Secretary (1913) Mrs Grant, Northwood, Queen's Road, Ryde, Isle of Wight.

RYLAND, BERTHA (1882–alive 1963) Lived in Birmingham, a member of a prominent Edgbaston family. In 1908, with her mother, she joined the WOMEN'S SOCIAL AND POLITICAL UNION and then ran the newly founded Midlands regional office. In January 1910 she established a WSPU base in Lichfield and in the first four months of 1911 canvassed for support in Walsall, Stafford and Hanley. In November 1911 she took part in London in the WSPU window-smashing raid, was sentenced to seven days' imprisonment and returned to repeat the experience in March 1912, breaking windows in Bond Street. This time she was sentenced to six months' hard labour, spent four months in Winson Green Prison, went on hunger strike, was forcibly fed and then released. In June 1914, in Birmingham Art Gallery, she damaged, with a cleaver, *Master Thornhill*, a painting by Romney. While on remand she went on hunger strike and was forcibly fed. She then accepted bail, was too ill to stand trial at the July assizes and had not been sentenced by the time that war broke out and amnesty was granted to suffragettes. She suffered permanent kidney damage as a result of her treatment in prison. In 1936 she executed the calligraphy for a poem that V.H. FRIEDLANDER contributed to a book, inscribed with the names of all their friends, given to Frederick and Emmeline PETHICK-LAWRENCE. In 1945 Bertha Ryland contributed a tribute to the memoir of Dorothy EVANS written by Monica Whately.

Address: (1913) 19 Hermitage Road, Birmingham; (1928) 61 High Street, Hampstead, London NW.

S

SAFFRON WALDEN (branch of the LONDON SOCIETY FOR WOMEN'S SUFFRAGE) Was in existence in 1906 when its honorary secretary was Miss Mitchell, The Training College, Saffron Walden, Essex.

ST ALBANS (NUWSS) In 1913 the society was a member of the EASTERN COUNTIES FEDERATION OF THE NATIONAL SOCIETY FOR WOMEN'S SUFFRAGE. Secretary (1913) Miss Lee, 1 Lemsford Road, St Albans, Hertfordshire.

ST ANDREWS committee of the NATIONAL SOCIETY FOR WOMEN'S SUFFRAGE Formed in 1871 when the honorary secretary was Mrs Baynes. In 1913 the local society was a member of the SCOTTISH FEDERATION OF THE NATIONAL UNION OF WOMEN'S SUFFRAGE SOCIETIES. Secretary (1913) Mrs Finlay, New Halls, St Andrews, Fife.

ST ANDREWS branch of the SCOTTISH UNIVERSITY WOMEN'S SUFFRAGE UNION Secretary (1913) Miss J.M. Benson, St Andrews University Women's Suffrage Society, The University, St Andrews, Fife.

ST BEES (NUWSS) In 1913 the society was a member of the NORTH-WESTERN FEDERATION OF THE NATIONAL UNION OF WOMEN'S SUFFRAGE SOCIETIES. Secretary (1913) Miss Florence Walker, 2 Victoria Terrace, St Bees, Cumberland.

ST GEORGE'S, HANOVER SQUARE (branch of the LONDON SOCIETY FOR WOMEN'S SUFFRAGE, NUWSS) Secretary (1913) Mrs Bertram, 38 Palace Mansions, Addison Bridge, London W.

ST HELEN'S (NUWSS) In 1913 the society was a member of the WEST LANCS, WEST CHESHIRE, AND NORTH WALES FEDERATION OF THE NATIONAL UNION OF WOMEN'S SUFFRAGE SOCIETIES. Secretary (1913) Miss Christine Pilkington, The Hazels, Prescot, Lancashire.

ST IVES (NUWSS) In 1913 the society was a member of the SOUTH-WESTERN FEDERATION OF THE NATIONAL UNION OF WOMEN'S SUFFRAGE SOCIETIES. Secretary (1913) Mrs F. Crichton Matthew, 9 Draycott Terrace, St Ives, Cornwall.

ST JOHN, CHRISTOPHER MARIE (pseudonym of Christabel Marshall) (c. 1875–1960) Educated at Somerville College, Oxford, gaining third-class honours in Modern History. She was for a short time secretary to Mrs Humphry Ward, and afterwards to both Lady Randolph Churchill and, at intervals, to her son Winston Churchill. Intent on becoming a dramatist, she spent three years on the stage, worked on occasion as secretary to Ellen Terry and from 1899 lived with Edith CRAIG. Although a feminist and admirer of militant tactics, she did not formally join the WOMEN'S SOCIAL AND POLITICAL UNION until 1909; she had previously worked for both the WOMEN WRITERS' SUFFRAGE LEAGUE and the ACTRESSES' FRANCHISE LEAGUE. In 1909 she saw the dramatic possibility in a short story, *How The Vote Was Won*, written by Cicely HAMILTON which had been published as a pamphlet, with illustrations by C. Hedley Charlton, by the WWSL. Christopher St John turned the story into a play and it was first performed at an Actresses' Franchise League matinée in April 1909, played at the WSPU Prince's Skating Rink Exhibition in May and was to prove very popular with suffrage societies throughout the country. On 29 June she took part in the WSPU deputation to the House of Commons, contributing an article "Why I Went on the Deputation" to *Votes for Women*, 9 July 1909. In November 1909 Christopher St John played the woman-soldier, Hannah Snell, in Cicely Hamilton's *Pageant of Great Women*, directed by Edith Craig.

With Cicely Hamilton she also wrote *The Pot and The Kettle*, 1909, and with Charles Thursby, *The Coronation*, 1912. Her play *The First Actress*, "celebrating the struggle of women in the theatre against sex discrimination", was performed in May 1911 as the first presentation of Edith Craig's company, the Pioneer Players. Christabel Marshall had earlier converted to Roman Catholicism, at which point she took the surname "St John", and in 1912 she presented a BANNER to the CATHOLIC WOMEN'S SUFFRAGE SOCIETY, becoming a member of the society's committee in 1913.

In 1915 Christopher St John published an autobiographical novel, *Hungerheart*, on which she had been working since 1899. It draws on her relationship with Edy Craig and describes her involvement in the suffrage campaign. From 1921 until 1931 Christopher St John was music and drama critic for Lady RHONDDA's feminist journal *Time and Tide*, and in 1935 she wrote a biography of Christine MURRELL.

Address: (1901) Priest's House, Smallhythe, Kent; (1906, 1913) 31 Bedford Street, Strand, London WC; (1928) Smallhythe, Kent.

Photograph: in J. Holledge, *Innocent Flowers: Women in the Edwardian Theatre*, 1981.

Bibliography: *Votes for Women*, 2 July 1909; E. Adlard (ed.), *Edy: Recollections of Edith Craig*, 1949; J. Holledge, *Innocent Flowers: Women in the Edwardian Theatre*, 1981; S. Stowell, *A Stage Of Their Own: Feminist Playwrights of the Suffrage Age*, 1992.

ST PANCRAS (WSPU) Secretary (1906) Miss Rozier, 9 Bartholomew Road, Camden Road, London NW.

ST PANCRAS (EAST) (branch of the LONDON SOCIETY FOR WOMEN'S SUFFRAGE, NUWSS) In 1906 its chairman was Miss McKEE. Secretary (1913) Miss Rinder, 14 Westgate Terrace, Earl's Court, London SW.

ST PANCRAS (SOUTH) (branch of the LONDON SOCIETY FOR WOMEN'S SUFFRAGE, NUWSS) Secretary (1909, 1913) Mrs Bertram, 38 Palace Mansions, Addison Bridge, London W.

SALE (GROUP) By 1912 the society was a member of the MANCHESTER AND DISTRICT FEDERATION OF THE NATIONAL UNION OF WOMEN'S SUFFRAGE SOCIETIES. Secretary (1913) Miss Geiler, Thornlea, Wardle Road, Sale, Cheshire.

SALISBURY (NUWSS) In 1913 the society was a member of the SURREY, SUSSEX, AND HANTS FEDERATION OF THE NATIONAL UNION OF WOMEN'S SUFFRAGE SOCIETIES. Secretary (1913) Miss Hardy, Harncroft, Old Blandford Road, Salisbury, Wiltshire.

SALTBURN (NUWSS) In 1913 the society was a member of the NORTH AND EAST RIDINGS FEDERATION OF THE NATIONAL UNION OF WOMEN'S SUFFRAGE SOCIETIES. Secretary (1913) Miss Leakey, 9 Leven Street, Saltburn-by-the-Sea, Yorkshire.

SANDERS, BEATRICE, MRS (c. 1874–1932) née Martin Financial secretary of the WOMEN'S SOCIAL AND POLITICAL UNION (at a salary in 1913 of £3 a week). Her husband, a Fabian Society lecturer, was a London County Council alderman (a fact which did not pass unremarked by the Home Office in 1913) and in 1908 was Labour parliamentary candidate for Portsmouth. He was secretary of the Metropolitan District Council of the ILP and contributed a short article to the first issue of Frederick PETHICK-LAWRENCE's journal the *Labour Record* in March 1905. Beatrice Sanders was a member of the FABIAN WOMEN'S GROUP in 1911, and was still a member in 1920. In February 1907 she was sentenced to 14 days' imprisonment after taking part in the deputation from the first Women's Parliament in Caxton Hall to the House of Commons. Her husband was chairman of the breakfast held at the Eustace Miles Restaurant on 3 April to celebrate the release of the suffragette prisoners. On 21 June 1908 Beatrice Sanders was chief marshal of the section that included the Portsmouth WSPU contingent in the procession to Hyde Park. Mabel TUKE in a letter to Isabel SEYMOUR on the arrangements for this procession wrote waspishly of Mrs Sanders, "her husband of course doing all the work, she taking the glory!" In November 1910 Beatrice Sanders was sentenced to one month's imprisonment in Holloway after taking part in a stone-throwing raid to protest against the treatment of women on "Black Friday". In June 1913 she was sentenced to 15 months' imprisonment on a charge of conspiring with the other members of the WSPU administration and with Edwy CLAYTON to commit

damage to a property and inciting others to do so. She was sent to Lewes prison and, after hunger striking, was released six days later. Beatrice Sanders and her fellow conspirators were much heartened by local supporters, who gathered each day to sing suffragette songs on the Downs near to the prison.
Address: (1906) 18 Brynmaer Road, Battersea, London SW; (1929) c/o 129 Sandy Lane South, Wallington, Surrey; (1932) 42 Salcott Road, Battersea, London SW.
Photograph: in the *Suffragette*, 20 June 1913.
Archival source: The Suffragette Fellowship Collection, Museum of London.

SANDERSON, AMY, MRS (?–?) Born at Belshill, Scotland, married in 1901, she joined the WOMEN'S SOCIAL AND POLITICAL UNION in Forfar in 1906. She took part in the deputation in February 1907 from the first Women's Parliament in Caxton Hall to the House of Commons and as a result was imprisoned in Holloway. She was actively campaigning for the WSPU in Scotland in September 1907 but in October was one of those who broke away to found the WOMEN'S FREEDOM LEAGUE, becoming a member of its executive committee, on which she remained for three years. In February 1908 she took part in a deputation to Asquith at his house in Cavendish Square and as a result was sentenced to one month's imprisonment. By 1909 she was living in Castleford, where her house was the headquarters for the South Yorkshire branch of the WFL. Amy Sanderson spoke at hundreds of public meetings (at 97 in 1909 alone) and in 1910 was the member of the executive committee deputed to take over at the London headquarters from Edith How MARTYN, while the latter was on holiday. Amy Sanderson was one of the principal speakers taking part in the "Woman's March" from Edinburgh to London, organized by Florence DE FONBLANQUE in November 1912. She later travelled to America and Australia, lecturing under the auspices of the Workers' Educational Association.
Address: (1913) Mizpah House, Castleford, Yorkshire.
Photograph: in L. Leneman, *A Guid Cause: The Women's Suffrage Movement in Scotland*, 1991.
Archival source: The Suffragette Fellowship Collection, Museum of London.

SANDERSON, [JULIA SARAH] ANNE COBDEN, MRS (1853–1926) Fourth daughter of Richard Cobden and his wife Kate, who was one of the signatories to the 1866 women's suffrage petition. In 1882 Anne Cobden married James Sanderson and became the mother of a son and a daughter. Her husband was a scholar and idealist, who gave up his practice as a barrister to study applied art and, at the suggestion of William Morris, a close friend and neighbour, became a bookbinder, eventually founding first the Doves Bindery and then, from 1901, the Doves Press. His wife's money helped finance the enterprise and she gave practical help with the sewing of the books. Anne Cobden Sanderson, although brought up in such a famously Liberal family, joined the Independent Labour Party. She was one of the five women delegates in February 1906 at the sixth annual conference of the Labour Representation Committee, at which the motion in favour of women's enfranchisement under the terms then obtaining to men, was defeated. She was a poor law guardian in Hammersmith from 1910 until 1922.

The Cobden sisters (*see also* Jane Cobden UNWIN and Ellen Cobden SICKERT) were life-long supporters of the cause of women's suffrage and, although too young to have signed the first petition, Anne Cobden attended the Women's Suffrage Conference held in London in April 1871. In 1903 she gave to Elizabeth Wolstenholme ELMY a copy of *The Life and Work of Susan B. Anthony*, published by her brother-in-law T. Fisher Unwin. Although a close friend of Millicent Garrett FAWCETT, she was the first prominent constitutional suffragist to defect to the militants, joining the WOMEN'S SOCIAL AND POLITICAL UNION in 1906. In an article, *Why I Want The Vote*, published in the *Vote* on 26 March 1910, she described how the ejection of Christabel PANKHURST and Annie KENNEY from the Free Trade Hall in October 1905 galvanized her into action. With, among others, Mary GAWTHORPE, Charlotte DESPARD and Emmeline PANKHURST, Anne Cobden Sanderson held a protest meeting in the Lobby of the House of Commons on 23 October 1906 and as a result was sentenced to two months' imprisonment. "We have talked so much for the Cause now let us suffer for it", she is reputed to have said on this occasion, and at her trial declaimed that "I am a law breaker because I want to be a law maker". Millicent Fawcett, to refute scurrilous press reports, wrote to *The Times*, 27 October 1906, "I have known

Mrs Cobden Sanderson for 30 years. I was not in the police-court on Wednesday when she was before the magistrate, but I find it absolutely impossible to believe that she bit, or scratched, or screamed, or behaved otherwise than like the refined lady she is." Twenty years later, in an obituary letter, Rose Lamartine YATES noted that it was due to Anne Cobden Sanderson's intervention, as a result of her prison experience, that clean bedding was provided in cells and a vegetarian diet was introduced. The prisoners were released on 24 November, having served only half their term. Before sanctioning the release of the prisoners the Home Office, on 14 November, requested the opinion of the law officers as to the power of the Crown to remit a term of imprisonment passed in default of those found guilty not being willing to enter into a recognizance to keep the peace and deemed the matter sufficiently important to then hold a conference with the attorney and solicitor general. The interpretation put upon this leniency was that a by-election was taking place at the time in Huddersfield and it was not deemed politic for the newly elected Liberal government to be seen to be holding suffragettes in prison, particularly one whose name held such historic Liberal resonance. The Home Office papers couch the case in terms of "Annie Cobden-Sanderson and others" and were originally considered sufficiently sensitive to be closed for 100 years. As it was, on her release, Anne Cobden Sanderson went straight to Huddersfield to take part in the by-election campaign. On 11 December she was a guest of honour at a dinner, organized by Millicent Fawcett and held at the Savoy, to celebrate the release of the suffrage prisoners. This occasion does seem to have had the effect of easing many erstwhile constitutional suffragists into the militant camp; presumably the combination of the political and social credentials of such ex-prisoners as Anne Cobden Sanderson and such socially acceptable surroundings worked their magic. In 1906–7 Anne Cobden Sanderson and her husband between them gave £108 to the WSPU. In 1907, when planning a visit to the USA, she wrote to Harriot Stanton BLATCH, offering to speak for her Equality League. The latter, by stressing Mrs Cobden Sanderson's prison credentials, engendered handsome publicity for the speaking tour.

However, by the autumn of 1907, Anne Cobden Sanderson, who had presumably become disenchanted by both the autocracy of the Pankhursts and, being an ILP supporter, by the WSPU's break with the Labour Party, took a very active part in the formation of the WOMEN'S FREEDOM LEAGUE. Elizabeth Wolstenholme Elmy, writing to Harriet MCILQUHAM in January 1908, waspishly remarked of Anne Cobden Sanderson, a traitor to the WSPU, "I have three times heard her speak. She has no clear strong message to deliver, but each time she has solemnly made a pause towards the middle of her speech and then begun, 'My father, Richard Cobden –' and then solemnly paused again for a cheer. I wonder if she always does it."

The Cobden Sandersons obviously did not bear any personal animosity against the Pankhursts because in January 1909 they presented Emmeline, on her release from prison, with an address written on white vellum in purple and green ink and bound by the Doves Bindery. Anne Cobden Sanderson proved one of the WFL's most tireless campaigners, speaking at outdoor meetings and continuing to take part in militant protests. She was arrested on 19 August 1909 while picketing the door of No. 10 Downing Street in order to present a petition to Asquith. Her fine was paid without her knowledge or consent, thereby depriving her of another short term of imprisonment. Sylvia Pankhurst recounts that during the fracas in Parliament Square on "Black Friday" in November 1910, Winston Churchill, who knew Anne Cobden Sanderson well, when he encountered her in the melée, called a policeman and ordered, "Drive that woman away!" The structure of society must indeed have seemed perilously close to crumbling when such an action was deemed necessary against a friend of one's family and erstwhile hostess.

When it was founded in 1909 Anne Cobden Sanderson became a member of the committee of the TAX RESISTANCE LEAGUE and represented that society at the Sixth Congress of the INTERNATIONAL WOMAN SUFFRAGE ALLIANCE, which was held in Stockholm in June 1911. She rallied round when the goods of TRL members were sold in lieu of tax; in September 1911 she attended the sale of Rosina SKY's chattels at Southend-on-Sea and on 29 June 1912 wrote to Maud Arncliffe SENNETT to say that she would not be able to visit Katherine GATTY, who had just been released from prison, because she had to go to Southend for an afternoon sale (again of Mrs Sky's goods) and an evening meeting. In 1911 Anne Cobden Sanderson subscribed to the Hawkins's Legal Fund (see Alice HAWKINS) organized by the MEN'S POLITICAL UNION. In 1912 she subscribed to the NUWSS Election Fighting Fund; she maintained her close association with the ILP, being particularly friendly with Keir HARDIE, for whom she had campaigned at Merthyr during the January 1910 general election. In 1913 she supported the NATIONAL POLITICAL LEAGUE and later that year, with her daughter Stella, undertook another suffrage speaking tour in America. In 1914 Anne Cobden Sanderson signed the Open Christmas Letter to the Women of Germany and Austria and during the war was an active member of the BRITISH DOMINIONS WOMAN SUFFRAGE UNION, chairing its final large meeting on 6 June 1918. In January 1918 she supported Charlotte Despard when she stood as the Labour Party candidate at North Battersea and in December attended the Women's Exhibition, organized by Sylvia Pankhurst and put on at the Caxton Hall by the EAST LONDON FEDERATION OF SUFFRAGETTES, the UNITED SUFFRAGISTS and the SUFFRAGETTES OF THE WSPU. Anne Cobden Sanderson was present, a few days before she died, at a dinner given to celebrate the PETHICK-LAWRENCES' silver wedding anniversary.

Address: (1888) Goodyers, Hendon, London NW; (1912) 15 Upper Mall, Hammersmith, London W; (1926) 319 St James's Court, London SW.
Photograph: in the *Vote*, 26 March 1910.
Archival source: Elizabeth Wolstenholme Elmy Papers, British Library; Hammersmith and Fulham Archives and Local History Centre; Home Office Papers, Public Record Office.

SANDHURST, MARGARET, BARONESS (c. 1828–92) née Fellowes Married in 1854 Sir William Mansfield, later Lord Sandhurst, a distinguished Indian administrator. She was the mother of several sons and a daughter and, having been widowed, became a spiritualist. An "advanced Liberal", she founded the Marylebone Women's Liberal Association in 1887, becoming its president. She ran a home for crippled or "incurable" children in the Marylebone Road. In 1889 she was a member of the council of the WOMEN'S FRANCHISE LEAGUE and in that year supported the formation of the Women's Trade Union Association and in January was elected to the London County Council, returned by Brixton. Having taken her seat and addressed herself to the problem of baby farms, her election was in March declared void because she was a woman, on the petition of Beresford Hope, the Conservative losing candidate. In 1890 Lady Sandhurst was president of the SOCIETY FOR PROMOTING THE RETURN OF WOMEN AS COUNTY COUNCILLORS and from 1889 was a member of the executive committee of the CENTRAL NATIONAL SOCIETY FOR WOMEN'S SUFFRAGE. She wrote at least two pamphlets, one of which, *Conversations on Political Principles*, was published by the WOMEN'S LIBERAL FEDERATION.

Address: (1892) Sandhurst, Berkshire.
Bibliography: *Woman's Herald*, 9 January 1892; P. Hollis, *Ladies Elect: Women in English Local Government, 1865–1914*, 1987.

SBARBORO (or SBARBARA), JANE, MRS (1842–1925) Described by Sylvia PANKHURST (who spelled her name "Sparborough" in *The Suffragette*, 1911) as an "old needlewoman". She was a member of the Bromley-by-Bow branch of the WOMEN'S SOCIAL AND POLITICAL UNION and on 19 June 1906 was arrested, with Annie KENNEY, Teresa Billington (see Teresa BILLINGTON-GREIG) and Mrs KNIGHT, after taking part in a WSPU deputation to Asquith's house in Cavendish Square. Sylvia Pankhurst describes Mrs Sbarboro's offence as rebuking laughing bystanders, reminding them of an occasion when Asquith had ordered out the army to deal with a trades dispute. At her trial, to an enquiry from the prosecuting counsel as to why she was involved in such a demonstration, she replied, "Because we want the vote. We see the misery you men have done for years and we want to alter it . . . You would have sympathy if you lived down Bow-common and saw the misery there. I think women can undo the tangle you men have made" (*The Times*, 4 July 1906). Mrs Sbarboro was sentenced to six weeks' imprisonment, writing from Holloway, "one blessing we have no fleas and no flies in prison". On 11 December 1906 she attended the banquet at the Savoy organized by Mrs FAWCETT to celebrate the release from prison of a subsequent batch of prisoners. After her imprisonment she became a "tea lady" at Clement's Inn, but it is not clear how long she remained there once the WSPU became a more professional and middle-class organization. Mrs Sbarboro took the trouble to write to Minnie BALDOCK when the latter was in hospital in 1911 and clearly remained in contact with one strand of the militant movement; she was one of the signatories to the memorial book presented by the UNITED SUFFRAGISTS to Evelyn SHARP in March 1918.

Address: (1906) Fairfort Road, Bow, London E; (1925) 28 St George's House, Whitechapel, London E.

SCARBOROUGH branch of the MEN'S POLITICAL UNION FOR WOMEN'S ENFRANCHISEMENT Founded in 1910.

SCARBOROUGH (WSPU) Organizer (1910) Miss Adela PANKHURST; honorary secretary, Miss Suffield, 23 Barwick Street, Scarborough; treasurer, Dr Marion Mackenzie, 7 The Valley, Scarborough. Secretary (1911) Dr Mackenzie; (1913) Miss N. Vickerman, 33 St Nicholas Cliff, Scarborough. In 1911 the WSPU had a shop at 39 Huntriss Row (photograph in *Votes for Women*, 6 October 1911).

SCARBOROUGH Women's Suffrage Society Affiliated to the CENTRAL NATIONAL SOCIETY (probably because of association with Florence BALGARNIE). Founded in 1888, the society was refounded in 1904, as a member of the NATIONAL UNION OF WOMEN'S SUFFRAGE SOCIETIES, reinvigorated in 1908, and by 1913 was a member of the NORTH AND EAST RIDINGS FEDERATION OF THE NATIONAL UNION OF WOMEN'S SUFFRAGE SOCIETIES. Secretary (1909) Mrs Daniel, 14 Royal Crescent, Scarborough, and Miss Kitson, May Lodge, Scarborough, Yorkshire; (1913) The Secretary; Office, 8 Falconer's Chambers, Huntriss Row, Scarborough, Yorkshire.

SCATCHERD, ALICE ELIZABETH CLIFF, MRS (1842–1906) The wife of Oliver Scatcherd, a textile factory owner and civic dignatory of Morley near Leeds, where his family had been settled for 200 years. The Scatcherd family had a history of involvement in such radical causes as Catholic Emancipation and the repeal of the Corn Laws. Alice Scatcherd's radicalism centred upon women's causes and was particularly directed against the Church of England marriage service which, to applause, on 25 July 1889 at the inaugural meeting of the WOMEN'S FRANCHISE LEAGUE, she maintained did "much to keep up the subjection of women in our land. It lends the sanction of religion to much that is degrading and wrong in married life. I, for one, can never sanction that Service by my presence." Her own marriage appears to have been happy and childless; she chose not to wear a wedding ring. She and her husband were very active in all good causes in Morley, championing, for instance, the Morley Friends' Adult School, the Morley Temperance Association, and the local branch of the Women's Co-operative Guild, the inaugural meeting of which was attended by Sarah REDDISH in June 1894. In November 1896, with Alice Scatcherd in the chair, Isabella FORD gave a lecture to the Morley Co-operative Women's Guild. In 1897 Alice Scatcherd launched a scheme, the Nursing Association, to employ trained nurses for Morley. Alice Scatcherd was attuned to the socialist aesthetic; when, in 1898, to celebrate the end of her husband's mayoralty year she presented a new mace to the council, it was one that was designed by Walter Crane and made by Alexander Fisher.

Alice Scatcherd was a member of the Campaign to Repeal the Contagious Diseases Acts and in 1873 spoke in Birmingham at the Third Annual Meeting of the Personal Rights Association. She still presided over meetings of the PRA in 1897. She helped to found branches of the National Union of Women Workers in Yorkshire, and to organize a six-week lock-out by women workers in Dewsbury in 1875.

In 1873–4 Alice Scatcherd, as secretary of the YORKSHIRE SOCIETY FOR WOMEN'S SUFFRAGE and chairwoman of meetings at Hunslet and Leeds, sent in petitions in favour of the Women's Disabilities Bill. In 1876 she was a member of the executive committee of the MANCHESTER NATIONAL SOCIETY FOR WOMEN'S SUFFRAGE (still a member of the committee in 1895) and in 1877 was present at a conference organized in Birmingham by the CENTRAL COMMITTEE OF THE NATIONAL SOCIETY FOR WOMEN'S SUFFRAGE, of which she was by now a member of the executive committee. Alice Scatcherd was particularly keen on involving working-class women in the suffrage agitation. At some point in the 1870s she had encountered Jessie CRAIGEN and, recognizing the latter's power over an audience, used her as a speaker at many suffrage meetings. Alice Scatcherd was herself an active and fluent speaker; she spoke at six of the Grand Demonstrations of Women held in the early 1880s. In addition she chaired a meeting held to accommodate the overflow from the Sheffield Grand Demonstration on 27 February 1882 and, the week before, addressed a drawing-room meeting, intended as a "warm-up", which was held at the home of Mrs Henry Wilson, wife of the Sheffield radical, a leading agitator for the abolition of the Contagious Diseases Acts, and who in 1885 became radical Liberal MP for Holmfirth. In the 1882 annual report of the Manchester National Society for Women's Suffrage Alice Scatcherd is particularly singled out for the work she had done to promote the Grand Demonstrations. In November 1882 she organized the testimonial to mark the passing of the Married Women's Property Act, from the National Society for Women's Suffrage that was presented to Ursula BRIGHT and Elizabeth Wolstenholme ELMY at the final meeting of the Married Women's Property Committee. Alice Scatcherd, representing the Morley Liberal Club, was one of only nine women delegates who attended and spoke at the Conference of Liberal Associations held in Leeds in October 1883. On this occasion she met, at the home of Emily and Isabella Ford, Susan B. Anthony, who had attended the Conference. Alice Scatcherd had often in the past worked with their mother, Hannah Ford, for instance in the Protest of Leeds Women Against the Industrial Schools Amendment Act in 1880. In 1886 she spoke at the inaugural meeting of the Newcastle Women's Liberal Association, at which Henrietta MULLER was also a speaker and Mrs Spence WATSON took the chair. However, by 1893 Alice Scatcherd was supporting Labour Party candidates in municipal elections.

In 1889 Alice Scatcherd was, with Elizabeth Wolstenholme Elmy and Harriet MCILQUHAM, one of the founders of the Women's Franchise League, becoming its treasurer and, with Ursula Bright, its financial mainstay. She did not follow Elizabeth Wolstenholme Elmy into the WOMEN'S EMANCIPATION UNION and, after the death of Jacob BRIGHT in 1899, appears to have been the League's main support. In 1897 the Women's Franchise League appears to have become a constituent member of the newly organized NATIONAL UNION OF WOMEN'S SUFFRAGE SOCIETIES. In 1898 Alice Scatcherd represented the Women's Franchise League at the funeral of Richard PANKHURST, giving an address at the graveside and lauding his work for women's causes. She subsequently subscribed £25 to the fund raised to support his widow and children. She was also present when a bust of Jacob Bright was unveiled at Manchester Town Hall in 1898. As well as such active involvement with the Women's Franchise League, Alice Scatcherd appears to have remained a member of the Central National Society for Women's Suffrage, speaking at its annual general meeting in 1896. She was very friendly with Elizabeth Cady Stanton who, with her daughter Harriot Stanton BLATCH, stayed at Morley Hall for a few days in 1890. Alice Cliff Scatcherd was also close to Jane Cobden UNWIN, writing to her in 1890 as "Dear Janey" and saying "I just long for a good talk with you". In 1891 Alice Scatcherd wrote to Annie Leigh BROWNE asking for written-out forms for petitions in support of the Women's County Council Bills and stating that "As a member of the Women's Franchise League I feel it is a duty to work as hard as I possibly can for WCC." In spite of all these efforts, in a letter written to Esther ROPER in 1901 Priscilla Bright McLAREN remarked, enigmatically, that Mrs Scatcherd "got spoiled" after joining the Women's Franchise League.

With her husband, Alice Scatcherd travelled widely. Together they took trips to Norway, Egypt, India and the Far East, and to southern Europe, and she published extensive descriptions of her travels in the local paper, the *Morley Observer*. Without her husband, but with Laura Ormiston CHANT, she sailed from Liverpool in 1888 as one of the delegates to the International Council of Women at Washington. In 1893, with Jane Cobden Unwin, she attended the World's Congress of Representative Women held in Chicago.

In 1903 Alice Scatcherd was elected to the Morley Education Board but in 1904 she was forced to resign all her public positions; according to Elizabeth Wolstenholme Elmy she had "suffered a loss of mental powers". She died intestate, her husband had predeceased her, and Morley Hall, which had been in the Scatcherd family for so long, was bought by Sir Charles Scarth, another prominent Morley citizen, and presented to the town as a maternity home, crèche, and public pleasure ground. It remained Morley's maternity home until 1972.

Address: (1880) 27 Virginia Road, Leeds; (1885) Morley Hall, Morley, near Leeds, Yorkshire.
Photograph: in Scatcherd Collection, Morley Public Library.
Archival source: Scatcherd Collection, Morley Public Library; Elizabeth Wolstenholme Elmy Papers, British Library.

SCHÜTZE, GLADYS, MRS (1884–1946) née Raphael A novelist who wrote as "Henrietta Leslie", born into a wealthy Jewish family, married in 1902 to Louis Mendl, she was taken on a WOMEN'S SOCIAL AND POLITICAL UNION deputation, probably around 1908, by a relation, the mother of J.E. Raphael (an active member of the MEN'S LEAGUE FOR WOMEN'S SUFFRAGE). Gladys Mendl subsequently joined the WSPU but was not a militant campaigner. After a divorce and remarriage in 1913 to Dr Harry Schütze, an Australian bacteriologist sympathetic to the feminist movement, her house in Glebe Place became a safe haven for suffragettes released under the "Cat and Mouse" Act. In February 1914 Mrs PANKHURST, during one of her periods out of prison, was hidden, with her bodyguard, at Glebe House and then addressed a large crowd from the house balcony, an episode that "Henrietta Leslie" records in amusing detail in her autobiography *More Ha'pence Than Kicks*. In April 1913, after Lincoln's Inn House had been raided by the police, the WSPU Information Department was secreted in Glebe House. On one occasion Gladys Schütze was asked by the WSPU to act as a messenger, carrying documents rolled into her hair to Christabel PANKHURST in Paris, incidentally meeting Ethel SMYTH in Christabel's flat. By the time the police did actually raid the house, in June 1914, all incriminating material had been removed. In March 1914 Dr Schütze examined Mrs Pankhurst some days after her arrest at the St Andrew's Hall in Glasgow, and wrote, with Dr Flora Murray, a letter to *The Times* cataloguing the injuries she appeared to have sustained at the hands, or, it is suggested, the feet of the police. Gladys Schütze took part in the 21 May 1914 deputation to Buckingham Palace, during the course of which she received a blow on the head from a truncheon and a kick from a police horse, from which she never properly recovered. "Henrietta Leslie's" "suffragette" novel, *A Mouse with Wings*, 1920, draws on her personal involvement in the militant campaign.

After the outbreak of war Gladys Schütze, disillusioned with the Pankhursts' pro-war and anti-German stance, became a pacifist and treasurer of the SUFFRAGETTES OF THE WSPU. Zoe PROCTER was her secretary at this time. After the war "Henrietta Leslie", as well as continuing with her novel writing, became a journalist on the *Weekly Herald* and active in PEN.

Address: (1913) Glebe House, Glebe Place, Chelsea, London SW.
Photograph: in H. Leslie, *More Ha'pence Than Kicks*, c. 1944.
Bibliography: H. Leslie, *More Ha'pence Than Kicks*, c. 1944; Z. Procter, *Life and Yesterday*, 1960; C.B. Hale, *A Good Long Time*, 1973.

SCOTT FAMILY Arabella Charlotte Scott (1886–post 1946) (later Mrs Colville-Reeves), Unitarian, born in Dunoon, Argyllshire, the daughter of an officer in the Indian army. She took her degree at Edinburgh University and then taught in Leith. She was a member of the WOMEN'S FREEDOM LEAGUE in 1908 and in the summer, with her sister, helped Hannah MITCHELL when she came to East Fife to campaign on behalf of the WFL. Under the auspices of the WFL Arabella Scott delivered a petition to Downing Street on 23 July 1909. She was arrested, charged with obstruction, sentenced to three weeks' imprisonment in Holloway and went on hunger strike. During this period she was visited by Rev. HANKINSON. After her release she continued working as a speaker with the WFL until in 1913, by now describing herself in the *Suffrage Annual* as a "strong advocate of Militant methods". She was found guilty in Edinburgh on 19 May of attempting to set fire to the racecourse at Kelso and sentenced to nine months' imprisonment. She went on hunger strike and was released under the "Cat and Mouse" Act after five days. She was recaptured in June only to win her release, by hunger striking after a few days. She was recaptured in London in August, sent back to Calton gaol in Edinburgh, where she added a thirst strike to the hunger strike. After four days she was released, protesting that she would not leave under the "Cat and Mouse" Act, but wanted an unconditional release. This was not granted but she evaded recapture, working in the south of England under an assumed name (probably "Catherine Reid"), as a WSPU organizer until in May 1914 she was recaptured in Brighton, again returned to Edinburgh, imprisoned, repeated the hunger and thirst strike and was quickly released. She was re-arrested in London a month later and this time was sent to Perth prison, where she was forcibly fed between 20 June and 26 July. She later married and emigrated to Australia, where, in 1946, living in Sydney, she was an active member of the Australian branch of the SUFFRAGETTE FELLOWSHIP.

Muriel Eleanor Scott (1888–?), born in India, also took her degree at Edinburgh University and, with her sister, joined the WFL and was imprisoned in July 1909 and went on hunger strike in Holloway after taking a petition to Downing Street. She, like her sister, later sympathized with the WSPU and militancy. She does not herself appear to have committed acts of violence but when her sister was being forcibly fed in Perth prison she organized an emotional picket outside.

Address: (1913) 88 Marchmont Road, Edinburgh.
Bibliography: L. Leneman, *Martyrs in Out Midst: Dundee, Perth and the Forcible Feeding of Suffragettes*, 1993.

SCOTTISH CHURCHES LEAGUE FOR WOMAN SUFFRAGE

Founded in 1912, uniting members, both men and women, from all the Scottish churches, in order "to express the recognition by the churches of the spiritual equality of the sexes, and the justice of the principle of their political equality" (*Suffrage Annual and Women's Who's Who*, 1913). The League lobbied cabinet members and Scottish MPs, as well as holding devotional services at which addresses in support of women's enfranchisement were delivered. Its vice-presidents, besides members of the clergy, included S.E.S. MAIR and Louisa Lumsden. Elsie INGLIS, Chrystal MACMILLAN, Frances Simson and Frances Melville were included on the League's general council. The League participated in the NATIONAL UNION OF WOMEN'S SUFFRAGE SOCIETIES' victory celebration on 13 March 1918.

President (1913, 1917) Lady Frances BALFOUR; honorary secretary, Annie G. Ferrier, 11 Howe St., Edinburgh; honorary treasurer, Sterling Craig, Esq., 130 Princes Street, Edinburgh.
Bibliography: L. Leneman, "The Scottish Churches and 'Votes for Women'", in *Records of the Scottish Church History Society*, 1992.

SCOTTISH FEDERATION OF THE NATIONAL UNION OF WOMEN'S SUFFRAGE SOCIETIES

Formed in 1909 from an idea proposed by the GLASGOW AND WEST OF SCOTLAND ASSOCIATION FOR WOMEN'S SUFFRAGE. This federation predated the reorganization of the English societies under a similar scheme in 1910. The Scottish Federation was divided over the implementation of the NATIONAL UNION OF WOMEN'S SUFFRAGE SOCIETIES' Election Fighting Fund policy after 1912. The element represented by the Edinburgh society was for it, and the Glasgow element against. It was the Scottish Federation that in October 1914 decided to aid the war effort by organizing a Scottish Women's Hospital. By 1916 the Scottish Federation included 65 Scottish suffrage societies.

President (1910, 1915) S.E.S. MAIR; chairman (1910) Andrew Ballantyne; (1915) Chrystal MACMILLAN, 46 Cranley Gardens, London SW; honorary treasurer (1913) Mrs Hope, Sunwick, Berwickshire; (1915) Mrs Laurie, Red House, Greenock; secretary (1910–15) Dr Elsie INGLIS; honorary parliamentary secretary (1915) Miss Henderson, Broughty Ferry; honorary press secretary (1915) Miss A. Stuart Paterson, Glasgow; organizing secretary (1916) Alice Crompton.
Address: 2 St Andrew Square, Edinburgh.
Archival source: 5th annual report of the Scottish Federation, 1915, Fawcett Library.
Bibliography: L. Leneman, *A Guid Cause: The Women's Suffrage Movement in Scotland*, 1991.

SCOTTISH (SCATTERED) (WFL)
Secretary (1913) Miss Eunice MURRAY, Moore Park, Cardress, Dumbarton.

SCOTTISH UNIVERSITY WOMEN'S SUFFRAGE UNION

Founded in 1909, its object the extension of the parliamentary franchise to women on the same terms as to men. It was open to both men and women who held a university degree from any university, either at home or abroad, and also to women whose names were on the medical register. Undergraduates at the four Scottish universities could be affiliate members. In 1912 there were 307 members of the former and 23 of the latter class. There were branches of SUWSU at St Andrews, Glasgow, Aberdeen and Edinburgh. The society's main effort it described as one of propaganda in far-flung districts of Scotland. In 1910 and 1911 Frances PARKER undertook speaking tours for the SUWSU, in 1911 travelling by CARAVAN. The SUWSU participated in the victory celebrations organized by the NATIONAL UNION OF WOMEN'S SUFFRAGE SOCIETIES on 13 March 1918.

President (1913) Frances Simson, 31 George Square, Edinburgh; honorary secretary (1913) Chrystal MACMILLAN, Ladies' Caledonian Club, 39 Charlotte Square, Edinburgh, (1917) 46 Cranley Gardens, London SW; honorary treasurer (1913) Alice Smith, 9 Hermitage Place, Leith.

SCOTTISH WOMEN'S SOCIAL AND POLITICAL UNION Had a brief flowering, with Helen FRASER as its organizer, in the first half of 1908. Its headquarters were established in Glasgow and a branch was opened in Edinburgh in May 1908. The "Convenor of the Committee" was Mrs John Hunter, who was probably the Mrs Hunter who had subscribed to the WOMEN'S EMANCIPATION UNION in 1896 and with whom Elizabeth Wolstenholme ELMY, as she wrote to Harriet McILQUHAM on 16 September 1908, had "spent a delightful Sunday & Monday at Bridge of Allan". Mrs Elmy continued that she "had long talks with Lady Steele, Miss METHVEN and Miss Chrystal MACMILLAN, it is delightful to have come thus fully into touch with the younger workers in the North. Helen Fraser has begun the work". The past tense in her last sentence was apposite. By this time Helen Fraser had resigned from the WSPU and joined the NATIONAL UNION OF WOMEN'S SUFFRAGE SOCIETIES as its organizer in Scotland. The final report in *Votes for Women* that was accorded the full heading of the "Scottish Women's Social and Political Union" appeared in the issue of 9 July 1908. Clement's Inn may have seen the Scottish base as a potential rival; the Scottish WSPU intended to launch its own version of *Votes for Women* and, as Helen Fraser noted in her report on 21 May, was resolved on being a self-supporting union, appealing for funds that were to be directed to their work only. Although there were afterwards separate WSPU branches in Scotland, there was never any other attempt to establish an umbrella organization north of the border to rival that in London. The effusive thanks given, in the 27 August 1908 issue of *Votes for Women*, by Emmeline PETHICK-LAWRENCE to the member of the Glasgow branch who had had a leaflet printed and distributed in Glasgow, publicizing the (London) *Votes for Women* and giving details of which local bookstalls stocked it, and the very elaborate "Scottish" demonstration accorded Mary PHILLIPS on her release from Holloway in September 1908 could be interpreted as signs of the WSPU leadership's determination to pull control of Scotland firmly back into Clement's Inn.

SCURR FAMILY Julia Scurr (1873–1927) née O'Sullivan, born in Cardiff, probably married John Scurr in Woolwich in 1899. In June 1905, with Keir HARDIE, Dora MONTEFIORE and George LANSBURY, she was involved in arranging the march of 1000 destitute women from the East End to Prime Minister Balfour. By 1907, inspired, as she told Sylvia PANKHURST, by the suffragettes, she had become a member of the Poplar Board of Guardians. In 1913 Julia Scurr was a supporter of the National Political League and in June 1914 led a deputation of six East End women, who included Daisy PARSONS, to Asquith, the only such deputation he ever received. Later that year she joined the UNITED SUFFRAGISTS, becoming one of the society's vice-presidents and intent on putting on its behalf the working-woman's point of view. During the First World War she was a pacifist. She was a councillor in Poplar from 1919 until 1925 and, with her husband and fellow councillors, was imprisoned in 1921 as a result of the Poplar Rates Dispute.

John Scurr (1876–1932), born with the surname "Rennie" in Brisbane, Australia, was the son of a captain in the British merchant navy. After his mother's early death he was adopted by her brother John Scurr, and took his surname. Scurr grew up in Poplar, worked as a clerk and by 1897 was secretary of the Poplar Labour League. In 1902 he joined the Social Democratic Federation, as did his friend George Lansbury, and by 1910 was its secretary.

In 1910–11, during the dock strike, John Scurr was district chairman of the dockers' union and soon afterwards was employed by George Lansbury on the *Daily Herald*. From 1913 Scurr supplied dockers to act as bodyguards to protect WSPU and, later, United Suffragist, speakers in Hyde Park. In 1913 he was charged under a statute of Edward III, as had been, on another occasion, George Lansbury and Flora Drummond, with incitement to violence when making a speech in support of women's suffrage in Norwich. Like the others, he was never made to serve the sentence. In 1914 Scurr was a member of the committee of the United Suffragists and was a stalwart supporter of Sylvia Pankhurst in both her suffrage and welfare work and, like her, was a pacifist during the First World War. Scurr stood for parliament as a Labour candidate on several occasions both before and after the First World War and was eventually elected, in 1923, for Stepney Mile End, holding the seat until 1932.

Photograph: of Julia Scurr in R. Taylor, *In Letters of Gold*, 1993.

Bibliography: R. Taylor, *In Letters of Gold: The Story of Sylvia Pankhurst and the East End Federation of the Suffragettes of Bow*, 1993.

SEAFORD (NUWSS) In 1913 the society was a member of the SURREY, SUSSEX, AND HANTS FEDERATION OF THE NATIONAL UNION OF WOMEN'S SUFFRAGE SOCIETIES. Secretaries (1913) Miss Ottley, The Chalet, Seaford, Sussex and Miss Casson, Seaford, Sussex.

SEAFORTH (NUWSS) In 1913 the society was a member of the WEST LANCS, WEST CHESHIRE, AND NORTH WALES FEDERATION OF THE NATIONAL UNION OF WOMEN'S SUFFRAGE SOCIETIES. Secretary (1913) *pro tem* Miss Bell, Lyndhurst, Norma Road, Waterloo, Lancashire.

SELKIRK (NUWSS) In 1913 the society was a member of the SCOTTISH FEDERATION OF THE NATIONAL UNION OF WOMEN'S SUFFRAGE SOCIETIES. Secretary (1913) Miss Mary Sorrie, MA, c/o Miss Gray, Tower St., Selkirk, Selkirkshire.

SENNETT, [ALICE] MAUD MARY ARNCLIFFE, MRS (1862–1936) née Sparagnapane   Born in London, the daughter of an Italian immigrant wholesale confectioner who died in 1877; she was the elder sister of Florence DE FONBLANQUE. She became an actress, using the stage name "Mary Kingsley" and played throughout Britain and, for a year, in Australia. She became engaged to Henry Arncliffe Sennett while playing Helen in *The Lady of the Lake* in Edinburgh and they were subsequently married in London in 1898, with Gerald du Maurier as one of the witnesses. She and her husband, who had no children, ran her family's firm "G. Sparagnapane & Co, The Oldest Established Manufacturers of Christmas Crackers and Wedding Cake Ornaments", for some years living on its premises off Old Street, on the borders of Clerkenwell and the City. Maud Arncliffe Sennett became interested in the women's suffrage movement in January 1906 after reading in *The Times* a letter from Millicent Garrett FAWCETT advising the public not to denounce the new militancy. She joined the NATIONAL UNION OF WOMEN'S SUFFRAGE SOCIETIES and attended the banquet given at the Savoy by Mrs Fawcett on 11 December to celebrate the release of the WOMEN'S SOCIAL AND POLITICAL UNION prisoners. She described how each of those present was given an "emblematic picture representing Queen Boadicea driving in a chariot, waving a flag inscribed 'Votes for Women'" and noted in her autobiography that hers was signed by all the leaders except Emily Davies. As Emily Davies was not present at the banquet this was hardly surprising. However, Maud Arncliffe Sennett continues, "To make up the deficiency of the great name of this great little lady, I was persuaded by my husband to finish up the signatures with my own . . .". If this was not autobiographical licence it shows a desire, early in her involvement with the suffrage cause, to position herself at the centre of things. She was a member of the committee formed by the LONDON SOCIETY FOR WOMEN'S SUFFRAGE to organize the "Mud March" held in February 1907 and supplied, through her firm, 7000 red and white rosettes to be worn by the marchers. She herself carried the banner of South Hackney. For whatever reason, soon afterwards she drifted from the constitutionalists into the WSPU. She gave a donation towards "the housing of the provincial women" who arrived in London to attend the second Women's Parliament held in Caxton Hall on

20 March 1907. In May 1907 she gave £100 at the beginning of Emmeline Pethick-Lawrence's drive to raise funds for the WSPU. Her dramatic training made her a very successful speaker and she was much in demand. She notes that it was around this time that she sloughed off the Conservative politics with which she had been brought up. In June 1908 she resigned from the WSPU, feeling that her talents were being overlooked. The final straw came when it became clear that she was not to be included among those invited to speak at the "Women's Sunday" demonstration in Hyde Park. She returned to the NUWSS, in time to carry the banner depicting Queen Victoria in the Business section of its 13 June procession. She appears to have remained a member of the London Society for Women's Suffrage for some time; she certainly subscribed in 1910. There must, however, have been a hiatus in her membership because she tried to rejoin the London Society in September 1911 and was unable to sign a declaration that she would abjure from militant activity.

Immediately on leaving the WSPU, as well as rejoining the constitutionalists, Maud Arncliffe Sennett joined the committee of the Women's Freedom League. In her autobiography she writes that Teresa Billington-Greig was not popular, describing her as "A brilliant, but, I think, weak secretary [who] held the fort for the absent leader and kept grip of the machine herself. Mrs Despard, the popular reformer, did not organize; she was president and a sort of flaming torch that toured London and the country". She remained on the committee for two years but "wearying of the waste of time, talk and mock procedure, and of the lack of grip at the head (&, indeed, a strong woman must inevitably have ousted the irritable and absent one in the north) . . . loathing squabbles between the secretary and the treasurer [Sarah Benett], a tiresome and quarrelsome woman, I resigned and was now a free lance". She resigned from the WFL in July 1910 and joined the Actresses' Franchise League, quickly becoming a member of its committee. She describes how "there was more peace and harmony among these gracious women, and more generosity of mind and less jealousy than one had seen in the other groups". Maud Arncliffe Sennett was present during the "Black Friday" fracas in Parliament Square in November 1910 and reported that the policeman who arrested her was not sober. In 1910 she gave a donation to the Men's Political Union for Women's Enfranchisement. In November 1911 she took part, with members of nine suffage societies, in a deputation to Asquith and Lloyd George, representing actresses in, as she put it, "their dual capacity of wage earners and human beings". A few days later Maud Arncliffe Sennett was found guilty of using threatening behaviour after breaking a window in the office of the *Daily Mail*, angered that the paper had failed to report anything of the WSPU rally held a few days earlier in the Albert Hall, at which over £4000 had been raised. A charge of using threatening behaviour was substituted for that of window breaking when it was heard that she had warned that she would smash all windows within reach. At her trial Mrs Arncliffe Sennett declaimed:

Sir, I broke the windows of the *Daily Mail* as a protest against the corruption of the Press for withholding, with malice aforethought, the truth about the suffrage movement from the great British public. I am an employee of male labour, and the men who earn their living through the power of my poor brain, the men whose children I pay to educate, whose members of Parliament I pay for, and to whose old-age pensions I contribute – these are allowed a vote, while I am voteless.

She was sentenced to a fine or seven days' imprisonment; her fine was paid by Lord Northcliffe, the proprietor of the *Daily Mail,* and her stay in Holloway lasted only three hours. Typically, she retained the receipts for the hammer, dog whip and chair which she used to carry out her window-breaking and these she pasted into her scrapbook.

In December 1911 Maud Arncliffe Sennett was "Toast Mistress" at the John Hampden Dinner organized by the Tax Resistance League. In December 1912 she organized the reception into London of the "Women's March" which was the brainchild of her sister Florence de Fonblanque, and took the chair at the final meeting in Trafalgar Square. In April 1912 she had given £25 to the WSPU Legal Defence Fund, the receipt for which was stamped by the Hampstead branch. In January 1913 she accepted an invitation from this branch to join its committee. In June 1913 she gave £100 to the *Daily Herald* funds and in the same month, for an unspecified reason, resigned from the committee of the AFL. During the previous years her published pamphlets included *The State and the Woman*, 1910 and *Make Way for the Prime Minister!*, which was published by the *Gazette* office, Eastbourne, in 1912, and an article, "Why I Want The Vote", published in the *Vote*, 26 February 1910.

In her autobiography Maud Arncliffe Sennett describes how she attended Emily Wilding DAVISON's funeral in London on 14 June 1913 and then, on the spur of the moment, accompanied the coffin on the train north to Morpeth. Inspired by the spectacle and the emotion of the occasion and having met at Morpeth an Edinburgh businessman, Alexander Orr, who thought that other men would be keen to press for women's suffrage, Maud Arncliffe Sennett decided to organize another march on parliament from the north. She tried in vain to get support for this from leaders of the London-based societies. She remarks in her autobiography that when she had previously suggested to Christabel PANKHURST that they should enlist the help of men voters, she received the reply that it was best for women to win freedom by themselves. However, with the help of two members of the Edinburgh WFL, the sisters Jessie and Nannie Brown, she mustered enthusiastic support among businessmen and councillors in Edinburgh and Glasgow for a deputation to the prime minister. Nannie Brown had walked all the way from Edinburgh in the "Women's March" and her friendship with Maud Arncliffe Sennett lasted through the years until, after the latter's death, she was left a bequest in her will.

The NORTHERN MEN'S FEDERATION FOR WOMEN'S SUFFRAGE (non-party and constitutional) was founded in July 1913, with the purpose of organizing a deputation to London. Maud Arncliffe Sennett was described as "founder and honorary organizer of the Federation" and Alexander Orr (32 Fettes Row, Edinburgh) was honorary secretary of the deputation, which was timed to coincide with the arrival in London of the NUWSS Pilgrims (*see* PILGRIMAGE). Asquith made it clear, in three separate statements, that he would not receive the deputation, but the NMF went ahead with it anyway. The men assembled at the offices of the NATIONAL POLITICAL LEAGUE and proceeded to Downing Street where Asquith, true to his word, was absent from No. 10. The men had prepared in advance a pamphlet, *Scotchmen at Downing Street: Speeches of the Delegates, 18 July 1913*, in which are set out their speeches. They then attended a lunch given for them by Lady COWDRAY at Carlton Terrace and an evening reception hosted jointly by the MEN'S LEAGUE FOR WOMEN'S ENFRANCHISEMENT, the National Political League, and the Actresses' Franchise League. Maud Arncliffe Sennett drummed up support for the NMF from such seasoned suffrage workers as Ruth Cavendish-BENTINCK, Janie ALLAN and Lilian HICKS, who became the new society's London organizer. However, Maud Arncliffe Sennett was by now certain that militancy would not further the suffrage cause and there was some doubt as to whether or not Janie Allan could take up the Glasgow secretaryship of the NMF if she still supported militancy. After her experience with the WFL, Maud Arncliffe Sennett put little faith in committees and she herself appears to have controlled and carried out the NMF's policy. She applied herself to raising funds for her new campaign, although by this stage it had become difficult to squeeze money out of the usual benefactors and from reading the replies to her requests one cannot but think that she must have been rather disappointed by the response. She was, as always, herself prepared to give very generously for the cause in which she believed. At the end of 1913 she did offer to hand over the NMF to the Pethick-Lawrences, but they turned down as impracticable the idea of running a Scottish-based society from London. In 1914 she became one of the UNITED SUFFRAGISTS' vice-presidents and on 29 June was present with her husband at the Costume Dinner given by the Actresses' Franchise League and the WOMEN WRITERS' SUFFRAGE LEAGUE at the Hotel Cecil. Henry Arncliffe Sennett had in 1911 written a play, *An Englishwoman's Home*, that proved very popular when presented by members of the AFL. In 1914 Maud Arncliffe Sennett had her portrait, as "Mary Kingsley" playing Joan of Arc in *Henry VI*, painted by Gilbert Pownall. She is still on display, magnificent in full armour, in the gallery at the Swan Theatre, Stratford-on-Avon. It was doubtless not coincidence that Maud Arncliffe Sennett chose the suffrage movement's patron saint as the character in which she chose to be immortalized.

During the First World War Maud Arncliffe Sennett continued the suffrage campaign, through the NMF, the WFL, the United Suffragists and as a contributor to the *Suffragette News Sheet*, the paper published by the SUFFRAGETTES OF THE WSPU, to which she may have belonged. At Christmas 1914, in a characteristically flamboyant gesture, she had supported Sylvia PANKHURST and the EAST LONDON FEDERATION OF THE SUFFRAGETTES by giving a Christmas tree for a children's party in Bow. In mid-1916, after a suggestion had been made that the NMF should have an executive committee, Maud Arncliffe Sennett first agreed to this and then tendered her resignation as president. Needless to say this was not accepted by her "bairns" (as those Glaswegian councillors and baillies referred to themselves) and no executive committee materialized. At the end of that year she wrote her "Manifesto on Venereal Disease", subtitled "Women's Suffrage and Parliamentary Morals", and for the rest of the duration of the war campaigned vigorously against the Contagious Diseases Acts contained in 40D DORA.

The NMF was not included among the suffrage societies working in a joint committee with the government to negotiate the final granting of the limited franchise to women in 1918. Maud Arncliffe Sennett was herself invited to the celebratory dinner held on 28 January 1918 at the Lyceum and chaired by Dora MONTEFIORE, but the NMF was not included among the organizations invited to the NUWSS's Queen's Hall celebrations on 13 March. Instead, in the same month, the NMF held its own commemoration dinner in Edinburgh and presented Maud Arncliffe Sennett with a silver rose bowl in recognition of her part in the suffrage campaign. The society, at her instigation, now changed its name to the Northern Men's Federation for Women's Suffrage and Land Reform and she drafted a "Land Charter". Difficulties of keeping a non-party stance arose, the membership faded away and in September 1919 the NMF's remaining funds were passed to the WFL. There was a suggestion that Maud Arncliffe Sennett should stand for parliament at the first general election after being granted the vote, but her husband apparently objected and she was never a candidate. Maud Arncliffe Sennett guaranteed the *Suffragette News Sheet* 10/– a month for six months, to be raised to £1 if five others could be found to give the same amount, in May–June 1918 subscribed to its "Emily Davison Memorial" number and around this time gave a talk to the Emily Davison Club (*see under* CLUBS) on how it was Emily Davison's death that had inspired the founding of the NMF. She remained in touch in the following years with Ruth Cavendish-Bentinck, and Nannie Brown, but does not appear to have had much more involvement in the continuing feminist campaigns. In the 1930s she discovered a new cause and was the founder and director of the Midhurst-Haselmere Anti-Vivisection Society. After she died, having been ill for some time with tuberculosis, her husband before remarrying the next year, organized the publication of her autobiography *The Child*, and gave to the British Museum her scrapbooks, which construct the suffrage campaign as she experienced it. Neither the autobiography nor her papers fail to conceal the notice Maud Arncliffe Sennett took of the slights and wounds she felt she sustained during her suffrage campaigns. In *The Child* she wrote, "No one but those in the reform movement can realize the sort of wound one can get from one's 'helpers', who are, maybe either jealous or ambitiously disloyal".

Address: (1906) 43 Mitchell Street, Ironmonger Row, London EC; (1911) 6 Wellington Road, St John's Wood, London NW; (1918) 42 Belsize Park Gardens, London NW3; (1936) Eversheds, Midhurst, Sussex.

Portrait: by Gilbert Pownall, as "Mary Kingsley" playing Joan of Arc, 1914, in the Swan Theatre gallery, Stratford-on-Avon, reproduced in L. Leneman, *A Guid Cause: The Women's Suffrage Movement in Scotland*, 1991; print of portrait drawing by Stewart Carmichael, 1914, in John Johnson Collection, Bodleian Library, Oxford.

Photograph: by Lena Connell in Arncliffe Sennett Papers, British Library; in the *Vote*, 26 February 1910.

Archival source: Maud Arncliffe Sennett Papers, British Library.

Bibliography: M. Arncliffe Sennett, *The Child*, no date (1938); L. Leneman, *A Guid Cause: The Women's Suffrage Movement in Scotland*, 1991; C. Eustance, "Citizens, Scotsmen, 'bairns': manly politics and women's suffrage in the Northern Men's Federation, 1913–20", in A.V. John and C. Eustance (eds), *The Men's Share?*, 1997.

SERUYA, SIME (*c.* 1876–1955) Born in Lisbon, Portugal, an actress. She joined the WOMEN'S SOCIAL and Political Union soon after its arrival in London. She appears to have been a woman of independent means; she gave £100 to the WSPU in the first half of 1907. In February 1907 she was sentenced to 14 days' imprisonment having taken part, on 13 February, in the deputation from the first Women's Parliament from Caxton Hall to the House of Commons. Later in 1907 she sided with the faction that founded the Women's Freedom League, becoming an honorary organizer. In February 1909 she was again arrested, after taking part in a deputation to Downing Street. She was imprisoned in Holloway where, in March, she was visited by Rev. Hankinson, having claimed him as her minister of religion. She was imprisoned once again before 1913. In 1910 she was honorary organizer of the WFL contingent in the 18 June women's suffrage procession.

In the autumn of 1908 Sime Seruya was the founder, with Winifred Mayo, of the Actresses' Franchise League. In 1909 she was a member of the first committee of the Tax Resistance League, from which she resigned in November 1911. In 1910 she opened the International Suffrage Shop (see shops) in a room in Bedford Street, off the Strand, lent to her by Edith Craig, with whom she worked closely in both the WFL and the AFL, and as an ordinary member of the Pioneer Players, 1911–14 and a member of its advisory committee, 1911–12. In 1910 Sime Seruya, who was a member of the ILP, attended the International Socialist Congress in Copenhagen. In *The Suffragette Movement*, Sylvia Pankhurst describes how on the return journey Sime Seruya, whom she terms a "Socialist-Suffragette", offered Keir Hardie £1000 towards the cost of setting up a Socialist daily paper. The scheme did not progress. Although apparently unmarried, at some point in her later life she had a son, to whom her entire estate was left.

Address: (1907) 13 Pembridge Crescent, London W; (1955) 1 The Gables, Vale of Health, Hampstead, London NW3.

SEVENOAKS (NUWSS) In 1913 the society was a member of the Kentish Federation of the National Union of Women's Suffrage Societies. Secretary (1909) Miss Crosbie Hill, 2 South Park, Sevenoaks, Kent; (1913) Miss Portlock, 70 High Street, Sevenoaks, Kent.

SEYMOUR, ISABEL MARION (1882–?) A friend of the Pethick-Lawrences, she joined the Women's Social and Political Union office in September 1906. Until the summer of 1909 she acted as hospitality secretary, organizing billets for country members when they came to London to take part in deputations. She appears to have been a fluent German speaker because she went to Berlin in 1909 to talk at a meeting of the Berlin branch of the Prussian National Association for Women's Suffrage about the militant tactics adopted by the WSPU. She undertook a similar speaking tour in Austria and Russia in February 1910. In January 1913 she was still working at Clement's Inn, now organizing bail for arrested WSPU members. Before 1930 Isabel Seymour spent eight years in Canada, returning to England after the death of the friend with whom she lived, and was elected to the Hampshire County Council. Emmeline Pethick-Lawrence remained a friend all her life, leaving Isabel Seymour a bequest in her will. Antonia Raeburn interviewed Isabel Seymour when writing *The Militant Suffragettes*, 1973, and includes lively reminiscences of life at Clement's Inn.

Address: (1930) 5 Clifton Terrace, Winchester, Hampshire; (1950) Woodstock Cottage, Wallingford, Berkshire.

Bibliography: A. Raeburn, *The Militant Suffragettes*, 1973.

SHANKLIN (NUWSS) In 1913 the society was a member of the Surrey, Sussex, and Hants Federation of the National Union of Women's Suffrage Societies. Secretary (1913) Miss E. De B. Griffith, Snowden, Shanklin, Isle of Wight.

SHARP, EVELYN JANE (1869–1955) (later Mrs Nevinson) Daughter of James Sharp, a London slate merchant and Jane Boyd, whose father had been a lead merchant. She had three sisters and seven brothers, of whom Cecil Sharp, the leader of the folk-dance revival, was the eldest. She was educated at home and then at Strathallan House in Kensington, leaving school when she was barely 16. She remained at home for the next six years, studying for university local examinations and writing short stories, until in 1894, with her family's disapproval although with no actual opposition, she left home in order to live on her own in London. She undertook daily tutoring while continuing with her writing. Her work was accepted by the *Pall*

Mall Gazette and attracted the attention of Henry Harland, editor of The Yellow Book, to which she became a contributor. In 1935 she annotated the letter, dated 10 November 1894, from John Lane of the Bodley Head accepting her novel, The Relton Arms, as "The most 'thrilling' letter of my life". By 1897 her teaching occupied her for two full days and until 2 pm three days a week. She also wrote for the girls' magazine Atalanta and was a member of the Women Writers' Society. She was particularly friendly with Netta Syrett, Percy and Mabel Dearmer, Alice Meynell and Laurence Housman, whom she described in an 1897 letter as "a strange, weird person". Her novel The Making of a Prig, published by John Lane in 1897, achieved a measure of success. It was obviously based on her personal experience. The young heroine finds work in London as a teacher, impressing the principal of her school with a lecture on "Gothic Architecture'; Evelyn Sharp's remaining papers include notes for lectures on Gothic Architecture in England, with a note that they were rewritten in October 1897. Another, not entirely sympathetic, character in the novel is a middle-aged "most active of political women", who "spoke upon platforms; . . . harried the rate-payers until they elected her favourite county councillor; . . . canvassed in the slums for the candidate who would vote for women's suffrage". After a time spent sorting out family affairs after her father's death in 1903, Evelyn Sharp dropped teaching and devoted herself to full-time writing, expanding into journalism to buy time to write childrens' novels and fairy tales. She was introduced by H.W. Nevinson to the Manchester Guardian, to which she became a contributor for more than 30 years, being on particularly friendly terms with its editor, C.P. Scott.

Evelyn Sharp joined the Women's Social and Political Union in 1906, inspired by hearing, in the course of her journalistic duties, Elizabeth Robins deliver her first suffrage speech. They became life-long friends. Evelyn Sharp joined the Kensington branch of the WSPU and became an active speaker and writer in support of women's suffrage. The impression she made as a speaker can be gauged from a letter she received from an unconverted male member of the audience after she had spoken in Paisley in April 1909:

Your face was of the Italian madonna type and your voice was exceedingly pleasant... You spoke as if you spoke from the heart, with a kind of steady girlish earnestness that was very impressive... You represented yourself as a simple, earnest, meek little lamb who was cruelly illused by men whose nervousness made them lose their heads and their manners, merely because you asked a civil and legitimate question, but all the time one could have sworn that you were a demure little imp of mischief who made the teasing of poor old cabinet ministers a fine art, and hugely enjoyed the row you raised...

Evelyn Sharp's sister Bertha was secretary for the Kensington contingent at the 21 June 1908 WSPU procession. In September Evelyn was one of the "horses" pulling Vera Wentworth, Elsie Howey and Maud Joachim from Holloway to the breakfast held to celebrate their release from prison. In 1909 she was sent by the WSPU to Denmark to lecture there on the militant suffrage movement. In January 1910 she was WSPU organizer for Kensington (North) in the general election campaign and with Louise Eates organized the East Procession for the 23 July 1910 WSPU demonstration. In January 1911 Evelyn Sharp succeeded Mrs Eates as the honorary secretary of the Kensington branch of the WSPU. In 1910 A.C. Fifield published Evelyn Sharp's Rebel Women, a series of vignettes of suffragette life. In these she demonstrates a good eye for the idiosyncracies to which living for the cause introduced her, such as selling Votes for Women in the street and running the Kensington WSPU shop. The book was reissued, with a new introduction by Elizabeth Robins, in late 1915. Among Evelyn Sharp's papers is a scrapbook of newspaper cuttings, which she described as "The book of the Woman, being historical, statistical, economic, entertaining, amazing and stuffy. Compiled in moments of frenzied enthusiasm (snatched from a life of underpaid toil)." Hitherto Evelyn Sharp's affection for her mother, who was appalled to think of her daughter being imprisoned, had prevented her from volunteering to join any of the WSPU deputations, but at the end of 1910 her mother absolved her from her promise. A letter from Constance Lytton to Evelyn Sharp dated 27 January 1911 intimates that she was to join the next deputation, but she certainly was not arrested until 11 November 1911 when she took part in the protest against the "torpedoing" of the Conciliation Bill. She was sentenced to 14 days in Holloway for breaking windows at the War Office. While she was in prison Nevinson wrote to her, saying "No one can say how we all miss you. Day and night we long for Saturday to come. Be sure we shall be at the gates to receive you. I am in touch with Dr Garrett Anderson every day, and she will come to take you straight away to her home to breakfast". He revealed that, in her absence, he had reviewed some girls' books for the *Nation*: "Heaven help us all!"

In March 1912 Evelyn Sharp undertook to edit *Votes for Women*, when the Pethick-Lawrences were arrested on the charge of conspiracy. In November she contributed to George LANSBURY's expenses when he stood as a suffrage candidate. In July 1913 she was again arrested, with Lady Sybil Smith and Emmeline PETHICK-LAWRENCE, after taking part, as a delegate from the WOMEN WRITERS' SUFFRAGE LEAGUE, in a protest at the Caxton Hall against the "Cat and Mouse" Act. She was sentenced to 14 days' imprisonment but, after going on hunger strike, the sentence was reduced to four days and, with her companions, she was released unconditionally. She attributed this strategy by the authorities to the fact that she was arrested with a lady of title. While she was in prison Louisa Garrett ANDERSON was driven by Vera HOLME in Evelina HAVERFIELD's car to the Sharp family home at Hammersmith in order to reassure Evelyn Sharp's mother of her well-being. By 28 July Evelyn Sharp was recuperating at Hertha AYRTON's house. In 1913 H.W. Nevinson wrote of Evelyn Sharp to Sidney Webb, "She has one of the most beautiful minds I know – always going full gallop, as you see from her eyes, but very often in regions beyond the moon, when it takes a few seconds to return. At times she is the very best speaker among the suffragettes, and Holloway knows her, for savage rage tears her heart. Now she edits and writes *Votes for Women* with Pethick-Lawrence, having given up all the 'arts' she loved, to fight for the Cause." Evelyn Sharp was assistant editor of *Votes for Women*, remaining loyal to the Pethick-Lawrences after the split with the Pankhursts. She does not, however, appear to have resigned from her position in the Kensington branch of the WSPU until August 1913. She was a founder of the UNITED SUFFRAGISTS in 1914 and became sole editor of *Votes for Women*. On 29 June 1914 it was in the character of Elizabeth Barrett Browning that she attended the WWSL costume dinner at the Hotel Cecil. During the First World War Evelyn Sharp continued working for the cause of suffrage and, a pacifist, supported the movement towards the founding of the Women's International League for Peace and Freedom. In 1916 she was a member of the executive committee of the newly formed NATIONAL COUNCIL FOR ADULT SUFFRAGE. Although not a member of the committee of the TAX RESISTANCE LEAGUE, Evelyn Sharp determinedly refused to pay tax and in 1917 was forced into bankruptcy, her furniture taken away, her correspondence intercepted and her earnings seized. The members of the United Suffragists compiled a book of signatures, decorated in the society's colours of purple, white and orange, and presented it to Evelyn Sharp "– from her comrades in the Long Fight" on 16 March 1918.

Evelyn Sharp wrote for the *Herald* in 1915 and between 1918 and 1923 was on the paper's staff. She had long been a friend of Barbara Ayrton GOULD, whose husband was the *Herald*'s proprietor. After Hertha Ayrton's death, Barbara Gould asked Evelyn Sharp to write Hertha's biography. Evelyn Sharp was also very friendly with Gertrude Baillie-WEAVER, writing in her commonplace book after she had seen her for the last time, shortly before Gertrude's death, "She was so pleased when I told her what she had been to me and how she had helped me." Evelyn Sharp wrote articles about Emmeline PANKHURST in the *New Leader* (which was edited by H.N. BRAILSFORD), June 1928, and in *The Nineteenth Century*, 1930. However, after the partial enfranchisement of women was achieved in 1918 she was ready to move on to new causes, working for a short time with the Relief Committee of the Society of Friends in Berlin, and then at home using the tool of journalism to draw attention to social problems. In 1933, six months after his wife's death, she married her long-time friend, Henry Nevinson.

Address: (1894) Brabazon Hostel, Store Street, London WC; (1897?) New Victorian Club, Sackville Street London

W (*see* CLUBS); (1896) Manor House, Wooton Turville, Tring, Herts and 19 Parkside, Albert Gate, London SW; (1897) 14 Marjorie Mansions, Fulham Road, London SW; (1901, 1914) 15 Mount Carmel Chambers, Duke's Lane, Kensington, London W; (1914) 38 Doughty Street, Mecklenburgh Square, London WC; (1915) 16 John Street, Bedford Row, London WC1; (1927) 24 John Street, Bedford Row, London WC1; (1932) 104 Guilford Street, London WC1; (1933) 4 Downside Crescent, London NW3; (1940) Campden, Gloucestershire; (1942) 23 Young Street, London W8.

Photograph: in E. Sharp, *Unfinished Adventure*, 1933.

Archival source: Papers of Evelyn Sharp, Bodleian Library, Oxford; Papers of H. W. Nevinson, Bodleian Library, Oxford.

Bibliography: E. Sharp, *Unfinished Adventure*, 1933.

SHEFFIELD (WFL) Founded in December 1908. Secretary (1913) Miss Macdonald, 21 Harcourt Road, Sheffield.

SHEFFIELD Women's Suffrage Society Founded in 1882 as a branch of the MANCHESTER NATIONAL SOCIETY FOR WOMEN'S SUFFRAGE, soon after the Grand Demonstration of Women was held in the city. The secretary and treasurer was Mrs Templeton. The society appears to have been refounded in 1903 when its secretary was Miss Peacock, 282 Attercliffe Common, Sheffield. Christabel PANKHURST addressed the society in November 1903. In 1913 the society was a member of the WEST RIDING FEDERATION OF THE NATIONAL UNION OF WOMEN'S SUFFRAGE SOCIETIES. Secretary (1909) Mrs Earp, 37 Cliffe Field Road, Meersbrook, Sheffield; (1913) Mrs Gill, 19 Southgrove Road, Sheffield.

SHEFFIELD (WSPU) Secretary (1906) Mrs Whitworth, 70 Wath Road, Sheffield. Organizer (1910) Miss Adela PANKHURST, 45 Marlborough Road, Sheffield. Secretary (1913) Miss Schuster, 26–28 Chapel Walk, Sheffield.

SHEFFIELD FEMALE POLITICAL ASSOCIATION Initiated in 1851 by Anne KNIGHT, who wrote to Mrs Rooke of Sheffield, a member of the National Charter Association. Anne Knight had been given Mrs Rooke's name by Isaac Ironside, the Sheffield Chartist leader. In this letter, which is now in the collection of York City Library, Anne Knight urged the ladies of Sheffield to band together to demand their political rights. A first meeting was held on

Taken on the occasion of the "Grand Demonstration" held in Sheffield in 1882, (*left to right, seated*) Alice Cliff Scatcherd and Mrs McCormick; (standing) Miss Carbutt, Mrs David Vero, Mrs Ellis and Helena Downing (Mrs Shearer). Taken from the Fawcett Library and reproduced by kind permission of the Mary Evans picture library.

26 February 1851 at the Democratic Temperance Hotel, 33 Queen Street, Sheffield, and unanimously adopted an "Address to the Women of England", which constitutes the first manifesto dealing with the suffrage ever formulated by a meeting of women in England. That year Anne Knight helped to form the Sheffield Female Political Association, based at 84 Pond Street, Sheffield. The Council of the Association comprised Mrs S. Turner, Mrs S. Bartholomew, Mrs E. Stephenson, Mrs M. Whalley, Mrs E. Rooke and Mrs E. Wade. Mrs C. Ash was president *pro tem*, Mrs E. Cavill was treasurer, Mrs M. Brook was financial secretary and Mrs Abiah Higginbottom was corresponding secretary. A peti-

tion signed by Mrs Higginbottom was sent to the House of Lords, where it was presented by the 7th Lord Carlisle. The SFPA received support from all over England and from France. Anne Knight visited Sheffield and addressed the SFPA in November 1851. In February 1852 it was agreed to establish a national Women's Rights Association. At the year ending 25 February 1853 Anne Knight was its president, the vice-president was Mrs Carr, the treasurer was Mrs Turner, the financial secretary was Mrs Brook and the corresponding secretary was Mrs Higginbottom. However, after 1853 there are no more reports of the SFPA in the local papers. Presumably its collapse was associated with that of the Chartist movement.

Bibliography: C. Rover, *Women's Suffrage and Party Politics 1866–1914*, 1967 (which contains the text of the 1851 "Address"); J.H. Copley, *The Women's Suffrage Movement in South Yorkshire*, 1968 (thesis), Local Studies Department, Sheffield City Library.

SHERBORNE (NUWSS) Founded at a meeting in May 1909 at which the speakers included Lady Frances BALFOUR. Secretary (1909, 1910) Hon. Mrs Evelina HAVERFIELD, Stock Gaylard, Sturminster Newton, Dorset. It was apparently no longer in existence by 1913, Evelina Haverfield having by then firmly sided with the WOMEN'S SOCIAL AND POLITICAL UNION.

SHETLAND (NUWSS) In July 1910 Miss Lamond (see Elizabeth ABBOTT), organizer for the SCOTTISH FEDERATION OF THE NATIONAL UNION OF WOMEN'S SUFFRAGE SOCIETIES visited Shetland in order to address the society, which was a member of the Federation. Secretary (1913) Miss Christina JAMIESON, Twagios, Lerwick, Shetland.

SHILDON AND DISTRICT (NUWSS) In 1913 the society was a member of the NORTH-EASTERN FEDERATION OF THE NATIONAL UNION OF WOMEN'S SUFFRAGE SOCIETIES. Secretary (1913) Miss Alice Robson, Sunnydale, Shildon, Co. Durham.

SHIPLEY (NUWSS) In 1913 the society was a member of the WEST RIDING FEDERATION OF THE NATIONAL UNION OF WOMEN'S SUFFRAGE SOCIETIES. Secretary (1913) Miss I.M. Miller, Inglewood, Stavely Road, Shipley, Yorkshire.

SHOPS, OFFICES AND BAZAARS In May 1845 many of the women who subsequently were active in the nineteenth-century women's suffrage campaign took part in the Anti-Corn Law League bazaar, held in the Covent Garden theatre, of which *The Times* wrote that, as well as looking gorgeous (based on a Norman cathedral) it was

> a manifestation of moral power, ... without parallel in the world's history. There were aggregated there ladies who, for 17 days, had devoted their time, their toil, and we fear their health, with unwonted assiduity to advance the great cause of humanity and justice. They were not conscious of the capabilities they possessed until they found them developed in action by the force of circumstances ... collected together from all parts of the British islands, those who had never seen or heard of each other in their lives found themselves encircled by friends, though surrounded by strangers, community of feeling being the basis for community of affection ... women went about fearless of insult, and children without danger of injury. It was a striking evidence of the moral feeling which the discussions and instructions of the League had infused into the public mind. (quoted in J.B. Mackie, *Life of Duncan McLaren*, 1888)

It may be difficult for us now to recognize the unparalleled moral power of a bazaar but on a practical level the occasion did bring together, as the newspaper report suggests, like-minded women, working for a common purpose, and was a precursor of all the bring-and-buy sales, reports of which sit beside those of processions, window breaking and arson in the twentieth-century suffrage journals. However, once the women's suffrage campaign was underway it is clear that not all women thought a bazaar a worthwhile endeavour. In 1871 a heralded "Bazaar and Exhibition in Aid of the Funds of the Manchester National Society for Women's Suffrage" was rendered unnecessary because, as the *Women's Suffrage Journal* reported, friends of the movement, one of whom was Lilias Ashworth HALLETT, "desirous to relieve the committee from the labour and responsibility of the undertaking, and of setting free their energies for more direct work, have generously come forward to guarantee the amount of £500 which the committee hoped to raise by the bazaar". These "friends", at least, were not convinced of the moral power of fancy goods; nor of the necessity to unite women for a purpose merely secondary to the true cause. However, after over 30 years of campaigning, the women's suffrage movement in the twentieth-century rediscovered the joy of the bazaar, the WOMEN'S SOCIAL AND POLITICAL UNION putting immense efforts into its Women's Exhibition held at the Prince's Skating Rink in May 1909, the Scottish Exhibition a year later, the 1911 Christmas Fair at the Portman Rooms and the Summer Fair in June 1913; the WOMEN'S FREEDOM LEAGUE holding its Green and Gold Fayres; and the NATIONAL UNION OF WOMEN'S SUFFRAGE SOCIETIES its Oriental Bazaar and Women's Kingdom Exhibition.

The WSPU's June 1908 Hyde Park demonstration introduced "the colours" to the country and launched a merchandizing offensive. POSTCARDS, GAMES, JEWELLERY, badges, bags and belts quickly followed and it was natural that shops should be opened to channel these goods, together with the movement's proselytizing books and pamphlets, to the public. The KENSINGTON branch of the WSPU, always innovative, was the first to open a shop, at 143 Church Street, Notting Hill Gate, in January 1909. Rachel Ferguson, herself a member of the PURPLE, WHITE, AND GREEN CLUB, described the shop as "tiny, wedge-shaped, you sidled round purple, white and green posters of Mr Two-Faced Asquith, brassards, badges, buttons, scarves, pamphlets (called 'literature'), hatpins made of stained fish-bones, portraits of the leaders of the W.S.P.U., and the current number of *Votes for Women*". A year later the WSPU had several other shops in London, at Croydon, Lewisham, Hammersmith, Kilburn and in the Fulham Road. *Votes for Women,* 10 July 1909, carried a very full description of the latter:

> The shop has been rented from a photographer, and consists of a window and office on the first floor, with a bow window and balcony useful for displays of flags, posters, etc, a kitchen with the necessary fittings, and three rooms above, which are being fitted up as club-room, dressing-room etc. Two ladies are chief shopkeepers, and about 20 of their members take their turn. A timetable of shop assistants has been drawn up. The stock is checked every morning, and the sales are entered in the sales book. The treasurer attends once a week to receive subscriptions, send out receipts, etc, and the Literature Secretary at the same time orders in new stock, and generally overlooks the literature. The rent, £1 per week (inclusive) is partly raised by weekly subscriptions from 3d to 1s from members, and occasional social evenings are held to add to the funds. . . . A lending library is part of the scheme, books relating to woman suffrage, and presented by members, being lent at 1d per week. . . . The shop is a rallying ground for members and a centre for communication, thus effecting a considerable saving of postage. It is also a centre from which speakers and workers go out to open-air meetings . . . and it is, in addition, a storage place for banners, temporary platforms, etc.

In the course of the next year many similar shops and offices opened around the country. *Votes for Women,* 6 October 1911, carries an account of the shops at Scarborough, Clacton and Bath. Mary BLATHWAYT's diary gives an idea of the *longueurs* (dusting, doing accounts, counting "literature") and petty annoyances involved in any kind of shopkeeping, even suffrage, but also describes how the Bristol shop was a meeting place for the local activists, fresh from chalking pavements or speaking on the Downs. In addition to these semi-permanent premises, shops were often taken for a mere couple of weeks at a time from which to conduct by-election or holiday campaigns.

As the militant campaign intensified, the WSPU shops were an obvious target for retaliation. The Bristol shop in Queen's Road, where Mary Blathwayt had been such a diligent shopkeeper, was attacked in October 1913 by students from the university. Photographs of the destruction were issued as postcards, on one of which the writer has described how "They painted the sign 'Votes for Women' over with red paint and left 'Varsity' on the blind or what was left of it. . . . The students burnt the fittings and furniture." Newcastle WSPU had a shop in Shield Road and in 1909 showed magic lantern slides of the WSPU campaign onto a sheet in the window, causing such interest from passers by that the police had to be called to clear the pavement. By February 1910 the shop and office had moved to larger premises at 77 Blackett

The International Suffrage Shop, 15 Adam Street, Strand, London. The left-hand window is broken, in what was described at the time as "a case of 'Tit for Tat'", the day after a WSPU window-smashing campaign, probably during March 1912. (Author's collection)

Street, where its windows were broken on at least three occasions and the shop ransacked after suffragette arson attacks in Newcastle. The main WSPU London shop opened at 156 Charing Cross Road in May 1910 (see *Votes for Women*, 13 May, for a very full description of the shop and the offices of the Woman's Press). The premises were leased from Alice and Edith Harvey of Morden Villa, Seven Sisters Road, Finsbury Park; Frederick PETHICK-LAWRENCE took over the remainder of the lease from George Allen (see under PUBLISHERS AND PRINTERS) for a rent of £250 per annum. The shop remained at these premises until, after the break with the Pethick-Lawrences, Mrs PANKHURST moved it into Lincoln's Inn House in September 1912. By no means all the branches had designated shops. Birmingham became the centre for the Midlands region of the WSPU in September 1908; Gladice KEEVIL was organizer and quickly rented an office at 14 Ethel Street. Work expanded and larger premises were taken in 1909 at 33 Paradise Street. In September 1910 the office moved again, to 97 John Bright Street, to larger rooms at double their previous rent. Although WSPU merchandise was doubtless sold there, the premises are always referred to as an office rather than a shop. In 1914 as a retaliation for damage done by WSPU members to the Cathedral the windows of the WSPU office were broken.

The WOMEN'S FREEDOM LEAGUE was as keen as the WSPU on merchandizing. Its Glasgow WFL shop, at 302 Sauchiehall Street, opened on 1 December 1909. The *Vote*, 9 December, carried a description of its ground-floor shop, hall and kitchen, and offices: "The centre is decorated throughout in colours of the League, white predominating." The "artistic" hall served as tea-room, meeting-place and showroom for women artists' work. On another occasion mention was made of "an Artistic Goods Department, where scarfs, ties, sashes, belts, blouses, buckles, hat-pins, pendants etc in the colours of the League" were on sale.

When the NATIONAL SOCIETY FOR WOMEN'S SUFFRAGE was founded it was only the MANCHESTER SOCIETY, under Lydia BECKER, that opened a designated office; Birmingham, Edinburgh and London continued to operate from the "private sphere", the homes of their honorary secretaries. What was perceived as the vacuum at the heart of the "public sphere" was filled in 1871 by the CENTRAL COMMITTEE OF THE NATIONAL SOCIETY, which, after a brief period of operating from the Hyde Park Gate home of Mr and Mrs PENNINGTON, opened a London office at 9 Berners Street, the premises of the Berners Club (see under CLUBS). Until 1885 the Central Committee continued to be located around Oxford Street, a "feminine" area close to shops, dressmakers, photographers, women's clubs and, indeed, the homes of many of the society's members, an area that had been associated for 25 years with the women's movement. In 1885 the Central Committee boldly moved into the male preserve of Westminster, closer to the parliamentary goal. After the split in the society in 1888, both the resulting societies and their eventual successor, the NUWSS, remained in Westminster. The NUWSS did not open a London shop; dignified Westminster was hardly a suitable district for such a venture.

The BRISTOL AND WEST OF ENGLAND branch of the National Society for Women's Suffrage had opened its first office in 1873, but it was only in 1909 that it added a shop to its current premises. This shop was clearly a success because in early 1912 it was the Bristol Society that was requested by the CAMBRIDGE WOMEN'S SUFFRAGE ASSOCIATION to give full details of how they ran their shop. The reply revealed that the Bristol Society paid rent of £42 for premises comprising a shop, office, kitchen and smaller offices. The premises were kept open from 11.30 am to 6.30 pm, except for a dinner-hour (1 pm to 2.30 pm) and were closed on Saturday afternoons. The paid secretary of the Bristol Society kept the shop, and lived next door to it. An office boy, who also delivered all notices, was employed. Weekly debates and lectures were held on the premises, to which admission was fixed at 6d, and the premises were let to other bodies for meetings. The Cambridge Women's Suffrage Association had rented its first permanent committee room and shop, providing "literature" and information, in Benet Street in early 1911; presumably it was because they thought that this service could be improved that they were seeking advice.

It was only in 1912–13 that most NUWSS societies placed themselves firmly in the high street. In March 1913 the BEDFORD SOCIETY rented as an office two rooms over a shop at 39 St Peter's for three months at £8 per annum. The society arranged for a sign, indicating its presence, to be fixed at the entrance on street level. However, emboldened, it then in August opened a shop at 83 Harpur Street and painted "Women's Suffrage Society" on the outside of the shop, although to be on the safe side it was suggested that "Non Militant" and "Non Party" should be added. The first-floor front room was to be used as a club room, where books, papers and leaflets would be available, for members paying an annual subscription of 2/6. The shop was open from 11 am to 1.30 pm and 3 pm to 6.30 pm daily. The secretary of the local Church League for Women's Suffrage was allowed to use the rooms during the lunchtime closure. The society continued running the shop until the winter of 1914.

The BIRMINGHAM WOMEN'S SUFFRAGE SOCIETY had an office as early as 1877, at 10 Broad Street Corner. However, when the NUWSS society, although it had a continuous existence, reopened an office c. 1908 at 10 Easy Row, it was noted in the society's minutes that it had not had an office for some years. The new office, open 10 am–1 pm, 2 pm–5 pm; Saturdays 10 am–1 pm, was comfortably furnished with gifts of curtains, china, vases, pictures, fire-irons, door mat, hearthrug, tea infusers, teapots, a rolltop desk and a typewriter. Small meetings were held there and all the suffrage papers were taken. In 1909 the office regularly subscribed to 100 copies of the *Common Cause* (60 for free distribution) and four copies of the *Englishwoman*.

The GLASGOW AND WEST OF SCOTLAND ASSOCIATION FOR WOMEN'S SUFFRAGE opened a new office at 58 Renfield Street in April 1909, which was to be open on a Tuesday and Thursday between 12 noon and 2 pm and on Saturday from 4 pm to 6 pm. The

Committee agreed that meetings should be held each Saturday from 4 to 6 pm for the purpose of discussion and practice in speaking. By early 1911 it was felt necessary to move to a more convenient office and a room at 202 Hope Street was rented at £36 per annum. In 1912 even the GWSAWS, one of the most undemonstrative of the NUWSS societies, felt that the office opening hours should be extended; they were now open 10 am–1 pm and 2 pm–5 pm daily except Saturdays, when it was open 10 am–1 pm. At the same time they arranged for Durrant's Press Cuttings service to be used at the cost of £11s and for a card index system, seen in the London office, to be imported to Glasgow. Because the office was open all day it was agreed in November 1912 that the secretary's salary be raised to £80 pa. A year later her salary was increased to £100 pa and, such was the increase in NUWSS activity, an assistant was engaged, presumably part time, at a salary of £1 per week. After the outbreak of war in 1914 one room in the GWSAWS office was used by the Scottish Women's Hospitals organizer.

In 1910 Sime SERUYA opened the International Suffrage Shop at 31 Bedford Street (third floor), in a room lent to her by Edith CRAIG. On 27 March 1911 the shop was able to move into more suitable premises at 15 Adam Street, Strand, where there was a large room to be let for meetings (a "picture lamp and sheet" could be hired to provide an accompaniment to talks). The shop was described as "The Only Feminist Bookshop" and, besides offering for sale all kinds of feminist as well as general literature, modern plays on social questions, art and children's books, pictorial posters, badges and colours of all the societies, foreign, American and English newspapers, photographs and postcards, it also organized public meetings, the one at the end of March 1911 being a debate between Cicely HAMILTON and G.K. Chesterton held at the small Queen's Hall. As well as selling, the shop also acted as publisher for Cicely HAMILTON's *Pageant of Great Women*, 1910, and as a lecture agency, and provided a book-search service. As militancy increased, the shop was an obvious target for retaliation. Helena SWANWICK described how the shop was harassed by medical students who "used to hover about and drop in, giggling and making rude remarks. She [the manager] remained calm and courteous, but she could not get rid of them without shutting up the shop." Helena Swanwick was at a meeting one evening held in the basement of the shop when windows were smashed and medical students broke in and threw books about. The police on this occasion would do nothing to help. It seems unlikely that the shop was ever a thriving commercial concern; Sime Seruya presumably underwrote it. An article in the *Daily Herald*, 24 January 1913, revealed that:

At present it is very much struggling for existence.... it is quite refreshing to look round at the shelves and tables of literature of all the Suffrage Societies. Almost every work that is vital, that means anything to all, is on sale. And the best photographs of leading Suffragists, dramatists, thinkers, and agitators adorn the place.... We have to move in June on account of the widening of the Strand.... A new feature, and certain to be popular, is the organisation of a lending library on a very moderate subscription basis. This will be open at the end of the month.

At this time the shop's advisory committee included Lilian HICKS and Marie LAWSON. It came close to closure in August 1913, but managed to carry on, appealing for funds in February 1915, but unlike the shops run by the suffrage societies, remaining open throughout the First World War. In April 1918 the proprietor of the International Suffrage Shop, now at 5 Duke Street, Adelphi, was threatened with bankruptcy and an appeal for contributions was sent out. The shop's manager was then Miss A.W. Trim.

Archival source: Documents relating to the Bedford Society for Women's Suffrage, Bedfordshire Record Office; Papers of the Birmingham Women's Suffrage Society, Birmingham Archives and Local History Library; Blathwayt Diaries, Dyrham Park (The National Trust), Avon; Records of the Cambridge Women's Suffrage Association, County Record Office, Cambridge; Minutes of the Glasgow and West of Scotland Association for Women's Suffrage, Department of Rare Books and Manuscripts, Mitchell Library, Glasgow.

Bibliography: H. Swanwick, *I Have been Young*, 1935; R. Ferguson, *Royal Borough*, 1950.

SHORE SISTERS Arabella Shore (c. 1823–1901), daughter of Rev. Thomas Shore, who acted as a tutor to young men preparing for college. She lived at home with her younger sister, Louisa. Another sister, Emily, died in 1839 and Arabella and Louisa Shore edited her *Journal* for publication in 1891. In the course of a visit to her friend Bessie Rayner PARKES, one day in December 1855 Arabella Shore was shown the draft petition calling for a change in the position of married women; it is not known if she signed it. Neither of the Shore sisters signed the 1866 women's suffrage petition, but in 1870-71 Arabella subscribed to the MANCHESTER SOCIETY FOR WOMEN'S SUFFRAGE and was probably still a member in 1880-81. In 1875 she and her sister subscribed to the CENTRAL COMMITTEE OF THE NATIONAL SOCIETY FOR WOMEN'S SUFFRAGE. In 1874 she gave a series of lectures on constitutional history at the office of the Women's Education Union, in which she highlighted the need of women to a constitutional right to the franchise. She wrote *The Present Aspect of Women's Suffrage Considered*, 1877, and *What Women Have A Right To*, 1879. Arabella Shore delivered a lecture with the latter title to members of the Women's Protective and Provident League in 1879 and gave a lecture on "The Political and Social Condition of Women" to the Central Committee of the National Society for Women's Suffrage in January 1879. She was later a member of the Bucks Women's Liberal Association. In 1890 she subscribed to the CENTRAL NATIONAL SOCIETY FOR WOMEN'S SUFFRAGE.

Louisa Shore (1824–1895) was a Liberal and a suffragist. In August 1861 Emily Hall wrote in her diary of Louisa Shore, "She is a curious specimen, not at all happy, indeed she is miserable . . . It is mournful to hear her lament her passing youth, to feel that the remedy lies in her own hands . . . if she would work, work, work, she would have no time to think . . . She cannot even take pleasure in doing the affairs of the house, a woman's province and which ought to be a woman's pride . . . [her father] admitted that she longs to be married and have a family". Louisa Shore obviously carried on thinking and in 1874 wrote "The Citizenship of Women Socially Considered", first published in the *Westminster Review* and then issued as a pamphlet, in which she discusses with verve and at length the nature of contemporary marriage. Arabella Shore, in a memoir written of her sister, describes the pamphlet as "written with much masculine vigour", but reveals that "the labour and excitement of its preparation prostrated her, and she uttered from the sofa to which weakness too often consigned her, a resolution never again to attempt a serious prose work, and she kept her word". Both sisters, separately and together, wrote poetry, being particularly fond of verse dramas.

Address: (1870) Firgrove, Sunninghill, Berkshire; (1890s) Orchard Poyle, near Taplow, Buckinghamshire; Arabella (1895) 16 Hillside, Wimbledon, Surrey.

Bibliography: L. Shore, *Poems*, with a Memoir by her sister, Arabella Shore, and an Appreciation by Frederic Harrison, 1897; O.A. Sherrard, *Two Victorian Girls: With Extracts from the Hall Diaries*, 1966; A. Shore, "The present aspect of women's suffrage considered", 14 May 1877 and L.S. [Louisa Shore], "The citizenship of women socially considered", both included in J. Lewis (ed.), *Before The Vote Was Won; Arguments For and Against Women's Suffrage 1864–1896*, 1987; J. Rendall, "Citizenship, culture and civilization", in C. Daley and M. Nolan (eds), *Beyond Suffrage: International Feminist Perspectives*, 1994.

SHOREHAM AND OTFORD (NUWSS) In 1913 the society was a member of the KENTISH FEDERATION OF THE NATIONAL UNION OF WOMEN'S SUFFRAGE SOCIETIES. Secretary (1913) Miss Dorothy Scott, Shoreham, nr Sevenoaks, Kent.

SHOTLEY BRIDGE (NUWSS) In 1913 the society was a member of the NORTH-EASTERN FEDERATION OF THE NATIONAL UNION OF WOMEN'S SUFFRAGE SOCIETIES. Secretary (1913) Miss A.C.E. Walton-Wilson, Derwent Dene, Shotley, Northumberland.

SHREWSBURY committee of the LONDON NATIONAL SOCIETY FOR WOMEN'S SUFFRAGE Founded in 1871. The secretary was Miss McKEE, Claremont Hill. The Shrewsbury society associated itself with the new CENTRAL COMMITTEE OF THE NATIONAL SOCIETY FOR WOMEN'S SUFFRAGE in 1872. A women's suffrage society was in existence in Shrewsbury in 1909, as a constituent of the NATIONAL UNION OF WOMEN'S SUFFRAGE SOCIETIES. Secretary (1909) Mrs Timpany, St Winifrede's Gardens, Shrewbury, Shropshire. In 1913, as the Shropshire Society, it was a member of the MIDLAND (WEST) FEDERATION OF THE NATIONAL UNION OF WOMEN'S SUFFRAGE SOCIETIES. Secretary (1913) Miss Hills, 12 Butcher Row, Shrewsbury, Shropshire.

SHREWSBURY (WSPU) Organizer (1913) Miss Marwick, 37 High Street, Shrewsbury, Shropshire.

SICKERT, ELLEN MELICENT COBDEN, MRS (1848–1914) Daughter of Richard and Kate Cobden, sister of Anne Cobden SANDERSON and Jane Cobden UNWIN. The latter's nephew by marriage, Sir Stanley Unwin, described Ellen Cobden Sickert as a more balanced personality than his aunt (although that may tell us more about Sir Stanley than it does about the sisters). In 1885 Ellen Cobden married the painter Walter Sickert, whom she had met through her friendship with his sister, Helena SWANWICK. Sickert was 12 years her junior and during the course of their marriage she supported him financially. Indeed, it was only with the safety-net of her wealth that he was able initially to devote himself to painting. As a consequence of his bohemian infidelity they separated in 1896, after an attempt to save the marriage had been made at a Venetian flat, lent to them by Barbara BODICHON's sister, Nannie Leigh Smith. However, this failed and, always remaining friendly, they divorced in 1899. As a novelist Ellen Cobden Sickert was able to put her marital experience to use in *The Wistons*, 1901.

In 1888, after the split in the CENTRAL COMMITTEE OF THE NATIONAL SOCIETY FOR WOMEN'S SUFFRAGE, Ellen Cobden Sickert supported the CENTRAL NATIONAL SOCIETY, in 1905–6 the CENTRAL SOCIETY FOR WOMEN'S SUFFRAGE and the WOMEN'S SOCIAL AND POLITICAL UNION in 1907 and 1908. She made strenuous, although fruitless, attempts to attend the trial of her sister, Anne Cobden Sanderson, in October 1906 and was present at the banquet at the Savoy on 11 December to celebrate Anne's release from prison. She gave a donation towards the expenses of the WSPU Prince's Skating Rink Exhibition in May 1909 and took part in the suffrage procession held on 18 June 1910. In 1914, shortly before she died, Ellen Cobden Sickert wrote, as "Miles Amber", *Sylvia Saxton, Episodes in a Life*, which was published by T. Fisher Unwin. This novel contains references to the suffrage movement and is dedicated to the painter Emily Osborn (*see* Barbara BODICHON) and her companion Mary Elizabeth Dunn, to both of whom Ellen Cobden Sickert left a small legacy, "as a token of love", in her will.

Address: (1885) 54 Broadhurst Gardens, Hampstead, London; (1907) 29 Buckingham Gate, London SW.
Portrait: by Whistler, *Green and Violet: Mrs Walter Sickert*, Fogg Art Museum, Cambridge, Mass., USA, reproduced in D. Sutton, *Walter Sickert*, 1976.

SIDLEY, MARGUERITE ANNIE (1886–?) Born in Nottingham, as a child went with her family to live in London. Her parents were theosophists but Marguerite, although for a time a member, had lapsed by 1908. She did, however, remain a lifelong vegetarian. She was educated at Camden School for Girls and then learnt shorthand and typing, taking first place in the country in the Royal Society of Arts typewriting examination. While she was employed as a shorthand-typist in a large firm of electrical engineers in October 1906 there was much discussion in the office about the arrest in the Lobby of the House of Commons of Anne Cobden SANDERSON and Edith How MARTYN and Marguerite Sidley determined to find out more about the suffrage movement. Two months later her health broke down and, threatened with consumption, she gave up work. In January 1907 she went with her mother to a meeting at which Mrs PANKHURST, Christabel PANKHURST and Mary GAWTHORPE were speaking and, with her mother, immediately joined the WOMEN'S SOCIAL AND POLITICAL UNION. Having been unable to take part in the Women's Parliament in Caxton Hall, she went to Clement's Inn and offered her office skills free to the cause for as long as her savings lasted. On 20 March 1907 she took part in a deputation to the House of Commons and as a result spent 12 days in Holloway. On her release she was offered paid employment as shorthand-typist and chief clerk in the WSPU office. However, because of difficulties with her health, she had to transfer to what she termed "the outdoor staff" and went first to Hull to campaign at a by-election and then to Lancashire where she worked with Adela PANKHURST, Gladice KEEVIL, Mary LEIGH and Jennie BAINES at the Rossendale by-election. She travelled round the country for the next year on behalf of the WSPU, carrying out both by-election and educational campaigns. In the summer of 1908, however, both she and her mother broke with the WSPU and joined the WOMEN'S FREEDOM LEAGUE, for which Marguerite Sidley worked until 1916.

Marguerite Sidley's first task with the WFL was to take over from Alison NEILANS the suffrage CARAVAN tour in the summer of 1908. For the next three years she spent between eight and ten weeks in the summer travelling around the country in the WFL caravan, usually in the company of a Miss M.J. Henderson and of Annie Roff, who was in 1912 to be, with Florence DE FONBLANQUE, one of the instigators of the "Women's March". Issues of the *Vote* for July and August 1910 carry detailed accounts of Marguerite Sidley's caravan adventures. In February 1909 she spent one month in Holloway after, so she described, merely going to the House of Commons to ask to see her Member of Parliament; there presumably was some accompanying disturbance of the peace. Later that year she spent six months working for the WFL around Glasgow and in 1910 she was appointed a WFL organizer in Scotland. In 1911 she had charge of the census protest in Edinburgh and drummed up much publicity for this in the local press. However, by the end of 1911, she found "outdoor work" too strenuous and in 1912 joined the WFL office staff. In March 1914 Marguerite Sidley was arrested for speaking from the steps of the Board of Trade offices in Whitehall and spent a further four days in prison.

Address: (1909) Strathleven, Oakleigh Park, London, N (which was the address of the MEN's COMMITTEE FOR JUSTICE TO WOMEN).

Photograph: of Marguerite Sidley was issued as a postcard by the Women's Freedom League, wearing her WFL enamel flag brooch (see JEWELLERY AND BADGES).

Archival source: The Suffragette Fellowship Collection, Museum of London.

SIDMOUTH AND DISTRICT (NUWSS) In 1913 the society was a member of the SOUTH-WESTERN FEDERATION OF THE NATIONAL UNION OF WOMEN's SUFFRAGE SOCIETIES. Secretary (1913) Lady Lockyer, 16 Pen-y-wern Road, London SW. (Lady Lockyer was sister of Annie Leigh BROWNE; their mother's family came from Sidmouth.)

SILLOTH (NUWSS) In 1913 the society was a member of the NORTH-WESTERN FEDERATION OF THE NATIONAL UNION OF WOMEN's SUFFRAGE SOCIETIES. Secretary (1913) Miss Wilson, 4 Hilton Terrace, Silloth, Cumberland.

SINCLAIR, MAY [MARY AMELIA ST CLAIR] (1863–1946) Novelist and poet, was converted to the cause of women's suffrage in 1908, writing to *Votes for Women* on 1 March, "I can only say that it is impossible to be a woman and not admire to the utmost the devotion, the courage, and the endurance of the women who are fighting and working for the Suffrage today". In the same month she took part in the WOMEN's SOCIAL AND POLITICAL UNION Self-Denial Week, with Violet Hunt, Evelyn SHARP and Clemence HOUSMAN collecting money in Kensington High Street. In 1908 May Sinclair was a member of the WOMEN's FREEDOM LEAGUE; in 1910 she supported the TAX RESISTANCE LEAGUE and was also a member of the WOMEN WRITERS' SUFFRAGE LEAGUE, by 1912 being one of its vice-presidents; and in 1913 she supported the NATIONAL POLITICAL LEAGUE. On 18 June 1910 she took part in the Writers' section of the suffrage procession and in the same month signed a Writers' memorial sent to Asquith to urge the claims of a women's suffrage bill. She wrote *Feminism*, which is dated 31 March 1912 and was published by the Women Writers' Suffrage League as a spirited refutation of Sir Almroth Wright's *Unexpurgated Case Against Women's Suffrage* (see Lady Almroth WRIGHT). On 29 June 1914 she attended, as "Jane Austen", the WWSL's costume dinner at the Hotel Cecil. One of her novels, *The Tree of Heaven*, published in 1917, contains suffrage scenes and characters.

Address: (1908) 4 Edwardes Square Studios, London W (next door to Olive HOCKIN); (1914) 1 Blenheim Road, St John's Wood, London NW.

Photograph: in T.E.M. Boll, *Miss May Sinclair: Novelist*, 1973.

Bibliography: T.E.M. Boll, *Miss May Sinclair: Novelist*, 1973.

SINGH, SOPHIA ALEXANDROWNA DULEEP, PRINCESS (c. 1876–1948) Daughter of Maharajah Duleep Singh, who, after the annexation of the Punjab, was granted a pension of £40 000, became a naturalized Englishman, a close friend of Queen Victoria, and settled in Norfolk. Her mother was a daughter of L. Muller of Alexandria, Egypt. According to Mrs BLATHWAYT, Princess Sophia had first been converted to the views of the WOMEN's SOCIAL AND POLITICAL UNION at the home of Una DUGDALE. She took part in the first deputation to the House of Commons on "Black Friday", 18

November 1910, and regularly spoke at meetings of the Richmond, Surrey, branch of the WSPU. She was a member of the TAX RESISTANCE LEAGUE and in 1910 had a diamond ring impounded against a 6/– non-payment of rates; it was bought at auction by a member of the TRL and returned to her. In March 1913 Princess Sophia chaired a meeting of the Kingston and District branch of the WSPU and in 1914 was again fined for refusing to pay taxes; a pearl necklace and gold bangle were seized under distraint and auctioned at Twickenham Town Hall. She was a supporter of the NATIONAL POLITICAL LEAGUE in 1913. In July 1915, still attached to the Pankhursts, she took part in the Women's War Work procession. After Mrs PANKHURST's death Princess Sophia was president of the committee charged with the responsibility of providing flowers for her statue. In her entry to the 1934 edition of *Women's Who's Who* she gave as her only interest, "The Advancement of Women". Her sister, Princess Catherine Duleep Singh, was a member of the NATIONAL UNION OF WOMEN'S SUFFRAGE SOCIETIES and, also living at Hampton Court, was associated with the Esher and Molesey branch. She was involved, appropriately, with the organization of the 1912 NUWSS Oriental Bazaar and opened the NUWSS East Midland Federation Christmas Bazaar in Nottingham. In 1914 their sister-in-law, Princess Anne Duleep Singh, became a theosophist, sponsored by Harold and Gertrude Baillie-WEAVER.

Address: (1912 and 1948) Faraday House, Hampton Court, Middlesex (a "grace-and-favour" residence); (1945) "Rathenrae", Penn, Buckinghamshire.
Photograph: in the *Suffragette*, 18 April 1913.
Bibliography: G.D. and J. Heath, *The Women's Suffrage Movement In and Around Richmond and Twickenham*, 1968.

SKY, ROSINA, MRS (1858–1928) Born in Soho, London, daughter of David Posener, in 1878 married William Sky, who left her a widow in 1892, after which she worked to support herself and her three children by running a tobacconist and fancy goods shop in Southend. In 1907 she collected 400 of the eventual 257 000 signatures in favour of votes for women, which were included in the Suffrage Declaration drawn up by Clementina BLACK (*see* WOMEN'S FRANCHISE DECLARATION COMMITTEE). Rosina Sky then approached the LONDON SOCIETY FOR WOMEN'S SUFFRAGE, of which she was a member, with the intention of opening a branch in Southend, but nothing seems to have come of this suggestion. In 1910 she subscribed to the NEW CONSTITUTIONAL SOCIETY FOR WOMEN'S SUFFRAGE and in the same year was treasurer of a new branch of the WOMEN'S SOCIAL AND POLITICAL UNION in Southend. She made a point, as a head of household, of spoiling her census form, writing, "No votes for women, no information from women" across it. She also joined the newly founded TAX RESISTANCE LEAGUE and had goods distrained in lieu of tax. She posted the notice of the penalty in her shop window. In September 1911 her goods were again put up for auction; Margaret Kineton PARKES and Anne Cobden SANDERSON and the Southend and Westcliffe branch of the WSPU came to give support. The process was repeated in June 1912. Mrs Sky made it clear that she could not afford to go to prison because she had to work to support herself. She continued to run her shop until 1922 and died at Hathersage, Derbyshire.

Address: (1906) 28 Cliftown Road, Southend-on-Sea, Essex.
Bibliography: N. Bonney, *Essex Women and the Campaign for Female Suffrage (1850–1914)*, Brentwood College of Education thesis (held in Fawcett Library), 1971

SLOUGH (NUWSS) Formed in 1914. Its chairman was Mrs Cyril Battock and the honorary secretary was Miss Hartopp Nash.

SMITH, CAROLINE, MRS (*c.* 1821–?) Sister of George HOLYOAKE and a close friend of Elizabeth Wolstenholme ELMY. She was a member of the BIRMINGHAM NATIONAL SOCIETY FOR WOMEN'S SUFFRAGE in 1872; in 1889, with her daughter (Caroline) Julia (b. 1859), attended the inaugural meeting of the WOMEN'S FRANCHISE LEAGUE; and in 1891 followed Mrs Elmy into the WOMEN'S EMANCIPATION UNION. In 1892 Caroline Smith paid £20 of the expenses of the conference, organized by Julia, which was held by the WEU in Birmingham.

Address: (1892) 19 Carpenter Road, Edgbaston, Birmingham.
Photograph: in Fawcett Library Collection.

SMITH, [ELIZABETH] DOROTHEA CHALMERS, DR (*c.* 1874?–1944) née Lyness Graduated in medicine from Glasgow University in 1894, worked at the Royal Samaritan Hospital for Women in Glasgow, and *c*. 1901 married Rev. William Chalmers Smith, minister of Calton Church, Glasgow, eventually becoming the mother of six children. The latter fact may explain why she does not appear to have taken part in the suffrage movement until 1912–13, although her sister, Jane Lyness, was a member of the Glasgow WOMEN'S SOCIAL AND POLITICAL UNION. In July 1913 Dorothea Chalmers Smith was caught, with Ethel MOORHEAD, attempting to set fire to a house in Glasgow. She went on hunger strike while on remand and was released under the "Cat and Mouse" Act after five days. While in hiding she wrote to Maud Arncliffe SENNETT offering her support and congratulations for her work with the NORTHERN MEN'S FEDERATION. She evaded recapture until October, was tried in Glasgow on 15 October and sentenced to eight months' imprisonment, again went on hunger strike and was again released. On 24 November the Glasgow Chief Constable noted that Dorothea Chalmers Smith had disappeared from her house, where she was thought to have remained since her release. The Criminal Record Office circulated her photograph and description (5' 6", hair dark, eyes grey, oval face, nose slightly aquiline, medium build, married, has children) but made no mention of the fact that she was a doctor. Dorothea Chalmers Smith was never recaptured, became a member of the UNITED SUFFRAGISTS and eventually resumed her practice as a doctor. She left her husband, taking her four daughters with her; her two sons, whom she was not allowed to visit, remained with her husband.

Address: (1944) 3 Melrose Street, Glasgow.
Photograph: in L. Leneman, *A Guid Cause: The Women's Suffrage Movement in Scotland*, 1991.
Bibliography: L. Leneman, *A Guid Cause: The Women's Suffrage Movement in Scotland*, 1991.

SMITH, LOUISA MARIA, MRS (1835–67) Elder sister of Elizabeth (*see* Elizabeth Garrett ANDERSON), Millicent Garrett FAWCETT and Agnes GARRETT, and cousin of Rhoda GARRETT. With Elizabeth she was educated for two years at the Miss Brownings' Academy at Blackheath, leaving around 1851. She then remained at home in Aldeburgh until in 1857 she married James Smith, the brother of school friends, and eventually became the mother of four children. For the rest of her short life she lived in London, first in Bayswater, then in Manchester Square and, finally, in Maida Vale, where she was constantly visited by her sisters. In the 1860s Elizabeth Garrett lived with the Smiths in Manchester Square while pursuing her medical education and by 1861 Louisa Smith was involved with the group of feminists, which included Barbara BODICHON and Emily FAITHFULL, centred on the office of the Society for Promoting the Employment of Women in Langham Place. In 1865 Louisa Smith was a member of the KENSINGTON SOCIETY and in 1866 signed the women's suffrage petition. She became honorary secretary of the ENFRANCHISEMENT OF WOMEN COMMITTEE, which was established on 23 November, with assistance from Harriet COOK. It was deemed politic for the Committee to be headed, on paper at least, by a married woman. Her involvement was, however, cut short; she died of appendicitis in February 1867.

Address: (1866) 2 Warrington Crescent, Maida Vale, London NW.
Archival source: Mill–Taylor Papers, London School of Economics and Political Science.
Bibliography: L. Garrett Anderson, *Elizabeth Garrett Anderson*, 1939.

SMYTH, ETHEL MARY, DAME (1858–1944) Daughter of a major-general in the Royal Artillery. An established composer, she joined the WOMEN'S SOCIAL AND POLITICAL UNION in 1910, drawn into it after attending a suffrage meeting addressed by Emmeline PANKHURST at the home of Lady Brassey. She was taken to the meeting by the latter's sister-in-law, a friend of her childhood, Muriel, Lady DE LA WARR. In 1909 Lady de la Warr's close friend Mary Dodge had financed both the first London production, conducted by Thomas Beecham, of Ethel Smyth's opera *The Wreckers,* and the building of her Surrey house, "Coign". Ethel Smyth soon became a devoted friend of Mrs Pankhurst and resolved to put herself and her musical skills at the service of the cause for a period of two years. She had, apparently, before meeting Mrs Pankhurst, never seriously considered the merits of the suffrage cause, although she had in her youth much admired Rhoda GARRETT. Ethel Smyth composed the tune "The March of the Women", to which Cicely HAMILTON fitted the words, which was published by Breitkopf and Hartel and played for the first time on Saturday 21 January 1911, at the Suffolk Street Galleries, at a social evening held to welcome the release from prison of those who had been sentenced after protesting at the events following "Black Friday" in November 1910. The issue of *Votes for Women* of 20 January 1911 describes how "The fiery spirit of revolution united with religious solemnity, the all-conquering union of faith and rebellion which makes the strength of the militant movement, is expressed in Dr Smyth's Marching Song. It is at once a hymn and a call to battle." "The March of the Women" appealed to constitutionalists as well as to militants. On 19 June 1911, commenting on the Coronation Procession, Ethel Smyth wrote to Millicent Fawcett to say "how very delighted I was at the Nat. Union Bands playing my march". "The March of the Women" was the third of three pieces for unaccompanied chorus (the others being "Laggard Dawn" and "1910") that comprised "Songs of Sunrise" which was given its première, at which Ethel Smyth was herself the conductor when Thomas Beecham failed to appear as promised, at a WSPU rally in the Queen's Hall in April 1911. Her biographer mentions that Ethel Smyth composed at least two other works inspired by the suffrage movement. One, *The Boatswain's Mate*, 1913–14, a comic opera, for which she also wrote the libretto based on a short story by W.W. Jacobs (whose wife was a member of the WSPU), was eventually performed in London in January 1916. The other, *A Medley for Choir and Orchestra*, for which she set to music her own words depicting a suffragette raid in Trafalgar Square, is described by Christopher ST JOHN as "a complete flop". Elizabeth Woods cites three further works as having been inspired by Smyth's suffrage involvement: a song, "Hey Nonny No", 1910, dedicated to Violet Woodhouse; the finale of her *String Quartet in E Minor*, 1913; and *Three Songs*, for solo female voice, 1913, at least one of which is based on a poem by Ethel Carnie and was originally published in *Votes for Women*, 21 April 1911.

Ethel Smyth enjoyed accompanying Emmeline Pankhurst, both disguised, on excursions to see Christabel PANKHURST in Paris. In March 1912 she took part in the WSPU window-smashing raid. On 22 March the *Daily Herald* reported that Ethel Smyth "said that she threw a stone through Sir Lewis Harcourt's window because he had made 'the most objectionable remark about Women's Suffrage she had ever heard'. He said 'I don't object to women having the vote if they were all as intelligent and well-balanced as my wife.' Witness thought this the most impertinent thing she had ever heard." Ethel Smyth was sentenced to two months' imprisonment; she was given a cell next to Mrs Pankhurst in Holloway, and did not serve the full term. The deputy medical officer committed his opinion to paper that "She is mentally unstable and is highly histerical [sic] & neurotic". During this period Thomas Beecham recorded visiting Holloway and seeing "the noble company of martyrs marching round it and singing lustily their war-chant while the composer, beaming approbation from an overlooking upper window, beat time in almost Bacchic frenzy with a toothbrush". On 27 May she delivered four bottles of Chateau Lafite to Holloway, "alleging" (as a Home Office official put it) that wine was necessary to Mrs Pankhurst's health. In July 1912 Ethel Smyth was arrested on suspicion of having, with Helen CRAGGS, intended to set fire to Nuneham House, which belonged to Lewis Harcourt. She was released without charge.

Having given the allotted two years to the suffrage movement, in mid-1913 Ethel Smyth returned to her musical career. She maintained her close friendship with Emmeline Pankhurst and on occasion sheltered her at "Coign" when she was evading recapture after being released from prison under the "Cat and Mouse" Act. The two were together in France, Mrs Pankhurst having escaped there after her tenth hunger strike, when war was declared in August 1914. A rift, however, developed between the two; Ethel Smyth did not sympathize with Christabel Pankhurst's excessively patriotic reaction to the outbreak of war nor with Mrs Pankhurst's plans for a Home for War-Babies. During the First World War Ethel Smyth trained as a radiographer and was attached to XIIIth Division of the French army. In 1921, having criticized Christabel in a letter to Emmeline Pankhurst, the latter severed all further communication. When she tried four years later to re-establish the friendship with Ethel Smyth, she was rebuffed; the magic had evaporated. However, Ethel Smyth performed a final service when, wearing her Holloway medal, she conducted the Metropolitan Police Band in "The March of the Women" at the unveiling ceremony of the statue of Emmeline Pankhurst in Victoria Tower Gardens on 6 March 1930.

Address: Coign, near Woking, Surrey.

Archival source: Home Office Papers, Public Record Office.

Bibliography: E. Smyth, *A Final Burning of Boats*, 1928; E. Smyth, *Female Piping in Eden*, 1933; E. Smyth, *Impressions That Remained*, 1919; E. Smyth, *As Time Went On*, 1936; C. St John, *Ethel Smyth: A Biography*, 1959; E. Woods, "Performing rights: a sonography of women's suffrage", *Musical Quarterly*, 4, 1995.

SNOWDEN, ETHEL, MRS (1880–1951) née Annakin Born in Harrogate, the daughter of a well-to-do builder. She and Mary GAWTHORPE were pupil-teachers together around 1894 and, after a formal teacher training at Liverpool Training College, Ethel Annakin held a teaching position at Nelson in 1904. She was already a lecturer for the Independent Labour Party and in 1905 married the ILP's chairman, Philip Snowden. Isabella FORD and her sister Bessie were the only witnesses to the wedding. On 11 December 1906 Ethel Snowden was present at the banquet given at the Savoy by Millicent FAWCETT to celebrate the release from prison of Anne Cobden SANDERSON and the other WOMEN'S SOCIAL AND POLITICAL UNION prisoners. She joined the NATIONAL UNION OF WOMEN'S SUFFRAGE SOCIETIES, believing that women's enfranchisement had to precede the establishment of socialism, and became an active suffrage speaker, both in Britain and the USA. She converted her husband to the women's suffrage cause and, after being elected MP for Blackburn in 1906, he became a valuable supporter inside parliament. He was prepared to support women's enfranchisement on the same terms as it was granted to men, rather than to follow the Labour Party line, which supported women's suffrage only as part of an adult suffrage measure. In 1913 he was a vice-president of the MEN'S LEAGUE FOR WOMEN'S SUFFRAGE. In 1912 Ethel Snowden was a member of the first Election Fighting Fund Committee, formed by the NUWSS to support Labour Party candidates. In July 1912 she signed a public letter of protest against WSPU militancy. In July 1913 Ethel Snowden was one of the speakers at the rally in Hyde Park at the end of the NUWSS PILGRIMAGE. Harriet Blessley, a "pilgrim" with the Portsmouth branch of the NUWSS, described Ethel Snowden as "my favourite of favourite speakers", and described her speech on this occasion as an "impassioned, grand little speech". Ethel Snowden wrote *The Woman Socialist*, 1907, and *The Feminist Movement*, 1913, and a pamphlet, *Woman Suffrage in America: A Reply to Mrs Humphry Ward*, 1909.

During the First World War Ethel Snowden was a pacifist, a member of the faction within the NUWSS that was prepared to join with the Union of Democratic Control. She also supported the Women's Peace Crusade and was a member of the British section of the Women's International League for Peace and Freedom. After the end of the war she was briefly a member of the Labour Party national executive. From 1926 until 1932 she was a governor of the BBC.

Address: (1913) Elberton, Woodstock Road, Golders Green, London N.

SOCIETY FOR PROMOTING THE RETURN OF WOMEN AS COUNTY COUNCILLORS Founded by Annie Leigh BROWNE in November 1888 in order to sponsor the candidature of Jane Cobden (*see* Jane Cobden UNWIN) and Lady SANDHURST at the London County Council election. The society was intended only to be temporary; notepaper was not printed with the society's address until 1890. The society's committee included Mrs Sheldon AMOS, Florence BALGARNIE, Annie Leigh Browne, Mary Kilgour, with Eva MCLAREN as treasurer. Members of the society's general committee included Mrs Anna BATESON and Mrs Corrie Grant (*see* Clementia TAYLOR) and the society's members included Lady CARLISLE, Isabella FORD and Mrs FAWCETT. In 1893 the society changed its name to the WOMEN'S LOCAL GOVERNMENT SOCIETY.

SOCIETY FOR PROMOTING THE RETURN OF WOMEN AS POOR LAW GUARDIANS Also known as the Women Guardians Society, it was founded in 1881 by Miss Ward Andrews, Caroline Ashurst BIGGS, Laura Ormiston CHANT and Eva Muller (*see* Eva MCLAREN).

Archival source: Annual reports of the society, Blackburn Collection, Girton College, Cambridge.

SOLIHULL AND DISTRICT (NUWSS) Secretary (1913) Miss Wright, Sutton Lodge, Solihull, Warwickshire.

SOLOMON FAMILY Mrs Georgiana Margaret (1844–1933) née Thomson, born in Edinburgh, emigrated to South Africa and became first principal of the Good Hope seminary. In 1874 she married Saul Solomon, who from 1854 had been a member of the first legislative assembly of Cape Colony and who eventually became governor-general. He was a liberal in politics and opposed to all discrimination. She was a temperance worker, first president of the Social Purity Alliance in Cape Town and led the campaign there against the reintroduction of the Contagious Diseases Acts, which had been repealed by her husband in 1872. In later years one of their daughters, Daisy, presented the Women's Service Library (now the Fawcett Library) with a copy, bearing the ownership inscription "Saul Solomon, Clarensville, Cape Colony", of the first edition (1792) of Mary Wollstonecraft's *Vindication of the Rights of Woman*, testifying in a tangible form to the family's long-held interest in the women's cause. After he died in Scotland in 1892 Mrs Solomon and her six children remained in Britain. In the 1890s she was in touch with Jane Cobden UNWIN, both being members of the Anti-Slavery and Aborigines Protection Society. In 1916 the two women were members of a conference held to consider General Botha's Native Land Policy and caused sufficient trouble to be considered obstreperous by other members of the committee.

In 1906 Mrs Saul Solomon was a delegate from the Sidcup Women's Liberal Association, of which she was president, to the annual meeting of the WOMEN'S LIBERAL FEDERATION and in 1907 was, with her daughter, a member of the LONDON SOCIETY FOR WOMEN'S SUFFRAGE. In 1908, with Daisy, she joined the WOMEN'S SOCIAL AND POLITICAL UNION; in early 1909 she also gave a donation to the WOMEN'S FREEDOM LEAGUE. On 30 March 1909 Mrs Solomon led a deputation to the House of Commons from the Women's Parliament in Caxton Hall. She was received at the House, but was refused an interview with the prime minister. She was arrested after taking part in the deputation to the House of Commons on 29 June 1909. She was a member, with Mrs PANKHURST and Elizabeth Garrett ANDERSON, of the first deputation to the House of Commons on "Black Friday" in November 1910 and was involved in the subsequent fracas in Parliament Square, claiming, in a letter to Dora MARSDEN, that she had endured sexual assault from the police. In March 1912, after taking part in the WSPU window-smashing campaign, she was served a term of a month's imprisonment in Holloway. In November 1912 she contributed towards George LANSBURY's expenses when he stood as a suffrage candidate at Bow. In 1913 she resigned from the WSPU, apparently as a result of the expulsion of the PETHICK-LAWRENCES, and later became a member of the UNITED SUFFRAGISTS.

Daisy Dorothea Solomon (?–alive 1963 in South Africa) was born in South Africa, daughter of Saul and Georgiana Solomon. She joined the WSPU with her mother in 1908. She featured in one of the WSPU's publicity stunts, sent as a "human letter", price threepence, to 10 Downing Street to publicize a suffragette deputation to the House of Commons on 24 February 1909 and was subsequently arrested after taking part in the deputation, with Emmeline Pethick-Lawrence, Lady Constance LYTTON and Caprina FAHEY, and sentenced to a month's imprisonment. She later said that she paused to help the elderly lady whom she was accompanying, and the police thought she was not moving sufficiently quickly and arrested her. She became organizing secretary of the Hampstead branch of the WSPU, certainly holding that position in 1912–13. In the early years of the First World War, until 1916, she is listed as one of the secretaries of the WSPU. In 1918 she was a member of the UNITED SUFFRAGISTS and literature secretary of the British Dominions Women Citizens' Union (see BRITISH DOMINIONS WOMAN SUFFRAGE UNION) and in 1923, as a representative of the British Commonwealth League, she attended the conference of the International Alliance of Women for Suffrage and Equal Citizenship in Paris. In 1926 she was honorary secretary of the EQUAL POLITICAL RIGHTS CAMPAIGN COMMITTEE, working to extend the vote to women of 21 and over. She was still living in England in 1948 but probably later returned to live in South Africa.

Address: (1906) Campsie, Station Road, Sidcup, Kent; (1913) Les Lunes, Sumatra Road, West Hampstead, London

NW; Mrs Solomon (1926) Clarensville, 7 Helenslea Avenue, Golders Green, London NW11; Daisy Solomon (1913) 178 Finchley Road, London NW, which was the address of the Hampstead branch of the WSPU; (1918) 64 Pattison Road, London NW2; (1923) Clarensville, 7 Helenslea Avenue, Golders Green, London NW11.
Photograph: Mrs Solomon in *Votes for Women*, 9 July 1909; Daisy Solomon in *Votes for Women*, 26 February 1909.
Bibliography: W.E. Gladstone Solomon, *Saul Solomon: The Member for Cape Town*, 1948.

SOMERVILLE COLLEGE (NUWSS) By 1913 the society was part of the OXFORD WOMEN STUDENTS SOCIETY. Secretary (1909) Miss Eckhard, Somerville College, Oxford.

SONGS, MUSIC AND POETRY Included in Helen BLACKBURN's scrapbook is a ballad, "The Ladies' Franchise", written by J. Ritchie, which was sold in the streets after the women's suffrage meeting held at St George's Hall, Langham Place, in May 1875. It begins, "Husbands and uncles, and brothers,/ With open ears attend;/ As well as all true hearted lovers,/ And hear us to the end." Doubtless this was not the earliest ballad associated with the campaign. "The March of Reform", which had been written by the Chartist leader Thomas Attwood, and was first sung at meetings in Birmingham in 1832, was adapted to be sung at women's suffrage meetings, probably before the end of the nineteenth century. It began, "God is our Guide, and in His name/ From hearth, from workshop, and from loom,/ We come, our ancient rights to claim,/ Those rights, with duties, to resume./ Then sisters, raise from sea to sea,/ The sacred watchword 'Liberty'." One version of the famous old comic song "The Two Obadiahs", the type that accommodated topical allusions, was published, probably in the 1870s/1880s, as a broadside that included the lines, "For englishmen all know what are really woman's rights,/ And ain gulled by Lydia Beckers, nor by Mrs Jacob Brights...".

The WOMEN'S SOCIAL AND POLITICAL UNION in its early days, before the split in the autumn of 1907, had published a "Votes for Women" pamphlet containing seven decidedly militant songs. They were: "International Anthem: English version" – "Arise! Oppressed of the earth" by Maude Fitzherbert; "Song of the Suffragists" – to the tune of "Hiawatha" – "There's a tramp of many feet" by Theodora MILLS; "Rise Up Women" – to the tune of "John Brown" – "Rise Up Women! For the fight is hard and long" – by Theodora Mills; "The Women's Battle Song" – to the tune of "Onward, Christian Soldiers" – "Forward sister women!" by Theodora Mills; "Women of England" – to the tune of "Men of Harlech" – "See we come with banners flying" by Theodora Mills; "In the Morning" – to the tune of "John Peel" – "Do you hear the rise of a mighty rushing sea?" by Theodora Mills; "Women, Arise!" adapted from "England, Arise" – "Sisters, Arise! The long, long night is over...". Before April 1908, that is while Campbell-Bannerman was still prime minister, an anonymous song, "Votes for Women", was in circulation, which was sung to the tune of "Bonnie Dundee" and ended with the call "Break down all barriers and let us go free,/ For we'll get 'Votes for Women' of Britain, you'll see". After May 1908 the WSPU issued another song sheet, leading with "The Women's Marseillaise", including some of the songs written by Theodora Mills, and introducing an anonymous ditty, "As I Came Through Holloway", sung to the tune of "The Keel Row", and having for its chorus, "We're wearing their colours, the green, white and purple,/ We're wearing their colours and joining in the shout;/ Back up the women, the women, the women,/ Back up the women and turn the Liberals out".

By October 1908 the revived women's suffrage campaign had inspired Miss Alicia Adelaide Needham, "the well-known composer", to write, publish, and advertise in *Votes for Women* four "Suffragette songs": "Marching On", "Daughters of England", "Fight On" and "Clipped Wings". Christianna Beake published in Sheffield a song, "The Brave Suffragette". More usually, however, the writers and composers were active members of the movement. Francis Bather of the Wimbledon WSPU wrote "Blue-Bell", "Christabel", "A Free Field" and "Freedom of Speech" *c.* January 1909. Laura Morgan-BROWNE, who had been campaigning since the end of the nineteenth century, wrote "The Purple, White & Green", to be sung to the tune of "The Wearing of the Green", which ends "For it is the grandest movement the world has ever seen,/ And we'll win the Vote for Women, wearing purple, white and green". Margaret O'Shea, sister of Norah O'SHEA of the Portsmouth NUWSS, wrote "Forward, brave and dauntless/ Daughters of the earth". Florence MACAULAY, a WSPU organizer, had written, before February 1909, "The Women's Marseillaise", setting her words, "Arise ye daughters..." to the well-known tune. The "Purple, White and Green March", with words by Reginald Pott, treasurer of the MEN'S LEAGUE FOR WOMEN'S SUFFRAGE, music by Mr Vivian Hatch, was specially composed for the 18 June 1910 WSPU procession.

The LONDON SOCIETY FOR WOMEN'S SUFFRAGE published, c. 1910, *Women's Suffrage Songs*, which included "In the Same Boat", words by H. Crawford, to the tune of "Here's to the Maiden"; "Onward" by Lady STRACHEY, to the tune of "Love will find out the way"; "Good Queen Bess" by H. Crawford, to the tune of the "Vicar of Bray"; "By and Bye" by Lady Strachey, to the tune of "Come, Lasses and Lads"; "Song for the Anti-Suffragists", to the tune of "Lady Frances Neville's Delight"; "What Women Mean to do" by H. Crawford, to the tune of "The Song of the Western Men"; "Shoulder to Shoulder" by Miss S.J. Tanner, to the tune of "Men of Harlech"; "Rule, Britannia" by Lady Strachey, to the tune of "Rule, Britannia"; "The Coming Day" by Miss S.J. Tanner, to the tune of "Hungarian Air"; "Our Hard Case" by Miss S.J. Tanner, to the tune of "Comin' thro' the Rye"; "Auld Lang Syne" by Lady Strachey, to the tune of "Auld Lang Syne".

Ethel SMYTH's "March of the Women", with words by Cicely HAMILTON, was published by Breitkopf and Hartel and played for first time in public on Saturday 21 January 1911 at a social evening at Suffolk Street Galleries to welcome those imprisoned after the events following "Black Friday", November 1910. The preview in *Votes for Women*, 20 January 1911, reported that "The fiery spirit of revolution united with religious solemnity, the all-conquering union of faith and rebellion which makes the strength of the militant movement, is expressed in Dr Smyth's Marching Song. It is at once a hymn and a call to battle". The "March of the Women" appealed to constitutionalists as well as militants. The CAMBRIDGE WOMEN'S SUFFRAGE ASSOCIATION ordered 50 copies for the June 1911 Procession and had a practice of the song at Mrs Stewart's house on 15 June. At a party given by BEDFORD WOMEN'S SUFFRAGE SOCIETY in March 1912 "A choir of ladies accompanied by the Bedford Town Band sang 'The March of the Women' at the beginning and Suffrage Songs during tea". Of Ethel Smyth's concert at Queen's Hall, 1 April 1911, which included "Songs of Sunrise", comprising "Laggard Dawn", "1910: a Medley" and "March of the Women", *Votes for Women* wrote, "For the first time this movement will be typified in music".

Laurence HOUSMAN's song "Women, Join Hands", set to music by Selwyn Lloyd, was published in aid of the suffrage movement by Messrs Bach, 1912, and in 1913 the NUWSS PILGRIMAGE inspired Henry Daw Ellis. He wrote a series of songs called, collectively, "The Suffrage Pilgrims" (sonnets 9d per doz from the Author). Sonnet IV was titled, "The North-Western Pilgrimage" and VI was "To a Woman Chain Maker". The Watling Street Route Committee chose for their theme tune, "Song of the Suffrage Pilgrims", set to the tune of the "Song of the Western Men". Harriet Blessley, a participant in the Pilgrimage from Portsmouth, noted *en route* that they sang "Suffrage Song" and the "Pilgrim's Song".

The women's suffrage movement appears to have inspired only three popular, that is, commercially published, songs. The earliest is "Bother The Men", written by Henry Walker and published by Metzler & Co., which probably dates from the 1880s. It includes the lines, "Only let Government bring in a bill,/ To give us the franchise and have it we will!/ Women we'll send into Parliament then,/ O ye shall see how they'll bother the men". A "Humourous One or Two-Step" by Montague Ewing was published by Phillips and Page in 1913 and shows on its cover jolly suffragettes, in purple, white and green. The most commercially successful song, "That Ragtime Suffragette" by Harry Williams and Nat D. Ayer, was American, published by B. Feldman, and seen and heard on Broadway in the Ziegfeld Follies, 1913. With its catchy tune and memorable lines, "Oh dear! Oh dear! Just look, look, look who's here... That Ragtime Suffragette. Ragging with bombshells and ragging with bricks, Hagging and nagging in politics", it was sufficiently successful to inspire two British records, one by The Three Rascals (Jumbo Records) and the other by Warwick Green (Phoenix). Comic songs titled "The Suffragette" were recorded by Harry Nelson on the Regal label in 1914 and by Will Evans for Zonophone; it is not clear whether or not these were the same song. Another song, "The Suffragee" (it being explained that this is the term for one who suffers from a suffragette) was recorded on Homochord by Jock Mills, a Scottish comedian.

Most of the suffrage-inspired "poems" published in the suffrage journals were merely ditties to mark an occasion and, apart from their lack of musical accompaniment, differ little from the rhymes above. Laurence Housman's "Woman This and Woman That", a parody of Kipling's "Tommy" ("For it's woman this, and woman that, and 'Woman, wait outside'/ But it's 'Listen to the Ladies!' when it suits your Party's side") was the best-known of this type and a staple of suffrage entertainments. Eva GORE-BOOTH, although feminism runs through her work, did not write many overtly "suffrage" poems, although "Women's Trades on the Embankment" was inspired by the disappointment of the deputation to Campbell-Bannerman in May 1906. *A Book of Verses of J.R.*, by John Russell, published by the Garden City Press in 1914 (probably, therefore, paid for by the author) contained some suffrage verses: "The March of the Women, February 9th 1907", "Parliament Square 20–25, 1913" and "Euston Road, June 14, 1913". *Holloway Jingles*, edited by N. John, and published by the Glasgow Branch of the WSPU in 1912–13 was born of shared prison experience. The title was well chosen, the poems themselves a still-intriguing mixture of reflective introspection and shared hardship lightened by limerick. Sylvia Pankhurst's collection of prison poems, *Writ on Cold Slate*, was published in 1922.

Archival source: Helen Blackburn Collection, Girton College; Papers of the Cambridge Women's Suffrage Association, Cambridge County Record Office; Documents relating to the Bedford Society for Women's Suffrage, Bedfordshire Record Office.

Bibliography: G. Norquay, *Voices & Votes: A Literary Anthology of the Women's Suffrage Campaign*, 1995; E. Wood, "Performing rights: a sonography of women's suffrage", *Musical Quarterly*, 4, 1995; D. Tyler-Bennett, "Suffrage and poetry: radical women's voices", in M. Joannou and J. Purvis (eds), *The Women's Suffrage Movement*, 1998.

SOUTH SHIELDS (NUWSS) In 1913 the society was a member of the NORTH-EASTERN FEDERATION OF THE NATIONAL UNION OF WOMEN'S SUFFRAGE SOCIETIES. Secretary (1913) Miss M.E. Sedcole, 17 Westoe Road, South Shields, Co. Durham.

SOUTH SHIELDS (WFL) Secretary (1913) Mrs Revel, 13 Hepscott Terrace, South Shields, Co. Durham.

SOUTH WALES AND MONMOUTH FEDERATION OF THE NATIONAL UNION OF WOMEN'S SUFFRAGE SOCIETIES In 1913 the Federation comprised the societies at ABERGAVENNY, ABERYSTWYTH, BARGOED, BRECON, BRIDGEND, CARDIFF, CARMARTHEN, KIDWELLY, LAMPETER, LLANELLY, MERTHYR, PONTYPRIDD, RHONDDA FACH, SWANSEA and the FARMERS DISTRICT. Decidedly pro-Liberal, the Federation was opposed to the NUWSS Election Fighting Fund policy. The Federation was wound up at the end of 1919. Honorary secretary (1912) Miss Janet Price, 159 Newport Road, Cardiff; organizing secretary (1913) Mrs Streeter.

SOUTHAMPTON (WSPU) Secretary (1913) Miss Cumberland, Naini Tal, College Place, Southampton, Hampshire.

SOUTHAMPTON Women's Suffrage Society Founded in 1870 as a branch of the MANCHESTER NATIONAL SOCIETY FOR WOMEN'S SUFFRAGE, when its secretary was Mrs Sawyer of Thanet House, Bevois Road. In 1872 the Southampton society associated itself with the CENTRAL COMMITTEE OF THE NATIONAL SOCIETY FOR WOMEN'S SUFFRAGE.

The National Union of Women's Suffrage Societies, Southampton Branch, was in existence by 1905, when Mrs Janie TERRERO chaired a drawing-room meeting for the society, which was by now a committee of the LONDON SOCIETY FOR WOMEN'S SUFFRAGE. The only extant minute book of the Southampton society covers the period 1911–14. It would appear that the Southampton society worked in association with, and was to some extent subordinate to, the PORTSMOUTH WOMEN'S SUFFRAGE SOCIETY. Norah O'SHEA was certainly a force in overseeing its activities.

In July 1911 the Southampton branch entrusted its secretary, Miss Cooper, with the production of a BANNER to be carried by the Southampton contingent in the Coronation procession. When in December 1911 H.N. BRAILSFORD was offered as a speaker for a meeting the Southampton society, although very conservative, did actually consider whether to co-operate with the WOMEN'S SOCIAL AND POLITICAL UNION in organizing the meeting. Although the idea was eventually rejected, members of WSPU and other societies were invited to attend the meeting. The society met once a month; when a visiting ORGANIZER suggested that, in order to maximize effect, meetings should be held once a fortnight, the suggestion was rejected. After the resignation of Miss Cooper in late 1911 the society does seem to recover some vigour. It was decided in December 1911 that when members represented the society outside the city their expenses should be paid, a box was taken by the society at the Albert Hall for the NUWSS mass meeting in February 1912 and, in the same month, they were addressed by Mr Lipson, the honorary secretary of the Portsmouth MEN'S LEAGUE FOR WOMEN'S SUFFRAGE. In April 1912, after the WSPU window-smashing raids, the society resolved to "send a letter of protest to the Home Secretary expressing indignation with the inhuman way he allowed the militant suffragists in prison to be treated".

In May 1912 the Southampton society resolved "not to support any new policy the Union might bring forward which would alter the Non-party basis of the Society", an indication that they were not prepared to support the NUWSS Election Fighting Fund policy. However, by February 1914, the society was pleased to join with the local ILP in canvassing voters on their attitudes to women's suffrage. After being warned, in September 1912, by Norah O'Shea that the "Anti-Suffragists" were going to concentrate their attentions on Southampton that winter, the society did organize a special campaign. They held a social evening for members in October, for which one dozen copies of *Votes for Women* was ordered. Because the local MP, Col Phillipps, did not support the women suffrage amendment to the 1913 Reform Bill, the committee of the Southampton society wrote to him, sent a deputation and then proposed that Miss O'Shea should send him some suitable literature and ask him to read it. In September 1913 Miss Godfrey's Orchestra was hired, at a cost of £2 2s, to play at a reception attended by Maude ROYDEN. The society's programme of autumn meetings also included one to be given by Mrs Kineton PARKES on tax resistance. By 1913 the society was a member of the SURREY, SUSSEX, AND HANTS FEDERATION OF THE NATIONAL UNION OF WOMEN'S SUFFRAGE SOCIETIES. Although at this time the Southampton society could not afford to rent premises to use as an office, later in the year they did take rooms at 194a Above Bar. Miss Dutton, an NUWSS organizer, spent two months from February 1914 in Southampton and conducted a "Lightning Campaign", for which Maude Royden and Muriel MATTERS were much in demand as speakers. A public meeting, for which the Southampton society had managed to secure Maude Royden, was held in April 1914; 5000 handbills were printed to publicize it. The committee of the society felt that definite progress had been made during 1913–14 and that the tone of the local press towards women's suffrage had improved. Having, on 24 July 1914, been planning the autumn suffrage campaign, two weeks later the society offered itself, as a provider of relief work, in the service of the town. The society's minute book was given to the Southampton Archives in 1977 by Miss Spencer, who had been a member of the Southampton Women's Suffrage Society in 1913, and secretary of the local Unitarian church.

Secretaries (1909) Mrs Welch, 61 Oxford St, Southampton and Miss M. Boswell, 109 Alma Road, The Avenue, Southampton; (1911) Dorothy M. Cooper; (November 1911) Miss Horton; (1913) Mrs E.E. Dowson, The Chestnuts, Sarisbury, Southampton.

Archival source: National Union of Women's Suffrage Societies, Southampton branch Minute Book, 1911–14, Southampton Archives Service.

SOUTHEND AND WESTCLIFF (WSPU) Secretary (1913) Miss N. Fripp, Beaumont, Torquay Drive, Leigh-on-Sea, Essex.

SOUTHEND AND WESTCLIFF-ON-SEA (NUWSS) In 1913 the society was a member of the EASTERN COUNTIES FEDERATION OF THE NATIONAL UNION OF WOMEN'S SUFFRAGE SOCIETIES. Secretary (1913) Mrs Webb, Briar Cottage, Salisbury Road, Leigh-on-Sea, Essex.

SOUTHPORT branch of the UNITED SUFFRAGISTS Formed in 1915. Honorary secretary: Mrs Shipman, 14 Manchester Road, Southport, Lancashire.

SOUTHPORT (WSPU) Organizer (1910) Miss Dora MARSDEN, 13 Nevill Street, Southport. Secretary (1913) Miss G. Duxfield, 13 Ash Street, Southport. Office: 1 Post Office Avenue, Lord Street, Southport, Lancashire.

SOUTHPORT Women's Suffrage Society Joined the NATIONAL UNION OF WOMEN'S SUFFRAGE SOCIETIES in 1898 and by 1913 was a member of the WEST LANCS, WEST CHESHIRE, AND NORTH WALES FEDERATION. Secretary (1900) Mrs Thew, 7 Trafalgar Road, Birkdale, Southport, Lancashire; (1913) Miss Margaret Bickett, 98 Forest Road, Southport, Lancashire.

SOUTHPORT GUILD OF THE UNREPRESENTED Founded in 1886 by women rate-payers keen to draw attention to the question of women's disenfranchised status. The Guild started by holding discussions in the afternoon, for the benefit of women who were unable or unwilling to go out at night, but interest was such that soon public meetings were arranged, the first of which was chaired by the mayor and attended by 500 to 600 people. In 1887 meetings were addressed by Lydia BECKER, in January, and Eva MCLAREN, in May. Secretary (1887) Mrs Sherbrooke, 17 Alexandra Road, Southport, Lancashire.

SOUTHWELL (NUWSS) In 1913 the society was a member of the MIDLANDS (EAST) FEDERATION OF THE NATIONAL UNION OF WOMEN'S SUFFRAGE SOCIETIES. Secretary (1913) Miss V. Smith, Vicars Court, Southwell, Nottinghamshire.

SOUTH-WESTERN FEDERATION OF THE NATIONAL UNION OF WOMEN'S SUFFRAGE SOCIETIES Honorary secretary (1912) Mrs Penry, Heles School, Exeter, Devonshire.

SOUTHWOLD (NUWSS) In 1913 the society was a member of the EASTERN COUNTIES FEDERATION OF THE NATIONAL UNION OF WOMEN'S SUFFRAGE SOCIETIES. Secretary (1909) Miss Kate Kirton, The Bungalow, Southwold, Suffolk; (1913) *pro tem* Mrs Charles Toster, Southwold, Suffolk.

SOWERBY BRIDGE (NUWSS) Founded in 1904 and by 1913 was a member of the WEST RIDING FEDERATION OF THE NATIONAL UNION OF WOMEN'S SUFFRAGE SOCIETIES. Secretary (1913) Mrs Johnson, School House, Sowerby, Sowerby Bridge, Yorkshire.

SPECIAL APPEAL COMMITTEE Formed in 1892 for the sole purpose of collecting signatures for "An Appeal from Women of All Parties and All Classes" to be placed before parliament. The idea originated as a by-product of the near success in 1892 of Sir Albert Rollit's "widows and spinsters" bill. Inspired by the closeness of the defeat, a meeting was held in Westminster Town Hall, Isabella FORD and Mrs FAWCETT being among the speakers, at which it was decided to organize the appeal in the belief that parliament could not be unmoved by such evidence of large-scale united support in favour of the enfranchisement of women. It was thought that conventional petitions had become so commonplace that little notice was taken of them.

The following groups combined to organize the Appeal: the CENTRAL COMMITTEE OF THE NATIONAL SOCIETY FOR WOMEN'S SUFFRAGE, the CENTRAL NATIONAL SOCIETY FOR WOMEN'S SUFFRAGE, the WOMEN'S LIBERAL FEDERATION, the PRIMROSE LEAGUE, the WOMEN'S LIBERAL UNIONIST ASSOCIATION, the World's Women's Christian Temperance Union and the British Women's Temperance Association. Among the members of the Special Appeal Committee were Mrs Fawcett, Lady Frances BALFOUR, Helen BLACKBURN, Lady KNIGHTLEY, Eva MCLAREN, Mrs MASSINGBERD, Clara MORDAN, Mona TAYLOR, the Countess of ABERDEEN, Priscilla Bright MCLAREN, Jessie METHVEN, Flora and Louisa STEVENSON and Eliza WIGHAM.

The Appeal opened by stating, "Many of the women who sign this appeal differ in opinion on other political questions, but all are of one mind that the continued denial of the franchise to women, while it is at the same time being gradually extended amongst men, is at once unjust and expedient." It drew attention to the fact that women's lack of enfranchisement "In the factory and workshop... places power to restrict women's work in the hands of men who are working alongside of women whom they too often treat as rivals rather than as fellow-workers." Small books in which were to be collected the signatures of women of all classes and conditions were circulated throughout the country. When they were returned to the Appeal office they were sorted by parliamentary constituency and pasted onto sheets, so as to be formed into volumes county by county. One hundred and forty meetings were held, in drawing rooms, cottages and public halls and 3500 people helped to collect the 248 000 signatures by the agreed deadline, 31 March 1894. Esther ROPER, the newly appointed secretary to the NORTH OF ENGLAND SOCIETY FOR WOMEN'S SUFFRAGE, had carried the Special Appeal to women working in the cotton trade in Lancashire and Cheshire and continued to concentrate on this aspect of the suffrage campaign.

There had been much discussion as to how the Appeal should be drawn to the attention of MPs. It was finally agreed that the Appeal would be presented as an accompaniment to a Registration Bill to which Viscount Wolmer had tabled an amendment to include women. The Speaker gave permission for the Appeal to be displayed in the Library of the House of Commons. However, the Registration Bill did not proceed and the Appeal was laid to one side to await a more propitious occasion.

This came when the Appeal was revived to accompany Mr Faithfull Begg's "Parliamentary Franchise (Extension to Women) Bill in 1896, by which time the number of signatures had increased to 257 796. The Speaker now withheld his consent to the use of the Commons' Library and the Appeal was, instead, displayed in Westminster Hall on 19 May, the day before the bill was due to be debated. This debate did not take place; the day was, instead, given up to government business. Although the suffrage societies were disappointed by the lack of response to the work of the Appeal Committee, the knowledge that they had combined successfully on such a project led the Central Committee and Central National Society to agree to organize a Special Fund to pay for a lecture campaign during autumn and winter of 1896. They also formed a joint parliamentary sub-committee to lobby for the Faithfull Begg bill. All this joint activity led to the holding of a conference in Birmingham in October 1896 at which it was agreed to divide the country into areas of influence and, eventually, in 1897, to the formation of the NATIONAL UNION OF WOMEN'S SUFFRAGE SOCIETIES. As to the Special Appeal, the EDINBURGH NATIONAL SOCIETY asked for the Scottish signatures to be returned to them, the Central Committee kept those of the Home Counties, and the Central National those of Wales and the Metropolitan constituencies.

Archival source: Minutes of the Central National Committee, 1896 to April 1897 (miscatalogued as minutes of the Women's Franchise League), in The Papers of Sylvia Pankhurst, Internationaal Instituut voor Sociale Geschiedenis, Amsterdam.

Bibliography: H. Blackburn, *Women's Suffrage: A Record of the Women's Suffrage Movement in the British Isles*, 1902.

SPENDER, EMILY (1841–1922) Novelist, daughter of Dr John Cottle Spender, who ran a long-established family medical practice in Bath. She was a cousin of Crabb Robinson the diarist; her brother-in-law William Saunders was a radical politician, supporter of Henry George and founder of the *Eastern Morning News* and of the *Western Morning News*, of which he made her brother, Edward Spender, editor. Edward Spender subscribed to the CENTRAL COMMITTEE OF THE NATIONAL SOCIETY FOR WOMEN'S SUFFRAGE in 1875. One nephew, J.A. Spender, became editor of the *Westminster Gazette* and another, Harold Spender, was a journalist on the *Daily News* and the author of an article, "The Revolt of the Women", published in support of the women's cause in the *Albany Review*, 1908. In 1871 Emily Spender was honorary secretary of the newly founded BATH COMMITTEE OF THE NATIONAL SOCIETY FOR WOMEN'S SUFFRAGE and a member of the executive committee of the CENTRAL COMMITTEE OF THE NATIONAL SOCIETY FOR WOMEN'S SUFFRAGE. In the same year she published anonymously, or at least as "By the Author of *Son and Heir*", a novel, *Restored*, the printed dedication of which runs, "To L.S.A. My Honoured Chief and Dear Friend, who is all that I aspire to be, and who has, unconsciously, inspired much that I have written." *Restored* treats of the women's cause (*see* NOVELS) and "L.S.A." was undoubtedly Lilias Sophia Ashworth (*see* Lilias Sophia HALLETT) who lived in Bath and was already an active committee member of the BRISTOL AND WEST OF ENGLAND SOCIETY. In 1884 Emily Spender signed the Letter from Ladies to Members of Parliament from women heads of households in support of their inclusion in the government's franchise bill. In 1885 she put her name to a petition to the House of Lords in support of the Women's Suffrage Bill.

In 1890 it appears to have been the attention of Emily Spender's brother, Dr John Kent Spender, surgeon to the Mineral Hospital at Bath, that Lydia BECKER sought when in need of treatment shortly before her death. Emily Spender's sister-in-law, Mrs Litz [Lilian] Spender, wife of Dr Spender and mother of J.A. Spender, also wrote novels, attended a conference organized by the Central Committee in 1893 and was an advocate of furthering women's employment opportunities. In 1908 Mary BLATHWAYT attended a meeting at which Emily Spender read a paper on "Women's Work and Wages". In 1911 Emily Spender was the co-compiler of *The Patriot's Year Book*, which comprises patriotic verse, culled almost entirely from male poets, and was printed by the Western Morning News. Emily Spender spent much of her later life in Italy; one of her novels, *A Soldier for a Day*, 1901, is subtitled "A Story of the Italian War of Independence", and *The Law Breakers*, 1903, paints the lamentable position of a middle-class, middle-aged unmarried woman trapped at home with her mother in Bath, until death and inheritance release her to discover the pleasures of Vicenza.

Address: (1922) 13 Springfield Place, Bath.
Photograph: in Helen Blackburn Collection, Girton College Archives.

SPIRITUAL MILITANCY LEAGUE Sent as its representative to the congress of the INTERNATIONAL WOMAN SUFFRAGE ALLIANCE at Budapest in 1913 Margaret Wetzlar Coit, daughter of Adela COIT. The League was still in existence in 1916.
Address: (1913) 46 Queen's Road, Bayswater, London W.

SPONG FAMILY Dora Spong (later Mrs Beedham) (1879–1969) was born in Wandsworth into a Liberal family. By the time she was 24 she held certificates as a sanitary inspector and as a midwife, had worked among the poor in Tottenham and Battersea and had become a vegetarian and interested in socialism. She joined the WOMEN'S SOCIAL AND POLITICAL UNION in 1908 and was arrested for obstruction after taking part in the deputation to the House of Commons on 30 June. She was sentenced to one month's imprisonment, but became ill and was released before the end of her term. She was arrested on "Black Friday" in November 1910 in Parliament Square, but along with the other women so arrested, she was discharged. She took part in the WSPU window-smashing campaign in March 1912 and was sentenced to two months' imprisonment, with hard labour. Dora Spong was married by November 1910; her husband was sympathetic to the cause and she eventually became the mother of a son and a daughter.

Florence Spong was "a weaver and artistic dressmaker" and had studied lace-making in Spain and wood-carving under Herkomer. She was arrested, accused of stone throwing, after taking part in the WSPU deputation on 29 June 1909, and sentenced to a month's imprisonment. She went on hunger strike and was released early from Holloway. In November 1910 she was sentenced to two months' imprisonment (without the option of a fine) after taking part in the stone throwing that resulted from the disgust felt by WSPU members at the way women, who had included her sister, Dora, were treated in Parliament Square on "Black Friday".

Irene Spong advertised as a singer in the pages of *Votes for Women*, gave concerts for the cause and gave lessons to WSPU members in singing and voice production. Another sister, Annie, and their mother, attended WSPU demonstrations and processions.

Address: Spong family: (1906) 34 Prince's Avenue, Muswell Hill, London N; (1909) 66 Adelaide Road, London NW; Dora Beedham (1951) 90 Brim Hill, Finchley, London N; (1969) Langmead, Pirbright, Woking, Surrey.
Archival source: The Suffragette Fellowship Collection, Museum of London.

SPROSON, EMMA, MRS (1867–1936) Born in West Bromwich, worked as a "half-timer" from the age of 9, left school when she was 13 and then worked in domestic service. She took the trouble to educate herself and become articulate. She married Frank Sproson in 1896 and had three children. Her husband, a postman and artist, was secretary of the Wolverhampton branch of the Independent Labour Party and was proud and supportive of her. Emma Sproson, who for 20 years supported the constitutional suffrage movement, was also a member of the ILP. In October 1906 her husband invited Mrs PANKHURST to address a meeting of the branch at which Emma acted as chairman. Mrs Pankhurst stayed overnight with the Sprosons and Emma subsequently joined the WOMEN'S SOCIAL AND POLITICAL UNION. She waged a campaign, espousing the cause of women's suffrage, through the columns of the local papers. On 13 February 1907, having left at home two young children, one of whom was only six months old, she attended the meeting of the Women's Parliament organized by the WSPU in Caxton Hall. She was arrested and sentenced to 14 days' imprisonment. Her autobiographical notes give details of her prison experiences. She was suffering from engorged breasts because she had been forced so abruptly to stop breast feeding; she obviously had not expected to be away from home for so long. On 10 September 1908 she sent Edith How MARTYN a postcard, "In memoriam of 13 Feb. 1907". Although now knowing what might be the result, in March 1907 she took part in another deputation from Caxton Hall and this time was sentenced to one month's imprisonment. On her release from prison on 20 April she attended, and spoke at, the celebratory lunch held at the Holborn Restaurant. On her return to Wolverhampton she held, with Jennie BAINES, a meeting in the market place, and then spent the rest of the year touring Black Country towns, speaking on the subject of sweated labour and the need for women to obtain a fair wage for their work.

After the break with the WSPU, Emma Sproson joined the WOMEN'S FREEDOM LEAGUE, becoming the chairman of the Wolverhampton branch, and by 1 February 1908 she was a member of the national executive, regularly attending meetings in London. She undertook extensive speaking tours, including ones in Wales and Scotland. Alexia Jack wrote in the *Vote*, 29 July 1911, that the flourishing condition of the WFL's Edinburgh branch was largely due to the influence of Emma Sproson. She had the distinction of being summonsed on a charge of pavement-chalking, apparently the only time that the law was invoked, and was fined 5/–.

In May 1911, as a member of the TAX RESISTANCE LEAGUE, Emma Sproson was sentenced to seven days' imprisonment in Stafford Gaol for refusing to pay for a dog licence. After she went on hunger strike she was reclassified from being a third-division to a first-division prisoner. Her dog, however, was shot by the police. On 18 November she took part in a deputation to the prime minister with Charlotte DESPARD and three other members of the WFL. However, by April 1912 Emma Sproson had tired of what she perceived to be Charlotte Despard's autocratic leadership, and she resigned from the national executive of the WFL. Thereafter she had no further involvement in suffrage politics and instead turned her attention to improving social conditions. In 1919 and 1920 she stood, unsuccessfully, as a Labour Party candidate in the local council elections. She was finally elected in Wolverhampton in 1921, and was re-elected in 1924. After standing as an Independent, again unsuccessfully, in 1927, she retired from politics.

Address: (1913) Kelmscott, Wolverhampton, Staffordshire; (1936) 56 Castlecroft Road, Finchfield, Wolverhampton, Staffordshire.
Photograph: in G.J. Barnsby, *Votes for Women: The Struggle for the Vote in the Black Country, 1900–1918*, 1995.
Archival source: Emma Sproson's Papers in Wolverhampton Central Library.
Bibliography: S.P. Walters, *Emma Sproson: A Black Country Suffragette*, unpublished MA thesis, University of Leicester, 1993; G. Barnsby, *Votes for Women: The Struggle for the Vote in the Black Country, 1900–1918*, 1995.

STACY, ETHEL MAUD, DR (1877–1938) After qualifying in medicine in London in 1904 she had set up practice in Bedford by 1907–8. It was at her house in 1908 that the first meeting was held to discuss the formation of a BEDFORD SOCIETY FOR WOMEN'S SUFFRAGE. She held positions of both honorary secretary and honorary treasurer of the society, and was still a leading member when the society agreed to dissolve in 1918. She was in practice with Dora MASON, to whom in her will she left her midwifery bag and instruments, and at the time of her death ran a nursing home from her address in Bedford. In 1934 she was president of the Bedford Soroptimist Club. In her will she left china and glass to Dr Jane Walker, close friend of Millicent Garrett FAWCETT.

Address: 34 Kimbolton Road, Bedford, Bedfordshire.

STAFFORD (NUWSS) In 1913 the society was a member of the MIDLAND (WEST) FEDERATION OF THE NATIONAL UNION OF WOMEN'S SUFFRAGE SOCIETIES. Secretary (1913) Miss G. Sproston, 31 Newport Road, Stafford, Staffordshire.

STAMFORD HILL (WFL) Secretary (1913) Mrs Thomson, 7 East Bank, Stamford Hill, London N.

STANSFELD, CAROLINE ASHURST, MRS (c. 1816–85) Unitarian, daughter of William Ashurst, who was a solicitor, a member, with P.A. Taylor (see Clementia TAYLOR), of the National Association for the Promoting of the Political and Social Improvement of the People, patron of Robert Owen, Garibaldi, George HOLYOAKE and all radical causes of the mid-nineteenth century. She was the sister of Emilie VENTURI and Matilda Ashurst BIGGS. In 1844 when she married James Stansfeld, another radical, the wedding was conducted by W.J. Fox. In 1851 Stansfeld was a member, with P.A. Taylor, David MASSON and Francis NEWMAN, of The Friends of Italy. In 1859 he was elected Liberal MP for Halifax. Caroline Stansfeld was a member of the committee of the Ladies' London Emancipation when it was formed in 1863. In 1866 she was a member of the first general committee of Elizabeth Garrett's (see Elizabeth Garrett ANDERSON) St Mary's Dispensary for Women and Children.

In 1866 Caroline Stansfeld signed the women's suffrage petition and joined the LONDON NATIONAL SOCIETY FOR WOMEN'S SUFFRAGE in 1867. In July 1869 her husband was one of the speakers at the first public meeting held in London to discuss women's enfranchisement. However, as an active member of the campaign for the Repeal of the Contagious Diseases Act, she broke with the London National and in 1871 became a member of the executive committee of the newly founded CENTRAL COMMITTEE OF THE NATIONAL SOCIETY FOR WOMEN'S SUFFRAGE.

Address: (1866) 35 Thurloe Square, London SW; (1885) Stoke Lodge, Hyde Park, London SW.
Bibliography: F. Richards (ed.), *Mazzini's Letters to an English Family, 1920–22*; J.L. and B. Hammond, *James Stansfeld: A Victorian Champion of Sex Equality*, 1932.

STEINTHAL, SAMUEL ALFRED, REV. (1826–1910) Unitarian, the son of a German merchant who left Germany in 1809 and became a naturalized British subject. In 1849, after an engineering apprenticeship, he entered Manchester New College to prepare for the ministry. When qualified he went as minister to Bridgwater, which was then a centre of refugee Poles and Hungarians. He sympathized strongly with the anti-slavery movement in America and was in touch with its leaders. In 1857 he moved to Liverpool and in 1864 to Manchester, where, in 1870, he became the colleague of the Rev. William Gaskell at the Cross Street Chapel. By 1864 Steinthal was a member of the Council of the National Association for the Promotion of Social Science. He also became the local secretary for the National Education League, was chairman of the Manchester Geographical Society and a supporter of the Froebel movement. He was honorary secretary of the General Hospital and Dispensary for Sick Children at Pendlebury, to which Louis BORCHARDT acted as physician. In January 1867 Rev. Steinthal was present at the meeting at which the women's suffrage society in Manchester was refounded and he and his wife Sarah (c. 1831–1902), who had signed the 1866 women's suffrage petition, were members of the Manchester Committee for the Enfranchisement of Women, which soon became the MANCHESTER NATIONAL SOCIETY FOR WOMEN'S SUFFRAGE. After Mathilde Kyllmann resigned as treasurer to the society at the end of 1868, in support of her sister-in-law Philippine KYLLMANN, and despite Lydia BECKER's preference for Ursula BRIGHT, as a woman, to take her place, Rev. Steinthal succeeded to the position, which he held, nearly continuously, until 1905. In 1871 he was a member of the executive committee of the newly founded CENTRAL COMMITTEE OF THE NATIONAL SOCIETY FOR WOMEN'S SUFFRAGE. In 1882 he wrote, "I feel very deeply that until woman's citizenship is recognized, by her admission to the vote, we shall not carry the thorough measures of reform which are needed to save the world from the wretched system of unequal balances with which human actions are weighed". Between 1889 and 1891, having resigned as treasurer of the Manchester National Society, he was a member of the executive committee of the CENTRAL NATIONAL SOCIETY FOR WOMEN'S SUFFRAGE. In 1894 he was a supporter of the WOMEN'S EMANCIPATION UNION. In 1905 he resigned from both his position of treasurer and as a member of the NORTH OF ENGLAND SOCIETY, in support of Christabel PANKHURST. It is not clear whether he then joined the WOMEN'S SOCIAL AND POLITICAL UNION; the brief mention of his death in *Votes for Women*, 13 May 1910, does not claim him as a member.

Address: (1872) 107 Upper Brook Street, Manchester; (1882) The Limes, Nelson Street, Manchester; (1889) Heathfield, 40 Wilmslow Road, Withington, Manchester.
Photograph: in *Manchester Faces and Places*, 1891.

STEPHEN, JESSIE (1894–?, post-1977) Born in Glasgow, one of 11 children of a tailor. After a period as a pupil-teacher she was forced to leave school when her family's finances could no longer support her and went to work in domestic service in Glasgow. She was a member of a Socialist Sunday School before joining the Independent Labour Party and the WOMEN'S SOCIAL AND POLITICAL UNION in 1910. In January 1912 she was the youngest member of the Glasgow delegation that took part in the WSPU Deputation of Working Women to Lloyd George. In Glasgow she took part, surreptitiously, in the militant campaign. She described how she "walked from my place of service in my uniform and dropped the acid container in the pillar-box and made my way back without interruption by anyone. A few minutes later the contents were aflame."

During the First World War she was in London, working with Sylvia PANKHURST and the EAST LONDON FEDERATION OF SUFFRAGETTES, organizing for them a branch in Hackney. She then went to Lancashire, where in 1917 she set up for the Workers' Suffrage Federation (as the ELFS had become) in Nelson. She returned to East London where she worked as an ILP organizer. After failing to be selected as an ILP parliamentary candidate, she was elected as a Labour borough councillor for Bermondsey in November 1922.

Archival source: B. Harrison taped interview with Jessie Stephen, 1 July 1977, Fawcett Library.
Bibliography: J. Stephen, "Memories of militancy", in E. Malos *et al.*, *Enough (or Not Enough)?: A Look at Woman's Situation*, no date (1970s?); L. Leneman, *A Guid Cause: The Women's Suffrage Movement in Scotland*, 1991.

STEPHENSON, [SARA] JESSIE (1873–1966) Born in Louth, Lincolnshire, she records in her autobiographical manuscript, written for the SUFFRAGETTE FELLOWSHIP, that "Despite her parents' rigid views that a woman's sphere must be limited to domesticity [she] gained their consent to spend two years in Germany and afterwards in France". She paid her way by teaching English and writes that she was for a time secretary to Josephine Butler. In 1907 she gave £50 to the WOMEN'S SOCIAL AND POLITICAL UNION and at the end of June was campaigning, with Nellie Alma MARTEL, Mrs PANKHURST and Mary GAWTHORPE, for the WSPU at the Jarrow by-election. On 21 June 1908 she was the chief marshall of the Paddington section of the WSPU rally in Hyde Park, speaking from platform 20. She describes how she prayed the night before that the day would be fine and that "my milliner and dressmaker took endless pains with my attire. A white lacy muslin dress, white shoes and stockings and gloves and, like an order, across the breast, the broad band in purple, white and green emblazoned 'Votes for Women', a white shady hat trimmed with white." She also had "two grand pendants – one 'Chief Marshall' and the other 'Speaker' – all very grand". A few days later she was chosen to take part in a WSPU deputation to the House of Commons, and she relates that she managed to enter the House of Commons, and almost succeeded in entering the Central Hall. She was not, however, among the women arrested on this occasion. She continued working for the WSPU, speaking at meetings around London. In January 1910 she contributed £5 to the WSPU general election fund and in November 1910 was arrested after breaking a window to protest at the way women had been treated in Parliament Square on "Black Friday". She was sentenced to one month's imprisonment and from Holloway sent a scribbled note to Margaret Travers SYMONS, asking for "some news of the outside world – carefully concealed either in a [?] or book. We may have no newspapers or letters or anything – at this time too!! I believe there is f.f. [forcible feeding] going on here, Love S. Jessie Stephenson." The chaplain in Holloway obtained for her, at her specific request, a copy of *Lola Montez*. At the Christmas luncheon held on 23 December for the prisoners on their release Jessie Stephenson sat next to Christabel PANKHURST, on whom she obviously doted. Her speech, "Thank God for Mrs Pankhurst", was reported in *Votes for Women*, 30 December 1910. In 1911 she went as a WSPU ORGANIZER to Manchester and there, in April, organized the census night protest. It seems that, in her absence, Christabel Pankhurst rented Jessie Stephenson's flat in Staple Inn.

Address: (1963) 3 Alexandra Road, Sheringham, Norfolk.
Archival source: The Suffragette Fellowship Collection, Museum of London.

STERLING, [LILIAN] BERTHA, MRS (c. 1845–1906)

Daughter of the artist Frank Stone, who was, with Clementia TAYLOR, in the 1840s involved with the Whittington Club and was art tutor to Eliza Ashurst, the elder sister of Matilda Ashurst BIGGS, Caroline STANSFELD and Emilie VENTURI. Her brother, Marcus Stone, was one of the most popular of the Victorian genre painters. In 1868 Bertha Stone married an artist, Edward Sterling, son of the poet John Sterling, who had been a loyal friend to John Stuart MILL and Harriet TAYLOR. Edward Sterling had been a member of the committee supporting Mill's election at Westminster in 1865. In 1878 the Sterlings commissioned Alfred Waterhouse to build for them a house, later to be described by Pesvner in *Buildings of England* as embodying "Gothic gloom". Moncure Conway in *Travels in South Kensington*, 1882, however, singles out Bertha Sterling's house for its aesthetic qualities and Morris wallpaper. She was a member of the CENTRAL COMMITTEE OF THE NATIONAL SOCIETY FOR WOMEN'S SUFFRAGE at its formation in 1871, remaining, after the split in 1888, a member of its executive committee. By 1899 Mrs Sterling was treasurer of the CENTRAL AND EAST OF ENGLAND SOCIETY and, after the amalgamation of this society with the CENTRAL AND WEST OF ENGLAND SOCIETY in 1900, remained treasurer of the resulting CENTRAL SOCIETY until her death. By 1903 she was a member of the executive committee of the NATIONAL UNION OF WOMEN'S SUFFRAGE SOCIETIES and in 1905, with her daughter, Frances STERLING, was a delegate to the NUWSS annual convention. Her sister, the artist Ellen Stone, signed the 1866 women's suffrage petition, in 1889 was a member of the general committee of the Central Committee, in 1897 was one of the initiators of the founding of the National Union of Women's Suffrage Societies and in 1900 was honorary secretary of the South Kensington branch of the Central Society.

Address: (1871) 45 Bedford Gardens, Camden Hill, London W; (1876) 38 Sheffield Terrace, London W.
Bibliography: E. Clayton, *English Female Artists*, 1876.

STERLING, FRANCES MARY (1869–1943)

Born in London, daughter of Edward and Bertha STERLING. She followed in the family's artistic footsteps and from 1893 until 1900 she exhibited at the Royal Academy genre paintings with such titles as *A Singing Lesson* and *Grandmamma's Picture Book*. She does not appear to have exhibited anywhere after 1900 and from 1902 devoted herself entirely to the cause of women's suffrage. In 1897 she had prepared an allegorical design representing the progress of women, which provided the framework for an "address to the Queen" submitted by the CENTRAL COMMITTEE OF THE NATIONAL SOCIETY FOR WOMEN'S SUFFRAGE on the occasion of Victoria's Jubilee. From 1903 until 1908 Frances Sterling was a member of the executive of the CENTRAL SOCIETY (renamed in 1907 the LONDON SOCIETY FOR WOMEN'S SUFFRAGE), from 1903 until 1909 she was joint honorary secretary of the NATIONAL UNION OF WOMEN'S SUFFRAGE SOCIETIES (for some of the time as second honorary secretary to Frances Hardcastle and then to Edith Dimock) and after 1909 was a member of its executive committee. She stood in the election for honorary secretary again in January 1911, but was defeated by Kathleen COURTNEY.

Frances Sterling attended the INTERNATIONAL WOMAN SUFFRAGE ALLIANCE in Amsterdam in 1908. She travelled round the country as a speaker for the NUWSS. In May 1907 Mary BLATHWAYT attended in Bath a women's suffrage meeting addressed by Frances Sterling and confided to her diary that "She is very nice looking and spoke very well". In 1909 Frances Sterling was the speaker at the first public meeting held by the BEDFORD WOMEN'S SUFFRAGE SOCIETY. She was president of the Falmouth branch of the NUWSS, in 1913 was chief speaker for the West of England contingent of the PILGRIMAGE, a member of the executive of the SURREY, SUSSEX, AND HAMPSHIRE FEDERATION and of the Election Fighting Fund.

In 1910 Frances Sterling was a member of the executive committee of the CHURCH LEAGUE FOR WOMEN'S SUFFRAGE and in that year the inaugural meeting of that society's Kensington branch was held at her house. She was a peripatetic speaker for this society as well as for the NUWSS. In 1912 she spoke at a meeting of the CLWS in Bromley, and at a public meeting, organized by the GLASGOW AND WEST OF SCOTLAND ASSOCIATION FOR WOMEN'S SUFFRAGE, on "The Religious Aspect of the Woman's Suffrage Movement".

During the First World War she was treasurer of the Maternity Unit for Refugees in Russia and by 1923, until 1935, was treasurer of the International Woman Suffrage Alliance. In 1934 she was a vice-president and a member of the executive committee of the National Council for Equal Citizenship.

Address: (1910) 38 Sheffield Terrace, Kensington, London W; (1926, 1943) Home Wood, Upper Hartfield, Sussex.

STEVENSON FAMILY Flora Clift Stevenson (1840–1905) was the younger daughter of Jane and James Stevenson, senior partner in the Jarrow Chemical Company. With her sister Louisa, she spent her childhood in South Shields before the family moved to Edinburgh. She was educated privately and at classes of the Edinburgh Association for the University Education of Women. In 1866 she signed the women's suffrage petition. In 1872, at the first elections for which women were eligible, she was elected to the Edinburgh School Board, and held the seat until her death. She acted as convenor of some of the most important committees of her Board, often travelling to London to transact parliamentary and other business. In 1900, the first woman to be so, Flora Stevenson was unanimously elected chairman of the Board. In 1901 she was selected as the only woman to sit on the committee set up in Scotland to consider the provisions of the the 1898 Inebriates' Act. She was a member of the CENTRAL COMMITTEE OF THE NATIONAL SOCIETY FOR WOMEN'S SUFFRAGE on its formation in 1871, subscribed to the EDINBURGH NATIONAL SOCIETY FOR WOMEN'S SUFFRAGE in 1872 and in 1884 signed the Letter from Ladies to Members of Parliament, asking for the inclusion of women heads of households in the government's Franchise Bill. In 1896 Flora Stevenson was a member of the SPECIAL APPEAL COMMITTEE and was a speaker at the annual general meeting of the CENTRAL NATIONAL SOCIETY FOR WOMEN'S SUFFRAGE. In December 1902, with Lady Frances BALFOUR, Flora Stevenson spoke at the first public meeting held by the GLASGOW AND WEST OF SCOTLAND ASSOCIATION FOR WOMEN'S SUFFRAGE. The minutes of the Association record that the meeting "was very successful over 200 ladies and gentlemen being present". Flora Stevenson was also vice-president of the Edinburgh Women's Liberal Unionist Association, vice-president of the Women's Free Trade Union and vice-president of the National Union of Women Workers. She was made an honorary LLD of Edinburgh University.

Louisa Stevenson (1835–1908), elder sister of Flora, was born in Glasgow. She was a founder of the Edinburgh School of Domestic Economy and secretary of the Edinburgh Association for the University Education of Women. A practical supporter of medical and university education for women, she paid for her niece, Alice KER, to spend a year studying medicine at Berne University, and by 1877 was a member of the governing council of the London School of Medicine for Women and became a member of the managing committee of the New Hospital for Women (later the Elizabeth Garrett ANDERSON Hospital). In the 1880s Louisa Stevenson was a member of the Edinburgh Ladies' Debating Society. In 1896, with her sister, she was a member of the Special Appeal Committee. In 1897 she was the first honorary secretary of Masson Hall (named for David MASSON), the first hall of residence for women students, financed by donations from, among others, Elizabeth Garrett Anderson, Emily DAVIES and Louisa Lumsden, at Edinburgh University. Louisa Stevenson was a founding member of the CENTRAL COMMITTEE OF THE NATIONAL SOCIETY FOR WOMEN'S SUFFRAGE in 1871, subscribed to the Edinburgh National Society in 1871, and by 1899 was a member of the executive committee of the NATIONAL UNION OF WOMEN'S SUFFRAGE SOCIETIES, still holding that position in 1902. In 1902 Louisa Stevenson was a delegate from the NUWSS to the annual general meeting, held in Edinburgh, of the National Union of Women Workers. In 1906 she was a vice-president of the CENTRAL SOCIETY. She, too, received an honorary doctorate from Edinburgh University. By the terms of her will she made certain that the daughters (who included Alice Ker) of her two married sisters received double the share of her estate given to her other nieces and nephews.

The Stevenson sisters were members of a clan in which Stevensons and Andersons were closely intermingled. They were cousins of J.G.S. Anderson, who in 1871 married Elizabeth Garrett. One of their brothers was the architect J.J. Stevenson, a leading proponent of the "Queen Anne" style. It was in the office of one of his pupils, J.M. Brydon, that Rhoda and Agnes GARRETT received their architectural instruction. J.J. Stevenson was the architect of the Cambridge house of Mary WARD and of many of the new schools commissioned by the London School Board, of which Elizabeth Garrett Anderson was a member. Another of their brothers, J.C. Stevenson, was Liberal MP for Morpeth, 1868–75, and a parliamentary supporter of women's suffrage. His father-in-law, Rev. James Anderson, conducted Elizabeth Garrett's marriage service.

Address: (1866, 1908) 13 Randolph Crescent, Edinburgh.
Portrait: of Flora Stevenson by Alexander Roche, presented to her in 1904, and bequeathed by her to the Scottish National Portrait Gallery.
Photograph: of Flora Stevenson in Helen Blackburn Collection, Girton College Archives; of Louisa Stevenson in T. Begg, *The Excellent Women*, 1994.
Bibliography: T. Begg, *The Excellent Women: The Origins and History of Queen Margaret College*, 1994.

STIRLING committee of the NATIONAL SOCIETY FOR WOMEN'S SUFFRAGE   Formed in 1871 when the honorary secretary was Mrs Harvey, Bridge Street, Stirling. In 1913 the Stirlingshire and District Society was a member of the SCOTTISH FEDERATION OF THE NATIONAL UNION OF WOMEN'S SUFFRAGE SOCIETIES. Secretary (1909) Miss Mary Kerr, Holmhurst, Bridge of Allan; (1913) Mrs Alec Morrison, Roselea, Bridge of Allan, Stirlingshire.

STOCKPORT (NUWSS)   Formed in 1911 and joined the MANCHESTER AND DISTRICT FEDERATION OF WOMEN'S SUFFRAGE SOCIETIES. Secretary (1913) Miss Andrew, 2 Victoria Grove, Heaton Chapel, Stockport, Cheshire.

STOCKTON-ON-TEES (NUWSS)   In 1913 the society was a member of the NORTH-EASTERN FEDERATION OF THE NATIONAL UNION OF WOMEN'S SUFFRAGE SOCIETIES. Secretary (1913) Miss D. Davison, Springholme, Stockton-on-Tees, Co. Durham.

STOKE-ON-TRENT committee of the LONDON NATIONAL SOCIETY FOR WOMEN'S SUFFRAGE   Formed in 1871 when its secretary was Mrs Ambrose Bevington, 47 Windsor St., Hanley. A Hanley correspondent of J.S. MILL, William Wood, "a working man in the Potteries", in 1869 had collected signatures locally to a petition in favour of women's enfranchisement. There was a suggestion that he might organize a meeting in Hanley, possibly to be addressed by Millicent Garrett FAWCETT. Once formed, the society associated itself with the CENTRAL COMMITTEE OF THE NATIONAL SOCIETY FOR WOMEN'S SUFFRAGE in 1872. In 1913 the Stoke-on-Trent and Newcastle-under-Lyne Society was a member of the MIDLAND (WEST) FEDERATION OF THE NATIONAL UNION OF WOMEN'S SUFFRAGE SOCIETIES. Secretaries (1913) Miss M. Barke, Stoke Lodge, Trentham Road, Stoke-on-Trent, and Miss Bakewell, Mount Pleasant, Newcastle-under-Lyne, Staffordshire.

STOKE-ON-TRENT (WSPU)   Founded in September 1908 by Adeline Redfern-Wilde.

STOPES, CHARLOTTE CARMICHAEL, MRS (1846–1929)   Born in Edinburgh. In 1874 she was one of the first three women (Flora MASSON was another) who received a special certificate having taken classes in literature, philosophy and science held by the Edinburgh Ladies' Educational Association. She married Harry Stopes, and in 1880 her daughter Marie was born. From 1888 she wrote for the *Rational Dress Gazette*, which was edited by Constance Wilde, and in that year she held a drawing-room meeting for the EDINBURGH SOCIETY OF THE NATIONAL SOCIETY FOR WOMEN'S SUFFRAGE. In 1894 she wrote *British Freewomen: Their Historic Privilege*, which was published by Swan Sonnenschein (see PUBLISHERS AND PRINTERS). In May, having read it, Elizabeth Wolstenholme ELMY, a knowledgeable and exacting critic, wrote to Harriet McILQUHAM that Mrs Stopes

> seems to be either wholly ignorant of – or deliberately to ignore the immense changes of position of the married women effected by the M.W.P. [Married Women's Property] Acts – the Clitheroe judgment – recent judicial decisions (Markham & Prentice) as to voting rights, and the L.G. [Local Government] Bill of last Session . . . I wish you could see Mrs Stopes – and talk the whole thing over with her. Surely she cannot seriously propose this [enfranchisement for widows and spinsters only].

Mrs Stopes replied in a letter to Mrs McIlquham that she was hoping to bring out a book devoted to married women and their disabilities, "which are, even yet, a disgrace to a civilised community". In 1895 Mrs Stopes drew thanks from the WOMEN'S EMANCIPATION UNION; she had obviously remained on friendly terms with Mrs Wolstenholme Elmy despite the latter's criticism of her work. *British Freewomen* was a popular book. Mrs Stopes remarks in the same letter to Mrs McIlquham that the 1000 copies first printed were ordered before it had even left the printers and that another 1000 were immediately reprinted. Sales of the book were boosted after the turn of the century as interest in the cause of women's suffrage grew and societies, with their associated lending libraries, mushroomed. *British Freewomen* was the first title that the new GLASGOW AND WEST OF SCOTLAND ASSOCIATION FOR WOMEN'S SUFFRAGE, after its formation in 1902, agreed to buy. Mrs Stopes obviously believed in the proselytizing effect of her work because, in April 1895, she sent John Ruskin, who was not noted for his support for women's suffrage, a presentation copy of *British Freewomen*. By 1909 the book had run through four editions (May, July 1894, October 1907 and August 1909) and was then taken over, with Swan Sonnenschein, by George Allen and Unwin.

In October 1896 Charlotte Stopes read a paper, "The Woman's Protest", at the London conference of the Women's Emancipation Union. She published in the *Humanitarian* an article that was reprinted in 1897, in an 18-page pamphlet, as *Women's Suffrage in the "Queen's Year"*. In 1901 she was a member of the CENTRAL SOCIETY FOR WOMEN'S SUFFRAGE and in 1906, by now living in Birkenhead, she was a delegate from the NATIONAL UNION OF WOMEN'S SUFFRAGE SOCIETIES to the annual conference of the National Union of Women Workers. In 1907 T. Fisher Unwin published another pamphlet by Mrs Stopes, *The Sphere of "Man" in Relation to That of "Woman" in the Constitution*. An article first published in the *Fortnightly Review*, in which she espoused the cause of woman's suffrage as exemplified in the Bible, was reprinted as a four-page leaflet, *Woman and Revelation*. In 1908 she wrote *The Constitutional Basis of Women's Suffrage*, which was published in the *Fortnightly Review* in September 1908 and then republished as a 15-page pamphlet by the Darien Press in Edinburgh, in which she argued, from precedent, for militant methods in pursuing the cause of women's enfranchisement.

According to Elizabeth Wolstenholme Elmy she and Mrs Stopes were present on the same platform at the June 1908 WSPU Hyde Park rally.

Address: (1908) 53 Stanley Gardens, Hampstead, London NW.
Photograph: in K. Briant, *Marie Stopes*, 1962.
Archival source: Elizabeth Wolstenholme Elmy Papers, British Library.

STOURBRIDGE (NUWSS) In 1913 the society was a member of the MIDLAND (WEST) FEDERATION OF THE NATIONAL UNION OF WOMEN'S SUFFRAGE SOCIETIES. Secretary (1913) Miss E. Downing, Elm Lodge, Hagley, nr Stourbridge, Worcestershire.

STRACHEY FAMILY Jane Maria Strachey, Lady (1840–1928) daughter of Sir John Grant of Rothiemurchus, in 1859 married Major (later Lt-Gen. Sir) Richard Strachey, and eventually had 13 children. In 1859 she read *On Liberty* and was henceforward a disciple of John Stuart MILL. Elizabeth French Boyd in *Bloomsbury Heritage*, 1976, relates that Lady Strachey, living in Edinburgh at the time, "enthusiastically circulated the first petiion to Parliament for votes for women, securing quantities of signatures, which petition was presented to Parliament in 1868 by John Stuart Mill himself". It is doubtful if it can have been, in fact, the "first petition" for which she was working. This was, of course, presented to Parliament by J.S. Mill in May 1866 and the printed version of the petition does not contain her signature. In her entry in the *Suffrage Annual*, 1913, Lady Strachey notes that she signed a petition in support of women's suffrage presented to parliament by John Stuart Mill in 1867. The EDINBURGH NATIONAL SOCIETY certainly organized a petition, in line with those from the Manchester and London societies, which was presented to parliament as she describes. Her peripatetic life, the birth of 13 children, three of whom died in infancy, domestic duties and literary pleasures may have precluded active involvement in the suffrage cause during the remainder of the nineteenth century, although from 1880 she was a supporter of Elizabeth Garrett Anderson's New Hospital for Women. From 1901 she subscribed to the re-formed CENTRAL SOCIETY FOR WOMEN'S SUFFRAGE; on 11 December 1906 she attended the banquet given at the Savoy by Millicent Garrett FAWCETT to celebrate the release from prison of members of the WOMEN'S SOCIAL AND POLITICAL UNION; and on 9 February 1907, with Millicent Fawcett and Lady Frances BALFOUR, she headed the Central Society's "Mud March". Lady Stocks recorded Lady Strachey as remembering that after this march she had to boil her skirt. Sir Richard Strachey was also a member of the LONDON SOCIETY FOR WOMEN'S SUFFRAGE in 1907. On 13 June 1908 Lady Strachey headed the NATIONAL UNION OF WOMEN'S SUFFRAGE SOCIETIES Procession on its way to Hyde Park. Between 1907 and 1909 she wrote a number of pamphlets for the NUWSS, including *Reduced to the Absurd*, a series of humorous syllogisms, and around 1910 she wrote the words for several rollicking songs, which were, with others, published as a pamphlet by the London Society as *Women's Suffrage Songs* (*see* SONGS, MUSIC AND POETRY). When it was founded in 1909 Lady Strachey, along with Mary LOWNDES, Cicely HAMILTON, and Lady Frances Balfour, was a member of the editorial committee of the *Englishwoman*. By 1909 she was president of the WOMEN'S LOCAL GOVERNMENT SOCIETY, still holding that position in 1917. By 1913 she had served as a member on the executive committee of the NATIONAL UNION OF WOMEN'S SUFFRAGE SOCIETIES. On 29 June 1914 she attended the Costume Dinner given by the WOMEN WRITERS' SUFFRAGE LEAGUE and the ACTRESSES' FRANCHISE LEAGUE at the Hotel Cecil; Lady Strachey sat at the same table as Ivy Compton Burnett. On 13 March 1918 Lady Strachey attended the celebrations at the Queen's Hall organized by the NUWSS to mark the (limited) enfranchisement of women and continued her support for the London Society for Women's Service and the Women's Service Bureau.

Philippa Strachey (1872–1968), one of the five daughters of Lady Strachey, was by 1906 a member of the executive committee of the Central Society for Women's Suffrage. In 1907 she became secretary of the LONDON SOCIETY FOR WOMEN'S SUFFRAGE (as the Central Society had been renamed), succeeding Edith PALLISER. In February 1907 she was one of the main organizers of the NUWSS "Mud March". She ensured that Strachey friends and relations played their part on the day; John Maynard Keynes was detailed to open Exeter Hall, the March's destination. Keynes, whose father had in 1888 acted as auditor for the CAMBRIDGE WOMEN'S SUFFRAGE ASSOCIATION, took his support for the suffragists seriously. When in 1912, after much heart-searching, he bought a bas-relief by Eric Gill originally inscribed "Votes for Women", Keynes only did so after those three words were physically removed by Gill's dealer. Keynes was apparently uncomfortable with the title, doubtless perceived to be mocking; the sculpture depicts a copulating couple – the woman on top. Gill, although no supporter of the cause, was clearly *au fait* with current notions of feminism, having contributed a mischievous correspondence to early issues of the *Freewoman* (December 1911). Keynes's friend and Philippa's brother, Lytton Strachey, who was named for his godfather, the father of Lady Constance LYTTON, was also sympathetic to the cause; in 1909 he is recorded as composing a humorous piece of writing on the suffrage movement. Her cousin, Duncan Grant, won a prize of £4 for a poster, "Handicapped", designed in 1909 for the ARTISTS' SUFFRAGE LEAGUE and in the January 1910 general election he canvassed a Hampstead polling station on behalf of the suffragists. As late as 1925 Lytton Strachey gave the proceeds of a play, *The Son of Heaven*, with sets designed by Duncan Grant and music by William Walton, to the LONDON AND NATIONAL SOCIETY FOR WOMEN'S SERVICE. Another of the Strachey brothers, James, in 1920 married Alix, daughter of Mary Sargant FLORENCE. Philippa Strachey remained as secretary of the London and National Society for Women's Service until retiring in 1951. Her sister Pernel, after her retirement as principal of Newnham, worked as a volunteer in the offices of the London and National Society. Another sister, Marjorie, had many years before gone as an NUWSS organizer to aid the founding of the BEDFORD WOMEN'S SUFFRAGE SOCIETY in March/April 1909.

Ray [Rachel] Strachey (Mrs Oliver Strachey) (1887–1940) was the daughter of Mary Costelloe (later Mary Berenson) and the granddaughter of Hannah Whittall Smith, a Philadelphian Quaker and feminist. At the end of the nineteenth century Mary Costelloe was president of the Westminster, Chelsea and Guildford Women's Liberal Associations. In 1889 both Mary Costelloe and her mother signed the Declaration in Favour of Women's Suffrage organized by the CENTRAL COMMITTEE OF THE

NATIONAL SOCIETY FOR WOMEN'S SUFFRAGE. Mary, with her sister Alys (who was later to marry Bertrand Russell), her parents and her husband, in the 1890s subscribed to the CENTRAL NATIONAL SOCIETY FOR WOMEN'S SUFFRAGE. In March 1890 Alice SCATCHERD mentioned in a letter to Harriet McILQUHAM that Mr Costelloe was a "warm friend" to the WOMEN'S FRANCHISE LEAGUE. Ray Costelloe was brought up, after her mother left the family in order to live in Italy with Bernard Berenson and after her father's death in 1899, by her grandmother. She was educated at Kensington High School and at Newnham College, Cambridge, 1905–8. While at Newnham she was an active member of the CAMBRIDGE UNIVERSITY WOMEN'S SUFFRAGE SOCIETY and in the summer of 1908, with F. Elinor RENDEL and Gwen Williams (1882–1952), who was secretary of the West of England Women's Suffrage Societies 1908–18, she took part in a suffrage CARAVAN tour of the Lake District. Through her school friendship with Elinor Rendel, Ray Costelloe had long been acquainted with the Strachey family. In 1911 she married, as his second wife, Oliver, one of Lady Strachey's five sons, and eventually had two children. The Fawcett Library holds a photograhic postcard of Julia Strachey, Oliver's daughter from his first marriage, leading a NUWSS procession in Littlehampton on 19 July 1913; the postcard is annotated, "A chip off the 'old block'". In 1913 Ray Strachey was chairman of the London Society for Women's Suffrage. From 1916 until 1921 she was honorary parliamentary secretary of the NUWSS, responsible for supervising the passage of the 1918 Reform Bill, and was chairman, from 1916 until 1934, of the Women's Service Bureau, which originated in the war work of the London Society for Women's Suffrage. Ray Strachey stood unsuccessfully for parliament, as an independent, in 1918, 1922 and 1923. After the end of the First World War she was editor of the *Common Cause* and then of its successor, the *Woman's Leader*, 1920–23, and acted as political private secretary to Lady Astor after the latter's election to parliament. Ray Strachey wrote *Women's Suffrage and Women's Service: The History of the London and National Society for Women's Service*, 1928; *The Cause*, 1928, a history of the women's movement, social and educational as well as political; and *Millicent Garrett Fawcett*, 1931, a biography of her mentor. From 1935 she ran the Women's Employment Federation and subsequently published *Career Openings for Women*, 1935, and the section "Changes in Employment" in *Our Freedom and its Results*, a collection of essays she edited, published in 1936 by Virginia and Leonard Woolf's Hogarth Press.

Address: Lady Strachey (1880) Stowey House, Clapham Common, London SW; (1913) 67 Belsize Park Gardens, London NW; Philippa Strachey (1934) 51 Gordon Square, London WC1; Ray Strachey, 41 Gordon Square, London WC1.

Portrait: of Lady Strachey by [Dora] Carrington, 1920, in Scottish National Portrait Gallery. Many self-portraits by Ray Strachey in National Portrait Gallery Reserve Collection. Photograph of Marjorie Strachey by Lizzie Caswell Smith in National Portrait Gallery. Photograph of Philippa Strachey in National Portrait Gallery.

Bibliography: M. Stocks, *My Commonplace Book*, 1970; E. French Boyd, *Bloomsbury Heritage: Their Mothers and Their Aunts*, 1976; B. Strachey, *Remarkable Relations*, 1980; P. Stansky, *On Or About December 1910: Early Bloomsbury and Its Intimate World*, 1996.

STRATFORD-ON-AVON (NUWSS) Secretary (1913) Mrs Cameron Stuart, The High School, Stratford-on-Avon, Warwickshire.

STRATFORD-ON-AVON (WSPU) Secretary (1913) Miss M. East, Fairview, Stratford-on-Avon, Warwickshire.

STREATHAM branch of the UNITED SUFFRAGISTS Formed in 1915. Honorary secretary: Mrs Gregory, 7 Ambleside Gardens, London SW; (from June 1915) 6 Gibson's Hill, West Norwood, London SE.

STREATHAM (WSPU) Secretary (1913) Miss Leonora TYSON, 5 Shrubbery Road, Streatham, London SW.

STREET branch of the MEN'S LEAGUE FOR WOMEN'S SUFFRAGE Founded in 1912. Its leading members were Mr Thompson Clothier and Laurence HOUSMAN.

STREET (NUWSS) Secretary (1913) Mrs Esther CLOTHIER, Leigh Holt, Street, Somerset. The society's BANNER is held in the Fawcett Library Collection. *See also* Alice CLARK; Helen Bright CLARK.

The Street Women's Suffrage Association, possibly photographed around the time of the NUWSS Pilgrimage, July 1913. This is typical of many gatherings, posing for the camera to announce solidarity of purpose in a garden setting. (Author's collection)

STROMNESS committee of the Edinburgh National Society for Women's Suffrage   Formed in 1871 as a result of the speaking tour undertaken by Jane Taylour and Agnes McLaren. Its convenor was Mr James Spence, of Pon.

STROUD branch of the London National Society for Women's Suffrage   Founded in 1870. Lady Amberley was a member of the executive committee and Lord Amberley was a member of the general committee. The secretary was Mrs P.C. Evans of Brimscombe Mills. The Stroud society associated itself with the Central Committee of the National Society in 1872.

STROUD branch of the United Suffragists   Founded in mid 1914. Secretary: Miss S. Edelman, Whiteway, Nr Stroud, Gloucestershire.

STRUCHR, Aberdeenshire, committee of the National Society for Women's Suffrage   Formed in 1873.

STURGE, ELIZA MARY (1843–1905)   Quaker, born in Birmingham, daughter of Charles Sturge, a friend of John Bright, and niece of Joseph Sturge, who, although a renowned abolitionist and social reformer, had not been prepared to include women in any proposed extension of the suffrage and who opposed the inclusion of women delegates at the World Anti-Slavery Convention in 1840. Eliza Sturge was a cousin of Elizabeth, Emily and Helen Sturge, of Bristol, and also related to the Clarks of Street. Eliza Sturge, although she had not signed the 1866 women's suffrage petition, subscribed to the Enfranchisement of Women Committee in 1866–7. In 1871 she succeeded Mary Johnson as secretary of the Birmingham Society for Women's Suffrage. She was an active speaker for the suffrage movement. In April 1871 she attended the Women's Suffrage conference held in London and in February 1872 she spoke in Bristol at the annual public meeting of the Bristol and West of England Society for Women's Suffrage and later in the same month addressed a suffrage meeting in Rochdale. A speech she gave on "Women's Suffrage" at Birmingham Town Hall on 6 December 1872 was reprinted as a pamphlet. In April 1873 she spoke at the public meeting on women's suffrage organized by the CENTRAL COMMITTEE OF THE NATIONAL SOCIETY FOR WOMEN'S SUFFRAGE at the Hanover Square rooms in London and between 1880 and 1881 addressed four of the Grand Demonstrations. A Liberal, who in the early 1870s despaired of the Liberal Party's lack of interest in the woman's cause, she was a delegate from the Birmingham Women's Liberal Association to the National Reform Union conference held in Manchester in December 1875. In 1875 she was a member of the executive committee of the Central Committee of the National Society for Women's Suffrage, of which society she had been a member since its formation in 1871. In 1873 Eliza Sturge was elected as the first woman member of the Birmingham School Board and in 1902 became a member of the Worcestershire Education Committee. She was also a pacifist and temperance worker. She died at the home of Dr Mary Sturge, an active member of the Birmingham Society for Women's Suffrage, who was presumably her niece and to whom she left her entire estate.

Address: (1871) 17 Frederick Street, Birmingham; (1905) 28 Bank Hill, Bewdley, Worcestershire; 45 Hagley Road, Birmingham.

Bibliography: E.M. Sturge, "Women's Suffrage", in J. Lewis (ed.), *Before The Vote Was Won: Arguments For and Against Women's Suffrage 1864–1896*, 1987.

STURGE SISTERS Quakers, they were daughters of Charlotte and William Sturge, a prosperous, self-made man, a land surveyor in Bristol. Elizabeth Sturge (1849–1944) educated at Weston-super-Mare and at Belmont House School, Leicester, attended from 1868 the newly founded series of lectures for ladies in Bristol and, after May 1876, lectures given at University College in Bristol. She later remembered that, as a girl, she attended a suffrage meeting in Bristol, chaired by Professor Francis NEWMAN, at which Eliza STURGE of Birmingham was chief speaker. This was probably the meeting held in February 1872. In 1878, after the death of Mary Carpenter, Elizabeth Sturge was invited to join the board of managers of the Red Lodge, the reformatory school for delinquent girls, and was soon appointed its honorary secretary. Between 1888 and 1891 she worked voluntarily for Octavia Hill, managing houses in London. In 1891 she returned to the family home in Bristol, her mother having died in 1890, remaining until her father's death in 1905. The family house was then sold and with Helen, the one other sister remaining at home, she first had a holiday and then returned to devote herself to the constitutional suffrage cause. She recorded that "We of the 'Old Guard', who were followers of Mrs Fawcett, could not adopt the methods of the Pankhursts, but we recognized their enthusiasm and heroism in facing imprisonment for themselves and their followers, and we felt that it was up to us to lend the whole weight of our influence in pushing forward the cause by every constitutional means."

Emily Sturge (1847–92) in 1868, with her sister Elizabeth, enrolled at the "Lectures for Ladies" organized by the Clifton Association for Promoting the Higher Education of Women. From 1878 until her early death, the result of a riding accident, she was honorary secretary of the BRISTOL AND WEST OF ENGLAND SOCIETY FOR WOMEN'S SUFFRAGE. For the previous ten years she had been an intrepid speaker for the suffrage cause, travelling out of Bristol to speak at meetings in the west country and even, by invitation, in Belfast and Dublin. In 1881 she was, with Anna Maria PRIESTMAN, one of the founders of the Bristol Women's Liberal Association, the first in the country. By 1891 she was a member of the executive committee of the CENTRAL NATIONAL SOCIETY FOR WOMEN'S SUFFRAGE. In 1878 she attended evening classes run by the newly opened University College in Bristol. In 1880 she was elected a member of the Bristol School Board, holding her place until her death. In 1883 she became the first woman on the council of Redland High School for Girls; Elizabeth succeeded her in 1896.

Helen Maria Sturge (1858–1945), younger sister of Elizabeth and Emily, was educated at home, and by attending lectures at the University College of Bristol. In 1890 she was assistant honorary secretary of Bristol Women's Liberal Association. In 1908 she stood, unsuccessfully, for the first city council elections for which women were eligible. In 1913 she spoke at a meeting held by the York branch of the CHURCH LEAGUE FOR WOMEN'S SUFFRAGE.

Address: (1864–1905) Chilliswood, Tyndalls Park, Bristol; Helen Sturge (1933) 2 Durdham Park, Bristol 6.
Photographs: of Elizabeth, Emily, and Helen Sturge in M. Goodbody, *Five Daughters in Search of Learning: The Sturge Family 1820–1944*, 1986.
Bibliography: E. Sturge, *Reminiscences of My Life*, 1928; M. Goodbody, *Five Daughters in Search of Learning: The Sturge Family 1820–1944*, 1986.

SUFFRAGE ATELIER Founded in February 1909 as "An Arts and Crafts Society Working for the Enfranchisement of Women". The constitution of the Atelier stated that "The object of the Society is to encourage Artists to forward the Woman's movement, and particularly the Enfranchisement of Women, by means of pictorial publications. Each Member of the Society shall undertake to give the Society the first refusal of any pictorial work intended for publication, dealing with the Woman's Movement. In return the Artist shall receive a certain percentage of the profits arising from the sale of her or his work." The Atelier, unlike the ARTISTS' SUFFRAGE LEAGUE, encouraged artists, who did not need to have been professionally trained, to submit suitable work to its exhibitions. The Atelier was particularly keen to attract designs for cartoons, postcards and posters, as well as "Pictures, Statuary, Black & White work & Craft work". Laurence and Clemence HOUSMAN were co-founders of the Atelier, which had probably been formed as a result of the co-operation enjoyed by members of the KENSINGTON branch of the WOMEN'S SOCIAL AND POLITICAL UNION, who worked together to make the Housman "From Prison to Citizenship" BANNER for the WSPU 21 June 1908 demonstration. This work had been carried out in the Housmans' garden studio and from 1910 their address was that used by the Atelier. Members of the Atelier included Catherine Courtauld (*see* COURTAULD FAMILY), Edith CRAIG, Isobel Pocock, Gladys Letcher and A.E. Hope Joseph, who in 1912 lived at the same address as Miss Willis.

The Atelier, unlike the ASL, was associated with the militant suffrage societies; one of its first requests was for work with which to stock the Art Stall at the WSPU's Prince's Skating Rink Exhibition in May 1909. In practice, however, the Suffrage Atelier worked mainly with the WOMEN'S FREEDOM LEAGUE. In November 1909 the Atelier's honorary secretary, Miss Willis, offered to help with advice regarding the decoration of the Albert Hall for the WFL "Yuletide Festival".

In December 1909 the Suffrage Atelier designed a banner, "Let Glasgow Flourish", for the Glasgow (Central) WFL, and one for Glasgow (West), probably the work of Miss Willis. The Atelier was also commissioned to supply the banner to be carried by members of the TAX RESISTANCE LEAGUE, an offshoot of the WFL, in the 18 June 1910 procession. In the Women's Coronation procession of 17 June 1911 members of the Atelier carried their own banner, which depicted Athene with her symbols the owl, olive, cock, serpent, sphinx, the Victory and medusa head. In 1912 the Suffrage Atelier provided coloured inserts given away with copies of the *Vote*. In addition to providing support for the fairs organized by other societies, the Suffrage Atelier also held its own, for instance in October 1910. In February 1912 the Suffrage Atelier held an exhibition at a meeting of the HAMMERSMITH branch of the WSPU, at which Frances ROWE was welcomed back after her release from Holloway. *Votes for Women*, 23 February 1912, noted that "The cartoons and posters made a very appropriate decoration to the walls" and Miss Willis was there, selling literature "in her little kiosk". Much of the work of the Suffrage Atelier, on both its posters and postcards, of which there were at least 16 designs, employed woodcuts, giving a strong, urgent stamp to their message. The Suffrage Atelier had an educational element; classes were given in life drawing and printing and work was submitted for criticism. The Atelier appears to have ceased work on the outbreak of war in August 1914.

Honorary secretary: (1909–14) Miss E.B. Willis. Secretary (1912) Katherine GATTY.
Address: (1909) 53 Broadhurst Gardens, London NW; (1910–1912) 1 Pembroke Cottages, Edwardes Square (address of Clemence and Laurence Housman); (1912–14) 4 Stanlake Villas, Stanlake Road, Shepherd's Bush (address of Miss E.B. Willis and A.E. Hope Joseph); (1913–14) also had address at 2 Robert Street, Adelphi (address of Minerva Publishing Co., publisher of the WFL's the *Vote*).
Archival source: The Fawcett Library collection, the Suffragette Fellowship collection, Museum of London and the Communist Party Archives all include Suffrage Atelier postcards and posters; the John Johnson Collection, Bodleian Library, Oxford, includes some Suffrage Atelier postcards.

Bibliography: L. Tickner, *Spectacle of Women: Imagery of the Suffrage Campaign, 1907–14*, 1987.

"SUFFRAGE FIRST" COMMITTEE Founded in November 1913. The object of the committee was to secure from electors a pledge that, at the next election, unless women had been already enfranchised, they would use their vote in such a way as to "put Woman Suffrage first". By its very nature the Committee intended to direct its campaign at men. Frederick PETHICK-LAWRENCE agreed to act as temporary honorary secretary.
Address: 4–7 Red Lion Court, Fleet Street, London EC.

SUFFRAGETTE FELLOWSHIP Founded, as the "Suffragette Club", by Edith How MARTYN in 1926 in order "to perpetuate the memory of the pioneers and outstanding events connected with women's emancipation and especially with the militant suffrage campaign, 1905–14, and thus keep alive the suffragette spirit". By 1947 the Fellowship had widened its aims "To perpetuate the memory of the pioneers and outstanding events connected with women's emancipation and especially with the militant suffrage campaign 1905–14. To secure women's political, civil, economic, educational and social status on the basis of equality of the sexes, and [co-operate] from time to time with other organisations working to the same end". When first set up, the Suffragette Club was to be open to "All Suffragette prisoners, unless they desire not to be; all members of militant suffrage societies between 13 October 1905 and 4 August 1914; direct descendants of Suffragette Prisoners; pioneer women and men by invitation of the Council, who declare their sympathy with the militant campaign and the suffragette spirit." The Suffragette Fellowship maintained an annual programme of commemorations, the birthday of Emmeline PANKHURST on 14 July, the first militant protest, 13 October 1905, and the suffrage victories of 1918 and 1928, celebrated in February and January respectively, and instituted a "Suffragette Lecture", all of which were occasions for reunion. Flora DRUMMOND and Katherine GATTY were among the earliest members of the Council of the Suffragette Club.

The Suffragette Club also at its inception set up a fund, from which it was intended to lend money to needy ex-(suffragette) prisoners. It may in part have been the difficulty of identifying whether or not an applicant had actually been imprisoned (there is evidence of fraudulent claims) that lay behind the concept of a "Book of Suffragette Prisoners", the idea being to include for each a short biographical piece and an accompanying photograph. This never materialized, although all the information submitted now forms a substantial part of the Suffragette Fellowship Collection. In the 1950s the Fellowship did produce a list of suffragette prisoners, containing, rather surprisingly, a substantial number of inaccuracies (*see* ALIASES).

Soon after its formation the Suffragette Club undertook to create a formal archive in order to house relics and memoirs of the militant movement. In 1933 the exhibits were kept in Geraldine LENNOX's house (*Daily Sketch*, 28 October 1933). By 1934 Mary PHILLIPS was the Fellowship's custodian and *c*. 1937 a "Women's Record Room" had been opened in the Minerva Club (*see* CLUBS). In May 1939 Rose Lamartine YATES opened new premises for the Record Room at 6 Great Smith Street, Westminster, where weekly meetings of the Suffragette Fellowship were also to be held. However, on the outbreak of war these premises were vacated, some of the material being taken for safe-keeping to the country home of Una DUVAL. The Suffragette Fellowship did keep a London presence during the war at 43 Black Lion Lane, Hammersmith, the home of Helen Atkinson. After the end of the war a "Suffragette Museum" was reopened in February 1947 at 41 Cromwell Road, London W. The Committee of the Record Room included Una Duval, Helen ARCHDALE, Edith How Martyn, Winifred MAYO, Marian Reeves, Stella NEWSOME, Marian LAWSON and Enid Goulden Bach, niece of Emmeline Pankhurst. Charlotte MARSH and Theresa GARNETT, Minnie BALDOCK, Janet Barrowman, May BILLINGHURST, Lillian Dove-WILLCOX (now Mrs Buckley), Nellie CROCKER, Ada FLATMAN, Mary GAWTHORPE, Margaret McPHUN, Princess Sophia Duleep SINGH, Margaret and Mary THOMPSON, Rachel BARRETT, Teresa BILLINGTON-GREIG, Emmeline PETHICK-LAWRENCE, Rosamund MASSY, Lady RHONDDA and Daisy SOLOMON all contributed in 1947 towards either the Fellowship or towards the setting up of the Record Room. Not only did the Fellowship have a natural desire to display its trophies for their general interest, but at this time the suffragette movement was to some degree being rediscovered by journalists and film-makers and the archive was used as a basis for newspaper articles, television programmes and the 1947 film of Howard Spring's *Fame is the Spur*. From 1951, the running of a museum presumably proving too arduous and expensive for a group of by now elderly women, the Suffragette Fellowship Collection was taken over by the London Museum, then at Kensington Palace, now in the Barbican.

The Suffragette Fellowship published a newsletter between 1947 and 1971, *Calling All Women*, which provides useful information about the Fellowship's activities and the later lives of its members. It also published, over the years, several pamphlets of reminiscences, including Thelma Cazalet Keir's *I Knew Mrs Pankhurst*, the costs of which were borne by Marie LAWSON. In 1970 the Suffragette Fellowship was responsible for the erection of a memorial, unveiled by Lilian LENTON, in Christchurch Gardens, between Victoria Street and Caxton Hall, the site of so many "Women's Parliaments". Made of glass fibre, bronzed, 13 feet high, in the shape of an unfolding scroll, its inscription reads: "This tribute is erected by the Suffragette Fellowship to commemorate the courage and perseverance of all those men and women who in the long struggle for votes for women selflessly braved derision, opposition and ostracism, many enduring physical violence and suffering." On the underside are replicas of both the WOMEN'S SOCIAL AND POLITICAL UNION'S and the WOMEN'S FREEDOM LEAGUES' "Holloway" prison badges (*see* JEWELLERY AND BADGES).

Address: (1947) 41 Cromwell Road, London SW. Chairman (1926) Edith How Martyn; honorary secretary (1926) Elsa GYE; vice-chairman (1947) Marian Reeves; honorary secretary, Stella Newsome.

Bibliography: L. E. Nym Mayhall, "Creating the 'Suffragette Spirit': British Feminism and the Historical Imagination", *Women's History Review*, 4, 3, 1995.

SUFFRAGETTES OF THE WOMEN'S SOCIAL AND POLITICAL UNION Formed as the result of a meeting, chaired by Rose Lamartine YATES in the Caxton Hall on 22 October 1915, which produced a resolution addressed to Emmeline and Christabel PANKHURST, expressing dismay at their abandonment of the cause of women's suffrage and asking for the presentation of the last two years' accounts for the WOMEN'S SOCIAL AND POLITICAL UNION. No reply was received and the erstwhile members of the WSPU set up a new society to revive the suffrage campaign. "The Suffragettes of the WSPU" was a democratic body with an executive and officials elected by and accountable to their members. The Committee in 1916 comprised Emily DUVAL, Gladys Evans, Miss A. Gilliat, Dr Helena Jones, Miss Metcalfe (author of *Woman's Effort*, 1917), Mrs TYSON and Rose Lamartine Yates. The group issued the *Suffragette News Sheet*, described as "An official account of the activities of The Suffragettes of the WSPU", to which Frederick PETHICK-LAWRENCE, Maud Arncliffe SENNETT and Alice ABADAM contributed. The May–June 1918 issue was designated as an "Emily Davison Memorial" number, reflecting the particular friendship that had existed between Emily Wilding DAVISON and Rose Lamartine Yates. Subscribers to this issue included Maud Arncliffe Sennett, Miss Peacock (*see* PORTSMOUTH WSPU), Mrs Frances SWINEY, Lilian HICKS, Janie ALLAN and Nannie Brown, who was the Edinburgh secretary of the NORTHERN MEN'S FEDERATION FOR WOMEN'S SUFFRAGE. The Suffragettes of the WSPU intended to carry on the campaign after the vote was partially won in 1918, working "on educational lines from our standpoint".

Address: (1917) 145 High Holborn, London WC1; (1918) Emily Davison Lodge Rooms (*see* CLUBS), 144 High Holborn, London WC1 (this was an address shared with the WOMEN'S FREEDOM LEAGUE).

SUFFRAGIST CHURCHWOMEN'S PROTEST COMMITTEE Honorary secretary (1913, 1917) Mrs Alice M. Kidd, 21 Downside Crescent, Hampstead, London NW.

SUFFRAGISTS' VIGILANCE LEAGUE The formation of this League, aimed at those not satisfied with the social and political condition of women, was advertised in the suffrage press in October 1909. The publication of "Propaganda Cartoons" was an enticement, but it is not clear whether or not either the League or cartoons materialized. It is likely that the single published issue of the *Suffragist* (*see* NEWSPAPERS AND JOURNALS) was the only manifestation of the League, to which Frances SWINEY, Mrs

Howey (*see* Elsie HOWEY) and Sarah BENETT had been among the contributors.
Address: (1909) Albert Buildings, 49 Queen Victoria Street, London EC.

SUNDERLAND (NUWSS) In 1913 the society was a member of the NORTH-EASTERN FEDERATION OF THE NATIONAL UNION OF WOMEN'S SUFFRAGE SOCIETIES. Secretary (1909) Mrs Baillie, 36 Otto Terrace, Sunderland, Co. Durham; (1913) Mrs Johnson and Miss Johnson, 2 Grey Road, Sunderland, Co. Durham.

SUNDERLAND (WFL) Secretary (1913) Mrs Palliser, 10 Fox Street, Sunderland, Co. Durham.

SUNLEY, AGNES, MRS (*c.* 1849–1924) Born at Wortley, Leeds, wife of George Sunley, an illiterate packer in an asbestos factory. By 1880 Agnes Sunley was a member of the MANCHESTER NATIONAL SOCIETY FOR WOMEN'S SUFFRAGE. In 1882 she, presumably as an ORGANIZER for that society, undertook a canvass in Leeds of women householders, asking them to sign a petition in support of their enfranchisement. She had a letter protesting against Mr Woodall's clause, limiting any proposed franchise to unmarried women and widows, published in the *Personal Rights Journal* in January 1887. The placing of this letter was probably not unconnected with her association with Elizabeth Wolstenholme ELMY; by 1889 Agnes Sunley was organizing agent for the WOMEN'S FRANCHISE LEAGUE, in April, for instance, writing to 32 MPs urging them to oppose the Woodall bill. For this work she received a small salary, paid to her on behalf of the WFL by Alice SCATCHERD, the treasurer. Elizabeth Wolstenholme Elmy knew only too well how important prompt payment was to those who relied on it and in a letter to Harriet MCILQUHAM of 13 January 1890 wrote of Mrs Sunley's salary, which had been due at the end of the year, "and Agnes has not received one penny for all the work she has done for the League ... and she will *never* get it till Mrs S[catcherd] is compelled in obedience to our mandate to pay it". When a few months earlier Agnes Sunley had been ill, Mrs Wolstenholme Elmy wrote on 11 August 1889 that, even though "she will need good care for some time yet, but she is worth all we can do for her". For her convalescence Agnes Sunley went to stay in Gloucestershire with Harriet McIlquham. In 1890 Agnes Sunley gave a lecture on Robert Burns to the Leeds Women's Co-operative Guild at a meeting chaired by Alice Scatcherd and later that year was present at a meeting of the LEEDS SUFFRAGE SOCIETY. In 1891, obviously classed as one of Mrs Wolstenholme Elmy's "earnest workers" for the woman's cause, Agnes Sunley was one of the founders of the WOMEN'S EMANCIPATION UNION. In 1892 at the Birmingham WEU conference she proposed that women of mature years and established position should be allowed to remain in the law courts when cases of indecent assault were being tried, in order that they might support the complainant by their presence. In 1891 in a letter to Harriet McIlquham, she had suggested, apropos the right of married women to be included on the local register, that "the claimant should commit contempt of court by *persistently* claiming the right until a technical assault is committed by some officer of the court, effecting her removal. This would draw the attention of the whole country to the injustice of denying m[arried] women the same rights as widows and spinsters without incurring the risk of an adverse decision". It would seem that by this time the idea of infringing the law, however "technical" the breach, was not inconceivable. It was at the Women's Emancipation Union meeting in 1892 that Mary COZENS suggested that the vote could be won by physical force.

In 1899, after the dissolution of the WEU, there was some discussion as to whether Agnes Sunley might stand for election as a poor law guardian. However, Elizabeth Wolstenholme Elmy pointed out in a letter to Harriet McIlquham of 22 September, "The real difficulty is, she has no money. The *inevitable* expenditure has been keenly felt by some of our proud Women Guardians. It has been a great sorrow to me, that the WEU was never able to employ her as a paid agent. She would have done splendid work in Yorkshire – and the pay would [have] enabled her to do other work also, such as standing as a Guardian". In another letter to Harriet McIlquham written in September 1899, Mrs Wolstenholme Elmy reported that "I had two hours with Mrs Sunley in Leeds, and am very sorry

to find her so painfully depressed. Her life is indeed a hard one, with little relief or encouragement, and one is so powerless to help her". Agnes Sunley's death certificate records "Exhaustion" as one of the causes of her death.
Address: (1894) 15 Castleton Place, Armley, Leeds.
Archival source: Elizabeth Wolstenholme Elmy Papers, British Library; Harriet McIlquham Papers, Autograph Collection, Fawcett Library.

SURREY, SUSSEX, AND HANTS FEDERATION OF THE NATIONAL UNION OF WOMEN'S SUFFRAGE SOCIETIES Honorary secretary (1913) Miss Norah O'SHEA, The Cottage, Cosham, Hampshire. The Federation's BANNER, designed by Mary LOWNDES and made by the ARTISTS' SUFFRAGE LEAGUE in 1910, is now held in Worthing Museum and Art Gallery.

SUSSEX (CENTRAL) (NUWSS) By 1913 the society had branches at Cuckfield, Haywards Heath, Horsted Keynes and Hurstpierpoint and was a member of the SURREY, SUSSEX, AND HANTS FEDERATION OF THE NATIONAL UNION OF WOMEN'S SUFFRAGE SOCIETIES. Secretary (1913) Miss E.C. Beavan, Horsgate, Cuckfield, Sussex.

SUSSEX MEN'S LEAGUE FOR WOMEN'S SUFFRAGE Honorary secretary (1910) Adrian Brunel, 61 Norway Street, Portslade, Sussex.

SUTTON (branch of the LONDON SOCIETY FOR WOMEN'S SUFFRAGE, NUWSS) Secretaries (1913) Mrs Stephens, St Moritz, Cambourne Road, Sutton, and Mrs Corelli, Umballa, London Road, Worcester Park, Surrey.

SUTTON COLDFIELD (NUWSS) In 1913 the society was a member of the MIDLAND (WEST) FEDERATION OF THE NATIONAL UNION OF WOMEN'S SUFFRAGE SOCIETIES. Secretary (1913) Mrs Raymond Gough, Weatheroak, Upper Holland Road, Sutton Coldfield, Warwickshire. Corresponding secretary, Mrs H. Butcher, Ashurst, Streetly, Birmingham.

SWANSEA (NUWSS) In 1913 the society was a member of the SOUTH WALES AND MONMOUTH FEDERATION OF THE NATIONAL UNION OF WOMEN'S SUFFRAGE SOCIETIES. Secretary (1913) Miss Aaron Thomas, Dolgoy, West Cross, Glamorgan, Glamorganshire.

SWANSEA (WFL) The society was formed in March 1909 at a meeting at which Mary A. Manning BA took the chair. The society's BANNER was designed in late 1909 by Miss Dorothy Salmon and was made, in green, white and gold, possibly with "Dare to be Free" on it, by a sewing party. Mary Mcleod CLEEVES was the first secretary, succeeded by 1913 by Miss Hutton, 9 Sketty Road, Uplands, Swansea.

SWANWICK, HELENA MARIA LUCY, MRS (1864–1939) CH Born in Bavaria, daughter of Oswald Sickert, a liberal German artist of Danish descent, and an Englishwoman of romantically vague origin. Helena Swanwick was sister to Walter Sickert and, therefore, became sister-in-law to Ellen Cobden SICKERT. The Sickert family left Germany for England in 1868, living first in Bedford before moving to London. Helena Sickert was educated, when very young, as a boarder at the school at Neuville which her mother had attended, before returning to London to be educated at home. When 14, she was allowed to join Notting Hill High School for Girls, where her closest friends were Margaret Burne-Jones and the daughters of William Morris, friendships which introduced her to the domestic lives of the Pre-Raphaelite Brotherhood and sowed in her mind the seeds of socialism. Among family friends were Johnston Forbes Robertson and Oscar Wilde, who commissioned her, still an undergraduate, to contribute an article to the *Woman's World*, of which he was editor. From school she proceeded, despite family opposition and with financial assistance from her godmother, to Girton to read the moral science tripos and, after graduating with a second-class degree, was appointed lecturer in psychology at Westfield College, London. During this time she was taken to Scalands by Maggie Cobden, an old school friend and sister of Ellen Cobden Sickert, to visit Barbara BODICHON, who was by now an invalid. In 1888 Helena Sickert married Frederick Swanwick, a lecturer in mathematics at Owen's College, and moved to Manchester. The marriage was, to her regret, childless. She relates in her autobiography that the woman who impressed her most during her 12 years in Manchester was Rachel Scott (*see* Harriet Cook), the Girton Pioneer and wife of C.P. Scott, editor of the *Manchester Guardian*. Helena Swanwick also became part of Susan Dacre's circle of friends. She obtained sporadic work lecturing, including to members of the Women's Co-operative Guild, but devoted most of her time to running two social clubs for men and women and one for working girls, and joined the Women's Trade Union Council.

Helena Swanwick began writing for the *Manchester Guardian*, first as a reviewer and then was asked to contribute articles on domestic subjects. She records how "Hundreds of books, which otherwise I would not have dreamt of reading, passed through my hands and my horrified mind", opening her eyes to the way in which men, in general, viewed women. She relates that at this time, although approving the principles of the Liberal Party she did not care for its personnel, more greatly respecting individual Conservatives, such as Lord Salisbury and A.J. Balfour. She took it for granted that all political parties were equally dishonest to women. Although approving in principle of the movement for women's enfranchisement, Helena Swanwick, for reasons that she does not specify, felt unable to join either the Manchester National Society for Women's Suffrage or its successor, the North of England Society for Women's Suffrage. However, after Christabel Pankhurst and Annie Kenney made their stand at the Free Trade Hall in Manchester on 13 October 1905, she immediately subscribed to the Women's Social and Political Union and in January 1906 wrote to the *Manchester Guardian* in support of the "insurgent women's" right to heckle candidates at the general election. However, after the first flush of enthusiasm, she knew that she would be unable to work with the Pankhursts; in her autobiography her deft delineations of Mrs Pankhurst, Christabel, and Sylvia relieve her of the necessity of spelling out her objections. In general she could not condone the use of physical force to attain any goal, although admiring and remaining friendly with such individual WSPU activists as Mary Gawthorpe and Emmeline Pethick-Lawrence. Although not greatly attracted to the prospect of involvement in the suffrage movement and having little illusion as to the effect that women voters would have on the political machine, her conscience now compelled her to play her part. She joined the North of England Society for Women's Suffrage, becoming its honorary secretary in 1907, and formed a branch at Knutsford, where she was living. She was a very active speaker for the National Union of Women's Suffrage Societies, addressing 150 meetings all over England and Scotland in 1908, as well as attending committee meetings in Manchester and London. As a reporter for the *Manchester Guardian* she attended the WSPU's "Women's Parliament" in 1908 and the Women's Liberal Federation meeting in the Albert Hall on 5 December 1908, appalled to witness the treatment meted out on WSPU hecklers by the Liberal stewards.

In April 1909 Helena Swanwick became editor-manager of the newly launched *Common Cause*, which was at first an independent weekly newspaper promulgating NUWSS policy. Her friendship with C.P. Scott stood her in good stead and, although a novice, she was able to produce a newspaper. By 1911 it was clear that the paper would benefit from being published in London and so, with her husband's retirement due, Helena Swanwick resigned as honorary secretary of the Manchester Society for Women's Suffrage (as the North of England Society had become) and moved back to London, becoming a member of the NUWSS's press committee. By now a member of the NUWSS executive committee, she was one of its representatives in the deputation to Asquith on 17 November 1912, unimpressed by the performance of the WSPU delegates. Helena Swanwick, a stickler for historical truth, records that a few days later Lloyd George rehearsed to her the speech he was to give to the Liberal rally in Bath on 24 November. When she objected to his phrase, "torpedoing the Conciliation Bill", he agreed to remove it. Of course he did not, later claiming that its insertion had been an impromptu piece of rhetoric, unleashing on the Liberal government outrage from the NUWSS and a renewal of militancy from the WSPU. Helena Swanwick wrote in her autobiography, "Words fail me to describe how unutterably weary I became of both the Liberal Government and the W.S.P.U., and of the impossible task of getting existing politicians to deal with our case on its merits." She marks the

Liberal Party's procrastination and vacillation over the subject of women's suffrage as the beginning of its disintegration. As for the WSPU, she felt that the renewal of militancy had destroyed any chance for the women's suffrage cause in that parliamentary session. Because NUWSS policy was to avoid public criticism of the WSPU, Helena Swanwick resigned as editor of the *Common Cause* in June 1912, although remaining a member of the NUWSS executive committee. A supporter of the Election Fighting Fund policy, in January 1913 she edited a special suffrage supplement of the *Labour Leader*, which was paid for by the EFF and copies of which were distributed both with the *Common Cause* and to delegates at the Labour Party conference. In June 1913 she was an NUWSS delegate to the INTERNATIONAL WOMAN SUFFRAGE ALLIANCE conference in Budapest. On 22 November 1913 she sent to Sir John Simon, an influential Liberal whom the NUWSS hoped was being converted to their cause, a copy of *The Future of the Woman's Movement*, her new book, to which Mrs Fawcett had contributed a foreword.

On 4 August 1914 Helena Swanwick was the speaker representing the NUWSS at the women's peace meeting held at the Kingsway Hall. As she had been "driven" to join the suffrage movement, so she was to be "driven" to oppose war. She signed the "Open Christmas Letter to the Women of Germany and Austria" in 1914 and in April 1915 was one of the women who, before the Channel was closed to shipping, planned to travel to the Women's Peace Congress at the Hague. Disagreeing with the majority of the NUWSS executive which did not support the antiwar campaign, Helena Swanwick resigned from the NUWSS. She was chairman of the Women's International League when it was formed at the end of 1915, remaining in that position for the next seven years. She joined the Union of Democratic Control and was subjected to telephone tapping and to the interference of her mail. In 1919, after excessive delays in supplying her with a visa, she managed to attend the end of the Women's Peace Congress at Zurich. She was editor of *Foreign Affairs*, the organ of the UDC, 1924–8 and was a member of the British Empire Delegation to the League of Nations in 1924 and 1929. She committed suicide in the early days of the Second World War.

Among her books are *The Small Town Garden*, 1906; *Some Points of English Law Affecting Working Women as Wives and Mothers*, Women's Co-operative Guild, 1914; *Women in a Socialist State*, published by the ILP, 1921; *Builders of Peace*, 1924 (a history of the UDC).
Address: (1913) 26 Lawn Crescent, Kew Gardens, Surrey; (1934) Satis, Maidenhead, Berkshire.
Photograph: in *Common Cause*, 4 November 1909.
Bibliography: H.M. Swanwick, *I Have been Young*, 1935; S.S. Holton, *Feminism and Democracy: Women's Suffrage and Reform Politics in Britain, 1900–1918*, 1986; J. Vellacott, *From Liberal to Labour with Women's Suffrage: The Story of Catherine Marshall*, 1993.

SWINDON AND NORTH WILTS (NUWSS) In 1913 the society was a member of the WEST OF ENGLAND FEDERATION OF THE NATIONAL UNION OF WOMEN'S SUFFRAGE SOCIETIES. Secretaries (1913) Miss Askew, St Hilaire, Bath Road, Swindon, and Miss Kathleen Ainsworth, Summerville, Bath Road, Swindon, Wiltshire.

SWINEY, [ROSA] FRANCES EMILY, MRS (1847–1922) Born in India, daughter of Major John Biggs, in 1871 married Major-General John Swiney and eventually became the mother of two daughters and four sons. In 1899 she wrote *The Awakening of Woman, or Woman's Part in Evolution*, which was reviewed in the July issue of the *Westminster Review* by "Ignota" (Elizabeth Wolstenholme ELMY), who praised the book as a "comprehensive and cogent plea for the full enfranchisement of women". By 1903 Frances Swiney was president of the CHELTENHAM WOMEN'S SUFFRAGE SOCIETY. In October 1906 she was present in London at the meeting, chaired by Mrs PANKHURST, at which the constitution of the WOMEN'S SOCIAL AND POLITICAL UNION was discussed and in 1907 and 1908 contributed money to the WSPU. However, this did not appear to preclude her continued attachment to the constitutional movement; she records in her entry in the *Suffrage Annual* that on 7 December 1907 she was given by the Cheltenham Suffrage Society a large revolving bookcase "in token of their esteem and appreciation of her work". She later subscribed to the WOMEN'S FREEDOM LEAGUE. She wrote articles on women's suffrage for the *Anglo-Russian* and the *Christian Commonwealth*. She was a theosophist, the founder and president of the League of Isis, and a vice-president of the Cheltenham Food Reform and Health Association. In 1913 she supported the NATIONAL POLITICAL LEAGUE and in 1918 she was a member of the SUFFRAGETTES OF THE WSPU. Among her other writings are *Woman and the Natural Law*, first published in 1906, 2nd edn 1912; *The Esoteric Teaching of the Gnostics*, 1909; *The Cosmic Procession*, 1906; *The Bar of Isis*, 1907; and *The Mystery of the Circle and the Cross*, 1908.

Address: (1913) Sandford Lawn, Cheltenham, Gloucestershire.
Photograph: In E. Hill and O.F. Shafer, *Great Suffragists – and Why*, 1909.
Bibliography: E. Hill and O.F. Shafer, *Great Suffragists – and Why*, 1909.

SWYNNERTON, ANNIE LOUISA, MRS (1844–1933) Artist, born in Kersal, near Manchester, one of seven daughters of Francis Robinson, a solicitor. After the family finances suffered a setback, Annie Robinson painted watercolours for money. She studied at Manchester School of Art and went, with Susan DACRE, to study in Rome for two years from 1874 and then, on their return to Manchester, joined her in founding the Manchester Society for Women Painters. From 1877 until 1880, again with Susan Dacre, she studied in Paris at the Académie Julien. Her loving portrait of Susan Dacre was painted at this time and was given to Manchester City Art Gallery in 1932. In 1882 two of her paintings were included in the summer exhibition of the Grosvenor Gallery. In 1883 Annie Robinson married Joseph Swynnerton (d. 1910), an English sculptor whom she had met in Rome. In 1889 Annie Swynnerton signed the Declaration in Favour of Women's Suffrage and in 1897 signed the claim for women's suffrage, both published by the CENTRAL COMMITTEE. In October 1891 the Central Committee hoped to commission a marble memorial to Lydia BECKER from Joseph Swynnerton; nothing appears to have come of the plan. In 1893 Annie Swynnerton sent a canvas, *Florence Nightingale at Scutari*, to the Women's Exhibition at Chicago. In June 1911 she headed the section of Chelsea artists in the Coronation Procession organized by the women's suffrage societies. Annie Swynnerton was obviously close to the Garrett family, painting the portrait of Agnes GARRETT in 1885 while staying with her in her cottage at Rustington in Sussex, and that of Louisa Garrett, wife of the youngest Garrett brother. On her death, Mrs Garrett left five paintings by Annie Swynnerton to Manchester City Art Gallery, to which bequest her sister added two more. In 1930 a portrait by Annie Swynnerton of Millicent Garrett FAWCETT was bought by the Chantrey Bequest and is now held by the Tate Gallery. In 1953 her portrait of Louisa Garrett ANDERSON was offered to, but refused by, the National Portrait Gallery. Among her other sitters were the two young sons of Christiana HERRINGHAM; the daughters of Hubert Parry, who was a close friend of the Garretts; the Rev. William Gaskell, widower of the novelist; and Henry James. She was elected ARA in 1922, strongly backed by John Singer Sargent, and was still exhibiting at the Royal Academy in the year of her death. In a codicil to her will she left a bequest to the artist Francis Dodd, in memory of Susan Dacre.

Address: (1880) 77 Park Street, Greenheys, Manchester; (1882) 5 Langham Chambers, London W; (1908 and 1933) 1a The Avenue Studios, 76 Fulham Road, London SW; 2E Via Montebello Macao, Rome.
Photograph: in E. Lang, *British Women of the Twentieth Century*, 1929.
Portrait: Mrs Swynnerton and Mrs Charles Hunter, by John Singer Sargent (photograph in National Portrait Gallery Archive). Mrs Hunter was the sister of Ethel SMYTH and patron and friend to Annie Swynnerton.
Bibliography: *Paintings by Mrs Swynnerton, ARA*, catalogue of exhibition at Manchester City Art Gallery, 1923.

SYMONS, MARGARET TRAVERS–, MRS (1873–?) née Williams Daughter of an architect who lived and practised in Alexandria. She was married to a New Zealander who by 1906 had deserted her. Maggie Symons was a journalist and from 1902 secretary to Keir HARDIE. For a brief period in early 1906, before Emmeline PETHICK-LAWRENCE took over the position, Margaret Travers-Symons was honorary treasurer of the newly formed London committee of the WOMEN'S SOCIAL AND POLITICAL UNION. On 13 October 1908 she caused consternation and much subsequent press coverage by entering the Chamber of the House of Commons and calling out, "Attend to the women's questions", while suffragettes barracked from Parliament Square. She eventually, as a punishment, had her permitted access to the precincts of the House revoked. After one year and nine months she apologized to the Speaker in July 1910 and had her permission reinstated. She was friendly with Jessie STEPHENSON and with Christabel PANKHURST. In December 1911 she was sentenced to five days' imprisonment after refusing to leave her WSPU companion when the latter was arrested after breaking a window. Around January 1913 she returned to Egypt, working there as a journalist during and after the First World War.

Archival source: Emrys Hughes Papers, National Library of Scotland.
Bibliography: C. Benn, *Keir Hardie*, 1997.

T

TAIN committee of the NATIONAL SOCIETY FOR WOMEN'S SUFFRAGE Was in existence in 1872 when E. McLardy, Esq. was honorary secretary. In 1913 the society was a member of the SCOTTISH FEDERATION OF THE NATIONAL UNION OF WOMEN'S SUFFRAGE SOCIETIES. Secretary (NUWSS) (1913) Miss F. Maclean, Sunnyside, Tain, Ross and Cromarty.

TANNER, MARGARET PRIESTMAN, MRS (1817–1905) Quaker, born in Newcastle, sister of Anna Maria and Mary PRIESTMAN, aunt of Helen Bright CLARK and of Anne ASHWORTH and Lilias Ashworth HALLETT. She was particularly friendly with John Bright, the widower of her elder sister Elizabeth. In 1846 she married Daniel Wheeler, a Bristol Quaker, and moved south. He died in 1848 and in 1855 she married Arthur Tanner of Sidcot, who died in 1869. There were no children of either marriage. Thereafter she lived with her sisters, who moved from Newcastle to Bristol. Margaret Tanner was involved in all feminist radical causes espoused by other members of her kinship network (see Appendix). In 1866 she signed the women's suffrage petition and in 1866–7 subscribed to the ENFRANCHISEMENT OF WOMEN COMMITTEE. By 1872 she was a member of the committee of the BRISTOL AND WEST OF ENGLAND branch of the NATIONAL SOCIETY FOR WOMEN'S SUFFRAGE. She was a member of the Bristol Women's Liberal Association, the first in the country, founded by her sister Anna Maria Priestman in 1881. With her other sister Mary, she was a leading member of the Ladies' National Association to Repeal the Contagious Diseases Acts and in 1895 attended, at Colmar, a meeting of the International Society of that campaign. In the 1890s Margaret Tanner was also president of the Western Temperance League (her sister-in-law Margaret Bright LUCAS was a leading temperance reformer) and headed the poll in the election to the parish council of Winscombe, where she had a country house. She spoke in support of the claim of women members of the Society of Friends to be accepted as an integral part of the Society's Yearly Meeting. She was friendly with Emily FORD, who in 1883 introduced her to Susan B. Anthony. From 1890 Margaret Tanner was a member of the executive committee of the CENTRAL NATIONAL SOCIETY FOR WOMEN'S SUFFRAGE.
Address: (1855–1905) Oakridge, Yatton, Somerset; (1870–1905) 37 Durdham Park, Bristol.
Photograph: carte de visite in Josephine Butler Collection, Fawcett Library.

TAUNTON (NUWSS) In 1913 the society was a member of the WEST OF ENGLAND FEDERATION OF THE NATIONAL UNION OF WOMEN'S SUFFRAGE SOCIETIES. Secretary (1913) Rev. F.W. Percy; assistant secretary, Miss Greswell, 2 Haines Hill Terrace, Taunton, Somerset.

TAX RESISTANCE LEAGUE Formed in October 1909 to conduct a campaign of constitutional militancy and organized resistance by women to taxation. The TRL was the culmination of a venerable tradition dating back to 1870, which was employed by workers in the cause of women's enfranchisement; Charlotte BABB, Rose Ann Hall, the PRIESTMAN SISTERS, Henrietta MULLER and Dora MONTEFIORE had all sought to highlight the anomaly of women, although unfranchised, being subject to tax. The TRL was founded at a meeting held at the invitation of Dr Louisa Garrett ANDERSON. Others present at this meeting, which was chaired by Margaret Wynne NEVINSON, were Mr Herbert Jacobs, Mary Sargant FLORENCE, Dr Elizabeth WILKS, Dr Kate Haslam, Dr Winifred Patch, Cicely HAMILTON, Edith How MARTYN, Clemence HOUSMAN, Mrs Wells, Mrs Ayres Purdie, Sarah BENETT, Gertrude ANSELL, Lady HARBERTON, Anne Cobden SANDERSON, Lilian

Hicks, Miss Carr Shaw, Sime SERUYA, Mrs Kate Freeman and Margaret Kineton PARKES. By 1910 the committee comprised Louisa Garrett Anderson, Mary Sargant Florence, Dr Kate Haslam, Evelina HAVERFIELD, Amy HICKS; Clemence Housman, Anne Cobden Sanderson, and Sime Seruya.

At the founding meeting Cicely Hamilton moved the resolution that the society should be entirely independent from any existing suffrage society. An amendment was introduced, but not carried, to the effect that, although separate as regards committee and finance, the society should remain under the auspices of the WOMEN'S FREEDOM LEAGUE. It was suggested that there should be two classes of member, those willing to resist taxation at the first opportunity and those willing to resist if 500 other women did the same. Those less brave were probably never put to the test; by July 1910 the TRL had 104 members. The motto adopted by the TRL was simple: "No Vote No Tax!". Mrs Kineton Parkes, who was involved with the Women's Freedom League, was allowed by that society to work for the TRL for at least three months. She remained as secretary for the entire life of the TRL.

By its very nature the TRL appealed mainly to middle-class women, in particular circularizing medical and other professional women. However, it was open to members who were not necessarily liable to income tax. Emma SPROSON, having refused to pay for a dog licence, was imprisoned and went on hunger strike in 1911; the dog was shot. However, the League was well aware of its natural sphere of influence. In October 1912 the TRL decided not to co-operate with the WOMEN'S SOCIAL AND POLITICAL UNION in its East End demonstrations, "as the Committee did not feel it worth while to do propaganda in that region".

When bailiffs seized goods belonging to women in lieu of tax, the TRL made the ensuing sale the occasion for a public or open-air meeting in order to spread the principles of women's suffrage and to rouse public opinion to the injustice of non-representation meted out on tax-paying women. Members of the TRL rallied round on these occasions and bought in the distrained goods and returned them to their owners. The case brought by the authorities against Mark Wilks, deemed responsible for the payment of his wife's tax, received widespread publicity. A scrapbook, presumably compiled by Dr Wilks, containing newspaper cuttings of the case is now held in the Suffragette Fellowship Collection of the Museum of London. In another gesture at defying bureaucracy, the TRL was at the forefront of the resistance to the census in April 1911.

The TRL was intent on spreading its message to both militant and constitutional societies; meetings were held in premises belonging to both the WSPU and the NATIONAL UNION FOR WOMEN'S SUFFRAGE SOCIETIES. The TRL took a platform at the WSPU Hyde Park demonstration on 23 July 1910. Around the country surviving minute books bear witness to Mrs Kineton Parkes's persistence in offering herself as a speaker to local societies. The GLASGOW AND WEST OF SCOTLAND ASSOCIATION FOR WOMEN'S SUFFRAGE repeatedly refused opportunities to support the TRL; this reluctance appears to have been due to the perceived illegality of its policy. The SOUTHAMPTON branch of the NUWSS, although phrasing its refusal of Mrs Kineton Parkes's proffered invitation to address them in 1912 rather more tactfully, in reality were not prepared to pay the required fee.

The TRL held its first conference, at Alan's Tea Rooms, in November 1910. On 12 December 1911 they held the "John Hampden dinner" at the Hotel Cecil. Guests were received by Maud Arncliffe SENNETT and Eva MOORE; the speakers were Charlotte DESPARD, Anne Cobden Sanderson, Alice ABADAM, Mrs Fagan, Margaret Kineton Parkes, Earl Russell, the Rev. Hugh Chapman, Frederick PETHICK-LAWRENCE and Laurence HOUSMAN. Another conference was held, this time at the International Suffrage Shop, in May 1912, to which delegates came from 12 suffrage societies. The primary object of the conference was to ask how many suffrage societies were prepared to adopt tax resistance as part of their policy. It was noted that members of the LONDON SOCIETY FOR WOMEN'S SUFFRAGE would have to resign from it if they wanted to adopt tax resistance.

In 1912 the TRL affiliated with the FEDERATED COUNCIL OF WOMEN'S SUFFRAGE. In 1913 the Duchess of Bedford, perhaps influenced by her experience as a prison visitor to the suffragette prisoners in Aylesbury prison in 1912, became a member of the TRL; her goods were distrained against unpaid taxes. On 10 June 1913 the League undertook a deputation, comprising Mrs Louis Fagan, Lena Ashwell, Adelaide Chapman, Dr Elizabeth Wilks, Mrs Ayres Purdie, Amy Hicks and Margaret Kineton Parkes to the Chancellor of the Exchequer, Lloyd George. The League suspended its activities at a meeting on 26 August 1914, although one section, led by Clemence Housman, thought that, although campaigning should be suspended, resisters should carry on refusing to pay taxes, in spite of the national crisis. Evelyn Sharp, brought to bankruptcy by the legal costs against her as a result of her continual refusal to pay tax, was the last tax resister.

In 1910 Mary Sargant Florence designed the League's BANNER, which bore the figure of John Hampden, based on the statue to him in the House of Commons, and it was made by the Suffrage Atelier. It was executed in the League's colours of grey and silver, with black poles and silver cords and is now in the Museum of London Collection. In 1911 Mary Sargant Florence designed and donated another banner to be carried in the Coronation Procession. It was made out of white silk in the colours of the League, bearing the motto "Pay the Piper call the Tune".

Secretary (1910, 1917) Margaret Kineton Parkes; treasurer, Elizabeth Wilks.

Address: (1910) 10 Talbot House, St Martin's Lane, where the TRL took a flat as office and residence of the secretary; (1917) 3 Gloucester Walk, Kensington W8.
Archival source: Tax Resistance League Papers, Fawcett Library.
Bibliography: H. Frances, "'Pay the piper, call the tune!': The Women's Tax Resistance League", in M. Joannou and J. Purvis, *The Women's Suffrage Movement: New Feminist Perspectives*, 1998.

TAYLOR, CAROLINE WATSON, MRS (1817–98) Daughter of Edwin Shute of Bristol, in 1852 she married William Taylor (1825–1903), brother of P.A. Taylor (*see* Clementia Taylor). She had two sons who died young, and three daughters, one of whom became Catherine Osler. Caroline Taylor was a member of the Society for Promoting the Employment of Women in 1867. In 1866, while living in Bridgwater, she signed the women's suffrage petition and in 1869, having moved to Birmingham, she was first treasurer of the newly founded Birmingham National Society for Women's Suffrage, becoming its president in 1873. She presided over a conference held in Birmingham in January 1874 by the National Society for Women's Suffrage and her name was appended to the long Memorial, intended for Gladstone, subsequently sent from the conference to Disraeli, who became prime minister in February, asking for support to the measure proposed by Jacob Bright to remove the electoral disabilities of women.

Address: (1870) 10 Chad Road, Edgbaston, Birmingham.
Archival source: Memorial to Gladstone, Birmingham Archives and Local History Library.
Bibliography: E.C. Stanton, S.B. Anthony and M.J. Gage (eds), *History of Woman Suffrage*, Vol. III, 1886.

TAYLOR, CLEMENTIA, MRS (1810–1908) Unitarian, one of the 12 children of John Doughty of Brockdish, Norfolk, a farmer and tanner. Through a Unitarian connection she obtained employment as a governess to the daughters of the Rev. J.P. Malleson, who ran a Unitarian boarding school at Hove. Frank, the brother of her charges, was, in 1857, to marry Elizabeth Whitehead (*see* Elizabeth Malleson). Clementia Doughty, who was always known as Mentia, was in 1842 married in Lewes by the Rev. Malleson to Peter Taylor, cousin to Frank Malleson and his sisters. The marriage was childless. P.A. Taylor, as he was invariably known, was a member of the Courtauld family and himself became a partner in the firm, which at that time was making its fortune by manufacturing mourning crape. Incidentally, 60 years later the Women's Social and Political Union's paper, *Votes for Women*, was to benefit from the extensive advertising for mourning crape taken in its pages by Courtaulds. P.A. Taylor's parents were very friendly with William Johnson Fox, MP for Oldham and the leading spirit of the South Place Chapel; Peter Taylor Snr had taken part in the Anti-Corn Law agitation. Mentia and P.A. Taylor carried on the radical tradition and were involved in the main social and political movements of the day (*see* Appendix). From 1845 Mentia Taylor was a close friend of Mazzini, helping to organize concerts and bazaars to raise funds for the school for poor Italian children he had established. Her husband was chairman of the committee of the Society of the Friends of Italy. They were both active in the campaign to abolish slavery and took Sarah REDMOND into their home. On the outbreak of the American Civil War Mentia Taylor formed the Freedmen's Aid Association and in 1863 became honorary secretary of the newly formed Ladies' London Emancipation Society.

After their marriage the Taylors first lived above the Courtauld premises in the City of London, then moved to leafy Sydenham, and in 1860 rented Aubrey House on Campden Hill in Kensington, which in the eighteenth century had been the country home of Lady Mary Coke; they bought the freehold (of what in the late-twentieth century is one of the most expensive properties in London) in 1863. From 1862 until 1884 P.A. Taylor was the "advanced" Liberal MP for Leicester and Aubrey House became a centre for radical movements. Elizabeth Malleson wrote:

> Those monthly [other sources say fortnightly] parties during the London season were unique and very enjoyable, for Mentia and her husband in her wake were admirably free of class prejudice in persons and opinions, so that all kinds of literary people – refugees from several countries – artists and humble lovers of social enjoyment, mingled with supporters of "causes" of all kinds and occasionally with M.P.s in court dress from the Speaker's dinner. No "amusements" were needed, and little or no supper, but the large rooms were filled with cheerful groups and couples engaged in every moment in the very real enjoyment of conversation.

George HOLYOAKE was, from 1861, a regular attender at Aubrey House, noting in his diary the appointed evenings for several months ahead. Those who went to "Mrs Taylor's evenings" did tend to remark them and mention them in their autobiographies; a picture can be built up from scattered fragments of reminiscences. It was at a party at Aubrey House, on the day that news of Lincoln's assassination belatedly reached England, that Millicent Garrett first met Henry FAWCETT; Moncure Conway in his autobiography mentions that he also was there that evening. On 2 June 1866 A.J. Munby recorded that he met at Aubrey House "an American lady from Boston, a Miss Allcot [sic]". Louisa M. Alcott, writing in *Shawl Straps: An Account of a Trip to Europe*, 1873, described her visit:

> Buckingham Palace is all very well . . . but I much prefer to be going to the house of a radical M.P., who is lending a hand to all good works. Mrs T. is a far more interesting woman to me than Victoria, for her life is spent in helping her fellow-creatures. I consider her a model Englishwoman – simple, sincere and accomplished; full of good sense, intelligence and energy. Her house is open to all, friend and stranger, black and white, rich and poor. Great men and earnest women meet there; Mazzini, and Frances Power Cobbe, John Bright, Jean Ingelow, Rossetti the poet, and Elizabeth Garrett the brave little doctor. . . . Though wealthy and living in an historical mansion . . . the hostess [is] the simplest dressed lady. Their money goes in other ways, and the chief ornament of that lovely spot is a school, where poor girls may get an education. Mrs T. gave a piece of her own garden for it, and teaches there herself, aided by her friends, who serve the poor girls like mothers and sisters.

The Pen and Pencil Club, a literary society, from 1864 met at Aubrey House and among the contributors to a privately published selection of papers given at its meetings were Frances Power COBBE, Mazzini, Joseph Biggs, Sheldon AMOS, Arthur Munby, Caroline Ashurst BIGGS, Adelaide Manning and Edward Carpenter.

A.J. Munby records in his diary another visit to Aubrey House in January 1866, writing, "The house stands on the hill top near the water tower, and with drive and gardens in front and parklike grounds behind, is thoroughly rural. . . . It was amusing to see how rooms and hall were made to express the owner's politics. Busts of Cromwell, portraits of Mazzini, memoirs of Abraham Lincoln, instead of Landseers and so on".

On 23 May 1866 Munby noted that he met at the Taylors' Barbara BODICHON, who was embroiled in the production of the petition for women's suffrage. The Taylors had supported the early emanations of the embryonic women's movement. In 1859 Peter Taylor was a shareholder in the *English Woman's Journal*; Mentia, as a married woman, could not hold shares. She was, however, from 1865 to 1870, a member of the committee of the Society for Promoting the Employment of Women. She was not a member of the KENSINGTON SOCIETY and not

Clementia Taylor (1810–1908). Reproduced from Stanton, Anthony and Gage, History of Women's Suffrage, vol. III, taken from the Fawcett Library and reproduced by kind permission of the Mary Evans Picture Library.

involved in the very earliest discussions about the desirability of producing a women's suffrage petition. However, when consulted by Barbara Bodichon in mid-May 1866, she promised that she would do all in her power to help. It was in Aubrey House that the 1499 signatures were collated from the petition sheets. On 10 June Mentia Taylor wrote to Helen TAYLOR that she was willing to take part in any further committee to promote the cause of women's suffrage. Around 20 June there was a meeting, evocatively described as the "acacia-tree party", held at Aubrey House between Emily DAVIES, Helen Taylor, Barbara Bodichon, Isa CRAIG Knox and Mentia Taylor, at which it appears to have been decided to press ahead with petitions but not actually to form a society. However, the situation was fluid; Mentia Taylor invited Helen Taylor and J.S. MILL to dinner at Aubrey House on 30 June, together with Henry Fawcett and other supportive MPs, adding that "in the evening several ladies will come for a conference upon the best mode of working for our objects". Mentia Taylor's role appears to have been that of a facilitator; she did not, as did Helen Taylor and Emily Davies, take firm stands on aspects of organization and policy. On 8 August she did, however, suggest to Helen Taylor that the proposed petition, which was being drafted by the latter, should expressly exclude married women in order that women should work their way slowly to universal enfranchisement, noting that "we women have many stumbling blocks because of man-made laws". However, she and Emily Davies, who shared this view, were overridden by Mill and Helen Taylor. With Barbara Bodichon, Mentia Taylor also opposed the view of Mill and Helen Taylor that the committee should consist only of women; she had 20 years' experience of working successfully on mixed committees. Between June and October 1866 Mentia Taylor acted as treasurer to the LONDON PROVISIONAL PETITION COMMITTEE and then, after the COMMITTEE FOR THE ENFRANCHISEMENT OF WOMEN was constituted on 23 November, became its treasurer. However, Mentia Taylor appears quickly to have become disillusioned with the work of the new Committee. On 4 March 1867 she wrote to Helen Taylor to suggest that after the presentation of the petitions which the Committee were preparing, "there should be a large meeting of the earnest friends of the cause to decide upon future work, organisation etc *and* form a new committee – have a paid Secretary – officials – such a Committee as *you* will be induced to join – and in which I shall not feel myself as a Pariah". She felt that Emily Davies was too conservative in her approach and presumably felt, like Jessie BOUCHERETT, that Lydia BECKER and the MANCHESTER SOCIETY were more effective.

Mentia Taylor was prepared to undertake the secretaryship of a new London society and was keen that a national society should be formed, the societies in London, Manchester, Edinburgh and Dublin combining strategy while maintaining their separate identities, in her own words "united but independent". Mentia Taylor was very friendly with Priscilla McLAREN, who with her husband often stayed with the Taylors during the parliamentary session. Friendship oiled the machinery of organization; agreement over consistency in naming the Edinburgh and London societies was reached during a morning call on 8 August by Mrs Taylor on Mrs McLaren. The first meeting of the LONDON NATIONAL SOCIETY was held in Aubrey House on 5 July 1867 and the Taylors gave £50 to the new society that year. Mentia Taylor was particularly keen that working men and women should not be excluded from the society and ensured that subscribers of less than 1/– per annum should receive all circulars and be able to attend all meetings. Mentia Taylor was treasurer of the London National Society and was, with Caroline Ashurst Biggs, its rather reluctant secretary until 1871. In 1868 Mentia Taylor wrote to Helen Taylor that Caroline Biggs, while still using the Aubrey House address, was to become sole secretary of the London National. However, Helen Taylor insisted that Mentia Taylor should remain as secretary *de jure* even though Caroline Biggs was secretary *de facto*. It was one of Mill's principles that the official secretary of the society should be a married woman, even though the actual work was done by a spinster.

In July 1869 Mentia Taylor took the chair at the first public meeting to discuss women's suffrage held in London and, again, at the meeting held in the Hanover Square Rooms in March 1870. In April 1871 she presided over a large suffrage meeting in Hackney Town Hall at which Elizabeth Malleson, Moncure Conway and Mrs Fawcett spoke. In 1871 the Taylors gave £50 each in support of the London National Society's lecture fund. Later in the year, however, Mentia Taylor resigned from the executive committee of the London National Society, hurt that, although she had been asked to sign the invitations to it, she had not been invited to speak at a conference of the suffrage societies organized by Jacob and Ursula BRIGHT and Lydia Becker. It was not that Mentia Taylor's views on the main issue under discussion differed from that of the Manchester National Society; unlike the majority of the executive committee of the London National Society, she was a supporter of Josephine Butler's campaign to repeal the Contagious Diseases Acts. After the conference the Brights asked all suffrage societies except the London National Society to a meeting to form the CENTRAL COMMITTEE. Mentia Taylor then wrote "I knew that all possibility of harmony existing between Manchester and London was over – and nothing but my retirement from office – *though most painful to me* – could pacify and set at rest Mrs B[right]'s jealousy of me and my position – not lessened I fancy by the opinions expressed by almost every Committee in England, Scotland, and Ireland, that I was the leader – that I founded their Societies". George Eliot, a close friend, wrote to Mentia Taylor at this time, "Welcome back from your absorption in the franchise! Somebody else ought to have your share of work now, and you ought to rest." However, Mentia Taylor remained an active suffrage worker; she was still a member of the London National Society and in 1873 again chaired a suffrage meeting at the Hackney Town Hall. In 1874 she resigned from the London National Society, withdrawing her annual subscription of £10. She probably soon after joined the Central Committee; certainly by 1878 she was a member of its executive committee. She was opposed to the exclusion of married women from the franchise bill supported by William Woodall and in 1889 was a member of the council of the WOMEN'S FRANCHISE LEAGUE. Although invited to do so, she was unable to take the chair at the inaugural meeting of the WFL and in November 1889 Elizabeth Wolstenholme ELMY urged her to come and chair the second meeting, explaining in a letter to Harriet MCILQUHAM, 7 October, "I want [the Taylors'] presence, sympathy and money help", and because, as Liberal Unionists, they would balance the Gladstone Liberals and the Conservatives, who were also represented on the council. Mentia Taylor, nearly 90 years old, was a member of the WOMEN'S EMANCIPATION UNION in 1897. She had been a member of the committee of the Whittington Club, a "radical Unitarian" venture founded in 1846 to provide working people with rational recreation and amusement. Its libraries, reading rooms, lecture halls, dining rooms and drawing rooms provided the setting for the discussion of progressive causes, from vegetarianism to women's enfranchisement. In 1869 the Taylors opened the Aubrey Institute, their own attempt to provide education and rational recreation for workers. Mentia Taylor gave up her carriage and the coach house and coachman's rooms in the grounds of Aubrey House were adapted as an evening institute. The Taylors supplied more than 500 volumes to form a lending library and reading room, which was opened on Sunday afternoon to young people of both sexes. The 1871 census shows that Mary

Grant was employed as a teacher at the Institute. Her husband, J.B. Grant, described by Elizabeth Wolstenholme Elmy as "a man of great intelligence and judgment", had been imprisoned for non-payment of church rates and had lost his business; P.A. Taylor then employed him as his secretary. In the autumn of 1867 Mentia Taylor paid Mary Grant to act as a canvasser in Southwark, collecting names for the petition organized by the London National Society. Mary Grant wrote a pamphlet, *The Franchise: An Educational Test, a Remedy for the Degeneracy of the House of Commons*, which was published by William Ridgeway in 1878. Their son, Corrie Grant, was later a radical Liberal MP and Clementia Taylor's executor; his wife was in 1898 a member of the executive committee of the Women's Liberal Federation. The Taylors' friends, many eminent, were volunteer lecturers at the Institute, which continued successfully until the Taylors were forced, by P.A.'s ill-health, to sell Aubrey House in 1873 and move to Brighton. They kept a London house in Westminster. Mentia Taylor carried on her philanthropic work by establishing in 1875 a Home for Young Women Servants in Pimlico.

In the 1870s and 1880s Mentia Taylor was treasurer of the Vigilance Association for the Defence of Personal Rights, of which Elizabeth Wolstenholme Elmy was secretary; in 1871 she was a member of the general committee of Elizabeth Garrett Anderson's newly founded Women's Hospital; and in 1876–82, with her husband, was a member of the executive committee of the Married Women's Property Committee. In a reminiscing letter (29 April 1908), occasioned by Mentia Taylor's death, Elizabeth Wolstenholme Elmy mentioned to Harriet McIlquham that "while he [P.A. Taylor] was in the House he was one of my best and most faithful helpers. When I was living in London he and Mr Thomas Sexton were my dearest helpers in the big fight". In 1869 Mentia Taylor was active in forming the Ladies' Educational Association to press for the admission of women students to University College, London.

From Mentia Taylor's will we can catch a glimpse of the objects remarked by Munby 30 years earlier as manifesting, in the decoration of Aubrey House, the Taylors' politics. The document itself embodies the satisfying consonance of Mentia Taylor's politics, possessions, friends and relations. Among many specific bequests, she left to Elizabeth Malleson a portrait of Eliza Flower (devoted friend of William Johnson Fox), a cenci brooch, and a volume of *In Memoriam* given to her by George Eliot; to her sister-in-law, Mrs William Taylor Malleson (Katie Ellen, sister of P.A.) she left a small round table that formerly belonged to Mr Fox; to Catherine Goodwin (a cousin of P.A. Taylor, who had, as Catherine Malleson, signed the 1866 suffrage petition) her gold brooch with Mazzini's ring in it, Mazzini's *Works*, Ruskin's *Modern Painters* and her bust of Mazzini; to Catherine OSLER her Italian necklace with Mazzini's portrait in it; to Mrs Emily Taylor her portrait in oil by Emilie VENTURI and a portrait in oil of W.J. Fox. Although the book is not specifically mentioned in the will, Elizabeth Wolstenholme Elmy revealed in a letter that the Taylors did possess a copy of *Woman Not Inferior To Man, or A Short and Modest Vindication of the Natural Right of the Fair-Sex to a Perfect Equality of Power, Dignity, and Esteem, with the Men* by "Sophia", a "Person of Quality", an extremely scarce tract published in 1739. Doubtless their library, long dispersed, contained many more works of similar interest.

Address: (1860) Aubrey House, Campden Hill, Kensington, London W; (1875) 22 Marine Parade, Brighton, Sussex; 22 Ashley Gardens, Westminster, London SW; (1908) 18 Eaton Place, Brighton, Sussex.
Portraits: of Clementia Taylor by Emilie Venturi, by Miss Fox, by Eaton, by Venables – all untraced.
Photograph: carte de visite in Josephine Butler Collection, Fawcett Library; in F.M. Gladstone, *Aubrey House, 1698–1920*, 1922; in E.C. Stanton, S.B. Anthony and M.J. Gage (eds), *History of Women's Suffrage*, Vol. III, 1886.
Archival source: Mill–Taylor Papers, London School of Economics and Political Science; Elizabeth Wolstenholme Elmy Papers, British Library.
Bibliography: P.A. Taylor, M.P. (compiler and editor), *Some Account of the Taylor Family*, printed for private circulation, 1875 (George Eliot was lent one of the 100 copies printed); *Auld Lang Syne: Selections from the Papers of the "Pen and Pencil Club"*; F.M. Gladstone, *Aubrey House, 1698–1920*, 1922; E.C. Stanton, S.B. Anthony and M.J. Gage, *History of Women's Suffrage*, Vol. III, 1886; *Englishwoman's Review*, 15 July 1908; G. Haight (ed.), *Letters of George Eliot*, 9 vols, 1954, 1955.

TAYLOR, HARRIET, MRS (1807–58) (Mrs John Stuart Mill) Unitarian, born in Walworth, daughter of Thomas Hardy, "surgeon and man midwife", married John Taylor in 1826 and had two sons and one daughter, Helen TAYLOR. Harriet Taylor and her husband formed part of the radical and decidedly feminist South Place Chapel circle, which also included William Johnson Fox, and the Flower and Gillies sisters. Through Fox, Harriet Taylor was introduced in 1830 to John Stuart MILL, with whom she soon developed a devoted friendship. At the end of 1833 Harriet Taylor, having negotiated a trial separation from her generous and affectionate husband, went to Paris, where Mill joined her for six weeks. The marriage was, however, resumed, preserving the outward proprieties while allowing Harriet Taylor to continue her friendship with Mill. This was based on shared sympathies, particularly those concerning the position of women. In the early years of their acquaintance, probably in 1832, they each wrote for the other an essay on the condition of women and of marriage, which Mill describes as "the subject which, of all connected with human Institutions, is nearest to [the] happiness" of "She to whom my life is devoted". In her essay Harriet Taylor was adamant that if women had entire equality, civil and political, with men, and if the marriage laws were abolished, "women would not then have children without considering how to maintain them. . . . Public offices being open to them alike, all occupations would be divided between the sexes in their natural arrangements. Fathers would provide for their daughters in the same manner as their sons". In his *Autobiography* Mill acknowledges that Harriet Taylor made a conspicuous contribution to the writing of *Political Economy*, 1848, and had had, from 1846, a share in writing his newspaper articles. In 1849 John Taylor died and in April 1851 Mill and Harriet Taylor were married. A month before the wedding, which was performed at a Dorsetshire register office, Mill wrote out a formal promise, abrogating all claims to the rights accorded to a man by the law of marriage. In July 1851 an article on "The Enfranchisement of Women", prompted by the Convention of Women held in Ohio in October 1850, was published in the *Westminster Review (see* NEWSPAPERS AND JOURNALS). At the time it was assumed to be the work of Mill, who, needless to say, had been the one to offer the article to W.E. Hickson, the editor of the *Westminster Review*. Doubts were, however, expressed by such perceptive contemporaries as Charlotte Brontë and it is clear that Harriet Taylor was in fact the author. Mill claimed only that he acted as "editor and amanuensis"; Harriet's writing had not acquired the polish derived from years of writing for publication. In 1866 Helen Taylor wrote firmly to Jessie BOUCHERETT that the essay was by her mother. In 1854 Mill turned down the opportunity, offered by John Chapman, editor of the *Westminster Review*, of reprinting the essay, intimating that he and Harriet were working further on the subject. In 1856 George HOLYOAKE reprinted the essay as a pamphlet titled *Are Women Fit for Politics?* and incurred Mill's wrath for not obtaining Harriet's permission. Holyoake claimed that this he had done. In 1868 the article was again reprinted as a pamphlet, this time by the LONDON NATIONAL SOCIETY FOR WOMEN'S SUFFRAGE.

An article on the necessity of protecting women and children from brutal husbands, published in the *Morning Chronicle* on 28 August 1858, and a pamphlet on the same subject published for private circulation in 1853, were described by Mill as being joint productions with his wife, his part, again, being little more than amanuensis. Mill gave credit to his wife for contributing "all that is most striking and profound" to *The Subjection of Women*, on which they were working during the latter years of her life, and which he finished in 1861 and published in 1869. Harriet Taylor, suffering from tuberculosis, spent her remaining years in a restless search for a suitable climate. She died at Avignon on her way to winter in the south of France.

Address: (1851) 1 Blackheath Park, London SE.
Portrait: by an unknown artist, *c.* 1834, in National Portrait Gallery.
Archival source: Mill–Taylor Papers, London School of Economics and Political Science.
Bibliography: F.A. Hayek, *John Stuart Mill and Harriet Taylor: Their Friendship and Subsequent Marriage*, 1951; J. Kamm, *John Stuart Mill in Love*, 1977.

TAYLOR, HELEN (1831–1907) Daughter of John and Harriet TAYLOR, step-daughter of John Stuart MILL. She saw little of her father and was educated at home, and on frequent continental travels, by her mother. From the age of 12 she was intent on going on the stage and from 1856 took lessons from an experienced actress. As "Miss Trevor", Helen Taylor went first to Newcastle, then to Doncaster and Glasgow, to serve her apprenticeship in the provincial theatre. Two years later, after her mother's death, she gave up all hankerings after dramatic glory and devoted herself to caring for John Stuart Mill, acting as both his housekeeper and secretary. Frances Power COBBE noted that Mill's attitude towards Helen was "beautiful to witness, and a fine exemplification of his own theories of the rightful position of women". Through Mill's friendship with George and Harriet GROTE, Helen Taylor became friendly with Kate AMBERLEY, to whom she in 1866 introduced Elizabeth Garrett (*see* Elizabeth Garrett ANDERSON). The Amberleys in 1872 asked Helen Taylor to be godmother to their son, Bertrand Russell. The day after he was born his father wrote to Helen Taylor, "I hope he will turn out mentally not unworthy of your regard". Mill, despite his lack of religious conviction, agreed to act as godfather. In 1907 Bertrand Russell, brought up in the Mill tradition, stood at a by-election in Wimbledon as a Women's Suffrage candidate. In 1864 Helen Taylor gave a donation of £12 to the Society for Promoting the Employment of Women and in 1865 she joined the KENSINGTON SOCIETY, invited to do so by Alice WESTLAKE. In November 1865 Helen Taylor, who with Mill was wintering in Avignon beside her mother's grave, sent in a paper to the Kensington Society in reply to that month's set question, "Is the extension of the Parliamentary suffrage to women desirable, and if so, under what conditions?"; Emily Davies expressed herself rather disappointed with the essay.

In 1866 members of the Kensington Society were vociferous in their support for the election of Mill as MP for Westminster and on 25 April 1866 a meeting between Mill, Helen Taylor and Emily Davies convinced the latter that the time, while discussion of the Reform Bill was taking place in parliament, was right for some agitation on the part of women for inclusion in any measure of enfranchisement. Barbara BODICHON wrote to Helen Taylor on 9 May suggesting that a petition from women, to be presented to parliament by Mill, would be an effective weapon of campaign (*see* WOMEN'S SUFFRAGE PETITION COMMITTEE). Helen Taylor replied giving her strong endorsement to the idea, and tacitly that of Mill. On 21 August, after the petition had been successfully drafted, signed and presented, Jessie BOUCHERETT wrote to Helen Taylor stressing that it was the latter's wholehearted backing for the initial suggestion that had given the idea reality. In January 1867 Helen Taylor published anonymously an article, "The Ladies' Petition", in the *Westminster Review*. In May the Manchester Society asked her to reprint the article as a pamphlet, offering £5 towards the expense. Helen Taylor did organize its publication, through Trubner, but entirely at her own expense. The pamphlet was titled "The Claims of Englishwomen to the Suffrage Constitutionally Considered". Even before the petition was presented, Helen Taylor suggested that the protest should be continued, with more petitions from "qualified" women being presented to parliament, and the LONDON PROVISIONAL PETITION COMMITTEE appears to have been her scheme for putting this into effect. She was concerned with the minutiae of the organization of a putative women's suffrage society, making it clear that she thought that the issue of enfranchisement should not be confused with any other aspect of the woman's cause. She and Mill were constantly consulted by Emily Davies and made it clear that they would only be associated with a society that was prepared to ask for the vote for married women, as well as for widows and spinsters; that these women should be property-owners, on the same terms as enfranchised men, was understood. By midsummer, however, it appeared that the idea of a society had been abandoned. Helen Taylor was in Avignon when the ENFRANCHISEMENT OF WOMEN COMMITTEE was finally established in the autumn; it is possible that her absence may have facilitated the process. She and Mill were adamant that such a committee should consist only of women and, when Barbara Bodichon and Clementia TAYLOR refused to exclude men, Helen Taylor wrote that she did not, therefore, intend to subscribe to the Committee as she wished to retain an independent voice. She handed over to the Committee the petitions on which she had been working. There appears to have been a rift between Emily Davies and Helen Taylor, whose opinion was not consulted in the months during which the former was running the Enfranchisement of Women Committee. There are no letters in Helen Taylor's papers from Emily Davies on suffrage matters between December 1866 and June 1867, when she wrote to tell Helen Taylor that the Committee was dissolved. Emily Davies was, however, fully aware that other factions had for the previous six months kept up a steady flow of information to Avignon. As early as March 1867 it became clear, in a letter from Mentia Taylor to Helen Taylor, that the Committee suffered from internal dissension and that the two women were in agreement as to the necessity of forming a new committee. This metamorphosed into the LONDON NATIONAL SOCIETY FOR WOMEN'S SUFFRAGE, which by late summer 1867 had been formed, from names suggested by Helen Taylor, with an all-women executive committee. Helen Taylor declined Mentia Taylor's request that she herself should join the committee, pleading her frequent absences abroad. In July she had given the new society £26 1s. Helen Taylor and Mill proposed that the London, Manchester and Edinburgh societies should band together as one. In the event the London Society was not willing to risk being compromised by any action taken by the other two and the eventual union was looser than Helen Taylor had envisaged.

Initially both Helen Taylor and Mill were members of the MANCHESTER NATIONAL SOCIETY as well as of the London National Society. Helen Taylor gave the Manchester Society £20 in November 1867. They both, however, resigned in December 1868 after being solicited for money by Lydia BECKER, who they afterwards learned had not had authorization from the committee of the Manchester Society, to support Philippine KYLLMANN's case in the Court of Common Pleas. The support that the "Bright and Becker set" gave to the campaign to repeal the Contagious Diseases Acts consolidated the rift between the Manchester and London societies. Mill and Helen Taylor became certain that the suffrage cause could only be harmed by its association in any way with "woman" in her less seemly condition. Helen Taylor was not, however, opposed to the CDA campaign *per se*; she gave £5 to the London National Association at its very inception in 1870 and there is a suggestion that she was for a short time a member of the committee of the LNA. The London National Society did not join with the 24 other local societies that pledged their support in 1871 to Jacob BRIGHT's CENTRAL COMMITTEE OF THE NATIONAL SOCIETY FOR WOMEN'S SUFFRAGE.

Helen Taylor gave her maiden speech in the suffrage cause at the public meeting held by the London National Society in the Hanover Rooms on 26 March 1870. Other women speakers that evening were Harriet Grote, Millicent Garrett FAWCETT and Katherine HARE. The occasion was witnessed by Catherine Winkworth who in a letter to her sister Emily (Mrs William Shaen) wrote, "Miss Helen Taylor made a most remarkable speech. She is a slight young woman, with long, thin, delicate features, clear dark eyes and dark hair, which she wears in long bands on her cheeks, fashionably dressed in slight mourning; speaks off the platform in a high, thin voice, very shyly with an embarrassed air; *on* the platform she was really eloquent". Helen Taylor's obituarist in *Women and Progress* remarked that when she began speaking on woman's suffrage in the 1870s "her remarkable oratorical powers became apparent. Her speeches, whatever the subject she dealt with, were always lucid, logical, convincing and inspiring". Kate Amberley's comment on Helen Taylor's performance that first evening was "a long & much studied speech; it was good but too like acting".

After the setting up of the Central Committee the policy of the London National Society, as dictated by Mill and Helen Taylor, appears to have been one of inaction, merely waiting for Jacob Bright's policy to fail. They both frequently threatened to resign if the London society were to support in any way the work of the Central Committee. After Millicent Garrett Fawcett had been forced by this policy to resign and join the Central Committee, Helen Taylor agreed to take her place on the executive committee of the London National Society. She was then able to use this position to continue to enforce a policy of inaction. When asked in January 1874 by the honorary secretary, Charlotte BURBURY, if she would speak at a large public meeting to be organized by the London National Society in the spring, Helen Taylor replied that she would pay £50 to the society not to have a meeting; that a successful meeting would take far longer than they were allowing to arrange; and that she thought they should continue Mill's policy of doing very little until after a dissolution and the election of a new House of Commons, by which time the circumstances would be so altered as to give reasonable cause for the adoption of a new plan of action. In the next month she intimated that she would retire if any joint effort were made by the London National Society with any other committee. In 1877, however, she attended the annual general meeting of the London National Society at which it was eventually agreed to join with the Central Committee; Jacob Bright had retired as parliamentary spokesman for the suffrage cause and his successor, Leonard Courtney, was considered more acceptable. Two years later Helen Taylor was included on the Central Committee's list of potential speakers; in May 1880 she addressed the Grand Demonstration held at the St James's Hall in London and in November 1881 that held in the Albert Hall, Nottingham. In 1880 with Florence Fenwick MILLER, she spoke at meetings, including one in Londonderry, organized by the Northern Ireland branch of the National Society for Women's Suffrage. By 1885 Helen Taylor was a member of the executive committee of the Central Committee.

In 1876, standing as a radical, Helen Taylor was elected to the Southwark seat on the London School Board, and re-elected in 1879 and 1882. In the early 1880s she was an active exponent of the Irish Ladies' Land League, organizing an English branch and using Jessie CRAIGEN as a speaker. She also supported the Land Reform Union and the League for Taxing Land Values. In 1884, with Michael Davitt, she founded the *Democrat* to further these causes. In 1881 she took part in the discussions that led to the formation of the Democratic Federation (from 1883 the Social Democratic Federation) and was a member of its first executive committee. In 1885 she was invited by the Camberwell Radical Association to stand as a parliamentary candidate for the North Camberwell seat. George HOLYOAKE offered her his support, the only man sitting on the platform at one of her meetings. Richard PANKHURST, who was standing at Rotherhithe, went over to Camberwell to speak in her support. Sylvia PANKHURST, in *The Suffragette Movement*, 1931, reports that Helen Taylor wore trousers on this occasion and that "Mrs Pankhurst was distressed that her husband should be seen walking with the lady in this garb, and feared that his gallantry in doing so... would cost him many votes" when the campaigning support was reciprocated. In 1866 Helen Taylor had had an interesting correspondence with Elizabeth French of Staplehurst, Kent, who most definitely was a trouser-wearer and proud of it. Helen Taylor's nomination was rejected by the returning officer and the campaign, which had received no support from the women's suffrage societies, dissolved.

By the late 1880s Helen Taylor was spending most of her time at Avignon. In 1888 both Elizabeth Cady Stanton and Priscilla Bright McLAREN attempted to persuade her to attend the first International Council of Women at Washington. Helen Taylor refused the invitation; there is a suggestion that she objected to the presence of Mrs Ashton DILKE as a fellow delegate. Helen Taylor was cared for in her later years by her niece, Mary Taylor. One of her last tasks, as recorded by Mary Taylor, was "making petticoats for the wives and children of the unemployed in West Ham". Shortly before her death she arranged for 1500 volumes from Mill's library to be given to Somerville College. During her lifetime she had been generous in her support of other women. In 1873–4, keen for women to test entry to the legal profession, she paid £75 for Eliza ORME to work as a pupil to a barrister in Lincoln's Inn. In 1882, having been alerted by Eliza Orme, Helen Taylor gave £25 to enable Hertha Marks (*see* Hertha AYRTON) to study for a scholarship to Girton. Mary Taylor, carrying on the family involvement, was among the women arrested in Parliament Square on "Black Friday", 18 November 1910.

Address: (1866) 1 Blackheath Park, London SE; (1873) 10 Albert Mansions, Victoria Street, Westminster, London SW; (1882) 13 Harrington Gardens, South Kensington, London SW; (1907) Babbacombe, Devonshire.
Photograph: in P. Hollis, *Ladies Elect: Women in English Local Government, 1865–1914*, 1987.
Archival source: Mill–Taylor Papers, London School of Economics and Political Science.
Bibliography: M.J. Shaen, *Memorials of Two Sisters: Susanna and Catherine Winkworth*, 1908; J. Kamm, *John Stuart Mill in Love*, 1977; P. Hollis, *Ladies Elect: Women in English Local Government, 1865–1914*, 1987; H. Taylor, "The claim of Englishwomen to the suffrage constitutionally considered", in J. Lewis (ed.), *Before the Vote was Won: Arguments For and Against Women's Suffrage 1864–1896*, 1987.

TAYLOR, [MARIA] MONA, MRS (*c.* 1852–1936) née Gulph Married to Thomas Taylor, a coal owner; she lived in a thirteenth-century castle, 11 miles from Hexham, and was a general benefactor in her area of Northumberland. She had two sons and two daughters; her household in the 1891 census consisted, besides her immediate family, of her mother, a governess, a lady's maid, a cook, two house maids, a laundry maid, a kitchen maid, a nurse, a nurse-maid, a footman, a coachman and his wife and grandson, who acted as a general domestic servant, plus a gardener and his family. In an article published in *Votes for Women*, 23 September 1910, Mona Taylor noted that she first attended a woman's suffrage meeting with her parents when she was 20, in 1872. It was held at St George's Hall and addressed by Lydia BECKER, Mrs FAWCETT and Rhoda GARRETT. In the 1880s Mona Taylor helped to promote the Guardianship of Children Act, which was eventually passed in 1886. In 1889 she gave £2 to the CENTRAL COMMITTEE OF THE NATIONAL SOCIETY FOR WOMEN'S SUFFRAGE and signed its Declaration in Favour of Women's Suffrage. In the 1890s she appears to have been a member of the executive committee of both the CENTRAL NATIONAL SOCIETY and the Central Committee. In 1890 she wrote to Jane Cobden (*see* Jane Cobden UNWIN), after the latter had lost *De Souza* v. *Cobden*, offering to collect what money she could towards the £110 judgment of costs, saying "I will give £20 myself. Forgive me if this proposal seems impertinent to you. I look on your action and the consequent 'costs' as a public matter and not a private or personal one." She did, however, advise that Jane Cobden should not appeal against the result, and was clear that her £20 should not be used to underwrite any such appeal. In 1890 she was a member of the council of the WOMEN'S FRANCHISE LEAGUE, but wrote a letter published in the *Woman's Herald*, 9 April 1892, in which she objected to the League's policy of opposing any women's suffrage bill that excluded married women. In the same year she wrote a letter to the *Hexham Herald* advising women in the Hexham Division to campaign for any candidate sympathetic to women's suffrage. In 1893–4 she wrote *Why Women Want the Suffrage*, 45 000 copies of which, produced as a leaflet by the Central National Society, were sent out in its first year.

Mona Taylor first joined the WOMEN'S LIBERAL FEDERATION in an attempt to galvanize it from within. She was one of the first 11 members to join the UNION OF PRACTICAL SUFFRAGISTS and became that society's honorary treasurer. In 1899 and 1900 she was a member of the executive committee of the NORTH OF ENGLAND SOCIETY FOR WOMEN'S SUFFRAGE. Between 1894 and 1896 she was an active promoter of the SPECIAL APPEAL COMMITTEE, which combined the efforts of the Central Committee, the Central National Society, the Women's Liberal Federation, the Primrose League and the British Women's Temperance Association and in 1896 presented a petition of 257 796 names. Mona Taylor commented that although MPs showed little interest in the petition, the experience led to the formation of the NATIONAL UNION OF WOMEN'S SUFFRAGE SOCIETIES, of which she became a member of the executive committee. She herself had been the driving force in drafting a proposal for the federation. In 1901 she published a pamphlet, *War Taxation and Women*.

In 1900 Mona Taylor became secretary of the newly founded NEWCASTLE AND DISTRICT WOMEN'S SUFFRAGE SOCIETY. By July 1908 tensions in the NUWSS over support for Liberal and Labour candidates at by-elections led to a proposal that the Newcastle society should withdraw its affiliation to the NUWSS and join the WOMEN'S SOCIAL AND POLITICAL UNION. The Newcastle society had twice, at Mona Taylor's instigation, asked the NUWSS to oppose all government candidates. When this motion was outvoted, Mona Taylor and 12 other members withdrew and formed the Newcastle WSPU. She was very active on behalf of the new branch; she ordered 1000 copies of the 29 October 1908 edition of *Votes for Women* to be given away "to men and women who cannot always afford the paper". In February 1910 she opened the WSPU shop in Newcastle. She eventually resigned from the WSPU in September 1912, after the PANKHURSTS had split with the PETHICK-LAWRENCES. Among her reasons for so doing was her inability to oppose Labour candidates who had given support to the suffrage campaign. She joined the NATIONAL POLITICAL LEAGUE FOR MEN AND WOMEN and became chairman of its North-Eastern Centre, of which Laura AINSWORTH was organizer and Violet Taylor, Mona's daughter, was treasurer. In her will she left a bequest to "my friend Laura Frances Ainsworth", who at that time was living in the same village.

Address: (1890, 1936) Chipchase Castle, Northumberland.
Archival source: Jane Cobden Unwin Papers, University of Bristol.
Bibliography: D. Neville, *To Make Their Mark: The Women's Suffrage Movement in the North East of England, 1900–1914*, 1997.

TAYLOUR, JANE E. (?–alive 1901) Scottish, described by Clementia TAYLOR as "the energetic little woman who came from Stranraer" to the women's suffrage meeting held by the LONDON NATIONAL SOCIETY in London in July 1869. In December 1869 Mentia Taylor wrote to her asking her to undertake a tour of some northern towns; this resulted in a lecture tour of Newcastle-on-Tyne and South Shields in February 1870. In March 1870 Jane Taylour gave more suffrage lectures in Aberdeen, Peterhead, Inverness, Cupar, Angus, Blairgowrie and Dundee and sent in a petition in favour of Jacob BRIGHT's bill to remove women's electoral disabilities. In January 1871, accompanied by Miss Burton of the EDINBURGH NATIONAL SOCIETY FOR WOMEN'S SUFFRAGE, Jane Taylour gave an hour-long lecture in Wigton on the progress of the suffrage movement. Of this the *Women's Suffrage Journal* commented, "Miss Taylour has all the requisites of a public lecturer. Her composition is chaste and elegant, her voice distinct and agreeable, and her manner attractive and graceful". She also spoke at Castle Douglas and in Glasgow, and the next month at Dumbarton, Rothesay and Greenock. She attended the Women's Suffrage Conference held in London in April 1871. In October Jane Taylour spoke at Wick, accompanied by Agnes McLAREN, who remarked that she had been asked to go north because everything had been done in Edinburgh that could be done; the city and county members had voted for the Women's Suffrage Bill, the town council had petitioned in its favour, and a very numerously signed petition had also been forwarded by the inhabitants. They carried on their northern tour to Tain, Dingwall, Forres, Elgin, Banff, Invergordon, Nairn and Dunkeld; women's suffrage committees were formed in these towns as a result of their campaign.

At the end of 1872 Jane Taylour is recorded by Helen Blackburn as having left Scotland to live in England, after delivering 139 lectures characterized, according to the *Women's Suffrage Journal*, January 1873, "by much care, thought, and talent, which have awakened interest not only in the question of granting Parliamentary suffrage to women, but also in the higher development of women generally". However, at the fifth annual meeting of the Edinburgh society, held in January 1873, Eliza Wigham announced that Miss Taylour had just been appointed secretary; she held that position jointly with Agnes McLaren until 1876. Jane Taylour was a member of the executive committee of the CENTRAL COMMITTEE OF THE NATIONAL SOCIETY FOR WOMEN'S SUFFRAGE in 1875, signed its Declaration in Favour of Women's Suffrage in 1889, was still a member of its general committee of the Central Committee in 1893 and was a vice-president of the NATIONAL UNION OF WOMEN'S SUFFRAGE SOCIETIES in 1901.
Address: (1874) 54 Rankeillor Street, Edinburgh; (1875) St Catherine's Place, Edinburgh.
Photograph: in H. Blackburn, *Women's Suffrage: A Record of the Women's Suffrage Movement in the British Isles*, 1902.

TAYSIDE (NUWSS) In 1913 the society was a member of the SCOTTISH FEDERATION OF THE NATIONAL UNION OF WOMEN'S SUFFRAGE SOCIETIES. Secretary (1913) Mrs E. Valentine, Ashcliff, Wormit-on-Tay.

TEIGNMOUTH (NUWSS) In 1913 the society was a member of the SOUTH-WESTERN FEDERATION OF THE NATIONAL UNION OF WOMEN'S SUFFRAGE SOCIETIES. Secretary (1913) Miss Clodd, St Agnes, Bitton Street, Teignmouth, South Devon, who had, in 1866 while living in Framlingham, signed the 1866 women's suffrage petition.

TERRERO, JANIE, MRS (1858–1944) née Beddall Born in Braintree, Essex, the daughter of a gentleman farmer. In her entry in the *Suffrage Annual* she noted that she had been a suffragist since the age of 18. While living in Southampton she was a member of the NATIONAL UNION OF WOMEN'S SUFFRAGE SOCIETIES in 1905 and in 1907 gave a drawing-room meeting for the LONDON SOCIETY FOR WOMEN'S SUFFRAGE. In 1885 she had married Manuel Terrero, who in 1906 chaired a meeting of the NUWSS in Southampton and who was a member of the MEN'S POLITICAL UNION in 1910. In 1908 Janie Terrero joined the WOMEN'S SOCIAL AND POLITICAL UNION and, after moving to Pinner, formed a branch there in 1910, becoming its honorary secretary. She and her husband were lavish with their hospitality and there were frequent WSPU garden parties in the grounds of their house.

Janie Terrero was arrested on 1 March 1912 after taking part in the WSPU window-smashing campaign and was sentenced to four months' imprisonment in Holloway. She took part in two hunger strikes and was, towards the end of June, forcibly fed until the prison doctor called a halt and released her a few days before the end of her sentence. The Southampton branch of the NUWSS sent her a letter "expressing sorrow that Mrs Terrero has had to suffer imprisonment for the sake of the Woman's Cause". She left extensive notes of her prison experience, which are now held as part of the Suffragette Fellowship Collection. In 1912 she refused to sign a petition to Mrs PANKHURST in protest against the break with the PETHICK-LAWRENCES. By the terms of her husband's will, Janie Terrero gave, as the Terrero Bequest, 2000 books from their library to that of the Working Men's College. Unfortunately the library was disbanded in the early 1990s, and this memorial to the Terreros' social and political interests was dispersed. In her will Janie Terrero left £500 to the council of the Working Men's College as an endowment for the upkeep of the Terrero Bequest.

Address: (1907) Fir Tree Lodge, Southampton; (1913) Rockstone House, Pinner, Middlesex; (1944) 62 Hillfield Court, Belsize Park, London NW.

Archival source: The Suffragette Fellowship Collection, Museum of London; Minutes of the Southampton Women's Suffrage Society, Southampton Archives.

TEWKESBURY AND DISTRICT (NUWSS) In 1913 the society was a member of the WEST OF ENGLAND FEDERATION OF THE NATIONAL UNION OF WOMEN'S SUFFRAGE SOCIETIES. Secretary (1913) Miss Rosie Livens, Timber House, Winchcombe, Gloucestershire.

THANET WOMEN'S SUFFRAGE SOCIETY See under CANTERBURY WSPU.

THEOSOPHICAL SOCIETY Many suffrage workers were members of the theosophical society, which in March 1914 formed a League to promote the cause of women's suffrage and to further the women's movement generally. Its intention was to co-operate with all organizations and individuals working for the same object and to take a neutral attitude as to tactics. Harold Baillie-Weaver was chairman; Gertrude Baillie-WEAVER, Charlotte DESPARD, Miss Townend (probably Gertrude Townend, partner, with Nurse PINE in the Pembridge Gardens nursing home) were among the members of the League's executive council, which arranged to meet each month at 19a Tavistock Square, London WC.

THETFORD (NUWSS) In 1913 the society was a member of the EASTERN COUNTIES FEDERATION OF THE NATIONAL UNION OF WOMEN'S SUFFRAGE SOCIETIES. Secretary (1913) Miss Leach, The Girls' Grammar School, Thetford, Norfolk.

THOMASSON, ELIZABETH LAWTON, MRS (c. 1876–1927) and **FRANKLIN THOMASSON** (1873–1941) Son and daughter-in-law of John Pennington THOMASSON, they married in 1895. In 1900 Franklin Thomasson had, with his father's financial backing and through negotiations conducted by Lloyd George, become one of the proprietors, with the Quaker manufacturer George Cadbury, of the *Daily News*, with the intention that it should become a London-based Liberal newspaper, as the *Manchester Guardian* was in the north. In July 1904, while Elizabeth Wolstenholme ELMY and Susan Anthony were staying with Katherine THOMASSON, the former wrote to Harriet McILQUHAM:

> Mr Franklin Thomasson and his wife joined us at dinner. I read them all Miss Pankhurst's letter to the *Daily News*, whereupon Mr FT did promise & vow (1) to give prominence to WS [women's suffrage] in his election address & speeches, (2) to secure that a strong WS Resolution was sent up in full time for consideration at the next meeting of the Gen[eral] Com[mittee] of the Liberal Fed[eration]. We had great talks about ways & means & methods of working – & we all, including Mrs [Katherine] Thomasson, agreed that the best results for our cause were to be looked for from the Textile Workers' movement & the establishment of a Press Bureau, on similar lines to that of the American WSS [Women's Suffrage Society] – supplying the papers steadily with

information and arguments on the woman question. Mrs [Katherine] Thomasson will, I think, adequately finance these 2 things, as soon as Somerset House enables her to do so [i.e. once probate had been granted on her husband's will]. Anyhow she is quite certain to help them both generously.

In early 1905 Franklin Thomasson withdrew his candidature as a Liberal MP on the grounds of ill-health. He was the proprietor of the *Tribune*, which in 1906 replaced the *Echo* as the radical Liberal paper. The *Tribune* was not successful; the journalist Philip Gibb gave a fictional portrait of its troubled life and its proprietor in *The Street of Adventure*, 1909 (*see under* NEWSPAPERS AND JOURNALS). Elizabeth Wolstenholme Elmy suspected, probably correctly, that the Thomassons were "Liberals above all, and Women suffragists a long way after" (*see* Appendix). In February 1907 the Thomassons followed the "Mud March" in their motor car; Mrs Thomasson was then president of the LEICESTER WOMEN'S SUFFRAGE SOCIETY and in 1913 was a vice-president of the LONDON SOCIETY FOR WOMEN'S SUFFRAGE.

Address: (1910) 36 Gloucester Square, London W; (1922) 91 Park Street, Mayfair, London W.

THOMASSON, JOHN PENNINGTON (1841–1904) Unitarian, son of Thomas THOMASSON, educated at the Pestalozzian School at Worksop and at University College, London. In 1867 he married Katherine Lucas (*see* Katherine THOMASSON), daughter of Margaret Bright LUCAS (*see* Appendix). He and John Bright were trustees for the daughters of Richard Cobden. J.P. Thomasson became a public benefactor to Bolton, giving the Mere Hall estate to the town (the house to be used as library and museum), a board school and £1000 a year for 20 years in student scholarships. In 1880 Thomasson was elected Liberal MP for Bolton; a fellow Bolton MP was J.K. Cross, brother-in-law of Anne ASHWORTH. A Liberal Unionist, Thomasson lost his seat in 1885, but remained an important Liberal supporter, giving £2500 to its election fund in 1903. With P.A. Taylor and Jacob BRIGHT, he was an active member of the Vigilance Association for the Defence of Personal Rights.

J.P. Thomasson was a subscriber to the ENFRANCHISEMENT OF WOMEN COMMITTEE, 1866–7, in the 1870s subscribed to the BIRMINGHAM NATIONAL SOCIETY FOR WOMEN'S SUFFRAGE, and in 1886 attended the annual general meeting of the MANCHESTER NATIONAL SOCIETY FOR WOMEN'S SUFFRAGE. With his wife, he was a generous supporter of both the Manchester society and the CENTRAL COMMITTEE. After the split in the latter society, in 1889, although a Liberal Unionist, he gave £200 to the newly formed CENTRAL NATIONAL SOCIETY. In 1890 he gave £50 to the WOMEN'S FRANCHISE LEAGUE on condition that they pledged not to oppose any franchise bill whatever, "even one which explicitly and in set terms excluded married women". After Elizabeth Wolstenholme ELMY and the committee of the WFL refused the money on these terms, he, according to Mrs Elmy, "gracefully gave way". He had initially supported the NATIONAL UNION OF WOMEN'S SUFFRAGE SOCIETIES but had presumably become disillusioned about the lack of progress because in 1901 Priscilla Bright McLAREN informed Esther ROPER that she had written "to John Thomasson to say as he withdrew his subscription to the Cause because the women did not show themselves anxious for suffrage, I hoped now he would help to get up the needful money to carry on this work in Cheshire and Yorkshire".

J.P. Thomasson's sister, Emma Winkworth, signed the 1866 women's suffrage petition as did her sister-in-law, Susanna Winkworth, who also subscribed to the Enfranchisement of Women Committee, and was an old friend of Elizabeth Wolstenholme Elmy, who, in 1906, was trying to persuade her to join the WSPU.

Address: (1902) Woodside, Bolton, Lancashire.
Photograph: carte de visite in Josephine Butler Collection, Fawcett Library; of Mr and Mrs J.P. Thomasson in Scatcherd Collection, Morley Public Library.
Archival source: Elizabeth Wolstenholme Elmy Papers, British Library; Priscilla Bright McLaren Papers, National Library of Scotland.

THOMASSON, KATHERINE, MRS (1842–1932) Daughter of Samuel Lucas and Margaret Bright LUCAS. Her marriage to John Pennington THOMASSON in 1867 was the occasion for a grand reunion of the Bright clan. The ramifications of the family network (*see* Appendix) are exemplified in the experience of her cousin, Helen McLaren, daughter of Priscilla Bright McLAREN, who came from

Edinburgh to attend the wedding and then went on to visit her cousin, Helen Bright CLARK and her family in Somerset, before staying with her step-sister, Catherine Oliver (daughter of Duncan McLaren by his first marriage), in Bournemouth. When it became clear that Catherine was dying of tuberculosis, the PRIESTMAN SISTERS immediately wrote inviting Helen McLaren to stay with them at Bristol. On her way back to Edinburgh, she then stayed with her aunt Ursula BRIGHT in London.

Katherine Lucas in 1866 signed the women's suffrage petition and in 1870 subscribed to the MANCHESTER NATIONAL SOCIETY. In 1871 she gave the society £30, and her husband gave a further £20, in order to relieve the society from the necessity of holding a fund-raising bazaar. In 1872 she gave £105 to the society and was elected to its executive committee. In 1873 she and her husband together gave £50 to the Manchester Society and £50 to the CENTRAL COMMITTEE. In 1874 she gave £50 to the Manchester Society and £50 to the Central Committee and, with her husband, a further £50 to the Manchester Society. This pattern of generous support continued. In February 1882 Katherine Thomasson was invited by Mrs Henry Wilson to a drawing-room meeting intended as a warm-up before the Grand Demonstration held the next week in the Albert Hall, Sheffield. After the split in the Central Committee in 1888 she, like the majority of the Bright clan, left to join the CENTRAL NATIONAL SOCIETY FOR WOMEN'S SUFFRAGE, of which, from 1889, she was a member of the executive committee. In 1901 she joined the executive committee of the NORTH OF ENGLAND SOCIETY FOR WOMEN'S SUFFRAGE.

After her husband's death in May 1904 Katherine Thomasson continued to be active in the women's movement. In July 1904, when Susan B. Anthony was in Britain after her visit to the International Congress of Women in Berlin, she, with Elizabeth Wolstenholme ELMY, stayed with Mrs Thomasson in Bolton. Repeating the pattern of Helen McLaren's experience 37 years earlier, Susan Anthony was planning then to visit Priscilla Bright McLaren in Edinburgh, the Priestmans in Bristol and Helen Bright Clark in Street. In September Mrs Thomasson attended a White Slavery conference in Zurich and then went to Dresden to an international conference on the Contagious Diseases Acts. In a letter of 7 October 1904 Elizabeth Wolstenholme Elmy wrote of Mrs Thomasson:

> I do hope she may soon be able to give effective help to the Women Textile Workers – who deserve much, as you will see from Miss PANKHURST's letter, a magnificent stand against the anti-suffrage fine ladies ... who call themselves the Council of the Manchester and District Women's Trade Union League Council. ... When we were together at Bolton she seemed eagerly interested – if she will finance them adequately, the whole body of women workers of the North and the Midlands may be effectively organized for WS [women's suffrage] within the next few months – the speakers are ready, the organizers are ready, – but they are under present circumstances, not able to find all the money, – though many of them are practising the severest self-denial to do what they can make possible.

Later that month Mrs Elmy reported that in the course of a visit to Eva GORE-BOOTH and Esther ROPER, she had learned that Mrs Thomasson was very depressed, "talks as if she had only £300 a year to live on", and was going to travel for six months in the USA with her son and daughter-in-law. In the meantime, "however, she will give them nothing till her return though the money is wanted for immediate work – & then only pledged herself to give what Mr Thomasson promised before his death". Although it was confirmed a month later that Mrs Thomasson was not prepared to support the Special Appeal campaign with £1000 that had previously been mentioned, this withdrawal was only temporary and a year later, in December 1905, Elizabeth Wolstenholme Elmy noted that Mrs Thomasson was giving generous support to Eva Gore-Booth and Esther Roper and the Women's Trade and Labour Council. When Eva Gore-Booth and Esther Roper broke with the NESWS at the end of 1905 Katherine Thomasson gave them £210 towards the cost of setting up the NATIONAL INDUSTRIAL AND PROFESSIONAL WOMEN'S SUFFRAGE SOCIETY, of which, in 1913, she was still a member of the executive committee. She did not, however, succumb to Elizabeth Wolstenholme Elmy's requests, made c. 1906, to give financial support to the WOMEN'S SOCIAL AND POLITICAL UNION.

By 1913 she was also a member of the NATIONAL UNION OF WOMEN'S SUFFRAGE SOCIETIES, a vice-president of the LONDON SOCIETY FOR WOMEN'S SUFFRAGE, and in 1911 had given a donation to the NEW CONSTITUTIONAL SOCIETY FOR WOMEN'S SUFFRAGE. Besides supporting so generously the women's suffrage movement, Katherine Thomasson also worked for the higher education of women, for social purity and for the abolition of the Contagious Diseases Acts; she gave £250 to the London Hospital for Women in 1877 and a large donation to the Maria Grey Training College in 1891.

Address: (1902) Woodside, Bolton; (1910) 16 Sussex Square, Hyde Park, London W.
Photograph: carte de visite in Josephine Butler Collection, Fawcett Library.
Archival source: Priscilla Bright McLaren Papers, National Library of Scotland; Elizabeth Wolstenholme Elmy Papers, British Library.

THOMASSON, THOMAS (1808–76) Quaker, but converted to Church of England after marrying a sister of Frederick PENNINGTON; another of his sisters-in-law was the mother of Ursula BRIGHT. He was a cousin of Thomas Ashworth, the father of Lilias (*see* Lilias Ashworth HALLETT) and Anne ASHWORTH. His son, John Pennington THOMASSON, continued his business and the Liberal family tradition (*see* Appendix). Thomas Thomasson was a mill owner in Bolton, friend of John Bright, involved in the Free Trade agitation, one of the founders of the Anti-Corn Law League, and a supporter of the Chartists. He was a town councillor in Bolton for 18 years, a member of the local Board of Guardians, and a supporter of the Mechanics' Institute and Bolton Infirmary. Thomasson was an important member of the MANCHESTER NATIONAL SOCIETY FOR WOMEN'S SUFFRAGE, of which his daughter Emma Winkworth was one of the founding members. He gave £10 to the society in 1867, £125 in 1870, £250 in 1872 and £130 in 1873. In 1873 he presided at its annual meeting. In addition, in 1873 he gave £100 to the CENTRAL COMMITTEE and £100 to the EDINBURGH NATIONAL SOCIETY FOR WOMEN'S SUFFRAGE. In 1874 he gave £50 to the Edinburgh Society and £105 to the Manchester Society. In the year he died he gave £100 to Sophia Jex-Blake's scheme for University Endowment for Women.

Address: (1870) Bolton-le-Moors, Bolton, Lancashire.

THOMPSON SISTERS Margaret Eleanor Thompson (1864–1957) and Mary Dawes Thompson (1866–1960) were born in Northumberland into a family of seven daughters and five sons. Six of the daughters became teachers, none of whom married. Mary Thompson was educated at Berwick Corporation's Academy, at a private school, and at Royal Holloway College, 1889–92, graduating with a distinction in Latin and the Driver Prize for Latin Prose. When she visited one of her brothers in Australia in 1902–3 he emphasized to her the fact that Australia, by giving the vote to women, was in advance of Britain. On her return, while teaching classics at South Hampstead School, she attended a suffrage talk given at the school, on 9 May 1904, by Emily DAVIES and immediately joined the NATIONAL UNION OF WOMEN'S SUFFRAGE SOCIETIES, as did her sister Margaret. On 22 February 1909 Margaret went to a WOMEN'S SOCIAL AND POLITICAL UNION meeting at the Queen's Hall and, inspired by Emmeline PETHICK-LAWRENCE's speech, volunteered to take part in a deputation to the House of Commons on 24 February. She was arrested and sentenced to one month's imprisonment. She was again arrested in November 1911 after taking part in the WSPU window-smashing campaign and sentenced to 10 days' imprisonment. Undeterred, she repeated the performance in March 1912 and, after being held on remand for 10 days, was, at the end of April, sentenced to six months' imprisonment in Holloway. She went on hunger strike on 19 June and was forcibly fed from 22 June to 6 July, when she was released early from her sentence. In the book of reminiscences that she wrote with her sister many years later, Margaret Thompson gives full details of her prison experiences and records the names of many of the other suffragettes who were imprisoned with her. The WSPU published as a pamphlet, titled *Adam and Eve*, a lecture she gave to the Croydon branch in January 1912.

In February 1912 Mary Thompson was arrested for playing a barrel-organ in Oxford Street during WSPU Self-Denial Week. She was sentenced to a fine, refused to pay, and was due to have goods distrained in lieu. However, the chairman of the Girls' Public Day School Trust (South Hampstead, where she still taught, is a GPDST school) sent her a letter and the money to pay the fine; Mary Thompson felt unable to refuse.

Both sisters joined the UNITED SUFFRAGISTS, remained in touch with the SUFFRAGETTE FELLOWSHIP and both contributed towards the plaque designed by Ernestine MILLS that recorded the BRACKENBURYS' association with "Mouse Castle".

Address: (1893) 4 Summer Hill, Berwick-on-Tweed; (1899) 37 Antrim Mansions, Haverstock Hill, London NW; (1913) 10 Stanley Gardens, Hampstead; (1950) Linden House, Eye, Suffolk.

Bibliography: M.E. and M.D. Thompson, *They Couldn't Stop us! Experiences of Two (usually Law-abiding) Women in the Years 1909–1913*, 1957.

THREE TOWNS AND DISTRICT (NUWSS) In 1913 the society was a member of the SOUTH-WESTERN FEDERATION of the NATIONAL UNION OF WOMEN'S SUFFRAGE SOCIETIES. Secretary (1909, 1913) Dr Mabel Ramsay, 4 Wentworth Villas, North Hill, Plymouth, Devonshire.

THURSO committee of the EDINBURGH NATIONAL SOCIETY FOR WOMEN'S SUFFRAGE Formed in 1871 as a result of the tour undertaken by Agnes MCLAREN and Jane TAYLOUR. Its convenor was Mr J.W. Galloway.

TIVERTON (NUWSS) In 1913 the society was a member of the SOUTH-WESTERN FEDERATION OF THE NATIONAL UNION OF WOMEN'S SUFFRAGE SOCIETIES. Secretary (1913) Mrs Jefford, Bank House, Tiverton, Devonshire.

TOBERMORY committee of the NATIONAL SOCIETY FOR WOMEN'S SUFFRAGE Formed in 1872.

TOLLEMACHE SISTERS Aethel Tollemache (c. 1875–1955) and Grace Tollemache (?–?) were daughters of the Rev. Tollemache, who after ministering in India had retired c. 1894 to Batheaston, Somerset. They were vegetarians and friends of Mary BLATHWAYT, whom Aethel accompanied on 8 November 1907 to their first WOMEN'S SOCIAL AND POLITICAL UNION meeting, which was addressed by Annie KENNEY, Emmeline PETHICK-LAWRENCE and Christabel PANKHURST, at the Victoria Rooms in Bristol. In February 1908, again with Mary Blathwayt, Aethel went to London to take part in the Women's Parliament at Caxton Hall. She worked in both Bath and Bristol, helping organize meetings for Annie Kenney. On the night of the census in April 1911 the Tollemache sisters entertained the protesting suffragettes who evaded the count in an empty house in Lansdowne Crescent, Bath; Grace played the violin, with Aethel accompanying her on the piano. In November 1911 Aethel was sentenced to 14 days' imprisonment after breaking a window at the National Liberal Club. At her trial she is reported in *Votes for Women* as saying that "she disliked very much destroying property, but they were forced into the position of soldiers, as Garibaldi was, by the circumstances, and she hoped the stone would be a protest against the abuse of British freedom". Mrs Blathwayt commented to her diary, "I wonder if she will come out madder than when she went in". On 5 December Mary Blathwayt sent the prisoner the first four parts of *Marvels of the Universe*, to help pass the time in Holloway. Grace Tollemache joined the WSPU window-smashing campaign in March 1912 and was sentenced to two months' hard labour. Mary Blathwayt sent her oranges and dates and Mrs Kineton PARKES, of the TAX RESISTANCE LEAGUE, visited her in Holloway. Mrs Tollemache had refused to pay tax; in 1911 some of her furniture was sold at auction in Batheaston and in 1912 and 1913 some silver. The items were bought by sympathizers and restored to her. The Tollemache sisters protested at several meetings held by cabinet ministers in Bristol and its neighbourhood, including one at Trowbridge for which they disguised themselves as what Mary Blathwayt described as "market women", and made a protest against forcible feeding in Bristol Cathedral during the service of enthronement for a new bishop. Grace Tollemache, who had joined the WSPU in 1910, was by 1913 secretary of the Bath branch. In January 1913 Aethel was sentenced to seven days' imprisonment in Holloway for wilful damage. After the Blathwayts resigned from the WSPU the Tollemaches took over their position as providers of hospitality to visiting WSPU speakers; in January 1914 Mrs DRUMMOND stayed with them. Both sisters were arrested outside Buckingham Palace after taking part in the deputation to the King on 21 May. Grace received a sentence of only one day's imprisonment, but Aethel was dealt with more harshly and went on a hunger-and-thirst strike in Holloway. Soon afterwards Grace Tollemache, with another suffragette, smashed a window at Buckingham Palace during a banquet, but the King chose not to press charges.

By December 1914 the Tollemache sisters were, literally, ploughing their own field, fully committed to doing their part to support the war effort. As Mrs Blathwayt noted, "They wish to produce food for times of scarcity". However, Aethel, at least, revised her opinion, became a pacifist, joined the EAST LONDON FEDERATION OF SUFFRAGETTES, and in 1917 was held for questioning in Leytonstone while canvassing for names for the "Peace Memorial".

Address: (1910) Batheaston Villa, Batheaston, Somerset.
Archival source: Blathwayt Diaries, Dyrham Park (The National Trust), Avon.
Bibliography: B.M.W. Dobbie, *A Nest of Suffragettes in Somerset*, 1979.

TONBRIDGE (NUWSS) In 1913 the society was a member of the KENTISH FEDERATION OF THE NATIONAL UNION OF WOMEN'S SUFFRAGE SOCIETIES. Secretary (1913) Mrs Ridgway, Greatham, 8 London Road, Tonbridge, Kent.

TONDU (GLAMORGAN) (WSPU) Secretary (1906) Mrs Doyle, 22 Coronation Street, Tondu, Mid-Glamorgan.

TOPSHAM (NUWSS) In 1913 the society was a member of the SOUTH-WESTERN FEDERATION OF THE NATIONAL UNION OF WOMEN'S SUFFRAGE SOCIETIES. Secretary (1913) Mrs Frood, Little Broadway House, Topsham, Devonshire.

TORQUAY AND PAIGNTON (WSPU) Secretary (1913) Mrs Fausten, Chalet la Rosaire, Livermead, Torquay, Devonshire.

TOTNES (NUWSS) In 1913 the society was a member of the SOUTH-WESTERN FEDERATION OF THE NATIONAL UNION OF WOMEN'S SUFFRAGE SOCIETIES. Secretary (1913) Mrs Ulyat, Port Meadow, Totnes, South Devon.

TOTTENHAM (branch of the LONDON SOCIETY FOR WOMEN'S SUFFRAGE, NUWSS) Was in existence in 1906 when its honorary secretary was Mrs Munks, 7 Beaufoy Road, Church Road, Tottenham. It does not appear to have been in existence in 1913.

TOTTENHAM (WFL) Secretary (1913) Miss F. Eggett, 30 Lausanne Road, Hornsey, London N.

TOWER HAMLETS (branch of the LONDON SOCIETY FOR WOMEN'S SUFFRAGE, NUWSS) Secretary (1913) Mrs Foulkes, 1 Bolingbroke Mansions, Bolingbroke Grove, Wandsworth Common, London SW.

TOWNSEND SISTERS Caroline Townsend (1870–1941) and Hannah Townsend (1868–alive 1939). They shared a house, with another sister, Alice, and both subscribed to the WOMEN'S SOCIAL AND POLITICAL UNION in 1907. On 24 February 1909 Caroline was arrested in Old Palace Yard after taking part in a deputation to the House of Commons and was sentenced to a month's imprisonment in Holloway. She was joint honorary secretary of the Lewisham branch of the WSPU, a member of the CHURCH LEAGUE FOR WOMEN'S SUFFRAGE, and remarked in the *Suffrage Annual* that she particularly enjoyed "out-door work – speaking, paper-selling, poster-parading". Hannah, a teacher and member of the National Union of Teachers, was a founding member and honorary secretary of the WOMEN TEACHERS' FRANCHISE UNION. In 1914 the Lewisham Women's Suffrage Club, to which they both belonged, published a pamphlet, *The Woman Teacher's Own Fault?* In her will Caroline Townsend left to Elsa GYE and the SUFFRAGETTE FELLOWSHIP "all my books and photographs and the two framed addresses referring to Women's Suffrage".

Address: (1913) 27 Murillo Road, Lee, London SE; (1939) Gravel Pit Farm, Gomshall, Surrey.
Photograph: of Hannah and Caroline Townsend in the Suffragette Fellowship Collection, Museum of London.

TUKE, MABEL KATE, MRS (1871–1962) née Lear Born at Plumstead, where her father was clerk of works in the Royal Engineers Department. In 1901 she married a captain in the South African Constabulary. After her husband's early death she returned in 1905 to England, meeting on the boat Emmeline PETHICK-LAWRENCE, who held her interest with a description of her work with the Espérance Girls' Club in Somers Town. Through this friendship Mabel Tuke was introduced to the embryonic WOMEN'S SOCIAL AND POLITICAL UNION and from 1906 until the outbreak of war in 1914 was its honorary secretary. She was particularly close to Christabel and Emmeline PANKHURST, to whom she was "Pansy". On 1 March 1912, with Emmeline Pankhurst and Kitty MARSHALL, Mabel Tuke went to Downing Street and threw a stone through the window of No. 10. For this she received a sentence of three weeks' imprisonment and while in Holloway was charged, along with Christabel and Emmeline Pankhurst and the Pethick-Lawrences, with conspiracy. She was, however, dismissed from the case on 4 April. Her health deteriorated after this experience and in the autumn, after the break with the Pethick-Lawrences, she embarked on a recuperative sea journey to South Africa. She frequently visited Christabel Pankhurst in Paris; she was certainly there in May and in December 1913.

In 1925 Mabel Tuke took part, with Emmeline and Christabel Pankhurst, in the ill-fated scheme to run a tea-shop (the English Tea-Shop of Good Hope) at Juan-les-Pins on the French Riviera. Mrs Tuke provided most of the capital and did the baking.

Address: (1962) The Rectory, Shadforth, Co. Durham.
Photograph: in the Suffragette Fellowship Collection, Museum of London.

TUNBRIDGE WELLS (NUWSS)   Had by December 1910 opened a shop "for the sale of literature and information and as a meeting place". At the end of November the committee had found a house, with a shop front, in Crescent Road, just opposite the entrance to the stables of the Calverley Hotel. They were able to afford the rent because one of their members, Ethel Sargant, sister of Mary Sargant FLORENCE, rented the top floor in which to store her books. Ethel Sargant (1863–1918) was a respected botanist, a fellow of the Linnaean Society and the first woman to serve on its council. She had been very friendly with Helena SWANWICK when they were both at Girton, and it was to the College that she eventually left all those books. She lived with her mother in Tunbridge Wells and it is through the latter's letters to Mary Sargant Florence that we can catch sight of the workings of the Tunbridge Wells Women's Suffrage Society. Mrs Sargant wrote to Mary Sargant Florence in early December 1910:

They took possession [of the shop] at once, not waiting for renovation, when they got it and the window is entirely filled with posters some of yours among them. . . . Yesterday Ethel was there when a delegate arrived from the central office to do what was possible at the election here (tomorrow is polling day) and Ethel offered a bed to the lady, whose name we have not yet grasped. . . . Ethel has hired a splendid motor car today decked in front with Liberal colours and our guest and the energetic young secretary are off I believe to Tonbridge to stir up voters . . .

On 13 March 1911 she wrote, "This is doing Ethel all the good in the world and throwing her with young and interesting women. . . . Ethel has had a good many meetings (suffrage) lately. The shop is getting much appreciated and several ladies have given 'teas' there so we hope it will be quite a centre." Mary Sargant Florence and her daughter, Alix, were invited to a theatrical suffrage event in Tunbridge Wells on 9 May 1911; Ethel and the committee were very anxious that the Opera House should be filled. Mary Sargant Florence was unable to attend but her mother reported on "what a success the play had been and now that all is settled up, the receipts just covered expenses which is very satisfactory. The notices in the local papers most complimentary particularly as to the goodness of the acting." Ethel went to London to take part in the suffrage Coronation Procession in June 1911. By 1913 the society was a member of the KENTISH FEDERATION OF THE NATIONAL UNION OF WOMEN'S SUFFRAGE SOCIETIES.

Secretary (1909, 1910) Mrs Tattershall Dodd, Grosvenor Lodge, Tunbridge Wells, Kent; (1913) Mrs Dodd and Miss Moseley. Office: 18 Crescent Road, Tunbridge Wells, Kent.

Photograph: of the Tunbridge Wells NUWSS shop (by Harold H. Cambury) in Fawcett Library.
Archival source: Sargant Florence Papers, Birmingham City Archives.

TUNBRIDGE WELLS AND EAST GRINSTEAD (WSPU)   Secretary (1913) Miss Olive WALTON, 11 The Pantiles, Tunbridge Wells, Kent.

TURNER, MINNIE SARAH (c. 1867–1948)   For 12 years the honorary secretary of a branch of the Brighton Women's Liberal Association, but in 1908 left, because the Liberal government refused women the vote, and joined the WOMEN'S SOCIAL AND POLITICAL UNION. In 1910 Minnie Turner noted that the years since she joined the WSPU had been the happiest of her life. She ran her home as a boarding-house, being particularly keen to cater for suffragettes, advertising from June 1910 in *Votes for Women*, then in the *Vote*, the *Suffragette*, the *Woman's Dreadnought*, the *Workers' Dreadnought* and, finally, until 1940, in the *Women's Freedom League Bulletin*. Her advertisement in *Votes for Women*, 19 August 1910 ran: "Suffragettes spend your holidays in Brighton, central. Terms moderate – Miss Turner N.W.S.P.U.". She was later to remember that "more of our leaders, speakers, 'Cat and Mouse' prisoners etc. have stayed with me than in any other home. My guests included Mrs PANKHURST, 3 of her sisters and other members of her family, Lady Constance LYTTON, Mrs PETHICK-LAWRENCE, Annie KENNEY, Mrs DRUMMOND, Marie NAYLOR, Ada Cecile WRIGHT, Mary LEIGH, Mary PHILLIPS, Elsa GYE, Helen Atkinson and Vera WENTWORTH". Suffragettes stayed with her while recovering from illness caused by overwork, or to recover from imprisonment, or, indeed, while working as organizers on the south coast. Mary CLARKE lived at "Sea View" in 1910, while based as WSPU ORGANIZER in Brighton, and it was from there that she went with Minnie Turner to London to take part in her final demonstration; Minnie BALDOCK stayed at "Sea View" while recuperating from her operation in 1911; and Emily Wilding DAVISON recovered there in July 1912 from her experiences in Holloway. By 1912 "rest cures", "home-made bread", "meals served in garden when weather permits" and "out-door sleeping accommodation" were among the lures offered by Minnie Turner. She also kept a suffrage lending library, which was doubtless available to her guests as well as to members of the local Brighton branch of the WSPU. A few of the books, distinctively covered, survive in the Suffragette Fellowship Collection in the Museum of London (*see* LIBRARIES).

In November 1910 Minnie was arrested, with Mary Clarke, after taking part in the deputation to Downing Street to protest against the treatment women had received on "Black Friday"; she was discharged. In November 1911 she took part in the organized WSPU campaign, breaking a window in the Home Office and receiving a sentence of 21 days' imprisonment. While preparing for imprisonment, she was also organizing working parties at her home for the Brighton stall (embroidery, lace and art metal work) at the WSPU Christmas Fair.

In March 1912 Minnie Turner received a postcard warning her that, as a retaliation for the WSPU window-smashing campaign, she, as a known activist, was likely to have her windows broken. A stone was indeed thrown through her front bay window; a photograph still exists, showing the holed pane. In May 1912, as a supporter of the TAX RESISTANCE LEAGUE, she had goods distrained and sold at auction in lieu of tax. After the First World War Minnie Turner was elected to the Brighton Board of Guardians. It was at her house in 1933 that Dr Elizabeth KNIGHT died after she had been involved in a traffic accident while on her way to "Sea View". She also kept in touch with Annie Kenney, who during the Second World War sent Minnie Turner a photograph of her son in naval uniform, and with Ada FLATMAN, who attended her funeral. In her entry in the *Suffrage Annual*, 1913, Minnie Turner gave her recreation as "collecting Suffrage photographs and autographs". Some of her photographs and postcards, although not grouped as her collection, are now held by the Museum of London; a scrapbook there does have "Minnie" on the cover.

Address: (1910, 1948) "Sea View", 13 (and later 14) Victoria Road, Brighton, Sussex.
Archival source: The Suffragette Fellowship Collection, Museum of London.

TYNEMOUTH (NUWSS) In 1913 the society was a member of the NORTH-EASTERN FEDERATION OF THE NATIONAL UNION OF WOMEN'S SUFFRAGE SOCIETIES. Secretary (1913) Mrs Scott, 5 Priors Terrace, Tynemouth, Northumberland.

TYSON FAMILY Mrs Helen Tyson (*c.* 1846–?) and her daughter Leonora Tyson (*c.* 1884–1959) joined the WOMEN'S SOCIAL AND POLITICAL UNION in 1908. In February 1908 Mrs Tyson and Leonora were arrested while taking part in the deputation to the House of Commons. From February 1910 Leonora Tyson was honorary secretary of the Lambeth branch of the WSPU and then of the Streatham branch. In 1911 she edited and printed by hand, from stencils by Alice B. Woodward, Pamela C. Smith, Ada P. Ridley, and others, *The Anti-Suffrage Alphabet* written by Laurence HOUSMAN. In October 1911, a fluent German speaker, she represented the WSPU at the Women's Congress in Hamburg. At the end of November she took part, with, among others, Annie KENNEY and Mabel CAPPER, in a protest in Bath, heckling Lloyd George from the roof of a four-storeyed building. She had intended to undertake a speaking tour in Germany in February and March 1912, but instead, after taking part in the window-smashing campaign she was imprisoned in Holloway from 8 March to 8 May 1912. She kept there an autograph album signed by her fellow prisoners, which, with letters she sent from prison, is now held in the Museum of London. Leonora Tyson, dressed in white, carrying a madonna lily, acted as a group captain of Section D at Emily Wilding DAVISON's funeral. When Leonora Tyson was travelling in the USA in 1954 she wrote to Christabel PANKHURST, who was living in California, and received a distant but polite letter in reply thanking the Tysons for their efforts on behalf of the WSPU all those years before.

Address: (1910) 37 Drewstead Road, Streatham, London SW; Leonora Tyson (1953) 26 Newlands Park, Streatham, London SW; (1959) 35 Montpelier Road, Purley, Surrey.
Photograph: of Leonora Tyson in the Suffragette Fellowship Collection, Museum of London.
Archival source: The Suffragette Fellowship Collection, Museum of London.

U

ULVERSTON (NUWSS) In 1913 the society was a member of the NORTH-WESTERN FEDERATION OF THE NATIONAL UNION OF WOMEN'S SUFFRAGE SOCIETIES. Secretary (1913) Miss L. Stirling, Skelfleet, Ulverston, Lancashire.

UNION OF PRACTICAL SUFFRAGISTS Finally formed within the WOMEN'S LIBERAL FEDERATION in 1896. At a council meeting of the WLF in 1893 Anna Maria PRIESTMAN had moved an amendment to the suffrage resolution, in favour of the "test question", that is, that potential Liberal candidates should be questioned as to their intention of supporting women's enfranchisement if elected. The corollary was that Women's Liberal Associations would then only campaign for candidates who could affirm their support. This amendment was defeated and in 1894 those in favour of putting the test question formed themselves into a small organization, with Anna Maria Priestman as president and Miss Tanner as secretary. By 1895 the group called itself the "Practical Suffragists"; Miss Julia Cameron and Miss Gertrude Woodward were its secretaries. Elizabeth Wolstenholme ELMY invited the Practical Suffragists to a drawing-room meeting of the WOMEN'S EMANCIPATION UNION in December 1896. In 1896 the Test Question Resolution was again drawn up before the WLF council meeting. However the Southport WLF, whose president was Eva McLAREN, had tabled such a resolution, which although different was to much the same effect, and this was adopted by the Practical Suffragists and moved by Lady GROVE. The motion was lost; on 10 June 1896 a meeting was held at which the "Practical Suffragist Committee" was merged in the existing "Union of Practical Suffragists within the WLF". The Union's objective was "To induce Women's Liberal Associations to work for no Liberal Candidate who would vote against Women's Suffrage in the House of Commons". As Valentine Munro-Ferguson wrote in a leaflet published by the UPS in 1896, "We have shown enough benevolence in politics, let us now make Woman's Suffrage the price of Woman's Work". In 1897 after the women's suffrage bill had passed its second reading by a large majority the committee decided with reluctance not to bring a test resolution that year at the WLF meeting. In 1898 a number of associations sent up resolutions to the annual WFL council meeting in favour of "Union" policy. The one that appeared on the agenda was that put forward by the Cuckfield WLA. It was moved by Florence BALGARNIE, supported by Lady Grove and Eva McLaren, and Mrs Mill Colman (sister to John Stuart MILL). It was again defeated, although by less than anticipated.

In 1898–9 the executive committee of the Union of Practical Suffragists comprised Ursula BRIGHT, Annie Leigh BROWNE, Mrs Gardner, Alison GARLAND, Lady Grove, Mary Kilgour, Miss Lile, Eva McLaren, Louisa MARTINDALE, Laura Morgan-BROWNE, Mary PRIESTMAN, Miss Ryley, Harriot Stanton BLATCH, Miss Tanner, Jane Cobden UNWIN, "Gwyneth Vaughan" and Mrs Williams. The Union issued a flood of pamphlets including ones by Ursula Bright, Dora MONTEFIORE and Mary Kilgour. Anna Maria Priestman's pamphlet *Women and Votes* was published c. 1896. In 1903 the Union of Practical Suffragists was dissolved after the WLF agreed to give its support only to candidates who were in sympathy with women's enfranchisement. However, this success was short-lived, for two years later the debate over the test question was reopened and in 1908, with the same objective, the FORWARD SUFFRAGE UNION was formed.

President (1898–9) Anna Maria Priestman; honorary treasurer (1898–9) Mona TAYLOR, Chipchase; honorary secretary (1898–9) Mrs Leeds, Tower House, Birdhurst Road, Croydon, Surrey, who with her husband had been in the previous years a member of the executive committee of the CENTRAL NATIONAL SOCIETY FOR WOMEN'S SUFFRAGE.

Bibliography: H. Leeds, *Origin and Growth of the Union of Practical Suffragists*, 1898.

UNITED SUFFRAGISTS Formed on 6 February 1914, open to both men and women, militants and non-militants. Its leaders had all been supporters and generous benefactors of the WOMEN'S SOCIAL AND POLITICAL UNION. Gerald Gould, H.W. NEVINSON and Evelyn SHARP were members of the first committee of the US, which by November also included Lena ASHWELL, Mr A.W. Evans (who had been honorary secretary of the BIRMNGHAM branch of the MEN'S LEAGUE FOR WOMEN'S SUFFRAGE), Agnes Harben (*see* Henry HARBEN), John SCURR and Elaine Whelan. Among the US vice-presidents were Hertha AYRTON, Dr Louisa Garrett ANDERSON, Evelina HAVERFIELD, Mr and Mrs George LANSBURY, Edith and Israel ZANGWILL, Laurence HOUSMAN, Maud Arncliffe SENNETT, William de Morgan, Beatrice HARRADEN, Louisa Jopling ROWE, Julia Scurr, Mrs Bernard Shaw and Harold and Gertrude Baillie-WEAVER. The PETHICK-LAWRENCES were members of the United Suffragists, supporting the continuing suffrage campaign from America in 1914–15. They had on 21 August 1914 given *Votes for Women,* of which Evelyn Sharp was editor, to the United Suffragists as their official paper. The work of the US can be followed through the issues of *Votes for Women;* branches were quickly formed in Amersham, Stroud and Edinburgh and campaigning carried out at the Poplar and Bethnal Green by-elections. After the outbreak of war the US continued its single-issue suffrage campaign, combining it with philanthropic work by opening a club for working women in Southwark, which was for a time run by Mary PHILLIPS. Funds for this purpose were raised by concerts given by Mary NEAL's Espérance Club. Branches were steadily added throughout the country, at the instigation of both former members of the WSPU (for instance in Birmingham) and of the NATIONAL UNION OF WOMEN'S SUFFRAGE SOCIETIES (for instance in Portsmouth). By 1917 the executive committee of the US had been augumented by, among others, Bertha Brewster and Ruth Cavendish-BENTINCK; Lady Rhondda (the former Mrs D.A. Thomas, not her daughter, *see under* Lady RHONDDA) and Lady Emily Lutyens had become vice-presidents. The United Suffragists participated in the NUWSS victory celebrations on 13 March 1918 at the Queen's Hall and held their own victory celebrations in the Caxton Hall, redolent of memories of past battles, on 16 March 1918. At this party Evelyn Sharp was presented with a book containing the signatures of many members of the United Suffragists; these ranged from Henry Nevinson to Mrs SBARBORO, once the WSPU tea lady. The United Suffragists then neatly fulfilled its motto, "Usque ad finem", by immediately winding up both itself and *Votes for Women.*

The United Suffragists published a pamphlet by Anna Martin, *Mothers in Mean Streets; or, The Toad under the Harrow,* with a preface by Gerald Gould. Laurence Housman designed a banner for the United Suffragists, which was then made by Clemence Housman. One of the society's BANNERS, featuring its colours and a device of two snakes entwining a flaming torch, is held in the Museum of London; it is not clear whether or not this is the Housmans'. A banner for the Manchester branch of the United Suffragists is held in Manchester Central Library Archives.

Honorary secretary (1914) Barbara Ayrton GOULD; honorary treasurer (1914) Mr H.J. Gillespie; secretary (1914) Mr Charles Gray.

Address: (1914) 3 Adam St, Strand, London WC; (June–October 1915) c/o VfW office 4–7 Red Lion Court, Fleet Street, EC; (October 1915–March 1918) 27 Chancery Lane, London WC.

Archival source: Evelyn Sharp Papers, Bodleian Library, Oxford.

Bibliography: K. Cowman, "'A party between revolution and peaceful persuasion': a fresh look at the United Suffragists", in M. Joannou and J. Purvis (eds), *The Women's Suffrage Movement: New Feminist Perspectives*, 1998.

UNWIN, [EMMA] JANE [CATHERINE] COBDEN, MRS (1851–1947) Daughter of Richard Cobden, sister of Anne Cobden SANDERSON and Ellen Cobden SICKERT. Her mother Kate signed the 1866 women's suffrage petition. The Cobden sisters were friendly in their youth with Barbara Leigh Smith (*see* Barbara BODICHON) and her sisters. Barbara Bodichon left Jane Cobden in her will a watercolour, *Shepherd and Sheep*, which she in her turn bequeathed to Girton College. It seems that Jane Cobden attended the Women's Suffrage conference held in London in 1871, by 1879 was a member of the finance committee of the CENTRAL COMMITTEE OF THE NATIONAL SOCIETY FOR WOMEN'S SUFFRAGE and by 1880 was its treasurer. In May 1880 she was one of the speakers at the Grand Demonstration held at St James's Hall in London and in 1881 at that held at Bradford. In 1883 she was, with Helen Bright CLARK, one of the women delegates to the Reform Conference held in Leeds by the Liberal Party. At this a resolution was passed in favour of women's suffrage. After the 1888 split she, like most of the women from established radical Liberal families, stayed with the CENTRAL NATIONAL SOCIETY and by 1890 was a member of its executive committee.

In 1889 Jane Cobden stood as a candidate, at Bow and Bromley, for the London County Council, sponsored by the SOCIETY FOR PROMOTING THE RETURN OF WOMEN AS COUNTY COUNCILLORS, which body had selected her from a short-list of three. She attracted sharp words on 9 January 1889 from the *Women's Penny Paper*, to whom she had declined to give an interview – "One so greatly indebted as yourself to the generosity & activity of Women is justly expected to respond to their efforts on her behalf, for it is the least she can do". Her successful campaign was organized by George LANSBURY, under the auspices of the Bow and Bromley Liberal and Radical Association. Unlike Lady SANDHURST, Jane Cobden held on to her seat because her defeated opponent declined to take legal action against her. She remained nominally on the LCC, although she was advised not to take part in committee work for the first year in order to ensure the validity of the remainder of her term of office. However, once she began actively to participate in committee work, devoting herself to the interests of children held in reformatories, a writ was filed and in 1891 *De Souza v. Cobden* was heard in the Court of Appeal. Her membership of the council was held valid but her participation invalid. The case attracted attention from suffrage workers throughout the country. Mona TAYLOR wrote to Jane Cobden offering to raise money towards her legal expenses and in March 1891 Elizabeth Wolstenholme ELMY wrote to Harriet McILQUHAM that she had spent "five quiet hours in the Manchester law library" reading up this case, "with all the cases therein referred to, and many others". Jane Cobden was debarred from standing for re-election.

Jane Cobden was a member of the council of the WOMEN'S FRANCHISE LEAGUE when it was founded in 1889 and presided over one of the sessions of the WFL's International Conference when it was held in London in July 1890. She was particularly friendly with Alice SCATCHERD and, with her and Agnes SUNLEY, in 1891 spoke at a meeting of the Morley Women's Co-operative Guild "to shew why women ratepayers should be allowed to vote for members of Parliament". In 1893 Jane Cobden attended the World's Congress at Chicago and there read to one of the sessions Ursula BRIGHT's paper on the Women's Franchise League, reported on the activities of the WOMEN'S LIBERAL FEDERATION (of which she was by then a member of the executive committee), and gave a paper on "Women's Legitimate and Illegitimate Influence on Politics". From the 1890s she was friendly with Mrs Saul SOLOMON, both being members of the Anti-Slavery and Aborigines Protection Society. Jane Cobden was, like Helen TAYLOR, involved with the Irish Land League and was elected a member of the council of the Home Rule Union. She edited a study of the Irish famine, *The Hungry Forties*, 1904, of which the publisher's nephew, Sir Stanley Unwin, waspishly remarked in his autobiography that it was "a volume members of the staff were never allowed to forget". In 1892 she had married Thomas Fisher Unwin (*see* PUBLISHERS AND PRINTERS), who had himself subscribed to the CENTRAL NATIONAL SOCIETY in 1890. Stanley Unwin described her as "the power behind the throne . . . a forceful personality, but highly emotional and unreliable in her judgments. Her enthusiasm for such causes as Women's Suffrage, the Protection of Aborigines, anti-vivisection, was unbounded." Two of Fisher Unwin's brothers had married sisters of Mrs Louisa MARTINDALE. In 1898 Jane Cobden Unwin was a member, with Mrs Martindale, of the executive committee of the UNION OF PRACTICAL SUFFRAGISTS and was president of the Brighton Women's Liberal Association, of which Mrs Martindale was also an active member. In 1899 Jane Cobden Unwin opened a debate on women's suffrage at the Pioneer

Club (*see under* CLUBS). In 1906, a vice-president of the NATIONAL UNION OF WOMEN'S SUFFRAGE SOCIETIES, Jane Cobden Unwin attempted to attend the trial of her sister, Anne Cobden Sanderson, but under a pretext was removed from the court, and not allowed to return. With her husband she attended the banquet held at the Savoy on 11 December to celebrate the release of her sister and the other WOMEN'S SOCIAL AND POLITICAL UNION prisoners. She subscribed to the WSPU in 1907 and in 1909–10. The Fisher Unwins' "New Year Day" card for 1907 used a design by Sylvia PANKHURST of working women with a banner streaming "Votes ..." and the heading "Women Demand the Right to Vote: The Pledge of Citizenship and Basis of All Liberty". In February 1907 Jane Cobden Unwin held an "At Home" at which Christabel PANKHURST spoke on "What the Woman Movement Means". In November 1907 she gave her support to the WSPU's new venture, *Votes for Women*. Jane Cobden Unwin does not appear to have followed Anne Cobden Sanderson into the WOMEN'S FREEDOM LEAGUE, although in 1912 she was a supporter of the TAX RESISTANCE LEAGUE. In June 1911 she organized the Indian contingent in the Women's Coronation Procession. In November 1909 she resigned her membership of the Rochdale Women's Liberal Association, as a protest against the government's treatment of women suffragists. In 1913 she was a vice-president of both the LONDON SOCIETY FOR WOMEN'S SUFFRAGE and of the FREE CHURCH LEAGUE FOR WOMEN SUFFRAGE and a supporter of the NATIONAL POLITICAL LEAGUE.

Jane Cobden Unwin was a very close friend of the artist Emily Osborn (*c*. 1828–1925) and was living at her house in 1889. Emily Osborn signed the Declaration in Favour of Women's Suffrage organized by the Central Committee of the National Society for Women's Suffrage in 1889. Emily Osborn, who had in 1884 painted a portrait of Barbara Bodichon, did the same service for Jane Cobden. Her portrait was exhibited at the Society of Lady Artists in April 1891 and in it the sitter is depicted with a fur draped in a manner not dissimilar to that used in the Bodichon portrait. This portrait hung in the Committee Room of the London County Council until the early 1980s when, while in the care of the London Residual Body during the winding up of the GLC, it was cut from its frame and stolen.

Address: (1880) 14 York Place, Baker Street, London W; (1884) 10 Oxford and Cambridge Mansions, London W; (1885, 1887) 17 Canfield Gardens, South Hampstead, London NW; (1889) 10A Cunningham Place, London NW (address of Emily Osborn); (1900) 10 Hereford Square, London SW; (1907) Oatscroft, Heyshott, Midhurst, Sussex; (1907) 3 Adelphi Terrace, Strand, London WC.
Portrait: photograph of portrait by Emily Osborn in archives of Guildhall Art Gallery; photograph of same portrait in the *Woman's Herald*, 4 February 1893.
Archival source: Jane Cobden Unwin Papers, Bristol University Library; Cobden Papers, West Sussex Record Office.
Bibliography: The *Woman's Herald*, 4 February 1893; P. Hollis, *Ladies Elect: Women in English Local Government, 1865–1914*, 1987.

V

VARLEY, JULIA (1871–1952) Granddaughter of a Chartist, she was a half-timer working in a mill when she was 12, later becoming a weaver. She joined the Bradford branch of the Weavers and Textile Workers' Union and was soon its secretary. She was a member of the WOMEN'S FRANCHISE LEAGUE in 1889, attending its public meeting in November at the Westminster Palace Hotel, subscribed to the WOMEN'S EMANCIPATION UNION in 1893, and in February 1899 is recorded by Elizabeth Wolstenholme ELMY as attending one of that society's meetings. From 1899 until 1906 Julia Varley was the first woman member of the executive committee of the Bradford Trades Council. From 1904 until 1907 she was a poor law guardian in Bradford. She was a member of the WOMEN'S SOCIAL AND POLITICAL UNION and imprisoned in Holloway for two weeks in February 1907, having been arrested during the demonstrations surrounding the Women's Parliament on 13 February, and was in Holloway again in April 1907, probably as a result of the disturbances surrounding the deputation from the second Women's Parliament on 20 March. Her sister, Mrs Barrett, was also arrested on 13 February. In 1908 Julia Varley joined the staff of the National Federation of Women Workers as an organizer, setting up a branch in Cadbury's Bournville factory. In 1909 she was elected a delegate to the Birmingham Trades Council and in 1911 stood as a Socialist candidate in Kings Norton in the election for the new town council of Greater Birmingham. Julia Varley does not appear again as a WSPU activist; she doubtless disagreed with the WSPU's break with the Labour Party shortly after her last imprisonment. However, in 1912 she was a member of the BIRMINGHAM WOMEN'S SUFFRAGE SOCIETY, presumably influenced by the NUWSS Election Fighting Fund policy, by which support was given to Labour Party candidates. In the 1920s she was a vice-chairman of the joint committee of the Industrial Women's Organizations and regularly addressed meetings of Lady RHONDDA's Women's Industrial League.
Address: (1952) 42 Hay Green Lane, Bourneville, Birmingham.
Bibliography: L. Middleton (ed.), *Women in the Labour Movement: The British Experience*, 1977.

VENTURI, EMILIE (?1826–93) Daughter of W.H. Ashurst, sister of Matilda Ashurst BIGGS and Caroline STANSFELD, friend of Mazzini and George HOLYOAKE. She signed the 1866 women's suffrage petition, and subscribed to the ENFRANCHISEMENT OF WOMEN COMMITTEE, 1866–7. She was a member of the executive committee of the CENTRAL COMMITTEE OF THE NATIONAL SOCIETY FOR WOMEN'S SUFFRAGE on its formation in 1871, and was probably the anonymous author of *The Rights of Women*, 1875, and, as "A Looker On", of a very interesting pamphlet, *Women's Rights as Preached by Women*, in which, acknowledging that her position is rather apart from the main suffrage society, she criticizes the suffrage campaign in the light of the ideals set for it by eighteenth-century radical women such as Mary Wollstonecraft and "Sophia" (*see under* PUBLISHERS AND PRINTERS). In 1890 she became a member of the committee of the WOMEN'S FRANCHISE LEAGUE. However, Emilie Venturi's main efforts for the woman's movement were directed not towards suffrage but as a member of the executive committee of the Married Women's Property Committee, 1876–82, of the Personal Rights Association and of the Ladies National Association for the repeal of the Contagious Diseases Acts. She was the editor of that campaign's journal, *The Shield*, from 1871 to 1886. Among her other activities Emilie Venturi was a painter, indeed on the 1871 census she gives her occupation as "artist painter", perhaps taught by Frank Stone, the father of Bertha STERLING, who had certainly taught her elder sister Eliza. Among the known subjects of her portraits were Mazzini (now in the Casa Mazzini in Genoa), George Holyoake and Clementia TAYLOR.

Address: (1871) 14 Milborne Grove, Gilston Road, West Brompton, London W; (1888) Carlyle Cottage, 318 King's Road, Chelsea, London SW.

Bibliography: E.F. Richards (ed.), *Mazzini's Letters to an English Family 1844–54*, 1920–22; J.L. and B. Hammond, *James Stansfeld: A Victorian Champion of Sex Equality*, 1932.

VOTES FOR WOMEN FELLOWSHIP Formed by Emmeline and Frederick PETHICK-LAWRENCE on 1 November 1912 after their break with the PANKHURSTS and their consequent withdrawal from the WOMEN'S SOCIAL AND POLITICAL UNION. As may be surmised from the name of the organization, it was built around the weekly suffrage paper, *Votes for Women*, which since its inception in 1907 had been owned and edited by the Pethick-Lawrences. The "Fellowship" was aimed at promoting *Votes for Women* as a suffrage paper, independent of all societies. By doing so it would be, in Emmeline Pethick-Lawrence's words, "giving full expression to the awakened militant spirit of womanhood; that they should associate themselves in various plans for carrying the message far and wide, until in every town and village of this land women realise that they are a living part of a spiritually militant sisterhood that is at war under the triple banner of liberty, compassion, and purity against every form of evil dominance" (*Votes for Women*, 8 November 1912). The Fellowship described itself as a common meeting ground for members of all suffrage societies, whether militant or non-militant, and its purpose as one of education, based on the message contained in *Votes for Women*. The Fellowship's emblem depicts a lady with a lamp and the motto "To spread the Light". Laurence HOUSMAN, Gertrude Colmore (*see* Gertrude Baillie-WEAVER), Christopher ST JOHN and Cicely HAMILTON were regular contributors to the paper, of which Evelyn SHARP was joint editor. *The Man's Share*, the pamphlet containing Frederick Pethick-Lawrence's speech from the dock during the May 1912 conspiracy trial, was reissued by the Votes for Women Fellowship. There does not appear to have been an overwhelming rush to join the VFWF; subscription lists each week are short and by the end of September 1913 the fund stood at only £862. By contrast, according to the *Suffragette* (26 September 1913), the WSPU garnered £357 in the period 13–25 August 1913 alone. Some familiar names appear among the list of those giving subscriptions to the VFWF: Mrs Mackworth (*see* Lady RHONDDA), Georgiana SOLOMON, Amy HICKS, Margaret and Mary THOMPSON and Henry NEVINSON. This lack of obvious success and the formation, at the beginning of 1914, of the UNITED SUFFRAGISTS, appealing to a similar audience, probably explains why the Pethick-Lawrences gave *Votes for Women* to that society in July as its official paper. It would be a mistake to construe the United Suffragists as a direct descendant of the Votes for Women Fellowship.

Address: (1912–14) 4–7 Red Lion Court, Fleet Street, London EC.

W

WAKEFIELD committee of the NATIONAL SOCIETY FOR WOMEN'S SUFFRAGE was in existence in 1872 when its honorary secretary was Miss Julia BARMBY, Westgate Parsonage. The Wakefield Women's Suffrage Society was refounded in 1904 as a member of the NATIONAL UNION OF WOMEN'S SUFFRAGE SOCIETIES and by 1913 was a member of the WEST RIDING FEDERATION. Secretary (1913) Miss F.M. Beaumont, Hatfield Hall, Wakefield, Yorkshire.

WALKDEN (WFL) Secretary (1913) Mrs Rogerson, 33 Westminster Road, Walkden, near Manchester, Lancashire.

WALKER AND WALLSEND (NUWSS) In 1913 the society was a member of the NORTH-EASTERN FEDERATION OF THE NATIONAL UNION OF WOMEN'S SUFFRAGE SOCIETIES. Secretary (1913) Miss M. Ellis, 613 Welbeck Road, Walker-on-Tyne, Northumberland.

WALLASEY (WSPU) Secretary (1913) Miss Lee, 58 Belvedere Road, Wallasey, Cheshire.

WALLASEY AND WIRRAL (NUWSS) In 1913 the society was a member of the WEST LANCS, WEST CHESHIRE, AND NORTH WALES FEDERATION OF THE NATIONAL UNION OF WOMEN'S SUFFRAGE SOCIETIES. Secretary (1909) Miss McPherson, 16 Newland Drive, Liscard, Cheshire; (1913) *pro tem* Miss J. Ward Platt, Warrendene, New Brighton, Cheshire.

WALLINGTON (WSPU) Secretary (1913) Mrs De Vere Mathew, Dinham, Hillside Gardens, Wallington, Surrey.

WALSALL (NUWSS) In 1913 the society was a member of the NORTH-WESTERN FEDERATION OF THE NATIONAL UNION OF WOMEN'S SUFFRAGE SOCIETIES. Secretary (1913) *pro tem* Mis Lowry, 74 Lysways Street, Walsall, Staffordshire.

WALSALL (WSPU) Address (1911) Field House, Buchanan Road, Walsall.

WALMSLEY, AMY (1868–1928) From 1895 the forceful and business-like principal of Bedford Kindergarten Preparatory Schools and Kindergarten Training College, which were run according to Froebel principles and which, under the previous headmistress (who had signed the 1889 Declaration in Favour of Women's Suffrage organized by the CENTRAL COMMITTEE OF THE NATIONAL SOCIETY FOR WOMEN'S SUFFRAGE) had advertised in the *Women's Penny Paper*. In 1903 Amy Walmsley was elected a member of the borough education committee and a governor of Luton Modern School. In 1908 she was instrumental in the refounding of the BEDFORD WOMEN'S SUFFRAGE SOCIETY, was its honorary secretary in 1909 and its chairman from 1913, many of the meetings of the society being held at her house. After that society was dissolved in 1918 she founded, in 1920, the Bedford branch of the National Council of Women Workers. In 1918 she stood, unsuccessfully, as parliamentary candidate at a by-election.
Address: (1908) 74 Ashburnham Road, Bedford; (1928) 10a Oaklands Road, Bedford.
Photograph: in R. Smart, *Bedford Training College, 1882–1982*, 1982.
Bibliography: R. Smart, *Bedford Training College, 1882–1982*, 1982.

WALTHAMSTOW (WSPU) Was in existence in early 1908. Secretary (1913) Miss Hart, 11 Sylvan Road, Walthamstow, London E.

WALTON, OLIVE GRACE (1886–1937) One of four children of Charles Walton, a retired wine merchant, by his second wife. He was in his 70s when Olive was born and died when she was seven years old. The children were then brought up in a somewhat puritanical household by their mother, who before her marriage had been a missionary in Africa, working there with a daughter of her husband's first marriage. Olive Walton attended a small private school and, with her family, spent two years in Germany, an experience from which she derived little educational benefit. Her brother and one of her sisters went to Oxford, but Olive Walton was unacademic and considered a misfit in the family. After attending cookery and art classes she was sent to London to do social work. She joined the Tunbridge Wells branch of the WOMEN'S SOCIAL AND POLITICAL UNION and, once living in London, was drawn into increasingly militant activity. Her niece believed that Olive Walton's involvement in the WSPU was "a godsend" for her. She was imprisoned in November 1911 for seven days and then, as a result of taking part in the window-smashing campaign, spent March to June 1912 in Aylesbury prison, where she went on hunger strike and was forcibly fed. Her family were horrified by such a disgrace; her brother and a sister went to court to bail her, but she refused any assistance. Her younger sister, in spite of Olive's request, refused to meet her on her release from prison. Olive Walton apparently kept a diary while in prison, but its whereabouts is now unknown.

After spending the early part of 1913 as WSPU ORGANIZER in Tunbridge Wells, from November until the outbreak of war in August 1914 Olive Walton was WSPU organizer in Dundee. In July 1914, during the visit of King George and Queen Mary to Scotland, Olive Walton threw a rubber ball, to which was attached a petition requesting the King to put a stop to the forcible feeding of suffragettes, into the royal carriage. She was arrested, but Queen Mary sent word to the police station in which she was held, asking that she should not be prosecuted. A few days later Olive Walton was able to repeat the appeal, again by throwing a rubber ball, when the Queen was leaving St Giles's Cathedral in Edinburgh.

Shortly after the outbreak of war, Olive Walton, with Dora Meeson COATES and Mary ALLEN, was one of the first to enrol in the Women Police Volunteers. She became one of the four inspectors in the headquarters staff of the Women Police Service and in 1920, as a member of the Women's Auxiliary Service, was drafted to Dublin to work with the Royal Irish Constabulary. She was eventually forced to leave the police force after being badly injured while riding her motorbike. Her niece described how Olive Walton had no interest in frivolous clothes, cut her hair short "like a man's" and wore a costume suit with shirt and tie. She became a Christian Scientist and vegetarian, voted Labour and worked as an almoner in a London East End hospital. She very much wanted to have a child and, despite a slowly developing bone cancer thought to have been triggered by her accident, adopted a daughter, named "Christabel". In her will she specifically left to her adopted daughter her "suffrage medal, brooch, address together with the bound copies of *Votes for Women* and any other books on the Women's Movement".

Address: (1935) Almora, West Runton, Norfolk; Flat 8, The Drive, Fulham Road, London SW.
Photograph: in Fawcett Library Collection; in D. Atkinson, *Suffragettes in Pictures*, 1996.
Archival source: B. Harrison, taped interview with Mrs Margaret Dunnett, niece of Olive Walton, 1976, Fawcett Library.
Bibliography: M. Allen, *The Pioneer Policewoman*, 1925.

WALTON-ON-THAMES (branch of the LONDON SOCIETY FOR WOMEN'S SUFFRAGE, NUWSS) Secretary (1909, 1913) Miss May Hawes, Edradour, Walton-on-Thames, Surrey.

WANDSWORTH (branch of LONDON SOCIETY FOR WOMEN'S SUFFRAGE, NUWSS) Secretaries (1909, 1913) The Misses Hill, Roseneath, 3 Blenkarne Road, Wandsworth Common, London SW.

WANDSWORTH (WSPU) Secretary (1913) Mrs Chapman, 57 Gorst Road, Wandsworth Common, London SW.

WANSBECK (NUWSS) In 1913 the society was a member of the NORTH-EASTERN FEDERATION OF THE NATIONAL UNION OF WOMEN'S SUFFRAGE SOCIETIES. Secretary (1909) Miss Pindar, Delaval Road, Whitby Bay, and Mrs T. Baird, New Hurst, Ashington; (1913) Mrs Tomlinson, Lilleville, Monkseaton, Northumberland.

WARD, MARY, MRS (1851–1933) Born in Armagh, one of the 12 children of a Congregational minister.

She had no conventional schooling, merely spending one year, when she was 15, as a pupil-teacher in Hampstead. From that time, until she went to Newnham in 1876, she was self-supporting. One of her brothers offered to pay her living expenses at Cambridge if she gained a Higher Local Examination Scholarship. This having been accomplished, she graduated from Newnham in 1879, the first woman to have achieved the equivalent of Class I in the Moral Science Tripos. She was resident lecturer in Moral Sciences at Newnham from 1880 until 1884 and, after her marriage in 1884 to James Ward, later to become Professor of Mental Philosophy and Logic, continued for many years to lecture for the college. The Wards had three children, one son and two daughters. They had a house built for them in Selwyn Gardens, very close to Newnham, by J.J. Stevenson, the brother of Flora and Louisa STEVENSON.

Mrs Ward signed the Declaration in Favour of Women's Suffrage compiled by the CENTRAL COMMITTEE FOR WOMEN'S SUFFRAGE in 1889 and became a very active suffragist, secretary of the CAMBRIDGE WOMEN'S SUFFRAGE ASSOCIATION from 1905 until 1915, and a member of the standing committee of its successor, the Cambridge branch of the National Union of Societies for Equal Citizenship, from 1918 until 1925. She was the author of a suffrage propaganda PLAY, *Man and Woman*, described in *Votes for Women*, 30 April 1908, as a "drama... frankly intended to promote the cause of woman's suffrage among working men and women". It was first performed in London in May 1908 and proved very popular with suffrage societies throughout the country over the next few years. The minutes of the Cambridge Association record that a performance of the play in Cambridge on 26 October 1911 realized a profit of £10, which was promised to the Eastern Counties Federation, to which in that year Mary Ward had been selected as Cambridge representative. She took part in the 1913 NUWSS PILGRIMAGE, marching through unfriendly crowds from Barnwell junction to Midsummer Common. In that year she resigned her membership of the Liberal Party in protest against the government's treatment of militant suffrage prisoners. Her last effort for the Cambridge Association was to organize a Market Place sale, in order to raise funds, in 1914. Failing health compelled her to resign the secretaryship in 1915. One of her daughters, Olwen Ward Campbell, was in 1952 the author of the *Report of a Conference on the Feminine Point of View*. Among the members of this conference were Teresa BILLINGTON-GREIG and Margery Corbett ASHBY.

Address: (1905) 6 Selwyn Gardens, Cambridge.
Archival source: Records of the Cambridge Association for Women's Suffrage, County Record Office, Cambridge.

WARRINGTON (NUWSS)   In 1913 the society was a member of the WEST LANCS, WEST CHESHIRE, AND NORTH WALES FEDERATION OF THE NATIONAL UNION OF WOMEN'S SUFFRAGE SOCIETIES. Secretary (1909) Miss L.F. Waring, Latchford House, Warrington, Lancashire; (1913) Mrs H. Pemberton, Bentley, Ellesmere Road, Stockton Heath, Warrington, Lancashire.

WARWICK AND LEAMINGTON (NUWSS)   In 1913 the society was a member of the MIDLAND (WEST) FEDERATION OF THE NATIONAL UNION OF WOMEN'S SUFFRAGE SOCIETIES. Secretary (1909) Miss M.L. Vellacott, Langton House, Leamington, Warwickshire; (1913) Mrs A. Hill, St Bees, Northumberland Road, Leamington, Warwickshire.

WATSON, ELIZABETH SPENCE (1838–1919) Quaker, born in Newcastle-upon-Tyne, third daughter of Edward and Jane Richardson. She was educated at the Quaker Lewes School and then studied at art school in Newcastle under William Bell Scott. She married Robert Spence Watson, a solicitor, in 1863. He was a close friend of Jonathan Priestman, brother to Anna Maria and Mary PRIESTMAN and Margaret TANNER, and, a radical who never stood for parliament, he led the Liberal Party in Newcastle and became president of the National Liberal Federation. He remembered that when he was a boy Charles Lennox Remond, brother of Sarah REMOND, was entertained to dinner by his parents. His interest in the anti-slavery movement led to a correspondence, when he was a young man, with Elizabeth Pease NICHOL and her husband. Both he and his father were friendly with George HOLYOAKE. The Watsons had six children; one of their daughters, Mabel, was a particularly close friend of Esther Bright CLOTHIER. Elizabeth Spence Watson was a poor law guardian, a president of the local Women's Liberal Association, which she helped to found, and was a member of the Newcastle and Gateshead Vigilance Association, the British Women's Temperance Association, and a prime mover, with her husband, in founding the High School for Girls in Gateshead. In 1890 she was a member of the council of the WOMEN'S FRANCHISE LEAGUE and in 1900 was one of the founders of the NEWCASTLE AND DISTRICT WOMEN'S SUFFRAGE SOCIETY, beoming an active member of its executive committee.

Address: (1900) Bensham Grove, Gateshead.
Photograph: in P. Corder, *Robert Spence Watson*, 1914.
Archival source: Friends' Library, London.
Bibliography: P. Corder, *Robert Spence Watson*, 1914; *Reminiscences of the late Rt. Hon. Robert Spence Watson*, 1969.

WATTS, HELEN KIRKPATRICK (1881–alive 1965) Daughter of Rev. A.H. Watts, vicar of Lenton, Nottingham. She had some association with the Girls' Realm Guild, sending in essays in response to competitions run by the *Girls' Realm*, and may actually have been employed by the Guild. She joined the WOMEN'S SOCIAL AND POLITICAL UNION after hearing Christabel PANKHURST speaking at a meeting in Nottingham in early December 1907. She was arrested on 24 February 1909 and charged with wilfully obstructing the police after taking part in a deputation from Caxton Hall to the House of Commons. She had not told her parents that she was intending to take part, but in the event they were very supportive. She enjoyed a welcoming supper organized by Nottingham members of the WSPU at Morley's Cafe on 24 March, the day of her release. On 29 April at the Albert Hall she received one of the illuminated scrolls, commemorating her imprisonment for the cause. In September 1909 she was again arrested, this time in Leicester after protesting outside a meeting being held by Winston Churchill. She went on hunger strike for 90 hours in Leicester Gaol and was released. Caprina FAHEY, with whom she had been imprisoned in Holloway a few months previously, wrote to congratulate her. In a talk she gave, again at Morley's Cafe, after her release, Helen Watts remarked:

> "Votes for Women" will not be won by drawing-room chatter. It has got to be fought for in the market-places, and if we don't fight for it, no-one else will. . . . The open-air meeting is a symbol of the principles, the method, and the spirit of the most vigorous movement towards Woman Suffrage in England today. The Suffragettes have come out of the drawing room, the study, and the debating hall, and the committee rooms of Members of Parliament, to appeal to the real sovereign power of the country – THE PEOPLE.

Interestingly, in view of the emphasis Helen Watts places on speaking at outdoor meetings, Col BLATHWAYT, with whom she stayed at Batheaston in April 1911, noted of her, "She is a nice girl, but difficult to talk with because besides being very deaf herself she speaks so that it is very difficult to understand her". She obviously did not let any possible disability deter her; she spoke at meetings at Midsomer Norton, 27 November 1909, in Birmingham, 18 May 1909, as well as at many places around Nottingham, even addressing a meeting of the NOTTINGHAM WOMEN'S SUFFRAGE SOCIETY. She does not appear to have been involved in any further militancy after January 1910 when she was arrested after being involved in a protest outside a meeting being held in Nottingham by Herbert Samuel; on this occasion her case was dismissed. She did some nursing and by 1912 was studying. It seems likely that Helen Watts was working in February 1914 for the WOMEN'S FREEDOM LEAGUE, organizing their campaign at the Poplar by-election. During the First World War she was first a nurse, working at the Mineral Water Hospital in Bath, and later in both the War Office and the Ministry of Labour. She emigrated to Vancouver in 1965. With her brother she published *Poems by a Brother and Sister*, 1906 (a copy of which she sent to the Blathwayts in 1911) and *The Nevilles: a story for Girls*, 1912.

Address: (1908) Lenton Vicarage, Lenton, Nottingham.
Photograph: in B.M. Willmott Dobbie, *A Nest of Suffragettes in Somerset*, 1979.
Archival source: Helen Watts Papers, 1909–14, Nottinghamshire Record Office.

WEAVER, GERTRUDE BAILLIE-, MRS (1855–1926) née Renton Quaker, a prolific novelist, who wrote as "Gertrude Colmore". Her first novel was published by Fisher Unwin (*see* PUBLISHERS AND PRINTERS) in 1888. She was educated in Frankfurt, Paris and London and was first married to a barrister, H.A. Colmore-Dunn. In 1901 she married Harold

Baillie-Weaver, another barrister. Harold Baillie-Weaver became an active member of the MEN'S LEAGUE FOR WOMEN'S SUFFRAGE and Gertrude was an early member of the WOMEN'S FREEDOM LEAGUE and spoke at WOMEN'S SOCIAL AND POLITICAL UNION meetings, particularly in Wimbledon where her friend Rose Lamartine YATES was secretary and treasurer of the local WSPU. Gertrude Baillie-Weaver was probably a member of the WOMEN WRITERS' SUFFRAGE LEAGUE, wrote many fictional sketches published in *Votes for Women* and the *Suffragette*, and a novel, *Suffragette Sally*, 1911, which draws directly on the militant suffrage movement (*see* NOVELS). In 1913 she wrote *The Life of Emily Davison*, which was published by the Woman's Press to commemorate the sacrifice of her friend, Emily Wilding DAVISON. On 29 June 1914 she and her husband were present at the Costume Dinner organized by the Women Writers' Suffrage League and the ACTRESSES' FRANCHISE LEAGUE at the Hotel Cecil. On 15 July Gertrude Baillie-Weaver wrote to Lord Robert Cecil to tell him that she was writing to MPs, bishops and men of influence, asking them to rally round Mrs Pankhurst, who was on release from prison, in order to escort her to a WSPU rally to be held the next day. It was, of course, a hopeless plea; Lord Robert merely forwarded her letter to the Home Office. In 1914 the Baillie-Weavers were founders of a THEOSOPHICAL SOCIETY suffrage league and joined the VOTES FOR WOMEN FELLOWSHIP and later the UNITED SUFFRAGISTS; Gertrude was much admired by Evelyn SHARP. The Baillie-Weavers also continued supporting the WFL.

Gertrude Baillie-Weaver joined the Theosophical Society in 1906 and was a close friend of Esther, daughter of Ursula BRIGHT. In 1915 she and her husband became particularly attached to Krishnamurti, thought by theosophists to be Christ reborn, and his younger brother Nitya, and lived with them in a house in Wimbledon. This house had been found for them by Countess DE LA WARR, who was also by then living nearby. During the war Gertrude Baillie-Weaver was a pacificist, stoned in 1914 while speaking in Saffron Walden against the imminent war. She and her husband founded the National Council for Animals Welfare Work which, after the First World War, was instrumental in the opening at Letchworth of Britain's first humane abbatoir. A statue, of a woman with a lamb and the inscription "To All Protectors of the Defenceless", sited in the garden of St John's Lodge, Regent's Park, commemorates the Baillie-Weavers' anti-vivisection work. Esther Bright wrote of the Baillie-Weavers, "they were pacifists at heart, but could be extremely warlike in defence of any weak or exploited creature".

Address: (1917) The West House, Widdington, Newport, Essex; (1925) Eastward Ho, Wimbledon Common, London SW19.
Bibliography: Lady E. Lutyens, *Candles in the Sun*, 1957; A. Morley and L. Stanley, *The Life and Death of Emily Wilding Davison* (including a reprint of G. Colmore, *The Life of Emily Davison*), 1988.

WEBSTER, [JULIA] AUGUSTA, MRS (1837–94) Born at Poole, Dorset, daughter of Vice-Admiral George Davies, chief constable of Huntingdonshire and his wife Julia (née Hume). She was educated at school in Banff, and at Cambridge, Paris and Geneva. In 1860 she published her first book of poems, *Blanche Leslie, and Other Poems* and in 1864 an acclaimed translation of Aeschulus's *Prometheus Bound*. In 1878 she published *A Housewife's Opinion*, a collection of essays about married women. A volume of selections from her verse, published in 1893, survives with a special "In Memoriam 5th September 1894" page inserted, this particular copy inscribed to "Mrs Bateson", doubtless Mary BATESON with whom she was likely to have been friendly during her time in Cambridge. In 1863 Augusta Davies had married Thomas Webster, law lecturer at Trinity College, Cambridge and became the mother of a daughter. He was an active supporter of the women's suffrage movement, had subscribed to the ENFRANCHISEMENT OF WOMEN COMMITTEE, on occasion chairing meetings of the CENTRAL COMMITTEE OF THE NATIONAL SOCIETY FOR WOMEN'S SUFFRAGE. In 1871 Augusta Webster was a member of the first executive committee of this society and was also a member of the LONDON NATIONAL SOCIETY FOR WOMEN'S SUFFRAGE, speaking at a meeting in Greenwich in 1876. Although a Liberal, she stood as an independent in Chelsea for the London School Board in 1879, becoming the first woman writer of note to hold elective office. Priscilla Bright McLAREN had written to Helen TAYLOR in July 1879, before the election, "I have no doubt many will work for

Mrs Webster but I wonder *she* should think herself fit for the work, she is often so delicate and subject to bronchial attacks". Whatever her health problems Augusta Webster completed her first three-year term of office and then, after a break of three years, was again elected for Chelsea in 1885. She supported the introduction of technical education in elementary schools until finally losing her seat in 1888. In May 1880 she spoke at the Grand Demonstration organized by the Central Committee in St James's Hall in London and in May 1884 she signed the Letter from Ladies to Members of Parliament asking for the inclusion of women heads of households in the government's franchise bill.

Address: (1894) Springfield, Kew Gardens Road, Kew, Surrey.
Photograph: in *Selections from the Verse of Augusta Webster*, 1893.
Archival source: Mill–Taylor Papers, London School of Economics and Political Science.
Bibliography: P. Hollis, *Ladies Elect: Women in English Local Government 1865–1914*, 1987; A. Webster, "Parliamentary franchise for women ratepayers", originally published in the *Examiner*, 1 June 1878, reprinted in J. Lewis (ed.), *Before the Vote Was Won: Arguments For and Against Women's Suffrage, 1864–1896*, 1987.

WEDNESBURY (NUWSS) In 1913 the society was a member of the MIDLAND (WEST) FEDERATION OF THE NATIONAL UNION OF WOMEN'S SUFFRAGE SOCIETIES. Secretary (1913) Mrs Thomas, 1 Loxdale Street, Wednesbury, Staffordshire.

WELLINGBOROUGH (WFL) Secretaries (1913) Miss V. Sharman, Ivy Lodge, Wellingborough and Mrs England Smith, Newstead, Hatton Park, Wellingborough, Northamptonshire.

WELLINGTON (NUWSS) In 1913 the society was a member of the MIDLANDS (EAST) FEDERATION OF THE NATIONAL UNION OF WOMEN'S SUFFRAGE SOCIETIES. Secretaries (1913) Mrs Clemson, Leahurst, Constitution Hill, Wellington, Shropshire, and Mrs Van-Homrigh, Vine Cottage, Wellington, Shropshire.

WELLS (NUWSS) In 1913 the society was a member of the WEST OF ENGLAND FEDERATION OF THE NATIONAL UNION OF WOMEN'S SUFFRAGE SOCIETIES. Secretary (1913) Miss A. Church, The Liberty, Wells, Somerset.

WENTWORTH, VERA (1890–1957) (born Jessie Spinks) When she joined the WOMEN'S SOCIAL AND POLITICAL UNION in 1908 she was working in a shop. Her brother, Wilfred Spinks, was the leader of an unsuccessful unofficial strike of women workers in the East End of London and it was through him that Vera, then still "Jessie", met Fenner Brockway. She was arrested in February 1908 after taking part in the WSPU's "pantechnicon" raid on the House of Commons. She was sentenced to six weeks' imprisonment and lost a day's remission by cutting "Votes for Women" into her cell wall. Mary BLATHWAYT met Vera Wentworth at the breakfast given at the Eustace Miles Restaurant to celebrate her release and that of her fellow prisoners. Mary Blathwayt describes in her diary how with the released prisoners she went to campaign at the Peckham by-election and how she came back with Vera Wentworth, "at one time walking arm in arm with her". Vera was arrested again after taking part on 30 June 1908 in another deputation to the House of Commons and was released in September after serving a three-month sentence. She wrote an article, "Should Christian Women Demand the Vote", for a September edition of the *Christian Commonwealth* and, the next week, "Three Months in Holloway", a description of her prison experience. Fenner Brockway contributed a description of her release from prison, in which he participated, in the same issue. In September it was her turn to wait outside Holloway's gates; she drove the open landau, garlanded in tartan, that met Mary PHILLIPS on her release.

In the autumn of 1908 and in 1909 Vera Wentworth worked, with Annie KENNEY and Elsie HOWEY, for the WSPU in the west of England. On occasion she stayed with the Blathwayts at Eagle House, Batheaston, and Mary Blathwayt read the *Christian Commonwealth* articles. At the end of April 1909 Vera Wentworth was put in charge of the WSPU campaign in Plymouth and in August, with Elsie Howey and Mary Phillips, was arrested while leading a protest crowd of 2000 to the doors of a meeting about the budget being conducted by Lord Carrington in Exeter. The crowd tried to prevent their arrest and troops were called in. As a consequence Vera Wentworth spent six days on hunger strike in Exeter Jail. On 5 September, with Elsie Howey and Jessie KENNEY, she accosted Asquith as he left

Vera Wentworth wearing an apron to advertise a WSPU London procession, probably that of 21 June 1908. (Author's collection)

Lympne church and made the remainder of his country weekend a misery. In November she was arrested in Bristol after breaking windows of the Liberal Club as Churchill was due to speak. Thus, by November 1909 she had been arrested four times, had hunger struck and had been forcibly fed. A year later, like so many other women, she was arrested after taking part in the "Black Friday" debacle in Parliament Square. Fenner Brockway wrote in his autobiography that he had been very friendly with Vera Wentworth, had been waiting at the gates on the occasions when she was released from prison, and accompanied her to Parliament Square on "Black Friday". However, as the militant campaign escalated into arson, his sympathies with the WSPU decreased and he lost touch with Vera. She took part in the March 1912 window-smashing campaign, was sentenced to six months' imprisonment and joined the hunger strike. She had written a one-act play, *An Allegory* (published in 1913 by the ACTRESSES' FRANCHISE LEAGUE) and this was presented in March in Holloway by the prisoners, coached by Mrs PETHICK-LAWRENCE.

Later in 1912 Vera Wentworth matriculated at St Andrews University as a first-year arts student, attending classes in General Modern History and General Political Economy. In 1913–14 she again attended, as an unqualified student, classes in Honours Economic History and Special Political Economy. She had obviously not given up her interest in suffrage matters and in May 1913 was in correspondence, from University Hall, St Andrews, with Hugh FRANKLIN. In 1914 Vera Wentworth was one of the women who interrupted Asquith's holiday at Clovelly. After that Vera Wentworth disappears from view for a number of years. During the Second World War she worked in London in the ARP and became a supporter of non-violence. She died in the Elizabeth Garrett Anderson Hospital, left her body to medical research and her small estate to Daisy Carden, who lived at the same address.
Address: (1909) Derby House, Hendon (*see also* Caprina FAHEY); (1957) White Heather House, Cromer Street, London WC1.
Photograph: in Fawcett Library Collection.
Archival source: Blathwayt Diaries, Dyrham Park (The National Trust), Avon.
Bibliography: F. Brockway, *Towards Tomorrow*, 1977.

WEST BROMWICH (NUWSS) In 1913 the society was a member of the MIDLANDS (EAST) FEDERATION OF THE NATIONAL UNION OF WOMEN'S SUFFRAGE SOCIETIES. Secretary (1913) Mrs Langley Browne, Moor House, West Bromwich, Staffordshire.

WEST HAM (WSPU) Secretary (1913) Miss Hooper, 49 Junction Road, West Ham, London E. V. FRIEDLANDER helped to make the society's BANNER, which was adapted from a design by Sylvia PANKHURST and probably dates from 1910. It is now held in the Museum of London Collection.

WEST HARTLEPOOL (WSPU) Secretary (1906) Mrs Norman, 3 Queen's Terrace, Seaton Carew, West Hartlepool, Co. Durham.

WEST LANCS, WEST CHESHIRE, AND NORTH WALES FEDERATION OF THE NATIONAL UNION OF WOMEN'S SUFFRAGE SOCIETIES Secretary (1912) Miss Jessie Beavan, 12 Ullet Road, Liverpool.

WEST OF ENGLAND FEDERATION OF THE NATIONAL UNION OF WOMEN'S SUFFRAGE SOCIETIES Secretary (1912) Miss Ethel Wheelwright, 52 Sydney Buildings, Bath.

WEST RIDING FEDERATION OF THE NATIONAL UNION OF WOMEN'S SUFFRAGE SOCIETIES Secretary (1912) Mrs Bauer, 8 Springwood Terrace, Bradford, Yorkshire.

WESTLAKE, ALICE, MRS (1842–1923) Daughter of Thomas HARE; an artist, she exhibited at the Royal Academy and at the Paris Salon. In 1865 she was a member of the KENSINGTON SOCIETY and in 1866 signed John Stuart MILL's women's suffrage petition. In 1864 she married John Westlake, QC, a Liberal, a founder of the Working Men's College, a subscriber to the Society for the Promotion of the Employment of Women, a member of the Law Amendment Society, of the National Association for the Promotion of Social Science and a supporter of the women's suffrage movement from its earliest days. In 1904 he was a member of a Committee to Secure the Admission of Women to the Legal Profession formed in Manchester by Christabel PANKHURST. The Westlakes had no children. Both Alice Westlake and her husband subscribed to the ENFRANCHISEMENT OF WOMEN COMMITTEE, 1866–7. She was active in its successor, the LONDON NATIONAL SOCIETY FOR WOMEN'S SUFFRAGE; in 1876 she addressed, with Madame RONNIGER and Charlotte BURBURY, a meeting of the Chelsea branch. By 1882 Alice Westlake was a member of the CENTRAL COMMITTEE OF THE NATIONAL SOCIETY FOR WOMEN'S SUFFRAGE. In the 1890s she was a member of the executive committee of the Women's Liberal Unionist Association. The Westlakes' main involvement with the women's movement was with Elizabeth Garrett's (see Elizabeth Garrett ANDERSON) hospital for women. Alice Westlake was a member of the first managing committee of the St Mary's Dispensary for Women and Children, becoming treasurer of its successor, the New Hospital for Women, and John Westlake was, with the husband of Louisa SMITH, one of the trustees. In 1922 Alice Westlake was still a vice-president of the hospital. An able administrator, she succeeded to Elizabeth Garrett Anderson's Marylebone seat on the London School Board, holding the position from 1876 until 1888.

Address: The River House, 3 Chelsea Embankment, London W.
Photograph: of Alice Westlake, taken in 1887, in *Memories of John Westlake*, 1914.
Portrait: of John Westlake by Alice Westlake, c. 1896–7, National Portrait Gallery. Of John Westlake by Marianne Stokes, 1902, given to the National Portrait Gallery by Alice Westlake, 1920. Of John Westlake by unknown artist in Trinity College, Cambridge (photograph in National Portrait Gallery Archive). A joint portrait of John and Alice Westlake at one time hung in the boardroom of the Elizabeth Garrett Anderson Hospital; its whereabouts is now unknown.
Bibliography: *Memories of John Westlake*, 1914.

WESTMINSTER (branch of the LONDON SOCIETY FOR WOMEN'S SUFFRAGE, NUWSS) Secretary (1909, 1913) Mrs Bertram, 38 Palace Mansions, Addison Bridge, London W.

WESTMINSTER (WSPU) Opened in December 1912. Its premises were strategically placed, midway between Caxton Hall and Parliament Square, and offered afternoon tea to those who had been lobbying at the House of Commons. It was decorated in the COLOURS and in June 1914 for a short time provided a haven for the main WSPU office after Lincoln's Inn House had been raided by the police.
Address: (1912) 17 Tothill Street, London W.

WESTON-SUPER-MARE (NUWSS) In 1913 the society was a member of the WEST OF ENGLAND FEDERATION OF THE NATIONAL UNION OF WOMEN'S SUFFRAGE SOCIETIES. Secretary (1913) Mrs Youngman, Torre House, Edinburgh Place, Weston-super-Mare, Somerset.

WEYBRIDGE AND DISTRICT (NUWSS) In 1913 the society was a member of the SURREY, SUSSEX, AND HANTS FEDERATION OF THE NATIONAL UNION OF WOMEN'S SUFFRAGE SOCIETIES. Secretary (1906 and 1913) Miss Agnes Gardiner, Heathfield, Weybridge, Surrey.

WHALEY BRIDGE (NUWSS) In 1910 the society joined the MANCHESTER AND DISTRICT FEDERATION OF THE NATIONAL UNION OF WOMEN'S SUFFRAGE SOCIETIES. Secretary (1913) Miss C.D. Simpson, Lynton, Whaley Bridge, Derbyshire.

WHARRY, OLIVE (1886–1947) Artist, daughter of a doctor, the only child of his first marriage; she later had three much younger half-brothers and a half-sister. She grew up in London but on her father's retirement the family moved to Devon and Olive trained at the School of Art in Exeter. In 1906, with her mother and father, she travelled around the world. By November 1910 she was active in the WOMEN'S SOCIAL AND POLITICAL UNION and was a member of the CHURCH LEAGUE FOR WOMEN'S SUFFRAGE. In November 1911 she was arrested after taking part in a WSPU window-smashing campaign and, after being released on bail guaranteed by Frederick PETHICK-LAWRENCE and Mrs Saul SOLOMON, was sentenced to two months' imprisonment. During this and her subsequent periods of imprisonment she kept a diary, which includes autographs of her fellow suffrage prisoners. She was arrested, again after window-breaking, in March 1912 and was sentenced to six months' imprisonment. She was held in Winson Green Prison in Birmingham and again kept an autograph album, signed by, among others, Constance BRYER. Olive Wharry took part in the hunger strike and was released in July, before the end of her sentence. In late November she was rearrested as "Joyce Locke", along with Frances PARKER, Ethel MOORHEAD and Marion Pollock, in Aberdeen after being involved in a scuffle at a meeting at which Lloyd George was speaking. She was sentenced to five days' imprisonment, during the course of which she broke her cell windows. On 7 March 1913 she was sentenced, as "Joyce Locke", with Lilian LENTON, for setting fire to the tea pavilion in Kew Gardens. She was released on 8 April after having been on hunger strike for 32 days, apparently without the prison authorities noticing. Her usual weight was 7st 11lbs; when released she weighed 5st 9lbs. Her release, immediately before the passing of the "Cat and Mouse" Act, was unconditional. Olive Wharry was re-arrested in May 1914, after taking part in the deputation to the King. She was sentenced to one week's imprisonment. By now, however, it was a matter of honour not to complete any prison sentence and, after going on hunger-and-thirst strike, she was released after three days. The next month she was tried at Carnarvon after breaking windows at Criccieth during a meeting being held by Lloyd George. She was held on remand, went on hunger strike and was released. She was re-arrested, as "Phyllis North" in Liverpool in June. She was brought back to Carnarvon, where she received a prison sentence of three months on 2 July. She was sent to Holloway where she remained, on hunger strike in solitary confinement, until being released on 10 August into the care of Dr Flora MURRAY under the amnesty of suffrage prisoners. Home Office medical reports make clear that one doctor at least regarded Olive Wharry as having been mentally unstable since 1912, blaming the ideas she had imbibed from the WSPU for bringing her to the brink of insanity. Olive Wharry's prison notebook contains no hint of insanity. It is full of delightful drawings of prison life, along with poems, satirical and amusing, and a photograph of her trial for arson, held at Richmond in 1913. It was given to what was then the library of the British Museum by the beneficiaries of the will of Geraldine LENNOX. In Olive Wharry's own will she asked to be cremated and "the ashes scattered on the high open spaces of the Moor between Exeter and Whitstone", and appointed Constance Bryer as one of her executors and left her an annuity of £200, two prints of her etchings, most of her books and her suffrage medal. This medal, with two bars commemorating her March 1912 and February 1913 hunger strikes, is now held in a private collection, still together with that belonging to Constance Bryer, despite the vicissitudes of time and travel.

Address: (1911) 7 Cambridge Gate, Regents Park, London NW; (1946) Courtlands, Newlyn Road, Torquay, Devonshire.

Portrait: sketch by E.S. Klempner in *Votes for Women*, 14 March 1913.

Archival source: Home Office Papers, Public Record Office; Olive Wharry's prison notebook, British Library Additional Manuscripts.

WHATELY, [MARY] MONICA (d. 1960) Born in London, daughter of Capt. Reginald Pepys Whately, educated at home, honorary treasurer of the CATHOLIC WOMEN'S SUFFRAGE SOCIETY in 1911. A journalist and public lecturer, she was in the 1920s and 1930s an active member of the Six Point Group, of which she later became chairman, the Open Door Council, the Society for Women in the Ministry and St Joan's Social and Political Alliance. In 1929 she

stood, unsuccessfully, as a Labour candidate for St Albans at the general election. She was a close friend of Dorothy EVANS.
Address: (1913) 75 Harcourt Terrace, Redcliffe Square, London SW; (1934) 31 Brookfield Mansions, West Hill, London N6.

WHITBY Suffrage Society   Affiliated to the NUWSS in 1905 and by 1913 was a member of the NORTH AND EAST RIDINGS FEDERATION OF THE NATIONAL UNION OF WOMEN'S SUFFRAGE SOCIETIES. Secretary (1909) Miss Pringle, The Abbey House, Whitby, Yorkshire; (1913) Miss Thornton, Sleights, Yorkshire.

WHITEHAVEN (NUWSS)   In 1913 the society was a member of the NORTH-WESTERN FEDERATION OF THE NATIONAL UNION OF WOMEN'S SUFFRAGE SOCIETIES. Secretary (1913) Miss I.C. Brown, 1 Lowther Street, Whitehaven, Cumberland.

WICK committee of the EDINBURGH NATIONAL SOCIETY FOR WOMEN SUFFRAGE   Formed as a result of the tour of Jane TAYLOUR and Agnes MCLAREN in 1871. Its convenor was Mr G.M. Sutherland. Secretary (1913) Miss Elizabeth Grant, 2 Moray Street, Wick.

WIDNES (NUWSS)   In 1913 the society was a member of the WEST LANCS, WEST CHESHIRE, AND NORTH WALES FEDERATION OF THE NATIONAL UNION OF WOMEN'S SUFFRAGE SOCIETIES. Secretary (1913) Miss Grace M. Morrison, Wellfield, Farnworth, Widnes, Cheshire.

WIGAN branch of the MANCHESTER NATIONAL SOCIETY FOR WOMEN'S SUFFRAGE was formed in 1870 when the secretary was Mrs Leech of Fair View, Pemberton. The society associated itself with the CENTRAL COMMITTEE OF THE NATIONAL SOCIETY FOR WOMEN'S SUFFRAGE in 1872. The Wigan and District Women's Suffrage Society (NUWSS) was formed in 1911 and joined the MANCHESTER AND DISTRICT FEDERATION OF THE NATIONAL UNION OF WOMEN'S SUFFRAGE SOCIETIES. Secretary (1913) Mrs James Ainscow, 224 Manchester Road, Higher Ince, Wigan, Lancashire; (1914) Mrs Helen Fairhurst (née Silcock, a Wigan textile worker, from the 1890s a member of Wigan Trades Council executive).

WIGHAM, ELIZA (1820–99)   Quaker, born in Edinburgh, daughter of a "webster", a manufacturer of shawls. Her mother, Jane Richardson, died in 1830. Her father remarried; Eliza Wigham was very fond of her stepmother and cared for her in old age. In 1840 Eliza Wigham attended the world's Anti-Slavery Convention in London, and became secretary of the Edinburgh Ladies' Emancipation Society. She wrote, in 1863, *The Anti-Slavery Cause in America and Its Martyrs*. She was a member of the executive committee of the CENTRAL COMMITTEE OF THE NATIONAL SOCIETY FOR WOMEN'S SUFFRAGE in 1871 and by 1872 was a member of the executive committee of the EDINBURGH NATIONAL WOMEN'S SUFFRAGE SOCIETY, to which her stepmother also subscribed. In 1882 and 1884 Eliza Wigham spoke at the Grand Demonstrations of Women in Glasgow and Edinburgh, in 1896 was a member of the SPECIAL APPEAL COMMITTEE and in 1899 was a member of the executive committee of the NATIONAL UNION OF WOMEN'S SUFFRAGE SOCIETIES. Among other women-centred causes, Eliza Wigham was a member of the executive committee of the Ladies' National Association and was one of 19 women who in 1869 signed a public protest against the Contagious Diseases Acts. In 1878 she was a governor of the London School of Medicine for Women and in 1892 was a member of the Ladies' Edinburgh Debating Society. From 1859 she ran for nearly 40 years a Penny Savings bank in Edinburgh and a Women's Working Society for Mothers' Meeting for 37 years from 1860. In 1887 Elizabeth Pease NICHOLL and Priscilla Bright MCLAREN organized the presentation to Eliza Wigham of a sum of money, testimonial to her work for philanthropic causes. When she left Edinburgh to spend the last few months of her life with her brother's family in Dublin, the Scottish Christian Union (part of the British Women's Temperance Association) presented her with an album containing photographs of the ladies associated with her in this work.
Address: (1871) 5 South Gray Street, Edinburgh.
Photograph: carte de visite in Josephine Butler Collection, Fawcett Library.
Bibliography: E.M. Mein, *Miss Eliza Wigham*, typescript in Edinburgh City Library.

WILKS, ELIZABETH, MRS (1866?–1956) née Bennett   Qualified as a doctor in London in 1894 and was for a time, before 1903, assistant physician at the New Hospital for Women. She married Mark Wilks, a London elementary school teacher, in 1894 and had one daughter. In 1907–9 Elizabeth Wilks subscribed to the LONDON SOCIETY FOR WOMEN'S SUFFRAGE. In June 1907 she organized a garden party in Clapton which was a joint venture between the CENTRAL SOCIETY, the North Hackney Women's Liberal Association and the WOMEN'S SOCIAL AND POLITICAL UNION, at which Mrs PETHICK-LAWRENCE and Christabel PANKHURST were the main speakers. When it was founded in 1910 Elizabeth Wilks became honorary treasurer of the TAX RESISTANCE LEAGUE. Realizing that, as a married woman, she was not liable to taxation, she informed the tax authorities that the relevant tax claim should be sent not to her, but to her husband. When this was done, Mark Wilks declared that he had no way of obtaining the information necessary to complete the tax form, and did not, in any case, have the means to pay what would be demanded. He was then imprisoned for debt. The Tax Resistance League took up the case, ensuring maximum publicity; Bernard Shaw was the principal speaker at a meeting held at the Caxton Hall to discuss the case. Their adopted daughter, Helen Wilks, also became a doctor and was working at the Endell Street hospital run by Louisa Garrett ANDERSON and Flora MURRAY when she died unexpectedly in 1919. Elizabeth Wilks was still in practice, in Harley Place, London NW1, in 1923.

Address: (1903) 24 Lower Clapton Road, London E; (1956) Openlands, Headley Down, Hampshire.
Photograph: in Fawcett Library Collection.
Archival source: Wilks Case Scrapbook, Museum of London.

WILLCOX, LILLIAN MARY DOVE-, MRS (1875–1963) (later Mrs Buckley) née Dugdale Born in Bedminster, Bristol, her mother had been a suffragist throughout the second half of the nineteenth century. Widowed, by 1908 Lillian Dove-Willcox was a member of the west of England branch of the WOMEN'S SOCIAL AND POLITICAL UNION, hostessing an "At Home" in Bristol in October. On 29 June 1909 she was arrested after taking part in the WSPU deputation to the House of Commons and was sentenced to a month's imprisonment. She went on hunger strike and was released. She was subsequently charged, with Theresa GARNETT, with having, during her imprisonment, struck a wardress. She was sentenced to a further ten days' imprisonment, again went on hunger strike, and was again released. Her father-in-law, who had subscribed to the BRISTOL AND WEST OF ENGLAND SOCIETY FOR WOMEN'S SUFFRAGE in 1886, wrote to *Votes for Women* on 3 September 1909 to the effect that, although he supported the enfranchisement of women, he was against militancy and repudiated the actions of his daughter-in-law. After Annie KENNEY left Bristol in autumn 1911, Lillian Dove-Willcox became honorary secretary of the Bristol branch of the WSPU. She had a country cottage on a hill overlooking the Wye and Tintern where many suffragettes, including Mary RICHARDSON, went to recuperate from imprisonment. Lillian Dove-Willcox was a stalwart supporter of the Pankhursts, writing a letter to the second issue of the *Freewoman* to protest against what she considered to be an attack on Christabel, and later joining Mrs Pankhurst's bodyguard. She was present at the meeting at St Andrew's Hall in Glasgow on 9 March 1913 when Mrs Pankhurst was re-arrested. Having outwitted the police, she managed to board, at Carlisle, the train taking Mrs Pankhurst back to Holloway and was able to talk a little with her. She herself was arrested on 11 March while attempting, with others, to present a petition to the King at the opening of parliament. She was sentenced to a month's imprisonment. In 1915 she was a member of the EAST LONDON FEDERATION OF THE SUFFRAGETTES and in 1963, as Mrs Buckley, subscribed to the Pethick-Lawrence Memorial Appeal Fund. In her will she left £10 to the SUFFRAGETTE FELLOWSHIP.

Address: (1947) 15 Lyndhurst Road, London NW3; (1963) 44 The Park, Ealing, London W.
Photograph: by Muriel Darton in *Votes for Women*, 6 August 1909; by Col Blathwayt in B.M. Willmott Dobbie, *A Nest of Suffragettes in Somerset*, 1979.

WILLESDEN (branch of the LONDON SOCIETY FOR WOMEN'S SUFFRAGE, NUWSS) Secretary (1906) Mrs Eleanor Penn GASKELL, 12 Nicoll Road, Willesden, London NW; (1909) Mrs J. Granger Evans, MD, 75 Craven Park Road, Willesden Junction, London NW; (1913) Mrs Macgregor, 9 Grange Road, Willesden, and Miss Blake, 37 Staverton Road, Willesden Green, London NW. (*See also* HARROW).

WILLIAMS, ANNIE (c. 1860–1943) Described herself as Cornish, a teacher who had experience in council schools in various parts of England. Two of her close relatives, Edith Williams and Mrs Anne Perks, were also members of the WOMEN'S SOCIAL AND POLITICAL UNION. Annie Williams joined the WSPU in 1907 and spent the summer of 1908 working for the WSPU in Bristol and at this time met there Lettice FLOYD. In September 1908 she returned to her post in Cornwall but kept in touch with the WSPU, observed by Mary BLATHWAYT to have attended an "At Home" in Plymouth in November. Annie Williams had a poem published in *Votes for Women*, 14 May 1909, and at the end of the academic year gave up her post as headmistress in order to become a full-time WSPU ORGANIZER. She immediately took part in the 29 June deputation to the House of Commons, was arrested, and released. On August Bank Holiday she was mobbed in Canford Park, Dorset, while speaking for the WSPU. By January 1910 she was the WSPU organizer for the general election campaign in Newcastle-upon-Tyne, remaining there until July 1911. Lettice Floyd left her Midlands home to live with her. Annie Williams then moved to work as an organizer in Huddersfield and Halifax and in 1912 was appointed WSPU organizer in Wales, based in Cardiff. In March she was sentenced, with Lettice Floyd, to a month's imprisonment in Holloway after taking part in the WSPU window-smashing campaign. Annie Williams' sister was WSPU secretary for Cornwall in 1913. By January 1914 Annie Williams had, according to Mary Blathwayt's diary, visited Christabel PANKHURST in Paris. In July 1914 she spoke at a WSPU garden party organized by the TOLLEMACHE SISTERS at Batheaston. She probably lived with Lettice Floyd until the latter's death in 1934, inheriting from her £3000 and an annuity of £300.
Address: (1913) 27 Charles St, Cardiff; and c/o Miss E. Williams, Glanafon, Devoran, Cornwall.

WILLIAMS, ETHEL MARY NUCELLA, DR (1863–1948) Born at Cromer, educated at Norwich High School and at Newnham, Cambridge, 1882–5, although she did not take a degree. She then went to London where she took an MB in 1891, an MD in 1895 and returned to Cambridge to study for a diploma in public health in 1899. After working as a medical officer at Clapham Maternity Hospital and at the Dispensary for Women and Children at Blackfriars, she went to Newcastle as the city's first woman doctor, eventually joining in practice with Ethel BENTHAM. In 1889 Ethel Williams signed the Declaration in Favour of Women's Suffrage organized by the CENTRAL COMMITTEE OF THE NATIONAL SOCIETY. She was secretary of the Newcastle Women's Liberal Association and became president of the NEWCASTLE AND DISTRICT WOMEN'S SUFFRAGE SOCIETY (NUWSS). Ethel Williams took part in the "Mud March" in February 1907. Although by no means militant, in 1912 she became a tax resister, witholding her taxes until the fate of the Conciliation Bill was known and then refusing payment when hopes were dashed. By 1915 she was chairman of the NORTH-EASTERN FEDERATION OF THE NUWSS. She broke with the Liberal Party just before the First World War, although it is doubtful if she went so far as to join the Labour Party. During the war Ethel Williams joined the Union of Democratic Control, was secretary of the Newcastle Workers' and Soldiers' Council, and was a founding member of the Women's International League for Peace and Freedom, of which she was secretary of the Newcastle branch in 1934.

In 1906 Ethel Williams was the first woman in the north-east to drive a car, in 1909 was appointed a member of the senate of Durham University, became a member of the Newcastle Education Committee and a justice of the peace, and in 1917 co-founded the Northern Women's Hospital.
Address: (1913) 3 Osborne Terrace, Newcastle; (1934) Bramble Patch, Low Bridge, Stocksfield-on-Tyne.
Photograph: in N. Todd, "Ethel Williams: medical and suffrage pioneer", *North East Labour History*, Bulletin no. 30, 1996.
Bibliography: N. Todd, "Ethel Williams: medical and suffrage pioneer", *North East Labour History*, Bulletin no. 30, 1996.

WILLIAMS, HENRIA HELEN L. (1867–1911) Originally from Glasgow, she lived in Upminster, Essex, and was a member of the WOMEN'S SOCIAL AND POLITICAL UNION. She was arrested after taking part in the deputation to the House of Commons on 29 June 1909, but released. In 1910 she joined the TAX RESISTANCE LEAGUE. Henria Williams was present as a member of the deputation to the House of Commons on "Black Friday", 18 November 1910, was mauled in the melée, and received medical attention. She never recovered and died of a heart attack two months later. Her statement of her experience in Parliament Square, included in the Memorandum compiled by H.N. BRAILSFORD and Dr Jessie Murray, describes how

> One policeman after knocking me about for a considerable time, finally took hold of me with his great strong hand like iron just over my heart. He hurt me so much that at first I had not the voice power to tell him what he was doing. But I knew that unless I made a strong effort to do so he would kill me. So collecting all the power of my being, I commanded him to take his hand off my heart... Yet that policeman would not arrest me and he was the third or fourth who had knocked me about.

Bibliography: C. Morrell, *"Black Friday": Violence Against Women in the Suffragette Movement*, 1981.

WILMSLOW, STYAL, AND ALDERLEY EDGE (NUWSS) Formed in 1911 and joined the MANCHESTER AND DISTRICT FEDERATION OF THE NATIONAL UNION OF WOMEN'S SUFFRAGE SOCIETIES. Secretary (1913) Mrs Forest Hewit, Overhill, Wilmslow Park, Wilmslow, Cheshire.

WILTSHIRE (WSPU) Secretary (1913) Mrs Harris, 28 Innox Road, Trowbridge, Wiltshire.

WILTSHIRE (SOUTH) (NUWSS) In 1913 the society was a member of the WEST OF ENGLAND FEDERATION OF THE NATIONAL UNION OF WOMEN'S SUFFRAGE SOCIETIES. Secretary (1913) Mrs Peart, Fovant, Salisbury, Wiltshire.

WIMBLEDON (WSPU) Secretary (1913) Mrs Lamartine YATES, 9 Victoria Crescent, Broadway, Wimbledon, London SW. Founded in 1908, the Wimbledon branch was very active, providing a regular series of lectures as well as the usual fund-raising activities. The Wimbledon WSPU held meetings on Wimbledon Common in 1913, despite attempts to prevent them being held in such public places, and attracted crowds of 5000. Local feeling ran so high against militancy that a Retaliation League was formed which vowed that "every act of violence perpetrated by these women, whether to persons, or public or private properties, will be answered by this league by attacks on the private houses or properties of Militant Suffragettes". The society's BANNER is now held in the Fawcett Collection.

Bibliography: G. Hawtin, *Votes for Wimbledon Women*, 1993; John Innes Society, *Dorset Hall 1906–1935*, 1994.

WIMBLEDON (NORTH) (branch of the LONDON SOCIETY FOR WOMEN'S SUFFRAGE, NUWSS) Secretary (1909) Miss Hughesdon, 10 Spencer Hill, and Mrs L. Hobhouse, 2 Lansdowne Road, Wimbledon, London SW; (1913) Miss E.E. Webster, 9 Ridgeway Gardens, Wimbledon Common, London SW.

WIMBLEDON (SOUTH) (branch of the LONDON SOCIETY FOR WOMEN'S SUFFRAGE, NUWSS) Secretary (1909) Mrs Beatty, 5 Elm Grove, Wimbledon, London SW; (1913) Mrs Threlfall, 246 Coombe Lane, Wimbledon, London SW.

WIMBLEDON PARK (WSPU) Secretary (1913) Mrs Scarborough, 3 Marguerite Villas, Copse Hill, London SW.

WINCHELSEA, ASHFORD, AND RYE branches of the NEW CONSTITUTIONAL SOCIETY FOR WOMEN'S SUFFRAGE Organizer (1913) Maud White, Magazine House, Winchelsea, Sussex.

WINCHESTER (NUWSS) In 1913 the society was a member of the SURREY, SUSSEX, AND HANTS FEDERATION OF THE NATIONAL UNION OF WOMEN'S SUFFRAGE SOCIETIES. Secretary (1913) Mrs Walter Carey, The Lodge, Bereweeke Road, Winchester, Hampshire.

WINDSOR (branch of the LONDON SOCIETY FOR WOMEN'S SUFFRAGE, NUWSS) Secretary (1909) Mrs Gibb, 3 Claremont Road, Windsor, Berkshire; (1913) Miss Miller, Crescent Lodge, Windsor, Berkshire. The society's BANNER is now held in the Fawcett Collection.

WINSCOMBE (NUWSS) In 1913 the society was a member of the WEST OF ENGLAND FEDERATION of the NATIONAL UNION OF WOMEN'S SUFFRAGE SOCIETIES. Secretary (1913) Mrs Tanner, Fordlynch, Winscombe, Somerset.

WINSFORD (NUWSS) By 1912 the society was a member of the MANCHESTER AND DISTRICT FEDERATION OF THE NATIONAL UNION OF WOMEN'S SUFFRAGE SOCIETIES. Secretary (1913) Miss Mary Walsh, The Hollies, Winsford, Cheshire.

WISBECH Women's Suffrage Society (NUWSS) Founded *c.* 1909 by Miss Woodgate and by 1913 was a member of the EASTERN COUNTIES FEDERATION OF THE NATIONAL UNION OF WOMEN'S SUFFRAGE SOCIETIES. Secretaries (1913) Miss E. King, Tydd, St Giles' Rectory, Wisbech, and Mrs Ransford, 8 Colville Road, Wisbech, Cambridgeshire.

WOBURN SANDS (NUWSS) In 1913 the society was a member of the OXON, BERKS, BUCKS, AND BEDS FEDERATION OF THE NATIONAL UNION OF WOMEN'S SUFFRAGE SOCIETIES. Secretary (1909, 1913) Miss E. Woods, Firdale, Woburn Sands, Bedfordshire.

WOKING (NUWSS) In 1913 the society was a member of the SURREY, SUSSEX, AND HANTS FEDERATION OF THE NATIONAL UNION OF WOMEN'S SUFFRAGE SOCIETIES. Secretary (1913) Miss Davies-Colley, Briarwood, Woking, Surrey.

WOKING (WSPU) Secretary (1913) Mrs Barrett, Maybury Croft, Heathside, Woking, Surrey.

WOKINGHAM (NUWSS) In 1913 the society was a member of the OXON, BERKS, BUCKS, AND BEDS FEDERATION OF THE NATIONAL UNION OF WOMEN'S SUFFRAGE SOCIETIES. Secretary (1913) Miss Violet Eustace, Montague House, Wokingham, Berkshire.

WOLVERHAMPTON (NUWSS) Secretary (1913) Mrs F. Taylor, 107 Waterloo Road, Wolverhampton, Staffordshire.

WOLVERHAMPTON (WFL) Secretary (1913) Mrs Cresswell, 25 Rugby Street, Wolverhampton, Staffordshire.

WOLVERHAMPTON (WSPU) Secretary (1906) Mrs Emma SPROSON, Kelmscott, Wolverhampton, Staffordshire; (1911) secretary, 117 Dunstall Road, Wolverhampton.

WOMEN SANITARY INSPECTORS' SUFFRAGE SOCIETY
Address: (1913) 83 Sutherland Avenue, London W.

WOMEN TEACHERS' FRANCHISE UNION Formed at a meeting held in the Essex Hall, Strand, London in July 1912. Its aims were "To get fair play for women teachers in the educational world; to organise women teacher suffragists and sympathisers so as to make their point of view felt in their own organisations" (*Suffrage Annual and Women's Who's Who*, 1913). The society included women from the NATIONAL UNION OF WOMEN'S SUFFRAGE SOCIETIES, the WOMEN'S SOCIAL AND POLITICAL UNION, and the WOMEN'S FREEDOM LEAGUE, prepared to unite in order to exert pressure on the National Union of Teachers to persuade it to support women's suffrage. By 1916 the WTFU was concentrating its efforts on securing equal pay for men and women teachers.
Honorary secretary (1913, 1917) Hannah M. Townsend, 27 Murillo Road, Lee, London SE (*see* TOWNSEND SISTERS).
Bibliography: H. Kean, *Deeds Not Words: The Lives of Suffragette Teachers*, 1990.

WOMEN WRITERS' SUFFRAGE LEAGUE Founded in 1908 by Cicely HAMILTON and Bessie HATTON. Its aim was to obtain the vote for women on the same terms as it is or may be granted to men and its method was to employ the pen to achieve this. Among its first members were Beatrice HARRADEN, Violet Hunt, Elizabeth ROBINS, Evelyn SHARP and Olive Schreiner. In 1913 its vice-presidents included Marie Belloc Lowndes (daughter of Bessie Rayner PARKES), Margaret Woods, Alice Meynell and Edith Ayrton ZANGWILL. The WWSL held large entertainments at which speeches were made and at which propaganda written by its members was sold. With the ACTRESSES' FRANCHISE LEAGUE it staged such suffrage plays as *A Pageant of Great Women* by Cicely Hamilton and *Votes for Women* by Elizabeth Robins, and held a "Costume Dinner", which the guests attended in fancy-dress, at the Hotel Cecil in June 1914. Members of the WWSL presented signed copies of their books to be auctioned in order to raise funds. Although, as its name implied, the WWSL was a women's society, it did have honorary men associates, among whom were John Masefield, Laurence HOUSMAN and H.N. BRAILSFORD. The League's first BANNER, designed by Mary LOWNDES and worked by Christiana HERRINGHAM, was carried in turn by Cicely Hamilton, Evelyn Sharp, Sarah Grand, Beatrice Harraden and Elizabeth Robins in the NUWSS 13 June 1908 procession. This banner is now held in the Museum of London collection. In 1909 W.H. Margetson, Bessie Hatton's brother-in-law, designed a new banner, depicting Prejudice and blindfolded Justice, which was carried in the Coronation Procession of June 1911. The WWSL also issued this design as a postcard. Among its other publications were *How the Vote Was Won*, 1909, by Cicely Hamilton and C. Hedley Charlton; *The Suffrage Question*, 1909, by M.L. Ryley; *A Pageant of Great Women*, 1909, by Cicely Hamilton; *Women's Cause*, 1909, a poem by Laurence Housman; *Why*, 1910, by Elizabeth Robins; *Lady Geraldine's Speech*, 1910, by Beatrice Harraden; *Woman's Plea*, 1911, a poem by Lilian Sauter; *Under His Roof*, 1912, by Elizabeth Robins; and *Feminism*, 1912, by May SINCLAIR. After the partial enfranchisement of women in 1918 the WWSL drew its existence to a close.

President (1908–12) Elizabeth Robins; (1912) Flora Annie Steel. Honorary secretary (1908–17) Bessie Hatton; (1917–18?) Mrs Romanne-James. Treasurer (1908) Margaret Wynne NEVINSON.

Address: (1909–12) 55 Berners Street, London W; (1913–17) Goschen Buildings, 12 & 13 Henrietta Street, London WC; (1917–18) 42 West Cromwell Road, London SW5.

WOMEN'S ELECTION COMMITTEE Formed in 1920 to support those women candidates in parliamentary elections who would make economic and social equality one of their platforms. President: Dr Christine MURRELL.

WOMEN'S EMANCIPATION UNION "An Association of Workers to Secure the Political, Social and Economic Independence of Woman" was founded by Elizabeth Wolstenholme ELMY as a breakaway group from the WOMEN'S FRANCHISE LEAGUE in 1891. The word "workers" would have been carefully chosen. It carried no connotation of "working-class", rather that Elizabeth Wolstenholme Elmy's experience with other organizations had made her particularly keen to be associated only with those who were prepared to *work* for emancipation. The WEU claimed for women "Equality of right and duty with men in all matters affecting the service of the community and of the State. Equality of opportunity for self-development by the education of the schools and of life. Equality in industry by equal freedom of choice of career. Equality in marriage and equality of parental rights." The Union was not "a mere Suffrage society" but wanted the parliamentary vote for women on the same terms as men, "for as at once the security for what measure of justice has already been achieved, the leverage by which further reforms can be most speedily effected, and the efficient mechanism by which that womanly and motherly influence, as necessary in the great household of the nation as in the lesser group of the family, can be brought to bear upon the stirring social and political problems of the time" (WEU Final Report, 1899).

The WEU's first Council included Mona CAIRD, Lady Florence Dixie, Harriet MCILQUHAM, Agnes SUNLEY and Agnes POCHIN; all but the last are known to have been members previously of the Women's Franchise League. In July 1891 Elizabeth Wolstenholme Elmy was writing to Harriet McIlquham of "the baby Union" – the council to consist of *"real* workers only". "I do not want to make a more *formal* organization than we have at present, till we see who are the *real workers* – not promises *only*, but I would be glad to have one other names [sic], *pro tem* as well as my own to give". She had received £5 from Mrs Margaret ILLINGWORTH, a promise of £5 from Mrs Russell Carpenter, and was hoping to get a promise of £20 from John Bayly (her hopes were exceeded; he gave £25 at the end of the year). She continues, "I have a whole set of ideas as to the ... management of the Union, and am determined it shall *not* be wrecked as was the League. We have about 40 active devoted working members – and shall add very much more rapidly, as soon as I have time to send out more of our forms – with our programme of work". Elizabeth Wolstenholme Elmy stated that she would offer her own services free of charge for six months, but after that, if funds were available, would request a salary of not more than £100 a year. On 21 November she was able to write, "We shall be a real power presently as all the earnest workers are certain gradually to drift to us." She was prepared to accept "earnest workers" of any political persuasion, keen to attract Primrose Leaguers as well as Liberals, and was emphatic about the non-party allegiance of the WEU. In early 1892 the Unionist candidate for Houghton-le-Spring (Durham), Sir Edward Sullivan, joined the WEU.

At the conference held by the WEU at the Grand Hotel in Birmingham in October 1892, attended by among others Mrs Ashford, Harriet McIlquham, Agnes Sunley and Laura Morgan-BROWNE, Elizabeth Wolstenholme Elmy proposed a memorial to the president of the Council of Education praying that women be appointed to the office of inspector of schools. Mona Caird wrote "Why Do Women Want the Franchise?" to be read at the conference. The WEU had already issued one article she had written, on "The Position of Women", as their "Emancipation of Women (no 2) leaflet" (1s per 100, post free). The Birmingham conference attracted to it Catherine OSLER, who proposed a resolution supporting the inclusion of women in any reformed scheme for local government. After the end of the conference a public meeting in support of women's enfranchisement was held in the Masonic Hall. At the March 1893 conference, held in London, papers were read by Emilie Ashurst Holyoake (*see* George HOLYOAKE) and by Isabella FORD on "Married Women in Factories", and Elizabeth Wolstenholme Elmy spoke on "Women in the Civil Service". The WEU, unlike the Women's Franchise League, was prepared to give the benefit of the doubt and its support to the women's suffrage bill to be introduced by Sir Albert Rollit, construing it as likely to convey at least "a large instalment of justice".

The 1894 WEU conference was held in Bedford. One of the papers was given by Mrs E.O. Fordham, who was also a member of the WOMEN'S LIBERAL FEDERATION and the Women's Franchise League. Another of the papers, in this year when duly qualified married women gained the local government vote, was given by Harriet McIlquham on "Women's Work in Local Government". The WEU brought pressure to bear on 400 MPs to support the amendment to the Local Government Bill; Keir HARDIE was later thanked by the WEU for his support. By the next year 11 members of the WEU were already members of local administrative bodies; Elizabeth Wolstenholme Elmy was certainly successful in attracting to her cause women who were "earnest workers". The WEU Council in 1894 comprised Mrs Ashton Saunderson, Mr Charles Beaumont, Mr Boyd Kinnear, Mona Caird, Miss Colby (who later was a subscriber to the WOMEN'S SOCIAL AND POLITICAL UNION), Mary COZENS, Lady Florence Dixie, Mrs J.G. Grenfell, Mrs Langdon Down, Mrs McKinnel, Harriet McIlquham, Agnes Pochin, E.A.E. Schaw Protheroe, Caroline and Julia SMITH, Agnes Sunley, Mrs Jessy Williams, Elizabeth Wolstenholme Elmy and Miss Anna Young. In 1895 a circular from the Union particularly stressed the fear of "restriction by law of the wage-earning power of women ... designed to crush out the free, individual development of woman, and thereby to reduce her once more to a state of absolute economic dependence on man". In this year the WEU had branches in Birmingham, Coventry, Dumbartonshire, Edinburgh, Glasgow, Islington, Lees, Oxford, Creetown and Newton Stewart.

On 1 January 1896 the WEU sent a memorial to Balfour, pointing out anomalies in the local government qualification for voting. In May 1896 the WEU sent out 2000 leaflets requesting the recipients to write to their MP asking them to support the bill to be introduced in parliament by Mr Faithfull Begg (nephew of Emily FAITHFULL). It had in February passed its second reading by a majority of 71. In order to lobby for the bill "a little practical working group in London" was set up, with Louisa MARTINDALE as its president; when the bill was eventually talked out Elizabeth Wolstenholme Elmy was furious. The WEU conference held in London on 14 and 15 October 1896 adopted the following resolution:

That this Conference claims for women, on equal terms with men, the protection and power of the Parliamentary vote, pledges itself to use every legitimate means to secure this, and urges the like duty on all who seek to promote social and political justice: and that a copy of this resolution shall be sent to every member for a Metropolitan Borough, with a request that he will do his utmost to secure during the coming Session, a full and fair discussion of the urgent claim of women to the Parliamentary Franchise.

In the 24 October 1896 edition of Keir Hardie's paper, the *Labour Leader*, Isabella Bream Pearce, a regular contributor as "Lily Bell" and a close friend of Elizabeth Wolstenholme Elmy, gave a most favourable report of the Women's Emancipation Union conference, writing "I have attended a good many meetings in my time representing all sorts and shades of opinions and convictions, but in none of them have I had more pleasure and satisfaction than in those of the WEU at which I was able to be present in London last week". In this year subscribers to the WEU included Lady Florence Dixie, Mrs Langdon Down, Agnes Pochin, Mrs Selous, Miss Gibson, Louisa Martindale, Mr and Mrs Tebb, Mr and Mrs Samuel Prout Newcombe (*see* Bertha NEWCOMBE), Miss Dismore, Miss Spicer (probably a sister of Louisa Martindale), Mrs Hunter, Mr Edward Maitland, Miss Alice Read, Mr Albert Spicer MP (brother of Louisa Martindale), Mrs Pariss, Mrs Wood, Miss Abney Walker, Miss Adderly, Mrs Moore, Miss M. Scaife, Mrs Stevenson, Mr W. Lewin, Miss G. Western, Miss Varty-Smith and Miss Cecil Wray.

In September 1898 Elizabeth Wolstenholme Elmy wrote that "I feel that to give up the work of the Union at the present crisis would simply be to make fruitless a very great part of what it has already done. It is quite useless to trust to the Suffrage Societies, for Suffrage will never be won by them. Not merely have they made no attempts to secure a good ballot for next Session, but I cannot stir them up to the absolutely necessary duty of educating the constituencies of the recalcitrant Cabinet Ministers." However, the WEU's perilous financial position was difficult to ignore; Mrs Russell Carpenter from Bridport, who had given £200 of the £1000 donated to the WEU in its lifetime, had died in March 1898. The final meeting of the WEU was organized for 1 July 1899, at 81 Harley Street (the home of Mrs Langdon Down), to coincide with the quinquennial Women's International Congress. The chair was taken by Harriet McIlquham and the meeting was addressed by Dr Aletta Jacobs, Louisa Martindale, Charlotte Carmichael STOPES, Harriot Stanton BLATCH, Mrs Wynford Philipps and Elizabeth Wolstenholme Elmy.

The WEU had throughout its short life placed great emphasis on its pamphleteering; by 1894 over 200 000 had been distributed. Emile Ashurst Holyoake contributed one on "The Organization of Women". In the final report of the WEU it was noted that "It was ... soon found that this educational work was of prime necessity. Comparatively few women had previously had the opportunity of taking part in direct parliamentary action and agitation. The educational work of the Union has been very great, carried on mainly through meetings, discussions, and the distribution of literature". After its demise the WEU owed about £45 to its printers. Margaret Illingworth, Louisa Martindale, Harriet McIlquham and Caroline Smith were mainly reponsible for clearing the debt. The WEU's income from its inception in September 1891 until 1894 was £411 8s 2d, its income for the 12 months beginning 1 July 1897 was £90, £40 of which was contributed by four benefactors.

Honorary secretary (1891–9) Elizabeth Wolstenholme Elmy, Congleton, Cheshire; treasurer (1892) Mr W.B. Smith, 19 Carpenter Road, Edgbaston, Birmingham; (1899) Caroline Smith, 19 Carpenter Road, Edgbaston, Birmingham.

Archival source: WEU Annual reports, British Library; Elizabeth Wolstenholme Elmy Papers, British Library; John Johnson Collection, Bodleian Library, Oxford; Fawcett Library.

Bibliography: S.S. Holton, *Suffrage Days: Stories from the Women's Suffrage Movement*, 1996.

WOMEN'S FRANCHISE DECLARATION COMMITTEE

Formed by Clementina BLACK in November 1906. The declaration, which asked for the franchise for women on the same terms as it was or might be granted to men, was drawn up in order to disprove the statement that women did not want the vote. It was not associated with any political party or existing suffrage organization and the executive committee included women of many different shades of opinion. The *Tribune*, newly launched by Franklin THOMASSON, from the first opened its columns to reports of the movement (*see* NEWSPAPERS AND JOURNALS). Work began in Hampstead, where Clementina Black lived; a Declaration Form was to be sent to every woman in the district who was listed in the post office directory as carrying on a business or profession. Local committees were set up around the country and the forms were eventually signed by 257 000 women. An interim report issued in March 1907 stated that of the 30 849 signatures then collected, an analysis of 25 000 revealed 5692 to be engaged in work of education, 450 to be medical women (out of a possible 700 in the country), 1500 to be women involved in art, music, drama and in science, 2000 were engaged in social and philanthropic work, over 1100 were clerks or secretaries, 3300 were engaged in trades and factories, 2769 were "domestic" and 5000 were unclassified, thought to be women of independent income and ratepayers. Members of the general committee of the Franchise Declaration Committee included Lady Frances BALFOUR, Mrs Benson, Lady Burne-Jones, Mrs Patrick Campbell, Rosalind, Countess of CARLISLE, Millicent Garrett FAWCETT, Isabella FORD, Lady KNIGHTLEY, Elizabeth Garrett ANDERSON, Beatrice HARRADEN, Eva McLAREN, Edith PALLISER, Margaret PENNINGTON, Elizabeth ROBINS, Lady STRACHEY, Katherine THOMASSON, Alice WESTLAKE, Walter McLaren, and Israel ZANGWILL. Mary Home, who had worked for the Women's Franchise Declaration Committee, joined the WOMEN'S SOCIAL AND POLITICAL UNION office staff at the beginning of 1908.

Address: c/o Offices of the *Tribune*, 23 Bouverie Street, London EC.

WOMEN'S FRANCHISE LEAGUE Founded in the first half of 1889; by 12 July its printed notepaper was in use. The printed objects of the WFL were "To extend to women, whether married, unmarried, or widowed the right to vote at parliamentary, municipal and local and other elections on the same conditions which qualify men. To establish for all women equal civil and political rights with men". The stress on the marital status of potential women voters reveals the reason for the formation of the League. It had been clear since 1872 that there was a very real difference of opinion between those in the suffrage movement who thought that married women should not be excluded from enfranchisement and those who thought that for pragmatic political reasons the couverture clause should be retained. By 1889 both the CENTRAL COMMITTEE OF THE NATIONAL SOCIETY, resolutely, and the CENTRAL NATIONAL SOCIETY, with some waverers, were in the latter camp. The Women's Franchise League had at its core a group of former members of the MANCHESTER NATIONAL SOCIETY. Elizabeth Wolstenholme ELMY, Alice Cliff SCATCHERD and Harriet McILQUHAM were the activists who transformed philosophy into action. On 21 February 1889 Elizabeth Wolstenholme Elmy led a deputation to Jacob BRIGHT asking him to introduce a suffrage bill that would include married women. For the annual meeting of the Central National Society in March 1889 she put together a petition of 40 to 50 names to publish a protest against William Woodall's bill, which excluded married women from a proposed franchise. Elizabeth Wolstenholme Elmy wrote to Harriet McIlquham on 17 March 1889 that, "if the Central Committee will not come to the side of common-sense and justice we are now in a position to outflank them by the formation of a new Society stronger than either of the others, which will go on the broadest lines from the very first. I hope it may not be needed, but if it must be done, it shall be done". After the Central National Society failed to remove its support for the Woodall clause, on 1 April 1889 she wrote that, "I am asking the P.A. Taylors [*see* Clementia TAYLOR] and Jacob Brights, with Mrs VENTURI to join the Committee, and all who have signed our Protest to join the League.... Every one will help.... Do please join the Committee and get everybody you can to join the League." On 4 April she wrote that she had prepared a draft bill which "is now being considered by 4 good lawyers". This was the Women's Disabilities Removal Bill, to give the vote to those women, whether married or single, who possessed the relevant qualifications. It was introduced by Richard Haldane, Sir Edward Grey (who 16 years later, by refusing to answer questions from Christabel PANKHURST and Annie KENNEY in the Free Trade Hall in Manchester, sparked off the militant suffrage campaign), and Thomas Ellis on behalf of the WFL in August 1889. Elizabeth Wolstenholme Elmy, ever hopeful, had remarked in April that it was important to get it brought in at once. "If the new League follows the example of the old M.W.P. [Married Woman's Property] Committee, not many Committee *meetings* will be needed. We seldom had more than 4 or 5 a year, even then we were doing most work. The two W.S. Societies seem to me to spend all their energies in perfecting the mere machinery, whilst wasting and destroying their motive power. Over-organizing may very easily weigh down effort."

By May 1889 Elizabeth Wolstenholme Elmy no longer expected Jacob and Ursula Bright to join the WFL, feeling that their loyalty to Gladstone was greater than that to women, and they do not appear to have attended the inaugural meeting which was held on 25 July 1889 at the house of Mr and Mrs Tebb, 7 Albert Road, Regents Park. Mrs McIlquham took the chair and among those present were Dr PANKHURST, Alice Cliff Scatcherd, Harriot Stanton BLATCH, William Lloyd Garrison (the younger), and Dr Kate Mitchell. The Provisional Executive Committee comprised Florence Fenwick MILLER, Harriet McIlquham, Mr H.N. Mozley, Richard and Emmeline PANKHURST, and Mr and Mrs P.A. Taylor. The Council of the League proposed at the inaugural meeting included Mrs Ashton Saunderson (from Hull), Rev. Canon and Mrs (Josephine) Butler, Mr John Bayly, Mrs Colby and Miss Cordelia Colby (from Cheltenham), Mr Elmy and Mrs Wolstenholme Elmy, Mrs Fenwick Miller, Mr C.J. Fleming, Mr John Gibson (the editor of the *Cambrian News*), Miss Sara Hennell (friend of George Eliot), Mrs Stephenson Hunter (Oxford), Mrs John James (Aberystwyth), Mrs McIlquham, Mr H.N. Mozley, Mr and Mrs William Malleson (*see under* Elizabeth MALLESON), Dr Pankhurst and Mrs Pankhurst, Mrs Alice Cliff Scatcherd, Mrs Agnes SUNLEY, Mrs Caroline SMITH and Miss Julia Smith, Dr Kate Mitchell and Dr Julia Mitchell, Harriot Stanton Blatch, Mr and Mrs P.A. Taylor, Mr and Mrs Tebb (they had been supporters of the Central Committee of the National Society at its formation in 1871, he was chairman of the London Society for the Abolition of Compulsory Vaccination, and both were members of the Vigilance Association for the Defence of Personal Rights), Mrs Venturi, Mrs Spence WATSON and Mrs Emma Wood. Many of the people had been associated with Elizabeth Wolstenholme Elmy in her campaign that led to the passing of the 1886 Infants Act. On 7 November the League held a meeting at the Westminster Palace Hotel in support of the Women's Disabilities Removal Bill. Harriet McIlquham was in the chair and among the League's speakers were Elizabeth Wolstenholme Elmy, Florence Fenwick Miller and Alice Scatcherd. Ursula and Jacob Bright did not join the Council of the WFL until February 1890. By that time fellow members of the League's Council included Cunninghame Graham, a flamboyant radical Liberal MP, who in 1887 had been Keir HARDIE's main sponsor as a Liberal candidate in North Ayrshire, Jane Cobden (*see* Jane Cobden UNWIN), Lady SANDHURST, Elizabeth Cady Stanton, Mrs Busk, BA, the Countess of CARLISLE, Mrs Colby and Miss Cordelia Colby (Cheltenham), Mr C.J. Fleming (Manchester), Mr F.A. Ford (husband of Florence Fenwick Miller), Lady Mary Murray (daughter of the Countess of Carlisle) and Professor Gilbert Murray, the Hon. Dadabhai Naoroji (the first Indian member of the House of Commons), Mr Hodgson Pratt, Miss E.M. Schaw Protheroe, Dr R.D. Roberts, Mrs King Roberts, the Countess Schack, Mr A. Sidgwick and Mrs Mona TAYLOR.

By early 1890 the WFL had 140 members and £70 in the bank. Lady Florence Dixie and Mary de Morgan, sister of William and daughter of Sophia de Morgan who had signed the 1866 women's suffrage petition, both joined. Drawing-room meetings were planned; Elizabeth Wolstenholme Elmy mentioned that Mona CAIRD, and possibly her father-in-law, Sir James Caird, might act as hosts. In March 1890 a public meeting organized by the Women's Franchise League at the South Kensington Liberal Club, with Jane Cobden in the chair, included among its speakers Elizabeth Cady Stanton, Florence Fenwick Miller, Alice Cliff Scatcherd, Elizabeth Wolstenholme Elmy, Harriot Stanton Blatch and Richard Pankhurst. On 3 May Elizabeth Wolstenholme Elmy wrote to Harriet McIlquham that "The league is already a young giant". However, the serpent had already entered this paradise. In April Sir Charles Dilke (*see* Lady DILKE) had given £10 to the WFL. He had not asked to become a member but there was obviously considerable doubt, at least in Elizabeth Wolstenholme Elmy's mind, as to whether, if the money were accepted, the League would not be compromised. On 31 March 1890 Alice Scatcherd had written to Harriet McIlquham describing a drawing-room meeting of the League held on 25 March at the Pankhursts' house in which she mentioned that "Lady Dilke [was] present but left after the first two speakers

... She said she would send a subscription and if we take her money and she seeks a place on Council we cannot refuse". Elizabeth Wolstenholme Elmy came to think that Ursula Bright and the Pankhursts were forcing Dilke on the League as a way of re-establishing his political career. In 1894 Elizabeth Wolstenholme Elmy's distrust of Dilke was vindicated when he reneged on a commitment to include women in his Registration Bill and party loyalties caused dissension within the WFL. On 20 May 1890 Ursula Bright, Mona Caird, Jane Cobden, Mrs Fagan, Countess Schack and Emilie Venturi were elected to the WFL committee (Harriet Stanton Blatch was added a little later). Mrs Elmy was very wary of the Brights' strong commitment to the Liberal Party, writing on 22 May to Ursula Bright:

> The League was framed on strictly non-party lines. Amongst its members are even women of every shade of political opinion, Conservatives, Unionists, Gladstonian Liberals, Advanced Radicals, and Socialists. Its one great object is "to establish for all women equal civil and political rights with men" and this object the League must pursue irrespective of all party consideration, subordinating to it all other questions. This is and must be the attitude of the League, as a League, the claims of women are to it paramount, and neither hope, nor fear, favour nor affection must sway it from its steadily balanced course.

The WFL annual report for 1890 specifically mentions that it was on this same day, 22 May, that Mrs Elmy verbally intimated her intention of retiring from the secretaryship. On 26 May 1890 Elizabeth Wolstenholme Elmy resigned as the secretary of the Women's Franchise League, which since the previous November had been a paid position, unable to tolerate what she perceived as the insulting behaviour of Florence Fenwick Miller. The annual report on the one hand implicitly criticizes her for her sudden resignation, and on the other notes that with the secretaryship now based in London, rather than Congleton, the League would be strengthened and "practical work" promoted.

At a time of considerable personal financial difficulty, Mrs Elmy remained a hard-working member of the League, arranging the International Conference. In a July letter to Harriet McIlquham she writes of "interesting communications from Switzerland, Italy, Spain, and Germany and [of hoping] to have present several representatives of each of these nationalities, as well as of Russia, Armenia, India, North and South America. I have just a little hope, as to which please say nothing, that we may get the Empress Frederick to give her countenance to the Conference". On 16 and 17 July this International Conference on the Position of Women in All Countries was held at Westminster Town Hall. Jacob Bright presided over the first sitting, Jane Cobden over the second. The League held "advanced" views not just on suffrage, but on life in general, advocating co-education, marriage law reform, trade unionism, internationalism, the defence of oppressed races, and the abolition of the House of Lords. It was closely associated, both in membership and ideals, with the Vigilance Association for the Defence of Personal Rights. A joint meeting was held in December 1890 by the two societies, at the St Pancras Reform Club, with Ursula Bright in the chair, to debate "Women and Politics". The very diversity of the WFL's views did lead to problems in keeping all its members happy all of the time. The League lost, as Alice Scatcherd revealed in a letter to Harriet McIlquham, the Colbys "because of Home Rulers and Socialists on the committee" and "the Mallesons because of divorce".

By 1891 Elizabeth Wolstenholme Elmy, having been disappointed in her belief that the council of the WFL would support her against Florence Fenwick Miller, had left the League, taking with her some supporters, and in 1892 set up the WOMEN'S EMANCIPATION UNION. At the beginning of December 1891 the Women's Franchise League held a conference, over a period of three evenings, at the Pankhursts' house in Russell Square. The first evening was devoted to the "Economic Position of Women", the second to the "Political Rights and Duties of Women" and the third to "The Programme of the League and the Bills it has promoted and supported". Among the speakers at the conference were James Stansfeld, Ursula Bright, Harriot Stanton Blatch, J.H. Levy, Herbert Burrows, Mrs Wynford Phillips and Alice Cliff Scatcherd. Mention of the meeting, accompanied by a charming engraving of the scene, appeared in the *Graphic*. Rather surprisingly Florence Fenwick Miller made no mention of the conference in her column in the

Graphic's rival, the *Illustrated London News*. In 1893 the League held an "At Home" at the house of Baroness de Pallandt in Bryanston Street, which was attended by, among others, Mr Arnold (who by 1895 was chairman of the London County Council), Dr Alice Vickery, Ursula Bright and Marie CORBETT. In 1892 the League actively opposed the bill put forward by Sir Albert Rollit, the Parliamentary Franchise (Extension to Women) Bill, which while not expressly excluding married women, was so drafted that women under couverture were unlikely to be included. In April members of the League, led by Herbert Burrows, disturbed a joint meeting of suffrage societies, organized in support of the bill by the WOMEN'S SUFFRAGE DEMONSTRATION COMMITTEE, a breakaway group from the WFL, at St James's Hall. J.H. Levy, who had chaired the meeting, described the WFL in a letter to Dr Pankhurst as "a mere annexe to the Fabian Society". In March 1893 Ben Elmy wrote to the *Woman's Herald* protesting against the WFL's opposition to the bill. He took the opportunity of reminding readers that he was the "very coiner of the name of the League ... The principle was to treat every political or party feeling as of minor importance compared with the one, great object, of obtaining the franchise for women on the same terms as for men".

In 1893 Ursula Bright delivered a paper on the origins and aims of the League to the Council of Representative Women at the Chicago Exposition. Alice Cliff Scatcherd and Jane Cobden also attended the Exposition. On 9 June 1894 the League, together with the Temperance Society and Lady Henry Somerset, organized a women's suffrage meeting in the Queen's Hall, London. Ursula Bright personally sent out 250 handbills advertising the meeting to working men's clubs. Lady Henry Somerset was in the chair and Herbert Burrows, Ursula Bright, Alice Cliff Scatcherd ("She is a brick" wrote Ursula Bright to Emmeline Pankhurst when she knew that Mrs Scatcherd would come to the meeting) and Harriot Stanton Blatch addressed the meeting. In 1894 members of the League also supported a large meeting in the Free Trade Hall, Manchester, which was organized by the Manchester National Suffrage Society. Mrs Pankhurst drummed up support prior to the meeting, which was addressed by Alice Cliff Scatcherd. The passing of the Local Government Act in that year, by which married women with the appropriate qualifications were enabled to vote at local elections, owed much to the League's efforts. Ursula Bright certainly looked upon the passing of this Act as a very necessary preliminary to the passing of a suffrage bill which would include married women. Her reasoning was that with married women enfranchised locally it would be impossible to carry a "Parliamentary Spinsters Bill".

After this triumph Ursula Bright put some thought into the way in which the League should continue with its campaign. There is a suggestion in a letter to Emmeline Pankhurst that the suffrage question could now be left to the societies specifically devoted to that issue, while the WFL tackled a wider programme of social reforms affecting women. She wrote to Emmeline Pankhurst that "We might issue lots of literature. It is the cheapest way of agitating. Meetings are soon forgotten. . . . Our leaflets should go to all the WLAs. The League is exceedingly strong, simply because our Programme is all but universally accepted by working people. They won't take the trouble to come to meetings. Why should they?" She was increasingly drawn towards socialism, but, in a letter to Emmeline Pankhurst, regretted that "we [i.e. the League and the Independent Labour Party] cannot unite on *one thing*. I have been doing my best to concentrate efforts on the abolition of the House of Lords. That would suit all advanced parties. It is quite on our lines, being a sex privilege as well as an hereditary one". The WFL employed as an ORGANIZER, certainly in 1895, Mrs McCormick, who was also secretary to the Cheshire and Lancashire Union of Women's Liberal Associations and who had a long association with Alice Cliff Scatcherd. On 30 May 1895 the League held a conference at Aberystwyth. By this time the executive committee included Mrs Behrens, Ursula Bright, Miss Bright (who may have been Esther, the Brights' daughter), Mrs Brownlow, Mr Herbert Burrows (a member of the Social Democratic Federation), Dr Clark, MP, Mrs Hunter of Matlock Bank, Mrs E. James (Aberystwyth), Mr H.N. Mozley, Dr and Mrs Pankhurst, Alice Cliff Scatcherd, Countess Schack and Jane Cobden Unwin. By 1895 there was a branch of the League in Australia.

The Women's Franchise League was subsumed into the newly organized NATIONAL UNION OF WOMEN'S SUFFRAGE SOCIETIES in 1897. There is no correspondence that covers this event; it merely appears as "the Franchise League" amongst the amalgamating societies. The WFL's reliance on strong personalities rather than on a committee structure probably contributed to its demise. The Pankhursts had moved towards the Independent Labour Party, Jacob Bright was ill and Ursula Bright was increasingly involved in theosophy. Presumably Alice Cliff Scatcherd felt unable to continue alone, particularly as the NUWSS, as well as giving hope of greater activity, would be competing for members and funds.

Secretary (1889) Elizabeth Wolstenholme Elmy; honorary secretaries (July 1890) Countess Schack and Emmeline Pankhurst; (1891) Ursula Bright and Harriet Stanton Blatch; treasurer (1889, 1895) Alice Cliff Scatcherd; organizing agent (1889) Agnes Sunley; (1890) Mrs McCormick. Mrs Sibthorp (a theosophist) was honorary secretary of the Highbury Branch.

Illustration: *Mrs Pankhurst at Home*, WFL conference at the Pankhursts' house in Russell Square, reproduced from the *Graphic*, December 1891, in A. Bott and I. Clephane, *Our Mothers*, 1932.

Archival source: 1895 6th Annual report, Fawcett Library; Elizabeth Wolstenholme Elmy Papers, British Library; Correspondence between Ursula Bright and Emmeline Pankhurst and Women's Franchise League pamphlets in the Papers of Sylvia Pankhurst, Internationaal Instituut voor Sociale Geschiedenis, Amsterdam; Harriet McIlquham Papers, Autograph Collection, Fawcett Library.

Bibliography: F. Fenwick Miller, "The Ladies Column", *Illustrated London News*, 31 August 1889; F. Fenwick Miller, *On the Programme of the Women's Franchise League: An Address Delivered at the National Liberal Club*, 1890; S.S. Holton, "Now you see it, now you don't: the Women's Franchise League and its place in the contending narratives of the women's suffrage movement", in M. Joannou and J. Purvis (eds), *The Women's Suffrage Movement: New Feminist Perspectives*, 1998.

WOMEN'S FREEDOM LEAGUE Was formed as a result of dissension within the WOMEN'S SOCIAL AND POLITICAL UNION that reached a crisis in September 1907. The immediate cause of the break was the wish of one group, led by Teresa BILLINGTON-GREIG, Charlotte DESPARD, Edith How MARTYN and Caroline Hodgson, to run the WSPU under a democratic constitution, an arrangement that the PANKHURSTS and PETHICK-LAWRENCES thought would be detrimental to the militant operation they were developing. There were also ideological and personality differences. In April, at the ILP conference, Charlotte Despard and Anne Cobden SANDERSON publicly repudiated the WSPU election policy, by which government candidates were to be attacked and by which Labour Party candidates were specifically not to be supported. In addition, as Sylvia PANKHURST set out in *The Suffragette Movement*, Christabel PANKHURST considered Teresa Billington-Greig "a wrecker". At a members' meeting on 10 September 1907 Mrs PANKHURST announced that in future the governing power of the WSPU would be vested in a committee chosen and appointed by herself. She also announced that the forthcoming annual conference was to be abandoned, and that there would be no further need for conferences attended by delegates from the provincial branches, because henceforward these were to become local autonomous unions. The outcome was that on 13 September a notice appeared in *The Times*, under the names of Charlotte Despard, Edith How Martyn and Caroline Hodgson saying, "We wish it to be made known that we have found it necessary to withdraw from WSPU in consequence of the unconstitutional method of a section of the committee. Our views with regard to the great questions that affect women have not, in the least, changed and we are ready and anxious to work for women's enfranchisement with any who, disliking as we do unrepresentative government of any kind are willing to join us." On 16 September a further notice appeared in *The Times* from Edith How Martyn, calling on Mrs Pankhurst to hold the annual WSPU conference and stating that if they did not hear from her by 17 September, "duly elected delegates will assemble on October 12 for the transaction of business". The implication was that the breakaway group was the "true" WSPU and for a time it kept the name "Women's Social and Political Union", the Pankhurst society renaming itself the "National Women's Social and Political Union". However, the breakaway group, which had no control over the original society's finances or premises, in November 1907 voted to call itself "The Women's Freedom League". At the October

Conference 31 out of the 52 WSPU branches then established were represented, but it is not clear how many of these committed themselves outright to the WFL.

In its constitution the WFL stated that it proposed to act entirely independent of all political parties; to agitate "upon lines justified by the position of outlawry to which women are at present condemned"; and to educate "public opinion by all the usual methods". Furthermore it stated that, although a militant organization, it did not approve of injury or attack on persons or property. The WFL's National Executive Committee was to meet once a month, with final power vested in the annual conference, to which each branch sent delegates. From 1908, when it took part in 13 by-elections, the WFL's policy as stated in its constitution was, like that of the WSPU and despite the ideological commitment of its leaders to the Labour Party, to oppose the government candidate "on lines sanctioned by the annual or a special conference". The policy was altered in 1912 after a referendum of the branches, to one of supporting the Labour candidate in a three-cornered fight.

The first WFL committee comprised: president and honorary treasurer, Mrs Despard, honorary organizing secretary Mrs Billington-Greig, honorary secretary Mrs How Martyn, with Mrs Coates Hansen, Miss Hodgson, Irene MILLER, Miss Fitzherbert, Mrs Drysdale, Miss ABADAM, Mrs Winton-Evans, Mrs Dick, Mrs Cobden Sanderson, Mrs Bell, Mrs HOLMES and Miss Mansell. The WFL's intention was that its protests should be designed to highlight women's lack of citizenship. Its first was made at the opening of parliament, on 29 January 1908, when several members attempted to present a petition to the King. On the same day ten WFL members were imprisoned after taking part in deputations to Cabinet ministers. On 13 June 1908 the WFL was the only militant society invited by the NATIONAL UNION OF WOMEN'S SUFFRAGE SOCIETIES to take part in its procession to Hyde Park. On 28 October Muriel MATTERS, Violet Tillard and Helen Fox carried out one of the very public protests that has been incorporated into "suffragette" mythology, by chaining themselves to the grille that protected MPs from spectators in the Ladies' Gallery. They were supported by 200 members of the WFL who had gathered in the Lobby of the House of Commons. Fourteen women were arrested and the galleries of the House were subsequently closed. In February 1909, when no mention was made of women's suffrage in the King's speech at the opening of parliament, an attempt was made to carry a resolution of protest to Asquith. Mrs Despard and 25 other women were arrested, as was Joseph Clayton, a journalist, whose wife was a WFL member. Muriel Matters had hired an airship and dropped handbills explaining the constitutional nature of the protest. In general the WFL's main policy might be described as political passive resistance. The "militant" aspect was defined as any protest without violence that involved the risk of imprisonment.

In the middle of the year, Asquith, who had refused to receive a deputation from the WSPU, also refused to receive one from the WFL. While, in response, the WSPU escalated its attack on police and property and introduced the hunger strike, the WFL undertook "The Great Watch", a continuous picket of the House of Commons that continued, while it was sitting, from July to November 1909. A picket was also instituted during the summer outside No. 10 Downing Street, occasioning ten arrests, including those of Mrs Despard and Anne Cobden Sanderson. In October 1909 the WFL's philosophy of civil disobedience was embodied in the setting-up of a sister organization, the TAX RESISTANCE LEAGUE. Until the outbreak of war it was by a refusal to pay a variety of taxes and, after 1910, the dues under the Insurance Act, with the attendant publicity, that WFL members were most "militant". In April 1911 the WFL was the instigator of an imaginative civil resistance, which historians will soon regret, when women householders either failed to complete or spoilt their census returns. What A.E. Metcalfe refers to as "this sin against [statistical] science", which will hide from history many of the period's most interesting women, was considered to have such a negligible affect at the time on the accuracy of the statistics that no prosecutions ensued.

Teresa Billington-Greig in an untitled fragment, "We were not then aware...", wrote how, in the early days of the WSPU in Manchester, she had suggested that militancy should take the form of intervention in elections and gave a few examples of methods she had considered. In October 1909, during the Bermondsey by-election, two WFL members, Alice Chaplin and Alison NEILANS, put suggestion into practice when they destroyed ballot papers. This protest, which was directly linked with the prime minister's continued refusal, despite the "Great Watch", to receive a WFL deputation, coincided with the launching of the WFL's own paper, the *Vote*, so that the editorial of 4 November was able to broadcast the point that "We shall make it [a protest] where our right is denied – in the polling booth where women ought to be voting." After the general election of January 1910, the WFL joined the WSPU in a truce in response to Asquith's indication that the government was prepared to make the introduction of a woman suffrage amendment to any future franchise bill the subject of a free vote. At their annual conference in January 1910 the WFL ruled that members of any other militant society should not be members of any WFL committee.

The WFL entered with gusto into the planning, with the WSPU, of the joint procession to Hyde Park on 18 June 1910. As a society it was particularly associated with the SUFFRAGE ATELIER, whose members, led by Edy CRAIG, produced the WFL contribution to the spectacle. WFL branches were keen to stage Cicely HAMILTON's *Pageant of Great Women*, with which Edy Craig was also associated. This form of political education, by means of which a message might be communicated, funds raised and members brought together in a common purpose, was very typical of WFL activity. From 1910 the *Pageant* was staged by the WFL at Beckenham, Sheffield, Ipswich, Middlesborough, Sunderland, Eastbourne and Swansea. On 17 June 1911, during another period of truce, the WFL took part in the Coronation Procession. In November it was at last received, with the other suffrage societies, in a deputation to Asquith. On this occasion Mrs Despard had the doubtful satisfaction of being complimented by Asquith on the stating of her case. In May 1912, shortly after the NUWSS adopted the Election Fighting Fund policy, the WFL announced that it would henceforward support Labour candidates in three-cornered fights. In January 1913, after the Speaker's ruling on the inadmissibility of the proposed amendment to the franchise bill, the WFL ended its truce with the government. WFL branches across the country organized bill-posting campaigns and protests in courts against the forced exclusion of women when cases concerning assault were discussed. This was by no means a new issue; as long ago as 1892 Agnes SUNLEY had proposed at a WOMEN'S EMANCIPATION UNION conference that suitable women should be allowed to remain in the law courts when cases of indecent assault were being tried, in order to support the alleged victim. The WFL, which unlike the WSPU had maintained its interest in challenging all barriers to women's emancipation, rather than restricting itself solely to agitation for the vote, might be seen as an inheritor of the WEU philosophy.

After the break with the WSPU in late 1907 the WFL had to build up its own network of branches. In 1910 those in England were considered sufficiently numerous to be allocated to specified districts, each with an honorary district organizer, who was usually a member of the National Executive Committee. The WFL had a strong Scottish base in Glasgow, where Teresa Billington-Greig lived, and where Anna MUNRO was organizer. The Scottish Council was reconstructed in early 1910, and was then composed of an honorary secretary and an honorary treasurer and the secretary, or delegate, from each branch. The main Welsh WFL society was founded in 1909 in Swansea. By 1913 the WFL had 60 branches, with new ones constantly being formed. After 1910 the WFL had a "Propaganda" department, devoted to organizing meetings, advertising and special campaigns. This department had charge of the CARAVAN tours for which the WFL was renowned. They had at least two caravans and organizers such as Muriel Matters and Marguerite SIDLEY spent their summers touring, holding meetings and dispensing literature. In 1910 the WFL's head office in London stayed open until 9 pm and welcomed members to call in. A suffrage library was run by the Literature Department. Marie LAWSON formed the Minerva Publishing Company in 1909 in order to publish the *Vote*, which, although smaller than the *Common Cause* and *Votes for Women*, continued publishing until 1933. In 1913 and 1914, as the WSPU's arson campaign escalated, the *Vote*, unlike *Votes for Women* and the *Suffragette*, gave little coverage to stories of suffragette arson.

The WFL's income was always very much smaller than that of the WSPU; in 1908–9 it was £6103 compared to the WSPU's £31 686. The WFL never held the demagogic mass meetings that engendered the heady atmosphere in which promises of large sums of money were made. Instead the WFL had to rely on raising money in the usual ways open to women's societies, jumble sales and bazaars, "Yuletide Festivals" and "Green and Gold Fayres". A glance at the "Our Treasury" list of donations in any issue of the *Vote* reveals names of women who were also subscribing to other militant and constitutional suffrage societies. A study of the "Branch Notes" in the *Vote* reveals that many of the talks given to the branches emphasized the connection between the vote and social reform. A few random examples from 1910 include "Marriage, Separation and Divorce", given by Cecil Chapman (*see* Adeline Chapman); "Citizens' Duty to Elementary School Children" by Mrs Lovibond; and "Women in Municipal Work", by Margaret Wynne Nevinson. After listening to a talk given by Emma Sproson at Upper Ettingshall in December 1910 one man in the audience was moved to say that he "had never before taken the Suffragettes as serious people, but after listening to the able address of Mrs Sproson he fully realised the importance of Women's Suffrage". It was this presentation and response that the WFL aimed to produce.

During the First World War the WFL suspended active militant activity and concentrated on continuing its proselytizing campaign and effecting the social reforms that war conditions, by loosening the cement of society, now revealed to be possible. In August 1914 the WFL inaugurated the Women's Police Volunteers after the Home Office refused to enrol women as special constables. The WFL argued that, as women were deprived of the protection of the men of their family and as so many regular police officers were drafted into the trenches, it was desirable for a women's police force to be formed. This was, however, the culmination of a campaign that Nina Boyle had run before the war in the pages of the *Vote*. By 1915 the women's police force had split into the Women's Police Service under Miss Dawson, which was prepared to enforce government wartime restrictions on women's movements and behaviour, and the Women's Police Volunteers, which was not and which reverted to being an organization under the aegis of the WFL. The WFL also founded a Woman Suffrage National Aid Corps, which aimed to help women whose financial support had been undermined by the war. They founded a Settlement at 1 Everett Street, Nine Elms in Battersea, which was organized by Isabel Tippett (the mother of Michael Tippett, the composer) and which supplied about 200 vegetarian meals a day. The Settlement also ran a children's play club and a guest house for children, where they might be cared for, for short periods while their mothers were unable to look after them. In north London the WFL opened the Despard Arms, first at 50 Cumberland Market (which was also the address of the Espérance Club, *see* Mary Neal) and then at 123 Hampstead Road. This was a temperance public house, with a restaurant and club room, and with three furnished bedrooms which were available to let to women. In 1915 the WFL founded its National Service Organization, run by Frances Parker and Ethel Moorhead, who had been two of the WSPU's most "active" Scottish members. The National Service Organization specialized in matching women who were looking for work with employers who had never previously employed women. It was not the WFL's policy to encourage women to refuse to enrol under the National Registration Act; it allowed its members to act as their conscience dictated. However, because resistance to the government without consent had been the constant tradition of the WFL, the columns of the *Vote* carried notices of such protests made by their members.

In 1916 the WFL, with the Suffragettes of the WSPU and the Independent WSPU, organized a picket of the Electoral Reform Conference, while it was taking place in the House of Commons. In December 1916 a deputation organized by the WFL, which included representatives of the League of Justice, the Free Church League for Women's Suffrage, the Suffragettes of the WSPU, the Women's International League, the British Dominions Woman Suffrage Union, the Actresses' Franchise League, the Hastings and St Leonards Women's Suffrage Propaganda League, Hendon Women's Franchise Society and the Independent WSPU, to the Home Secretary protesting against the compulsory notification, treatment and detention of women suffering from venereal disease.

The WFL took part in the NUWSS victory celebrations held at the Queen's Hall on 13 March 1918 to celebrate the passing of the Representation of the People Act, enfranchising those women over 30 who fulfilled the property criteria. The WFL then determined to fight on until all women were enfranchised on the same terms as men. It also demanded that women should be made commissioners of prisons; that all professions should be open to women; that women should be entitled to equal pay with men; that a woman should have the right to retain her own nationality on marriage; and that women peers in their own right should be eligible to sit and vote in the House of Lords. In 1923 the WFL had 30 branches and as a feminist lobbying society it remained in operation until 1961.

By the summer of 1908 the Women's Freedom League had a BANNER, designed by Mary LOWNDES, made from black velvet with the gates of Holloway prison embroidered on it in grey and the inscription "Stone walls do not a prison make". There is now no trace of this banner. However, two other WFL banners, one probably dating from late 1909, and the other probably made c. 1908, by Mary Sargant FLORENCE, are now in the Fawcett Library Collection. Two made for the Hampstead branch of the WFL are in the Museum of London. Another, with the motto "Jus Suffragii" is held in the People's Palace, Glasgow, and that for the Partick branch is in the National Museum of Antiquities of Scotland, Edinburgh.

President (1907–18) Mrs Despard; (1926–35) Emmeline Pethick-Lawrence. Honorary organizing secretary (1907–10) Teresa Billington-Greig; (1918) Alice Schofield COATES. General secretary (1907–11) Edith How Martyn; (1911–post 1938) Miss F.A. Underwood. Head of militant and political department (1907–10) Teresa Billington-Greig; (1911–12) Edith How Martyn; (1916) C. Nina Boyle. Treasurer (1907–9) Mrs Despard; (1909–10) Sarah Benett; (1910–13) Miss C.V. Tite; (1913–33) Dr Elizabeth KNIGHT.

Address: (1907) 18 Buckingham Street, Strand, London WC; (1908–15) 1 Robert Street, Adelphi, London WC; (1915–1961?) 144 High Holborn, London WC.

Archival source: annual reports of the WFL, Fawcett Library.

Bibliography: M. Wynne Nevinson, *Five Years' Struggle for Freedom: A History of the Suffrage Movement from 1908 to 1912*, WLF, c. 1912/13; S. Newsome, *The Women's Freedom League 1907–1957*, 1960; C. McPhee and A. FitzGerald (eds), *The Non-Violent Militant: Selected Writings of Teresa Billington-Greig*, 1987; C. Eustance, "Meanings of militancy: the ideas and practice of political resistance in the Women's Freedom League, 1907–14", in M. Joannou and J. Purvis (eds), *The Women's Suffrage Movement: New Feminist Perspectives*, 1998.

WOMEN'S LIBERAL FEDERATION The suggestion of forming a federation of Women's Liberal Associations was first mooted in 1886 and formalized at a meeting held at the Metropole Hotel in London in February 1887. The first Women's Liberal Association had been founded in Bristol by Anna Maria PRIESTMAN and Emily STURGE in 1881, and had been followed by others in Darlington and York. Mrs PANKHURST averred that the founding of the Women's Liberal Federation was a shrewd manoeuvre on Gladstone's part to sidetrack the suffrage movement. Certainly, although a resolution in favour of women's suffrage was, from 1886, brought forward each year at the annual council meeting of the Women's Liberal Federation, it was not until 1890 that it was passed. An attempt at the annual council meeting in 1896 to commit the Federation to work only for those Liberal candidates who did not oppose women's suffrage was defeated in favour of adherence to local autonomy. This led to the formation of a "forward" group, the UNION OF PRACTICAL SUFFRAGISTS. By 1902 the WLF had an official organizer whose role was only to work for candidates supporting women's suffrage. This momentum was not maintained and when it became clear, after the Liberal government was elected in 1906, that women's suffrage was a priority neither for the government nor the Women's Liberal Federation, another pressure group, the FORWARD SUFFRAGE UNION, was formed.

Bibliography: D. Rubinstein, *Before the Suffragettes: Women's Emancipation in the 1890s*, 1986; L. Walker, "Party political women: a comparative study of Liberal women and the Primrose League, 1890–1914", in J. Rendall (ed.), *Equal or Different: Women's Politics 1800–1914*, 1987.

WOMEN'S LIBERAL UNIONIST ASSOCIATION Formed in 1886, a female reflection of the split in the Liberal Party over the question of home rule for Ireland. Among its members were Caroline Ashurst BIGGS, Lady GOLDSMID, Lady Frances BALFOUR and Mrs FAWCETT, who spoke at its first annual general meeting. Never a body enthusiastic in support of women's suffrage, by 1909–10, by which time it had become the Women's Unionist Association, its policy was one of neutrality.

President, Mary, Lady Ilchester; chairman, Hon Mrs Maxse (who was anti-suffrage); vice-chairman, Mrs Arnold Foster.

Bibliography: D. Rubinstein, *Before the Suffragettes: Women's Emancipation in the 1890s*, 1986; L. Walker, "Party political women: a comparative study of Liberal women and the Primrose League, 1890–1914", in J. Rendall (ed.), *Equal or Different: Women's Politics 1800–1914*, 1987.

WOMEN'S LOCAL GOVERNMENT SOCIETY The renamed SOCIETY FOR PROMOTING THE RETURN OF WOMEN AS COUNTY COUNCILLORS.

Address: (1898, 1917) 19 Tothill Street, Westminster, London SW. President (1898) the Countess of Aberdeen; (1905) Louisa Twining; chairman of committee, Lady Strachey; president (1917) Lady Strachey (*see* STRACHEY FAMILY); honorary treasurer Lady Lockyer (sister of Annie Leigh Browne), honorary secretary Annie Leigh BROWNE, deputy secretary M.S. Kilgour.

WOMEN'S NATIONAL LIBERAL ASSOCIATION Formed in 1892 by those members of the WOMEN'S LIBERAL FEDERATION who felt that, because women's suffrage was not a Liberal party issue, it should not be included in the Women's Liberal Federation programme. Among the WNLA's leading members were Mrs Theodore (Sophia) Fry, of Darlington, and Eliza ORME.

Bibliography: D. Rubenstein, *Before the Suffragettes: Women's Emancipation in the 1890s*, 1986.

WOMEN'S PARTY From 1917 the successor to the WOMEN'S SOCIAL AND POLITICAL UNION. Its manifesto included demands for equal opportunities of employment, equal pay, equal marriage and divorce laws, equality of parental rights and the raising of the age of consent, alongside a blueprint for a national-socialist state. At its victory celebration in the Royal Albert Hall on 16 March, three days after that held at the Queen's Hall by the NATIONAL UNION OF WOMEN'S SUFFRAGE SOCIETIES, Mrs PANKHURST, Christabel PANKHURST, Annie KENNEY and Flora DRUMMOND were the speakers. At the 1918 general election Christabel Pankhurst, standing in Smethwick as the Women's Party candidate, backed by the Coalition "coupon", was defeated. Her election manifesto was not particularly feminist. Her two main platforms were: "a Victorious Peace based on material guarantees against German aggression" and "True Social Reform and especially Industrial Salvation". Although in 1919 Christabel Pankhurst announced that she was standing as the Women's Party candidate for the Abbey division of Westminster in the general election, her campaign petered out and by the end of the summer the Women's Party had ceased to exist.

Honorary secretary (1917) Annie Kenney.

Address: (1917) 114 Great Portland Street, London W; (1918–1919) 4 William Street, Knightsbridge, London SW.

WOMEN'S PROGRESSIVE SOCIETY A letter from Mrs Warner Snoad in the *Women's Penny Paper*, 26 July 1890, suggested "Why do not women combine to prevent the return of men, by supporting those candidates only who will vote for us?" There was a very positive response to this suggestion in subsequent issues of the paper, leading to the foundation later that year of the Women's Progressive Society, which affiliated to the CENTRAL NATIONAL SOCIETY. Among the society's objects were the promotion of any measure in favour of granting women the parliamentary vote and campaigning support for only those parliamentary candidates who pledged themselves to vote for women's suffrage. The society's remit was, therefore, very close to that of the UNION OF PRACTICAL SUFFRAGISTS, although not so overtly associated with only the Liberal Party. In 1892–3 the executive committee of the WPS included Mrs MASSINGBERD, Laura Morgan-BROWNE (whose daughter was the WPS's honorary librarian) and Mrs Sibthorpe, editor of *Shafts*. Vice-presidents included Matilda Blind, Sara Hennell (friend of George Eliot), Henrik Ibsen, Henrietta MULLER, and Elizabeth Cady Stanton. President (1892–3) Mrs Warner Snoad; honorary secretary Mrs Grenfell, 12 John Street, Bedford Row, London WC; (1897) Mrs Brownlow, 30 Theobald's Road, London WC.

WOMEN'S REFORM UNION President (1909) Anna Maria PRIESTMAN; chairman Miss Tanner; treasurer Mrs Perry; honorary secretary Mrs W. Cross; secretary Mrs Willis.
Address: (1909) 104 Whiteladies Road, Clifton, Bristol.

WOMEN'S SILENT CO-OPERATION FOR FREEDOM
The movement was formed in 1913 as the outcome of a suggestion made in a letter from the Society of Silent Unity (for Practical Christianity): "If the women desiring their freedom knew the power of concentrated thought they could do more in Silent Co-operation than in outward demonstration ... England could not long stand out against the spiritual and mental agreement of power of five hundred women if they could only realize that 'the battle is the Lord's' and trust Him to bring it all about". The "thought" was held daily at 12 noon and was orchestrated from Eastbourne by Sibella Jones.
Address: (1913) 10 Southfields Road, Eastbourne, Sussex.
Archival source: *The Women's Silent Co-operation for Freedom*, leaflet received by the British Museum on 13 August 1913, British Library.

WOMEN'S SOCIAL AND POLITICAL UNION founded on Saturday, 10 October 1903 in Manchester at a small gathering of women, all of whom belonged to the Manchester Independent Labour Party. The meeting was called by Emmeline PANKHURST and was held at her home at 62 Nelson Street. The name first chosen, the "Women's Labour Representation Committee", was, according to Sylvia PANKHURST in *The Suffragette Movement*, vetoed by Christabel PANKHURST, who was not at that first meeting, as being too similar to that of the LANCASHIRE AND CHESHIRE WOMEN TEXTILE AND OTHER WORKERS' REPRESENTATION COMMITTEE, which had recently been founded by Eva GORE-BOOTH and Esther ROPER. The second, and final, choice of name was not a synonym for the first. Mrs Pankhurst in her autobiography omits any mention of the first choice, and states that the meeting "voted" for the title "Women's Social and Political Union". Sylvia Pankhurst wrote that Mrs Pankhurst "selected instead: 'The Women's Social and Political Union'". In her autobiography Mrs Pankhurst glosses the title of the new group as chosen to emphasize its democracy (in the light of its later history, she appeared oblivious of this irony) and as defining its object as "political rather than propagandist". By this latter term she presumably meant that a political solution was actively to be sought rather than that a proselytizing campaign should be undertaken. Sylvia Pankhurst described the name as uniting her mother's desire to "conduct social as well as political work". It is not entirely clear if this meant that the society was merely to work for social as well as political reform, or if, as "a social union", it was to act as a friendly society. The term "political union" had resonances from the early 1830s, when Chartists in the major cities so organized themselves during the Reform Bill agitation. Sylvia Pankhurst further adds that her mother's intention in 1903 was that the organization should be composed mainly of "working women" (as was LCWTOWRC) and should, as her first choice of name indicated, be "a women's parallel to the I.L.P., though with primary emphasis on the vote". By 31 October, when Rachel Scott, the first secretary, wrote to the *Labour Leader* to announce the formation of the Women's Social and Political Union, with its object to secure complete equality with men, social and political, both its name and its intended audience were defined.

From its very beginning the new organization had historic and philosophical roots in both the suffrage campaign and the "great crusade", the agitation to repeal the Contagious Diseases Acts. Mrs Pankhurst had been a member of the executive committee of the Married Women's Property Committee and of the MANCHESTER NATIONAL SOCIETY FOR WOMEN'S SUFFRAGE. In the 1890s she had been deeply involved with the WOMEN'S FRANCHISE LEAGUE, which had taken an absolutist stand against the introduction of a bill that would have excluded married women from the franchise. She was not a committed party woman, but always put the cause of women first. She had been a member of the Fabian Society from 1890 to 1900, of the ILP since 1894, and in 1902 had been one of the founder members of the ILP Central Manchester branch; she had previously been a member of the executive committee of the Lancashire and Cheshire Union of the Women's Liberal Association. A momentum of experience influenced the formation of the WSPU, the initial aim of which was to win the vote for duly qualified women on the assumption that social reform would then follow.

The WSPU never fell into the political trap of aiming to enfranchise all women. The qualifying distinction between married women and "spinsters and widows" had been eliminated by the passing of the 1894 Local Government Act; distinction based on the property qualification still remained. In this case Mrs Pankhurst was quite prepared to adopt "the half-a-loaf" principle and aim only to enfranchise women on the same terms as men. The adult suffrage cause was considered even more hopeless than the enfranchisement of propertied women. Although many individual MPs, both Conservatives and Liberals, pledged their support to women's enfranchisement, no political party had ever brought it forward as a party measure. A reading of the parliamentary reports in *The Times* of any debate on women's enfranchisement in the first years of the twentieth century makes it clear that, 40 years after J.S. MILL had introduced his amendment to the 1866 Reform Bill, the culture of the House of Commons precluded any rational debate on the subject. The idea of women as active participants in the political system, other than, of course, canvassers for men, was considered risible. Women were, if middle-class, too noble, too sensitive, or too frivolous, and if working-class, too ignorant to cast a vote. Among other well rehearsed arguments for maintaining the *status quo* were: that, because they were more numerous, women electors would outnumber men; that, being unable to carry arms in defence of the state, women did not qualify for citizenship; that, in spite of the innumerable petitions presented to parliament in the past 40 years, there was no proof that women wanted the vote; that, if they were able to vote, there would be no reason to bar women from sitting in parliament; and that, if that were so, there would be no reason why a woman might not become Speaker of the House of Commons. The latter was usually the last arrow that the MP pulled from his quiver, in order that he might resume his seat to the sound of the House in full throat.

It was natural that the founders of the WSPU should place their faith in the fledgling Labour party, which was the party of the disenfranchised. It had been galling to realize that MPs such as John Burns, once a member of the Socialist Democratic Federation but now a Liberal, and David Shackleton, whose parliamentary salary was in the main paid for by the contributions of women textile workers, were no more prepared actively to champion the cause of women at Westminster than any Liberal or Conservative. The WSPU's initial political campaign was to influence the Labour Party to include in its programme the enfranchisement of women, based on the Women's Disabilities Removal Bill drafted by Richard PANKHURST over 30 years previously. The ILP's National Administrative Council, despite Mrs Pankhurst's membership of its executive committee, was naturally inclined to support adult suffrage, rather than the interests of what were perceived as propertied women. An attempt was made, using very unscientific criteria, to gather statistics from ILP branches to see how many women who could be classed as "working women voters" were entitled to the municipal vote, the basis of the parliamentary franchise. Keir HARDIE and the WSPU deemed themselves happy with the result that "proved" that 82 per cent of the women who would thus be enfranchised were "working women". The Labour Representation Committee was less convinced and in January 1905 voted to back a policy of adult suffrage. The WSPU, nevertheless, continued to work in close association with the ILP, and its speakers, who by now included Teresa Billington (*see* Teresa BILLINGTON-GREIG), Hannah MITCHELL, Alice Milne and Annie KENNEY, travelled widely around the north, addressing a variety of radical societies. After nearly two years' existence the WSPU succeeded to some degree in raising the profile of the cause in its home territory. However, in the summer of 1905 Nellie MARTEL, visiting from London, noted that its membership then was less than 30.

Teresa Billington-Greig has left a very plausible description of life as experienced by these first members of the WSPU. Although a secretary, Mrs Rachel Scott (Woodbine, Flixton, Manchester), who had been present at the first meeting, had been appointed, the post changed frequently. It is doubtful if minutes were taken at those early meetings in Manchester; certainly none have survived. The WSPU had no office; all correspondence was carried out from 62 Nelson Street. This, for the first two years of the WSPU's existence, was in the main limited to the booking of speakers to address the local Socialist, trade union, and ethical society meetings. The WSPU was then a means of communicating its message, not intent on promoting itself. Christabel Pankhurst had several letters on the subject of women's suffrage published in both general newspapers and in Labour journals in which, although she stressed the need to remove the electoral disabilities that stood in the way of women's enfranchisement, she did not particularly emphasize the existence of the WSPU. On 25 July 1904 an article by Christabel Pankhurst, "Woman's Rights: an American reformer in Manchester" appeared in the *Daily Dispatch*, Manchester's newspaper. The article concerns itself with Susan Anthony's life and beliefs and mentions that she would that day be in Manchester, but does not give notice that she was to address a meeting of the WSPU. That meeting, held in a room above a warehouse in Portland Street, was sufficiently momentous for it to be remembered 73 years after the event by a frail Alice Schofield COATES.

Although Mrs Pankhurst had travelled to London on the occasion of the opening of the new parliament in February 1904 to take part in the traditional NUWSS interview with sympathetic MPs, and had questioned Sir Charles McLaren as to whether the parliamentary supporters of women's enfranchisement would act, rather than merely resolve, to bring it about, it is doubtful if her new position as leader of the WSPU was a matter of any import to other suffrage campaigners. The WSPU waited a year, until the opening of the 1905 session of parliament and then, with every encouragement from Keir Hardie, who had himself been unsuccessful in the ballot for a place for a private members' bill, lobbied to find another member to introduce their bill. They were eventually successful in persuading Bamford Slack, a Liberal MP whose wife was a member of the executive committee of the NATIONAL UNION OF WOMEN'S SUFFRAGE SOCIETIES. The bill was due to be heard on 12 May 1905. Members of the WSPU, led by Mrs Pankhurst and Elizabeth Wolstenholme ELMY, travelled down from Manchester, meeting up in Westminster with members of the NUWSS, including Millicent Garrett FAWCETT, Isabella FORD, Florence BALGARNIE, Emily DAVIES, and with Dora MONTEFIORE and Nellie Alma Martel, who was accompanied by a large number of members of the Co-operative Women's Guild. The bill was "talked out"; the WSPU leaders held an impromptu protest meeting and signed a resolution, drawn up by Elizabeth Wolstenholme Elmy, condemning the procedures of the House of Commons. Eight years previously, as secretary of the WOMEN'S EMANCIPATION UNION, Mrs Elmy had presented a similar petition. Mrs Pankhurst later dated the beginning of militancy to this demonstration.

The use of coercion against those in power was not a concept totally unconsidered in suffrage circles. Mary COZENS had, in 1892, suggested at a conference of the WOMEN'S EMANCIPATION UNION that the use of guns and dynamite would bring women the franchise within a week. This debate was widely reported in the suffrage press and, although doubtless the notion was mentioned only for effect, it had, nevertheless, been voiced. In the summer of 1905 the power of mass demonstrations, both in London where they were orchestrated by, among others, George LANSBURY and Dora Montefiore, and in Manchester, was shown to bring results; the Unemployed Workmen Bill was passed despite the government's lack of interest in it. The obvious lesson was drawn by the WSPU. Christabel Pankhurst put two elements of militant policy to the test on 13 October 1905. One constituent was publicly to interrogate Liberal politicians, not an act that hitherto would have been expected of women. On that evening Annie Kenney and Christabel Pankhurst interrupted the meeting being held by Sir Edward Grey at the Free Trade Hall, asking "Will the Liberal Government give women the vote?" The other was, in the process, to court imprisonment and, hence, notoriety and publicity, in order to draw attention to the WSPU's cause. Christabel Pankhurst and Annie Kenney effected their imprisonment, the former on a charge of assault after spitting at a policeman, the latter for obstruction. The WSPU strategy of incurring imprisonment had an obvious precursor in the stand taken by Emmeline Pankhurst at Boggart Hole Clough in 1896; her co-resisters Leonard Hall and John Harker had indeed gone to prison. Even earlier, in 1891 Agnes SUNLEY, a working-class member of the Women's Emancipation Union, had suggested in a letter to Harriet MCILQUHAM that, in order to draw attention to her cause, a woman should induce an official (she was talking of the demonstration taking place in a court of law) to commit a technical assault against her. It is very likely that over the years many such suggestions had been made in private, gathering a momentum of possibility. Both Leonard Hall and John Harker, whose wives were members of the WSPU (Mrs Harker was its first treasurer), were with Keir Hardie and Elizabeth Wolstenholme Elmy on the platform at the Free Trade Hall on 20 October to join in the rapturous welcome to the two released prisoners. While they had been in Strangeways Teresa Billington had orchestrated a very successful publicity campaign. The national press covered the event, which seized the popular imagination in a way that 40 years of petitioning had failed to. On Monday 16 October, beneath an account of the death of Sir Henry Irving, which had also taken place on 13 October, *The Times* reported the appearance of Christabel Pankhurst and Annie Kenney in the police court on 14 October, describing them as "two prominent upholders of women's rights" and reporting that the prosecuting solicitor had described their conduct as "instead of being what was expected of educated ladies [as] like that of women from the slums". The two women were quoted as saying "that as they were denied votes, making a disturbance was the only way they could put forward their claim to political justice". *The Times* continued with a short report of an open-air protest that had been held that evening at which Mrs Pankhurst said "she was proud that her daughter had taken so courageous a stand. The Liberal party desired to keep the question in the background. These noble girls had undeceived the Liberal women as to the intentions of the Liberal party". The 20 October 1905 issue of the *Labour Leader* noted that the ILP would not endorse the action taken by Christabel Pankhurst and Annie Kenney, but would stand by them. Of Christabel Pankhurst the paper wrote:

> She is full of fire and energy for it [women's suffrage]. She feels that unless someone forces it ahead – forces it in our own movement, no less than outside it – the question will remain in utter neglect. And she is right. To anyone who really believes in Socialism and political equality, the almost complete apathy, if not opposition, outside the ranks of the ILP, to the civic enfranchisement of women, is but an index of the fact that the power of conservatism, of egotism, and privilege is as manifest in respect to women's rights as women, as to the workers' rights as workers.

On 21 October, besides celebrating the centenary of Trafalgar, *The Times* gave a lengthy obituary notice of Jessie Boucherett, a report of the NUWSS annual convention, a very full description of Sir Henry Irving's funeral and coverage of the welcome to the released WSPU prisoners the evening before. Christopher St John has described in her memoir of Edy Craig how she saw her first suffrage demonstration on the occasion of Sir Henry's funeral. *The Times* makes no mention of such a demonstration at Westminster, where the funeral took place. It is possible that Christopher St John elided the memory of the funeral with an awareness of the suffrage heroics in Manchester. A mere week after the first recognizably militant stand the suffrage question had become so newsworthy that *The Times* would not have failed to mention any such activity if it had impinged on the funeral of the first knight of the theatre.

According to Mrs Pankhurst's autobiography, the WSPU slogan, "Votes for Women", originated as a by-product of the 13 October 1905 meeting when a large BANNER with the inscription, "Will the Liberal Government Give Votes for Women?" proved too large to take into the meeting and was cut down to the final three words. Christabel Pankhurst remembered that the banner read "Will you give votes for women?" and commented of the wording, "It was so obvious and yet, strange to say, quite new." This may be so, but "Votes for Women" had been used the previous year as a heading on a flyer issued by the Kensington Committee of the Central Society for Women's Suffrage. The coincidence is doubtless an indication that at the beginning of the new century the revived suffrage movement, in both its constitutional and militant aspects, was able to see the advantage of a snappy slogan. A photograph of the 20 October celebration shows Annie Kenney and Christabel Pankhurst seated at the dinner in their honour, flanked by Nellie Martel and Jennie Baines, with behind them a printed poster, "Women's Social and Political Union. Votes for Women".

On 4 December 1905, Balfour the Conservative prime minister resigned, and Campbell-Bannerman, the Liberal leader, was called to form an administration prior to a general election in January 1906. The Manchester WSPU liaised with like-minded women in London to take the hectoring of the Liberals to the capital. Elizabeth Wolstenholme Elmy had introduced Dora Montefiore to the Pankhursts at Easter 1904, when there was a suggestion that she would represent the WSPU that summer at the Berlin conference of the Congress of the International Council of Women. Sylvia Pankhurst, now a student at the Royal College of Art in South Kensington, had been in touch with Mrs Montefiore, speaking with her at an open-air suffrage meeting in west London. Although Sylvia had been present with her mother at the various lobbyings of parliament in 1905 she had not attempted, in the midst of her studies, to build up any support for WSPU policy in London. In mid-December Annie Kenney and Teresa Billington came to London, stayed with Sylvia Pankhurst and made arrangements with Dora Montefiore, who introduced them to Minnie BALDOCK, to infiltrate the Queen's Hall on 19 December. On this occasion Asquith, under the auspices of the London Liberal Federation, was to give his support to the Liberal candidates for north London constituencies. According to *The Times* at least three women interrupted the proceedings. Although they were promised by the stewards that an answer to the question, "I want to know whether the Liberal government will give women their votes?", would be forthcoming, it was not. Two days later a Liberal rally at the Albert Hall, the first platform appearance of Campbell-Bannerman as prime minister, at which he was accompanied by most members of the cabinet and of the ministry outside the cabinet and which was attended by an audience of 9000, was a suitable occasion on which to draw attention to the WSPU cause. Two banners were produced. One, saying "Votes for Women", was suspended upside down from the balcony, to general derision, another was then unfolded which bore the legend, "Will the Liberal Government give Working Women A Vote?" Two women were ejected; *The Times* reported that they were the same women who had created the disturbance at the Queen's Hall. The next day, 22 December, Annie Kenney, Minnie Baldock, Teresa Billington and a Mrs Fennell followed up their demonstration by calling on Campbell-Bannerman at his house at 39 Belgrave Square, to ask him for an interview. He replied that he would be dealing sometime in the future with the question of women's suffrage. The fact that newspaper reports were created that allow us to reconstruct the first footsteps of the long campaign is evidence enough of the efficacy of demonstration.

The general election campaign was launched in earnest at the beginning of 1906. WSPU policy, which it is assumed was directed by Christabel Pankhurst, was to oppose government candidates. This contrasted with the NUWSS policy of actively supporting suffragist candidates. The purpose was to harass the government until WSPU demands were met. The lesson was said to have been learnt from Parnell's success in influencing the Gladstone administration to introduce a Home Rule Bill for debate in the House of Commons. At the 1906 general election the WSPU did not have the troops to take its campaign into every constituency. It restricted its opposition to Liberal cabinet ministers. Winston Churchill, who had lately repudiated Conservatism, was the Liberal candidate for North-West Manchester and as such was the focus of the WSPU's attention. A manifesto, written by Christabel who, under the terms of her promise given to the Manchester University authorities, could not herself take part in the heckling, asked constituents "to vote and work" against Churchill. On 6 January his meeting was interrupted by Sylvia Pankhurst, waving a "Votes for Women" banner; she was then asked to ascend the platform and put her question. After she had been removed from the hall, Churchill self-righteously told the audience that "he was not so hostile to the proposal as he had thought it right to say just now, but he was not going to be henpecked". His evening meeting on 9 January was interrupted by Hannah Mitchell who, after unfurling a banner, was invited to address the audience from the platform. Her speech was then subjected to constant interruption from an impatient audience and she was forced to give up and leave the room. ILP women elsewhere in the country followed the lead of the WSPU and heckled Liberal ministers. Ivor Guest had his meeting in Cardiff interrupted,

Asquith was heckled at Huddersfield and Campbell-Bannerman vociferously so at Liverpool. At the latter meeting the stewards were already sufficiently alert to the danger, they were issued with photographs in order to identify the leading agitators, who had been shadowed beforehand and were thrown out of the meeting. Flora DRUMMOND, with an entourage, travelled to Glasgow to heckle Campbell-Bannerman there. Despite the general policy of negative campaigning, Mrs Pankhurst and Annie Kenney did work actively for Keir Hardie at Merthyr Tydfil. With the Women's Co-operative Guild, the Lancashire and Cheshire Women's Textile and other Workers' Representation Committee, the MANCHESTER AND SALFORD WOMEN'S TRADE AND LABOUR COUNCIL, the WOMEN'S LIBERAL FEDERATION, the National British Women's Temperance Association, the ILP, the Northern Counties Weavers, the Amalgamated Felt Hat Trimmers and Wool Formers Association and the Operative Bleachers, Dyers and Finishers Association, the WSPU issued a "United Manifesto in favour of votes for women" calling on all parliamentary candidates to declare in favour of women's suffrage – and if returned to bring influence with the government to introduce legislation. It was with this manifesto in her hand that Minnie Baldock attended a meeting held in Poplar by Sydney Buxton in early January 1906. Although she was promised that she could question him about his attitude to women's suffrage, she was never called. Her companion Irene MILLER did, however, stand on her chair, waving her red and white "Votes for Women" flag until she was asked onto the platform. The manifesto represented the final formal co-operation between the WSPU and the Labour movement.

The efficacy of the WSPU campaign did not pass unnoticed by the constitutional suffrage movement. In January Mrs Fawcett issued an open letter:

> We have conducted ourselves with perfect propriety in our middle-class way, and have got nothing for our pains. A new element has come upon the scene – working women. They are conducting the campaign in their own way. Their way is not our way; it is possible that it may be a better way than ours. Let me counsel all friends of women's suffrage not to denounce the flag-waving women who ask questions about women's suffrage at meetings, even to the risk of rough handling and jeers. It is proving to men what many have not realised – that women are in earnest...

The campaign also had its effect on the Labour movement. The profile of women's concerns was so raised that in its February 1906 issue the *Labour Leader* launched "Our Women's Outlook". This women's interest page was not universally welcomed; both Isabella Ford and Hannah Mitchell wrote in to complain that separating women's and men's interests was a retrograde step. A month later, in the March issue of the *Labour Leader*, came the first announcement of the founding of the Women's Labour League. It is now clear that the idea of such a body, a sister organization to the Labour Representation Committee, had been under discussion since the end of 1904. The timing of its appearance, as the WSPU had accrued recognition as the women's society linked to the ILP, looked like a spoiling manoeuvre and there was discussion in the "Our Women's Outlook" column in the first few months of 1906 as to which of the groups "our women" would favour. It is worth noting that the WLL was formed before there was any evidence that the WSPU would repudiate its association with the Labour movement.

After the election the Liberal landslide had brought into power a party that had, with its radical element, traditionally been less averse to women's enfranchisement than had the Conservatives. The prime minister was known to be personally in favour, as were perhaps four members of the cabinet. The Labour Representation Committee, now to be known as the Labour Party, had 29 MPs. The WSPU's policy had always been to achieve a political solution, the seat of government was in London, and it was to there that the campaign had to move. Annie Kenney, a deceptively unlikely tool of history, was sent to rouse London at the end of January.

In her 1908 articles in *Votes for Women*, on which was based *The Suffragette*, 1911, and in *The Suffragette Movement*, 1931, Sylvia Pankhurst wrote that Annie Kenney had come to her in London without instructions and dwelt on the frailty and helplessness of the two girls and the enormity of their task. Daunting it certainly was, but they were not without advice and influential friends. Keir Hardie suggested that they should book the Caxton Hall; W.T. Stead, an old friend and associate of Mrs Elmy, was approached to give support and publicity and, with Isabella Ford and Walter Coats, secretary to the Vacant Lands Cultivation Society, paid the hire cost. Fleet Street editors were approached; the WSPU was already news and the *Daily Mirror*, recently launched, not unsurprisingly offered publicity for the meeting. A photograph, which was later issued as a postcard, of the "Women Who Want Votes", together with a news item, appeared in its issue of 20 February. The handbill printed to advertise the Caxton Hall meeting gave the address of the organizer as Miss Annie Kenney (Late member District Committee Card and Blowing Room Operatives' Association, Oldham) and her address as 45 Park Walk, Chelsea. The leaflet was issued by the Women's Social and Political Union, 10 Clifford's Inn, London WC, which was the address of Frank Smith, a journalist (who was later the Lambeth member of the LCC), and was printed by the Women's Printing Society. Dora Montefiore in *From Victorian to a Modern*, 1927, contested Sylvia Pankhurst's presentation of events. Whether or not Mrs Montefiore's recollections were entirely accurate, she certainly must have been involved in the arrangements. She was a forceful, effective, experienced campaigner whose advice and help the two young women could have ill afforded to ignore. There seems no doubt that in the mere two or three weeks between Annie Kenney's arrival in London and the opening of parliament she spent some time, on the advice of Dora Montefiore, with Minnie Baldock in the East End of London. It was from there that the newly formed London Committee of the WSPU, consisting of Annie Kenney, Sylvia Pankhurst, her aunt, Mary CLARKE, and her landlady, Mrs Roe, planned to draw its support in order to fill the 700 seats of the Caxton Hall. In the week or two before 19 February the London Committee was aided by Nellie Martel, and by Mrs Pankhurst, Teresa Billington, Jessie KENNEY and Flora Drummond, all of whom came from Manchester to help. On 19 February 300 or 400 women travelled from the East End by tube, arriving at St James's Park station, where they were met by the organizers. "Votes for Women" banners had been made both in Canning Town and in Park Walk; the police did not allow them to be unfurled during the procession to Caxton Hall. Once there they were joined by others, whom Sylvia Pankhurst described as "women of all sorts and conditions", meaning, it seems, that many were middle- and upper-class suffragists. The *Daily Mirror* reporter put the number of women in attendance at 3000 and commented on the number of babies and "the greatest good humour [that] prevailed, some being convulsed with laughter at the novelty of marching in the streets". Dora Montefiore and Lady CARLISLE were among those who addressed the meeting which, when it was reported that the King's Speech made no mention of women's suffrage, resolved to turn itself into a "lobbying committee", as had the Women's Franchise League on occasions over ten years before, and to march to the House of Commons to persuade members to introduce a suffrage measure. Initially they found that the government had given instructions that no women were to be allowed inside the House, but after representations, groups of 20 women at a time were allowed into the Lobby. The remaining crowd waited outside in the rain and February cold. The WSPU reaped its full measure of publicity from this endurance.

On 22 February Mrs Pankhurst, Sylvia Pankhurst, Annie Kenney and Mrs Stanton COIT were among those attending the sixth annual conference of the Labour Representation Committee (now the Labour Party). The subject of extending men's franchise rights to women as they stood was to be debated, but became confused by a declaration made in favour of adult suffrage. There was a mix-up over the votes, the women's cause was declared lost, although a correction to the number of votes cast in their favour, which would have altered the result, was afterwards made. In the course of the same busy month Mrs Pankhurst was also present at a meeting of the Metropolitan Council of the ILP, alongside Kropotkin, Isabella Ford, Mrs DESPARD and the council's chairman, William Sanders. Annie Kenney was in February appointed the WSPU's first ORGANIZER, at £2 a week, and on 27 February the first London branch was founded, at Canning Town. There followed a rather confusing period as new arrangements took shape. Printed notepaper in use at this time shows the honorary secretary of the

London committee of the WSPU to be Mrs Roe and the honorary treasurer to be Margaret Travers-Symons, Keir Hardie's secretary, and her address as 10 Clifford's Inn. However, Keir Hardie introduced Mrs Pankhurst to Emmeline PETHICK-LAWRENCE, who agreed to become the WSPU's treasurer; her formal appointment can be dated to 1 March, the beginning of the WSPU fiscal year. Keir Hardie and Frederick PETHICK-LAWRENCE paid off the WSPU's debts and introduced Alfred Sayers to act as auditor. The Central London Committee by the end of February comprised Sylvia Pankhurst as honorary secretary, Mrs Pankhurst, Flora Drummond, Mary NEAL (introduced by Emmeline Pethick-Lawrence), Mrs Roe, Mary Clarke, Nellie Martel and Irene Miller. In a letter published in the *Labour Leader* on 23 March, Frances ROWE, while urging women to join the WSPU rather than the newly announced Women's Labour League, gave the name of the general secretary of the WSPU as Mrs Dean, 6 Gerald Road, Lower Broughton, Manchester. A few pages later in the same issue a formal notice gives the personnel of the WSPU as Sylvia Pankhurst as honorary secretary and Emmeline Pethick-Lawrence as treasurer. Obviously events moved so fast that even devotees could not keep abreast. At this stage, too, the WSPU had not realized that it was entirely a single-issue campaign. In May, at the instigation of Emmeline Pethick-Lawrence, the London committee sent a resolution to the government calling for a commission of inquiry into the unrest in the Natal; that same month the Glasgow branch attempted to interview the president of the Local Government Board on behalf of the unemployed; and in the summer Adela Pankhurst, working as an organizer for the WSPU, organized strike pickets in support of textile workers in Yorkshire. Once Christabel Pankhurst took complete control of policy in the summer, such digressions were eliminated.

By the association with the Pethick-Lawrences the WSPU not only gained professional management but a platform. The April issue of the Pethick-Lawrences' *Labour Record and Review* carried a profile of Annie Kenney, and the May issue a plea by Emmeline Pethick-Lawrence for trade union women to join the WSPU and for "volunteers for active service", canvassers, "volunteers for the front", with mention of "danger work" and active agitation. The July issue contained a profile of Teresa Billington, who had moved to London as organizer in late March after giving up her position with the ILP, and a programme of future WSPU events. The transatlantic network ensured that the WSPU received publicity in America; the *New York Literary Digest,* 2 June 1906, carried an article on "The British Women's Suffrage Movement" and photographs of Emmeline and Christabel Pankhurst and Annie Kenney. It was around this time that Sylvia Pankhurst resigned her secretaryship, being succeeded by Edith How MARTYN and Charlotte Despard, who held the position jointly. The work of the WSPU was moved from Park Walk to 4 Clement's Inn, where the Pethick-Lawrences lived and from where they published the *Labour Record.* A formal WSPU office was opened in October. At the beginning of July, after she had completed her degree course at Manchester University, Christabel Pankhurst came to London as chief organizer, living in Clement's Inn with the Pethick-Lawrences. With Beatrice SANDERS, wife of the chairman of the ILP's Metropolitan Council, as financial secretary and, from September, Harriet KERR in charge of office administration, the backbone of the WSPU organization was in place.

After their success in attracting publicity on 19 February, the WSPU kept up the momentum by organizing deputations to the prime minister. The first was on 2 March, the day that the second reading was to take place of Sir Charles Dilke's Adult Franchise Bill. Dora Montefiore, Frances Rowe, Minnie Baldock, Flora Drummond and Annie Kenney went to see Campbell-Bannerman at No. 10 Downing Street. Although he could not see them, they made sure that their presence on the doorstep was recorded; a photograph of the occasion (wrongly captioned "3 March", the day that the photograph appeared on the front page of the *Daily Mirror*) is reproduced in Dora Montefiore's autobiography. They returned in force a week later; the *Daily Mirror* had obviously been primed to send along a photographer. Annie Kenney, Irene Miller and Flora Drummond were arrested, although at Campbell-Bannerman's request they were released without charge and were asked to make a formal application for him to receive a deputation. After receiving their caution the three women went straight to the House of Commons, where they saw two Labour MPs, Will Crooks and Will Thorne. *The Times* had obviously been searching for an explanation for this commotion and, presumably, had asked the CENTRAL SOCIETY FOR WOMEN'S SUFFRAGE if their members had been responsible. The Central Society took the opportunity of disclaiming in the newspaper "any connexion between that association or its affiliated societies and the demonstrators. Nothing is known by the association of the women's visit to Downing Street, and they strongly disapprove of such methods being employed." However, the parliamentary women's suffrage committee did liaise with the WSPU with the result that the prime minister did agree to receive a joint deputation on Saturday 19 May. This was held in the large hall at the Foreign Office and among the MPs present were Sir Charles McLaren, Corrie Grant (*see* Clementia TAYLOR), Keir Hardie, Philip Snowden and H.Y. Stanger. The societies represented were the National Union of Women's Suffrage Societies, Lancashire and Cheshire Women's Suffrage Societies, the HAMMERSMITH WOMEN'S SUFFRAGE SOCIETY, the Women's Liberal Federation, the Scottish Women's Liberal Federation, the Metropolitan Radical Association, the Women Textile Workers' Representation Committee, the WSPU, the Manchester and Salford Trade and Labour Council, the General Union of Weavers and Textile Workers, United Cigarette Workers and Tobacco Cutters, the Society of Women Employed in Bookbinding, the Scottish Christian Union of the North British Women's Temperance Association, Women Graduates of Universities, the Society for the State Registration of Trained Nurses, the Registered Nurses' Society, the National Union of Women Workers, the Women's Industrial Council, the Fabian Society, the Freedom of Labour Defence League and the Queen Square Club (*see under* CLUBS). Appeals were made by the women's representatives, who included Emily Davies, Mary BATESON and Elizabeth Wolstenholme Elmy. Emmeline Pankhurst stated that WSPU members were, for enfranchisement, "prepared to sacrifice . . . everything they possessed, their means of livelihood, their very lives, if necessary". To all these women Campbell-Bannerman said that "He had only one thing to preach to them, and that was the virtue of patience."

The disappointed deputation reconvened at the Exeter Hall where, at a meeting chaired by Sir Charles McLaren, Keir Hardie urged that the government should be compelled to give a leading place on its programme to women's suffrage and that suffragists should not repudiate the "fighting element in their ranks". The WSPU delegation, which included Mrs Elmy and Annie Kenney dressed as a mill girl in clogs and shawl, together with women from the East End, then advanced to Trafalgar Square where they held their first large open-air meeting in London. The next day, a rainy Sunday, the working women who had come down from Lancashire to support their delegations marched in procession to Hyde Park, carrying trade union banners, and were met there by WSPU women from Canning Town. On 20 February Eva Gore-Booth and Esther Roper had spoken at the weekly meeting of what was then the "Unemployed Women of South-West Ham" and not quite yet the Canning Town branch of the WSPU, to ask them to support a Hyde Park demonstration at the end of May. Sarah Dickenson, Sarah REDDISH and Selina COOPER were among the speakers on 20 May. Although the press covered this meeting and although it included women who saw themselves as WSPU members, none of the Pankhurst histories mention it; the Canning Town element was already being sidelined.

Parliament had been given its chance of supporting women's suffrage when on 25 April Keir Hardie introduced a resolution, "that sex should cease to be a bar to the exercise of the Parliamentary franchise". Under new rules that had come into operation only on the previous day, the debate was due to end at 11 o'clock. Some of the WSPU women, caged in the Ladies' Gallery, were under the misapprehension that the vote itself had to be taken by 11 and as that time approached and the House was subjected to a filibuster they grew impatient and began to protest. The Speaker ordered the gallery to be cleared and the debate ended without a vote having been taken. Sylvia Pankhurst was bitter that Keir Hardie, whom she appreciated was doing his best for them, should have his work destroyed. W.T. Stead, according to Elizabeth Wolstenholme Elmy, thought that the disturbance in the Ladies' Gallery was the best thing that had happened for a long time. In truth it was unlikely that the Speaker would have allowed a vote in any event. Even if he had it would have meant little; favourable votes had been taken in the past to no avail. The idea was that a good majority in favour of the resolution would have allowed Campbell-Bannerman on 19 May to give greater encouragement to the suffrage deputation. It appears that this fiasco marked the end of attempts to sway the House of Commons through its individual members. WSPU policy was now to concentrate on converting the cabinet, the heart of power, to the cause.

The WSPU did not use gentle persuasion; the policy was to confront intransigent ministers. Of these Asquith, then Chancellor of the Exchequer, was seen as the most obdurate. On 19 June Teresa Billington and Mrs Baldock led a contingent of about 30 East End women to his house in Cavendish Square. The resulting altercation led to the arrest of Teresa Billington, Adelaide KNIGHT, Mrs SBARBORO and Annie Kenney. The last three received prison sentences of six weeks, although they were released after a month. Teresa Billington was sentenced to two months, which was, after representations in parliament, cut to one month; her fine was then paid against her will. Christabel Pankhurst saw her policy bringing its rewards. In *Unshackled*, 1959, she laconically remarked, "Militancy had now begun in London. The first prisoners for the vote were in Holloway Gaol."

The full scope of the WSPU's by-election policy was revealed at Cockermouth in August, where a Labour candidate was among the contestants. Rather than supporting the Labour candidate and, merely in consequence, opposing the Liberal, Christabel Pankhurst's policy was certainly to oppose the Liberal but neither would the WSPU actively support any other party. At this by-election the Conservative won and the Labour Party candidate came a poor third. There seems to have been little objection to the policy at this time from WSPU members, most of whom were still those who had been drawn into the WSPU through association with the ILP. Mary GAWTHORPE was, indeed, excluded from the WSPU platform at Cockermouth because she campaigned for the Labour candidate; but she was not at that time a WSPU member. She converted from the Women's Labour League shortly afterwards.

The organization of the WSPU had until then evolved to meet situations as they developed. An attempt was made in October 1906 to fit a constitution around the existing structure. Elizabeth Wolstenholme Elmy described the meeting, which was held in Clement's Inn on 20 October and attended by 64 delegates, in a letter, dated 3 November, to Harriet McIlquham. There is no suggestion other than that the meeting was amicable, Mrs Pankhurst a fair chairman, and the constitution democratically discussed and adopted. However, clauses concerning the setting up of an accountable national executive council were never put into effect and the Pankhursts and Pethick-Lawrences continued to direct the WSPU throughout the next year.

At this same meeting, plans were made for a demonstration to take place in the Lobby of the House of Commons at the opening of parliament on 23 October. This was the last WSPU demonstration at which women from the East End were present in large numbers. The police were on the look-out for them. At 12.30 pm on 23 October the police at Plaistow sent a telegram to Cannon Row police station to let the Metropolitan Police know that "about 30 women suffragettes now leaving Plaistow Station by 12.20 train to Westminster Bridge Station, with the intention of going to House of Commons". Cannon Row then sent one of their plain-clothes men to meet the train, alerted the sergeant at arms at the House of Commons and, as the superintendent recorded, "strengthened the approaches with some of my staff". At the House of Commons 20 women were allowed into the Central Lobby and 25 into St Stephen's Hall; the remainder had to wait in Old Palace Yard. At 4 pm, after the women had seen various MPs, the police recorded that they began a demonstration. They singled out as the principals: "Mrs Pankhurst, Despard, Lawrence, Montefiore, and Sanderson". Among those who succeeded in getting arrested were Minnie Baldock, Teresa Billington, Mary Gawthorpe, Annie Kenney, Edith How Martyn, Irene Miller, Dora Montefiore, Adela PANKHURST, Emmeline Pethick-Lawrence and Anne Cobden SANDERSON. Sylvia Pankhurst was subsequently charged with obstruction and abusive language for protesting against the arrests. The imprisonment of Cobden's daughter sent a frisson through socially and politically aware middle England. The prison sentences meted out brought in publicity (an "Indignation Meeting", addressed by W.T. Stead, was held in the Caxton Hall on the afternoon of the convictions), converts and money, and marks the point at which the WSPU gathered to it a growing middle-class membership. In a gesture of solidarity Mrs Fawcett and the NUWSS organized a banquet at the Savoy on 11 December 1906 to celebrate the release of the WSPU prisoners. Mrs Fawcett was reported in *The Times* as stating of the ex-prisoners that "the example which they had set of courage, endurance and self-sacrifice had fanned in every one of them a keener flame of idealism, a greater desire to serve, to spend and be spent in the cause which they had at heart". Elizabeth ROBINS proposed "Success to the Woman Suffrage Cause", supported by Isabella Ford; Anne Cobden Sanderson and Teresa Billington responded. Each guest was given an emblematic picture of Queen Boadicea driving in a chariot, waving a "Votes for Women" flag. Many women who had been campaigning within the law for many years were present that night and henceforward subscribed to the WSPU. Guests were stirred by the sacrifice made for the cause by the ex-prisoners, most of whom were of their class. Both Minnie Baldock and Annie Kenney, who might have been deemed not to be, have left descriptions of the effort that went into choosing the right outfit for that evening. Thus refreshed, some of the ex-convicts took their fame to help the WSPU campaign at the Huddersfield by-election. Before the end of the year another 20 women were serving prison services for similar raids on parliament. On 16 December Dora Montefiore warned Adelaide Knight that working women should not rely on the WSPU. "It was perhaps foolish to believe that the W.S & Pol. Union was *really* democratic, but is governed by a clique, and that clique will allow no inside criticism, so that any one that criticises, even in the best spirit, must go."

The "clique" was now adept at marshalling its forces. On the evening of 12 February, the day on which parliament reassembled, a WSPU "At Home" was held in the rooms of the Royal Society of British Artists, Suffolk Street, to greet provincial delegates to what *The Times* described as the "Votes for Women" convention to be held the next day. It was reported that the guests, who numbered about 400, were received by Emmeline Pethick-Lawrence. The next day the Caxton Hall was again the scene of a Women's Parliament, with the Exeter Hall, which a week before had held the NUWSS at the end of their "Mud March", hired to house an overflow meeting. From there a deputation set forth, Mrs Despard carrying the meeting's resolution to the prime minister, calling on the House of Commons to give precedence to a women's suffrage measure. Elizabeth Wolstenholme Elmy suggested to the WSPU leaders that a request should be conveyed from Caxton Hall to the Speaker, asking for a hearing at the Bar of the House, a refusal of which would justify stronger action. (This tactic was eventually carried out in 1912 by the Actresses' Franchise League.) After news of the first arrests was conveyed back to Caxton Hall, Christabel Pankhurst was reported in *The Times* as urging "the audience to repeat the experiment of the afternoon, to march again to the House of Commons and insist on admission. She advised them not to be afraid of the police, to link arms, not to break up their ranks, and if they lost sight of their leaders to become leaders themselves." The police were in readiness. It was estimated that there were 300 to 400 suffragettes in the vicinity of the Palace of Westminster; arrests took place about 9 pm, the police refuting allegations of brutality. Fifty-six women were sentenced to terms of imprisonment. The only man arrested, A.R. Orage from Leeds, was discharged. A month later, on 20 March, the women were back at the House of Commons. On 8 March W.H. Dickenson's women's suffrage bill had been talked out, a fate that so often overtook the private member's bill. This time it was Viscountess HARBERTON who led the deputation to the House of Commons. Sixty-seven women went to prison as a result. On 9 April the Pankhursts were among the audience at the Court Theatre to witness the first night of Elizabeth Robins's play, *Votes for Women*, based on their campaign and a signal *coup de théâtre* for an organization not yet four years old.

By the end of its first financial year, March 1907, the number of WSPU branches had increased from 3 to 47 (by August the number had risen to 70), the leading organizers had spoken at more than 1200 public meetings in a year and nearly £3000 had been received in voluntary subscriptions. However, during March, April and May 1907 the WSPU spent £2000. As Emmeline Pethick-Lawrence wrote to Maud Arncliffe Sennett in July, "This sum can only be raised by persistent organisation; by getting as many people as possible on this particular business of raising money and widening our circle of supporters." She then specifically asked Mrs Arncliffe Sennett to make a list of women in the Paddington area who were likely to contribute. This direct approach was replicated tirelessly. In parallel with the move towards those who had money was the move away from those who had not. In the early summer Emmeline and Christabel Pankhurst resigned from the ILP. At the ILP conference in April Charlotte Despard and Anne Cobden Sanderson issued a statement saying that they would not campaign at by-elections, unless it was to support a Labour candidate, which was tantamount to a rejection of WSPU election policy. This created one of the strands of disagreement that led, in September, to the splintering of the WSPU. Apart from loyalty shown to the Labour Party, the major dissension was over the organization of the WSPU. Natural democrats such as Teresa Billington-Greig, who was now based in Glasgow, objected to the autocratic control of Clement's Inn. She wished to see the constitution enforced and members of the national council elected by the branches and responsible to them. Elizabeth Wolstenholme Elmy, from Congleton, wrote on 20 August 1907 to Harriet McIlquham:

> I am most troubled at what you tell me of her [Mrs Rowe's] notion that no paid officers of the WS & PU should be members of its Executive. This means that Mrs Pankhurst and Christabel who created the WS & PU and have sacrificed everything for the woman's cause, should be degraded and insulted. If such a folly . . . is ever carried into effect, farewell to all hope of success for another quarter of a century or more. I for one would have nothing more to do with such an organization, which would be in the hands and under the control of a few impractical women, who have done little or nothing for the cause.

On 13 September she wrote:

> I am delighted that the leaders and executive of the WSPU have dealt so promptly and vigorously with the schismatics. They have done just what I ought to have done in the matter of the Women's Franchise League, and should have done but for Mrs Stanton Blatch (Must tell you what *she* did one day) and thus effectively prevented that Society from being degraded into a mere party tool. I suspect Mrs Despard will lead the dissidents into the arms of the Social Democratic Federation, the most unsatisfactory (and, so far as women are concerned, actively mischievous of socialist groups in the country, hot for prohibition of women's *paid* labour). London is the hotbed of intrigue and treachery; and I have been expecting something of this kind ever since it was made head quarters. I am sorry Mrs Rowe has gone so hopelessly wrong in this matter. The bare idea of superseding the Pankhursts, who have erected and sustained the movement, by Mrs Despard, who has neither political knowledge nor practical wisdom to guide – is too monstrously silly, to say nothing of its base ingratitude for a moment's consideration by any one who knows the facts.

The decisive meetings had taken place on 10 September. At the first, held in the afternoon for organizers, Mrs Pankhurst revealed that henceforward all members would have to sign a pledge by which they agreed not to support parliamentary candidates of any political party. Mrs Despard and Caroline Hodgson refused to sign. That evening, at the Essex Hall, many WSPU members were, like Marie LAWSON, shocked to discover that the WSPU was no longer to have a constitution. For a time the breakaway group, led by Charlotte Despard, kept the name "Women's Social and Political Union" on the grounds that it had kept faith with the constitution that had been accepted in 1906. The Pankhurst/Pethick-Lawrence majority was then known as the "National Women's Social and Political Union", although always colloquially referred to as the "WSPU". The Despard-led group soon renamed themselves the WOMEN'S FREEDOM LEAGUE. The NWSPU retained about 80 per cent of the membership. On 11 October Mrs Elmy wrote to Sylvia Pankhurst: "I am delighted to tell you that at Wednesday night's meeting of the Manchester Branch (The Mother Branch) of the WSPU the motion proposed to send a delegate to the separatists Convention tomorrow was resolutely negative

– only 3 voting for it whilst the Resolution of Love & Devotion to, and confidence in our dear leader, Mrs Pankhurst, was carried *unanimously* and with deepest feeling."

Although the split had ideological overtones, it would be a mistake to think that the WFL removed the Socialist element from the WSPU. Very many of those who remained with the WSPU saw themselves as Socialists then and, once they were enfranchised, demonstrated this by voting Labour and standing as Labour candidates for elections. In 1907, however, they were prepared to put the women's cause before party interest. In reply to a letter from a Socialist Scottish organizer Mary PHILLIPS, who wrote for *Forward*, asking what she should do to explain the split, Emmeline Pankhurst wrote on 21 September, "Thanks for your letter and for your confidence in us. I do not think what is happening now is of general public interest. It concerns the members of the Union solely. All that is good for the general world outside is the assurance that our policy is unchanged and that our political independence is stronger than ever . . . I am resolutely refusing to reply to any 'personal' statements made by the seceders. The sooner the incident is closed the better it will be for the women's cause." The NWSPU was given a titular committee comprising Annie Kenney, Mary Gawthorpe, Mary Neal, Elizabeth Robins and Elizabeth Wolstenholme Elmy. Mrs Pankhurst and Mabel TUKE were joint secretaries, Emmeline Pethick-Lawrence was treasurer and Christabel Pankhurst was organizing secretary. Although, according to Elizabeth Robins's diary, the committee did for a time hold weekly meetings in Clement's Inn, it was never a serious channel of decision-making. As Clara CODD put it succinctly in her autobiography, "By this time, Mrs Despard had left us and our committee was replaced by a dictatorship. As a fighting unit this was immeasurably superior for a committee can never fight."

The WSPU's Intermediate Report for the six months ending 31 August 1907 showed that it had in that time conducted campaigns at seven by-elections (Hexham, Stepney, Rutland, Jarrow, Colne Valley, North-West Staffordshire and Bury St Edmunds). In June, before the split in the WSPU, a Scottish Council of the WSPU had been set up in Glasgow. Teresa Billington-Greig had been its honorary secretary, Mrs J.D. Pearce its treasurer and Helen FRASER the Scottish organizer. After Teresa Billington-Greig had left to found the WFL, Mrs Pearce, with Grace Paterson, became joint honorary secretary of the Scottish WSPU. Scotland witnessed its first large-scale suffrage demonstration on 5 October; the WSPU worked in co-operation with the constitutional societies to stage a procession in Edinburgh. In London the Monday afternoon "At Homes" at Clement's Inn proved so popular that a parallel series was launched on Thursday evenings. The latter were intended to bring in to the movement women who had to earn their own living. Clement's Inn soon proved too small to accommodate the numbers who wished to attend and in February 1908 the meetings moved to the Portman Rooms. A Literature Department had been inaugurated at the beginning of 1907 and in October the Pethick-Lawrences launched *Votes for Women*, which they owned and edited, giving the WSPU an excellent medium through which to advertise its policy and campaigns and the means whereby members could gain assurance that they were part of a national movement. The local unions were encouraged to send in news of their meetings and fund-raising exploits. Donations were recorded by name, thereby both assuring the donors that their mites were appreciated and encouraging others to follow suit. The paper was available by post, through newsagents, and also from WSPU members who undertook to sell it in the streets. A middle-class woman standing in the gutter (to stand on the pavement was to court arrest for obstruction), with a newspaper satchel across her shoulder, offering to sell passers-by *Votes for Women,* was construed by the Edwardian public as a denial of all that was womanly. Many women, long after the event, recorded the calumny to which they were subjected while thus exposing themselves to the public gaze. It appears, however, to have had the effect of innoculating them against further public obloquy; pavement-chalking, sandwich-board and poster parades, heckling, and speaking from the backs of carts, the target of verbal and physical missiles, became rapidly part of the everyday life of such erstwhile sheltered members of the WSPU as Mary BLATHWAYT.

At the beginning of 1908 Christabel Pankhurst was able to use the January issue of *Votes for Women* to broadcast her plans for that year's national campaign. Her article records that extra office space had been taken in Clement's Inn, the staff there increased by four, and that their paid organizers, who were sent out around the country, now numbered 14. A three-day Women's Parliament was planned for 11, 12 and 13 February, a woman's demonstration in the Albert Hall on 19 March and a mass meeting in Hyde Park on 21 June. All this activity was to impress on the cabinet that women were in earnest. Individuals were also intent on ensuring that members of the government could not ignore women; Flora Drummond and others padlocked themselves to the railings of No. 10 Downing Street on 19 January, an event that is now a cornerstone of suffragette mythology. The WSPU by-election policy was also bearing fruit. The Liberals were defeated in January at South Devon and such was the animosity against the WSPU who were, presumably, therefore given the credit for having affected the outcome, that Emmeline Pankhurst and Nellie Alma Martel were knocked to the ground by incensed Liberals. The Women's Parliament followed the set pattern. Once it was established that women's suffrage was not included in the King's Speech, a march set out from Caxton Hall to the House of Commons. On 11 February this was the occasion of the "pantechnicon raid", an attempt to emulate the Trojan horse by bringing a furniture van, in which were concealed 21 women, up to the gates of the Palace of Westminster. They then attempted to rush into the Lobby. Most of the women were members of the Chelsea and Kensington WSPU and, by no means all young, were to play an increasingly daring part in the WSPU campaign. On 13 February Mrs Pankhurst, still lame from her treatment in Devon, led the deputation to the House of Commons. With eight of the women who accompanied her, she was arrested and was sentenced to six weeks' imprisonment in the second division. Sylvia Pankhurst described in *The Suffragette*, 1911, how, as news came back to Caxton Hall of the arrests, Emmeline Pethick-Lawrence, "our ever thoughtful treasurer", made an appeal for funds and that over £400 had been raised by the time the prisoners were released on bail. A photograph of Emmeline Pankhurst, carrying a scroll of paper on which was written the resolution of the meeting, limping at the head of the deputation, reveals her as an icon of injured, pleading womanhood. The WSPU issued the photograph as a postcard. The archetype had been perfected; militancy and martyrdom were to be encouraged. By this means money was brought in to finance the dignified mass demonstrations that were to be a contrasting feature of the WSPU campaign and to pay for the increasingly numerous band of organizers who were hard at work throughout the country. During 1906–7 WSPU members served the equivalent of 191 weeks in prison, in 1907–8 this had increased to 350 weeks and in 1908–9 to over 960 weeks. At the mass demonstration held in the Albert Hall on 19 March, to which Mrs Pankhurst came direct from Holloway, over £7000 was raised. In 1908 the WSPU's income was over £20 000.

By the middle of the year the WSPU's policy seemed vindicated. H.Y. Stanger's women's suffrage bill, which was similar to Dickinson's 1907 bill, and to Keir Hardie's 1906 resolution, resulted in a division giving a larger majority (179) for the bill than any that had been achieved previously. The government refused, in spite of a deputation on 20 May from 60 Liberal MPs, to grant facilities to further the debate. After Campbell-Bannerman's resignation, due to ill health, the consequent cabinet reshuffle led to a series of by-elections. Christabel Pankhurst headed the campaign against Churchill at North-west Manchester; he was defeated. It is not clear to what extent this was due to the WSPU campaign, but the WSPU certainly thought that without their intervention he would have been returned. The Hyde Park demonstration on 21 June, a week after the NUWSS had staged a similar display, was perceived as a triumph, a tribute to the Pethick-Lawrences' ability as organizers. Widespread and ingenious methods were used to advertise the demonstration. It was for this occasion that Emmeline Pethick-Lawrence devised the WSPU regalia, setting the precedent for all contemporary and subsequent suffrage societies to burst into a rainbow of adopted COLOURS. The purple, white and green of the WSPU was omnipresent, on the sashes, programmes, flags and banners. Women from 70 provincial centres arrived in London, many on specially hired trains, and were marshalled into seven processions. Speakers addressed an audience of at least a quarter of a million from 20 platforms. Elizabeth Wolstenholme Elmy has left a touching description of what it felt like to be one of the fêted. Christabel Pankhurst rushed to Asquith the demonstration's resolution, asking the government what it proposed to do to implement the demand for women's suffrage. On 20 May he had told the deputation of MPs that he required evidence that there was support from the women of the country as well as from men. On 23 June he responded to the Hyde Park resolution, the result of so much time, energy and good will, not to mention its £4314 staging cost, by merely saying that he had nothing to add to the statement he had made on 20 May.

The WSPU's response was to renew the call to militancy. Another Women's Parliament was organized for 30 June at Caxton Hall, from whence a deputation led by Emmeline Pankhurst, Emmeline Pethick-Lawrence, Clemence HOUSMAN and eight other women set out for the House of Commons. The police locked all the other women in Caxton Hall. Asquith refused to receive the deputation. That evening, when they left Caxton Hall, the women encountered a crowd of about 100 000 people, controlled by 1700 policemen, massed in Parliament Square. There were many arrests and 25 women were subsequently sentenced to between one and three months' imprisonment. In addition Mary LEIGH and Edith NEW took the opportunity, by throwing stones through the windows of No. 10 Downing Street, to escalate the demands of active service. They were both sentenced to two months' imprisonment. The allocation of suffragette prisoners to the second division, with all the indignities this incurred, was the subject of much debate both in and outside the House of Commons. Throughout the summer large meetings were held in all provincial cities and in London the weekly "At Homes" outgrew the Portman Rooms and moved into the Queen's Hall, Langham Place, which had a capacity of 1000. It was estimated that the WSPU held 10 000 meetings throughout the country in 1908.

The resumption of the parliamentary term in October 1908 was the occasion of another mass meeting. This time a preliminary meeting was held on 11 October in Trafalgar Square at which Mrs Pankhurst, Christabel Pankhurst and Flora Drummond asked the public to assist them on 13 October in "rushing" the House of Commons. This brought a charge of conduct likely to provoke a breach of the peace and their arrest. The "raid" on the House of Commons was led, in their absence, by Marion Wallace-DUNLOP, and resulted in the arrest of 24 women and 12 men, and the appearance in the chamber of the House of Commons of Margaret Travers-SYMONS, Keir Hardie's secretary, to the consternation of the members. The trial of the leaders at Bow Street was a publicity coup for the WSPU. Christabel Pankhurst, the suffragette Portia, subpoenaed and cross-examined Lloyd George and Herbert Gladstone, Mrs Pankhurst recounted the many years of social and political work that now resulted in her standing in the dock and Mrs Drummond assured the magistrate, Mr Curtis Bennett, that nothing would stop the movement. The WSPU published *The Trial of the Suffragette Leaders* as a 50-page pamphlet and included in it Christabel Pankhurst's cross-examination of Lloyd George and Herbert Gladstone. Flora Drummond and Mrs Pankhurst were sentenced on 24 October to three months' imprisonment, Christabel Pankhurst to ten weeks. It was the last occasion on which she was to go to prison; she thought that a waste of her time. On 29 October another mass meeting held in the Albert Hall raised £3000.

During the rest of the autumn the WSPU continued to heckle cabinet ministers. A rally held by Lloyd George in the Albert Hall to convince the Women's Liberal Federation that the party had their interests at heart was continuously interrupted by WSPU infiltrators, some of whom revealed themselves, under their cloaks, to be resplendent in second-division prison attire. The Liberal stewards dealt viciously with the hecklers; Helen OGSTON used her dog-whip. Teresa Billington-Greig, in *The Militant Suffrage Movement*, criticized this demonstration as an "act of madness" on the part of the WSPU, who thereby alienated an audience of women who were intrinsically in favour of enfranchisement. A few days later the government introduced the public meetings bill, which provided for a fine of £5 or imprisonment for one month for anyone convicted of disorderly conduct at a meeting.

The WSPU grew steadily throughout the year 1908–9. By the end of February 1909 it employed 30 organizers throughout the country, and a staff of 45 in Clement's Inn. It had opened 11 regional offices in eight provincial districts. Each of these districts was in the charge of a paid organizer. In February 1909 Annie Kenney was organizer in the West of England (which had offices in Bristol and Torquay), Mary Gawthorpe in Lancashire (with headquarters in Manchester and offices in Preston and Rochdale), Gladice KEEVIL in Birmingham, Charlotte MARSH in Leeds and Bradford, Edith New in Newcastle, Gertrude CONOLAN in Glasgow, F.E.M. MACAULAY in Edinburgh and Ada FLATMAN in Aberdeen. Unlike the NUWSS structure, the WSPU did not organize through a committee system at the local level, any more than it did at a national level. Organizers moved into districts as appointees from headquarters and put into effect WSPU policy as it emanated from Clement's Inn. It is because there were no branch minutes or branch delegates that local WSPU histories have been so long in emerging. The history of the WSPU has been, perforce, the history of individuals.

The established pattern of conduct continued in 1909; militancy mingled with rhetoric and spectacle. A Women's Parliament was held on 24 February, a week after the opening of the men's parliament. It must be presumed that there had been some co-operation between the WSPU and the WFL, whose turn it was to use the occasion of the opening of parliament to attempt to present a resolution of protest to Asquith. On 24 February the WSPU deputation, led by Emmeline Pethick-Lawrence, headed for the House of Commons and, with Lady Constance LYTTON, Daisy SOLOMON, Caprina FAHEY and 25 others, was arrested and imprisoned. A private member's bill introduced by Geoffrey Howard, son of Lady Carlisle, had its second reading on 19 March. The result was a majority of only 34 and, because it was not granted government facilities for further discussion, the bill passed into oblivion. On 30 March the WSPU organized another Caxton Hall meeting and a deputation, led by Mrs Saul SOLOMON, called at the House of Commons, to be told that the prime minister was not there. In the process 20 women were arrested. On 29 April, two days after the LONDON SOCIETY FOR WOMEN'S SUFFRAGE had entertained there delegates to the International Women's Suffrage Congress, the WSPU held another mass meeting in the Albert Hall. In May the WSPU held a very successful exhibition at the Prince's Skating Rink in Knightsbridge, in which the political, artistic, theatrical and domestic elements of women's sphere were charmingly and professionally represented. It marked a decided advance in WSPU propaganda and marketing. However, although increasing numbers of women were being brought into the movement the political solution was no nearer achievement. The cabinet had neither been won over nor worn down by the WSPU campaign.

The Caxton Hall meeting held on 29 June 1909 marked a watershed in the militant campaign. The WSPU had sent out to its branches around the country a call for volunteers to take part in the deputation. This was tantamount to asking for volunteers for imprisonment, and was seen as such. There was no shortage of respondents. Lady Frances Balfour, who with Lady Betty Balfour attended the meeting in Caxton Hall, described the occasion in a letter written that evening to Millicent Fawcett:

> We slowly battled our way to the west side of Parliament Square and up to Whitehall, here we saw several arrests, the women all showing extraordinary courage in the rough rushes of the crowd round them . . . [At the Treasury] two women exactly in front of us threw stones at the windows. Poor shots, I dont think the glass was cracked. A policeman flew on them, and had his arms round their necks before one could wink. Crowd and police made a rush together, and B. and I were both knocked flat, falling in a rather ignominious heap! . . . The courage that dares this handling, I do admire . . . There is a fine spirit but whether it is not rather thrown away on these tactics remains a doubt in my mind.

For the first time, as leader of the deputation, Mrs Pankhurst, after receiving a written refusal from Asquith to a request to interview him, invited arrest by striking a police inspector in the face. She and the Hon Evelina HAVERFIELD, also arrested, stood trial on 30 June. Mrs Haverfield's defence was that she had been arrested while exercising a constitutional right of petitioning. They were found guilty, but in order to test the law, an appeal was allowed which, when heard in December, went against them. On 29 June after a prolonged struggle, the 3000 policemen present succeeded in arresting 108 women and 14 men, although charges against them were not proceeded with. Later that evening a group of women attacked the windows of government buildings with stones; they were all arrested. The action had not been organized by WSPU headquarters, but was afterwards condoned and brought within the range of tactics available. In a letter to Mary Phillips, dated 21 September 1909, Emmeline Pethick-Lawrence gives an insight into the WSPU's method of working at this time. She wrote:

> I can assure you that every part of the militant policy is thought out and controlled by Headquarters as much as is humanly possible. I do not say that evey detail is sanctioned beforehand, very often we are filled with surprise at the ingenuity and resourse [sic] of the women. In individual cases where some one goes just a little too far, they are told that the action does not meet with our approval, but at the same time, they know the limit beyond which they must on no account go and have always observed it honourably.

"Headquarters" was presumably suitably surprised and gratified when Marion Wallace-Dunlop went on hunger strike in Holloway. She was arrested on 22 June while attempting, with the help of Hugh FRANKLIN, to print an extract from the Bill of Rights on the wall of St Stephen's Hall, and on 2 July was sentenced to a month's imprisonment and was refused first-division treatment. This new weapon in the militant's armoury was not one that had been suggested by the WSPU leadership but when, after three days' fasting, Marion Wallace-Dunlop was released, its efficacy was acknowledged. Those who had thrown stones on 29 June were convicted on 12 July and when they arrived at Holloway demanded to be accorded first-division treatment, as political prisoners. When this was refused, they went on hunger strike and, after six days, were released. This weapon against the government, demonstrably effective, was used by WSPU prisoners in London, Liverpool, Manchester and Newcastle throughout the summer to secure their early release from prison sentences. In September the Home Office gave instructions that the suffragette prisoners, who included Mary Leigh, held in Winson Green Prison in Birmingham should be fed against their will. Keir Hardie kept the subject of the women's treatment alive in the House of Commons. A memorial signed by 116 medical practitioners, including Charles Mansell-Moullin (see Edith MANSELL-MOULLIN), was presented to Asquith, deploring the practice, a sentiment confirmed by both the *British Medical Journal* (2 October) and the *British Journal of Nursing* (9 October). The press, on the whole, condoned the government's policy. Many erstwhile Liberal women, such as Catherine OSLER, were, however, horrified and resigned their membership of the Women's Liberal Federation, in protest, often after a lifetime of service. The government's obduracy was matched by that of the WSPU. The adoption of the hunger strike became WSPU policy. Alice PAUL in an interview recorded in 1976 remembered, "the WSPU would say, 'Now if you want to go, we want you to hunger strike or not go'. And so you went in with that understanding." Martyrdom meant money; at an Albert Hall meeting held on 7 October £2300 was raised and at another on 9 December, at which Mary Leigh, recently released from Winson Green, was fêted, £2000 to fund the WSPU general election campaign was guaranteed.

The general election of January 1910 was the result of the rejection by the House of Lords of Lloyd George's 1909 budget. The Liberal government was returned with a greatly reduced majority, and was in future dependent on the Labour Party and the Irish Nationalists, whether separately or in combination, to ensure the passage of legislation. The WSPU had campaigned against the government candidate in 40 constituencies, taking the credit for unseating the Liberal in 18 of these. The women's cause was, however, only one of the many fronts on which the Liberal government was attacked and, as with previous campaigns, it is difficult to apportion the influence of one interest group. On 31 January, jubilant at its perceived success, relieved to postpone the question of further militancy, and prepared to take at face value the assurance that had been given by Asquith to a meeting of the National Liberal Federation on 10 December that if the Liberal government were returned, and if it introduced a reform bill, it would make the question of a women's suffrage amendment the subject of a free vote, the WSPU declared a truce.

The Conciliation Committee formed by H.N. BRAILSFORD, with Lord Lytton as chairman, drew

The "Arts" banner carried by university graduates in the West Procession, 23 July 1910. (Author's collection)

support from all the political parties and all the suffrage societies in order to draft a private member's bill, "To Extend the Parliamentary Franchise to Women Occupiers". This, with its property qualification, which could not, of course, be used by both husband and wife for the same property, tacitly excluded most married women. Even though it was in effect a "widows and spinsters" bill, likely to enfranchise more Conservative voters than Liberal or Labour supporters, time had eroded opposition from radical suffrage and political factions. It was now accepted that women's enfranchisement would have to be achieved by instalment. The bill was introduced by David Shackleton, the Labour MP, on 14 June, at a time at which the mood of the country was subdued by the death of Edward VII. On 18 June, the day after the nation emerged from public mourning, the WSPU, in co-operation with the Women's Freedom League, staged a major demonstration in support of the bill. This, the first held in London since the summer of 1908, was known as "The Prison to Citizenship" Procession, the theme inspired by Laurence HOUSMAN's banner.

The WSPU section of the procession emphasized the nobility of the 617 women who had gone to prison for their cause. They themselves, or proxies, marched in the Prisoners' Pageant, dressed in white, wearing their medals, and each carrying a standard topped by a broad arrow, the emblem of imprisonment. The entire procession, comprising between 10 000 and 15 000 women wended its way from the Embankment to Kensington, where the WSPU held its meeting in the Albert Hall. After speeches from Emmeline and Christabel Pankhurst, Emmeline Pethick-Lawrence, Annie Kenney and Lord Lytton, who explained the work of the Conciliation Committee, the audience contributed £5000 to WSPU funds. The Conciliation Bill passed its second reading on 12 July, with a majority in favour of 110, but was then referred to a committee of the whole House, rather than to a grand committee, precluding any likelihood that the government would give it facilities for further discussion during the course of that parliamentary session. Another WSPU demonstration, which was originally to have taken place in conjunction with the NUWSS but which fell foul of distrust and misunderstandings between the two societies, took place on 23 July. In the week leading up to this date, around 35 meetings were held each day throughout London. On 23 July a mass meeting was held on Calton Hill in Edinburgh and similar demonstrations in support of the Conciliation Bill were also made in Bristol, Liverpool, Nottingham, Manchester, Birmingham and Glasgow. The planning for the London demonstration, the date of which marked the anniversary of the day in 1867 on which men demonstrating for their inclusion in the Reform Bill pulled down the railings in Hyde Park, was given impetus by the favourable majority given to the vote on the Conciliation Bill. Two processions were organized. That approaching from the west was designed by the WFL with a Roman theme, focusing on Victory and Justice, that from the east, the responsibility of the WSPU, was "Oriental". The two converged on Hyde Park, where 150 speakers addressed a crowd, estimated at between 12 000 and 20 000, from 40 platforms. Its splendour is now given poignancy by the knowledge that, on the day it took place, Asquith informed Lord Lytton that the Conciliation Bill would progress no further that parliamentary session.

In her editorial in the 29 July 1910 issue of *Votes for Women* Christabel Pankhurst promised that if, once parliament reassembled, the Conciliation Committee was unable to persuade the House of Commons to overturn the government's veto:

> The opposition which the Women's Social and Political Union have offered to the Liberal government during the past five years will be renewed, and redoubled in its energy. . . . Unless Members of Parliament have in the meantime secured the necessary facilities, a great concourse of women will, immediately after Parliament reassembles in the Autumn, proceed to Westminster to demand of the Government that the Suffrage Bill be forthwith carried into law. The ordinary, conventional means of agitation being entirely ignored, this more vigorous action will be necessary to bring pressure to bear upon the Government.

After conducting their usual imaginative summer holiday campaigns around the country, members of the WSPU reconvened in Caxton Hall on 18 November (later to be known as "Black Friday"), to hear that, the two houses of parliament being locked in a battle for supremacy, a dissolution was to take effect on 28 November. There was no mention that women would be enfranchised before then so, as Christabel Pankhurst had prognosticated and Emmeline Pankhurst had reiterated at a mass meeting in the Albert Hall on 10 November, a deputation of over 300 women, divided into groups of 10, set out from Caxton Hall for the House of Commons. These women were volunteers for "active service"; 150 had already enrolled for the deputation by 27 October. The first detachment comprised doyennes of the suffrage movement, Mrs Pankhurst, Elizabeth Garrett ANDERSON, Annie Cobden Sanderson, Hertha AYRTON, Dorinda NELIGAN, Mrs Saul Solomon, Mrs BRACKENBURY and the Princess Duleep SINGH. A promise was extracted from Asquith that he would the next week state in parliament his government's intentions towards women's enfranchisement. This dubious satisfaction was moderated by the violence endured by women during the course of the afternoon and evening in battles with the police in Parliament Square. Instead of using their powers of arrest the police physically forced control. In the event 115 women and four men were arrested; the next day all charges against them were dropped on the instructions of the Home Secretary, who was doubtless embarrassed by the tales that a court case would reveal. H.N. Brailsford and Dr Jessie Murray collected evidence of police brutality, produced a memorandum, and called for a public inquiry.

Asquith's promised statement, made the following Tuesday, gave little hope of satisfaction. He stated that the government, if returned to power at the election, would introduce a franchise bill, which would be so framed as to allow a free amendment to include women. This was to be introduced sometime in the course of the next parliament, not necessarily in the next session. The WSPU retaliated by sending 200 women to Downing Street. A lesson had been learned from "Black Friday"; it was better to commit an act of damage to property which would bring with it the certainty of a swift arrest, than to risk further painful tussles with the police. Stones were thrown at Asquith's car and at windows of government offices and 159 women were arrested, to be followed over the course of the next two days by a further 47. A total of only 75 women were convicted, on charges of damaging property or assault. Rule 243A, introduced by Churchill in March 1910 during, it may be noticed, the period of truce, had ameliorated prison conditions for suffragists and the necessity of hunger striking in order to achieve political prisoner status had lessened. Nevertheless two women went on hunger strike, only to have their fines paid by friends. Among the women arrested in November, two subsequently died: Mary Clarke on Christmas day, two days after her release from prison, and Henria WILLIAMS, who had been arrested but not prosecuted, on 2 January 1911.

During the general election the WSPU maintained a non-militant campaign against Liberal candidates in 50 constituencies. In ten of these the Liberal candidate was defeated. The Liberals were returned, the balance of power in the House of Commons being much as it had been in the previous parliament. No Caxton Hall Women's Parliament was held to coincide with the reopening of parliament. The WSPU waited for MPs to make the next move. This came when Sir George Kemp procured the first place in the ballot for private members' bills and proposed to introduce a new Conciliation Bill, a "Bill to Confer Parliamentary Franchise to Women". This passed its first reading and its second was set for 5 May. During its year of truce the WSPU had expanded its organization throughout the country. It now had 110 employees in London, who were based in 23 rooms in Clement's Inn and at 156 Charing Cross Road, which housed the WSPU shop and the Woman's Press. Predictably, without the frisson of daring deeds to part sympathizers from their money, its income had dropped slightly to £29 387. During the couple of months before the second reading of the bill the WSPU maintained its truce, working to educate its membership on the contents of the bill. However, plans were in readiness to carry on the fight if the government tampered with its progress. From February Christabel Pankhurst's initials appeared under a call in *Votes for Women* for 1000 volunteers to join a deputation in the event of the bill failing and WSPU members joined with gusto in the census resistance in April. This second Conciliation Bill did pass its second reading, but on 29 May Lloyd George announced that the government was unable to allot further time to the bill that session but would in the next, after another second reading, allocate a week for it to pass through subsequent stages. The WSPU still had the members of its deputation on call. In *Unshackled*, Christabel Pankhurst stresses that the WSPU might then have resumed its militant policy but was relieved that, by accepting Asquith's assurance to Lord Lytton that "The Government though divided in opinion as to the merits of the Bill are unanimous in their determination to give effect, not only in the letter but in the spirit, to the promise in regard to facilities which I made on their behalf before the last General Election", it did not have to undertake the painful duty of causing disruption during the coronation of George V. On 17 June the WSPU joined with 28 other suffrage societies in staging the Women's Coronation Procession and a mass meeting in the evening at the Albert Hall. The message at this meeting was that, although it was necessary still to be vigilant, victory was within the grasp. In a letter to Mary PHILLIPS dated 4 July 1911 Christabel Pankhurst wrote that she was keen to force Lloyd George, who though presenting himself as a suffragist was suspected of working behind the scenes against the Conciliation Bill, to be seen to take a stand on women's suffrage. She asked Mary Phillips to persuade the Leeds Women's Liberal Association, with whom she was on friendly terms, to invite Lloyd George to address them during the course of the summer. As she wrote, "the real thing is to drag Lloyd George out on to the public platforms so that the necessity of restoring cabinet unity may become imperative. The more he has committed himself to WS the more difficult it will be for the cabinet quietly to shelve the question". The WSPU also, for this period, modified its by-election policy and campaigned actively for those candidates, even if they were Liberals, who gave the most satisfactory pledges in support of the Conciliation Bill.

It was the near certainty that, in spite of being aware of Lloyd George's machinations, the cause was about to be won that made Asquith's announcement on 7 November, that the government intended to introduce a manhood suffrage bill which might, if the House of Commons desired, be amended to include women, such a bitter blow. Plans for the deputation were activated; 400 volunteers were enrolled within a week. On 16 November, at another Albert Hall meeting, the WSPU declared that war would be renewed on the government unless it was prepared to withdraw its manhood suffrage bill and substitute one giving equal franchise rights to men and women. As a result of the meeting the WSPU raised £4250 for its "war chest". On 17 November Christabel Pankhurst, Annie Kenney, Mabel Tuke, Lady Constance Lytton, Elizabeth Robins and Mrs Pethick-Lawrence (Mrs Pankhurst was still on a speaking tour in the USA) comprised the WSPU delegation in a joint deputation from all suffrage societies to Asquith and Lloyd George. This was the first occasion that the two militant societies, the WSPU and the WFL, had been received by Asquith. It would appear from the verbatim report as recorded in *Votes for Women*, which may, of course, have distorted the balance of the speeches, that Christabel Pankhurst and Annie Kenney dominated the interview. Asquith was reduced to telling Annie Kenney that he knew more about parliamentary procedure than she did. On 21 November, while Mrs Pethick-Lawrence led a deputation from Caxton Hall to the House of Commons, another body of women, armed with bags of stones, set about breaking the windows of government offices and business and shop premises. During the course of the evening 220 women and three men were arrested and the next day around 150 of these were sentenced to periods of between five days' and two months' imprisonment. Lloyd George who had, through the columns of the *Daily News* on 18 November, maintained that he would personally be prepared to introduce a women's suffrage amendment to the proposed manhood suffrage bill, in the course of a speech to the annual congress of the Liberal Federation in Bath on 24 November declared, complacently, that the Conciliation Bill had now been "torpedoed". This was in spite of Asquith's protestations that the manhood suffrage bill would not affect the progress of the Conciliation Bill. As Christabel Pankhurst had suggested in her letter to Mary Phillips of 4 July, it was on the public platform, lulled in the bosom of Liberal supporters, that the reality of Lloyd George's thinking was clarified. She had then been working on exposing a potential split in the cabinet; it was now clear that, although for different reasons, both Lloyd George and Asquith were united in opposition to women's suffrage. The 1 December 1911 issue of *Votes for Women* carried a cartoon which was captioned, "TORPEDOED!", depicting Lloyd George, the gunner of "HMS Devastation", scoring a hit on the foundering ship "Conciliation Bill", while the sturdy destroyer "WSPU" steams onto the scene. For her leading article Christabel Pankhurst took an excerpt from Lloyd George's Bath speech in which he stated, "I will tell you what has been a menace to property. When power was withheld from the democracy, when they [men] had no voice in the Government, when they were oppressed, and when they had no means of securing redress, except by violence – then property has many times been swept away." He could not have delivered himself of more apt incitement. During the course of the next month the WSPU manifested its contradictory aspects; on the one hand it was arming for war, putting out calls for volunteers to make the next protest, and, on the other, the pages of *Votes for Women* were full of descriptions and photographs of its Christmas Fair, held at the Portman Rooms, for which the stall holders dressed in eighteenth-century costumes devised by Sylvia Pankhurst. As Lady Sybil Smith was recorded as saying, "the Fair would prove that Suffragettes loved beauty as well as justice".

A few days after the fair ended, on 15 December Emily Wilding Davison fired the first pillar box. She had told the authorities of her intention, was caught in the act and was sentenced to six months' imprisonment. At the end of January vigorous disturbances were made at meetings held by cabinet ministers; McKenna, Runciman, Samuel and Hobhouse all suffered repeated interruptions. Harcourt informed a deputation, led by Annie Kenney, in his Rossendale constituency, that if all women were like his wife they would have the vote, thereby inviting Ethel SMYTH a month later to break his house windows. On 16 February 1912, at a dinner of welcome for the prisoners released after the 21 November demonstration, Mrs Pankhurst told members of the WSPU that "the argument of the broken pane of glass is the most valuable argument in modern politics". A protest was advertised to take place in Parliament Square on 4 March. This demonstration was, however, pre-empted and

The Women's Social and Political Union Christmas Bazaar in the Portman Rooms, 4–9 December 1911. Stall holders were dressed in a version of eighteenth-century costume designed by Sylvia Pankhurst. Taken from the Fawcett Library and reproduced by kind permission of the Mary Evans Picture Library.

WSPU policy put into practice on 1 March when, without prior warning, 150 women armed with hammers and instructions as to their use and timing, broke shop and office windows in the West End of London. Police investigation discovered that two dozen hammers had been bought on 22 or 23 February from Melhuish in Fetter Lane by "a well set up intellectual lady. She was evidently a lady: her manner was not assumed". Stones, which the police thought had been gathered with premeditation from a beach, were carried in specially made suspended bags. Some of the window smashers had picked up these bags from Edith DOWNING's studio in Chelsea. The police estimated that the window-smashing campaign had created £6600 worth of damage. Home Office papers contain a complete list of the 270 premises which had their windows broken. Around 220 arrests were made on 1 March and on subsequent days, most attracting sentences of from seven days to two months. Those women who had managed to cause more than £5 worth of damage were tried at Newington Sessions and their sentences ranged from four to six months. Mrs Pankhurst, who had driven in a taxi with other women to No. 10 Downing Street, where they broke four windows, was sentenced to two months' imprisonment. On 5 March she, the Pethick-Lawrences, Mabel Tuke and Christabel Pankhurst were then also charged with conspiracy to commit damage under the Malicious Injury to Property Act. The cover cartoon for the *Votes for Women* dated 8 March passed the responsibility for incitement over to Hobhouse who, at a meeting in Bristol on 16 February, had said that there was obviously insufficient demand for women's suffrage because in 1832, when men had been agitating for it, they had been so moved as to burn Nottingham Castle and in 1867 to destroy the railings of Hyde Park. The same issue carried dramatically blank spaces, including the entirety of the column to be occupied by Christabel Pankhurst's leading article, where, it was alleged, the printers had deemed material to be too inflammatory to publish. Christabel Pankhurst evaded arrest and escaped to Paris. The leadership devolved onto Annie Kenney. A meeting at the Albert Hall on 28 March, the day that Sir Almroth Wright's (*see* Lady WRIGHT) intemperate letter was published in *The Times*, was addressed by Annie Kenney, Elizabeth Robins, Annie Besant, Evelyn SHARP and Israel ZANGWILL and raised £10 500 in promises.

The imprisonment of a large number of suffragettes caused considerable disruption to the prison service. Most of the women were held in Holloway, but some were dispersed to Aylesbury and Winson Green in Birmingham. On 5 April the 28 WSPU members held in Aylesbury went on hunger strike, their example soon followed by the remainder in London and Birmingham. The women were fed by force. The conspiracy trial of their leaders took place in May; Mrs Tuke had earlier been acquitted. It was an occasion on which, from the dock, they were able to give full vent to their political grievances, but, despite a plea for clemency from the jury, when found guilty were sentenced to nine months' imprisonment in the second division, with the full costs of the prosecution to be borne by Frederick Pethick-Lawrence and Mrs Pankhurst. In anticipation, the WSPU had emptied its bank account; £7000 was made out in a cheque, dated 1 March, to Hertha Ayrton, leaving only £341 in the account. By 20 March this was reduced to £75.

It was quickly announced, at yet another mass meeting in the Albert Hall, that if all WSPU prisoners did not receive first-division status, a hunger strike, to include the leaders, would be instigated. The leaders were given first-division status on 10 June, but it was withheld from the rest of the prisoners, who were treated under Rule 243A. The Home Office was obdurate, despite representations from 104 MPs and a succession of questions in the House, and on 19 June all prisoners, including the leaders, went on hunger strike. Most prisoners, including the Pethick-Lawrences, were forcibly fed; Mrs Pankhurst was not. By 6 July all the hunger strikers were released, having thereby reduced their sentences by about two months. During the period of their imprisonment local WSPU branches had mounted vociferous open-air campaigns and had made much of the government's treatment of the prisoners during the course of the Hythe and North-West Norfolk by-elections. In London another Albert Hall meeting was the occasion for less than subtle appeals for more money. The advertising message, ostensibly from Christabel Pankhurst, ended, "Remembering how finely and freely the prisoners are giving themselves and their liberty, those who have hitherto from choice or necessity kept to smoother paths will be glad of the opportunity that will be theirs on June 15 to give at least money to further the Union's great work." On the night £6000 was promised. The WSPU had, however, now lost the support of one of its earliest and oldest workers. *Votes for Women*, 26 July 1912, carried a public letter of protest against militancy, on the grounds that it would jeopardize the amendments proposed for the enfranchisement bill, which was signed by, among others, Elizabeth Wolstenholme Elmy. On 14 July, Bastille Day and Mrs Pankhurst's birthday, Sylvia Pankhurst and Flora Drummond organized a demonstration, in co-operation with other suffrage societies and the ILP, in Hyde Park, at which red caps of liberty atop banners made their first appearance. Keir Hardie and George Lansbury were among the speakers. It is thought that this type of demonstration was no longer part of Christabel Pankhurst's policy and marked a divergence in the policy of the two sisters. All this activity was set against the background of the second reading of the government's despised Franchise and Registration Bill (Manhood Suffrage Bill) which was shepherded through the Commons by J.A. Pease and Lewis Harcourt, both unreconstructed anti-suffragists. Militancy now, as on previous occasions, was propelled from the ranks. On 13 July Helen CRAGGS was arrested in the grounds of Lewis Harcourt's house in Oxfordshire. She was equipped with inflammable material and matches, and a note to say that "I have accepted the challenge given by Mr Hobhouse at Bristol, and I have done something drastic." Her companion escaped. On 18 July Mary Leigh, in Dublin, threw a hatchet into a carriage in which Asquith and Redmond, the leader of the Irish Nationalists, were riding. She and Gladys Evans then, that evening, attempted to set fire to a Dublin theatre. They were subsequently sentenced to five years' penal servitude. Jennie BAINES, who was also arrested on a minor charge, was sentenced to seven months' hard labour. All three went on hunger strike; Jennie Baines was released, ill, and the other two were forcibly fed, the first time that this operation had been carried out in an Irish prison. Mary Leigh and Gladys Evans were eventually released on "ticket of leave". After protracted legal arguments, the cases were dropped, the two women having between them served only 16 weeks of their five-year sentences.

After their release from prison the Pethick-Lawrences departed to recuperate in Canada; Mrs Pankhurst to Paris. The WSPU announced that it would be leaving Clement's Inn; the premises had been repossessed by the landlord. The 13 September issue of *Votes for Women* revealed "Where Christabel is" and reassured its readers that Christabel had always been at the helm and that from now on she would sign her articles, which had previously appeared anonymously. As the statement revealed, there had been "contemptible critics" who had "taunted Miss Pankhurst with evading her responsibilities". The next week's issue unveiled the WSPU's new home in Lincoln's Inn House in Kingsway, together with six photographs of Christabel.

An Albert Hall meeting for 17 October had been announced as far back as 19 July, at which Mrs Pankhurst and the Pethick-Lawrences were to be welcomed on their return. In the event the Pethick-Lawrences were told by Mrs Pankhurst, the day after they returned from Canada, that, as Emmeline Pethick-Lawrence recorded it, "she had severed her connection with me". A committee meeting of the WSPU held on 14 October rubber stamped the decision. Mary Neal and Elizabeth Robins attempted to protest but were told by Mrs Pankhurst that as they had not attended meetings regularly they were not sufficiently well informed to form a view. Christabel returned from Paris to confirm to them that she alone intended to control the WSPU. The break appears to have been caused by a difference of opinion over the efficacy of militant methods. Frederick Pethick-Lawrence recorded in his autobiography that he felt that by directing its members to make increasingly dangerous attacks on public property the WSPU would create a new hostility to itself. He felt that by living in Paris Christabel was out of touch with the mood of the country; he assumed she would return. Christabel Pankhurst makes it clear in her autobiography that she had resolved very soon after her escape that she would not return to Britain until the vote was won. She saw herself as the only one capable of controlling affairs from a distance and of reading "the mind of particular Cabinet Ministers and of the Government in general". It had been arranged that the Pethick-Lawrences keep *Votes for Women*; the WSPU immediately launched a new paper in its stead, the *Suffragette*, the first issue of which, dated 18 October, was actually available for sale on the 17th.

At the Albert Hall meeting, besides announcing the departure of the Pethick-Lawrences, Mrs Pankhurst stated that the WSPU would now work in direct opposition to the Labour and Irish Nationalist parties, members of which, in March, had not supported the second reading of the Conciliation Bill. George Lansbury was one Labour member who had voted for the bill, against his party's direction. In November, with encouragement from Emmeline and Christabel Pankhurst, he resigned his seat at Bromley and Bow, in order to stand as an Independent Labour candidate, making his main platform the suffrage issue. Sylvia Pankhurst had, since the Bastille Day Hyde Park demonstration, been building up support in the East End of London and might have expected to direct the Bromley and Bow campaign. However, Grace ROE, whom Sylvia Pankhurst castigates in *The Suffragette Movement*, was sent from headquarters to organize the WSPU's involvement in the campaign. Lansbury was defeated by the Unionist candidate and WSPU members responded by carrying out a nationwide "pillar-box campaign", the perpetrators escaping arrest. Previously most of those who had committed damage had not seriously attempted to evade arrest. It was the fact that damage to property brought with it publicity and, it was hoped, public sympathy, that had been the mainspring of militant policy. Damage was now to be done, as the *Suffragette*, 26 December 1912, elucidated, "to make the electors and the Government so uncomfortable that, in order to put an end to the nuisance, they will give women the vote".

Hostilities were momentarily suspended in January during the debate of the Franchise Reform Bill and on 23 January Flora Drummond and Annie Kenney led a deputation of working women to see Lloyd George and Sir Edward Grey, both ostensibly pro-suffrage; Asquith had refused to meet them. Although Lloyd George was mollifying, four hours later, in the House of Commons, the Speaker indicated that an amendment to introduce women into the bill would so change it that it would have to be reintroduced as a new bill. When the ruling was confirmed on 27 January the arson campaign gathered momentum. Flora Drummond and Annie Kenney had had a further meeting with Lloyd George on Sunday 26 January. They had followed close on the heels of a small deputation to him from the NUWSS, one member of which, Kathleen COURTNEY, had asked them if they would abandon militancy if all other suffrage societies united to demand a government measure for women's enfranchisement. The WSPU refused to consider the proposal.

In her stirring speech at the Albert Hall on 18 October 1912 Mrs Pankhurst had declared, "I incite this meeting to rebellion". On 10 January 1913 she distributed a circular to WSPU members, instructing them that "To be militant in some way or other is a moral obligation. It is a duty which every woman will owe to her own conscience and self-respect, to other women who are less fortunate than she is herself, and to all those who are to come after her. If any woman refrains from militant protest against the injury done by the Government and the House of Commons to women and to the race, she will share the responsibility for the crime". The police were already attending all London WSPU meetings and forwarding verbatim reports to the Home Office, where a note was taken of all incitements to break the law. However, to quote a minute made by one official on 31 January 1913, "both Mrs Pankhurst and Miss Kenney were I think clearly guilty of inciting to commit crime – but as we cannot punish, I suppose it is useless to prosecute". The police underlined, in a report of a meeting on 4 February, Mrs Pankhurst's statement, "for what women do in the future, short of taking human life, I take full personal responsibility". On 19 February a Home Office minute on a report of a speech given by Mrs Pankhurst at Cromwell Hall, Putney, is marked, "This is the speech for which Sir C. Mathews wishes to prosecute". However, the Home Office waited until, at a meeting at the Cory Hall, Cardiff on 19 February, Mrs Pankhurst stated that she accepted full responsibility for the destruction, on 18 February, of Lloyd George's house in Surrey. This meeting was attended by a police superintendent, in plain clothes, who had under his direction, in uniform, one chief inspector, one inspector and 30 constables. Twenty of the police were in the basement of the building, hiding out of sight in case of an emergency. The police superintendent especially singled out for the attention of the Head Constable Mrs Pankhurst's words, "we have not yet got all the members of the present government in prison, but we have blown up the Chancellor of Exchequer's house" and "For all that has been done in the past I accept responsibility. I have advised, I have incited, I have conspired." The speech was taken down by an employee of the *Western Mail*, whose editor wrote on 20 February to assure the Chief Constable that the shorthand taker had kept his original notes and would be available to give evidence, if required. A Home Office minute on the papers notes that the Secretary of State had seen the report that morning, 21 February, and had discussed with his officials the action to be taken. The decision was then taken to prosecute Mrs Pankhurst for procuring and inciting women to commit offences contrary to the Malicious Injuries to Property Act, 1861. The significance of the Home Office minute of 31 January became clear when, in the course of a bitter attack in the House of Commons on the Home Secretary, McKenna revealed that he had been considering how he could prevent the hunger strike circumventing the law's punishment. His suggestion of letting such prisoners out on licence was drafted as a bill. The Prisoners (Temporary Discharge for Ill-Health) Bill, to be colloquially known as the "Cat and Mouse" Act, passed its second reading on 2 April. It was no coincidence that a day later, on 3 April, Mrs Pankhurst was found guilty of incitement and sentenced to three years' penal servitude. The bill received its royal assent on 25 April, demonstrating how quickly the House of Commons could move if so minded. The WSPU issued its seventh annual report on 31 March and it was sent to subscribers with a letter from Emmeline Pankhurst, writing, as she said, on the eve of her trial and urging members to attend the Albert Hall rally on 10 April and raise "such a sum of money for the war-chest that we shall be able to extend our agitation and at the same time give the enemy another proof of our strength". The accounts for the year ending 28 February 1913 show an increase in subscriptions of about £4000 over the previous year. This information was not lost on the Home Office; a police constable was deputed to buy from Lincoln's Inn House the copy of the annual report that now lies among the Home Office papers.

On 8 April Annie Kenney was arrested under an obscure statute dating from the reign of Edward III. The *Suffragette* responded in its issue of 11 April by carrying the headline "The Women's Revolution – A Reign of Terror – Fire and Bombs" over successive news items relating arson, telephone wire cutting, raids on art galleries and the wrecking of municipal flower beds. The Edward III statute was then invoked against both George Lansbury and

Flora Drummond. After a final rally in the Albert Hall on 10 April, its management subsequently refused to let it to the WSPU. On 15 April the WSPU was proscribed by the Metropolitan Police from holding meetings in public parks, a notice that was to be served on "Annie Kenney or any other woman who was in control of the business of the Union". On 30 April the police raided Lincoln's Inn House and arrested the chief office organizers, Harriet Kerr, Beatrice Sanders, Rachel BARRETT, Geraldine LENNOX, Agnes Lake and Flora Drummond. The next day Annie Kenney, who was out on bail, was arrested after returning from France. Her flat had been raided and as a consequence Edwy CLAYTON, a chemist, was arrested. Grace Roe took over Annie Kenney's position as chief organizer. The police removed from Lincoln's Inn House a pantechnicon full of papers, which were never returned, thereby creating a vacuum which historians of the WSPU have been forced to fill from material that came to rest outside the organization's centre. The new printer of the *Suffragette* was arrested, but WSPU activists, with the help of Gerald Gould (*see* Barbara Ayrton GOULD) saw to it that it appeared that week, 2 May, as usual, with the dramatic headline "Raided" printed across the stark front cover. On 2 May the Home Office requested the General Post Office to cut off all telephone communication with Lincoln's Inn House; but the GPO replied that it was not entitled to do so. The police pursued printers of the *Suffragette*; the manager of the National Labour Press was arrested on 9 May, the day on which the first issue printed by that press appeared. J.E. Francis of the Athenaeum Press (*see* PUBLISHERS AND PRINTERS), who from 1907 until 1911 had published *Women's Franchise*, took on the responsibility of printing the *Suffragette*, ensuring that he escaped prosecution by deleting material he thought might be actionable. In July 1913 police raided the WSPU's Manchester office.

As the WSPU's legitimate political operation was curtailed and erstwhile non-combatants such as Harriet Kerr and Beatrice Sanders were removed, the void was filled by even more extreme words and deeds. As they were forced underground, WSPU activists, such as Lilian LENTON and Kitty MARION, adopted guerrilla tactics, moving from area to area, committing damage, adopting disguises, ALIASES (which besides confusing the police later confused members of the Suffragette Fellowship), and avoiding arrest. Repression bred solidarity and bonds were at this time created between women, such as Ethel MOORHEAD and Frances PARKER, that lasted the rest of their lives. On 25 April, under the headline "Human Life in Danger", Christabel Pankhurst's leading article concluded, "A Militant woman may be killed, but her cause will live and triumph". On 9 May a column headline in the *Suffragette* read "W.S.P.U. Strengthened by Persecution". On 4 June Emily Wilding DAVISON put the Leader's thoughts into practice when she rushed onto the Derby race course and was killed. On 14 June the WSPU reached its apotheosis in the staging of a martyr's funeral.

Although the 9 May 1913 issue of the *Suffragette* contained a lengthy report of the second reading debate of W.H. Dickenson's "Representation of the People Bill", for which Asquith had promised facilities after the withdrawal of the government's bill in January, Christabel Pankhurst's leading article declared that, whereas once the second reading of such a bill would have been a red-letter day, "now such proceedings are regarded with cold contempt by all Suffragists". The defeat of the bill was a foregone conclusion; most of that issue of the *Suffragette* is taken up with the news of WSPU prisoners, trials, and arson, the plans for the summer fair, and an article by Christabel Pankhurst on Joan of Arc. The political process had been relegated and, significantly, a whole-page article, "The Falling Birthrate", by "A Medical Woman", in which she implicated the spread of syphilis, is given full prominence. This article refers back to an article written by Christabel Pankhurst, "To Cure White Slavery. A Medical Question", in the 25 April issue. Two weeks earlier, in the April 11 issue, which carried a full-page photograph of Mrs Pankhurst and the caption "Three Years' Penal Servitude" on its front cover, Christabel Pankhurst devoted her leading article not to her mother but to "The War Against Slavery". The "slavery" was, of course, of women and its "chief fruit is the Social Evil" (prostitution). W.T. Stead who had campaigned against "white slavery" for the previous 30 years had died in April 1912, drowning with the *Titanic*. He had been extremely helpful to the WSPU in its early years in London and his history and dramatic campaigning experience must have made an impact on Christabel Pankhurst's thinking. Between 15 July and 26 September she published each week in the *Suffragette* articles dealing with prostitution and venereal disease, eventually published as *The Great Scourge*, counterpointed with the realities of vice and the law's lenient treatment of it, as exemplified by the Piccadilly Flat Case then being tried. The argument that the social evil would never be eliminated while men made the laws had been reiterated at length by Olive HOCKIN at her trial, reported in the *Suffragette*, 11 April 1913.

Mrs Pankhurst served little of her prison sentence, successively hunger striking and being released under the "Cat and Mouse" Act until, in October, with the full knowledge of the Home Office, she sailed to the USA to undertake a lecture tour. It is likely that, as well as keeping her out of reach of imprisonment, fund-raising for the WSPU was necessary. Contributions, as recorded in the *Suffragette*, were declining. During the period 2–30 July contributions, in the aftermath of the spectacular funeral, amounted to £1856; for 31 July–12 September the amount raised was only £846, which included one large donation, of £55, from Mrs D.A. Thomas (*see* Lady RHONDDA). It appears, from studying the local reports in the *Suffragette*, that fewer paid organizers were in operation. Many of those in charge of districts are by now described as "honorary secretary". At least one organizer, Mary Phillips, was treated at this time to dismissal and a decidedly intemperate letter from Christabel Pankhurst. During the summer, the *Suffragette* ran a vigorous campaign to increase its circulation, photographs of its paper sellers at holiday resorts around the country contrasting oddly with those of the very real destruction wrought by the guerrilla fighters. Many of these latter were escaped "mice" who, in later autobiographical reminiscences, although they were still reticent about the actual damage for which they were responsible, recalled with glee the strategies they had employed to outwit the police. Annie Kenney, Flora Drummond and six others who had been arrested in May were tried for conspiracy in June, found guilty, sentenced to between six and 21 months in the third division and each ordered to pay a seventh of the prosecution costs. They, of

A neat corner of a WSPU office/shop. Note the piles of "literature" and the shelf of books, possibly the branch's lending library. (Author's collection)

course, successively went on hunger strike, were released under the "Cat and Mouse" Act and evaded the police. Between them, out of the 66 months to which they were sentenced, only 4 months was served before the outbreak of war in August 1914. For much of this time the police made no attempt to re-arrest them. On Mrs Pankhurst's return from America in December elaborate plans were made to arrest her at the quayside, and the Home Office did make some effort to keep her in prison; she was on hunger strike four times between March and her final release before the war, on 18 July 1914. It would appear, however, that the intention was to harass rather than to make certain that she served her full term. The police, arriving in force at the St Andrew's Hall in Glasgow on 9 March to re-arrest her, met with stiff resistance from her appointed bodyguard. Janie ALLAN is reputed to have fired a starting pistol on this occasion. Each of Mrs Pankhurst's re-arrests was the occasion for fresh retaliation from such militants as Mary RICHARDSON. Likewise, anonymous reprisals were carried out by friends of hunger strikers in response to the treatment they received. For instance, in February 1914 Frances Parker fired Whitekirk, a destruction that at the time caused very real outrage and £10 000 worth of damage, in response to the injury done by forcible feeding to Ethel Moorhead.

By the beginning of 1914 Christabel Pankhurst was undergoing a degree of internal criticism for her handling of the WSPU. At least two influential members, Beatrice HARRADEN and H.D. HARBEN, are known to have, quite separately, written to her at the beginning of the year, censuring her for being out of touch. They felt that WSPU loyalists were being mistreated, both through carelessness and by indifference to the reality of their suffering, by a leader who was herself removed from the struggle. It is only chance that has preserved the evidence for these two reproaches; they are not, of course, contained in the main Suffragette Fellowship collection. However, in *Unshackled*, writing of this time Christabel Pankhurst comments, in the context of describing the government's attempts to threaten subscribers to WSPU funds, that "It did not cost much money to commit a militant deed, it did not cost much money to do a hunger-and-thirst strike or to be forcibly fed." It is salutary to contrast this cool assessment with the messy and painful reality of the twice-daily prison reports, now lying among the Home Office papers, of the forcible feeding of such women as Olive WHARRY. It would be very unlikely that Christabel Pankhurst did not receive more such complaints. She demonstrated the inflexibility of her position by ejecting the EAST LONDON FEDERATION OF THE SUFFRAGETTES, under her sister Sylvia, from the WSPU in January 1914. Another group of erstwhile supporters broke away to found the UNITED SUFFRAGISTS in February 1914. Both groups included many of the men, such as H.D. Harben, H.W. NEVINSON, George Lansbury and Gerald Gould, who had been stalwart supporters for many years, providing funds, advice and publicity. The WSPU had since the summer of 1913, in tandem with its moral crusade, been unwilling to allow men to be involved in its affairs, or to work with any organization that included men. Maud Arncliffe SENNETT recorded in her autobiography that some time prior to the summer of 1913 Christabel Pankhurst had rejected her suggestion that more men should be involved in the suffrage campaign, saying that she thought it best if the women fought their own fight. Maud Arncliffe Sennett then formed the NORTHERN MEN'S FEDERATION FOR WOMEN'S SUFFRAGE. Through March, April and May 1914 the damage escalated, churches, mansions, grandstands, golf links, paintings in the National Gallery and the Royal Academy were damaged or destroyed. On 21 May police raided a flat at Lauderdale Mansions in Maida Vale, uncovering material that could have been used in attacks on property. There was a certain historical aptness that among the women arrested in this flat was the wife of Leonard Hall, who in 1896 had inspired Emmeline Pankhurst to make a stand at Boggart Hole Clough, and her daughter Nellie HALL. On the same day Emmeline Pankhurst was re-arrested while leading a deputation to the King. This was no staged spectacle such as had celebrated his Coronation in 1911. Women, armed with clubs, battled with the police. The next day, by which time the National Gallery, Tate Gallery and the Wallace Collection were closed until further notice, the police raided Lincoln's Inn House. Grace Roe, by then in charge of the WSPU's organization, was arrested on a charge of conspiracy. The Home Office was determined this time to deprive the WSPU of its telephone. A Home Office minute records that "There is no doubt that the telephone is used in the campaign of lawlessness the WSPU are directing and as there seems to be little hope of introducing legislative measures to strengthen our hands or cripple theirs, why should not so simple an expedient as cutting off telephonic communication with all WSPU offices be adopted?" Herbert Samuel, the Postmaster General, did not feel able to comply, writing "Deprivation of telephones would of course inconvenience them but I fancy the actual work of organizing outrage is done from semi-private premises like the Lauderdale Mansions flat and they would have little difficulty in setting up telephone centres in private houses." In the end the Home Secretary decided not to apply to the Postmaster General to cut off the telephones from Lincoln's Inn House, writing on 16 June that the police would soon have to give back the building. The police seized all mail that arrived at Lincoln's Inn House while they were in possession, noting that the "contents are useful". While the police were in possession, the WSPU moved to the premises at 17 Tothill Street which housed its Westminster and St George's branch, where Mrs Louie Hatfield, who had been Annie Kenney's housekeeper since 1910, was put in charge of the office. Police raided and seized these premises on 8 June. The WSPU then moved to "Mouse Castle", the Brackenburys' house in Campden Hill Square, followed by the police who again, on 12 June, raided and seized all WSPU papers. Olive BARTELS, disguised as a young widow and living in a Bloomsbury hotel, succeeded Grace Roe as organizer. Grace Roe was not released, in spite of hunger striking both before and after sentencing, until 10 August, under the government amnesty. The Home Office was now insistent that prisoners would serve their term; perhaps practice had made the prison officials more skilful at administering forcible feeding without causing damage. It is clear that the personal suffering endured was not a concern of the government, which was far more affected by the state of Ireland than that of women. Christabel Pankhurst's hope that the WSPU would be taken as seriously as the militant Ulster Unionists was a chimera. If it was the example of Irish Nationalists, under Parnell, that had influenced the formation of the original WSPU policy of militancy, it was the perceived success, by employing similar methods, of the Irish Unionists under Carson that had lured Christabel Pankhurst deeper into an intransigence from which it is difficult to see any logical conclusion other than disappointment.

A letter written on 9 June 1914 by Mrs Pankhurst, who was then in hiding at 6 Blenheim Road, London NW, has survived. It is a direct plea for money, addressed to Mrs Badley, the wife of the founder of Bedales School, cousin of Millicent Fawcett, and a long-standing supporter of the WSPU. Christabel Pankhurst had made a similar request to Mrs Badley in November 1913. In her 1914 letter, Mrs Pankhurst gives clear instructions for money to be sent to her at the Blenheim Road address, made out to "Miss Howard". Although the letter was handwritten, it has the overtones of a circular. It is very likely that other such requests were despatched as the business organization and conventional fund-raising of the WSPU succumbed to police harassment. The annual accounts for March 1913 to February 1914 had shown that subscriptions had increased to over £28 000 but it is very likely that the disruption caused by police harassment had eaten into the WSPU's cash reserve and inhibited both the giving and the receipt of further donations. Towards the end of July the Home Office attempted to cut off the WSPU's proselytizing medium, and its potential to raise its latest "Great Protest Fund", by sending a letter to newsagents, threatening that they might be liable for prosecution if they distributed the, now sadly lean, *Suffragette*. Mildred MANSEL, assumed as cousin of the chief Liberal Whip to be immune from arrest, was responsible for organizing the WSPU's last large meeting, held at the Holland Park Hall on 16 July 1914. Mrs Pankhurst was arrested when, lying on a stretcher, she left Nurse Pine's nursing home in order to attend the meeting. Annie Kenney, in disguise, managed to evade the police and appear on the platform; apparently £16 350 was promised as a result of this meeting. However, it is doubtful if all these promises were called in before the outbreak of war.

On 10 August all WSPU prisoners, as well as men who were in prison as a consequence of strike activities, were granted an amnesty by the government. They were not required to make an undertaking to refrain from further militant activity; confidence was expressed that they would "respond to the feelings of their countrymen and countrywomen in this time of emergency". On 13 August Emmeline Pankhurst sent a circular letter to members of the WSPU:

Even the outbreak of war could not affect the action of the WSPU so long as our comrades were in prison and under torture. Since their release it has been possible to consider what should be the course adopted by the WSPU in view of the war crisis. It is obvious that even the most vigorous militancy of the WSPU is for the time being rendered less effective by contrast with the infinitely greater violence done in the present war not to mere property and economic prosperity alone, but to human life. As for work for the vote on the lines of peaceful argument, such work is we know futile even under ordinary conditions... How much less therefore will it avail at this time of international warfare. Under all the circumstances it has been decided to economise the Union's energies and financial resources by a temporary suspension of activities. The resumption of active work and the reappearance of the *Suffragette* whose next publication will be also temporarily suspended will be announced when the right time comes.

As regards the war, the view the WSPU expresses is this:– we believe that under the joint rule of enfranchised women and men the nations of the world will, owing to women's influence and authority find a way of reconciling the claims of peace and honour and of regulating International relations without bloodshed; we nevertheless believe also that matters having come to the present pass it was inevitable that Great Britain should take part in the war and with that patriotism which has nerved women to endure torture in prison cells for the national good, we ardently desire that our country shall be victorious... I want in conclusion to thank with all my heart the generous and devoted women who have supported the WSPU until now, and to assure them of my confidence that at the present time and later when we resume active work, that support will be continued.

Thus the militant campaign ended.

When Christabel Pankhurst returned to England and made her first public appearance on 8 September, addressing her audience of erstwhile WSPU members on "The War Crisis", it became clear that Christabel and Emmeline Pankhurst, loyally assisted by Annie Kenney and Grace Roe, intended to transform the WSPU organization into a jingoist machine. This was not a move that proved acceptable even to the loyal membership that the WSPU retained into the first year of the war. On 22 October 1915, at the Caxton Hall, Rose Lamartine YATES chaired a meeting, criticizing the Pankhursts' policy and the lack of financial accounts, that led to the foundation of the SUFFRAGETTES OF THE WSPU. In March 1916 other WSPU members, who included Charlotte Marsh, formed themselves into the INDEPENDENT WSPU. In August 1916, as a response to a speech by Asquith in which he declared himself, at last, to be in principle in favour of women's enfranchisement, the WSPU accused him of putting votes for women before that of disenfranchised fighting men. As Sylvia Pankhurst commented in *The Suffragette Movement*, this was a curious position for Christabel and Emmeline Pankhurst to hold. In March 1917 Mrs Pankhurst wrote to Millicent Fawcett asking if they might meet in order to discuss the political situation as it affected the suffrage cause. Mrs Fawcett did suggest an appointment but it is not known if it took place or, if it did, what Mrs Pankhurst's suggestions were for the "wise and limited action" she mentioned. In November 1917, in anticipation of the near reality of women's enfranchisement, the Pankhurst rump renamed itself "THE WOMEN'S PARTY".

Hon. Organizer Christabel Pankhurst; Treasurer (1903) Mrs Harker; (1906–12) Emmeline Pethick-Lawrence; (1912–17) Emmeline Pankhurst.

See also POLICE; PRISONS.

Address: (1903–6) 62 Nelson Street, Manchester; (1906) 45 Park Walk, Chelsea; (1907–12) 4 Clement's Inn, London WC; (1913–17) Lincoln's Inn House, Kingsway, London WC.

Archival source: Annual Reports, WSPU, 1907–14, Fawcett Library; Elizabeth Wolstenholme Elmy Papers, British Library; Papers of Sylvia Pankhurst, Internationaal Instituut voor Sociale Geschiedenis, Amsterdam; Mary Phillips Papers, Camellia plc; Home Office Papers, Public Record Office; Millicent Garrett Fawcett Papers, Fawcett Library.

Bibliography: S. Pankhurst, *The Suffragette*, 1911; A.E. Metcalfe, *Woman's Effort: A Chronicle of British Women's Fifty Years' Struggle for Citizenship (1865–1914)*, 1917; C. Rover, *Women's Suffrage and Party Politics in Britain, 1866–1914*, 1967; A. Rosen, *Rise Up Women: The Militant Campaign of the Women's Social and Political Union, 1903–1914*, 1974; B. Harrison, *Peaceable Kingdom: Stability and Change in Modern Britain*, 1982; J. Marcus (ed.), *Suffrage and the Pankhursts*, 1987.

WOMEN'S SUFFRAGE DEMONSTRATION COMMITTEE Led by Mary COZENS in 1892. It had its origin in a "Hyde Park Demonstration Committee" originally organized by the WOMEN'S FRANCHISE LEAGUE and mentioned in passing by Sylvia Pankhurst in *The Suffragette Movement*, 1931. The plan had been to hold an open-air demonstration in

Hyde Park on 29 May 1892, to which the following resolution was to be put: "That in the opinion of this meeting of men and women, the time has arrived when all local municipal and parliamentary franchises should be granted to women, whether married or unmarried, on the same terms as they are granted to men." This resolution was to be sent to all MPs. However, by April the Committee had split and, instead, one section, with Mary Cozens as its secretary and treasurer, organized a meeting at St James's Hall, in support of Sir Albert Rollit's suffrage bill. This was held in opposition to the views held on that bill by the Women's Franchise League and members of the League, led by Herbert Burrows, and apparently backed by Alice SCATCHERD and Richard and Emmeline PANKHURST, caused sufficient disruption for the meeting to be prematurely abandoned.

Address: 21 Earl's Court Gardens, London SW.

WOMEN'S SUFFRAGE PETITION COMMITTEE
The meeting of the KENSINGTON SOCIETY held in November 1865 had discussed the question, "Is the extension of the Parliamentary suffrage to women desirable, and if so, under what conditions?" After the meeting Emily DAVIES wrote to H.R. Tompkinson that "some people are inclined to begin a subdued kind of agitation for the franchise ... She [Barbara BODICHON] thinks (and so do I) that more women care for the suffrage than is supposed, and that more still would care if they thought about it." At this juncture Emily Davies could not agree with Barbara Bodichon's suggestion that a committee should be formed to pursue the goal of women's suffrage. However, after Disraeli declared on 27 April 1866 that he saw no objection in principle to women's enfranchisement, Barbara Bodichon, Emily Davies, Bessie Rayner PARKES, Jessie BOUCHERETT, Elizabeth GARRETT and Jane Crow did form a small, very informal committee to promote a petition that John Stuart MILL, newly elected to parliament, was prepared to present. This called for "the representation of all householders, without distinction of sex, who possess such property or rental qualifications as your honourable House may determine". What Barbara Bodichon described as this "very bare sharp statement" was carved out of a petition quickly drafted by Helen TAYLOR. The committee then organized the printing of the petition sheets and sent them to contacts throughout the country. The accompanying letter explained that:

An impression is widely prevalent that the extension of the Parliamentary suffrage to women, whether it would be in itself desirable or not, is at any rate not desired by women. In the hope of in some way removing this impression, it is proposed to present to the House of Commons, at an early date, a Petition briefly expressing the opinion of women on this point. The grounds on which the franchise is desired are very various. Arguments which, to some people, appear irresistible, with others carry little weight. The Petitioners do not attempt to enumerate the reasons which might be urged in support of their claim, and by which they are severally influenced. They simply adopt what appears to be the most direct method of expressing their wishes on a matter which they hold to be of great importance. The co-operation of all who concur in the general object of the Petition is respectfully invited.

Elizabeth Garrett lent her drawing room as an office, and the returned petitions were sent there. Emily Davies wrote, much later, in her *Family Chronicle*, "I have a distinct recollection of the party of friends who met at Miss Garrett's house from day to day and worked it." From an analysis of the 1499 names and addresses on the petition it is clear that the women contacted gathered signatures from their relations, friends and neighbours, many of whom were teachers, shop-keepers, or dressmakers, and from the wives of their butchers, booksellers, brushmakers, greengrocers, blacksmiths and cabinet makers. In a letter to *Votes for Women* on 18 March 1910 Elizabeth Wolstenholme ELMY remarked that she herself had collected 300 of the signatures for the petition. Ann Dingsdale has concluded that those canvassing were more likely to gain support for the petition from women who were heads of their household, or from women who lived in such households.

The returned petition sheets were collated in Aubrey House, the home of Clementia TAYLOR, and the whole was ready to be presented, in the name of "Barbara L.S. Bodichon and others", on 7 June. On 6 June Helen Taylor wrote to Barbara Bodichon that "Mr Mill himself will present the petition tomorrow, (if that is still the wish of the ladies) and it should be sent to the House of Commons to arrive there before two p.m. tomorrow, Thursday June 7th, directed to Mr Mill, and 'petition' written on it. It is indeed a wonderful success. It does honour to the energy of those who have worked on it and promises well for the prospects of any future plan for furthering the same objects."

The work of the petition committee was not yet finished. Emily Davies wrote to Helen Taylor on 9 June that:

> the printer promises revised proofs of the Petition with the list of names, in slip, by Monday evening. These will do for sending to newspaper writers. Miss King, the Sec of the Society for the Employment of Women, has written to the proprietor of the Standard, and will see the Editor of the Atheneum, whom she knows intimately. I have asked Miss Boucherett to call on Harriet Martineau and see what she will do about the Daily News, in which she writes pretty regularly. Miss Bostock will look after the Spectator, and Miss Garrett will I think try the Scotsman. I am going to write to Mr Courtney, who is on the staff of The Times, tho without much hope of his being able to do anything. If there is any one to whom you would like the list of names sent on Tuesday, perhaps you will kindly let me know. We shall not get copies in the pamphlet form till some days later, but the slips can be used in the meantime.

They were, however, ill-served by their printer and it was only on 18 July that Emily Davies was able to write to Helen Taylor that she had that day sent the finished pamphlet copies of the Petition to all the weekly papers of any consideration, "that in case they take any notice, they may know what they are commenting upon". Notice of the petition was certainly taken by the *Pall Mall Gazette*, the *Record*, the *Law Times* and the *Working Man*. Emily Davies proposed sending reprints of this latter extract to Miss Horsburgh, secretary of the Working Men's Club in the Strand, "for her to send out to her friends among working men".

An anonymous article, "The Ladies' Petition", now identified as written by Helen Taylor, appeared in the *Westminster Review* in January 1867. In it she commented that the number signing the petition might be small:

> But if we reflect a little on the peculiar position of women and their usual ways of thinking – on their habitual reticence on all subjects which they are accustomed to consider as beyond their own sphere, their timidity and dread of exposing their names to public observation, their deference ever to the most unreasonable prejudices of those who have any claim on their affections, their clinging to old association, and their regard for the opinion of all who are ever remotely connected with them. We shall see reason to think that these 1500 ladies, who have not hesitated to affix their names to a public document, and to pronounce a decided opinion, open to the controversy and criticism, must represent an extraordinarily important phase of thought.

The article suggests that, although for every one woman who signed there were ten who because of timidity and family hindrances did not feel able to, "there can be no doubt that the class of independent women is a continually increasing one in this country and their admission to the franchise is therefore continually becoming, by the natural course of events, a question of greater practical importance". The article concludes, "If the possession of a vote should induce more women to extend their interest to the comfort and happiness of other homes besides their own, it will certainly not have exercised a deteriorating influence on their character." By the time this article appeared the women's suffrage campaign was indeed gathering momentum. It is clear that both Barbara Bodichon and Helen Taylor had assumed, even before the petition was presented, that the committee would continue in some form. The LONDON PROVISIONAL PETITION COMMITTEE emerged as the body hoping, rather tentatively, to capitalize on the interest engendered by Mill's petition.

Archival source: Mill–Taylor Correspondence, London School of Economics and Political Science.
Bibliography: B. Stephens, *Emily Davies and Girton College*, 1927; A. Dingsdale, *"Generous and Lofty Sympathies": The Kensington Society, the 1866 Women's Suffrage Petition and the Development of Mid-Victorian Feminism*, 1995 (thesis), in Fawcett Library.

WOODLOCK, PATRICIA (*c.* 1878–alive 1930) Daughter of an Irish artist, David Woodlock, who had settled in Liverpool in the mid-nineteenth century. He was a Socialist and gave moral support to his daughter, who was an active member of the Liverpool Independent Labour Party and a founding member of the Liverpool branch of the WOMEN'S SOCIAL AND POLITICAL UNION. She was on occasion described as an artist, but nothing is known of her career and she does not appear to have exhibited at any of the galleries that accepted work from her father. On 13 December 1906 she came to London, a member of a WSPU deputation of Lancashire women, was arrested in Parliament Square and sentenced to 14 days' imprisonment in Holloway. In February 1907 she was again arrested, after taking part in a deputation from Caxton Hall to the House of Commons, and was this time sentenced to one month's imprisonment. On 20 March 1907, a week after her release, she was again arrested, having been a member of the deputation, in which Lancashire was strongly represented, from the second Women's Parliament in Caxton Hall to the House of Commons. She again served a month's imprisonment. By early 1909 she had become WSPU organizer in Liverpool and was described in the 2 April 1909 issue of *Votes for Women* as "one of Miss Mary GAWTHORPE's most untiring workers, and a brilliant speaker". On 30 March 1909 Patricia Woodlock was arrested while taking part in a deputation from the eighth Women's Parliament and, a persistent offender, sentenced to three months' imprisonment. Her release from Holloway in June was the occasion for a cover cartoon on the 18 June issue of *Votes for Women*, a breakfast at the Inns of Court Hotel in Holborn and an evening procession to Hyde Park, followed by receptions in Manchester and Liverpool. In September 1909 she took part with Mary LEIGH, Charlotte MARSH and Mabel CAPPER in the disturbances during Asquith's visit to the Bingley Hall in Birmingham. She joined the hunger strike with her fellow suffragette prisoners in Winson Green but, according to the Visiting Committee report, when she saw the preparations being made to forcibly feed her, consented to "take food in the ordinary way". In July 1910 she was one of the platform speakers at the WSPU Hyde Park demonstration. Like so many other WSPU members she was arrested on "Black Friday" in November 1910 but was released without charge. She did not join the Liverpool contingent that took part in the March 1912 window-smashing campaign, having apparently been advised against it. This may be because the WSPU now considered it inadvisable for paid organizers to risk arrest. She certainly continued working for the WSPU in Liverpool, speaking at meetings (for instance at the Liverpool and District branch of the Catholic Women's Suffrage Society in June 1912) and selling newspapers.

Address: (1907) 27 South Hunter Street, Liverpool.
Photograph: in *Votes for Women*, 11 June 1909.
Archival source: Visiting Committee of HM Prison Winson Green, Birmingham Archives and Local Studies Library.

WOOLPIT (GROUP) (NUWSS) Secretary (1913) Mrs Foster, Lawn Farm, Woolpit, Bury St Edmunds, Suffolk.

WOOLWICH (WSPU) Secretary (1913) Miss Clifford, 4 Heathwood Gardens, Charlton, London SE.

WORCESTER (NUWSS) Secretary (1909) Miss Power, 5 Field Terrace, Bath Road, Worcester, Worcestershire; (1913) Miss N.M. Williams, 19 Droitwich Road, Worcester, Worcestershire.

WORKINGTON AND DISTRICT (NUWSS) In 1913 the society was a member of the NORTH-WESTERN FEDERATION OF THE NATIONAL UNION OF WOMEN'S SUFFRAGE SOCIETIES. Secretary (1913) Mrs E.H. Holden, MA, 25 Curwen Street, Workington, Cumberland.

WORTHING (NUWSS) In 1913 the society was a member of the SURREY, SUSSEX, AND HANTS FEDERATION OF THE NATIONAL UNION OF WOMEN'S SUFFRAGE SOCIETIES. Secretary (1913) Miss Helen Wright, 31 Warwick Street, Worthing, Sussex.

WORTHING (WSPU) Secretary (1913) Miss M. Douglas, Fox Down, Findon, Sussex.

WREXHAM (NUWSS) In 1913 the society was a member of the WEST LANCS, WEST CHESHIRE, AND NORTH WALES FEDERATION OF THE NATIONAL UNION OF WOMEN'S SUFFRAGE SOCIETIES. Secretary (1913) Miss Price, 76 Beechley Road, Wrexham, North Wales.

WRIGHT, ADA CECILE GRANVILLE (*c.* 1862–1939) Born at Granville, France, she attended the Slade and, at University College, physics lectures given by Margaret Whelpdale, half-sister to Octavia Hill, and English lectures given by Edward Aveling. She then spent a short time at an educational institution in Bonn and on her return to England expressed an interest in taking up social work. Her father refused to allow her to do so. She then accompanied her father and sister in travels through Europe and North Africa until the family eventually returned to England, settling in Sidmouth in 1885. She was now left to her own devices and worked at what she described as "a social centre", presumably a settlement, alongside a niece of Elizabeth Barrett Browning. It was in Sidmouth at this time that she first became interested in the movement for women's suffrage, joining the local suffrage society, and in 1886 helping to collect signatures for a petition. However, when she realized how ineffective the petition was, her enthusiasm waned.

Ada Wright eventually left Sidmouth and joined the West London Mission, worked with the Hon. Maude Stanley in running a club for working girls in Greek Street, Soho, and then became a probationer nurse at the London Hospital. In 1896, however, she had to return home in order to nurse her father. She continued to support the Women's Liberal Association and "progressive" candidates in county council and London School Board elections. Having moved to Bournemouth, she joined the local branch of the NATIONAL UNION OF WOMEN'S SUFFRAGE SOCIETIES. In October 1905, inspired by the arrest of Christabel PANKHURST and Annie KENNEY at the Free Trade Hall in Manchester, Ada Wright withdrew all she possessed, £12, from her post-office savings account and sent it to them. When she next paid a visit to London, in February 1906, she attended a meeting of the WOMEN'S SOCIAL AND POLITICAL UNION and in March 1907 she joined the deputation from the Women's Parliament in Caxton Hall to the Houses of Parliament, was arrested and imprisoned for two weeks. During the course of 1907 she gave £30 to the WSPU. In October 1908 she was imprisoned for a month after taking part in the attempt to "rush" the House of Commons. In February 1909 she sent a contribution to the *Women's Franchise* and in April gave £20 to the WSPU. She took part in the deputation to the House of Commons on 29 June and was arrested after throwing two stones through the window of a government office in Whitehall. She later wrote that "to a woman of culture and refinement the throwing of a stone as a protest required a great deal of moral courage – and it was almost a relief to be arrested". She was sentenced to a month's imprisonment and, refusing to be treated as a criminal, broke the windows in her cell. She went on hunger strike for six days and was then released.

For the next year Ada Wright worked continuously, voluntarily, for the WSPU, speaking at meetings all over the country, both in halls and at street corners, working at by-elections, and heckling and being thrown out of Liberal meetings. In April 1910 she gave a further £15 to the WSPU and later that year also subscribed to the NEW CONSTITUTIONAL SOCIETY FOR WOMEN'S SUFFRAGE. She was organizer for the "Colonial and Foreign Contingents" of the 18 June 1910 WSPU Procession. On "Black Friday", 18 November 1910, Ada Wright took part in the WSPU demonstration in Parliament Square. She later remarked that orders had been given from WSPU headquarters that there was to be no retreat. She was knocked to the ground several times, had her arm severely twisted by a policeman and suffered, she recorded, a great sense of humiliation. The front-page picture of the *Daily Mirror* of 19 November shows Ada Wright lying on the ground, a tiny cowering figure. The chief commissioner of police expressed the opinion that he thought from the smiling expression of a boy seen in the background, and from the fact that there was not a dense crowd around the police, that the woman had simply sunk to the ground exhausted with struggling with the police. The picture in the 25 November issue of *Votes for Women* shows that the police are holding back a large crowd, a man who had come to Ada Wright's aid has been seized by the police, and another policeman is bending over her, apparently about to grasp her by her upheld arm. Ada Wright's predicament produced the iconic image of "Black Friday". She reported that the government suppressed copies of the *Daily Mirror* and ordered negatives of the photographs to be destroyed. The WSPU made full use of its moral advantage and used a photograph of the incident in Leaflet 75 – "Plain Facts About Suffrage Deputations".

Ada Wright gave a donation to the MEN'S POLITICAL UNION and in January 1911, while staying with a friend in Switzerland, wrote to Hugh FRANKLIN on his release from prison. He had served a sentence for taking a whip to Churchill, whom he held responsible for the police brutality on "Black Friday". Ada Wright had taken fruit to him in Pentonville. Ada Wright herself was arrested on 21 November 1911 for breaking a window in the disturbances surrounding the WSPU protest at the government's "torpedoing" of the Conciliation Bill and was sentenced to 14 days' imprisonment. Before joining the deputation that day she wrote a letter from the Inns of Court Hotel to Maud Arncliffe SENNETT in which she remarked that before any militant activity "the suspense always tries me terribly". In March 1912 she took part in the window-smashing campaign and, when her previous record was taken into account, received a sentence of six months' imprisonment. She was sent to Aylesbury prison, went on a secret hunger strike, and was then forcibly fed for ten days until orders came from the WSPU headquarters that the hunger strike should cease. After three months the hunger strike was resumed. Ada Wright became very ill, was taken to the prison hospital and then, on 6 July, released. Philip Snowden had, at Maud Arncliffe Sennett's behest, asked a question in the House of Commons about Ada Wright's condition and she assumed that this intervention had led to her release after the completion of only four months of her sentence. She went with Charlotte MARSH and two other suffragette ex-prisoners to Switzerland to recover from her ordeal. In November 1912 she contributed to George LANSBURY's expenses when he stood at Bromley and Bow as a suffrage candidate.

On 1 May 1913 Mrs Pankhurst, released from Holloway under the "Cat and Mouse" Act, was taken to Ada Wright's flat in Westminster. On 15 June, having just sailed from Queenstown on her way to conduct family business in the United States, Ada Wright wrote from the RMS *Carmania* to Maud Arncliffe Sennett, describing to her the part she had played just over a week earlier in the drama surrounding the death of Emily Wilding DAVISON. Ada Wright had, with Mrs Green, in whose house Emily Davison had been living, travelled to Northumberland to give Mrs Davison comfort and a personal report on her daughter's condition. Emily Davison was at that time alive but unconscious. Ada Wright wrote that "We were three days and two nights on that journey and we did not take off our clothes or even have a decent wash for all the time we were on it as we travelled by night and came back by night and day." While she was in the US, Mrs Pankhurst was to have the use of her flat.

In 1914, after her return from the USA, Ada Wright continued to work for the WSPU. She was arrested on 10 February in a scuffle surrounding the escape of Mrs Pankhurst from "Mouse Castle" in Campden Hill and sentenced to 14 days' imprisonment. She was standing with Princess Duleep SINGH when Mrs Pankhurst addressed a crowd from the balcony of Gladys SCHÜTZE's house in Glebe Place. She was arrested, the Princess was not. In May 1914 she went with Mrs Pankhurst on the deputation to the King at Buckingham Palace. Again she was arrested, but her fine was paid without her consent. She only discovered years later that it was her sister, fearing the result to her health of more forcible feeding, who had paid the fine.

During the First World War Ada Wright groomed horses, worked in canteens and drove hospital motor ambulances. She remained in touch with Christabel Pankhurst, who when in England during the 1920s and 1930s stayed with her in Bayswater. Ada Wright was a pallbearer at Mrs Pankhurst's funeral. She was a member of the International Franchise Club (*see under* CLUBS), the WOMEN'S FREEDOM LEAGUE and the SUFFRAGETTE FELLOWSHIP, and was a supporter of its Record Room. In her will she named Ernest Lowy (*see* LOWY FAMILY) as one of her trustees and left bequests of £1600 to Christabel Pankhurst, £500 to Rosamund MASSY, £200 to Flora DRUMMOND, £150 to Nina BOYLE, £100 to Evie Hammill, sister of Cicely HAMILTON, £60 to Nurse PINE and £50 to the Suffragette Fellowship.

Address: (1907) Brankstone Wood Road, Bournemouth, Hampshire; (1909) 30 Ridgemount Gardens, London WC; (1913) 51 Westminster Mansions, Great Smith Street, Westminster, London SW; (1939) 20 Talbot House, St Martins Lane, London WC.

Photograph: in *Votes for Women*, 25 November 1910; photograph by Gertrude Salaman (née Lowy) in the Suffragette Fellowship Collection, Museum of London.

Archival source: Suffragette Fellowship Collection, Museum of London; Maud Arncliffe Sennett Papers, British Library.

WRIGHT, JANE GEORGINA MACKAY, LADY (*c.* 1860–1926) née Wilson Born in Co. Kildare, in 1889 married Almroth Wright (1861–1947), who by 1903 was professor of pathology at the Army Medical School and was knighted in 1906. The couple had two sons and a daughter. She subscribed to the National Society for Women's Suffrage in 1897 and to the CENTRAL SOCIETY FOR WOMEN'S SUFFRAGE in 1900, 1906 and 1907. In the summer of 1909 she contributed to the cost of the summer WOMEN'S SOCIAL AND POLITICAL UNION campaign in Lowestoft and in 1910 made a handsome donation to the MEN'S POLITICAL UNION. Her sister, Rebecca Wilson, died in 1912 and left £4000 to the NATIONAL UNION OF WOMEN'S SUFFRAGE SOCIETIES. In 1913, the year in which Lady Wright is recorded as a vice-president of the NATIONAL POLITICAL LEAGUE, her husband published *The Unexpurgated Case Against Woman Suffrage* "to show that the Women's Suffrage Movement has no real intellectual or moral sanction, and that there are very weighty reasons why the suffrage should not be conceded to women". He attributed the conduct of suffragettes to hysteria; his own drew remonstrances from fellow anti-suffragists. The couple had, unsurprisingly, by then been separated for several years.

As though to disprove any suggestion of hysteria, Lady Wright had built up a library of feminist books which, as the "Edward Wright Library", named for her son who died in 1913 while a student at Trinity College Dublin, was in 1922 combined with the Cavendish-Bentinck Library, and in 1931 became part of the Women's Service Library, and is now contained in the Fawcett Library (*see* LIBRARIES).

Address: (1925) 3 Park Square, West Portland Place, London.

WRIGHT, LOUISA (1849–1916) Born at Witchford, near Ely, inspired in 1872 by Lydia BECKER, she began suffrage activity, signing petitions and collecting signatures, in Darlington. In February 1882 Louisa Wright was invited to a drawing-room meeting organized by Mrs Henry Wilson as a prelude to the Sheffield Grand Demonstration of Women. After moving to Mansfield in the 1880s she began similar work there and became president of the MANSFIELD SOCIETY FOR WOMEN'S SUFFRAGE when it was formed in 1893. In 1889 she signed the Declaration in Favour of Women's Suffrage organized by the CENTRAL COMMITTEE OF THE NATIONAL SOCIETY FOR WOMEN'S SUFFRAGE and on 17 June 1911 took part in the Coronation Procession organized by the suffrage societies.

Address: (1882) Forest Hill, Mansfield, Nottinghamshire; (1916) 87 West Hill Drive, Mansfield, Nottinghamshire.

WRIGHT SISTERS Alexandra Wright (1879–1942) (later Signora Gambardella) Educated at Notting Hill High School, then graduated with a chemistry degree from Bedford College in 1903. After a short period of research at Bedford College, she worked as a research student at University College with Karl Pearson and with him co-published a paper. She was a member of the executive committee of the North Kensington Liberal Association, but left the Liberal Party in 1907 as a protest against the brutal manner in which women were ejected from a meeting in the Albert Hall organized by the WOMEN'S LIBERAL FEDERATION. A member of the LONDON SOCIETY FOR WOMEN'S SUFFRAGE, she was elected a member of the executive committee of the NATIONAL UNION OF WOMEN'S SUFFRAGE SOCIETIES in 1909, but resigned, unhappy with its election policy. She then joined the committee of the NEW CONSTITUTIONAL SOCIETY FOR WOMEN'S SUFFRAGE, becoming its honorary organizing secretary. In 1933, at Brompton Oratory, she married Cavaliere Crescenzo Gambardella. She died in Italy.

Her sister, [Frances] Gladys Wright (b. 1884) attended Bedford College for only the first term of the 1902 academic year, but by 1907 had merited a BA degree. Her political career followed that of her sister. In 1907 she was honorary secretary of the Kensington (North) branch of the London Society for Women's Suffrage and of the local Liberal Association, but resigned from the NUWSS to become honorary secretary of the New Constitutional Society for Women's Suffrage.

Address: (1913) 27 Pembridge Crescent, London W.

WYLIE, BARBARA FANNY (*c.* 1862–1954) One of four sisters, all of whom were very active members of the WOMEN'S SOCIAL AND POLITICAL UNION. Barbara Wylie joined the WSPU in 1909, was an organizer at the Camberwell by-election in April 1910, and then worked for the WSPU in Glasgow from September 1910 for at least a year. In 1912 she undertook a suffrage speaking tour across Canada. In April 1914 she was present, and was injured, in the fracas in St Andrew's Hall, Glasgow, while attempting to help Mrs PANKHURST evade arrest. On 22 May 1914 Barbara Wylie was arrested outside His Majesty's Theatre in London, during a visit of the Czar of Russia and King George and Queen Mary. Barbara Wylie remained faithful to the Pankhursts, working for their WOMEN'S PARTY at the end of the First World War and was a pallbearer at Mrs Pankhurst's funeral.

Address: (1914) 6 Blenheim Road, London NW; (1952) 67 Holland Road, London W.

Photograph: *Votes for Women*, 20 September 1912.

Y

YARMOUTH (NUWSS) In 1913 the society was a member of the EASTERN COUNTIES FEDERATION OF THE NATIONAL UNION OF WOMEN'S SUFFRAGE SOCIETIES. Secretary (1913) Miss Teasdel, Martelsham, Southtown, Gorleston, Norfolk.

YATES, ROSE LAMARTINE, MRS (1875–1954) Born in Brixton of French parentage, educated at Clapham and Truro High Schools, at Kassel and at the Sorbonne. In 1896 she entered Royal Holloway College, studying modern languages. She left before the end of her final year, but passed the Oxford final honours examination in modern languages and philology. In 1900 she married a solicitor, Tom Lamartine Yates. They were both keen cyclists and had met through the Cyclists Touring Club, to the council of which Rose was in 1907 elected as its first woman member. When she stood for this election she publicly stated that she was not a suffragette. However, a year later, in a speech titled "How I became a Suffragist", she wrote "on looking into the matter seriously I find I have never been anything else . . . and . . . I came to realise that I was and must remain one at whatever personal cost". She joined the Wimbledon branch of the WOMEN'S SOCIAL AND POLITICAL UNION soon after it was founded in January 1909, and quickly joined its committee.

For her birthday in January 1909 her husband gave Rose Lamartine Yates a letter containing the sentence, "The present I give thee is not gold or silver but permission freely and gladly, to offer up thy liberty for the benefit of downtrodden women." On 24 February 1909 Rose Lamartine Yates was a member of the deputation led by Emmeline PETHICK-LAWRENCE from Caxton Hall to the House of Commons. She was arrested and, despite her husband acting for her defence at her trial, was sentenced to one month's imprisonment. Her son was eight months old at the time. On her release she and 25 other suffragette prisoners were escorted in procession by WSPU members to a breakfast at the Inns of Court Hotel. She then returned to Merton; her home had been decorated in the WSPU colours to mark the occasion. At the end of April 1909 she was presented with one of the new illuminated addresses given to all WSPU members who had served at least one week's imprisonment and a "Holloway brooch" (*see* JEWELLERY), both of which had been designed by Sylvia PANKHURST. Rose Lamartine Yates continued as a very active member of the Wimbledon WSPU, chairing local meetings, indoors and on Wimbledon Common, often as the principal speaker. "A Month in a Common Gaol for the Faith" was the title of one of her popular talks and she gave a lantern lecture, "A true story of the militant campaign", "illustrated by actual photographs of events". In September 1909 she went on a brief lecture tour to Monmouth and Bath, probably staying with the BLATHWAYTS at Eagle House, Batheaston. She certainly planted an Austrian pine in "Annie's Arboretum". Rose Lamartine Yates supplied flowers, eggs, fruit and vegetables from her large garden to be sold at the Wimbledon WSPU SHOP. For her birthday in 1910 her husband's present to her was 48 chairs for the meeting room attached to the shop. In the course of the year she became treasurer and organizing secretary of the Wimbledon WSPU. In 1911 her husband's present was a clock for the WSPU shop. Wimbledon attracted a steady stream of eminent speakers from all the suffrage societies. Among regular visitors were Georgina BRACKENBURY, Mary GAWTHORPE, Emily Wilding DAVISON, Dr MANSELL-MOULLIN, George LANSBURY, Anne Cobden SANDERSON, who in 1913 spoke on "Women in the Workhouse", Ernest Duval who gave a talk on "Mary Astell", and H.D. HARBEN.

Rose Lamartine Yates spent summers with her son at the family's cottage in Seasalter near Whitstable and, with a fellow WSPU worker, Gertrude Wilkinson, who stayed nearby, carried on a suffrage campaign in that area. Tom Lamartine Yates, a member of the MEN'S POLITICAL UNION FOR WOMEN'S ENFRANCHISEMENT, was arrested during the demonstrations on 21 November 1911, protesting against the "torpedoing" of the Conciliation Bill. He was not prosecuted, but the publicity adversely affected his firm. He often acted as legal adviser for WSPU prisoners and in June 1913 he represented the Davison family at the inquest into the death of Emily Wilding Davison. Rose was the "first guard of honour" to Emily Davison's coffin on its journey between Epsom and King's Cross.

Until the outbreak of war in August 1914 Rose Lamartine Yates and the Wimbledon WSPU maintained a very active militant suffrage campaign. When the Home Secretary tried to prevent the WSPU from holding public meetings in open spaces Rose Lamartine Yates maintained the right of free speech on Wimbledon Common, in spite of facing hostile crowds and 300 police drafted in to control them.

At the beginning of the First World War the Wimbledon WSPU converted its meeting room and shop into a soup kitchen and then opened another in Merton. Rose Lamartine Yates was treasurer of the Distress Kitchens. Her record of loyalty to the Pankhursts came to an end when on 22 October 1915 she chaired a meeting of the WSPU at Caxton Hall, attended by members from many parts of the country, which produced a resolution addressed to Emmeline and Christabel PANKHURST, protesting at their abandonment of the cause of women's suffrage and calling for a statement of the WSPU accounts. No reply was received. Rose Lamartine Yates then became one of the committee members of the SUFFRAGETTES OF THE WSPU and a member of the Emily Wilding Davison Lodge (*see under* CLUBS). In 1928, at the dinner held to celebrate the final victory of enfranchisement, Rose Lamartine Yates and her husband specifically asked to be seated at Sylvia Pankhurst's table. In 1915 Paul Lamartine Yates had been the solicitor consulted by Sylvia Pankhurst over a family legal matter.

Rose Lamartine Yates was, with Una DUGDALE Duval, one of the prime movers behind the setting-up of the Suffragette Record Room (*see* SUFFRAGETTE FELLOWSHIP), performing the opening ceremony in May 1939. After the outbreak of war in September she ensured that the suffragette relics were packed up and removed to the country. Some of Emily Wilding Davison's papers that she had held since 1913 were not included in the Suffragette Fellowship Collection but were eventually inherited by her daughter-in-law, who donated them to the Fawcett Library.

Address: (1906) Dorset Hall, Merton, London SW.
Photograph: in John Innes Society, *Dorset Hall 1906–1935*, 1994.
Bibliography: A. Morley and L. Stanley, *The Life and Death of Emily Wilding Davison*, 1988; G. Hawtin, *Votes for Wimbledon Women*, 1993; John Innes Society, *Dorset Hall 1906–1935*, 1994.

YEOVIL (NUWSS)   In 1913 the society was a member of the WEST OF ENGLAND FEDERATION OF THE NATIONAL UNION OF WOMEN'S SUFFRAGE SOCIETIES. Secretary (1913) *pro tem* Miss Beatrice Brooke Smith, The Knoll, Yeovil, Somerset.

YORK (WFL)   Secretary (1913) Mrs Robinson, 30 Ratcliffe Street, York, Yorkshire.

YORK (WSPU)   Organizer (1913) Miss Key-Jones, Colby Chambers, Coppergate, York, Yorkshire.

YORKSHIRE SOCIETY FOR WOMEN'S SUFFRAGE Formed in 1873 when its honorary secretary was Mrs Buckton, 1 Victoria Chambers, South Parade, Leeds. She was succeeded by Mrs Alice SCATCHERD. The society was refounded as the York Women's Suffrage Society in 1889 and affiliated with the CENTRAL NATIONAL SOCIETY FOR WOMEN'S SUFFRAGE. By 1899 the work of the society was to all intents suspended. On 1 March 1901 a drawing-room meeting was held for the purpose of considering the position. Esther ROPER attended the meeting, and pointed out the need for patience and perseverance. She strongly urged the society to take up the work in York again. Shortly afterwards the committee met and appointed Miss Nield, MA, The Mount School as treasurer, Mrs Rawlings, 47 Wentworth Road as secretary, and Mrs Wilkinson, Dringhouses Manor as president. In 1901 the society asked to join the NATIONAL UNION OF WOMEN'S SUFFRAGE SOCIETIES and by 1913 it was a member of the NORTH AND EAST RIDINGS FEDERATION. Secretary

(1909) Miss Mary Cudworth, Butt's Close, Mount Villas, York; (1913) Mrs E.R. Meyer, The Nook, Huntingdon, York; Office 10 Museum Street, York, Yorkshire.

YOUNG HOT BLOODS A group of younger members of the WOMEN'S SOCIAL AND POLITICAL UNION, founded in 1907. The members, who included Grace ROE, Jessie KENNEY, Elsie HOWEY and Vera WENTWORTH, were under 30 years old, had to sign a pledge not to divulge the meaning of the letters "YHB", and were prepared to undertake "danger duty". Of the older members of the WSPU only Mrs PANKHURST was allowed to attend their meetings, which were held at a tea shop in the Strand. In 1908 a YHB choir sang each evening outside Holloway to keep up the morale of their fellows inside. The YHB was the idea of Mary Home, who before joining the WSPU office had worked for the WOMEN'S FRANCHISE DECLARATION COMMITTEE. She was responsible for clipping newspapers for information relevant to the WSPU campaign and it was presumably through her association with press agencies that the YHB was able to prepare for the Prince's Skating Rink exhibition in 1909 a history of the suffrage movement as seen through the eyes of the press photographers. A catalogue of the "Y.H.B. Photographic Exhibit" which, although unillustrated, gives the title of each photograph and name of the photographer (or his paper), is now held in the Fawcett Library Collection.

YOUNG PURPLE, WHITE, AND GREEN CLUB Aimed "to put it in the way of the young supporters of the Union [WOMEN'S SOCIAL AND POLITICAL UNION] to show real practical sympathy". The Club, which might have been a successor to the DRUMMERS' UNION, was in operation by June 1910 when it staged two suffrage plays, *The Reforming of Augustus* by Irene McLeod and *How Spring Came to Nutte Alley* at Greenwich Borough Hall. On 25 February 1911 the Young Purple, White, and Green Club presented a card "in grateful recognition of his services to the Womans Cause" (*sic*) to Hugh FRANKLIN. The card was signed by Rachel Ferguson (later a novelist and contributor to *Punch*) (Treasurer), Roma Ferguson (Property manager), Margaret Douglas, Jessie Bartlett (who may have been the daughter of Frances BARTLETT), Irene McLeod (b. 1891) (Stage manager). Other members of the Club were Helena Fraser, Norah Trowell, Helena Reinold, Ruth Lowy (*see* LOWY FAMILY), Gladys Larad, Violet George, Iris and Gwenda Rowe, and Winifred Walker. Patrons of the Club were Mrs McLeod, Mrs Ferguson (who was an active member of the Kensington WSPU), Isabel SEYMOUR and Isabel Green.

Bibliography: R. Ferguson, *Royal Borough*, 1950.

YOUNG SUFFRAGISTS Founded in 1926 to represent the young women who were still waiting to be enfranchised. It was associated with the WOMEN'S ELECTION COMMITTEE, and was prepared to adopt at least one strategy attempted by the WOMEN'S SOCIAL AND POLITICAL UNION, that of breaking into Buckingham Palace in order to present a letter to the King. President: Barbara Wootton.

YOUNGER SUFFRAGISTS An associate society of the NATIONAL UNION OF WOMEN'S SUFFRAGE SOCIETIES in 1910. Secretary Miss Dunlop, 10 Westminster Mansions, Great Smith Street, London SW.

Z

ZANGWILL, EDITH CHAPLIN, MRS (*c.* 1879–1945) Born in Japan, daughter of Professor W.E. Ayrton and his first wife, and cousin, Dr. Matilda Chaplin Ayrton (1846–83). Her maternal grandmother, Mrs Matilda Chaplin, who lived in Blandford Square close to Barbara BODICHON, signed the 1866 women's suffrage petition. After her mother's death Edith Ayrton was cared for in Sussex by Mrs Ayrton Chaplin, who was her father's cousin and her mother's sister-in-law, until her father's marriage to Hertha AYRTON. In November 1903 Edith Ayrton married Israel Zangwill; they eventually had three children. She took part in the "Mud March" in February 1907 and was a member of the NATIONAL UNION OF WOMEN'S SUFFRAGE SOCIETIES, until leaving to join the WSPU in 1909. In 1910 she gave a donation to the NEW CONSTITUTIONAL SOCIETY FOR WOMEN'S SUFFRAGE and in 1913 supported the NATIONAL POLITICAL LEAGUE. In 1914 she became a leading member of the UNITED SUFFRAGISTS. Edith Zangwill contributed a short story to the first issue of the *Freewoman*, edited by Dora MARSDEN and Mary GAWTHORPE, but publicly disassociated herself from the paper in the next issue, objecting to what she considered to be an attack on Christabel PANKHURST. Among her novels, *The Call*, published by Allen and Unwin in 1924 and dedicated "To all those who fought for the Freedom of Women", which centres on the militant suffrage struggle and on the experiences of a woman scientist in the First World War, is very clearly based on the life of her step-mother.

Address: (1913) Far End, East Preston, Sussex.
Photograph: in the *Vote*, 8 January 1910.
Bibliography: E. Hill, "Mrs Israel Zangwill", in the *Vote*, 8 January 1910; E. Sharp, *Hertha Ayrton*, 1926.

ZANGWILL, ISRAEL (1864–1926) Jewish, novelist, Zionist, and staunch supporter of the women's suffrage movement. He bought his house in Sussex from Henry Holiday, artist and fellow suffrage supporter, *c.* 1906–8. He was present at the banquet given on 11 December 1906 at the Savoy by Millicent Fawcett to celebrate the release of WOMEN'S SOCIAL AND POLITICAL UNION prisoners. Two of his speeches, "One and One are Two" and "Talked Out!", given at the Exeter Hall on 9 February and 8 March 1907 respectively, were published as an appendix to Brougham Villiers (ed.), *The Case for Women's Suffrage*, 1907. In April 1907 Zangwill joined the MEN'S LEAGUE FOR WOMEN'S SUFFRAGE. Among his other speeches, that given at the Queen's Hall on 7 June 1909 was published as "Old Fogeys and Old Bogeys", by the Woman's Press, that delivered at a WSPU rally on 10 November 1910 was published by the Garden City Press as "The Sword and the Spirit", and "The Hithertos", given to the WSPU on 28 March 1912, was also published by the Garden City Press. In 1913 Zangwill was a vice-president of the Men's League and in 1914 supported the UNITED SUFFRAGISTS.

Address: (1913) Far End, East Preston, Sussex.
Portrait: by Walter Sickert, Scottish National Gallery of Modern Art, Edinburgh.
Photograph: in the *Vote*, 16 January 1909.
Bibliography: E. Hill, "Mr Israel Zangwill", in the *Vote*, 16 January 1909.

Appendix: The Radical Liberal Family Networks

APPENDIX: THE RADICAL LIBERAL FAMILY NETWORKS

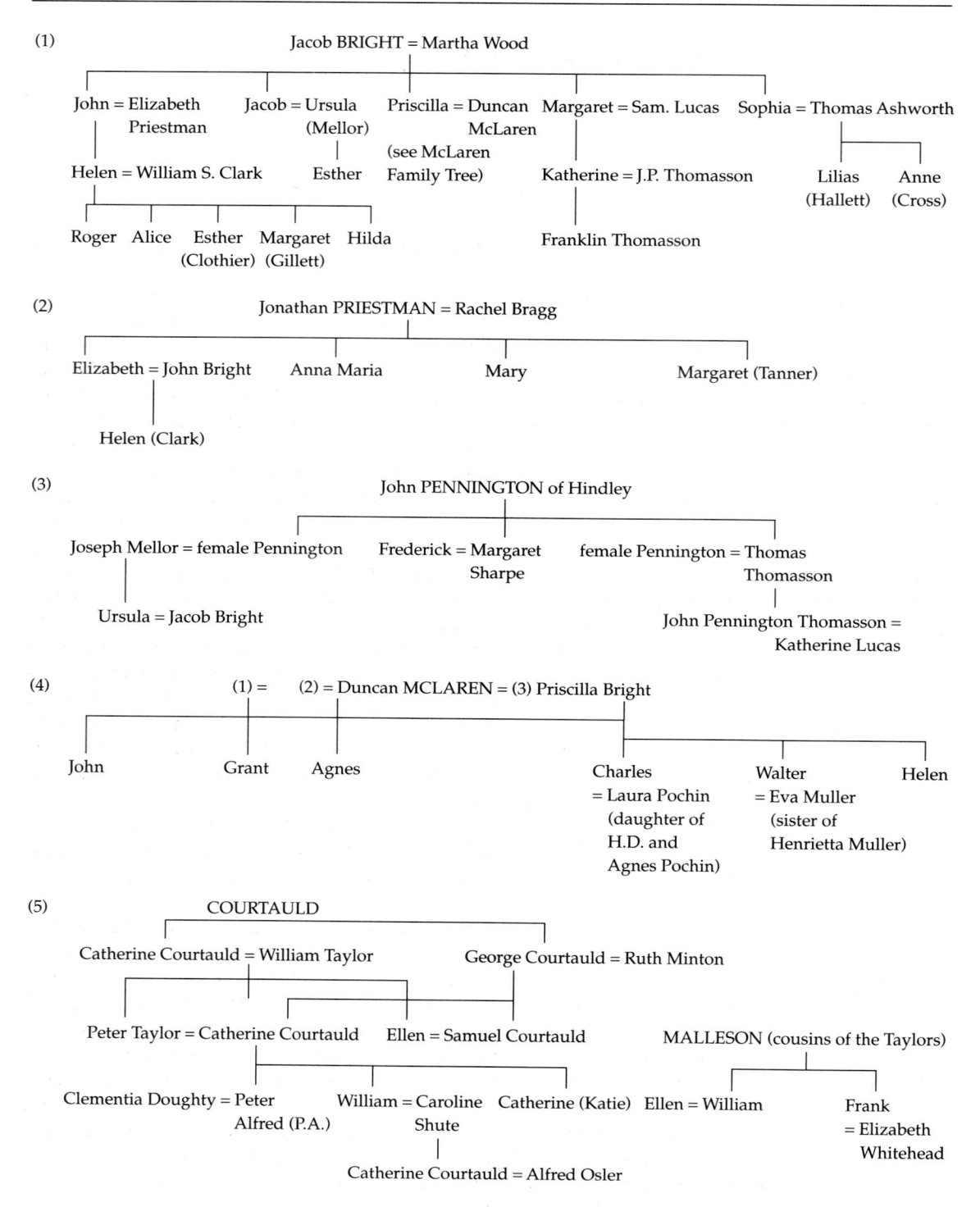

(1)

Jacob BRIGHT = Martha Wood

- John = Elizabeth Priestman
  - Helen = William S. Clark
    - Roger, Alice, Esther (Clothier), Margaret (Gillett), Hilda
- Jacob = Ursula (Mellor)
  - Esther
- Priscilla = Duncan McLaren (see McLaren Family Tree)
- Margaret = Sam. Lucas
  - Katherine = J.P. Thomasson
    - Franklin Thomasson
- Sophia = Thomas Ashworth
  - Lilias (Hallett), Anne (Cross)

(2)

Jonathan PRIESTMAN = Rachel Bragg

- Elizabeth = John Bright
  - Helen (Clark)
- Anna Maria
- Mary
- Margaret (Tanner)

(3)

John PENNINGTON of Hindley

- Joseph Mellor = female Pennington
  - Ursula = Jacob Bright
- Frederick = Margaret Sharpe
- female Pennington = Thomas Thomasson
  - John Pennington Thomasson = Katherine Lucas

(4)

(1) =   (2) = Duncan MCLAREN = (3) Priscilla Bright

- John
- Grant
- Agnes
- Charles = Laura Pochin (daughter of H.D. and Agnes Pochin)
- Walter = Eva Muller (sister of Henrietta Muller)
- Helen

(5)

COURTAULD

- Catherine Courtauld = William Taylor
- George Courtauld = Ruth Minton

- Peter Taylor = Catherine Courtauld
- Ellen = Samuel Courtauld
- MALLESON (cousins of the Taylors)

- Clementia Doughty = Peter Alfred (P.A.)
- William = Caroline Shute
  - Catherine Courtauld = Alfred Osler
- Catherine (Katie)
- Ellen = William
- Frank = Elizabeth Whitehead

Acknowledgements

I was delighted by the excellent response to a letter asking for details of material relating to the women's suffrage campaign that I sent to all the record offices and main libraries in England, Scotland and Wales. Even if they did not hold any manuscript material many of the librarians took the trouble to photocopy relevant reports in local papers, which have proved very useful in spotting the campaigners as they travelled around the country. The following institutions do hold relevant material and I am indebted to their staff for the helpfulness and efficiency I experienced in the course of my visits, and, where relevant, for permission to quote from papers in their possession: Aberdeen Art Gallery; Bedfordshire Record Office; Birmingham Central Library, Archives Division; Bishopsgate Institute Library; Bodleian Library, Department of Special Collections and Western Manuscripts, Oxford; Bolton Archive Service; British Library, Department of Manuscripts; British Library of Political and Economic Science; Bristol University Library; Cambridgeshire County Record Office, Cambridge; Camden Local History Unit, Holborn Library; Camellia plc; Colindale Newspaper Library; Dundee District Archive and Record Centre; Dyrham Park, The National Trust; Friends' Library, London; Essex Record Office; Fawcett Library, London; Girton College Archive, Cambridge; Glamorgan Record Office, Cardiff; Guildhall Library, City of London; Hammersmith and Fulham Archives; Kensington and Chelsea Local Studies Library; Lancashire Record Office; London Metropolitan Archives; Manchester Central Library, Local Studies Unit; Manchester City Art Gallery; Marx Memorial Library, London; Mitchell Library, Glasgow; Morley Reference Library; National Film Archive; National Portrait Gallery Archive; Newnham College Archive, Cambridge; Trustees of the National Library of Scotland, Edinburgh; North-West Sound Archive, Greater Manchester County Record Office Listening Station; Nottinghamshire Archives; Oldham Local Studies Library; Portsmouth City Records Office; Rochester upon Medway City Archives; Scottish Record Office, Edinburgh; Sheffield Archives, Sheffield Central Library; Southampton Archives Services; Victoria and Albert Museum Library and Print Room; West Sussex Record Office.

I have been particularly grateful for the service offered by the Public Record Office, Kew; the Family Record Centre; the Principal Registry of the Family Division; the Museum of London; David Doughan and the staff, past and present, of the Fawcett Library; and the staff and architect of the British Library, who have made working in the new building such a pleasure.

I am grateful to the following who have been generous with their time and with information; their interest and kindness has been appreciated: Lord Aberconway; Donald Bedford; Allan Bland; James Blewitt; Jim and Phyllis Bratt; Miss Elizabeth Bushnell, for detective work in the Eastern Cemetery, St Andrews; Irene Cockcroft; Krista Cowman; Ann Dingsdale; jay Dixon; Carol Dyhouse; Mr G. Fong; Livia Gollancz; Philip and Myrna Goode; Dr Sheila Hamilton; Pam Hirsch; Fred Hunter; Judy Goodman of the John Innes Society, Wimbledon; Leah Leneman; Jill Liddington; Terence Pepper, Curator of the Photographic Collection, National Portrait Gallery; Dr Mary Prior; Christine Pullen; June Purvis; Michael Rubinstein; Virginia Russell; Dr Anne Sutherland; Ruth Tomalin; Claire Tylee; Rosemary van Arsdel; Teresa Vanneck-Murray; Dr I.M. Webb; Colin White; and the archivists of University College, London, of St Andrews and Aberdeen Universities, of Lady Margaret Hall, Somerville, and Royal Holloway Colleges, of St Bartholomew's Hospital, Birmingham Museums and Art Gallery, Southampton Art Gallery; and librarians at Grantham, Orkney and Great Yarmouth.

A welcoming screen-saving message from my children, Agnes, Edmund, and Beatrice, has been my affectionate companion in archives and libraries around the country and reminded me, as I recreated in my mind the past, that life is also the here and now.

Archival Sources

I have given accession numbers when the papers may be difficult to identify; most of the manuscript material consulted is easy to locate in archive listings.

Aberdeen Museums and Art Gallery: Papers of Caroline Phillips.

Bedfordshire Record Office: Documents relating to the Bedford Society for Women's Suffrage, 1908–18.

Birmingham Central Library, Archives Division: Birmingham Women's Suffrage Society, 1900–1921; National Union of Women Workers, Birmingham branch; Birmingham Society for Promoting the Election of Women on Local Governing Bodies, 1907–21; letters of Mary S. Florence; Minutes of the Visiting Committee of HM Prison, Winson Green.

Bishopsgate Institute Library, London: Diaries and Papers of George Jacob Holyoake.

Bodleian Library, Department of Western Manuscripts, Oxford: John Johnson Collection (which among a wide and random variety of interesting leaflets includes material issued by the Women's Emancipation Union not found anywhere else); Papers of Evelyn Sharp; Papers of H.W. Nevinson.

Bolton Archive Service: Minute books of Bolton Women's Suffrage Association, 1908–20; Minute books of Bolton Women Citizen's Association 1923–8; Haslam Papers.

Bristol University Library: Papers of Jane Cobden Unwin.

The British Library, London: Maud Arncliffe Sennett Collection; Archives of Kegan Paul, Trench, Trubner and Henry S. King, 1858–1912; Archives of Swan Sonnenschein & Co., 1878–1911; *The Times* (all on microfilm).

The British Library, London: Additional Manuscripts Collection: Elizabeth Wolstenholme Elmy Papers; Harben/Pankhurst correspondence; Olive Wharry's Prison Diary; Balfour Papers (correspondence with Christabel Pankhurst and Annie Kenney).

Cambridgeshire County Record Office, Cambridge: in particular Minutes of the Cambridge Women's Suffrage Association 1884–1930.

Camellia plc, London: papers of Mary Phillips; Minute book of the Central Committee of the National Society for Women's Suffrage, 1896–8.

Carmarthen Record Office: Minute book of the Carmarthen Women's Suffrage Society.

Dundee District Archive and Record Centre: Memories of Miss I. Carrie.

Dyrham Park, Avon (The National Trust): diaries of Mary and Emily Blathwayt.

Essex Record Office, Chelmsford: Eliza Vaughan on the Pilgrimage (T/Z 11/27); Miss G.M. Alderman on life in Holloway (T/Z11/27); copy of letter from Anne Knight, Chelmsford, about franchise for women (T/Z 20/47).

Family Record Centre, London: holds volumes containing records, by quarter, of all births, marriages and deaths in England and Wales since 1837. One can also book a link to the very much more efficient Scottish system, which has been computerized. The FRC also holds microfilm of the English and Welsh censuses 1841–91.

Fawcett Library, Guildhall University, London: Autograph letter collection; taped interviews by Brian Harrison; a very wide range of printed and manuscript material relating to individual suffrage societies; microfilms of archives held elsewhere (including, in particular, the Manchester Suffrage Collection, the Suffragette Fellowship Collection (Museum of London) and the Papers of Sylvia Pankhurst (Internationaal Instituut voor Sociale Geschiedenis, Amsterdam); artefacts related to suffrage societies; and the photographic collection, which contains images of a very wide range of suffrage personalities and events.

Friends' Library, London: biographical details of members of the Society of Friends; papers of Anne Knight; papers concerning the Friends' League for Women's Suffrage.

General Register Office (Scotland), Edinburgh: holds registers of births, marriages and deaths in Scotland since 1855 and of all Scottish parish registers earlier than 1855.

Girton College Archive, Cambridge: Helen Blackburn Collection and Library; papers of Bessie Rayner Parkes.

Glamorgan Record Office, Cardiff: Minutes of the Cardiff and District Women's Suffrage Society; Minutes of the Penarth branch of NUWSS 1910–15.

Hammersmith and Fulham Archives: letter from Anne Cobden Sanderson (1907) and cuttings relating to her (DD/375/11); duplicated list of officers and committee of the NUWSS Central Society for Women's Suffrage, Shepherd's Bush Executive (DD/375/382); cuttings concerning demonstration of Mrs Montefiore, 1906.

Lancashire Record Office, Preston: Papers of Selina Jane Cooper; NUWSS Clitheroe branch treasurer's book, 1912–21.

London Metropolitan Archives: papers relating to the Elizabeth Garrett Anderson Hospital.

London School of Economics and Political Science, Archives Division: Mill–Taylor Papers; Fabian Society Archives.

Museum of London: The Suffragette Fellowship Collection (some of which has been microfilmed and is also available in the Fawcett Library), together with its accompanying photographic collection; the David Mitchell Collection.

Scottish Record Office, Edinburgh: in particular Scottish Office Prison Commission files. The SRO has produced a leaflet as a guide to suffrage material in its holding.

Manchester Central Library, Local Studies Unit: Papers of the Manchester branch of the National Union of Women's Suffrage Societies and the North of England Society for Women's Suffrage; Papers of Millicent Garrett Fawcett (the Fawcett Library now holds microfilm copies of these papers); Biographical index of local personalities.

Manchester City Art Gallery: papers relating to Annie Swynnerton.

Marx Memorial Library, London: typescript autobiography of Helen Crawfurd.

Morley Reference Library: Scatcherd Papers.

Mitchell Library, Glasgow: Glasgow and West of Scotland Association for Women's Suffrage minute books, 1902–18, letter books 1913–18; Minute Books of Scottish Women's Hospitals and Glasgow and West of Scotland Association for Women's Suffrage Hospitals Committee, 1915–19.

National Film Archive, London: a source sheet lists newsreel films relating to the women's suffrage campaign – many of the films can be viewed by appointment.

National Library of Scotland, Edinburgh, Department of Manuscripts: Janie Allan Papers; Emrys Hughes Papers (son-in-law of Keir Hardie), which contain material on Margaret Travers-Symons; WSPU album assembled by Miss E.M. Gorrie; some WSPU postcards; Men's League for Women's Suffrage, Glasgow branch; Roland Muirhead Papers; Papers of Priscilla Bright McLaren.

National Portrait Gallery Archive, London: the "Sitters' Boxes" contain a wide variety of images, of portraits and photographs in the main collection but also of items that are not – for example, copies of portraits that have been offered to the Gallery but refused, images culled from auction catalogues, and copies of portraits held in private collections.

Newnham College Archive, Cambridge: Newnham College Newsletters.

North-West Sound Archive, Greater Manchester County Record Office Listening Station: the Archive's catalogue lists interviews and radio items relating to the women's suffrage campaign.

Nottinghamshire Archives: Minute books of the Mansfield Women's Suffrage society, 1893–1918; Minute books of the Nottingham and Nottinghamshire branch of the NUWSS 1909–24; Dowson Papers; Papers of Helen Watts.

Oldham Local Studies Library: Lees Family Papers.

Portsmouth City Records Office: collection of books from the library of the NUWSS Portsmouth branch; Harriet Blessley's manuscript account of her participation in the NUWSS Pilgrimage; Lancelot Surry's transcript recollections of his mother's involvement in the Portsmouth branch of the WSPU.

Principal Registry of the Family Division, London: holds volumes containing entries of wills that have been entered for probate.

Public Record Office, Kew: provides a useful checklist, "Source Sheet no 16 – Suffragettes", giving brief details of likely files. HO 144 Home Office Registered Papers: Supplementary – I looked at a wide selection of files in this category but will mention in particular: /847/149245 Suffragettes' prosecution at Westminster in connection with the procession to the House of Commons (1907); /837/145641 Complaints of Treatment in Prison by Suffragettes (Anne Cobden Sanderson *et al.*) 1906; /1041/183189 Release of hunger-striking suffragettes from a Manchester prison (1909); /1255/234788 Lilian Lenton (1913–14); /1261/236533 "Phyllis Brady" (Elsie Duval, 1913–14); /1254/234646 Emmeline Pankhurst (1913–17); /1038/180782 Prison treatment of suffragettes (1908–10); /1041/182749 and /1052/187234 Suffragettes in Liverpool prison (1909–10); /1205/221999 Hunger strikes at Aylesbury prison; /1268/238215 Sydney Drew (printer) found guilty of publishing articles inciting suffragettes to commit arson; /1318/252288 Police raid on WSPU headquarters.

MEPO 2/ Metropolitan Police Papers: under this category I will draw attention in particular to: /1016 The Suffragette movement: disturbances and convictions (1906–7); /1308 Suffragette disturbances: instructions to police (1910); /1438 Suffragette demonstrations: police procedure (1911); /1488 Suffragettes: arrest of 200 for assaults on police and other offences (1911–12); /1551 Suffragettes: accident involving His Majesty's horse and jockey (1913).

PCOM 8/ Registered Papers: Supplementary Series 1 in particular: /174 Emily Wilding Davison "Derby Outrage" (1912–13); /175 Emmeline Pethick-Lawrence (1912–14); /228 Suffragettes: Instructions to Prison Governors (1912).

TS 27/ Treasury Solicitor Papers: in particular /28 Fraudulent assignment for sale of his furniture by Edwy Clayton, which also includes material on Olive Hockin.

I would also like to draw attention to the PRO's holdings of information on companies with which women were involved; these are an extremely useful and hitherto untapped source of evidence of individual and group involvement in interesting enterprises.

Rochester upon Medway City Archives: material relating to Vera Conway Gordon.

Scottish Record Office, Edinburgh: wills of Scotswomen.

Sheffield Archives: Pamphlets and correspondence on women's suffrage, 1872–82, held as part of the correspondence of H.J. Wilson; Minute book of the Barnsley Women's Suffrage Society, 1913–33.

Sheffield Central Library, Local Studies Department: J.H. Copley, *The Women's Suffrage Movement in South Yorkshire* (unpublished thesis) (324.4274 SQ).

Southampton City Archives Office: Minute book of the Southampton branch of the NUWSS 1911–14.

West Sussex Record Office, Chichester: Papers of Jane Cobden Unwin.

Westminster Archives: Papers of the Ladies' Residential Dwellings Company.

Guildhall Library; London Metropolitan Archives; Bishopsgate Institute: a wide variety of Post Office and street directories.

NEWSPAPERS AND JOURNALS

Colindale Newspaper Library: *Britannia; Clarion; Conservative & Unionist Women's Franchise Review; Graphic; Illustrated London News; Independent Suffragette; Journal of Vigilance Association for the Defence of Personal Rights; Forward;* the *Freewoman; Labour Leader; Labour Record and Review; Shafts,* the *Suffragist; Women's Dreadnought; Woman; Woman's Opinion; Women's Franchise; Women's Gazette; Women's Penny Paper; Women's Suffrage; Women's Suffrage News. Deacon's Newspaper Handbook; May's Press Guide* (late nineteenth-century editions).

Fawcett Library: *Awakener; Calling All Women;* the *Catholic Citizen;* the *Coming Day;* the *Common Cause; Englishwoman; English Woman's Journal; Englishwoman's Review; Free Church Suffrage Times; Men's League for Women's Suffrage; Suffragette News Sheet;* the *Vote; Votes for Women; Woman's Herald; Woman's Leader; Women's Suffrage Journal; Woman's Signal; Woman's Tribune.*

Select Bibliography

Aberdeen, Lord and Lady, *"We Twa": Reminiscences*, Collins, 1925.

Adam, R., *A Woman's Place 1910–1975*, Chatto & Windus, 1975.

Adams, P., *Somerville for Women: An Oxford College 1879–1993*, Oxford University Press, 1996.

Adlard, E. (ed.), *Edy: Recollections of Edith Craig*, Muller, 1949.

Alberti, J., *Beyond Suffrage: Feminists in War and Peace, 1914–28*, Macmillan, 1989.

Alberti, J., *Eleanor Rathbone*, Sage Publications, 1996.

Acres, E.L., *Helen Hanson*, H.R. Allenson, no date (c. 1927).

Alcott, L.M., *Shawl Straps*, Sampson Low & Co., 1873.

Alexander, S. (ed.), *Women's Fabian Tracts*, Routledge (Women's Source Library), 1988.

Alexander, S., *Becoming a Woman: And Other Essays in 19th and 20th Century Feminist History*, Virago, 1994.

Allen, M., *The Pioneer Policewoman*, Chatto & Windus, 1925.

Allen, M., *Lady In Blue*, Stanley Paul, 1936.

Allen, M. and Heyneman, J., *Woman at the Cross Roads*, The Unicorn Press, 1934.

Altick, R.D., *The Cowden Clarkes*, Oxford University Press, 1948.

Anderson, L. Garrett, *Elizabeth Garrett Anderson*, Faber, 1939.

Anderson, N.F., *Women against Women in Victorian England: A Life of Eliza Lynn Linton*, Indiana University Press, 1987.

Andrews, S., *Crested China: The History of Heraldic Souvenir Ware*, Springwood Books (Horndean), 1980.

Anstruther, I., *Coventry Patmore's Angel: A Study of Coventry Patmore, His Wife Emily and* The Angel in the House, Haggerston Press, 1992.

Armstrong, R.A., *Henry William Crosskey: His Life and Work*, Cornish Bros (Birmingham), 1895.

Ashby, Dame Margery Corbett, *Memoirs*, with additional material by Dr Michael Ashby, M.G. Ashby, 1996.

Ashwell, L., *Myself a Player*, Michael Joseph, 1936.

Askwith, B., *Lady Dilke: A Biography*, Chatto & Windus, 1969.

Atkinson, D., *Mrs Broom's Suffragette Photographs: Photographs by Christina Broom 1908 to 1913*, Nishen Photography, no date, 1980s.

Atkinson, D., *The Purple, White, and Green: Suffragettes in London, 1906–14*, Museum of London, 1992.

Atkinson, D., *The Suffragettes in Pictures*, Sutton Publishing/Museum of London, 1996.

Baedeker, K., *London and its Environs*, Dulau & Co., 1881.

Baker, M., *Our Three Selves: A Life of Radclyffe Hall*, Hamish Hamilton, 1985.

Balfour, B. (ed.), *Letters of Constance Lytton*, William Heinemann, 1925.

Ballantyne, J. (ed.), *Researcher's Guide to British Newsreels*, British Universities Film and Video Council, 1983.

Banks, O., *Faces of Feminism*, Martin Robertson, 1981.

Banks, O., *The Biographical Dictionary of British Feminists*, vol. 1, *1800–1930*, Harvester, 1985; vol. 2: *A Supplement, 1900–1945*, Harvester, 1990.

Banks, O., *Becoming a Feminist: The Social Origins of "First Wave" Feminism*, 1986.

Banks, O., *The Politics of British Feminism, 1918–1970*, Edward Elgar, 1993.

Barrow, M., *Women 1870–1928; A Select Guide to Printed and Archival Sources in the United Kingdom*, Mansell Publishing, 1981.

Barry, K., *Susan B. Anthony: A Biography*, New York University Press, 1988.

Barnsby, G.J., *Votes for Women: The Struggle for the Vote in the Black Country 1900–1918*, Integrated Publishing Services, 1995.

Baylen, J. and Gossman, N.C., *Biographical Dictionary of Modern British Radicals*, 1984.

Beddoe, A.M., *The Early Years of the Women's Suffrage Movement*, Bradford-on-Avon, 1911.

Begg, T., *The Excellent Women*, John Donald Publishers (Edinburgh), 1994.

Belchem, J., *Popular Radicalism in Nineteeth-Century Britain*, Macmillan Press, 1996.

Bellamy, J. and Saville, J., *Dictionary of Labour Biography*, Macmillan, 1970s–1990s.

Benn, C., *Keir Hardie*, Richard Cohen Books, 1997.

Bennett, D., *Emily Davies and the Liberation of Women*, Deutsch, 1990.

Bentwich, H., *If I Forget Thee: Some Chapters of Autobiography 1912–1920*, Elek, 1973.

Biggs, C.A., "Great Britain", in Stanton, E.C., Anthony, S.B. and Gage, M.J. (eds), *History of Woman Suffrage*, Vol. III *(1876–1885)*, 1886.

Blackburn, H., *A Handbook for Women Engaged in Social and Political Work*, J.W. Arrowsmith, 1881.

Blackburn, H., *Women's Suffrage: A Record of the Women's Suffrage Movement in the British Isles, with Biographical Sketches of Miss Becker*, Williams and Norgate, 1902.

Blackburn, H., "Great Britain", in Anthony, S.B. and Harper, I.H. (eds), *History of Woman Suffrage*, Vol. IV *(1883–1900)*, 1902, reprinted Arno and The New York Times, 1969.

Blain, V., Clements, P. and Grundy, I. (eds), *Feminist Companion to Literature in English: Women Writers from the Middle Ages to the Present*, Batsford, 1990.

Bland, L., *Banishing the Beast: English Feminism and Sexual Morality 1885–1914*, Penguin, 1995.

Blatch, H.S. and Lutz, A., *Challenging Years; The Memoirs of Harriot Stanton Blatch*, G.P. Putnam's Sons, 1940.

Boll, T.E.M., *Miss May Sinclair: Novelist*, Fairleigh Dickinson University Press, 1973.

Bolt, C. and Drescher, S. (eds), *Anti-Slavery, Religion and Reform*, Dawson & Sons, 1980.

Bolt, C., *The Women's Movements in the United States and Britain from the 1790s to the 1920s*, Harvester Wheatsheaf, 1993.

Boon, J., *Under Six Reigns: The House of Waterlow* [Waterlow Bros and Layton], 1925.

Boyle's Court Guide, 1910.

Bosch, M., *Politics and Friendship: Letters from the International Woman Suffrage Alliance, 1902–1942*, Ohio State University Press, 1990.

Branca, P., *Silent Sisterhood: Middle-class Women in the Victorian Home*, Croom Helm, 1975.

Bright, E., *The Ancient One*, Theosophical Publishing House, 1927.

Bright, E., *Old Memories and Letters of Annie Besant*, Theosophical Publishing House, 1936.

Bright, Mrs J. (ed.), *An Evil Law Unfairly Enforced*, E.W. Allen, 1885.

Bright, Mrs J. (ed.), *Speeches of Jacob Bright*, Simpkin, Marshall & Co., 1885.

Brittain, V., *Pethick-Lawrence: A Portrait*, George Allen & Unwin, 1963.

Brockway, F., *Towards Tomorrow*, Hart-Davis MacGibbon, 1977.

Brookes, P., *Women at Westminster; An Account of Women in the British Parliament 1918–1966*, Peter Davies, 1967.

Brown, L., *Victorian News and Newspapers*, Clarendon Press, 1985.

Brownlow, K., *Behind the Mask of Innocence: Films of Social Conscience in the Silent Era*, Jonathan Cape, 1990.

Bryant, M., *The Unexpected Revolution: A Study in the History of Education of Women and Girls in the Nineteenth Century*, University of London Institute of Education, 1979.

Buckley, J., *Joseph Parkes of Birmingham*, Methuen, 1926.

Bullock, I. and Pankhurst, R. (eds), *Sylvia Pankhurst: From Artist to Anti-Fascist*, Macmillan, 1992.

Burkhauser, J. (ed.), *Glasgow Girls: Women in Art and Design 1880–1912*, Canongate, 1990.

Burman, S. (ed.), *Fit Work for Women*, Croom Helm, 1979.

Burton, H., *Barbara Bodichon 1827–1891*, John Murray, 1949.

Burton, K., *According to the Pattern: The Story of Dr Agnes McLaren and the Society of Catholic Medical Missionaries*, Longmans, 1946.

Bussey, G. and Tims, M., *Pioneers for Peace: Women's International League for Peace and Freedom 1915–1965*, 2nd edn, 1980.

Caine, B., *Victorian Feminists*, Oxford University Press, 1992.

Caine, B., *English Feminism, 1780–1980*, Oxford University Press, 1997.

Callen, A., *Angel in the Studio: Women Artists of the Arts and Crafts Movement, 1870–1914*, Astragal Books, 1979.

Camp, J., *Holloway Prison: The Place and the People*, David & Charles, 1974.
Carter, H., (ed.), *Women's Suffrage and Militancy*, Frank Palmer, 1912.
Casteras, S.P. and Denney, C., *The Grosvenor Gallery: A Palace of Art in Victorian England*, Yale University Press, 1996.
Cherry, D., *Painting Women: Victorian Women Artists*, Routledge, 1993.
Chew, D.N. (ed.), *Ada Nield Chew: The Life and Writings of a Working Woman*, Virago, 1982.
Clarke, P., *Lancashire and the New Liberalism*, Cambridge University Press, 1971.
Clayton, E., *English Female Artists*, Tinsley Brothers, 1876.
Clayton, F.H., *The Claytons Since 1800 A.D.*, privately published, 1959.
Clayton, K., *Memoir of Bishop Clayton: Some Personal Reminiscences Written in 1917*, Cambridge University Press, 1927.
Cline, S., *Radclyffe Hall: A Woman Called John*, John Murray, 1997.
Coates, D., *George Coates: His Art and His Life*, Dent, 1937.
Cobbe, F. Power, *The Life of Frances Power Cobbe by Herself*, Houghton, Mifflin & Co., 1894.
Cockin, K., *Edith Craig (1869–1947): Dramatic Lives*, Cassell, 1998.
Codd, C., *So Rich a Life*, Institute for Theosophical Publicity, 1951.
Cole, M., *Women of Today*, Nelson, 1938.
Cole, M., *Growing Up in to Revolution*, Longmans, 1949.
Collette, C., *For Labour and For Women: The Women's Labour League, 1906–18*, Manchester University Press, 1989.
Colville, J., *Strange Inheritance*, Michael Russell (Salisbury), 1983.
Conway, M., *Travels in South Kensington*, Trubner, 1882.
Corder, P., *Robert Spence Watson*, Headley Bros, 1914.
Cossart, M. de, *The Food of Love, Princesse Edmond de Polignac (1865–1943) and her Salon*, Hamish Hamilton, 1978.
Courtauld, S.L., *The Huguenot Family of Courtauld*, privately printed, 1957.
Courtney, J.E., *The Women of My Time*, Lovat Dickson, 1934.
Covert, J.T. (ed.), *Memoirs of a Victorian Woman: Reflections of Louise Creighton, 1850–1936*, Indiana University Press, 1994.
Crane, W., *Cartoons for the Cause*, Twentieth Century Press, 1896.
Crawford, A., *C.R. Ashbee: Architect, Designer and Romantic Socialist*, Yale University Press, 1985.
Crofton, E., *The Women of Royaumont: A Scottish Women's Hospital on the Western Front*, Tuckwell Press, 1997.
Crunden, C., *A History of Anstey College of Physical Education 1897–1972*, Anstey College (Sutton Coldfield), 1974.
Cunningham, H., *Leisure in the Industrial Revolution*, Croom Helm, 1980.
Daims, D. and Grimes, J., with editorial assistance of Doris Robinson, *Towards a Feminist Tradition: An Annotated Bibliography of Novels in English by Women 1891–1920*, Garland, 1982.
Daley, C. and Nolan, M. (eds), *Suffrage and Beyond: International Feminist Perspectives*, Auckland University Press, 1994.
Dangerfield, G., *The Strange Death of Liberal England*, Constable, 1936.
Daniels, E.A., *Jessie White Mario: Risorgimento Revolutionary*, Ohio University Press, 1972.
Darley, G., *Octavia Hill: A Life*, Constable, 1990.
David, E. (ed.), *Inside Asquith's Cabinet: From the Diaries of Charles Hobhouse*, John Murray, 1977.
Davidoff, L. and Hall, C., *Family Fortunes: Men and Women of the English Middle Class 1780–1850*, Hutchinson, 1987.
Davies, M. Llewellyn, *The Women's Co-operative Guild, 1883–1904*, Women's Co-operative Guild, 1904.
Dee, L. and Keineg, K. (eds), *Women in Wales*, Women Unite Press, 1987.
Dennis, B. and Skilton, D. (eds), *Reform and Intellectual Debate in Victorian England*, Croom Helm, 1987.
Dennis, R., *Catalogue of an Exhibition of Doulton Stoneware and Terracotta, 1870–1925*, Richard Dennis, 1971.
Dewar, D.L., *History of the Glasgow Society of Lady Artists' Club*, Maclehose, 1950.
Dictionary of National Biography, Oxford University Press.
Dobbie, B.M. Willmott, *A Nest of Suffragettes in Somerset*, The Batheaston Society, 1979.

Doughan, D. and Sanchez, D., *Feminist Periodicals 1855–1984: An Annotated Critical Bibliography of British, Irish, Commonwealth and International Titles*, Harvester, 1987.

Dove, I., *Yours in the Cause: Suffragettes in Lewisham, Greenwich and Woolwich*, Lewisham Library Services and Greenwich Libraries, 1988.

Dubois, E.C., *Harriot Stanton Blatch and the Winning of Woman Suffrage*, Yale University Press, 1997.

Dunford, P., *A Biographical Dictionary of Women Artists in Europe and America since 1850*, Harvester Wheatsheaf, 1990.

Dunham, J., *Amy K. Browning*, Boudicca (Saxmundham), 1995.

Dyhouse, C., *Feminism and the Family in England 1880–1939*, Basil Blackwell, 1989.

Dyhouse, C., *No Distinction of Sex? Women in British Universities, 1870–1939*, UCL Press, 1995.

English Woman's Year Book, 1889–1916.

Eoff, S.M., *Viscountess Rhondda: Equalitarian Feminist*, Ohio University Press, 1991.

Fawcett, M.G., *Women's Suffrage: A Short History of a Great Movement*, T.C. & E.C. Jack, 1912.

Fawcett, M.G., *The Women's Victory – and After: Personal Reminiscences, 1911–1918*, Sidgwick and Jackson, 1920.

Fawcett, M., *What I Remember*, T. Fisher Unwin, 1924.

Ferguson, R., *Royal Borough*, Jonathan Cape, 1950.

Ferris, P., *The House of Northcliffe: The Harmsworths of Fleet Street*, Weidenfeld and Nicolson, 1971.

Fladeland, B., *Abolitionists and Working-Class Problems in the Age of Industrialization*, Louisiana State University, 1984.

Fletcher, S., *Maude Royden: A Life*, Basil Blackwell, 1989.

Flint, K., *The Woman Reader 1837–1914*, Clarendon Press, 1993.

Forster, M., *Significant Sisters: The Grassroots of Active Feminism 1839–1939*, Secker & Warburg, 1984.

Francis, J.C., *John Francis, Publisher of the Athenaeum: A Literary Chronicle of Half a Century*, R. Bentley, 1888.

Francis, J.E., *Dick and JEF*, Joseph Sault, 1939.

Franklin, M.L., *The Case for Woman Suffrage: A Bibliography*, National College Equal Suffrage League, 1913.

Fraser, H., *Women and War Work*, Shaw (New York), 1918.

Fry, A., *Conversations with Alice Paul*, University of California, Bancroft Library, 1976.

Fulford, R., *Votes for Women*, Faber, 1957.

Gaddes, B., *Evelina: Outward Bound from Inverlochy*, Merlin (Braunton), 1995.

Gaffin, J. and Thoms, D., *Caring & Sharing: The Centenary History of the Co-operative Women's Guild*, Co-operative Union Ltd, 1983.

Gardner, V. and Rutherford, S. (eds), *The New Woman and Her Sisters: Feminism and Theatre 1850–1914*, Harvester, 1992.

Garner, L., *Stepping Stones to Women's Liberty: Feminist Ideas in the Women's Suffrage Movement 1900–1918*, Heinemann Educational, 1984.

Gates, G.E. (ed.), *The Woman's Year Book, 1923–1924*, Women Publishers Ltd, 1924.

Gaur, A. and Tuson, P. (eds), *Women's Studies*, British Library Occasional Papers 12, British Library, 1990.

Gifford, D., *The British Film Catalogue, 1895–1985: A Reference Guide*, David and Charles, 1986.

Girouard, M., *Sweetness and Light*, Clarendon Press, 1990.

Girton College Register, 1869–1946, privately printed, 1948.

Gladstone, F.M., *Aubrey House*, A.L. Humphreys, 1922.

Glage, L., *Clementina Black: A Study in Social History and Literature*, Carl Winter, 1981.

Gleadle, K., *The Early Feminists: Radical Unitarians and the Emergence of the Women's Rights Movement, 1831–51*, St Martin's Press, 1995.

Goldman, H., *Emma Paterson*, Lawrence and Wishart, 1974.

Goodbody, M., *Five Daughters in Search of Learning: The Sturge Family 1820–1944*, published by the author, 1986.

Gordon, M., *Penal Discipline*, George Routledge, 1922.

Gould, B., *Daniel Cottier*, Naples Press, 1969.

Gould, F.J., *The Pioneers of Johnson's Court: A History of the Rationalist Press Association from 1899 onwards*, Watts & Co., 1929.

Graves, C.L., *Hubert Parry: His Life and Works*, Macmillan, 1926.

Graves, P., *Labour Women: Women in Britain Working-Class Politics 1918–1939*, Cambridge University Press, 1994.

Griffiths, D. (ed.), *The Encyclopaedia of the British Press, 1422–1992*, Macmillan, 1992.
Grigg, J., *Lloyd George, the people's champion, 1902–1911*, Eyre Methuen, 1978.
Grimes, J. and Daims, D., *Novels in English by Women, 1891–1920: A Preliminary checklist*, Garland, 1981.
Gwynn, S. and Tuckwell, G., *The Life of the Rt Hon Sir Charles W. Dilke*, John Murray, 1917.
Haight, G.S. (ed.), *Letters of George Eliot*, 9 vols, Oxford University Press, 1954, 1955.
Haight, G.S., *George Eliot and John Chapman: With Chapman's Diaries*, Archon Books, 1969.
Hale, C.B., *A Good Long Time*, Regency Press, 1973.
Hallinan, L., *British Commemoratives: Royalty, Politics, War and Sport*, Antique Collectors' Club, 1995.
Hamilton, C., *Marriage As A Trade*, Chapman Hall, 1909.
Hamilton, C., *Life Errant*, J.M. Dent, 1935.
Hammond, J.L., *C.P. Scott of the Manchester Guardian*, G. Bell & Sons, 1934.
Hammond, J.L. and Hammond, B., *James Stansfeld: A Victorian Champion of Sex Equality*, Longmans, 1932.
Hannam, J., *Isabella Ford*, Basil Blackwell, 1989.
Hargrove, E.C., *The Garden of Desire*, Grafton & Co., 1916.
Harris, W., *J.A. Spender*, Cassell, 1946.
Harrison, B., *Separate Spheres: The Opposition to Women's Suffrage in Britain*, Croom Helm, 1978.
Harrison, B., *Peaceable Kingdom: Stability and Change in Modern Britain*, Clarendon Press, 1982.
Harrison, B., *Prudent Revolutionaries: Portraits of British Feminists between the Wars*, Clarendon Press, 1987.
Harrison, J.F.C., *A History of the Working Men's College 1854–1954*, Routledge, 1954.
Harrison, J.F.C. and Thompson, D., *Bibliography of the Chartist Movement 1837–1976*, Harvester Press, 1978.
Hartnell, R., *Pre-Raphaelite Birmingham*, Brewin Books, 1996.
Hawkins, D. (ed.), *The Grove Diaries: The Rise and Fall of an English Family, 1809–1925*, Dovecote Press, 1995.
Hawtin, G., *Votes for Wimbledon Women*, published by the author, 1993.
Hayek, F.A., *John Stuart Mill and Harriet Taylor: Their Friendship and Subsequent Marriage*, Routledge and Kegan Paul, reissued, 1969.

Heath, G.D. and J., *The Women's Suffrage Movement in and around Richmond and Twickenham*, Borough of Twickenham Local History Society, 1968.
Heath, H.J.B., *Margaret Bright Lucas*, published for the author, 1890.
Henley, D., *Rosalind Howard: Countess of Carlisle*, The Hogarth Press, 1958.
Herstein, S.R., *A Mid-Victorian Feminist: Barbara Leigh Smith Bodichon*, Yale University Press, 1985.
Hesketh, P., *My Aunt Edith*, Peter Davies, 1966.
Hill, E. and Shaffer, O.F. (eds), *Great Suffragists – and Why*, Henry J. Drane, 1909.
Hill, R. And F. Davenport, *The Recorder of Birmingham: A Memoir of Matthew Davenport Hill*, Macmillan, 1878.
Hirsch, P., *Barbara Leigh Smith Bodichon: Feminist, Artist, and Rebel*, Chatto & Windus, 1998.
Hobhouse, H., *Lost London*, Macmillan, 1971.
Holcombe, L., *Victorian Ladies At Work: Middle-class Working Women 1850–1914*, David & Charles, 1973.
Holcombe, L., *Women and Property: Reform of the Married Women's Property Law in 19th Century England*, Toronto University Press, 1983.
Holledge, J., *Innocent Flowers: Women in the Edwardian Theatre*, Virago, 1981.
Hollis, P. (ed.), *Pressure from Without in Early Victorian England*, Edward Arnold, 1974.
Hollis, P., *Ladies Elect: Women in English Local Government 1865–1914*, Clarendon Press, 1987.
Holroyd, M., *Lytton Strachey*, Chatto & Windus, 1994.
Holt, R.V., *The Unitarian Contribution to Social Progress in England*, 2nd edn, The Lindsey Press, 1952.
Holtby, W., *Woman in a Changing Civilization*, John Lane, 1934.
Holton, S.S., *Feminism and Democracy: Women's Suffrage and Reform Politics in Britain, 1900–1918*, Cambridge University Press, 1986.
Holton, S.S., "The suffragist and 'the average woman'", *Women's History Review*, 1, 1992.
Holton, S.S., *Suffrage Days: Stories from the Women's Suffrage movement*, Routledge, 1998.
Holyoake, G.J., *Sixty Years of an Agitator's Life*, T. Fisher Unwin, 1906.
Hopkins, J., *Michael Ayrton: A Biography*, Deutsch, 1994.
Horstman, A., *Victorian Divorce*, Croom Helm, 1985.

Houghton, W.E. (ed.), *The Wellesley Index to Victorian Periodicals*, University of Toronto Press, 1966–89.

Housman, L., *The Unexpected Years*, Cape, 1937.

Hudson, D., *Munby: Man of Two Worlds*, John Murray, 1972.

Hume, L.P., *The National Union of Women's Suffrage Societies, 1897–1914*, Garland, 1982.

Hunt, K., *Equivocal Feminists: The Social Democratic Federation and the Woman Question 1884–1911*, Cambridge University Press, 1996.

Hutchinson's Woman's Who's Who, Hutchinson, 1934.

Huxley, G., *Lady Denman, GBE, 1884–1954*, Chatto & Windus, 1961.

Ingram, A. and Patai, D. (ed.), *Rediscovering Forgotten Radicals 1889–1939*, University of North Carolina Press, 1993.

Ireland, N.O., *Index to Women of the World from Ancient to Modern Times: A Supplement*, Metuchen, 1988.

Irwin, I.H., *The Story of Alice Paul and the National Woman's Party*, Denlinger's Publishers, 1977.

Jalland, P. (ed.), *Octavia Wilberforce: The Autobiography of a Pioneer Woman Doctor*, Cassell, 1989.

Jeffreys, S., *The Spinster and her Enemies: Feminism and Sexuality 1880–1930*, Pandora, 1985.

Jenkins, R., *Sir Charles Dilke: A Victorian Tragedy*, revised edn, Collins, 1968.

Jenkins, R., *Asquith*, 3rd edn, Collins, 1986.

Jenkins, R., *Gladstone*, Macmillan, 1995.

Joannou, M. and Purvis, J. (eds), *The Women's Suffrage Movement: New Feminist Perspectives*, Manchester University Press, 1998.

John, A.V. (ed.), *Our Mother's Land: Chapters in Welsh Women's History 1830–1939*, University of Wales Press, 1991.

John, A.V., *Elizabeth Robins: Staging a Life, 1862–1952*, Routledge, 1995.

John, A.V. and Eustance, C. (eds), *The Men's Share?: Masculinities, Male Support and Women's Suffrage in Britain, 1890–1920*, Routledge, 1997.

Johnson, N.C. (ed.), *Tea and Anarchy!: The Bloomsbury Diary of Olive Garnett 1890–1893*, Bartletts Press, 1989.

Jones, A., *Powers of the Press: Newspapers, Power and the Public in Nineteenth-century England*, Scolar, 1996.

Jones, D., *Chartism and the Chartists*, Allen Lane, 1975.

Kean, H., *Deeds Not Words: The Lives of Suffragette Teachers*, Pluto Press, 1990.

Kamester, M. and Vellacott, J., *Militarism versus Feminism: Writings on Women and War*, Virago, 1987.

Kamm, J., *Rapiers and Battleaxes: The Women's Movement and its Aftermath*, Allen & Unwin, 1966.

Keir, T.C., *I Knew Mrs Pankhurst*, published for the Suffragette Fellowship by Marian Lawson, 1945.

Kelly, A., *Lydia Becker and the Cause*, Centre for North-West Regional Studies, 1992.

Kent, S. Kingsley, *Sex and Suffrage in Britain, 1860–1914*, Princeton University Press, 1987.

Kenney, A., *Memoirs of a Militant*, Edward Arnold, 1924.

Kerr, R., *The Gentleman's House; or, How to Plan English Residences from the Parsonage to the Palace*, John Morray, 1864.

King, E., *The Thenew Factor: The Hidden History of Glasgow's Women*, Mainstream Publishing, 1993.

Kirk, J.F., *A Supplement to Allibone's Critical Dictionary of English Literature and British and American Authors*, Gale Research, 1965.

Koss, S., *The Rise and Fall of the Political Press in Britain*, vol. 2, *The Twentieth Century*, Hamish Hamilton, 1984.

Koss, S., *Asquith*, Hamish Hamilton, 1985.

Lacey, C.A. (ed.), *Barbara Leigh Smith and the Langham Place Group*, Routledge (Women's Source Library), 1987.

The Lady's Who's Who, 1938–1939, Pallas Publishing, 1939.

Lago, M., *Christiana Herringham and the Edwardian Art Scene*, Lund Humphries, 1996.

Lang, E.M., *British Women in the Twentieth Century*, T. Werner Laurie, 1929.

Law, C., *Suffrage and Power: The Women's Movement, 1918–1928*, I.B. Tauris, 1997.

Lawrence, M., *Shadow of Swords: A Biography of Elsie Inglis*, Michael Joseph, 1971.

Lee, A.L., *The Origins of the Popular Press 1855–1914*, Croom Helm, 1976.

Leighton, D. (pseud. of Dorothy Forsyth), *Disillusion*, Henry & Co., 1894.

Leneman, L., *Martyrs in Our Midst: Dundee, Perth and the Forcible Feeding of Suffragettes*, Abertay Historical Society, 1993.

Leneman, L., *In the Service of Life: The Story of Elsie Inglis and the Scottish Women's Hospitals*, Mercat Press, 1994.

Leneman, L., "A Guid Cause": The Women's Suffrage Movement in Scotland, Aberdeen University Press, 1991 (rev. edn, Mercat Press, 1995).

Leslie, H. (pseud.), More Ha'pence Than Kicks, Being Some Things Remembered, Macdonald, no date (1940s).

Leventhal, F.M., The Last Dissenter: H.N. Brailsford and His World, Clarendon Press, 1985.

Levine, P., Victorian Feminism, 1850–1900, Hutchinson, 1987.

Levine, P., Feminist Lives in Victorian England: Private Roles and Public Commitment, Basil Blackwell, 1990.

Lewis, G., Eva Gore-Booth and Esther Roper, Pandora, 1988.

Lewis, J., Women in England, 1870–1950: Sexual Divisions and Social Change, Wheatsheaf, 1984.

Lewis, J. (ed.), Before the Vote was Won: Arguments For and Against Women's Suffrage 1864–1896, Routledge, 1987.

Liddington, J. and Norris, J., One Hand Tied Behind Us: The Rise of the Women's Suffrage Movement, Virago, 1978.

Liddington, J., The Life and Times of a Respectable Rebel: Selina Cooper 1864–1946, Virago, 1984.

Liddington, J., The Long Road to Greenham: Feminism and Anti-militarism in Britain since 1820, Virago, 1989.

Linklater, A., An Unhusbanded Life: Charlotte Despard: Suffragette, Socialist, and Sinn Feiner, Hutchinson, 1980.

Lock, J., The British Policewoman, Robert Hale, 1979.

Lord, F., Christian Science Healing: Principles and Practice with Full Explanations for Home Students, G. Redway, 1888.

Lovett, W., The Life and Struggles of William Lovett, Trubner, 1876.

Lown, J., Women and Industrialization: Gender at Work in 19th century England, University of Minneapolis Press, 1990.

Lumsden, L., Yellow Leaves: Memories, William Blackwood, 1933.

Lutyens, Lady E., Candles in the Sun, Hart-Davis, 1957.

Lynn Linton, E., In Haste and at Leisure, William Heinemann, 1895.

Lytton, C., Prisons and Prisoners: Some Personal Experiences, William Heinemann, 1914.

Lytton, C., I Constance Lytton, privately printed, 1987.

MacCabe, J. (ed.), Life & Letters of George Holyoake, Watts & Co., 1908.

MacKenzie, M., Shoulder to Shoulder, Penguin, 1975.

Mackie, J.B., The Life and Work of Duncan McLaren, Nelson, 1888.

Malleson, E., Notes on the Early Training of Children, Sonnenschein & Co., 1885.

Malleson, E., Elizabeth Malleson, 1828–1916, Autobiographical Notes and Letters. With a memoir by Hope Malleson, printed for private circulation, 1926.

Malleson, H., A Woman Doctor: Mary Murdoch of Hull, Sidgwick and Jackson, 1919.

Malmgreen, G., Neither Bread Nor Roses: Utopian Feminists and the English Working Class, 1800–1859, John L. Noyce, 1978.

Malmgreen, G. (ed.), Religion in the Lives of English Women, 1760–1930, Croom Helm, 1986.

Malos, E., "Bristol women in action, 1839–1919", in Bild, I., (ed.) Bristol's Other History, Bristol Broadsides, 1983.

Manchester Faces and Places, John Heywood, 1891.

Manton, J., Elizabeth Garrett Anderson, Methuen, 1965.

Mappen, E., Helping Women at Work: The Women's Industrial Council 1889–1914, Hutchinson, 1985.

Marcus, J. (ed.), Suffrage and the Pankhursts, Routledge (Women's Source Library), 1987.

Markievicz, Countess, Prison Letters of Countess Markievicz, Sebestyn, A., intro., Virago, 1987.

Marks, D.W. and Lowy, Rev. A. (eds), Memoir of Sir Francis Henry Goldsmid with a Preface by Louisa Goldsmid, Kegan Paul, 1879.

Marryat, F., At Heart A Rake, H. Cox, 1895.

Martindale, H., From One Generation to Another, 1839–1944, George Allen & Unwin, 1944.

Martineau, H., Harriet Martineau's Autobiography, Chapman, M.W. (ed.), Houghton, Mifflin & Co., 1877.

Mason, B., The Story of the Women's Suffrage Movement, Sherrat and Hughes, 1912.

Masson, D., Memories of London in the 'Forties, Blackwood, 1908.

Masson, F., Victorians All, W. & R. Chambers, 1931.

Mathews, V. Laughton, Blue Tapestry, Hollis & Carter, 1948.

May, J. & J., Commemorative Pottery, 1780–1900, Heinemann, 1972.

Maynard, M. and Purvis, J. (eds), *Researching Women's Lives from a Feminist Perspective*, Taylor and Francis, 1994.

Mayne, E.C., *The Life and Letters of Anne Isabella, Lady Noel Byron*, Charles Scribner's Sons, 1929.

McCarthy, L., *Myself and My Friends*, Thornton Butterworth, 1933.

McCormack, P., *Women Stained Glass Artists of the Arts and Crafts Movement*, William Morris Gallery, 1985.

McDonald, I., *Vindication!: A Postcard History of the Women's Movement*, Bellew, 1989.

McHugh, P., *Prostitution and Victorian Social reform*, Croom Helm, 1980.

McPhee, C. and FitzGerald, A. (eds), *The Non-Violent Militant: Selected Writings of Teresa Billington-Greig*, Routledge and Kegan Paul (Women's Source Library), 1987.

McLaren, E. Shaw, *A History of the Scottish Women's Hospitals*, Hodder & Stoughton, 1919.

McWilliams-Tullberg, R., *Women at Cambridge: A Man's University – though of a Mixed Type*, Gollancz, 1975.

Melman, B., *Women and the Popular Imagination in the Twenties: Flappers and Nymphs*, Macmillan Press, 1988.

Melville, J., *Ellen and Edy*, Pandora, 1987.

Metcalfe, E., *Memoir of Rosamond Davenport Hill*, Longmans, 1904.

Meynell, Dame A., *What Grandmother Said: The Life of Alice Dowson*, Colt Books, 1998.

Middleton, L. (ed.), *Women in the Labour Movement: The British experience*, Croom Helm, 1977.

Midgley, C., *Women Against Slavery: The British Campaign 1780–1870*, Routledge, 1992.

Miles, L. Eustace, *Untold Tales of War-Time London: A Personal Diary*, Cecil Palmer, 1930.

Mill, J.S., *The Subjection of Women*, and Taylor, H., *Enfranchisement of Women*, with introduction by Kate Soper, Virago, 1983.

Miller, J.E., *Rebel Women: Feminism, Modernism, and the Edwardian Novel*, Virago, 1994.

Milliken, H.T., *The Road to Bodnant*, Morten, 1975.

Mills, J., *From Tinder-Box to the "Larger" Light: threads from the life of John Mills Banker . . . Interwoven with Some Early Century Recollections by His Wife*, Sherrat & Hughes, 1899.

Mills, J. Travis, *John Bright and the Quakers*, Methuen, 1935.

Mineka, F.E. and Lindley, D.N., *The Later Letters of John Stuart Mill 1849–1873*, Routledge & Kegan Paul, 1972.

Mitchell, D., *Women on the Warpath: The Story of the Women of the First World War*, Jonathan Cape, 1966.

Mitchell, D., *The Fighting Pankhursts: A Study in Tenacity*, Jonathan Cape, 1967.

Mitchell, D., *Queen Christabel*, Macdonald, 1977.

Mitchell, H., *The Hard Way Up: The autobiography of Hannah Mitchell, Suffragette and Rebel*, Faber, 1968.

Moffat, G., *Join Me in Remembering*, Winifred Moffat, 1955.

Montefiore, D., *Prison Reform: From a Social-Democratic Point of View*, Twentieth Century Press, 1909.

Montefiore, D., *From a Victorian to a Modern*, E. Archer, 1927.

Moore, E. [Mrs Eva Jack], *Exits and Entrances*, Chapman and Hall, 1923.

Moore, L., *Bajanellas and Semilinas: Aberdeen University and the Education of Women, 1860–1920*, Aberdeen University Press, 1991.

Moorhead, E. and Walsh, E. (eds), *This Quarter*, 1 and 2, 1925; 3, 1927; 4, 1929.

Morgan, D., *Suffragists and Liberals: The Politics of Woman Suffrage in Britain*, Basil Blackwell, 1975.

Morgan, K.O., *Keir Hardie: Radical and Socialist*, Weidenfeld and Nicolson, 1975.

Morley, A. and Stanley, L., *The Life and Death of Emily Wilding Davison: with Gertrude Colmore's The Life of Emily Davison*, The Woman's Press, 1988.

Morley, E., *The Life and Times of Henry Crabb Robinson*, J.M. Dent, 1935.

Morrell, C., *"Black Friday": Violence against Women in the Suffragette Movement*, Women's Research and Resources Centre, 1981.

Moyes, H., *Woman in a Man's World*, Alpha Books, 1971.

Mulvihill, M., *Charlotte Despard: A Biography*, Pandora, 1989.

Mumby, F.A., *The House of Routledge, 1834–1934*, Routledge, 1934.

Mumby, F.A. and Stallybrass, F.H.S., *From Swan Sonnenschein to George Allen & Unwin Ltd*, Allen and Unwin, 1955.

Munn, G.C. and Gere, G., *Artists' Jewellery: Pre-Raphaelite to Arts and Crafts*, Antique Collectors' Club, 1989.

Murray, F., *Women as Army Surgeons: Being the History of the Women's Hospital Corps in Paris, Wimereux and Endell Street, September 1914–October 1919*, Hodder & Stoughton, 1920.

Neale, R.S., *Class and Ideology in the Nineteenth Century*, Routledge, 1972.

Neville, D., *To Make Their Mark: The Women's Suffrage Movement in the North East of England, 1900–1914*, Centre of Northern Studies, University of Northumbria, 1997.

Nevinson, H.W., *Fire of Life*, James Nisbet with Victor Gollancz, 1935.

Nevinson, M. Wynne, *Life's Fitful Fever: A Volume of Memories*, A. & C. Black, 1926.

Newman, F.W., *Memoir and Letters of Francis W. Newman*, Sieveking, I. Giberne (ed.), Kegan Paul, 1909.

Newnham College Register, 1871–1950, Cambridge, 1965.

Newsome, S., *The Women's Freedom League*, [WFL], 1960.

Newton, S.M., *Health, Art & Reason: Dress Reformers of the 19th Century*, John Murray, 1974.

Norquay, G., *Voices and Votes: A Literary Anthology of the Women's Suffrage Campaign*, Manchester University Press, 1995.

Oldfield, A., *Woman Suffrage in Australia: A Gift or a Struggle?*, Cambridge University Press, 1992.

Oram, A., *Women Teachers and Feminist Politics 1900–39*, Manchester University Press, 1996.

Orr, C. Campbell (ed.), *Women in the Victorian Art World*, Manchester University Press, 1995.

Overton, J. and Mant, J., *A Suffragette Nest: Peaslake, 1910 and after*, Hazeltree Publishing, 1998.

Pankhurst, C., *The Great Scourge, and How to End It*, The Woman's Press, 1913.

Pankhurst, C., *The Militant Methods of the NWSPU*, 2nd edn, The Woman's Press, 1913.

Pankhurst, C., *Unshackled: The Story of How We Won the Vote*, Hutchinson, 1959.

Pankhurst, E., *The Trial of the Suffragette Leaders*, The Woman's Press, 1908.

Pankhurst, E., *The Importance of the Vote*, 8th edn, The Woman's Press, 1913.

Pankhurst, E., *My Own Story*, Eveleigh Nash, 1914.

Pankhurst, E.S., *Writ On Cold Slate*, Dreadnought Publishers, 1922.

Pankhurst, E.S., *The Suffragette Movement: An Intimate Account of Persons and Ideals*, Longmans, 1931.

Pankhurst, E.S., *The Home Front*, Hutchinson, 1932.

Pankhurst, E.S., *The Life of Emmeline Pankhurst: The Suffragette Struggle for Women's Citizenship*, T. Werner Laurie, 1935.

Pankhurst, R., *Sylvia Pankhurst: Artist and Crusader*, Paddington Press, 1977.

Pankhurst, S., *The Suffragette: The History of the Women's Militant Movement*, Sturgis & Walton, 1911.

Pankhurst, S., contribution to Asquith, M. (ed.), *Myself When Young*, 2nd edn, Muller, 1938.

Pankhurst, S., *A Sylvia Pankhurst Reader*, Dodd, K. (ed.), Manchester University Press, 1993.

Pascoe, C.E., *London of To-day*, Sampson Low, 1888.

Peacock, S., *Votes for Women: The Women's Fight in Portsmouth*, Portsmouth Papers, no. 39, 1983.

The *Pelican*: A Quarterly Magazine, Simpkin Marshall, 1874–75.

Pentland, M., *A Bonnie Fechter: The Life of Ishbel Marjoribanks, Marchioness of Aberdeen and Temair, 1857–1939*, B.T. Batsford, 1952.

Petersen, M.J., *Family, Love, and Work in the Lives of Victorian Gentlewomen*, Indiana University Press, 1989.

Pethick-Lawrence, E., *My Part in a Changing World*, Gollancz, 1938.

Pethick-Lawrence, F., *Fate Has been Kind*, Hutchinson, no date (1943).

Phillips, M., *The Militant Suffrage Campaign in Perspective*, The Suffragette Fellowship, no date (c. 1960).

Postgate, R., *George Lansbury*, Longmans, 1951.

Pratt, E.A., *Pioneer Women in Victoria's Reign: Being Short Histories of Great Movements*, George Newnes, 1897.

Priestley, P., *Victorian Prison Lives: English Prison Biography, 1830–1914*, Methuen, 1985.

Procter, Z., *Life and Yesterday*, The Favil Press, 1960.

Pugh, M., *Electoral Reform in War and Peace, 1906–18*, Routledge & Kegan Paul, 1978.

Pugh, M., *Lloyd George*, Longmans, 1988.

Pugh, P., *Educate, Agitate, Organize: 100 Years of Fabian Socialism*, Methuen, 1984.

Purvis, J., *Women's History: Britain, 1850–1945*, UCL Press, 1995.

R., A.J. (ed.) *The Suffrage Annual and Women's Who*, Stanley Paul, 1913.

Radzinowicz, L. and Hood, R., *A History of English Criminal Law*, vol. 5, *The Emergence of Penal Policy*, Clarendon Press, 1986.

Rae, L. Milne, *Ladies in Debate: Being a History of the Ladies' Edinburgh Debating Society 1865–1935*, Oliver and Boyd, 1936.

Raeburn, A., *The Militant Suffragettes*, Michael Joseph, 1973.

Raeburn, A., *The Suffragette View*, David & Charles, 1976.

Ramelson, M., *Petticoat Rebellion*, Lawrence & Wishart, 1976.

Ratcliffe, S.K., *The Story of South Place*, Watts, 1955.

Reed, J.W., Jr (ed.), *An American Diary: Barbara Leigh Smith Bodichon, 1857–8*, Routledge and Kegan Paul, 1972.

Reid, M., *A Plea for Women*, Polygon, 1988 (reprint of 1843 edition, with introduction).

Rendall, J., *The Origins of Modern Feminism: Women in Britain, France, and the United States, 1780–1860*, Macmillan, 1985.

Rendall, J. (ed.), *Equal or Different: Women's Politics, 1800–1914*, Basil Blackwell, 1987.

Rhondda, Viscountess, *This Was My World*, Macmillan, 1933.

Richards, E.F., *Mazzini's Letters to an English Family, 1844–1854*, John Lane, 1920.

Richards, G., *Author Hunting*, Hamish Hamilton, 1934.

Robinson, H. Crabb, *The Diary of Henry Crabb Robinson*, Hudson, D. (ed.), Oxford University Press, 1967.

Richardson, M., *Laugh a Defiance*, Weidenfeld & Nicolson, 1953.

Roberts, E. (ed.), *Louisa: Memoirs of a Quaker Childhood*, Friends Home Service Committee, 1970.

Robins, E., *Way Stations*, Tauchnitz, 1913.

Robins, E., *The Convert*, with introduction by Jane Marcus, The Woman's Press, 1980.

Robinson, D., *Women Novelists 1891–1920: An Index of Biographical and Autobiographical Sources*, Garland, 1984.

Romero, P., *E. Sylvia Pankhurst: Portrait of a Radical*, Yale University Press, 1987.

Roper, E., Biographical Introduction to *Poems of Eva Gore-Booth*, Longmans, 1929.

Rosen, A., *Rise Up Women!: The Militant Campaign of the Women's Social and Political Union, 1903–1914*, Routledge, 1974.

Rosenbaum, S.P., *Victorian Bloomsbury: The Early Literary History of the Bloomsbury Group*, Macmillan Press, 1987.

Ross, A., *British Documentary Sound*, Scottish Council for Educational Technology, 1976.

Rover, C., *Punch Book of Women's Rights*, Hutchinson, 1967.

Rover, C., *Women's Suffrage and Party Politics*, Routledge, 1967.

Rover, C., *Love, Morals, and the Feminists*, Routledge & Kegan Paul, 1970.

Rowbotham, S., *Hidden from History: 300 Years of Women's Oppression and the Fight Against it*, Pluto Press, 1974.

Royden, M., *A Three-Fold Cord*, Gollancz, 1947.

Royle, E., *Victorian Infidels: The Origins of the British Secularist Movement 1791–1866*, Manchester University Press, 1974.

Royle, E., *Radicals, Secularists and Republicans: Popular Freethought in Britain, 1866–1915*, Manchester University Press, 1980.

Rubinstein, D., *Before the Suffragettes: Women's Emancipation in the 1890s*, Harvester Press, 1986.

Rubinstein, D., *A Different World for Women: The Life of Millicent Garrett Fawcett*, Harvester, 1991.

Rupke, N.A. (ed.), *Vivisection in Historical Perspective*, Routledge, 1982.

Russell, B. and P. (eds), *The Amberley Papers: The Letters and Diaries of Lord and Lady Amberley*, Hogarth Press, 1937.

Ruston, A., "Clementia Taylor", *Transactions of the Unitarian Historical Society*, 20, 1, April 1991.

Rutter, F., *Since I Was Twenty-Five*, Constable, 1927.

Ryan, M.V., *Dr Agnes McLaren*, Catholic Biographies, vol. 24, London, 1915.

Schwarzkopf, J., *Women in the Chartist Movement*, St Martin's Press, 1991.

Scott, J.W. Robertson, *The Story of the Women's Institute Movement*, The Village Press (Idbury), 1925.

St John, C., *Christine Murrell*, Williams and Norgate, 1935.

St John, C., *Ethel Smyth: A Biography*, Longmans, 1958.

Sennett, M. Arncliffe, *The Child*, C.W. Daniel, no date (1938).

Sewall, M.W. (ed.), *The World's Congress of Representative Women*, Chicago, 1894.
Shaen, M.J. (ed.), *Memorials of Two Sisters: Susanna and Catherine Winkworth*, Longmans, 1908.
Shanley, M.L., *Feminism, Marriage, and the Law in Victorian England 1850–1895*, I.B. Tauris, 1989.
Sharp, E., *Hertha Sharp, 1854–1923*, Edward Arnold, 1926.
Sharp, E., *Unfinished Adventure*, John Lane, 1933.
Shattock, J. and Wolff, M., *The Victorian Periodical Press: Samplings and Soundings*, Leicester University Press, 1982.
Shepherd, A., *Cartooning for Suffrage*, University of New Mexico Press, 1994.
Sherrard, O.A., *Two Victorian Girls: With Extracts from the Hall Diaries*, Frederick Muller, 1966.
Shiman, L.L., *Women and Leadership in Nineteenth-Century England*, Macmillan, 1992.
Shore, L., *Poems*, with a Memoir by her Sister, Arabella Shore, and an Appreciation by Frederic Harrison, Grant Richards, 1897.
Sigerson, G., *"Custodia Honesta": Treatment of Political Prisoners in Great Britain*, with an introduction by Henry W. Nevinson, Woman's Press, 1912.
Simon of Wythenshawe, Lady, *Margaret Ashton and Her Time*, The Margaret Ashton Memorial Lecture for 1948, Manchester University Press, 1949.
Smart, R., *Bedford Training College 1882–1982*, Bedford Training College Publication Committee, 1982.
Smith, H.L. (ed.), *British Feminism in the Twentieth Century*, University of Massachusetts Press, 1990.
Smyth, E., *Impressions That Remained*, Longmans, 1919.
Smyth, E., *A Final Burning of Boats*, Longmans, 1928.
Smyth, E., *Female Piping in Eden*, Peter Davies, 1933.
Smyth, E., *As Time Went On*, Longmans, 1936.
Solomon, W.E.G., *Saul Solomon*, Oxford University Press (Cape Town), 1948.
Spencer, I., *Walter Crane*, Studio Vista, 1975.
Spender, D., *Women of Ideas and What Men Have Done to Them*, Routledge, 1982.
Spender, D., *Feminist Theorists*, Woman's Press, 1983.
Spender, D., *Time and Tide Wait For No Man*, Pandora, 1984.
Spender, D. and Hayman, C., *How the Vote was Won, and Other Suffragette Plays*, Methuen, 1985.
Srebrnik, P.T., *Alexander Strahan, Victorian Publisher*, University of Michigan Press, 1986.

Staars, D., *The English Woman: Studies in her Psychic Revolution*, trans. from the French and abridged by J.M.E. Brownlow, Smith, Elder, 1909.
Staff, F., *The Picture Postcard and its Origins*, 2nd edn, Lutterworth Press, 1979.
Stansky, P., *On or About December 1910: Early Bloomsbury and its Intimate World*, Harvard University Press, 1996.
Stanton, E.C., *Eighty Years and More (1815–1897): Reminiscences of Elizabeth Cady Stanton*, Source Book Press, 1970 (reprint of 1898 American edition).
Stanton, T. (ed.), *The Woman Question in Europe*, Sampson Low, 1884.
Steele, T., *Alfred Orage and the Leeds Arts Club, 1893–1923*, Scolar Press, 1990.
Steen, M., *A Pride of Terrys: A Family Saga*, Longmans, 1962.
Stocks, M., *Eleanor Rathbone*, Gollancz, 1949.
Stocks, M., *My Commonplace Book*, Peter Davies, 1970.
Stoddart, A.M., *Life and Letters of Hannah E. Pipe*, William Blackwood, 1908.
Stowell, S., *A Stage of Their Own: Feminist Playwrights of the Suffrage Era*, Manchester University Press, 1992.
Strachey, R., *Women's Suffrage and Women's Service: The History of the London & National Society for Women's Service*, LNSWS, 1927.
Strachey, R., *"The Cause": A Short History of the Women's Movement in Great Britain*, G. Bell, 1928.
Strachey, R., *Millicent Garrett Fawcett*, John Murray, 1931.
Strachey, R. (ed.), *Our Freedom and its Results*, Hogarth Press, 1936.
Strauss, S., *"Traitors to the Masculine Cause": The Men's Campaigns for Women's Rights*, Greenwood Press, 1982.
Sutherland, J.A., *Victorian Novelists and Publishers*, Athlone Press, 1976.
Swanwick, H., *I Have Been Young*, Gollancz, 1935.
Tanner, S.J., *How the Women's Suffrage Movement Began in Bristol Fifty Years ago*, The Carlyle Press (Bristol), 1918.
Taylor, B., *Eve and the New Jerusalem: Socialism and Feminism in the 19th Century*, Virago, 1983.
Taylor, M., *Some Notes on the Private Life of John Stuart Mill*, in *The Letters of John Stuart Mill*, Elliot, H.S.R. (ed.), Longmans, 1910.

Taylor, R., *In Letters of Gold: The Story of Sylvia Pankhurst and the East London Federation of the Suffragettes in Bow*, Stepney Books, 1993.

Taylor, S., *The Great Outsiders: Northcliffe, Rothermere and the Daily Mail*, Weidenfeld and Nicolson, 1996.

Thomas, C., *Love and Work Enough: The Life of Anna Jameson*, University of Toronto Press, 1967.

Thomis M.I. and Grimmett, J., *Women in Protest 1800–1850*, Croom Helm, 1982.

Thompson, D.M., *Nonconformity in the Nineteenth Century*, Routledge, 1972.

Thompson, M.E. and M.D., *They Couldn't Stop Us! Experiences of Two (Usually Law-abiding) Women in the Years 1909–1913*, W.E. Harrison & Sons, 1957.

Thompson, T., *Dear Girl: The Diaries and Letters of Two Working Women, 1897–1917*, Woman's Press, 1987.

Tickner, L., *The Spectacle of Women: Imagery of the Suffrage Campaign 1907–14*, Chatto & Windus, 1987.

Tolles, F.B. (ed.), *Slavery and "The Woman Question": Lucretia Mott's Diary, 1840, Journal of the Friends' Historical Society*, supplement 23, 1952.

Tulloch, G., *Mill and Sexual Equality*, Harvester Wheatsheaf, 1989.

Tyler, M. Coit, *Glimpses of England, Social, Political and Literary*, G.P. Putnam & Sons, 1898.

Van Helmond, M., *Votes for Women: The Events on Merseyside 1870–1928*, National Museums and Galleries on Merseyside, 1992.

Vellacott, J., *From Liberal to Labour with Women's Suffrage: The Story of Catherine Marshall*, McGill–Queen's University Press, 1993.

Vicinus, M. (ed.), *A Widening Sphere: Changing Roles of Victorian Women*, Indiana University Press, 1977.

Vicinus, M., *Suffer and Be Still: Women in the Victorian Age*, Methuen, 1980.

Vicinus, M., *Independent Women: Work and Community for Single Women 1850–1920*, Virago, 1985.

Villiers, B. (ed.), *The Case for Women's Suffrage*, T. Fisher Unwin, 1907.

Walkowitz, J.R., *Prostitution and Victorian Society: Women, Class and the State*, Cambridge University Press, 1982.

Walkowitz, J., *City of Dreadful Night: Narratives of Sexual Danger in late-Victorian London*, Virago, 1992.

Walsh, E., *Poems and Sonnets: with a Memoir by Ethel Moorhead*, Harcourt Brace, 1934.

Webb, C., *The Woman with the Basket: The Story of the Women's Co-operative Guild, 1883–1927*, Women's Co-operative Guild, 1927.

Webb, I.M., *History of Chelsea College of Physical Education*, forthcoming.

Weinreb, B. and Hibbert, C., *The London Encyclopaedia*, Macmillan, 1983.

Weir, C., *Women's History in the Nottinghamshire Archives Office 1550–1950*, Nottinghamshire Archives Office, 1989.

Weller, K., *"Don't be a Soldier!": The Radical Anti-War Movement in North London, 1914–1918*, Journeyman Press, 1985.

Westlake, J., *Memories of John Westlake*, Smith, Elder, 1914.

Wheatley, V., *The Life and Work of Harriet Martineau*, Secker & Warburg, 1957.

Whitlaw, L., *The Life and Rebellious Times of Cicely Hamilton*, The Woman's Press, 1990.

Whittick, A., *Women Into Citizen*, Athenaeum with Frederick Muller, 1979.

Who Was Who, A.C. Black.

Widdowson, F., *Going Up Into the Next Class: Women and Elementary Teacher Training 1840–1914*, Hutchinson, 1983.

Wiltsher, A., *Most Dangerous Women: Feminist Peace Campaigners of the Great War*, Pandora, 1985.

Wohl, A.S. (ed.), *The Victorian Family*, Croom Helm, 1978.

Women Artists' Slide Library, A Second Viewing: An Exhibition of Suffragette Banners, Posters, and Photographs from the Fawcett Library, 1986.

Women's Who's Who, 1934–5, Shaw Publishing, 1934.

Yevonde, *In Camera*, The Women's Book Club, 1940.

Young, J.D., *Women and Popular Struggles: A History of Scottish and English Working-Class Women*, Mainstream, 1985.